ENCYCLOPEDIA OF THE DEAD SEA SCROLLS

ENCYCLOPEDIA OF THE DEAD SEA SCROLLS

Lawrence H. Schiffman
James C. VanderKam
EDITORS IN CHIEF

VOLUME 1

OXFORD
UNIVERSITY PRESS

2000

OXFORD
UNIVERSITY PRESS

Oxford New York
Athens Auckland Bangkok Bogotá Buenos Aires Calcutta
Cape Town Chennai Dar es Salaam Delhi Florence Hong Kong Istanbul
Karachi Kuala Lumpur Madrid Melbourne Mexico City Mumbai
Nairobi Paris São Paulo Singapore Taipei Tokyo Toronto Warsaw

and associated companies in
Berlin Ibadan

Published by Oxford University Press, Inc.
198 Madison Avenue, New York, New York 10016
www.oup.com

Library of Congress Cataloging-in-Publication Data
Encyclopedia of the Dead Sea scrolls /
Lawrence H. Schiffman and James C. VanderKam, editors in chief
p. cm.
Includes bibliographical references and index.
1. Dead Sea scrolls—Encyclopedias.
I. Schiffman, Lawrence H. II. VanderKam, James C.
BM487.E53 2000
296.1′55′03—dc21 99-055300

ISBN 0-19-508450-0 (set)
ISBN 0-19-513796-5 (vol. 1)
ISBN 0-19-513797-3 (vol. 2)

Publisher: Karen Casey
Commissioning Editor: Claude Conyers
Development Editor: Marion Osmun
Managing Editor: Matthew Giarratano
Project Editor: Kathy Moreau
Production Manager: Nancy Hoagland
Production Editor: Cynthia Garver
Indexer: Catherine Goddard
Book Designer: Joan Greenfield

3 5 7 9 8 6 4 2

Printed in the United States of America
on acid-free paper

Contents

Preface

The fifty years since the discovery of the Dead Sea Scrolls have seen an immense development in our understanding of biblical studies, the history of Judaism, and the rise of Christianity—the result of what has been called by many the most important archaeological discovery of the century. Recent years have seen an intensification of research and publication relating to the scrolls. The purpose of the *Encyclopedia of the Dead Sea Scrolls* is to present to scholars and interested lay people the results of this half century of research and to reveal to them this trove of information that highlights a period in the history of our civilization the importance of which cannot be overstated. The documents discussed in this encyclopedia, as well as the historical sites and circumstances, were formative in shaping the Western religious tradition as we know it. It is therefore no accident that these scrolls have engendered such great enthusiasm on the one hand and much controversy on the other. The encyclopedia aims to provide an up-to-date account of all aspects of these important finds.

As understood in this encyclopedia, the Dead Sea Scrolls are a set of collections of texts found in the Judean Wilderness, an area east and south of Jerusalem and west of the Dead Sea. Although the term *Dead Sea Scrolls* is usually used to designate only the texts found in the eleven caves of Qumran, this encyclopedia also includes the texts found in Wadi ed-Daliyeh, Wadi Murabbaʿat, Naḥal Ḥever and related sites, Masada, and Khirbet Mird. Taken together, scholars usually designate these collections as the Judean Desert texts. These materials range in date from the fourth century BCE to the seventh century CE. While these collections are often described using the terms *scrolls*, *texts*, or *documents*, most of the parchment and papyrus scraps are but fragmentary representations of what once constituted complete scrolls. Those few scrolls that survive in full-length copies are often missing sections or break off at certain points. The reconstruction of the original texts is one of the most difficult tasks for scholars and has been compared to assembling a jigsaw puzzle with most of the pieces missing. Nevertheless, through reconstruction and interpretation, the Dead Sea Scrolls provide textual evidence for a variety of topics, including the history of the text of the Hebrew Bible, background for the New Testament and early Christianity, and evidence for the development of Second Temple and Rabbinic Judaism.

Although research began on the scrolls shortly after their discovery in the late 1940s and 1950s with the intent of publishing all the texts, scholarship slowed in the 1960s and was revived only in the 1980s. At that time, there were protests about the paucity of texts that were available for study. Those that had not been published remained in the possession of the editors, who at times denied other researchers access to them. The decade of the 1990s opened with the "liberation" of the scrolls and continued by making all the texts available to the public in several formats. This encyclopedia could not have been conceived until this development in the history of scrolls scholarship had taken place. At the end of the 1990s, it is particularly appropriate to encapsulate this new knowledge in an encyclopedia written by experts, each of whose field of study now has been greatly enhanced by access to these materials. Even as this encyclopedia goes to press, editions and translations of the remaining unpublished texts are in progress in the Oxford University Press series Discoveries in the Judaean Desert.

To be sure, the centerpiece of this encyclopedia is the Qumran scrolls. These scrolls, along with the other documents, illuminate the several centuries preceding Jesus' life and extending until shortly after his death, a very significant period for understanding the history of both Judaism and Christianity. During this era, Judaism consisted of a varied group of sects and movements that rivaled one another for supremacy. Echoes of these can be found in the Qumran texts, which shed light on the Essenes, Pharisees, Sadducees, Boethusians, and other Second Temple groups. This was the period of the rise of Talmudic Judaism. Further, these texts reverberate in the literature of the Karaites, Talmudic rabbis, and early Christians through their exposition and interpretations of Jewish law, their polemic against other groups, and their own theological and ritual construction of Judaism. The Dead Sea Scrolls are a unique record of this period, for they constitute the only contemporary manuscripts of these centuries outside the Bible itself and some passing references in the works of the first-century Jewish historian Josephus. In past research, Josephus was the key to understanding the events of the period. Now, with the eight hundred fifty or so documents found in the caves of Qumran as primary material, the previously available sources must be reinterpreted in light of the scrolls.

The Collections

Since the discovery of the first scrolls in 1947 at Qumran, a variety of collections from different sites in the Judean Desert have been found, sold, and published. For the most part, these collections have been studied separately in secondary scholarly literature. They are included together in this encyclopedia for a number of reasons. First, they all share a similar history of discovery, publication, and research. Second, they often throw light on one another when studied together. Third, the history and archaeology of the region in which they have been discovered are shared ones. Thus, these several collections together are the basis of this encyclopedia. At the same time, the quantitative size of the Qumran collection, the important research that has been done on it, and its overarching significance in historical terms have led us to give greater emphasis to it. Nevertheless, we do not wish to diminish the significance of the other material.

The collections included in this encyclopedia are as follows.

Qumran Scrolls

The most extensive collection is that of Qumran on the western shore of the Dead Sea. Here, in caves associated with the ruins of a nearby settlement, from 1947 on, remnants of more than eight hundred texts have been unearthed, for the most part by bedouin. These texts had been brought to the settlement or copied at Qumran between the third century BCE and the first century CE.

The texts may be divided almost equally into three divisions by their contents: biblical books, other books read at the time throughout the Land of Israel, and sectarian writings describing the beliefs and religious practices of the people who authored them. While this sect has been identified with many previously known groups, it is certain that it was a Jewish sect with a rather strict construction of Jewish law, a strong messianic belief, and a cohesive communal organization. Most scholars have identified this sect with the Essenes, and some recent scholarship has pointed to relations of the group with the Sadducean priestly sect.

The excavation of the site of Qumran has yielded a building complex that virtually all archaeologists agree served the community that collected the scrolls and hid them in the caves. This site was occupied from sometime after 134 BCE through 68 CE and includes a complex water system that fed a variety of installations, including ritual baths, as well as rooms for public assembly and dining. Most scholars therefore judged these facilities to have served a group such as that described in the sectarian scrolls found in the nearby caves.

Samaria Papyri

In 1962, bedouin located two caves at Wadi ed-Daliyeh, northeast of Jericho, that yielded Samarian legal papyri from the fourth century BCE, clay bullae, coins, and signet rings. Roman coins of the early second century CE and later remains from the Arabic and Mameluke periods were also located. The Samaria Papyri, as the documents from this site have been termed, testify to the legal usages and state of the Aramaic language in the fourth century BCE. Further, these texts have helped reconstruct the history of Samaria in the Persian period.

Bar Kokhba Texts

Beginning in 1951 bedouin unearthed texts and ostraca from caves located along the shore of the Dead Sea at Murabbaʿat, south of Qumran and north of Masada, ranging from the Iron Age to the Byzantine period and including texts written in Hebrew, Aramaic, Nabatean, Greek, Latin, and Arabic. The most important finds were the so-called Bar Kokhba texts, which were brought to the caves by Jewish refugees during the Bar Kokhba Revolt of 132–135 CE. Among them were Jewish, Greek, and Nabatean legal documents. In addition, some ostraca and coins were found. The scroll of the Twelve Minor Prophets found there is extremely significant.

The Israel Department of Antiquities undertook a survey of the caves of Naḥal Ḥever, between Wadi Murabbaʿat and Masada, in 1953. In addition to Chalcolithic potsherds, many remnants of everyday life in the Roman period were uncovered—clothing, shoes, vessels, textiles, knives and other utensils, baskets, keys, bullae, coins, and skulls. Additional documents from the Bar Kokhba period were also found. Legal documents in the possession of a woman named Babatha were written in Nabatean, Aramaic, and Greek. Hebrew land contracts from ʿEin Gedi were another important find, and personal letters from none other than the leader of the revolt of 132–135 CE, Bar Kokhba himself, were found addressed to members of his administration. Another cave, excavated in 1955, and known as the Cave of Horror, contained numerous skeletons of women and children, everyday utensils, and remains of foodstuffs. A further excavation of this cave in 1961 located fragments of a scroll of the Greek text of the Twelve Prophets. Those texts listed as coming from Naḥal Ṣeʾelim actually derive from Naḥal Ḥever. Taken together, this collection of texts gives us a valuable window on life in Judea and the Roman province of Arabia in the second century CE, as well as illuminating the history of Jewish law and the state of the Greek, Hebrew, and Aramaic languages in use at the time.

Masada

In 1955 and 1956, excavations were carried out at Masada by the Hebrew University, the Israel Exploration Society, and the Israel Department of Antiquities. Here were found extensive architectural remains from the Chalcolithic period, the Iron Age, and the time of Herod the Great. The most dramatic evidence concerns the destruction of the site in 73 CE and includes the Roman siege works surrounding the plateau. The site also yielded finds indicative of its occupation by a Roman garrison after 73 and a later Byzantine church. In addition to the remains of the Jewish occupiers of the palace during the revolt against Rome (66–73 CE), including several biblical and a variety of apocryphal-type texts on parchment, there were many coins, more than seven hundred ostraca, and more than twenty documents on papyrus. The Hebrew and Aramaic texts, though few in number, include some of the same texts found at Qumran. This collection contributes to an understanding of the history of the biblical text and to the nature of the groups that revolted against Rome in 66–73 CE.

Khirbet Mird

Khirbet Mird, also called Horqaniah, yielded forty Greek and ten Christian Palestinian Aramaic documents, as well as more than one hundred fifty Arabic papyri from the Byzantine period. These texts were found by bedouin in the ruins of a Byzantine monastery in 1952. This last collection has been given the least attention but is of great importance. It testifies to the religious situation in the last years of Byzantine Palestine. Further, biblical fragments in this collection are valuable witnesses to the Aramaic biblical texts of the time and the state of the Greek Bible. The Arabic papyri also contain much interesting information for social historians.

The Purpose and Design of the *Encyclopedia of the Dead Sea Scrolls*

This work aims to encompass all scholarship on the scrolls to date, making use of the research of many scholars of international reputation. It includes the details of the discovery of the scrolls, a review of the archaeological context in which the scrolls were found, descriptions of the various fragments and scrolls, and a discussion of their contents. The written material and artifacts from each site, the history of the site, and the more general historical context of the texts and other finds are the subjects of the articles. Each article stresses the relevance of the corpus to biblical scholarship, its wider historical significance, and, in the case of the Qumran texts, how it contributes to the reconstruction of the Qumran community through an understanding of sectarian rulings, prayer, and rituals. Discussions emphasize the later impact of the material on Judaism, Christianity, and other related groups. The various articles constitute a reference work that unites the fields of historical geography, archaeology, paleography, biblical studies, history, law, theology, and religious studies.

While there is a vast and ever-growing literature on the sites in the Judean Desert and the material discovered there, the *Encyclopedia of the Dead Sea Scrolls* is the first and only reference work that brings all the information together in one place. It goes far beyond the various extant introductions to the scrolls in two significant ways. First, it provides much more detailed information and greater background material; second, it encompasses all the collections of Judean Desert texts, not just the Qumran scrolls.

Studies of these sites, or at least some of them, are often included in other reference works, the principal concern of which is the Bible or ancient Near Eastern archeology. While our sites are only a minor set of topics in such works and serve as background material in them, they are the primary focus of the *Encyclopedia of the Dead Sea Scrolls.* Consequently, the content and design of the encyclopedia are not driven by the concerns that govern, say, an encyclopedia of the Bible. The material from each of our sites is the heart and soul of what is presented here and what gives structure to the work as a whole. Many biblical and Bible-related topics fall within the purview of the encyclopedia and are treated here, but they are included only when they are relevant to the discoveries in the Judean Desert.

In planning the work, the editors attempted to organize the large amount of information available about the sites and to do so with the aim of making the contents of the encyclopedia accessible to a wide audience. The authors of the articles were carefully selected to write within their areas of specialization, but they wrote their entries with the goal of setting forth the material in such a way that educated readers, clergy, and scholars in related fields will be able to profit from the contributions.

In planning a reference work such as this, there is always a danger that selection of the contributors will reflect the biases of those who organize it. In order to counter this problem, a sincere effort has been made to avoid endorsing any specific views and to include a wide spectrum of opinion. The many contributors represent the diversity and international character of modern scholarship on the material. They also come from varied religious backgrounds and have been given the freedom to write their articles in ways that reflect their own scholarly points of view. The *Encyclopedia of the Dead Sea Scrolls* advances no unified ideology about the ancient sites and finds. Authors were given scope descriptions of the articles that they were invited to contribute, but they were also encouraged, as experts in their particular fields, to develop their articles according to their best judgment. The initial descriptions provided were meant only as guides, not as restrictions on the contributors' thinking. The authors were assigned word limits for their articles; these ranged from about five hundred to five thousand words.

The origins of the encyclopedia can be traced to a suggestion by Eric Meyers, editor in chief of *The Oxford Encyclopedia of Archaeology in the Near East*, that Oxford University Press be approached about publishing an encyclopedia of the Dead Sea Scrolls. Lawrence H. Schiffman of New York University was the first to be involved in the project, and Marlene Schiffman drafted a proposal that was submitted to and accepted by Oxford University Press in 1992. James C. VanderKam of the University of Notre Dame was invited to become the other editor in chief along with Schiffman. The next step in the planning was to appoint an editorial board of experts in a range of subdisciplines connected with scrolls research. Those who served in this capacity are George J. Brooke of the University of Manchester, John J. Collins of the University of Chicago, Florentino García Martínez of the University of Groningen, Eileen M. Schuller of McMaster University, Emanuel Tov of the Hebrew University, and Eugene Ulrich of the University of Notre Dame.

The editors in chief and the editorial board also were assisted by Ephraim Stern of the Hebrew University, who served as a consultant primarily in archaeological matters, and by four advisers, Joseph A. Fitzmyer, the late Jonas C. Greenfield, Émile Puech, and Hartmut Stegemann, who contributed their expertise both in the initial definition of articles and their scope and, once the articles began to be submitted, on specific topics and problem areas.

In the complicated process of planning the hundreds of articles to be included in the encyclopedia, the editors and advisers began with eight conceptual categories that were broken down into smaller areas and eventually into individual topics under each. Those conceptual categories are:

1. places and archaeological sites (both places of general importance in the period covered and archaeological sites with written remains)
2. material remains (the architectural and artifactual material from the sites included in the work)
3. written materials discovered in the Judean Desert
4. related ancient texts (Jewish, Christian, and other)
5. history (political, military, religious, and economic)
6. beliefs, institutions, and practices
7. figures (individuals in ancient history)
8. scrolls research (research, publication, preservation, tools, methods, important individuals, and institutions).

Naturally, the articles are arranged in alphabetical order, but these were the categories that allowed the editors to plan the work and to make the coverage as systematic, detailed, and efficient as possible. Each member of the editorial board was assigned to supervise articles within certain conceptual categories and fields of interest.

How to Use the *Encyclopedia of the Dead Sea Scrolls*

Articles are titled in such a way that the reader will have access to information from several different angles, whether from the textual or artifactual side or through more general articles. In addition, articles have been included that provide necessary background material for understanding the Judean Desert texts and the research that has centered on them. There are three kinds of headwords, or article titles: independent entries, composite entries, and blind entries.

1. *Independent entries* were selected as the most likely term or phrase under which a person would look for an article on the particular subject.
2. *Composite entries* are headings under which groups of related topics are gathered in order to provide appropriate contexts for comparison and to make comparison more convenient. For example, the composite article on Qumran consists of two headings, Archaeology and Written Materials. Each is an independent article written by a different author, and each has its own bibliography.
3. *Blind entries* appear in their appropriate, alphabetical place and simply refer the reader to the independent or composite entry under which the subject is treated. This reference allows the reader who searches for an article under a particular title to find the information needed, even if the article is actually presented under a different title.

The articles are also supplied with a series of cross-references to related material. In this way the diverse contents of the encyclopedia are made more readily available. Readers will find that they can begin reading articles of a more general character and be guided by the cross-references and the index to progressively more detailed and more technical articles, which when read in such a fashion will make sense to people with different levels of previous knowledge.

The editors and authors of the encyclopedia are aware of the changing nomenclature and numeration of texts that plagues the still-developing field of Dead Sea Scrolls studies. Some texts are known by more than one name, as is the case with the text originally called the Zadokite Fragments, now more generally known as the Damascus Document. In some cases, there are both English and Hebrew names, so that the Hodayot Scroll is the Hebrew designation for the Thanksgiving Scroll. A few texts also have French or Arabic titles. We have developed a standardized set of titles for the encyclopedia and carefully followed the numeration assigned by the International Team for the Publication of the Dead Sea Scrolls. Occasionally, however, we had no choice but to deviate somewhat and use differing titles. Further, as research has been progressing, and since the texts were being published while this encyclopedia was being prepared, changes were taking place in some aspects of numeration of texts, fragments, columns, and lines. We have made every attempt to update the encyclopedia to the greatest extent possible in this regard, but users may occasionally find that recent publications have adopted titles or numerations that are different from those here. For example, we have attempted to follow the new numbering system for columns and lines in the Hodayot Scroll, but most readers will find that the editions and translations available still follow the old system. The simple fact is that because this field is making so much progress, we could not avoid such problems short of delaying the appearance of the encyclopedia for years. We trust that readers will concur in our decision to proceed as we have and to live with these minor inconsistencies and inconveniences for the sake of disseminating the progress that has made in the study of this field.

The articles are meant to appraise the reader of the latest scholarship on the topics treated. To that end they include bibliographies, the lengths of which are normally proportional to the importance of the topic. These bibliographies are not meant to be exhaustive but to inform the reader of the basic studies, such as where a text was published or where the standard archaeological report(s) about a site are to be found. The bibliographies, which are less complete for publications in languages other than English, are in many cases annotated by the authors of the articles in order to increase their usefulness.

At the end of the encyclopedia is a comprehensive topical index and a synoptic outline of the contents, as well as a list of the Judean Desert texts according to the official numeration, specifying their titles as used in the encyclopedia which occasionally differ from those in the official publications.

At the turn of the millennium, it is especially appropriate that the *Encyclopedia of the Dead Sea Scrolls* make its appearance, renewing our acquaintance with texts that were composed over two millennia ago. With access to all of the Dead Sea Scrolls, there has been a flowering of interest and research, and more people than ever are involved in scrolls scholarship and study, in academic, religious and informal circles. The volumes of this encyclopedia are meant to establish a reciprocal relationship between the synthesis of scholarship assembled herein and future study, summarizing past research and stimulating further investigation. Scholars in other fields will be able to find here material relating to their interests and to share in the significant progress that has been made since the early years of Qumran Studies in which scholars were occupied so heavily with piecing together the fragments. Here at last, there is an attempt to bring together into one place all the critical texts, introductions, articles, and studies into one widely accessible work for scholars in the field, students of related fields, clergy, and interested lay persons. This encyclopedia sums up all the wonderful accomplishments of recent years and points to the tasks still awaiting future efforts in this exciting field. In the process, it fully delineates the Dead Sea Scrolls as a field of study in its own right with great contributions to make to the history of Western civilization and to the modern quest for an understanding of our collective human past.

ACKNOWLEDGMENTS We have been blessed with the support and encouragement of numerous people throughout this project, which could never have been completed without the cooperation of a large group of dedicated editors, consultants, and authors, and the members of the staff of Oxford University Press. Our area editors—George J. Brooke, John J. Collins, Florentino García Martínez, Eileen M. Schuller, Emanuel Tov, and Eugene Ulrich—have contributed unstintingly to the planning and execution of the encyclopedia. We benefited greatly from the advice of Ephraim Stern, Joseph A. Fitzmyer, Émile Puech, Hartmut Stegemann, and Jonas C. Greenfield (of blessed memory). The friendship and collegial cooperation of these leaders in the Dead Sea Scrolls field have made our task much easier and certainly more pleasant. It is an honor to work with them.

The members of the staff of Oxford University Press have worked with us at every stage to bring this project from dream to reality, even when the overcommitment of scrolls scholars to the publication of the scrolls and to the celebration of the fiftieth anniversary of their discovery always seemed to slow us down. They also lived with the changing details which resulted from the steady publication of the texts and from the progress the field has been experiencing while we were putting this encyclopedia together. Claude Conyers, then editorial director of the scholarly reference division of Oxford University Press, initially expressed confidence in this project and oversaw its development and progress until his retirement in 1998. It was from him that we learned how to plan the intellectual structure of an encyclopedia, and his patient prodding and sage advice were major factors in the success of the project. He was succeeded by Karen Casey, whose administrative talents were a major factor in bringing the encyclopedia to publication. Marion Osmun led us through the planning of the entries and the organization of the project. Scott Lenz and Jeffrey Edelstein handled much of the administrative editorial work, and their help is greatly appreciated. The project came together under the editorial guidance of project editor Kathy Moreau, who managed the editorial and organizational tasks.

One of the great pleasures of being in the field of Dead Sea Scrolls studies has been working closely with students who constitute the next generation of scholars. We have been privileged to involve in this project a number of our students in various bibliographic and editorial tasks. We express our appreciation to Eric Mason, Kelley Coblenz Bautch, Tobin Rachford, and Monica Brady of the University of Notre Dame, and to Michael Rand and Kevin Osterloh of New York University.

On a personal note, the editors have had an international and ecumenical experience and have learned a great deal from both writing articles and editing the work of colleagues. The encyclopedia has helped us to keep abreast of all the new research in areas other than our specific interests. We hope that it serves as a stimulus to further discoveries in the wealth of materials left to us from the Judean Desert in Late Antiquity.

New York, New York
Notre Dame, Indiana
December 1999

L.H.S.
J.C.V.

A

AARON. The figure of Aaron, his ancestry, and his rise to priestly prominence is treated rather tersely in the Bible. Though he stems from the lineage of Levi (Levi, Kohath, Amram, Aaron; *Ex.* 6.16–20), he must be distinguished from the secondary class of temple servants who also come from that tribe and more properly bear the name *Levites*. [*See* Levi.] The account of Aaron's elevation over his Levitical brothers is not recorded in the Bible, but we do have the Korah story, in which his prominent role amid the other Levites is contested (*Nm.* 16–17); his investiture as chief priest also is described (*Ex.* 29).

When we turn to the Second Temple sources found at Qumran we find a surprising dearth of interest in the figure of Aaron as a narrative character. Though the name *Aaron* occurs numerous times, it almost always refers to the category of Aaronic priests, rarely to the biblical person himself. Many of the more important references of this kind are to be found in the Rule of the Community from cave 1 (1QS). [*See* Rule of the Community.] Here we find the community itself broken down into two composite parts: the "Sons of Aaron" and the "majority of the members of the Community." There is some variation here as to how the priestly element is named. Alongside the title "Sons of Aaron" (1QS v.21) one also can find "Sons of Zadok" (1QS v.2, v.9), and simply "the priests" (1QS vi.19). These different titles for the priestly element of the sect must be understood as synonymous. [*See* Zadok, Sons of.]

Interest in the role of the Aaronic priests also is prominent in the War Scroll (1QM vii.10, xvii.2); here the biblical role of Aaron in raising up the militia of Israel (*Nm.* 1ff.) is drawn upon. In Temple Scroll[a] (11Q19) there is frequent reference to Aaron as the person to whom Israel's sacrificial legislation was first entrusted (11Q19 xxii.5, xxxiv.13). [*See* Temple Scroll.] Finally, one must note the interest the scrolls show in a messianic figure from the line of Aaron, nearly always paired with a messianic figure from the line of David (e.g., Damascus Document, CD xix.11). [*See* Damascus Document; Messiahs.]

This lack of interest in Aaron's narrative character is counterbalanced by the very significant attention the figure of Levi receives in Second Temple sources (cf. *Jub.* 30–32; *Testament of Levi*; Aramaic Levi [1Q21], Aaronic Text A (bis) [4Q540], and Aaronic Text A [4Q541]; *Heb.* 7.9). [*See* Levi, Aramaic; Testaments.] Nearly all of Aaron's priestly attributes (and their anticipated return) are funneled into stories about Aaron's ancestor Levi. Indeed, in much of this literature the relationship envisioned for the restoration of a royal and priestly office is expressed through the figures of Judah and Levi.

Alongside the question of the restoration of an Aaronic messiah is the very complicated question of what constituted authentic Aaronic lineage. This question cannot be addressed without some consideration of the figure of Zadok. [*See* Zadok.] The biblical picture portrays Zadok as one of David's two leading priests (*2 Sm.* 8.17). Eventually Zadok emerged as the leading priest in Jerusalem, once the Temple was built. The foundation story of Zadok's elevation is to be found in *1 Samuel* 2.27–36. Here the house of Eli, the other major priestly family in David's kingdom, is condemned to lose its priestly status. The historical origins of Zadok and his genealogical relationship to Aaron are contested issues in biblical scholarship. But however that historical problem is to be solved, the Bible's own solution is clear: Zadok is given an Aaronic ancestry (*1 Chr.* 5.27–34). The position of Zadok reaches extreme heights in the *Book of Ezekiel* (44.15–26). For this prophet claimed that, as a result of the priestly errors that led to the exile, only priests of Zadokite descent would be qualified for service at the altar.

The question of how these biblical categories of priestly superiority functioned in the Second Temple period is very complicated. On one level, the name of one particular priestly party was transformed into the title of a much broader political constituency in the affairs of this Second Commonwealth, that of the Sadducees (the Hebrew term for Sadducees is derived from the name *Zadok*). [*See* Sadducees.] Yet on another level, the figure of Zadok continued to serve as the person from whom all legitimate high priests would trace their ancestry. This is made quite clear by Josephus (*Jewish Antiquities* 11.347) when he notes that the ancestry of the Oniad family could be traced back to the last high priest mentioned in the Hebrew scriptures, Jaddua (*Neh.* 12.22). Much of the political intrigue related to currying favor with the Seleucid rulers in Syria involved rival claims to priestly power. [*See* Seleucids.]

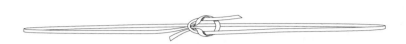

The Dead Sea Scrolls themselves make ample use of the polemical biblical texts about Aaron and Zadok. But frequently these allusions do not presume the specific polemical import of their biblical origins. Aaron and Zadok function as ciphers for the sect as a whole. For example, *2 Samuel* 2.35, which points toward the rise of the house of Zadok and the "sure house" he would build for Israel, is alluded to in the Damascus Document (CD iii.19) when the writer describes the sect itself as the "sure house" God has built within Israel. In a more obvious fashion, the text of *Ezekiel* 44.15 is quoted verbatim just a few lines later in the Damascus Document (CD iii.21–iv.4). Here again the priestly titles "Levite," "Sons of Aaron," and "Sons of Zadok" are given metaphoric value. The Aaronic priests are the "penitents of Israel"; the Levites are those who "accompanied" (a wordplay on "Levi" in Hebrew) those "penitents" into exile; and the Zadokites are the "chosen ones of Israel."

The ability to trace a clear and pure Aaronic pedigree back to the specific figure of Zadok was an especially important matter in the second century BCE. With the rise of Antiochus IV Epiphanes and the large-scale persecution of those who desired to remain true to the demands of the Torah, there arose yearnings for a return to more ancient and customary forms of religious observance. [*See* Antiochus IV Epiphanes.] Among those desires was the restoration of the true Aaronic priests and their proper Zadokite leader. Hopes must have been raised quite high when the Maccabees appeared on the scene, restored a modicum of independence, and, most importantly, rededicated the Temple. Yet those hopes were quickly dashed when the first two Hasmonean rulers, Jonathan (152 BCE) and Simon (143 BCE), both laid claim to the office of the high priest (*1 Mc.* 14.41), a claim that could only be viewed as illegitimate by religious traditionalists. [*See* Jonathan; Simon.] Most likely it was the traditionalists of this stripe who formed the backbone of the group at Qumran; the history traced above accounts for the strong asseveration of the priestly role of Aaron and Zadok in the Qumran sect's documents of self-definition.

BIBLIOGRAPHY

Collins, John J. *The Scepter and the Star*. New York, 1995. An excellent discussion of Aaron, his messianic role in the scrolls, and the relationship of this role to the testamentary literature of Levi.

Licht, Jacob. *Megillat ha-Serakhim*. Jerusalem, 1965. The best commentary on the Rule of the Community ever produced. It contains several excellent summary discussions of Aaronic priesthood at Qumran.

Schiffman, Lawrence H. *The Halakhah at Qumran*. Leiden, 1975. Fine discussion of the problem of Zadok.

Schiffman, Lawrence H. *Reclaiming the Dead Sea Scrolls: The History of Judaism, the Background of Christianity, the Lost Library at Qumran*. Philadelphia, 1994. Schiffman makes a strong argument for the relationship of Sadducees to the sect at Qumran.

VanderKam, J. *The Dead Sea Scrolls Today*. Grand Rapids, Mich., 1994. Argues against Schiffman's claim of Sadducean origin and reasserts the classic Essene hypothesis.

GARY A. ANDERSON

ABRAHAM (Heb., *Avraham*) or Abram (Heb., *Avram*) is the name of the progenitor of the Hebrew people. At first he is called Abram (*Gn.* 11.26–27, 12.1), perhaps meaning "exalted father." (This form of the name occurs some sixty-one times in the Hebrew scriptures, all but two of them in *Genesis*.) Later his name becomes Abraham (*Gn.* 17.5), meaning "father of a multitude." (This form of the name occurs some 175 times in the Hebrew scriptures). Abraham's story is told in *Genesis* 12–25. Among the many noteworthy episodes in his life were his calling (*Gn.* 12.1–9), his battle with the tribal kings (*Gn.* 14), his covenant with God (*Gn.* 15), and his willingness to sacrifice his son Isaac (*Gn.* 22). His most surprising failing was his fear and deceit with regard to his wife Sarah (with Pharaoh, *Gn.* 12.10–20; with Abimelech, *Gn.* 20). In subsequent books of the Hebrew scriptures Abraham, the "friend of God" (*Is.* 41.8; *2 Chr.* 20.7; cf. *Jas.* 2.23), emerges as the most venerable of all Jewish figures (*Jos.* 24.2–3; *Is.* 29.22, 51.2; *Ezek.* 33.24; *Mi.* 7.20; *Sir.* 44.19–23). It was this great respect for Abraham that led to much of the interpretation and embellishment found in later Jewish and Christian sources.

Abraham is often mentioned as the ideal example of Jewish piety and orthodoxy; his election is a subject of great interest in many of these sources. Whereas Abraham's virtues and accomplishments are often greatly magnified, his failings are explained or even justified. Although by no means a major character in the Dead Sea Scrolls, Abraham does figure significantly in a few passages.

The name *Abraham* (or *Abram*) is found some eighty times (including restorations) in the Dead Sea Scrolls published thus far. About one third of these occurrences are found in the Genesis Apocryphon (where he is called Abram). These appearances in the Scrolls cohere with other early Jewish traditions.

Abraham in the Dead Sea Scrolls. There are three extended treatments of the figure of Abraham among the Dead Sea Scrolls. One is found in the Commentary on Genesis A (4Q252), a fragmentary Hebrew scroll; another is in the Genesis Apocryphon (1QapGen, 1Q20), a poorly preserved Aramaic scroll; and the third is found in Pseudo-Jubilees[a] (4Q225), a paraphrase of portions of *Genesis* and *Exodus*. All three scrolls are similar to *Jubilees* in that they are dependent on *Genesis*, yet they take certain liberties with the text. This is especially so in the Genesis Apocryphon.

Commentary on Genesis A. According to the Commentary on Genesis A (4Q252), God "gave the land to Abraham, his beloved. Terah was one hundred and [for]ty years old when he left Ur of the Chaldees and came to Haran; and Ab[ram was se]venty years old. Abram lived five years in Haran, and afterwards [Abram] went [to] the land of Canaan" (4Q252 1.ii.8–10). At this point the text breaks off, making it impossible to discern what interpretive slant, if any, might have been given to the story. Column iii (6–7) treats briefly the events of Genesis 22: "Abraham stretched out his hand . . . your only . . . ," but again too little of the scroll has been preserved.

Genesis Apocryphon. Columns ii, xii, and xix–xxii of the Genesis Apocryphon (1QapGen) are substantially preserved. Column xviii, which is lost, probably introduced Abram, who becomes the principal figure in the remainder of the scroll. Columns i–xvii had dealt with the ancient patriarchs, leading up to Noah. The surviving portion of column xix begins with Abram's building an altar and confessing that God is eternal. Sometime later, famine forces Abram to travel to Egypt. But shortly after entering the country, he has a dream: "And I, Abram, had a dream in the night of my entering into the land of Egypt and I saw in my dream [that there wa]s a cedar, and a date palm (which was) [very beautif]ul; and some men came intending to cut down and uproot the cedar but leave the date palm by itself. Now the date palm remonstrated and said, 'Do not cut down the cedar, for we are both from one family.' So the cedar was spared with the help of the date palm, and [it was] not [cut down]" (xix.14–16). Perhaps attempting to mitigate the patriarch's deception, the dream, in which Abram is the cedar and Sarah the date palm, implies that Abram's life was in danger and that Abram and Sarah (or Sarai) were blood relatives. The story goes on to tell of Pharaoh Zoan's infatuation with the beautiful Sarah and the adventure to which this leads. There is nothing about the Genesis Apocryphon that suggests that it was composed at Qumran or by an Essene.

Pseudo-Jubilees[a]. Perhaps the most interesting paraphrase of the story of Abraham is found in Pseudo-Jubilees[a] (4Q225). Most of the extant material is concerned with "[the covenant that] was made with Abraham" (1.4). According to this scroll, God tested Abraham in *Genesis* 22 because of "Prince Mastemah" (2.i.9–11). The introduction of Mastemah, who is Satan (he is called Belial in 2.ii.14), coheres with Jewish interpretive lore found elsewhere (cf. *Jub.* 17.15–16; B.T., *San.* 89b) and probably owes its origin to *Job* 1.6–12.

Abraham in Jewish Piety and Theology. There are several important aspects of Abraham's life that became foundational for later Jewish ideas regarding piety. Abraham's faith, moreover, is viewed as exemplary and informs later Jewish and Christian doctrine concerning righteousness and justification (being declared righteous or guiltless by God).

Conversion of Abraham. The Damascus Document presents Abraham as the ideal convert and supreme example of a proselyte. This is because "Abraham did not walk in (the stubbornness of his heart), but was counted as a friend for keeping the precepts of God and not following the desire of his spirit. And he passed (the precepts) on to Isaac and to Jacob" (CD iii.2–3). Appropriately, the true faith may be called the "covenant of Abraham" (CD xii.11; cf. 4Q225 1.4). This idea is followed up later in the Damascus Document. "And on the day which a man undertakes to be converted to the Law of Moses, the angel of hostility will depart from him if he fulfills his promises. For this reason Abraham circumcised himself on the day of his knowledge" (CD xvi.4–6). The scrolls offer other references to the life and example of Abraham, but the fragmentary condition of the materials makes it impossible to tell what points are being made.

God's election of Abraham. Several explanations in Jewish lore and legend are given for God's election of Abraham (*Jub.* 12.12–22; Josephus, *Jewish Antiquities* 1.7.1, 154–157; Pseudo-Philo, *Biblical Antiquities,* 6.1–8.3; *Ap. Ab.* 8.1–6). All these traditions, which introduce fire in various ways, are ultimately based on a wordplay involving "Ur of the Chaldees." Vocalized differently, it can mean "fire of the Chaldees" (cf. *Tg. Neofiti Gn.* 11.31).

The Dead Sea Scrolls may shed light on Paul's emphasis on faith and how it is supported by what is said of Abraham in *Genesis* 15.1–6. According to Paul, "one is not justified by works of the Law [*erga nomou*] but through faith . . . thus, Abraham 'believed [*episteusen*] God, and it was reckoned to him as righteousness [*elogisthē autō eis dikaiosunēn*]'" (*Gal.* 2.16, 3.6). According to Pseudo-Jubilees[b] (4Q226), "Abraham was recognized as faithful to [G]o[d . . .] that he might be accepted. And the Lord blessed [him . . .]" (7.1–2). The word translated as "faithful" is from the same root as the word "believe" in *Genesis* 15.6. Pseudo-Jubilees[b] is saying that Abraham's faith led to his acceptance. Here we seem to have agreement with Paul's position. But in Miqtsat Maʿasei ha-Torah (MMT; 4Q394–399) a different understanding of *Genesis* 15.6 is expressed, possibly very similar to the one opposed by Paul. Near the end of the letter the author writes: "Now, we have written to you some of the works of the Law, those which we determined would be beneficial for you and your people . . . . And it will be reckoned to you as righteousness, in that you have done what is right and good before him, to your own benefit and to that of Israel" (4Q398 2.ii.2–3, 7–8 = 4Q399 1.i.10–11; 1.ii.4–5). The words "will be reckoned to you as righteousness" echo *Genesis* 15.6. Yet it is performing the "works of the Law" (*maʿasei ha-torah* = *erga [tou] nomou* in Greek) that will lead to one's being reckoned as righteous before God. This concept may parallel *1 Maccabees* 2.51–52: "and remember the works [*ta erga*] of the fathers, which they did in their time, and received great honor and an eternal name. Was not Abraham found faithful [*pistos*] when tempted, and it was reckoned to him as righteousness?" These materials, especially as seen in MMT, probably reflect the theology against which Paul so vigorously argues in *Galatians*.

[*See also* Genesis Apocryphon; Miqtsat Maʿasei ha-Torah; *and* Sarah.]

BIBLIOGRAPHY

Evans, Craig A. "The Genesis Apocryphon and the Rewritten Bible." *Revue de Qumrân* 13 (1988), 153–165. Compares the rewriting techniques of the Genesis Apocryphon with those of other writings, such as *Jubilees* and Josephus's *Jewish Antiquities*.

Fitzmyer, Joseph A. *The Genesis Apocryphon of Qumran Cave I: A Commentary*. Biblica et Orientalia, 2d. ed., vol. 18a. Rome 1966. Critical study; provides Aramaic text, English translation, and notes on the Genesis Apocryphon.

Kuiper, G. J. "A Study of the Relationship between *A Genesis Apocryphon* and the Pentateuchal Targumim in Genesis 14.1–12." In *In memoriam Paul Kahle*, edited by Matthew Black and Georg Fohrer, pp. 149–161. Beihefte zur Zeitschrift für die alttestamentliche Wissenschaft, 103. Berlin, 1968.

Lehman, Manfred R. "1Q Genesis Apocryphon in the Light of the Targumim and Midrashim." *Revue de Qumrân* 1 (1958–1958), 249–263.

Millard, Alan R. "Abraham." In *Anchor Bible Dictionary*, edited by David Noel Freedman, vol. 1, pp. 35–41. New York, 1992. Helpful overview of major issues.

Qimron, Elisha. "Towards a New Edition of the Genesis Apocryphon." *Journal for the Study of the Pseudepigrapha* 10 (1992), 11–18. Observes that new photographic techniques will enable scholars to produce a better and fuller edition of the Genesis Apocryphon.

Steiner, Richard C. "The Heading of the *Book of the Words of Noah* on a Fragment of the Genesis Apocryphon: New Light on a 'Lost' Work." *Dead Sea Discoveries* 2 (1995), 66–71. Discusses the words *ktb mly nwḥ*, concluding that they should be read "the book of the words of Noah."

van Seters, John. *Abraham in History and Tradition*. New Haven, 1975. Scholarly study of the stories of Abraham in *Genesis*.

Wacholder, Ben Zion. "How Long Did Abram Stay in Egypt?: A Study in Hellenistic, Qumran, and Rabbinic Chronology." *Hebrew Union College Annual* 35 (1964), 43–56.

CRAIG A. EVANS

ABSALOM, HOUSE OF. The only reference to the phrase *house of Absalom* in the Dead Sea Scrolls appears in Pesher Habakkuk (1QpHab v.9), where its position in a dispute between two religious leaders is described as follows:

> Why are you staring, traitors, but are silent when a wicked man swallows up one more righteous than he? [*Hb*. 1.13b). Its interpretation concerns the House of Absalom and the men of its council, who kept silent at the reproach of the Teacher of Righteousness and did not help him against the Man of the Lie, who rejected the Law in the midst of their whole con[gregation].
> (1QpHab v.8–12)

The author of the *pesher* is disappointed by the attitude of the house of Absalom toward the Teacher of Righteousness, this group or family's behavior appearing to result in its alignment with the policies of the man of the Lie, or the Liar.

The historical identification of the house of Absalom and the meaning of the title are open to dispute. William H. Brownlee (1948) and those who agree with his position see here a cryptic reference to a religious party given the name of Absalom who rebelled against his own father, thereby symbolizing its unfaithfulness to the Teacher of Righteousness. By contrast, David N. Freedman (1949) and those who follow him see this as a reference to an actual historic figure named Absalom and his family or partisans. They suggest a historical family such as that mentioned in *1 Maccabees* 11.70 and 13.11; a historical figure such as the one mentioned in *2 Maccabees* 11.17 (Freedman); or even a later figure to whom Josephus refers in *Jewish Antiquities* (14.4. 4 [71]; Dupont-Sommer, 1964). The latter set of hypothetical identifications is not likely, and nominal identifications of specific persons are not customary in the scrolls. Conversely, in light of the terminology used in the scrolls, Brownlee's suggestion may be supported in the following way: Terms such as *house* (*bayit*) and the like are used in the scrolls to symbolize a definite group or party (Flusser, 1965). For example, we find the title, the *house of Judah*, and similar titles, referring to the Yaḥad (Qumran) community (Pesher Habakkuk, 1QpHab viii.1; CD iv.11; xx.10.13; cf. 1QS v.6; viii.5, 9; ix.6) and the *house of Peleg*, another cryptic name given to an opposing group (Damascus Document, CD xx.22–24; Pesher Nahum, 4Q169 3–4.iv.1), in which the name *Peleg* is used to symbolize a schism (cf. *Gn*. 10.25, *Jub*. 8.8).

This suggestion is supported by another term, the *men of their council* (*ʿetsah*), used here to define the members of the house of Absalom rather than their followers. The term *ʿetsah* is used in the Hebrew scriptures for "counsel," but in the Qumran scrolls it acquires the additional meaning of "council": either "the council of the Yaḥad" (1QpHab xii.4; Rule of the Community, 1QS vi.14) and its members (1QpHab ix.10; Pesher Psalms[a], 4Q171 1–2.ii.18; Rule of the Congregation, 1Q28a i.3; Hodayot[a], 1QH vi.11, 13), or the council of their opponents, the "seekers after smooth things" (4Q169 3–4.iii.7–8).

Various identifications have been suggested for the historical event mentioned here, most of them related to the historical identification of the Man of the Lie and his partisans. One must nevertheless recognize that all identifications are only theoretical. Groups such as the house of Absalom or the house of Peleg, which separated from their parent body and attached themselves to others, may have been one of the socioreligious consequences of the dispute among religious leaders concerning which halakhic precepts should prevail in Israel. The existence of such groups reflects the dangerous situation of schism among the followers of the Teacher of Righteousness (cf. 1QpHab ii.1–4; CD xix.32–35; xx.10–12, 22–26) and within Second Temple Judaism as a whole.

[*See also* Peleg, House of; Pesher Habakkuk; *and* Teacher of Righteousness.]

BIBLIOGRAPHY

Brownlee, William H. "The Jerusalem Habakkuk Scroll." *Bulletin of the American Schools of Oriental Research* 112 (1948), 8–18. See especially page 17, n.36.

Brownlee, William H. *The Midrash Pesher of Habakkuk*, pp. 91–98. Society of Biblical Literature, Monograph Series, 24. Missoula, Mont., 1979.

Dupont-Sommer, André. *The Essene Writings from Qumran*. English version of *Les écrits esséniens découverts près de la Mer Morte*, 3d. ed., 1964. Translated by G. Vermes. Gloucester, Mass., 1973.

Flusser, D. "The Dead Sea Sect and Pre-Pauline Christianity." In *Aspects of the Dead Sea Scrolls*, edited by Chaim Rabin and Yigael Yadin. Scripta Hierosolymitana, 4, pp. 215–266. Jerusalem, 1965. See especially pages 233ff.

Freedman, David N. "The 'House of Absalom' in the Habakkuk Scroll." *Bulletin of the American Schools of Oriental Research* 114 (1949), 11–12.

Nitzan, Bilha. *Pesher Habakkuk. A Scroll from the Wilderness of Judea (1QpHab)*, pp. 52–53, 166–167 (Hebrew). Jerusalem, 1986.

Worrell, J. "'Counsel' or 'Council' at Qumran?" *Vetus Testamentum* 20 (1970), 65–74.

BILHA NITZAN

Translated from Hebrew by Jonathan Chipman

ACTS OF A GREEK KING. The scroll fragment Acts of a Greek King (4Q248), previously also Pseudohistory, is now called Historical Text. It is approximately 8 by 8 centimeters in size and ought to be dated paleographically to between 30 and 1 BCE. Stitching holes on the right margin testify to the existence of at least one sheet to the right of our column. It is written in late Second Commonwealth Hebrew. Our fragment preserves nine of ten lines, all dealing with events connected with King Antiochus IV Epiphanes: his first invasion of Egypt, the first siege of Alexandria, selling Egyptian land, and the capture of Jerusalem and the conquest of Cyprus. An interesting fact mentioned here but not recorded in other sources is that the Seleucid king sold Egyptian land for lucre. This agrees closely with the data about Antiochus's rapacity. It also explains a difficult verse in *Daniel* concerning this monarch: "and he shall distribute land for a price" (*Dn.* 11.39). A passage in Acts of a Greek King, "And when the shattering of the power of the ho[ly] people [comes to an end] then all these things [be fulfilled]," is identical to *Daniel* 12.7. Acts of a Greek King refers to events that took place between 170 and 168 BCE, and its author does not know yet of the persecutions of 167 BCE. The *Book of Daniel*, which has ample references to the persecutions (*Dn.* 7.25, 11.30–33, and 12.1) and refers also to the victory over Xerxes, king of Armenia, which took place in 166 BCE, could not have been edited before this year. Therefore our text should be regarded as one of the sources of *Daniel*.

BIBLIOGRAPHY

Broshi, Magen, and Esther Eshel. "The Greek King Is Antiochus IV (4Q248)." *Journal of Jewish Studies* 48 (1997), 120–129.

MAGEN BROSHI

ACTS OF THE APOSTLES is the second volume of a two-volume work, *Luke-Acts*, which relates the story of the early church in ways that are strikingly similar to the structure and practices of the Qumran community.

Acts of the Apostles. The two treatises, *Luke* and *Acts*, relate the story of Jesus and the early church. Although there is no manuscript evidence that the two ever circulated together in antiquity and there are differences between them, factors such as the use of the double preface (*Lk.* 1.1–4, primary preface; *Acts* 1.1–2, secondary preface), the unified narrative, and intertexual connections (e.g., *Acts* 6.14 appears to have been in mind when the author wrote the trial scene in *Lk.* 22.54–71; cf. *Mk.* 14.53–65, especially 58 and *Mt.* 26.57–68, especially 61) suggest that the two were planned as one work. A third generation Christian who is distinct from Luke, the sometime traveling companion of Paul, probably composed the work in the last twenty years of the first century CE. The empire-wide perspective of the work makes the identification of the locale for the author and first readers uncertain.

Acts begins where *Luke* began and ended: Jerusalem. The author provides a rough table of contents indicating the geographical expansion of Christianity out from Jerusalem. Jesus says to the apostles (1.8), "You will be my witness in Jerusalem" (2.1–8.3), "in all Judea and Samaria" (8.4–12.25), "and to the ends of the earth" (13.1–28.31). The work thus chronicles Christianity's expansion from Jerusalem to Rome or from an exclusively Jewish base to a predominately gentile base. The work attempts to provide Christians with a new sense of identity as members of an ethnically and geographically diverse movement. One important consequence of this orientation is the conscious effort to Hellenize earlier traditions in an attempt to make the story reflect the historical reality of Christianity's presence in the wider world. Another is the replacement of the apocalypticism of earliest Christianity, which contained the expectation of an imminent parousia, with a new form of salvation history, which offers the Spirit in the present and situates the parousia in the distant future. At the same time, the text goes to great lengths to anchor this movement in Judaism.

Acts and the Dead Sea Scrolls. If we consider *Acts* from the perspective of its terminus, we find that the text stands at a considerable remove from the world of the Judean Desert, especially from the Covenanters at Qumran. On the other hand, if we consider *Acts* from the viewpoint of the effort to anchor the movement in Judaism and to depict Jewish Christianity as the earliest form of Christianity, there are three broad areas of agreement.

The first has to do with the concept and structure of the movements. *Acts* used the word "Way" (Greek, *hodos*) both absolutely (9.2; 19.9, 23; 22.4; 24.22) and with modifiers (16.17; 18.25, 26) to describe Christianity as a "sect" within Judaism (24.14). The closest analogy is the use of "way" (Hebrew, *derekh*) in the Dead Sea Scrolls where it appears both absolutely (e.g., in the Rule of the Community, 1QS ix.17–18; x.21; CD i.13; ii.6; and the War Scroll, 1QM xiv.7) and with modifiers (e.g., CD xx.18) to mean the strict observance of the law in contrast to deviation from the law to another "way" (1QS viii.13–15; cf. also iii.17–21). Both probably took their inspiration from *Isaiah* 40.3 in order to establish self-identity, but developed it with different nuances. Similar analogies exist for specific units within the movements. Both *Acts* and the Dead Sea Scrolls use the word "many" as a technical term to denote the full assembly (*Acts* 6.2, 5; 15.12, 30 and 1QS vi.7, 7–9, 11–18 etc.). Each community has a group of twelve: in *Acts* they are the apostles (6.2; cf. 1.15–26) and at Qumran twelve laymen, along with three priests, constitute the community council (1QS viii.1–4). Apparently each group found the number of the twelve tribes of Israel to be important for their identification as a reconstituted Israel, although again with different applications. Finally, each has a similar leader: *Acts* knows of "bishops" (*episkopoi*) who shepherd the flock (*Acts* 20.28–35) just as the Damascus Document compares the inspector (*mevaqqer*) of the camp to a shepherd (CD xiii.7–13) who functions in very similar ways.

The second area of agreement comprises the common practices of the two groups. Both practiced communal meals, which had some eschatological significance, although the seating arrangements at Qumran would have been foreign to early Christians (*Acts* 2.26; 1QS vi.4–6; Rule of the Congregation [1Q28a] ii.11–22). Both practiced baptism and associated it with repentance, cleansing from sins, and entry into the community (e.g., *Acts* 2.38, 41 and 1QSa iii.6–9), although Christians understood it as an unrepeatable act while the residents of Qumran practiced it not only in initiation (1QS iii.4–12, v.13–14) but also as an ablution (CD x.10–13). The most striking practice that they shared is the community of goods (*Acts* 2.44–45; 4.32–35 along with 4.36–37; 5.1–11 and 1QS i.11–13, v.2, vi.16–25). The Dead Sea Scrolls may help to explain a famous conundrum in *Acts* where there is a tension between the sharing of goods in the narratives (4.36–27; 5.1–11) and the common treasury in the summaries (2.44–45; 4.32–35). Although the residents of Qumran surrendered their property to the congregation, they did maintain some control (1QS vii.6–7, 27–28). It is thus possible to have a common treasury without surrendering all personal control of the property.

The third area is the exegesis of scripture (a Greek text for *Acts* and generally a Hebrew text for Qumran). *Acts* sometimes uses a text that is closer to the text circulating at Qumran than to the underlying Masoretic Text or the Septuagint (e.g., *Am.* 9.11 in *Acts* 15.16 and Florilegium [4Q174] i.12). Like the Qumran Essenes, the Christian author understands the text eschatologically, though the Christian writer looks to the past and present while the Essenes look to the present and future (e.g., *Acts* 2.17; 3.24; 10.43; and Pesher Habakkuk [1QpHab]). They share a similar hermeneutic including the use of the same introductory formulae (e.g., *Acts* 1.20, 23.5, and CD xi.20; *Acts* 7.42, 13.33, and 4Q174 i.2). In some cases they use the same texts, although their interpretations vary (see table 1). Furthermore, for years New Testament scholars have thought that New Testament authors used *testimonia* in their expositions of the sacred scriptures such as we find in the speeches of *Acts*. They based this position on phenomena such as incorrect attributions of quotations and composite citations. What they lacked was a pre-Christian example. We now have examples in Testimonia (4Q175) and Florilegium (4Q174).

The Essenes and Jewish Christianity in Acts. These similarities have led some to look for a direct connection between the Essenes (following the view that the Qumran sect is to be identified with the Essenes of Greco-Roman sources) and Jewish Christians as they are presented in *Acts*. Perhaps the most interesting of these hypotheses has been the argument that one group of Jewish Christians sprang directly from the Essenes. This argument requires the postulation of an Essene community in southwest Jerusalem during the first century (cf. *The Jewish*

ACTS OF THE APOSTLES. TABLE 1. *Major Texts and Parallels with Dead Sea Scrolls and* Acts.

SACRED TEXT	DEAD SEA SCROLLS	*ACTS*
Deuteronomy 18.15, 18–19	1QS ix.11; 4Q175 5–8	7.37; 3.22–23
Amos 5.26–27	CD vii.14–15	7.43
Amos 9.11	CD vii.16; 4Q174 i.12	15.16
Habakkuk 1.5	1QpHab [i.17]–ii.10	13.41

War 5.145) at the site where a small second-century Christian community is known to have resided (cf. Epiphanius, *On Measures and Weights*, 14). The primary link between the two is the common practice of the sharing of goods. As interesting as this hypothesis is, it rests on a very tenuous tie between a postulated group of Essenes and later Christians who, if they were similar to the Jewish Christians of *Acts* or later Ebionites, were very different in many important ways. It also requires that the summary statements in *Acts* reflect actual practices. It is more likely that they are authorial generalizations based on the traditions in the surrounding narratives. They make the same claim for the early Jerusalem community that Philo and Josephus did for the Essenes, and this claim may have been made with the Essenes in mind.

Others have argued that the Hellenists in *Acts* 6.1–8.3 who opposed the Temple were related to the Essenes. This argument is also problematic on several grounds. The speech of Stephen in *Acts* 7.2–53 is an authorial composition, which certainly presents the author's perspective, but may or may not provide information about the earlier Hellenists. Even if it does, the grounds for opposition are quite different: the Essenes opposed the Jerusalem Temple as ritually polluted; the Hellenists of *Acts* opposed the Temple as the sole locus of God's presence. Similarly, some have suggested that the priests who are reported to have converted to Christianity were Essenes (*Acts* 6.7). However, the text calls them priests in a context devoted to the Jerusalem Temple. It is difficult to imagine how they could have been Essenes. [*See* Essenes.]

Along a different line, some have argued that there are New Testament manuscripts among the unclassified fragments found in Cave 7, including a small fragment of *Acts* 27.38 (7Q6 frag. 2). The problem with this identification is that there are only three unambiguous letters in the published photograph and three more reconstructed letters in the published edition, hardly enough to warrant a firm identification. Even if the case is eventually made for the identification of some of the other fragments with New Testament texts, the identification of 7Q6 fragment 2 will remain questionable at best since the fragment is so small and Cave 7 contains copies of texts other than the New Testament. The manuscript evidence at Khirbet Mird is a different story. Here we have a fragment from *Luke* (3.1, 3–4) and two manuscripts of *Acts*: a fifth-century Greek uncial (0244 [*Acts* 11.29–12.1 and 12.2–5]) and a sixth-century Christian-Palestinian Aramaic manuscript (*Acts* cpa [*Acts* 10.26b–29, 32c–41a]). These, however, come from a Christian monastery founded in 492 CE. [*See* Mark, Gospel of; Mird, Khirbet.]

Our present evidence then does not warrant us to believe that there was a direct connection between the Essenes and Jewish Christianity or *Acts*. It is far more likely that both movements sprang from a common milieu of which they are the best attested representatives.

BIBLIOGRAPHY

Black, Matthew. *The Scrolls and Christian Origins: Studies in the Jewish Background of the New Testament*. London, 1961. One of the most important discussions of parallels.

Braun, Herbert. *Qumran und das Neue Testament*. 2 vols. Tübingen, 1966. Volume 1 works through the parallels systematically in the order of the text of *Acts*; volume 2 deals with the material thematically.

Brooke, George J. *Exegesis at Qumran: 4QFlorilegium in Its Jewish Context*. Journal for the Study of the Old Testament Supplement, 29. Sheffield, 1985. Important discussion of exegesis at Qumran with discussions of parallels in *Acts*.

Capper, Brian J. "Community of Goods in the Early Jerusalem Church." *Aufstieg und Niedergang der römischen Welt* 2.26.2 (1995), 1730–1774. Discussion of the community of goods in Jerusalem. See also the German article by R. Raisner on pp. 1775–1922, which provides a comprehensive bibliography.

Conzelmann, Hans. *Acts of the Apostles*. Philadelphia, 1987. Rich in history of parallels between religions, including references to the scrolls.

Fitzmyer, Joseph A. *The Semitic Background of the New Testament: Combined Edition of Essays on the Semitic Background of the New Testament and A Wandering Aramean; Collected Aramaic Essays*. Biblical Resource Series. Grand Rapids, Mich., 1997. The most important collection of essays addressing a large number of similarities.

Haenchen, Ernst. *The Acts of the Apostles: A Commentary*. Philadelphia, 1971. Although dated, still the standard critical commentary.

Mayer, Bernhard, ed. *Christen und Christliches in Qumran?* Eichstätter Studien, 32. Regensburg, 1992. The most important recent collection of essays on direct ties between Jewish Christians and Qumran.

Sterling, Gregory E. "'Athletes of Virtue': An Analysis of the Summaries in Acts (2:41–47; 4:32–35; 5:12–16)." *Journal of Biblical Literature* 113/114 (1994), 679–696. Attempts to situate the summaries within the larger tradition of presenting religious/philosophical groups to the Greco-Roman world.

Waard, J. de. *A Comparative Study of the Old Testament Text in the Dead Sea Scrolls and in the New Testament*. Studies on the Texts of the Desert of Judah, 4. Leiden, 1966. A study of the type of text cited in *Acts*.

GREGORY E. STERLING

ADAM. In the literature and religion of the Hebrew scriptures, Adam plays almost no role. The story of his transgression and eviction from the garden of Eden is recounted in a mere two chapters and never addressed again. One can understand the figure of Adam only in light of the wider narrative of the primeval history of *Genesis* 1–11, which documents the slow but inexorable decline of humanity that provides the background for the call of Abraham (*Gn*. 12.1).

Second Temple sources are divided as to where they wish to locate the moment of man's fall within this primeval history. One set of sources locates that moment in the sin of Adam; another, in the myth of the "Fall of the Watchers" (*Gn.* 6.1–4). In the former category we would include the writings of Paul, *4 Ezra*, and, perhaps, Philo. If one is willing to include sources beyond the Second Temple period, one could also mention Gnostic materials and the *Life of Adam and Eve*.

The other manner of depicting origins of evil within the world is through the myth of the "Fall of the Watchers." This myth can be found in *1 Enoch*, *Jubilees*, and the Dead Sea Scrolls. The Enoch literature is the best place to turn for the full elaboration of the tale. But the Dead Sea Scrolls allude to it in an indirect manner. In the Damascus Document (CD ii.14–21), the writer summarizes all the most important moments in human history up to the rise of the sect. Significantly, the section begins with the "Fall of the Watchers"; Adam's sin is passed over in silence.

One very prominent problem in assessing the role of Adam in the Dead Sea Scrolls is the ambiguity of the term *adam* in Hebrew. The term can mean "man," or "mankind" in general, or it can specify the figure of Adam. In the Hebrew scriptures the former meaning is far more common than the latter. We would expect and, in fact, do find a similar situation in the Dead Sea Scrolls. For example, in the Damascus Document (CD x.8) the diminution of human longevity—a clear result of the sins of Noah's generation (*Gn*. 6.1–4)—is ascribed to the sin of "man." The Hebrew term used in this text is *adam*, but the historical figure of *Genesis* 2–3 is certainly not intended. All translations of the text rightly opt for the more standard meaning in Hebrew, "man," that is, "humanity." In other, more ambiguous cases, it is probably wiser to opt for the banal translation of "man" than to presume the rarer meaning "Adam." Thus, in the Damascus Document (CD iii.20), just after the failures and achievements of all human creation have been narrated and Adam has been conspicuously passed over in silence, the writer concludes by asserting: "those who remain steadfast will gain eternal life, and all the glory of man will be theirs." In light of the overall context of the passage, the translation of "man" is preferred. Yet, many scholars prefer to translate the line "the glory of Adam."

It is a well-known fact among scholars that the scrolls found at Qumran can be divided into two groups: those authored by the members of the sect (most likely at the site of Qumran) and those authored by other groups. The latter texts were ones that the sectarians clearly respected or showed some interest in, but they do not necessarily represent, in every detail, the thought of the sect itself. In light of this, it is certainly worth noting that several of these nonsectarian texts show substantial interest in the biblical figure of Adam. As Esther Chazon (1997) has shown, three of these texts, Paraphrase of Genesis-Exodus (4Q422), Words of the Luminaries[a] (4Q504), and Sapiential Work A[e] (4Q423), exhibit numerous parallels, though the closest ones are between the first two texts. In particular, these first two texts evidence an interest in Adam's rule over all creation, a theme that shows an interpretive decision to regard *Genesis* 1–3 as one complete narrative; a tendency to base this rule on the diction of *Psalms* 8.7 ("you set him as ruler over the works of your hands") instead of *Genesis* 1.27; and an interest in correlating the sin of Adam with that of the generation of Noah, especially in regard to the presence of an "evil inclination."

The most interesting text among these three is the Words of the Luminaries[a], because this text was a set of prayers for each day of the week. Thus, the fall of Adam would have been read in a weekly fashion as a part of this liturgy, and it certainly would have become a central topos in the imagination of those who recited it in prayer.

Finally, I should mention the important text published by Joseph Baumgarten (1994), Serekh Damascus (4Q265). This text shows a very close relationship to *Jubilees* in the matter of Adam and Eve's process of purification after childbirth. In *Jubilees*, Adam and Eve must wait forty and eighty days, respectively, in order to purify themselves, prior to entering the garden of Eden. This period of time is drawn from *Leviticus* 12, a legal text about purification after childbirth. A parallel of this level of specificity can come about only as a result of some form of very close contact and/or borrowing. This is hardly surprising, however, in light of the close filiation between the Qumran material and the *Book of Jubilees*. Perhaps it is significant and worth noting that although *Jubilees* ascribes halakhic import to the life and times of Adam and Eve, it shows little interest in highlighting their glorious state prior to the sin or the sin itself; there is little more than the bare biblical narrative. The sectarian writings from Qumran seem to share this more pedestrian evaluation of Adam and his sin.

In the New Testament, in *Romans* 5.12–21, Paul uses the Adam-Christ typology to proclaim that, as sin and condemnation came through Adam, life came through Christ. In *1 Cor.* 15.45–47 Adam is the ancestor through whom all have a physical body; Christ's resurrection guarantees that believers will rise with a spiritual body (*1 Cor*. 15.22, 15.45). In *1 Timothy* 2.13–14, Adam's creation, prior to that of Eve, who sinned first, grounds the authority of men and denies it to women (cf. *1 Cor.* 11.9).

Among the Nag Hammadi texts, an *Apocalypse of Adam* appears. Adam, in the year of his death, tells Seth about his life (creation and fall), about a special race who have knowledge of God, about attempts to destroy them in the Flood, and about the coming of the Illuminator.

Extrabiblical traditions about Adam also figure in rabbinic texts. Some concern his nature or appearance when first created (he was androgynous [*Gn. Rab.* 8.1]; he was a fully developed man of twenty years [*Gn. Rab.* 14.7]). Although angels questioned whether he should be created, once he was made, they had to be commanded not to worship him (*Gn. Rab.* 8.10). There were discussions about which laws were revealed to Adam; it was recognized that he was not born circumcised and that he had not been commanded to keep the Sabbath (*Gn. Rab.* 11.6, 24.5). He is also said to have learned the power of repentance from Cain and to have recited *Psalm* 92 (*Gn. Rab.* 22.13).

BIBLIOGRAPHY

Anderson, G. "The Status of the Torah in the Pre-Sinaitic Period: St. Paul's Epistle to the Romans." In *Biblical Perspectives: Early Use and Interpretation of the Bible in Light of the Dead Sea Scrolls*, edited by Michael E. Stone and Esther Chazon, pp. 1–23. Proceedings of the First International Symposium of the Orion Center for the Study of the Dead Sea Scrolls and Associated Literature, 12–14 May 1996. Leiden, 1998. A consideration of how Adam figures in Romans 5.12ff. and how this representation is related to legal thought at Qumran.

Baumgarten, J. "Purification after Childbirth and the Sacred Garden in 4Q265 and *Jubilees*." In *New Qumran Texts and Studies: Proceedings of the First Meeting of the International Organization for Qumran Studies, Paris, 1992*, edited by George J. Brooke with Florentino García Martínez, pp. 3–10. Studies on the Texts of the Desert of Judah, 15. Leiden, 1994. Discusses the relationship of this fragment to *Jubilees*.

Chazon, E. "The Creation and Fall of Adam in the Dead Sea Scrolls." In *The Book of Genesis in Jewish and Oriental Christian Interpretation*, edited by J. Frishman and L. van Rompay. Louvain, 1997. Fine discussion of the figure of Adam in nonsectarian texts from Qumran.

Collins, J. "The Creation of Humankind and the Origin of Sin. The Interpretation of *Genesis* 2–3 in *Ben Sira* and Qumran," forthcoming. Similar in some respects to Chazon's article but extends it more broadly to the book of *Ben Sira*.

Levison, John R. *Portraits of Adam in Early Judaism: From Sirach to 2 Baruch.* Journal for the Study of the Pseudepigrapha Supplement Series, 1. Sheffield, 1988. General survey of Second Temple Jewish literature on the figure of Adam.

Vermes, G. "Genesis 1–3 in Post-Biblical Hebrew and Aramaic Literature before the Mishnah." *Journal of Jewish Studies* 43 (1992), 221–225. Fine survey of recent literature and discoveries.

Stone, Michael E. *A History of the Literature of Adam and Eve.* Atlanta, 1992. A survey of literature about the Adam books (*Life of Adam and Eve*) and their purported origins in the Second Temple period. A good methodological discussion about the difficulties in dating this type of literature.

GARY A. ANDERSON

AEMILIUS SCAURUS, MARCUS, first-century BCE Roman aristocrat; Pompey's quaestor during the annexation of Syria and conquest of Judea, also Pompey's brother-in-law and husband of Pompey's (divorced) third wife; first Roman governor of Syria. According to Josephus (*Jewish Antiquities* 14.29–33; *The Jewish War* 1.127–130), while Pompey was still in Armenia campaigning against Tigranes he sent Scaurus ahead to Syria. That would place Scaurus's mission no later than 66 BCE, but the rest of Josephus's account seems to indicate that it is instead to be placed in 65 BCE. Perhaps Josephus meant to refer to Mithradates VI of Eupator Pontus, whose death he indeed reports somewhat later (*Antiquities* 14.53). When Scaurus discovered that Damascus had already been taken by Roman forces, he proceeded down to Judea. He arrived during one of the critical junctures in the struggle between Hyrcanus II and Aristobulus II, the two sons of King Alexander Jannaeus (died 76 BCE) and Queen Shelamzion Alexandra (died 67 BCE): Hyrcanus, with the assistance of Nabatean forces, was besieging Aristobulus in Jerusalem. Both brothers appealed to Scaurus for assistance, employing various arguments and bribes, and Scaurus decided in favor of Aristobulus. An ultimatum from Scaurus forced the Nabateans to lift their siege, and then, after Scaurus withdrew to Damascus, Aristobulus inflicted a major defeat on his enemies.

At this point there is some disruption in Josephus's narrative in *Jewish Antiquities,* apparently due to the juxtaposition of material from Strabo (cited explicitly) and another source. Perhaps as a result, the next stage of the story (*Antiquities*, 14.34–38; *The Jewish War* 1.131–132) is less than clear. Josephus reports that when Pompey himself arrived in Syria (64 BCE), both Hyrcanus and Aristobulus sent envoys to him, and Nicodemus, Aristobulus's envoy, for some reason saw fit to accuse Scaurus of having accepted a bribe from Aristobulus. Naturally, this strange move is said to have made Scaurus turn against Aristobulus, and, indeed, we may surmise that it played some role in Pompey's decision to favor Hyrcanus. Certainly Scaurus's continued influential position, in Pompey's eyes, is shown by the fact that when Pompey left the region after the conquest of Jerusalem (in the summer of 63), Scaurus remained, as the governor of Syria (*Antiquities* 14.79; Appian, *Syrian Wars* 51). In this capacity, Scaurus undertook a campaign against the Nabateans, but upon failing to take Petra he came to a financial arrangement with them and withdrew (*Antiquities* 14.80–81; *The Jewish War* 1.159). After he was replaced in Syria by Marcius Philippus (c.61 BCE; Appian, *Syrian Wars* 51), Scaurus returned to Rome. His subsequent career began with a succession of high positions (aedile, praetor, governor of Sardinia) but ended in exile after he was convicted of corruption.

A fragmentary text from Qumran apparently refers to Scaurus and tantalizingly suggests a supplement to the story summarized above. Calendrical Document C^{d} from Cave 4 at Qumran (4Q324a) seems to read *hrg ʾmlyws* at the ends of lines 4 and 8 of fragment 2. In both cases, the name appears fairly clearly, the word *hrg* less so. *ʾMlyws* is most probably a transcription of Aemilius. Since other fragments of this text refer to Hyrcanus, Aristobulus, and Shelamzion, it is reasonable to infer that "Aemilius," too, is a historical character of the seventies and sixties of the first century BCE. Scaurus is our only candidate, although it is remarkable that this Qumran text refers to him by his nomen, in contrast to the Greek and Latin texts, which prefer his cognomen scaurus. As for *hrg*, it apparently means that on both of the dates mentioned, which were in the late summer (end of the sixth month and fifteenth of the seventh, that is, the first day of the festival of Sukkot), Scaurus was responsible for the killing of some important Jew or Jews. It seems most likely that both references are to the killing of more than one individual, for if only one individual had been killed, the fact that the event was listed in the calendar would indicate that he was quite important—but in that case his name would have been expected. There seems to be no space for such a name in the text.

Our sources do not supply a reference to any killing, much less massacre, perpetrated by Scaurus. We may assume that he participated in Pompey's campaign against Aristobulus II and in the conquest of Jerusalem, but we do not know why any massacres in that context would have been associated with his name and not with Pompey's. Of course, we know very little about these events, and any suggestion here is necessarily speculative. As Michael Wise has already proposed, nevertheless, it is attractive to imagine some connection between our text and the conundrum mentioned above: Why would Aristobulus's agent accuse Scaurus of having accepted the bribe from Aristobulus? It is likely that this reflects a falling-out between the two, and it is just possible that our text alludes to events in that process. Wise suggests, furthermore, that memorializing such a (perhaps perfidious) massacre by Scaurus might indicate Qumran support for Aristobulus. However, it may be no more than just another item in a general Qumran picture of Roman cruelty, such as that painted more fully in Pesher Habakkuk (1QpHab ii–vi).

[*See also* Alexander Jannaeus; Hasmoneans; Pesher Habakkuk; Rome; *and* Shelamzion Alexandra.]

BIBLIOGRAPHY

Klebs, Elimar. "Aemilius (141)." In *Paulys Real-encyclopädie der classischen Altertumswissenschaft,* vol. 1. Halbband 1 (1893), cols. 588–590.

Milik, J. T. *Ten Years of Discovery in the Wilderness of Judaea.* Studies in Biblical Theology, 26. London, 1959. See page 73 for short account of the Calendrical Document.

Schürer, Emil. *The History of the Jewish People in the Age of Jesus Christ, 175 B.C.–A.D. 135,* vol. 1. English ed. by Geza Vermes and Fergus Millar. Edinburgh, 1973. See pages 236–245 for Judean history of the period.

Shatzman, Israel. *Senatorial Wealth and Roman Politics,* Collection Latomus, 142. Brussels, 1975. See pages 290–292 on Scaurus.

Wise, Michael O. "An Annalistic Calendar from Qumran." In *Methods of Investigation of the Dead Sea Scrolls and the Khirbet Qumran Site: Present Realities and Future Prospects,* edited by Michael O. Wise et al. Annals of the New York Academy of Sciences, 722, pp. 389–408. New York, 1994. This paper, which offers a full text and translation of 4Q322–324c, as well as historical commentary, appeared in a fuller version in Wise's *Thunder in Gemini: And Other Essays on the History, Language, and Literature of Second Temple Palestine,* pp. 186–221. Journal for the Study of the Pseudepigrapha, Supplement Series, 15. Sheffield, 1994.

DANIEL R. SCHWARTZ

AENEID. A fragment with a line from the *Aeneid*, the sonorous Roman epic and "principal secular book of the Western World" (Knight, 1958, p. 23), was found on top of Masada near fragments of the Bible, the principal religious book of the Western world.

Publius Vergilius Maro (70–19 BCE), after composing his *Eclogues* (or *Bucolics*) in 37 BCE and *Georgics* in 30 BCE, worked for the remaining decade or so of his life on composing the *Aeneid*. Based on the *Iliad* and the *Odyssey*, it tells the story of the heroic Trojan warrior and paragon of moral virtues, Aeneas, son of Anchises and Venus, who, despite all obstacles and with the help of the gods, reaches Italy and prepares the way for the might and grandeur of Rome.

The small papyrus fragment, Virgil's *Aeneid* (recto; Mas721r), was found in Locus 1039 and bears the inventory number 1039-210. On the recto is part of a line that contained *Aeneid* 4.9, while on the verso is a similar fragmentary line with three words presumably from another poet (Mas721v). It is inscribed in large and elegant letters characteristic of the Old Roman Cursive script (also called Capital Cursive), with parallels to scripts in the Latin papyri from Egypt and the Roman fort at Vindolanda in North Britain (Cotton and Geiger, 1989, pp. 28–29). It was found alongside various scraps of other Latin and Greek papyri as well as biblical and religious fragments (Cotton and Geiger, 1989, pp. 18–19), and the archaeological, numismatic, and historical indicators point to a date "shortly before Spring of 73 or 74 CE" (Cotton and Geiger, 1989, p. 27). Thus this papyrus "may be the earliest [extant] MS witness to Virgil, and is certainly the earliest that can be dated with any certainty" (Cotton and Geiger, 1989, p. 33). It probably belonged to a soldier in the *Legio X Fretensis* (cf. Josephus, *The Jewish War* 7.5) or its auxiliaries.

The scanty text preserved on the recto, with reconstruction, is:

]NA[ ]OR[ ]RQUAEMESUSP[

[An]na [s]or[o]r quae me susp[ensam insomnia terrent] (*Aen.* 4.9)
= "Anna, my sister, what dreams terrify me and leave me helpless!"

After her great banquet welcoming the storm-tossed Trojans, Queen Dido of Carthage has listened through the night to the lengthy story of Aeneas's escape from Troy and his adventurous travels. As dawn nears, Dido, overcome by Cupid's machinations, begins her passionate speech confiding to her sister the strength of her love.

The editors of the fragment suggest that the papyrus was not part of a roll (Cotton and Geiger, 1989, p. 31), but neither does it appear to be simply a writing exercise (Cotton and Geiger, 1989, pp. 33–34). They see it as an isolated line and thus wonder whether it could be "addressed to someone called Anna," or whether it might "reflect the writer's feelings of horror at what he had witnessed on Masada" (Cotton and Geiger, 1989, p. 34).

It is uncertain whether one should focus on the fragment or the opus. Did the Roman soldier have only a few lines, or Book 4, or the entire *Aeneid*? Was he simply dreaming dactylic hexameter daydreams of his contemporary counterpart for *forma pulcherima* Dido (*Aen.* 1.496)? Or was he a worthy counterpart for his Jewish opponent atop Masada? The fragment invites contemplation of the two scenes at the top and at the foot of that majestic mountain, of soldiers and their books. As the Roman soldier eyed that towering fortress, was he remembering the *altae moenia Romae* (*Aen.* 1.7), confident that his gods would effect the destined victory, despite the resistance from other divine forces, just as they had done for *pius Aeneas* (*Aen.* 6.176)?

BIBLIOGRAPHY

Cotton, Hannah M., and Joseph Geiger, eds. *Masada II: The Yigael Yadin Excavations 1963–1965: Final Reports, The Latin and Greek Documents*. Jerusalem, 1989. The critical edition and photograph of the Masada fragment are on pages 31–35 and plate 1.

Knight, W. F., trans. *Virgil: The Aeneid*, rev. ed. Baltimore, 1958. An English translation with an introduction.

Pharr, Clyde, ed., *Virgil's Aeneid Books I–VI*, rev. ed. Boston, 1964. Latin text and study edition of the epic.

EUGENE ULRICH

AGES OF CREATION. The title *Ages of Creation* was given by the first editor, John M. Allegro, to several Hebrew fragments. [*See biography of Allegro*.] They stem from at least four columns of the original scroll and are copied in a late Herodian formal hand (thus John Strugnell). However, as observed by Strugnell, the title fits only the content of fragment 1 but not that of the remaining fragments. A more suitable title would be the one provided by the work itself (4Q180 1.1): Pesher on the Periods. All together, eight decipherable fragments are assigned to this scroll (Strugnell's corrected number). Four other tiny fragments are hardly readable. The largest and best preserved is fragment 1. It comes from the right section of a column, preserving both the upper and bottom margins, and the upper corner of the right margin. It thus produces the entire height of a column. This column seems to contain the beginning of the work, or at least of a major section, since it opens with a formula introducing the subject: Pesher on the Periods. The *pesher* seems to have been divided into units, marked by blank spaces at the end of each paragraph, as is the practice in many Qumran manuscripts. Such a blank space of a word or two is visible in Ages of Creation (4Q180) 2–3.ii.3. In Ages of Creation (4Q180) 1.6 an entire line was left blank, apparently to mark the end of the introductory section and to indicate a new paragraph.

The first paragraph of Ages of Creation opens with the title, followed by a general description of the subject matter, namely the Periods, as divinely preordained and engraved on the Heavenly Tablets. It is formulated in typical sectarian terminology, especially when introducing the subject in general terms. For instance, Ages of Creation (4Q180) 1.2–3 says: " . . . before he created them he set up their activities." Compare Ages of Creation (4Q180) with 1QHodayot[a] (1QH[a]) i.7 and Damascus Document (CD) ii.7 [*See* Damascus Document; Hodayot.] This description refers to a concept of history as a sequence of precisely defined periods, a concept occurring in other community writings (Rule of the Community, 1QS iii.15 and 23, iv.13; 1QH[a] i.24; Pesher Habakkuk, 1QpHab vii.13) and in ancient Jewish apocalypses (e.g., *Dn.* 9.24–27; the "Animal Apocalypse" [*1 En.* 85–90]; the "Apocalypse of Weeks" [*1 En.* 91.11–17, 93.1–10]) [*See* Pesher Habakkuk; Rule of the Community.] The general description of the Periods concludes with a reference to a sequence or order (the term *serekh* is employed), after which the text breaks off. The following line speaks of "twenty." Given the context of the Periods and the mention of Isaac's birth in the following line (4Q180 1.5), the order may refer to the twenty generations from Adam to Abraham, which represent the first two Periods. Such an explanation accounts for the fact that all the events alluded to in the surviving fragments concern episodes that fall within these two Periods: the sin of the angels (4Q180 1.7–8; see *Gn.* 6.1–4), the change of Abraham's name (4Q180 2–3.i.3–5; see *Gn.* 17.3–5), the visit of the three angels to Abraham (4Q180 2–3.ii.3–4; see *Gn.* 18.2), and the destruction of Sodom and Gomorrah (4Q180 2–3.ii.5–7; see *Gn.* 18.20–21). All these events took place before the birth of Isaac, which marks the beginning of the next series of ten generations.

Following the general first section, the second paragraph (4Q180 1.7–10) introduces a *pesher* "on Azazel and the angels." Mention of the giants in the next line connects the allusion to the episode of the sinful angels who fathered giants by mortal women (*Gn*. 6.1–4). Several aggadic expansions of this biblical episode are known from early Jewish sources, roughly contemporary with the Qumran scrolls, chiefly *1 Enoch* (6–16, 89–90) and *Jubilees* (5, 7.20–25, 10.1–11). One of the main divergencies among these versions concerns the name and character of the sinners' leader. The Ages of Creation identifies the leader of the sinful angels with the demon Azazel. In this it agrees with one of the traditions recorded in *1 Enoch* (8.1–2; 10.4–6; 54.5), but differs from another tradition found in other sections of *1 Enoch*, where the angel Shemiḥazah is mentioned as the leader (6.3–7; 7.1–4; 69.2).

The remaining decipherable fragments 2–3 and 5–6 concern episodes from the life of Abraham. Clearly identifiable are the change of his name (4Q180 2–3.i.3–5; see *Gn*. 17.3–5), the three men who visited Abraham (4Q180 2–3.ii.3–4; see *Gn*. 18.2), and the destruction of Sodom and Gomorrah (4Q180 2–3.ii.5–7; see *Gn*. 18.20–21). This passage also contains an explicit quotation of *Genesis* 18.20–21. Since fragments 2–3 are materially connected and preserve remains of two successive columns, they establish the sequence of the description: first the change of Abraham's name, then the visit of the angels, and finally the destruction of Sodom and Gomorrah. Such an order clearly follows the biblical sequence of episodes as it is told in *Genesis* 17–18. The biblical order of events seems, therefore, to be the underlying structural principle of the *pesher*, as indeed is the case in other contemporary Jewish apocalypses that present early history (the "Apocalypse of Weeks," the "Animal Apocalypse"). [*See* Apocalyptic Texts.] If the biblical sequence is to be maintained, the mention of Mount Zion in Ages of Creation (4Q180) 2–3.ii.1–2 therefore should be linked to an event preceding the angels' visit to Abraham. It may have to do with *Genesis* 13.14–17, where Abraham is promised the land that was not chosen by Lot. That would also account for the mention of Lot in this context (4Q180 2–3.ii.2) and for the fact that the story about the destruction of Sodom and Gomorrah follows directly.

The badly preserved fragments of Ages of Creation 4Q180 5–6 have been placed by most of the editors after fragments 2–3. But these fragments mention Pharaoh (4Q180 5–6.5), which may refer to the earlier sojourn of Abram in Egypt (*Gn*. 12.10–20; see 4Q180 5–6.2–4). If, however, the principle of biblical sequence is to be maintained throughout the *pesher*, fragments 5–6 should precede fragments 2–3 and perhaps be placed at the upper right section of Ages of Creation (4Q180) 2–3.i. It should further be noted that fragment 4, which contains general predestination phraseology, was placed by the first editor at the bottom of fragment 3. However, it does not fit there materially or contextually, and therefore this joining cannot be retained.

Although the extant fragments deal only with episodes related to antediluvian and postdiluvian events, the original work may have included details about other, later periods, perhaps even of the entire historical sequence. Lists of historical events or precedents also occur in other contemporary writings (*Sir*. 16.7–10, *1 Mc*. 2.51–61). A particularly close parallel to the Pesher on the Periods is provided by the "Apocalypse of Weeks" (*1 En*. 93.1–10, 91.11–17), an Aramaic copy of which was found in Cave 4 at Qumran (Enoch[a] [also = Letter of Enoch] 4Q212), and where the entire history is described in terms of periods of *shemiṭot* (units of seven years). [*See* Enoch, Books of.]

The Pesher on the Periods should be considered as belonging to the peculiar literature produced by the Qumran community, since it contains ideas and terminology typical of the community's writings. In fact, the *pesher* presents the Periods within the framework of predestination characteristic of the community's thought (4Q180 1.1–3, 1.3,4,9–10; cf. 1QS iii.15, CD ii.10). Moreover, it may be alluding to the dualism embedded, according to the Qumranites' belief, in the present world structure (see Caquot, 1973, p. 391), since it describes both sinners and righteous. In itself the use of the term *pesher* indicates a sectarian provenance, since the *pesher* is a typical product of the Qumran community. Nevertheless, the Pesher on the Periods is unique in that it introduces comments on a conceptual theme, the Periods, rather than on biblical prophecy, as is the practice in all other extant *pesharim*. This, however, does not prevent the author from citing biblical texts concerning various details in a manner typical of the *pesharim* (4Q180 3–4.i.3–5 quoting *Gn*. 17.3–4; 4Q180 3–4.ii quoting *Gn*. 13.8 and *Gn*. 18.20–21; and 4Q180 5–6.6 quoting *Gn*. 12.17). The *pesher* even seems to employ actual *pesher* formulas, such as *pesher ha-davar* ("the meaning of the matter," 4Q180 2–4.ii.7) or *va-'asher katuv* ("and as for what is written," 4Q180 5–6.5).

Preserved in only one copy, it is difficult to determine whether the *pesher* is an autograph or a copy, yet the Pesher on the Periods falls well within the typical sectarian style and ideology. It may therefore be assumed that it reflects a major ideological teaching of the Qumran community. At the same time the *pesher* betrays a considerable affinity to the worldview espoused by ancient Jewish apocalypses. Such an affinity suggests close links between the two corpora, perhaps even similar origins. This conclusion is corroborated by the fact that a number of works containing apocalypses, such as *Jubilees*, *1 Enoch* and the Aramaic Levi, were also found at Qumran.

What is the relationship between Ages of Creation 4Q180 and 4Q181? In his first edition, Allegro published the two as separate texts, without commenting on the close similarity between lines 4Q180 1.8 and 4Q181 2.2, referring to the birth of giants. [*See* Giants, Book of.] This phenomenon has not yet been satisfactorily explained. For Józef Milik (1972, pp. 112–124) 4Q180 and 4Q181 are two copies of the same work, a work that, in his opinion, dealt with the activities of angels through the Periods. He combined the two texts to create one document, a combination adopted by Émile Puech and J. J. M. Roberts. In Milik's opinion Melchizedek (11Q13) constitutes a third copy of the same work. A connection between 4Q180–181 and Melchizedek should be discarded on material as well as contextual grounds (see Puech, 1987, p. 509). Considerations of a similar nature disprove the proposed identity between 4Q180 and 4Q181 (see Dimant, 1979, pp. 89–91). 4Q180 and 4Q181 each have a distinct subject matter and literary structure and forms. Their material combination, attempted by Milik, is problematic. As for the close parallel line concerning the giants, it is well integrated into the context of 4Q180, whereas it stands out in 4Q181 2. If one of these works was commenting on the other, it was 4Q181 commenting on 4Q180 and not, as suggested by Strugnell, the other way around. Perhaps both refer to a third source, or to a biblical episode well known in the circles of Qumran. 4Q180 and 4Q181 should then be treated as copies of two distinct works.

BIBLIOGRAPHY

Allegro, John M., ed. *Qumran Cave 4, I (4Q158–4Q186)*. Discoveries in the Judaean Desert, 5. Oxford, 1968. See pages 77–79.

Caquot, André. "Hébreu et araméen." *Annuaire de Collége de France* 73 (1973), 389–392.

Dimant, Devorah. "The 'Pesher on the Periods' (4Q180 and 4Q181)." *Israel Oriental Studies* 9 (1979), 77–102.

Milik, Józef Tadeusz. "Milkî-ṣedeq et Milkî-reša' dans les anciens écrits juifs et chrétiens." *Journal of Jewish Studies* 23 (1972), 109–124.

Milik, Józef Tadeusz. *The Books of Enoch: Aramaic Fragments of Qumran Cave 4*. Oxford, 1976. See pages 248–252.

Puech, Émile. "Notes sur le manuscrit de 11QMelkisédek." *Revue de Qumrân* 12 (1987), 508–509.

Puech, Émile. *La Croyance des esséniens de la vie future immortalite, resurrection, vie eternelle? Histoire d'un croyance dons le judaisme ancien*. Études bibliques, n. 5. 21–22. Paris, 1993. See pages 526–529.

Roberts, J. J. M. "Wicked and Holy (4Q180–4Q181)." In *The Dead Sea Scrolls*, edited by J. H. Charlesworth, vol. 2, pp. 204–213. Tübingen, 1995.

Strugnell, John. "Notes en marge du volume V des 'Discoveries in the Judean Desert of Jordan.'" *Revue de Qumrân* 7 (1970), 252–254.

Weiss, Raphael. "Fragments of a Midrash on Genesis from Qumran Cave 4." *Textus* 7 (1969), 132–134.

DEVORAH DIMANT

AGRICULTURE. The landscape of the Judean Desert consists of four mountainous escarpments descending to the east. The uppermost and lowest escarpments are composed of hard limestone, the middle two of soft chalky hills. The peaks of the Judean Hills stand at altitudes of 800–1,000 meters above sea level; the Dead Sea lies approximately 400 meters below the level of the Mediterranean Sea. The climate of the Judean Desert is unlike that of the other deserts in the Land of Israel, which lie at subtropical latitudes, since the Judean Desert lies on the leeward side of the Judean Hills and constitutes a local desert. The Judean Hills have a Mediterranean climate—rainy in winter and dry in summer. The Judean Desert is therefore suitable for select sheep breeding. This eastern arid region of the Judean Hills consists of three long climatic strips: a Mediterranean climate in the highest part of the Judean Hills, which, in its easternmost border region, receives some 400 millimeters of rain per annum, favoring the cultivation of wheat; a very narrow strip of steppe climate in the middle part of the desert, which receives some 200–300 millimeters of rain per annum, where barley is grown; and an arid climate in most of the lower region, which receives some 100–200 millimeters of rain per annum and is suitable for sheep- and goat-raising.

The Judean Desert never lacks water entirely and—to a lesser extent—food, as the peaks of the Judean Hills receive some 600–700 millimeters of precipitation each winter, which flows rapidly down to the Judean Desert and the Dead Sea, filling cisterns in the chalk hills and potholes in valleys and canyons, and replenishing the groundwater in the desert. A few rather meager springs may be found in the upper slopes of the desert, while some large springs, the most plentiful in the Judean Hills, flow at the foot of the Dead Sea cliffs in the east.

Sheep-Raising. The Judean Desert is the most suitable part of the country for raising sheep and goats, in view of the favorable lithological and climatic conditions, its proximity to Jerusalem and the Temple, and the efficient settlement geography of the Judean Hills. Grazing in the Judean Desert depends on an annual cycle of migration, with the animals moving down from the wooded peaks of the Judean Hills to the Judean Desert and the Dead Sea and back. This cycle assures the animals of a favorable climate and readily available grass, fodder, and water in each season of the year. In winter the shepherds bring their flocks down from the villages in the hills to the Dead Sea coast, where grass grows early in the floodplains of the wadis and springs, nourished by heavy floods and the high temperatures at the Dead Sea, which never freezes. In spring the flocks climb westward to the chalky hills, which support the low, thin grass known in Hebrew as *revi'ah* (B.T., *Ta'an*. 6a), the first vegetation after the rainy season; here the animals can drink water from the many cisterns and potholes in the valleys. In summer the animals feed on stubble in the barley fields, fertilize the fields with their excreta, and drink water from cisterns and potholes in the valleys. Finally, in autumn the livestock graze on wheat stubble and fertilize the wheat fields, also eating acorns from oak trees and sycamore figs (*Am.* 7.14), as well as forest weeds; in addition, the livestock receive straw from the local village farmers and drink spring water.

Flocks were mixed, about three-quarters of the animals being sheep, which produce a variety of dairy products and have tasty meat and soft and pleasant fleece; the remaining quarter consisted of goats, which produce abundant milk but little meat and coarse fleece (*1 Sm.* 25.2). The Israelite flock was improved by importing fat and purebred rams from the rainy, wooded hills of southern Moab (*2 Kgs.* 3.4), as well as purebred rams and goats from the high hills of Edom (*2 Chr.* 17.11).

It is noteworthy that pilgrims to the Jerusalem Temple in the Second Temple period made more than a quarter of a million animal sacrifices on each of the three pilgrimage festivals (Josephus, *The Jewish War* 6.9.2); a small proportion of these animals were reared in the Judean Desert.

Sheep and goats provided a major livelihood for the Israelite peasants living in the hilly areas, thanks to their highly varied range of produce, as one reads in the Babylonian Talmud: "Whoever wishes to become wealthy should keep sheep and goats" (B.T., *Ḥul.* 84b). There was a close economic relationship between the people of the towns at the edge of the Judean Desert and the shepherds. The latter received supplies and fodder from the townspeople while providing them, particularly residents of Jerusalem, with dairy produce. Thanks to the proximity of the animals, these Judean towns developed a wide range of dairy-based industries: from cooked sheep's butter they prepared fat for cooking and frying food; sheep's and goat's flesh was eaten and used as sacrifices at festivities and festivals; the fleece provided the only fabric for winter clothing (the "hairy mantle" of *Zechariah* 13.4 was a warm fur made from sheep's hide); the animals' wool was used to weave rugs, tents (*Ex.* 26.7), and sacks for the transportation of grain; the hides were used to make harnesses and shoes, while the skins of lambs and kids provided vessels for water (*Jgs.* 4.19), oil, and wine (*Jos.* 9.13), as well as the parchment on which the Holy Scriptures were written (J.T., *Meg.* 71d; see Har-El, 1977).

Irrigated Farming. The types of agriculture practiced by the people and sects of the Judean Desert depended primarily on flood crops and irrigated crops in three centers: Jericho, Khirbet Qumran, and ʿEin-Gedi. Irrigated farming in the Judean Desert began in Canaanite Jericho; it continued apace during the years of the monarchy of Judea and Israel and reached its peak in the Hasmonean and Herodian periods.

The main irrigated crops grown in the Jericho region were dates and flax since the Late Bronze Age, and balsam since the Second Temple period.

The date palm and its special uses. The date palm, the Judean Desert's only local fruit tree, provided the local people with an important source of nourishment (B.T., *Ket.* 10b). The palm's fruit, the date, is rich in carbohydrates and easily preserved in arid conditions. Dates may be eaten either fresh and moist or dried; and wine, honey, and an intoxicating liquor can be made from them. The palm grows in nature in oases, where high groundwater is available, and thrives in soil with a salt content of as much as 20 percent. Palm branches can be used to make baskets, mats, and fibers for string, rope, and hats (*Ber. Rab.* 41).

Jericho's dates were already famous in Second Temple times, as stated in the Tosefta (T., *Bik.* 1.5): "No dates may be brought as first fruits, save the dates of Jericho"; and Pliny writes that Judea was famous for its date palms, especially those of Jericho (*Natural History* 13.6.26; 9.44). Josephus states that the groves of Jericho extended for some 21 square kilometers, yielding an abundance of dates, balsam, balm, myrrh, and camphor (*The Jewish War* 1.6.6; 4.8.3). According to data published by the Israel Hydrological Service, the amount of water supplied to Jericho's orchards by the springs of Naḥal Perat (Wadi Qilt), Naʿaran, and ʿEin-Duk reaches some 1,500 cubic meters per hour.

Flax. Flax was grown in the land of Israel in two climatic regions: as a dry farm crop in the Mediterranean region, which produced rather poor-quality flax; and as an irrigated crop in arid regions—Beth-Shean and Jericho—where the yield is of good quality. Flax is associated with Jericho in the biblical story of Rahab, who concealed Joshua's spies under some "stalks of flax" (*Jos.* 2.6).

Examination of linen objects discovered in the Qumran caves has dated them to between 167 BCE and 237 CE, in good agreement with archaeological findings (Yadin, 1957, pp. 53–56, 161–162). Excavating the Cave of the Letters in Naḥal Ḥever in the Judean Desert, Yadin discovered many dyed fabrics from the time of the Bar Kokhba Revolt (132–135 CE; see Yadin, 1993, p. 830). In addition, Stern mentions a dye plant from the First Temple period discovered in excavations at ʿEin-Gedi (Stern, 1979, p. 247).

The blue dye indigotin was extracted from the plant *Isatis*, mentioned in the Mishnah, which grew in the vicinity of Jericho, Zoar, and Beth-Shean; the dye itself is mentioned in the Mishnah and in the Tosefta (*Shevi.* 7.1; *Shab.* 5.9; *Meg.* 4.7; T., *Shab.* 9.7). E. L. Sukenik (Sukenik 1956, p. 7, lines 10–11) cites the description in one of the Dead Sea Scrolls of clothing made of blue, purple, and scarlet yarns.

Balm and balsam. Balm from Gilead is mentioned in the Bible as early as the period of the Patriarchs (*Gn.* 37.25; *Jer.* 8.22, 46.11); it was probably grown in the Sukkot Valley in the Jordan Plain. During the reign of King Solomon it was probably cultivated for use in the Temple, in "the King's Garden" (*Neh.* 3.15) in the Kidron Valley (Har-El, 1987).

Benjamin Mazar, excavating at ʿEin-Gedi, discovered equipment used in the manufacture of perfumes: barrels, bowls, dishes, juglets, balance pans, and *sheqel* weights from the First Temple period (Mazar, 1993, pp. 401–402).

The balsam trees of Jericho are mentioned by Josephus: "The soil [in Jericho] is the most fertile in Judaea and provides abundance of palms and balsam-trees; the stems of the latter are cut with sharp stones and the balsam is collected at the incisions, where it exudes drop by drop" (*The Jewish War* 1.6.5 [Loeb ed.]; see also 4.8.3). Strabo, too, describes the palm groves in a fertile, abundantly watered area near Jericho, near which are also "the palace and the balsam park" (*Geography* 16.2.41 [Loeb ed.]). This palace was excavated by Ehud Netzer, who discovered, north of the palace, a farm, 450,000 square meters in area, fed by aqueducts from Naḥal Perat and the Duk Spring. Netzer believes that the Hasmoneans grew date palms, persimmon, and balsam trees there (Netzer, 1992, pp. 690–691). To the west of the farm, Netzer exposed two large winepresses, which he presumes were used to make date wine and date honey. At the edge of the farm were various workshops with pools, ovens, treading pavements, drainage channels, and a square (12 by 12 meters) building used to store liquids. These industrial installations were used, Netzer believes, to produce balsam from the Hasmonean period to the first half of the first century CE.

An indication of Judean Desert priests' cultivation of perfumes at Jericho and ʿEin-Gedi may be found in the Rule of the Community: "To offer up a pleasing odor . . . and may be received willingly to atone for the land" (Habermann, 1952, p. 8, lines 9–10).

Grain. Jericho was a center of Levites, who served the pilgrims to the Jerusalem Temple. They were organized in accordance with the twenty-four priestly courses (or divisions) from the entire Holy Land, twelve of which stayed at Jericho while the other twelve came to Jerusalem from all over the country (*baraita* in B.T., *Taʿan.* 27a). Cultivation of grain at Jericho, to be brought to the Temple for the offering of the first sheaf, is referred to in the Mishnah: "The men of Jericho did six things: for three they reproved them and for three they did not reprove them. And these are the things for which they did not reprove them: they grafted palms [on the fourteenth of Nisan] the whole day, they did not make the prescribed divisions in the *Shemaʿ*, they reaped and stacked before the *Omer* . . ." (*Pes.* 4.8 [trans. Danby]).

Agriculture at Khirbet Qumran. The members of the Judean Desert sects strictly observed the laws of ritual purity, immersing themselves in water before any prayer or meal. They would not touch bread baked by outsiders and ate only vegetables from their own fields (Josephus, *The Jewish War* 2.8.5, 8). Philo of Alexandria writes of the Essenes: "Some of them labour on the land and others pursue such crafts as co-operate with peace and as benefit themselves and their neighbours" (*Every Good Man Is Free*, chap. XII [Loeb ed.]). The Rule of Community hints at the sect's wheat-growing and sheep-raising: "The time of harvest is in summer, the time of sowing is the time of grass" (Habermann, 1952, p. 10, line 7).

The people of Khirbet Qumran, therefore, cultivated flood crops and irrigated crops.

Flood crops. Evidence of the cultivation of flood crops comes from the Hyrcanium Valley, about 5 kilometers west of Qumran. The valley is 12 kilometers long and 2–3 kilometers wide, providing about 7 million square meters of fertile alluvial soil and loess. The precipitation amounts to approximately 150 millimeters per annum, which floods the valley's fields in winter. Three Iron Age settlements were discovered in the valley itself, and a fortress was built on the hills to the west (Hyrcanium, today Khirbet Mird). It was here, most probably, that the sectarians grew grain and perhaps also legumes and vines.

Irrigated farming. The sect's irrigated fields lay to the east of Qumran, on the Dead Sea shore, where there are several abundant springs: ʿEin-Ghazal (Qumran), some 1.5 kilometers away, with a yield of 420 cubic meters per hour; and ʿEin-Tannur, 2.5 kilometers away, yielding 260 cubic meters per hour. Both springs have a salinity of 2,000–4,000 milligrams chlorine per liter, and their temperatures in the months of December and January are 25–28 degrees Celsius. Channels and pools that were clearly used for agriculture have been discovered at both springs. The sectarians probably grew date palms here, since they can grow in salty water. They may also have grown vegetables, and presumably also bathed in the warm spring water.

Some 3 kilometers southeast of Qumran lie the largest springs of the western Dead Sea shore, ʿEin-Feshkha or ʿEnot Tsuqim. Their total yield reaches some 50 million cubic meters per annum, and their salinity varies from 1,500 to 4,000 milligrams chlorine per liter. Remains similar to those of Khirbet Qumran have been unearthed in the region, dating from the reign of Alexander Jannaeus to the Bar Kokhba Revolt (de Vaux, 1993, pp. 1240–1241). According to de Vaux, this was the site of an agricultural and industrial settlement that served the Qumran congregation, one of its industries being tanning, which needs abundant water. The sectarians spent their time writing scrolls of the law and other scrolls (Yadin, 1957), which must be written, according to Jewish law, on parchment (J.T., *Meg.* 71d).

Agriculture at ʿEin-Gedi. The settlement at ʿEin-Gedi had 1.3 to 1.4 million square meters of land, on hill terraces and the estuaries of the David and ʿArugot (ʿAreijah) streams, which are fed from springs with a yield of 350 cubic meters per hour, and a salinity of 63–78 milligrams per liter. The inhabitants of this oasis raised sheep and goats (as indicated by the name ʿEin-Gedi = Spring of the Kid) and grew dates (another biblical name of the site is "Hazazon-tamar" wherein *tamar* = date; *2 Chr.* 20.2), camphor (*Song* 1.14), balm (Eusebius, *Onomastikon*, s.v. "ʿEin-Gedi"), and vines (*Song Rab.* 1.14). Pliny writes: "On the west side of the Dead Sea, but out of range of the noxious exhalations of the coast, is the solitary tribe of the Essenes, which is remarkable beyond all the other tribes in the whole world . . . and has only palm-trees for company. . . . Lying below the Essenes was formerly the town of Engedi, second only to Jerusalem in the fertility of its land and in its groves of palm-trees . . ." (*Natural History* 5.15.73–74 [Loeb ed.]). Among Yadin's discoveries in the Cave of the Letters were letters that Bar Kokhba had sent to the commander of the ʿEin-Gedi region, urging him to send him wheat, salt, palm branches, citrons, myrtles, and willow branches—all the produce of ʿEin-Gedi and its environs (Yadin, 1993, p. 832).

BIBLIOGRAPHY

de Vaux, Roland. "Qumran, Khirbet, and ʿEin Feshkha." In *The New Encyclopedia of Archaeological Excavations in the Holy Land*, vol. 4, pp. 1235–1241. Jerusalem, 1993.

Habermann, Abraham Meir. *Megillat ha-Serakhim. ʿEdah we-ʿEdut*, (Hebrew). Jerusalem, 1952. Habermann published the text of the Rule of the Community with vowel points and punctuation, as well as the Pesher Habbakuk and the Damascus Covenant. He also identified the relevant biblical verses, adding indexes and notes.

Har-El, Menashe. "Sheep-Raising in Semi-Desert." In *Studies in Settlement Geography* (in Hebrew), pp. 529–538. Jerusalem, 1977. An account of the migrations of sheep in the Judean Desert between the Judean Hills and the Dead Sea, as determined by geographical structure, lithological and climatic conditions, and water sources through the seasons of the year.

Har-El, Menashe. "Water for Purification, Hygiene and Cult at the Temple in Jerusalem." In *Eretz Israel* (in Hebrew), vol. 19, pp. 310–313. Jerusalem, 1987. Water was brought from the Hebron Hills along the ʿEin-ʿArub aqueduct to the Temple of Jerusalem, at a rate of 60 cubic meters per hour, to cleanse the sacrifices, provide drinking water for pilgrims, irrigate the "King's Garden," and clean the public conveniences in Jerusalem, thus preventing outbreaks of disease.

Mazar, Benjamin. "En-Gedi." In *The New Encyclopedia of Archaeological Excavations in the Holy Land*, vol. 2, pp. 399–405. Jerusalem, 1993.

Netzer, Ehud. "Tulul Abu el-ʿAlayiq." In *The New Encyclopedia of Archaeological Excavations in the Holy Land*, vol. 2, pp. 682–691. Jerusalem, 1993.

Stern, Ephraim. "Craft and Industry." In *World History of the Jewish People: The Age of the Monarchies—Culture and Society*. Jerusalem, 1979.

Sukenik, E. L. *The Dead Sea Scrolls of The Hebrew University* (in Hebrew). Jerusalem, 1956.

Yadin, Yigael. *The Message of the Scrolls*. New York, 1957. An account of the discovery of the Dead Sea Scrolls; the excavations at Khirbet Qumran and in the Bar Kokhba archives at Wadi Murabbaʿat; description of the Isaiah and Hodayot scrolls, the *pesharim* of Habbakuk, Psalms, and Nahum, Rule of the Community and the Damascus Covenant, the War of the Sons of Light against the Sons of Darkness, the Genesis Apocryphon and the Copper Scroll, and identifications of the scrolls.

Yadin, Yigael. "Cave of the Letters." In *The New Encyclopedia of Archaeological Excavations in the Holy Land*, vol. 3, pp. 829–832. Jerusalem, 1993.

MENASHE HAR-EL

ALBRIGHT INSTITUTE OF ARCHAEOLOGICAL RESEARCH. *See* American Schools of Oriental Research.

ALEXANDER JANNAEUS, king and high priest of Judea from 103 to 76 BCE. There are those who suppose that he was the first Hasmonean to bestow upon himself the title *king*.

Alexander Jannaeus was the third son of John Hyrcanus I. His Hebrew name was Jonathan as can be learned from his coins, which were inscribed with *King Alexander* written in Greek on one side and *Jonathan High Priest* on the other. During the days of his brother Aristobulus's rule, he was incarcerated. Upon the death of his brother, he was released from prison by his brother's wife Shelamzion Alexandra, who most likely became Alexander Jannaeus's wife following levirate marriage.

The twenty-seven years of Alexander Jannaeus's rule were characterized by never-ending wars. In his conquests Alexander Jannaeus had expanded the borders of Judea and forced his sole rule as a Hellenistic king in every way upon his subjects. Josephus subdivided the rule of Alexander Jannaeus into three periods. During the first period, 103–95 BCE, Alexander Jannaeus completed the conquest of the coast of Palestine from the Carmel to the border of Egypt (excluding Ashkelon) amid fierce struggle in the Hellenistic cities and against their ally Ptolemy Lathyrus, king of Cyprus. Alexander Jannaeus was aided in his battle by Ptolemy's mother, Cleopatra III, queen of Egypt. During this period he began his attempt to conquer Transjordan as well.

The second period, 95–83 BCE, was marked by overt conflict between Alexander Jannaeus and the Pharisees, while he fought the Nabateans in the east and Demetrius III in the north. During these years, Alexander Jannaeus suffered severe defeats from these kings and was compelled to relinquish territories to the Nabateans. In the third period, 83–76 BCE, Alexander Jannaeus resumed his wars in Transjordan upon the cities of the Decapolis; however, when he besieged the city of Ragaba, he fell ill and died.

Events from the era of Alexander Jannaeus's reign are mentioned in three *peshers* from Qumran Cave 4: Pesher Isaiah[a] (4Q161) on the verses from *Isaiah* 10.28–34 describes an enemy advancing from the northeast toward Jerusalem, almost conquering the city, but compelled to retreat due to divine intervention. In light of Josephus's description in *The Jewish War* 1.86 and *Jewish Antiquities* 13.324–355, it appears that this enemy could be identified with Ptolemy Lathyrus. In 103 BCE, Ptolemy waged war against Alexander Jannaeus, conquered the city of Shiḥin in the Upper Galilee, and advanced southward in the direction of Jerusalem. Alexander Jannaeus was defeated, but Ptolemy was forced to retreat from Judea when his mother Cleopatra III embarked with her army for Palestine in order to stop him. In Pesher Isaiah[a], Ptolemy's retreat from Judea was explained as the fulfillment of this prophecy of Isaiah.

Events of 88 BCE are alluded to in Pesher Nahum (4Q169). Here, the Seekers after Smooth Things, identified as the Pharisees, invited Demetrius to Jerusalem. However, the Lord protected Jerusalem, which did not fall into the hands of gentiles from the days of Antiochus until the Roman conquest. Later on, the "Lion of Wrath" hanged the Seekers after Smooth Things (the Pharisees) alive on the tree.

In *The Jewish War* 1.92–98 and *Jewish Antiquities* 13.376–383, Josephus relates that the enemies of Alexander Jannaeus summoned Demetrius to invade Judea and promised him aid. Demetrius invaded Judea, camped near Shechem, and defeated Alexander Jannaeus in battle. After this defeat, the majority of the Jews abandoned the camp of Demetrius, and he returned to Syria. Then, Alexander Jannaeus caught eight hundred of the Jewish leaders who rebelled against him and crucified them in Jerusalem. In light of the similarity between the descriptions of Josephus and Pesher Nahum, it is accepted that the nickname of Alexander Jannaeus in the *pesharim* is the "Lion of Wrath," and that the *pesher* relates to the events of 88 BCE. The proof from Pesher Nahum that Alexander Jannaeus hanged the rebels alive is significant since some scholars had doubted it and were of the opinion that it was invented by Nicolaus of Damascus, historian of Herod the Great and a source for Josephus.

The Temple Scroll (11Q19 lxiv.6–9) states that whoever turns his nation over to a foreigner must be hung on a tree. Thus, Yigael Yadin suggested that Alexander Jannaeus executed his enemies according to the laws appearing in the Temple Scroll, and concluded that Pesher Nahum, therefore, does not criticize Jannaeus. This suggestion cannot be accepted since the author of the *pesher* alluded to *Deuteronomy* 21.23: ("You shall not leave his corpse overnight on the tree but you shall bury it on that day") when he wrote "for the hung on the tree shall be called living. . . ." Hence, he assumed that Alexander Jannaeus violated the law of the Pentateuch in the manner in which he executed the rebels or by not interring those who were hanged immediately. It is possible to see in Pesher Hosea[b] (4Q167) an allusion to the events of 88 BCE as well. In this composition, fragments of a pesher on *Hosea* 5.13–14 were preserved:

> Ephraim saw its illness and Judah its wound and Ephraim went to Assyria and sent for an enemy king, and he will not be capable of curing you or remove your wound. For I will be as a lion to Ephraim and a cub to the house of Judah, I will prey upon and will go and will take, and there will be no savior.

The cub that will harm Ephraim and the house of Judah without a savior is understood by the author of the *pesher* to be speaking of the execution of the rebels by the "Lion of Wrath," designating Alexander Jannaeus.

An additional scroll from Qumran that probably mentioned Alexander Jannaeus is Apocryphal Psalm and Prayer (4Q448). This scroll contains a prayer for the safety of "King Jonathan" and his kingdom. It is probable that the king mentioned in Apocryphal Psalm and Prayer is Alexander Jannaeus, the only king whose Hebrew name was Jonathan. The prayer also thanks the Lord for his having saved King Jonathan on a day of war. On the basis of the description of Josephus, it is possible to suggest three events in which it is feasible to attribute Jonathan's rescue to divine intervention. The first is Alexander Jannaeus's war against Obedas I in 95 BCE, in which the Jewish forces were driven by the Nabatean army into a deep valley and Alexander Jannaeus barely succeeded in escaping. Another possibility is the rescue in 103 BCE when Ptolemy Lathyrus retreated from Jerusalem. The third possibility is the retreat of Demetrius from Jerusalem in 88 BCE. It is also quite possible that the author referred to a different event in the course of Alexander Jannaeus's life for which we have no details.

BIBLIOGRAPHY

Amusin, J. D. "The Reflection of Historical Events of the First Century B.C. in Qumran Commentaries (4Q161, 4Q169, 4Q166)." *Hebrew Union College Annual* 48 (1977), 123–134.

Eshel, E., H. Eshel, and A. Yardeni. "A Qumran Composition Containing Part of Ps 154 and a Prayer for the Welfare of King Jonathan and his Kingdom." *Israel Exploration Journal* 42 (1992), 199–229.

Flusser, D. "Pharisäer, Sadduzäer und Essener im Pescher Nahum." In *Qumran*, edited by K. E. Grozinger et al., pp 121–166. Darmstadt, 1981.
Stern, M. "Judea and Her Neighbors in the Days of Alexander Jannaeus." *Jerusalem Cathedra* 1 (1981), 22–26.
Yadin, Yigael. "Pesher Nahum (4QpNahum) Reconsidered." *Israel Exploration Journal* 21 (1971), 1–12.
Vermes, G. "The So-Called King Jonathan Fragment (4Q448)." *Journal of Jewish Studies* 44 (1993), 294–300.

HANAN ESHEL

ALLEGORY OF THE VINE. *See* Wisdom Texts.

ALLEGRO, JOHN MARCO (1923–1988), scholar, author, and scrolls editor, attended the University of Manchester after wartime service and received a bachelor of arts degree in Oriental Studies (1951) and a master of arts degree (1952). In 1954 he became Lecturer in Comparative Semitic Philology in Manchester, but in 1953 had already been sent to join the editorial team in Jerusalem responsible for the Cave 4 texts. Here he worked, chiefly with Józef Milik, on the texts containing biblical interpretation. [*See biography of Milik*.] Having once been a candidate for the Methodist ministry, his linguistic studies and work on the scrolls nevertheless convinced him that established views on the origins of Christianity were wrong. He concluded that the Qumran community anticipated much of the history and doctrines of early Christianity and his popularizing of these views created friction with his editorial colleagues, culminating in a letter by his colleagues to the *London Times* after a radio broadcast in English in which Allegro claimed to have proof for his conclusions in the texts he was editing. Allegro came to believe that the delay in publication of the Cave 4 materials was due to a policy of suppression, and that he was being victimized.

Allegro succeeded in bringing the Copper Scroll (3Q15) to Manchester for opening, which took place in 1956. [*See* Copper Scroll.] Convinced that this was a genuine treasure list, he suspected his colleagues' claim that it was folkloric arose from dislike of him and from fear of instigating a bedouin treasure hunt. Although its official translation was entrusted to Milik, Allegro finally lost patience with Milik's procrastination and published his own edition (although Milik's preliminary edition did appear before Allegro's publication). Allegro's opinion of the genre of this text is now generally accepted.

Allegro was enthusiastic and enterprising: during the digs at Qumran he made his own small excavation and took numerous photographs of the site and the texts, which are invaluable and have now been published in microfiche form. He later organized other excavations at and near Qumran in the hope of discovering more caves and more texts, possibly some of the Copper Scroll treasures. An indefatigable broadcaster and writer, he made a documentary in 1957 for the British Broadcasting Corporation (broadcast in 1959).

He published most of the Cave 4 texts entrusted to him quickly in journals, and finished his assignment, aided by his Manchester colleague Arnold Anderson, in 1966. The edition has been criticized as careless, and it is clear that Allegro was more interested in the wide dissemination of the contents of the scrolls. By contrast, his more careful colleagues did not publish their texts at all. His resignation from Manchester in 1970 coincided with publication of his notorious book, *The Sacred Mushroom and the Cross*, which identified Christianity as a cult based on a hallucinogenic mushroom, and he later developed this in *The Dead Sea Scrolls and the Christian Myth* (1981) in which he traced what he saw as key ideas and practices in the scrolls into Christianity and gnosticism, arguing for a common mystical tradition (connected with the hallucinogenic mushroom) from which the myth of Jesus arose. In an appendix to this book he published a text (4QTherapeia) that he took to be an account of a healing, but which has since been claimed to be a meaningless writing exercise. Allegro's subsequent writings on the history of Judaism and on religion and medicine evidence a widening of interests. Despite general academic scorn, Allegro has maintained a large popular following (there is a John Allegro Society), and his views on the scrolls and Christianity have been voiced by a small number of scholars and journalists. His personal charm, enthusiasm, range of interests, dislike of academic cliques, and open-mindedness contrast with the widespread image of him as a cynical sensationalist.

BIBLIOGRAPHY

Allegro, John M. *The Dead Sea Scrolls: A Reappraisal*. Harmondworth, 1956; rev. ed. 1959.
Allegro, John M. *The Treasures of the Copper Scrolls*. London, 1960.
Allegro, John M., ed. *Qumran Cave 4, I (4Q158–4186)*. Discoveries in the Judaean Desert, 5. Oxford, 1968.
Allegro, John M. *The Sacred Mushroom and the Cross*. London, 1970.
Allegro, John M. *The Dead Sea Scrolls and the Christian Myth*. London, 1981.
Allegro, John M., with D. N. Freedman. *The People of the Dead Sea Scrolls*. London and New York, 1958/1959.

PHILIP R. DAVIES

ALPHABETS. Alphabetical inscriptions have been in existence since the Canaanites of Palestine first invented the consonantal script under the influence of the Egyptian script in about 2000 BCE. The earliest pieces of evidence for consonantal alphabetical inscriptions are the cuneiform consonantal alphabet of Ugarit from the fourteenth century BCE (27+3 letters: *ʾ[aleph]bgḫdhwzḥṭykšlmḏnẓsʿ[ayin]pṣqršġt + ius̀*; the traditional alphabetical order can already be recognized, *p* after ʿ [*ayin*]), and the Old Canannite cuneiform alphabet of Beth-Shemesh (thirteenth century BCE), which gives evidence of the south-Semitic alphabetical order in Palestine (*hlḥmqwśrġtšknḫspʾ[aleph]ʿ[ayin]źgdbṭẓḏyṯṣ/ṯ*) (A. Lundine, Le Muséon 100, 1987, pp. 243–250). Evidence for the twenty-two-letter consonantal script in the traditional order in Syria-Palestine comes from the twelfth century BCE in old Canannite script at ʿIzbet Tsartaḥ in Judea (ʿ [*ayin*] after *p*); the eighth century BCE in paleo-Hebrew script at Kuntillet ʿAğrud in Sinai (ʿ [*ayin*] after *p*) and at Lachish and Qadesh Barnea; in Aramaic script at Deir ʿAlla, outside Palestine at Tell Ḥalaf (ʿ [*ayin*] after *p*); seventh century BCE in Phoenician script outside Palestine at Salamis; and also in Etruscan and Greek script.

The alphabets were written on stone, limestone, jars, potsherds (ostraca), and seals. The inscriptions were the result of school exercises (Lemaire, 1981; Haran, 1988) or the work of apprentices in seal cutting, or perhaps even the result of apotropaic magic rites (the latter being even more likely when the inscriptions were part of grave donations or ossuary inscriptions such as were found at Beth-Shemesh and Jericho), or on magic bowls, in use from the fourth century CE. Some inscriptions were likely also created for the purpose of votive and memorial inscriptions, such as those that have been found at Hatra and Dura Europos.

Alphabetical inscriptions in the Jewish square script were found in the following places: the ruins of Khirbet Qumran, one ostracon, about 30 BCE (de Vaux, *Revue biblique* 61 [1954], 229; *p* after ʿ [*ayin*], this ostracon, in addition to the inkwells and the writing tables, is one of the indications for a writing school at Qumran); Murabbaʿat, four ostraca (Mur 73, 78–80) and two fragments of leather (Mur 10 11), all in a formal bookhand, and all from about 100 CE except for Mur 73 (which is from about 50 BCE). Mur 73 (Discoveries in the Judaean Desert, 2, p. 175, pl. LII) consists of personal names arranged in nonalphabetical order, Mur 78 (Discoveries in the Judaean Desert, 2, p. 178, pl. LIV) is a palimpsest with each letter being written two times, Mur 79 (Discoveries in the Judaean Desert, 2, p. 178, pl. LV) exhibits *p* after ʿ [*ayin*] and medial as well as final letterforms with the exception of final *mem*, Mur 80 (Discoveries in the Judaean Desert, 2, p. 179, pl. LV), Mur 10 (Discoveries in the Judaean Desert, 2, pp. 90–92, pl. XXVI) is a palimpsest (originally an account) that also exhibits *p* after ʿ [*ayin*] and medial as well as final letterforms, Mur 11 (Discoveries in the Judaean Desert, 2, p. 92, pl. XXVII) is perhaps a palimpsest; Masada, two ostraca, about 74 CE, in a formal bookhand, Mas606 with *p* after ʿ [*ayin*] and Mas607, Greek (Mas782 and Mas783) and Latin (Mas983) and bilingual Greek-Latin (Mas941); alphabetical inscriptions were also found at Masada, from about 74 CE; Herodion, one ostracon was found from the end of the first century CE, the front and back of it being in a formal bookhand, a personal name follows beginning with ʾ [*alef*]; at Naḥal Michmash (Wadi Tsuweniṭ, about 10 kilometers northeast of Jerusalem), were found, in addition to other inscriptions, two-wall inscriptions with alphabets written by Jewish refugees in a formal bookhand from perhaps 70 CE with *p* after ʿ [*ayin*].

Alphabetical order is evident in lists of personal names on several ostraca from Masada, Mas608 and Mas609 (74 CE), and on one ostracon of unknown provenance after an alphabetical inscription as well as on a list of proper names from Qumran Cave 4 (4Q341) composed as part of a writing exercise in Herodian script (cf. also Greek of Mur 122). Use of the alphabet as an aspect of poetic style is found in the acrostic psalms and hymns in the manuscripts of the Dead Sea Scrolls. In addition to the traditional order with ʿ [*ayin*] after *p* in Lamentations from Qumran Cave 4 (4Q111) 1 and Lamentations[b] (5Q7) 4, the following are written as acrostics: Psalms[b] from Qumran Cave 4 (4Q84) 112; 1Q10; Psalms[g] (4Q89) 119; Psalms[h] (4Q90) 119; Psalms from Qumran Cave 5 (5Q5) 119; Psalms[a] from Qumran Cave 11 (11Q5; hereafter 11QPsalms[a]) 119, only partly 11QPs[a] col. xxiv (equals *Psalm 155*); Lamentations from Qumran Cave 3 (3Q3) 1 and 3; Lamentations[b] (5Q7) 4; not written as acrostics are Psalms[a] from Qumran Cave 4 (4Q83) 25 and 34; Psalms[c] from Qumran Cave 4 (4Q85) 37; Psalm 37 in Pesher Psalms[a] (4Q171); 11QPsalms[a] 145; Lamentations[a] (5Q6) 4; in Pesher Nahum (4Q169) 1; Mur 88, XII Nah 1; *Sir.* 51 in 11QPsalms[a] col. xxi; Apostrophe to Zion in 11QPsalms[a] col. xxii and in Psalms[f] (4Q88).

Letters of the alphabet in the paleo-Hebrew and in the Jewish square script are attested as ciphers and numeral signs from the end of the second century BCE: within the dates on coins of Alexander Jannaeus, 103–76 BCE (cf. the Greek legend); for counting pages and columns, in the ostracon Mur 72 (120 BCE), in Rule of the Community[b], 4Q256 (=4QS[b]). Paleo-Hebrew *W* is used as a division marker in paleo-Leviticus[a] (11Q1); paleo-Exodus[m] (4Q22); Psalms[b] from Qumran Cave 4 (4Q84; below col. v before the beginning of col. vi, the beginning of Psalm 94; and perhaps above col. xxi, cf. Aramaic ʾ [*alef*] used to separate one saying from the other in Aḥiqar, sixth/fifth century BCE; J. M. Lindenberger, *The Aramaic Proverbs of Ahiqar*, Baltimore, 1983, p. 305ff.).

BIBLIOGRAPHY

Beyer, Klaus. *The Aramaic Language, Its Distribution and Subdivisions*. Göttingen, 1986. See pages 56ff.

Freedman, David Noel. "Acrostic Poems in the Hebrew Bible: Alphabetic and Otherwise." *Catholic Biblical Quarterly* 48 (1986), 408–431.

Haran, Menahem. "On the Diffusion of Literacy and Schools in Ancient Israel." *Supplements to Vetus Testamentum*, vol. 40. Leiden, 1988. See pages 81–95.

Lemaire, André. *Les écoles et la formation de la Bible dans l'Ancien Israel*. Göttingen, 1981. See pages 7–33.

Lemaire, Andre. *Studi epigrafici e linguistici sul Vicino Oriente Antico* 1 (1984), 131–143.

Naveh, J. *Early History of the Alphabet: An Introduction to West Semitic Epigraphy and Palaeography*. Jerusalem, 1987.

Tov, E. "Special Layout of Poetical Units in the Texts from the Judean Desert." *Give Ear to My Words: Psalms and Other Poetry in and around the Hebrew Bible: Essays in Honour of Professor N. A. van Uchelen*, edited by J. Dyk, pp. 115–128. Amsterdam, 1996.

Tov. E. "Scribal Markings in the Texts from the Judean Desert." *Current Research and Technological Development on the Dead Sea Scrolls*, edited by Donald W. Parry and Stephen D. Ricks, pp. 41–77. Leiden, 1996.

G. WILHELM NEBE

AMERICAN SCHOOLS OF ORIENTAL RESEARCH. A scholarly organization founded in 1890 by a consortium of twenty-one institutions of higher learning, the original purpose of the American Schools of Oriental Research (ASOR) was, according to the founding committee's circular of 1895, to establish an overseas school in Jerusalem:

> . . . The object of the school would be to afford graduates of American theological seminaries, and other similarly qualified persons, opportunities to prosecute Biblical and linguistics investigations under more favorable conditions that can be secured at a distance from the Holy Land . . . to gather material for the illustration of the Biblical narratives; to settle doubtful points in Biblical topography; to identify historic localities; to explore and, if possible, excavate sacred sites.
>
> (King, 1983, p. 26)

The bibliocentric attitude reflected in this circular was a direct result of the legacy of nineteenth-century explorers, travelers, and missionaries, whose rediscovery of the Holy Land led ultimately to the establishment of the most important national schools of archaeology, the British, French, German, and American schools in Jerusalem. The high point of America's nineteenth-century accomplishments was the signal achievement of Edward Robinson, who first visited Palestine in 1838 and whose exploration and identification of sites with biblical connections made him America's first biblical archaeologist.

Instrumental in the establishment of ASOR were three parent societies: the Society of Biblical Literature (SBL), founded in 1880 as the Society for Biblical Literature and Exegesis, whose president in 1895, Joseph Henry Thayer, promoted the effort that resulted in the circular quoted above; the American Oriental Society (AOS), which formally endorsed the idea in 1896; and the Archaeological Institute of America (AIA), which endorsed the proposal in 1898 and had previously established overseas centers in Athens (1882) and Rome (1895). The broad backing of such diverse bodies led in time to a restatement of goals and objectives that extended the ASOR's purview beyond the Levant into the greater Near East and its historical reach and focus beyond the biblical world.

ASOR opened its Jerusalem School in 1900 with Charles C. Torrey, Professor of Old Testament at Yale, as its first director. Its quarters were in a large room of a hotel near the Jaffa Gate inside the Old City, where lectures were given and field projects planned. The first long-term director of the Jerusalem School was William F. Albright, who served from 1920 to 1929 and from 1933 to 1936. The first major field project was the expedition to Samaria between 1908 and 1910 led by George A. Reisner, Clarence S. Fisher, and David G. Lyon. During these early years the Jerusalem School was run by a managing committee in the United States; reports of the school's activities were normally presented at meetings held in conjunction with the annual meeting of the AIA and the SBL. ASOR and the Jerusalem School were one and the same until the opening of the Baghdad School in 1923. Anticipating that event, ASOR was incorporated in the District of Columbia in 1921 with the plural "Schools" in the title, a title that was reaffirmed in the annual meeting of the Corporation in Philadelphia on 18 November 1995. In 1923 the Egyptian ankh, symbol of life, inside of which was the sign of the deity, the eight-pointed Babylonian star, became the symbol of ASOR.

ASOR and the Dead Sea Scrolls. ASOR played a major role in the recovery, publication, and dissemination of information about the Dead Sea Scrolls from their earliest discovery. Four of the scrolls were brought first to the Jerusalem School in 1948 to John Trever, who was acting director on behalf of Millar M. Burrows. Burrows was also president of ASOR and happened to be away on official business at the Baghdad School. Trever recognized the scrolls' importance, photographed them, and sought the advice of Albright at Johns Hopkins University. Albright responded in the following letter:

> My heartiest congratulations on the greatest manuscript discovery of modern times! There is no doubt in my mind that the script is more archaic than that of the Nash Papyrus. I should prefer a date around 100 B.C. . . . What an absolutely incredible find! And there can happily not be the slightest doubt in the world about the genuineness of the manuscript.
>
> (King, p. 116)

ASOR was granted full rights to publish those first manuscripts; and Millar Burrows made the first public announcement of the discovery. Among the first scrolls published by ASOR were the Isaiah[a] manuscript (1QIsa[a]), the Rule of the Community (1QS), and Pesher Habakkuk (1QpHab). In 1972 ASOR published *Scrolls from Qumran Cave I,* edited by Frank Moore Cross, Jr., et al., which contained Trever's first color photographs.

As a result of the 1948 War of Independence, the Jerusalem School wound up in the Hashemite Kingdom of Jordan, where it remained until 1967. Excavations at Qumran and the adjacent caves were conducted between 1949 and 1956, led by Roland de Vaux of the École Biblique et Archéologique Française and Gerald Lankester Harding of the Department of Antiquities of Jordan. American scholars Frank Moore Cross, Jr., and Patrick W. Skehan were assigned key roles in the publication of all new materials discovered in these years by virtue of their official role in the administration of the Palestine Archaeological Museum in Jerusalem, home of the Department of Antiquities of Jordan. Publication of Psalms[a] (11Q5) in 1965 by James A. Sanders was also an effort in which ASOR was active.

The debate over public access to the scrolls and their publication reached its zenith in the early 1990s. In this connection, ASOR called upon its vice president for archaeological policy, Walter E. Rast, to prepare a policy statement in consultation with the Standing Committee on Ancient Manuscripts chaired by James C. VanderKam, which was adopted with some revisions at the November 1992 meeting of the board of trustees in San Francisco. Unlike statements of policy such as the one by the SBL, ASOR's policy takes into account both written and nonwritten archaeological remains and reaffirms the right of the host country to regulate access and guarantee proper site preservation (Meyers, 1994, pp. 458–459).

> We the members of ASOR affirm the priority of national antiquities authorities to manage and regulate cultural remains. As an organization of scholars devoted to recovery of the cultures of Middle and Near Eastern lands, we reaffirm the principles of scholarly integrity and ethics with respect to retrieval, preparation, preservation, and timely publication of material remains, including texts.
>
> 1. Publication
>
> Before assignment of finds to an excavator(s) or editor(s) by the responsible authorities (be they the licensed excavator(s) or the antiquities authority) and their scholarly advisors, these groups should determine what constitutes a reasonable time for publication. In the case of major finds, it is desirable that preliminary editions be promptly published. In the interval between assignment and publication, the excavator(s) or editor(s) should be encouraged to cooperate with interested scholarly parties.
>
> 2. Access
>
> a. Recognizing that the responsible antiquities authorities and their scholarly advisors will be concerned with securing and preserving the finds, it is likely that scholarly access to the originals, after publication, will still be necessary. Such access will be regulated by the responsible antiquities authorities and their scholarly advisors.
>
> b. After the reasonable time limit (see no. 1 above) has passed, the materials, photographs, and documentation should be made generally accessible within the limits of the requirements for preservation and laws of the host country.

New Centers. Because of the political division of Jerusalem, Nelson Glueck, past director of the Jerusalem School and the president of Hebrew Union College (HUC) in Cincinnati, established an HUC campus in west Jerusalem in 1964, which he envisioned as a successor to the Jerusalem School. The 1967 Arab-Israeli War resulted in the unification of the city and an Arab boycott of all scholars who worked in Israel. ASOR's response to this development led to the reorganization of the Jerusalem School into the W. F. Albright Institute of Archaeological Research (AIAR) in 1969 and to the establishment of the American Center of Oriental Research (ACOR) in Amman in 1970. George Ernest Wright, president of ASOR at the time, took these steps to preserve ASOR's historic position of political neutrality, thereby enabling ASOR scholars to work on both sides of the Jordan River. Another research center, the Cyprus American Archaeological Research Institute (CAARI), was established in 1978, four years after Wright's death. Today, all three centers are independently incorporated and administered by individual boards of trustees, though this was not the original intent. The Albright Institute has had as fellows numerous important scroll scholars and has sponsored many lectures and seminars on the Dead Sea Scrolls as well.

The decentralization of ASOR has had a profound and lasting impact on the society. ASOR's historic role in fostering overseas fieldwork today is reflected in the oversight work of the Committee on Archaeological Policy, which acts as an accrediting agency. In recent years this committee has also turned its attention to broader policy questions such as ethical issues concerning the preservation of sites, trade in antiquities, and responsibility to the public. ASOR's Committee on Publications monitors all the society's journals and monographic publications. Important articles dealing with the scrolls have appeared in ASOR's publications *Biblical Archaeologist* and *Bulletin of the American Schools of Oriental Research.* The home office provides assistance to the overseas centers as needed, including library exchanges. Various lectures on the scrolls and the archaeology of Qumran have been presented at ASOR's annual meetings. ASOR also offers scholarships to students and faculty among the approximately 140 colleges, universities, seminaries, and museums that make up the ASOR consortium.

ASOR is the major international scholarly organization dedicated to promoting research in the Middle East. Its record of political neutrality has earned it widespread respect from nearly all the countries in the area. Effective 1 July 1996, ASOR administrative offices were relocated to the campus of Boston University adjacent to the offices of the Archaeological Institute of America.

[*See also* Discovery and Purchase; Publication; *and* Scrolls Research.]

BIBLIOGRAPHY

Burrows, M., et al. *The Dead Sea Scrolls of St. Mark's Monastery.* New Haven, 1950.

Cross, Frank Moore, Jr., et al. *Scrolls from Qumran Cave I.* Albright Institute of Archaeological Research and the Shrine of the Book. Jerusalem, 1972.

King, P. J. *American Archaeology in the Mideast: A History of the American Schools of Oriental Research.* Philadelphia, 1983.

Meyers, E. M. "Ethics of Publication of the Dead Sea Scrolls: Panel Discussion." In *Methods of Investigation of the Dead Sea Scrolls and the Khirbet Qumran Site,* edited by M. O. Wise, N. Golb, J. J. Collins, and D. G. Pardee, pp. 455–460. New York, 1994.

Meyers, E. M. "The American Schools of Oriental Research." In *The Oxford Encyclopedia of Archaeology in the Near East,* vol. 2, pp. 94–98. New York, 1997.

Meyers, E. M. "History of the Field: An Overview." In *The Oxford Encyclopedia of Archaeology in the Near East,* vol. 3, pp. 37–42. New York, 1997.

ERIC M. MEYERS

AMMAN MUSEUM. The National Archaeological Museum on the Citadel in Amman is the principal archaeological museum in Jordan. The museum has long been associated closely with the Jordanian Department of Antiquities, which played a central role in the discovery, purchase, preservation, and publication of the Qumran scrolls until 1967. Along with other national treasures, fragments of at least twenty scrolls are housed in the museum, including the whole of the Copper Scroll (3Q15). These materials were transferred from the Palestine Archaeological Museum (now Rockefeller Museum) in Jerusalem before 1967 for an exhibition.

The complete list of fragments housed at the National Archaeological Museum is as follows:

Scroll	Fragment	Amman Museum No.
1Q13 Phylactery	1–58	J 5926 A, J 5926 C
1Q17 Jubilees[a]	1	No number assigned
1Q18 Jubilees[b]	1–5	No number assigned
1Q19 Noah	1, 3	No number assigned
1Q20 Genesis Apocryphon	1–8	No number assigned
1Q22 Words of Moses	1–28, 31, 33–37, 41–45, 47–49	J 5928
1Q23 Enoch Giants[a]	1–22, 24–31	J 5928
1Q27 Mysteries	1–17	J 5928
1Q28a Rule of the Congregation	Cols i–ii	No number assigned
1QM War Scroll	1–2	J 5928
1Q34 Liturgical Prayer	1	J 5928
1Q35 Hodayot[b]	1–2	J 5928 (Numbered 1Q33 on the museum plate)
1Q36 Hymns	1–18, 20–25	J 5928
1Q37 Hymnic Compositions?	1–6	J 5928
1Q70 Unclassified fragment	1–32	J 5928
3Q15 Copper Scroll	23 segments	
4Q22 paleo-Exodus[m]	11	No number assigned
4Q109 Qoheleth[a]	1–6	No number assigned
4Q162 Pesher Isaiah[b]	1	No number assigned
4Q175 Testimonia	Single col.	No number assigned

The fragment numbers are given here according to the principal published edition of each manuscript in the Discoveries in the Judaean Desert (of Jordan) series (Oxford, 1955–). In some of the museum plates the fragments are numbered differently; this is especially the case for Words of Moses, Mysteries, and Hymnic Compositions.

In addition to these fragments, a group of uninscribed and unidentified fragments not listed in any catalogue is given the Amman Museum number J 5927. A glass plate in the museum containing some linen with very neat edging is labeled AF 33.

The collection in the museum in Amman is representative of the Qumran finds as a whole. There are examples of texts written on leather, papyrus (e.g. 1Q70), and copper. There are examples of Hebrew, Paleo-Hebrew (1Q35), and Greek script (in the Copper Scroll). Most of the texts are in Hebrew; two are in Aramaic (1Q20, 1Q23). There are examples of all kinds of scribal practices, including marginal marks (4Q175), paragraphing, and cancellation dots (4Q162).

The principal exhibit in the museum is the Copper Scroll. [*See* Copper Scroll.] This was originally sawed into strips in Manchester in 1955 and 1956 and was exhibited in the museum in cases built shortly afterward. In the early 1990s it was agreed between the Jordanian and

French authorities that the scroll should be conserved in the laboratories of Electricité de France. In 1997 the conserved scroll, together with a facsimile, was formally received back for the Jordanians by Her Majesty Queen Noor at a ceremony in the Louvre, Paris. After being exhibited in Paris and in Manchester, the scroll returned to the National Archaeological Museum in Amman where it is now on permanent display in specially constructed mounts, together with one of the facsimiles.

In addition, two scrolls from Cave 4 form part of the permanent display in the museum: Pesher Isaiah[b] and Testimonia, which is a single column containing four quotations: *Exodus* 20.21, *Numbers* 24.15–17, *Deuteronomy* 33.8–11, and a passage that is either quoted from or quoted in the Apocryphon of Joshua[b] (cf. 4Q379 22 ii.7–15). Some artefacts from Qumran are also on display. A large collection of silver coins from Qumran is also held in the Amman Museum.

Apart from the official publications, the best photographs of many of the fragments in the National Archaeological Museum have been taken by Bruce and Kenneth Zuckerman of West Semitic Research during a project completed in association with Princeton Theological Seminary.

BIBLIOGRAPHY

Arif, Aida S. *A Treasury of Classical and Islamic Coins: The Collection of Amman Museum*, pp. 15–21, 192–199. London, 1986.

Brooke, George J. "The Jordanian Dead Sea Scrolls." *Inter-Faith Quarterly* 14 (1996), 332–335. A brief survey of the principal characteristics of the collection in the National Archaeological Museum, Amman.

Brooke, George J. "The Dead Sea Scrolls in the National Archaeological Museum, Amman." *al-Nadwah (Al al-Bayt University Journal)* 8 (1997), 23–35. The most comprehensive listing and description of the fragments that are currently stored or on exhibition in the museum.

Reed, Stephen A. *The Dead Sea Scrolls Catalogue: Documents, Photographs and Museum Inventory Numbers*, revised and edited by Marilyn J. Lundberg with the collaboration of Michael B. Phelps. SBL Resources for Biblical Study, 32. Atlanta, 1994. The most accessible listing of the scroll fragments in Amman, but with some minor mistakes.

GEORGE J. BROOKE

AMOS, BOOK OF. *See* Minor Prophets.

AMRAM. Appearing frequently in genealogical lists of the Hebrew scriptures, Amram is a son of Qahat (Kohath) and father of Aaron, Moses, and Miriam (*Ex.* 6.18, 6.20; *Nm.* 26.58–59); his wife was Jochebed, his father's sister. Amram is also prominent in a number of Second Temple writings. In Pseudo-Philo's *Biblical Antiquities* (9.1–10) he is the hero of a significant incident before the birth of Moses. In *Jewish Antiquities* (1.210–216), Josephus writes of visions vouchsafed to Amram before the birth of Moses. In a later work, *Sefer ha-Razim*, a Hebrew magical text originating from the first millennium CE, Amram, together with Qahat and Levi, figures in the book's chain of transmission from Noah to Moses. Interestingly, Amram plays no major part in *Jubilees*, which is generally linked to Aramaic Levi (1Q21, 4Q213–4Q214a) and the Testament of Qahat (4Q542).

Significantly, in view of Josephus's writings, five copies of the Visions of Amram were found in Cave 4 at Qumran. Although this number of copies suffices to show that the work must have had some importance for the Qumran covenanters, no references to it occur in sectarian literature. In 1972, Józef T. Milik published a substantial fragment of the Visions of Amram[b] (4Q544) and claimed that Origen had alluded to it. Milik recognized six copies (4Q543–548?). Émile Puech thinks that the same scribe copied the Testament of Qahat and the Visions of Amram[a]. Moreover, he notes that the Testament of Qahat starts on a piece of leather with a join on the right, and he even speculates that this work and the Visions of Amram[a] might have formed part of the same manuscript. Details about the other manuscripts of the Visions of Amram are not yet known.

Milik dates Visions of Amram[b] to the second century BCE. His view that it may come from the earlier part of that century has been challenged, however, and the manuscript most probably comes from the latter part of the century. The published text is written in Late Literary Aramaic of the type familiar from the other Aramaic documents found at Qumran.

The beginning of the work has survived, and its superscription reads: "Copy of the Book of the Words of the Visions of Amram." The word *copy* may be compared with the term *copy* used in *Ezra* 4.11, while "Book of the Words of . . . Amram" resembles the recently deciphered phrase "Book of the Words of Noah" in the Genesis Apocryphon (1QapGen, col. v). The book is clearly a testament, recounting Amram's words to his children "on the day of his death, in the 136th year, the year of his death." Although the title "Testament of Amram" would fit its contents, in fact, the work is known as "The Visions of Amram."

The full contents of the work remain unknown because part of it is lost; some substantial fragments have been published. Column i, lines 10–15, as reconstructed by Milik (1972) from fragments of three manuscripts, tells of a dream vision in which Amram sees two angels. One is like a serpent, and his garment is multicolored and dark, while the other has a happy visage. They rule over all humans, and the two beings are struggling over Amram. In a second, fragmentary column, Amram is called upon to make a decision between these two beings. Milik thinks that this fragmentary second column is column 2 of the manuscript. It identifies one figure as Melchiresha' and associates him with darkness, while the speaker is the angel who rules over light. The name of the ruler of light has been lost, but it is often reconstructed as Melchizedek. Other names found in the text are "ruler of light" and "ruler of darkness" (cf. 1QS iii.16 20, CD v.16 18, etc.). In the next column, apparently, Amram asks the ruler of light a question. Milik calculates that these three columns comprise approximately one-third of the book.

In the Bible, Melchizedek was the mysterious king of Salem encountered by Abraham (*Gn.* 14.18), as well as the type of a priest (Ps. 110.4), and a type of Christ (*Heb.* 5.6). In the Melchizedek scroll found in Cave 11 at Qumran (11Q13), Melchizedek appears as a heavenly figure, as he does in Gnostic texts, such as the Nag Hammadi Codex (9.1). He was the object of much (chiefly heretical) speculation in early Christian circles, where his priestly function is combined with his eschatological role.

The dualism of light and darkness in the Visions of Amram is notable. It is, of course, very typical of the sectarian documents. However, the dualism of the two spirits is already present in Aramaic Levi, which clearly antedates the Visions of Amram (and the Qumran sect). This does not necessarily demonstrate that the Visions of Amram was written by the Qumran sect; a pre- or extra-Qumran origin is quite possible. On the other hand, in reference to Aramaic Levi, it is generally accepted that the sectarian community did not compose Aramaic documents, but this factor is not necessarily determinative.

The three sacerdotal writings, Aramaic Levi, the Testament of Qahat, and the Visions of Amram, form a series of priestly instructions. Aramaic Levi is the oldest of the works and the one on which the other two depend, although the exact relationship between them cannot be determined. The Testament of Qahat and the Visions of Amram were composed in addition to the existing Aramaic Levi in order to legitimate the continuity of the priestly line and its teaching. This theme is stressed in Aramaic Levi and particularly in the Testament of Qahat.

Milik (1978) has suggested that the conflict among the angels over Abraham's soul described in Origen (Homily 25 on Luke) derives from the Visions of Amram. That view is based on his emendation (editorial alteration) of Origen's *Abraham* into *Amram*. A very similar conflict between Michael and the devil over Moses' body is mentioned in *Jude* 9, while the theme of two conflicting angels is found elsewhere, for example, in Hermas (*The Shepherd*, Mandates 6.2.1) and the Armenian pseudepigraphical work, *Questions of Ezra*. Thus, Origen's acquaintance with the Visions of Amram is not definitely demonstrated.

Milik suggested, moreover, that the works of "the three patriarchs" (Gk. *Ton g' patriarchon*) mentioned in *Apostolic Constitutions* 6.16.3, connected with "the apocryphal books," are Aramaic Levi, the Testament of Qahat, and the Visions of Amram. This view has not been widely accepted, and, unless it is, there is no assured reference to the Testament of Qahat beyond the single manuscript from Qumran. Nonetheless, it seems quite correct to emphasize the relationship between Aramaic Levi, the Testament of Qahat, and the Visions of Amram, works associated with the descendants of Levi, down to Aaron, the direct father of the priestly line of Israel.

[*See also* Aaron; Levi, Aramaic; Miriam; Moses; Priests; Qahat; Testaments; *and* Visions].

BIBLIOGRAPHY

de Jonge, M. "'The Testament of Levi' and 'Aramaic Levi'." *Revue de Qumrân* 13 (1988), 367–385. Discusses textual and literary issues.

Milik, J. T. "4Q Visions de 'Amram et une citation d'Origène." *Revue Biblique* 79 (1972), 77–97. Edition and translation of the published fragments.

Milik, J. T. "Écrits préesséniens de Qumrân: de Hénoch à 'Amram." In *Qumrân: Sa piété, sa théologie et son milieu*, edited by M. Delcor, pp. 91–106. Bibliotheca ephemeridum theologicarum lovaniensium, 46. Louvain, 1978. Puts the early literature at Qumran into context.

Puech, É. "Le testament de Qahat en araméen de la grotte 4 (*4QTQah*)." *Revue de Qumrân* 15 (1991), 23–54. Discusses, *inter alia*, the relationship of the Qahat and Amram documents.

MICHAEL E. STONE

ANGELIC LITURGY. *See* Songs of the Sabbath Sacrifice.

ANGELS. Originally, Hebrew *mal'ak* and Greek *angelos* were terms that indicated messengers, be it between humans or between God/the gods and humans. During the Second Temple period the divine messenger was identified with other heavenly beings, like the seraphim, the holy creatures, and so forth, and thereby became by itself a designation for heavenly beings, which may have some contact with humans. Jerome took the Greek *angelos* for the translation of heavenly messengers only, hence the modern European term *angel*.

Angels play an important role throughout the Dead Sea Scrolls as well as in other Jewish writings of the time. Josephus notes the Essene practice of keeping angelic names secret (*The Jewish War* 2.142). Yet, even without identifying the members of the Qumran community with the Essenes as described by Josephus, the development of Jewish angelology during the last centuries before the destruction of the Second Temple is most remarkable.

Luke's short notice concerning the Sadducees' denial of the existence of angels (*Acts* 23.8; cf. Daube, 1990) needs further consideration, especially in light of recent attempts to stress a more Sadducean character of some Qumran writings. [*See* Sadducees.]

However, a specific, coherent doctrine of angelology within the Qumran community cannot be easily defined because of the nature of the sources and our lack of knowledge concerning the provenance of Qumran writings and their literary development. Fragments from *1 Enoch* and *Jubilees*, for example, have been found at Qumran, and these works are, among others, major sources of angelology. Though it seems that the works did not originate within the community, the fact that they were copied so often shows that their angelology was acceptable in the Qumran community.

The different works attributed to the Qumran community show sometimes quite disparate beliefs and motifs concerning angels, though at times allusions in one work find a closer explanation in another. A work like the Songs of the Sabbath Sacrifice (4Q400–407, 11Q17, Mas1k) is a classical source for a fully developed angelology; Temple Scroll[a] (11Q19) in contrast, does not mention heavenly beings at all. Some *pesharim* use angelic terms (4Q174, 4Q177, 4Q182, 11Q13) whereas others do without (4Q169; cf. Davidson, 1992, pp. 136–141).

Combining different sources is highly problematic and might produce an artificially coherent picture. There are many differences between the sources, and yet some connections can be made. The Dead Sea Scrolls mostly reflect aspects and problems of beliefs in angels commonly shared in the Judaism of the period: Angels rule over nature, serve God, watch over the tree of knowledge, and so forth. The scrolls mention several angels by name. These (and many more) are known from the Jewish literature of the time.

Terminology and Interpretation. The first aspect to be stressed is an exegetical one. Jewish literature of the Second Temple period identified more and more Biblical Hebrew terms as angels regardless of earlier probable meanings. Designations for God or terms that survived from polytheistic myth were now understood as angelic designations. The "sons of God" (*Gn.* 6.1–4) become "divine beings"—angels—as already in the Septuagint. Dead Sea Scroll literature is especially rich in angelic terms derived from combinations with the words *El* ("God") or *Elim*; for example, the War Scroll (1QM x.8).

The same holds true for certain biblical references to "holy ones," which are quite often understood as angels (again as in the Greek translation). According to the War Scroll (1QM i.16), "holy ones" appear at God's side to destroy the sons of darkness (following Yadin's reconstruction; cf. *Zec.* 12.5). The War Scroll also offers a play on the words "holy ones," referring to angels and human beings side by side (1QM x.10–12 and xii.1–7, as in Hodayot[a], 1QH[a] xix.9–11 [xi.6–8]). This kind of double usage has its clearest parallels in *1 Enoch*'s "Book of Parables" (*1 En.* 37–71), where both meanings change constantly. Yet, some commentators stress the interpretation of the "holy ones" as mere human beings. The question has given rise to much discussion among scholars (mostly related to the explanation of *Daniel* 7; see Di Lella, 1977).

One of the more interesting features of angelology in the Dead Sea Scrolls is the development of the meaning "angel" for the Hebrew term *ruaḥ* (though still maintaining a series of other connotations, including "spirit"; see Davidson, 1992, pp. 155–156; Sekki, 1989, pp. 145–171). Here, too, a double meaning is very common, for example: "And a perverted spirit you purified from great violation, so that it might stand in rank with the host of holy ones, and so that it might come together with the congregation of the sons of heaven. And you cast for man an eternal lot with the spirits of knowledge" (1QH[a] xi.22–23 [iii.21–22]). *Holy ones* and *sons of heaven* are typical terms for angels in the Dead Sea Scrolls; they are paralleled here by the term *spirits of knowledge*. A few other texts attribute limited knowledge to the angels (1QH[a] ix [i]). Yet, the person joining their congregation has been a perverted spirit: *spirit*, like *holy one*, can designate in the same context angels and human beings. Some scrolls refer to angels as "spirits of knowledge" (*Elei daʿat*; Newsom, 1985, pp. 23–24; cf. Mach, 1992, pp. 133–144).

The Dead Sea Scrolls use the term "prince" or "commander" (*sar*) quite frequently (cf. *Daniel* 12.1). It seems that this term replaces another biblical expression for "messenger" (*tsir*) found in *Isaiah* 63.9. The passage from *Isaiah* seems to be used in the War Scroll (1QM xiii.14), yet its importance is much greater: A certain reading of the prophet's Hebrew words allowed for the term *Angel/s of the Presence*, which is attested quite often in the Qumran writings.

Following such exegetical practices, the Dead Sea Scrolls offer a full range of comparable terms for angels that often derive from former divine designations (Newsom, 1985, pp. 23–29; Noll, 1979, pp. 216–240; Yadin, 1962). Scholars often have tried to identify angelic beings mentioned in the scrolls with specific angels such as Michael. However, such identifications serve mostly modern needs for systematizing an otherwise quite unsystematic literature. The "Prince of Light" in the Rule of the Community from Qumran Cave 1 (hereafter, 1QRule of the Community, 1QS iii–iv) need not be the archangel Michael (Davidson, 1992, p. 148; Segal, 1992) or Uriel.

The Visions of Amram[a–f] (4Q543–548) are of special interest in this regard: the angel who appears seems to have three names. Józef Milik (1972) discusses the possible names for the angel and his evil counterpart (4Q544 2.3, 3.2), as does Paul Kobelski (1981). It seems clear that angels might have had more than one name at a time.

The Melchizedek scroll (11Q13) places Melchizedek in opposition to Belial (the "evil one") and his angels, making Melchizedek a savior figure for the end time. The identification of Melchizedek with Elohim (perhaps 11Q13 ii.24–25) is not completely certain; however, Melchizedek clearly is depicted as a heavenly figure, a priestly savior (Milik, 1972; Kobelski, 1981).

Another aspect of the interpretative activity of the Qumran community is the introduction of angels into the biblical text, whether by identifying biblical terms as angels or by adding angels to the biblical story. The Genesis Apocryphon (1QapGen), for example, speculates about whether the wonderful appearance of the newborn Noah is a sign that his parents are indeed the watchers (angels who descended according to *1 Enoch*). The three men who visit Abraham after his circumcision in *Genesis* 18 are understood, it seems, explicitly as angels in the Ages of Creation (4Q180).

Duality and Communion with Human Beings. A major characteristic of the belief in angels in Qumran, however, is the so-called communion with the angels, which has to be seen in connection with certain dualistic tendencies that are more prominent in the Dead Sea Scrolls than in most of the contemporary literature. In a variety of works, this communion of members of the Qumran community with the angels is either presumed or expected (especially in Hodayot[a]). In the dualistic partitioning of humanity into the Sons of Light and the Sons of Darkness, who are allotted to the principal angelic Princes of Light and Princes of Darkness, respectively, communities are matched with the corresponding angelic host; the motif is formulated primarily in terms of the communion of the Qumranites and the Angels of Light only. The dualistic division of humanity is broadly formulated in the Treatise on the Two Spirits, now part of 1QRule of the Community (1QS iii.13–iv.26). The text is still under discussion because of its theological difficulties. The precise form of the dualism is at issue as well as the question whether and when some terms indicate a more personal angelic being or, to the contrary, might still be understood as nouns designating human situations and/or behavior. Yet, the idea of a common future battle of the Prince of Light and the Sons of Light (i.e., the Qumranites) against the forces of darkness (angels as well as humans) is clearly linked to the dualistic division.

Following biblical and later traditions, the communion of humans with angels in the eschatological battle against Belial and his angels is especially developed in the War Scroll. From the beginning of that scroll, angels from both sides seem to form part of the armies together with the humans (1QM i.10–11, ix.14–16, xii.1–9). For this battle the names of the archangels will be written on the shields of the towers (1QM ix.14–16). Accordingly, the War Scroll prohibits certain people from staying in the camp, "for the angels of holiness are in the camp, together with their hosts" (1QM vii.6). Elsewhere, the idea of the presence of the angels in the camp produces similar prohibitions that need not be understood as total expulsion from the group. They might exclude a member from certain meetings or tasks (Schiffman, 1989, pp. 51–52).

The author of Hodayot gives thanks for his elevation to the rank of the angels or expects that elevation in the near future (1QH[a] xiv.12–13 [vi.9–10], xix.13 [xi.10], and more often in the fragments of this scroll). The close relation to the angels has a revelatory aspect (as in 1QH[a] xix.4–13 [xi.2–10]), since the communion here is clearly linked to the salvation hidden from others, that is, outsiders. The purpose of such a communion is the common praise of God as in "You cast eternal destiny for man with the spirits of knowledge, to praise your name together in celebration and to tell of your wonders before all your work" (1QH[a] xi.20–23 [iii.19–22]; cf. 1QM xii.1–2). The liturgical communion of the members of the Qumran community with the angels is still the most plausible explanation for the function of the Songs of the Sabbath Sacrifice (4Q400–407).

In light of this liturgical communion, one might surmise that other texts have a specific liturgical character, too, as suggested recently by Bilhah Nitzan (1995) for Berakhot[a–e] (4Q286–290). If her interpretation is right, the angels did attend the yearly liturgy of the renewal of the covenant. According to the Rule of the Blessings, that communion may be expected as a future blessing: the "words . . . to bless the Sons of Zadok the priest" (1Q28b iii.25–26). At the same time, the priests are supposed to bless in that way, and they themselves are described as sharing the angelic communion (1Q28b iv.23–26).

On various other occasions, angels are involved not only with the fulfillment of eschatological and liturgical tasks; it seems that they also struggle for the future of individuals as in the Visions of Amram[a–b] (4Q543 3, 6; 4Q544 3.12–14, 6.2–3). In a text that was published just recently, a fragment mentioning Zedekiah (4Q470), Erik Larson (1994) suggests an active role for the angel Michael in the rehabilitation of Judean king Zedekiah.

Recently, these expectations of sharing a common future with the angels or even living with them have raised the question of whether the Qumranites believed in a transformation of the just into angelic beings. The theory has been advocated by Morton Smith with respect to the

War Scroll[a] (4Q491), which appears to speak of a figure enthroned in heaven. It has some parallels in other writings of the period (e.g., *Dn.* 12, *1 En.* 104; Segal, 1992; Mach, 1992, pp. 163–173). It has been opposed, however, by other scholars (e.g., Davidson, 1992, p. 156). The continuation of the same song that suggests the idea of a common lot with the angels in Hodayot[a] (1QH[a] xi.20–23 [iii.19–22]) shows the author's awareness of the dissimilarity between himself and the angels. The communion with them might, at least according to this text, be expected, but it is not always conceived of as having already been accomplished.

Judgment against Angels. At one point it seems that the author of Hodayot is following a different biblical or postbiblical tradition that allows for a certain critique against at least some of the angels (1QH[a] xviii.34–35 [x.32–33]). God is in dispute with the angels and seeks justice among them. According to the same text, the angels' knowledge of God seems to be limited and they are unable to stand before his wrath. Punishing angels are mentioned several times in the scrolls, but their precise role is disputed. [*See* Demons.]

[*See also* Hodayot; Michael; Songs of the Sabbath Sacrifice; *and* War of the Sons of Light against the Sons of Darkness.]

BIBLIOGRAPHY

Daube, David. "On Acts 23: Sadducees and Angels." *Journal of Biblical Literature* 109 (1990), 493–497.

Davidson, Maxwell J. *Angels at Qumran: A Comparative Study of 1 Enoch 1–36, 72–108 and Sectarian Writings from Qumran*. Journal for the Study of the Pseudepigraphic Supplement Series, 11. Sheffield, 1992. Especially important for Qumran angelology, working through each document separately.

Di Lella, Alexander A. "The One in Human Likeness and the Holy Ones of the Most High in Daniel 7." *Catholic Biblical Quarterly* 39 (1977), 1–19. Summarizes the discussion regarding the identity of the "Holy Ones," stressing the interpretion of the phrase as relating to humans.

Kobelski, Paul J. *Melchizedek and Melchireša'*. Catholic Biblical Quarterly Monograph Series, 10. Washington, D.C., 1981. Gives a full discussion of the texts and scholarly literature regarding the two figures up to 1980.

Larson, Erik. "4Q470 and the Angelic Rehabilitation of King Zedekiah." *Dead Sea Discoveries* 1 (1994), 210–228.

Mach, Michael. *Entwicklungsstadien des jüdischen Engelglaubens in vorrabbinischer Zeit*. Texte und Studien zum Antiken Judentum, 34. Tübingen, 1992. General overview about angelological developments from the Old Testament to the end of the second century CE. Bibliography up to the end of 1991.

Milik, J. T. "4Q Visions de 'Amram et une citation d'Origène." *Revue biblique* 79 (1972), 77–97. Important for the text and reconstructions.

Milik, J. T. "Milkî-ṣedeq et Milkî-reša' dans les anciens écrits juives et chrétiens." *Journal of Jewish Studies* 23 (1972), 95–144. Offers different readings for the Melchizedek text and interpretation.

Newsom, Carol A. *Songs of the Sabbath Sacrifice: A Critical Edition*. Harvard Semitic Studies, 27. Atlanta, 1985.

Nitzan, Bilhah. "4QBerakhot[a–e] (4Q286–290): A Covenantal Ceremony in the Light of Related Texts." *Revue de Qumrân* 16 (1995), 487–506.

Noll, Stephen F. "Angelology in the Qumran Texts." Ph.D., diss., Manchester University, 1979. Important discussions of the texts.

Schiffman, Lawrence H. *The Eschatological Community of the Dead Sea Scrolls: A Study of the Rule of the Congregation*. Society of Biblical Literature Monograph Series, 38. Atlanta, 1989.

Segal, Alan F. "The Risen Christ and the Angelic Mediator Figures in Light of Qumran." In *Jesus and the Dead Sea Scrolls*, edited by James H. Charlesworth, pp. 302–328. New York, 1992.

Sekki, Arthur Everett. *The Meaning of Ruaḥ at Qumran*. Society of Biblical Literature Monograph Series, 110. Atlanta, 1989. Detailed discussion of the occurrences of the term in the Dead Sea Scrolls.

Smith, Morton. "Two Ascended to Heaven—Jesus and the Author of 4Q491." In *Jesus and the Dead Sea Scrolls*, edited by James H. Charlesworth, pp. 290–301. New York, 1992.

Stuckenbruck, Loren T. *Angel Veneration and Christology: A Study in Early Judaism and in the Christology of the Apocalypse of John*. Tübingen, 1995. Pages 150–164 discuss angel veneration in Qumran.

MICHAEL MACH

ANOINTING. The Dead Sea Scrolls provide a valuable link between the biblical tradition of anointed kings and other special individuals and later Christian and rabbinic definitions of "the anointed one" or messiah. Terms for anointing in the scrolls include *mashakh* and *sukh*. Both terms indicate pouring, rubbing or smearing oil upon someone or something. *Mashakh* usually is used in ritual contexts, while *sukh* is confined to ordinary situations, for example, smearing oil on the body for medicinal or cosmetic purposes.

The sectarians understood anointing in the manner described in the Bible, where it was performed for the inauguration of a king, priest, certain prophets, and others who were chosen as God's agents. Anointing could be literal, as in the cases of Saul and David, or symbolic, as in the case of the prophet who exclaims, "The Spirit of the Lord has anointed me to . . ." (*Is.* 61.1; cf. *Is.* 45.1). Anointing sanctifies, or separates, such persons from the normal sphere of human activity, elevates them above their fellow human beings, and empowers them for sacred service. By anointing, God endows his agent with his spirit (*1 Sm.* 16.13–14), providing the person with protection (Ps. 105.15), strength (Ps. 89.20–21), honor (Ps. 45.7), and wisdom (*Is.* 11.2). Thus, a special relationship between God and his anointed is forged. Objects that are anointed are separated for sacred use and become dangerous to those who encroach upon them unworthily (*Ex.* 30.29–33, 40.9; *Nm.* 4.15).

Oil for sacred purposes differed from ordinary oil. It was composed of a special recipe that included various aromatic spices mixed with fine olive oil (*Ex.* 30.23–25). It was not to be used for any noncultic purposes. By reserving this aromatic oil for his use, God claims its fragrance as his own; those anointed with it become associated with him as his special representatives.

Among Israel's neighbors anointing was also significant. When Egyptian officials were anointed by the king, they were given authority and protection to act as his agents. Rubbing oil on the body solidified legal contracts in Mesopotamia, signifying the commitment of each party. At weddings, the groom poured oil on the head of his bride, probably emphasizing his selection of her.

In the pseudepigrapha, we find a heavenly anointing that transforms individuals by endowing them with divine glory. According to the *Testament of Levi* (8.4–5) the patriarch Levi was anointed by an angel to serve as high priest. After the angel Michael anoints Enoch, he becomes virtually indistinguishable from the angels (*2 En.* 22.8–10). In addition, oil is considered a source for strength and healing (cf. *Apocalypse of Moses* 9.3).

In the Dead Sea Scrolls, as in the Bible, the term "anointed" refers to kings, priests, and prophets. Like other Jews of the Second Temple period, the sectarians clearly awaited a messiah, an anointed Davidic king who would restore the political and moral condition of Israel (cf. *Ps. Sol.* 17.3, 18.5–8; *Mt.* 11.3; *Jn.* 1.41). He is referred to as the "Messiah of Justice" in the Commentary on Genesis A (4Q252 5.3), the "Branch of David" in the Florilegium (4Q174 1.11), "Messiah of Israel" in the Rule of the Congregation (1Q28a ii.14), the "Holy Messiah" in a liturgical text? (1Q30 i.2) [partially restored] and "the Anointed of the Spirit" in Melchizedek (11Q13 ii.18). The Davidic Messiah described in the Scrolls is clearly a human being. There appears to be no influence from the heavenly "son of man" tradition found in Enochic literature and elsewhere (*1 En.* 46.1–3, 48.2–10; cf. *4 Ezr.* 13.1–53).

"Anointed" in the scrolls also refers to consecrated priests. In the description of the eschatological battle, the priests are told not to come near those who are severely wounded so as not to "desecrate the oil of their priesthood" with the slain (War Scroll[c] 4Q493 1.5; cf. 1QM ix.7–9). The community expected an anointed high priest as well as the anointed Davidic ruler. The Rule of the Community from Cave 1 (hereafter, 1QRule of the Community) refers to the coming "Messiahs of Aaron and Israel" (1QS ix.11). The priestly Messiah will be preeminent in the community; he is "at the head of the whole congregation" and the key figure in the eschatological battle (War Scroll, 1QM ii.1, xvi.13, xviii.5; cf. CD vii 7.18–21).

Finally, the prophets are considered by the sectarians to be the anointed of God. The Damascus Document refers to those "anointed ones" (for example, prophets) who had taught Israel throughout her history by God's Holy Spirit (Damascus Document, CD ii.12; cf. CD v.21–vi.1). The War Scroll honors God for providing military wisdom through the agency of his anointed prophets: "By the hand of your anointed ones, seers of decrees, you taught us the times of the wars of your hands, to fight to cover you with glory, with our enemies to fell the hordes of Belial . . ." (1QM xi.7–8).

Although they emphasize two future messiahs, the Dead Sea Scrolls represent an outlook on the biblical tradition that is fairly similar to that of rabbinic literature. Like the sectarians, the rabbis expected a messianic era in which the temple and the Davidic kingdom would be restored. The Shemoneh ʿEsreh, a first-century rabbinic text containing eighteen benedictions, includes a prayer to God to be merciful to David, his anointed, and to restore the fortunes of Israel to Jerusalem. Within the priesthood of the period, however, sacred anointing apparently had been abandoned. The Mishnah implies that the high priest was consecrated by investiture only (*Meg.* 1.9, *Hor.* 3.4). According to the Talmud, the sacred anointing oil was hidden by Josiah, King of Judah (seventh century BCE) and never used again (B.T., *Hor.* 11b–12a).

In contrast to the Dead Sea Scrolls and rabbinic teachings, the New Testament regards Jesus as the embodiment of Jewish messianic expectations. He is referred to as the Christ (in Greek, "Anointed One"), who has been elevated and enthroned in heaven due to his obedience to God as a sinless sacrifice for humanity (*Heb.* 1.9). By extension, Christians—those who identify with Christ—partake of his anointing and become his fragrance (*1 Jn.* 2.27; *2 Cor.* 1.21, 2.14–16). The New Testament, like the scrolls, connects anointing with empowerment by the Holy Spirit (*Acts* 1.8, 10.38; *Lk.* 4.18). Anointing with oil was also used by the early church in acts of exorcism and healing (*Mk.* 6.13, *Jas.* 5.14–15).

[*See also* Messiahs; Priests.]

BIBLIOGRAPHY

Collins, John J. *The Scepter and the Star.* Anchor Bible Reference Library. New York, 1995.

de Jonge, M. "The Use of the Word 'Anointed' in the Time of Jesus." *Novum Testamentum* 8 (1966), 132–148.

de Jonge, M. "Messiah." In *The Anchor Bible Dictionary,* edited by David Noel Freedman, vol. 4., pp. 777–788. New York, 1992.

Dudley, Martin, and Geoffrey Rowell. *The Oil of Gladness: Anointing in the Christian Tradition.* London, 1993.

Houtman, C. "On the Function of the Holy Incense (*Exodus* 30.34–38) and the Sacred Anointing Oil (*Exodus* 30.22–33)." *Vetus Testamentum* 42 (1992), 458–465.

LaSor, William Sanford. "The Messianic Idea in Qumran." In *Studies and Essays in Honor of Abraham A. Neuman,* edited by Meir Ben-Horin, pp. 343–364. Leiden, 1962.

Licht, Jacob. "Meshiḥah." In *Encyclopedia Biblica,* vol. 5, pp. 526–531. Jerusalem, 1968 (Hebrew).

Milgrom, Jacob. "Anointing." In *Encyclopedia Judaica,* vol. 3, pp. 27–28. Jerusalem, 1972.

HANNAH K. HARRINGTON

ANTIOCHUS IV EPIPHANES, son of Antiochus III "the Great," succeeded his brother Seleucus IV as king of the Seleucid empire in 175 BCE, and ruled over that kingdom until his own death in late 164 BCE. Antiochus's image is etched in the collective memories of Jews and Christians as the Syrian despot who imposed a systematic religious persecution on the Jews of Judea, setting in motion the Hasmonean uprising that ultimately led to Jewish political independence, thereby effecting a major turning point in the history of the Jewish people.

Antiochus's personality is projected by classical historians as eccentric and contradictory, at once generous and gregarious while also tyrannical. On his coins he employed the epithet [*Theos*] *Epiphanes* ("God manifest"), but Polybius (26.10) is often cited for his mocking rendering of the king's surname as *Epimanes* ("mad"). Antiochus inherited an empire in decline, following his father's defeat at the hands of the Romans, and his espousal of a fierce Hellenizing policy, evinced through the founding of more Greek *poleis* than all his Seleucid predecessors, is frequently interpreted as a step toward restoring the kingdom to its earlier prominence as the leading force in the Hellenistic East. Antiochus encouraged this process in Jerusalem as well, by deposing the high priest Onias and appointing his brother Jason (*2 Mc.* 4.7–10), who proceeded to introduce a variety of Hellenistic institutions into the city, and ultimately transformed the city into a Greek *polis* called "Antioch" (*2 Mc.* 4.9; the precise meaning of the text in *2 Maccabees* has been fiercely debated by scholars—see Tcherikover, 1959, pp. 161–169). Subsequently, Jason was also deposed by the king in favor a more docile pro-Hellenist, Menelaus (*2 Mc.* 4.23–27). In retrospect, this interference by Antiochus in the most sensitive areas of Jewish religious life was a harbinger of future events.

Antiochus embarked on two campaigns against Ptolemaic Egypt: in 170–169 BCE and again in 168 BCE. Neither expedition led to the king's ultimate goal of outright conquest, with the initial successes of the second campaign only to be thwarted by Roman intervention leading to Antiochus's retreat. It is unclear precisely when and in what sequence (compare *1 Mc.* 1.20–24, *2 Mc.* 5.11, and Josephus, *Jewish Antiquities* 12.242–250; see Mørkholm, 1966, p. 142; Tcherikover, 1959, pp. 473–474), but in close proximity to these campaigns disturbances broke out in Jerusalem, possibly encouraged by the perception of a Seleucid defeat and even the king's death (*2 Mc.* 5.5), and these were cruelly put down in the course of a visit (or visits) to the city by the Seleucid king himself. Within months, the king's steps toward neutralizing any Jewish opposition culminated in the imposition of religious persecution; under penalty of death, the Jews were required "to depart from the laws of their fathers and to cease living by the laws of God. Further, the sanctuary in Jerusalem was to be polluted and called after Zeus Olympius" (*2 Mc.* 6.1–2). Antiochus's expeditions to Egypt, as well as his "raging against the holy covenant," the desecration of the Temple, and the establishment therein of "the appalling abomination" are all described in great detail in the *Book of Daniel* (11.21–45). To this we might possibly now add Acts of a Greek King (4Q248), which has been interpreted (see Broshi and Eshel, 1997) as alluding to the actions undertaken by Antiochus both in Egypt and in Jerusalem, and which has even been dated earlier than *Daniel* and described as the possible source for the reference there (*Dn.* 11.39) to the king who "will distribute land for a price."

Antiochus did not personally devote his remaining years to the implementation of Seleucid policy against the Jews. The dwindling financial resources of his empire forced Antiochus to turn eastwards, and in 164 BCE he began an expedition with the intention of sacking one of the wealthy temples in Elymais. He died at Tabae, a city situated between Persis and Media, shortly before 20 November 164 BCE.

BIBLIOGRAPHY

Broshi, Magen, and Esther Eshel. "The Greek King Is Antiochus IV (4QHistorical Text=4Q248)." *Journal of Jewish Studies* 48 (1997), 120–129. The identification of a scroll fragment as a historical composition alluding to the Egyptian campaigns and steps against the Jews taken by Antiochus IV. A valuable summary of the questions and various solutions proposed to establish an accurate sequence of Antiochus's activities in the area, with major implications for the redactional relationships between Qumran material and the later books of the Hebrew scriptures.

Mørkholm, Otto. *Antiochus IV of Syria*. Copenhagen, 1966. A definitive study of the reign of Antiochus, with a complete chapter (pages 135–165) devoted to Seleucid policy in Judea.

Tcherikover, Victor. *Hellenistic Civilization and the Jews*. Philadelphia, 1959. A study of the events leading to the Hasmonean uprising, with particular attention to the prehistory of Hellenization in Jerusalem, and an analysis of all the theories addressing the nature and causes of the Antiochean persecution of the Jews.

ISAIAH M. GAFNI

APOCALYPTIC TEXTS. Writings that are governed by a worldview in which the revelation of divine secrets is constitutive of salvation from an alien or threatening world are referred to as apocalyptic.

Definitions: Traditional Terminology. The establishment of *apocalyptic* as a common term in the Western world is the result of nineteenth-century Christian historical and theological discourse, which took its cue from the initial Greek word of the New Testament *Book of Revelation, apokalypsis* ("revelation"). The noun *apocalypse* designated writings like *Revelation,* which claimed to reveal secrets about the future or the hidden parts of the cosmos. The adjective *apocalyptic* denoted the kind of dualistic eschatology presented in *Revelation*—the clash of divine and demonic powers that would be resolved in an imminent final judgment ending the present evil age and ushering in a new age and the return of primordial bliss. The adjective *apocalyptic* was also used as a noun that designated the worldview and theology that permeated the *Book of Revelation* and its Jewish precursors and that comprised such elements as the divine control of history, a developed angelology and demonology, eschatology, messianism, and resurrection (Russell, 1964). In popular parlance (the) *apocalypse* came to refer to the eschatological clash depicted in the *Book of Revelation*. In much of this scholarly and popular usage, the element of revelation inherent in the term *apocalyptic* faded or disappeared in favor of an emphasis on violent and dualistic eschatological cataclysm.

New Terminology. By the middle of the present century the variety of connotations and nuances applied to the term *apocalyptic* had created such semantic confusion that some scholars suggested the word should be discarded. The discovery of the Qumran scrolls further complicated the issue but also catalyzed a new discussion that has helped to clarify the apocalyptic phenomenon and its place on the religious and social horizon of Second Temple Judaism.

The new discussion was initiated by Klaus Koch (1972), who proposed that a good starting point would be an investigation of texts that most scholars would agree are apocalypses. Taking his cue from Koch, Paul D. Hanson (1976) distinguished the literary genre *apocalypse*, the *apocalyptic eschatology* found in such writings, and *apocalypticism*, the worldview expressed in apocalypses and embodied in social movements.

In a discussion of *1 Enoch*, Michael Stone (1978) drew attention to this work's great interest in cosmology, indicated its parallels in Israelite sapiential texts, and thus argued that Judaism of the Persian and early Hellenistic periods was more diverse than had been assumed in studies of apocalyptic literature that focused on the prophetic roots of its eschatology.

Further refining this discussion, a subgroup of a Society of Biblical Literature task force on genres examined the corpus of Jewish, Christian, and pagan texts that arguably could be called *apocalypses* and developed a definition and a detailed typology of the morphology of the texts. According to John Collins, an apocalypse is "a genre of revelatory literature with a narrative framework, in which a revelation is mediated by an otherworldly being to a human recipient, disclosing a transcendent reality which is both temporal, insofar as it envisages eschatological salvation, and spatial insofar as it involves another supernatural world" (Collins, 1979, p. 9). By emphasizing the activity of an otherworldly mediator and revealer, the presence of a "transcendent eschatology," and the frequent occurrence of cosmological revelations, the definition helped to distinguish the apocalypses from some of their biblical prophetic counterparts. Later, Collins added a statement about function: an apocalypse is "intended to interpret present, earthly circumstances in the light of the supernatural world and of the future, and to influence both the understanding and the behavior of the audience by means of divine authority" (1991, p. 19).

The distinction between the genre apocalypse, on the one hand, and apocalyptic eschatology and apocalypticism, on the other hand, significantly clarified discussion of biblical texts; nonetheless, the retention of the root *apocalyp-* in the latter cases allows some terminological confusion to remain. Paul D. Hanson finds "apocalyptic eschatology" (the eschatology found in apocalypses) already in promises of a new creation in "Third Isaiah." Collins (1992) distinguishes between the genre apocalypse and apocalypticism, which is a worldview with two components: a heightened interest in otherworldly regions and supernatural beings and an eschatology in which belief in the judgment of the dead transcends the eschatology of the later prophets. At the same time, he supposes that this worldview preceded and gave rise to the literary phenomenon of apocalypse. The terminological confusion in both instances involves the use of the term *apocalyptic* or *apocalypticism* in the absence of the revealer and the mechanisms of revelation that are central to the apocalypses.

Apocalyptic Collections from the Greco-Roman Period. The present discussion focuses on two early collections of apocalypses, *1 Enoch* and *Daniel*, which then provide a basis of brief comparison with other texts, mainly from the Qumran corpus, that may be said to be apocalypses or to reflect an apocalyptic worldview.

1 Enoch. This lengthy collection of revelatory texts is an appropriate starting point for several reasons. It contains all the elements comprised by an apocalyptic worldview and presents them within the framework of an explicit claim to revelation. The traditions contained in the work are among the oldest in apocalyptic literature and are, thus, potentially helpful in tracing the origins of the phenomenon. The complexity of the corpus discourages oversimplifying definition.

Composed in Aramaic between the fourth century BCE and the turn of the era, the components of this gradually evolving corpus claim to record revelations that were received by the ancient patriarch mentioned in *Genesis* 5.18–24. Although no part of *1 Enoch* seems to have been composed at Qumran, its popularity there is attested by eleven fragmentary manuscripts from Cave 4, which preserve bits and pieces of four of its five major sections.

The book *1 Enoch* is appropriately called an apocalyptic writing because mediated revelation is not only present in the text but is essential to its dualistic worldview (Nickelsburg, 1991). A temporal dualism opposes the present time of experience to a hidden future or a remote past; a spatial dualism counterpoises the inhabited world and the rest of the cosmos. A complex of ontological dualisms is folded into both temporal and spatial dualisms. Humanity, distinct from the superhuman realm of God, angels, and demons, is inextricably bound up with their activity, and God and God's angels are pitted against the demonic powers. These respective dualisms are mitigated by the apocalypticists' revelations, which unveil the hidden future and penetrate the inaccessible parts of the cosmos. The revelations effect salvation by enabling people to endure the present time and world of evil experience in the knowledge that God's will is being done in the heavenly throne room and out in the cosmos, and that divine justice will be effected among humans when the final judgment obliterates evil and the new age becomes present reality.

The imminent arrival of this judgment is the dominant theme of *1 Enoch*. Judgment is necessitated by the present pervasive state of injustice, which is manifested variously in the gentiles' victimization of Israel, the persecution and oppression of the righteous poor by rich and powerful "sinners," and the success of false teachers in leading many astray from the correct interpretation of God's commandments (Nickelsburg, 1985, pp. 336–339). In the judgment, the respective groups will receive the just recompense that hitherto has been lacking. As a function of this judgment, the righteous who have died unjustly will be rewarded in spite of death, and the prosperous sinners will be punished after they have died.

The message of judgment of *1 Enoch* places the present world of evil, suffering, and injustice in relation to their future resolution in the judgment and the new creation that will follow it. This viewpoint is "eschatological" because it envisions an end (Gr., *eschaton*) to the present order and the beginning of a qualitatively new state of affairs. The temporal axis of *1 Enoch* also projects backward into primordial times, when angelic revolt originated the violence, sexual promiscuity, and some of the false teachings that are focal in the authors' portrayal of evil.

The spatial dimension reinforces *1 Enoch*'s temporal axis. In contrast to the evil and injustice that pervade the world, in heaven God's angels record human deeds in preparation for the judgment and plead the cause of the righteous. Beyond the inhabited world, on the mountain of the dead, the souls of the righteous and wicked are separated for reward and punishment, and at the ends of the earth the pits of hell are stoked. Running through the accounts of Enoch's cosmic journeys and related sections of *1 Enoch* is the belief that the Creator has built order and justice into the structure and operation of the cosmos, which are securely under the control of God's angelic deputies and aides.

All this information is explicitly presented as revelation, that is, the divine unveiling of hidden things: the events of the future and their timing and the periodized structure of human history; the places beyond the inhabited world and the activities that occur in them. Even in the "Book of the Luminaries" (chaps. 72–82), which contains information that could be gathered from empirical observation, the author claims to have seen these things in the company of an interpreting angel. Revelation in *1 Enoch* is always visual and usually auditory as well. Enoch sees the enthroned Deity and hears the divine oracle of judgment. Traveling around the world, he sees cosmological phenomena and hears the accompanying angel interpret them. The angel commands him to look at the book of human deeds and read and learn what is written in it (81.1–4) so that he can recount the structure of human history (93.1–2). Dream visions are especially important in this text: Enoch's ascent to heaven occurs in a dream vision (chaps. 13–16). Chapters 17–32 imply that Enoch's cosmic journeys took place within that dream vision, as angels led him away from the heavenly throne room (17.1), although the narrative at the conclusion of these journeys depicts a physical return to his house rather than an awakening from sleep (81.5). The dream visions in chapters 83–84 and 85–90 differ from the others in not having an otherworldly figure interpret what Enoch has seen (although chapters 85–90, reflecting chapters 12–36, depict Enoch traveling in the company of angels).

The components of *1 Enoch* are cast in a wide variety of literary forms that are paralleled in biblical and postbiblical Israelite literature and in non-Israelite literature. These include a prophetic oracle (chaps. 1–5); an account of a heavenly prophetic commissioning that is especially reminiscent of *Ezekiel* 1–2 and 40–48 (chaps. 12–16); journeys to the underworld that recall both the Greek *nekyia* ("journey to the underworld") and *Ezekiel* 40–48 and *Zechariah* 1–6 (chaps. 17–36); symbolic dream visions (chaps. 83–90); and an epistle (chaps. 92–105) that comprises, in turn, oracles of woe, beatitudes, predictions of what will happen "in those days," and proverbial two-ways ethical instruction (cf. chap. 91). In addition, the narrative thread that organized the penultimate form of *1 Enoch* (chaps. 1–32, 81.1–81.3, chaps. 91–105) is shaped in the well-known genre of a testament, which presents the text as Enoch's last words delivered to his son Methuselah in order to be transmitted to his children—the righteous who will live in the last days (Nickelsburg, 1981, pp. 150–151).

The prophetic forms support the authors' claims to be presenting revelation. Other forms typical of Israelite sapiential literature are qualified so as to indicate the revealed character of their content. Enoch presents his two-ways instruction as a corollary of the revelations he has received about the future (91.1). He cites and alludes to his visions in support of his admonitions (103.1–4; cf. 98.7–8, 104.1–2, 104.7–8). He defines his testament—a traditional form found in many contexts—as the written, earthly deposit of heavenly "wisdom" that will function as a testimony for future generations (81.6–82.3, 104.12–105.2). Twice he alludes to its contents with the formula "wisdom shall be given" (5.8, 93.10), and the revelatory "Book of Parables" is explicitly presented as "wisdom" (37.1–4).

The Enochic claims to revelation provide or refer to several kinds of salvific knowledge: instruction about the right calendar; a range of other mandates, necessary for salvation, implied in admonitions to walk in the path of uprightness (cf. 99.10, 100.6); belief in God's justice, which enables one not to apostatize in the face of oppression and persecution.

The revelation of this Enochic wisdom constitutes an exclusive eschatological community of the chosen, who will survive the coming judgment. Who these people were is impossible to know. The evidence does not allow us to identify them with any known group in Judaism, though they appear to have been historical predecessors of the Qumran community, who preserved their literature. The identity of the authors of the texts is hinted at in two ways: the leaders of the righteous are called "the wise" (98.9, 99.10), and Enoch is described as a "scribe" (12.4, 15.1, 92.1).

Daniel. This second major work of the pre-Christian era (composed c.165/64 BCE), which was also found in multiple manuscripts in the Qumran caves, manifests important similarities to *1 Enoch* and significant differences from it. The biblical books *1 Enoch* and *Daniel* (especially *Daniel* 7–12) are substantially similar in their worldview and the form, function, and some of the content of their revelations. The latter half of Daniel posits a sharp opposition between the divine and demonic realms and sees human history as a mirror of events on this level. Visionary eschatological revelations mediated by angels to a figure of the past—who is both sage and seer—penetrate the hidden realms of time and space. The three visions in chapters 7, 8, and 10–12 (as well as the one in chapter 2) recount the determined course of history from the fictional author's time to the great judgment and the new age, which are expected in the real author's time (cf. *1 En.* 85–90, 93.1–10, 91.11–17). Chapters 2 and 7 are dream visions, and the contents of chapters 2, 7, and 8 are symbolic, like *1 Enoch* 85–90, although chapters 7 and 8 are interpreted by angels. The promise of an imminent judgment and resurrection encourages the faithful to stand fast despite persecution. Chapter 7 schematizes latter-day history into four periods that have a counterpart in the four periods of demonic activity in *1 Enoch* 89.59–90.19 (cf. also *Daniel* 2). In addition, *Daniel* 7 draws on the tradition of the throne vision in *1 Enoch* 14–15 and, in turn, informs the vision about the "Son of Man" in *1 Enoch* 46–48. The vision in *Daniel* 10–12, which recounts the course of history inscribed in the heavenly "book of truth," is presented as a kind of prophetic commissioning that is to be recorded in a written document to be revealed in the end time (12.9; cf. *1 En.* 14–15). Like *1 Enoch, Daniel* has sapiential features. Its heroes are sages, skilled in dream interpretation, and their latter-day counterparts are "the wise" (Heb., *maskilim*).

Daniel also differs from *1 Enoch.* Its account of the archdemon's revolt against heaven (chap. 8) draws on *Isaiah* 14 rather than *Genesis* 6 (cf. *1 En.* 6–11) and identifies the revolt with the demon's present rather than primordial activity. Although *Daniel*'s eschatology posits a great judgment that separates the present evil time from a new creation, the Danielic authors indicate no interest in the cosmological information that dominates *1 Enoch* and reinforces its eschatological message. Apart from the dream visions and a commissioning account, *Daniel* lacks the literary forms that constitute much of the Enochic text. Similarly, the biographical narratives that introduce the recipient of revelation and his friends (chaps. 1–6) do not constitute a testamentary framework but recount a set of traditional court tales that exemplify the wisdom and faithfulness of Daniel and his friends. The book's audience appears to have been faithful Israelites in general and not an exclusive group who saw their adherence to a particular interpretation of the Torah as constitutive of their status as the chosen. [*See* Court Tales.]

Early Apocalyptic Writings. Our findings allow some conclusions about the form, content, and function of early apocalyptic writings and offer some hints about their origin.

Shared peculiarities. Although *1 Enoch* and *Daniel* contain much material that is paralleled in the Hebrew scriptures, and especially their prophetic and sapiential books, the peculiar contour of the two works lies in a unique cluster of substantial and formal elements. Their worldview is governed by a dualism that emphasizes the origin and activities of an immense demonic realm that victimizes human beings and clashes with God and God's angels. Both works speculate about the ordered structure of human history and feature an enhanced eschatology, with a final judgment that will end the demonic hold on humanity and a new creation that is epitomized in a resurrection or its equivalent. They embody all this in accounts of visionary eschatological revelations received in dreams or in cosmic journeys, and they attribute these revelations to sages and seers from the past who were not biblical prophets of record. They also employ sapiential self-designations, terminology, and literary forms.

Rationale and function of the apocalyptic synthesis. This cluster of elements has an integrity. The demonic mythology is consonant with the experience of persecution and acute sense of victimization that pervades these books; evil is perceived as too massive to be attributed merely to humans. Speculation about the structure of the cosmos in *1 Enoch* and the periodization of history in both works is related to their demonology. Historically, speculation has supported the hope for an imminent end to evil times, and cosmologists have found order in a chaotic universe, attributing ultimate power to the Creator of a cosmos that the Hellenistic world found to be much larger than had been supposed. Their perception of the immensity of the cosmos and the consequent remoteness of God helps explain their multiplication of angels with cosmic functions and the stipulation of other angels as intercessors who provided access to that God. Their appeal to revelation attested the veracity and authority of their own worldview. Thus, the apocalyptic synthesis functioned to alleviate the threat of a world that was experienced as chaotic, unjust, hostile, and threatening. It maintained that, in the final analysis, the divine King and his entourage were in control, and order and justice would prevail over evident chaos and experienced injustice. In some respects, this synthesis paralleled contemporary philosophical systems, astrological speculation, and magical practice.

Roots and provenance of apocalypticism. Like much of the religious and cultural syncretism of the Hellenistic age, the roots of apocalypticism are diverse, multicultural, and often difficult to disentangle. Elements in the demonic mythology and its dualism were drawn from Greek and Near Eastern religions. Speculation about the ordered structure of history derived from Mesopotamian sources, although many elements in the eschatology of *1 Enoch* and *Daniel* hark back to the prophets. The sense of cosmic order in *1 Enoch* has many parallels in contemporary Israelite sapiential literature, although the data that underlie these texts surely reflect the activity and observations of both non-Israelite and Israelite sages. While the claims to revelation in *1 Enoch* and *Daniel* are carried in forms that derive from the prophetic corpus, their embodiment in accounts and interpretations of dream visions is beholden to the sapiential tradition attested in the Joseph cycle of *Genesis* and also reflects broader currents in Mediterranean and Near Eastern antiquity. Thus, it is not by accident that Daniel and his friends are counterpoised to Babylonian sages and that the figures of Enoch and Daniel have Mesopotamian counterparts.

The provenance of apocalypticism is more difficult to identify because it is masked by the pseudepigraphic attribution of these works. Nonetheless, the cluster of elements in these texts suggests some inferences, which will need much more detailed consideration and explication. The creators and masters of the apocalyptic synthesis were members of a learned class of scribes and sages, who were the keepers and interpreters of the sacred Israelite tradition that was in the process of becoming the Hebrew scriptures and were knowledgeable also in the religious and intellectual traditions of their non-Israelite neighbors. In this respect, Ben Sira's description of the scribe is suggestive (*Sir.* 39.1–5). Moreover, his concern about right conduct and its consequences, his interest in the cosmic order (42.15–43.33), and his respect for the prophets (39.1; chaps. 45–49) indicate that we may look among such sages for the sapiential-prophetic synthesis found in the apocalyptic writings (Argall, 1995).

These similarities notwithstanding, the apocalyptic authors differed substantially from scribes such as Ben Sira in their epistemology, their understanding of revelation, and their appropriation of the prophetic tradition. For Ben Sira the regularity of the cosmos could be perceived by empirical observation, even if it revealed the power of the Creator (41.15–43.33). Moreover, though he claimed to "pour out teaching like prophecy" (24.32–33), he viewed the prophetic corpus as an extant body of ancient tradition that was to be interpreted, and he severely criticized divination from dream visions (34.1–8). Finally, the prophetic vision of the future was interpreted without reference to the activity of opposed divine and demonic realms.

The authors of *1 Enoch*, to the contrary, intensified prophetic eschatology and incorporated it into a dualistic worldview that counterpoised the present and the future and the divine and demonic realms. They presented this worldview in accounts of revelation, and they anchored their assertions about the order of the cosmos in accounts of revelatory journeys (cf. 2.1–5.3 for an exception). Their pseudepigraphic ascription notwithstanding, the Enochic authors' use of prophetic revelatory forms and accounts of dream visions suggests that they saw themselves as latter-day representatives of the prophetic tradition.

Apocalypticism Outside of the Apocalypses. If a particular claim to revelation is integral to the worldview of the apocalypses, one should exercise caution in the use of the term *apocalyptic* with respect to texts that do not explicitly make that claim. Of course, a text that presents a dualistic worldview with a radical eschatology may, in fact, have derived this from an apocalypse and, thus, may presume an apocalyptic notion of revelation. Here a close exegesis of specific relevant texts may provide answers to some difficult questions. Which is prior: the account of the activity of the two spirits in Rule of the Community from Cave 1 (hereafter, 1QRule of Community; iii.13–iv.26) or the pseudepigraphal account of a vision of the confrontation of these spirits in the Visions of Amram? Does the language in 1QRule of the Community (1QS xi.3–9) presume apocalyptic accounts like *1 Enoch* or even claim that the author had such visions? Does 1QHodayot[a] ix.24 (1QH[a] i.24) presume something like Enoch's vision of the heavenly tablets (*1 En.* 81.1–3)? What is the relationship of the Ages of Creation (4Q180–181) to the Enochic "Apocalypse of Weeks" and its claim to be based on a reading of the heavenly tablets?

One can postulate the existence of heavenly tablets or armies of angels and hordes of demons without claiming to have seen them or before any one claimed to have seen them. One can believe in a resurrection without claiming that this was revealed by an angel. If this is the case, what are the roots, precipitating causes, and specific functions of texts that ascribe these beliefs to a particular kind of revelation? Historical and conceptual clarity will be helped by a distinction that reserves the term *apocalyptic* for the revelatory embodiment of the beliefs.

Revelation in the Qumran Community. Clarity on these issues may provide a context for a broader discussion of revelation in the Qumran community. Pesher Habakkuk (1QpHab vii.1–8) asserts that God revealed the time of the end to the Teacher of Righteousness. What were the mechanisms of revelation, and how does this eschatological speculation compare and relate to revelation in the apocalypses? 1QRule of the Community (1QS v.9) posits a revealed interpretation of the Torah, the observance of which is necessary for salvation. A similar notion appears in the Damascus Document (CD vi–vii). What, again, were the actual and claimed mechanisms of such revelation, and how did the claim relate to *Jubilees* 23.26 and to *Jubilees'* assertion that its Torah derives from an angelic revelation of laws inscribed on heavenly tablets?

The Genre Apocalypse at Qumran. Many questions remain about the role that the genre apocalypse played in Qumran piety. How, precisely, were *Daniel, 1 Enoch, Jubilees,* and the Vision of Amram used at Qumran? What other Qumranic texts might be identified as apocalypses or apocalyptic? In addition to *1 Enoch,* García Martínez identifies the following as "apocalyptic" texts composed at Qumran: Elect of God (4Q534); Prayer of Nabonidus (4Q242); Pseudo-Daniel (4Q243–245); Aramaic Apocalypse (4Q246); and New Jerusalem (1Q32, 2Q24, 4Q232, 4Q554–555, 5Q15, 11Q18). Because of the fragmentary character of these works, it is difficult to decide whether the designation is appropriate. It is not sufficient to point to the oracular form and eschatological content of some of them, and one must remember that the heavenly Jerusalem has a parallel in *Ezekiel* 40–48. How one deals with these issues and how one decides whether any of these works was likely composed at Qumran will affect our understanding of the character of revelation at Qumran and the propriety of referring to the community as "apocalyptic."

[*See also* Amram; Daniel, Book of, *article on* Pseudo-Daniel; Enoch, Books of; Eschatology; Messianic Apocalypse; New Jerusalem; Revelation; Revelation, Book of; *and* War of the Sons of Light against the Sons of Darkness.]

BIBLIOGRAPHY

Argall, Randall. *1 Enoch and Sirach: A Comparative Literary and Conceptual Analysis of the Themes of Revelation, Creation, and Judgment.* Society of Biblical Literature, Early Judaism, and Its Literature, 8. Atlanta, 1995.

Collins, John J., ed. *Apocalypse: The Morphology of a Genre. Semeia,* 14. Missoula, Mont., 1979.

Collins, John J. *The Apocalyptic Imagination: An Introduction to the Jewish Matrix of Christianity.* New York, 1984. Excellent introduction to Jewish apocalyptic literature, its forms, contents, settings, and functions.

Collins, John J. "Apocalyptic Literature." In *Early Judaism and Its Modern Interpreters,* edited by Robert A. Kraft and George W. E. Nickelsburg, pp. 345–370. Philadelphia and Atlanta, 1986. Review of the scholarly discussion of apocalyptic literature.

Collins, John J. "Genre, Ideology, and Social Movements in Jewish Apocalypticism." In *Mysteries and Revelations: Apocalyptic Studies since the Uppsala Colloquium,* edited by John J. Collins and James H. Charlesworth, pp. 11–32. Journal for the Study of the Pseudepigrapha, Supplement Series, 9. Sheffield, 1991.

Collins, John J., and Adela Yarbro Collins. "Apocalypses and Apocalypticism: Early Jewish Apocalypticism" and "Early Christian." In *The Anchor Bible Dictionary,* edited by David Noel Freedman, 1, pp. 282–292. 6 vols. New York, 1992. Discussion of Jewish and Christian apocalyptic literature and their contexts.

Collins, John J. *Daniel: A Commentary on the Book of Daniel.* Hermeneia. Minneapolis, 1993.

García Martínez, Florentino. *Qumran and Apocalyptic: Studies on the Aramaic Texts from Qumran.* Studies on the Texts of the Desert of Judah, 9. Leiden, 1992. Collection of articles.

Hanson, Paul D. *The Dawn of Apocalyptic.* Philadelphia, 1975. Study of Third Isaiah and Deutero-Zechariah.

Hanson, Paul D. "Apocalypticism." In *Interpreter's Dictionary of the Bible, Supplementary Volume,* edited by Keith Crim, 28–34. Nashville, 1976.

Hellholm, David, ed. *Apocalypticism in the Mediterranean World and the Near East: Proceedings of the International Colloquium on Apocalypticism, Uppsala, August 12–17, 1979.* Tübingen, 1983. Important collection of papers.

Koch, Klaus. *The Rediscovery of Apocalyptic: A Polemical Work on a Neglected Area of Biblical Studies and Its Damaging Effects on Theology and Philosophy.* Studies in Biblical Theology, 2. Naperville, Ill, 1972. See page 22.

Nickelsburg, George W. E. *Jewish Literature between the Bible and the Mishnah.* Philadelphia, 1981. See pages 47–55, 90–94, 145–151, and 214–223 for introductory material on *1 Enoch.*

Nickelsburg, George W. E. "Revealed Wisdom as a Criterion for Inclusion and Exclusion: From Jewish Sectarianism to Early Christianity." In *To See Ourselves as Others See Us: Christians, Jews, "Others" in Late Antiquity,* edited by Jacob Neusner and Ernest S. Frerichs, pp. 73–91. Atlanta, 1985.

Nickelsburg, George W. E. "The Apocalyptic Construction of Reality in *1 Enoch.*" In *Mysteries and Revelations: Apocalyptic Studies since the Uppsala Colloquium,* edited by John J. Collins and James H. Charlesworth, pp. 51–64. Journal for the Study of the Pseudepigrapha, Supplement Series, 9. Sheffield, 1991.

Rowland, Christopher. *The Open Heaven: A Study of Apocalyptic in Judaism and Early Christianity.* London and New York, 1982. Rightly emphasizes centrality of revelations and importance of cosmological material.

Russell, D. S. *The Method and Message of Jewish Apocalyptic.* Old Testament Library. Philadelphia, 1964. Early handbook reflecting traditional approach to this literature.

Stone, Michael. "1 Enoch and Judaism in the Third Century B.C.E." *Catholic Biblical Quarterly* 40 (1978), 479–492. Important historical study.

GEORGE W. E. NICKELSBURG

APOCRYPHA AND PSEUDEPIGRAPHA. The word *Apocrypha* means "hidden things," but the term is used traditionally to refer to those books included in the Old Testament of the Latin Vulgate translation but not in the Hebrew scriptures. The category embraces fifteen books or portions of books: *1 Esdras, 2 Esdras, Tobit, Judith, Additions to Esther, Wisdom of Solomon, Ben Sira, I Baruch, Letter of Jeremiah, Prayer of Manasseh, 1 Maccabees, 2 Maccabees, Prayer of Azariah and the Song of the Three Young Men, Susanna,* and *Bel and the Dragon* (the last three items are known collectively as the *Additions to Daniel*). The books *3 Maccabees* and *4 Maccabees* sometimes are included, as is *Psalm 151* (these books are found in the Greek Bible). The *Psalms of Solomon* also is found in manuscripts of the Greek Bible but is not traditionally classified with the Apocrypha.

All these writings originally were composed between 200 BCE and 150 CE. All at some point were regarded as canonical scriptures, although some were more widely accepted than others. Older scholarship explained this more inclusive collection of scriptures by positing an "Alexandrian canon," that is, by supposing that the Jews of Alexandria had a more inclusive collection of scriptures than their Palestinian counterparts. The idea of an Alexandrian canon was discredited by the work of Albert Sundberg, who showed that Judaism before 70 CE had a fixed canon of Torah and Prophets, but an open-ended collection of Writings. The Christian Old Testament canon continued to fluctuate for some centuries. Jerome (c.400) distinguished sharply between the books found in the Hebrew scriptures and those that were not, but he translated the Apocrypha into Latin nonetheless. The Protestant Reformers excluded the Apocrypha from the canon, but the Roman Catholic church at the Council of Trent accepted them (excluding *1* and *2 Esdras* and the *Prayer of Manasseh*). Those books that are accepted by the Roman Catholic church but rejected by Protestants are called "deutero-canonical."

The word *pseudepigrapha* means "falsely attributed writings." In this case there is no quasi-canonical collection, and the period of composition cannot be delimited firmly. The "Old Testament pseudepigrapha" primarily are books attributed to figures that appear in the Old Testament (Adam, Enoch, Abraham, Moses, etc.), but the category also is extended to Jewish works ascribed to pagan authors, such as the *Sibylline Oracles*. None of these works is older than the Hellenistic period. Many of them, however, are of uncertain date and provenance, and some of them were composed by Christians. The most important Jewish pseudepigrapha are *1 Enoch, 2 Enoch, Jubilees,* the *Psalms of Solomon,* the *Testament of Moses* or *Assumption of Moses, 4 Ezra, 2 Baruch, 3 Baruch,* the *Sibylline Oracles,* and the *Letter of Aristeas.* The *Prayer of Manasseh,* usually classified with the Apocrypha, is also a pseudepigraphon. The *Testaments of the Twelve Patriarchs* are Christian in their final form but contain much Jewish material and may have originated as a Jewish composition. Unlike the Apocrypha, most of the pseudepigrapha were never accepted as scripture, but *1 Enoch* and *Jubilees* were regarded as authoritative in some circles and subsequently became canonical in the Ethiopian church.

Apocrypha. All the books of the Apocrypha were transmitted in both Greek and Latin. Only in the case of *Ben Sira* was a significant portion of a Hebrew text preserved.

Ben Sira. Several Hebrew citations from that book are known from rabbinic literature. At the end of the nineteenth century several leaves of the book, representing four distinct manuscripts, were found at Cambridge University in the materials recovered from the Cairo Genizah. Fragments of two more manuscripts were later discovered, one at the Jewish Theological Seminary of America in New York and one in Cambridge. These fragments are all of medieval origin and include most of chapters 3–16 and fragments of chapters 18–36. The Dead Sea Scrolls yielded much older fragments, from around the turn of the era. Two fragments of *Ben Sira* from Cave 2 (2Q18) contain only four complete words and some letters from chapter 6, but the Psalms Scroll from Cave 11 contains *Ben Sira* 51.13–20 and the last two words of verse 30b. Finally, twenty-six leather fragments from one scroll were found at Masada. These date to the first century BCE and contain portions of chapters 39 through 44. In general, these fragments confirm the antiquity of manuscript B from the Cairo Genizah and indirectly enhance the credibility of the other fragments. The fragment of *Ben Sira* 51 found in the Psalms Scroll is not part of a manuscript of *Ben Sira*. This is an autobiographical poem in praise of wisdom. It is in the form of an acrostic and makes some use of erotic imagery. Opinion is divided as to whether this poem is the work of Ben Sira and reflects his autobiography or is simply a wisdom poem that became attached secondarily to the book.

Book of Tobit. The *Book of Tobit* is represented at Qumran by four Aramaic manuscripts and one Hebrew manuscript. These copies show that Tobit was composed in a Semitic language, although they leave open the question as to whether it was Hebrew or Aramaic. Current opinion favors the priority of the Aramaic. The Semitic fragments support the long form of the text of *Tobit* that is found in Codex Sinaiticus over the short form found in Codices Vaticanus, Alexandrinus, and Venetus. [*See* Tobit, Book of.]

Only two other compositions traditionally associated with the Apocrypha have been found at Qumran: *Psalm 151* and the *Letter of Jeremiah.*

Psalm 151. Present in the Septuagint and also preserved in Syriac as one of five apocryphal psalms, *Psalm 151* is found in Hebrew in the Psalms Scroll from Cave 11 as two separate psalms (*Psalm 151 A* and *151 B*). *Psalm 151 B* is poorly preserved. Only the heading, half of verse 1, and a few letters of verse 2 survive. The heading seems to correspond to verses 6 and 7 in the Greek and Syriac versions. The Greek *Psalm 151,* on which the Syriac depends, is a conflation and condensation of the two Hebrew psalms. Where the Hebrew is preserved it shows a fuller and longer text. Verses 5 and 6 of *Psalm A* are not represented in the Greek and Syriac versions. These verses say that the mountains and hills do not bear witness to God, and some scholars think that they were omitted intentionally. Other scholars, however, interpret these verses as questions ("do not the mountains bear witness to me?") and so render them theologically unobjectionable.

Letter of Jeremiah. A polemic against idols, the *Letter of Jeremiah* is sometimes found after *Lamentations* in the Greek manuscripts and sometimes after *Baruch.* From the time of Jerome, the *Letter of Jeremiah* has been consistently appended to *Baruch* as chapter 6. Most scholars think that the *Letter of Jeremiah* was composed in Hebrew, but the fragment found at Qumran (7Q2) is in Greek. The manuscript dates from about 100 BCE. It contains only verses 43 and 44.

Omissions. The majority of the writings that came to constitute the Apocrypha have not been found at Qumran. In some cases, their absence is not surprising. The Qumran settlement was destroyed before *2 Esdras* and *4 Maccabees* were written. The *Wisdom of Solomon* and *3 Maccabees* were most probably composed in Alexandria close to the middle of the first century CE, too late to have found their way to Qumran. In some cases, the absence of specific books may be due to ideological considerations. The *First Book of Maccabees* was almost certainly composed in Hebrew, before the end of the second century BCE. And although it certainly was current in Israel at the time when many of the Dead Sea Scrolls were being written, no trace of it is found among them. The absence of *2 Maccabees* is less remarkable since it was abridged from the history of Jason of Cyrene in the Diaspora. The lack of any literature about the Maccabees is surely significant as regards the ideology of the people who hid the scrolls and shows that they were not supporters of the Hasmoneans in general. The *Book of Judith,* which celebrates the defeat of a foreign invader, also may be regarded as pro-Maccabean and is missing from the scrolls, although it too was probably written no later than the first century BCE.

In other cases, however, the absence of apocryphal writings can be explained by neither unavailability nor ideological reasons. The additions to *Daniel* (the *Prayer of Azariah and the Song of the Three Young Men, Susana, and Bel and the Dragon*) are similar in genre to stories and prayers that are found in the Dead Sea Scrolls. The *Prayer of Azariah* is thought to date from Maccabean times. *Bel and the Dragon* contradicts the canonical *Book of Daniel* by making Daniel a priest, and so is likely to have been composed before the biblical book had become established as authoritative. Yet none of these writings has been found in the caves. (Józef Milik tentatively identified 4Q551 as a fragment of *Susana,* but the identification is not persuasive.) Similarly, the Old Greek of *Daniel* 4–6 is very different from the text of the Hebrew scriptures and is widely believed to be based on a different Semitic text. Yet no trace of such a textual tradition has been found at Qumran. In these cases, we can only conclude that the writings in question were not known or transmitted universally. Furthermore, there is no evidence that *Ben Sira* and *Tobit* had the status of sacred scripture at Qumran. The apocryphal psalms in the Psalms Scroll are not differentiated from the psalms that have been traditionally recognized as canonical. Some scholars have argued that this was a liturgical collection, but the lack of differentiation is still significant. There is no example of a *pesher* or formal interpretation of an apocryphal psalm, but then we have such interpretations for only a few of the canonical psalms. The status of the apocryphal psalms at Qumran remains uncertain.

Pseudepigrapha. Among the pseudepigrapha, the books of *Enoch* and *Jubilees* are most prominent at Qumran. The *Apocalypse of Enoch, 1 Enoch,* is fully preserved only in Ethiopic, with some fragments in Greek. It is a composite book containing five major works: the "Book of Watchers" (chapters 1–36); the "Similitudes" (37–71); the "Astronomical Book" (72–82); the "Book of Dreams," including the "Animal Apocalypse" (83–90); and the "Epistle," including the "Apocalypse of Weeks" (91–105). Appended at the end are a brief "Book of Noah" (106–107; see below) and a discourse on the last judgment, addressed to Methuselah (108). Aramaic fragments of all sections except the "Similitudes" and the concluding discourse have been found at Qumran. The "Astronomical Book" was copied separately, and is found in four copies (4Q208–211). Seven manuscripts contain fragments of the other sections.

Enoch. Enoch^{a} and Enoch^{b} (4Q201 and 202) contain only fragments of the "Book of Watchers." Enoch^{d} and Enoch^{e} (4Q205 and 206) combine fragments of the "Book of Watchers" and the "Book of Dreams." Enoch^{c} (4Q204) contains fragments of the "Book of Watchers," the "Book of Dreams," the end of the "Epistle," and the "Book of Noah" (104–107). Enoch^{f} (4Q207) contains a fragment of the "Book of Dreams"; and Enoch^{g} (4Q212) contains fragments of the "Epistle." Moreover, there are allusions to the Enoch literature in sectarian compositions (for example, the Damascus Document [CD ii.18] refers to the story of the "Watchers." The motif of planting in *1 Enoch* 93.10 is echoed in the Damascus Document i.7 and other passages).

Jubilees. This work is even more prominent in the scrolls than the Enoch literature. The book is fully preserved in Ethiopic, but fragments of the Hebrew original have now been found in fourteen (possibly fifteen) manuscripts from Qumran: two from Cave 1, 1Q17 and 18; two from Cave 2, 2Q19 and 20; one from Cave 3, 3Q5; eight or possibly nine from Cave 4, 4Q176a and 4Q216–224; and one from Cave 11, 11Q12. There are also three fragments that have been dubbed Pseudo-Jubilees (4Q225, 226, and 227). All three mention Moses and have parallels to material dealt with in *Jubilees* but do not correspond to the Ethiopic text of *Jubilees.* There appears to be an explicit reference to *Jubilees* in the Damascus Document, CD xvi.3–4, where it is called "the book of the divisions of the periods according to their jubilees and their weeks." Another fragment, 4Q228, may also refer to *Jubilees* as an authority or source of information. The sheer number of manuscripts is significant. Only *Genesis, Exodus, Deuteronomy, Isaiah,* and *Psalms* are represented by more manuscripts than the pseudepigrapha of *Enoch* and *Jubilees.* It is very likely that they were regarded as authoritative scripture at Qumran. Both these books became canonical in the church of Ethiopia; *1 Enoch* may have been more widely regarded as canonical (cf. *Jude* 14–15, Epistle of Barnabas 16.5).

Testaments of the Twelve Patriarchs. Materials have also been found at Qumran that relate to the *Testaments of the Twelve Patriarchs.* In this case, the relationship of the Qumran fragments to the Greek pseudepigraphon is much more complex, in part because there is no consensus on the provenance of the Greek Testaments. The presence of Christian elements is undeniable, but there has been a long-standing debate as to whether the *Testaments of the Twelve Patriarchs* is a Christian composition (M. de Jonge) or a Jewish work that was later interpolated by Christians (Charles). The fragments found at Qumran do not preserve the distinctive elements of the literary form of testaments and should probably be regarded as source documents for the Greek Testaments rather than as fragments of Testaments themselves.

The most important fragments relate to the *Testament of Levi.* The Aramaic fragments, 1Q21, 4Q213, and 4Q214, are part of a Levi apocryphon that coincides partially with material in the Greek Testaments and partially with Aramaic fragments found in the Cairo Genizah, which themselves partially overlap with the Greek Testaments. The Aramaic fragments from Qumran and the Cairo Genizah also overlap with additional material found in a Greek manuscript of the Testaments from Mount Athos but not in most manuscripts of the Testaments. From these fragments it is possible to reconstruct an Aramaic Levi apocryphon that corresponds in large part to chapters 2–15 of the *Testament of Levi*, with some additional material, notably the "Prayer of Levi," which is also found in Greek in the Mount Athos manuscript. Milik and Puech have argued that other fragments (4Q540, 541, 548) correspond to passages in the *Testament of Levi* 17–19. While these fragments bear some similarity to the Testament, however, the similarity is not enough to warrant identification.

Milik has also tentatively identified fragments of the *Testaments of Judah* (3Q7, 4Q484, 4Q538) and *Joseph* (4Q539), but in these cases the identifications are very doubtful. A Hebrew fragment (4Q215) parallels a passage in the *Testament of Naphtali* but again may be a source on which the author of the Greek Testaments drew rather than part of a Hebrew testament. A much later, medieval Hebrew *Testament of Naphtali* is known, but it is not clear whether there is any relationship between that work and the Qumran fragment (Milik, 1978, p. 97).

Book of Giants and Book of Noah. Two other pseudepigrapha, previously known but not usually listed among the Jewish pseudepigrapha of the intertestamental period, are also attested at Qumran. These are the *Book of Giants* and the "Book of Noah." Milik claimed to have identified "ten, if not some twelve," copies of the *Book of Giants,* which was previously known as a Manichaean work of the third century CE (Milik, 1976, p. 4; cf. 2Q26, 4Q203, 4Q530–533, 6Q8). One of these manuscripts was copied by the same scribe as Enoch[a] (4Q201), and Milik has argued that it was originally part of an Enochic pentateuch and that it followed the "Book of Watchers." We do not, however, have any fragments that actually show that the *Book of Giants* was copied in the same manuscript as any of the Enochic writings.

The "Book of Noah" was known only indirectly before the discovery of the scrolls. There is mention of such a book in *Jubilees* (10.13, 21.10), in the Mount Athos manuscript that contains the apocryphal Levi material and in the *Chronography of Syncellus.* Fragments have been identified in *1 Enoch,* notably in chapters 106 and 107, but there is no agreement as to how much material in *1 Enoch* can be ascribed to this book. In the scrolls, too, fragments of the "Book of Noah" can only be identified tentatively because of their content; no composition clearly identified as a book of Noah has been found. The most likely candidate is the text known as the Elect of God (4Q534). Initially thought to chart the horoscope of the Messiah, it more plausibly has been explained as referring to the birth of Noah. It is also possible that the section of the Genesis Apocryphon dealing with Noah is a summary of the lost "Book of Noah" (García Martínez, 1992, p. 40). Fragments of the book may also be found in 1Q19 and 6Q8, although Milik regards the latter as a copy of the *Book of Giants.*

Other Compositions. The scrolls include several other apocryphal and pseudepigraphic compositions, previously unknown, but not obviously or necessarily of sectarian origin. These include patriarchal testaments with apocalyptic elements, written in Aramaic, ascribed to Jacob (4Q537), Amram (4Q543–548), and Qahat (4Q542). 4Q541, which we have mentioned already in connection with the Levi Apocryphon, also belongs to a priestly apocryphal text, but the beginning and end are missing and the exact identification is uncertain. Also in Aramaic are several compositions related to the *Book of Daniel:* the Prayer of Nabonidus (4Q242), the pseudo-Daniel texts (4Q243–245), the so-called Aramaic Apocalypse or Son of God text (4Q246), and the Four Kingdoms text (4Q552–553). The so-called Proto-Esther text (4Q550) resembles several of these Danielic writings insofar as it has a court setting. The Aramaic Genesis Apocryphon (1Q20) is a rewriting of narrative material from *Genesis* that is partly related to the "Book of Noah." Another Aramaic text purports to give the words that Michael spoke before the angels of God (4Q529).

Apocryphal and pseudepigraphal writings in Hebrew include prophetic-apocalyptic texts that are apparently in the names of Moses (1Q22; 4Q385[a], 387[a], 388[a], 389, 390) and Ezekiel (4Q385, 386, 387, 388, 391) and a narrative work related to Jeremiah (4Q383, 384, 385[b], 387[b], 389[a]). Another Hebrew apocryphon (2Q22) appears to describe the battle between David and Goliath. The Apocryphon of Joshua (4Q378–379) is cited in the Testimonia (4Q175). The so-called messianic apocalypse in 4Q521 resembles the apocalyptic pseudepigrapha in its content, but it is not possible to say on the basis of the surviving fragments whether it was attributed to an ancient author. Noncanonical Psalms A and B (1Q380 and 381) contain psalms attributed to specific biblical characters, including Obadiah and Manasseh (Schuller, 1986, pp. 27–32, argues that the pseudepigraphic attributions were secondary). The psalm attributed to Manasseh at Qumran does not appear to bear any relationship to the Greek *Prayer of Manasseh,* which is sometimes included in the Apocrypha.

Omissions. It is not possible here to survey all the fragmentary literature that may be derived from apocryphal or pseudepigraphal compositions. The examples cited show a considerable literature of this sort that was unknown before the discovery of the Dead Sea Scrolls. At the same time, only a fraction of the pseudepigrapha that were transmitted in Greek and other languages has been found at Qumran. The standard edition of the pseudepigrapha of the Hebrew scriptures (Charlesworth, 1985) includes more than fifty works. Of these, only *Jubilees,* the various sections of *1 Enoch,* and the apocryphal parallels to the *Testaments of the Twelve Patriarchs* are found at Qumran. (Charlesworth also includes the apocryphal psalms from the Cave 11 Psalms Scroll). The great majority of the works included by Charlesworth were composed too late to be found at Qumran. The absence of Greek compositions such as the *Sibylline Oracles* is also unsurprising. There are, however, a few works that generally are believed to have circulated in Palestine, in Hebrew or Aramaic, before 70 CE, that have not been found at Qumran. These are the *Psalms of Solomon,* the *Testament of Moses,* and the "Similitudes" of *1 Enoch.* The *Psalms of Solomon* are often thought to be Pharisaic, and no Pharisaic literature has been found in the scrolls. The absence of the "Similitudes" could be due to a late composition date. It has also been suggested that the near equality of sun and moon in *1 Enoch* 41 might have been unacceptable at Qumran. No plausible reason has been found for the absence of the *Testament of Moses*, which dates from the turn of the era. None of the previously known Apocrypha and pseudepigrapha found at Qumran can be dated later than the second century BCE.

[*See also* Apocryphal New Testament; Ben Sira, Book of; Cairo Genizah; Enoch, Books of; Giants, Book of; Jubilees, Book of; Levi, Aramaic; Noah, Texts of; Psalms Scroll; Testaments; *and* Twelve Patriarchs, Testaments of the.]

BIBLIOGRAPHY

Charles, R. H. *The Apocrypha and Pseudepigrapha of the Old Testament.* 2 vols. Oxford, 1913. This was for many years the standard English edition of the Apocrypha and Pseudepigrapha.

Charlesworth, James H. *The Old Testament Pseudepigrapha.* 2 vols. New York, 1985. A much larger collection than that of Charles. It includes some works that may be as late as the ninth century CE.

Dimant, Devorah. "Apocalyptic Texts at Qumran." In *The Community of the Renewed Covenant*, edited by Eugene C. Ulrich and James C. VanderKam, pp. 175–191. Notre Dame, 1994. Survey of texts that are even loosely related to apocalyptic literature.

Dimant, Devorah. "Apocrypha and Pseudepigrapha at Qumran," *Dead Sea Discoveries* 1 (1994), 151–159.

García Martínez, Florentino. *Qumran and Apocalyptic: Studies on the Aramaic Texts from Qumran.* Studies on the Texts of the Desert of Judah, 9. Leiden and New York, 1992. Studies of the "Book of Noah," the Aramaic fragments of *Enoch*, the *Book of Giants*, the Prayer of Nabonidus, the pseudo-Daniel literature, 4Q246, and the New Jerusalem text.

Hollander, H. W., and M. de Jonge. *The Testaments of the Twelve Patriarchs: A Commentary.* Studia in Veteris Testamenti pseudepigrapha, 8. Leiden, 1985. Full commentary on the Testaments, with translations of the relevant Qumran fragments.

Metzger, Bruce M. *The Apocrypha of the Old Testament.* Revised standard version, expanded edition containing the *Third* and *Fourth Books of the Maccabees* and *Psalm 151.* New York, 1977. Annotated translation of the apocryphal books that are sometimes considered canonical.

Milik, Józef T. *The Books of Enoch: Aramaic Fragments of Qumrân Cave 4.* Oxford, 1976. The official edition of the Enoch fragments, and one fragment of the *Book of Giants.*

Milik, Józef T. "Écrits préesséniens de Qumrân: d'Hénoch à Amram." In *Qumrân: Sa piété, sa théologie et son milieu*, edited by M. Delcor, pp. 91–106. Bibliotheca Ephemeridum Theologicarum Lovaniensium, 46. Paris, 1978. Review of nonsectarian, noncanonical writings associated with Enoch, the patriarchs, and Amram.

Moore, C. A. *Tobit.* Anchor Bible 40A. New York, 1996. Up-to-date commentary on *Tobit*, informed by the Qumran manuscripts.

Puech, Émile. "Fragments d'un apocryphe de Lévi et le personnage eschatologique. 4QTestLévi^{c-d} (?) et 4QAJ^{a}." In *The Madrid Qumran Congress: Proceedings of the International Congress on the Dead Sea Scrolls, Madrid, 18–21 March 1991*, edited by Julio Trebolle Barrera and Luis Vegas Montaner, pp. 635–648. Studies on the Texts of the Desert of Judah, 12. Leiden, 1992. Publication of 4Q540, 541, and 537 (apocryphal texts related to the Levi tradition and the *Testament of Jacob*).

Sanders, James A., ed. *The Psalms Scroll of Qumran Cave 11.* Discoveries in the Judaean Desert, 4. Oxford, 1965. Publication of the Psalms Scroll from Cave 11.

Schuller, Eileen, M. *Non-Canonical Psalms from Qumran.* Harvard Semitic Studies, 28. Atlanta, 1986.

Skehan, Patrick W., and Alexander A. DiLella. *The Wisdom of Ben Sira.* Anchor Bible 39. New York, 1987. The most up-to-date commentary on *Ben Sira*, with full cognizance of the Qumran fragments.

Sparks, H. F. D. *The Apocryphal Old Testament.* Oxford, 1984. A smaller collection of pseudepigrapha than that of Charlesworth, it has superior treatments of *1 Enoch* and the *Testaments of the Twelve Patriarchs.*

Sundberg, Albert C. *The Old Testament of the Early Church.* Cambridge, Mass., 1964. Groundbreaking work on the formation of the canon.

VanderKam, James C. "The Jubilees Fragments from Qumran Cave 4." In *The Madrid Qumran Congress: Proceedings of the International Congress on the Dead Sea Scrolls, Madrid, 18–21 March 1991*, edited by Julio Trebolle Barrera and Luis Vegas Montaner, pp. 635–648. Studies on the Texts of the Desert of Judah, 12. Leiden, 1992. Presentation of the Jubilees fragments from Qumran.

JOHN J. COLLINS

APOCRYPHAL NEW TESTAMENT. The title *Apocryphal New Testament* is commonly applied to collections of early Christian writings that were not included in the canon of authorized scripture. In general, the term covers literature composed in imitation of the genres of writing found in the New Testament proper, such as the Gospels and *Acts of the Apostles* or stories concerned with characters who appear in the New Testament. [*See* John, Gospel and Letters of; *and* Luke, Gospel of.] Modern scholars normally exclude other early Christian writings, like the so-called Apostolic Fathers and the bulk of Gnostic texts from such collections. [*See* Apostolic Fathers.]

This umbrella title, *Apocryphal New Testament*, though convenient and widely understood, is less than ideal. First, many of the so-called apocryphal texts do not in fact match New Testament genres. [*See* Apocrypha and Pseudepigrapha.] Second, few of the writings are apocryphal in the literal meaning of "hidden." Third, and most important, the title gives the erroneous impression that we are dealing with a recognizable fixed body of literature, comparable to the New Testament or parallel to the Apocrypha. Modern editors, who gather collections of writings under a general title, such as the *Apocryphal New Testament*, are all too aware that they are making a selection from an amorphous and vast range of texts. Even the most comprehensive collections that have been published (such as Erbetta's or Moraldi's) do not claim to be exhaustive.

The Apocryphal New Testament comprises writings that range in age from the second (and some would argue first) century CE to the Middle Ages. Some texts are richly represented in numerous extant manuscripts. Others have survived in a single fragment or in lone patristic citations. The provenance and original language of the writings range from the Latin West through the Greek of the Mediterranean areas to the Syriac East and to the Coptic and Ethiopic writings of Africa. In addition, Armenian and Arabic texts are included. Given the fact that several texts are known today from manuscripts written in different centuries, it is clear that we are dealing with a popular form of religious literature that endured for many hundreds of years.

Although the common denominator of these apocryphal writings may be loosely described as the events and personalities of the New Testament world, the contents cover a variety of genres and topics, such as birth and infancy stories (of Mary and of Jesus), passion gospels, narratives about various New Testament characters (especially Pontius Pilate), collections of sayings (such as the *Gospel of Thomas*), narratives about the founding fathers of early Christian communities (the Acts of Peter, the Acts of Andrew, for example), scenes of the other world, and dialogues between the risen Jesus and his disciples. There are treatises, novels, hymns, poems, letters, and apocalypses. Some of the contents seem to be tinged with what were claimed to be heresies by the wider church, including Gnosticism or Encratism [*See* Gnosticism.]; others fit comfortably with "orthodox" Christian teaching. Many texts, especially the apocryphal Acts, are characteristic of popular folk religion, full of entertaining, albeit highly magical or superstitious, miracles and improbable legends.

Various ecclesiastical authorities, particularly in the fourth century, set out in their lists of approved texts those books that by then were recognized throughout Christendom as the foundation documents of the Christian faith, that is, the canonical New Testament. Those books not on a list of authorized reading were branded as apocryphal. It is surprising that these rejected books ever survived official opprobrium. In some cases, especially the apocryphal Acts, expurgated Catholicized versions of the stories were produced; these usually enhanced the deaths, typically martyrdoms, of the apostles, and eventually these rewritings became the accepted hagiographies of the Church's heroes. Nevertheless, a sufficient number of the original texts have survived in clandestine copies (now locked in libraries) for modern scholars to be able to reconstruct, albeit often only partially, many of the second- and third-century Acts, Gospels, and other texts.

It is obvious that we are dealing here with a range of literature a world away from the Dead Sea Scrolls. The contrast between the Apocryphal New Testament and the scrolls could not on the face of it be wider. The latter represent the literary remains of an exclusive Jewish sect, probably largely removed from the mainstream of society; most of its extant literature was composed in pre-Christian times. [*See* Essenes.] The origins and inspiration of the Apocryphal New Testament texts are Christian (however deviant on occasion); much of the literature seems to have been written for an educated readership whose background was pagan and secular; and the outlook in most of the texts is universal—inclusive and all-embracing. Unlike the Dead Sea Scrolls, where little historical interest in the founders of the sect is expressed, the apocryphal New Testament writings owe their raison d'être to the inquisitiveness, and imagination, of Christian communities about the founders of their faith and church. Another obvious difference is that many of the concerns of the Qumran sectarians, such as community rules, hardly surface in the New Testament—and even less so in the Apocryphal New Testament.

Certain structural features found in the Dead Sea Scrolls, such as the insertion of hymns, prayers, and poetic passages, are also to be found in some of the apocryphal texts, but these are common features of religious writing in general and the Hebrew scriptures in particular. [*See* Psalms, Hymns, and Prayers.] There is no obvious reason to look to the scrolls for such influences on Christian writers.

Nevertheless, some links and parallels may be observed. Certain Apocryphal New Testament texts betray the exclusivity and insight characteristic of the Qumran sectarians (e.g., *Gospel of Thomas* 23: "Jesus said, 'I shall choose you, one from a thousand, and two from ten thousand, and they shall stand as a single one'"; or Gospel of Thomas 67: "Jesus said, 'He who knows the All but fails to know himself lacks everything.'" Such ideas may be compared with Hodayot[a] [1QH[a]]). [*See* Hodayot.] In these hymns a constant theme is that salvation is assured for those with knowledge; the sectary gives thanks for the insight into the divine mysteries. But it is improbable that one should detect any direct literary or social influence of the Dead Sea Scrolls on the Apocryphal New Testament. A more rewarding search would seek these common links in Gnosticism.

If the Qumran sectarians believed that they, as privileged initiates, were living in the end time, awaiting the fulfillment of the Kingdom, they shared aspirations comparable to those of Christians as expressed both in the New Testament and in the apocryphal texts, such as the *Apocalypse of Paul*, of *Peter*, or of *Thomas*. Although the apocalyptic literary genre is rare in the Qumran writings, the fact that *Enoch*, parts of the *Testaments of the Twelve Patriarchs*, and *Jubilees* were discovered there shows that the sectarians found such literature congenial. Eschatological texts also are found at Qumran. Again, we may conclude that this interest in apocalyptic matters at Qumran and among early Christians is due to their shared background.

Teaching about the sovereign power of God and the need for humanity to rely and depend exclusively on that power is fundamental to the Dead Sea Scrolls. This is a unifying and dominant theme throughout the otherwise amorphous Apocryphal New Testament, too, and is a theme arguably more consistently stressed than in the New Testament itself. But such faith and fervor inevitably characterize much religious literature, and it is a more rewarding exercise to study how those beliefs are expressed in differing literary vehicles within various traditions than to seek parallels for the Christian apocrypha exclusively within the Qumran literature. In our examples the links may be traced to a shared, Jewish, or, more specifically, Hebrew biblical heritage. Jewish, and particularly sectarian Jewish, influence on the writings in the Apocryphal New Testament would have reached Christians predominantly through the books that eventually were accepted into the New Testament proper.

There are, nevertheless, some areas where it might be legitimate to look for a specific influence of the scrolls on extracanonical Christian literature, however secondhand and filtered that influence may have been.

Jewish-Christian Gospels. Although manuscripts of Gospels, such as the *Gospel of the Ebionites*, the *Gospel of the Nazareans*, and the *Gospel according to the Hebrews*, have not survived from the Jewish Christian groups allegedly responsible for them, certain citations in the works of the church fathers are attributed to these sources. Even though only a few samples survive, one detects that a feature of this Jewish Christianity was an asceticism comparable to that found in the Qumran community. [*See* Jewish Christians.] Vegetarianism is described in the Gospel of the Ebionites, as known from Epiphanius (*Refutation of All Heresies* 30.13), where it speaks of John the Baptist's food as being not locusts and wild honey but only "wild honey, which tasted like manna, formed like cakes of oil" (cf. *Refutation of All Heresies* 30.22). [*See* Epiphanius.]

The asceticism apparent in the *Gospel of the Ebionites* surfaces elsewhere in the Apocryphal New Testament, especially in the *Acts.* A common theme in the Acts is that of the apostle who endures great deprivation, hardship, and poverty, and whose life is contrasted with the wealth and position enjoyed by his main, usually pagan, protagonists. The message of the apostle is that money, beauty, possessions, and power are transient. Marriage is railed against (e.g., in the *Acts of John* 113), and sexual relations even within marriage are to be avoided, according to the apostles' teaching. Acts of Thomas 12 presents negative and uncompromising teaching about procreation. It is no wonder that Encratite groups found such texts congenial. A common chord between such material and the monasticism in the Qumran community may be detected, but, once more, there is no evidence that the Qumran material directly influenced authors of the Apocryphal New Testament. [*See* Ebionites; Encratites.]

Insofar as attempts have been made from time to time to identify the Qumran sectaries with the Ebionites, it is worth noting that, despite some superficial similarities of practice between the two movements (e.g., purificatory baths, Sabbath observance, circumcision, and a shared communal meal), from what we know about the Ebionites in the writings of Irenaeus, Tertullian, Epiphanius, and other church fathers, as well as in the Pseudo-Clementine literature, it seems that the Ebionites, unlike the Qumran community, did not accept the whole of the Pentateuch and rejected prophets of the Hebrew scriptures, the practices of sacrifice, and the institution of priesthood. [*See* Ebionites.] In these matters and in their teachings about dualism, the Ebionites differed so fundamentally from the Qumran sectarians that it is illusory to look in the Gospel of the Ebionites for direct evidence of influence from the Dead Sea Scrolls. In any discussion of the identification of the Qumran sect with the Ebionites, it must be remembered that the Ebionite movement was Christian and post-Qumran.

Messianism. The Apocryphal New Testament obviously does not share the teaching of the Dead Sea Scrolls about the expected Messiahs. [*See* Messiahs.] However, the quasi-magical powers attributed to Jesus and to those who confess their faith in him through these Christian texts are similar to those described in the Messianic Apocalypse (4Q521), in which healing and resurrection are linked with the coming of the kingdom of God ("He will heal the wounded and revive the dead. . . ."). The effectiveness of healing miracles became an incessant theme in many apocryphal tales; in the apocryphal Acts, in particular, miracles characterize and in effect justify apostolic activity. But, again, we might more profitably seek the shared background for ideas found in the Messianic Apocalypse, the New Testament, and the Apocryphal New Testament in the Hebrew scriptures, especially in *Isaiah* 61 or Psalm 146.

Apocalypse of Peter 4.7–9 (Ethiopic) and Apocryphon of Ezekiel. A plausible attempt has been made by Richard Bauckham to link the citation in the *Apocalypse of Peter* 4.7–9 (Ethiopic), the only formal scripture citation in the apocryphon, with Pseudo-Ezekiel[a] (4Q385). [*See* Ezekiel, Book of, *article on* Pseudo-Ezekiel.] The quotation in the *Apocalypse of Peter*, based on *Ezekiel* 37.7–8, parallels the wording in Pesudo-Ezekiel[a] in several ways, most convincingly in "bone to its bone" and the reference to "joints," which mark significant variants from the canonical *Ezekiel.* If the Qumran fragments of Pseudo-Ezekiel (4Q385, 386, 387, 388, and, perhaps, 391) belong to the so-called *Apocryphon of Ezekiel*, of which there exist five fragments (none paralleling the Qumran passages) in patristic citations and in Chester Beatty Papyrus 185, then the source of the quotation in the Apocalypse of Peter may well be from an apocryphon that circulated more widely than Qumran. Such a conclusion would therefore make a direct link from a Qumran text to a Christian apocalypse less likely. (An alternative, but less probable, explanation would be that the *Apocalypse of Peter* was quoting from a form of canonical *Ezekiel* differing from the Masoretic Text, on which Pseudo-Ezekiel also depends.) That the *Apocryphon of Ezekiel* was known in Christian circles from an early date may be confirmed by the apparent citation from it (frg. 2) in *Epistle of Barnabas* 12.1, which is attributed to "another prophet." The *Apocryphon of Ezekiel* was Jewish, but its themes of repentance, resurrection, and judgment made it a popular text for Christians. Tertullian (*De carne Christi* 23.2) also seems to have known the *Apocryphon of Ezekiel*, as does Justin (*Dialogue with Trypho* (*1 Apologies* 52.5–6) and Tertullian (*De resurrectione mortuorum* 32.1), whose quotations of *Ezekiel* 37.7–8 seem to know a form of wording that agrees with Pseudo-Ezekiel[a].

Hymn of the Bride. Yiphtah Zur (1993–1994, pp. 103–107) has raised the possibility of links between the "Hymn of the Bride," inserted into *Acts of Thomas* 6–7, and Wiles of the Wicked Woman (4Q184). [*See* Wiles of the Wicked Woman.] These include the length, structure, and meter of the poems, and textual parallels. The Qumran text in effect lampoons the panegyric in the *Acts of Thomas*, a not unfamiliar form of satire. If the suggestion is correct, the Hymn of the Bride must have had an earlier Jewish (Hebrew) prototype. This is not impossible, given the practice of Apocryphal New Testament texts (especially the *Acts*) to import hymnic material into a narrative. Such a link does not, of course, betray any direct influence of a Qumran text on the author of the apocryphal *Acts*, merely that a hypothetical prototype of the Hymn of the Bride permeated sectarian Judaism and, later, Christian congregations.

Apostolic Fathers. If we stray outside the Apocryphal New Testament, as commonly understood nowadays, and turn to the Apostolic Fathers, in particular the *Epistle of Barnabas* and the Didache, we find that the Doctrine of the Two Ways (the Way of Darkness/Death; the Way of Life/Light) in these two books reflects a common Jewish source, which has interesting links with the Rule of the Community (1QS). Such material, however, has a long ancestry in Jewish writings, going back to *Deuteronomy* 30.15–16, Psalm 1, and *Jeremiah* 21.8. [*See* Apostolic Fathers.] More rewarding comparisons lie outside the Doctrine of the Two Ways: *The Epistle of Barnabas* and the Qumran community share a common interest in covenant; both hold to the centrality of scripture and see scriptural truths as their own possession and referring to their own community. Both identify the understanding of scripture as knowledge and attribute to it a strong ethical meaning (compare *Barnabas* 2.2–3, "The auxiliaries of our faith are fear and endurance, while patience and self-control fight alongside us. While these allies remain in a pure state in relation to the Lord, there rejoice with them wisdom, understanding, knowledge, and Gnosis," with the Damascus Document [CD ii.2], "God loves knowledge. Wisdom and understanding he has set before him, and prudence and knowledge serve him. Patience and much forgiveness are with him toward those who turn from transgression").

Other links between teachings found in the Dead Sea Scrolls and in the Apostolic Fathers may be noted, but, as with the Apocryphal New Testament, there are no unambiguous or definitive parallels that demand the direct literary or other influence of the Dead Sea Scrolls on early Christian noncanonical writings. A shared cultural and religious heritage and a common background of ideas are responsible for those links that have been identified.

BIBLIOGRAPHY

Elliott, J. K. *The Apocryphal New Testament: A Collection of Apocryphal Christian Literature in English Translation.* Oxford, 1993. Translations of the most important texts, with introductions and full bibliographies.

Elliott, J. K. *The Apocryphal Jesus. Legends of the Early Church.* Oxford, 1996. A selection of the most influential noncanonical stories about Jesus and the apostles.

Fitzmyer, Joseph A. "The Qumran Scrolls, the Ebionites and Their Literature." *Theological Studies* 16 (1955), 335–372, reprinted in Joseph A. Fitzmyer, *Essays on the Semitic Background of the New Testament*. London, 1971. A magisterial and detailed examination. See pages 435–480.

Strugnell, John, and Devorah Dimant. "4Q Second Ezekiel." *Revue de Qumrân* 13 (1988), 45–58. See M. Kister and E. Qimron, "Observations on *4QSecond Ezekiel,*" *Revue de Qumrân* 15 (1992), 595–602.

Zur, Yiphtah. "Parallels between Acts of Thomas 6–7 and 4Q184." *Revue de Qumrân* 16 (1993–1994), 103–107.

J. K. Elliott

APOCRYPHON OF ______. *See under latter part of name.*

APOSTOLIC CONSTITUTIONS. Near the end of the fourth century CE an anonymous author, perhaps living in Syria (not ancient Palestine), collected into one work diverse laws and hymns. Despite John Chrysostom's support of its apostolic authenticity, it was rejected as spurious by the Council of Trullo in 692. It is certainly pseudepigraphical (see, for example, the claim that James the son of Zebedee is the composer of a constitution [8.2.12]). The collection is thus erroneously labeled the *Apostolic Constitutions*, because of its pseudonymous title, "Constitutions of the Holy Apostles." Divided into eight books, and preserved in its full form only in Greek, Latin, and Coptic, it is a late-fourth-century church manual of ecclesiastical rules and liturgical compositions.

As a collection of rules that to a certain extent concludes with liturgical texts, it is reminiscent of the Rule of the Community from Qumran. Like the compiler of the Qumran book, the author of the *Apostolic Constitutions* compiled a manual of instruction including rules and liturgical compositions. And like the texts composed at Qumran, especially the Rule of the Community and the *pesharim*, the *Apostolic Constitutions* depends upon the Hebrew scriptures, interprets them legalistically, and considers them holy and perfect (6.4.19); but—of course—the *Apostolic Constitutions* is a Christian composition and so depends upon and interprets with equal rigor the books of the New Testament (except *Revelation*). Like the Wiles of the Wicked Woman from Qumran (4Q184), sections of the compilation exhort devotion to Lady Wisdom and warn about the wicked woman who will seduce and mislead (1.2.7), and like the author of the Temple Scroll[a] (11Q19), the compiler of the *Apostolic Constitutions* values the priesthood over kingship (2.5.34). [*See* Temple Scroll; Wiles of the Wicked Woman.] But unlike the Qumran theology, the compiler (or author of a section) warns against writings that others deem sacred (1.2.5–6) and exhorts his readers not to observe ritual lustrations (6.4, preface). In Book 2 (2.3.22) the compiler excerpts from the *Prayer of Manasseh*, one of the books in the Old Testament Pseudepigrapha, but it is not related to the "Prayer of Manasseh" found in Noncanonical Psalms B (4Q381 33 + 35.8–11). The compiler of the *Apostolic Constitutions* knows the Essenes (who are most likely to be identified with the members of the Qumran community) as those who are separated from others and observe different laws (6.2.6). As these observations, which pertain to Books 1 through 6, show, there is no reason to imagine, let alone posit, any direct influence of the Qumran scrolls upon the *Apostolic Constitutions*. While influence is possible even with authors of vastly different perspectives, it is essential, in assessing possible links between this Christian compilation and the Qumran scrolls and related Jewish compositions, to recognize that the compiler of the *Apostolic Constitutions* thought the Jews had crucified Christ (5.3.17) and were now rejected by God (6.2.5).

Most important for a perception of its relation to the Dead Sea Scrolls are the final two books, numbers seven and eight. Book 7 presupposes the concept of "Two Ways," which was first definitively developed into a light–darkness paradigm in Jewish theology only in the Rule of the Community (1QS iii.13–iv.26). The source of the compiler's thought is *Deuteronomy*, which he explicitly quotes; and it is based on *Deuteronomy* 30.15 that he emphasizes the two ways: the way of life and the way of death. This dualism is appreciably different from and in no way clearly influenced by the ideas peculiar to and developed in the Qumran scrolls. Conspicuously absent in the *Apostolic Constitutions* are the terms found in the Qumran scrolls, such as *Sons of Light* and *Sons of Darkness*, and the light–darkness dualism. Any link between the way of life and good works (7.1.12) or the way of death and wicked deeds (7.1.18) of the *Apostolic Constitutions* and similar lists found in the Rule of the Community (1QS iii.13–iv.26) is not because of direct Qumran influence; the similarity is caused because of the subject matter and the dependence of both works on the books of the Hebrew scriptures.

Books 7 and 8 clearly are an epitome or selection of some early Jewish compositions. For example, they contain the Qedushah. Book 8, in section 3, 18–41, may also preserve Jewish hymns which may derive from an otherwise unknown Jewish collection or hymn book (Kohler, 1924; Charlesworth, 1986; Fiensy, 1985). These hymns are Jewish but they are not clearly influenced by Qumran compositions or Qumran theology; none of the Qumran technical terms and no ideas peculiar to Qumran appear in them. If the Qumran scrolls are any indication of Essene thought, as most Qumran experts have concluded, then there are abundant reasons to disagree with K. Kohler, who asserted that the Jewish hymns excerpted in Book 7.33–38 derive from a pre-Christian Essene group.

[*See also* Rule of the Community.]

BIBLIOGRAPHY

Charlesworth, James Hamilton. "Jewish Hymns, Odes, and Prayers (ca. 167 BCE–135 BCE)." In *Early Judaism and its Modern Interpreters*, edited by Robert A. Kraft and George W. E. Nickelsburg, pp. 411–436. Philadelphia, 1986.

Donaldson, James, ed. "Constitutions of the Holy Apostles." In *The Ante-Nicene Fathers*, vol. 7, pp. 387–508. New York, 1926. Grand Rapids, Mich., 1951, 1970. Contains W. Whiston's translation from the Greek, with significant alterations, of the *Apostolic Constitutions*.

Fiensy, David. *Prayers Alleged to be Jewish: An Examination of the* Constitutiones Apostolorum. Brown Judaic Studies, 65. Chico, Calif., 1985. In the definitive treatment of the Jewish prayers excerpted in the *Apostolic Constitutions*, Fiensy concludes that the Jewish prayers in this collection were redacted by a Christian, that their form postdates the first century, and that generally they are an example of Syrian synagogal Sabbath morning services that are theologically similar to rabbinic thought.

Kohler, Kaufmann. "The Origin and Composition of the Eighteen Benedictions with a Translation of the Corresponding Essene Prayers in the *Apostolic Constitutions*." *Hebrew Union College Annual* 1 (1924), 387–425. Kohler argues, unpersuasively (pp. 410–425), that the *Apostolic Constitutions* preserves a collection of prayers from an Essene synagogue; yet, he demonstrates that this Christian collection preserved the first six of the seven benedictions of the Amidah that were recited on the Sabbath in some synagogues.

James H. Charlesworth

APOSTOLIC FATHERS. The collection known as the *Apostolic Fathers* consists of several Christian works written from the late first through the late second century. A letter written by the leaders of the Roman community to Corinth, *1 Clement* probably dates from the last decade of the first century or first decade of the second. It attempts to mediate a dispute within the Corinthian community in which some elders had been deposed from office. The *Letters of Ignatius* were written by the bishop of Antioch while he was being transported to Rome for execution under the emperor Trajan (98–117). They address churches along the way to Rome, as well as the Roman community itself, encouraging unity under episcopal leadership, and resistance to "Judaizing" and to docetism, or the denial of the full humanity of Jesus. The *Didache* is a book of church order probably composed in Syria in the late first or early second century. [*See* Didache.] It contains admonitions to follow the "way of life," instructions for celebrating baptism and eucharist, and guidance on fasting and support of itinerant and residential leaders. *Barnabas* is a polemical treatise probably composed around the time of the Bar Kokhba Revolt (132–135 CE), interpreting scripture in order to support Christian claims and inculcating a life of ethical perfection. The *Shepherd of Hermas* is a lengthy apocalypse written in Rome, probably in the second quarter of the second century. In the form of symbolic visions, it offers guidance for the Roman community on various ethical and doctrinal issues. The fragments of Papias preserve tidbits of tradition collected by an important elder of the church in Asia Minor in the early second century. The *Letter of Polycarp* contains admonitions to fidelity to the church at Philippi from the bishop of Smyrna, martyred in 155, an event recorded in the *Martyrdom of Polycarp.* The letter also accompanied copies of letters of Ignatius that Polycarp sent to the Philippians. The work *2 Clement* is a homiletic letter of uncertain date inculcating a high Christology, a virtuous life, and belief in resurrection. The *Epistle to Diognetus* is an apologetic work probably dating from the late second century. Most of the disparate collection thus consists of Christian works concerned with ecclesiastical issues of the second century.

The *Didache* offers the most interesting parallels to material from the scrolls in its teaching of the Two Ways theology (*Didache* 1.1–6.2), although a direct connection to the scrolls is unlikely. Instead, both Rule of the Community (1QS) and the *Didache* draw on a widespread form of ethical instruction. Instructions on baptism (*Didache* 7.1–4) and eucharist (9–10) show acquaintance with some Jewish forms, but also divergence from the fragmentary prayer text Baptismal Liturgy (4Q414) and from Grace after Meals (4Q434a), a blessing over food. No specific connection to the scrolls is likely.

Barnabas 18.1–20.2 contains another version of the Two Ways schema, close to but not derived from the *Didache*. The extensive scriptural citations in *Barnabas* use texts that may derive, at least in part, from collections of "testimonies" or proofs for messianic claims. Two such collections are found in the scrolls, Florilegium (4Q174) and Testimonia (4Q175). Related is Catena[a] (4Q177), a commentary on Psalms 6–17, which draws upon other scriptural texts as well. The parallels are largely formal, although often with eschatological thrust, and for Barnabas the materials are oriented to his "Christian" interests. Parallels in detail, for example, Pseudo-Ezekiel[a] (4Q385) to *Barnabas*, are infrequent, although both Pseudo-Ezekiel[a] 2.9–10 and *Barnabas* 12.1 contain the same image of a tree bending over and straightening up in answer to the question of when certain events will occur. While there may be borrowing here on the part of *Barnabas*, it may be the case that the two works share a common exegetical tradition (cf. also *Barn.* 4.3 and 4Q385 3). The scrolls have probably not provided the sources of *Barnabas* but offer analogies from a community that took seriously the need to interpret scripture.

The concern in *Hermas* for the welfare of the poor recalls the desire of the Teacher of Righteousness to proclaim to the poor in Hodayot[a] (1QH[a] xviii.14), who are the object of God's special care (1QH[a] ii.32–35). The allegory of the tree (*Herm.* 67–77 [*Similitudes* 8]) resembles the imagery of 1QH[a] vi.8–28 and viii.1–12.

The *Epistle of Polycarp to the Philippians* 2.2 contains the principle "to love all that he has chosen and to hate all that he has despised," reminiscent of the stark dichotomy of Rule of the Community (1QS i.9–10). Direct dependence, however seems unlikely.

In general, there were numerous paths for transmission of Jewish and Semitic sources to eastern and western Christian writers. These included both contact between living communities that transmitted texts and traditions about *Enoch*, the *Testaments of the Twelve Patriarchs, Jubilees*, the *Ascension of Isaiah*, and other materials. They also included "archeological" discoveries such as Origen's use of Greek Bible translations found mysteriously "in jars" at Nicopolis near Actium (Eusebius, *HE* 6.16.2–3; the *Dialogue of Timothy* and *Aquila* 3.10 locate the discovery in Palestine). [*See* Origen.] Hence, it remains possible that material from the Dead Sea Scrolls could have been used by Christian authors. Yet hypotheses that some of the works among the Apostolic Fathers were written by converts from Qumran are unconvincing. Nothing sufficiently concrete is known about these authors or their sources to provide external evidence for any connections with the Dead Sea Scrolls, and the internal evidence is too ambiguous to make a strong case for direct or even for significant indirect dependence. Themes common to *Barnabas*, the *Didache*, and *Hermas*, especially associated with the Two Ways instruction, have echoes in the Dead Sea Scrolls, but they are more likely commonplace Jewish views rather than uniquely Dead Sea Scrolls influences.

The possible use of collected "testimonies" in *Barnabas* (also to some extent in *1 Clement*, but absent from the *Didache* and *Hermas*) may have some remote connection with a practice attested in the Dead Sea Scrolls but probably not unique to them. Whether the "logia of the Lord" mentioned by Papias have any connection to this kind of collection is a matter of conjecture. The larger context is the variety of approaches to scriptural interpretation, from restatement to anthologizing to explicit commentary, in early Jewish and Christian circles. Finally, the very idea of the *Didache* as a "rule book" (and along with it, the Two Ways genre of instruction) resembles the similarly directive Dead Sea Scrolls materials such as the Rule of Community and the Damascus Document, but such regulatory literature is unlikely to be unique to the scrolls. Connections between the Dead Sea Scrolls and early Christian literature are possible, but, in the case of the Apostolic Fathers, they are generally improbable.

BIBLIOGRAPHY

GENERAL

Audet, J.-P. "Affinités Littéraires et Doctrinales du Manuel de Discipline." *Revue biblique* 59 (1952), 219–238; 60 (1953), 41–82.

Braun, Herbert. *Qumran und das Neue Testament*, 2 vols. Tübingen, 1966.

Flusser, David, *Judaism and the Origins of Christianity*. Jerusalem, 1988.

DIDACHE AND THE TWO WAYS TRADITION

Bergman, J. "Zum Zwei-Wege-Motif: Religionsgeschichtliche und exegetische Bemerkungen." *Svensk Exegetisk Arsbok* 41–42 (1976–1977), 27–56.

Danielou, Jean. "Une source de la spiritualité chrétienne dans les manuscrits de la Mer Morte: La doctrine des deux exprits." *Dieu vivant* 25 (1953), 127–136.

Delcor, Mathias. "Doctrines des Esséniens: Instruction des deux Esprits." *Dictionnaire de la Bible Supplément* 9 (1978), 960–970.

Kraft, Robert A. *Barnabas and the Didache*. New York, 1965.

Rordorf, W. "Un chapitre d'éthique judéo-chrétienne: Les deux voies." *Revue des sciences religieuses* 60 (1972), 109–128.

Suggs, M. Jack. "The Christian Two Ways Tradition: Its Antiquity, Form, and Function." In *Studies in New Testament and Early Christian Literature: Essays in Honor of Allen P. Wikgren*, edited by David E. Aune, pp. 60–74. Novum Testamentum Supplements, 33. Leiden, 1972.

HERMAS

Ford, J. M. "A Possible Liturgical Background to the Shepherd of Hermas." *Revue de Qumrân* 6 (1969), 531–551.

Hanson, A. T. "Hodayoth vi and viii and Hermas Sim. VIII." *Studia Patristica* 10 (Berlin, 1970), 105–108.

Osiek, Carolyn. *Rich and Poor in the Shepherd of Hermas*. Catholic Biblical Quarterly Monograph Series, 15. Washington, D.C., 1983.

POLYCARP

Flusser, David. *Judaism and the Origins of Christianity*. Jerusalem, 1988.

ROBERT A. KRAFT
JAMES C. VANDERKAM

APOSTROPHE TO ZION. *See* Psalms Scroll.

AQUEDUCTS. *See* Water Systems.

ARABIA (PROVINCIA ARABIA). The term *Arabia* has been variously applied in both modern and ancient times to refer to a vast territory stretching from the borders of the Fertile Crescent in northern Syria to the tip of the Arabian Peninsula, and from the borders of the Euphrates to the fertile regions near the Jordan River. Under this general rubric, all the Judean Desert sites in which manuscript discoveries have been made fall within the territory of Arabia, although at the time the texts were written the area was not known by this name. During the time of Roman domination of the area, when Roman Arabia was known as *Provincia Arabia*, the discovery sites were in territories under Roman domination.

For the ancients, this vague term, *Arabia*, referred to the dwelling places of the varieties of South Semitic speakers lumped together under the term *Arab*. For speakers of Hebrew and Aramaic, the term *Arab* (*ʿarabi*) carried the semantic notion of the desert or the wilderness (*ʿarabah*), since the Arabs they encountered were primarily the nomadic and seminomadic desert dwellers engaged in long-distance commerce, animal husbandry, or the supply of cavalry troups to imperial armies. The meager textual evidence available to us shows that in pre-Islamic times many of the northern Arabs used Aramaic and Hebrew as well as varieties of Arabic. After the rise of Islam, however, the Arabic of northwest Arabia, the region of the Hijaz, became the dominant language of the Arabs, and it, along with its cognate dialects, became the Arabic known today.

Among the important pre-Islamic pastoral nomads of the region were the Nabateans, who, by the time of the arrival of Roman imperial presence in the region, dominated the region's trade from around Damascus to the Hijâz. Settled in their heartland around Petra, the Nabateans plied their trade through the areas of Transjordan, across the Wadi ʿArabah to Gaza and al-ʿArîsh (Rhinocolura). There is also evidence that they used the interior route of the Wadi Sirhân to carry goods to Bostra for distribution to Damascus and beyond. Nabatean wealth and influence attracted the Romans into an unsuccessful invasion of Arabia in 26 BCE, and the Nabateans were able to resist Roman domination until 106 CE, when *Arabia Nabataea* became a Roman province. In later history, the name *Nabatean* became identified with irrigation and agriculture, because the Nabateans are credited with the development of hydraulic technology in the region. In modern Arabic, "Nabatean" (*nabati*) refers to vernacular poetry in the ancient style.

By 106 CE, the Romans dominated most of the former territories of the Nabateans and the adjacent Syrian cities of Gerasa and Philadelphia (modern Jarash and Amman in Jordan), creating a province through the formal annexation of the Nabatean kingdom under the Roman emperor Trajan. *Provincia Arabia* was bounded by the western coast of the Sinai Peninsula, the present Syrian-Lebanese border to a line south of Damascus, and the eastern coast of the Red Sea as far as Egra (Madaʿin Salih in the Hijaz). Gaza prospered as a major seaport and outlet for the province's commerce. This trade continued under Roman domination, and the borders were fortified by semipermeable lines of fortifications and client states. Under the Romans, Bostra (Bozrah; now Busrâ ash-Shâm) in the north became the capital around a legionary camp. Petra remained a religious center until the penetration of Christianity into the area. The construction of a highway, the Via Traiana Nova, linking Damascus, via Bostra, Gerasa, Philadelphia, and Petra, to Aelana on the Gulf of Aqaba, set the border of Arabia *(Limes Arabicus)* along the lines of an ancient biblical route. Paved by Claudius Severus, the first governor of *Provincia Arabia*, in approximately 114 CE, the highway improved communication and established a modicum of control over the influx of pastoral nomads into settled territory. More importantly, the road insured the increase in prosperity of the cities along the route.

At the end of the third century, the Roman emperor Diocletian divided Arabia into a northern province, enlarged by the Palestinian regions of Auranitis and Trachonitis, with Bostra as the capital, and a southern province, with Petra as the capital. The southern province, united to Palestine by the emperor Constantine I the Great, became known as *Palaestina Salutaris* (or *Tertia*) when detached again in 357–358 CE. The cities of both provinces enjoyed a marked revival of prosperity in the fifth and sixth centuries but fell into decay following the Arab conquest after 632 CE.

During the period in which the Judean Desert finds were deposited in the caves, the area containing the discovery sites remained off the main conduits of trade and communication, and it is this remoteness that, for the most part, provided value to the caves as retreats from the demands of the central settled world. The practice of using the Judean Desert caves as *genizot* continued from the time of the Roman Wars through as late as the eleventh century CE. The presence of Byzantine Greek and Arabic texts (Arabic texts were found in the caves of the Wadi Murabbaʿat and Khirbet Mird) indicates that the local populations both knew of the presence of the caves and made use of them as depositories for important documents. This fact has had important implications in discussions about the presence of copies of the Damascus Covenant found in the Cairo Genizah. [*See* Arabic; Cairo Genizah.] The texts, particularly the texts from the Byzantine and Islamic periods, indicate that the inhabitants of the region who deposited the finds were well connected not only to Palestine but also to Egypt and the larger world of the Mediterranean.

The Roman province of Arabia is mentioned in a number of Greek texts from the Bar Kokhba period: 5/6Ḥev 12, 14, 15–18, 20, 22, 27, and 37; XḤev/Se 62, 64, and 65. The city of Maoza, from which both Babatha and Salome Komaïse came, was located within this province. The texts also attest the change of the province's name to "the new province of Arabia" in 127 CE and to the census that occurred in the same year (see XḤev/Se 62, 64, and 65 for the name, and XḤev 62 for the census).

BIBLIOGRAPHY

Benoit, P., J. T. Milik, and R. de Vaux. *Les grottes de Murabbaʿat.* Discoveries in the Judaean Desert, 2. Oxford, 1961.

Bowersock, G. W. *Roman Arabia.* Cambridge, Mass., 1983.

Cotton, Hannah M. and Ada Yardeni, eds. *Aramaic, Hebrew and Greek Documentary Texts from Naḥal Ḥever and Other Sites.* Discoveries in the Judaean Desert, 27. Oxford, 1997. Publication of the XḤev/Se texts mentioning the province of Arabia.

Erder, Yoram. "When Did the Karaites First Encounter Apocryphic Literature Akin to the Dead Sea Scrolls?" *Cathedra* 42 (1987), 54–68.

Grohmann, Adolf. *Arabic Papyri from Khirbet el-Mird.* Louvain, 1963.

Lewis, Naphtali, ed. *The Documents from the Bar Kokhba Period in the Cave of Letters: Greek Papyri.* Judean Desert Studies. Jerusalem, 1989. Publication of the 5/6Ḥev texts mentioning the province of Arabia.

Parker, S. Thomas. *The Roman Frontier in Central Jordan: Interim Report on the Limes Arabicus Project, 1980–1985.* Oxford, 1987.

Segal, Arthur. *Town Planning and Architecture in Provincia Arabia.* Oxford, 1988.

Shahid, Irfan. *Rome and the Arabs: A Prolegomenon to the Study of Byzantium and the Arabs.* Washington, D.C., 1984.

GORDON D. NEWBY

ARABIC. Arabic texts, mostly on papyrus but five on paper, have been discovered at two sites in the Judean desert. Over a hundred texts and fragments were discovered at Khirbet Mird (*khirbat al-mird*) and five at Wadi Murabbaʿat. [*See* Mird, Khirbet; Murabbaʿat, Wadi.] The majority of the texts date from the first two Islamic centuries (seventh and eighth centuries CE), but some can be dated as late as the eleventh century CE, in a context of artifacts that have been dated as late as the fourteenth century. Most of the texts are damaged, some being only scraps, but the texts yield important paleographic data even when many add little to our literary and historical knowledge. The collection from Khirbet Mird represents the largest cache of Arabic papyri found outside Egypt and demonstrates both the close connection between Egypt and Palestine in the early Islamic period and that the Judean desert area was on a literary par with Egypt.

It also demonstrates the continued use of the Judean caves as *genizot* well into Islamic times.

The five texts from Wadi Murabbaʿat are on paper and date from the fourth century AH/tenth century CE. One text is a receipt, one a fragment of a contract, and three are magical texts. A magical text fragment (Mur 171) has numerous magical signs, a drawing of a figure, and three lines of Greek characters. While this should not be construed as a bilingual text, the use of Greek letters indicates the conservative nature of magic and the perseverance of older cultural forms in the Islamic context. An amulet of fifty lines (Mur 173) adds to the limited corpus of early Arabic magical texts. [*See* Magic and Magical Texts.] This text, a palimpsest in which the underlying text is illegible, also exhibits transconfessional features, mentioning God, both in Arabic and in an Arabic rendering of the Tetragrammaton, Muḥammad, Satan, Solomon, and some apparently pagan names.

The corpus of texts from Khirbet Mird represents the range of written materials one would expect from an archive found within the borders of the important district of Aelia Capitolina, the borders of which were taken over by the Umayyad administration and maintained for the first four Islamic centuries. In the Bilingual Protocols (APHM 1–4), we see linguistic and conceptual interplay between Arabic and Greek in which the usual Islamic Arabic introductory formulas are transformed into a Greek calque (APHM 2: *theos monos Mamet apostolos theou*), and possibly in APHM 3 Greek letters are used to transliterate Arabic, as is the case in texts from other sites. The rendering of the name Muḥammad as Mamet suggests a phonetic transformation dependent on a spoken dialect.

There are a number of letter fragments in the *jalîl* ("majestic") script that was used by the Umayyad caliphs for foreign imperial correspondence and for official signatures (APHM 10–17). The Umayyad caliph Umar II allowed this very old script style to be used by provincial governors at the close of the first Islamic century. [*See* Letters.] The fragments are too incomplete to give an indication of the content of the originals. The official letters, administrative texts, and economic documents not in the monumental script (APHM 18–41) show, where the texts are complete enough, an expected range of topics: domestic violence, divorce, robbery, taxes on grain, lists of personnel, and lists of commodities. In the economic texts, Greek characters are used for calculation as is usual in this early period.

The private letters (APHM 42–70) are fragmentary and offer only slight glimpses into the lives of the individuals mentioned within them. Most of the letters seem to be written to and by Muslims, but APHM 45 and 46 are a letter from a Father Anbâ Magnille, who was probably an abbot of a monastery near Khirbet Mird, and the reply from Habban ben Yûsuf. The letter starts with an apparently Monophysite statement, "In the name of the Father, and the Son, and the Holy Spirit in one nature." The correspondence, dating from the eighth century CE, exhibits some unusual diacritical marks on some of the letters. What little remains of the letters hints at unfulfilled promises and urgent requests, but careful matching of the fragments has failed to produce extensive texts.

There is one fairly extensive literary text in the corpus, APHM 71, which consists of a fragmentary notice of a historian's account of the names of the participants with Muḥammad at the Battle of Badr in 2 AH/624 CE. Such lists were important for social and financial reasons in the early Islamic world because proof of the participation by one's ancestors at the Battle of Badr afforded both prestige and a share in the distribution from the public dole. Such notices were often family- and clan-specific. Unscrupulous historians would sometimes extort money from families by threatening to claim that their ancestors were not at Badr, thus requiring written proof. Another literary text, APHM 72, like APHM 11, appears to be a pen trial by a scribe who wrote a portion of the first chapter of the Koran and possibly the first verse of chapter 20.

The discovery of Arabic texts in the Judean Desert caves gives us a clear indication that the caves were used regularly through the Byzantine and early Islamic periods, with some use attested until at least the eleventh century CE. Therefore, it is plausible to assume that access in early Islamic times to some of the pre-Islamic materials in the caves did indeed occur. In a letter of the Nestorian catholicos of Baghdad, Timotheus, to a priest in charge of the area of Elam named Sergius, he tells of the discovery around 805 CE of a chamber in the Judean Desert filled with ancient books. When Jews from Jerusalem investigated, they declared that the books were heretical. Some scholars have linked this ninth-century discovery in the Judean Desert caves to the copies of the Cairo Damascus Document found in the Cairo Genizah and their putative association with the origins of Karaism and the Karaite use of vocabulary and concepts parallel to what has been found among Judean Desert scrolls. While all this remains speculative, and while the discovery of ancient texts in caves stands as a distinctive literary topos, it is clear that the premodern inhabitants had as much possibility of access to the materials as have modern bedouin and scholars. [*See* Cairo Genizah; Damascus Document.]

BIBLIOGRAPHY

Benoit, P., J. T. Milik, and R. de Vaux. *Les grottes de Murabbaʿat.* Discoveries in the Judaean Desert, 2. Oxford, 1961.

Erder, Yoram. "When Did the Karaites First Encounter Apocryphic Literature Akin to the Dead Sea Scrolls?" *Cathedra* 42 (1987), 54–68.

Gil, Moshe. *A History of Palestine 634–1099*. Translated by Ethel Broido. Cambridge, 1992.
Grohmann, Adolf. *Arabic Papyri from Khirbet el-Mird*. Louvain, 1963.
Wieder, Naphtali. *The Judean Scrolls and Karaism*. London, 1962.

GORDON D. NEWBY

ARAMAIC. Qumran texts and other Judean Desert texts have been recovered that are written in Aramaic, the most commonly used language in Judea in the last three centuries BCE and the first two centuries CE. This is not surprising since Aramaic had been the lingua franca of the ancient Near East for centuries prior to the conquest of Alexander the Great (334–324 BCE).

Aramaic Language. Aramaic is one of the two chief branches of the Northwest Semitic family of languages used in the ancient Near East. The other branch, Canaanite, embraced Amorite, Ugaritic, Phoenician/Punic, Moabite, and Hebrew.

Aramaic was the language spoken by Aramaeans, the people living in Aram, the area around Damascus and in northern Syria between the Tigris River and the Taurus Mountains. Nomads from the Syrian-Arabian Desert, the Aramaeans gradually settled in city-states in northern Syria in the late twelfth century BCE. In the Assyrian annals of the fourth regnal year of Tiglath-pileser I (c.1115–1076 BCE) the Aramaeans are mentioned for the first time. Ancestral traditions recorded in the Hebrew scriptures refer to Aramaeans who lived in Paddan-Aram (*Gn*. 25.20), Aram-Naharaim, and the city of Nahor (*Gn*. 24.10; Nahor, brother of Abraham, *Gn*. 11.27). Although Aramaeans are traced to the end of the twelfth century BCE, only in the ninth century BCE do Aramaic texts begin to appear.

From the ninth century BCE until the Middle Ages, Aramaic remained basically one language, although it underwent development and various phases of it must be distinguished. Unfortunately, names for the phases have not been uniformly agreed upon. One reason for the lack of agreement in terminology is that prior to the twentieth century almost the only known Aramaic texts were either biblical, targumic, or rabbinical, whereas the bulk of extrabiblical Aramaic texts known today, and even some *targumim*, have come to light only in the last seventy-five or eighty years. Sometimes the designation of phases of Aramaic begins as chronological and then shifts to geographical, with little rhyme or reason. The following attempt to designate five main phases of Aramaic is intended solely in a chronological sense. When geographical designations appear, they are subdivisions of the main phases.

Old Aramaic. Dating roughly from 900 to 700 BCE (or perhaps to 613, the fall of Nineveh), this phase is represented by inscriptions from northern Syria, Mesopotamia, and Israel, written in the borrowed Phoenician alphabet. These texts, which are not entirely uniform, represent an archaic form of the language that is sufficiently homogeneous to mark it off from contemporary Canaanite and Phoenician. In some instances there are features in this phase of the language that are Canaanitisms (e.g., infinitives used as infinitives absolute in Hebrew, Phoenician, and Ugaritic, or *vav*-conversive forms, both of which disappear in subsequent phases); there are also remnants of ancient case endings (masculine plural forms ending in *vav* [= nominative?] or *yod* [= genitive?]). The chief feature of the language, however, which distinguishes it from Canaanite, is the postpositive article. Whereas Hebrew prefixes *ha'*, "behold," to the stem *malk*, "king," and *ha'malk* becomes *ham-malekh* (with assimilation of the *alef* to the *mem* and an anaptyptic vowel breaking up the consonantal cluster), then *ham-melekh* (with vocalic assimilation), "the king," Aramaic affixes it: *malkay* + *ha'* becomes *malkayya'* then *malkayya(')*, "the kings." The feature that distinguishes texts of this phase from subsequent phases is the way Aramaic interdental and sibilant consonants are represented in the borrowed Phoenician alphabet. When Aramaeans borrowed the alphabet, they were still pronouncing these consonants in the proto-Semitic way: the interdental fricative was still pronounced like *th* (in *the*), a sound for which the Phoenician alphabet had no character. Consequently, the Phoenician *z* was used to represent it as well as the Aramaic *z*. The result was that *z* stood for two sounds. As Aramaic developed, the fricative shifted to a stop and fell together with the *d*, both being represented by *d*. Thus, the relative pronoun was written in Old Aramaic as *zy* and it persisted in the writing in the early part of the following phase, even when it was already being pronounced *di*; eventually it was written as *dy*.

Another characteristic of Old Aramaic is its orthography. Phoenician was written in consonants only and had not developed a system of writing vowels; its diphthongs usually were contracted and represented as zero in writing. At an early stage Aramaeans began to use certain consonants to represent vocalic sounds, which at first was confined to final long vowels and uncontracted diphthongs: *yod* = long *i* or the diphthong *ay*; *vav* = long *u* or the diphthong *au*. Gradually, it spread to medial positions. The occasional contraction of *ay* to *e* was represented in final positions by *h*. In this phase *aleph* was treated as a consonant: the emphatic state ended in *-a'* (e.g., *malka'*, "the king"). Later the *aleph* quiesced, and the vowel was lengthened in a compensatory manner, becoming *-a*.

Standard or Official Aramaic. Dating roughly from 700 (or 613) to 200 BCE, Standard Aramaic sometimes is called *Reichsaramäisch*, or Imperial Aramaic, and originally denoted the Aramaic used during the dominance of the Persian empire; but its use is now traced back to the late Neo-Assyrian period. It was employed not only for communication between officials in the Assyrian and Persian empires, but even for communication between ordinary Jews and Aramaeans. It is called Standard Aramaic because it became the classic form of the language that would persist, despite later local dialectal differences, as long as the language remained alive. During this period this form of Aramaic became the lingua franca, used from the Indus Valley (modern Afghanistan and Pakistan), across the ancient Fertile Crescent (Babylonia and Armenia) into Asia Minor and to southern Egypt; examples even have been found in Greece. To this phase belong the twenty-eight Samaria papyri and fragments from Wadi ed-Daliyeh and the Biblical Aramaic of *Ezra* and probably even that of *Daniel*. Sometime during this period the short vowel in a pretonic open syllable was reduced to a shewa, which became another characteristic of Aramaic: the earlier *shalam*, "peace," became *shelam*. The vast corpus of Standard Aramaic comprises letters written on skin and papyrus, contracts, deeds, legal documents, literary texts (e.g., *Aḥiqar*), inscriptions, inscribed ostraca, wooden labels, and clay tablets. In this phase some scholars have sought to distinguish a western and an eastern form of the language; that is a debatable issue, since evidence for the distinction is so meager.

Middle Aramaic. During this phase, which dates roughly from 200 BCE to 200 CE, Standard Aramaic develops, and one detects the emergence of five local dialects.

The Palestinian or Judean Aramaic dialect remained closest to Standard Aramaic and is found in inscriptions on Jerusalem ossuaries and tombstones, in literary texts from Qumran, in letters and documents from the Judean Desert, and in Aramaic words preserved in the Greek of Josephus and the New Testament.

Nabatean Aramaic was used by Arabs in Transjordan between the Hejaz and Damascus. Its center was Petra (from which the majority of Nabatean inscriptions come). It was a local dialect of Aramaic with Arabic interference, especially Arabic vocabulary. Outside Petra, Nabatean inscriptions have been found along caravan routes leading to South Arabia, Hauran, and even Judea.

Palmyrene Aramaic was the dialect of the caravan city of Palmyra (Tadmor) in the Syrian Desert and its environs. The earliest text in this dialect is from about 32 BCE (*PAT* 1067). The vast majority of these texts are sepulchral or dedicatory inscriptions from the heyday of Palmyra under Odaenathus and Queen Zenobia (130–270 CE).

Hatran Aramaic was the dialect used by the people of Hatra (modern Al-Hadhr), a town in Parthian-controlled Mesopotamia, fifty miles south of Mosul, where an Aramaean dynasty constructed a caravan town serving northern Syria and the Persian Gulf. Its heyday was about 100 CE. Its dialect is related to Palmyrene with Iranian loanwords.

Old Syriac was used by people in Edessa, Serrin, Dura, and other Syrian towns. The extant Old Syriac texts are pagan Aramaic inscriptions written in a script related to Palmyrene that began developing toward that of the early Christian Syriac scripts. The texts represent the kind of Aramaic spoken during the Achaemenid domination of the area, a development of Standard Aramaic, which had not yet adopted the characteristics of later literary Syriac, used by Christians. The third singular masculine imperfect form still begins with *yod*, not *nun*, as in classical Syriac, although the *n* form starts to appear sporadically. The proto-Semitic *ś* is represented by *shin*, whereas it falls together with *s* in classical Syriac. The inscriptions are for the most part memorial, sepulchral, and dedicatory.

Late Aramaic. Dated between approximately 200 and 700 CE, these Aramaic texts of various geographical areas and dialects have further peculiarities that distance them from Standard Aramaic even more than those in the Middle Aramaic phase. They fall into two large geographic subdivisions, Western and Eastern. The Western subdivision consists of dialects of Jewish Palestinian Aramaic (sometimes called Galilean Aramaic), to which belong the so-called Palestinian Targums, literary texts of the tannaitic and amoraic periods, and synagogal and funerary inscriptions (*MPAT*, appendix, A1–A56); Samaritan Aramaic; and Christian Syro-Palestinian Aramaic. The Eastern subdivision consists of dialects of Syriac (further divided into a western form [Jacobite] and an eastern form [Nestorian]), Babylonian Talmudic Aramaic, and Mandaic.

The cutoff date of this phase is not easily set. Seven hundred CE is taken as a round number close to the Muslim conquest and the consequent spread of Arabic, which brought an end to the active use of Aramaic in areas of the Near East. Neither Aramaic nor Syriac, however, completely died out at this time. Aramaic continued to be spoken among Jews until the end of the geonic period in Palestine and Babylonia (end of the eleventh century), and Syriac continued among Christians even to the end of the thirteenth century (Bar Hebraeus and his contemporaries).

Noteworthy in this phase not only is the *liqtul* and *neqtol* form of the third singular masculine imperfect *peal* in Babylonian Talmudic Aramaic and Syriac (respectively), but also the waning use of the absolute and construct states of the noun: *malka'* can mean either "a king" or "the king"; instead of the construct state of nouns, one uses the determinative pronoun *de-*. Also characteristic of this phase is the piling up of pronominal forms; the widespread use of the possessive pronoun, *dil-*; and the introduction of many Greek words into all the dialects.

Modern Aramaic. Sometimes called Neo-Aramaic, Modern Aramaic still is spoken in northern Syria, Iran, Iraq, and related areas: in the west in villages of the Anti-Lebanon region, north of Damascus (Maʿlūla, Jubbʿaddîn, Baḫʿā), and in several areas of the east (Ṭûr ʿAbdîn, the region between Lakes Urmia and Van, and in northern Iraq, around Mosul). The dialects spoken in these areas are a remnant of Late Aramaic or Syriac, heavily influenced by other local languages (e.g., Arabic, Turkish, or Kurdish).

Aramaic of Judean Desert Texts. The Aramaic of the Qumran and Murabbaʿat texts belongs to the dialect called Palestinian or Judean. A few documents, however, from Naḥal Ḥever are written in Nabatean. In either case, they are part of the corpus of Middle Aramaic texts, representing a transitional form between the Aramaic of *Daniel* (c.165 BCE) and that of the classical Targums of Onkelos and Jonathan, which are not earlier than 200 CE. These Middle Aramaic texts give us an idea of the language commonly spoken in Judea in the time of Jesus and the early Christians and provide the background for the study of Aramaic words preserved in the Greek texts of Josephus and the New Testament.

About 120 fragmentary texts (some still unpublished) from eleven Qumran caves were composed in Aramaic. Among them are eight biblical manuscripts, six Targumic and deuterocanonical texts, and many parabiblical texts from Qumran.

That some Aramaic texts are found in multiple copies at Qumran and that some have been copied in scribal hands already known from the site indicate that these texts were copied at Qumran itself. In most instances, however, little in the Aramaic texts classes them as sectarian; the bulk of the Aramaic documents represents texts that Essenes read or studied but that were not composed by them. Moreover, because most of the sectarian literature at Qumran was composed in Hebrew, the scarcity of sectarian tenets in Aramaic texts supports the view that the use of Hebrew was something that Qumran Essenes had restored because of their high regard for *leshon ha-qodesh*, "the language of the sanctuary."

Grammatical analysis of the Judean Desert Aramaic texts depends to a certain extent on their vocalization. The texts are written in consonants with matres lectionis. In many cases the vocalization is certain, because their vocabulary uses standard words well known in earlier or later Aramaic or in cognate Semitic languages. Many of the words occur in Biblical Aramaic. Although its vocalization is later than its consonantal text, the Masoretic vocalization can be adopted, provided that the consonantal text of these documents tolerates it. The same must be said about vocalizations derived from later pointed texts of Jewish Palestinian Aramaic or from Syriac and Babylonian Talmudic Aramaic. In using Biblical Aramaic, however, one must realize that the Masoretic tradition has at times Hebraized some Aramaic forms (e.g., *melekh*, "king," instead of *mĕlēkh*, as in the Targums and Syriac; see Blake, 1951, pp. 81–96.

Orthography. Scribes who copied Judean Desert Aramaic texts made abundant use of consonants as matres lectionis. Such scriptio plena is known from Qumran Hebrew texts (see Tov, 1986, 1988). Occasionally, some texts preserve historical orthography: *zi* for *di*, *zenah* for *denah*.

Phonology. Sibilants and interdentals are the same as in Biblical Aramaic; the proto-Semitic *ḍ* always is represented by *ʿayin*. *Nun* at the end of a closed syllable often is assimilated to the following consonant, but not always; *lamed* similarly is assimilated at times. Doubled consonants are at times resolved by the use of liquids, especially *nun* (*yiddaʿ* becomes *yindaʿ*; *Dammeśeq* becomes *Darmeśeq*).

Morphology. In this Palestinian Aramaic the three states of the noun (absolute, construct, and emphatic) are still alive. There is the shift of *haphel* to *ʾaphel* in the causative conjugation; a shift of the pronouns from *di* to *de* and from *denah* to *den*, "this." The third plural masculine pronoun passes from *himmô(n)* to *innun*. The conjunction "if" shifts from *hēn* to *ʾin*. The sign of the accusative often still is *le-*, though *yat(-)* begins to appear. Hebraisms occur (*ʾim* for *ʾin*; ending *-im* for *-in*).

BIBLIOGRAPHY

Beyer, Klaus. *The Aramaic Language.* Translated from the German by J. F. Healey. Göttingen, 1986. A translation of the introduction of Beyer's *Die aramäischen Texte vom Toten Meer samt den Inschriften aus Palästina, dem Testament Levis aus der Kairoer Genisa, der Fastenrolle und den alten talmudischen Zitaten* (1984), pp. 20–153. To the latter, Beyer has added *Ergänzungsband* (1994), updating his collection. Beyer's work contains a valuable bibliography, but one must always check his readings against official editions or photographs and query many of his vocalizations.

Blake, F. R. *A Resurvey of Hebrew Tenses: With an Appendix, Hebrew Influence in Biblical Aramaic*. Rome, 1951.

Drijvers, H. J. W. *Old Syriac (Edesean) Inscriptions Edited with an Introduction, Indices and a Glossary.* Semitic Study Series 3. Leiden, 1972. Convenient collection of Old Syriac inscriptions.

Fitzmyer, Joseph A., and Daniel J. Harrington. *A Manual of Palestinian Aramaic Texts (Second Century B.C.–Second Century A.D.).* Biblica et Orientalia 34. Rome, 1978. Presents one hundred fifty Aramaic texts with translations and bibliography, many of them from Qumran, Murabbaʿat and Naḥal Ḥever; in an appendix are fifty-six Palestinian texts from the Late Aramaic phase (third to sixth centuries CE) for comparison.

Fitzmyer, Joseph A. "The Phases of the Aramaic Language." In *A Wandering Aramaean: Collected Aramaic Essays*, pp. 57–84. Society of Biblical Literature Monograph Series 25. Missoula, Mont., 1979. Explanation of and justification for the division of Aramaic into five main phases.

Fitzmyer, Joseph A., and Stephen A. Kaufman. *An Aramaic Bibliography: Part I, Old, Official, and Biblical Aramaic.* Publications of the Comprehensive Aramaic Lexicon Project. Baltimore, 1992. Detailed bibliography of all known Aramaic texts of the phases mentioned.

Greenfield, Jonas C. "Aramaic and Its Dialects." In *Jewish Languages: Theme and Variations*, edited by H. H. Paper, pp. 29–43. Cambridge, Mass., 1978.

Greenfield, Jonas C. "The Languages of Palestine, 200 B.C.E.–200 C.E." In *Jewish Languages: Theme and Variations*, edited by H. H. Paper, pp. 143–54. Cambridge, Mass., 1978.

Hillers, Delbert R., and Eleonora Cussini. *Palmyrene Aramaic Texts.* Publications of the Comprehensive Aramaic Lexicon Project. Baltimore, 1996. Collection of all known Palmyrene texts with glossary.

Kaufman, Stephen A. "Languages (Aramaic)." In *The Anchor Bible Dictionary*, edited by D. N. Freedman, vol. 4, pp. 173–178. New York, 1992. A good survey of the Aramaic language.

Koffmahn, Elisabeth. *Die Doppelurkunden aus der Wüste Juda: Recht und Praxis der jüdischen Papyri des 1. and 2. Jahrhunderts n. Chr. samt Übertragung der Texte und deutscher Übersetzung.* Studies on the Texts of the Desert of Judah 5. Leiden, 1968. Comprehensive study of double documents published up to the date of Koffmahn's book, including Aramaic texts from Murabbaʿat (Mur 18–20, 23, 26) and Naḥal Ḥever (5/6Ḥev 36).

Kutscher, E. Y. "Aramaic." In *Linguistics in South West Asia and North Africa*, pp. 347–412. Current Trends in Linguistics 6. The Hague, 1971. Valuable survey of the Aramaic language.

Lewis, Naphtali. *The Documents from the Bar Kokhba Period in the Cave of Letters: Greek Papyri.* Judean Desert Studies 2. Jerusalem, 1989. Includes the Aramaic and Nabatean subscriptions and signatures of these Greek documents, studied by Jonas C. Greenfield.

Segert, Stanislav. "Bedeutung der Handschriftenfunde am Toten Meer für die Aramaistik." In *Bibel und Qumran: Beiträge zur Erforschung der Beziehungen zwischen Bibel- und Qumranwissenschaft: Hans Bardtke zum 22.9.1996*, edited by S. Wagner, pp. 183–87. Berlin, 1968. Discusses contributions made by Qumran texts published up to 1966 to the study of Aramaic.

Sokoloff, Michael. "The Current State of Research on Galilean Aramaic." *Journal of Near Eastern Studies* 37 (1978), 161–167. A study of Late Aramaic texts from Judea.

Tov, Emanuel. "The Orthography and Language of the Hebrew Scrolls Found at Qumran and the Origin of These Scrolls." *Textus* 13 (1986), 31–57.

Tov, Emanuel. "Hebrew Biblical Manuscripts from the Judaean Desert: Their Contribution to Textual Criticism." *Journal of Jewish Studies* 39 (1988), 5–37.

JOSEPH A. FITZMYER, S.J.

ARAMAIC APOCALYPSE. Known as the Aramaic Apocalypse (4Q246) or the Son of God Text, this skin fragment (14.1 by 8.8 centimeters) preserves the end of nine lines on column i and the complete nine lines of column ii, with upper and lower margins (photo PAM 43.236). It is from the middle of a document, of which neither the beginning nor the end is preserved. Written in Herodian script, this copy is dated from approximately 25 BCE and is derived from a pre-Christian source of ancient Judea. It is written in the Palestinian form of Middle Aramaic known from other Qumran texts. [*See* Aramaic.]

The text is called an apocalypse because it tells of a coming era of peace, when God's people will arise after a period of distress, war, and carnage. [*See* Apocalyptic Texts.] A seer(?) falls before the throne of a king, whom he addresses with a message of reassurance. The seer explains that distress will come from enemies called (historically? symbolically?) Assyria and (perhaps) Egypt, whose domination, however, will be short-lived. An individual will arise, who "will be called great" and "will be hailed as the Son of God"; they will call him "Son of the Most High." "His (*or* Its [God's people's]) reign will be an everlasting kingdom . . . ; he (*or* it) will judge the land with truth, and everyone will make peace. The sword will cease from the land, and all provinces will pay him (*or* it) homage, (because) the great God is his (*or* its) might."

Column ii is easily read; the restoration of column i is problematic, and there is no certainty about its width. Line 9 reads: [ ]*baʾ yitqereʾ u-vi-shemeh yitkaneh*. The possible restoration is: [*ve-huʾ bar El rab*]*baʾ* . . . , "[and he] will be called [son of] the [gr]eat [God]; by his name will he be named." *ʾEl rabbaʾ* occurs in Aramaic Apocalypse 2.7. Milik read the verbs as middle passive/passive voice, restoring [*bar malkaʾ rab*]*baʾ*, "will call himself [son of] the [gr]eat [king]," which he took to refer to Alexander Balas, who pretended to be son of Antiochos IV Epiphanes. But would a Jewish writer give a pagan Seleucid king the titles "Son of God," "Son of the Most High"? Puech preferred [*bar maryaʾ rab*]*baʾ*, "[son of] the [gr]eat [Sovereign]." Who is this person? The answer is debated. For David Flusser, he is an antichrist, a human exponent of satanic forces of evil, claiming such titles. For Florentino García Martínez, he is an eschatological savior of heavenly character, someone like Melchizedek. For Martin Hengel, the titles are collective (equivalent to the Jewish people), like Son of Man (*Dn.* 7.13). For Émile Puech and John J. Collins, the titles are those of a messiah, but that interpretation imports gratuitously yet another title into the text. It may simply refer to an awaited Jewish ruler, a successor to the Davidic throne, not envisaged as a messiah, since the text does not use that title. [*See* Messiahs.]

This text supplies an important Palestinian Jewish background for the titles *Son of God* and *Son of the Most High* used for Jesus in *Luke* 1.32 and 1.35.

BIBLIOGRAPHY

Collins, John J. "The 'Son of God' Text from Qumran." In *From Jesus to John: Essays on Jesus and the New Testament Christology in Honour of Marinus de Jonge*, edited by Martinus C. de Boer, pp. 65–82. Journal for the Study of the New Testament. Supplement Series, 84. Sheffield, 1993.

Fitzmyer, Joseph A. "4Q246: The 'Son of God' Document from Qumran." *Biblica* 74 (1993), 153–174.

Fitzmyer, Joseph A. "The Aramaic 'Son of God' Text from Qumran Cave 4." In *Methods of Investigation of the Dead Sea Scrolls and the Khirbet Qumran Site: Present Realities and Future Prospects*, edited by Michael O. Wise et al., pp. 163–178. Annals of the New York Academy of Science, 722. New York, 1994. These articles give the history of publication and earlier bibliography.

Flusser, David. "The Hubris of the Antichrist in a Fragment from Qumran." *Immanuel* 10.1 (1980), 31–37.

Hengel, Martin. *The Son of God*. Philadelphia, 1976. See page 45.

García Martínez, Florentino. "The Eschatological Figure of 4Q246." In *Qumran and Apocalyptic: Studies on the Aramaic Texts from Qumran*, pp. 162–179. Studies on the Texts of the Desert of Judah, 9. Leiden, 1992.

Milik, Jósef T. "Les modèles araméens du livre d'Esther dans la grotte 4 de Qumran." *Revue de Qumrân* 15 (1991–1992), 321–399, especially p. 383.

Puech, Émile. "Fragment d'une apocalypse en araméen (4Q246 = pseudo-Dan[d]) et le 'Royaume de Dieu.'" *Revue biblique* 99 (1992), 98–131. The preliminary publication of the text, on which Puech has published further notes, *Revue biblique* 101 (1994), 533–558.

Puech, Émile. "246 4QApocryphe de Daniel ar." In *Qumran Cave 4, XVII: Parabiblical Texts, Part 3*, pp. 165–184. Discoveries in the Judaean Desert, 22. Oxford, 1996. The *editio princeps*.

JOSEPH A. FITZMYER, S.J.

ARAMAIC LEVI. *See* Levi, Aramaic; Testaments.

ʿARAQ EN-NAʿSANEH CAVE. *See* Daliyeh, Wadi ed-.

ARCHAEOLOGICAL SURVEYS of the Judean Desert can be divided into two groups: bedouin explorations and controlled surveys (see table 1).

Bedouin Explorations. Although by no means official or scientific, the explorations and clandestine excavations by Taʿamireh bedouin have yielded by far the largest part of the ancient, written material from the Judean Desert. Sites from which the bedouin recovered epigraphic materials include Wadi en-Nar (Naḥal Qidron), Wadi Sdeir (Naḥal David), Wadi Ghweir (Naḥal Qaneh), Wadi ed-Daliyeh, Wadi Murabbaʿat, and the Qumran Caves.

Controlled Surveys. A variety of archaeological organizations have sponsored numerous surveys and excavations in the Judean Wilderness.

Survey of the cliffs. In March 1952, in conjunction with the excavation of Qumran Cave 2, a survey of the cliffs 4 kilometers north and south of Wadi Qumran was carried out by R. de Vaux and W. Reed, director of the American School of Oriental Research in Jerusalem (now known as the Albright Institute), and assisted by D. Barthelélemy, J. T. Milik, and M. Henri de Contenson. Through 230 soundings, forty caves containing archaeological remains were found, including Cave 3. Twenty-six caves yielded pottery identical to that of Cave 1 and Khirbet Qumran. The dig was stopped due to heat.

Judean Desert Survey. Following news that many manuscripts sold by bedouin in Jerusalem had come from Judean Desert sites on the Israeli side of the green line, a series of surveys and minor excavations were conducted by Y. Aharoni between 1953 and 1960 at sites ranging from ʿEin-Gedi to Masada. In the wake of Aharoni's findings, the Judean Desert Survey of 1960 and 1961 was organized. Four archaeologists were assigned to direct the units. N. Avigad was in charge of Group A (the southern bank of Naḥal Ṣe'elim and Naḥal David); Y. Aharoni, Group B (the northern bank of Naḥal Ṣe'elim, Naḥal Harduf, and Naḥal Ḥever); P. Bar-Adon, Group C (Naḥal Mishmar, Naḥal ʿAsahel, southern bank of Naḥal Ḥever); and Y. Yadin, Group D (northern bank of Naḥal Ḥever and Naḥal Arugot). This survey was aided by personnel and equipment of the Israel Defence Forces.

Copper Scroll Expedition. In the spring of 1960, J. M. Allegro directed the "Copper Scroll Expedition," which excavated various sites in the Judean Wilderness believed to contain items mentioned in the Copper Scroll (3Q15) from Qumran Cave 3, including Khirbet Mird and Khirbet Mazin.

Operation Scroll. From November 1993 to January 1994 a joint survey was undertaken by the Israel Antiquities Authority (IAA) and the Military Authority of Judea and Samaria, directed by A. Drori, director of the IAA, and Y. Magen, staff officer for archaeology of the Military Authority of Judea and Samaria. The survey covered an extensive area from Jericho to ʿEin-Gedi and involved many archaeologists. Caves and archaeological sites (including Qumran) were surveyed and excavated, yielding finds ranging from the Chalcolithic to Islamic periods. Although no new sites produced epigraphic remains, the Wadi el-Mafjar Cave of Avior (also known as Ketef Jericho) produced additional papyrus fragments related to those found earlier by H. Eshel.

Recent surveys of Qumran environs. Surveys conducted in the 1980s and 1990s by J. Patrich, J. Eisenman, V. Jones, and M. Broshi and H. Eshel have added in varying degrees to the knowledge of the region, but have not yielded any written material.

Epigraphic Remains from Surveys and Excavations. The epigraphic remains found at the Judean Desert sites vary in materials, eras, language, and content. The following section organizes these finding according to era and location.

First Temple period

Wadi Murabbaʿat (Naḥal Dargah): one papyrus.

Khirbet Qumran: *la-melekh* jar handles.

ʿEin-Gedi: *la-melekh* jar handles and seal impressions.

Persian-Hellenistic period (fourth century BCE)

Wadi ed-Daliyeh Caves: Discovered by bedouin in February 1962 in the Abu Shinjeh Cave were at least twenty-eight papyrus legal documents, nearly one hundred clay bullae, several coins, and two gold sig-

ARCHAEOLOGICAL SURVEYS. TABLE 1. *Excavations and Surveys.*

Site	Uncontrolled Excavations	Survey or Excavation Director	Date	Sponsoring Institutions
Wadi en-Har (Naḥal Qidron)	bedouin			
Wadi Sdeir/Naḥal David	bedouin	G. D. Sandel;	1905;	
		Y. Aharoni (Judean Desert Survey);	1956;	Israel Department of Antiquities
		N. Avigad	1960, 1961	
Wadi ʿEin-Ghweir (Naḥal Qaneh)	bedouin	P. Bar-Adon	1960, 1961	
Wadi ed-Daliyeh	bedouin (1962)	P. Lapp; Y. Magen	1963; 1964; 1980	American Schools of Oriental Research
Wadi Murabbaʿat (Naḥal Dargah)	bedouin (1951)	R. de Vaux	1952	JDA/Palestine Archaeological Museum/EB
Qumran Cave 1	bedouin	G. L. Harding, R. de Vaux	1949	JDA/Palestine Archaeological Museum/EB
Qumran Cave 2	bedouin	R. de Vaux, W. Reed (Survey of Cliffs)	Feb. 1952	JDA/Palestine Archaeological Museum/EB; American Schools of Oriental Research
Qumran Cave 3		R. de Vaux, W. Reed (Survey of Cliffs)	Feb. 1952	JDA/Palestine Archaeological Museum/EB; American Schools of Oriental Research
Qumran Caves 4, 6	bedouin	G. L. Harding, R. de Vaux	Sept. 1952	JDA/Palestine Archaeological Museum/EB
Qumran Cave 5		J. T. Milik	Sept. 1952	JDA/Palestine Archaeological Museum/EB
Qumran Caves 7–10		R. de Vaux	Feb. 1955	JDA/Palestine Archaeological Museum/EB
Qumran Cave 11	bedouin	R. de Vaux	Feb. 1956	JDA/Palestine Archaeological Museum/EB
Khirbet Qumran		Baramki;	Dec. 1940;	Brit. Mandate;
		S. Husseini; R. de Vaux	April 1946; 1951, 1953, 1954, 1955, 1956;	Brit. Mandate; JDA/Palestine Archaeological Museum/EB
Caves		P. Bar-Adon; M. Broshi; J. Eisenman; H. Eshel; V. Jones; Y. Patrich	1980s–1990s	
Qumran		A. Drori; Y. Magen; J. Strange		
ʿEin-Feshkha		R. de Vaux	1958	JDA/Palestine Archaeological Museum/EB
Khirbet Mird	bedouin (1952)	Copper Scroll Expedition (J. M. Allegro); R. de Langhe	1953, 1960	JDA/Palestine Archaeological Museum/EB
Khirbet Mazin		Copper Scroll Expedition (J. M. Allegro); R. de Langhe		
Naḥal Ḥever (Wadi Khabra)		Y. Aharoni;	1953;	Israel Department of Antiquities
		Y. Yadin	1960, 1961	

(*continued*)

ARCHAEOLOGICAL SURVEYS. TABLE 1. *Excavations and Surveys (continued).*

Site	Uncontrolled Excavations	Survey or Excavation Director	Date	Sponsoring Institutions
Cave of the Letters				
Naḥal Ḥever (Wadi Khabra)		Y. Aharoni	1953, 1955, 1961	Israel Department of Antiquities
Cave of Horror				
Naḥal Mishmar (Wadi Mahras)		P. Bar-Adon	1960, 1961	Israel Department of Antiquities
Cave of Treasure				
Naḥal Se'elim (Wadi Seiyal)		N. Avigad; Y. Aharoni	1960; 1960	Israel Department of Antiquities
Naḥal Harduf (Wadi Maradif)		Y. Aharoni		
ʿEin-Gedi		B. Mazar; Y. Aharoni, J. Naveh; B. Mazar, I. Dunayevsky, T. Dothan; Y. Hirschfeld	1949; 1956, 1957; 1961–1965; 1996–1998	Israel Exploration Society
Masada		M. Avi-Yonah, N. Avigad, Y. Aharoni, I. Dunayevsky, S. Gutman;	1955, 1956;	HU/Israel Exploration Society/Israel Department of Antiquities
		Y. Yadin	1964, 1965	ICRC/SPNI
Wadi el-Mafjar (Cave of Avior)		H. Eshel	1986	

net rings. Found in 1963–1964 during two seasons of excavations directed by P. Lapp on behalf of the American Schools of Oriental Research (ASOR) were five papyrus manuscripts, four clay bullae, coins, and shards in Greek (as well as Middle Bronze, Iron Age II, Late Persian, Early Roman, Arabic, and Mameluke remains). Found in December 1980 in ʿAraq en-Naʿsaneh by Y. Magen (Israel Defence Forces, archaeological staff officer, Judea and Samaria) were similar remains and a hoard of seventeen Roman coins (second century CE).

Wadi el-Mafjar, the Cave of Avior: A wooden comb found by A. Frumkin in 1984 and similar to others from the Judean Desert led to the 1986 excavation by H. Eshel on behalf of the Israel Cave Research Centre and Ofra Field School of the Society for the Preservation of Nature in Israel (SPNI). Epigraphic remains include a list of names in Aramaic (fourth century BCE), and legal documents in Aramaic and nonliterary documents in Greek (second century CE). During "Operation Scroll," Eshel once more found fragmentary papyri associated with this cave.

ʿEin-Gedi: jar handles with seal impressions.

Hasmonean-Hellenistic period (Second Temple period; third–first centuries BCE). While bedouin were responsible for the original discovery of several of the Qumran scroll caves (1, 2, 4a and 4b, 6, and 11; all later officially excavated), others were discovered by methodical surveys and explorations (Caves 3, 5, 7–10).

Qumran Cave 1: Early in 1947 bedouin discovered Cave 1, taking seven scrolls from the cave and selling them on the antiquities market. The official excavation was conducted in February/March 1949 by G. L. Harding and R. de Vaux on behalf of the Jordan Department of Antiquities (JDA), the Palestine Archaeological Museum (PAM), and the École Biblique et Archéologique Française (EBAF), jointly. The finding of "scroll" jars and fragments from at least one of the seven scrolls confirmed the cave as the source of the scrolls. All remains were from the Hasmonean and Early Roman periods.

Qumran Cave 2: In February 1952 bedouin discovered Cave 2 and offered numerous fragments for sale. None of the thirty-three manuscripts found was complete. The discovery of this new cave prompted the authorities to undertake the survey of the cliffs (see above).

Qumran Cave 3: The only scroll cave discovered during the 1952 survey contained the fragmentary remains of nine manuscripts and the Copper Scroll (3Q15).

Qumran Cave 4: In September 1952, close to the site of Khirbet Qumran, bedouin discovered three new caves containing manuscript fragments. These became known as Caves 4 (4a and 4b) and 6. Unfortunately, the bedouin mixed the manuscripts from Caves 4a and 4b (which were only seven meters apart) and, accordingly, de Vaux decided to record all fragments coming from both caves as 4Q. Within two days of the bedouin offering fragments for sale, the authorities found the caves, stopped the illicit digging, and began a controlled excavation under de Vaux and Harding. Fragments of about one-fourth of the approximately six hundred fragmentary manuscripts identified as having come from Cave 4 were identified among those found in the excavation. An ink-inscribed jar and an object were also recovered.

Qumran Cave 5: During the excavations of Cave 4 a partially collapsed cave (5) was discovered about 25 meters to the north. At least fifteen manuscripts were recovered in the excavation carried out by J. T. Milik.

Qumran Cave 6: No manuscripts were found in the de Vaux excavation but bedouin produced fragments of at least twenty-one manuscripts from this cave, mainly on papyrus.

Qumran Caves 7, 8, 9, and 10: During the fourth season of excavation at Khirbet Qumran (February 1955), it was decided to investigate possible collapsed caves spotted along the cliffs on the southern end of the terrace. Three caves containing fragmentary manuscripts were discovered and designated caves 7, 8, and 9. Cave 7 contained fragments of at least five manuscripts, numerous Greek papyrus fragments, a jar inscribed *roma* and objects; Cave 8 contained fragments of five texts as well as thongs and reinforcing tabs; and Cave 9 contained only one badly worn papyrus fragment. Cave 10, discovered during the excavations when worn steps leading to a possible collapsed cave were noted near Cave 4, revealed a woven mat, date pits, and an ostracon.

Qumran Cave 11: This cave was discovered by bedouin in January 1956, who cleared it of manuscripts. Shortly after their sale to the PAM, de Vaux and his team excavated the cave, prior to their fifth season of excavation at Qumran. From the excavation, an unidentified, blackened, cigar-shaped document and several small fragments of paleo-Leviticus[a] (11Q1) were recovered; from the bedouin, nine biblical manuscripts (including paleo-Leviticus[a]), one *targum*, two apocryphal or pseudepigraphic texts, and eight sectarian documents were recovered.

Khirbet Qumran: Surveys in December 1940 by Baramki and in April 1946 by S. Husseini made note of the ruined buildings, reservoir, boundary walls, and cemeteries with a consensus that the site dated to the Byzantine and Arab periods.

R. de Vaux, returning to the site in late 1951, made a test sounding in the middle of the tell. Pottery matching that from Cave 1 (1 kilometer to the north)—including the cylindrical "scroll" jars—was found, confirming the relationship of the site to the cave. As a result, several seasons of thorough excavation were launched, directed by R. de Vaux on behalf of the JDA, PAM, and EBAF, jointly. During the first season (24 November–12 December 1951), loci 1–4 in the main building and a few graves in the main cemetery were opened. During the second season (9 February–24 April 1953), the remainder of the main building and its tower (loci 5–53) were uncovered. The third season (13 February–14 April 1954) saw the clearing of loci 54–99, which included the dining room/assembly hall, "pantry," and potters workshop. During the fourth season (2 February–6 April 1955) the entire western sector and remainder of the water system were excavated (loci 100–142). The fifth season (18 February–28 March 1956) was used for rechecking the stratigraphy of the site and determining the extent and makeup of the nearby cemeteries. Remains from the Iron II period, second century BCE to first century CE (four phases), and second century CE (Bar Kokhba Revolt) were found. No writing on skins or papyrus was recovered from the strata contemporary with the scroll caves (third century BCE to first century CE), although inscribed jars, ostraca, ink wells, and (possibly) writing tables were found.

Epigraphic remains included a jar with an inscription, a jar neck fragment with an etched name in Greek, *IOSIPOS*, more than twenty Hebrew ostraca (mainly names), an abecedary, one Greek ostracon, and more than seven hundred coins.

During the winter of 1996 J. Strange excavated a deep trench just south of the ruins of Khirbet Qumran on the esplanade. During the clean-up work at the end of the excavation, fragments from two ostraca were discovered in the recesses of the north-south enclosure wall (excavated earlier by de Vaux).

ʿEin-Feshkha (ʿEnot Ṣuqim): A test sounding was made during the fifth season of excavation at Khirbet Qumran. Ceramic and numismatic finds confirmed that the site was contemporary with Khirbet Qumran and one season of excavation (25 January–21 March 1958), directed by R. de Vaux, was conducted as a result. Inscriptional remains were limited to an inscribed stone weight, an inkwell, and sixty-two coins.

Masada: During 1955 and 1956 two seasons of archaeological survey were carried out at Masada by M. Avi-Yonah, N. Avigad, Y. Aharoni, I. Dunayevsky, and S. Gutman on behalf of the Hebrew University (HU), Israel Exploration Society (IES), and Israel Department of Antiquities (IDA), jointly. At this time, the entire mound, its visible structures, and its water system were mapped and drawn. Special attention was paid to the northern palace, which was partially excavated. One ostracon, one papyrus fragment, one graffito on plaster, and three coins were recovered. Y. Yadin directed two seasons of excavation at Masada in 1963–1964 on behalf of the HU, IES, and IDA. The extensive architectural and material remains, exposed in their entirety, dated primarily from the time of Herod the Great until the site's destruction in 73 CE (including Roman army camps and siege works built around the site). A limited occupation by a Roman garrison during the post-destruction years followed. Evidence of Chalcolithic, Iron, and especially the Byzantine period occupation (including the remains of a church) was also found. From the Roman period several biblical and other texts on parchment were recovered as well as many coins, more than seven hundred ostraca, and more than two hundred Roman secular documents on papyrus.

Second Revolt (Bar Kokhba Period; second century CE)

Wadi Murabbaʿat (Naḥal Dargah): This site was originally discovered in 1951 by bedouin who eventually offered large quantities of fragmentary manuscripts of texts and ostraca (mostly dating to the Bar Kokhba Revolt) in Hebrew, Aramaic, Nabatean, Greek, Latin, and Arabic to the PAM (with a few items from other periods ranging from the Iron Age to the Byzantine period). Controlled excavations in 1952 directed by R. de Vaux on behalf of the JDA, PAM, and EBAF, yielded four caves with archaeological remains; of these, only adjacent Caves 1 and 2 produced epigraphic remains. Shepherds found a fifth cave in March 1955, which yielded a single document: the scroll of the Twelve Prophets.

Naḥal David (Wadi Sdeir), The Cave of the Pool: This area was surveyed by G. D. Sandel in 1905 and Y. Aharoni in 1956 and excavated by N. Avigad (1960–1961) with archaeological remains coming from the Chalcolithic period, Iron Age, and Bar Kokhba Revolt (including a plastered pool). Epigraphic remains consist of two coins from the Bar Kokhba Revolt.

Naḥal David (Wadi Sdeir), Unidentified Cave: Bedouin offered Aramaic and Greek documents purported to be from this cave, along with fragments of a copy of *Genesis*.

Naḥal Ḥever (Wadi Khabra) Cave 5/6, The Cave of the Letters: This area was first investigated by Y. Aharoni in 1953 on behalf of the IDA, at which time traces of illicit digging were found. Aharoni dated the remains of the cave and the Roman camp on the plateau above to the Bar Kokhba Revolt. During two seasons of excavation (1960–1961), Y. Yadin recovered from the cave Roman period remains including linen clothing, shoes, bronze vessels, glassware, knives, wooden utensils, matting, baskets (one with skulls), door keys, two bullae with impressed images of Hercules, and a number of coins.

Three archives derived from this cave: (1) Legal documents from the personal archive of a certain Babatha, many of which were "double documents" written in Nabatean, Aramaic, and Greek; (2) Land contracts written at ʿEin-Gedi mainly in Hebrew; (3) Personal letters written by Shimʿon Bar Kokhba, mainly to two administrators at ʿEin-Gedi.

Naḥal Ḥever (Wadi Khabra) Cave 8, The Cave of Horror: Cave 8 was first noticed by Y. Aharoni in 1953 while investigating Cave 5/6 directly across the ravine. In 1955 Aharoni entered the cave and found pottery from the Early Bronze and Roman periods. Among the remains (all dated to the Bar Kokhba Revolt) were clothing, shoes, dehydrated fruit, wooden utensils, matting and ropes, together with numerous skeletons of primarily young people and children (thus the name of the cave). The only epigraphic find was a Hebrew ostracon.

In 1961, Aharoni fully excavated the cave, finding more remains from the Roman period, including fragments of the Dodekapropheton (Greek Minor Prophets) scroll (8Ḥev 1), papyrus fragments with Greek or Jewish script, ostraca in Jewish script (two legible, others illegible), and four coins.

Naḥal Mishmar (Wadi Mahras) Cave 1, Cave of the Treasure (Scouts Cave): Two seasons of excavation by P. Bar-Adon (1960, 1961) yielded finds from the Chalcolithic and Roman periods, including a large cache of bronze and bone objects from the Chalcolithic period.

Naḥal Ṣeʾelim (Wadi Seiyal): In the spring of 1960, two excavation teams centered their attention on the cliffs and area around Naḥal Ṣeʾelim. N. Avigad and his crew worked on the southern cliffs of the wadi and its tributaries and found only a few potsherds from the Chalcolithic period and no inscriptional material.

Y. Aharoni excavated several sites and caves along the northern cliffs, and found remains from the Chalcolithic, Iron II, and Bar Kokhba periods. Only three adjacent caves produced epigraphic remains.

Naḥal Ṣeʾelim (Wadi Seiyal) Cave 31, Cave of the Arrows: Roman period remains included a lamp, storage jars, cooking pots, iron tipped arrows, and a coin of the emperor Trajan.

Naḥal Ṣeʾelim (Wadi Seiyal) Cave 32, Cave of the

Skulls: The bedouin thoroughly explored this cave before the excavators arrived. Left behind were seven skeletons in secondary burial, potsherds from the Chalcolithic and Roman periods, some cloth, and a coin of the emperor Trajan.

Naḥal Ṣe'elim (Wadi Seiyal) Cave 34, Cave of the Scrolls: Remains mainly from the Bar Kokhba Revolt include a wooden comb, game pieces, and fragments of various documents, as well as two coins from the early third century CE.

Naḥal Ḥarduf (Wadi Maradif) Cave 40, Cave of the Reservoir: In a tributary of the Naḥal Ṣe'elim Aharoni found, in the Cave of the Reservoir, Chalcolithic and Roman period potsherds, a Bar Kokhba coin, and a plastered cistern.

ʿEin-Gedi: In 1949 trial excavations and survey were conducted by B. Mazar at Tell Goren and in the oasis on behalf of the IES. In 1956–1957 an extensive archaeological survey was conducted by Y. Aharoni and J. Naveh, which yielded remains from the Chalcolithic, Iron, Hellenistic, Roman, and Byzantine periods. Epigraphic remains from the Hellenistic, Roman, and Byzantine periods included coins and mosaic inscriptions. The land contracts found in Naḥal Ḥever's Cave of the Letters deal with plots of land at ʿEin-Gedi: these and other documents found in the cave must have derived from this town. Between 1961 and 1965 five seasons of excavations at ʿEin-Gedi-Tell Gorden were conducted by B. Mazar, I. Dunayevsky, and T. Dothan.

Byzantine-Islamic Periods

Wadi Murabbaʿat (Naḥal Dargah): In addition to the fragments from earlier periods (see above), fragments of several manuscripts from the Byzantine-Islamic period were found in the caves of the Wadi Murabbaʿat.

Khirbet Mird (Ḥorqaniah): In July 1952 bedouin found manuscripts in Christian Palestinian Aramaic, Greek, and Arabic in a room in the ruins of a Byzantine monastery at this site. The Belgian archaeological expedition under R. de Langhe recovered additional manuscript fragments in a cistern in 1953. Finds include more than forty Greek documents, at least ten Christian Palestinian Aramaic texts, as well as more than 150 Arabic papyri.

Khirbet Mazin (Copper Scroll Expedition): Excavated by R. de Langhe on behalf of J. Allegro, the site yielded Second Temple and Byzantine period remains.

BIBLIOGRAPHY

Aharoni, Y. "Expedition B." In *The Expedition to the Judean Desert, 1960*, pp. 11–24. Jerusalem, 1961.

Aharoni, Y. "Expedition B: The Cave of Horror." In *The Expedition to the Judean Desert, 1961*, pp. 186–214. Jerusalem, 1962.

Avi-Yonah, M., N. Avigad, Y. Aharoni, I. Dunayevsky, and S. Gutman. *Masada: Survey and Excavations, 1955–1956*. Jerusalem, 1957.

Baillet, M., J. T. Milik, and R. de Vaux. *Les "petites grottes" de Qumran*. Discoveries in the Judaean Desert, 3. Oxford, 1962.

Bar-Adon, P. "Expedition C." In *The Expedition to the Judean Desert, 1960*, pp. 25–35. Jerusalem, 1961.

Bar-Adon, P. "Judean Desert Caves: The Naḥal Mishmar Caves." In *Encyclopedia of Archaeological Excavations in the Holy Land*, edited by M. Avi-Yonah and E. Stern, vol. 3, pp. 683–90. Jerusalem, 1977.

Barag, D., et al. *Masada IV: Lamps, Textiles, Basketry, Cordage and Related Artifacts, Wood Remains, Ballista Balls*. The Yigael Yadin Excavations 1963–1965, Final Reports. Jerusalem, 1994.

Barthélemy, D., and J. T. Milik. *Qumran Cave 1*. Discoveries in the Judaean Desert, 1. Oxford, 1955.

Benoit, P., J. T. Milik, and R. de Vaux. *Les grottes de Murabbaʿat*. Discoveries in the Judaean Desert, 2. Oxford, 1961.

de Vaux, R. "Qumran Excavation Reports: First Season." *Revue biblique* 60, 83–106; Second Season, *Revue biblique* 61 (1954), 203–236; Third–Fifth Seasons, *Revue biblique* 63 (1956), 533–577; ʿEin-Feshkha, *Revue biblique* 63 (1956), 575–577, and *Revue biblique* 66 (1959), 225–255.

de Vaux, R. *Qumran Grotte 4.II: Archéologie*. Discoveries in the Judaean Desert, 6. Oxford, 1977.

Humbert, J.-B., and A. Chambon. *Fouilles de Khirbet Qumrân et de Aïn Feshkha*. Göttingen, 1994.

Mazar, B., T. Dothan, and I. Dunayevsky. "En-Gedi: The First and Second Seasons of Excavations, 1961–1962." *ʿAtiqot V* (English Series). Jerusalem, 1966.

Netzer, E. *Masada III: The Buildings, Stratigraphy and Architecture*. The Yigael Yadin Excavations 1963–1965, Final Reports. Jerusalem, 1992.

Pfann, S. J. "History of the Judean Desert Discoveries." In *Companion Volume to the Dead Sea Scrolls Microfiche Edition*, edited by E. Tov with the collaboration of S. J. Pfann, 2d ed., pp. 97–108. Leiden, 1995.

Pfann, S. J. "Sites in the Judean Desert Where Texts Have Been Found." In *Companion Volume to the Dead Sea Scrolls Microfiche Edition*, edited by E. Tov with the collaboration of S. J. Pfann, 2d ed., pp. 109–119, and extensive bibliography therein. Leiden, 1995.

Yadin, Y. *The Finds from the Bar Kokhba Period in the Cave of Letters*. Judean Desert Studies, 1. Jerusalem, 1963.

Yadin, Y. *The Excavation of Masada, 1963/64: Preliminary Report*. Jerusalem, 1965.

STEPHEN J. PFANN

ARCHAEOLOGY. In the nineteenth century and the first half of the twentieth century, scholars were mainly attracted to explore the unique geographical features of the Dead Sea. The first surveys were undertaken by F. de Saulcy (1853), V. Guérin (1869), and Conder and Kitchener (1881–1883), while the monastic remains in the Judean Desert and in the Valley of Jericho were recorded by Tobler (1853–1854), Schick (1877), and J. L. Federlin (1902–1904).

Exploration of Caves. A new interest in archaeological exploration of the Judean Desert caves and ruins was instigated by the discovery of the first scrolls in Cave 1 at Qumran by a bedouin shepherd from the Taʿamireh tribe in the spring of 1947. Because of the political circumstances prevailing in that region at that time, scholarly exploration was delayed. Systematic excavations were carried out in Cave 1 at Qumran only in February–March 1949, on behalf of the Department of Antiquities of Jordan, The École Biblique et Archéologique Française in Jerusalem, and the Palestine Archaeological Museum in Jerusalem (now the Rockefeller Museum). In 1951 excavations began at Khirbet Qumran, which was interpreted then as a Roman military post. In January–March 1952, following rumors of new scrolls having been discovered by bedouin of the same tribe in the area farther to the south, the directors of the Qumran excavations—G. L. Harding and R. de Vaux, together with D. Barthélemy—excavated four caves at Wadi Murabbaʿat. The first group of Bar Kokhba letters was discovered in these caves. In 1960 another group of Bar Kokhba letters was retrieved by Y. Yadin in the Cave of the Letters in Naḥal Ḥever.

Meanwhile, in February 1952 the bedouin discovered Cave 2Q. This prompted the archaeologists to extend their investigations by conducting a systematic survey along the 8-kilometer long limestone cliffs extending from ʿEin-Feshkha to their northern end, beyond Khirbet Qumran. The survey, in March 1952, was directed by Harding, de Vaux, and W. L. Reed. The most outstanding find in this survey was the Copper Scroll (3Q15), found in Cave 3Q. It was again first the bedouin who in September 1952 discovered Cave 4Q—the richest of the Qumran caves. They managed to extract most of its content before de Vaux and J. T. Milik, with the assistance of the Department of Antiquities of Jordan, could begin their systematic excavation, which lasted seven days. Cave 5Q was subsequently found nearby, and Cave 6Q farther to the west, near the fall of Wadi Qumran at its outlet to the valley. Finds from Cave 6Q were already purchased earlier from the bedouin. Caves 7Q–10Q were discerned only in the spring of 1955, during the fourth season of the Qumran excavations, at the edge of the marl plateau to the south of the site. Cave 11Q, the last to yield scrolls, was discovered early in 1956. It is assumed that the Temple Scroll (11Q19 and 11Q20), brought to scholarly attention only after the 1967 war, was originally found by the bedouin there. Caves 1Q, 4Q, and 11Q are considered to be the most important of the Qumran caves in terms of inscribed finds.

Khirbet Mird (Hyrcania) papyri were also first found in 1952 by the bedouin. In 1953 the site was explored by an expedition from Louvain University, directed by R. de Langhe and Lippens.

On the Israeli side of the border it was Y. Aharoni who devoted special efforts, already in the end of 1953 and again in the springs of 1955 and 1956, to explore the caves of Naḥal Ḥever and Naḥal David on behalf of the Israel Department of Antiquities and Museums. As a result of Aharoni's finds, and due to rumors during the late 1950s that papyri originating from caves in the Israeli part of the Judean Desert had reached the antiquities market in Jordanian Jerusalem, an Israeli campaign began. In January 1960 Aharoni went on a ten-day survey to Naḥal Ṣe'elim. This was followed in March–April 1960 and March 1961 by four expeditions headed by Y. Aharoni, P. Bar Adon, N. Avigad, and Y. Yadin, on behalf of the Hebrew University of Jerusalem, the Israel Exploration Society, and the Israel Department of Antiquities and Museums. The territory explored extended between ʿEin-Gedi and Masada, encompassing the cliffs of Naḥal Ṣe'elim, Naḥal Mishmar, Naḥal Ḥever, and Naḥal David. The papyrus documents from the Cave of the Letters in Naḥal Ḥever also included, besides the Bar Kokhba letters, the archive of Babatha, a wealthy Jewish matron of ʿEin-Gedi.

In 1963 and 1964, an expedition headed by P. W. Lapp and N. L. Lapp, on behalf of the American School of Oriental Research in Jerusalem, explored two caves in Wadi ed-Daliyeh, northeast of Jericho. This time, as well, bedouin preceded the archaeologists. The major finds included papyri and bullae from the end of the Persian period.

In 1983, a systematic archaeological survey of the Judean Desert caves was initiated by J. Patrich in collaboration with Y. Yadin, on behalf of the Hebrew University of Jerusalem. The survey, conducted in the fall and winter of each year until 1987, was followed by trial soundings, especially in some of the Qumran caves. The area surveyed extended from Naḥal Og (Wadi Mukellik) in the south to Wadi Auja in the north. The limestone cliffs of Qumran and ʿEin-Feshkha were subjected to a careful reexamination (Patrich, 1995).

In 1983 a cave yielding unique Pre-Pottery Neolithic B finds was excavated by O. Bar Yosef and D. Alon in Naḥal Hemar. Other caves in the Judean Desert were explored in the 1980s by the Israel Cave Research Center of the Society for the Preservation of Nature, directed by A. Frumkin. In the course of this survey, the caves at Wadi ed-Daliyeh were reexamined; Wadi Makukh and Wadi Khareitun were explored; and in 1986, excavations by H. Eshel at Avior Cave at Ketef Jericho revealed several papyri fragments from the Persian and Bar Kokhba periods. The terrace below this cave was excavated by Eshel in 1993 in the framework of "Operation Scroll," yielding more papyri. In 1991 a cave in the upper section of Naḥal Ḥever was excavated by D. Amit and H. Eshel (1993), yielding finds typical of other Bar Kokhba Revolt caves (including one silver coin of "year three," but without inscribed documents, except two fragmentary ostraca). At the site of Hiam el-Saqha, north of Murabbaʿat, Bar Adon found a cemetery consisting of twenty graves, which he claimed to be of the Qumran type. Two of them were excavated by H. Eshel and Z. Greenhut (1993).

"Operation Scroll," on behalf of the Israel Antiquities Authority and the staff officer for archaeology in Judea and Samaria, started in mid-November 1993 and lasted until January 1994 (Drori, et al., 1994). The area explored extended along approximately 100 kilometers of canyons in the Jordan Valley, from Wadi ed-Daliyeh in the north to Naḥal Dragot in the south. Most cliffs had been explored already on a more modest scale by other expeditions. The area was divided into six zones. The cliffs of Qarantal and Qumran were divided into secondary zones. Approximately 650 caves were surveyed, and approximately 70 were excavated. A separate numeration system, different from those used by earlier expeditions, was employed. New excavations also took place at Khirbet Qumran at that time. The work was undertaken by a team of approximately one hundred archaeologists, assistants, and volunteers, and approximately 170 workers from Shechem and Jericho were employed in the excavations. A systematic, expert use of a metal detector proved to be most fruitful. The finds included fifteen papyri from the Ketef Jericho caves (Eshel and Zissu, 1995); an ostracon from Cave 38 near Qarantal, overlooking Jericho; thousands of fragmentary clay vessels, flint tools, metal objects, glass, coins, cloths, leather, basketry; and foodstuff such as dates, almonds, olive stones, etc. No new scrolls were found. The periods of occupations attested were similar to those already known in this region: Neolithic, Chalcolithic, Early Bronze I, Iron Age (few finds), and a wealth of finds from the Persian, Hellenistic (mainly Hasmonean), and Roman (end of Second Temple and Bar Kokhba) periods. In Khirbet Qumran the flat area on the south was excavated, uncovering Iron Age pits and the surface of a date press adjacent to a *miqveh.* Soundings were opened in various rooms and in later years the area along the water channel extending northward was entirely excavated as well.

Other Surveys and Excavations. In conjunction with the Qumran scroll finds, and de Vaux's excavations at Qumran and ʿEin-Feshkha in the years 1951–1956, the Iron Age sites in the Buqeia (Hyrcania Valley) were excavated by Cross and Milik in 1954 and 1955. The agricultural installations associated with them were further explored by Stager in 1972. On the Israeli side of the Judean Desert, biblical ʿEin-Gedi (Tell Goren) was first surveyed in 1949 by B. Mazar, A. Reifenberg, and T. Dothan. Later surveys were carried out by Y. Aharoni and J. Naveh. Five seasons of excavations were conducted during the years 1961–1965 by an expedition of the Hebrew University and the Israel Exploration Society, headed by B. Mazar. The ʿEin-Gedi Synagogue and adjacent area was excavated in 1970–1972 by D. Barag and Y. Porath, and in 1993 by G. Hadas. The excavations at the site were resumed in 1996 by Y. Hirschfeld. The agricultural installations were studied by J. Navah, Y. Porath, and more recently by G. Hadas.

In 1955 and 1956 two comprehensive archaeological surveys were undertaken at Masada, but large-scale excavations at the site took place only in the years 1963–1965 on behalf of the Hebrew University of Jerusalem and the Israel Exploration Society, headed by Y. Yadin. Excavations at the site were resumed in 1989 by E. Netzer and in 1995–1996 by E. Netzer and G. Stiebel. On the Jordanian side of the Judean Desert, the Herodian palace-fortress of Herodium was excavated in the years 1962–1967 by V. Corbo on behalf of the Studium Biblicum Franciscanum in Jerusalem. [*See* Herodium.] The excavations at the site were continued in the years 1967–1970 by G. Foerster, and since 1970 Lower Herodium has been exposed by an expedition of the Hebrew University headed by E. Netzer. Netzer had also excavated Cyprus and Nuseib Uweishirah, on either side of Wadi Qilt, overlooking Jericho, in conjunction with his large scale excavation at the site of the Hasmonean-Herodian palaces and agricultural estate of Jericho. Other Hasmonean-Herodian fortresses were mainly surveyed or excavated on a small scale by Israeli scholars (Tsafrir, 1982). [*See* Hasmoneans; Herodians.] The siege systems around these fortresses were studied mainly by Meshel, while the siege system of Masada was studied by Schulten long before. [*See* Roman Camps.]

W. R. Farmer, who had assisted Cross and Milik in the Buqeia survey, excavated in 1957 at Khirbet Zaraniq on behalf of the American School of Oriental Research at Jerusalem. The site turned out to be the monastery of Jeremias, known from Byzantine sources. In the winter of 1961 J. M. Allegro and R. de Langhe excavated for three weeks at Khirbet Mazin. In 1964–1966 I. Blake conducted surveys and excavations at several Iron Age and Byzantine sites (ʿEin el-Turabeh, ʿEin el-Ghweir, and El Kuseir-Sousakim), on behalf of the British School in Jerusalem.

Following the 1967 war, an "Emergency Archaeological Survey" was launched in 1968 on behalf of the Israel Department of Antiquities. In this framework and in the following years Bar-Adon (1972, 1989) explored many Judean Desert sites and caves, mainly on the fault escarpment and along the Dead Sea shores.

Comprehensive archaeological surveys all over the Judean Desert were conducted during the 1980s on behalf of the Archaeological Survey of Israel by Y. Hirschfeld (1985), J. Patrich (1995), U. Dinur, N. Feig, H. Goldfus, A. Golani, and O. Sion (Finkelstein, 1993). In this period two Iron Age II sites were also excavated (Eitan, 1992).

A Broad Survey of the Finds and Settlement Patterns. In all periods the Judean Desert served as a land of pasture for nomadic tribes. Typical installations of nomadic and semi-nomadic societies are tent encampments, burial grounds, water cisterns, stone cairns (Chalcolithic and/or Early Bronze I), and cave shelters. The desert was also a place of seclusion and wandering for hermits and pious people of high spirituality. The desert caves, adjacent to the settled land, always served also as places of refuge in times of war and oppression. To such hideouts the refugees would bring with them their most precious belongings, including judicial documents and sacred writings.

Prebiblical and biblical periods. The beginnings of a walled settlement at Jericho go back to Pre-Pottery Neolithic A period. The most interesting finds of the Pre-Pottery Neolithic B period, including textiles and basketry, were found in Naḥal Hemar Cave. Finds from this period were also found in Cave 24 to the north of Qumran (Patrich, 1995). Chalcolithic shards are common in any survey in the Judean Desert. The main Chalcolithic settlement exposed so far in the Judean Desert is at ʿEin-Gedi, where a large temple was found. The Naḥal Mishmar treasure was presumably taken from this temple. Early Bronze I finds are common as well. The finds from Cave 13 in the lower Wadi Makukh ("The Warrior Cave"), excavated in the framework of "Operation Scroll," are of particular interest: an Early Bronze I burial of a warrior, laid on a mat, wrapped by a cloth. A flint blade, approximately 30 centimeters long, an arch cut into two pieces with the string attached to it, a wooden bowl painted red, a worked stick, and four arrows were laid next to him, and his sandals were placed near his legs.

Jericho and ʿEin-Gedi, abounding with spring water, were the chief settlements of the Judean Desert throughout history. In biblical and postbiblical times they were royal estates. Other prominent Iron Age II sites include the settlements and agricultural estates of the Judean Kings Jehoshaphat and Uzziah (*2 Chr.* 17.21; 26.10), or Josiah in the Buqeia, and along the Dead Sea (Qumran, Khirbet Mazin, ʿEin el-Turabeh, ʿEin el-Ghweir). [*See* Agriculture; Buqeia.] These sites were identified with the cities mentioned in *Joshua* 15.61–62 in the wilderness of Judea: Middin, Secacah, Nibshan, and Ir-Melaḥ (City of Salt), between Beth-Arabah in the north and ʿEin-Gedi in the south. Eshel has suggested the identification of the City of Salt with the Iron Age II site of Mezad Gozal, adjacent to the salt rock of Mount Sodom, farther south than ʿEin-Gedi (1995). To these Iron Age II sites we can add the royal fortresses of Horvat Shilha, excavated by Amit and Ilan, adjacent to the road leading from Michmash to Jericho, and that of Vered Jericho, excavated by Eitan (1983) to the south of Jericho. The road system leading from the settled land of Judea to Jericho, Qumran, the Dead Sea, ʿEin-Gedi, and Zoara on the southern shore of the Dead Sea, across the Judean Desert, is quite well known due to the intensive surveys and excavations.

Second Temple period. The Hasmonean and Herodian initiative for agricultural exploitation of the Jordan Valley and ʿEin-Gedi oasis is attested at the sites of Phasaelis, Archelais, Naʿaran, Jericho, Qumran, and ʿEin-Gedi. [*See* Agriculture.] Rujum el Bahr and Qatsr el-Yahud (Khirbet Mazin) are two Hasmonean maritime docks on the shores of the Dead Sea. The Hasmonean/Herodian fortresses of Masada, Herodium, Hyrcania, Cyprus, Dok and Aleksandryon, and Machaerus (on the other side of the Dead Sea), with their water supply systems (Amit et al., in press), are the most comprehensive settlement initiative of the Late Hellenistic and Early Roman periods in the confines of the Judean Desert (Tsafrir, 1982). [*See* Water Systems.] Late Roman and Byzantine fortresses and military posts of Provincia Palaestina at ʿEin-Boqeq (Gihon, 1993) and Mezad Zohar are located south of Masada.

The sectarian site at Qumran. *Qumran* was the chief settlement of the Dead Sea sect. [*See* Qumran; Qumran Community.] Another settlement associated with it is in ʿEin el-Ghweir, where a similar cemetery was exposed. Recently (early 1998), Hirschfeld claimed that approximately twenty-five huts and simple shelters he had excavated above ʿEin-Gedi, on the northern bank of Naḥal Arugot, rather than Qumran, should be identified with the location of the Essenes mentioned by Pliny the Elder (*Natural History* 5.15.73). A similar agglomeration of thirteen poor huts, already traced by Bar Adon (1972, p. 126, site 114) at the outlet of Wadi en-Nar, above Khirbet Mazin, was excavated by U. Dahari in the framework of "Operation Scroll," without arguing for any association between them and the Essenes.

Following the original interpretation of Qumran by de Vaux as a monastic site of the Dead Sea Sect, various other suggestions were put forward. Most agree that, at least in its last phase, Qumran was a sectarian settlement. According to H. Stegemann, Qumran was an educational and study center, where the manuscripts of the Essenes were also copied and stored. According to J. B. Humbert (1994), it was a religious cultic center of the Essenes, where sacrifices took place, and according to E. M. Cook (1996), it was their main ritual purification center. Others, ignoring or misinterpreting the archaeological evidence as a whole, deny its sectarian character. According to N. Golb it was a military post, but there is no real fortification wall. According to R. Donceel and P. Donceel-Voûte it was a Hasmonean or Sadducean winter *villa rustica*, but their reconstruction of its triclinium is farfetched. According to A. Crown and L. Cansdale, it was a commercial entrepôt, and for Y. Hirschfeld (1998), it was an agricultural manor (Cook, 1996; Humbert, 1997).

In terms of architecture, as was pointed out by Hirschfeld, Qumran shares some basic features with a group of Hasmonean and Herodian farms equipped with a fortified tower that served as a stronghold. At the beginning it might also have had a military function. The various workshops, warehouses, and installations indicate that it was indeed a busy place, presumably engaged in the manufacture of date and balsam products cultivated in the terraced fields extending along the shore between ʿEin-Feshkha and Qumran, and irrigated by a network of built channels. On the other end, the sectarian character of Qumran, suggested by the scrolls found in caves in its immediate vicinity, is even more evident due to its unique archaeological features, which set this site apart from any other site uncovered so far in the Judean Desert or elsewhere in Israel: the multiplicity of ritual baths (*miqva'ot*) equalling ten in number, hall 77 (the "refectory" and assembly hall), the elongated hall on the second story above locus 30 (the "scriptorium"), the inkwells, and the vast and well-organized cemetery that demonstrates shaft burials completely different from the *kokhim*, rock-cut, family burials, so common in the necropoleis of Jerusalem or that of Jericho and ʿEin-Gedi.

The limited space for dwellings within the walls indicates that the permanent population at the site did not exceed a few dozen inhabitants. In spite of claims by Eshel and Broshi (1997), extramural dwelling quarters in tents or caves, large enough to accommodate a population of 150 inhabitants or more, have not been traced (Patrich, 1997 and 1998). Yet, some features point to a larger population: the refectory could have served approximately 150 inhabitants or more, the ten *miqva'ot* could as well serve a much larger group than the small permanent population at the site. Similarly, the cemetery is much larger in size relative to the small settlement.

These seemingly contradictory data might be resolved if we assume that sect members from Jerusalem and elsewhere used to come here on feast days, to celebrate together, according to the calender and liturgy of the sect, which were different from the official Jewish practice in the Jerusalem temple. Qumran should be conceived as an integral part of the Essene community of Jerusalem.

Hideouts in the desert caves. Biblical and postbiblical literary references, as well as the archaeological finds, attest that the desert caves—mainly those not too remote from the settled land on the west, or from ʿEin-Gedi and Jericho on the east—had served as hideouts. For the late Persian and early Hellenistic periods this is attested by the finds of Wadi ed-Daliyeh, Ketef Jericho, and other caves to the west of Jericho. A hoard of tetradrachmas of Alexander the Great found near Jericho should also be associated perhaps with the early Greek conquest of the country. The Hasmonean period is attested by caves to the west of Jericho, which were explored in the framework of "Operation Scroll." The desert of Samaria also served as a land of refuge for the rebellious Hasmoneans (Schwartz and Spanier, 1991). For the end of the Second Temple period this phenomenon is attested by the hideouts in ʿEin-Fara and Naḥal Michmash, and by the Qumran caves (Patrich, 1995). In the cliffs near ʿEin-Fara the cave encampment set up by Simeon Bar Giora, one of the leaders of the First Jewish Revolt against the Romans, was found; this same camp was mentioned by Josephus. [*See* ʿEin-Fara.] Aramaic inscriptions and painting of menorahs and a pentagram were found in one of the caves in Naḥal Michmash. Hideouts from the Bar Kokhba Revolt were found in Naḥal David, Naḥal Ṣe'elim, Naḥal Harduf, Naḥal Ḥever (including the Sela Cave), Murabbaʿat, Herodium, Ketef Jericho, Naḥal Michmash, Wadi Makukh, and Wadi ed-Daliyeh. El-Massaiyah Cave, from the same period, was excavated in upper Naḥal Dargot. A defense network, which included three towers and a defensive wall, was found on the banks of the wadi surrounding this cave.

Manuscript finds. Discoveries of ancient manuscripts in caves in the Jericho region are recorded in ancient sources. According to a colophon for the *Hexapla* of Origen, a Greek version of *Psalms* was found in a jar in the Jericho region, together with other Greek and Hebrew manuscripts, during the reign of the emperor Caracalla. A note on another cave discovery in this region, in about 785 CE, of biblical and other works in Hebrew script, is preserved in a letter by the Nestorian patriarch Timotheus I to Sergius, the metropolitan of Elam. The *Pentateuch*, called the *Jericho Pentateuch* by the Masoretes, probably was discovered in such a cave. A papyrus of the end of the Judean monarchy (Bordreuil and Pardee, 1990), was presumably found at an unknown site near Jericho. In one cave south of Naḥal Yishai an inscription from the biblical Judean monarchy was found.

Manuscripts, on parchment or papyrus, other than the Dead Sea Scrolls from the Qumran caves, were found at Wadi ed-Daliyeh, Ketef Jericho, Khirbet Mird, Murabbaʿat, Masada, Naḥal David, Naḥal Ḥever, Naḥal Mishmar, Naḥal Ṣe'elim, and ʿEin-Boqeq (Gichon, 1993). [*See entries for place names in this paragraph.*]

The Byzantine Period. The Byzantine period in the Judean Desert and in the Valley of Jericho is characterized by monasteries and hermitages. At that time, monks settled many ravines all over the Judean Desert, establishing there lauras and cenobia. Churches were erected near the site of baptism at the Jordan, and in other centers of pilgrimage. [*See* Monasteries.]

Archaeological Techniques and Methods Used in the Dead Sea Sites. Unlike a regular survey and excavations, archaeological explorations of caves require some special equipment: mountaineering equipment to get access to those caves that are located on steep cliffs, lighting, dust masks, and ventilation equipment.

Aerial photographs are of a limited help for the designation of caves located on steep cliffs. Horizontal shootings are preferable in these cases.

In some areas and caves adjacent to Qumran, special electronic equipment measuring electrical conductivity and resistivity or electromagnetic resonance, or similar remote sensing equipment, was used in order to trace still hidden underground spaces, but to no avail.

A new method of carbon-14 analysis invented in the mid-1980s—Accelerator Mass Spectrography (AMS), requiring just 5–10 milligrams of organic material in order to be applied—was utilized to analyze manuscripts in two separate laboratories: the Institut für Mittelenergiephysik in Zurich and the NSF Arizona Accelerator Mass Spectrometry Facility, University of Arizona, at Tucson. Twenty samples from fourteen dated and undated manuscripts written on leather and papyrus were examined in the first laboratory (Bonani et al., 1991), and fifty-three samples from eighteen inscribed leather scrolls and two linen textiles were examined in the second (Jull et al., 1996). The resulting dates nicely corroborated dates attributed to these scrolls and documents earlier by paleography, and established once and for all that the sectarian writings preceded Christ by many decades. Linen textiles used as wrapping for the scrolls were subjected to carbon-14 probes already in 1951 (Libby, 1951). Weaving and dyeing aspects of these fabrics have been subjected to particular study as well (Bélis, 1997).

Another field of scientific application, still under operation, is to determine the DNA of the scroll parchments to recover genetic information about the animals from which the skins were taken. A comparison with animal bones retrieved from excavations in Qumran and the adjacent caves may establish relations between the scrolls and local herds of sheep, goats, or other animals. This method may thus determine whether the scrolls were written or copied at Qumran or elsewhere. It may also enable researchers to trace fragments that originally had belonged to the same text. This field, still under development, has been undertaken by a team of scholars, headed by P. Smith and G. Kahila from the School of Medicine of the Hebrew University of Jerusalem at Hadassah Hospital, in collaboration with S. R. Woodward (1996) of Brigham Young University, Utah.

New methods of analysis were also applied to the study of the pottery, in addition to the regular typological-chronological comparative study. Petrographical and Neutron Activation analyses conducted on clay vessels from Qumran and ʿEin el-Ghweir proved the clay to be of two different sources (Broshi, 1992), raising some difficulty concerning the usual interpretation of ʿEin el-Ghweir as a sectarian site.

BIBLIOGRAPHY

Amit, D., and H. Eshel. "Selaʿ Cave." *Excavations and Survey in Israel* 13 (1994), 107–108.

Amit, D., J. Patrich, and Y. Hirschfeld, eds. "The Ancient Aqueducts of Judaea-Palaestina." *Journal of Roman Archaeology Supplement Series,* in press.

Bar Adon, P. "The Judaean Desert and Plain of Jericho." In *Judaea, Samaria and the Golan: Archaeological Survey 1967–1968,* edited by M. Kochavi, pp. 92–152. Jerusalem, 1972.

Bar Adon, P. "Excavations in the Judean Desert." *ʿAtiqot* 9 Hebrew Series (1989).

Bélis, M. "Des étoffes de lin pour protéger les manuscrits." *Le Monde de la Bible* 107 (1997), 32.

Blake, I. "Dead Sea Sites of 'the Utter Wilderness.'" *Illustrated London News,* 4 March 1967, pp. 27–29.

Blake, I. "El Kuseir: A Hermitage in the Wilderness of Judea." *Palestine Exploration Quarterly* 101 (1969), 87–93.

Bonani, G., M. Broshi, I. Carmi, S. Ivy, J. Strugnell, and W. Wölfli. "Radiocarbon Dating of 14 Dead Sea Scrolls." *ʿAtiqot* 20 (1991), 27–32.

Bordreuil, P., and D. Pardee. "Le papyrus du Marzeah." *Semitica* 38 (1990), 49–68.

Broshi, M. "The Archaeology of Qumran: A Reconsideration." In *The Dead Sea Scrolls: Forty Years of Research,* edited by D. Dimant and U. Rappaport, pp. 103–115. Jerusalem 1992.

Cook, E. M. "A Ritual Purification Center." *Biblical Archaeology Review* 22/6 (November/December 1996), 39, 48–51, 73–75.

Drori, A., et al. "Operation Scroll." In *Twentieth Archaeological Conference in Israel: Abstracts* (in Hebrew). Jerusalem, 23–24 March 1994, pp. 12–17.

Eitan, A. "Vered Jericho." *Excavations and Surveys in Israel* 2 (1983), 106–107.

Eshel, H. "Archaeological Research in the Judean Desert between 1967–1992" (in Hebrew). In *Judea and Samaria Research Studies,* [proceedings of the fourth annual meeting, 1994], edited by Z. H. Erlich and Y. Eshel, pp. 103–120. Kedumim-Ariel, 1995.

Eshel, H. "A Note on Joshua 15.61–62 and the Identification of the City of Salt." *Israel Exploration Journal* 45 (1995), 37–40.

Eshel, H. "New Data from the Excavations at Qumran." *American Schools of Oriental Research, Newsletter* 46.2 (1996), 28.

Eshel, H., and M. Broshi. "The Archaeological Remains on the Marl Terrace around Qumran" (in Hebrew). *Qadmoniot* 30.2 (1997), 129–133.

Eshel, H., and Z. Greenhut. "Hiam El-Sagha: A Cemetery of the Qumran Type, Judaean Desert." *Revue biblique* 100 (1993), 252–259.

Eshel, H., and B. Zissu. "Ketef Jericho, 1993 [Operation Scroll]." *Israel Exploration Journal* 45 (1995), 293–295.

Farmer, W. R. "Soundings at Khirbet Wadi ez-Zaraniq." *Bulletin of the American Schools of Oriental Research* 147 (1957), 34–36.

Finkelstein, I., ed. *Archaeological Survey of the Hill Country of Benjamin,* sites no. 511, 527, 539. Jerusalem, 1993.

Gichon, M. "En Boqeq." In *The New Encyclopedia of Archaeological Excavations in the Holy Land,* edited by E. Stern, pp. 395–399. Jerusalem, 1993.

Gichon, M. *En Boqeq I.* Mainz, 1993.

Hirschfeld, Y. *Archaeological Survey of Israel: Map of Herodium (108/2) 17–11.* Jerusalem, 1985.

Hirschfeld, Y. "Early Roman Manor Houses in Judaea and the Site

of Khirbet Qumran." *Journal of Near Eastern Studies* 57.3 (1998), 161–189.
Humbert, J.-B., "L'espace sacré à Qumrân." *Revue biblique* 101–102 (1994), 161–214.
Humbert, J.-B. "Les différentes interprétations du site de Qumran." *Le Monde de la Bible* 107 (1997), 20–25.
Jull, A. J. T., D. J. Donahue, M. Broshi, and E. Tov. "Radiocarbon Dating of Scrolls and Linen Fragments from the Judean Desert." *ʿAtiqot* 33 (1996), 1–7.
Libby, W. F. "Radiocarbon dates II." *Science* 114 (1951), 291–296.
Patrich, J. "Khirbet Qumran in Light of New Archaeological Explorations in the Qumran Caves." In *Methods of Investigation of the Dead Sea Scrolls and the Khirbet Qumran Site*, edited by M. O. Wise, et al., pp. 73–95. Annals of the New York Academy of Sciences, 722. 1995.
Patrich, J. *Archaeological Survey in Judea and Samaria: Map of Deir Mar Saba (109/7)*. Jerusalem, 1995.
Patrich, J. "Did Extra Mural Dwelling Quarters Exist at Qumran?" *Proceedings of the International Congress: The Dead Sea Scrolls—Fifty Years after Their Discovery*. Jerusalem, 1999.
Patrich, J. "Was There an Extra Mural Dwelling Quarter at Qumran?" (in Hebrew). *Qadmoniot* 31 (1998), 66–67.
Patrich, J., et al. " Judean Desert Caves." In *The New Encyclopedia of Archaeological Excavations in the Holy Land,* edited by E. Stern, pp. 820–837. Jerusalem, 1993.
Reed, R. "The Examination of Ancient Skin Writing Materials in Ultra-Violet Light." *Proceedings of the Leeds Philosophical and Literary Society: Scientific Section* 9 (10 August 1965), 257–276.
Reed, S. A. *The Dead Sea Scrolls Catalogue: Documents, Photographs and Museum Inventory Numbers*. SBL Resources for Biblical Study, 32. Atlanta, 1994.
Schwartz, J., and J. Spanier. "On Mattathias and the Desert of Samaria." *Revue biblique* 98 (1991), 252–271.
Tsafrir, Y. "The Desert Fortresses of Judaea in the Second Temple Period." In *The Jerusalem Cathedra* 2, edited by L. I. Levine, pp. 120–145. Jerusalem and Detroit, 1982.
Woodward, S. R. "The Use of DNA Analysis to Identify Parchment Pages." *American Schools of Oriental Research, Newsletter* 46.2 (1996), 29.

JOSEPH PATRICH

ARCHITECTURE. While climatic conditions did not generally make the Judean Desert into an obvious choice for settlers, major architectural activities did nevertheless materialize throughout this area. Being a marginal area, regular settlements came into being in this arid zone only in places where water was available, either in the form of perennial springs, as in the oases of Jericho, ʿEin-Gedi, ʿEin-Buqeq, and Zoar, or as a result of human efforts to collect such water by means of aqueducts, dams, or cisterns.

Building activities were primarily a result of the presence of groups that had withdrawn into the Judean Desert for a variety of reasons, and under differing historical circumstances. One such group that had severed its ties with contemporary society and made the desert its home was the community at Qumran. Early Christian monks who took up residence in the area starting in the fourth century CE were another group that purposely created a boundary between itself and its contemporaries.

During both the First and Second Revolts against Rome (66–74 and 132–135 CE), the Judean Desert served as a base of operations (Herodium, ʿEin-Gedi, Masada) and as a last refuge (Judean Desert caves), and these events also resulted in a strong, although mostly temporary, Roman military presence in the region, which has left considerable architectural traces. At Masada, where a series of opulent palaces had been constructed by Herod, the choice of the site had likewise been dictated by the wish to facilitate withdrawal to a safe and faraway desert fortress in times of crisis.

In the Judean Desert, the most conspicuous architectural remains cannot, therefore, be described in terms of a slow, evolutionary process. They rather should be seen as reflecting the history of different groups of people, whose presence in the area was limited in both time and space as it was being dictated by very specific concerns. Despite the relative isolation in which such people chose to live, the architecture they produced and the artifacts they used were nevertheless very similar to the architecture and artifacts common in other parts of Hellenistic, Roman, and Byzantine Palestine. Architectural remains from the Judean Desert thus help to document the complex, yet interactive relationship between people residing in this desert and those living elsewhere in ancient Palestine.

The Road System. In antiquity, only a few roads were constructed in the inhospitable and mountainous Judean Desert. The main road, on the northern fringe of the Judean Desert, was the one leading from Jerusalem to Jericho, from where it went on to Heshbon and Philadelphia (Amman). This road, along which watchtowers were erected beginning in Hellenistic times, continued to be in use throughout antiquity and beyond, as indicated by archaeological evidence dating mainly to the Mamluk period discovered in Nebi Musa.

Further roads in the Judean Desert should be considered as desert tracks rather than actual roads. One such track, which was partially surveyed by P. Bar Adon in 1968, led from Jerusalem to Bethlehem and Tekoa, from where it continued into the Judean Desert to ʿEin-Gedi, and from there along the coast of the Dead Sea through Wadi ʿArabah down to Aila (Eilat). A second important track, which began in Hebron, joined the Jerusalem-Aila track in the Judean Desert. Defense and watchtowers, as well as remains of caravanserais, were discovered along this track during a recent survey. They permit us to date the main activities along this track to the time of the Iron Age and the Byzantine era. Still another major track connected Gaza-Maiumas on the Mediterranean coast with ʿEin-Buqeq on the Dead Sea.

Settlements located on the shores of the Dead Sea were accessible via harbors as well. Such harbors probably existed in ʿEin-Gedi as well as at Rujm el Bahr.

Monumental Architecture. In the Judean Desert, a chain of fortress and palaces was constructed starting in the later second century BCE. Except for Herod's winter palace built along Wadi Qilt near Jericho, architectural remains at sites such as Cypros, Hyrcania, Herodium, and Masada show how, in the early Roman period, the wish to participate in supra-regional artistic trends was combined with a strongly felt need for security. Being located on inaccessible hilltops and having been equipped with a set of walls and defense towers, these sites were first developed under the Hasmoneans. It was not until the reign of King Herod, however, that they were turned into the splendid palace-fortresses visible at these sites today. Because they could easily be defended, palace-fortresses such as Masada and Herodium also played a prominent role in the First Jewish Revolt, and in case of the latter, the Bar Kokhba Revolt as well.

Recent study of architectural remains at Masada by E. Netzer (1991) and G. Foerster (1995), and of such remains at Jericho, has helped to document the extent to which Herod's architectural projects were indebted to local architectural and artistic traditions. Such study has also shown, however, how Herod's architects managed to integrate elements deriving from the larger world of the Hellenistic Near East in the terms of layout, construction techniques, and decorative schemes applied. Typically Roman architectural elements can best be seen in the form of characteristically Roman building techniques such as the use of *opus reticulatum* and *opus quadratum* at Jericho, or the construction of Roman-type baths at all the Herodian sites in question.

Evidence of specifically Jewish architectural practice survives in the form of *miqva'ot* (ritual baths), which appear at all these sites, while Hebrew letters carved into a series of seventy column drums discovered at Masada likewise seem to indicate that at least part of the workforce there may have been Jewish. In the particular case of Masada, Nabatean artistic influence can be detected in a series of Corinthian-Nabatean blocked-out capitals.

During the First Jewish Revolt, Herodium and Masada became important centers of resistance. The insurgents appropriated existing structures in such a way as to accommodate large groups of people. They also transformed existing buildings into synagogues. Herodium also played a role during the Bar Kokhba Revolt, when an extensive network of underground galleries was excavated in the partially artificial hill. Except for some isolated evidence of activity by monks in the Byzantine period, Herod's large palace-fortresses were not rebuilt in the post–135 CE era, nor did the Roman army occupy them for any significant length of time.

Industrial Complexes. In the ancient world, the area surrounding the Dead Sea was famous for its production of asphaltus, balsam, and perfumes. A workshop of 20 by 20 meters for processing products of this type has been excavated in ʿEin-Buqeq. It was probably already operative in the Hasmonean period and continued to function well into the second century CE. Similar workshops must also have existed at ʿEin-Gedi and at Jericho, where the production of dates constituted the single most important crop. In the latter town, evidence for the existence of a workshop for the production of balsam has survived to the north of Herod's palace. A complex for the large-scale processing of agricultural products was excavated by R. de Vaux (1973) at ʿEin-Feshkha—a site that may have been a dependency of Qumran. Workshops that satisfied local needs were probably also common. One such workshop (for the production of pottery) has been excavated in Qumran.

Domestic Architecture. Little is known about the history of domestic architecture in the Judean Desert on the basis of archaeological remains. Literary sources suggest that a large Jewish village existed in ʿEin-Gedi during the Roman and Byzantine periods, but except for individual finds, little is known about the formal appearance of the domestic architecture of the site. In Jericho, south of Herod's palace, evidence of houses dating to the Second Temple period and probably belonging to wealthy owners has also survived, but these houses too await further study. [*See* ʿEin Feshkha; ʿEin-Gedi.]

Qumran. The chronology and interpretation of individual buildings as proposed by R. de Vaux in the preliminary account of his archaeological discoveries in Qumran has recently been called into question. Where de Vaux had stressed the communal nature of most of the architectural spaces at Qumran, other scholars have lately suggested that the site functioned primarily as a fortress or as a villa. The final publication of the stratigraphy and architecture, which is in preparation, will probably help to settle these questions. [*See* Qumran, *article on* Archaeology.]

Caves. From prehistoric times onward, the hundreds of caves that can be found in the Judean Desert, in cliffs overlooking dry streambeds, have been a preferred site for human habitation. In the Roman period, it was not unusual for such caves to have been used for domestic purposes. Such caves were used especially intensively at two points in history, during the period of the revolts against Rome, when such caves were used for hiding, and in the early Christian era, when caves served as a retreat for anchorites. Much of what is known about the history of the Judean Desert derives from these caves and dates to these periods.

The caves found north of Masada in Naḥal Ṣe'elim, Naḥal Mishmar, Naḥal Ḥever, and Naḥal David, as well as the caves in Wadi Murabbaʿat have provided us with a wealth of written and artifactual evidence bearing on the Bar Kokhba Revolt. The general absence of architectural remains inside the caves mentioned attests that human activity there resulted from an emergency situation that accompanied the collapse of Bar Kokhba's reign. Something similar holds true for the caves that were used during the First Jewish Revolt, such as the caves at ʿEin-Fara, in the western part of Wadi Qilt, and Naḥal Michmash, which were studied by J. Patrich (1995) and, possibly, also the caves in Wadi Murabbaʿat. Architectural activity in these caves was limited to the construction of the cisterns (Cave of the Pool in Naḥal David, Miqveh Cave in Naḥal Harduf).

The caves in and around Qumran served various purposes. Some of these were used for storage and as a library, while others may have provided living quarters for members of the community. The caves finally also served to hide documents.

In the early fourth century, early Christian aescetics "turned the Judean Desert into a city." Taking up residence in desert caves, such ascetics made their caves into abodes in which they could dwell on a permanent basis (see below).

Water Systems. In the Judean Desert, survival was possible only in places where enough water could be acquired. Archaeological evidence suggests that much energy was spent on obtaining and preserving water. At sites where water was not locally available, it was brought in by means of aqueducts. Remains of aqueducts have been traced in and near Herodium, Wadi Qilt, and Wadi Nuʿeima (a total of five aqueducts), and Hyrcania. Aqueducts and plastered conduits that were fed by local sources can be found in ʿEin-Gedi and ʿEin-Buqeq. In ʿEin-Gedi, such aqueducts fed into cisterns that were used to water a series of terraced fields, which were located in the vicinity.

In Masada, Hyrcania, and Qumran, water from the surrounding wadis was collected and led to a series of reservoirs and cisterns in and around the settlements themselves. Huge cisterns that also served for the collection of run-off water were discovered at all of Herod's palace-fortresses. The later monks likewise relied on run-off water, as is evident, for example, from archaeological evidence uncovered at the monastery of St. Theodosius.

Miqvaʾot and Baths. Jewish ritual baths occur at Herodian sites such as Masada, Herodium (Upper and Lower), and Herod's winter palace along Wadi Qilt. We can only speculate as to why such *miqvaʾot* were included in Herod's palaces. One possible explanation is that these ritual baths should be dated to the period of the First and Second Revolts against Rome. In Qumran, a series of *miqvaʾot* has been excavated. They provide telling evidence for the importance attached to ritual purity by the members of the Qumran sect. [*See* Miqvaʾot.]

Roman architectural influence is most tangible in the form of a series of Roman-type bath complexes. All of the palace-fortresses—Masada and Lower Herodium in particular—contained one or more such baths. The same holds true for Herod's winter palace in Jericho. Remains of a Roman-style bath dating to the period between 70 and 135 CE also came to light near ʿEin-Gedi, in the plain between Naḥal David and Naḥal Arugot.

Funerary Architecture. Remains of several burial grounds have been excavated in the Judean Desert. According to Josephus, Herod was buried in Herodium, but his mausoleum has not been identified, despite efforts to do so. At the foot of Hyrcania, another of Herod's palace-fortresses, graves, which may contain the earthly remains of his political opponents, were found.

In Jericho, R. Hachlili (Hachlili and Killebrew, 1983) has excavated some 120 chamber tombs dating to the time of the Second Temple. These tombs, which contain vital evidence on the history of primary and secondary burial among Jews, are particularly interesting because of the remaining Hebrew, Aramaic, and Greek inscriptions as well as the wall paintings they contain. At ʿEin-Gedi, a series of similar chamber tombs dating to the second and first centuries BCE has been discovered, especially in the years 1984–1988. There too, remains of ossuaries, wooden coffins, and traces of wall paintings could be recovered. Wooden coffins dating to the Hasmonean period also came to light in the so-called burial caves in Naḥal David.

Physical remains of the supporters of Bar Kokhba who had been starved to death were encountered in the Cave of Horror and also in the Cave of the Letters, in Naḥal Ḥever.

A large cemetery with some 1,100 shaft graves, as well as two subsidiary cemeteries, were discovered in Qumran. During the excavations of fifty graves in these cemeteries, remains of males, females, and children were uncovered. Fifteen kilometers south of Qumran a similar, but much smaller cemetery was excavated at ʿEin el-Ghweir. [*See* Cemeteries.]

Roman Military Architecture. Regular Roman military forces were stationed in Jerusalem following the destruction of the city in 70 CE, and in Ramat Raḥel, where Roman barracks belonging to the same period have been discovered. In the fourth century CE, troops that were part of a defense line known as *Limes Palestinae* could be found in ʿEin-Buqeq, where a small fort of 16.5 by 16.5 meters has come to light.

The Roman military presence in the Judean Desert was mostly temporary in character. The largest and architecturally most interesting complex of Roman military architecture in this area is constituted by a series of two large and six smaller Roman camps built during the siege of Masada—camps that were interconnected by a long, continuous circumvallation wall. Architecturally, these camps, which have been only partially excavated, conform to the standard type of Roman military camp in terms of layout (four gates, two principal roads, *praetorium*, etc.).

Of special interest are the *contubernia* or mess-units, which served to accommodate the soldiers and which have survived in large numbers. Recent and still unpublished work on the siege ramp and on one of the Roman camps at the foot of this ramp should help to further clarify both the chronology and the nature of Roman military activity in and around Masada.

Evidence of a Roman military presence postdating the First Jewish Revolt also survives on top of Masada, and at other sites such as Qumran, but the evidence suggests that such a presence was but short-lived (until 111 CE and 73 CE respectively). A Roman garrison (*cohors I miliaria Thracum*) was probably also stationed in ʿEin-Gedi in the period between the two revolts.

Other Roman camps, dating mainly to the period of the Bar Kokhba Revolt, survive in the Judean Desert on plateaus that overlook the cliffs and caves where the supporters of Bar Kokhba had taken refuge. Such camps survive near Naḥal Ṣeʾelim near ʿEin-Anava, near Caves 1 and 2 in the Naḥal Mishmar (only shards), near Naḥal Ḥever over the Cave of the Letters and the Cave of Horror, respectively (extensive architectural remains), and, possibly, also in Wadi Murabbaʿat. Again, archaeological evidence suggests that such camps were but temporary structures that were deserted soon after the purpose of bringing the Bar Kokhba Revolt to an end had been accomplished. [*See* Roman Camps.]

Synagogues. The Judean Desert has preserved some of the earliest evidence bearing on the history of synagogue architecture. During the First Jewish Revolt, preexisting buildings in Masada and Herodium were turned into synagogues through the construction, along the walls, of benches, which consisted of reused materials. Although scholarly opinion on the identification of the buildings as synagogues is divided, the presence of fragments of a *Deuteronomy* and an *Ezekiel* scroll in the Masada synagogue seems to favor those who regard these buildings as early examples of Jewish religious architecture. It has been suggested that during the same general period there also existed a *beit midrash* ("house of study") at Masada.

In the late antique period, when the architecture of the synagogue had fully evolved, further synagogues were constructed at ʿEin-Gedi, Jericho (Tell es-Sulṭan), and Naʿaran. These synagogues are especially interesting because of their mosaic floors, which document how in the course of the sixth century naturalistic scenes were replaced by geometric ones, as at Jericho, or verbal transcriptions of the signs of the Zodiac and the months of the year, as at ʿEin-Gedi. [*See* Synagogues.]

Churches and Monasteries. Upon the rise of early Christian monasticism in the fourth century CE, the Judean Desert became a preferred spot for anchorites and cenobites who wanted to withdraw into the desert. As a result of the surveys and excavations carried out by Y. Hirschfeld (1992) and J. Patrich (1995), it has recently become possible to reconstruct the history of the monastic movement using archaeological evidence. Concentrations of early Christian monastic remains can be found in and around Wadi Qilt, where early in the fourth century Chariton founded the oldest laura in Palestine, at ʿEin-Fara. Along this wadi no less that sixty-five monastic sites dating to the Byzantine period have been identified. Another concentration can be found in the triangle Jerusalem-Bethlehem-Mar Saba (five Byzantine monasteries and forty-five hermitages associated with the activities of St. Sabas [439–532 CE]), as well as near Herodium-Tekoa (Wadi Charitum, after a monastery founded by Chariton). In the southern part of the Judean Desert there were considerably fewer monasteries and hermitages. Isolated spots such as Herod's old palace-fortresses, including Herodium, Dok, Cypros, Hyrcania, and Masada, were especially popular among early Christian monastics. [*See* Churches; Monasteries.]

BIBLIOGRAPHY

Corbo, Virgilio. *Herodion I: Gli edifici della Regia-Fortezza.* Jerusalem, 1989. Final report on the Franciscan excavations of Herod's mountain palace-fortress at Herodium.

de Vaux, Roland. *Archaeology and the Dead Sea Scrolls.* Schweich Lectures of the British Academy. London, 1973. Relatively detailed account by the excavator of Qumran of his archaeological excavations in and around Qumran.

Donceel, Robert. "Reprise des traveaux de publication de fouilles au Khirbet Qumran." *Revue biblique* 99 (1992), 557–573. Describes new insights gained while preparing for final publication R. de Vaux's excavations at Qumran.

Foerster, Gidon. *Masada V: Art and Architecture.* Jerusalem, 1995. Final excavation report with special emphasis on larger artistic context against which the architectural and artistic remains from Masada should be seen. Should be consulted in conjunction with *Masada III*.

Gichon, Mordechai. *En Boqeq: Ausgrabungen in einer Oase am Toten Meer.* Mainz, 1993. Final report of the excavations of a late antique castellum on the shore of the Dead Sea.

Grabercht, G., and E. Netzer. *Die Wasserversorgung des geschichtlichen Jericho und seiner königlichen Anlage (Gut. Winterpaläste).* Leichtweiss-Institut für Wasserbau der technischen Universität Braunschweig, Mitteilungen 115. Braunschweig, 1991. Detailed description of the waterworks in and around Herod's winter palace in Wadi Qilt.

Hachlili, Rachel. "Burial Practices at Qumran." *Revue de Qumrân* 16 (1993), 247–264. Critical evaluation of the archaeology of funerary practices in the Qumran area.

Hachlili, Rachel, and Ann Killebrew. "Jewish Funerary Customs during the Second Temple Period in the Light of the Excavations at the Jericho Necropolis." *Palestine Exploration Quarterly* 115 (1983), 109–139. Discusses how the discoveries in the Jericho necropolis throw new light on Jewish burial customs and questions of genealogy.

Hirschfeld, Yizhar. *The Judean Desert Monasteries in the Byzantine Period.* New Haven and London, 1992. Standard treatment concerning the development and archaeology of early Christian monasticism in the Judean Desert.

Humbert, J.-B., and A. Chambon. *Fouilles de Khirbet Qumrân et de Aïn Feshkha*, vol. 1. Göttingen, 1994. Contains the fieldnotes of R. de Vaux and is richly illustrated.

Magness, Jodi. "A Villa at Khirbet Qumran?" *Revue de Qumrân* 16 (1994), 397–419. Stresses the differences between the architectural evidence from Qumran and excavated villas in Judea and Idumea.

Netzer, Ehud. "Greater Herodium." *Qedem* 13 (Jerusalem, 1981). Report of the fieldwork carried out in Lower Herodium with special emphasis on the principles governing Herodian palatial design.

Netzer, Ehud. *Masada III: The Buildings, Stratigraphy, and Architecture.* Jerusalem, 1991. Final publication with detailed descriptions of the excavated architectural remains at Masada. Should be consulted in conjunction with *Masada V.*

Patrich, Joseph. *Sabas, Leader of Palestinian Monasticism: A Comparative Study in Eastern Monasticism, Fourth to Seventh Centuries.* Washington, D.C., 1995. Detailed archaeological study of the evidence bearing on one of the founding fathers of the monastic movement in Palestine.

Strobel, August. "Die Wasseranlagen der *Hirbet Qumran.*" *Zeitschrift des deutschen Palästinavereins* 88 (1972), 56–86. Detailed discussion of water management in Qumran and of the theological importance attached to ritual purity.

Yadin, Yigael. *The Finds from the Bar Kokhba Period in the Cave of Letters.* Jerusalem, 1963. Describes the archaeological context in which some of the most important discoveries in the Judean Desert caves were made.

Yadin, Yigael. *Bar-Kokhba: The Rediscovery of the Legendary Hero of the Last Jewish Revolt against Imperial Rome.* London, 1971. Popular account of the discoveries in the Judean Desert caves, including reports on the archaeology of Roman military camps in the area.

LEONARD V. RUTGERS

ARISTOBULUS II. *See* Alexander Jannaeus; Hasmoneans; *and* Shelamzion Alexandra.

ARUGOT, NAḤAL. Cutting through the Judean Desert, Naḥal Arugot flows southeast from the Judean Mountains to the Dead Sea, from about 1000 meters above sea level to 400 meters below sea level. Its length is 31 kilometers and its drainage area is about 220 square kilometers. Its western border is the Teqoʿa–Kefar Baruch (Bani-Naʿim) road.

It has three sections: Naḥal Arugot Elyon (upper) or Wadi el-Jihar, Naḥal Arugot Tikhon (middle) or Wadi el-Ghar, and Naḥal Arugot Taḥton (lower) or Wadi Areijeh.

Throughout history, Naḥal Arugot was the site of only roads and forts. Its location in the Judean Desert precluded permanent settlements, but nomads camped there for limited seasons. The middle and lower wadi belong to ʿEin-Gedi, which was a large Jewish village from before the fourth century CE (*Onomasticon* 428) through the sixth century CE, as shown by the synagogue located there. [*See* ʿEin-Gedi.]

The main road to Jerusalem from ʿEin-Gedi was via Teqoʿa. Along the road were forts built during the Iron Age and used during the Early Roman period (Bar-Adon 1972, pp. 93–4). At Rujum en-Naga architectural remains were found with pottery from the Iron Age, Hellenistic, and Early Roman periods (Bar-Adon, 1972, p. 93–94), and the remains at Mitspe ʿEin-Gedi can be dated to the Late Iron Age and are paralleled by those of Stratum V in Tel Goren (Ofer, 1986, 27).

The Teqoʿa-Hebron road runs north-south along Naḥal Arugot's western edge, along a chain of forts from the Byzantine period (Hirschfeld, 1985, p. 10*) such as Khirbet Sahba (Hirschfeld, 1985, pp. 57–58).

In upper Arugot, south of Teqoʿa, lies a connecting road between the two roads mentioned above, with towers and water cisterns established at the end of the Iron Age and reused in the Byzantine period (Amit, 1989, pp. 161–162).

Two ascents were built to cope with the 600-meter height, the Ascent of ʿEin-Gedi near the Israelite fort and the Ascent of the Essenes, built by Hadrian to serve the Roman siege camps above the caves in Naḥal Ḥever (Harel, 1967, pp. 21–23). [*See* Ḥever, Naḥal, *article on* Archaeology.]

Monasteries were built during the Byzantine period, only in Wadi el-Jihar: Nea Laura, which included a church with monks' cells around it, a garden with a dam, and a reservoir and cisterns (Hirschfeld, 1992, pp. 26–27; the Severianus monastery (Hirschfeld, 1992, pp. 46 and 49); and Khirbet ed-Deir, which included church and dining-hall complexes, residential quarters, and a garden. On the church floor is a Greek inscription taken from the Septuagint (Ps. 106.4–5). Another Greek inscription is taken from *1 Corinthians* 15.52–53 (Hirschfeld, 1991, pp. 39–42).

A number of settlement sites are located in the lower part of Wadi Areijeh, close to the Tell of ʿEin-Gedi. In the ravine are remains of aqueducts hewn out of the rock and a reservoir. Tombs were found at the mouth of the river with many wooden coffins and vessels dating from the second or first century BCE. There were primary burials in wooden coffins, secondary burials in large wooden coffins (Hadas, 1994, p. 30), and wooden ossuaries (Hadas 1994, p. 7).

On top of the desert plateau at Mitspe Arugot are twelve buildings and the remains of an ascent to the wadi dating from the sixth century CE (Bar-Adon, 1972, p. 145).

Even in the Arugot Cave, pottery from the Iron Age and Early Roman period was found. A jar handle imprinted in old Hebrew, *le-Naḥum ʿavdi* ("to Nahum my servant"), also was found (Hadas, 1983, p. 62).

[*See also* Archaeology; Qumran, *article on* Archaeology.]

BIBLIOGRAPHY

Amit, David. "Hebron–ʿEn Gedi, Survey of an Ancient Road." *Excavations and Surveys in Israel* 9 (1989/1990), 161–162.

Bar-Adon, P. "The Judean Desert and Plain of Jericho" (in Hebrew). In *Judea, Samaria, and the Golan, Archaeological Survey 1967–8*, edited by Moshe Kochavi, pp. 92–149. Jerusalem, 1972.

Hadas, Gidʿeon. "Nahal Arugot" (in Hebrew). *Ḥadashot Archeologiot* 82 (1983), 62.

Hadas, Gidʿeon. "Nine Tombs of the Second Temple Period at ʿEin-Gedi" (Hebrew). *Atiqot* 24 (1994), 1–8.

Harel, Menashe. "Israelite and Roman Roads in the Judean Desert." *Israel Exploration Journal* 17 (1967), 18–25.

Hirschfeld, Yizhar. "Map of Herodium." *Archaeological Survey of Israel*. Jerusalem, 1985.

Hirschfeld, Yizhar. *The Judean Desert Monasteries in the Byzantine Period.* London and New Haven, 1992.

Ofer, A. "ʿEn Gedi." *Excavations and Surveys in Israel* 5 (1986), 27–28.

GIDEON HADAS

ASSYRIA. Located on the west bank of the Tigris (Qalʿat Sherqat), forty miles south of the Upper Zab tributary, Assyria (Ashur) is the designation of a land and then an empire named after the old capital city of Ashur. The Assyrian heartland consists of a roughly triangular stretch of land around the upper Tigris embracing Ashur and the subsequent capital cities Kar-Tukulti-Ninurta, Kalhu (Nimrud), Dur Sharrukin (Khorsabad), and Nineveh (Kuyunjik). At the height of its power the Assyrian empire embraced the entire Fertile Crescent, extending from southern Armenia in the north, the Arabian Desert in the south, Egypt in the southwest, and the Persian Gulf in the east. Assyrian political power ended with the fall of Nineveh in 612 BCE, although certain elements of Assyrian culture and administrative practices lived on in various parts of the Neo-Babylonian and Persian empires that succeeded it.

Assyria became a factor in Israelite and Judean history in the ninth century BCE, perhaps under Shalmaneser III and certainly under Tiglath-pileser III, and remained a decisive force, bringing about the fall of Ephraim and its capital Samaria in 722 BCE and threatening Jerusalem and Judah until its own fall. Assyria, city and empire, and the kings Tiglath-pileser III, Shalmaneser V, Sargon II, Sennacherib, Esarhaddon, and Ashurbanipal are mentioned in the historical books of the Hebrew scriptures as well as in the prophecies of *Hosea, Amos, Micah, Isaiah, Nahum, Zephaniah, Obadiah, Jeremiah, Ezekiel,* and *Zechariah*, and the *Book of Psalms*.

As early as the seventh century BCE the Egyptians and Greeks used Assyria, and a shortened form, Syria, to designate all lands speaking Aramaic, which had become the official language of the Assyrian empire and its successors. This usage is reflected in the rabbinic designation of the Aramaic and late Hebrew script as Assyrian (*Ashurit*). Later on, Syria became the Greek designation of the Levant, while Assyria was used for Mesopotamia. *Ketubbot* 10b in the Babylonian Talmud identifies Assyria with Seleucia. The Dead Sea Scrolls refer to Assyria in its Hebrew form, Ashur, and even the attestations in Aramaic texts prefer this form to the Aramaic Attur. Assyria occurs in the Dead Sea Scrolls with two distinct meanings, reflecting the biblical meaning on the one hand and the later connotation on the other.

Assyria appears in the Qumran biblical scrolls as it does in the other versions. Noncanonical Psalms B (4Q381 33.8; Prayer of Manasseh, reflecting *2 Chr.* 33.10–19), Pesher Isaiah[c] (4Q163 7.2, a citation of *Is.* 10.12–13; 4Q163 40.1), and the Genesis Apocryphon (1QapGn xvii.8; cf. *Jub.* 9.1) also refer to the historical Assyria as known from the Hebrew scriptures. In these instances Ashur is a descendant of Shem. Describing the division of the earth among Noah's sons Shem, Ham, and Japheth, Genesis Apocryphon (1QapGn xvii.8) places the portion of Shem "to the west, to Assyria, until it reached the Tigris" (cf. *Gn.* 10.22 and *Jub.* 8.11–9.15). Certain nonbiblical passages also refer to Assyria as a descendant of Shem and in its historical borders. Thus, the War Scroll (1QM ii.12) reads "During the sixth and seventh years they shall wage war against all the sons of Ashur, and Persia, and the Eastern peoples up to the Great Desert."

A special meaning of Ashur, attested exclusively in the War Scroll, occurs in the expression *Kittiyyei Ashur*, "the *Kittim* of Ashur" (1QM i.2, i.6, xviii.2, xix.10). This term is an expanded and specialized form of the frequently attested *Kittim*, who were an enemy descended from Japheth destined to come from the Mediterranean. The *Kittim* in the Dead Sea Scrolls, once thought to be the Greeks, are now often identified with Rome, and the *Kittim* of Assyria are a subdivision of this group. Several biblical texts that speak of the historical Assyria are used as a basis for an apocalyptic predication concerning the *Kittim* (1QM xi.11, "From of old you foretold the moment of the power of your hand against the *Kittim*: Assyria will fall by the hand of no one, and the sword of nobody will devour it," based on *Is.* 31.8). A precedent for such identifications can be found in biblical texts such as *Ezekiel* 38.17, where the prophecy about Gog and Magog is based on *Isaiah* 14.24–27, a passage relating to Assyria. The War Scroll (1QM xix.10) reads: "And in the morning at the battlefield will arrive the heroes of the *Kittim* and the hordes of Assyria and the army of all the nations who gather with them, [and, lo, they are all] dead corpses [because] they fell there by the sword of God"; the expressions "in the morning" and "dead corpses" seem to reflect *2 Kings* 19.35 and *Isaiah* 37.36, while the "heroes of the *Kittim*" is related to *2 Chronicles* 32.21, which expands and refers to "every hero of valor, officer, and prince in the Assyrian camp." These passages are meant to apply the biblical texts concerning the fall of Sennacherib in the past to the expected demise of the *Kittim* in the future.

It has been suggested that the use of Ashur as a modifier of *Kittim* implies that the nature of the Kittian rule will resemble Assyrian domination (cf. *Gn. Rab.* 16.4: "Rav Huna in the name of Rav Aḥa said: all the empires are named after Nineveh because they adorn themselves at Israel's expense"). It is more likely, however, that the combination of Ashur and *Kittim* indicates that the *Kittim*, who occupy the islands of the sea and the Mediterranean coast, have a center to the north of Israel or would invade the land of Israel from the north. In fact, the War Scroll (1QM i.1–2) groups the *Kittim* of Ashur along with Israel's traditional biblical neighbors, Edom, Moab, Ammon, Philistia, and the "offenders against the covenant." In this passage, which may have been influenced by Psalm 83.7–9, the Assyrian *Kittim* are a northern enemy closing a ring around Israel. They are comparable, therefore, to the "nation from the north" mentioned in the prophecies of Jeremiah. Morever, the use of Assyria to designate the land north of Israel is certainly related to the later use of Assyria, or the shortened form, Syria, to designate the lands speaking Aramaic to the west of the Euphrates.

The locution *Kittiyei Ashur* and the use of the two words in parallelism may be related to the proximity between the two words found in Balaam's last blessing, a text of apocalyptic nature (*Nm.* 24.23–24). The lines "Ships come from the quarter of *Kittim*; they subject Ashur, subject Eber" may have been understood by the Qumran community as "Ships will come from *Kittim*; Assyria will afflict—they [Assyria] will afflict the descendants of Eber." Note also *Isaiah* 23.12–13: "Up, cross over to *Kittim*—even there you shall have no rest. Behold the land of Chaldea—this is the people that has ceased to be. Assyria which founded it for ships . . . has turned it into a ruin." *Ezekiel* 27.6 reads: "From oak trees of Bashan they made your oars; of *bat Ashurim* from the isles of *Kittim* . . . they made your decks"; here the enigmatic *bat Ashurim* should be read *bitashurim*, "with boxwood," but the reading preserved in the Masoretic Text already may have been known to the scribes who wrote the Dead Sea Scrolls.

[*See also* Kittim.]

BIBLIOGRAPHY

Frye, Richard N. "Assyria and Syria: Synonyms." *Journal of Near Eastern Studies* 51 (1992), 281–285.

Grintz, Yehoshua. "The Men of the Yaḥad, Essenes, Beth-(Es)sene" (in Hebrew). *Sinai* 32 (1953), 11–43. See especially page 26, note 34.

Nitzan, Bilhah. *Pesher Habakkuk: A Scroll from the Wilderness of Judaea (1QpHab)* (in Hebrew). Jerusalem, 1986. See pages 71–73.

Steiner, Richard C. "Why the Aramaic Script Was Called 'Assyrian' in Hebrew, Greek and Demotic." *Orientalia* 62 (1993), 80–82.

Yadin, Yigael. *The Scroll of the War of the Sons of Light against the Sons of Darkness.* Translated by Batya Rabin and Chaim Rabin. Oxford, 1962. See pages 21–26.

Zeitlin, Solomon. "The Alleged Antiquity of the Scrolls." *Jewish Quarterly Review* 40 (1949–1950), 57–78.

VICTOR AVIGDOR HUROWITZ

ASTROLOGY. *See* Horoscopes.

ATONEMENT. The term *kipper* ("atone") is associated with the Arabic term *kafara* ("cover") as well as with the Akkadian *kuppuru* ("purge" or "wipe"). In the Bible the term is often paralleled by words meaning "decontaminate" or "purify." The Septuagint translation of *kipper* is *hilaskomai* ("propitiate" or "appease"). The root also carries the meaning of "ransom." Sin and severe impurities must be purged lest the wrath of God fall on Israel. In order to be reconciled to God, the guilty party must bear the penalty of the violation or provide a ransom, that is, a prescribed substitute. Priests act as mediators between God and the sinner to atone for, or expiate, guilt through specific sacrificial rituals.

The community at Qumran attempted to fill the void caused by their withdrawal from the Jerusalem cult. They did not reject the cult on principle but rather decried its present corruption. They fully expected the pure cult to be reestablished and priests to expiate sin through sacrifices once again (cf. Temple Scroll[a], 11Q19 xxv.10–xxvii.10; War Scroll, 1QM ii.5). Even one of the expected Messiahs would be a priest (e.g., Damascus Document, CD xiv.19; Rule of the Community from Cave 1, hereafter, 1QRule of the Community, 1QS ix.11). However, lacking a temple, members of the Qumran community accomplished atonement "without the flesh of burnt offerings and without the fats of sacrifice"; prayer "in compliance with the decree" was "a pleasant aroma," that is, incense before God, and "correctness of behavior" was "acceptable like a free-will offering" (1QS ix.4–5).

The emphasis in the scrolls is on God as the provider of atonement. His holy spirit, compassion, and grace make atonement possible (1QH[a] xii.37 [iv.36]; CD ii.4–5). Though Israel had rebelled against him, God, "in his wonderful mysteries, atoned for their failings and pardoned their sins" (CD iii.18). In future days, God will again expiate the guilt of Israel (CD xx.34).

Atonement also depends on the penitent's humble obedience: "By the spirit of uprightness and of humility his sin is atoned. And by the compliance of his soul with all the laws of God his flesh is cleansed by being sprinkled with cleansing water. . . " (1QS iii.8–9; cf. CD ii.5). The "laws of God" include subjection to the community, and stiff discipline is enforced to keep the sect holy (1QS v.6–13; ix.3–4). Apparently, the repentant sinner makes a declaration of praise to God for his mercy (cf. "May you be blessed, [God of Israel, who forgave me all] my faults and purified me . . . and atoned . . ."; Ritual of Purification, 4Q512 29–32.vii.9, 21).

The atonement process was accompanied by water purifications by the members of the Qumran community as described above (cf. 1QS iii.9) It is no surprise that the efficacy of water is denied to the rebel: "He will not become clean by the acts of atonement, nor shall he be purified by the cleansing waters, nor shall he be made holy by the seas or rivers nor shall he be purified by all the water of the ablutions" (1QS iii.4–5; cf. v.13). The requirement of ritual purification for the sinner is not new in Israel. According to the Bible, the leper and individuals suffering from leprosy and gonorrhea are sinners, the diseases resulting from a curse (*Lv*. 14.34, *Nm*. 12.9–11, *Dt*. 28.27, *2 Chr*. 26.23; cf. 4Q272 1.2; 4Q274 1.1; T., *Neg*. 6.7; B.T., *Arakh*. 16a). Purification by water must accompany the atoning sacrifices (*Lv*. 14.8, 15.13; cf. also *Gn*. 35.2).

There is a sense in which the righteousness of the sect atones for the entire world as an appeasement to God, which brings about his fair distribution of justice and prevents indiscriminate destruction. The sectarians are "chosen by the will (of God) to atone for the earth and to render the wicked their retribution . . . and these will be accepted in order to atone for the earth and to decide the judgment of the wicked" (1QS viii.6–7; cf. 1Q28a 1.3). These holy ones will "appease (*va-yekhapru*) his [God's] will in favor of all those converted from sin" (Songs of the Sabbath Sacrifice, 4Q400 1.16). Israel's enemies will be punished instead of her: "Of the wicked you shall make our ransom while for the upright [you will bring about] the destruction of all our enemies." (Liturgical Prayers, 1Q34 3.i.5).

Another aspect of atonement is the presentation to God of the first fruits of the new wine and oil as "atonement" for the rest of these crops. In other words, these first fruits serve as a sort of "ransom" or propitiatory gift to God that releases the rest of these crops for human consumption. The notion of first fruits is biblical, but it is not linked to atonement. The term used in the Bible is *ḥillel* ("desanctify"; *Dt*. 20.6), in contrast to the sectarian term *kipper* (11Q19 xxi.7–9; xxii.15–16). [*See* Tithing.]

Yom Kippur, the annual day of repentance in Israel (*Lv*. 16), is outlined extensively in Temple Scroll[a] (11Q19 xxv.10–xxvii.19). The Levitical prescriptions are reorganized, and details are added from other parts of the Pentateuch. The day is to be observed by fasting and prayer (CD vi.19; Pesher Habakkuk, 1QpHab xi.8) not only for atonement but for the restoration of Israel (Festival Prayers[b], 4Q508 2.2).

The rabbis, like the sectarians, bewail the loss of the Temple cult and fully expect it to be reinstated in the messianic era. They focus on personal piety and good deeds as a substitute, much as the sectarians: "Now that we have no prophet or priest or sacrifice, who shall atone for us? In our hands is left only prayer" (*Tanḥuma* on va-Yishlaḥ 10), and "Prayer, repentance, and charity avert the evil decree" (J.T., *Ta'an*. 2.1, 65b).

In contrast to the sectarians, the New Testament writers do not consider the Temple cult necessary for atonement but rather affirm their faith in atoning for the death of Jesus (*Mt*. 26.26–29; *Mk*. 14.22–25). Nevertheless, the biblical language of atonement is used to interpret this event. Jesus "substitutes" his life as a "ransom" for penitent sinners (*Mk*. 10.45), "expiates" their guilt by his own sacrificial blood (*Heb*. 10.12), serves as their "propitiation" (*Rom*. 3.25; *1 Jn*. 2.2), and "reconciles" them to God (*Rom*. 5.10).

[*See also* Purity; Sacrifice; Sin; *and* Yom Kippur.]

BIBLIOGRAPHY

"Atonement." In *Encyclopedia Judaica*, vol. 1, pp. 830–832. Jerusalem, 1971.

Buechler, A. *Studies in Sin and Atonement in the Rabbinic Literature of the First Century*. London, 1928.

Lang, B. "Kippēr." In *Theological Dictionary of the Old Testament*, vol. 7, edited by G. Johannes Butterweck, translated by John T. Willis, pp. 288–303. Grand Rapids, Mich., 1995.

Levine, Baruch. *In the Presence of the Lord: A Study of Cult and Some Cultic Terms in Ancient Israel*. Leiden, 1974.

Milgrom, Jacob. "Kippēr." In *Leviticus*, vol. 1, pp. 1079–1084. Anchor Bible, vol. 3. Garden City, N.Y., 1991.

Tuckett, C. M. "Atonement in the NT." In *Anchor Bible Dictionary*, vol. 1, edited by David Noel Freedman, pp. 518–522. New York, 1992.

HANNAH K. HARRINGTON

ATONEMENT, DAY OF. *See* Yom Kippur.

AZAZEL. The name *Azazel* occurs in *Leviticus* 16.8, 10, 26 and in the Qumran texts Ages of Creation (4Q180), Enoch[a–c] (4Q201, 202, 204), Enoch Giants[a] (4Q203), and Temple Scroll[a] (11Q19). In the biblical text Azazel appears to be a desert demon, while in works found at Qumran he is a leader of the angels who sinned. [*See* Demons.]

The etymology of the name and the meaning, and the origin of the ritual in *Leviticus* 16, have been the subject of much discussion (Janowski and Wilhelm, 1993). Perhaps Azazel means "God is powerful." This form of the name (*Azaz'el*, without consonantal metathesis) appears to be the more original and is still preserved in Temple Scroll[a] (11Q19 xxvi.13) and Ages of Creation (4Q180 1.7–8). The masoretic form (*Aza'zeel*) is to be found in Enoch Giants[a] (4Q203 7.i.6). There are still other spellings, but they depict the same name: Enoch[a] (4Q201 iii.9) uses *ʿAsa'el*, while the parallel texts in Enoch[c] (4Q204 ii.26) and Enoch[b] (4Q202 ii.26–29) have *ʿAśa'e[l]*.

On the one hand, Azazel is the name of a desert demon. Within the ritual of Yom Kippur as described in *Leviticus* 16 (cf. 11Q19 xxvi.13; *Yoma* 4.1a, 6.2–6), one of the two goats prescribed by the biblical text is sacrificed for God, and the other carries the sins of Israel into the desert to Azazel. Instead of understanding Azazel as a proper name, the Septuagint and the Vulgate translate *Aza'zel* as *ez* ("goat") plus *zal* ("to go away")—*ho apopomaios* or *caper emissarius*, "scapegoat."

On the other hand, Azazel is one of the fallen angels who, according to *Genesis* 6.1–4, once descended to earth (*1 En.* 6.7; cf. 4Q201 iii.9, 4Q204 ii.26, which refer to Azazel as the tenth of twenty such angels). [*See* Angels; Enoch, Books of.] When he fell in love with human women, he taught them his knowledge of metals, diamonds, and colors (*1 En.* 7.1, 8.1; cf. 4Q202 ii.26–29). The archangel Michael is to announce God's sentence to these angels (*1 En.* 10.11): they will experience the deaths of their wives and of their "sons of prostitution" (cf. *1 En.* 10.9); then they will be chained for seventy generations in a valley of the earth (*1 En.* 10.12). Azazel is treated in a special way (*1 En.* 10.4–8): Raphael is to bind Azazel's hands and feet, and to heal the earth from the corruption of the angels. Azazel will find neither peace nor pity nor intercession (*1 En.* 13.1–2); his final destination and that of his adherents is eternal punishment (*1 En.* 55.4, 69.2).

In Ages of Creation, "a *pesher* on the periods that God made" (4Q180 1.1), Azazel stands at the head of the fallen angels (4Q180 1.7: "and the interpretation concerns Azazel and the angels"). They lead Israel astray to love iniquity, to possess wickedness, and to forget the commandment of purity. Since Ages of Creation seems to refer to God's providence for the period of the angels' fall as well as for the periods of the temptation of Israel, Azazel plays a role that is usually occupied in Essene-Qumran texts by Belial.

In the *Apocalypse of Abraham*, Azazel is portrayed as the opponent of the angel Jaoel. Azazel takes the form of an unclean bird who tries to keep Abraham away from sacrificing and to make him leave Jaoel (*Ap. Ab.* 13.2–4). Evil comes from Azazel over all generations of godless mankind (*Ap. Ab.* 13.8; cf. *Ap. Ab.* 14.4). As a serpent he had already tempted Adam and Eve (*Ap. Ab.* 23.6–8). Justice is his enemy (*Ap. Ab.* 14.4); he is personified wickedness (*Ap. Ab.* 13.6). His former position in heaven is now Abraham's (*Ap. Ab.* 13.12), but God allows Azazel to rule over the inhabitants of the earth (*Ap. Ab.* 13.7). As the chief of the fire-oven of hell (*Ap. Ab.* 14.3) he functions as an instrument of God's punishments.

In a medieval *midrash* about Shemiḥazah (another leader of the fallen angels) (Milik, 1976, pp. 321–331), Shemiḥazah repents of his deeds when the flood is near, but Azazel continues to tempt humankind. For this reason an animal is sent to Azazel to make him bear the burden of Israel's injustice.

The two aspects of Azazel, his role in an expiatory context (*Lv.* 16) and his position as one of the leading fallen angels (cf. *1 En.*), are combined from the first century BCE on. For example, in Enoch Giants[a] (4Q201 7.i.6) Azazel is punished for the sins of the giants.

Despite the traditions of Azazel as an evil figure, he also appears as one of God's good archangels. In some of the manuscripts of the *Sibylline Oracles* 2.215 he belongs to the four imperishable court angels (cf. Mandean *Ginza* 144.25, where Azazel is the head of the 444 Shekinas to the right, and 173.21, where Azazel is one of the watchers of the bound Ur). In magical literature Azazel plays an important role as a helpful angel; for example, by the name of Azazel the wind demon Lix Tetrax is thwarted (*T. Sol.* 7.7), and the name of Azazel is mentioned among the helpful forces on an Aramaic incantation bowl (Montgomery, 1913, no. 19.18). [*See* Magic and Magical Texts.]

BIBLIOGRAPHY

Janowski, Bernd. "Azazel" (in Hebrew). In *Dictionary of Deities and Demons in the Bible*, edited by Karel van der Toorn, Bob Becking, and Pieter W. van der Horst, pp. 240–248. Leiden and New York, 1995.

Janowski, Bernd, and Gernot Wilhelm. "Der Bock, der die Sünden hinausträgt: Zur Religionsgeschichte des Azazel-Ritus Lev 16, 10.21f." In *Religionsgeschichtliche Beziehungen zwischen Kleinasien, Nordsyrien und dem Alten Testament. Internationales Symposium Hamburg 17.–21. März 1990*, edited by Bernd Janowski, Klaus Koch, and Gernot Wilhelm, pp. 109–169. Orbis Biblicus et Orientalis, 129. Freiburg, 1993. Thorough study of the etymology of the name Azazel and the ritual of *Leviticus* 16, with bibliography.

Milik, Józef T. *The Books of Enoch: Aramaic Fragments of Qurmân Cave 4*. Oxford, 1976.

Montgomery, James Allen. *Aramaic Incantation Texts from Nippur*. University of Pennsylvania, Museum Publications of the Babylonian Section, 3. Philadelphia, 1913.

Tawil, Hayim. "ʿAzazel: The Prince of the Steepe [*sic*]: A Comparative Study." *Zeitschrift für die alttestamentliche Wissenschaft* 92 (1980), 43–59.

ALEXANDER MAURER

B

BABATHA, a Jewish woman who is the central figure in a group of papyrus documents of the early second century CE found in the Judean Desert at Naḥal Ḥever. The documents, designated 5/6Ḥev 1–35, are generally known as P.Yadin (less commonly P.Babatha) or as the Babatha archive. No particular connection between this archive and Qumran literature is apparent.

The Archive. The papyri were found in March 1961 in the course of the second season of the archaeological expedition led by Yigael Yadin, in the Cave of the Letters, located on the northern bank of Naḥal Ḥever about 5 kilometers southwest of ʿEin-Gedi. The cave was named for a cache of letters of Shimʿon Bar Kokhba that had been found during the previous year's excavations. The cave apparently served as the hideaway from the Romans for people of ʿEin-Gedi, including a commander in Bar Kokhba's forces, Yehonatan ben Beʿayan. In a corner of the innermost chamber, hidden in a crevice and covered by stone slabs, a basketful of various household objects and a carefully wrapped pouch containing the documents of the Babatha archive were found. Underneath the pouch were more household objects and a second purse with six additional documents dating from the first and third years of the Bar Kokhba Revolt, 132 and 134 CE. Babatha's pouch, then, could not have been placed there before November 134 CE. [*See* Bar Kokhba Revolt; ʿEin-Gedi.]

The Babatha archive is composed of legal documents, ranging in date from 93/94 to 132 CE and written in various languages: six documents are written in Nabatean, three in Aramaic, twenty-six in Greek. Of the Greek documents, nine have Aramaic or Nabatean subscriptions. Detailed descriptions of the documents in the Babatha archive were published by Yadin in 1962 and 1971. Three Greek documents, those later entitled 5/6Ḥev 15, 27, and 28, were published promptly by H. J. Polotsky. The Greek documents in their entirety were published after Yadin's death by Naphtali Lewis (1989); the Aramaic and Nabatean signatures and subscriptions were edited by Jonas C. Greenfield (Yadin and Greenfield, 1989). Of the remaining documents, only two in Aramaic have been published to date, 5/6Ḥev 7 and 10. Documents from the Babatha archive serve scholars concerned with various matters, including Roman legal procedure and provincial administration.

Personal History. Babatha's name, in one document spelled consistently as "Babtha," may be derived from the Aramaic word for "pupil of the eye," indicating someone especially precious. Her father was Shimʿon son of Menaḥem, her mother Miriam daughter of Yosef son of Menashe (5/6Ḥev 7.3, 24). Babatha is regularly identified as a Maozene, that is, of Maoza, also known as Maḥoz ʿEglatain, a port or town in the district of Zoara at the southern end of the Dead Sea in the Roman province of Arabia. Her family had lived in Maoza at least since 99 CE, when her father bought a palm grove there (5/6Ḥev 3). We do not know if she had siblings. By 120 CE she was married (5/6Ḥev 7.24–25) to Yeshua son of Yeshua son of Yosef Zaboudos, also of Maoza. If the skeletons of the eight women, between the ages of fifteen and thirty, found in the Cave of the Letters include that of Babatha, then she would have been sixteen or probably younger at the time of her marriage.

By the first half of 124 CE she had a son, Yeshua, who was quite young since he was still a minor eight years later, and her husband was dead. The city council at Petra, the metropolis of the region, assigned the orphan two guardians, one Jewish, one Nabatean. The guardians invested the boy's capital and gave Babatha an allowance for his support at the rate of one-half percent, two denarii per month, half the usual interest rate. In 124 and 125 CE, Babatha petitioned the provincial governor about this low rate and offered to triple the return if the boy's property would be entrusted to her and secured by her own property (5/6Ḥev 13–15). Her initiative appears to have failed, for in 132 CE the guardians were still giving Babatha an allowance for her son at the original rate (5/6Ḥev 27).

In 127 CE, for a provincial census, Babatha declared her ownership of four palm groves in Maoza, listing yields and taxes for each (5/6Ḥev 16). We are not told how these groves came into her possession. One grove appears to have belonged to her father and presumably was given to Babatha as a gift before he gave his remaining property to his wife (5/6Ḥev 4, 7). The same may be true of the other groves, or she may have received them as part of the settlement of her first marriage.

By February 128 CE, and possibly as early as October 125 CE, Babatha was remarried, to Judah son of Eleazar Khthousion son of Judah. His official residence was ʿEin-

Gedi, where his family lived and he owned a home, but he lived in Maoza, where he also owned property. Judah previously was married to Miriam daughter of Beianos of ʿEin-Gedi, perhaps the sister of the Bar Kokhba commander mentioned above. Contrary to the view of several modern scholars that Judah's marriages were polygamous, nothing in the documents indicates that he was still married to Miriam when he married Babatha. The Aramaic document recording Judah and Babatha's marriage (5/6Ḥev 10) matches the traditional Jewish marriage contract as it would have been at that period. In February 128 CE, Babatha deposited with her husband three hundred denarii, probably a loan without a fixed term (5/6Ḥev 17).

In April of that year, Judah gave his daughter from his previous marriage, Shelamzion, in marriage to Yehudah Cimber son of Ananias son of Somalos, of ʿEin-Gedi. Eleven days later he gave her his house in ʿEin-Gedi as a gift, half of it to take effect after his death. Two years later Judah was already dead when representatives of the orphans of his deceased brother Jesus conceded to Shelamzion rights to that house (5/6Ḥev 18–20). That Shelamzion's documents were found among the papers of her stepmother Babatha is consistent with her being a minor and indicates a notable measure of trust between the two women.

Babatha, now twice widowed, probably by the age of twenty-five years or less, took possession of at least three palm groves owned by Judah in satisfaction of obligations under their marriage contract or loan. In September 130 CE, Babatha disposed of the produce of these groves by selling the crop before the harvest (5/6Ḥev 21–22). Two months later she was summoned to the court of the Roman provincial governor in Petra by the guardians of Judah's nephews to answer their claim, presumably to these same groves. A plausible reconstruction of these events would be that the estate of Eleazar Khthousion, the father of Judah, Babatha's second husband, was never completely divided between Judah and his brother Jesus in their lifetimes, but held more or less in common, and that after their deaths representatives of the orphans of each came to a settlement in June 130 CE. The orphans of Jesus relinquished rights to the house in ʿEin-Gedi (5/6Ḥev 20); Shelamzion daughter of Judah relinquished rights to groves in Maoẓa (in a document that naturally would not be present in this archive). At the same time Babatha was embroiled in a suit with Miriam, Judah's first wife, over household goods of their late husband (5/6Ḥev 26). The outcome of neither litigation is known.

Representing the orphans of Jesus as *episkopos* ("overseer") was a woman named Julia Crispina daughter of Berenicianus. There has been considerable scholarly speculation about her identity. It has been suggested that she was the granddaughter of Queen Berenice and thus the last Herodian princess, or, alternatively, that she was no less than the daughter of C. Julius Alexander Berenicianus, scion of the house of Herod and Roman consul in 116 CE, and granddaughter of the notorious Crispinus, an Egyptian who rose to power and dubious fame in the late first century CE (cf. Juvenal, *Satires* 1.26–30, 4.1–33). If so, she would have made a formidable opponent for Babatha. However, she or her father could have been freedpersons of that family, and her function may have been little more than that of a nanny. Indeed, when challenged by Babatha, she denies having the capacity to do anything but deliver documents (5/6Ḥev 25, lines 59–63).

The documentation of these legal conflicts has led reviewers such as Martin Goodman (1991), to complain of Babatha's "enthusiasm for litigious confrontation." However, in two of the three suits recorded in the archive, it was not Babatha but her opponents who initiated the litigation. The facts as she presents them certainly raise the suspicion of corruption on the part of her son's council-appointed guardians. A picture of a very young widow of whom various parties try to take unfair advantage is equally plausible. Though evidently a woman of means, she was illiterate, apparently both in Greek and in Hebrew and Aramaic (5/6Ḥev 15.35, 22.34).

Significance. Babatha's place in Jewish society in her time has been the subject of controversy. Her archive contains neither pious phrases nor any explicit reference to the Jewish religion or to religious authority, except for an oblique reference to the Sabbath in a bequest of property (5/6Ḥev 7). Most of the documents were written in Greek, even when the principals were illiterate in that language but literate in Hebrew or Aramaic. Clearly, these documents were intended for presentation, if need be, to Roman rather than to rabbinic courts, in violation of the halakhic injunction against recourse to gentile courts. In the subscription written in Babatha's name to her property registration (5/6Ḥev 16), she is said to have taken an oath by the *tyche* ("genius") of the emperor. On the other hand, there are features of the documents, most notably in Babatha's marriage contract (5/6Ḥev 10), that appear to be read best in light of rabbinic literature. Since Babatha herself was illiterate, these features reflect less her own commitments and more those of her society and are better treated in a general discussion of contracts from the Judean Desert.

[*See* Contracts; Documentary Texts; Family Life; Ḥever, Naḥal, *article on* Written Material; Marriage and Divorce; *and* Women.]

BIBLIOGRAPHY

Bowersock, G. W. "The Babatha Papyri, Masada, and Rome." *Journal of Roman Archaeology* 4 (1991), 336–344.

Cotton, Hannah. "The Guardianship of Jesus, Son of Babatha: Ro-

man and Local Law in the Province of Arabia." *Journal of Roman Studies* 83 (1993), 94–108.
Cotton, Hannah. "Deed of Gift and the Law of Succession in the Documents from the Judaean Desert." *Akten des 21. Internationalen Papyrologenkongress, 13–19 August 1995*. Archiv für Papyrusforschung Beiheft, forthcoming.
Cotton, Hannah, and Jonas C. Greenfield. "Babatha's *Patria*: Maḥoza, Maḥoz ʿEglatain, and Zoʿar." *Zeitschrift für Papyrologie und Epigraphik* 107 (1995), 126–134.
Goodman, Martin. "Babatha's Story." *Journal of Roman Studies* 81 (1991), 169–175. Review-Article of P.Yadin.
Ilan, Tal. "Julia Crispina, Daughter of Berenicianus, A Herodian Princess in the Babatha Archive: A Case Study in Historical Identification." *Jewish Quarterly Review* 82. 3–4 (1992), 361–381.
Isaac, Benjamin. "The Babatha Archive: A Review Article." *Israel Exploration Journal* 42 (1992), 62–75.
Katzoff, Ranon. "Polygamy in *P.Yadin?*" *Zeitschrift für Papyrologie und Epigraphik* 109 (1995), 128–132.
Lewis, Naphtali. *The Documents from the Bar Kokhba Period in the Cave of Letters: Greek Papyri, Aramaic and Nabatean Signatures and Subscriptions*. Edited by Yigael Yadin and Jonas C. Greenfield. Jerusalem, 1989.
Polotsky, H. J. "Three Documents from the Archive of Babatha, Daughter of Simeon" (in Hebrew). *Eretz-Israel* 8 (1967), 51–96.
Yadin, Yigael. "Expedition D—The Cave of Letters." *Israel Exploration Journal* 12 (1962), 227–257. The first report of the content of the papyri.
Yadin, Yigael. *Bar-Kokhba: The Rediscovery of the Legendary Hero of the Second Jewish Revolt against Rome*. London and Jerusalem, 1971. The most detailed account of the expedition and the content of the papyri.
Yadin, Yigael, Jonas C. Greenfield, and Ada Yardeni. "Babatha's *Ketubba*." *Israel Exploration Journal* 44 (1994), 75–101.
Yadin, Yigael, Jonas Greenfield, and Ada Yardeni. "A Deed of Gift in Aramaic Found in Naḥal Ḥever: Papyus Yadin 7" (in Hebrew). *Eretz Israel* 25 (1996), 383–403.

RANON KATZOFF

BABYLON. A Mesopotamian city situated slightly southwest of the convergence of the Tigris and Euphrates Rivers, Babylon (Babel in Hebrew) is well known from textual and archaeological evidence. Babylon first rose to political prominence under King Hammurabi (1792–1750 BCE). It remained the dominant city in southern Mesopotamia (Babylonia) for about two hundred years until the invasion of the Hittite King Mursilis I in the early sixteenth century BCE. Its next rise to greatness came under Nebuchadnezzar I (ca. 1124–1103 BCE) when, after his defeat of Hultaludish-Inshushinak of Elam, it became the major power in southern Mesopotamia. Babylon's dominance faded again with the rise of Assyria. Babylon and Assyria remained rival forces until 609 BCE when Assyria and its capital Nineveh fell to Babylon, which had long since come under Chaldean (Aramean) domination. Babylon itself fell to the Persians under Cyrus the Great in 538 BCE, an event recorded in the prophecies of "Second Isaiah." The city of Babylon continued to exist for hundreds of years thereafter, finally disappearing with the advent of Islam.

Babylon first appears in the Bible as a city of Nimrod (*Gn*. 10.10). The legend about building the Tower of Babel explains the divine dispersal of humankind over the face of the earth and the proliferation of languages (*Gn*. 11). Babylon became a political factor in Judah under the reign of Merodach-baladan II (see *2 Kgs*. 20.12–21), but its real influence came under the reign of Nebuchadnezzar II (*2 Kgs*. 24), who destroyed Jerusalem and its Temple and sent the king, the nobility, and most of the populace of Judea into exile in Mesopotamia and Egypt. The prophecies of Jeremiah were spoken under the ascendancy and victory of Babylonia in the Levant, while Ezekiel was exiled and flourished in Babylonia itself. Babylonia and its kings form the backdrop of the *Book of Daniel*. The prophet Habakkuk complains that wicked Chaldean (Babylonian) dominance in the world is an affront to divine rule and a grave injustice. Babylon is mentioned occasionally in the books of *Isaiah, Micah, Zechariah, Psalms, Esther, Ezra-Nehemiah*, and *Chronicles*, most of these books being postexilic.

Apart from the biblical attestations of Babel, the city is mentioned in the Dead Sea Scrolls some seven times. In the Genesis Apocryphon (1QapGen 21.23) Babel is used rather than Shinar to describe the kingdom of Amraphel (cf. Targum Onkelos to *Gn*. 14.1). The Damascus Document (CD i.6) records the defeat of Israel by King Nebuchadnezzar.

In the Prayer of Nabonidus (4Q242 1–3.1) the healed and penitent last king of Babylon describes himself in ways reminiscent of Nebuchadnezzar as described in *Daniel* 3.31–4.34, thus confirming the suggestion that the author of *Daniel*, never having heard of Nabonidus, substituted the name of the well-known king for the unknown one.

Babel occurs in two *pesharim* to *Isaiah* in broken contexts. Whereas Pesher Isaiah[c] (4Q163 8.1) and Pesher Isaiah[e] (4Q165 8.1) speak of historical Babylon on the basis of *Isaiah* 14 and 39, Pesher Isaiah[c] (4Q163 6.ii.4) and Pesher Isaiah[e] (4Q165 8.1) seem to substitute the king of Babylon for the king of Assyria mentioned in *Isaiah* 10.13–19 and 30.31.

The Chaldeans mentioned in the *Book of Habakkuk* are identified in Pesher Habakkuk (1QpHab ii.11) as the *Kittim*, a code word for Rome. In this way a prophecy about an enemy world power from the time of the prophet is made applicable to the major foe contemporary with the writer of the *pesher*.

It has been suggested that the Land of Damascus where the exiles from Judah lived according to Damascus Document (CD vi.5) was actually Babylonia (see also CD viii.21, xix.33–34, xx.10–12). Since the covenanters claim that they organized in Damascus, they place their origin in the context of the exile. [*See* Damascus.]

BIBLIOGRAPHY

Beyer, Klaus. *Die aramäischen Texte vom Toten Meer*. Göttingen, 1984. See pages 223–224 for text and translation of the Prayer of Nabonidus.

Horgan, Maurya P. *Pesharim: Qumran Interpretations of Biblical Books*. Catholic Biblical Quarterly Monograph Series, 8. Washington, D.C., 1979.

Knibb, Michael Anthony. "Exile in the Damascus Document." *Journal for the Study of the Old Testament* 29 (1983), 99–117.

Milikowsky, Chaim. "Again: Damascus in the Damascus Document and in Rabbinic Literature." *Revue de Qumrân* 11/41 (1982), 97–106.

Murphy-O'Connor, Jerome. "A Literary Analysis of Damascus Document VI 2–VIII 3." *Revue biblique* 78 (1971), 210–232.

Nitzan, Bilhah. *Pesher Habakkuk: A Scroll from the Wilderness of Judaea (1QpHab)* (in Hebrew). Jerusalem, 1986.

VICTOR AVIGDOR HUROWITZ

BAILLET, MAURICE (1923–1998), French epigrapher. Born in Bordeaux, France, on 25 March 1923, Maurice Baillet studied there, where he obtained a Licence-ès-Lettres. He continued his studies in Toulouse and Tübingen; then in Paris, where he learned Biblical Hebrew, Aramaic, Syriac, Akkadian, Arabic, and modern Hebrew at the École Pratique des Hautes Études; in Jerusalem, where he arrived in 1952; and finally in Rome, where he obtained a Licentia in Sacra Scriptura. After several years of teaching in Toulouse (1955–1958), he arrived at the Centre National de la Recherche Scientifique in 1959, where he remained until 1993 as a research director.

In Jerusalem, between 1952 and 1953, Baillet worked on the texts that had been discovered in the caves at Qumran, at first the texts from the small caves, then, later, those from Cave 4. By this time, he had begun to show a strong interest in the Samaritans and their texts.

In 1953, at the Académie des Inscriptions et Belles-Lettres in Paris, Baillet presented his first thesis, in which he dealt with fragments from the Jeremiah scroll (2Q13). The following year he presented his second thesis, at the same institution in Paris, which dealt with the Aramaic New Jerusalem fragments from Cave 2 at Qumran (2Q24). [*See* New Jerusalem.] These fragments were published in 1955 in the *Revue Biblique*. This preliminary work led to the publication of the fragments that had been discovered in the small caves at Qumran, Caves 2, 3, 6, 7, and 10. The publication appeared in 1962, but the preface by Roland de Vaux dates back to 1959. The documents had been poorly preserved (the scrolls were torn and had been damaged by water, insects, and rodents), and Maurice Baillet's editing was a thankless task.

In this timely publication, a special place was given to the Greek fragments 7Q4–5, which led to some lively discussions, since some scholars have seen some traces of the New Testament in them. The editor intervened in the debate, but he was able to justify objectively his reading of the fragments. [*See* New Testament.]

In June 1958, Jean Starcky arranged to have Baillet join the Dead Sea Scrolls' editorial team. [*See biography of Starcky, Jean.*] At the same time, Baillet received five texts from Cave 4. In 1959, Roland de Vaux entrusted him with a collection of fragments on papyrus, among which was War Scroll[f] (4Q496). After many difficulties, about which Baillet made no secret in his preface, he received C. H. Hunzinger's collection in 1971. After much strenuous work, the manuscript intended to ensure the publication of all these texts was finished in 1976, but it was published only in 1982 because of the 1967 Arab–Israeli War. The appearance of this set of texts in volume 7 of Discoveries in the Judaean Desert bears witness to the role of Maurice Baillet in the publication of manuscripts from Qumran.

BIBLIOGRAPHY

Baillet, Maurice. "Textes de Grottes 2Q, 3Q, 6Q, 7Q a 10Q." In *Les 'Petites Grottes' de Qumrân (Textes)*, edited by Maurice Baillet. J. T. Milik, and Roland de Vaux, pp. 45–164. Discoveries in the Judaean Desert, 3. Oxford, 1962.

Baillet, Maurice. "Nouveaux phylacterès de Qumran (X Q Phyl 1–4). à propos d'une édition récente." *Revue de Qumrân* 7 (1970–71), 403–415. About a phylactery bought and edited by Yigael Yadin.

Baillet, Maurice. "Les manuscrits de la grotte 7 de Qumran et le Nouveau Testament." *Biblica* 53 (1972), 508–516. Discussion about biblical texts? 7Q4–5 as evidence for the New Testament.

Baillet, Maurice, ed. *Qumrân Grotte 4:* 4Q482–4Q520). Discoveries in the Judaean Desert, 7. Oxford, 1982.

JACQUES BRIEND

BARKHI NAFSHI. The texts entitled Barkhi Nafshi consist of five collections of fragments numbered 4Q434–438. These fragments contain a collection of hymns of praise to the Lord for delivering the righteous and of thanksgiving for his continued grace. Earlier discussions of these texts often included 4Q439, which is a lament and does not have any material or compelling thematic connection with Barkhi Nafshi; therefore it is probably not part of this collection. The editors have entitled it 4QLament by a Leader.

The texts of Barkhi Nafshi are all in Hebrew and are from five different scribal hands. Several examples of textual parallels and overlapping in the five collections of fragments demonstrate that all five manuscripts were originally copies of the same text. Barkhi Nafshi[a,c–d] (4Q434, 436, 437) contain significant portions of extant text whereas Barkhi Nafshi[b,e] (4Q435, 438) are very fragmentary. Paleographically Barkhi Nafshi[e] is the earliest manuscript, and the other four are more recent copies. John Strugnell identified the script of Barkhi Nafshi[e] as belonging to the late Hasmonean (150–30 BCE) or early Herodian period (30 BCE–70 CE). The rest of the fragments date to the Herodian period. There is no internal evidence for dating the original composition.

The title Barkhi Nafshi derives from the opening line of Barkhi Nafshi[a] 1.i.1 *barkhi nafshi et Adonai*: "Bless, O my soul, the Lord," a phrase known from Psalms 103 and 104, both of which begin and end with this expression (*Ps*. 103.1, 103.2, 103.22, 104.1, 104.35). The opening line is likely a deliberate imitation of the biblical psalms, suggesting thereby the existence of a genre of Barkhi Nafshi texts, but there do not appear to be any other texts from Qumran that contain this phrase. There exists a *Barkhi Nafshi* tradition in Judaism. Psalm 104, a hymn of praise to the Lord as creator, continues to be recited in the Ashkenazic tradition after *Minḥah* on Sabbath afternoon and in all the rites on *Rosh Ḥodesh* (the beginning of the Hebrew month). In the Sephardic tradition a supplicatory prayer called "Barkhi Nafshi," ascribed to Bahya ben Joseph ibn Pakudah from eleventh-century Spain, is read after *Musaf* (the additional service) on Yom Kippur.

In Barkhi Nafshi[a] and in the beginning of Barkhi Nafshi[c], the Lord is praised for his deliverance of a group of righteous people from Israel identified as the poor (*ebyon*), the humble (*ʿani*), and the helpless (*dal*). "In the abundance of his mercy" (4Q434 1.i.3) and "on account of his lovingkindness (*ḥesed*)" (4Q434 1.i.4) the Lord has preserved his people from their enemies, and "his angel encamped around them" (4Q434 1.i.12). In Barkhi Nafshi[c] the Lord is described as strengthening the heart of the contrite, comforting the poor, and giving knowledge to the wise. The poet addresses God in the second person and praises him for writing his law on his heart, for making his mouth like a sharp sword, and for giving him a pure heart. In Barkhi Nafshi[d] the poet continues blessing the Lord for delivering him from the gentiles and for rescuing his soul from the underworld.

Like much of the poetry from Qumran, the Barkhi Nafshi hymns imitate biblical psalms. The poetry is crafted from biblical language by verbatim citations of biblical passages, by paraphrase, and by allusion to biblical metaphors and imagery. Often the poet quotes two or more complete lines from a biblical passage, altering the wording and the order of the lines. Most of the biblical citations and allusions are from *Psalms*, *Isaiah*, and *Jeremiah*. Likewise, there is much language and imagery in these hymns that are also found in other Qumran texts—most notably the Hodayot.

A central and unifying theme of the Barkhi Nafshi texts is that of God implanting in his people and in the author a series of pious qualities. For example, in Barkhi Nafshi[a] the Lord opens his eyes to the helpless and hears the cries of the orphans, and in turn God opens their eyes to see his ways, and their ears to hear his teachings, and he circumcises the foreskins of their hearts (4Q434 1.i.3–4), "he set their feet to the way" (4Q434 1.i.4) and gave them "another heart" (4Q434 1.i.10). In Barkhi Nafshi[c] the author praises God because "my heart you have commanded and my inmost parts you have taught well, lest your statutes be forgotten" (4Q436 1.i.5); "and you have made my mouth like a sharp sword, and my tongue you have set loose to (utter) holy words" (4Q436 1.i.7); and "my foot you have strengthened" (4Q436 1.i.8). In Barkhi Nafshi[d] the poet blesses the name of the Lord, "for you have delivered me from the snare of the gentiles" (4Q437 2.i.4), "in your quiver you hid me . . . you made me into a sharp arrow, and in the shelter of your palm you hid me" (4Q437 2.i.8–9).

The sectarian origin of the poetic material at Qumran is notoriously difficult to prove because hymns and prayers do not always contain the terms distinctive to the sectarian literature. Nevertheless, the Barkhi Nafshi hymns contain a constellation of phrases and imagery found in other sectarian texts from Qumran: the designation of the community as the poor, the imagery of the circumcision and the giving of a new heart and of "walking in the way," and references to Psalm 37.15 (4Q434 1.i.5; 4Q437 2.i.3) closely resembling the interpretation given in the sectarian Pesher Psalms (4Q171[a] ii.19). An argument could be made for the sectarian origin of these hymns.

The Barkhi Nafshi hymns are important examples of early Jewish prayer. Moshe Weinfeld (1992) has identified in Barkhi Nafshi[a] 2 a series of phrases also found in the rabbinic prayer *Birkat ha-mazon la-ʾavelim* ("Grace after Meals for Mourners") and has argued that this fragment preserves an early form of Grace after Meals. The identification of the righteous as the poor, the theology of God's grace, and the imagery of internal conversion are significant themes for the study of Jewish and Christian theology.

BIBLIOGRAPHY

Kahl, Werner. "The Structure of Salvation in 2 Thess and 4Q434." *Qumran Chronicle* 5 (1995), 103–121. Argues that the definition and structure of salvation are identical in the two documents.

Seely, David Rolph. "The 'Circumcised Heart' in 4Q434 *Barkhi Nafshi*." *Revue de Qumrân* 65–68 (1996), 527–535. A review of the image of the circumcised heart in *Barkhi Nafshi*, the Bible, and other Qumran texts.

Weinfeld, Moshe. "Grace after Meals in Qumran." *Journal of Biblical Literature* 111 (1992), 427–440. Identifies 4Q434 2 as an early form of the rabbinic prayer Grace after Meals for Mourners.

Weinfeld, Moshe, and David R. Seely. *4Q434–438 Barkhi Nafshi* and *4QLament by a Leader*. Discoveries in the Judaean Desert, 29. Oxford, 1999.

DAVID ROLPH SEELY

BAR KOKHBA, SHIM'ON, leader of the second major Jewish revolt against Rome in the province of Judea, during the years 132–135 CE. This was the only revolt out of a long list of Jewish uprisings against foreign domination to be called by the name of its leader, and for good reason, as this revolt was characterized, among other things, by the confederation of all the revolutionaries under the banner of a single leader, Shim'on Bar Kokhba. Bar Kokhba not only was the military commander of the revolutionaries but also headed an independent Jewish polity that came into being during the course of the revolt.

The documentary evidence from the time of the revolt includes the Bar Kokhba letters, which were found in the caves of the Judean Desert near the Dead Sea, and which contribute materially to expanding the extant evidence for the Bar Kokhba Revolt in general, and for Bar Kokhba himself in particular. In 1952 various artifacts and documents from the time of the revolt were found in Wadi Murabba'at, including documents about leasing land in the name of Bar Kokhba. In 1961–1962 further finds were made in the Judean Desert, the most outstanding of which are letters from Bar Kokhba himself, found in a cave in the cliffs of Naḥal Ḥever.

Until the discovery of these documents even the very name of Bar Kokhba (more accurately, Bar Kokhva) had been uncertain, and it was not clear whether his name was Bar Kokhba with a letter *kaf* as it appears in the writings of the church fathers, or Bar Kozeba with a letter *zayin* as in Talmudic literature. Nor was it known whether the name Shim'on, which appears on some of the coins issued during the revolt, was the first name of Bar Kokhba, or of another leader. When Bar Kokhba's letters were found, together with the land-lease documents signed in his name, it became clear that his name was Shim'on bar Koseba, spelled with a letter *samekh* or *sin*. In the letters written in Greek his name appears as Chosiba. It is clear, then, that the name Bar Kokhba stems from a nickname given to him after Rabbi Aqiva proclaimed him the King Messiah, the realization of the biblical verse: "There shall come a 'star' (*kokhav*) out of Jacob" (*Nm.* 24.17). It was usual at the time to explain this verse as a prophecy about a king or leader as seen, for example, in the Damascus Document (CD vii.18–20). The form Bar Kozeba, with a letter *zayin*, may have been a derogatory nickname given to Bar Kokhba after the failure of the revolt, as related by Rabbi Yohanan: "Rabbi used to comment on 'There shall come a star out of Jacob': 'Do not read *kokhav* ('star') but *kozev* ('liar')'" (*Lam. Rab.* 2.4). However, it is more likely that this by-form was produced by a copyist's unintentional interchange of the letters *samekh* and *zayin*. It is also possible that Bar Kokhba's name connects his origins with a village called Kozeba, mentioned in the Bible (*1 Chr.* 4.22). This village has been identified with Khirbet Kuweizibe, in the area of Bethlehem, the birth place of King David (from whose descendants the Messiah was to come), situated about two kilometers south of 'Ein-'Arub, where finds from the time of the revolt have surfaced.

Bar Kokhba's title as it appears in the documents and letters from the caves of the Judean Desert, and on the coins of the revolt, is *Nasi* of Israel. In the Bible and in the language of the sages this title is used of a king. Rabbi Aqiva, when he saw Bar Kokhba, proclaimed "This is the *melekh mashiaḥ*" ("King Messiah") (J.T., *Ta'an.* 4.68d; *Lam. Rab.* 2.4), thereby relating him to the royal house of David. Aqiva is most likely using the term to describe an earthly military and political leader rather than an eschatological messiah who is seen as a savior and redeemer with supernatural qualities. Rabbi Aqiva's concept of redemption had no apocalyptic foundations, and was restricted to the hope for the realization of an earthly historical process, which would culminate in the rebuilding of the Temple that had been destroyed in 70 CE. This is spelled out in the parallel source in *Lamentations Rabbah*, which attributes immense physical strength to Bar Kokhba, as symbolized in his ability to catch Roman missiles on his knee and hurl them back at the Romans. On this the Midrash comments: "And it was about this that Rabbi Aqiva made his statement." In other words, Rabbi Aqiva's statement about Bar Kokhba's messianic nature was made because of his physical strength and military abilities. Other Talmudic sources also stress Bar Kokhba's great strength. To them must be added the description of Bar Kokhba's death by snake-bite in the Palestinian sources. The intention of this narrative is not only to show that Bar Kokhba's death was the result of divine intervention, but also to show that a charismatic and powerful hero like Bar Kokhba could not have been simply defeated on the battlefield. This is most clear from the version that relates that the snake was found curled around his knee (*Lam. Rab.*, ed. Buber, pp. 102–103). Like the biblical hero Samson, who could not be defeated until his hair, which contained his legendary power, was cut off, so Bar Kokhba could not be defeated until he was bitten on the knee, the same limb upon which he caught the Roman missiles, and which more than any other was a metaphor for his strength.

A tradition in the Babylonian Talmud tells that after Bar Kokhba proclaimed himself messiah he was put to the test by the sages, and when it was shown that his claim was unfounded they put him to death. (B.T., *San.* 93b). This tradition comes from a passage that is based on a debate between *amoraim* of the fourth generation, sages who lived in Babylonia in the mid-fourth century. It is therefore reasonable to assume that it is a product of the intellectual world of these sages, who were at the peak of their established strength in the fourth century, and found it hard to explain to themselves how the sages of Bar Kokhba's day did not see him for what he really was, a false messiah. From the Palestinian Talmudic literature it is clear that the sages as a group supported Bar Kokhba. It is possible that the sources which note the exaggerated numbers of Rabbi Aqiva's pupils and their untimely deaths are in fact dealing with Rabbi Aqiva's political followers, who were to be found among Bar Kokhba's soldiers. The Talmudic *aggadah* does indeed blame Bar Kokhba for opposing the divine will, obviously in order to explain his final defeat, but Bar Kokhba is still depicted by them as having taken account of the instructions of the sages. There is some reticence about Bar Kokhba's messianic nature among certain sages, as well as despair in the final stages of the revolt when it must have been clear that defeat was just around the corner. It is interesting to note that, although the Talmudic literature describes the Bar Kokhba Revolt after the event (for even the earliest material was edited after the revolt was over), its attitude to Bar Kokhba is still ambivalent, while Rabbi Aqiva, who proclaimed Bar Kokhba King Messiah, is accorded a central and wholly positive status among the *tannaim* without any word or hint of disapproval.

Only Christian traditions, in fact, give any evidence that Bar Kokhba surrounded himself with a halo of supernatural miracles and was not just renowned for his military prowess. For example, Eusebius writes:

> The Jews at the time were led by a man called Bar Chochebas, which means a star, a bloodthirsty bandit who on the strength of his name, as if he had slaves to deal with, claimed to be a luminary who had come down from heaven and was magically enlightening those who were in misery.
>
> (*Historia Ecclesiastica* 4.6.2)

Here we see a tendency to tarnish the image of Bar Kokhba and present him as a sort of Antichrist. In fourth century CE Christian eyes, Bar Kokhba appeared as the representative of Jewish extremist, nationalist messianism, at the opposite end of the spectrum from the pacifist, spiritual, universalistic Christian gospel.

Bar Kokhba's letters complement the picture obtained from Talmudic sources. Bar Kokhba appears as a pragmatic leader who tyrannizes his men, and is personally involved in running the daily life of the revolt. There is nothing in the letters that conveys even the slightest impression of messianic fervor. Bar Kokhba appears in them rather as a harsh and exacting leader of revolutionary bands, and not as a king. In one of the letters Bar Kokhba castigates Masabbalah and Yehonatan bar Baʿayan, the commanders of the base at ʿEin-Gedi: "Here you are, sitting in comfort, and eating and drinking away everything the Jews own, and not caring a damn for your fellows . . . from the ship which is with you and in the harbour" (Yadin, 1961, papyrus 12, p. 47). Just like units on the home front throughout history, the soldiers at ʿEin-Gedi preferred to take food for themselves from the supplies that reached them (which included supplies coming by ship from south or east of the Dead Sea) rather than pass them on to furnish the needs of the soldiers on the battle front, which would have involved effort and risk to themselves. Bar Kokhba's instructions are brief and to the point, and include threats of punishment for those who disobey. In one of the letters he threatens the soldiers in the unit commanded by Yeshuʿa ben Galgula that if they harm the Galileans among them: "I'll clap your legs in irons like I did to Ben ʿAflul" (Milik, no. 43, 1961, 159–161). In another letter, Bar Kokhba demands from Yehonatan and Masabbalah, the commanders of the base on the home-front at ʿEin-Gedi, to send him the men of Teqoʿa (near Herodium) and Tel ʾArazin (which has not yet been identified with certainty), who are staying with them in order to avoid serving on the battlefield, for if not: "You had better know that I'll get my own back on you" (Yadin, 1961, papyrus 14, p. 47–48).

Bar Kokhba's letters reveal his concern for religious observance among his soldiers. He makes a particular point of arranging for them to carry out the commandment of taking *Arbaʿat ha-Minim* ("the Four Species"):

> "Shimʿon to Yehudah bar Menasheh, to Qiriat ʿArbayah: 'I have sent you two donkeys so that you can send two men with them to Yehonatan bar Baʿayan and Masabbalah so they can pack and send palm branches and citrons to the camp, to you. And you are from your place to send others who will bring you myrtles and willows. See that they are tithed and send them to the camp. . . . Be well.'"
>
> (Yadin, 1961, papyrus 15, pp. 48–50)

The letter is addressed to Yehudah bar Menashe, who was presumably the commander of the unit stationed at Qiriat ʿArbayah, which was probably in the region of ʿEin-ʿArrub. Yehudah was to send messengers to the commanders at ʿEin-Gedi in order to bring *lulavim* ("palm branches") and *etrogim* ("citrons") from the Dead Sea area, and was further ordered to send people to gather *hadassim* ("myrtles") and *ʿarabot* ("willows"). Finally, he was told to take tithes from these *Arbaʿat ha-Minim* and to send them to Bar Kokhba's base. Bar Kokhba's concern for the proper observance of the commandments relating to *Arbaʿat ha-Minim* is more than merely a simple wish to observe the festival of *Sukkot* ("Tabernacles") according to religious law. For *Arbaʿat ha-Minim* do not merely represent the rejoicing of the community on the festival of *Sukkot*, but all community rejoicing, and especially rejoicing in victory. The taking of tithes appears in the Bar Kokhba deeds of lease, among the duties of the lessee. It is likewise understood in lease contracts that the parties will observe the laws of the sabbatical year.

Several other documents also demonstrate Bar Kokhba's concern for strict Sabbath observance in his army units. In one letter he orders the commanders at ʿEin-Gedi to send Elʿazar ben Ḥitta to him immediately, so that he will arrive at the base before the beginning of the Sabbath (Yadin, 1961, papyrus 8, pp. 44–45). In another letter he demands that Yeshuʿa ben Galgula should send him a certain quantity of corn, but that he should keep it with him over the Sabbath, and only after the Sabbath ends should he send it on (Milik, no. 44, 1961, pp. 161–163). The national importance of these religious observances to the revolutionaries was known to the Romans and they therefore included bans on taking the *lulav* and on observing the laws of Sabbath, tithes, and the sabbatical year in the *gezerot ha-shemad* ("repressive legislation") after the failure of the revolt.

Bar Kokhba emerges from the letters as someone close to the world and spirit of the sages. He accepted the way of the sages of Yavneh who, after the destruction of the Temple, had reconstructed religious observances so as to preserve the national framework of the Jewish people in their land. It is true that Talmudic sources present Bar Kokhba as someone who trusted in his own powers and was insolent before heaven, claiming that he did not need divine aid but only requested divine non-interference, but it is clear that these traditions were written after the event, in order to explain Bar Kokhba's downfall and death as being the result of his sinful behavior.

Among the documents from the Judean Desert caves are legal contracts that reveal a complex system of land leasing to various individuals by Bar Kokhba's staff, and with his permission. These land-leases seem to be dealing with some sort of state land, which may have previously been in Roman hands but which had been captured by the revolutionaries. Some of these contracts were drawn up at Herodium, which was also the place where the lessees had to bring their rent and their tithes. Archaeological finds from the time of the Bar Kokhba Revolt have been made at Herodium, and it is clear that the fortress was one of its administrative centers. Bar Kokhba may actually have had his headquarters there for some time. So not only did the activities of daily life continue during the revolt, but they were carried on under the aegis of the revolt leadership.

Thus Bar Kokhba was both a military and political leader during the revolt, heading a kind of independent polity, albeit short-lived, which even had its own coins. He has remained the subject of controversy up to the present day. There are those who see him as a false messiah who misled the people and caused them to suffer a terrible defeat. Others identify with his heroism, and see him as both the symbol of non-compromise with foreign governments and of the Jewish people's yearning for independence in their land.

BIBLIOGRAPHY

Alon, Gedalia. *The Jews in Their Land in the Talmudic Age*, vol. 1. Jerusalem, 1980.

Ben-Shalom, Israel, and David Goodblatt. "Bar-Kokhba's Position as a Leader of the Nation" (in Hebrew). *Cathedra* 29 (1983), 4–28.

Isaac, Benjamin, and Aharon Oppenheimer. "The Revolt of Bar Kokhba: Ideology and Modern Scholarship." *Journal of Jewish Studies* 36 (1985), 33–60.

Lewis, Naphthali et al. *The Documents from the Bar Kokhba Period in the Cave of Letters, Greek Papyri: Aramaic and Nabatean Signatures and Subscriptions*. Jerusalem, 1989.

Mildenberg, Leo. *The Coinage of the Bar Kokhba War*. Aarau, 1984.

Milik, Józef T. "Textes Hébrâux et Araméens." In *Les grottes de Murabbaʿât* by Pierre Benoit, Józef T. Milik, and Roland de Vaux, pp. 118–133. Discoveries in the Judaean Desert, 2. Oxford, 1961.

Mor, Menachem. *The Bar-Kokhba Revolt: Its Extent and Effect* (in Hebrew). Jerusalem, 1991.

Oppenheimer, Aharon. "Leadership and Messianism in the Time of the Mishnah." In *Eschatology in the Bible and in Jewish and Christian Tradition*, edited by Henning G. Reventlow, pp. 169–188. Sheffield 1997.

Reinhartz, Adele. "Rabbinic Perceptions of Simeon bar Kosiba." *Journal for the Study of Judaism* 20 (1989), 172–194.

Schäfer, Peter. *Der Bar Kokhba-Aufstand*. Texte und Studien zum Antiken Judentum, 1. Tübingen, 1981.

Schäfer, Peter. "Rabbi Aqiva and Bar Kokhba." In *Approaches to Ancient Judaism*, vol. 2, edited by William S. Green, pp. 113–130. Ann Arbor, Mich., 1980.

Schürer, Emil. *The History of the Jewish People in the Age of Jesus Christ (175 BC–AD 135)*, revised by Geza Vermes and Fergus Millar, vol. 1. Edinburgh, 1973.

Yadin, Yigael. "Expedition D." *Israel Exploration Journal* 11 (1961), 36–52; 12 (1962), 227–257.

Yadin, Yigael. *The Finds from the Bar Kokhba Period in the Cave of Letters*. Jerusalem, 1963.

AHARON OPPENHEIMER

BAR KOKHBA REVOLT. Both the high point of the Jewish revolutionary movement against Roman rule in Erets Yisraʾel and its breaking point, the Bar Kokhba Revolt (c.132–135 CE) was characterized by its large number of participants, apparently more than in the First Jewish Revolt (66–70 CE). The Jews of Erets Yisraʾel joined forces under one leader, Shimʿon Bar Kokhba, who gave his name to the revolt and, in its course, set up a kind of independent polity. Unlike other Jewish revolts, the Bar Kokhba Revolt did not provoke internal dissent, nor was it accompanied by internecine struggles like those of the Hellenizers and the Hasideans in the Maccabean Revolt (166–164 BCE), or the Peace Party and the Zealots in the First Jewish Revolt. Paradoxically, this was a result of the activities of Rabban Yoḥanan ben Zakkai, who had left Jerusalem at the height of the First Jewish Revolt in order to negotiate with the Romans. As head of the leadership institutions at Yavneh, he (and later Rabban Gamliel) had worked to unite the people in the severe crisis that followed the destruction of the Second Temple.

There is no ancient literary or historical record that describes the Bar Kokhba Revolt firsthand. The absence of a source of this kind means that the course of the revolt must be reconstructed from a mosaic of tiny pieces of evidence, often contradictory, sometimes biased, and frequently incomplete. This evidence is to be found in the Talmudic literature, in the works of Roman authors, in the works of the church fathers, and in the Samaritan chronicles. Archaeological finds must be added to this list, especially the unique source for the revolt contained in the discoveries from the Dead Sea area. In 1952, documents and artifacts from the time of the Bar Kokhba Revolt were found in Wadi Murabbaʿat. In 1961–1962, further finds were made in caves in the Judean Desert, of which the most outstanding were the letters from Bar Kokhba himself that were found in a cave in the cliffs of Naḥal Ḥever. These exciting finds evoked waves of scholarly and popular interest since they had an immediacy that is rare in research into the distant past.

The Roman historian Dio Cassius wrote his *Roman History* in the first half of the third century CE. There he ascribes the direct cause for the outbreak of the Bar Kokhba Revolt to the decision by the emperor Hadrian to rebuild Jerusalem as a pagan city, placing a pagan temple inside it and turning it into a colony called Aelia Capitolina (*Aelia* from Aelius, the name of the emperor's family or gens; *Capitolina* for the god Jupiter, whose temple stood on the Capitoline hill in Rome; *Roman History* lxix.12). In contrast, the fourth-century CE church father Eusebius writes that Jerusalem was refounded as Aelia Capitolina after the revolt. If this is so, then this was a consequence rather than a cause of the revolt (*Ecclesiastical History* iv.6). It would seem more likely that Aelia was founded before the revolt and that the revolutionaries confounded the Roman plans and probably took over the city, so that after the revolt the Romans had to rebuild it from its ruins. The author of the fourth-century CE *Historia Augusta* writes that the revolt took place because the Romans placed a ban on the religious practice of circumcision (*Vita Hadriani* xiv.2). It may well be that this was an additional reason for the outbreak of the revolt, although other sources place the ban on circumcision among the repressive legislation that was instituted after the revolt was put down.

The Bar Kokhba Revolt was no spontaneous uprising. It was preceded by careful preparations. Dio Cassius writes that the local population deliberately forged weapons that were not up to Roman military requirements, so that they would be rejected as substandard by the Romans who had ordered them and therefore would be left for the rebels to use. He also records the construction of fortifications and the excavation of complex underground hide-outs. His evidence has been confirmed by the discoveries of underground hide-outs in Judea and elsewhere. (There is still no agreement, however, on whether these hide-outs are exclusively connected with the Bar Kokhba Revolt.) The revolt was timed to break out only after Hadrian had left the country on his journey to Athens in 132 CE.

The documents from the Judean Desert may not provide all the information necessary to describe the central events of the revolt, but they do contain tiny vignettes full of fascinating details about what Bar Kokhba was like and even what his name was, as well as about the course of the revolt. It is possible to infer from them that there were people from Galilee in the unit that was active around the Hebron hill country. The documents also clarify the identity of the commanders of various units, and they tell of some of the revolutionaries who chose to leave the area where the battle was raging and found refuge in units on the home front. Information about ownership of land is contained in lease contracts found with the letters and also in the archive of Babatha, who brought a set of documents relating to her legal negotiations with family members with her when she took refuge in the caves.

Finds from the time of the revolt also have come to light in a cave in Wadi ed-Daliyeh, southwest of Phasaelis in the Jordan Valley; in the caves at ʿEin-ʿArrub between Bethlehem and Hebron; and in Ḥorvat ʿEqed, east of Emmaus. Finds from Herodium are particularly important in that they provide evidence for the activities of the Bar Kokhba revolutionaries in this fortress, for the base at Herodium also is mentioned in papyri that were found in Wadi Murabbaʿat. It is possible that for part of the period of the revolt, Bar Kokhba actually had his headquarters at Herodium, but at least the documents are evidence that Herodium served as an administrative center for the popular leadership during the revolt. Present research into the Roman roads of the province of Judea shows that there was widespread paving of official highways during the reign of Hadrian, although insofar as these roads can be dated, they were paved before the outbreak of the revolt. It should be noted that the archaeological and epigraphic evidence shows that the Roman army in the province was strengthened even before 120 CE, almost certainly in 117 CE. The main evidence for this is the promotion in rank of the governor and procurator of Judea, which points to the reinforcement of the standing army of the province, as well as the paving of military roads from Legio (the base for the legion that was now added to the Tenth Legion Fretensis) to Sephoris and from Akko/Ptolemaïs to Sephoris in 120 CE. This is a clear indication that unrest and terrorist activities against the Romans were endemic in Erets Yisra'el throughout the reign of Hadrian. However, there is also some evidence that Hadrian was popular with the Jews at the beginning of his reign, as can be seen from the praise of Hadrian in the fifth book of the *Sibylline Oracles* (1.46–50).

The sources do not provide a full picture of what happened during the revolt. It would seem that in the first stages the revolutionaries had the advantage. It is almost certain that Bar Kokhba and his men were able to take Jerusalem: at least this is the picture from the contemporary evidence of Appian (*Syriaca* 50, 252). The name of Jerusalem appears on a large number of Bar Kokhba coins, although in Jerusalem itself very few coins from the revolt have been found to date. There can be no doubt that the revolutionaries intended to rebuild the Temple, but there is no certain evidence that they managed to carry this out. One of the well-known coins of the revolt bears the image of the front of a sanctuary that can reasonably be identified with the Temple, but this coin may well express an idealistic hope rather than a historical fact. The main events of the revolt took place in Judea, and it is doubtful whether the Samaritans took any part in them, even though there is some basis for the contention that the Romans did not treat them too kindly at this time. It is clear that the scope and intensity of the revolt in Galilee did not approach that in Judea, but it is possible that there were sporadic outbreaks of rebellion there. The names of the settlements that appear in the documents from the time of Bar Kokhba, found in Wadi Murabba'at and Naḥal Ḥever, are all from Judea. However, this is not conclusive evidence for deciding the territorial extent of the revolt; it is reasonable to suppose that it was the people who lived close to the caves who used them as refuge, so that it is only natural that the names of settlements from the area where they lived and operated should appear in the documents that were in their possession.

The Romans were unable to get the better of the revolutionaries with two legions that were based in Erets Yisra'el, the Tenth Legion Fretensis in Jerusalem and the Sixth Legion Ferrata, which gave the name Legio to its base near Tel Megiddo. Attempts to regain control using legions from the neighboring provinces of Syria, Arabia (Transjordan), and Egypt were unsuccessful. The Twenty-second Legion Deiotariana, which came from Egypt, no longer appears in the roll call of the Roman legions after the revolt, and it may be that it was decimated by the revolutionaries or dispersed following its failure to put down the revolt. In the end, the Romans were forced to bring in soldiers from the Danube and to put at their head the governor of Britain, Julius Severus, their best general at the time. He was careful to avoid frontal conflict with the revolutionaries and preferred to use siege tactics, cutting off their lines of supply and slowly entrapping them.

Eventually, the revolutionaries were forced back to Betar and besieged there, in what became the final stage of the revolt. Betar, about 11 kilometers southwest of Jerusalem, was not merely a stronghold of the revolutionaries but a settlement that had grown up largely after the fall of Jerusalem in the First Jewish Revolt. During the Bar Kokhba Revolt, the leadership of the sages and the family of the patriarch himself were in Betar and may have moved there even before the revolt. It also is possible that preparations for the revolt were made in Betar, which could have served as a base for launching attacks on the Tenth Legion aimed at the control of Jerusalem. The Talmudic sources describe the fall of Betar in chilling terms, as symbolizing the failure of the revolt. Various traditions give an all-too-vivid tableau of the huge number of slain, including women and children, whose blood flowed as far as the Mediterranean and stained its waters. Bar Kokhba himself met his end at the fall of Betar, while the last of the revolutionaries found temporary shelter in the caves of the Judean desert. The Romans besieged these caves as well, and those hiding there were killed or starved. Cassius Dio stresses the large number of the slain, too, but notes that such a large number of Romans also died on the battlefield that Hadrian was unable to open his report to the senate with the usual formula: "If you and yours are well, it is well; I and the army are well" (*Roman History* lxix.14).

The Romans laid down various repressive bans on the Jews in order to undermine the religious base of their national identity. For example, they banned the reading of the Shema' prayer, which stresses the uniqueness of the Deity, and thus was a kind of threat to the cult of the emperor. Similarly, festival observances that had a national significance were outlawed, such as lighting Ḥanukkah lamps, eating unleavened bread on Passover, and taking palm branches on Sukkot. Naturally, the Romans banned the leadership institutions and public assemblies. These repressive bans are known in the Talmudic literature as *gezerot ha-shemad*. Jewish reactions to them varied. There were those who accepted the laws and others who even converted; the best known of these is the sage Elisha' ben Avuyah, who subsequently was called Aḥer ("another"). Some defied the bans openly and were prepared to die for the sake of the exact observance of religious law. The best known of these was Rabbi 'Aqiva', whose flesh was torn to shreds with iron claws but who still continued to declaim the Shema' until the end. The readiness to die "for God's name" became, with the passage of time, a model for Jewish martyrs throughout the generations. A historical and literary expression of this is the tradition of the Ten Martyrs in the Heikhalot literature and the *piyyutim*, although not all the sages in these lists (which are not all identical) were among the martyrs who died following the revolt. However, many of the people, influenced by the sages, made considerable efforts to observe the banned practices secretly or with changes, in order to preserve their Jewishness without being punished by the Roman authorities.

By the end of the revolt, large areas of Judea had been destroyed, many people had been killed or wounded, and many more had been taken into captivity. So many captives were sold as slaves that the price of slaves fell all over the empire, and one of the traditions tells that in the Hebron hill country one could buy a slave for the price of a bale of fodder for a horse. Many refugees fled from Judea to Galilee, which had been less involved in the revolt and thus was less subject to punishment. Others left for Babylonia, the only sizable Jewish community outside the Roman empire. At this time, partly as a result of this influx of refugees, the foundations were laid for the institutions of the exilarchate and the large rabbinic academies, the *yeshivot*, which characterized Babylonian Jewry of the Talmudic period (200–500 CE).

Most of the repressive legislation ceased with the death of Hadrian in 138 CE and the succession of the Antonine dynasty. There were some laws that remained in force longer; for example, a law banning Jews from living in Jerusalem. The self-governing leadership institutions, such as the patriarch and the council of sages, the Sanhedrin, were reconstituted in Galilee, which became the chief center of Jewish Life in Erets Yisra'el from then on.

The Bar Kokhba Revolt was the last attempt at achieving Jewish independence in Erets Yisra'el until 1948. Later uprisings were of a more local nature and were put down by police, rather than military, action. Later reactions to the revolt were, and remain, ambivalent: on the one hand, the Bar Kokhba Revolt was a failure with catastrophic results; on the other hand, there is a tendency to respect the valor of the revolutionaries, especially Bar Kokhba, and their desire for Jews and Judaism to survive unchallenged.

BIBLIOGRAPHY

Alon, Gedalia. *The Jews in Their Land in the Talmudic Age*. Vol. 1. Jerusalem, 1980.

Applebaum, Shimon. *Prolegomena to the Study of the Second Jewish Revolt (A.D. 132–135)*. British Archaeological Reports, Supplementary Series, 7. Oxford, 1976.

Bowersock, Glen, W. "A Roman Perspective on the Bar Kochba War." In *Approaches to Ancient Judaism*, edited by William S. Green, pp. 131–141. Brown Judaic Studies, 9. Ann Arbor, 1980.

Isaac, Benjamin. "Roman Colonies in Judaea: The Foundation of Aelia Capitolina." *Talanta* 12–13 (1980–1981), 31–54.

Isaac, Benjamin. "Cassius Dio on the Revolt of Bar Kokhba." *Scripta Classica Israelica* 7 (1983–1984), 68–76.

Isaac, Benjamin, and Aharon Oppenheimer. "The Revolt of Bar Kokhba: Ideology and Modern Scholarship." *Journal of Jewish Studies* 36 (1985), 33–60.

Lewis, Naphthali et al. *The Documents from the Bar Kokhba Period in the Cave of Letters, Greek Papyri: Aramaic and Nabatean Signatures and Subscriptions*. Jerusalem, 1989.

Mildenberg, Leo. *The Coinage of the Bar Kokhba War*. Aarau, 1984.

Milik, Józef T. "Textes Hébreux et Arameéns." In *Les Grottes de Murabba'at*, edited by P. Benoit, J. T. Milik, and R. de Vaux, pp. 118–133. Discoveries in the Judaean Desert, 2. Oxford, 1961.

Mor, Menachem. *The Bar-Kokhba Revolt: Its Extent and Effect* (in Hebrew). Jerusalem, 1991.

Schäfer, Peter. *Der Bar Kokhba-Aufstand*. Texte und Studien zum Antiken Judentum, 1. Tübingen, 1981.

Schäfer, Peter. "Hadrian's Policy in Judaea and the Bar-Kokhba Revolt—a Reassessment." In *A Tribute to Geza Vermes*, pp. 281–303. Journal of the Study of the Old Testament Supplement Series, 100. Sheffield, 1990.

Schürer, Emil. *The History of the Jewish People in the Age of Jesus Christ (175 B.C.–A.D. 135)*. Vol. 1. Revised by Geza Vermes and Fergus Millar. Edinburgh, 1973.

Yadin, Yigael. "Expedition D." *Israel Exploration Journal* 11 (1961), 36–52.

Yadin, Yigael. "Expedition D." *Israel Exploration Journal* 12 (1962), 227–257.

Yadin, Yigael. *The Finds from the Bar Kokhba Period in the Cave of Letters*. Jerusalem, 1963.

AHARON OPPENHEIMER

BARTHÉLEMY, DOMINIQUE (1921–), French epigrapher, was born in Nantes, France, on 16 May 1921. He entered the Dominican order in 1939, studying first in Paris and then in Jerusalem (1949–1951). It was at the École Biblique in Jerusalem that he began to work as a university teacher and researcher.

From 1957 to 1991, Barthélemy was professor of the Old Testament at the University of Fribourg in Switzerland, where he carried out research in the history of the Old Testament text. From 1969 to 1980, he was actively involved in the Hebrew Old Testament Project. As a result of this collaborative work, he became editor of a series of publications on the textual criticism of the Old Testament. Three of them were published in 1982, 1986, and 1992, respectively, and two more are being prepared.

Barthélemy was dean of the Theology Faculty from 1964 to 1965 and pro-vice chancellor of the University of Fribourg from 1970 to 1978. He retired from teaching in 1991, but he still continues his research in textual criticism of the Old Testament.

During his stay in Jerusalem, Barthélemy quickly became interested in the manuscripts and fragments that had been discovered in Cave 1 at Qumran. In 1950, his first article dealt with Isaiah[a], the main Isaiah scroll; he used photographic reproductions published by J. C. Trever to emphasize the special characteristics of this manuscript and its place in a tradition brought to light by what had been learned from more recent manuscripts.

In 1952, the work carried out on the manuscripts at Qumran enabled Barthélemy to take stock for the first time of the history of the Masoretic Text, of the origin of the Hebraic vocalization, and also of the origin of the Greek version. The biblical fragments from Qumran Cave 1 were published in Discoveries in the Judaean Desert, along with a Rule of the Congregation fragment (1Q28a), a well-known text with mention of a messiah (1955, pp. 108–118). From 1953 onward, there was a shift in Barthélemy's focus toward the Greek texts, following the discovery of important fragments from a Dodekapropheton (twelve prophets scroll) in a cave in the Judean Desert. The work on this new manuscript gave rise to an authoratative work, *Les devanciers d'Aquila*, which reopened the question of the history of the Greek versions and which became a point of departure for investigations into the Greek text of the Bible by other researchers. This Greek text received the initials 8ḤevXII gr (the Greek Minor Prophets) and was published by Emanuel Tov in 1990 (Discoveries in the Judaean Desert, 8). Thus, within a short number of years, the contribution of Barthélemy to the publication of texts discovered in the caves of the Judean Desert was not only swift but effective and authoritative.

BIBLIOGRAPHY

Barthélemy, D. "Le grand rouleau d'Isaïe trouvé près de la mer Morte." *Revue biblique* 57 (1950), 530–545. About Isaiah[a].

Barthélemy, D. "Notes en marge des publications récentes sur les manuscrits de Qumrân." *Revue biblique* 59 (1952), 187–218. About the manuscripts from Qumran Cave 1.

Barthélemy, D. "Redécouverte d'un chaînon manquant de l'histoire de la Septante." *Revue biblique* 60 (1953), 18–29. First paper on the Greek Minor Prophets (8ḤevXII gr).

Barthélemy, D. "Textes bibliques." In *Qumran Cave 1*, edited by Dominique Barthélemy and Józef T. Milik. Discoveries in the Judaean Desert, 1. Oxford, 1955.

Barthélemy, D. *Les devanciers d'Aquila: Première publication intégrale du texte des fragments du Dodecapropheton trouvés dan le désert de Juda*. Supplements to Vetus Testamentum, 10. Leiden, 1963.

JACQUES BRIEND

BASKETRY has survived the ravages of time in the Dead Sea region due to the arid climate. Fragments of baskets and mats, as well as some nearly complete articles, have been recovered from archaeological sites spanning the past nine thousand years. With the exception of that found at Masada and Jericho, the basketry in the Judean Desert was recovered from caves, in some cases the same caves that yielded ancient documents, though none in direct association.

The antiquity of basket-making in the region is also demonstrated by impressions on the bottoms of clay pots, and at Jericho, impressions of rush mats on Neolithic floors. Such evidence, however, lacks the heuristic potential inherent in original specimens that are replete with details of material, shape, size, technique, and style. Moreover, the organic composition of basketry renders it datable by radiocarbon testing, thus enhancing the scientific relevance of finds from cultural contexts that are ambiguous.

Despite often-cursory reporting, infrequent direct dating of basketry specimens, and the absence of information for some eras, existing data attest to techno-stylistic variation through time. The following chronologically ordered synthesis draws on personal observations as well as published accounts and is offered with the proviso that new discoveries may require revisions to the scheme.

Pre-Pottery Neolithic (Seventh Millennium BCE). The oldest basketry found to date in the Judean Desert is best known from the Naḥal Ḥemar collection, which features specimens of three types—twined, wrapped, and coiled—as well as remnants of basketlike containers made by coating cords with bitumen. The twined fragments, all woven in fine-gauge close simple twining, include some with color-contrast decoration. Other fragments represent matting made from rushes or grass with sumaclike wrapped rows. Only one example of coiling is reported for Naḥal Ḥemar. All three basketry types are also reported from other nine-thousand-year-old Judean Desert Neolithic contexts, including Jericho (soumak-style wrapping, coiling) and Netiv Hagdud (fine close twining). Wrapped fragments from mixed contexts at Wadi Murabbaʿat are likely of the same age.

Chalcolithic (Second Half of Fourth Millennium BCE). Basketry is known from Chalcolithic-age contexts in at least ten caves in the Judean Desert. In most cases, the specimens are associated with burials and comprise remnants of mats used to lay out or shroud the dead. Such mats are made from reeds or rushes laid side by side, close with no visible spaces, and attached at intervals by simple twining, or by passing a thin cord through pierced holes. The latter method is represented by a relatively intact specimen found in the Cave of the Treasure in Naḥal Mishmar, where it had been used to wrap a hoard of treasured objects. Mat fragments are also reported from Naḥal Mishmar Caves 2 and 3, Naḥal Ṣe'elim Cave 1, Cave of the Pool in Naḥal David, and Cave of Horror in Naḥal Ḥever. Caves at Masada and Wadi Murabbaʿat produced similar fragments that may be Chalcolithic. Two specimens have been radiocarbon dated, and both confirm assignment to the Chalcolithic era: samples from a mat associated with a burial in the Cave of Horror yielded a date of 5460 ± 125 BP; and three assays on samples from the mat wrapping the Naḥal Mishmar treasure gave an average age of about five thousand years.

Other types of basketry from apparent Chalcolithic-age contexts in the Judean Desert include remnants of containers or trays made by coiling from Naḥal Badir Cave 49 and from the Cave of the Treasure. The latter site also produced a sieve with coiled sides and a base woven in open checker plaiting.

Middle Bronze Age (Early Second Millennium BCE). Rush matting made in a plaiting technique was recovered from burial tombs at Jericho, as were coiled baskets. Kathleen Kenyon (*Digging Up Jericho*, 1960, p. 247) observes that the ancient mats were exactly like modern manufactures. Impressions of coiled baskets are reported for the Late Bronze Age at Jericho.

Roman (First Century BCE–Second Century CE). Basketry from the time of the Roman presence in the Judean Desert includes two comparatively large assemblages that have been analyzed and reported in detail (Cave of the Letters in Naḥal Ḥever and Masada). There are also small assemblages from the Cave of the Treasure, the Cave of the Pool, and others in Naḥal Mishmar; the Cave of Horror in Naḥal Ḥever; Naḥal David Cave 4; Qumran Caves 10, 11, 12; and Wadi Murabbaʿat. None has been radiocarbon dated.

The predominant type is made from flat braids of date-palm leaf in a combined coiling-plaiting technique. Several (usually nine) long, narrow leaflets are plaited on a bias in 2/2 interval twill, forming a strip that spirals from the center out and from the bottom upward. Successive courses are connected, apparently during construction, by passing a thin twisted cord through the folded edges of the weaving elements. The cord, though invisible, produces horizontal ridges on the basket wall. Both baskets and mats were made in this twill-braid technique. The baskets were strong, general-use containers. At the Cave of the Letters in Naḥal Ḥever, many twill-braid baskets contained secondary burials (human bones removed from their original place of deposit); one contained a cache of bronze vessels. One nearly complete twill-braid mat, measuring 62 by 80 centimeters, was recovered from Qumran Cave 12. Archaeologists speculated that it had been used to cover pottery jars.

Other types of basketry from Roman-era sites in the Judean Desert include variants of plaiting, coiling, and twining. The Masada collection features a sieve with an open-twined base. The Cave of the Letters produced a small cylindrical basket made in decorative wickerlike plaiting.

The incidence of basketry finds parallels that of other archaeological discoveries in the Judean Desert. Notably, there are two periods for which numerous findsites are known: the Chalocolithic and Roman eras. Although methods of construction vary over time, craft quality remains high. Moreover, even the earliest Pre-Pottery Neolithic specimens document a sophisticated technological expertise that obviously had much older roots. Basketry comprised an important and ubiquitous item of everyday life, serving in both mundane and ceremonial capacities for thousands of years. Where environmental conditions favor the preservation of basketry, its diagnostic potential and ready datability should encourage increased attention from archaeologists intent on reconstructing the past.

BIBLIOGRAPHY

Aharoni, Y. "Expedition B: The Cave of Horror." *Israel Exploration Journal* 12 (1962), 186–199. Summary of finds with radiocarbon date for Chalcolithic mat.

Bar-Adon, Pessaḥ. *The Cave of the Treasure: The Finds from the Caves in Naḥal Mishmar*. Jerusalem, 1980. Sections on basketry, pages 190–197, with good photographs; radiocarbon dates on page 199.

Bernick, Kathryn. "Basketry, Cordage and Related Artifacts." In *Masada IV: The Yigael Yadin Excavations 1963–1965; Final Reports*, pp. 283–317. Jerusalem, 1994. Detailed descriptive analysis with illustrations.

Crowfoot, Elizabeth. "Textiles, Matting and Basketry." In *Excavations at Jericho, Vol. 1: The Tombs Excavated in 1952–1954*, by Kathleen M. Kenyon, pp. 519–526 (appendix A). Jordan, 1960. Catalog of the basketry with brief descriptions mainly based on inspection of photos.

Crowfoot, G. M. and Elizabeth Crowfoot. "The Textiles and Basketry." In *Les grottes de Murabbaʿat*, edited by P. Benoit, J. T. Milik, and R. de Vaux, pp. 51–63. Discoveries in the Judaean Desert, 2. Oxford, 1961. Brief descriptions of basketry from at least two cultural contexts, not differentiated.

Schick, Tamar. Naḥal Ḥemar Cave: Cordage, Basketry and Fabrics. *ʿAtiqot* 18 (1988), 31–43. Preliminary report with radiocarbon dates.

Yadin, Yigael. *The Finds from the Bar Kokhba Period in the Cave of the Letters*. Jerusalem, 1963. Detailed descriptions of basketry, pages 136–156, with discussion of biblical references; also illustrations.

KATHRYN BERNICK

BATHS AND BAPTISM can only be understood and discussed in relationship to the system of purity and impurity, but it is not the aim of this article to discuss this system in detail. The basis of all Jewish understanding of purity is the biblical ordinances concerning purity, impurity, and the possibility of attaining cultic purity. The water rite as a means of regaining ritual purity following pollution (e.g., impurity through contact with corpses or carcasses, impurity of the parturient and the *ẓav*) is a common property of ancient Judaism. It is no surprise that we find in Josephus's account of the Essenes and the texts of the Qumran community the rituals of purity as a predominant trait of the religious and halakhic life. The excavations of Khirbet Qumran have revealed a water system that not only provided a supply of drinking water but also filled the pools that served for purification rites.

Purification Rites and Communal Life. As Josephus says in *The Jewish War* 2.129, purification is a prerequisite for the common meal. Ordinances[c] (4Q514) 1.i.5–7 states: "All those (who are) 'impure of days' shall on the day of their healing, bathe and launder in water, and become pure. And afterwards they may eat their food according to the purity precept. And he shall not eat anymore while in his initial impurity who has not begun to become pure from his source" (trans. Milgrom; see also lines 8–10). Temple Scroll[a] (11Q19) xlix.20–21 excludes the impure who are already in the process of purifying themselves from the communal meal (Harrington, 1993, p. 63). Excluding someone who is impure from the common meal is also prescribed in Rule of the Community (1QS v.13–14; i.25; vii.16ff.).

Repentance is the precondition for entry into the community and the effectiveness of the water rites (see 1QS ii.25–iii.12). In this paragraph we see that purity and atonement are bound together in a very distinctive way: "He cannot be purified by atonement, nor be cleansed by water of purification, nor sanctify himself in streams and rivers, nor cleanse himself in any waters of ablution. Unclean, unclean is he, as long as he rejects the judgments of God, so that he cannot be instructed within the Community of his (God's) counsel" (1QS ii.4–6; trans. Charlesworth). This correspondence of bath and atonement has often been related to the baptism of John the Baptist in order to show that he was or had been a Qumran-Essene. It is true that John preached and practiced a "baptism of repentance for the forgivenness of sins" (*Mk.* 1.4), but that is a unique, unrepeatable, symbolic, and prophetic ritual act as a salvific baptism before the last judgment. A characteristic feature of John is the title *the Baptist* (as Josephus also relates), which identifies this baptism as something inextricably his own. Even though Josephus, in his report about baptism (*Jewish Antiquities* 18.116–119), disputes the sacramental character of baptism in effecting the forgiveness of sins and allows it to be of use only for the purification of the body, such a negation of the atoning effectiveness of baptism nevertheless shows that Josephus knew the special significance of the baptism of John but desired to rank it within the common Jewish understanding of purity. It cannot be proved that John derived his baptism from the Qumran rituals.

Various Impurities and Their Respective Rites. Purification Rules A (4Q274) 1.i.1–9 offers legislation for individuals who are impure because of fluid discharges:

> An unclean person must remain at distance of twelve cubits from a pure person or dwelling. Anyone who is in the process of purification but comes in contact with an impure person must bathe in water and wash his clothes; only afterwards may he eat. For example, a woman who is purifying herself for seven days after the flow of blood may not touch a man who has a flux nor anything which he has touched. She should also not touch a menstruating woman or a man who has had an emission of semen. For whoever touches one of these impure persons during his period of purification must bathe and wash his clothes as though he had been in contact with a corpse.

Serekh Damascus (4Q265) 2.15–17 says about a woman who has given birth to a child:

> that if she has a boy, she remains impure for seven days as though she were menstruating and has a purification period of thirty-three days; for a girl, the first period is 14 days, and the second sixty-six days.

A *metsora*ʿ ("person with a skin disease") defiles those who touch him: "[Whoev]er of the impure persons to[uches] him shall bathe in water, launder his clothes, and afterwards he may eat of it (any food). This is what is meant by 'impure (to the) impure he shall call out' (*Lv.* 13.45)—all the days the [aff]liction is [in him]" (Purification Rules A, 4Q274 1,3). The *metsora*ʿ is recognized as a sinner in the Damascus Document (4Q266; 272; 268). "Thus, I conclude about the *metsora*ʿ that only after being forgiven by God, as evidenced by healing, can the purification process begin. The *metsora*ʿ can enter the ordinary city after bathing and laundering on the first day of the purification rituals . . . but must keep away from the members of the community so as not to defile them" (Harrington, 1993, pp. 82–93). (For the uncleanness of the leper see 11Q19[a] xlvii.14; xlix.19–21; CD xiii.5–6.)

Everyone who had contact with a corpse was barred from the common meal. The house of the dead is unclean for seven days (11Q19[a] xlix.5–6), but 11Q19[a] xlix.11–21:

> Temple Scroll[a] xlix.11–21 explains that a house in which a dead body was present must be cleansed from any liquids; the floor, walls, and doors must be scraped, and the locks, doorposts, and lintels must be washed with water. In addition, all the vessels of wood, iron, or bronze must be purified, and all clothing and skins must be washed. Any person who was in the house must bathe and wash his clothes on the first, third, and seventh days. On these last two occasions he must be sprinkled with the water of impurity. By the evening he will become pure and then be allowed to touch pure things.

Temple Scroll[a] and Miqtsat Maʿasei ha-Torah B state that the impure person is unclean to the end of the purification period; this means until after sunset of the last day of the purification. People in the process of purification are not considered clean. Purification Rules A (4Q274 1.i.4–5) says: "As for the woman who is discharging blood, for seven days she shall not touch a male with a genital flux, or any object [th]at he has either touched, l[ain] upon, or sat on. [And if] she has touched, she shall launder her clothes, bathe, and afterwards she may eat."

Ritual Baths of the Essenes according to Josephus. Daily after work until the fifth hour, the Essenes "assemble in one place and, after girding their loins with linen cloths, bathe their bodies in cold water. After this purification, they assemble in a private apartment which none of the uninitiated is permitted to enter, pure now themselves, they repair to the refectory, as to some sacred shrine" (*The Jewish War* 2.129). Also in the regulations for admission to the community, the laws of purity play a crucial role: After a year of probation the candidate "is brought into closer touch with the rule and is allowed to share the purer kind of water for purification" (*The Jewish War* 2.138). It has often been observed that there is some relationship between the Essene purification laws and the practice of Bannus (*Life* 11) of "using frequent ablutions of cold water, by day and night, for purity's sake." There is also some similarity between Josephus's accounts of the Essene immersion baths and his view of John the Baptist's baptism, in the use of *hagneia*, purification. This terminology is firmly rooted in the Essene accounts (this is hardly to be traced to its very rare usage in the Septuagint; *The Jewish War* 2,129.138.159; *Jewish Antiquities* 18.19; for Bannus, *Life* 11). [*See* John the Baptist.] More important still is the fact that in both the account of John's preaching and baptizing and the Essene section (*The Jewish War* 2.129) the life-change and ensuing righteous lifestyle precede the water rite. Only after a one-year probationary period is the candidate permitted to "share the purer waters for purification" (*The Jewish War* 2.138). Concerning John's baptism, it is expressly stated that virtue and righteousness are the "necessary preliminary if baptism was to be acceptable to God" (*Jewish Antiquities* 18.117).

There is another important note in *The Jewish War* 2.129. It is expressly stated that "they bathe their bodies." This also agrees with the explicit emphasis in the account of John the Baptist that the baptism did not serve "to gain pardon for whatever sins they committed, but as a purification (consecration) of the body implying that the soul was already thoroughly cleansed by right behaviour" (*Jewish Antiquities* 18.117). Josephus's view of the meaning of John's baptism is not in accordance with the New Testament accounts of John the Baptist (see above on 1QS ii.25–iii.12).

Later Developments in Jewish and Jewish-Christian Baptismal Movements. Many groups within early Judaism and Christianity practiced baptismal rites besides the Qumran-Essenes and the followers of John the Baptist. Two aspects are important for the understanding of their water rites: (1) the concept of a repeatable rite for the achievement of cultic purity and (2) the concept of a one-time baptism for the forgiveness of sins. They form the basic presuppositions for the later history of baptismal movements. Between these two aspects stands the proselyte baptism in rabbinic literature; it presents a first-time immersion for the achievement of cultic purity after which, according to cultic needs, other immersions may follow.

The reports about some of the baptists, hemerobaptists, and masbotheans are so scanty that only the name itself betrays a baptismal group. The hemerobaptists, according to Epiphanius, practiced a total immersion in water daily, both summer and winter. [*See* Epiphanius.] The *Apostolic Constitutions* portray them as corresponding to a Pharisaic ideal of purity (cf. *Mk.* 7). Usually brought into connection with them are the *tovlei Shaḥarit*, the "dawn baptizers" of Tosefta Yadayim 2.20. Their Pharisaic opponents disputed the effectiveness of purifying oneself by bathing every day even when a nocturnal defilement had not taken place.

Scattered reports about baptizing activities appear in connection with Bannus (Josephus, *Life* 11); *Sibylline Oracles* IV,161–169; *Life of Adam and Eve* 6–11; Epictetus (Diss II,9,21); and various adherents of John the Baptist (*Ephesus, Acts* 19.1–7; Rome?). In general, we find Jewish-influenced baptismal movements at the turn from the first to the second centuries; they are varied and are geographically widely distributed.

Irenaeus mentions Ebionite water rites only in connection with the eucharist (water instead of wine); however, the general information that they retained the Jewish law certainly includes rules concerning frequent purifying immersions. The Gospel of the Ebionites (reported by Epiphanius, *Heresies* 30.13) began with the appearance of John the Baptist and the baptism of Jesus. John is a vegetarian, like the Ebionites. Another Ebionite work portrays Peter as washing himself for purification every day, like an Ebionite. The Pseudo-Clementine literature confirms the general character of this information. It reports about baptism for salvation and purification rituals following sexual intercourse. [*See* Pseudo-Clementine Literature.] One must distinguish between the book of revelation of Elkesai and the preaching of Alcibiades. Hippolytus relates the Elkesaites teaching "that there was preached unto men new remission of sins in the third year of Trajan's reign," which was likened to a baptismal rite. A second baptism is especially required in cases of more serious sins, such as adultery, fornication, or false prophecy. The immersion is conducted while fully clothed and can be repeated up to forty times. These extensive water rites emerge later in the *Cologne Mani Codex*, where they are criticized. [*See* Elkesaites.]

The Mandaeans are a further model of a syncretistic baptismal sect. Their traditions are recent, but their origins are at home in the same baptismal-sectarian milieu as that of the Ebionites, the Elkesaites, and the other baptismal groups of Palestine. Every Sunday, the Mandaeans practiced a thrice-repeated signing of the forehead with water accompanied by a baptismal formula and a thrice-repeated drinking of water. In addition, there is a daily self-immersion performed as a morning washing by every member. The water rituals of the Mandaeans until the present have undergone a powerful ritualization and organization, but their origin is clearly from among the heretical Jewish and Jewish-Christian baptismal sects of the first two centuries.

The Jewish-Christian baptismal movements preserved the two basic possibilities of the use and understanding of water rites: self-immersion for the attainment of cultic purity; one-time baptism by a "baptist" as a "baptism of repentance for the forgiveness of sins," mediated through John the Baptist to primitive Christianity. Ebionites as well as Elkesaites practiced the water ritual in a double form: the one-time baptism as an initiation (for the Elkesaites, an additional second baptism for the forgiveness of sins) and repeatable baptism as a cultic-ritual washing following pollution.

BIBLIOGRAPHY

Badia, Leonard F. *The Qumran Baptism and John the Baptist's Baptism.* Lanham, Md., 1980.

Baumgarten, Joseph M. "The Essene Avoidance of Oil and the Laws of Purity." In *Studies in Qumran Law*, pp. 88–97. Studies in Judaism in Late Antiquity, 24. Leiden, 1977.

Baumgarten, Joseph M. "The Pharisaic-Sadducean Controversies about Purity and the Qumran Texts." *Journal of Jewish Studies* 31 (1980), 157–170.

Baumgarten, Joseph M. "Purification after Childbirth and the Sacred Garden in 4Q265 and Jubilees." In *New Qumran Texts and Studies: Proceedings of the First Meeting of the International Organization for Qumran Studies, Paris, 1992*, edited by George J. Brooke, with Florentino García Martínez, pp. 3–10. Studies on the Texts of the Desert of Judah, 15. Leiden, 1994.

Baumgarten, Joseph M. "Liquids and Susceptibility to Defilement in New 4Q Texts." *Jewish Quarterly Review* 85 (1994/95), 91–101.

Baumgarten, Joseph M. "The Laws about Fluxes in 4QTohora[a] (4Q274)." In *Time to Prepare the Way in the Wilderness: Papers on the Qumran Scrolls by Fellows of the Institute for Advanced Studies of the Hebrew University, Jerusalem, 1989–1990*, edited by Devorah Dimant and Lawrence H. Schiffman, pp. 1–8. Studies on the Texts of the Desert of Judah, 16. Leiden, 1995.

Black, Matthew. *The Scrolls and Christian Origins: Studies in the Jewish Background of the New Testament.* New York, 1961. Qumran baptismal rites and sacred meal.

Brownlee, William H. "John the Baptist in the New Light of Ancient Scrolls." *Interpretation* 9 (1955), 71–90. In *The Scrolls and the New Testament*, edited by Krister Stendahl, pp. 33–53. New York, 1957. Reprinted New York, 1992.

Charlesworth, James H., ed. *John and Qumran*. London, 1972.

Collins, Adela Yarbro. "The Origin of Christian Baptism." In *Cosmology and Eschatology in Jewish and Christian Apocalypticism*, pp. 218–238. Leiden, 1996.

Collins, John J. "Apocalyptic Eschatology as the Transcendence of Death." In *Visionaries and Their Apocalypses*, edited by Paul D. Hanson, pp. 61–84. Philadelphia, 1983.

Dunn, James D. G. "Spirit-and-Fire Baptism." *Novum Testamentum* 14 (1972), 81–92.

Dupont-Sommer, André. "Rules and Rites of the Community of the Covenant." *The Jewish Sect of Qumran and the Essenes: New Studies on the Dead Sea Scrolls*, translated by R. D. Barnett. London, 1954. ET pp. 77–103.

García Martínez, F. "Les limites de la communauté: Pureté et impureté à Qumrân et dans le Nouveau Testament." In *Text and Testimony: Essays on New Testament and Apocryphal Literature in Honour of A. F. J. Klijn*, edited by T. Baarda et al., pp. 111–122. Kampen, 1988.

Harrington, Hannah K. *The Impurity Systems of Qumran and the Rabbis: Biblical Foundations.* Society of Biblical Literature Dissertation Series, 143. Atlanta, 1993.

Harrison, R. K. "The Rites and Customs of the Qumran Sect." In *The Scrolls and Christianity: Historical and Theological Significance*, edited by Matthew Black, pp. 22–36. London, 1969.

Janowski, Bernd, and Hermann Lichtenberger. "Enderwartung und Reinheitsidee: Zur eschatologischen Deutung von Reinheit und Sühne in der Qumrangemeinde." *Journal of Jewish Studies* 34 (1983), 31–62.

Jaubert, A. "Le calendrier des Jubilés et les jours liturgiques de la semaine." *Vetus Testamentum* 7 (1957), 35–61.

LaSor, William S. "Discovering What Jewish Miqva'ot Can Tell Us about Christian Baptism." *Biblical Archaeology Review* (1987), 52–59.

Lichtenberger, Hermann. "The Dead Sea Scrolls and John the Baptist." In *The Dead Sea Scrolls: Forty Years of Research*, edited by Devorah Dimant and Uriel Rappaport, pp. 340–346. Leiden, 1992.

Lohfink, Gerhard. "Der Ursprung der christlichen Taufe." *Theologische Quartalschrift* 156 (1976), 35–54.

Milgrom, Jacob. "The Scriptural Foundations and Derivations of the Laws of Purity in the Temple Scroll." In *Archaeology and History in the Dead Sea Scrolls*, edited by Lawrence H. Schiffman, pp. 83–99. Sheffield, 1990.

Milgrom, Jacob. "On the Purification Offering in the Temple Scroll." *Revue de Qumrân* 16 (1993), 99–101.

Milgrom, Jacob. "The Concept of Impurity in *Jubilees* and the *Temple Scroll*." *Revue de Qumrân* 16 (1993), 277–284.

Newton, M. *The Concept of Purity at Qumran and in the Letters of Paul.* Society for New Testament Studies Monograph Series, 53. Cambridge, 1985.

Perrot, C. "Le mouvement baptiste en Palestine." *Bible et Terre Sainte* 180 (1976), 8–9.

Rowley, H. H. "The Baptism of John and the Qumran Sect." In *New Testament Essays: Studies in Memory of Thomas Walter Manson, 1893–1958*, edited by Angus John Brockhurst Higgins, pp. 219–229. Manchester, 1959.

Schiffman, Lawrence H. "Purity and Perfection: Exclusion from the Council of the Community in the *Serekh Ha-ʿEdah*." In *Biblical Archaeology Today: Proceedings of the International Congress on Biblical Archaeology, Jerusalem, April 1984*, edited by Janet Amitai, pp. 373–389. Jerusalem, 1985.

Schiffman, Lawrence H. "The Impurity of the Dead in the Temple Scroll." In *Archaeology and History in the Dead Sea Scrolls*, pp. 135–156. Sheffield, 1990.

Schiffman, Lawrence H. "Pharisaic and Sadducean Halakhah in Light of the Dead Sea Scrolls: The Case of Ṭevul Yom." *Dead Sea Discoveries* 1 (1994), 285–299.

Schüssler Fiorenza, Elisabeth. "Cultic Language in Qumran and in the NT." *Catholic Biblical Quarterly* 38 (1976), 159–177.

Schwartz, D. R. "On Quirinius, John the Baptist, the Benedictus, Melchizedek, Qumran and Ephesus." *Revue de Qumrân* 13 (1988), 635–646.

Scobie, C. H. H. "John the Baptist." In *The Scrolls and Christianity: Historical and Theological Significance*, edited by Matthew Black, pp. 58–69. London, 1969.

Stegemann, Hartmut. *The Library of Qumran: On the Essenes, Qumran, John the Baptist, and Jesus.* Grand Rapids, Mich., 1998.

Taylor, Joan E. *The Immerser: John the Baptist within Second Temple Judaism.* Grand Rapids, Mich., 1997.

Taylor, Joan E. "John the Baptist and the Essenes." *Journal of Jewish Studies* 47 (1996), 256–285.

Thiering, B. E. "Inner and Outer Cleansing at Qumran as a Background to New Testament Baptism." *New Testament Studies* 26 (1980), 266–277.

Webb, Robert L. *John the Baptiser and Prophet: A Socio-Historical Study.* Journal for the Study of the New Testament Supplement Series, 62. Sheffield, 1991.

Wood, Bryant G. "To Dip or to Sprinkle? The Qumran Cisterns in Perspective." *Bulletin of the American Schools of Oriental Research* 256 (1984), 45–60.

HERMANN LICHTENBERGER

BEATITUDES. A set of related Hebrew fragments, one of which contains five beatitudes, was found in Cave 4 at Qumran; it is known as Wisdom Text with Beatitudes (4Q525). The fragments originally were assigned for editing to Jean Starcky but were first published by Émile Puech. Puech continues to group other small fragments with the original core identified by Starcky, so that at this time final conclusions cannot be drawn about the extent of the text preserved. But it is the larger fragment (4Q525 2.ii.1–6) that deserves to retain the interest of students. This large fragment can be structured as a series of five beatitudes. Since the beginning is lost, what is extant could have been preceded by one or more other beatitudes. The first of the extant beatitudes is concerned with speaking the truth with a pure heart and avoiding slander. The second congratulates those who uphold (Wisdom's) statutes and avoid the paths of perversity. The third praises those who rejoice in Lady Wisdom and avoid the paths of folly. The fourth felicitates the one who seeks Wisdom with purity of hand and does not strive after her with a deceitful heart (mind). The fifth is much longer. It puts in parallel Wisdom and "the Law of the Most High." It praises Wisdom's devotee for his studiousness, his delight in accepting her corrections, and his fidelity to her even in affliction and in a time of distress. The last line reads "For on her [Wisdom] he mediates always, and in his misfortune he ponders on . . ." before breaking off. The whole last long beatitude bears a striking resemblence to Psalm 1, as the first four beatitudes remind one of Psalm 15.2–3.

The extant fragments are dated by Puech and George Brooke to between 50 BCE and 50 CE because they are written in Herodian script. The date of composition could be earlier. The sapiential values of the text do not mark much of a change from *Proverbs* and *Ecclesiastes* (i.e., the Persian period, so Puech). On the other hand, the signs of careful composition and conformity to a rigidly structured genre of beatitude series (which includes the exact counting of words) such as Puech finds in this Qumran text, as well as in Psalm 15, *Ben Sira* 14.20–27 and 15.1–10, and *Matthew* 5.3–10, argue for the Hellenistic or Herodian-Roman period, perhaps between 150 and 30 BCE. The language is a Hebrew similar to that of *Psalms*, with some suggestions of the influence of Aramaic vocabulary.

It is difficult to determine the exact origins of this text since the language is quite general. It is certain that the text comes from a wisdom circle, perhaps of scribes. There is nothing particularly sectarian about it. The crucial issue that has been debated is the absence (Viviano) or presence (Puech, 1993) of eschatology in the series of beatitudes. It is clear that the War Scroll (1QM) and the more recently published Danielic text Aramaic Apocalypse (4Q246) share an apocalyptic eschatology centered on the kingdom of God, and occasionally (in the War Scroll) mentioning the archangel Michael, with the *Book of Daniel* (and much of the New Testament). There is none of their special terminology in these beatitudes. Whatever implication there is of punishment or judgment in our text is the result of one's personal folly; it is immanent, not transcendent, with the possible exception of line 5, which mentions a "time of oppression" and days of "terror." The phrase "in a time of oppression," *be-ʿet tsuqah*, could be an echo of the phrase *uve-tsuq haʿitim*, literally "in an oppression/distress of times," that is, "in a troubled time" from the prophecy of seventy weeks in *Daniel* 9.25. This is quite apocalyptic, yet the same word *tsuqah* appears in a purely sapiential text, *Proverbs* 1.27. The word for terror, *paḥad*, is common throughout most of the Hebrew scriptures. This question remains unsettled. From another angle, one sees that the long final beatitude presupposes the identity of Wisdom with the Torah, a bold theological step first attested outside Qumran in *Ben Sira* 24.22(23), though anticipated in *Deuteronomy* 4.5–8 (cf. *1 Cor.* 1.24, 30). This datum suggests that our text represents late rather than early Israelite wisdom ideas, that is, from after 200 BCE.

Since the text is a unicum, any detection of redactional layers would be speculative. The author is so immersed in the phraseology of *Psalms* and wisdom books that they could be viewed as the earliest layers of the text. As it stands, however, it seems a unity, indeed, if Puech's word counts have validity, a tightly structured unity. There is no evidence that the work was used or viewed as an authoritative scriptural book.

As for relations with other works, besides those already mentioned, a parallel with Hodayot[a] from Cave 1 at Qumran (1QH 6.13–16) has been noted; also the idiom in line 3 (*be-vor kapayim*, with purity of hands, i.e., with clean hands) is found in Rule of the Community from Cave 1 (IQS 9.15) as well. [*See* Hodayot; Rule of the Community.] With the Hebrew scriptures note the following: line 1 is parallel to *Psalms* 15.3, "slander with the tongue"; in *Proverbs* 3.18, those who cling to wisdom are called happy; and *Proverbs* 4.4 says "keep my commandments, and live." Line 2 is parallel with *Proverbs* 5.5, neglect of wisdom leads to death and Sheol. Line 3 has a parallel in *Proverbs* 12.20's phrase "the heart of deceit" and in the use of the verbal root *nśg* to refer to attaining wisdom/the paths of life. For the rest, we can say that there is a biblical vocabulary, yet the phraseology is original, with an almost masochistic intensification in line 4, "delighting in wisdom's strokes." For the whole, see *Ben Sira* 14.20–27, which contains eight verses introduced by "happy is." This passage can be read (Puech, 1991) as one long eight-part beatitude that expresses an intellectual eros. *Ben Sira* 15.1–8 continues this sapiential eros in a series of maternal and bridal images. New Testament comparisons begin with *Matthew* 5.3–12, parallel to *Luke* 6.20–26, Jesus' list of beatitudes (the number varies from four to nine). The rest of the beatitudes in the New Testament are single, not in series. Qumran's first beatitude refers to sins of the tongue or speech; this is also the subject of *Matthew* 5.23–37 and 23.16–22, and *James* 3.1–12; for the purity of heart mentioned in this first Qumran beatitude, see *Matthew* 5.8, "blessed are the pure of heart." For Qumran's second beatitude, compare *Matthew* 5.17–20 and *Luke* 16.17, both passages concerned with observance of the Law. Qumran's third beatitude connects with *Matthew* 5.10–12, 7.13–14, 7.24–27, 25.1–13, and 25.14–30 in the sense that all these passages speak either of a contrast between wisdom and folly (the wise and the foolish) or between the way that leads to life and the way that leads to death; they move the reader to a choice or a decision. *Matthew* 11.25 and *1 Corinthians* 1.19 and 1.26–29 differ from these texts to the extent that they contrast the apparently wise (but really foolish) with the apparently foolish (but really wise). Compare the fourth beatitude from Qumran with *Matthew* 6.33, which lists the values one should most seek; compare Qumran's deceitful heart with *Matthew* 9.4, 5.28, 12.34, 13.15 (citing *Is.* 6.10), 15.8 (citing *Is.* 29.13), and 15.18–19, all heart texts. On the ready assumption of sinfulness, compare the Qumran text with *Matthew* 7.11. The Qumran beatitude text is important for the history of this literary genre, for the study of Hebrew wisdom literature, and for the analysis of the Sermon on the Mount/Plain (*Mt.* 5–7; *Lk.* 6).

[*See also* Wisdom Texts.]

BIBLIOGRAPHY

Brooke, G. J. "The Wisdom of Matthew's Beatitudes (4Qbeat and Matt 5:3–12)." *Scripture Bulletin* 19 (1989), 35–41. First English presentation.

Fabry, Heinz-Joseph. "Der Makarismus—mehr als nur eine weisheitliche Lehrform: Gedanken zu dem neu-edierten Text 4Q525." In *Altestamentlicher Glaube und Biblische Theologie* (FS H.D. Preus), edited by Jutta Hausmann and Hans-Jürgen Zobel, pp. 362–371. Stuttgart, 1992. Good on the Hebrew scriptures' literary background.

Fitzmyer, Joseph A. "A Palestine Collection of Beatitudes." In *The Four Gospels 1992: FS Frans Neirynck*, edited by F. Van Segbroeck et al., pp. 509–515. Louvain, 1992.

Puech, Émile. "Un hymne essénien en partie retrouvé et les béatitudes." *Revue de Qumrân* 13 (1988): 59–88. See especially pages 84–88. The earliest, partial publication of the Wisdom Text with Beatitudes.

Puech, Émile. "4Q525 et les péricopes des béatitudes en Ben Sira et Matthieu." *Revue biblique* 98 (1991), 80–106. This is the first publication of the text and remains fundamental.

Puech, Émile. "The Collection of Beatitudes in Hebrew and in Greek (4Q525, 1–4 and Matt 5, 3–12)." In *Early Christianity in Context: Monuments and Documents* (FS Emanuele Testa). Studium Biblicum Franciscanum Collectio Maior 38, pp. 553–568. Jerusalem, 1993. In this article Puech presents further readings of fragments connected to the Wisdom Text with Beatitudes, then his structural analysis with word counts, and his reply to his critics.

Viviano, Benedict Thomas. "Beatitutes Found Among Dead Sea Scrolls." *Biblical Archaeology Review* 18 (1992), 53–55, 66.

Viviano, Benedict Thomas. "Eight Beatitudes at Qumran and in Matthew? A New Publication from Cave Four." *Svensk Exegetisk Årsbok* 58 (1993), 71–84. Questions some of Puech's interpretations.

Viviano, Benedict Thomas. "Eight Beatitudes from Qumran," *The Bible Today* 31.4 (1993), 219–224.

BENEDICT T. VIVIANO

BELIAL. *See* Demons.

BEN GALGULA, YESHUʿA. According to three letters found at Wadi Murabbaʿat, a letter from Beit-Mashiko to Yeshuʿa ben Galgula (Mur 42) and two letters from Shimʿon Bar Kokhba to Yeshuʿa ben Galgula (Mur 34–44), Yeshuʿa ben Galgula is the name of one of the commanders in Bar Kokhba's army. Bar Kokhba's letters contain the names of several of his subordinate commanders, but Yeshuʿa ben Galgula is the only one whose army rank is specified. He is called "chief of the camp," although it is impossible to know from this his exact position in the hierarchy of command. The term *camp* also is used in another document to refer to Herodium, but in neither case is there any way of knowing the size of this unit, if indeed there was a standard size.

One of the letters (Mur 43) sent to Yeshuʿa ben Galgula by Bar Kokhba begins as follows: "From Shimʿon ben Kosibaʾ to Yeshuʿa ben Galgula and the men of *ha-Barukh*, peace." According to Józef T. Milik (Benoit, 1961, pp. 159–161), who edited the document, the unclear word *ha-Barukh* refers to Kefar ha-Barukh, a village near Hebron, where Yeshuʿa ben Galgula's camp must have been located. There is some support for identifying this word as a geographical place-name since other letters of Bar

Kokhba that were sent to local commanders begin by addressing the commander's men, specifying the place in which they are situated; for example: "from Shimʿon ben Kosibaʾ to the men of ʿEin-Gedi, to Masabbala [and] Yeho[n]atan b[ar] Baʿayan, peace" (Yadin, 1961, p. 47). However, others think the correct reading should be *ha-kerakh*, "the fort," or perhaps even *ḥevrekha*, "your company." A further text that associates Yeshuʿa ben Galgula with this geographical area is the remarriage contract of his sister Salome, which also was found at Murabbaʿat (Mur 115). This document dates from the year 124 CE and was drawn up in the toparchy of Herodium. It was written in Greek, so that from it we know the correct pronunciation of Yeshuʿa ben Galgula's name, which appears without vowels in the Hebrew and Aramaic documents.

In the letter to Yeshuʿa ben Galgula (Mur 43), Bar Kokhba appears to demand from him and his men that they not harm the Galileans in their unit; if they do, he will clap them in irons, as he once punished someone called ben Aflul. If this reading is correct, it provides evidence for the presence of soldiers from Galilee in Bar Kokhba's forces stationed in the area of the Hebron hill country, as well as evidence for local differences and tensions between the Galileans and the men from Judea. A further letter (Mur 44) from Bar Kokhba to Yeshuʿa ben Galgula deals with the supply of food (Benoit, 1961, p. 161).

The letter (Mur 42) in which the name of Yeshuʿa ben Galgula appears as chief of the camp was sent to him by the officials of the village of Beit-Mashiko, which was within his area of command. This name does not appear anywhere else in Jewish sources, but it is found in Nabatean and Palmyrene. Thus, Milik presumes that the village must have been in Southern Judea, an area that belonged to the Roman province of Arabia, according to Josephus. The officials demand that Yehosef ben Ariston return the cow that he took from Yaʾaqov ben Yehudah, a resident of Beit-Mashiko, who had bought it legally. They are unable to come to Yeshuʿa ben Galgula in person because of the Roman presence nearby. From this it is clear that, at the time, Bar Kokhba's units and the Roman units were very near each other (Benoit, 1961, pp. 155–159).

BIBLIOGRAPHY

Benoit, P., J. T. Milik, and Roland de Vaux, eds. *Les Grottes de Murabbaʿat.* Discoveries in the Judaean Desert, 2. Oxford 1961. See pages 169–163.

Kutscher, Eduard Y. "The Hebrew and Aramaic Letters of Bar Koseba and His Contemporaries" (in Hebrew). In *Hebrew and Aramaic Studies*, pp. 36–70. Jerusalem, 1977.

Yadin, Yigael. "Expedition D." *Israel Exploration Journal* 11 (1961), 36–52.

Yadin, Yigael. *Bar-Kokhba.* New York, 1971.

AHARON OPPENHEIMER

BEN SIRA, BOOK OF. The *Wisdom of Yeshua* (Jesus), *Ben Sira* in Hebrew (*Sirach* in Greek and *Ecclesiasticus* in Latin), is part of the Apocrypha and traditionally is included among those Jewish works called wisdom literature. It was composed in Hebrew in Jerusalem somewhere between 195 and 180 BCE by a scribe whose name is given as Jesus son of Eleazar, son of Sira (*Sir.* 50.27). This date can be confirmed by the inclusion in the book (chap. 50) of a paean to the high priest Simon II (219–196 BCE), during whose high priestly tenure the author lived and after whose death he most likely wrote, and the lack of awareness of the events under Antiochus IV Epiphanes that led to the Maccabean Revolt. The translator presents himself in the prologue as the author's grandson, who came to Egypt in the "thirty-eighth year of King Euergetes" (Ptolemy VIII, nicknamed Physcon Euergetes), in about 132 BCE (Prologue). There he translated the work into Greek, which became the book's primary language of transmission into modernity.

Transmission of the Text. Both the Hebrew manuscripts and the Greek translation have been transmitted in at least two different forms. The original Hebrew text of *Ben Sira* has been designated *HTI*, and a text or texts augmented with additional proverbs is known as *HTII*. The grandson's translation, *GI*, was made from *HTI*, and a second Greek recension, *GII*, was translated from *HTII*. The manuscripts from the Cairo Genizah witness both forms of the Hebrew text, and the quotations of *Ben Sira* contained in rabbinic literature also show awareness of this expanded text form. Additionally, all extant Greek manuscripts show a textual displacement in which the order of particular verses—30.25–33.13a and 33.13b–36.16a—has been switched.

Two other translations constitute important additional textual witnesses to the book. The Old Latin, which was eventually accepted into the Vulgate because Jerome did not make a new translation of the book, probably dates from the second century CE and rests on the expanded *GII*. The Syriac translation was made on the basis of *HTI* and *HTII*, but it also shows the influence of the Greek. It was most likely the product of Ebionites in the fourth century.

Even though a number of Ben Sira's proverbs are cited in rabbinic literature, the original Hebrew gradually fell into obscurity, presumably because the book was not included in the Jewish canon. It survived in Karaite communities well into the Middle Ages, perhaps after having been rediscovered as part of a find of Hebrew manuscripts in the area of the Dead Sea around 800 CE.

Hebrew Manuscripts. In 1896 Solomon Schechter of Cambridge University identified the first fragments of the Hebrew *Ben Sira* among the thousands of manuscript pieces found in the Cairo Genizah. To date, scholars have identified fragments of six manuscripts of the book, denoted A through F. None, unfortunately, encompasses the entire fifty-one chapters of the book. The following list provides those passages extant in the Cairo Genizah manuscripts.

MS A, 3.6b–16.26
MS B (written in stichometric form and including a subscription), 30.11–33.3; 35.11–38.27b; 39.15c–51.30
MS C (a compilation of citations), 3.14–18; 3.21–22; 4.21–23; 4.30; 4.31; 5.4–7; 5.9–13; 6.18b; 6.19; 6.28; 6.35; 7.1; 7.2; 7.4; 7.6; 7.17; 7.20; 7.21; 7.23–25; 18.31b–19.3b; 20.5–7; 20.13; 20.22–23; 25.8; 25.13; 25.17–24; 26.1–3; 26.13; 26.15–17; 25.8; 25.20–21; 36.27–31; 37.19; 37.22; 37.24; 37.26; 41.16
MS D, 36.29–38.1a
MS E, 32.16–34.1
MS F, 31.24–32.7; 32.12–33.8

More recently portions of the Hebrew text were found among the discoveries at Qumran and Masada. Small fragments from Cave 2 at Qumran (2Q18) preserve a few words from *Ben Sira* 6.14–15 (or 1.19–20) and 6.20–31. Maurice Baillet, the editor (1962, pp. 75–77) dates the fragments to the first century BCE. Although small, these fragments reveal that *Ben Sira* was copied at an early period in poetic stichometry (lines). The Psalms Scroll from Cave 11 (hereafter 11Q Psalms[a], 11Q5), which contains several compositions not in the Hebrew scriptures (Psalms 151, 154, 155, the Plea for Deliverance, Apostrophe to Zion, Hymn to the Creator, and David's Compositions), also includes *Ben Sira* 51.13–19 and 51.30. James A. Sanders (1965) argues that the Hebrew text of *Ben Sira* 51 in 11Q Psalms[a] is superior to that extant in the Cairo Genizah manuscripts.

The Ben Sira scroll found at Masada (Mas1h), discovered in casemate 1109, comprises the most extensive Judean Desert remains of the work. This scroll, the earliest Hebrew-manuscript evidence for the book, is written, according to Yigael Yadin (1965), in a "middle or late Herodian" hand and dates from the first century BCE. It encompasses *Ben Sira* 39.27–43.30. The text of the scroll is virtually identical with that of the Cairo Genizah manuscripts, and it is the closest among extant Hebrew copies to Ben Sira's original text (Yadin, 1965).

Contents of Ben Sira. The book contains sapiential material of a diverse nature. Ben Sira includes in his work both "recipe" or practical wisdom—advice for living a good life (e.g., *Sir.* 4.1–10)—and "existential" wisdom—those traditions that provide meaning for the difficulties of life (for example, *Sir.* 18.8–14). Several themes dominate the book, but Alexander Di Lella (1992) argues that the most dominant theme concerns acquiring wisdom by fearing the Lord and keeping his commandments. Wisdom is personified as a woman, who calls out to those seeking her and desires to be sought (for example, *Sir.* 14.20–15.8; 24; 51). The book concludes with a long section, usually called the Praise of the Ancestors, glorifying the heroes of Israel's past up through the high priest Simon II.

The book also provides a wealth of potential clues about the social world of Jewish Palestine and inner-Jewish religious tensions in the pre-Maccabean period. In what seems to be a polemic against Jewish groups that he does not countenance, Ben Sira warns his charges against the danger of speculating about the secrets of the universe (*Sir.* 3.21–24), and, in an apparent swipe at those who use a solar calendar, he goes beyond *Genesis* 1.14 and says that it is solely according to the moon that important days and times should be set (43.1–8).

[*See also* Cairo Genizah; Psalms Scroll; Wisdom Texts.]

BIBLIOGRAPHY

Baillet, Maurice. "Ecclésiastique." In *Les 'Petites Grottes' de Qumrân,* edited by Maurice Baillet, J. T. Milik, and Roland de Vaux, pp. 75–77. Discoveries in the Judaean Desert, 3. Oxford, 1962.

Beentjes, Pancratius C. *The Book of Ben Sira in Hebrew.* Supplements to Vetus Testamentum, 68. Leiden, 1997. A complete reconsideration and reedition of all the known Hebrew fragments.

Di Lella, Alexander A. *The Hebrew Text of Sirach: A Text-Critical and Historical Study.* Studies in Classical Literature, 1. The Hague, 1966. Establishes that the Cairo Genizah manuscripts are not translations from Syriac but substantially reflect the original Hebrew of the book.

Di Lella, Alexander A. "The Newly Discovered Sixth Manuscript of Ben Sira from the Cairo Geniza." *Biblica* 69 (1988), 226–238. Publication of manuscript F from the Cairo Genizah.

Di Lella, Alexander A. "Wisdom of Ben Sira." In *The Anchor Bible Dictionary,* vol. 1, edited by David Noel Freedman, pp. 931–945. New York, 1992.

Historical Dictionary of the Hebrew Language. *The Book of Ben Sira: Text, Concordance, and an Analysis of the Vocabulary.* Jerusalem, 1973. Contains all the Hebrew texts of Ben Sira except manuscript F. Includes extensive concordances to the Hebrew.

Lee, Thomas R. *Studies in the Form of Sirach 44–50.* Society of Biblical Literature Dissertation Series, 75. Atlanta, 1986. Focuses on the Praise of the Ancestors and argues that the section is written in the form of an encomium.

Mack, Burton L. *Wisdom and the Hebrew Epic: Ben Sira's Hymn in Praise of the Fathers.* Chicago Studies in the History of Judaism. Chicago, 1985. Analyzes the Praise of the Ancestors in *Sirach* 44–50. Focuses on the structure and signs systems of the poem, especially the offices held by the figures.

Sanders, J. A., ed. *The Psalms Scroll of Qumran Cave 11.* Discoveries in the Judaean Desert, 4. Oxford, 1965.

Skehan, Patrick, and Alexander A. Di Lella. *The Wisdom of Ben Sira.* Anchor Bible, vol. 39. Garden City, N.Y., 1987. The definitive commentary currently available. Very extensive and complete bibliography up to 1987.

Winter, M. M. "The Origins of Ben Sira in Syriac." *Vetus Testamentum* 27 (1977), 237–253, 494–507. Argues that the Syriac version was translated by Ebionite Christians.

Wright, Benjamin G. *No Small Difference: Sirach's Relationship to Its Hebrew Parent Text.* Septuagint and Cognate Studies, 26. Atlanta, 1989. An examination of the translation technique of the Greek version. Extensive bibliography.

Yadin, Yigael. *The Ben Sira Scroll from Masada*. Jerusalem, 1965.
Ziegler, Joseph. *Sapientia Iesu filii Sirach*. Vetus Testamentum graecum auctoritate societatis litterarum gottingensis editum, 12/2. Göttingen, 1965. The standard critical edition of the Greek text.

BENJAMIN G. WRIGHT III

BERAKHOT. The Hebrew work Berakhot has been preserved in Cave 4 at Qumran in .five manuscripts, known as Berakhot[a–e] (4Q286–290), dated paleographically between approximately 1 through 50 CE. The opening of the work is missing, and the overlap of text among the five manuscripts is slight. However, on the basis of the extant fragments, its length may be estimated at approximately sixteen columns of thirteen lines each.

The text of Berakhot consists of a series of liturgical blessings and curses and a series of laws. A ceremonial function is suggested by such opening rubrics as "[F]urther they shall bless the God" (4Q286 7.i.8) and by closing rubrics such as "the council of the Community, all of them will say together: Amen. Amen" (4Q286 7.ii.1 = 4Q287 6.1). These characteristics, together with such phrases as "year after year in orde[r]" (4Q287 4.1) and a law referring to the muster of the members of the community (4Q286 17ab), indicate an annual covenantal ceremony of the *yaḥad* (cf. Rule of the Community [hereafter 1QRule of the Community] 1QS i.16–iii.12). [*See* Rule of the Community.]

The sequence of the covenantal ceremony may have been as follows: a communal confession (4Q286 1.i.7–8 [and frg. 9?]); a series of blessings addressed to God (4Q286 1.ii–7.i and 4Q287 1–5); a series of curses against Belial and his lot (4Q286 7.ii [= 4Q287 6] and 4Q287 7–10); a series of laws (4Q286 20ab [= 4Q288 1] and 4Q286 13, 14, 15, 17ab); liturgy of expelling the willful sinner from the community (4Q289 [and 4Q286 9?]); and the conclusion of the ceremony (4Q290).

Generally speaking, this sequence from Berakhot is similar to that of the covenantal ceremony recorded in the Rule of the Community, both of them, according to the *yaḥad* sectarian outlook [*see* Covenant], being intended to renew the biblical covenant with Israel. Nevertheless, the two covenantal ceremonies differ in their liturgical course and in the content of the blessings and curses, thus representing different aspects of the same covenantal idea.

Although blessings, curses, and *amen* responses are recited in alternating sequence in Berakhot, these do not follow the pattern of *Deuteronomy* 27 and 1QRule of the Community (1QS) ii, which contain recitations by priests, Levites, and those who enter the covenant. Rather, the blessings and curses of Berakhot are set in a liturgical sequence of recitations by heavenly and earthly participants, to which the men of the *yaḥad* community then respond. Thus, the ceremonial system of blessings and curses evident in the literary form of Berakhot is based upon a broader concept of the covenantal ideology than that of 1QRule of the Community. Whereas the covenantal ceremony of 1QRule of the Community follows that of *Deuteronomy* (esp. chaps. 27–29) and of the priestly blessing of *Numbers* 6.24–26, which are of a national nature, the covenantal ceremony of Berakhot seems to reflect a cosmological approach, similar to that in the biblical psalmody concerning the kingdom of God (cf. Ps. 96–100, 103.19–22, 145). Following this tradition, the covenantal concept of Berakhot expresses the idea of the overall nature of the law of God as creator and king, who creates and unifies the entire universe (cf. Ps. 103.17–22). Thus Belial and his lot, pretending to rule by their antithetical laws, are cursed (cf. the Melchiresha' and Melchizedek concept in Visions of Amram[a–f]? [4Q543–548]; Melchizedek [11Q13]; War Scroll [1QM xiii.2–12]; and Curse [4Q280]). [*See* Amram; Melchizedek; *and* War of the Sons of Light against the Sons of Darkness.]

The antithesis between God and Belial appears in Berakhot as the antithesis between holiness and abomination. This concept of holiness is apparent in Berakhot through the invocation of God in the blessings recited by his angelic ministers in the heavenly sanctuaries (4Q286 1.ii–7.i, 4Q287 2). These angelic blessings are shaped by biblical and postbiblical motifs of the Merkavah tradition. Thus, the connection between the Sinai covenant and the angelic chariot, as shown in Psalm 68.18 and 68.34–36, may have influenced the idea of holiness in Berakhot (see 4Q286 2). However, the main concept expressed in Berakhot is that of the celestial holiness of the heavenly sanctuary, similar to that known in *Ezekiel* 1.26–28 and 8.2, *Daniel* 7.9b–10, *1 Enoch* 14, and the Songs of the Sabbath Sacrifice, possibly as an antithesis to the abomination of the pit, Abaddon, and Sheol, which are the dwellings of Belial (4Q286 7.ii.7–10 = 4Q287[b] 6.6–9). [*See* Songs of the Sabbath Sacrifice.] The blessings of the earthly realms, following the blessings of the angelic realms, express the hegemony of the laws of God the Creator over the whole universe (4Q286 5–7.i; 4Q287 3–5). Among them, the men of the *yaḥad*, "the . . . elect . . . who have knowledge" of the laws of God like "[the c]ouncil of elim [angels] of purification who have eternal knowledge" (4Q286 7.i.2–3 and 6), reflect the idea of commitment to the laws of God by all the faithful of the covenant (cf. *Ps.* 103.20–22).

Stylistically, the blessings of God and the curses of Belial (4Q286 1–7, 4Q287[b]) are structured as catalogs, in various forms of poetic parallelism and repetition of linguistic forms. The liturgical nature of this work is characterized both by its catalog structure and by poetic repetition (cf. *Ps.* 29, 103.20–22; *Prayer of Azariah and the Song of the Three Young Men*, 22; and esp. *Ps.* 148.7–13 and the

Sabbath hymn of the Words of the Luminaries[a] [4Q504 1–2.vii.4–9]). The antithetical curses are likewise rhymed in poetic parallelism, but of a different nature, similar to that of the War Scroll xiii.4–5, albeit versified in Berakhot in a more elaborate manner.

The series of laws preserved in Berakhot may be integrated with the same idea of the dualistic separation between the allies of God and the allies of Belial by the procedure of rebuking a sinning member of the *yaḥad* who may turn to the path of Belial (4Q286 20ab [= 4Q288 1] and 4Q286 13 and 14). These laws interpret *Leviticus* 19.17–18 as intended to prevent the unwitting sinner from deviation and elaborating the forensic procedure of punishment (cf. Damascus Document, CD ix). Thus, the sequence as a whole seems to lead toward the conclusion of expelling the willful sinner from the community (4Q289). There are parallels to this part of the annual covenantal ceremony in 1QRule of the Community ii.25b–iii.6a and Damascus Document[a] 4Q266 11.5b–18a (= Damascus Document[e] 4Q270 7.i.19c–ii.12a). [*See* Damascus Document.]

The ceremony concludes with a hope for the eschatological days, when wickedness vanishes and anger disappears (4Q290). Thus, the dualistic sectarian ideology is conclusively molded in ceremonial expression.

[*See also* Blessings and Curses.]

BIBLIOGRAPHY

Kobelski, Paul J. *Melchizedek and Melchireša'*. Catholic Biblical Quarterly Monograph Series, 10. Washington, D.C. 1981. See pages 42–48.

Milik, J. T. "Milkî-ṣedeq et Milkî-reša' dans les anciens écrits juifs et chrétiens." *Journal of Jewish Studies* 23 (1971), Pl. II, pp. 130–134. Entire article appears on pages 95–144.

Nitzan, Bilha. "4QBerakhot (4Q286–290): A Preliminary Report." In *New Qumran Texts and Studies: Proceedings of the First Meeting of the International Organization for Qumran Studies, Paris 1992*, edited by George J. Brooke with Florentino García Martínez, pp. 53–71. Studies on the Texts of the Desert of Judah, 15. Leiden, 1994.

Nitzan, Bilha. "Merkabah Descriptions in 4QBerakhot (4Q286–290)" (in Hebrew). In *Proceedings of the Eleventh World Congress of Jewish Studies*. Jerusalem, 1994. See pages 87–94.

Nitzan, Bilha. "Harmonic and Mystical Characteristics in Poetic and Liturgical Writings from Qumran." *Jewish Quarterly Review* (1994), 163–183.

Nitzan, Bilha. "Processes of Emergence of Sectarian Texts in Qumran" (in Hebrew). *Beth Mikra* 40/3 [142] (1995): 232–248.

Nitzan Bilha. "4QBerakhot[a-e] (4Q286–290): A Covenantal Ceremony in the Light of Related Texts." *Revue de Qumrân* 16/64 (1994), 487–506.

Nitzan, Bilha. "The Textual, Literary and Religious Character of 4QBerakhot (4Q286–290)" (in Hebrew). In *A Light for Jacob: Studies in the Bible and the Dead Sea Scrolls, In Memory of Jacob Shalom Licht*, pp. 227–253, edited by Y. Hoffman and F. Polak. Jerusalem, 1997.

Nitzan, Bilha. "The Laws of Reproof in 4QBerakhot[a,c] (4Q286, 4Q288) in Light of their Parallels in the Damascus Covenant and Other Texts from Qumran." In *Legal Texts and Legal Issues: Proceedings of the Second Meeting of the International Organization for Qumran Studies, Cambridge 1995, Published in Honour of Joseph M. Baumgarten*, edited by M. Bernstein, Florentino García Martínez, and John Kampen, pp. 149–165. Leiden, 1997.

BILHA NITZAN

BIBLE. *See* Scriptures, *article on* Texts.

BIBLICAL CHRONOLOGY is the name given to a papyrus manuscript of twelve or thirteen preserved fragments written in a late Hasmonean–early Herodian formal script with but a few cursive traces (50–30 BC). Only one copy (J. Starcky, 1956) from Qumran Cave 4 has survived, Biblical Chronology (4Q559). The text is written in Hasmonean Aramaic but does contain one Hebraism (*mimits[rayin]*). Ciphers are used throughout the text to designate numbers.

The chronology of the manuscript begins with Adam and Noah (or Abraham?). The end of the chronology is lost. Fragments 1 to 3 (and perhaps 6) contain a brief outline of biblical history from Isaac to Aaron, using primarily the phrasing formulas of the biblical genealogies (*Gn*. 5.1–32, 11.10–32): "X person begot, at Y years of age, so and so." The outline starts with Isaac's marriage (at the age of 40; *Gn*. 25.20), his fatherhood (at the age of 60; *Gn*. 25.26), Abraham's admonition to his sons (Isaac's age being 65; cf. *Jub*. 20), Isaac's sending his son Jacob to Mesopotamia, Jacob's years in Canaan (69; *Jub*. 19.13, 27.19), and the years of service that he traded for the hands of both Leah and Rachel (14 years; *Gn*. 31.41). Fragment 3 includes information about Levi's fatherhood (at the age of 35; Greek *Testament of Levi* 11), Qahat's age (29), Amram's age, Aaron's departure from Egypt together with 11,536 members of his family (this number's significance deriving from the fact that it is equal to half of 23,000 + 36 ?; cf. *Nm*. 3.26; *1 Chr*. 23.13–14). Fragments 4, 5, and 7 contain a brief historical outline from the departure from Egypt until the time of the Judges in Israel, interconnected via the repeated use of the formula "X person + the years of said person's reign." This outline details the Israelites' journey of forty years in the desert, their arrival at the Jordan River, their staying at another spot for thirty-five years (it is impossible to tell where), their coming to Gilgal, Joshua's time at Timnat Serah (20 years; cf. *Jos*. 24.30; *Jgs*. 2.9), the lives of the rulers of Israel after Joshua's death: Cush-rishathaim (8 years; *Jgs*. 3.8), Othniel (40 years; *Jgs*. 3.9–11), Eglon (18 years; *Jgs*. 3.12–14), Ehud (80 years; *Jgs*. 3.16–30), Shamgar (*Jgs*. 3.31). Fragment 5 also details the period of the dominance of the Midianites (7 years; *Jgs*. 6.1–10), Gideon (40 years; *Jgs*. 8.28), Thola (23 years, *Jgs*. 10.1–2); Abimelech is omitted. Fragment 7 deals with Jabin's twenty years (*Jgs*. 4.2), followed by Deborah's forty years (*Jgs*. 4–16;

5.31) or Abdon's eight years (*Jgs*. 12.14), followed by forty years of Philistine domination (*Jgs*. 13.1).

As mentioned, Biblical Chronology quotes its chronology from the biblical tradition. An Aramaic Targum (cf. frg. 1.1 with *Gn*. 25.20; frg. 2.3 with *Gn*. 29.18–20) should probably not be presupposed as the literary base of the manuscripts even though there is an obvious dependence on a Hebrew Bible tradition (the Hebraism *mi-mits* [*rayin*], and the geographical terminology for Land of Israel *Yardena*ʾ and *Gilgela*ʾ), perhaps stemming from a branch of the proto-Septuagint (cf. *Cush-rishathaim* frgs. 4, 6 and Septuagint *Jgs*. 3.8–10). In addition to the biblical tradition, Biblical Chronology quotes from other works such as *Jubilees*, *Testaments of Levi*, *Amram*, *Qahat*, and so on. Fragments 4, 5, and 7 quote from *Judges* in a way that ignores the Deuteronomistic framework. Enemies and saviors of Israel stand side by side without any precise characterization. The missing Deuteronomistic element argues against any Hasidean-Essene origin for the work, but the fact that fragments 1, 2, and 3 concentrate on the genealogy of priestly families is possibly the result of their being written by sacerdotal groups. The text is likely the work of a scribe or a school of scribes from the second or first century BCE, at the earliest from the third century BCE, that pursued a specific interest in abstract summaries of Jewish history.

BIBLIOGRAPHY

Eisenman, R., and M. Wise. *The Dead Sea Scrolls Uncovered*, 16. Dorset, 1992.

García Martínez, F. *Dead Sea Scrolls Translated*. Leiden, 1994. See page 228.

Maier, J. *Die Qumran-Essener*. Die Texte 2. Munich, 1995. See page 737.

Nebe, G.W. "4Q559 Biblical Chronology." In *Zeitschrift für Althebraistik* 10 (1997), 85–88.

Reed, S. A., ed. *Dead Sea Scrolls Catalogue*. Atlanta, 1994.

Richter, H. P., ed. *A Preliminary Concordance*. Göttingen, 1988.

Starcky, J. *Revue biblique* 63 (1956), 66.

Tov, E., ed. *The Dead Sea Scrolls on Microfiche*. Leiden, 1993.

VanderKam, J. C. "Das chronologische Konzept des Jubiläenbuches." *Zeitschrift für die Alttestamentliche Wissenschaft* 107 (1995), 80–100.

Wise, M. O. "To Know the Times and the Seasons: A Study of the Aramaic Chronograph, 4Q559." *Journal for the Study of Pseudepigrapha* 15 (1997), 3–51.

G. WILHELM NEBE

BIBLIOTHÈQUE NATIONALE DE FRANCE.

Founded in 1368 by King Charles V, the Bibliothèque Royale became the Bibliothèque Nationale during the French Revolution in 1789; in 1994, upon its amalgamation with the Bibliothèque de France, it took the name of Bibliothèque Nationale de France.

In 1953, at the request of Roland de Vaux, director of the École Biblique et Archéologique Française in Jerusalem, the Bibliothèque Nationale de France acquired 377 fragments from Cave 1 at Qumran, where excavations were carried out in 1949. The entire collection was given the number 18674 and was placed in the Oriental Section of the Manuscripts Department. As a result of this purchase, the publication of the texts from Cave 1 was made possible; the edition of the biblical texts (1Q1–13) was prepared by Barthélemy and that of the nonbiblical texts (1Q14–70) was undertaken by J. T. Milik. Their work was published in 1955 as the first volume of the series Discoveries in the Judaean Desert (Oxford).

The Bibliothèque Nationale de France houses the following fragments: Genesis (1Q1), Exodus (1Q2), paleo-Leviticus (1Q3), Deuteronomy[a] (1Q4), Judges (1Q6), Samuel (1Q7), Pesher Micah (1Q14), Pesher Zephaniah (1Q15), Pesher Psalms (1Q16), Enoch Giants[b] (1Q24), apocryphal prophecy (1Q25), wisdom apocryphon (4Q Sapiential Work A[f]) (1Q26), liturgical texts? (1Q30–31), New Jerusalem (1Q32), hymnic compositions? (1Q38–40), and unclassified fragments (1Q50–56 and 63–68).

[*See also* Department of Antiquities of Jordan; Discoveries in the Judaean Desert; Museums and Collections; *and* Scrolls Research.]

BIBLIOGRAPHY

Barthélemy, D., and J. T. Milik, eds. *Qumran Cave I*. Discoveries in the Judaean Desert, 1. Oxford, 1955.

JACQUES BRIEND

BLESSINGS AND CURSES. Numerous blessings and curses appear in the Qumran corpus. The source of their power is the deity; hence, these benedictions and maledictions may be considered prayers. [*See* Psalms, Hymns, and Prayers.] Their stylistic forms and usage follow those of the biblical blessings and curses. However, they are used in the life of the Qumran community on a limited number of occasions and adapted in terms of content and liturgical form to express sectarian dualistic ideas.

The counterpoising of blessings and curses plays a central role in the life of the Qumran community in ceremonies and literary compositions. These demonstrate the contrast between the *yaḥad*, as the chosen seed of Israel loyal to the Law, and those who violate the Law. At the same time they express the dualistic ideology of the *yaḥad* concerning the struggle between light and darkness. Counterpoised blessings and curses occur in covenantal ceremonies and in various expressions of the ideas of covenant and reward found in other texts. In some cases, there are only blessings or only curses.

Covenantal Ceremonies and Literature. Since the discovery of the covenant treaties and law codes of the peoples of the ancient Near East, it has become clear that counterpoising blessings against curses serves regularly as a legal formula of covenantal obligation. Their role is to assure loyalty to a political or religious authority by serving as judicial or religious sanctions (Mendenhall, 1954). The biblical covenant formulary between the Lord of Israel and his people follows these treaties in either ceremonial or literary contexts (*Dt.* 27, *Lv.* 26, *Jos.* 24, *1 Sm.* 12.6–19, *2 Kgs.* 22.22–23.5, *Neh.* 9–10).

An annual ceremony held by the *yaḥad* essentially follows the biblical covenantal formulary of renewing the covenant with God. Thus, juxtaposed blessings and curses appear in this ceremony (Rule of the Community from Cave 1 [hereafter 1QRule of the Community] 1QS ii.1–18 [Rule of the Community[b] 4Q256 1–4, 4Q257 1.i, 5Q11 1.i–ii]; Curse 4Q280 [fragmentary], Berakhot[a–e] 4Q286–290). [*See* Rule of the Community.] Nevertheless, although the biblical covenant formulary was followed, the role of the blessings and curses was changed in these Qumran writings in accordance with the particular character of the *yaḥad* covenant. The renewal of the covenant obliged the *yaḥad* to keep the Law of Moses according to its sectarian interpretation. In adapting for itself the designation of *Jeremiah* 31.31, a "new covenant" (Damascus Document, CD vi.19; viii.21; xx.12), the *yaḥad* community regarded its covenant as the eschatological renewal of the covenant between God and Israel. [*See* Damascus Document.] However, it did not apply to all Israel but only to those who had atoned for their sins and committed themselves to the laws of this "new covenant" (1QS i.24–ii.1; CD xx.28–34). They were blessed, whereas those who rejected these laws remained cursed (CD xx.8–13; cf. 1QS ii.5–18 and parallels).

Moreover, the covenantal blessings and curses of Qumran were intended not only to assure the observance of the covenant on the part of those who had committed themselves to it (1QS ii.11–18, CD viii.1–2 [= xix.13–14] and parallels) but also to draw a distinction between those who had undertaken the *yaḥad* covenant—"all the men of God's lot who walk perfectly in all His ways"—and those who had not done so—"all the men of Belial's lot who walk in the boundaries of darkness" (1QS ii.1–9 [= 4Q256 3–4, 4Q257 1.i], CD vii.4–10, War Scroll 1QM xiii.12). Thus, one may assume that these counterpoised blessings and curses primarily symbolize the ceremonial distinction between the two antithetical lots, that of those faithful to the laws of God and that of those faithful to the laws of Belial (cf. 1QM xiii.9–12 [= War Scroll[e] 4Q495 2]). Even if the covenantal custom of reciting blessings and curses per se was derived from the Bible, its aim was altered in the Qumran texts in accordance with the deterministic-dualistic worldview of the *yaḥad*. [*See* Determinism; Dualism.]

The Juxtaposition of Blessings and Curses in a Covenant Formulary appears in the Qumran writings in several versions of the annual covenantal ceremony of the *yaḥad*, thereby reflecting its textual development. One may discern three basic patterns upon which the covenantal blessings and curses of Qumran are based: the priestly blessing of *Numbers* 6.24–26 (in 1QS ii.2–9 and 4Q280 2.2–4b); the covenantal curse of *Deuteronomy* 29.17–20 (in 1QS ii.11–17 and 4Q280 2.1); and the counterpoised blessings and curses of the dualistic authorities, God and Belial, and their lots, found in the War Scroll (1QM xiii.2–6), Berakhot[a] (4Q286 7.ii [= 4Q287 6]), curse (4Q280 2 [2b?] 4c–7a). [*See* War of the Sons of Light against the Sons of Darkness.]

The Rule of the Community. An entire formulary of the annual covenantal ceremony of the *yaḥad* appears in 1QRule of the Community (1QS i.16–ii.18). Based on the covenantal formulary of *Deuteronomy* 27, it has counterpoised blessings and curses (cf. *Sotah* 7.5). However, as *Deuteronomy* 27 lacks blessings, the blessings in 1QRule of the Community (1QS ii.2–4) are based on the biblical priestly blessing of *Numbers* 6.24–26, which also became the model for the counterpoised curse in the scroll (1QS ii.5–9 and parallels). The curse of *Deuteronomy* 29.17–20 became the model for additional curses in 1QRule of the Community (1QS ii.11–17).

The circumstances for the recitation of the priestly blessing are not specified in the Hebrew scriptures; there is no allusion there to its recitation in a covenantal ceremony. Hence, its recitation in such a ceremony, where it is used to express the idea of dualistic separation between the lots of good and evil, may be considered an innovation. Besides the possibility that the blessing of *Numbers* 6.24–26 was chosen in order to assign the priests who recite it (1QS ii.1) a priestly blessing based on the Torah (cf. Berakhot 11Q14 1–2 [= War Rule 4Q285 1]), there may be an additional reason for this ordinance. [*See* Berakhot.] According to *Ben Sira* 50.19b–20 and the Mishnah (*Tam.* 5.1, 7.2; *Taʿan.* 4.1), it was customary to recite the priestly blessing following the sacrificial service, a custom based on *Leviticus* 9.22. As the *yaḥad* did not participate in the sacrificial service, which atoned for the sins of Israel but made atonement "for iniquitous guilt" by means of prayer (1QS ix.4–9; CD xi.18–21), one may assume that the confession that preceded the priestly blessing in the covenantal ceremony (1QS i.22–ii.1) of 1QRule of the Community was considered an act of repentance, by means of which those who entered the covenant were made deserving of the priestly blessing. To quote the words of 1QRule of the Community (1QS iii.11–12) addressed to those entering the covenant of the *yaḥad*: "Then he will be accepted by an agreeable atonement before God, and it shall be unto him a covenant of everlasting community."

As the biblical priestly blessing of *Numbers* 6.24–26 is not a covenantal blessing and there is no corresponding curse in the Bible, its adaptation into the covenantal formulary of the *yaḥad* required literary creativity. The blessing of *Numbers* 6.24–26 is retained in 1QRule of the Community (1QS ii.2–4) in its entirety and in its original order, with the exception of God's name, which is not used because of its sacredness. However, certain homiletical additions are attached to the verbs to indicate their desired benefit. These additions place the homiletical contents into the pattern of the biblical priestly blessing, suitable to the worldview of the *yaḥad*, as follows:

May He bless you with every good
And keep you from every evil;

May He enlighten your heart with immortal wisdom
and favor you with eternal knowledge;

May He lift up His merciful countenance upon you
for eternal peace.

The curse in 1QRule of the Community (1QS ii.5–9) is formulated with greater detail and greater freedom than the corresponding blessing, with several of its expressions being recited in parallel sentences. At the beginning of each sentence there is a verb of malediction, opposed to the verb of felicitation at the beginning of the corresponding sentence in the blessing; at the end there are words contrasting with the exegetical additions found in the corresponding blessings.

Cursed be you because of all your guilty deeds.
May God give you up to terror through all those who breathe vengeance;
May He visit upon you destruction through all those who take revenge.

Cursed be you without mercy for your deeds of darkness.
Damned be you in everlasting murky fire.
May God not be merciful unto you when you call.
May He not forgive by wiping out your iniquity.

May He lift up His angry countenance to wreak His vengeance upon you.
May there be no peace for you at the mouth of any intercessors.

The opposition between the blessings and the curses is characteristic of the dualistic contrasts applied by God's edict to both the deeds of the opposed lots and to their recompense. In the first pair the opposition is of good against evil; in the second, light against darkness; in the third pair the opposition is expressed in terms of an eternity of grace and peace over and against the denial of peace.

The additional curse of 1QRule of the Community (1QS ii.11–18) is directed against one who enters the covenant of the community insincerely. It imposes upon him the curse of *Deuteronomy* 29.18–20, directed against a man or woman of Israel who intentionally breaks the covenant. Such a member is cursed with the words "may God set him apart for calamity, that he may be cut off from all the Sons of Light" (1QS ii.16), and "may he put his lot among those who are cursed forever" (1QS ii.17), namely, he is considered to be cursed as one of those of Belial's lot.

Curse. The content suggests that the text Curse 4Q280 belongs to the annual covenantal ceremony as well. However, the extant fragments consist only of covenantal curses. Fragments 1 and 2, lines 1 and 7b, reflect the basic order of the last part of the curses of 1QRule of the Community (1QS ii.15–17, 25–26), dealing with a member of the *yaḥad* who has intentionally broken its covenantal laws. But this order is interrupted in lines 2–7a with an additional series of curses directed to Melchiresha', the leader of wickedness, and his lot.

The curse of Melchiresha' and his lot is arranged in two parts, based on two different patterns. In the first part (4Q280 2.2–4b), Melchiresha' himself is cursed with some of the imprecations directed in 1QRule of the Community (1QS ii.5–9) to the men of the lot of Belial, but in a shorter version, without the parallel bicolon found in 1QRule of the Community (1QS ii.5–9). In the second part (4Q280 2.4c–7a), Melchiresha' and his followers ("his lot") are cursed according to the pattern of the War Scroll (1QM xiii.2–6) and Berakhot[a–e] (see below). Nevertheless, this series as a whole is written consistently in one style, applying directly to the leader Melchiresha' and his lot, as follows:

(2) [*Cur*]sed be you Melchiresha' in all the sc[*hemes of your guilty inclination*].

[*May*] God [give you up] (3) to terror at the hand of avengers of vengeance.
May God not be merciful unto you when you call (on Him).
[May He lift up His angry face] (4) upon you for a curse.
May there be no peace for you at the mouth of any intercesso[*rs*].

[Cursed be you] (5) with no remnant and damned be you with no escape.
And cursed be those who execu[te their wicked schemes] (6) and those who confirm your purposes in their hearts, by plotting evil against the covenant of God [and. . . (7) against the word]s of all seers of [His] truth.

In light of the close relationship between the Curse scroll and 1QRule of the Community (1QS ii) on the one hand, and the partial similarity of Curse, 4Q280 2 4c–7a, to a curse in the Berakhot texts on the other (see below), the question of the origin of these curses must be raised. Considering the undeveloped liturgical form of the covenantal ceremony in the Curse scroll, in contrast to that of 1QRule of the Community (1QS ii) where rubrics for those who recite the blessings and the curses and the Amen responses are written systematically throughout the ceremony, one may assume that the Curse scroll represents an earlier stage of the covenantal ceremony. This conclusion may also be deduced from the fact that the Curse scroll, like the Rule scroll (5Q13) and the Rule of the Community from Cave 5 at Qumran (hereafter, 5QRule of the Community 5Q11), were all written by the same scribe in a "rustic semiformal hand" of the middle of the first century BC (Milik, 1972, p. 129) and may be related to "the evolution of compositions into what was eventually called the *Rule of the Community*" (Charlesworth, 1994, p. 105). If this assumption is correct, one may suggest that the editor of the Rule of the Community found the curse of Melchiresha' inappropriate to a covenantal ceremony concerned with human beings alone, unless it was ascribed to "the men of the lot of Belial."

Purification Rules B[a]. This fragmentary text (4Q275) contains a covenantal ceremony. It includes the procedure of cursing a member of the *yaḥad* in the presence of the elders with a priest [?] and the overseer (frg. 1). The curse probably referred to a member of the *yaḥad* who did not purify himself according to the purification laws of the group, whereas the blessed ones are those who keep the Law (frg. 2). The contrast between the curse and the blessing is apparent in their reference to the inheritance (*naḥalah*) granted by God to each person. The sinner is cursed by being expelled "from his inheritance forever" (4Q275 1.5), parallel to the curse "may he be cut off from the midst of all the sons of light" (1QS ii.16, 4Q280 2.1), whereas those faithful to the Law are blessed that "They will inherit in their inheritance" (4Q275 2.1–2; cf. CD i.7–8; Pesher Psalms[a] 4Q171 ii.4–5, 8–11). *Naḥalah* ("inheritance"), like its parallel *goral* ("lot"; cf. *Nm.* 26.56, *Jos.* 17.14), is used here metaphorically for the predestination of each person (see 1QS 4.16, 4.24). [*See* Pesher Psalms.]

Berakhot[a–e]. A specific example of the dualistic distinction between the lot of God and that of Belial appears in the covenantal ceremony of Berakhot[a–e] (4Q286–290). The blessings and curses of this text do not play the role of direct religious sanctions and do not even apply to those who do or do not enter the covenant. The blessings, to be recited by all the heavenly and earthly creatures faithful to the laws of Creation and by the covenanters faithful to the Law, praise God directly (4Q286 1–7.i and 4Q287 1–5), whereas the curses, to be recited by the "Council of the Community," apply to Belial and his lot, as maledictions for their "hostile schemes" and "evil purpose" (4Q286 7.ii = 4Q287 6). Thus, the dualistic distinction between the two antithetical authorities, that of God and of Belial, became the main focus of these counterpoised blessings and curses. [*See* Demons.] In this respect, the ceremonial blessings and curses of Berakhot[a–e] may be considered as a medium in the dualistic struggle between God and Belial, light and darkness, justice and evil, as in the War Scroll (1QM xiii.1–6) and Songs of the Sage[b] (4Q511 52–59).

Noteworthy is the absence in Berakhot [a–e] of blessings directly rewarding those who are faithful to the covenant of God. However, in the last section of the blessings of God (4Q286 7.i and 4Q287 5), those faithful to the covenant of God are described as "those who become clo[se]" to God, and probably "the offspring" of "the families of the earth to become [blessed)" (cf. *Is.* 61.9). In Berakhot[a] (4Q286 7.i.2–3) they are defined as "the elect" and "men who have knowledge of psalms." In these characteristics they are similar to the angels," [the c]ouncil of *elim* of purification . . . those who have eternal knowledge to bless and praise" the name of God (4Q286 7.i.6–7). Thus, considering their superior virtues, their reward is certain. The opposite description of those faithful to the lot of Belial in the following section of the curses (4Q286 7.ii [= 4Q287 6) reflects the antithetical recompense that will come to those unfaithful to the covenant of God. Thus, the dualistic distinction between the two opposite lots, as defined according to their deeds and reward, plays the same role as direct blessings and curses.

In light of another text representing the covenant formulary of Qumran, the absence of direct blessings and curses is not unique. In Damascus Document (4Q266 11.11–14), the priest recites a blessing to God while expelling the willful sinner from the community, saying:

> You chose the descendants of our fathers
> and gave them your truthful regulations
> and your holy precepts,
> so that man could carry them out and live,
> and you established frontiers for us,
> and you curse those who cross them
> and we are the people of your ransom
> and the flock of your pasture.
> You curse those who cross them
> but we have raised ourselves up.

Blessings and Curses in Dualistic Struggles. The transformation of the covenantal formula into a theology of dualistic struggle between the forces of light and darkness (i.e., good and evil) permits the use of counterpoised blessings and curses in other contexts as well. Thus, blessings and curses are used in the eschatological war (1QM xiii.1–6) and in magical poetry (4Q511 52–59).

***Songs of the Sage*[b].** Songs of the Sage[a] and [b] (4Q510–511) offer magical defense for the Children of Light against the injuries caused by the spirits and demons sent by Belial. Songs of the Sage[b] (4Q511 52–59) begins with the praise of God who brings blessing to those who fear him and curses to the wicked spirits. [*See* Songs of the Sage.] The words of curse and blessing (4Q511 11.4–6) are as follows:

> for from You comes judgment . . . [the curs]ed ones,
> and from you is the foundation of all those who fear you . . .
> [the ble]ssed one

These lines express God's dualistic edict to the two "lots." It follows that these curses and the corresponding blessings serve as a kind of magical weapon in the daily struggle of the children of light against the spirits of Belial in the era of the rule of wickedness. It is as if there were a certain magical power in the words said by a righteous sage.

War Scroll. This text (1QM xiii.2–6), which became a pattern for the dualistic distinction in Berakhot[a–e] and Curse, is to be recited in the eschatological war between the Children of Light and the Children of Darkness. It seems that the blessing of God in his holy plan, and with him all who serve him in justice, and the curse of Belial with his malicious plan, and together with him all his spirits whose deeds are full of filthy uncleanness, are used here either as a magical weapon against the hosts of darkness or as a symbol of the distinctive eschatological rewards decreed for the two opposite lots.

Blessings on Solemn Ceremonial Occasions. Blessings alone, without curses, are recited on solemn ceremonial occasions (e.g., Rule of the Blessings 1Q28b; War Rule 4Q285 1 [= Berakhot 11Q14 1–2]). Curses alone appear in magical poetry directed against evil spirits (4Q511 3.5, 11.3; Apocryphal Psalms[a] 11Q11 4.6ff., 3.4ff.). The occasions for reciting these magical texts are not clear. [*See* Magic and Magical Texts.]

War Rule. The blessing of the War Rule (4Q285 1 [= 11Q14]) occurs in this text about the eschatological victory of the Children of Light over the *Kittim*. [*See* Kittim.] The blessing, possibly recited by a priest, opens with praise of the God of Israel, by whose power the people of Israel are blessed. The blessings directed to Israel are based upon two of the priestly blessings (*Nm.* 6.24–25) and the elimination of the covenantal curses written in the Bible. The idea of the blessings, as deduced from the literary structure of its content, is "May God Most High bless you" with good wishes of heaven and earth (see 11Q14 1–2.6–10a [= 4Q285 3–7a]) "and make His face shine upon you" in removing all the curses and imprecations which come at the time of hiding of the face (see 11Q14 1–2.6, 10b–14 [= 4Q285 1.3, 7b–11]). While focusing on the content of the blessing itself, the restorative aspect of possessing the land of Israel, as based on the Deuteronomic covenant, is noticeable. Yet this aspect of the blessings is illuminated in light of the prophetic blessings of *Ezekiel* 34.25–29 and 36.29–30, which intended to eliminate the covenantal curses. In this way the blessings of the War Rule are integrated into the wider context of the War Rule, which deals with the fulfillment of the prophetic eschatological plan of Ezekiel and Isaiah.

Rule of the Blessing. This text (1Q28b) consists of blessings to all the members of the community, according to their status; these were to be recited at a solemn ceremony. There is no explicit reference to the particular occasion of the blessings. Nevertheless, as all the blessed ones are thought to remain constant to their holy covenant with God (1Q28b i.2, ii.25, iii.23–24, v.23), one may suggest that the solemn occasion is connected with a covenantal ceremony or perhaps an eschatological ceremony. Furthermore, the blessing of the Prince of the Congregation deals with an eschatological figure (1Q28b v.20–29), and the fact that no curses are mentioned also points to an eschatological time. The blessings are based mainly on the biblical priestly blessing (*Nm.* 6.24–26) and other biblical writings.

Blessings or Curses upon Individuals. Blessings or curses upon individuals hardly appear at all in the Qumran writings. This category is found only in the Testimonia (4Q175 21ff. [= *Psalms of Joshua*[b] 4Q379 22.ii.7ff.]). Here the curse of *Joshua* 6.26 is interpreted as applying to figures from the Second Temple period, one who is symbolically named "a man accursed, the one of Belial" and two others who "may be instruments of violence." Statements about the predestination of individuals, recorded in the *pesharim* and other sectarian writings (e.g., Pesher Psalms[a] 4Q171; Pesher Habakkuk 1QpHab viii.1–3, 13–15; x.3–5; CD i.16–18, viii.1–2), are not intended as curses or blessings but as presaging the recompense of particular figures. [*See* Pesher Habakkuk.]

Undefined Curses and Blessings. The Curses scroll (5Q141) includes curses directed alternatively to an individual person and to the group. There is no sectarian terminology in the preserved text, only biblical language. The content and style of the curses seem to be influenced by the covenantal curses of *Leviticus* 26, written in the second person plural, and *Deuteronomy* 28, written in the second person singular.

Only five small fragments of Benediction from Cave 6

at Qumran (6Q16) are preserved. In the text, copied in the first century CE, one may discern blessings (see frg. 3) and curses (see frg. 2), possibly referring to a sectarian covenant.

Stylistic Traits. Declarative forms using the passive participle, *barukh* ("blessed be") and *arur* ("cursed be") or *zaʿum* ("be execrated"), appear in Qumran writings in both the singular and plural. "Blessed be" is directed to God, denoting his praise, while the plural, *berukhim*, is directed to those who fear Him, denoting their reward. By contrast, *ʿarur* and *ʿarurim*, or *ʿarur ve-zaʿum* and *ʿarurim u-zeʿu-mim*, are directed to the leader of wickedness (Belial in his various names) and/or his lot, denoting their punishment (1QM xiii.1–6, 1QS ii.5–11 [= 4Q256 3–4, 4Q257 1.i.1–6], 4Q511 52–59.4–6, 4Q286–290, 4Q280, 4Q285 1 [= 11Q14 1–2], Purification Rules B^a 4Q275).

The one to be blessed or cursed is addressed primarily in the second person, in more or less fixed forms. Extensive use is made of the imperfect (jussive) form, as in: "may He bless you . . . and may He protect you . . ." (1QS ii.2–3); "may God give you up . . . may He visit upon you . . ." (1QS ii.5–6 [= 4Q257 1.i.2f., 5Q11 1.3); "may there be no peace for you" (1QS ii.9). In some cases the third person is used, such as "may God set him apart for calamity" (1QS ii.16, 4Q280 1 [cf. *Dt.* 29.20], 4Q275 1.5). Negation may be expressed by *ein* as in "there is no bereavement in your land nor any illness" (11Q14 1–2.10–11 [= 4Q285 1.7]; cf. *Lv.* 26.6, 26.17, etc.). The use of the imperative is quite rare. Such phrases as *ashre* ("blessed is/are" or "happy is/are") and *oy* ("woe") appear in wisdom writings (Wisdom Text with Beatitudes 4Q525 3.ii.1, sapiental work 4Q185 1–2.ii.8, 1–2.ii.13) and poetical works (Apocryphal Lamentations A 4Q179 1.i.4, 1.ii.1) in indirect blessings or curses.

BIBLIOGRAPHY

Baltzer, Klaus. *The Covenant Formulary in Old Testament, Jewish, and Early Christian Writings*. Translated from the German original (1957, 1964) by David E. Green. Oxford, 1971.

Charlesworth, James H. *Rule of the Community and Related Documents*. The Dead Sea Scrolls I: Hebrew, Aramaic, and Greek Texts with English Translations. Tübingen and Louisville, 1994. See page 105.

Kobelski, Paul J. *Melchizedek and Melchirešaʿ*. Catholic Biblical Quarterly Monograph Series, 10. Washington, D.C., 1981.

Licht, Jacob. *Megillat ha-Serakhim (The Rule Scroll)*. Jerusalem, 1965. See pp. 54, 64, 70–72, 99, 102, and 273–289.

Mendenhall, G. E. "Ancient Oriental and Biblical Law." *Biblical Archaeologist* 17 (1954), 26–46. Also in *Law and Covenant in Israel and the Ancient Near East*, Pittsburgh, Penn., 1955. See pages 54–76.

Milik, Józef T. "Milkî-ṣedeq et Milkî-rešaʿ dans les anciens écrits juifs et chrétiens." *Journal of Jewish Studies* 23 (1972), 95–144. See also pp. 126–137 Pls. I–II.

Newsom, Carol. "The Psalms of Joshua from Qumran Cave 4." *Journal of Jewish Studies* 39 (1988), 56–73. See pp. 68–73.

Nitzan, Bilhah. "Benedictions and Instructions from Qumran for the Eschatological Community (11QBer, 4Q285)." *Revue de Qumrân* 16/61 (1993), 77–90.

Nitzan, Bilhah. *Qumran Prayer and Religious Poetry*. Studies on the Texts of the Desert of Judah, 12. Translated by Jonathan Chipman. Leiden and New York, 1994. See pages 119–171.

Weinfeld, Moshe. "The Loyalty Oath in the Ancient Near East." *Ugarit Forschungen* 8 (1976), 379–414.

BILHA NITZAN

BOETHUSIANS. The Boethusians were a sect of Jews who thrived in the late Second Temple period and who differed greatly from the Pharisees (*Perushim*) or Sages of that era in their religious outlook and practices. They are known to us only from rabbinic literature and are referred to there as the *Baytusim*. These sources often cite the Boethusians in close proximity to the Sadducees (*Tseduqim*), and parallel rabbinic passages often interchange the names of the two sects. [*See* Sadducees.] As a result, the Boethusians have frequently been viewed as closely aligned with the Sadducees, and it is sometimes difficult to isolate the views of the Boethusians from those of the Sadducees.

Scholars of the last two centuries have generally assigned the origins of the Boethusians to the Herodian era (37–4 BCE). Josephus reports that after Herod decided to marry Mariamme (25–24 BCE), he promptly elevated his father-in-law, Simon ben Boethus, to fill the post of high priest. This appointment effectively inaugurated the Boethusians as a sect. This theory, however, is questionable because rabbinic sources never even intimate that there was a connection between the origins of the sect and the Herodian Simon. In fact, *Avot de-Rabbi Natan*, a late rabbinic source, traces the origins of both the Boethusians and Sadducees to students several generations after the tenure of Antigonus of Sokho. Since Antigonus was an early sage who presided during the first quarter of the second century BCE, the origins of the Boethusians would probably be traced—by *Avot de-Rabbi Natan*—to the reign of either John Hyrcanus (135/4–104 BCE) or Alexander Jannaeus (103–76 BCE). It is usually assumed that the Boethusians ceased to exist as a viable group after the destruction of the Second Temple (70 CE). One rabbinic source, however, records a discussion between a Boethusian and a rabbi of the mid-second century CE.

The Boethusians are usually depicted by historians as rich aristocratic priests who wielded considerable power in opposing the Pharisees. While the suggestion that they were wealthy finds little corroboration in rabbinic literature, the claim that they were dominated by priests appears rather certain. Indeed, several rabbinic sources portray a Boethusian in the position of high priest while others indicate serious involvement on the part of the sect with Temple-related matters.

The opponents of the Boethusians are most commonly identified simply as the *Sages*. Only one passage labels their opponents *Pharisees*. Although the Boethusians were always subdued by the Sages, they are viewed as having presented a serious threat to their authority. Indeed, the defeat of the Boethusians is sometimes connected to the commemoration of Second Temple semi-festival days.

The views of the Boethusians are recorded with respect to a wide array of issues. In the only theological dispute attributed to the Boethusians, they are portrayed as having denied the rabbinic doctrine of the resurrection of the dead. This accounted for their departure from the Sages. In one passage, the Boethusians apply a literalist approach to three biblical verses. These interpretations were rejected by the Sages because of their lack of adherence to the teachings of the Oral Law.

In three Temple-related matters, the disagreements and activities of the Boethusians are related. One of a set of parallel rabbinic passages relates that on Yom Kippur, a Boethusian high priest offered the incense outside of the Holy of Holies. This ran counter to the directives of the Pharisaic Sages. His action even drew rebuke from his Boethusian father. The Boethusians attempted to thwart the willow branch ceremony on the Festival of Tabernacles because they did not share the view of the Sages that the ceremony may be performed even on the Sabbath. Their plot was uncovered by the common people. A Boethusian priest is also accused of having poured water on his feet on that same festival in what seems to have been an attempt to mock the Sages' insistence on pouring the water libation on the altar. He was pelted with citrons by the people assembled in the Temple.

Two court procedures separated the Boethusians and their opponents. One of a set of parallel passages presents the Boethusians as having argued that the refuted (*zomemim*) witnesses may be killed by the court even after the adjudged had been executed. Another passage indicates that the Boethusians—in opposition to the Pharisees—argued on logical grounds that a daughter may inherit from her father. In both cases, their arguments were rejected.

The Boethusians are also presented as having disagreed with the Sages with regard to the determination of certain calendar dates: The reaping of the *ʿomer* was performed amidst great pomp and ceremony on the second day of Passover. This was done in accordance with the Sages' understanding that the biblical requirement to reap the *ʿomer* "on the morrow of the Sabbath" refers to the day after the festival day of Passover. The public ceremony was thereby aimed at refuting the claims of the Boethusians that the ceremony should not be done "at the conclusion of the festival." In two separate contexts, the Boethusians are presented as having insisted that the Festival of Pentecost must always fall on a Sunday. This was in opposition to the view of the Sages that Pentecost occurs fifty days from the second day of Passover, regardless of the day of the week.

The standard scholarly view is that the sectarians at Qumran employed the same calendar as that which was used by the authors of *Jubilees* and *1 Enoch*. This calendar consisted of 364 days, divided over twelve months, with eight months possessing 30 days and four months possessing 31 days. Each quarter of the year would always begin on a Wednesday. Likewise, Passover, falling on the fifteenth day of the first month, would also occur on a Wednesday. Consequently, if "on the morrow of the Sabbath" is taken as a reference to the first Sunday following Passover (that is, the day of the Paschal sacrifice and the seven-day festival of unleavened bread, which immediately follows it), Pentecost would consistently fall on the fifteenth day of the third month. Some scholars have argued that the calendar employed by the Boethusians was identical to that which was employed by *Jubilees*, *1 Enoch*, and the Dead Sea Scrolls. Others have rejected this equation, instead arguing that the Boethusians placed the reaping of the *ʿomer* on the Sunday of Passover itself.

Commentators and historians have frequently attempted to reveal some unifying theme among the views of the Boethusians. Consequently, they have often portrayed the Boethusians as having taken a literalist approach to the Bible and as having rejected the entire corpus of the Oral Law. The contention that the Boethusians took a consistently literalist approach, however, is difficult to sustain. The Boethusians offer scriptural proof in only three rabbinic passages. Moreover, in several cases, the view of the Boethusians is not more literal than that of their opponents. In point of fact, even some of the clearly literalist understandings of the Boethusians match tannaitic opinions elsewhere in rabbinic literature. Although the Boethusians clearly rejected the binding nature of the Oral Law in some circumstances, it remains unclear to what extent they went in their rejection. In all probability, they rejected laws passed down as oral traditions with absolutely no support in the biblical text. Some historians have offered sociological motives to explain the differences between the Boethusians and their opponents, but these remain, on the whole, unproven.

Rabbinic sources never equate the Boethusians with any other group. Nevertheless, the prevalent opinion—and that which has the clearest support in the sources—finds that the Boethusians had a close affinity with the Sadducees. Several scholars have also adopted the equation between the rabbinic Boethusians and the Herodians of the New Testament.

Some historians, however, have argued that the Boethusians are to be equated with the Essenes. These arguments have been bolstered primarily by the similarity between the term used for the Boethusians in rabbinic literature (*"Bet Sin"* or *"Betsin"*) and *"Esse'im"* (the presumed Hebrew that would lie behind *Essenoi* and *Essaioi* of Josephus and other Greek texts). [*See* Essenes.] In order to resolve the differences in practices and beliefs between the Essenes of Josephus and the Boethusians of rabbinic literature, it has been posited that there existed two groups of Boethusians: one group (described by Josephus) that lived in the outlying villages and another (cited in rabbinic literature) that moved to Jerusalem, came into conflict with the Pharisees, and altered its way of thinking and way of life.

The discovery and interpretation of the Dead Sea Scrolls has introduced a new dimension to the task of identifying the Boethusians. The dominant position has been that the Qumran sect is identical to the Essenes. Hence, shortly after the publication of the first scrolls, scholars began to assert that the Boethusians were one and the same with the Qumran sect.

More recently, some scholars have again advanced this argument on the basis of the contents of Miqtsat Maʿasei ha-Torah. On the one hand, the Pharisaic-type of laws that the author rejects and the Sadducean-type of laws that he advocates point to the decidedly Sadducean character of the scroll. On the other hand, the Essenes are presumed to be the composers of the Qumran scrolls. For these scholars, therefore, the Boethusians of rabbinic literature, followers of Sadducean traditions, were actually the Essenes of nonrabbinic literature, the composers of the Qumran scrolls.

Some scholars have resisted identifying the Boethusians with any of the contemporary sects, instead arguing that they formed a distinct group insistent on a literalist interpretation of the Bible and rejection of the Oral Law.

BIBLIOGRAPHY

Baumgarten, Joseph M. *Studies in Qumran Law*. Leiden, 1977. Some of the reprinted articles relate to the Qumran calendar and have a bearing on the Boethusian calendar.

Finkelstein, Louis. *The Pharisees: The Sociological Background of Their Faith*. 2 vols. Philadelphia, 1962. Thorough study of rabbinic sources related to the Pharisees and Sadducees with a decidedly sociological perspective.

Ginzberg, Louis. "Boethusians." *Jewish Encyclopedia*, vol. 3 (1909), 284–285. Overview article.

Grintz, J. M. "Anshe Ha-Yaḥad, Esseim, Bet [Es]sene." *Sinai* 32 (1953), 36–43. Early article (in Hebrew) linking the Boethusians to the Essenes and the Dead Sea Sect.

Herr, Moshe David. "Mi Hayu ha-Baytusim?" In *Proceedings of the Seventh World Congress of Jewish Studies: Studies in the Talmud, Halacha and Midrash*, pp. 1–20. Jerusalem, 1981. Hebrew article analyzing the major issues in the study of the Boethusians.

Jaubert, Annie. *La Date de la Cène*. Paris, 1957. Development of the now standard view regarding the calendar employed by the authors of *Jubilees* and *1 Enoch*. English translation: *The Date of the Last Supper*. Staten Island, 1965.

Lauterbach, Jacob Z. *Rabbinic Essays*. Cincinnati, 1951. Discussions of some controversies between the Pharisees and Sadducees, particularly surrounding the incense offering on Yom Kippur.

Le Moyne, J. *Les Sadducéens*. Paris, 1972. Thorough study of rabbinic and nonrabbinic sources regarding the Sadducees.

Qimron, Elisha, and John Strugnell. *Qumran Cave 4: Miqṣat Maʿaśe Ha-Torah*. Discoveries in the Judaean Desert, 10. Oxford, 1994. Sussman's groundbreaking essay identifying the Qumran sect with the Sadducees and the Boethusians appears here in English.

Saldarini, A. J. *Scholastic Rabbinism: A Literary Study of the Fathers According to Rabbi Nathan*. California, 1982. Useful for study of the origins of the Sadducees and Boethusians.

Schiffman, L. H. "The New Halakhic Letter (4QMMT) and the Origins of the Dead Sea Sect." *Biblical Archaeologist* 55 (1990), 64–73.

Schürer, Emil. *The History of the Jewish People in the Age of Jesus Christ (175 BCE–135 CE)*. Edited by G. Vermes and F. Millar, in collaboration with P. Vermes and M. Black. 3 vols. Edinburgh, 1973–1987. Classic work on ancient Jewish history. Sections on the Pharisees, Sadducees, and early rabbinic Sages.

Zeitlin, Solomon. *Studies in the Early History of Judaism*. 4 vols. New York, 1974. Several chapters deal with the Pharisees and Sadducees. Includes also short synopses of all the debates between the Sadducees and Pharisees.

RAYMOND HARARI

BONE ARTIFACTS. In the Judean Desert sites dating to the Roman period, artifacts fashioned out of bone are rare. Most of these objects were for personal or domestic use. The richest and largest collection of bone and ivory artifacts was found at Masada, inside the rooms of the casemate wall surrounding the hilltop palace-fortress site originally constructed by King Herod. These objects were dated by Yigael Yadin to the period of the First Jewish Revolt (66–70 CE) when these casemate rooms served as dwellings for Jewish rebels who reinhabited Masada following the fall of Jerusalem. The artifacts included domestic or cosmetic objects such as spindle-whorl and stick, a flat spatula, dice, a small shallow circular spoon, and a larger spoon richly decorated with an incised rosette pattern. These personal belongings were most likely the property of women and represent the last days of Jewish resistance at Masada against the Roman army.

In the Murabbaʿat caves, several bone objects were recovered by archaeologists following the illicit excavations of the cave by local bedouin. Although the archaeological context was largely disturbed, Roland de Vaux assigned them to the Roman period. Owing to the personal nature of the artifacts, it is likely that they belonged to refugees who occupied the caves during the Bar Kokhba Revolt (c.132–135 CE), and who were the owners of the documents from these caves. The finds included spoons (one incomplete example was a shallow bowl of a spoon decorated with an incised rosette pattern and concentric circles) and two circular objects termed "buttons" by de Vaux, one measuring approximately 4 centimeters in diameter and the other measuring 2 centimeters in diameter with a hole drilled through the center. The smaller button was decorated with several circles and triangles, while the larger one was richly ornamented with geometric designs consisting of incised circles, triangles, and diagonal lines. A bone blade with rounded edges served an unknown function. Bone dice, similar to those from Masada and Jason's Tomb in Jerusalem, complete the bone artifact assemblage.

Contemporary with the finds from the Murabbaʿat caves, a few bone objects were found in the Cave of the Letters. A shallow bowl of polished horn, part of a spoon, was found in the "Letters-skin" and was probably used for cosmetics. A second bone object from this cave was a handle formed out of polished bone, which was decorated with incised crisscross bands filled with an unidentified black substance. A similar decoration is found on a wood stylus from the Murabbaʿat caves.

Bone artifacts were especially rare in tombs from this period. In the Jericho Jewish cemetery dating to the Second Temple period, a bone spatula, resembling one from Masada, was found in a coffin tomb dating to the first century BCE. This object may have been used as a weaving tool.

At ʿEin-Gedi, in a burial cave situated in Naḥal David, one of the coffins was decorated with bone and wood inlays. These coffins are contemporary with those found in the Jericho cemetery and date to the first century BCE. The patterns formed by the inlays included circle, rosette, and pomegranate motifs, all typical designs of the Second Temple period.

BIBLIOGRAPHY

Aharoni, Yohanan, Nahman Avigad, Pessah Bar-Adon, and Yigael Yadin. "The Expedition to the Judean Desert, 1961." *Israel Exploration Journal* 12 (1962), especially pp. 181–183. A description of the artifacts found during the 1961 expedition to the Judean Desert, including a description of the wooden inlaid coffin from Naḥal David.

de Vaux, Roland. "Archéologie." In *Les Grottes de Murabbaʿat*, edited by P. Benoit, J. T. Milik, and R. de Vaux, pp. 29–48. Discoveries in the Judaean Desert, 2. Oxford, 1961. A report on the salvage excavations of the caves in Wadi Murabbaʿat. These caves had been previously cleared by illicit excavations.

Hachlili, Rachel, and Ann E. Killebrew. *Jericho: The Jewish Cemetery of the Second Temple Period*. Jerusalem, in press. A detailed final report of the salvage excavations in the Roman period Jewish cemetery at Jericho.

Yadin, Yigael. "The Wooden and Bone Objects." In *The Finds from the Bar Kokhba Period in the Cave of the Letters*, pp. 123–135. Jerusalem, 1963. Detailed descriptions of wooden and bone objects found during the second series of excavation in the Cave of the Letters.

Yadin, Yigael. *Masada: Herod's Fortress and the Zealots' Last Stand*. London, 1966. A popular report of the Masada excavations including a photograph of the bone artifacts.

ANN E. KILLEBREW

BRANCH OF DAVID. *See* Messiahs.

BUQEIA. The Hyrcania Valley, Buqeia, is a geological syncline at the northeastern edge of the Judean Desert above the fault escarpment dominating Qumran and ʿEin-Feshkha. It is approximately 9 kilometers long, extending from north-northeast to south-southwest, between Naḥal Og (Wadi Mukellik) and Naḥal Kidron. [*See* Wadi en-Nar.] It is 2 to 4 kilometers wide, its central zone being drained by two tributaries of Naḥal Qumran. Overlooking the valley on the west is the Hasmonean/Herodian fortress of Hyrcania (Khirbet Mird). The elevation of the valley is between 0 and 100 meters above sea level. It is an arid zone, with annual precipitation of 100 to 150 millimeters. Much of the valley is covered by local shallow and saline soil, unsuitable for agriculture, but over the wadi beds alluvial deposits have aggraded, forming chalky-marly soils that were deep enough and full of enough clay to store up winter rain and flood water to permit desert agriculture. The main north-south road was the shortest path of communication between Jericho and Hebron. The transversal roads lead from Jerusalem and Bethlehem to Khirbet Qumran and Khirbet Mazin via two steep ascents.

First visited by E. W. G. Masterman at the beginning of the century, the Buqeia ruins were explored by Frank Moore Cross and Józef T. Milik in 1954 and 1955, by Pessah Bar Adon in 1968, by Lawrence Stager in 1972, and by Joseph Patrich in 1981–1982.

There is a consensus about the identification of Buqeia with the biblical Valley of Achor (*Jos.* 7.24, 7.26, 15.7; *Hos.* 2.17; *Is.* 65.10). But according to a fourth-century Christian tradition the valley was located to the north of Jericho (Wadi Nuweiʾimeh). The ruins in the Valley of Achor are mentioned in the Copper Scroll (3Q15 i.1) (see also 3Q15 iv.6, where two tamarisk trees in the Valley of Achor are mentioned); opinions vary as to whether the reference is to the biblical valley or whether the later Christian tradition already had its roots in the Second Temple period (see Milik's commentary to the scroll; compare with Allegro's commentary).

The settlement in the valley flourished in the seventh century BCE (Iron Age II), when three village-fortresses and five associated farms with terraced fields and watchtowers were established along the valley, forming thirteen installations and paramilitary farming enterprise sites. This settlement was first attributed by Cross and Milik (1956) to the Judean kings Jehoshaphat and Uzziah (*2 Chr.* 17.12, 26.10), but a reexamination of the finds by Lawrence Stager and several soundings he has conducted have indicated that the sites were not occupied for more than several decades; Stager (1976) has suggested attributing the settlement to the time of King Josiah. The entire system was abandoned in the last days of the monarchy of Judah (Stern, 1994).

Pottery finds indicate that the ruins (mainly the northern one), were partially reoccupied in the Hellenistic and Roman periods (Second Temple period). Otherwise there is plenty of evidence of nomadic and seminomadic installations of various periods in the valley: tent encampments, cairns, burial places, etc. (Patrich, 1995).

The three Iron Age II village-fortresses were Khirbet Abu Tabaq in the north, Khirbet (or Karm) es-Samrah in the center of the valley, and Khirbet el-Maqari (or Makari) in the south. Each settlement was rectilinear in plan and surrounded by a wall 1.0 to 1.2 meters thick, with casemates on two or three sides and rock-cut tunnel-like cisterns. The largest settlement was Khirbet es-Samrah, 68 by 40 meters in dimension. Khirbet Abu Tabaq measured 59 by 30 meters, and Khirbet el-Maqari was a square of about 32 meters to a side.

Two *lmlk*, stamped jar handles from the second half of the seventh century BCE, were found in Khirbet es-Samrah, and an incised scarab with a seventh-century inscription reading "Of Badyahu son of M [. . .]" was found at Khirbet Abu Tabaq. An inscribed shard was found in Khirbet el-Maqari with parts of only two letters, *lamed* and *alef,* preserved.

Karm Atrad, the field adjacent to Khirbet Abu Tabaq, is the largest and best explored dam complex. Approximately 740 meters long and comprising approximately 100 dunams, it had seven transversal dams or terraces. It was encircled on the south, east, and north by a U-shaped enclosure wall and on the west by a 250-meter-long wall with sluice gates, installed in order to regulate the gushing floods. Three dam complexes were found in the neighborhood of Khirbet es-Samrah. The one to the north was 54 by 82.5 meters in dimension, the second was located to the west, and the third, called Kurum el-ʿAjuz, located about 1 kilometer to the west-southwest, was approximately 155 meters long and 57.5 meters wide. About 1.5 kilometers to the west of Khirbet el-Maqari were the remains of another dam complex, with a total of more than 1,000 meters of wall. Wheat, barley, and legumes were cultivated in the fields, and the surrounding area served as a grazing land for sheep and goats.

These three village-fortresses have been identified with the biblical Middin (Khirbet Abu Tabaq), Secacah (Khirbet es-Samrah), and Nibshan (Khirbet el-Maqari), three of the desert cities of Judea mentioned in *Joshua* 15.61–62 (Cross and Milik, 1956), unless these sites should be sought along the western shore of the Dead Sea, as was suggested by Bar Adon (1989).

BIBLIOGRAPHY

Bar Adon, Pessah. "The Judaean Desert and Plain of Jericho." In *Judaea, Samaria and the Golan: Archaeological Survey 1967–1968*, edited by Moshe Kochavi. Jerusalem, 1972. See pages 92–152.

Bar Adon, Pessah. "Excavations in the Judean Desert" *ʿAtiqot* 9 (1989), Hebrew Series.

Cross, Frank Moore. "Buqei'a." In *The New Encyclopedia of Archaeological Excavations in The Holy Land*, edited by E. Stern, vol. 1, pp. 267–269. Jerusalem, 1992.

Cross, Frank Moore, and Józef T. Milik. "Explorations in the Judaean Buqeʿah." *Bulletin of the American Schools of Oriental Research* 142 (1956), 5–17.

Masterman, E. W. G. "Notes on Some Ruins and Rock-Cut Aqueduct in the Wadi Kumran." *Palestine Exploration Fund Quarterly Statement* 35 (1903), 264–267.

Milik, Józef T. "Le rouleau de cuivre." In *Les 'Petites Grottes' de Qumrân (Textes)*, edited by Maurice Baillet, J. T. Milik, and Roland de Vaux. Discoveries in the Judaean Desert, 3. Oxford, 1962. See page 262.

Patrich, Joseph. *Archaeological Survey in Judea and Samaria: Map of Deir Mar Saba (109/7)*. Jerusalem, 1995.

Stager, Lawrence. "Farming in the Judean Desert during the Iron Age." *Bulletin of the American Schools of Oriental Research* 221 (1976), 145–158.

Stern, Ephraim. "The Eastern Border of the Kingdom of Judah in Its Last Days." In *Scripture and Other Artifacts: Essays in Honor of Philip J. King*, edited by M. D. Coogan, J. Cheryl Exum, and L. E. Stuyer, pp. 399–409. Louisville, Ky., 1994.

JOSEPH PATRICH

BURIAL. *See* Cemeteries.

C

CAIRO GENIZAH. The title *Cairo Genizah* is used to describe both the source and the contents of a collection of about 220,000 fragments of medieval Hebrew and Jewish writings. These were amassed in the *genizah* ("depository") of the Ben Ezra Synagogue in Old Cairo (Fustat) over a period of about nine hundred years and have in the past century found their way into various academic libraries in the Western world. In view of their large number and extensive range, as well as their dating from the tenth through thirteenth centuries, they constitute a unique source for the history, religion, and everyday life of the Mediterranean Jewish communities of the early Middle Ages. The manuscripts from the Cairo Genizah provide the only Hebrew paleographical links between texts from the time of Jesus and Hillel and the manuscript codices and early editions of the thirteenth through sixteenth centuries. The only other early manuscript source for some of the works found among the scrolls from the Judean Desert is the Cairo Genizah.

Discovery and Dispersal. During the last two decades of the nineteenth century, Cairo Genizah fragments first began to appear in the collections of booksellers, bibliophiles, and scholars. The minor officials of the Ben Ezra Synagogue had become aware that there was a market for such literary antiquities and were willing to supply it in return for some financial inducements. The material often passed through more than one pair of hands, and by the time it reached its final destination, its source was often obscure. Four personalities played major roles in the Cairo Genizah transfer from the East to West during the 1880s and early 1890s. A Jewish bookseller and editor from Jerusalem, Rabbi Solomon Aaron Wertheimer, was enthusiastic enough about some of his acquisitions to prepare them for publication but insufficiently prosperous to allow himself the luxury of retaining them. Reverend Greville Chester, an Anglican cleric and Egyptologist, on the other hand, presented a number of items to the Bodleian Library of the University of Oxford and to the University Library, Cambridge. The Imperial Public Library in Saint Petersburg, for its part, was enriched by the receipt of a substantial collection of Cairo Genizah documents from an archimandrite of the Russian Orthodox church in Jerusalem, Antonin, who lived in Jerusalem from 1865 until his death in 1894. Unlike others, the lawyer and bibliophile Elkan Nathan Adler, son of the British chief rabbi, Nathan Marcus Adler, did not operate through intermediaries but visited the Cairo Genizah himself in 1896 (for a second time) and came away with a sackful of archival spoils.

Adler's friend and scholarly rival, Solomon Schechter, then Reader in Talmudic Literature at the University of Cambridge, though probably already aware of the Chester and Adler finds, was more fully alerted to the possibilities of a major discovery by the exciting purchases of his Scottish Presbyterian associates in Cambridge, the widowed twin sisters Agnes Lewis and Margaret Gibson. Encouraged, financed, and recommended by Charles Taylor, master of Saint John's College, Schechter spent a few weeks in Cairo in the winter of 1896–1897 and ensured that Cambridge University Library obtained a large number of fragments, now comprising almost 70 percent of all Cairo Genizah material. Even after Schechter's efforts, there were still some spoils to be taken from the Ben Ezra Synagogue and the Bassatin Cemetery. The Jewish Mosseri family of Cairo, together with some scholarly acquaintances, also assembled a significant collection. Among other private collectors was the Haham of the Sephardi community in England, Moses Gaster, who purchased many Cairo Genizah fragments.

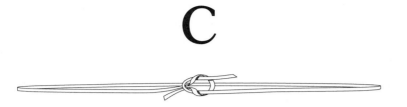

The activities of such individuals and the subsequent relocation of the precious texts that they had obtained resulted in the enrichment of a number of libraries around the world. More than 140,000 Cairo Genizah fragments are now housed at the Cambridge University Library and consist of items obtained from Chester and Wertheimer, Lewis and Gibson, and Taylor and Schechter, as well as from the bookseller Samuel Raffalovich, and from a few others between 1897 and 1982. The second most extensive collection is probably the one in the institution that has recently been renamed the Russian National Library in Saint Petersburg, which holds the Antonin Collection of some twelve hundred pieces and many thousands of manuscript remnants (yet to be precisely sorted and numbered) purchased from the nineteenth-century Karaite scholar Abraham Firkowitsch. The uncertainty arises out of doubts as to whether his material came from the Ben Ezra Synagogue or from another synagogue, possibly Karaite. A hoard of twenty-four thousand fragments, definitely from the Cairo Genizah, is in the possession of the Jewish Theological Seminary of America in New York City, having been purchased from Adler when financial pressures forced him to dispose of his library in 1923 and from his estate after his death in 1946. The Seminary also inherited fragments from what Schechter regarded as his private collection. Gaster's fragments were divided between the British Museum (now the British Library) in London and the John Rylands University Library of Manchester, the former buying some five thousand of the better-preserved pieces in 1924 and the latter about ten thousand of lesser quality in 1954. The Bodleian Library boasts a substantial Cairo Genizah collection (five thousand pieces), established at about the same time as that of Cambridge, as a result of purchases from Wertheimer and presentations by Chester and the Oxford Assyriologist and traveler, A. H. Sayce. Westminster College, the United Reformed Seminary in Cambridge, was presented with two thousand fragments by Lewis and Gibson. The Mosseri collection (four thousand pieces) remains in family hands in Paris. The city also is host to thirty-five hundred items at the Alliance Israelite Universelle, acquired early in the century by the Consistoire Israelite. Smaller collections are to be found in Strasbourg, Budapest, Philadelphia, Jerusalem, Cincinnati, Washington, D.C., Vienna, Birmingham (United Kingdom) and Kiev.

Origin and Literary-Historical Importance. Remarkable though it is as a historical archive, the Cairo Genizah was built neither with an eye to preservation nor the expectation of historical research. From as early as the eleventh century, when the Ben Ezra Synagogue was built on its current site, the communal authorities followed the practice of Jews worldwide in not destroying any text that might contain the name of God or a quotation from sacred literature. For almost nine centuries the religious functionaries in Cairo, however, appear to have interpreted the tradition more strictly, consigning to their *genizah* not only worn and damaged religious tracts but also a host of written items of purely mundane content. As the combined result of reverence for Jewish texts, the climate, and an undisturbed site, the Cairo Genizah has bequeathed to posterity a unique testimony to the medieval Jewish Mediterranean.

The earliest such testimony goes back four centuries before the founding of the Ben Ezra Synagogue, some texts having apparently been retained by previous generations and inherited by the founders; the latest dates from the end of the nineteenth century. The period best represented is that of the tenth through thirteenth centuries, when the community was still of central significance to the Jewries of both Egypt and the wider Jewish Orient. As the Jewish settlement in Fustat gave way to its successor in Cairo to the northeast, the importance of the Ben Ezra Synagogue declined. Nevertheless, the arrival of Jews expelled from Spain in the fifteenth and sixteenth centuries is variously documented, as is Judeo-Spanish literature. Such Jewish languages are another central feature of the Cairo Genizah materials, including as they do Judeo-Arabic, Judeo-Greek, Judeo-Persian, and Judeo-German (Yiddish), as well as (less surprisingly) Hebrew, Aramaic, and Arabic.

Intriguingly, Cairo Genizah texts represent the first evidence of Jewish compositions committed to writing after a gap of a number of centuries. This may be no more than an accident of archaeological history but can also be interpreted more innovatively. The rabbinic tradition was perhaps so overwhelmingly oral that only Torah scrolls and a few other items such as incantations, notes on matters of religious law, and synagogal poetry existed in written form. This is not to say that the rabbinic traditions were not being systematically compiled and edited; indeed there is the real and important possibility that such a process was essentially oral. If this suggestion is correct, the Cairo Genizah testifies to an explosion of written material among rabbinic Jews during the ninth and tenth centuries (given that there are some 220,000 items [some consisting of a number of folios] still in existence from the Cairo Genizah, many times this number of texts must simply have not survived). This trend may have been inspired by the need to respond to Islamic, Christian, and Karaite developments and was probably aided by the widespread adoption of the codex, in preference to the scroll and the individual folio. Once this new medium became widely employed, it influenced the format and transmission of texts, the nature of literacy, and the history of the book in many Jewish communities.

Content and Study. It is immediately apparent to the historian assessing almost a century of Cairo Genizah scholarship that the results represent a virtual rewriting of Jewish history for the early medieval period. Through letters and documents, detailed accounts have now been compiled of the social, economic, and religious activities of the vibrant Oriental Jewish communities during the tenth through thirteenth centuries. Studies of halakhic rulings, commentaries, and correspondence have demonstrated the development of Jewish law in the gaonic period (seventh through eleventh centuries) and the manner in which the Babylonian academies succeeded in establishing a centralized system of education, authority, and administration throughout the Islamic empire. The description of the biblical texts, Aramaic and Judeo-Arabic translations, and exegetical works have clarified how rabbinic interpretations met Karaite challenges and responded to Muslim and Christian theological notions. Previous knowledge about such leading personalities as Saʿadya ben Yosef Gaʾon, Shemuʾel ben Hofni, Moses Maimonides, Yehudah ha-Levi, and Yosef Karo has been significantly deepened. Texts have been found of both the Babylonian and Jerusalem Talmuds, and of many Midrashic works that predate by centuries the few manuscripts on which standard editions are based, permitting the restoration of more accurate versions. Historians of the Masoretic Text and Hebrew philology have been able to provide new insights into how the biblical text was carefully transmitted and how a number of systems of grammar were developed. The variety of Jewish liturgical rites, especially those of Babylonia and Palestine, contrast significantly with later standards, and thousands of unknown poems, sacred and secular, many by newly discovered poets, have been restored to Jewish lyrical history. A new era of Semitic linguistic study has been ushered in through the close examination of the Judeo-Arabic dialect. Also uncovered have been rare examples of Jewish artistic, musical, scientific, and medical self-expression.

These scholarly achievements have by no means been evenly spread over each of the last ten decades. The intensive preservation, sorting, and description of the collections in the early decades was followed by an era of relative neglect in the period of the two world wars. Since the 1950s, institutions have again given attention to the fragments and made them more widely available. As a result, there has been another flowering of Cairo Genizah scholarship, particularly in the past thirty years, in which Cambridge University Library, the Jewish Theological Seminary, the Institute of Microfilmed Hebrew Manuscripts at the Jewish National and University Library in Jerusalem, the Israel Academy of Sciences and Humanities, and the efforts of Shelomo Dov Goitein and his students have played major roles.

It was Goitein who brilliantly deciphered many of the mundane Cairo Genizah documents and was thus able to reconstruct the daily life of the Jew in the medieval Mediterranean area. Inspired by their teacher, his students have added many chapters to Oriental Jewish history in the Middle Ages.

Links with the Dead Sea Scrolls. There are a number of aspects of the Cairo Genizah story that are of particular relevance to the interpretation of the discoveries in the Judean Desert. It is clear that the consonantal texts of the earliest biblical material from the Cairo Genizah betray little variation from the famous medieval exemplars and confirm the accurate transmission of texts between the periods of Rabbi ʿAqiva and Maimonides. While that transmission no doubt included traditions of vocalization and cantillation, such traditions were systematized only in the early period of the Cairo Genizah, and a variety of methods were championed in different Jewish centers. Some Hebrew and Aramaic linguistic phenomena and apocalyptic and mystical texts may be traced back to the Second Temple period, but it is also clear that there are early medieval linguistic features.

As far as liturgy is concerned, the precise links between the Dead Sea Scrolls, the Talmudic traditions and the developments of the late geonic period are not yet clear. At Qumran, prayers, hymns, and benedictions on the one hand, and supplicatory formulas and incantations on the other, were already structured, communal, and an integral part of religious duties. The linguistic and contextual parallels with rabbinic prayer are striking, but the precise formulation is unique to each group, and it is an open question whether the rabbis were inspired by the Qumran practice to commit their prayers to writing and to standardization. It is clear that there was no Talmudic prayerbook as such, and that the way that rabbinic prayers were formulated, recited and transmitted in the first few centuries still left room for development. In that case, some communities may have followed more closely than others the texts and customs recorded at Qumran. What the Cairo Genizah fragments have demonstrated is that there was still considerable variety in the geonic period, either freshly encouraged by the liturgical poets in the post-Talmudic period, or a continuation of the earlier situation.

Special mention must be made of the fact that apocryphal and pseudepigraphal texts are represented among the Cairo Genizah material and have parallels in the texts from Qumran and Masada. The most important of these is the Damascus Document, the first and most extensive text of which was discovered by Schechter and published by him in his *Documents of Jewish Sectaries* (1910). It was puzzled over until a link could be made in 1947 with the literature from Qumran, including copies of this composition from Cave 4. Fragments of *Ben Sira* were also located and published by Taylor and Schechter, and later by others; one of the manuscripts is particularly close to the version discovered by Yadin at Masada. There are also texts of *Tobit* in Hebrew and the *Testament of Levi* in Aramaic, as well as sixth-century palimpsests of Greek Bible translations.

How is one to account for the survival of all this material from the second to the tenth century? It is possible that the rabbinic tradition was central during this period and was only lukewarm about such items, which found greater acceptance among Karaites, fringe groups, and non-Jewish communities and made only occasional, haphazard appearances in the more normative synagogues such as the Ben Ezra. In that case, either such items were consigned to the *genizah* of that synagogue precisely because they were regarded as heretical, or their origins are more accurately to be sought in a Karaite synagogue nearby. Alternatively, it may be that the rabbinic tradition was less central than it later imagined itself to have been, and historians should be working to uncover major Jewish religious trends during the first Christian millennium that manifest themselves in a variety of ideologies that were, for their part, unenthusiastic about rabbinic developments. It would have been natural for Talmudic Judaism to have played down the importance of alternative traditions and condemned alternative literature, perhaps not always with success. During periods of literary expansion, such as the one represented by the classic Cairo Genizah texts, the drive toward the adoption of written, and therefore authoritative and perhaps syncretistic, versions may have been one of the factors leading to the temporary acceptance within the Talmudic communities of a greater variety of compositions than that sanctioned in some earlier or later contexts.

[*See also* Ben Sira, Book of; Damascus Document; Levi, Aramaic; *and* Tobit, Book of.]

BIBLIOGRAPHY

Beit-Arié, Malachi. *Hebrew Codicology: Tentative Typology of Technical Practices Employed in Hebrew Dated Medieval Manuscripts.* Rev. ed. Jerusalem, 1981. One of a number of important books by Beit-Arié on various aspects of the study of Hebrew manuscripts.

Blau, Joshua, and Stefan C. Reif, eds. *Genizah Research after Ninety Years: The Case of Judaeo-Arabic.* University of Cambridge Oriental Publications, 47. Cambridge, 1992. A collection of essays that exemplifies the range of subjects written in one of the Jewish languages represented in the *genizah*.

Goitein, S. D. *A Mediterranean Society: The Jewish Communities of the Arab World as Portrayed in the Documents of the Cairo Genizah.* 6 vols. including the index volume by Paula Sanders. Berkeley and London, 1967–1993. An outstanding study of Oriental Jewish life in the Middle Ages based on *genizah* sources.

Kahle, Paul. *The Cairo Genizah.* 2d. ed. Oxford, 1959. Outdated in some respects and out of print, but not difficult to obtain and certainly important for the history of *genizah* research.

Khan, Geoffrey. "Twenty Years of Genizah Research." In *Encyclopedia Judaica Year Book 1983/1985,* edited by Geoffrey Wigoder, pp. 163–170. Jerusalem, 1985. A detailed assessment of recent *genizah* research and publication.

Lambert, Phyllis, ed. *Fortifications and the Synagogue: The Fortress of Babylon and the Ben Ezra Synagogue, Cairo.* London, 1994. An attractive collection of essays and plates on all aspects of the history of Ben Ezra as a building and a community in medieval and modern times.

Reif, Stefan C. *A Guide to the Taylor-Schechter Genizah,* 2d. ed. Cambridge, 1979. A useful booklet briefly introducing the history and contents of the collection, with some plates. Out of print, but still available online.

Reif, Stefan C. *Published Material from the Cambridge Genizah Collections: A Bibliography, 1896–1980.* Geniza Series, 6. Cambridge, 1988. Details of the books and articles published on the Cambridge Genizah, indexed according to classmark, author, and title.

Reif, Stefan C. "Aspects of Mediaeval Jewish Literacy." In *The Uses of Literacy in Early Mediaeval Europe,* edited by Rosamond McKitterick, pp. 134–155. Cambridge, 1990. A survey of the written material used by the Oriental Jewish Communities in the early Middle Ages and how it came to be extensive.

Reif, Stefan C. "Jenkinson and Schechter at Cambridge: An Expanded and Updated Assessment." *Transactions of the Jewish Historical Society of England* 32 (1992), 279–316. A critical account of the efforts of two major figures in the first decade of the *genizah* story.

Reif, Stefan C. "The Cairo Genizah and Its Treasures, with Special Reference to Biblical Studies." In *The Aramaic Bible: Targums in the Historical Context,* edited by Derek R. G. Beattie and Martin J. McNamara, pp. 30–50. Journal for the Study of the Old Testament, Supplement Series, 166. Sheffield, 1994. A summary of the *genizah's* importance for many aspects of biblical study.

Reif, Stefan C. "One Hundred Years of Genizah Research at Cambridge." *Jewish Book Annual* 53 (1995–1996), 7–28. A survey of the changing fortunes of the Cambridge Genizah material since its acquisition in the 1890s.

Richler, Benjamin. *Hebrew Manuscripts: A Treasured Legacy.* Cleveland and Jerusalem, 1990. A popular but informed introduction to the subject, with plates and samples of handwriting, and a chapter on the Cairo Genizah by Robert Brody.

Richler, Benjamin. *Guide to Hebrew Manuscript Collections.* Publications of the Israel Academy of Sciences and Humanities, Section of Humanities. Jerusalem, 1994. A most useful reference tool, providing details of all the major collections and personalities, as well as their history, with specific treatment of the *genizah* finds.

STEFAN C. REIF

CALENDARS AND MISHMAROT. The momentous importance that attaches to "proper chronology" and Temple watches (*mishmarot*) in the conceptual world of the "Community of the Renewed Covenant" is evinced by fragments of some twenty calendrical documents (4Q320–330, 4Q335–337, 6Q17), the tailpiece of a calendar preserved in one manuscript of Miqtsat Maʿasei ha-Torah[a] (4Q394; hereafter MMT[a]), and Otot (4Q319); a detailed exposition in Temple Scrolls[a and b] (11Q19–20); and calendar-related references in major works of the Qumran community—the Rule of the Community (1QS), the Damascus Document (CD), Pesher Habakkuk (1QpHab), Psalms[a] (11Q5; hereafter 11QPsalms[a]), Songs of the Sabbath Sacrifice (4Q400–407; 11Q17; and Mas1k) and other works, which presuppose this calendrical system. The covenanters' messianic-millenarian expectations depended upon a divinely ordained sequence of periods in history (*qitsei*; Pesher Habakkuk [1QpHab vii.12–13]), or eternal periods (*qitstsei ʿolamim* or *qitsei netsaḥ*; Hodayot[a] [1QH[a] ix.26–27] [i.24–25]; iv.16; War Scroll [1QM i.8–9]), which were expected to culminate in the "cutoff period" and establishment of the fervently awaited "new [age]" (*qets neḥ eratsah va-ʿasot ḥadashah*; Rule of the Community [1QS iv.25]).

The covenanters' calendrical works can be divided into four major categories.

Chronographical Schedules. These would include enumerations of days, weeks, months, and annual quarters in the Qumran community's 364-day solar calendar year and rotas of the annual cycle of "holy seasons"—Sabbaths and festivals. No document comprises all facets of the covenanters' calendar. The itemized roster of David's daily, Sabbath, and festival psalms in 11QPsalms[a] (11Q5 xxvii) comes indirectly closest to a comprehensive circumscription of it. However, by collating and combining various features extracted from diverse sources, a full picture of the Qumran community's calendar can be reconstituted (see Table 1).

Unlike the Jewish lunisolar calendar of 354 days, the covenanters' solar year holds 364 days (fifty-two weeks) and can be subdivided into four quarters of three months (thirteen weeks or ninety-one days each). The first two months of a quarter (*tequfah*, a term also used in rabbinic parlance) number thirty days each. The last month of the quarter, that is, the third, sixth, ninth, and twelfth months of the year, has one *yom nosaf* ("additional day") to which is attached a special cultic significance, and thus numbers thirty-one days. This basic structure is captured in the fragmentary but still restorable opening lines of what appears to be a mnemonic calendrical composition (6Q17 i.1–2): 1 "[The first month, in it 30 days; the] second, in it 30 [days]; 2 [the third month, in it 31 days]; and complete are the days [of the quarter]."

In this document and others, for example the Biblical Chronology (4Q559), figures are not spelled out but are expressed in numerical symbols. These are known from weights and Hebrew inscriptions of the First Temple period and from Aramaic papyri of the fifth–fourth centuries BCE from Elephantine in Egypt: a slanted stroke (\) signifies one; a hook (¬) stands for the number ten; two superimposed hooks (∃) indicate the number twenty. In some cases, the numbers three and four are presented as units of slanted strokes in opposite directions (/\\, /\\\).

Months are indicated by ordinal numbers, as in the ancient Israelite tradition (e.g., *Gn*. 8.4, 8.13, 8.14; *Ex*. 12.1; *Lv*. 23; *Hg*. 1.1; *Zec*. 1.1) and as occasionally seen in *Maccabees*, and not by Babylonian month names, which the returnees from the Babylonian exile are said to have brought back with them (J.T., *R. ha-Sh*. 1.56d) and which occur predominantly in postexilic books (e.g., *Zec*. 1.7; *Est*. 3.7, 3.13; *Neh*. 2.1), or by Canaanite appellations, some of which are preserved in biblical texts pertaining to the preexilic period (e.g. *Ex*. 13.4, 23.15, 34.18; *Dt*. 16.1; *1 Kgs*. 6.1, 6.37, 6.38, 8.2). However, Babylonian month names do occur in the fragmentary Zodiology and Brontology (4Q318) and the month name *Shevat* is mentioned once in a small fragment of Historical Work[c] (4Q333). In several Qumran documents the number of days in each of the recorded months is given. At times, these details are combined with a summary reference to the number of days in an annual quarter.

The sequence of the annual quarters parallels the progression of the four major agricultural seasons in the Rule of the Community: "the seasons of reaping to [that of] summer [fruits]; the season of sowing to the season of [cutting] green fodder" (1QS x.7). These terms echo the designations of the agricultural seasons in *Amos* 7.1–4 and 8.1–2 and in the Gezer Calendar (c.900 BCE). The beginnings of the quarters, possibly observed as festivals and marked by special prayers (cf. Liturgical Prayers [1Q34 and 34[bis.]], *Jub*. 6.23–25), coincide with the onsets of the astronomical seasons—vernal equinox, summer solstice, autumnal equinox, and winter solstice—which are paraphrastically referred to in *1 Enoch* 82.16–19: "these are the signs of the days . . . glowing heat and dryness . . . all the trees bear fruit . . . the wheat is ripe for harvest . . . the trees produce their fruits ripe and ready . . . and all the fruits of the earth are gathered in."

The covenanters' calendrical documents are not in almanac form. Only "holy seasons" are recorded and secular workdays are altogether omitted. This schema appears in fragments of an item, which seems originally to have contained thirteen extremely narrow columns with lines of between three and ten letters and spaces (MMT[a] [4Q394 i–ii]). In this document the dates of every single Sabbath throughout the year are registered, together with the dates of the covenanters' harvest festivals for the (New) Wine, the (New) Oil, and the "Wood Offering" (cf. Reworked Pentateuch[c] [4Q365 23.9]), which occur at intervals of fifty days and do not have an explicit biblical basis but are seemingly derived from pertinent scriptures

CALENDARS AND MISHMAROT. TABLE 1. *The* Enoch/Jubilees/*Qumran Solar Calendar.*

	Months		
Days of the Week	1, 4, 7, 10	2, 5, 8, 11	3, 6, 9, 12
Wednesday	1, 8, 15, 22, 29	6, 13, 20, 27	4, 11, 18, 25
Thursday	2, 9, 16, 23, 30	7, 14, 21, 28	5, 12, 19, 26
Friday	3, 10, 17, 24	1, 8, 15, 22, 29	6, 13, 20, 27
Saturday	4, 11, 18, 25	2, 9, 16, 23, 30	7, 14, 21, 28
Sunday	5, 12, 19, 26	3, 10, 17, 24	1, 8, 15, 22, 29
Monday	6, 13, 20, 27	4, 11, 18, 25	2, 9, 16, 23, 30
Tuesday	7, 14, 21, 28	5, 12, 19, 26	3, 10, 17, 24, 31

(*Nm.* 18.12; *Dt.* 18.4; *Neh.* 10.40, 10.35). In addition, summaries of the number of days in each annual quarter and of the total 364 days in the year are given:

> The twenty-third of it [the second month] is a Sabbath. The thirtieth [of it] is a Sabbath. The seventh of the third [month] is a Sabbath. The fourteenth of it is a Sabbath. The fifteenth of it is the Festival of Weeks. The twenty-[fir]st of it is the Sabbath. The twenty-eighth of it is a Sabbath. After it, the first and second day [of the week] a day is added and the quarter terminates [with] ninety-one days. . . . [The twenty-fir]st of it [the sixth month] is a Sabbath. The twenty-second of it is the Festival of the [New] Oil.

The 364-day system ensures the smooth rotation of the annual cycle of the holy seasons. The first and fifteenth days of the first month of each quarter fall invariably on the fourth day of the week. On this day God created the luminaries (*Gn.* 1.14–19), which are the indispensable bases of all calendrical schemata. The Sabbaths always fall on the same monthly dates, and each festival falls on the same weekday. The offering of the Passover lamb is celebrated as a separate feast late Tuesday afternoon on the fourteenth of the first month, and the festival of Passover is celebrated on Wednesday, the fifteenth of the month. Shavuʿot is observed on Sunday, the fifteenth of the third month (cf. *Jub.* 15.1, 16.13, 44.1–5), fifty days after Sunday, the twenty-sixth of the first month, which follows upon the first Sabbath (*Lv.* 23.11–16) after the Passover festival. Thus the date of Shavuʿot is aligned with the dates of Passover on the fifteenth of the first month and Sukkot on the fifteenth of the seventh month. Ro'sh ha-Shanah, on the first of the seventh month, and Sukkot, on the fifteenth, fall again on a Wednesday. Yom Kippur is observed on Friday, the tenth of the seventh month, immediately before the ensuing Sabbath. The covenanters probably hailed this propinquity as the most accurate realization of the term *shabbat shabbaton*, which designates this day in the Priestly code (*Lv.* 16.31, 23.32), presumably taking it to mean "double Sabbath" or "one Sabbath after the other."

In the documents of the Qumran community, only the first days of the week-long festivals of Passover and Sukkot are recorded. There is no mention of the last day designated throughout the Hebrew Scriptures (*Ex.* 12.16; *Lv.* 23.8, 23.36; *Nm.* 28.25, 29.35; *Dt.* 16.8; *Neh.* 8.18; *2 Chr.* 7.9). The last holy seasons fall in the seventh month of the covenanters' calendar: Ro'sh ha-Shanah on the first, Yom Kippur on the tenth, and Sukkot on the fifteenth. Ḥanukkah and Purim, which depends on the biblical book of Esther that is not extant among the Qumran finds of biblical books, observed by mainstream Judaism in the ninth and the twelfth months respectively, are not listed. [*See* Festivals.]

The fragments of chronological schedules discovered at Qumran are remains of documents or scrolls (e.g., Calendrical Document A [4Q320] and Calendrical Document B[a] [4Q321]) that contain a variety of calendrical rota and provide chronographic guidelines for the conduct of the individual and the community as a socio-religious entity. The correct observance of Sabbaths and festivals and the efficacy of ritual, foremost the sacrificial acts, depend on accurate timing. Since the schedule of sacrifices in the Jerusalem Temple was adjusted to the lunar year of 354 days, which mainstream Judaism followed, the covenanters abstained from participating in the Temple service. They filled the resulting void in their religious life by instituting prayers that were to be offered at prescribed times every day of the month, every Sabbath, and every festival by humans on earth and by angels in heaven (e.g., 1Q34; 4Q286–293, 400–407, 434–444, 449–457, 507–509).

An interesting consequence of the Qumran calendar is Annie Jaubert's thesis that the presentation of the Last Supper in the Synoptic tradition as the celebration of the Passover meal on the Tuesday evening of Holy Week conforms with its fixed date in the solar calendar of 364 days. In distinction, the *Gospel of John* dates the beginning of Passover to the Friday evening, presumably in accordance with the lunar calendar of mainstream Judaism. Critics have taken exception to the thesis on several counts. It has been argued that it clashes with the reports that Jesus and the disciples observed the festivals regularly in accord with the orthodox Jewish calendar and that adherence to a sectarian calendar would have totally divorced him and his followers from the mainstream community.

Mishmarot. This is the second category into which the covenanters' calendrical works can be divided. The covenanters considered their abstention from the Jerusalem Temple only a temporary state of affairs. They awaited fervently the rebuilding of a new Temple in which their own priesthood would conduct the holy service in accord with their solar calendar and their ritual rulings (Temple Scroll[a] [11Q19], New Jerusalem [1Q32]). The various tables of priestly "watches" or "courses"—the *mishmarot* cycle—relate to this area of cultic concern. The genesis of the schema is traced back in the Otot scroll to the very beginning of the world: "Creation [was] on the fourth [day] of Ga[mul]" (4Q319 i.11). This concept is echoed in Calendrical Document A; an account of the Creation culminates in a reference to the fashioning of the great luminaries on the fourth day (cf. *Jub.* 2.8–9). Only the closing remark, which speaks of the moon's "appearing from the east . . . in the midst of heaven . . . from evening until morning" (4Q320 1.1–3), is preserved. The cosmic event is immediately linked to a roster of concordant dates in the lunar and the solar calendar, with corresponding days in a three-year cycle of priestly watches, which opens (1.3–5): "On the fourth in the week [of service] of the sons of Gamul, in the first of the month, in the first year (2.i.1, 5 [the sons] of Gamul at the head of all years"). Through this linkage, the covenanters' system of *mishmarot* becomes a salient feature of the creation of the cosmos.

Mishmarot lists fall into several subcategories that answer to the particular requirements of the priestly hierarchy. Some are enumerations of the names of the priestly watches that serve a one-week rotation every half-year. Their names accord with the biblical roster of twenty-four priestly families (*1 Chr.* 24.7–19), although this roster causes difficulties when applied to the fifty-two weeks in the solar year of 364 days. The covenanters solved the problem by establishing a six-year cycle with a staggered rotation system. The four weeks by which the solar year exceeds the lunar year are covered by three watches that serve three times and two that are on duty for an additional half-week, one at the beginning of the year, and one at its end:

> Gamul [second half of his service] Delaiah Maaziah Joiarib Jedaiah Ḥarim Seorim Malkiah Mijamin Haqqots Abiah Jeshua Shekaniah Eliashib Jaqim Ḥuppah Jeshbeab Bilgah Immer Ḥezir Happittet Petaḥaiah Jehezkel Jakin Gamul Delaiah Maaziah Joiarib Jedaiah Ḥarim Seorim Malkiah Mijamin Haqqots Abiah Jeshua Shekaniah Eliashib Jaqim Ḥuppah Jeshbeab Bilgah Immer Ḥezir Happittet Petaḥaiah Jehezkel Jakin Gamul Delaiah Maaziah Joiarib Jedaiah [first half of his service].

This arrangement is reflected in the War Scroll (1QM ii.1–2): "The fathers of the community are fifty-two. The major priests shall be appointed after the high priest and his deputy in twelve courses to serve constantly before God. And twenty-six heads of courses shall serve in their appointed term." This seemingly baffling statement actually summarizes the turns of duty of twenty watches that served semiannually and covered forty weeks and of four that served three times and covered twelve weeks, fifty-two weeks in all; their "heads" are the "fifty-two fathers of the community."

In *1 Chronicles* 24.7–19 the priestly watches are listed by name and ordinal number: "the first [is] Joiarib, Joiada the second . . . Maaziah the twenty-fourth." In the Qumran community rosters, only the names of the *mishmarot* are given (Calendrical Document F[a] [4Q328 2, restored]). The ordinal numbers one through twenty-four of the biblical roster were presumably dropped because they did not tally with the twenty-six-watch system based on the solar calendar.

In some documents, years, quarters, months, and the first day of a quarter are identified by the name of the first priestly watch then on duty. In Calendrical Document F[a] and Calendrical Document F[b] (4Q329) a list of *mishmarot* that served at the beginning of the years in a six-year cycle is followed by a roster of priestly watches that officiated at the onset of each quarter:

> [In the first year Gamul, in the second Jedaiah, in the third Miyamin, in
> the fourth Shekaniah in the fifth Jeshbe]ab, in the sixth Happittet
> These are the (watches at the) beginnings of the years
> In the first [year] Gamul Eliashib Maaziah [Ḥuppah]
> [in the] second Jedaiah Bilgah Se[o]rim Ḥe[zir]
> [in the third] Miya[min Petahaiah Abi[ah Jakin
> [in the fourth Shekaniah De]laiah Jaqim Joia[rib
> [in the fifth Jeshbeab Ḥarim Immer] Malkiah
> in the si[xth Happittet Haqqots Immer Jeshua]

Calendrical Document A (contains a fragmentary register that details names of the *mishmarot* that served at the beginnings of the months in a given year, together with the number of days in each month: "the second thirty [Jedaiah], the third [thirty] one [Haqqots], the fourth thirty [Eliashib]." Calendrical Document C[d] (4Q324[a] 1.ii.3) specifies: "the fourth day [in] Malkiah this is the first in the tenth month" (cf. 4Q324[a] and Calendrical Document C[c] [4Q324 1.5]). Calendrical Document D (4Q325) lists the fifty-two annual Sabbaths that are named after the watches that enter the Temple on Saturday afternoon and begin their duties on Sunday morning, together with the "Beginnings of the Months," the special festivals of the "First Wine," the "First Oil," the "Wood Offerings," and the biblical "Festival of the (First) Grain," but without mentioning other biblical festivals. In contrast, Calendrical Document B[a] (4Q321 2.ii–iv) presents a roster of the first watch on duty in every single month of a six-year cycle, next to a list of the annual biblical festivals and the names of the *mishmar* in whose week of service each falls. Calendrical Document A (4Q320 4.ii), restored on the strength of evidence culled from other documents, does not record the covenanters' special festivals:

> 1 The first year (of the six-year cycle) <vacat> its feasts:
> 2 On the 3rd (day) in the week of the sons of Maaziah [falls] the Pesaḥ
> 3 On [the 1st in] Jeda[iah] the Swinging of the [Omer]
> 4 On the 5th in Seorim the [Second] Pesa[ḥ]
> 5 On the 1st in Jeshua the Feast of Weeks
> 6 On the 4th in Maaziah the Day of Remembrance
> 7 [On the six]th in Joiarib the Day of Atonement
> 8 [On the 10th in the] seventh <vacat>
> 9 [On the 4th in Jedai]ah the Feast of Booths

It should be noted that there is no mention between lines 2 and 3 of the Festival of Unleavened Bread, which falls on the fourth service day of Maaziah. Further, if the proposed text restoration is correct, the Day of Atonement—

and only this day—is identified by a calendrical date, the tenth day of the seventh month, in addition to the day on which it falls in the week of Joiarib.

Calendrical Document G (4Q329[a] 1) contains remains of a roster that pertains ostensibly to the "holy seasons" in one year of a six-year cycle but in fact records only the names of the priestly watches in whose week of service Passover falls:

> [The first year its festivals, on the third day in] the week of [Maaziah the Passover; the seco]nd (year) its fe[stivals, on the th]ird [day in Seorim the Passover; the th]ird (year) its festivals, on the third (day) [in the week of Abiah the Passov]er; the fourth (year) its festivals, on the third (day) of [Yakim the Pass]over; the fifth (year) its festivals, [on the third (day) of Immer the Passover]

In all *mishmarot* texts the dating by the name of a priestly watch and the day in the weeks of its service pertains to recurring features of the annual cycle of holy days. Only in the tiny fragment of Historical Work[c] (4Q333) is a one-time event dated in this fashion: "(x) killed (y) on the fif[th day] in Jedaiah."

Synchronization Tables. The third category into which the calendrical works of the community can be divided consists of synchronization tables of two phases of the moon's monthly revolution in a six-year cycle, identified by days in the week of service of the pertinent priestly course and by concordant dates in the solar year (4Q320 1.i–iii). In Calendrical Documents B[a] and B[b] (4Q321 and 4Q321[a]), the first phase, {a}, is defined by date alone, the second, {b}, by date and the otherwise unknown term *duqah* or *duqo[h]*. Most scholars (including J. Baumgarten, J. T. Milik, and J. VanderKam) derive the term from the words *duq* or *diq* ("exactitude") while S. Talmon connects it with *daq* (thinness). Calendrical Document B[a] (4Q321 i.1–2) illustrates this schema: "a, On the second [day] in [the week of] Abijah [which falls] on the twenty-fifth [of the eighth lunar month]; and *duqah*; b, on the third day in Miyamin [which falls] on the twelfth in it [the eighth solar month]." The alignment of only two specific days in every lunar month with dates in the solar calendar does not evince an intention to synchronize the solar year with the lunar year, singling out the propitious nights of the new and the full moon, as is the prevailing opinion. Rather, the two phrases pertain to the unfavorable phases of the moon's waning and total eclipse. These ominous days and dark nights are identified by dates in the solar calendar so that the covenanters would beware of them.

The terminology of calendrical and *mishmarot* texts is marked by a manifest dependence on biblical linguistic usage. Months are identified by numerals rather than by appellations. The prevalent employment of the word *qets*, signifying "period" rather than "end," parallels the Biblical Hebrew *ʿet* ("time") and *moʿed* ("seasons") found in *Ezekiel* and *Daniel* (e.g. *Ezek*. 7.6, 21.30, 21.34; *Dn*. 12.6–7, 8.19, 11.27, 11.35). The entrance of a priestly watch into the Temple on Saturday afternoon is called *biʾat yedaʿyah* in Calendrical Document C[b] and Calendrical Documents C[d–f] (4Q323, 4Q324[a–c]). This technical term echoes the biblical appellation of the incoming temple guard (*baʾei ha-Shabbat*), which spells the outgoing contingent (*yotsʾei ha-Shabbat*; *2 Kgs*. 11.7, 11.9). The completion of a time segment of a year or quarter is defined by derivatives of *shlm: ve-shalmah ha-shanah* ("the year is complete" in MMT[a] [4Q394 3–7.i]), *be-hishalem ḥoq tiqqunam* ("when the statute of their [the festivals] norm is completed" in Rule of the Community [1QS x.6–7]), and possibly *moʿed shillum[am]* ("the time [or festival] of their completion (in Festival Prayers[c] [4Q509 i.3]). This use of *shlm*, which also underlies diverse translational references to the solar calendar in *1 Enoch* 82.6 and *Jubilees* 6.30 and 6.32, appears to derive from *Isaiah* 60.20: *ve-shalmu yemei evlekh* ("the days of your mourning shall be ended").

Otot. Timetables of the Otot, the fourth category of Qumran calendrical works, cover fifty-year periods (jubilees) and are found in the Otot scroll (4Q319), in fragments of astronomical treatises in which the phases of the moon are recorded (4Q335–336), in Phases of the Moon (in Cryptic A script; 4Q317), and in Zodiology and Brontology (4Q318), which bear resemblance to the astronomical discourses in the Book of the Luminaries in *1 Enoch* 72–82.

The Calendar Controversy. The schism between the covenanters and mainstream Judaism is deeply rooted in the calendar controversy. The major features of the Qumran ephemeris are identical with those of the solar calendar propagated in *1 Enoch*'s Book of the Luminaries (*1 En*. 72–82) and *Jubilees*.

1 Enoch and Jubilees. According to *1 Enoch*, "The sun and stars (the moon is significantly omitted!) will bring in the years exactly so that they do not advance or delay their position by a single day unto eternity; but complete the years with perfect justice in 364 days" (*1 En*. 74.12; cf. 72.32).

This calendar is traced back to Enoch in Pseudo-Jubilees[c]: "He wrote [down] everything [concerning the] heavens and the ways of their hosts, [the mo]nths" (4Q227 2), "the days of appointed times in the four parts of the year" (*Jub*. 5.23; cf. *2 En*. 40.6), stating that "all the days . . . will be . . . fifty-two weeks" (*Jub*. 6.30). Enoch is said to have taught these details to his son Methuselah (*1 En*. 82). This knowledge was then divinely imparted to Noah, who transmitted it to his descendants: "Now you command the Israelites to keep the years in this number—364 days. Then the year will be complete" (*Jub.* 6.32).

In Commentary on Genesis A (4Q252 i–ii), as in the version of the Noah episode in *Jubilees* (*Jub.* 6.23–27), the story of the flood unfolds in accord with this timetable. The successive stages of the deluge, detailed in *Genesis* 7.6–8.19, are fitted into a framework of dates from the seventeenth of the second month in the sixth-hundredth year of Noah's life (i.3–4) to the seventeenth (the Masoretic Text says the twenty-seventh) of the second month in the next year, so that Noah left the ark after exactly 364 days, at the completion of one year (4Q252 ii.2–3).

The prologue of *Jubilees* (*Jub.* 1.4, 1.25, 1.29) reports that the calendar was transmitted down to the generation of Moses, engraved on "heavenly tablets" that were given to him on Sinai together with the tablets of the Decalogue:

> Moses remained on the mountain for forty days and forty nights while the Lord . . . related to him the divisions of all the times. . . . Now you write all these words which I tell you . . . what is to come during all divisions of time . . . in the weeks of their jubilees until eternity. . . . The angel of the presence . . . took the tablets [which told] of the divisions of the years . . . for the weeks of their jubilees, year by year in their full number.

The authors of *Jubilees* and the Book of the Luminaries extol the immutability of the sun, which never increases or decreases, favoring it over the instability of the moon, which is subject to a monthly process of waxing and waning (*1 En.* 73–74). The preeminence of the 364-day solar calendar is demonstrated by the fact that in this ephemeris the festivals always occur on the same days of the week, whereas in the 354-day lunar calendar they do not, and special computation is required to determine the day on which a festival will fall in a given year.

The opposition to the lunar calendar is at the very heart of the covenanters' controversy with mainstream Judaism, but since both the sun and the moon were divinely created, the moon too must be given attention (cf. Calendrical Document A [4Q320]). The author of the Rule of the Community (1QS x.4–6) indeed mentions the moon in the Song of the Seasons but seems to deny it any role in matters calendrical, which are exclusively tied to the sun. God had created the sun, "the great (luminary) for the Holy of Holies . . . for the beginning of appointed days . . . at the new years and at the period of their appointed times."

The author of *Jubilees* discusses the moon in reference to light and darkness, day and night, but at the same time he does not assign it any role in the revolution of the appointed seasons:

> And on the fourth day he (God) made the sun and the moon and the stars. And he set them in the firmament of heaven so that they might give light upon the whole earth. . . . And the Lord set the sun as a great sign upon the earth for days of Sabbaths, months, feast (days), years, sabbaths of years, jubilees, and for all the (appointed) epochs of years . . .

God then warned Noah:

> All the Israelites will forget and will not find the way of the years. They will forget the first of the month, the season[s] and the Sabbath[s]; they will err in respect to the entire prescribed pattern of the year. . . . There will be people who carefully observe the moon . . . it is corrupt (with respect) to the seasons. . . . Everyone will join together both holy days with the profane and a profane day with the holy day. . . and will not make a year (exactly) three hundred and sixty-four days.
>
> (*Jub.* 6.36–38)

This warning is echoed in Pseudo-Moses[e] (4Q390 i.8–10): "they will forget ordinance and appointed time, and Sabbath and covenant. And they will violate everything, and they will do what I consider evil. Consequently, I will hide my face from them. I will hand them over to the hand[s] of their enemies and deliver them to the sword" (cf. *Jub.* 1.12–14).

In contrast, praising God's mighty deeds at Creation, the author of Psalms 8.4–5 mentions the moon and the stars but omits any reference to the sun: "When I look up at thy heavens, the work of thy fingers, the moon and the stars, set in their place by thee, what is man that thou shouldst remember him?" In Psalms 104.19 the moon is explicitly lauded as the divinely appointed source of the seasonal cycle: "Thou hast made the moon to mark the seasons." *Ben Sira* also praises the role accorded to the moon at Creation; his praise is couched in terms that bring to mind the covenanters' calendrical vocabulary: "The moon prescribes the periods [*ʿitot*], [his is] the rule over appointed time [*qets*] and an everlasting sign [*ʾot ʿolam*]. His [is every] festival [*moʿed*] and from him [every] feast [*ḥag*]" (*Sir.* 43.6–7).

To the advocates of the solar calendar adherence to the lunar ephemeris meant walking "in the feasts of the Gentiles, after the errors and their ignorance" (*Jub.* 6.37). Rabbinic tradition turned the accusation around: "Israel reckons by the moon and the Gentiles reckon by the sun" (*Mekhilta de-Rabbi Yishmaʿel*, Tractate Pisḥa, ed. J. Z. Lauterbach, 1933). The Sages stressed the exclusive legitimacy of the lunar calendar by quoting Psalm 28.5:

> Because they regard not the works of the Lord nor the operations of his hands he shall destroy them: "the operation of his hands," these are the new moons, as is written, "he appointed the moons for seasons" (Ps. 104.19) . . . ("he shall destroy them") these are the heretics who do not reckon either ap-

> pointed days or periods. . . . He will destroy them in this world and will not build them up in the world to come."
> (*Midrash Psalms*, 1947, ed. Buber, p. 230)

Minor discrepancies between the covenanters' calendar and the *1 Enoch/Jubilees* ephemeris may have arisen from a variety of factors: scribal mistakes in the textual transmission of the apocryphal books or their original Hebrew texts, the translators' incomplete understanding of the ancient time register, or inaccurate renditions in the Greek and/or Ethiopic translations. Long before the discovery of the covenanters' writings, R. H. Charles cast doubt on the reliability of *1 Enoch* in matters calendrical: "The chronological system of this book is most perplexing. It does not in its present form present a consistent whole and probably never did" (Charles, p. 149). In contrast, the covenanters' calendar is wholly consistent. In some instances, Qumran texts actually enable us to recover an original Hebrew technical term that evidently underlies an Ethiopic reading or to resolve a textual difficulty and emend a misconceived calendar in *1 Enoch* or *Jubilees*.

There is, though, a telling difference between the covenanters' calendrical documents and calendar-related statements in the pseudepigraphal books. The authors of the pseudepigraphal books never tire of stressing the "indisputable" superiority of the 364-day solar calendar, holding it up as the only legitimate Jewish calendrical system, or of disenfranchising the 354-day lunar calendar that the mainstream community followed. Again and again they outline the essential principles of the solar calendar and its basic structure but do not delve into details of its application in daily life. The pseudepigraphal books are addressed to indeterminable groups of the "Enoch circles" type and not to a structured community that geared its everyday life and cultic observance to the 364-day solar calendar. In contrast, the authors of the Qumran calendrical documents give less attention to solar doxology, dwelling instead on select features that have an evident bearing on actualities of communal organization and cultic life, such as the Sabbaths and festivals. In their writings, the bitter calendar controversy of Second Temple period comes into full light. Whereas the pseudepigraphal books theorize, the Qumran documents breathe actuality.

A stemmatic arrangement of passages in the Damascus Document brings to the fore the dependency of the covenanters' calendrical system on the calendar propagated by *Jubilees* and the latter's dependency on *1 Enoch*. In the Damascus Document, the Book of Division of Times, undoubtedly the Book of *Jubilees* as we know it or a close version of that work, is juxtaposed to the Book of Moses: "Therefore a man shall impose upon [himself] by oath to return to the Law of Moses for in it everything can be learnt. And the exact statement of the epochs of Israel's blindness to all these, behold it can be learned in the Book of Division of Times into their Jubilees and Weeks" (CD xvi.1–4). This juxtaposition appears to echo a pertinent statement in the prologue of *Jubilees*: "These are the words regarding the divisions of the times of the law and of the testimony, of the events of the years, of the weeks of their jubilees throughout all the years of eternity as he related [them] to Moses on Mt. Sinai when he went up to receive the stone tablets."

The above reference in the Damascus Document proves that when the Damascus Document was written (by the middle of the second century BCE), *Jubilees* was already considered an authoritative source for calendrical matters. The book could not have attained such a distinctive status unless its teachings had been known for a considerable length of time—not less than two or three generations—and unless the intrinsic opposition to the lunar calendar that it reflects was also already in full force (*Jub.* 6.32–38). The author of *Jubilees* (*Jub.* 4.15–18) traces the roots of his solar calendar to the antediluvian patriarch Enoch (cf. Pseudo-Jubilees[c] [4Q227]) and to the book of *Enoch*:

> He (Enoch) was the first of mankind . . . who wrote down in a book the signs of the sky in accord with the fixed pattern of their months so that mankind would know the seasons of the years. . . . The weeks of the jubilees he related, and made known the days of the years; the months he arranged, and related the sabbaths of the years, as we had told him.

The reliance of *Jubilees* on *Enoch* in calendrical matters implies that in the author's days the Book of the Luminaries was as much appreciated as *Jubilees* was when the Damascus Document was composed. We may therefore conclude that the composition of the Book of the Luminaries cannot be dated later than the second half of the fourth century BCE.

Introduction of the lunar calendar. Thus the solar calendar of 364 days was not the covenanters' innovation but rather was rooted in Jewish tradition. In light of the Qumran discoveries, Annie Jaubert theorized that the biblical solar calendar was in fact identical with the covenanters' 364-day ephemeris. The application of this calendar to the dates in the biblical literature has surprising results. During their years of wandering in the desert following the Exodus from Egypt, the Israelites are credited with avoiding travel on Sabbaths and festivals by breaking camp on Sunday or after a "holy season" and arriving at the next station on Friday or before another "holy season." Although critics have pointed out events in the biblical sources that cannot be accommodated in this system, the theory still has merit.

The ten-day difference between the lunar and solar calendars necessitates periodical adjustments to keep the lunar and solar years from being thrown out of kilter. But nothing in the biblical or covenantal literature indicates that adjustments were effected systematically on the basis of astronomical computations. It has been suggested that Calendrical Document A (4Q320 2.i–iii) implies that a serviceable concordance was achieved through adding one month of thirty days at the end of every third lunar year. But this conclusion is doubtful. The author merely records in detail the loss of ten days per year in the lunar calendar vis-à-vis the solar year, without ever hinting at a need for, or the existence of, a fixed practice of intercalation. The author of *1 Enoch* similarly summarizes the difference between the two calendars for periods of three, five, and eight years, again without giving a reason for doing so (*1 En.* 74.10–17). We must therefore assume that, if intercalation was practiced at all, the lunar year was realigned with the solar year only when the divergence between them had become too great. Likewise, the Qumran documents do not contain any information concerning a calibration of the 364-day solar year with the true solar year of 365 days and six hours. Presumably intercalation was practiced by calibrating units of weeks and not of months, so as to maintain the proper functioning of the *mishmarot*. The 364-day calendar is kept in step with the seasonal year by adding one week every seven years and possibly by adding two weeks every twenty-eight years.

The question of whether the covenanters counted the day from the evening before, as in the lunar calendar of mainstream Judaism, or from the morning, as could be expected in solar ephemeris is still debated. Relying on the Daily Prayers scroll (4Q503), in which schedules proceed from evening to sunrise, some scholars reason that the covenanters followed a lunar calendar and that the day began for them with sundown. Others presume that the lunar calendar was introduced into the Jerusalem Temple during the Second Temple period. No definite information on this can be elicited from the sources at our disposal. The hypothesis that it occurred in the days of the Seleucid emperor Antiochus IV Epiphanes, who in approximately 167 BCE imposed the lunar calendar on the Jerusalem Temple, has little merit. It is highly improbable that the Jewish leadership and the sacerdotal establishment would have willingly submitted to a heathen ruler's imposition of such change in the Temple schedule. It stands to reason that the introduction of the lunar calendar into the Temple occurred at a much earlier date and that it was connected with an internal rift in Judaism. At some juncture in the fourth or third century BCE, a rival priestly house that adhered to the lunar calendar ousted the officiating priesthood that followed a solar ephemeris. The founding fathers or forerunners of the Qumran community remained loyal to the deposed priestly house, persevered in their adherence to the ancient solar calendar, and dissented from the community that acknowledged the new priesthood and acquiesced in the scheduling of Temple services according to the lunar calendar.

The considerable number of chronographic rota and calendar-related statements from the Qumran site stands out in comparison to texts discovered at various other Judean Desert sites. Remains of biblical books, apocryphal and liturgical compositions, and historical documents have turned up at Masada, Wadi Murabbaʿat, Naḥal Ḥever, and Naḥal Ṣeʾelim. But not a single fragment of a calendrical work was found at any one of these sites. The covenanters' intense preoccupation with the issue of the calendar has no parallel in Hellenistic, early Christian, or rabbinic reports about schismatic communities in Judaism at the turn of the era. The singular proliferation of calendar-related materials evinces their importance in the covenanters' communal and private life and highlights the pivotal role of the calendar in their increasingly hardening confrontation with mainstream Judaism. The 364-day solar calendar was the most significant and conspicuous boundary marker that separated the Qumran community from the other socio-religious enclaves during the Second Temple period.

The Teacher of Righteousness and the Wicked Priest. An early stage of the calendar controversy appears to be reflected in Miqtsat Maʿasei ha-Torah (MMT). The writer adduces a series of legal-cultic statutes over whose interpretation he and the addressees are divided, foremost among them being the 364-day calendar. It is significant that in the editors' reconstruction of MMT[a] (4Q394 3–7.i) this list is headed by the end of an account of a 364-day solar calendar. "[The twenty-eighth in it (viz. the twelfth month) is] a Sabbath. Un[t]o it after [th]e Sa[bbath the first and second day (of the week) a day] is [ad]ded. And the year is complete (in) three hundred and si[xty-four] days."

In MMT[c] the writer matter-of-factly states that because of these halakhic differences "we have separated ourselves from the multitude of the people" (4Q396 7–8). The rather conciliatory tone suggests that when MMT was composed, the covenanters were intent on winning others over. However, their estrangement from the mainstream community progressively intensified. Concomitantly, Qumran authors criticized their opponents' views and standards of behavior with an increasing passion and bitterness. It is remarkable that of all the theological and legal differences that come to the fore in the covenanters' writings, the calendar controversy emerges in Pesher Habakkuk as the crucial issue in the direct confrontation between the Teacher of Righteousness and his opponent the Wicked Priest. The words of the biblical prophet, "Woe to you who make your companions drink from the cup of your wrath, making them drunk" (*Hb.* 2.15), are interpreted in Pesher Habakkuk (1QpHab xi.4–8) as a proleptic reference to the Wicked Priest's pursuit of the Teacher of Righteousness to his (and his followers') "abode of refuge" (*abet galuto*) (literally "the place of his [self-imposed] exile")—Qumran: "at the appointed time of their rest, the Day of Atonement, he appeared before them to confuse them and to cause them to transgress the Day of Fasting," forcing them to eat and drink on that day. It is evident that the Wicked Priest would not have violated the holiest day of the year by traveling from Jerusalem to the shores of the Dead Sea. We must therefore conclude that his Day of Atonement did not coincide with the covenanters' "fast day of their rest" and that their observances of the holy seasons throughout the year were likewise differently timed.

The Wicked Priest rightly viewed the covenanters' adherence to a solar calendar as an act of religious and civil rebellion and set out to nip it in the bud. His violent interference brought their opposition to mainstream Judaism to a climax: "One may no longer join the house of Judah. Each must stand on his watchtower" (CD iv.11–12). The author exhorts "all who were brought into the covenant," to whom God had revealed "hidden things in which all Israel strayed—his holy sabbaths, the glorious appointed times, his righteous testimonies" (CD iii.13–15). They are "not to enter the sanctuary to light his altar in vain" (CD vi.11–12), so as not to be like their adversaries who offer sacrifices at the wrong times. Rather, the members of the Qumran community are admonished "to make known [the difference] between the holy and the profane . . . to observe the Sabbath day in its exact detail, and the appointed times and the day of the fast as ordained by those who entered the [re]new[ed] covenant in the land of Damascus" (CD vi.17–19). The rift is final: "the fence is built, the boundary extends far" (CD iv.12).

Rabbinic calendar controversy. The Yom Kippur episode related in Pesher Habakkuk invites comparison with a report in the Mishnah (*R. ha-Sh.* 2.8–9) of a calendar controversy between Rabban Gamliel II, leader of the Sanhedrin at Yavneh and Rabbi Joshua ben Ḥananiah at the end of the first century CE. Although astronomical computations of the moon's orbit were available (*B.T., R. ha-Sh.* 25a), the high court officially announced the onset of the new month when two reliable witnesses affirmed that they had actually sighted the new moon. On the strength of such a statement, Rabban Gamliel II proclaimed the beginning of the new month, evidently the first month of the year (Tishrei), and thus fixed the entire annual cycle of festivals. Rabbi Dosa ben Harkinas, himself a prominent sage, declared the witnesses to be liars because his own observation proved that on the crucial night the moon was still full: "How can one say of a woman that she has given birth and on the next day she is still visibly pregnant." Rabbi Joshua invalidated the men's evidence and demanded that the proclamation of the new moon be deferred. But Rabban Gamliel stood by his resolution. Apprehensive lest Rabbi Joshua's dissenting opinion cause a rift in the community, with some following Gamliel's decision and others fixing the holy days in accord with Joshua's opinion, Gamliel ordered Joshua to present himself before him in Yavneh on the day on which, according to Joshua's computation, Yom Kippur fell, carrying his staff and his purse, so as publicly to desecrate his Day of Atonement. The rather similar episodes differ however on two points. While Rabbi Joshua's dispute with Rabban Gamliel pertained to differences regarding the lunar calendar that both men followed, the clash between the Teacher of Righteousness and the Wicked Priest revolved around the lunar versus solar controversy. And whereas Rabbi Joshua followed the counsel of Rabbi Dosa ben Harkinas and acted as ordered, thus preserving the unity of Israel, the fact that the Teacher of Righteousness persevered in his adherence to a nonconformable ephemeris put the final touch on the Qumran community's schismatic dissent from mainstream Judaism.

[*See also* Miqtsat Maʿasei ha-Torah; Pesher Habakkuk; Psalms, Hymns, and Prayers; *and* Qumran, *article on* Archaeology.]

BIBLIOGRAPHY

Baumgarten, Joseph M. "The Calendar." In *Studies in Qumran Law*, pp. 101–144. Leiden, 1977.

Buber, Martin, ed. *Midrash Psalms*. New York, 1947.

Charles, R. H. *The Book of Enoch or 1 Enoch*. Oxford, 1912.

García Martínez, Florentino. "Calendars and Priestly Rotas." In *The Dead Sea Scrolls Translated: The Qumran Texts in English*, pp. 451–455. Leiden and New York, 1994.

Herr, Moshe David. "The Calendar." In *The Jewish People in the First Century: Historical Geography, Political History, Social, Cultural, and Religious Life and Institutions*, edited by Shmuel Safrai et al., vol. 2, pp. 834–864. Compendia Rerum Iudaicarum ad Novum Testamentum. Assen, Amsterdam, and Philadelphia, 1976.

Jaubert, Annie. "The Calendar of Qumran and the Passion Narrative in John." In *John and Qumran*, edited by J. H. Charlesworth, pp. 62–76. London, 1972.

Lauterbach, J. Z., ed. *Mehkilta de-Rabbi Yishma'el*, Tractate Pisḥa, vol. 1, pp. 18–19. Philadelphia, 1933.

Milik, J. T. *Ten Years of Discovery in the Wilderness of Judaea*, translated by J. Strugnell, pp. 107–113. London, 1959.

Nitzan, Bilhah. *Qumran Prayer and Religious Poetry*, translated by Jonathan Chipman. Studies on the Texts of the Desert of Judah, 12. Leiden and New York, 1994.

Talmon, Shemaryahu. "The Gezer Calendar and the Agricultural Cycle of Ancient Canaan." In *King, Cult, and Calendar in Ancient Israel*, pp. 100–103. Jerusalem, 1986.

Talmon, Shemaryahu. "The Calendar of the Covenanters of the Ju-

dean Desert." In *The World of Qumran from Within: Collected Studies*, pp. 147–185. Jerusalem, 1989.
Talmon, Shemaryahu. "The Emergence of Institutionalized Prayer in Israel in the Light of Qumran Literature." In *The World of Qumran from Within: Collected Studies*, pp. 186–199. Jerusalem, 1989.
VanderKam, James C. "The Origin, Character, and Early History of the 364-Day Calendar: A Reassessment of Jaubert's Hypotheses." *Catholic Biblical Quarterly* 41 (1979), 390–411.
Van Goudoever, J. *Biblical Calendars*. Leiden, 1959.

SHEMARYAHU TALMON

CANON. The term "canon" is derived from the Greek word *kanōn*, which in turn is related to the Hebrew *qaneh*, meaning a reed, a measuring instrument. It eventually acquired the sense of norm and in that meaning was used by Christians, beginning in the fourth century CE, to designate the list of inspired, authoritative books that made up the church's Bible. These constituted a norm in the sense that books on that list defined faith and practice and were the final authorities for settling matters in dispute. There appears to have been no corresponding term in Judaism in the Second Temple period, and thus, in asking which books were included in a canon at that time, one runs the risk of anachronism. Yet, while the term "canon" is not attested in the Jewish texts, the concept of inspired, authoritative books was present because many compositions document the idea that for the authors some works possessed supreme authority in the sense of defining teachings and practices and refuting opponents.

Definitions. Discussions of canon, especially in relation to Qumran, tend to be at cross-purposes owing to a lack of clear definitions, and so it is important to distinguish between an authoritative text, a book of scripture, the process toward formation of the eventual canon, the Bible, and the canon.

An authoritative text is a text (e.g., a law code or a sacred book) that a community, secular or religious, acknowledges to hold authority over the members; it is a guide for the conduct of life to which all are accountable. A book of scripture is a sacred authoritative text which, in the Jewish or Christian context, the community acknowledges as having authority over the faith and practice of its members. The process toward formation of the canon ("the canonical process") is the long journey from the community's first acknowledgment that a certain sacred text is binding for faith and practice to the final, largely agreed-upon decision that the collection of certain books, and only those books, is universally and permanently binding. The Bible, in the singular, usually carries the implication of a codex, that is, a book with a front cover, a back cover, and a defined table of contents, as opposed to the form that the scriptures would have had in the Qumran period, a collection of individual scrolls. Although the plural term "*ta biblia ta hagia*" (the holy books) does occur, for example, in *1 Maccabees* 12.9 in a subordinate clause, it seems to denote simply a collection of sacred books available (as in the Prologue to *Ben Sira*), not a restricted collection; at that time *Enoch* and *Jubilees*, for example, may well have been envisioned as part of that collection, but *Daniel* may not have been.

The term canon, though it is used loosely in a number of ways, is a religious *terminus technicus* with a specific meaning used over a long history. It means the established and exclusive list of books that hold supreme authoritative status for a community. There are three aspects of the techinical use of "canon" that are important (see Ulrich, 1992): (a) "Canon" represents a reflexive judgment; that is, the community may long guide its life according to certain authoritative books, but it is not until questions are raised, debates held, and communal or official agreements made defining the exact contents that a canon properly so called comes to be; (b) It concerns books, not the specific text form of a book; for example, it is the *Book of Jeremiah* that is canonical or "defiles the hands," regardless of whether it is the earlier, short edition as witnessed in the Septuagint or the later, longer, and rearranged edition witnessed in the Masoretic Text; (c) It denotes a closed list; the formation of the canon "was a task, not only of collecting, but also of sifting and rejecting" (Metzger, 1987). "The crucial element is the question of *closure*. . . . A 'canon' is thus by definition a way of setting *limits* to the books recognized as holy" (Barton, 1996).

When it is used in the context of Qumran, the question usually concerns one of two aspects: whether a certain work was acknowledged as having authoritative status as sacred scripture, or whether there existed a canon, that is, an acknowledged list of books with authoritative status as sacred scripture. This dichotomy gets to the root of the confusion: the active sense of "canonical" as *norma normans*, an authoritative book that governs faith and practice, in contrast to the passive sense as *norma normata*, the authoritative list of those books which do, in conscious exclusion of those which do not, hold supreme status as governing faith and practice. The answer to that first question is certainly positive. It is clear that certain works were long since established and acknowledged as possessing this status. But that certain books exercised authoritative status does not mean that there was a canon yet. The answer to the second question is negative: there is no evidence in the scrolls (or in wider Judaism prior to the fall of the Temple), of a considered, inclusive-and-exclusive list. The period from the early existence of some books with "canonical" (in the active sense) status to the decisions about a definitive list constitutes the process toward canon, but the canon itself is a post-biblical phenomenon. In fact, the halakhic disputes of the first century, together with the Roman threat of annihilation and the emergence of Christianity in the second, may well have been the stimuli that brought the canonical process on to the homestretch toward conclusion.

Clues in Jewish Texts. Several Jewish texts from the Second Temple period do indicate that at least for certain groups some traditional literature of the Jewish people merited special status and study, and in some cases they offer classifications of the texts. So, for example, Ben Sira (ca. 180 BCE), in praising Israel's famous ancestors in chapters 44–50 of his book, mentions characters and events from most works in the Hebrew scriptures, usually in the order that later became fixed. The list begins with Enoch and ends with the high priest Simon II (219–196 BCE). On the other hand, certain major figures and books are not mentioned. Three questions can be raised: (a) Whether it was the few verses in *Genesis* 5 or rather the greater Enochic literature that merited Enoch's inclusion; (b) Whether Ben Sira viewed his own book as scripture, since Simon does not appear elsewhere in the Bible; and (c) Whether Ben Sira viewed his laudatory parade of heroes as a rehearsal from scripture as such or rather from his nation's proud and wise literature.

Ben Sira's grandson (after 132 BCE), in his Prologue to the Greek translation of the book, refers three times to the law and the prophets and the other ancestral books. Some scholars interpret the third group as already regarded as scripture, and thus that the traditional sacred literature was already divided into three categories as it is today in the Hebrew Bible. Others, however, interpret Ben Sira's divisions as two classifications: scripture, that is, the Law and the Prophets, and the other books, not scriptural but helpful toward instruction and wisdom. Some of this latter group would later have been elevated to the rank of scripture, others would later be classified as the apocrypha or pseudepigrapha, and yet others would be simply lost. In support of the second interpretation is the absence for the next two centuries of awareness by any other author of a tripartite classification.

The author of *Luke-Acts* (ca. 90 CE) usually refers to the scriptures as the law (or Moses) and the prophets (*Lk.* 16.16, 29, 31; 24.27; *Acts* 26.22; 28.23), though *Luke* 24.44 speaks of the law of Moses, the prophets, and the psalms in a context where "everything must be fulfilled." *4 Ezra* 14.23–48 (ca. 100 CE) speaks of ninety-four inspired books, of which twenty-four (which may well coincide with the books of the Hebrew Bible) are said to be for all to read, whereas the other seventy are only for the wise. The latter number shows that for the author the number of inspired works was not limited to the ones in the Hebrew scriptures. This is instructive, for it illumines the danger of simply finding a single ancient reference and automatically retrojecting upon it our later categories and views. Finally, Josephus, writing at about the same time as *4 Ezra*, states the number of books that are "justly accredited" as twenty-two and even lists which they are: five books of Moses, prophetic histories covering events from the time of Moses to Artaxerxes in thirteen books, and four works of hymns and precepts (*Against Apion* 1.37–43). These twenty-two books do not easily coincide with the books of the traditional Hebrew Bible (Beckwith, 1985), and it is noteworthy that the division between the Prophets and the Writings does not coincide with the Masoretic division.

Evidence in the Scrolls. The writings composed by the group that inhabited Qumran have made a significant contribution to our knowledge of the topic by providing different kinds of first-hand data about which books were considered authoritative. Naturally, it is not valid to extrapolate from the Qumran evidence—just as it is not from the testimony of Ben Sira, Josephus, or *4 Ezra*—to the views held by all Jews at this time, but the texts from Qumran do demonstrate what one group representing a particular Jewish tradition thought about authoritative literature in the late Second Temple period. Moreover, just as the biblical scrolls were the product of general Judaism, not of the group at Qumran, so too much of the evidence in the texts found at Qumran is evidence for the views of broader Judaism.

No text from Qumran supplies a list of which books were considered uniquely authoritative, but a number of works from Qumran refer to the Law (or Moses) and the Prophets as special categories of revelation. An example is the Rule of the Community (1QS), which is based on the Law and the Prophets. The *maskil* (sage) is to teach them "to seek God with all their heart and with all their soul, to do that which is good and upright before him, just as he commanded through Moses and all his servants the prophets" (1QS i.1–3).

The Miqtsat Maʿasei ha-Torah (4Q394–4Q399 C.9–10) indicates the writers' knowledge of certain categories of books, which they wanted their opponents to understand: "[And also] we [have written] to you that you may have understanding in the book of Moses [and] in the book[s of the P]rophets and in Dav[id . . .]." We can be confident about which books were included in Moses' law and about many that would have been classified among the prophets; but exactly which other texts were subsumed under "prophets" is not obvious, and it is unlikely that "David" here refers to anything beyond *Psalms*. After "David" the damaged sequel in the fragments ("[. . .] generation after generation") may add yet another book or category—perhaps annals.

Since none of the scrolls gives a list of authoritative books, one must search for other ways of uncovering which books (leaving aside the issue of oral traditions) enjoyed supreme status at Qumran. A study of the texts shows that there is evidence for the authoritative status of a large number of books that would become part of the fixed Hebrew Bible at a later time and for the authoritative status of some other writings that did not find their way into the official Hebrew Bible.

1. One approach is to check which books are cited as authorities and how the citations are introduced. There is a series of Qumran texts in which the writers refer to a book and introduce it as the words of God. For instance, the Damascus Document introduces a quotation of *Ezekiel* 44.15 with "as God promised them by the prophet Ezekiel" (CD iii.20–21); and the same text prefaces a citation of *Isaiah* 24.17 with "just as God said by Isaiah the prophet, the son of Amoz, saying" (CD iv.13–14). See also CD vi.13–14 (*Malachi*); viii.9 (*Deuteronomy*); and ix.7–8 (*Leviticus*).
2. Another method is to check which books were considered worthy of commentary. To compose a commentary on a book, especially considering the amount of labor required for doing so in antiquity, was to attribute a high level of importance to it, and the *pesharim* among the scrolls provide even more evidence that the writers of the commentaries believed those books—the writings of God's servants the prophets—to have been revealed and to contain the keys for understanding the latter days in which they were living. The commentaries that have been indentified are on the books of *Isaiah* (six: 3Q4; 4Q161–65), *Hosea* (two: 4Q166–67), *Micah* (one: 1Q14; cf 4Q168), *Nahum* (one: 4Q169), *Habakkuk* (one: 1QpHab), *Zephaniah* (two: 1Q15; 4Q170), and *Psalms* (three: 1Q16; 4Q171; and 4Q173).
3. The number of copies found and the frequency of citation also provide, though not proof, some indication of status. The Pentateuch and the Prophets, including *Psalms* and *Daniel*, are heavily represented, as are *Enoch* and *Jubilees*. But the Writings are sparse and seldom quoted.
4. In addition to the cases in which books now in the Hebrew Bible are quoted or alluded to as authorities, there is a saturated and pervasive influence of the language of the scriptural books on the writings composed at Qumran.
5. There are also a number of indications that some books that did not become part of the Hebrew Bible were accorded lofty status at Qumran. First, the claim that all 4,050 of David's compositions, not just those in the Psalter, were spoken "through prophecy given him by the Most High" is made in 11QPsalms[a] (11Q5 27.11). The fact that these poetic works were considered prophecy harmonizes well with the existence of *pesharim* on parts of *Psalms*, as well as the New Testament's use of the *Psalms* as prophecy. Second, the commentary on *Habakkuk* states that the Teacher of Righteousness was the one "to whom God made known all the mysteries of the words of his servants the Prophets" (1QpHab vii.4–5). Third, there are several books that present themselves as revelations from God, are present in multiple copies at Qumran, and exercised noticeable levels of influence on other Qumran texts. The best examples are the booklets of *Enoch* (quoted as scripture in *Jude*) and the *Book of Jubilees* (quoted in the Damascus Document). A different type of case is the Temple Scroll (11Q19 and 11Q20), which presents itself as the direct speech of God to Moses and which embodies legal material that was accepted at Qumran.

The Jewish texts found at Qumran and those composed there give us a glimpse into the time between the two points when much of the "biblical" literature was written and when it was formally recognized in a canon of scripture. They provide evidence that many of the books that would become the Hebrew Bible were regarded as authoritative and were so used, but they also show that the boundaries and classifications of authoritative literature were not yet settled in Judaism.

BIBLIOGRAPHY

Barr, James. *Holy Scripture: Canon, Authority, Criticism.* Philadelphia, 1983. An insightful and careful discussion of canon and related issues.

Barton, John. "The Significance of a Fixed Canon of the Hebrew Bible." In *Hebrew Bible/Old Testament: The History of Its Interpretation,* edited by Magne Sæbø, vol. 1 part 1, pp. 67–83. Göttingen, 1996. A recent and thoughtful discussion of the implications of canonicity.

Beckwith, Roger. *The Old Testament Canon of the New Testament Church.* Grand Rapids, Mich., 1985. An impressive and highly useful accumulation of data covering many aspects of the canon of the Hebrew Bible, but maximalist in its interpretation of the data, pushing the formation of the canon centuries too early. Should be read with the review by Albert C. Sundberg, Jr., "Reexamining the Formation of the Old Testament Canon." *Interpretation* 42 (1988), 78–82.

Beyer, H. W. "κανών." In *Theological Dictionary of the New Testament*, vol. 3. Grand Rapids, Mich., 1965, pp. 596–602. A foundational and informative overview.

Leiman, Sid Z. *The Canonization of Hebrew Scripture: The Talmudic and Midrashic Evidence.* Hamden, Conn., 1976. A survey of the Talmudic and Midrashic evidence, offering a historical reconstruction of the closing of the biblical canon.

Metzger, Bruce. *The Canon of the New Testament: Its Origin, Development, and Significance.* Oxford, 1987. An excellent, balanced, and nuanced discussion primarily of the New Testament canon, but very useful for clear thinking about the canon of the Hebrew Bible.

Sanders, James A. "Canon." In *Anchor Bible Dictionary,* vol. 1, pp. 837–852. New York, 1992. A comprehensive and well-seasoned overview of the issues, including the scrolls.

Ulrich, Eugene. "The Canonical Process, Textual Criticism, and Latter Stages in the Composition of the Bible." In *"Sha'arei Talmon": Studies in the Bible, Qumran, and the Ancient Near East Presented to Shemaryahu Talmon,* edited by Michael Fishbane and Emanuel Tov with Weston W. Fields, pp. 267–291. Winona Lake, Ind., 1992. An attempt to sort out some of the issues of canon in light of the scrolls and the compositional process of the biblical texts.

VanderKam, James C. "Authoritative Literature in the Dead Sea Scrolls." *Dead Sea Discoveries* 5 (1998), 382–402. A richly detailed and judicious exposition of the period illuminated by the scrolls, when many of the scriptural books were authoritative but prior to the formal recognition of the canon of scripture.

EUGENE ULRICH

CANTICLE OF CANTICLES. *See* Five Scrolls.

CARBON-14 DATING. Radiocarbon testing is the primary method used by archaeologists for dating organic and other materials containing the radioactive carbon isotope C^{14}. All plant and animals absorb C^{14} from the environment. The C^{14} isotope is continually produced in a reaction from the bombardment of nitrogen atoms with cosmic radiation in the upper atmosphere. When an organism dies, it ceases to be in equilibrium with its surroundings (that is, ceases taking in new carbon). The C^{14} isotope at the point of death decays at a known half-life rate (about 5,700 years). By measurement of the ratio of today's remaining C^{14} compared to carbon isotopes that have remained stable, the amount of radioactive decay that has occurred since the death of the plant or animal can be calculated.

Since the amount of new C^{14} production in the atmosphere varies through time, a means of calibration is necessary to convert these measurements into calendar years. Radiocarbon measurements on dated tree-ring sequences provide such a means of calibration going back some 11,000 years before present. Radiocarbon measurements are expressed by laboratories in terms of one-sigma (68 percent confidence) and two-sigma (95 percent confidence) calibrated date ranges. These figures represent lab estimates of confidence that the true dates of samples are within the reported date ranges.

The method was discovered in 1949, about the same time as the discovery of the Dead Sea Scrolls, by Willard F. Libby at the University of Chicago. In the fall of 1950 Libby measured a sample of linen from Cave 1 at Qumran that had been used to wrap a scroll. Libby measured this linen (before calibration) as 1,917 radiocarbon years older than the year 1950, plus or minus 200 years.

Until the late 1970s radiocarbon dating of parchment or papyrus texts was not practical due to the amount of sample material required to be destroyed (5–10 gms of carbon). This changed with the development of Accelerator Mass Spectrometry (AMS) methods, which permitted dating of small samples on the order of milligrams. This method was applied to Dead Sea manuscripts in 1990 at a Zurich AMS facility. Fourteen texts were dated, including eight from Qumran, two from Masada, and four items from other Dead Sea sites bearing internal dates.

A second battery of scrolls radiocarbon dating (and a dating of Qumran Cave 4 linen) was undertaken at an AMS facility at Tucson, Arizona in 1994–1995. Of the Dead Sea texts dated between the two labs, seven had internal dates (none of these texts were from Qumran). The radiocarbon dates for six of these seven were in excellent agreement with these texts' true dates. For the literary texts from Qumran, a large number of calibrated date ranges fell in the first century BCE, indicating that text activity in that century is certain. A few of the texts (e.g., Isaiah[a] [1QIsa[a]]) appear from the radiocarbon dates to be older, perhaps in the second century BCE, whereas others gave dates that appear to be younger, in the latter part of the first century BCE or in the first century CE. For about 80 percent of the text datings there was overlap between some part of the radiocarbon date possibility range and paleographic date estimates. [*See* Paleography.]

When conducting radiocarbon datings of Qumran texts, samples are cut from margins of the columns so that writing is not destroyed. In the lab the samples are subjected to chemical pretreatment to remove contaminants. Finally, the sample is converted (by combustion) to carbon, and the carbon then measured for C^{14} and other relevant isotopes. Because of the sensitivity of AMS measurements to the presence of even minute amounts of contamination, radiocarbon scientists emphasize the importance of multiple measurements, the conducting of radiocarbon datings in batteries, and interpretation of patterns of date rather than reliance upon single radiocarbon measurements considered in isolation.

There are several hundred radiocarbon laboratories throughout the world engaged in a wide range of datings for archaeologists, museums, and research projects. International radiocarbon conferences are held every three years, and the journal *Radiocarbon* reports continuing research and applications of radiocarbon dating methods.

BIBLIOGRAPHY

Aitken, M. J. *Science-Based Dating in Archaeology*. London and New York, 1990.

Bonani, G., et al. "Radiocarbon Dating of the Dead Sea Scrolls." *'Atiqot* 20 (1991), 27–32.

Bowman, S. *Radiocarbon Dating*. London, 1990.

Doudna, G. "Dating the Scrolls on the Basis of Radiocarbon Analysis." In *The Dead Sea Scrolls after Fifty Years: A Comprehensive Assessment*, edited by P. Flint and J. VanderKam, vol. 1, pp. 430–471. Leiden, 1998.

Jull, A. J. Timothy, et al. "Radiocarbon Dating of Scrolls and Linen Fragments from the Judean Desert." *ʿAtiqot* 28 (1996), 85–91.

Pardee, D. "Report and Discussion Concerning Radiocarbon Dating of Fourteen Dead Sea Scrolls." In *Methods of Investigation of the Dead Sea Scrolls and the Khirbet Qumran Site: Present Realities and Future Prospects*, edited by M. Wise, N. Golb, J. Collins, and D. Pardee, pp. 441–453. New York, 1994. The same report as Bonani et al. 1991 but with discussion and comments from Qumran scholars afterward.

GREGORY L. DOUDNA

CARMIGNAC, JEAN. *See* Revue de Qumrân.

CATENA. Two manuscripts found in Qumran's Cave 4 have been labeled Catena (i.e., a "Chain" of quotations), 4Q Catena A (4Q177) and 4Q Catena B (4Q182).

Thirty-four fragments have been assigned to Catena A. Thirty of these were transcribed and published by J. M. Allegro (Allegro, 1968, pp. 67–74); to these, J. Strugnell added four more. The fragments have been reedited by Steudel (Steudel, 1994, pp. 57–124). She has convincingly placed twenty of them in five columns. Her reconstruction is based on the content of the fragments and their damage patterns. Several of the fragments preserve straight vertical breaks, with the result that one can visualize how a rolled scroll was flattened in antiquity and broke into pieces where it was creased. Fragment 11 preserves traces of stitching, so what remains of 4Q177 belongs to at least two sheets of parchment. Steudel has reckoned that the five extant columns come from the middle of a scroll, so she labels them columns 8–12. The preservation of both top and bottom margins in fragment 5 shows that the manuscript was written with sixteen lines per column.

The handwriting is "Rustic Semiformal" (Strugnell, 1970, p. 236), typologically from the early Herodian period. 4Q177 was probably penned in the second half of the first century BCE. The orthography of the manuscript is generally full.

Column i (5, 6, 8 Steudel, viii) begins in the middle of a sentence, and is therefore not the beginning of the scroll. It contains quotations from *Isaiah* 37.30 and 32.7 (parallel to Ps. 10.2, 10.7–11) which seem to conclude a discussion of Psalm 10 by describing the "boasters" and possibly "the man of scorn (*ish ha-latson*)" (cf. CD i.14, in the plural in CD xx.11; 4Q162 ii.6, ii.10; 4Q525 23.8) who are the enemies of the Qumran community. Then Psalm 11.1–2 is cited and interpreted with the aid of *Micah* 2.10–11. This unit describes the persecution of the honest. Psalm 12.1 is cited next, and is interpreted by reference to *Isaiah* 27.11, 22.13, and possibly *Jeremiah* 6.14; the context is too broken to understand.

The extant portion of column ii (7, 9, 10, 11, 20, 26 Steudel, ix) begins with a quotation of Psalm 12.7 interpreted through *Zechariah* 3.9 and *Isaiah* 6.10 (according to the Septuagint). The Sons of Light and the Interpreter of the Law (cf. 4Q174 1.i.11; CD vi.7, vii.18) will ultimately be protected against the men of Belial. Then Psalm 13.2–3 is used to explain the delay in divine intervention by asserting that it is due to the community's need to be purified. The enemy mentioned in Psalm 13.5 is identified with the Seekers after Smooth Things and then interpreted through *Ezekiel* 25.8.

Column iii (1, 2, 3, 4, 14, 24, 31 Steudel, x) opens with a quotation from *Deuteronomy* 7.15, which completes a section of interpretation before Psalm 16.3, which is in turn interpreted through *Jonah* 2.2 and *Nahum* 2.11. Then Psalm 17.1 is interpreted, partly through *Zephaniah* 3.4, with a long discourse on the blessings to come for those who have resisted Belial; such things are inscribed on tablets and confirmed through a citation of *Hosea* 5.8, whose trumpet is identified either as "the Book of the Law again" (Strugnell, 1970, p. 241; Steudel, 1994, p. 109; cf. 1QpHab v.9–12; 4QpIsa[c] 23 ii.14a) or as "the book of the Second Law," (Allegro, 1968, p. 68) which might be the Temple Scroll (Yadin, 1983, 1.396–7) or some other work.

Column iv (12, 13, 15, 19 Steudel, xi) contains quotations of *Ezekiel* 22.20 and *Jeremiah* 18.18 which lead into the citation of Psalm 6.2–6. Its interpretation describes the defeat of Belial and the rescue of the Sons of Light. Steudel's ordering of the fragments is most questionable in the case of this column. If the reconstruction is granted, then the presentation of Psalm 6 comes after that of Psalms 12–17 in the previous three columns. No *Psalms* manuscript from Qumran contains the Psalms in that order, though in the separate fragments of 4QPsalms[a] (4Q83) there are remains only of Psalms 5–6 and those after Psalm 31. Thus, rather than providing a running commentary on the *Book of Psalms*, some other matter is the principal motivation behind the whole composition.

Column v (Steudel, xii) survives in only a few lines on the left of fragment 13. Again the subject is Belial in the last days.

For Steudel, 4Q177 is a copy of the same composition as is found in 4Q174 and probably also in 4Q182, 4Q178, and 4Q183. She has labeled all five manuscripts "Eschatological Midrash." However, despite several similarities in form and content, none of these manuscripts contains any overlap with the others. 4Q177 is clearly sectarian as can be seen in phrases like "Sons of Light" (iv.12, iv.16),

"Seekers after Smooth Things" (ii.12; cf. 4QPesher Nahum 3–4.i.2, ii.2, ii.4, iii.3, iii.6–7), and "council of the community" (iii.5).

4Q177 is not a catena in the strict sense (a chain of quotations of either primary or secondary source material), since interpretative comments are given between the scriptural citations. It appears that the composition is a thematic commentary on a series of Psalms, some of which are cited merely by their opening verse(s), others more extensively. The Psalms are the principal texts in the commentary; *Deuteronomy* and the Prophets provide secondary supportive quotations. Both levels of quotation are formulaically introduced, the Psalms by some form of *amar* ("he said," i.e. David), the other quotations generally by *katuv* ("it is written"). The interpretations are also carefully structured. The term *pesher* is found twice (ii.9, iii.6) and is only used directly after a Psalms citation (as in 4Q174); the Psalms are viewed as unfulfilled prophecy. The structure is similar to that found in later *midrashim*, and it may not be entirely inappropriate to label the work *midrash*. The Psalms and Prophets are treated as if they have predicted present events; single words or phrases are identified atomistically; the original context of the proof-texts generally retains some relevance.

If Steudel's order of the fragments is correct, then it seems that 4Q177 is organized as a description of the sequence of events in the last days. The running narrative within the interpretation covers the flight of a persecuted community, description of various participants in the last days, a statement of the sure blessings that will be given to the Sons of Light, and the defeat of Belial and the men of his lot. The whole narrative is eschatological as the frequent use of the phrase "the last days" makes clear (ii.10, iii.5, iv.7, v.6), though there has been some dispute as to whether this term refers to the end time, the period before the end, or simply to the future.

Two small fragments are assigned to 4QCatena B (4Q182). They were associated with 4QCatena A for two reasons: Both fragments speak of "the last days," and fragment 1 contains part of a formulaic introduction to a quotation from *Jeremiah*. Steudel has proposed that 4Q Catena B should also be renamed "Eschatological Midrash" and that the fragments should be seen as yet another copy of the same composition.

BIBLIOGRAPHY

Allegro, John M., with the collaboration of Arnold A. Anderson. *Qumrân Cave 4.I (4Q158–4Q186)*. Discoveries in the Judaean Desert of Jordan, 5. Oxford, 1968. The official edition of 4Q177 is on pp. 67–74; eventually this will be revised by M. J. Bernstein, G. J. Brooke and F. H. Cryer.

Puech, Émile. *La Croyance des Esséniens en la vie future: immortalité, résurrection, vie éternelle? Histoire d'une croyance dans le judaïsme ancien*. Études Bibliques, 22. Paris, 1993. This detailed discussion of 4Q174 comments on parts of 4Q177 which like Steudel he considers to be another copy of the same composition.

Steudel, Annette. "Eschatological Interpretation of Scripture in 4Q177 (4QCatena[a])." *Revue de Qumrân* 14 (1989–1990), 473–481. A detailed consideration of the content of 4Q177.

Steudel, Annette. "4QMidrEschat: 'A Midrash on Eschatology' (4Q174–4Q177)." In *The Madrid Qumran Congress: Proceedings of the International Congress on the Dead Sea Scrolls, Madrid 18–21 March, 1991*, edited by J. Trebolle Barrera and L. Vegas Montaner, pp. 2.531–541. An English presentation of the main points of her thesis that 4Q174 and 4Q177 are two copies of the same composition.

Steudel, Annette. *Der Midrasch zur Eschatologie aus der Qumrangemeinde (4QMidrEschat[a,b]): Materielle Rekonstruktion, Textbestand, Gattung und traditionsgeschichtliche Einordnung des durch 4Q174 ("Florilegium") und 4Q177 ("Catenaa") repräsentierten Werkes aus den Qumranfunden*. Studies on the Texts of the Desert of Judah, 13. Leiden, 1994. The most comprehensive analysis concerning the reading and positioning of the fragments.

Strugnell, John. "Notes en marge du Volume V des 'Discoveries in the Judaean Desert of Jordan.'" *Revue de Qumrân* 7 (1969–1971), 163–276. Significant notes on the whole manuscript.

Yadin, Yigael. *The Temple Scroll*. Jerusalem, 1983. Understands 4Q177 to be referring to the Temple Scroll.

GEORGE J. BROOKE

CAVE OF ABU SHINJEH. *See* Daliyeh, Wadi ed-.

CAVE OF AVIʿOR. *See* Mafjar, Wadi el-.

CAVE OF HORROR. *See* Ḥever, Naḥal.

CAVE OF THE ARROWS. *See* Ṣeʾelim, Naḥal.

CAVE OF THE LETTERS. *See* Ḥever, Naḥal.

CAVE OF THE PAPYRI. *See* Daliyeh, Wadi ed-.

CAVE OF THE PARTRIDGE. *See* Qumran.

CAVE OF THE POOL. *See* Sdeir, Wadi.

CAVE OF THE RESERVOIR. *See* Ṣeʾelim, Naḥal.

CAVE OF THE SCROLLS. *See* Ṣeʾelim, Naḥal.

CAVE OF THE SKULLS. *See* Ṣeʾelim, Naḥal.

CAVE OF THE TREASURE. *See* Mishmar, Naḥal.

CELIBACY. Among Jewish groups of the Second Temple period, the only literary evidence for the practice of celibacy comes from the descriptions of the Therapeutae and the Essenes.

The Therapeutae were depicted by Philo as a small order of men and women living in a settlement near Alexandria, where they devoted themselves to a contemplative religious life "following the truly sacred instructions of the prophet Moses" (*On the Contemplative Life* 64). Although the women, seated separately, were equal participants in the ceremonial and philosophical activities of the group, they were not married to the men but were "most of them aged virgins, who have kept their chastity . . . of their own free will in their ardent yearning for wisdom" (*On the Contemplative Life* 68). We infer that a few women may have been previously married, but they were not devoted to the life of the spirit. Among men, too, the senior members were "those who from their earliest years have grown to manhood and spent their prime in pursuing the contemplative branch of philosophy" (*On the Contemplative Life* 67). It is noteworthy that the neglect of familial life is not viewed here as incompatible with Mosaic law, a perspective that may be compared with the blessing of the virtuous eunuch and barren woman in the *Wisdom of Solomon* 3.13–14. There is also no trace in Philo's laudatory description of the female Therapeutae of the mistrust of women that he elsewhere proffered (*Hypothetica* 11.14–17) as a rationale for celibacy among the Essenes.

The misogynic rationale for Essene celibacy was also introduced by Josephus into his account of their community (*The Jewish War* 2.120–121). However, unlike Philo who stated flatly that "no Essene takes a wife," Josephus reported the existence of "yet another order of Essenes" who did marry. They believed that failure to do so threatened "the chief function of life, the propagation of the race" (*The Jewish War* 2.160). The latter was for them the sole legitimate purpose of marriage; hence, they took pains to determine the fecundity of their prospective wives and forbade intercourse during pregnancy (*The Jewish War* 161).

The third major ancient writer to refer to the Essenes, Pliny the Elder, either did not know or chose to ignore the marrying Essenes. [*See* Pliny the Elder.] Instead, he offered readers of his *Natural History* the following dramatic depiction of Essene celibates:

> Gens sola, et in toto orbe prater ceteras mira, sine ulla femina, omne venera abdicata, sine pecunia, socia palmarum. . . . Ita per seculorum milia (incredibile dictu) gens aeterna est, in qua nemo nascitur.
>
> They are a lonely people, the most extraordinary in the world, [who live] without women, without love, without money, with the palm trees for their [only] companions. . . . So, through thousands of generations, hard though it is to believe, this people among which no one is born, has endured.
>
> (*Natural History* 5.17)

Despite the apparent chronological exaggeration, as we shall see, Pliny's description has a verbal parallel with a pivotal passage in the Damascus Document.

Celibacy at Qumran. The idea that celibacy was also found among the Qumran Covenanters emerged as an outgrowth of the widely held hypothesis that they were to be identified with the Essenes. Many similarities in organizational structure, in the sharing of goods, in the geographical location near the Dead Sea, as well as details concerning particular practices were noted by scholars as soon as the Rule of the Community was published. Moreover, although celibacy is nowhere mandated in the Rule of the Community from Qumran Cave 1 (hereafter, 1QRule of the Community, 1QS), its regulations and the penal code appear to reflect the discipline of an all-male "monastic" order: "And together they shall eat, together they shall recite benedictions, together they shall counsel" (1QS vi.2–3). Each man is seated according to his rank in the presence of the presiding priest (1QS vi.4). Wherever there are ten men, there must be one studying the Torah day and night, "each man relieving another" (1QS vi.7). Infractions of discipline are punished by reduction of the food allotment or suspension of the right to come in contact with the pure food of the many (1QS vi.25). Presumably, this presupposes that the men would not have the option of recourse to their own domestic board.

Women and children are nowhere mentioned in 1QRule of the Community. The blessing of "long life and fruitfulness of seed" (1QS iv.7) may be figurative. However, the education and marriage of young men in the End of Days figure prominently in the Rule of the Congregation (1Q28a). Here, twenty is set as the husband's minimal age for marriage, and the wife shares responsibility for keeping their marital relations within the bounds of the precepts of the Torah (1Q28a 1.11). This may well be an allusion to the restriction of nonprocreative intercourse, also found among the marrying Essenes. That women were instructed in the precepts of the Torah is implied by their required presence at the assembly where the Law was read (1QS i.4).

Unlike 1QRule of the Community, the law code of the Damascus Document embraces several rules pertaining to marriage and family life: marriage is limited to one spouse in one's lifetime, marriages between uncles and nieces are banned as incestuous, the right of a husband to annul the vows of his wife is elaborated, sexual relations in the city of the sanctuary are forbidden, and provision is made for the oath of the covenant by sons when they reach the age of twenty. Proponents of the identification of the Qumran community with the Essenes were thus led early on to attribute the Damascus Document to the marrying Essenes. However, in light of the additional texts now available from Cave 4, this dichotomy between 1QRule of the Community and the Damascus Document no longer appears as straightforward as was thought. Although we have manuscripts of the latter with additional laws pertaining to marriage, we also have substantial parallels to the penal code of 1QRule of the Community, which apparently was capable of being adapted to a nonmonastic setting. One previously unknown penal rule from Damascus Document[e] concerns "one who comes near to fornicate with his wife contrary to the Law" (4Q270 7.i.12–13), which we have suggested most likely refers to forbidden intercourse. Another sets a penalty for murmuring against the mothers (4Q270 7.i.14), thus indicating that the latter had an honored place in the congregation.

An Allusion to Men of Perfect Holiness. Despite these indications that marriage and family were considered normal in the law code of the Damascus Document, there is one passage that contains a significant allusion to celibacy as the lifestyle of an elitist element within the community. The Damascus Document (CD vi.11–vii.6) contains an extended list of duties incumbent upon "those that walk in the perfection of holiness." For their dedication they are assured that "the covenant of God shall stand faithfully with them to keep them alive for thousands of generations" (CD vii.6, xix.20). The latter phrase corresponds to Pliny's *saeculorum milia* ("through thousands of generations"). Immediately following we have an adversative provision: "And if they dwell in camps according to the order [*serekh*] of the land and take wives and beget children, they shall walk according to the Law" (CD vii.6–7). The conditional phrase "And if" indicates that the previously mentioned aspirants to perfect holiness did not dwell in scattered camps in the conventional manner of the land, did not take wives, and did not beget children. Yet, they too were assured existence for "thousands of generations" through the continuity of the *gens aeterna*, *ʿam ʿolamim* ("eternal people"; Ritual of Marriage, 4Q502 24.3).

If the celibate men of perfect holiness did not dwell in camps, where would one have found them? One possibility is that the practice of celibacy was confined to the communal center at Qumran and its environs. It has been estimated from the sampling of the graves in the cemeteries that 90 percent of the men lived here without their wives. This, however, may merely reflect temporary separation during the intensification of purity associated with the renewal of the covenant.

More pertinent to the reference to "camps" in the Damascus Document (CD vii.6) is Elisha Qimron's observation that in Miqtsat Maʿasei ha-Torah (MMT) texts found in Cave 4 at Qumran (4Q394–399), Jerusalem is distinguished from other "camps" as "the chief of the camps of Israel" (4Q395 62) and as "the holy camp" (4Q395 60). This finds expression in various stringencies in the laws of purity applicable to the city of the sanctuary, especially the ban on sexual relations (CD xiii.1). The Temple Scroll[a] (11Q19 xlv.11) excludes from the Temple city anyone who has had sex or a seminal flux during the preceding three days. The model for this severe restriction was probably found in the preparations of Sinai (*Ex.* 19.15), but its application to people living in Jerusalem would have made celibacy for them a practical necessity. Yet, the Damascus Document does not localize the residence of the men of perfect holiness to Jerusalem, which in the present "period of evil" would rather have been a place upon which "to close the door" (CD vi.12–14). Qimron therefore invokes the further hypothesis that the men of perfect holiness regarded themselves as a kind of substitute for Jerusalem.

The Qumran Concept of Marriage. Qumran writings reflect a markedly idealistic view of marriage as an exclusive covenant between one man and one woman "in their lifetime." This is in accord with the "foundation of creation" as found in *Genesis* 1.27, "male and female he created them."

It required full maturity on the part of the husband, attainable only after the age of twenty, "when he knows good and evil" (1Q28a i.11). The wife, too, was to be of unblemished character and knowledgeable of the laws applicable to marriage, although no minimal age is specified. Remarriage after the death of a spouse was condoned (11Q19 lvii.17–19) but apparently not after divorce. Polygamy was seen as one of Belial's traps.

The ideal relationship between husband and wife is alluded to in the Ritual of Marriage (4Q502), a fragmentary but significant text. One fragment alludes to "[Adam] and his wife." The pairing of male and female is further indicated by the word *reʿiyyatov* ("his companion"). Another fragment has an alternation of blessings. First a man extends a blessing to a woman for "long life amidst an eternal people." Then the woman invokes a similar blessing for longevity upon the man. The editor, Maurice Baillot, and other scholars assume this to be an exchange of vows between a bridegroom and his bride. This writer, however, noted that the ceremony takes place "in the council of elderly men and women" and that allusions to old men, collectively called "Brothers," and their female counterparts, called "Sisters," occur prominently in these fragments. This raises the question of whether the exchange of blessings rather might be between happily married senior members honored at some festive communal occasion. However this may be, the text shows clearly that women of virtue (one is called "Daughter of Truth"), rather than being denigrated, were honored for their longevity within the Qumran community.

In conclusion, there is no evidence that celibacy was ever made into a general norm at Qumran. To the contrary, marriage for the purpose of raising children "in the way of the land" was the general rule. This has been used as one of the major arguments against the identification of the Qumran community with the Essenes by Norman Golb and other critics of this widely held hypothesis.

However, the pervasive concern with purity in Qumran law could not have been without its consequences. Aside from the sharply dualistic ethic that contrasts spirit and flesh, those who aspired to perfect holiness would have found the practical maintenance of normal marital life difficult, if not impossible. A. Guillaumont has noted the tradition, found already in Philo, that Moses renounced all conjugal relations from the time that he began to prophesy. This has relevance to the Covenanters, who may not have viewed themselves as prophets but who lived with the constant expectation of revelations granted to those who were spiritually worthy. For many, this may have meant protracted periods of separation from their wives, especially when participating in the general sessions of the community. For a few, the men of perfect holiness, it apparently led to the renunciation of marriage and family life for a higher level of spiritual attainment.

[*See also* Family Life; Marriage and Divorce; Rule of the Community; *and* Rule of the Congregation.]

BIBLIOGRAPHY

Baumgarten, Joseph M. "The Qumran-Essene Restraints on Marriage." In *Archaeology and History in the Dead Sea Scrolls*, edited by Lawrence H. Schiffman, pp. 13–24. Sheffield, 1990.

Golb, Norman. *Who Wrote the Dead Sea Scrolls?: The Search for the Secret of Qumran*. New York, 1995.

Guillaumont, A. "A propos du célibat des Esséniens." In *Hommages à André Dupont-Sommer*, edited by André Caquot and Marc Philonenko, pp. 395–404. Paris, 1971.

Qimron, Elisha. "Celibacy in the Dead Sea Scrolls and the Two Kinds of Sectarians." In *The Madrid Qumran Congress: Proceedings of the International Congress on the Dead Sea Scrolls, Madrid, 18–21 March 1991*, edited by Julio Trebolle Barrera and Luis Vegas Montaner, pp. 287–294. Studies on the Texts of the Desert of Judah, 11. Leiden, 1992.

Schiffman, Lawrence H. "Women in the Scrolls." In *Reclaiming the Dead Sea Scrolls: The History of Judaism, the Background of Christianity, the Lost Library at Qumran*. Philadelphia, 1994. See pages 127–144.

Talmon, Shemaryahu. "The Community of the Renewed Covenant: Between Judaism and Christianity." In *The Community of the Renewed Covenant*, edited by Eugene Ulrich and James VanderKam, pp. 9–10. Notre Dame, Ind., 1994.

JOSEPH M. BAUMGARTEN

CEMETERIES. The Qumran and Wadi-Ghweir cemeteries reveal burial practices that differ considerably from the accepted normative Jewish customs found in Jerusalem, Jericho, and ʿEin-Gedi in the Second Temple period. The fundamental differences in placement and structure of the tombs and the demography of the cemeteries, as well as type of deposition, seem to reflect different attitudes toward death, with the Qumran community separating itself from mainstream Judaism. [*See* ʿEin-Gedi; Ghweir, Wadi; Jerusalem.]

Qumran. The Qumran cemetery was used during periods Ib–II of the Qumran settlement during the first century BCE until the destruction of the site in 68 CE, with intensive use for several years. This dating agrees with that of the community who lived at Qumran and its environs, probably in caves, huts, and tents. The Qumran cemetery was a central community burial place; however, these clearly are not family tombs. Although the number of excavated tombs is small, it is apparent that the Qumran community practiced primary burial with or without a wooden coffin in individual shaft graves. The burials also lack inscriptions. The graves are carefully dug out and arranged, which seems to rule out the assumption by some scholars that the tombs were dug in haste for a large group of dying people involved in the First Jewish Revolt against the Romans (66–70 CE). [*See* Rome.] Scholarly controversy exists about the question of identifying the Qumran community and cemetery with the Essene sect. [*See* Essenes.]

The main cemetery of Qumran is located 30–40 meters east of the settlement and contains about 1,100 graves. Only fifty-two tombs were excavated (forty-three by de Vaux and nine by Steckoll) in the main and secondary cemeteries. In the main cemetery (and its extensions) twenty-six tombs were excavated, in different parts of the cemetery. The tombs are arranged in neat, ordered rows, separated by two alleys into three plots. Nearly all the tombs are oriented on a north–south axis, and each grave is marked by a heap of stones on the surface. The tomb form is a shaft hewn as a rectangular cavity at the bottom, cut horizontally to accommodate the corpse. The dead were placed supine: the head oriented to the south with a stone beneath it or small stones beside it; arms stretched along the sides of the body or crossed on the pelvis. In three tombs remnants of wooden coffins were found. On the downward sloping hills, seven more tombs were found with less regularity of orientation.

In the main cemetery area all the excavated tombs contained males, while in the extended areas of the cemetery four of the six skeletons examined are female, and one is a child. Two female skeletons had beads and earrings, but no other objects were found in the tombs.

Two secondary cemeteries were found at Qumran. One cemetery, located north of Qumran, was the site of a group of twelve tombs, similar to the tombs in the main cemetery. The two that were excavated contained one male and one female skeleton, respectively. The other secondary cemetery is located to the south of Wadi Qumran and consists of a group of thirty tombs of varying orientations. Four tombs were excavated: one contained a woman, the others children. The burial of large numbers of males in the main cemetery and a much smaller number of women and children in the extensions of the main cemetery and in the secondary cemeteries may be significant.

Wadi Ghweir. The cemetery of Wadi Ghweir is contemporary with the Qumran cemeteries (first century BCE–first century CE). Seventeen tombs were excavated in this cemetery located 800 meters north of a building. The form of the tombs is similar to those at Qumran: their orientation is north–south, and each grave is marked by a heap of stones. The interred lay supine. Remains of twelve men and six women were discovered in the north hill tombs; a man and a child were found in the south hill tombs. Some broken vessels and potsherds were found placed on the tombs. Among the finds was a jar inscribed with the name Yehoḥanan.

The large building at Wadi Ghweir served for ceremonial and assembly purposes, much as the public center at Qumran, although the community members probably lived in caves, tents, and booths. The cemetery of Wadi Ghweir served the settlement's occupants. The inhabitants of Qumran and Wadi Ghweir seemingly belonged to the same sect.

Other Judean Desert Sites. Several tombs dated to the Second Temple period were excavated in the ʿEin-Gedi area. Six small caves were excavated at Naḥal David and used for primary burials and reinterments. These burials, probably of the inhabitants of ʿEin Gedi, are dated to the first century BCE, during the Hasmonean period. In Caves 1 and 4 remnants of wooden coffins were discovered, (one of them decorated with bone and wood inlays). Other finds included a wooden bowl and cup, basket remnants, and fruits. Also a wrapped skeleton was preserved, still with leather shoes. In Caves 2 and 3 bones, pottery vessels, and bronze ladles were found, and, in Cave 5, several skulls, cooking pots and a glass bottle. In the small Cave 6 only fragments were discovered.

The nine tombs found at ʿEin-Gedi (second–first centuries BCE) were badly eroded: some were found still with the sealed entrance intact. They consisted of loculi (burial recess hewn in tomb wall), a chamber, and central pit. The burial customs of the ʿEin-Gedi tombs show several modes of burial: the most prevalent was primary burial in wooden coffins. Others consisted of primary burial on the tomb floor with the corpse wrapped in mats or shrouds. Secondary burial was in wooden coffins or in stone or wooden ossuaries. These modes of burial are based on only a few examples, so it is difficult to describe the actual practices and their chronological development. It should also be noted that nothing was found to prove that the ʿEin-Gedi burials were Jewish, except for finds and customs similar to those found at the Jewish cemeteries of Jerusalem and Jericho.

About forty wooden coffins were found: rectangular chests with four small legs and gabled or flat lids, mostly made of sycamore and seldom decorated. The construction of the ʿEin-Gedi coffins consists of planks joined at the corners with uprights to function as legs, all joined by tapered wooden pegs and unlike the technique used for the coffins at Jericho.

Other finds in the ʿEin-Gedi tombs consisted of wooden vessels and bowls; cosmetics items (ointment bowls, combs, a kohl tube); bronze objects (a jug, ladles, and kohl sticks); pottery vessels; glass and stone beads; remains of palm mats and a basket; and remains of textiles, possibly burial shrouds. [*See* ʿEin-Gedi.]

The graves from other sites in the Judean Desert indicate that they were not from organized or designated cemeteries, like others of the Second Temple period. As the skeletal remains from these graves showed no signs of violence, the assumption is that they died of hunger and thirst during a long siege at the place they were hiding, probably in the second century CE, in connection with the Bar Kokhba Revolt.

At Masada, in the Cave of the Skeletons, a great heap of about twenty-five skeletons and bones (including women and children) was found above objects such as pottery and fragments of mats and remnants of food. They seem to have been tossed down haphazardly, probably at the end of the Masada siege in 73 CE. [*See* Masada, *article on* Archaeology.] Several graves were found in the Cave of Horror (Cave 8), with forty corpses, including women and children. The finds consisted of fragments of cloth and two iron awls which were found beside the pelvis of a complete skeleton; ostraca (inscribed pottery fragments), probably connected with the graves; three fragments of parchment with Hebrew writing. In the Cave of Letters, Burial Niche 2, in the eastern wall of Chamber III, included secondary burials in three groups: three baskets, each of which contained several skulls; a group of graves, in which some of the bones were wrapped in cloth; and a single grave covered by cloth. Some of the graves are of women and children. It is apparent that the bones were collected and placed in and among the baskets, possibly by refugees.

Cemeteries of the Second Temple Period. The Jerusalem and Jericho cemeteries constitute our data for funerary customs in the Second Temple period. Their location was outside the town limits, in accordance with Jewish law.

The Jerusalem cemeteries consisted of tombs surrounding the walls of the city, in three major areas to the north, south, and east. Several crowded burial quarters and plots exist in the present-day areas of Mount Scopus, Dominus Flevit and French Hill, Sanhedria, and other parts of Jerusalem. The majority of the tombs are loculi tombs and in many of them burial in ossuaries was found, as well as a few sarcophagi. A group of monumental rock-hewn tombs, such as the Kidron Valley tombs (the tomb of Zachariah, the Bene-Hezir tomb, and the Monument of Absalom), the Jason Tomb, and the Tomb of the Kings—probably belonging to prominent Jerusalem families—have a memorial (*nefesh*) in the shape of a pyramid or tholus standing above the ground and richly ornamented facades. In spite of the lavish ornamentation, burial was probably similar to that of the simpler, undecorated loculi tombs. Many of the tombs were found in a disturbed, looted state.

The Jericho cemetery was located outside the town, on the hills flanking the Jordan Valley. Approximately 120 rock-hewn loculi tombs were discovered containing either primary burials in wooden coffins or secondary collected-bone burials in ossuaries or in heaps.

The tomb forms. The tombs found in Jerusalem and Jericho consist of rock-hewn tombs cut into the hillsides. Two basic tomb plans exist: one is known as the loculi type (*kokhim*); the other, the arcosolia type. Both types of plans are found in the Jerusalem necropolis, but the Jericho cemetery consists of only loculi tombs. Occasionally, single-loculus tombs were constructed.

The form of the loculi tomb is square, often with a pit dug into its floor, deep enough for a man to stand upright. The rim of the pit forms three or four benches, along each side of the tomb. One to three arched loculi (1 meter high and 2 meters long) are hewn into three of the walls, the entrance wall being excepted. The entrance to the tomb is rectangular; in Jerusalem it sometimes has a forecourt and an ornamented facade. The entrance is closed either by a blocking stone, sometimes in the shape of a large "stopper," or by mud bricks and small stones.

The evidence from Jericho proves conclusively that loculi tombs were first designed and used for primary, that is, permanent, burial in wooden coffins. The same tomb plan continued to be used in the case of ossuary burials. The origin of the plan for the rock-cut loculi tomb of the Second Temple period in Judea is to be found in Egypt, particularly in Leontopolis, from as early as Hasmonean times.

A few tombs have a courtyard with benches and an attached *miqveh* (ritual bath where purification rites took place), which was used probably for mourning and for memorial services, as at the "eulogy place" mentioned in Jewish sources. Courtyards with benches dating to the third century are also found at Beth Shearim and probably served a similar purpose.

In the Jerusalem tombs a later type of burial is found: the *arcosolium*, which is a benchlike aperture with an arched ceiling hewn into the length of the wall. In several cases the deceased was interred in a trough grave hewn in the arcosolium.

Both types of burial, in the common loculi tomb, and in the arcosolia tomb, were in use at the end of the Second Temple period. These tombs served as family tombs, with provision for separate burial of each individual in the loculus or arcosolium and its container.

Several shaft (dug-out) tombs, similar to the Qumran tombs, were found in several locations in Jerusalem, especially Beit Zafafa. (In Jericho, however, the shaft tombs are reused Middle Bronze tombs.) Some scholars suggest that these tombs were burial places of individuals who belonged to the Dead Sea sect who lived in Jerusalem; others maintain that the shaft graves might have been in frequent use in Jerusalem and elsewhere, but did not survive as well as the rock-hewn tombs.

Wooden coffins were discovered in the Jericho, ʿEin-Gedi, and Qumran tombs. The form of the Jericho coffin was a wooden chest with a post at each corner, constructed by mortise and tenon joinery (that is, with wooden pegs which interlocked with rectangular-shaped cavities). The lid of the chest was usually gabled, and consisted of one plank on each side and a pediment at each end. One well-preserved example, however, has a hinged lid. Iron nails and knobs found with the coffins were probably used only for decoration or structural support. The coffins were decorated with red- and black-painted geometrical patterns and designs. The most common types of wood were sycamore, Christ's-thorn, and cypress. Earlier examples of similar wooden coffins, dating to the fourth century BCE, have survived in Egypt and South Russia.

It should be noted that the wooden coffins in Jericho were used for primary burials only and not as containers for secondary burials. This is in contrast to the wooden coffins at ʿEin-Gedi, which were also reused as ossuaries.

Ossuaries were hewn from one large block of limestone, usually in the shape of a small, rectangular box, often decorated, resting on four low legs, and measuring approximately 60 by 35 by 30 centimeters for adults, and less for children. A stone lid, flat, slightly curved, or gabled, was placed on top. Inscriptions on ossuaries, incised, scratched, or written, have been found on the front, back, sides, and lid. They usually contained the name of the interred person and his family relations; sometimes the inscriptions included a profession or a status. Special kinds of inscriptions were sometimes found—such as an alphabet—or objects, such as a unique, inscribed funerary bowl from an ossuary tomb at Jericho.

Dates for the burials are still the subject of debate. Nevertheless, the Jericho cemetery can provide a chronology for the two different types of burials: Primary burials in coffins can be dated from the mid-first century BCE to 10 CE, and secondary burials in ossuaries immediately followed, dating from 10 CE to 68 CE. Rahmani dates the practice of secondary burials in ossuaries in Jerusalem to 30/20 BCE–70 CE, continuing sporadically until 135 CE or even the third century.

Burial practices. Jewish burial practices of the late Second Temple period reveal a corresponding importance placed on both the individual and the family. At Jerusalem, Jericho, and ʿEin-Gedi, this is reflected in the plan of the loculi tomb and arcosolia tomb, which provided for individual burial in a coffin, in an ossuary, or in a separate loculus, yet allowing a family to be buried together in the same tomb. All strata of the population, not just the upper classes (as in the Israelite period), were accorded individual burials. This practice is probably related to the increasing importance placed on the individual in contemporary Hellenistic society, and to the Jewish belief in individual resurrection of the body. This belief is reflected in sources dating as early as the second century BCE. [*See* Death; Religious Beliefs, Qumran Sect.]

As far as deposition of the remains is concerned, the excavations in the extended Jerusalem necropolis and the Jericho cemetery reveal that two completely different burial customs, one chronologically following the other, were practiced by Jews of the Second Temple period. The earlier custom (first century BCE), found in Jericho, ʿEin-Gedi, and Qumran, is a primary individual burial in a wooden coffin. The second burial custom found later in Jerusalem and in the Jericho cemetery (and in some of the ʿEin-Gedi wooden coffins) is the deliberate secondary burial of the bones, either in communal burials in loculi or pits or in individual ossuaries; this practice lacks parallels with any other contemporary neighboring culture. This complete change in burial customs occurred during the beginning of the first century CE, simultaneously with a change in the political status of Judea, which then became a Roman province. [*See* Judea, *article on* History.] So far, no theory has been able to account for this drastic change in burial customs; unfortunately, all ancient sources dealing with ossilegia (the act of collecting bones and placing them in an ossuary) describe only the custom itself, without mentioning the reasons for its sudden appearance. Rahmani (1994, p. 53) suggests that ossuary burial began as an attempt to expiate sins through the decay of the flesh, which would then allow resurrection of the purified physical individual. This seems to be plausible, particularly in view of the historical events of the period.

The Judean Desert Documents and Burial Practices. The Temple Scroll (11QT) is the only document of the Dead Sea Scrolls in which burial customs are mentioned. [*See* Temple Scroll.] It deals with the commandments regarding uncleanliness contracted from the dead, discussing burial grounds (xlviii.11–14); the house of the dead person (xlix.5–21); uncleanliness of a grave (l.5–9). The scroll bans random burials in dwellings and cities, instead stipulating that one burial place should be assigned to every four cities (per tribe), so as not to pollute all the land. However, the archaeological finds indicate some different practices in this period: the cemetery of Qumran was found in the area east of the buildings: the excavated cemeteries of Jerusalem and Jericho of the Second Temple period are hewn on hills outside the cities.

The uncleanliness of the house, its residents and contents, and the manner of its purification and cleansing are treated in the Temple Scroll in detail (xlix.11–17). [*See* Purity.] Uncleanliness occurs also by contact or by touching the bone of a dead man, blood of a dead man, or a grave. Yigael Yadin asserts that the scroll intimates that all these proscriptions concerning uncleanliness contracted from the dead, usually only applied to the priests, should apply instead to all the people of Israel.

Thus there are no clear rules indicated by the Dead Sea manuscripts. As interpreted by Yadin and Lawrence H. Schiffman, they seem to follow the usual Jewish laws with some modifications. Significantly, the writings do not explain the significance of some of the Qumran burial customs.

[*See* Archaeology; Qumran, *article on* Archaeology.]

BIBLIOGRAPHY

Avigad, N., *Ancient Monuments in the Kidron Valley* (Hebrew). Jerusalem, 1954.

Avigad, N. "Expedition A, The Burial Caves of Nahal David," *Israel Exploration Journal* 12 (1962), 181–183.

Bennet, C. M. "Tombs of the Roman Period." In *Excavations at Jericho*, vol. 2, edited by K. M. Kenyon. London, 516–535.

de Vaux, Roland. "Fouilles de Khirbet Qumran, Le cimetière," *Revue biblique* 63 (1956), 569–572.

Hachlili, R. "Burial Practices at Qumran," *Revue de Qumrân* 62 (1993), 247–264.

Hachlili, R. "The Change in Burial Customs in the Late Second Temple Period, in Light of the Jericho Cemetery Excavation (Hebrew). In *Tombs and Burial*, edited by I. Singer, see 173–189. Tel Aviv, 1994.

Hachlili, R., and Killebrew, A. "Jewish Funerary Customs during the Second Temple Period, in Light of the Excavations at the Jericho Necropolis." *Palestine Exploration Quarterly* 115 (1983), 109–139.

Hachlili, R. and Killebrew, A. *Jericho—The Jewish Cemetery of the Second Temple Period* (in press).

Hadas, G. *Nine Tombs of the Second Temple Period at En Gedi* (Hebrew). *Atiqot* 24 (1994), English abstract, 1–8.

Kloner, A., "The Necropolis of Jerusalem in the Second Temple" (Hebrew) Ph.D. thesis, University of Jerusalem.

Rahmani, L. Y. *Catalogue of Jewish Ossuaries. In the Collections of the State of Israel*. Jerusalem, 1994.

Steckoll, S. H. "Preliminary Excavation Report in the Qumran Cemetery." *Revue de Qumrân* 6 (1968), 323–336.

RACHEL HACHLILI

CHILDREN. *See* Family Life.

CHRONICLES, FIRST AND SECOND BOOKS OF. The manuscript of Chronicles (4Q118), preserved in only one fragment, belongs paleographically to the late Hasmonean period (ca. 50–25 BCE). The portion of text contained in column ii corresponds to *2 Chronicles* 28.27–29.3. This sole surviving manuscript is enough to attest the presence of *Chronicles* in the Qumran library. The reading *veta'aleni* ("raise me") in column i, 1.3 does not have any counterpart in the Masoretic Text of *Chronicles* and *Kings* nor in the presumed original of Septuagint *Chronicles* (Trebolle). It suggests a psalmodic context (cf. *Ps*. 71.20, 102.25), raising the possibility that 4QChronicles is rather a historiographic work parallel to *Chronicles* that contains a prayer or psalm; also the Paraphrase of Kings et al. (4Q382) seems to intercalate prayers and prophecies (A. Rofé, private communication).

The author of *Chronicles* knew a text of *Samuel-Kings* similar to that attested by Samuel[a] (4Q51), the Old Greek and its proto-Lucianic recension of Samuel-Kings, and Josephus (Cross; Ulrich). The Greek translation (*Paraleipomena*) reflects this textual tradition. Many variants that were ascribed to the author(s) of *Chronicles*, particularly historical or theological changes, are rather to be explained as elements proper to that textual tradition of Samuel-Kings (Lemke; Klein). *Chronicles* preserves some readings that are older than the parallel in Masoretic Text Samuel/Kings, as *ish ba'al/ish boshet* (*1 Chr*. 8.33; *2 Sm*. 2.8).

As a reworking of inherited biblical material, *Chronicles* has been characterized as exegesis, targum, midrash, or "rewritten Bible." It is, however, a unique work. The unparalleled materials of *Chronicles* have always raised the question of possible extra-biblical sources. As for the section about the building of the Temple (*2 Chr*. 3), it has been suggested that, besides *1 Kings* 6–8, the author knew a text akin to that of the Temple Scroll (11QT [11Q19] v–vii) (Steins).

The Greek version, *Paraleipomena*, probably dated to second century Egypt, although extensively revised, is best preserved in manuscripts B (Vaticanus), S (Sinaiticus) and minuscule c_2 (Allen). Not a few of its many variants represent preferable readings to those of the Masoretic Text (*1 Chr*. 2.24, 4.15, 26.17; *2 Chr*. 1.13, 14.6, 19.8, 3.22, 32.22, and many more) (Japhet). It often agrees with the Masoretic Text or the Septuagint Samuel-Kings against the Masoretic Text *Chronicles*. The translator made use of the Greek version of *Kings*, possibly in a nonrevised form (Shenkel). The text of the supplements in *2 Paraleipomena* 35–36 is taken from the old, nonrevised Greek of *Kings*, or at least from an old pre-Lucianic recension (Klein). G. Gerleman and L. C. Allen argue, rather, in favor of a secondary assimilation of both Greek versions.

A "Prayer of Manasseh, king of Judah, when the king of Assyria put him in prison" is among the Noncanonical Psalms found at Qumran (4Q381, frg. 33.8; cf. *2 Chr*. 33). The *Second Book of Chronicles* 20.7 is alluded to in the Commentary on Genesis A (4Q252 ii.7–8) where the "tents of Shem" (*Gn*. 9.27) are identified as the land given "to Abraham, his beloved." Work with Place Names (4Q522) mentions the "rock of Zion" in a context similar to that of *1 Chronicles* 21.18–22.1.

BIBLIOGRAPHY

Allen, Leslie C. *The Greek Chronicles: The Relation of the Septuagint of I and II Chronicles to the Massoretic Text*. Supplements to Vetus Testamentum, 25 and 27. Leiden, 1974.

Cross, Frank Moore. "The Old Testament at Qumrân." In *The Ancient Library of Qumran*, pp. 121–142. 3rd ed. Biblical Seminar, 30. Sheffield, 1995.

Gerleman, Gillis. *Studies in the Septuagint: II Chronicles*. Lunds Universitets Årsskrift, N.F. Avd. 1, Bd. 44, Nr 5. Lund, 1946.

Japhet, Sara. *I & II Chronicles: A Commentary*. Old Testament Library. London, 1993.

Klein, Ralph W. "New Evidence for an Old Recension of Reigns." *Harvard Theological Review* 60 (1967), 93–105.

Klein, Ralph W. "Supplements in the Paralipomena: A Rejoinder." *Harvard Theological Review* 61 (1968), 492–495.

Lemke, Werner. "The Synoptic Problem in the Chronicler's History." *Harvard Theological Review* 58 (1965), 349–363.

Puech, Émile. "La pierre de Sion et l'autel des holocaustes d'après un manuscrit hébreu de la grotte 4 (4Q522)." *Revue de Qumrân* 15 (1992), 676–696.

Shenkel, James D. "A Comparative Study of the Synoptic Parallels in I Paralipomena and I–II Reigns." *Harvard Theological Review* 62 (1969), 63–85.

Steins, Georg. *Die Chronik als kanonisches Abschlussphänomen: Studien zur Entstehung und Theologie von 1/2 Chronik*. Bonner Biblischer Beiträge, 93. Bodenheim, 1995.

Trebolle, Julio. "Édition préliminaire de 4QChroniques." *Revue de Qumrân* 15 (1992), 523–529.

Ulrich, Eugene Charles. *The Qumran Text of Samuel and Josephus*. Harvard Semitic Monographs, 19. Chico, Calif., 1978.

Williamson, H. G. M. *1 and 2 Chronicles*. The New Century Bible Commentary. Grand Rapids, Mich., and London, 1987.

JULIO TREBOLLE BARRERA

CHURCHES. The emperor Constantine (died 337) and his mother Helena were the first to erect churches in Palestine. Earlier, Christians did not have a prayer house with distinctive architectural features. Their place of assembly was a *domus ecclesia*, a domestic building that was adjusted to serve this purpose. The erection of churches was a major domain of imperial enterprise.

Four churches were erected by Constantine: the Church of the Holy Sepulchre in Jerusalem, the Church of the Nativity in Bethlehem, the Church of Abraham's Oak at Mamre, and the Eleona Church on the Mount of Olives. Other churches were erected by later emperors, wealthy donors, and community members.

To date, about three hundred churches from the Byzantine period are known in Israel. But their number was much larger, since every Christian village and monastery possessed at least one church, and there were several in each town or city. The first effort toward a synthetic study of the churches of Palestine, done by Crowfoot (1941), was augmented and elaborated by Ovadiah's *Corpus of Byzantine Churches in the Holy Land* (1970), which was continually updated (Ovadiah and de Silva, 1981–1984). Other important contributions were made by Bagatti (1971), and more recently by Bottini, Di Segni, and Alliata (1990), and Tsafrir (1993).

The churches in the Judean Desert, known as the desert of the Holy City in the contemporary ecclesiastical sources, were mainly monastic chapels. [*See* Monasteries.] These include the chapels at Masada and the chapels in the monasteries of the desert of Zif near Capharbaricha (Bani Naim), the chapels in the desert of Natufa near Thecoa, the Sabas and Euthymius monasteries in the desert of Rouba to the east of Bethlehem and Jerusalem, and the monasteries of the desert of Jordan near Jericho. Hermitages of *laura* monks were regularly equipped with private chapels (Patrich, 1995; Tsafrir, 1993, pp. 233–243). Three small basilical churches were found in lower Herodium, and another monastic chapel was found on the hilltop (Bottini et al., 1990, pp. 165–176; Tsafrir, 1993, pp. 219–232).

Besides the daily prayers and the celebration of the Eucharist, the cult of relics of martyrs and saints took place in the church. Relics were generally held in a special stone or marble container shaped like a tiny sarcophagus, a reliquary. Generally, the relics were placed under the main altar, but more than one saint could have been venerated in a single church, and then one or both of the lateral rooms or apses flanking the central apse could have been used for this purpose. The baptismal rite was another function associated with a church. In the monastic context of the Judean Desert it was associated mainly with the conversion to Christianity of the Arab tribes of the desert (Bottini et al., 1990, pp. 501–522).

Pilgrims were attracted to monasteries, looking for counsel and healing from the monks, some of whom were venerated as holy men and workers of wonders. The original cave of the founder or his tomb was sometimes given an elaborate architectural shape that included a chapel. Holy sites associated with monastic events, possessing their own chapels, came into being along secondary routes running between the monasteries and the dispersed hermitages (Hirschfeld, 1993). From a spot adjacent to Capharbaricha (Jerome, *Epistle* 108.11.5) pilgrims used to have an overlook over the desert wastes, the Dead Sea, and the former sites of Sodom and Gomorrah.

In the Jericho Valley and near the Jordan River there were several important pilgrim churches associated with the site of baptism and with some traditions of the Hebrew scriptures and the New Testament, since as a rule a church was erected over a holy site, which soon became a center of pilgrimage. The road from Jerusalem to the Jordan River via Jericho was a busy pilgrimage route. Guesthouses along this route and elsewhere had chapels as well. A map of the monasteries and of the pilgrimage sites in the Judean Desert and the Dead Sea region thus matches the map of chapels and churches (see the map of churches in Tsafrir, 1993, and in Tsafrir et al., 1994).

From the early fourth century (Eusebius, *Onomasticon* 59.18) the baptismal site at Bethabara (Makhadet el Hajla) was the most important pilgrimage site near the Jordan. According to the pilgrim Theodosius (before 581 CE), the place where Christ was baptized was marked by a marble pillar on which an iron cross was set. The emperor Anastasius erected a church dedicated to John the Baptist nearby; it was supported by great vaults, high enough to withstand the Jordan floods. Each of the monks residing in this church received six gold coins (*solidi*) a year from the imperial treasury for his livelihood. The church at Bethabara is depicted on the sixth-century Madeba mosaic map. The Piacenza pilgrim (ca. 570) gives a detailed description of the Epiphany rite at the site of baptism, where on both banks there are steps leading down to the river. Near the site of baptism he mentions a very large monastery of Saint John, which had two guesthouses. Arculf's pilgrimage, from approximately 681 to 684, recounted by Adamnan at the end of the seventh century, gives further details on the site of baptism in his day: a tall wooden cross was set in the riverbed, near the western side. From this cross a stone causeway supported on arches stretched to the bank, and people could approach the cross going down the ramp and returning to the riverbank. Right at the river's edge stood a small rectangular church, supported by four stone vaults and with a tiled roof. According to the local tradition it was built at the place where Jesus' clothes were placed while he was baptized. Farther up, upon a hill overlooking the church, there was a great monastery. Enclosed within the masonry wall of the monastery was the church built in honor of Saint John the Baptist. According to a post-Byzantine tradition (Epiphanius), a stone on which John the Baptist stood when baptizing Christ was set in the apse of the Forerunner Church.

One mile north of Jericho was the site of Galgala (Juljulieh), with the twelve stones that the sons of Israel took up from the Jordan. The Jewish site of pilgrimage was taken over by the Christians in the early fourth century. A church depicted on the Madeba mosaic map is first mentioned by the Piacenza pilgrim, who relates that the twelve huge stones were shown in the basilica, behind the altar. In front of the basilica he mentioned a plain, the Lord's Field, which Jesus sowed with his own hands. The crop, reaped in February, was used for Communion at Easter.

The Piacenza pilgrim mentions a cave on the bank of the Jordan in which were cells for seven virgins who were placed there as small girls; when one of them died, she was buried in her cell, and another cell was hewn from the rock, so that another girl could be placed there to make up the number. They had people outside to look after them. Pilgrims went in to pray there, but they were not allowed to see the face of any of the virgins.

The church at the spring of Elisha, at the foot of biblical Jericho (Tell es-Sultan), depicted on the Madeba map, is first mentioned by Theodosius as being two miles from Byzantine Jericho. Another site indicated by him at Jericho is the house of Rahab the prostitute, who received the spies. According to the Piacenza pilgrim, the house had a guesthouse, and the bedroom where she hid the spies served as a chapel of Saint Mary. Not far from Jericho to the south, the Piacenza pilgrim was shown the tree that Zacchaeus the tax collector climbed in order to see Jesus. The tree had been surrounded by a chapel and grew through the chapel's roof, but it had already dried up in his day. The steep ascent of the road leading from Jericho to Jerusalem was known as the ascent of Zacchaeus (*Miracles of the Holy Virgin in Choziba* 1). Epiphanius the monk (750–800 CE) mentioned farther along this road, twelve miles from the monastery of Euthymius, the church where Adam stayed and wept at losing Paradise. Near this church was the House of Joachim, a monastery (Khan Saliba). Farther to the west, along the road leading to Jerusalem, at the site of Qasr Ali, another station along the road was identified as the Church of Saint Peter, founded by the empress Eudocia.

To the north of Jericho there were churches at Phaselis (Jon Moschus *Leimonarion* 92), Archelais (Khirbet Beiyudat, a basilical church), and Khirbet Umm. Zaquma (a chapel). Another church nearer to Jericho (excluding monastic churches and chapels) was found at Tell Matleb, identified by some authors with Galgala. (For references see Tsafrir et al., 1994, under site names.)

On the southern side of the Dead Sea, the sanctuary of Saint Lot depicted on the Madeba map near Zoara (Ghor es Safi) was identified with the basilical church discovered in the monastery at Deir Ain Abata. The pilgrim Theodosius knew about a pillar of stone interpreted as Lot's wife; the Piacenza pilgrim mentioned many hermits in this neighborhood, the region of Segor.

BIBLIOGRAPHY

Avi Yonah, Michael. *The Madaba Mosaic Map*. Jerusalem, 1954.

Bagatti, B. *The Church from the Gentiles in Palestine: History and Archaeology*. Jerusalem, 1971.

Bottini, G. C., Leah Di Segni, and Eugenio Alliata. *Christian Archeology in the Holy Land. New Discoveries. Essays in Honour of Virgilio C. Corbo*. Jerusalem, 1990.

Crowfoot, John Winter. *Early Churches in Palestine*. London, 1941.

Geyer, Paul, ed. *Itineraria et alia geographica, Corpus Christianorum, Series Latina 175*. Turnhout, Belgium, 1965. This volume contains the Latin texts of the pilgrim Theodosius, the Piacenza Pilgrim, and Arculf, edited by L. Bieler.

Hirschfeld, Yizhar. "Holy Sites in the Vicinity of the Monastery of Chariton." In *Early Christianity in Context: Monuments and Documents*, edited by Frederic Manns and Eugenio Alliata, pp. 297–311. Jerusalem, 1993.

Ovadiah, Asher. *Corpus of Byzantine Churches in the Holy Land*. Bonn, 1970.

Ovadiah, Asher, and C. G. de Silva. "Supplement to the Corpus of Churches in the Holy Land." *Levant* 13 (1981), pp. 200–261; 14 (1982), pp. 122–170; 16 (1984), pp. 129–165.

Patrich, Joseph. *Sabas, Leader of Palestinian Monasticism. A Comparative Study in Eastern Monasticism, Fourth to Seventh Centuries*. Washington D.C., 1995. See pages 82–106.

Politis, Konstantinos D. "Excavations at Deir Ain Abata." *Liber Annuus* 38 (1988), pp. 461–462, pls. 17–20; 40 (1990), pp. 475–476, pls. 77–78; 41 (1991), pp. 517–518, pls. 70–71; 42 (1992), pp. 374–377, pls. 48–49; 44 (1994), pp. 629–630, pls. 53–54; 46 (1996), pp. 413–414, pl. 42.

Politis, Konstantinos D. "Excavations at Deir Ain Abata." *Annual of the Department of Antiquities of Jordan* 33 (1989), pp. 227–233, 404–406; 34 (1990), pp. 377–388; 36 (1992), pp. 281–290; 37 (1993), pp. 503–520.

Prignaud, Jean. "Une installation monastique Byzantine au Khan Saliba." *Revue biblique* 70 (1963), pp. 243–254.

Tsafrir, Yoram, ed. *Ancient Churches Revealed*. Jerusalem, 1993.

Tsafrir, Yoram, Leah Di Segni, and Judith Green. *Tabula Imperii Romani, Judaea/Palaestina*. Jerusalem, 1994.

Wilkinson, John. *Jerusalem Pilgrims before the Crusades*. Jerusalem, 1977.

JOSEPH PATRICH

CISTERNS AND RESERVOIRS. A necessary component of water systems in the Judean wilderness in antiquity was a means of storing the water; this was accomplished with cisterns and reservoirs. Cisterns were small, private, water storage units, whereas reservoirs were larger in size and designed to store water for public use. Tsuk (1997, p. 112) defines a cistern as a water storage facility holding up to 100 cubic meters (3,532 cubic feet); something holding more than that amount would be considered a reservoir. Every household in the Roman-Byzantine period had a cistern with an average capacity of 30 to 50 cubic meters (1,059 cubic feet to 1,766 cubic feet), which would supply the family with water throughout the year.

In the Hellenistic and Roman periods cisterns and reservoirs were generally square or rectangular in shape. Cisterns were normally cut into bedrock and often covered for sanitation and to reduce evaporation loss. Reservoirs, because of their size, were usually partially cut into bedrock and partially built of stone, and lacked roofs. In order to be watertight, cisterns and reservoirs were lined with an impermeable plaster. The water supply was directed to a small settling basin adjacent to the storage tank to remove impurities. Water was drawn from a cistern by means of a jar or pail on a rope. Water from reservoirs, on the other hand, was usually directed to secondary facilities by means of channels or pipes.

The more remarkable of the Judean wilderness cisterns, pools, and reservoirs are to be found at Jericho, Qumran, and Masada.

Jericho. At the site of Tulul Abu el-ʾAlayiq, the Hasmonean and Herodian kings built a luxurious complex of palaces, villas, estates, and gardens. Of special interest are the swimming pools adjacent to the palaces. During the Hasmonean period, a total of seven swimming pools ranging in size from 7 by 7 meters to 12.5 by 20 meters (23 by 23 feet to 41 by 65.6 feet) were constructed at the site, a phenomenon unparalleled elsewhere in the Middle East. Five of the pools had steps along one side, while two did not. The pools were surrounded by patios, gardens, pavilions, and ritual baths. Many of the pools continued in use in the Herodian period, with the addition of a large 40 by 92 meters (131 by 302 feet) pool and a bathhouse. The most famous event to have taken place in a pool in the Judean wilderness occurred during the reign of Herod the Great. Josephus reports that the seventeen-year-old Hasmonean Aristobulus III, Herod's brother-in-law, high priest, and rival, was drowned in one of the palace pools:

> After a while, the young man, at the instigation of Herod, went into the water among them, while such of Herod's acquaintances he had appointed to do it, dipped him as he was swimming, and plunged him under the water, in the dark of the evening, as if it had been done in sport only; nor did they desist till he was entirely suffocated. (*Jewish Antiquities* 15.3.3)

East of the palace area was an enormous reservoir, Birket Mousa, which evidently served the practical needs of the palaces. The largest reservoir in Palestine, it measured 220 by 160 by 21.5 meters (722 by 525 by 70.5 feet) and had a capacity of 756,800 cubic meters (over 2 million cubic feet). [*See* Hasmoneans; Herod; *and* Josephus Flavius.]

Qumran. The most striking feature of the ruins at Qumran is the number of cisterns and reservoirs in close proximity. The settlers of Period Ia (third quarter of the second century BCE) refurbished a round cistern built in the Iron Age and also built two new cisterns. Both were rectangular, and both had steps at one end extending the full width of the cistern. The full-width steps are a unique feature of the Qumran cisterns, which suggests that they were used for communal ritual immersion. In Period Ib (late second century–first century BCE) one additional cistern, without steps, was constructed, along with three stepped cisterns, maintaining an approximate two-to-one ratio of cisterns with steps to cisterns without steps. One of the stepped cisterns was subsequently abandoned because of damage from the earthquake of 31 BCE. In Period II (first century CE), a wall was built across the middle of another of the stepped cisterns to create two cisterns out of one—one to continue as a ritual immersion facility, and the other to be used as a functional cistern for daily needs.

It is clear that the stepped cisterns at Qumran were used for communal ritual immersion as described by Josephus (*The Jewish War* 2.2, 5, 13) and in the Rule of the Community from Cave 1 at Qumran (1QS iii.4–5, 9, v.13–14). [*See* Rule of the Community.] Not only the design of the stepped cisterns would suggest this but also the capacity of the system. The amount of water needed for a community of approximately two hundred people and their pack animals, for the eight months of the year during which rainwater was not available, is around 258 cubic meters (9,112 cubic feet). System capacity, on the other hand, including allowance for evaporating losses, is approximately 578 cubic meters (20,413 cubic feet), more than twice what was needed. The water volume of the cisterns without steps, on the other hand, was around 259 cubic meters (9,147 cubic feet), more than enough to meet the practical needs of the community. [*See* Qumran, *article on* Archaeology.]

Masada. Herod ensured a secure water supply for his fortress atop Masada by having a well-engineered water system. Aqueducts delivered water from nearby wadis during the rainy season to twelve storage reservoirs located on the northwest slope of the mountain. The square-shaped reservoirs were cut into the slope of the rock in two parallel rows—eight in the upper row and four in the lower. The upper eight had a capacity of around 3,000 cubic meters each (105,348 cubic feet), while the lower four had a capacity of approximately 4,000 cubic meters (141,264 cubic feet) each, for a total capacity of some 40,000 cubic meters (over 1 million cubic feet). A number of large reservoirs were also cut into the summit on the north, south, and east sides. Water was transported from the northwest slope to the summit by means of human labor or pack animals. From the Snake Path on the northeast side and the Water Gate on the northwest side, water could be directed to the upper reservoirs by means of channels. Sufficient water was available to maintain bathhouses and a swimming pool on the summit. [*See* Masada.]

[*See also* Archaeology; Baths and Baptism; Miqva'ot; Purity; *and* Water Systems.]

BIBLIOGRAPHY

Hirschfeld, Yitzhar. *The Judean Monasteries in the Byzantine Period.* New Haven, 1992. Discusses cisterns and reservoirs on pp. 148–162.

Netzer, Ehud. *The Swimming Pools of the Hasmonean Period at Jericho.* Leichtwiess Institut für Wasserbau der Technischen Universität Braunschweig, Mitteilungen 89. Braunschweig, 1986.

Tsuk, Tsvika. "Cisterns." In *The Oxford Encyclopedia of Archaeology in the Near East*, edited by Eric M. Meyers, vol. 4, pp. 12–13, translated from Hebrew by Ilana Goldberg. New York, 1997.

Tsuk, Tsvika. "Pools." In *The Oxford Encyclopedia of Archaeology in the Near East*, edited by Eric M. Meyers, vol. 4, pp. 350–351, translated from Hebrew by Ilana Goldberg. New York, 1997.

Wood, Bryant G. "To Dip or Sprinkle? The Qumran Cisterns in Perspective." *Bulletin of the American Schools of Oriental Research* 256 (1984), 45–60. Presents evidence to show that the stepped cisterns at Qurman were used for religious purposes.

BRYANT G. WOOD

COFFINS. *See* Cemeteries.

COINS. *See* Numismatics.

COMMENTARY. *See* Interpretation of Scriptures.

COMMUNITY ORGANIZATION. [*This entry comprises three articles*: Community Organization in the Rule of the Community, Community Organization in the Damascus Document, *and* Community Organization in Other Texts.]

Community Organization in the Rule of the Community

The Qumran community (*ha-yaḥad*) was organized according to a strict and rigid hierarchy. Many scholars maintain that it was controlled, at least during the early period of its existence, by priests and Levites. However, 4QS[d], a copy of the Rule of the Community which dates from the later decades of the first century BCE (see Cross, 1996), may represent an earlier version than that of the Rule of the Community from Cave 1 at Qumran (hereafter, 1QRule of the Community; 1QS), the scroll in which the Rule of the Community is best preserved and which dates from approximately 100 to 75 BCE. 4QS[d] is conspicuously missing the words "the priests, the Sons of Zadok" (see Charlesworth and Strawn, 1996; Vermes and Metso correctly think 4QS[d] witnesses to "an earlier stage of the literary evolution of the Community Rule"). According to 4QS[d], "the men of the Community" are not "answerable to the Sons of Zadok, the priests who keep the covenant" (1QS v.2).

Foremost in the Qumran community is the overall concept of "oneness" (*yaḥad*); that is, the full members of the community held all things in common and were devoted in oneness to all responsibilities and the task of preparing the way for God's final act of judgment, the final war at the end of time, and to the coming of the Messiahs of Aaron and Israel, at least beginning in the first century BCE (1QS ix.11; this section of 1QRule of the Community seems to reflect a later period in the community's existence; it is not present in 4QS[d], which seems generally to be an earlier version; see Charlesworth in *Qumran Messianism* [1997] and Metso). They ate "(in) unity," said "benedictions (in) unity," and gave "counsel (in) unity" (1QS vi.2–3). All members of the community were predestined to be "the Sons of Light" in contrast to "the Sons of Darkness," who were all those who were not members of their sect, even (and especially during the first phase of the community's existence) the ruling priests in Jerusalem. It took at least two years to become a member of the community; during this probationary period the novices, "the Sons of the Dawn" (Words of the Sage to the Sons of Dawn 4Q298), were instructed by a *maskil* ("master") and eventually examined by the "examiner" (*mevaqqer*) regarding their knowledge and purity.

In the community the hierarchy was so strict that predetermined "lots" were discerned and then assigned, by discerning God's will; hence, love was measured out according to the lot of a Son of Light. That is, the members of the community are exhorted "to love all the Sons of Light each according to his lot in the council of God" (1QS i.9–10). At least during the early years at Qumran, the hierarchy, from the top down, consisted of the Righteous Teacher (Teacher of Righteousness) to whom God alone had revealed all the mysteries of the words of the prophets (Pesher Habakkuk, 1QpHab 7), the priests (the Sons of Zadok), the Levites, and then Israel (all members of the community). [*See* Teacher of Righteousness.] The hierarchy was centered upon the priests (1QS vi.3–4). During special ceremonies, as at the yearly ceremony for the renewal of the covenant, the hierarchic distinctions were strictly demanded and followed (1QS ii.19–25). Josephus was most likely thinking about this sect of Jews and this phenomenon when he reported that the Essenes were so hierarchical that a member lower in rank must not touch one above him; otherwise the latter must purify himself from the resulting pollution (*The Jewish War* 2.150). [*See* Josephus Flavius.]

Numerous technical terms designating social groups or leaders are found in the Rule of the Community. It is not wise to seek to systematize the meanings of all these terms and relate them, because this quintessential Qumran document reflects the evolutionary nature of the Qumran community; that is, the terms most likely had different meanings at different periods in the history of the community and perhaps also at the same time.

Technical Terms for Social Groups within the Community. The Qumranites called their group the "community" (*yaḥad*) and sometimes the "Community of God" (1QS i.12). The use of *yaḥad* in this sense is unique to Qumran. While in the Rule of the Community the term *serekh* denotes the "rule" that contains the regulations of the community, in the War Scroll (1QM) it designates the military organization of the Qumranites.

The "Council of the Community" (*ʿatsat ha-yaḥad*) usually indicates a group of twelve men, including three special priests (1QS viii.1, however, can also be read to mean twelve men plus three priests [see Weinfeld]). The council of the community had awesome responsibilities; it was "a most holy assembly for Aaron, (with) eternal truth for judgment, chosen by (divine) pleasure to atone for the land and to repay the wicked their reward" (1QS viii.5–7). These twelve leaders were to be "perfect in everything which has been revealed from the whole Torah" (1QS viii.1–2); thus each one was "to perform truth, righteousness, justice" and "merciful love," and to walk circumspectly "with his fellow" (1QS viii.2). According to some passages in the Rule of the Community the members of the "Council of the Community" seem to have been the judges (1QS viii.3, viii.10); but, according to other passages in this composite document, it is possible that they arrived at some judgments, while most jurisdiction within the community was not before the council but before the "Many" (1QS vi.1). Either the priests in the council of twelve men must be "Sons of Aaron," since they are the only leaders who administer justice and property according to the end of the Rule of the Community ("the Sons of Aaron alone shall rule over judgment and property"; 1QS ix.7), or the latter rule applied only to an earlier phase in the life of the community.

The "Many" (*rabbim*; 1QS vi.7–21) is the name of the whole assembly when it deliberates over the business of the community. It is not wise to attempt to distinguish always between *rabbim* and *yaḥad*; they are virtually synonyms. The "Many" constituted all who have remained faithful, the novices who have passed all requirements, and those members who have been reinstated in the community. They made judicial decisions and were responsible for excommunications and readmission (1QS viii.19–ix.2). Thus, although the community was controlled in the early years by the Righteous Teacher, in practice it was sometimes oligarchic and even democratic; it seems likely that after the death of its "Teacher," "the Priest," the community became less monarchical. The "Many" also gather together to worship and study: "The Many shall spend the third part of every night of the year in unity, reading the Book, studying judgment, and saying benedictions in unity." (1QS vi.7–8). During a session of the Many a member may not mention anything that is not pertinent to the Many (1QS vi.11).

The technical term *rabbim* does not appear in other Jewish literature that antedates 70 CE. It is, however, found in rabbinic literature. There it denotes a large gathering of Jews organized together for some business (i.e., *Qiddushin* 4.5; see also B.T., *Yev.* 86b, which Weinfeld suggests is close to Qumran usage).

Technical Terms for Leaders in the Community. "The Righteous Teacher" (*moreh ha-Tsedeq*) was the founder of the community. While he was alive he was the most important figure in the community. He was the bearer of God's special revelation (1QpHab), he was considered like Moses "the Lawgiver," he was the author of some of the hymns chanted in the community, and he most likely composed many of the rules to be memorized by members of the community (most likely, but not certainly, 1QS iii.13–4.16). It is unlikely that his office was inherited by others; rather, he was revered and praised by his followers far above any of his near or far contemporaries.

The "priests" (*ha-kohanim*) were the elite members of the community. They marched at the head of the yearly ceremony for covenant renewal (1QS ii.19–20). They were the first to sit in the session of the Many (1QS vi.8). Their authority was prescribed; a priest must be present when ten men gathered (1QS vi.3–4). The priest was to be the first to stretch out his hand to bless the bread and the new wine (1QS vi.5). The priests, as "the Sons of Aaron," "alone" were in charge of judgment and property (1QS ix.7).

All who joined the community swore to be "answerable to the Sons of Zadok, the priests who keep the covenant" (1QS v.2). The "Sons of Zadok" (*benei tsadoq*), who seem to be synonymous with the "Sons of Aaron" (*benei ʾaharon*), are, of course, priests. They are the ones who were in charge of almost everything, especially the interpretation of Torah. The "Interpreter of Torah" (*doresh be-Torah*) mentioned in 1QRule of the Community (1QS vi.6) is not necessarily a separate office but a function performed by a leader (in Testimonia 4Q175 1–3.11 he is a messianic figure who will arise "in the latter days"). Each leader was most likely empowered to interpret Torah, but there were probably ceremonial events in which a specially designated person was recognized as the "Interpreter of Torah," following the model of the Righteous Teacher, the interpreter of Torah par excellence for the members of the community.

The "elders" (*zeqenim*) are mentioned only in 1QRule

of the Community (1QS vi.8), and there they are second in authority and power only to the priests; that is, for the "session of the Many" the priests are to sit first, then the "elders," and finally all others. Because of this brief reference to the "elders," it is impossible to discern their functions at Qumran or compare them with the "elders" who were officials in synagogues and the Sanhedrin (cf. *Acts* 4.5, 4.8) or "the elders" (*hoi presbuteroi*) mentioned in the New Testament as heads of a church (i.e., *Acts* 15–16, *1 Tm.* 5.17, *Ti.* 1.5, *Js.* 5.14, 1 *Pt.* 5.1, *2 Jn.* 1, *3 Jn.* 1).

The "Examiner" (*mevaqqer*; 1QS vi.12, 20; CD xiii.6, 7, 13; xiv.13; xv.8, 11, 14) was the most important official and functioned as the head of the community (the president or General superior). He was responsible, perhaps with the counsel of the *maskil*, for examining the novices (Rule, 5Q13 frg. 4.1, CD xv.11). He controlled discussions (1QS vi.11–13) and presided at plenary sessions. His authority was not absolute and could not become autocratic, since a member who was not recognized to speak by the examiner could appeal to the Many, and if they allowed him to speak, then he could address them (1QS vi.11–13). The examiner recorded all that went into the common storehouse (1QS vi.20). He had to be between thirty and fifty years of age, according to the Damascus Document (CD xiv.8–9; cf. Rule of the Congregation 1Q28a i.14–18), but it is not clear if that rule applied to the Qumran community.

The "Overseer" (*paqid*) was most likely the second most important officer, although it is conceivable (especially because the "Community" and the "Many" tend to be synonymous) that one person sometimes performed the tasks assigned to the "Examiner" and the "Overseer." He was "at the head of the many." He also examined the insight and works of all those who wished "to join the council of the community"—here meaning anyone who wished to join the community (1QS vi.14). The "Overseer" was to be between thirty and sixty years of age, according to the Damascus Document (xiv.6–7; cf. 1Q28a i.14–18), but it is impossible to discern if that rule applied at Qumran.

The "Master" (*maskil*), a wise and learned man, was the officer who taught the novices (4Q298). The *maskil* is not "only another title for the *mevaqqer*" (against Trebolle Barrera, 1995, p. 57). He was the one who had mastered "all understanding" (1QS ix.12–14). He evaluated "the Sons of Righteousness" (Rule of the Community^{e} 4Q259), who are "the chosen ones of the end time" (1QS ix.14), which probably denoted the novices. He was responsible for their advancement (1QS ix.15–16). His major task was to guide the devotees and "instruct them in the mysteries of wonder and truth in the midst of the men of the community" (1QS ix.18–19). The most important lesson to be taught to "the Sons of Light" by the "Master" is the instruction regarding "the two spirits," by which all humans are influenced:

> It is for the Master to instruct and teach all the Sons of Light concerning the nature of all the sons of man, . . . From the God of knowledge comes all that is occurring and shall occur. . . . In a spring of light emanates the nature of truth and from a well of darkness emerges the nature of deceit. In the hand of the Prince of Light (is) the dominion of all the Sons of Righteousness; in the ways of light they walk. But in the hand of the Angel of Darkness (is) the dominion of the Sons of Deceit; and in the ways of darkness they walk. (1QS iii.13–21)

Structure of the Community. Men who wished to join the community faced at least two years of examination in knowledge and in conduct (1QS vi.21). If after the probationary period a novice passed all tests, he was admitted by the decree of the Many. He was then recorded and given a rank in the community. Finally, his property was placed in the common storehouse (1QS vi.22). Members could be punished, primarily by losing a portion of their food, be dismissed for a specified period of time, and even banished (1QS vi.25–7.18). Meals were eaten together, probably in one large room.

New Testament and Christian Origins. After the publication of the scrolls found in Cave 1, some New Testament specialists claimed that the *mevaqqer*—a term found at Qumran only in the Damascus Document and in the Rule of the Community, but nowhere else in other Jewish literature, including the apocryphal compositions and rabbinic writings—significantly helps explain the title and function of the bishop in the early church (Dupont-Sommer, 1950). The links, however, are not so persuasive, and the *mevaqqer* is not as dominant as the bishop seems to have been, and certainly became, in the church (Nötscher, 1961; Reicke, 1957). The parallel between twelve men with three special members is strikingly similar to the twelve men Jesus chose, among which were three special leaders (Peter, James, and John); but the number twelve symbolized Israel and its twelve tribes and the early synagogues may well have been led by twelve men. [*See* Twelve Patriarchs, Testaments of the.]

BIBLIOGRAPHY

Alexander, Philip S. "The Redaction History of Serekh ha-Yaḥad: A Proposal." *Revue de Qumrân* 17 (1996), 437–456.

Charlesworth, James H. "Challenging the Consensus Communis Regarding Qumran Messianism (1QS, 4QS MSS)." In *Qumran-Messianism,* edited by James H. Charlesworth, Hermann Lichtenberger, and Gerbern S. Oegema, pp. 120–134. Tübingen, 1998.

Charlesworth, James H. et al., eds. *The Dead Sea Scrolls: Hebrew, Aramaic, and Greek Texts with English Translations. Volume 1: Rule of the Community and Related Documents*. The Princeton Theological Seminary Dead Sea Scrolls Project. Tübingen and Louisville, 1994. This volume contains the critical texts, translations, and introductions to all the copies of the Rule of the Community. Translations of the document in this article are from this critical edition.

Charlesworth, James H., and Brent A. Stawn. "Reflections of the Text of *Serek ha-Yaḥad* Found in Cave IV." *Revue de Qumrân* 17 (1996), 405–435.

Cross, Frank M. "Paleographical Dates of the Manuscripts." Appendix to E. Qimron and James H. Charlesworth, "Cave IV Fragments." In *The Dead Sea Scrolls: The Rule of the Community*, edited by James H. Charlesworth, p. 57. Tübingen, 1994.

Dupont-Sommer, André. *Aperçus préliminaires sur les manuscrits de la mer morte*. Paris, 1950.

Maier, Johann. "Zum Begriff *yḥd* in den Texten von Qumran." In *Qumran*, edited by Karl Erich Grötzinger et al., pp. 225–248. Wege der Forschung, 410. Darmstadt, 1981.

Metso, S. *The Textual Development of the Qumran Community Rule*. Studies on the Texts of the Desert of Judah, 21. Leiden, 1997.

Nötscher, Friedich. "Vorchristliche Typen urchristlicher Ämter? Episkopos und Mebaqqer." In *Vom Alten zum Neuen Testament*, pp. 188–220. Bonner Biblische Beiträge 17. Bonn, 1961.

Reicke, Bo. "The Constitution of the Primitive Church in the Light of Jewish Documents." In *The Scrolls and the New Testament*, edited by Krister Stendahl with James H. Charlesworth, pp. 143–156. New York, 1957.

Trebolle Barrera, Julio. "System of Government." In *The People of the Dead Sea Scrolls: Their Writings, Beliefs, and Practices*, edited by F. García Martínez and Julio Trebolle Barrera, translated by Wilfred G. W. Watson, pp. 55–58. Leiden and New York, 1995. The presentation is confused because it is assumed, incorrectly, that the Rule of the Community and the Damascus Document should be read as if they pertain to the same community. Only the Rule of the Community describes the procedures for organization at Qumran; the Damascus Document applies to the Essenes who lived elsewhere.

Vermes, Geza. "Preliminary Remarks on Unpublished Fragments of the Community Rule from Qumran Cave 4." *Journal of Jewish Studies* 42 (1991), 250–255.

Vermes, Geza. "Qumran Forum Miscellanea I." *Journal of Jewish Studies* 43 (1992), 299–305.

Weinfeld, Moshe. *The Organizational Pattern and the Penal Code of the Qumran Sect: A Comparison with Guilds and Religious Associations of the Hellenistic-Roman Period*. Novum Testamentum et Orbis Antiquus, 2. Göttingen, 1986.

JAMES H. CHARLESWORTH

Community Organization in the Damascus Document

The discovery of fragments of eight manuscripts of the Damascus Document in Cave 4 at Qumran (4Q266–273) significantly increased our knowledge of the text of this work, which previously had been known only from two manuscripts found in the Cairo Genizah (CD MS A and MS B). Small fragments of the Damascus Document were also found in Caves 5 and 6 at Qumran (5Q12, 6Q15), but these were much less important. The Damascus Document consists of two sections, the Admonition and the Laws, but the Cave 4 discoveries showed that the text preserved in the Cairo Genizah manuscripts lacked the beginning of the Admonition, and the beginning and the conclusion of the Laws, as well as part of the Laws section itself. The corpus of Laws can now be seen to form about two-thirds of the entire work, and the Admonition essentially serves as an introduction to the Laws; it is within the Laws that the sections of the Damascus Document concerned with community organization are to be found.

The Laws section provides legislation for a community of Jews who lived among other Jews and gentiles, were married and had children, had male and female slaves, practiced agriculture, engaged in trade, had private income from which they were expected to contribute the wages of at least two days per month to support members of the community who were in need. They adopted a positive attitude toward the Temple, in that they were concerned about maintaining its purity and participated in its cult. In short, the legislation was intended for a group of Jews who were not cut off from society, even though they formed a separate community. It is assumed here that this community was Essene and that the legislation essentially was Essene legislation. But it has been widely recognized that the corpus of Laws is a composite and that it consists of two main types of material: general *halakhah* and interpretation of the Torah on the one hand, and communal laws on the other. The former is represented, for example, by the detailed regulations concerning the observance of the Sabbath (CD x.14–xi.18); this type of material appears to have been intended for all Israel (cf. CD xii.19–22) and may include interpretations of the Torah that go back to the time before the formation of the Essenes. The latter is represented above all by CD xii.22–xiv.19, which is set off in the manuscript by the heading "And this [is] the rule for the settlers of [the] c[amps]." Other parts of the corpus of Laws are also concerned with communal organization, particularly the passage concerned with admission procedures (CD xv.5–xvi.6), the list of punishments for infringements of community law (4Q266, 270), and a ritual for expulsion from the community (4Q266, 270).

The community legislation of the Damascus Document invites comparison with that of the Rule of the Community (hereafter, 1QRule of the Community; 1QS v–ix). The relationship between the two works has often been explained on the basis that the Damascus Document was intended for those members of the sectarian movement who lived in towns and villages among other Jews, while 1QRule of the Community, which appears to embody a stricter law, was intended for those Essenes living at Qumran itself. It is perhaps more accurate to say that the two documents belong to different, but related, communities, and that, whatever the chronological relationship between the Damascus Document as a whole and 1QRule of the Community, the legislation of the Damascus Document is older than that of 1QRule of the Community, dating in its final form from about 100 BCE.

The Damascus Document refers to the community with

which it is concerned as a "congregation" (*'edah*; e.g., CD x.4, 5, 8; 4QD[a] 8.i.9, 8.iii.4 4QD[e] 7.i.14), but it also uses the expressions "association" (*ḥever*; CD xiv.16; 4QD[a] 10.i.10) and "association (*hibbur*) of Israel" (CD xii.8). Like Israel in the wilderness period, the congregation is said to live in "camps" (*maḥanot*; e.g. CD ix.11; x.23; 4QD[a] 11.17; 4QD[e] 7.ii.14); behind the references to the term *camps* we should envisage groups of members of the community living among their fellow Jews in towns and cities—just as the Essenes were said to do by both Philo and Josephus. Each camp consisted of a minimum of ten men (cf. CD xiii.1), and each group was under the direction of a priest and an officer called "the overseer of the camp."

A summary of the duties of the priest (CD xiii.2–7) is introduced by the statement "And where there are ten, let there not be lacking a priest learned in the Book of Hagu" (CD xiii.2; cf. 1QS vi.3–4). What precisely is meant by the term the *Book of Hagu* (*Book of Meditation*) remains uncertain, but it may refer to the Torah or a collection of interpretations of the Torah. [*See* Hagu, Book of.] The priest was to exercise authority ("by his word shall they all be ruled" CD xiii.2–3); this probably refers to determining the interpretation of the Torah) and to hand down decisions in cases of skin disease (see *Lv.* 13). In interpreting the Torah, if the priest was "not experienced in all these [matters]" (CD xiii.3) and a Levite was, authority was to be exercised by the Levite. In cases involving skin disease, the priest was to be instructed in the interpretation of the law by the overseer; but even if the priest was ignorant, it was he who had to pronounce the legal decision. The application of the laws on skin disease was evidently a matter of concern to the members of the community, and more information on the role of the priest in applying the law is contained in a separate section on skin disease, which is preserved in fragmentary form in Damascus Documents[a,d,g,h].

The "overseer [*mevaqqer*] of the camp" is also referred to as "the overseer of the many" (CD xv.8) or simply "the overseer." His duties consisted of exercising pastoral oversight over members of the camp and being responsible for the admission of new members, in which he had the final word (CD xiii.7–13). The duties assigned to the overseer are similar to those assigned to the "wise leader" or "master" (*maskil*) in the Rule of the Community (1QS ix.14–21), which suggests that the two offices were related. It is worth noting that in 1QRule of the Community (1QS vi.12) the title *overseer over the many* is used, apparently to refer to the individual called elsewhere the "wise leader," and that in the Damascus Document the title *wise leader* occurs several times but only in contexts too fragmentary to interpret. The overseer also was assigned to keep a record of witness statements in cases where a capital offense was witnessed by a single individual, so that, if further offenses were committed, the requirement of the law of *Deuteronomy* 17.6 might be met by the cumulative record (CD ix.16–22). In a passage concerned with proper arrangements for marriages (Damascus Document[f] 4Q271 3) the overseer was responsible for the arrangements for confirming the good moral character of a prospective bride (3.14).

The procedure for admission to the community is treated in more detail in the Damascus Document (CD xv.5–xvi.6) and was much simpler than that described in the 1QRule of the Community (1QS vi.13–23). According to the Damascus Document a potential member first was examined as to his suitability by the overseer and then required to swear "the oath of the covenant that Moses made with Israel, the cove[na]nt to re[turn t]o the law of Moses with all [his] heart and [with all his] soul." Sons of members were also required to take the oath, at the age of twenty (cf. *Ex.* 30.14). Once the new member had taken the oath, the community was free of the blame incurred by him if he transgressed; but he was eligible to be instructed by the overseer for one year. Those who were mentally or physically impaired were not permitted to join the congregation "because the holy angels [are in their midst]" (Damascus Document[a] 4Q266 8i.6–9), the implication being that no person should be included who might offend the angels.

The section of the Damascus Document that is headed "The rule for the session of all the camps" is concerned with the organization of the entire community and describes the hierarchical order in which the members were to be registered and to conduct their meetings: "the priests first, the Levites second, the sons of Israel third, and the proselyte[s] fourth" (CD xiv.3–17). This passage also refers to two officers, "the priest who is appointed at the head of the many" and "the overseer of all the camps," whose responsibilities covered the entire congregation, not just an individual camp. The former, like the priest attached to each camp, had to be "learned in the Book of Hagu" in order to be capable of expounding the Torah. The latter, who was required to be master of "every secret of men and every language of their cla[n]s," was the ultimate source of authority in the congregation (CD xiv.9–17). He was responsible, together with the judges (see CD x.4–10), for receiving the contributions of at least two days' wages per member of the community, for the support of fellow members who were in need. With regard to commercial relations between members, in the Damascus Document it is said that they should not buy from or sell to fellow members, here called the "Sons of Dawn," except "hand to hand" (CD viii.14–15). Apparently, this means that they should not seek to profit from commercial dealings with fellow members of the community, but provide for their needs on the basis of exchange and mutual trust. They were not to make agreements for buying or selling without informing the overseer of the camp (CD xiii.15–16).

Communal discipline was enforced by a series of punishments, and a list of these is given near the end of the corpus of Laws. The beginning of the list survives in fragmentary form in the Cairo Genizah manuscript of the Damascus Document (CD xiv.20–23) but much more has been preserved in Damascus Document[a] and Damascus Document[e] (4Q266 10.i, ii; 4Q270 7.i). Similar lists of punishments are found in 1QRule of the Community (1QS vi.24–vii.25) and in the fragments of Serekh Damascus (4Q265). Punishments range from a penance of ten days for interrupting the speech of another member or for leaving the assembly three times without reason, to thirty days exclusion and ten days of penance for falling asleep in the assembly or for indecent exposure, to exclusion for one year and six months of penance for insulting a fellow member. The ultimate sanction—expulsion—was levied for at least five offenses: a malicious accusation in a capital case, slandering the community, fornication with one's wife in violation of the law (where the precise nature of the breach of the law is unclear), murmuring against "the fathers" (apparently an honorific applied to senior members of the community), and despising the communal law. A good deal remains unclear about the list of punishments, including the precise nature of the penance—whether it involved loss of rations or some other punishment, such as exclusion from communal deliberations—but the list provides a revealing insight into the issues that were important to members in relation to the internal working of the community.

As noted above, the punishment for those who despised the communal law was expulsion, and the final part of the corpus of Laws consisted of a ritual of expulsion for "everyone who despises these regulations in accordance with all the statutes that are found in the law of Moses." The ritual is preserved in Damascus Document[a] and Damascus Document[e] (4Q266 11; 4Q270 7.i, ii) and the expulsion occurred at the time of the annual ceremony of the renewal of the covenant in the third month (4Q266 11.17), almost certainly on the occasion of Shavu'ot. The ritual of expulsion includes a prayer uttered by "the priest who is appointed over the many" (4Q266 11.8). Those who were associated with the man being expelled were to leave with him, and a record was to be kept by the overseer, presumably the "overseer of all the camps" (4Q266 11.14–16). [*See* Cairo Genizah; Damascus Document; *and* Rule of the Community.]

BIBLIOGRAPHY

Baumgarten, Joseph M. "The 'Sons of Dawn' in *CDC* 13:14–15 and the Ban on Commerce among the Essenes." *Israel Exploration Journal* 33 (1983), 81–85.

Baumgarten, Joseph M. "The Cave 4 Versions of the Qumran Penal Code." *Journal of Jewish Studies* 43 (1992), 268–276.

Baumgarten, Joseph M. *Qumran Cave 4, XIII: The Damascus Document (4Q266–273)*. Discoveries in the Judaean Desert, 18. Oxford, 1996.

Hempel, Charlotte. *The Laws of the Damascus Document: Sources, Traditions, and Redaction*. Forthcoming in the series Studies on the Texts of the Desert of Judah. Analysis of the different layers within the Laws of the Damascus Document.

Knibb, Michael A. "The Place of the Damascus Document." In *Methods of Investigation of the Dead Sea Scrolls and the Khirbet Qumran Site: Present Realities and Future Prospects*, edited by Michael O. Wise et al., pp. 149–162. Annals of the New York Academy of Sciences, vol. 722. New York, 1994.

Qimron, Elisha. "The Text of CDC." In *The Damascus Document Reconsidered*, edited by Magen Broshi, pp. 9–49. Jerusalem, 1992. Recent edition of manuscripts A and B of the Damascus Document from the Cairo Genizah.

Vermes, Geza. *The Dead Sea Scrolls: Qumran in Perspective*. 3d., rev., pp. 85–99. London, 1994. Discussion of the community organization reflected in the Damascus Document and its relation to that reflected in the Community Rule.

MICHAEL A. KNIBB

Community Organization in Other Texts

The Rule of the Community from Cave 1 (hereafter, 1QRule of the Community, 1QS) and the Damascus Document (CD 4Q266–4Q273, 5Q12, 6Q15) are not the only texts found at Qumran that reflect something of the communal life of those responsible for the Dead Sea Scrolls. Three other texts deserve to be mentioned on account of their communal legislation: Serekh Damascus (4Q265), Rebukes by the Overseer (4Q477), and the Rule of the Congregation (1Q28a).

Serekh Damascus, which survives only in fragmentary form, reveals affinities with both 1QRule of the Community and the Damascus Document, but its legislation does not correspond exactly with that of either work. Thus, affinities with the 1QRule of the Community can be observed in the list of punishments, specifically the provision for a cut of half the food ration (4Q265 1.i, cf. 1QS vi.25) although the amount is not the same) in the procedure for admission (4Q265 1.ii, cf. 1QS vi.13–23), and in the provision for a council of fifteen men, the members of which would make atonement for the land (4Q265 2.ii, cf. 1QS viii.1–10; ix.3–6). The passages in 1QRule of the Community indicate that the atonement would be made, not by sacrifice, but by prayer and by proper observance of the Torah. On the other hand, the Sabbath legislation of Serekh Damascus (4Q265 2.i) is very similar to that of the Damascus Document (CD x.14–18).

The few small fragments of the work known as Rebukes by the Overseer preserve the remains of a record of rebukes of community members who had committed an offense. Both 1QRule of the Community (1QS v.24–vi.1) and the Damascus Document CD ix.2–8 refer to the duty of members to rebuke their fellows, apparently as a preliminary stage in the judicial process, and the Damascus Document (CD ix.16–20) provides that a record of such rebukes was to be kept by the overseer. Rebukes by the Overseer perhaps would be better entitled "The Overseer's Record of Rebukes." The offenses listed are essentially ones that affected the internal life of the community, such as being short-tempered or offending the spirit of the community, and the text is additionally important because it is the first in which the actual names of members are preserved.

1QRule of the Congregation is a short text that appears as a kind of appendix at the end of the version of the Rule of the Community found in Cave 1 at Qumran. It provides legislation for a community living "at the end of days," and it includes regulations for the common meals that would be eaten when the two messianic figures expected by the community, the priest and the Messiah of Israel, had appeared. But at the same time it seems very likely that the legislation contained in the document reflected the actual practice of the community that produced it. As in the case of the Damascus Document, the community with which the Rule of the Congregation is concerned is frequently described as a "congregation" (*'edah*; e.g., 1Q28a i.1, 6)—hence the title given to the work—but terminology familiar from the Rule of the Community, namely, "the council of the community" (see e.g., 1Q28a i.26, 27), is also used. The Rule of the Congregation legislates, again, like the Damascus Document, for a community whose members were married and had children: The first part of the document (i.6–25) is concerned with the education of children and the stages in the lives of members. Thus, at the age of twenty, members were registered in the community and were permitted to marry, and at the ages of twenty-five and thirty they achieved higher levels of seniority in the community; these thresholds were based on biblical precedent (cf. *Ex.* 30.14; *Nm.* 1.3; 4.3; 4.23; 8.24) and may be compared with the ages in the Damascus Document (CD x.6–10; xiv.6–10) and the War Scroll (1QM vi.13–vii.3).

The central part of the Rule of the Congregation (1Q28a i.25–ii.11) is concerned with procedure at assemblies of the congregation, from which those who were ritually unclean or who suffered from a physical defect were to be excluded. The reason given is the same as the reason given in Damascus Document[a] (4Q266 8.i.6–9) for exclusion from the congregation, namely, "because the holy angels are [in] their [congregat]ion." The final part of the text (1Q28a ii.11–22) contains the legislation for the communal meals to be eaten in the messianic age. At these meals the messianic priest, who no doubt is to be identified with the Messiah of Aaron in 1QRule of the Community, would have precedence over the Messiah of Israel. The legislation in the Rule of the Congregation concerned with the common meal of the messianic age bears an obvious similarity to the regulation in 1QRule of the Community, (1QS vi.4–5) which, although in much briefer form, is concerned with the common meals of the community responsible for that scroll; this suggests that the common meals were seen as an anticipation of the common meals that would be eaten in the messianic age.

The legislation in the Rule of the Congregation for the common meals ends as follows: "It is in accordance with this statute that they shall proceed at every me[al at which] at least ten men [g]ather" (1Q28a ii.21–22). The group of ten is referred to in both 1QRule of the Community (cf. 1QS vi.3–4, 6–7) and the Damascus Document (CD xiii.1–2) Josephus also refers to such a group of ten in his account of the Essenes, and the rabbinic writings likewise regard ten men as the minimum needed to perform certain religious activities.

The above texts reveal a number of interesting connections with the communal legislation of the 1QRule of the Community and the Damascus Document, which make it clear that all the texts stem, if not from the same community, at least from related communities. But it is also clear that no simple picture is likely to do justice to the complexities of the relationships between the texts or the communities that lie behind them.

The texts mentioned above are explicitly concerned with community organization. There are, however, a number of other legal texts which, although they consist primarily of interpretations or amplifications of biblical law, nonetheless do occasionally touch on matters of community organization. To mention just one example, Ordinances[a] (4Q159; cf. Ordinances[b–c] [4Q513, 4Q514]) has been described as an anthology of elaborations of biblical laws on diverse topics and has been thought to be close in style to parts of the corpus of Laws in the Damascus Document. Here, alongside laws on such topics as the amount of the harvest that the poor may garner (cf. *Dt.* 23.24–25) or on slavery (cf. *Lv.* 25.39–46), there is reference to a tribunal of twelve men, including two priests, which had the power to impose the death penalty. By contrast, the Damascus Document (CD x.4–10) provides for a tribunal of ten judges, four of whom were to be priests.

[*See also* Damascus Document; Rule of the Community; Rule of the Congregation; *and* Serekh Damascus.]

BIBLIOGRAPHY

Allegro, John M., ed. "Ordinances." In *Qumran Cave 4.* Discoveries in the Judaean Desert, 5. Oxford, 1968.

Baillet, Maurice. "Texte halachique." In *Qumran Grotte 4: 4Q482–4Q520.* Discoveries in the Judaean Desert, 7. Oxford, 1982.

Baumgarten, Joseph M. "The Cave 4 Versions of the Qumran Penal Code." *Journal of Jewish Studies* 43 (1992), 268–276. Includes discussion of the penal code of 4QSerekh Damascus (4Q265) in relation to the penal codes of the Damascus Document and the Community Rule.

Baumgarten, Joseph M. "Purification after Childbirth and the Sacred

Garden in 4Q265 and Jubilees." In *New Qumran Texts and Studies: Proceedings of the First Meeting of the International Organization for Qumran Studies, Paris, 1992*, edited by George J. Brooke and Florentino García Martínez, pp. 3–10, Pl. 1. Studies on the Texts of the Desert of Judah, 15. Leiden, 1994. Preliminary edition and study of parts of 4QSerekh Damascus.

Eshel, Esther. "4Q477: The Rebukes by the Overseer." *Journal of Jewish Studies* 45 (1994), 111–122.

Hempel, Charlotte. "Who Rebukes in *4Q477*?" *Revue de Qumrân* 16 (1995), 655–656.

Knibb, Michael A. *The Qumran Community*, pp. 145–155. Cambridge Commentaries on Writings of the Jewish and Christian World 200 BC to AD 200, 2. Cambridge, 1987. Translation of and commentary on the Rule of the Congregation.

Schiffman, Lawrence H. *The Eschatological Community of the Dead Sea Scrolls: A Study of the Rule of the Congregation*. Society of Biblical Literature, Monograph Series, 38. Atlanta, 1989.

MICHAEL A. KNIBB

CONSERVATION. The first of the Dead Sea Scrolls was discovered in 1947 and exploration continued in the area of Qumran until 1956. Some of the scrolls were found wrapped in linen cloths in jars, other in niches in the walls of caves or on the floor buried in dirt and partially disintegrated by the action of water, insects, and mold. By the end of 1959, most of the fragments that had been found, and those that had been bought from bedouin who searched the area as well, were arranged in the so-called Scrollery, on the premises of the Rockefeller Museum. After two thousand years in the caves, the scrolls began to be treated by the scholars under drastically different climatic conditions, raising a number of issues concerning the scrolls' conservation.

The majority of the scrolls are written on hides, the others on papyrus. The skin of the Dead Sea Scrolls is neither leather nor parchment, as we understand these terms today.

Previous Conservation. When the international team of scholars began preparing an edition of the Dead Sea Scrolls for publication, the scrolls were moistened, then flattened and sorted, according to the text. In the course of sorting, pressure-sensitive tape was used for backing and connecting. The flattened fragments of parchment and papyri were placed between sheets of ordinary window glass without framing. Fragments lay loose between glass plates, sometimes slipping out. These plates were piled one above the other, causing additional pressure on the fragments. Thus, the process of penetration of the greasy and sticky adhesive of the cellotape into the parchment was accelerated.

It is interesting to note the description of the state of the scrolls given by John M. Allegro, one of the first editors of the scrolls, in 1966: "On a recent visit to the Museum I saw for myself just how perilous is the situation. Fragile fragments, which have been out of their desert habitat now for more than fourteen years, are lying still between the glass plates where we left them many years ago, mostly unsecured, and in some cases, as I was horrified to see, subjected to intolerable pressure by the plates lying on top of one another in a large cabinet."

In 1955, Harold Plenderleith, the Keeper of the Research Laboratory of the British Museum, was approached about the matter. In his technical notes of that year he describes how he attempted to separate and analyze scroll fragments contained in three boxes that had been sent to London. "After many experiments the process eventually adopted was to expose the scroll fragments at 100% relative humidity for a few minutes and then to transfer them to a refrigerator for a like period. The degree of freezing was sufficient to congeal the surface of the black material while leaving the membrane sufficiently limp."

When Plenderleith came to Jerusalem in March 1962 he tried to unroll a rigid scroll. The method just described having failed, he carried out a dissection with appropriate tools, using as support the thinnest white silk, spread thinly with polyvinyl acetate and brought into intimate contact with the clean flat surface of the scroll. In 1963, Valerie H. Foulkes of the British Museum visited the Rockefeller Museum in order to prepare the scrolls for an exhibition in the British Museum. She wrote in her report: "It was a shock to discover the extent of the contamination caused by Scotch Tape. The cellotape was removed with trichloroethylene as recommended by Mr. Plenderleith. Gummed silk strips or gold beater skin was used in order to join the fragments, with polyvinyl acetate as adhesive. Special leather dressing was applied to the reverse."

Only in the 1970s and 1980s were some of the parchments and papyri (that were stored in glass plates) restored in the laboratories of the Israel Museum. According to documentation, the cellotape was removed with a scalpel, and greasy spots of adhesive with trichloroethylene. The fragments were treated with the disinfectant thymol. They were then backed with white lens tissue, using perspex glue as a solution in acetone and polyvinyl acetate glue. Some of the glass plates were replaced by acid cardboard, the kind available in Israel at that time.

Thus, the scrolls passed through many hands, were exposed to drastic environmental changes, and treated by various methods. Unsuitable treatments in the fifties, sixties and seventies—excessive humidity, leather dressing, polyvinyl acetate, and perspex solution—compounded the deterioration.

Current Methods. In 1991, a laboratory for the conservation of the scrolls was established by the Israel Antiquities Authority in the Rockefeller Museum. The state of the scrolls had deteriorated further. The fragments had been penetrated by the adhesive of the cellotape; they were darkened; on some, the text was no longer legible; and, worst of all, the edges of some of the fragments had already gelatinized. After experiments with blank samples of parchment, it was decided to exclude parchment glue and adhesives based on organic solvents because of the difficulty of reversibility and the creation of rigid surfaces. It was found that water-based adhesives such as methylcellulose could be used. This was placed on Japanese tissue in a thin layer, left to dry to form a film, and then applied in narrow strips with a little moisture.

It was realized by our team of four conservators that the removal of the pressure-sensitive tape and the stains would take many years and divert our attention from other tasks. It was therefore decided to start a "first-aid treatment" as an emergency measure, which meant removing the fragments from the acid boards and glass plates and placing them between acid-free cardboard. This was done as follows: First, a work record was made with full documentation of the condition of the fragment, which included a scheme showing its position and where it had been stuck with pressure-sensitive tape; second, a description was given of the damage suffered by the skin and the text; third, the kind of intervention that had been carried out previously was recorded; and fourth, the fragments were attached to lens tissue with hinges of Japanese tissue in the order shown on the original photographs taken by the scholars. This was a temporary measure to dispense quickly with the glass and acid board and is now completed.

Parallel with the first-aid treatment, an operation to remove the pressure-sensitive tape was started. The old and well-established method of protecting the recto side temporarily with Japanese tissue is laborious. Each fragment is checked and treated with the aid of a stereomicroscope. Delaminated areas of leather are reinforced with minute quantities of methylcellulose glue carefully introduced into every peeling. After the recto side has been reinforced, the pressure-sensitive tape is removed piece by piece by means of a heated surgical scalpel or a scalpel and a hot-air gun. A thick layer of greasy and sticky adhesive remains. In this case solvents are used in the form of vapors or a mineral powder (Fuller's Earth) dampened with a little methyl ethyl ketone or acetone. The operations cannot be standardized because of the varying extent of the adhesion of the tape and the amount of the dark and sticky residues that render the text illegible. After reinforcing the verso side, which has been freed of cellotape, the Japanese tissue, which had been applied temporarily to the recto side, is easily removed. The restored fragments are kept in acid-free passe-partouts and attached with hinges of Japanese paper.

When preparing the plates for exhibition, another method of mounting is used. Fragments are sewn between two layers of polyester net stretched in an acid-free cardboard. The polyester net is very thin and transparent, in various shades of color.

Preservation of Papyrus. At first glance, the state of preservation of papyrus seems to be much better than that of parchment. The sticky adhesive of the pressure-sensitive tape did not penetrate the papyri and remained on the surface, which makes its removal less troublesome. But removing the pressure-sensitive tape itself from such a fibrous material as papyrus without causing damage is a problematic undertaking.

A fair number of papyrus fragments have text on both sides; on them cellotape is glued on the script itself. This makes the process of removing tape extremely complicated. We attempted several methods—chemical means as well as laser rays. For the time being, the hot-air method seems to be the most appropriate. Tiny strips of Japanese paper with methylcellulose glue are used to fix and unite the papyrus fragments. This procedure is performed together with removing cellotape and is a permanent reinforcement. Cotton wads dampened with a solvent (methyl ethyl ketone acetone) are used to remove adhesive residues from the papyrus surface. The protruding papyrus fibers can then be softened with a brush dampened in distilled water, pressed down, and dried under a press.

Future Research. The Dead Sea Scrolls constitute an almost virgin field for research in conservation. Fortunately, a team of conservators and scientists from the Getty Conservation Institute came to our assistance. Since 1992, studies have aimed to determine the exact character of the damage to the scrolls and the changes that have occurred, and to answer questions about the climate in the caves, the origin of the minerals found in the scrolls, and the causes of physical, chemical, and biological deterioration.

Samples of damaged blank skins were analyzed in the laboratories of the Getty Conservation Institute before and after treatment. It was found that there is no loss of natural oils from the skins.

Studies are being carried out by the Getty Conservation Institute inside the Qumran caves where the scrolls were found. Temperature and Rh conditions were examined and will be published by the institute.

In the course of the joint project, samples of leather, ink, salt crystals, and mold fungi were examined and continue to be examined. Preliminary results show that the inks are carbon inks with traces of iron, copper, zinc, titanium, and manganese. Luckily the mold and fungi are in a passive state. A great quantity of salt crystals were found. Their presence evidently is the cause of the condition of the leather.

Unfortunately, the process of aging cannot be halted. We would be satisfied if we succeed in arranging to slow it down. We are trying to accomplish this with as little intervention as possible and by using reversible methods. We hope that our work contributes to the preservation for the future of these two-thousand-year-old treasures.

BIBLIOGRAPHY

Allegro, John M. Letter to the Editor of the "Observer," 11 December 1966.

Foulkes, Valerie H. Unpublished notes.

Ginell, W. S. "Report on Dead Sea Scrolls." The Getty Conservation Institute, 1993.

Plenderleith, Harold. Unpublished notes.

Schilling, Michael, and W. S. Ginell. "The Effects of Relative Humidity Changes on Dead Sea Scrolls Parchment Samples." Getty Conservation Institute, 1993.

ELENA LIBMAN
ESTHER BOYD-ALKALAY

CONTRACTS. About sixty-five published documents from the Judean desert are included in what loosely may be called contracts. One of the documents (farming contracts Mur 24) contains copies of at least eleven separate leases; two others (purchase of a date crop 5/6Ḥev 21; sale of a date crop 5/6Ḥev 22) are nearly identical documents written from the perspectives of each of the parties. Seventy-five transactions are represented. All are written on papyrus, as documents, in contradistinction to literary remains, which generally are on animal skin (contract? Mur 7; contract XḤev/Se 7; and probably *Eretz Israel* 20 [1989] 256 = *Journal of Jewish Studies* 45 [1994] 287). There are said to be three unpublished fragments of contracts written on leather classified among the material from Cave 4 at Qumran. Of the published documents, about a third are so fragmentary that they yield little or no sense of their contents beyond the fact that they are the remains of contracts.

Most were found in caves in Wadi Murabbaʿat and in Naḥal Ḥever, the same places in which correspondence of Shimʿon Bar Kokhba were found. Of those formerly ascribed to Naḥal Ṣeʾelim, certainly some, and probably all, in fact came from Naḥal Ḥever. In nearly all of them the parties, or at least one of the parties, to the contracts are Jewish, or, in a small number of instances, the documents relate to property subsequently owned by Jews. All but two or three (debt acknowledgment Mur 18, 55/56 CE; sale 5/6Ḥev 36, 56–69 CE; and recognition of debt Mur 114, possibly of 171 CE) are dated explicitly or by paleography to the years between 70 and 135 CE, that is, the period between the First Jewish Revolt and the Bar Kokhba Revolt, with the distribution heaviest toward the end of the period. The documents, it may be supposed, were brought to the caves by Jews who left their homes in the settled parts of the vicinity during the critical parts of the latter revolt and either met their death in the caves or, if they succeeded in escaping, left the documents behind.

Of the main texts of these documents, about half (counting Mur 24, the register of multiple leases in Hebrew, as one) are in Aramaic, the traditional language of the region for legal transactions; about a quarter are in Greek, the language of civil administration in the eastern provinces of the Roman Empire. Nine are in Hebrew, all from the years between 133 and 135 CE, that is, during the Bar Kokhba Revolt, and represent 60 percent of the contracts from those years (76 percent if the eleven contracts of Mur 24 are counted separately), a reflection of the nationalist revival of Hebrew associated with the revolt. Six contracts are in Nabatean, all written in the region of Arabia, all but one when that region was an independent Nabatean kingdom not yet a province of the Roman Empire. What governed the choice of language between Aramaic and Greek is not clear. The proportion of documents written in Greek is substantially higher for those written in the province of Arabia than for those written in Judea. At any rate, it was not the main language of the parties that determined the language of the documents, since in nearly half of the Greek documents the subscriptions of the parties were written in Aramaic, indicating that those parties themselves could not write Greek.

A peculiar feature of about half the contracts is the form in which they were drawn up, that of the double contract. The scribe of this sort of document wrote the text of the document twice on the same sheet of papyrus, one copy above the other. The lower copy was usually written first. The part of the sheet on which the upper copy was written was then folded in narrow horizontal strips from the top down to the end of the upper copy, tied with string looped and knotted at several points, and in at least one case (deed of sale Mur 29) sealed. Witnesses affixed their signatures on the back of the sheet, one next to each of the ties, perpendicular to the direction of the writing of the text on the front. The bottom copy would be similarly folded in horizontal strips from the bottom up, but neither tied nor sealed. The two copies are known, therefore, as the inner and outer (in 5/6Ḥev 12.3: *en tois exoterois*) copies, respectively. Presumably, the inner sealed copy would provide a check on the authenticity of the text in case it was claimed that someone had tampered with the unsealed outer text. This form of document is familiar from Greek documents found in Egypt mainly from the third century BCE. By the end of that century the practice had become attenuated in Egypt as registry in public archives of one sort or another replaced double documentation as the preferred method of authentication. The inner copy turned progressively more summary, becoming no more than symbolic, and by the time of the Roman conquest of Egypt in 31 BCE it had disappeared almost entirely. Where Greek double contracts have appeared elsewhere, as in Dura Europos, the inner copies also are abbreviated in varying degrees. It is remarkable, then, that when this form is used in contracts found in the Judean Desert, the inner text generally is a completely unabridged, occasionally even augmented, copy of the outer text (an exception is deed of sale of plot Mur 30), even when registry in a public archive is anticipated, as in writ of divorce Mur 19. It now is generally accepted that the double contract form did not originate with the Greeks but rather was adopted by them from the double contracts of their eastern, Semitic neighbors, for which cuneiform precedents have been adduced. The full use of this form by Jews even in Greek language contracts—the form is distributed among the languages in roughly the same proportions as the contracts in general—can be considered, then, an expression of their Jewish and Semitic heritage, rather than of Hellenization. This is likely the form of the sale document mentioned in *Jeremiah* 32.11 and 14, though the interpretation has been disputed. It apparently is the *geṭ mequshar* discussed in M. *Bava Batra* 10.1 and the associated pericopes in each Talmud. These documents confirm the interpretation of the Talmudic passages given by the thirteenth-century rabbi Me'ir Abulafia in *Yad Ramah*.

The contracts generally are signed by witnesses, in varying numbers. In the documents whose state of preservation allows determination of the number of witnesses, the most common number in contracts from Wadi Murabba'at is three and in the Naḥal Ḥever documents seven. The "IOU" published by Magen Broshi and Elisha Qimron (1989, 1994) has two witnesses, as does the confirmation of divorce, not properly a contract, XḤev/Se 13. (Naḥal Ḥever documents submitted to government authorities, not contracts, are signed by five witnesses.) In addition, the contracts generally are signed by at least one of the parties. Talmudic literature does not refer to this practice even though the law is insistent that only the signatures of the witnesses are legally determinative. In Talmudic literature it seems that such subscriptions by the parties took the form of a simple statement: "I, so-and-so, wrote this [the signature]." In the Greek papyri from Egypt, on the other hand, the subscription took the form of a summary of the transaction. In the contracts from the Judean Desert, the form of the subscription follows the language of the main body of the document. In documents whose main language is Aramaic, the subscription invariably is of the short form. In documents whose main language is Greek, the subscription is in the form of a summary, irrespective of whether the subscription itself is written in Greek or, as often, in Aramaic.

Of the Greek documents sufficiently preserved for investigation, most are couched in the form of a *homologia*, that is, a declaration by one (or less commonly by both) of the parties that he acknowledges that a binding transaction has taken place or that he has undertaken an obligation. Thus, the main body of the text begins with a form of the verb *homologeio* ("acknowledge"). Most of these are couched in "subjective style," that is, the verb *acknowledge* is in the first person, and references to the parties are thereafter in the first and second persons. A small number (remarriage contract Mur 115, deposit 5/6Ḥev 17, and perhaps marriage contract 5/6Ḥev 37) are couched in objective style, with the verb for *acknowledge* and all subsequent references to the parties in the third person, in *oratio obliqua*. Three Greek documents certainly are not homologies but rather assert directly in objective style that a transaction occurred. Two of these are marriage documents (marriage contract 5/6Ḥev 18 and double contract; marriage contract XḤev/Se Gr. 2; see Cotton, "A Cancelled Marriage Contract from the Judaean Desert," 1994); the third (deed of gift 5/6Ḥev 19) is a gift given on the occasion of the marriage in marriage contract 5/6Ḥev 18. A fourth document, marriage contract 5/6Ḥev 37, may well be of this form, even though Cotton (1997) confidently restores a form of the verb *acknowledge* where the original editor, Naphtali Lewis, more prudently declined to do so. The Hebrew and Aramaic documents are evenly divided in this respect. Those that are couched as a *homologia* have the verb for *say* in the third person and continue in the first and second persons of *oratio directa*. The others are in either objective, subjective, or mixed style. Two declarations of indebtedness, debt acknowledgment Mur 18 in Aramaic and the "Hebrew IOU Note" (see Broshi and Qimron, 1989, 1994), present an enigma because of anomalies at the beginning or end. I suggested taking the documents as straight homologies, closely modeled on the Greek, despite the anomalous placement of the parties' signatures at the end. Other scholars have followed Segal (1991) in taking the introductory verb *acknowledge* as a passive whose subject is the name of the creditor, despite the problematic syntax thus created and the separation from both Greek and Aramaic models of homology.

Several documents, deposit 5/6Ḥev 17, marriage contract 5/6Ḥev 18, concession of rights 5/6Ḥev 20, purchase of a date crop 5/6Ḥev 21, sale of a date crop 5/6Ḥev 22, marriage contract 5/6Ḥev 37, and XḤev/Se Gr. 5 (census declaration, rent or tax receipt, unclassified fragments; Cotton, 1995), end with a phrase to the effect that, having been asked, one or both of the parties to the transaction acknowledge that the transaction was done correctly. This is a declaration that the Roman *stipulatio* had taken place. That would have the effect in Roman law of turning the obligation into a unilateral *stricti juris* one. It certainly is doubtful whether a proper exchange of question and answer as required by the Roman *stipulatio* really took place in any of these cases, but it is significant in light of the extent of Romanization of the region that the scribes took the trouble to write the phrase into the written contracts, nearly a century before this was done in Egypt and in Dura Europos.

Some twenty of the contracts are for the sale, probably or certainly, of real estate, whether fields or houses. Sixteen, if those of farming contracts Mur 24 are counted separately, are leases of real estate. Eleven are contracts of deposit, loan, or acknowledgment of debt; nine are contracts of marriage or dowry. There also are scattered documents of purchase of crop, gift, sale of movables, concession of rights, and divorce.

On the whole, the language of the contracts in Hebrew and Aramaic is what may be expected on the basis of rabbinic literature. Marriage contract 5/6Ḥev 10, Babatha's *ketubbah*, is the most striking document in this respect. Similarly, the contracts written in Greek follow the conventions of Greek documents known from Egypt. I have argued, and A. Wasserstein and Hannah Cotton have vigorously denied, that even the Greek documents display elements drawn from the Jewish tradition.

BIBLIOGRAPHY

Benoit, P., J. T. Milik, and R. de Vaux, eds. *Les Grottes de Murabbaʿat*. Discoveries in the Judaean Desert, 2. Oxford, 1961.

Beyer, K. *Die aramäischen Texte vom Toten Meer*. Göttingen, 1984.

Broshi, Magen, and Elisha Qimron. "A House Sale Deed from Kefar Baru from the Time of Bar Kokhba." *Cathedra* 40 (1986), 201–213 (Hebrew) = *Israel Exploration Journal* 36 (1986), 201–214.

Broshi, Magen, and Elisha Qimron. "A Hebrew I.O.U. Note from the Second Year of the Bar Kokhba Revolt." *Eretz Israel* 20 (1989), 256–261 (Hebrew) = *Journal of Jewish Studies* 45 (1994), 286–294.

Cotton, Hannah. "A Cancelled Marriage Contract from the Judaean Desert (*XHev/Se Gr. 2*)." *Journal of Roman Studies* 84 (1994), 64–86.

Cotton, Hannah M. "Loan with Hypothec: Another Papyrus from the Cave of Letters?" *Zeitschrift für Papyrologie und Epigraphik* 101 (1994), 53–59.

Cotton, H. M., E. H. Cockle, and F. G. B. Millar. "The Papyrology of the Roman Near East: A Survey." *Journal of Roman Studies* 85 (1995), 214–235. The most useful list of individual documents.

Cotton, Hannah, and Ada Yardeni, eds. *Aramaic, Hebrew, and Greek Documentary Texts from Naḥal Ḥever and Other Sites, with an Appendix Containing Alleged Qumran Texts* (The Seiyal Collection II). Discoveries in the Judaean Desert, 27. Oxford, 1997.

Friedman, Mordechai A. "Babatha's *Ketubba*; Some Preliminary Observations." *Israel Exploration Journal* 46 (1996), 55–76.

Katzoff, Ranon. "Papyrus Yadin 18 Again: A Rejoinder." *Jewish Quarterly Review* 82 (1991), 171–176.

Katzoff, Ranon. "An Interpretation of P.Yadin 19: A Jewish Gift after Death." In *Proceedings of the Twentieth International Congress of Papyrologists, 23–29 August 1992*, edited by Adam Bülow-Jacobsen, pp. 562–565. Copenhagen, 1994.

Katzoff, Ranon. "Supplementary Notes." In *Legal Documents in the Talmud: In Light of Greek Papyri and Greek and Roman Law* (in Hebrew), by Asher Gulak, edited and supplemented by Ranon Katzoff. Jerusalem, 1994.

Koffmahn, Elisabeth. *Die Doppelurkunden aus der Wüste Juda. Recht und Praxis der jüdischen Papyri des 1. und 2. Jahrhunderts n. Chr. samt Übertragung der Texte und deutscher Übersetzung*. Studies on the Texts of the Desert of Judah, 5. Leiden, 1968.

Lehmann, Manfred R. "Studies in the Murabbaʿat and Nahal Hever Documents." *Revue de Qumrân* 4 (1963), 53–81.

Lewis, Naphtali, ed. *The Documents from the Bar Kokhba Period in the Cave of Letters, Greek Papyri*. Jerusalem, 1989.

Lewis, Naphtali, Ranon Katzoff, and Jonas C. Greenfield. "Papyrus Yadin 18." *Israel Exploration Journal* 37 (1987), 229–250. See pages 236–247.

Milik, J. T. "Deux documents inédits due désert de Juda." *Biblica* 38 (1957), 245–268.

Segal, Peretz. "The Hebrew IOU Note from the Time of the Bar Kokhba Period" (in Hebrew). *Tarbiz* 60 (1991), 113–118.

Starcky, J. "Un contrat nabatéen sur papyrus." *Revue biblique* 61 (1954), 161–181.

Wasserstein, A. "A Marriage Contract from the Province of Arabia Nova: Notes on Papyrus Yadin 18." *Jewish Quarterly Review* 80 (1989), 93–130.

Yadin, Yigael, Jonas C. Greenfield, and Ada Yardeni. "Babatha's *Ketubba*." *Israel Exploration Journal* 44 (1994), 75–101.

Yadin, Yigael, Jonas C. Greenfield, and Ada Yardeni. "A Deed of Gift in Aramaic found in Naḥal Ḥever: *Papyrus Yadin 7*" (in Hebrew). *Eretz Israel* 25 (1996), 383–403.

Yaron, Reuven. "The Murabbaʿat Documents." *Journal of Jewish Studies* 11 (1960), 157–171.

RANON KATZOFF

COPPER SCROLL. Often called the most enigmatic of the Dead Sea Scrolls, the Copper Scroll (3Q15) is a list of hidden treasures, inscribed in Hebrew on thin copper sheets. The text consists of sixty-four sections, arranged in twelve columns, each typically describing a hiding place and the treasure to be found there. A representative section is the first, which reads as follows: "In the ruins which are in the Valley of Achor, under the steps which go eastward, forty rod-cubits: a strongbox of silver and its vessels—a weight of seventeen talents." The hiding places listed appear to be mainly in and around Jerusalem, and the treasure described is enormous, consisting of many tons of silver and gold, as well as other valuables.

The Copper Scroll was discovered in Cave 3 (about 2 kilometers north of Qumran) on 20 March 1952 by archaeologists working under the joint auspices of the American School of Oriental Research, and École Archéologique Française de Jérusalem, and the Palestine Archaeological Museum. Since 1956, the Copper Scroll has been housed in the Archaeological Museum of Amman, Jordan. [*See* Amman Museum.]

Distinctive Features. The Copper Scroll stands out among the other Dead Sea Scrolls in a number of ways: writing material; script; orthography; subject matter; language; literary structure; and the inclusion of Greek letters.

Writing material. Whereas the other texts are written on parchment or papyrus, the Copper Scroll is inscribed on copper sheets. The original scroll consisted of three copper sheets riveted together, but it was found in two rolled-up pieces. Apparently one of the three sheets had become detached before the scroll was rolled up and hidden. The metal is of exceptional purity (99 percent copper) and thinness (about 1 millimeter), and would have been very costly. The size of the sheets (roughly 30 by 30 centimeters each), as well as the way they were attached to each other and inscribed in columns, indicated that the Copper Scroll is a replica of a standard parchment scroll. It is unclear why copper was chosen as the medium on which the text was inscribed; the choice may have been dictated by considerations of durability or ritual purity.

The uniqueness of the writing material had two important consequences. Firstly, the text of the Copper Scroll was not so much "written" by a trained scribe as "engraved" by one or more metalworkers, who may themselves have been illiterate. The letters of the text appear to have been hammered into the copper with a punch (each letter requiring several blows), with the result that they showed through on the reverse side of the thin copper. Secondly, during the period of almost two thousand years that the scroll lay hidden, the copper was completely oxidized. This meant not only that some parts of the scroll were completely destroyed by corrosion, but also that its two rolled-up pieces could not be unrolled without destroying them.

Script. The paleographical analysis of the Copper Scroll is complicated by the fact that the engraver or engravers were themselves likely illiterate, copying from a *Vorlage*. As a result, the shape of the writing looks rough and unpracticed, and many look-alike letters of the Hebrew alphabet are not distinguished at all, notably *bet* and *kap*, *dalet* and *resh*, *he* and *ḥet*, *waw* and *yod*. Despite these irregularities, it is possible to classify the script of the Copper Scroll as a "vulgar semiformal" variety of the late Herodian script. There are some indications that the *Vorlage* used cursive forms.

Orthography. The Copper Scroll has its own brand of Hebrew spelling, which conforms to neither the "Qumran orthography" characteristic of many of the literary Dead Sea Scrolls, nor to any other standard orthography. Some notable features are the use of *alep* instead of *he* to represent a final long *-a* (e.g., *ḥwm*ʾ, "wall," in ii.10), the use of *samek* instead of *śin* (e.g., *ʿsr*, "ten," in ii.9), and the occasional dropping of gutturals (e.g., *mrb* for *mʿrb*, "cave," in xii.1).

Subject matter. Whereas almost all the other Dead Sea Scrolls contain material which can be broadly classified as "religious" or "literary," the Copper Scroll appears to be an administrative document which simply enumerates, in a dry bookkeeping style, a series of physical locations and the valuables that are hidden there. In connection with its bookkeeping character, it should be noted that the Copper Scroll is one of the very few autographs among the Dead Sea Scrolls; almost all the others, heterogeneous as they are, appear to be copies of works belonging to a religious or literary canon.

Language. The Copper Scroll is written in an early form of Mishnaic Hebrew, and thus constitutes an invaluable linguistic link between Late Biblical Hebrew and the language of the Mishnah. Its affinity with Mishnaic Hebrew can be demonstrated in the areas of morphology (e.g., *-în* instead of *-îm* as the regular masculine plural ending), of syntax (e.g., the frequent use of *šel* to indicate the genitival relationship), and of lexicon (some fifty vocabulary items illustrate words or usages characteristic of Mishnaic Hebrew). Another feature which it shares with Mishnaic Hebrew, and which sets it off from the literary Hebrew of the other scrolls, is the frequent use of Greek loanwords (e.g., *prsṭlyn* for *peristylion*, "peristyle," in i.7). The language of the Copper Scroll, therefore, is important evidence that there was a form of Hebrew used around the turn of the era that already had clearly Mishnaic features, and that this Hebrew differed significantly from the classical language used in literary works. Linguistically speaking, the closest analogue to the Copper Scroll among the other Dead Sea Scrolls is 4QMMT, although the latter still differs in important respects from Mishnaic Hebrew (e.g. the absence of *-în* and *shel*).

Literary structure. Although the Copper Scroll is not "literary" in the sense of belonging to *belles lettres*, it does have a very specific structure by which its content is organized. In an unvarying pattern, the sixty-four sections present material in the following order: a designation of a hiding place, a further specification of the hiding place, a command to dig or measure, a distance expressed in cubits, a treasure description, additional comments, and Greek letters. Each of these standard slots has stereotypical features of its own. For example, the second slot regularly begins with *shel* plus a preposition, and the fourth typically consists of the word *ʾmwt*, "cubits," followed by a number written out in full. Although no section includes all seven slots, a section is always filled in the order indicated. As a result, the text as a whole reads like a bookkeeper's ledger.

Greek letters. The seventh slot consists of two or three Greek letters (e.g., KEN in section 1, and HN in section 6), and is found in only seven of the sixty-four sections, all of them in the first three columns. Although various theories have been offered to explain the Greek letters, they remain an enigma. It may be significant that they could in each case be the beginning of a Greek proper name.

Making the Text Available. Another way in which the Copper Scroll is unique is the way in which it was initially opened for reading, and its text subsequently published.

Opening the scroll. After their discovery in 1952, the two rolled-up pieces of the scroll remained unopened for three and a half years. They could not be unrolled, since the oxidized copper crumbled to the touch. During this time, scientists searched in vain for a way to reconstitute the original copper, so that the scroll could be unrolled in the ordinary way. In the end, the two pieces were successively brought to Manchester in 1955 and 1956, where they were opened by being coated on the outside with an adhesive, and then cut into narrow strips by means of a small circular saw. After cleaning, the concave side of the resulting twenty-three curved segments of oxidized copper revealed the inscribed text. This delicate operation was successfully carried out by H. Wright Baker at the Manchester College of Science and Technology. He was advised and assisted by John Allegro of the University of Manchester, a member of the international team of scholars entrusted with the publication of the Dead Sea Scrolls, who had arranged for the Copper Scroll to be brought from Jerusalem to Manchester, and who was the first to transcribe and translate the Hebrew text of the scroll as it became legible. [*See biography of Allegro.*]

Publishing the text. Although black-and-white photographs of the Copper Scroll segments have been published in Discoveries in the Judaean Desert, 3 (Oxford, 1962), these are virtually illegible, both because the indented letters do not stand out visually from the surrounding oxidized and corroded copper, and because the curvature of the segments makes reading difficult. In the absence of legible photographs, the text of the Copper Scroll has been made available in the form of hand-drawn facsimiles. Three of these have been published. The first was prepared in collaboration with Allegro by the Jordanian artist Muhanna Durra, who copied directly from the twenty-three segments in Amman. This is the text published by Allegro (1960). The second facsimile is that prepared by Wright Baker in Manchester, published in Discoveries in the Judaean Desert, 3 (*Planche* XLV), in 1962. This was based on various photographs of each segment, taken from different angles, and was checked against the original, but by someone without a knowledge of Hebrew. The third facsimile is a revision of the second done by the expert Hebraist J. T. Milik, who also had an opportunity to consult the original in Amman. [*See biography of Milik.*] His facsimile, which may be considered the most authoritative of the three, was also published in Discoveries in the Judaean Desert, 3 (*Planches* XLVIII–LXX). However, the many divergences between the three published facsimiles still introduce a significant element of uncertainty in the detailed textual study of the Copper Scroll.

Given this situation, and the fact that the twenty-three copper segments have experienced further deterioration since 1956, it is highly desirable that a reliable reproduction of the Copper Scroll text be made available as the basis for further scholarly study. An important step in this direction will be the publication of the original photographs made in Manchester, as well as the publication of the sophisticated new color photographs taken by Bruce and Kenneth Zuckerman in 1990.

Major Issues of Interpretation. Apart from many differences over questions of exegetical detail, scholarship on the Copper Scroll has been divided over three major issues which affect the overall interpretation of this enigmatic document.

Dating. Although Cross, in his paleographical excursus on the Copper Scroll in Discoveries in the Judaean Desert, 3, dated its script to the period 25–75 CE, some scholars have relied on the later paleographical dating proposed by Albright, namely 70–135 CE. Depending on the dating chosen, it is thus possible to associate the Copper Scroll either with the First Jewish Revolt of 66–70, or the Second Jewish Revolt of 132–135—or the period in between.

The archaeological evidence with respect to the dating question has also been interpreted in two different ways. If the Copper Scroll was deposited in Cave 3 at the same time as the fragmentary manuscripts and broken pottery which were also discovered there, it must be dated to the time around 68 CE. According to William Reed, who reported on the discovery of the Copper Scroll (*Bulletin of the American Schools of Oriental Research* 135 [1954], 10): it is "certain that the rolls were placed on the floor of the cave prior to 70 A.D." This has been the view of most scholars. However, some have argued that the archaeological evidence does not exclude the possibility that the Copper Scroll might have been a later deposit, and therefore had nothing to do with the other artifacts in Cave 3.

Authenticity. From the moment that the text of the Copper Scroll first became known, there has been scholarly disagreement about its authenticity. Could the enormous amounts of gold and silver, some of it buried at a depth of 17 cubits (about 9.3 meters), really be taken seriously as real treasure actually hidden in antiquity? Milik, followed by a number of other scholars, argued that they could not, and that the Copper Scroll therefore represented a kind of folklore, comparable to other legendary accounts of hidden treasure. The opposing viewpoint was taken by Allegro and others, who argued that a fictional account would not have been laboriously inscribed on such an expensive material, nor composed in such a dry bookkeeping style. Advocates of the latter view account for the high numbers in the scroll in different ways, either as historically plausible at face value, or as in fact representing smaller amounts. Most recent students of the scroll have adopted the view that it is realistic, partly because the legendary interpretation may originally have been influenced by political considerations, as well as a desire to discourage treasure hunters.

Relation to the other scrolls. If the documents found in the caves near Qumran all belonged to the "library" of a quasi-monastic group residing at Qumran, then the Copper Scroll can reasonably be taken to be a product of that same community, and should be interpreted in that light. However, because the Copper Scroll is so distinctive in many respects, it has been argued that it was a later deposit, which has no historical connection with the other scrolls found in the vicinity. Alternatively, if the Qumran scrolls are a heterogeneous collection emanating from Jerusalem, then the Copper Scroll may be of the same date as the other scrolls, but with no essential connection to them.

The Major Theories. Because of the different answers which students of the Copper Scroll have given to the question of its date, its authenticity, and its relation to the other scrolls, a number of distinct theories of interpretation have emerged. They can be classified under the following six headings (for bibliographic details, see Wolters, 1994, pp. 285–292).

1. The treasure is authentic, and belonged to the Qumran community before 70 CE. This view was defended in the 1950s by Dupont-Sommer, and, more recently, by Goranson (1992).
2. The treasure is authentic, and belonged to the Temple in Jerusalem before 70 CE. Prominent defenders of this view in the 1950s and 1960s were Roth, Rengstorf, Allegro, and Driver. This theory was revived by Golb in 1980, who has since been followed on this point by many scholars, including Wilmot (1984), McCarter (1994), Lefkovits (1993), Wise (1994), and Wolters (1994).
3. The treasure is authentic, and belonged to the Jewish rebels under Bar Kokhba around 135 CE. The French scholar Laperrousaz and the Israeli scholar Luria independently put forward this interpretation in the early 1960s, but they have had no followers.
4. The treasure is authentic, and represents undelivered temple contributions after the destruction of the Temple in 70 CE. This is the theory of Lehmann, who believes the Copper Scroll can be dated to the period 70 to 90–92 CE.
5. The treasure is legendary, and was part of the folklore of the Qumran community before 70 CE. This was the view of a number of scholars in the 1950s, including Harding, Cross, Silberman, and Mowinckel. It was also held by Milik and De Vaux before 1959.
6. The treasure is legendary, and was part of Jewish folklore around 100 CE, when the Copper Scroll was deposited in Cave 3. This view, which Milik adopted in 1959, is reflected in his authoritative edition of the Copper Scroll in Discoveries in the Judaean Desert, 3 (1962). Milik was followed by de Vaux and Rodrigues in the 1960s, but by virtually no one thereafter.

Evaluation. In assessing the various theories, it needs to be borne in mind that the burden of proof rests on those who assign a post-68 CE date to the Copper Scroll. It may be true (though this has been disputed by Pixner) that the archaeological evidence does not rule out the possibility that the Copper Scroll was a later deposit in Cave 3. However, there is no positive indication that this was in fact the case. In the absence of evidence to the contrary, it is methodologically preferable to assume that the material remains found in Cave 3 were all deposited there at the same time, probably around 60 CE. In other words, there is something inherently implausible about theories three, four, and six.

Furthermore, it is difficult to imagine any document less like folklore than the Copper Scroll, with its dry catalogue of locations and valuables. Besides, the attempt to classify it under that heading can be shown to have an identifiable political background (see Wolters 1990). These considerations count heavily against theories five and six.

The weight of the evidence therefore seems to point to the theories numbered 1 and 2 above: The treasure is authentic, and belonged, prior to 68 CE, to either the Qumran community or the Jerusalem temple. Almost all recent scholarship on the Copper Scroll (with the notable exceptions of Laperrousaz and Lehmann) has moved in this direction.

Two further considerations tip the scales in favor of linking the Copper Scroll with the Jerusalem temple rather than the Qumran community. The first is the enormous size of the treasure, which (if taken at face value) could only have come from the vast wealth of the temple. The second is the incidence of cultic terminology in the scroll, which is much higher than previously recognized. Many terms in the Copper Scroll, especially in the treasure descriptions, identify specifically temple-related items (for example, *maʿaser sheni*, "second tithe," in i.10 and *mnqyʾwt*, "libation bowls," in iii.3).

If the treasure of the Copper Scroll is indeed part of the legendary wealth of the Second Temple, and if it was hidden shortly before the destruction of the temple in 70 CE, then the most likely historical context for the scroll and its treasure is the military conflict between the Romans and the Zealot-led Jewish forces in Jerusalem.

BIBLIOGRAPHY

Allegro, John Marco. *The Treasure of the Copper Scroll.* London, 1960. The first complete edition of the text.

Golb, Norman. "The Problem of Origin and Identification of the Dead Sea Scrolls." In *Proceedings of the American Philosophical Society* 124 (1980), 1–24, especially 5–8. Argues that the Copper Scroll is pivotal for a new interpretation of the Qumran scrolls.

Goranson, Stephen, "Sectarianism, Geography, and the Copper Scroll." *Journal of Jewish Studies* 43 (1992), 282–287.

Laperrousaz, Ernest-Marie. *Qoumran. L'établissement essénien des bords de la Mer Morte. Histoire et archéologie du site.* Paris, 1976. The chapter on the Copper Scroll (pp. 131–147) is the fullest statement of Laperrousaz's theory.

Lefkovits, Judah K. "The Copper Scroll—3Q15, A New Reading, Translation and Commentary." Ph.D. dissertation, New York University, 1993. Detailed commentary in light of rabbinic sources.

Lehmann, Manfred R. "Where the Temple Tax Was Buried." *Biblical Archaeology Review* 196 (1993), 38–43. The most recent statement of Lehmann's controversial theory.

Luria, Ben-Zion. *Megillat ha-Neḥošet Mimidbar Yehuda.* Jerusalem, 1963. Reproduces Allegro's facsimile, and provides translation and extensive commentary in Modern Hebrew.

McCarter, P. Kyle. "The Copper Scroll Treasure as an Accumulation of Religious Offerings." In *Methods of Investigation of the Dead Sea Scrolls and the Khirbet Qumran Site: Present Realities and Future Prospects*, edited by Michael O. Wise, Norman Golb, John J. Collins, and Dennis G. Pardee, pp. 133–148. Annals of the New York Academy of Sciences, 722. New York, 1994. A preview of McCarter's edition of the Copper Scroll in the Princeton series of the Dead Sea Scrolls.

Milik, J. T. "Le rouleau de cuivre provenant de la grotte 3Q (3Q15)." In *Les "petites Grottes" de Qumran*, edited by M. Baillet et al., pp. 200–302. Discoveries in the Judaean Desert, 3. Oxford, 1962. The standard scholarly edition, with French translation.

Wise, Michael O. "The Copper Scroll." *Parabola* 19 (1994), 44–53.

Wolters, Al. "Apocalyptic and the Copper Scroll." *Journal of Near Eastern Studies* 49 (1990), 145–154. Examination and refutation of the legendary hypothesis.

Wolters, Al. "The Copper Scroll and the Vocabulary of Mishnaic Hebrew." *Revue de Qumrân* 14 (1990), 483–495. Identifies fifty lexical Mishnaisms in the Copper Scroll.

Wolters, Al. "Literary Analysis and the Copper Scroll." In *Intertestamental Essays in Honour of Jósef Tadeusz Milik. Vol. 1*, edited by Z. J. Kapera, pp. 239–252. Cracow, 1992. An investigation of the stereotypical patterns of the text.

Wolters, Al. "History and the Copper Scroll." In *Methods of Investigation of the Dead Sea Scrolls and the Khirbet Qumran Site: Present Realities and Future Prospects*, edited by Michael O. Wise, Norman Golb, John J. Collins, and Dennis G. Pardee, pp. 285–298. Annals of the New York Academy of Sciences, 722. New York, 1994. Extensive survey of the history of research, with additional evidence favoring authenticity.

Wolters, Al. "Cultic Terminology in the Copper Scroll." In *Intertestamental Essays in Honour of Józef Tadeusz Milik. Vol. 2*, edited by Z. J. Kapera. Cracow, 1996. Argues that the incidence of cultic terminology in the Copper Scroll is much higher than Milik recognized.

AL WOLTERS

COSMETICS during the Roman and Byzantine periods included expensive powders, ointments, perfumes, and fragrant oils, which were produced from various plants and resins mixed with vegetable oil or animal fat. Physical remains of cosmetic preparations are rare in the archaeological evidence from the Judean Desert. Numerous artifacts, however, associated with cosmetic use have been discovered at several Judean Desert sites, indicating their common usage. The widespread popularity and acceptance of cosmetics are also clearly reflected in later Roman period rabbinic sources: women were permitted by Jewish law to adorn their faces with kohl and rouge (B.T., *Moʿed Q.* 9b) and a husband was obliged to give his wife ten *dinars* for her cosmetic needs (B.T., *Ket.* 66b).

The containers and utensils associated with cosmetic application discovered in the Judean Desert include small containers made out of wood, glass, and pottery, shell and stone palettes, and metal cosmetic applicators. Other objects associated with personal beautification include mirrors and combs. The most complete sets of cosmetics utensils were found at Masada, associated with the later reuse of Herod's fortress-palace complex by the Sicarii during the First Jewish Revolt, and in the Cave of the Letters (Naḥal Ḥever), dating to the Bar Kokhba Revolt. Several items related to cosmetic use are known from the caves in Naḥal Ḥever, Naḥal David, Qumran, Murabbaʿat, and Naḥal Ṣeʾelim.

The most noteworthy cosmetic container is the cylindrical wooden box with a lid found in the Cave of the Letters. Traces of a reddish powder found in this box may be remnants of rouge. This *pyxis*, unusual due to the excellent state of its preservation, is a well-known cosmetic container form and imitates more expensive examples made out of metal. More common cosmetic containers include pottery perfume vials, such as those found at Masada. Small ceramic juglets and glass bottles, which are found at most Judean Desert sites and throughout Palestine, probably contained precious oils or substances as well.

Other typical items associated with cosmetics include kohl sticks and palettes. The kohl stick, used for painting the eyes, was thickened at one end, for applying the paint, while the other end was shaped like a little spoon or spatula, for extracting paint from the container. Several bronze kohl sticks have been found at Masada and in the ʿEin-Gedi tombs. Stone and shell cosmetic palettes were also among the personal items found in rooms inhabited by the Sicarii at Masada.

During the Roman and Byzantine periods, much attention was devoted to hair care among both men and women. Hair treatment included washing, combing, dyeing, and oiling, the latter practice mentioned in the New Testament (*Mt.* 26.7). Numerous wooden combs have been found at Masada, Cave 1 at Qumran, the Murabbaʿat caves, the Cave of Horror and the Cave of the Letters in Naḥal Ḥever, the Naḥal Ṣeʾelim caves, and the Cave of the Pool (Naḥal David). These combs, with fine teeth on one edge and coarser teeth on the other, were typical of a general type known throughout the Roman Empire. Several of these combs even revealed traces of lice and their eggs attached to them.

Mirrors were commonly used during this period. Two well-preserved handheld mirrors have been found among the personal belongings of the refugees from the time of the Bar Kokhba Revolt, in the Cave of the Letters in the Judean Desert. Each mirror was formed by a thin disk of polished tinned copper with a lead handle, one of which was decorated with a leaf design. The mirror was placed in a wooden case comprising two halves. The disk was fastened to one of the two halves, and the second half served as the lid. An additional mirror case made from bronze was recovered from Masada.

Though ancient sources and archaeological evidence are largely silent regarding cosmetic preparations, several classical authors, including Pliny, do provide some information about the cultivation of plants and recipes used to produce perfumes and ointments from them. The most famous and precious of all perfumes, balsam, was produced from a plant grown at ʿEin-Gedi and Jericho. The special climatic conditions of the Dead Sea area were especially suitable for the cultivation of this unique aromatic plant, whose production secrets were closely guarded. Pliny (*Natural History* XII.111), for example, records that as the army of Titus advanced through the balsam-growing area on its way to Jerusalem in 70 CE, Jews attempted to chop down the precious orchards to prevent them from falling into the hands of the Romans. However, the Roman army did capture the orchards and later Titus displayed balsam trees in his triumphal procession in Rome.

Balsam is also mentioned in several inscriptions from Masada. Two inscriptions were found on ceramic storage jars, one with the words *balsam balsama* on it in Aramaic and Hebrew, and a second inscribed *balsaneh*. Two papyrus fragments in Latin, also from Masada, mention *xylobasamum*—the inferior product of the balsam tree. This may indicate that the Roman soldiers stationed in that fortress were involved in the balsam trade.

One possible clue regarding the identity of the balsam plant, now extinct in the ʿEin-Gedi and Jericho regions, is the discovery in Cave 13 at Qumran of a ceramic juglet wrapped in palm fibers, which contained a small amount of a viscous plant oil. Chemical analysis failed to identify the fluid as any known vegetable oil, and scientists have suggested that it may be remains of the famous balsam oil.

The balsam industry may be alluded to in an inscription on a sixth-century CE mosaic pavement in the ʿEin-Gedi synagogue. This long inscription contains a curse on "whoever shall reveal the secret of the town to the gentiles." It has been suggested that the "secret" referred to in this inscription concerns the production of the perfume derived from balsam. During recent excavations at ʿEin-Gedi, a fortified towerlike structure in Naḥal Arugot has been suggested as one of the locations at which balsam was processed during the early Byzantine period.

Another indication of the importance of this region for the preparation of perfumes and cosmetics is the discovery at ʿEin-Buqeq of a first-century CE building complex, possibly a workshop for the production of fine fragrances, ointments, or other cosmetics.

The discovery of cosmetics containers and implements at Judean Desert sites, especially at locations associated with refugees during the First and Second Jewish Revolts, indicates the common use of cosmetics. Their importance to women—who, even during troubled times, were not willing to part with these items of personal beautification—is evident.

BIBLIOGRAPHY

Aharoni, Yohanan, Nahman Avigad, Pessah Bar-Adon, and Yigael Yadin. "The Expedition to the Judean Desert, 1960." *Israel Exploration Journal* 11 (1961), 3–52. Includes a description of the artifacts found during the 1960 expedition to the Judean Desert.

Aharoni, Yohanan, Nahman Avigad, Pessah Bar-Adon, and Yigael Yadin. "The Expedition to the Judean Desert, 1961." *Israel Exploration Journal* 12 (1962), 168–183, 186–199, 215–257. Includes a description of the artifacts found during the 1961 expedition to the Judean Desert.

Dayagi-Mendels, Michal. *Perfumes and Cosmetics in the Ancient World.* Exhibition Catalog, Israel Museum. Jerusalem, 1989. General introduction to perfumes and cosmetics in the ancient world.

Patrich, Joseph, and Benny Arubas. "A Juglet Containing Balsam Oil(?) from a Cave near Qumran." *Israel Exploration Journal* 39 (1989), 43–59. A detailed report of the juglet, which may contain balsam.

Yadin, Yigael. "The Wooden and Bone Objects." In *The Finds from the Bar Kokhba Period in the Cave of the Letters*, pp. 123–135. Jerusalem, 1963. Detailed description of wooden and bone objects found during the second series of excavation in the Cave of the Letters.

Yadin, Yigael. *Masada: Herod's Fortress and the Zealots' Last Stand.* London, 1966. Popular report of the Masada excavations including photographs of a cosmetic set.

ANN E. KILLEBREW

COURT TALES. A popular genre of the Persian and Hellenistic periods, court tales existed both outside and inside Judaism. As an international genre, it may be defined as a story of the adventures of a deserving person in the royal court, who (usually) achieves success through skill or wisdom. A good example of this genre is the Aramaic *Story of Aḥiqar,* which tells of the adventures of Aḥiqar, a courtier of the Assyrian king, who is persecuted by his nephew, narrowly escapes death, and is ultimately vindicated through his wit. Although Aḥiqar is not Jewish, this story must have been popular with the Jewish community, for it appears among the documents of the Jewish colony at Elephantine. Eventually it was translated into many languages used by the Christian church.

Within Judaism, the genre may be most widely defined as the story of the adventures of a Jew in the court of a foreign king. This tale takes two forms: the contest and the conflict. In the contest, a wise person of undistinguished status solves a problem, interprets a dream, and so forth, and as a result is elevated. In the conflict, a wise courtier begins in a respected position, is persecuted, suffers a fall, and is finally vindicated. The Hebrew scriptures and the Apocrypha contain several examples of both types of court tale. The Joseph story (*Gn.* 37–50), *Daniel 2, Daniel 4, Daniel 5,* and the story of Zerubbabel in *1 Esdras* 3–4 are all examples of the contest type, while *Esther, Daniel 3, Daniel 6,* and *Bel and the Dragon* are examples of the conflict type. A related type of tale uses the same basic structure but is not set in a royal court, for example, the story of *Susanna.* These tales often present ideals of Wisdom in popular narrative form. There was a natural association of the royal court with Wisdom (e.g., the figure of Solomon), and the tales are human rather than God centered; that is, it is the wit and wisdom of the protagonist that saves him or her rather than the direct intervention of God (*Daniel 3* and *Daniel 6* are exceptions).

The discovery of the Dead Sea Scrolls offers evidence that the court tale existed in Judaism outside the Hebrew scriptures and the Apocrypha. Of the biblical examples, several have been found at Qumran. The Joseph story has been found in fragmentary form in Genesis[c,e,f,j] (4Q3, 4Q5, 4Q6, 4Q9), Genesis-Exodus[a] (4Q1), and paleo-Genesis-Exodus[l] (4Q11). Fragments of *Daniel* 1–6 appear in Daniel[a] (1Q71, 4Q112) and Daniel[b] (1Q72, 4Q113) while the tale of Daniel and Susanna may appear in Daniel-Susanna? (4Q551). No manuscript of *Esther* has been found at Qumran.

At least two new compositions that are related to the court tale have been identified at Qumran. The first is the Prayer of Nabonidus (4Q242), an Aramaic composition dating to the late second or early first century BCE. Although the Prayer of Nabonidus itself does not take the form of a court tale, it is generally agreed that the text is the original form of the court tale now found in *Daniel* 4. The Prayer of Nabonidus concerns the last Babylonian emperor, Nabonidus (556–539 BCE), who, according to the text, was afflicted by an "evil ulcer" in Teima (Nabonidus's historical capital in Arabia). He was healed by an unnamed Jewish exorcist, who forgave his sins and commanded Nabonidus to recount the incident in writing, to glorify the name of God. The text breaks off at the beginning of Nabonidus's written statement. Evidently, the author of *Daniel* (or his predecessor) took this tale and recast it, changing the location to Babylon, switching the king's name to the much better known Nebuchadnezzar, and greatly expanding the account of the king's illness. Most importantly, the author of *Daniel* identified the unnamed Jewish exorcist of the Prayer of Nabonidus with his hero Daniel, thus bringing the tale into the Daniel cycle where it appears in *Daniel* 4 in the form of a contest tale.

The second composition uncovered at Qumrân is an Aramaic text officially named Proto-Esther[a–f] (4Q550), but which would be better entitled Tales of the Persian Court. This composition, which exists in three separate manuscript groups, dates paleographically to the late Hasmonean period. The story (or stories), set in the Persian court, bears certain similarities to the Hebrew and Greek versions of the *Book of Esther,* raising the possibility that the composition may have influenced the author of *Esther.* The first set of fragments (a–c) is set in the court of Xerxes I and involves an unnamed protagonist whose father, Patireza, was a servant of the royal wardrobe. One day the king has his father's annals read to him, in which is found, evidently, a record of the deeds of Patireza. The king then rewards the son for Patireza's good works. Although fragmentary, this story seems to take the form of a conflict tale, spread out over two generations. The story is not specifically Jewish.

The second set of fragments (d), again set in the Persian court, seems to tell the tale of a conflict between Bagasraw, a Jew, and Bagoshe, a gentile, in which Bagasraw triumphs. The king, evidently as a result of Bagasraw's triumph, venerates the Jewish God. This set of fragments bears certain similarities to *Daniel* 1–6 as well as to both the Hebrew and Greek versions of *Esther.*

The third set of fragments (e–f) are very broken, but the contents do not seem to take the form of a court tale. It is impossible to suggest a direct relationship between Proto-Esther[a–f] and the *Book of Esther,* but an indirect relationship is extremely plausible.

Other compositions found among the Dead Sea Scrolls share certain affinities with the court tale, although they are not court tales themselves. These include the Genesis Apocryphon (1QapGen) and Tobit (4Q196–200).

[*See also* Daniel, Book of, *article on* Pseudo-Daniel; Esther, Book of.]

BIBLIOGRAPHY

Crawford, Sidnie White. "Has the Book of Esther been found at Qumran? 4QprotoEsther and the Esther Corpus." *Revue de Qumrân* 17 (1996), 307–325.

Lange, Armin, and Marion Sieker. "Gattung und Quellenwert des Gebets de Nabonid." In *Qumranstudien. Vorträge und Beiträge der Teilnehmer des Qumranseminars auf dem internationalen Treffen der SBL: Münster, 25–26 Juli, 1993,* edited by H. J. Fabry, Armin Lange, and Hermann Lichtenberger, pp. 3–34. Göttingen, 1996.

Milik, J. T. "'Prière de Nabonide' et autres écrits d'un cycle de Daniel, fragments araméens de Qumrân 4." *Revue biblique* 63 (1956), 407–415. The original publication of 4Q242.

Milik, J. T. "Les modèles araméens du livre d'Esther dans la Grotte 4 de Qumrân." *Revue de Qumrân* 15 (1992), 321–399. See also plates which have no page number. The original publication of 4Q550.

Puech, Émile. "La Prière de Nabonide (4Q242)." In *Targumic and Cognate Studies: Essays in Honour of Martin McNamara,* edited by Kevin J. Cathcart and Michael Maher, pp. 208–228. Journal for the Study of the Old Testament, Supplement Series, 230. Sheffield, 1996.

Wills, Lawrence M. *The Jew in the Court of the Foreign King.* Minneapolis, 1990. A study of Jewish court tales.

SIDNIE WHITE CRAWFORD

COVENANT. A contractual agreement between parties, a covenant in Jewish literature is primarily made between God and his people or God and an individual.

Covenant in the Hebrew Scriptures. The Hebrew scriptures describe covenants between the deity and Noah (*Gn.* 9), Abra(ha)m (and his children; *Gn.* 15 and 17), Israel (*Ex.* 19–24), Levi (*Mal.* 2.4–5), Phinehas (*Nm.* 25), and David (*2 Sm.* 7). While some covenants are called eternal, and promises in the form of grants without conditions are given to Abraham, Phinehas, and David, agreements normally include conditions imposed on the human party. The most prominent example is the covenant between God and Israel at Mount Sinai. The laws of this covenant, found between *Exodus* 20 and *Numbers* 10, are intended to give concrete shape to ongoing life in community with God and neighbors. The arrangement is sanctioned by promised blessings for obedience and curses for disobedience (*Dt.* 27–28). The prophetic books contain complaints about Israelite violations of the covenant and threats that the penalties, including exile from the land, would be implemented if no changes occurred. Jeremiah refers to a new or rather renewed covenant between God and his people in which he would place his "law within them" (*Jer.* 31.31–34). *Nehemiah* 9–10 recounts an occasion on which the postexilic inhabitants of Jerusalem confessed their sins and those of their ancestors and made an agreement to adhere to the divine law.

Covenant in the Apocrypha and Pseudepigrapha. The author of *1 Baruch* confesses that the nation has not upheld the covenant yet holds out the hope that repentance in exile will lead to an everlasting covenant that will be obeyed, so that God would never again remove the people from their land (*1 Bar.* 1.15–3.8). The *Prayer of Azariah and the Song of the Three Young Men*, part of the *Additions to Daniel*, also offers a confession and a plea that God not annul his covenant (*Sg. of 3* 11). In *Ben Sira* 24.23, wisdom is identified as "the book of the covenant of the most high God, the law that Moses commanded us"; the author also refers to the covenants with Noah (*Sir.* 44.18), Abraham (*Sir.* 44.20–21), Isaac (*Sir.* 44.22), Jacob (*Sir.* 44.23), Moses (*Sir.* 45.5), Aaron (*Sir.* 45.7, 15, 25), Phinehas (*Sir.* 45.24), and David (*Sir.* 45.25, 47.11; cf. Commentary on Genesis A, 4Q252 v.4). The *Books of the Maccabees* describe a time when Jewish people fought to preserve the covenant against the threat posed by both Jewish apostasy and Antiochus IV Epiphanes' decrees (175–164 BCE) outlawing the Jewish religion. The *First Book of the Maccabees* says that certain Jews who "removed the marks of circumcision . . . abandoned the holy covenant. They joined with the gentiles and sold themselves to do evil" (*1 Mc.* 1.15). Under Antiochus IV Epiphanes, "[a]nyone found possessing the book of the covenant, or anyone who adhered to the law, was condemned to death by decree of the king" (*1 Mc.* 1.57). The faithful, however, "chose to die rather than to be defiled by food or to profane the holy covenant; and they did die" (*1 Mc.* 1.63). When he sounded the cry of revolt, Mattathias said: "Let every one who is zealous for the law and supports the covenant come out with me!" (*1 Mc.* 2.27; cf. 2.20). He exhorted his sons from his deathbed to "show zeal for the law, and give your lives for the covenant of our ancestors" (*1 Mc.* 2.50). According to *2 Maccabees* 1.2, the Jews of Judea wrote to their kindred in Egypt asking that God remember his covenant with the patriarchs. In the story about the martyrdoms one learns that the brothers who made the supreme sacrifice received "everflowing life, under God's covenant" (*2 Mc.* 7.36; cf. 8.15).

Among the pseudepigrapha, covenant is a central theme in *Jubilees*, a significant precursor of Qumran thought and a popular book among the sectarians. The covenant serves as a framework within which the author views biblical history from its beginnings until the people of Israel arrived at Mount Sinai. The first chapter places *Jubilees* in a covenantal context by dating the revelation to Moses to the sixteenth day of the third month, that is, the day after the ceremonies ratifying the covenant. The overarching significance of the covenant is indicated by God's declaration that the history revealed in the book would prove that he had been more faithful than the people of Israel, who had abandoned the covenant and suffered punishment (*Jub.* 1.5–6). Once the people repented in their places of exile, God would restore them to their land and to proper covenantal relations with him (*Jub.* 1.15–18, 1.22–25). As *Jubilees* begins with the covenant, it ends with the story about the covenant at Mount Sinai.

In *Jubilees* the covenant is made initially between the Lord and Noah with his sons on the occasion of Noah's sacrifice after the Flood, a sacrifice dated to the first of the third month (*Jub.* 6.1, 4). The law against consuming blood was then revealed (*Jub.* 6.11). The Angel of the Presence connects the later Sinaitic covenant with the Noachic one:

> During this month he made a covenant before the Lord God forever throughout all the history of the earth. For this reason he [God] told you [Moses], too, to make a covenant—accompanied by an oath—with the Israelites during this month on the mountain and to sprinkle blood on them because of all the words of the covenant which the Lord was making with them for all times. (*Jub.* 6.10–11)

The passage, by connecting the first and last covenantal ceremonies in the book, shows that Sinai marked a renewal and updating of the ancient covenant that also was made in the third month. The same chapter stipulates for *Shavuʿot*, to be celebrated on the fifteenth day of the third month: "For this reason it has been ordained and written on the heavenly tablets that they should celebrate the Festival of Weeks during this month—once a year—to renew the covenant each and every year" (*Jub.* 6.17). The writer also indicates that Abram's covenant (*Gn.* 15) was made in the middle of the third month (*Jub.* 14.1, 18; cf. 48.8) and identifies this agreement with Noah's covenant (*Jub.* 14.20). The covenant of circumcision (*Gn.* 17) was concluded on the same date (*Jub.* 15.1–14) some twenty-two years later. The Lord also reaffirmed the covenant with Isaac, who was born in the middle of the third month (*Jub.* 16.13–14; see 15.19, 21, 24.11; cf. 24.22–23). Abraham prayed during one celebration of *Shavuʿot* (*Jub.* 22.1) that the same covenant would be renewed with Jacob and his descendants (*Jub.* 22.15, 30; cf. 27.21–25). [*See* Shavuʿot.]

For the author of *Jubilees*, the covenant involves not only promises of land and progeny but also laws that are progressively revealed. The first was given to Noah and his sons, and that law was later supplemented with commands about circumcision (*Jub.* 15), sacrificial procedure (*Jub.* 21), separation from the gentiles (*Jub.* 30), and so on. A person could not be condemned for violating a law that had not yet been revealed (see *Jub.* 33.15–17).

Covenant in the Qumran Texts. The concept of covenant is an important one in several of the documents found at Qumran, among them the Rule of the Congregation (1Q28a), the Rule of the Blessings (1Q28b), the War Scroll (1QM), Liturgical Prayers (1Q34), Hodayot[a] from Qumran Cave 1 (hereafter, 1QHodayot[a], 1QH[a]), Apocryphal Lamentations B (4Q501), the Words of the Luminaries[a] (4Q504), and Temple Scroll[a] (11Q19), but especially in the Rule of the Community (1QS, 4Q255–264a, 5Q11) and the Damascus Document (CD, 4Q266–273, 5Q12, 6Q15). In general, the covenant mentioned in these works is considered the same agreement as the one made and renewed in the Hebrew scriptures (Talmon, 1994, p. 13). It is the ancient covenant, the one made with the ancestors (see CD i.4; viii.17–18; xix.30–31; 1QM xiii.7; xiv.8; xviii.7; cf. 11Q19 xxix), and it is eternally valid (1QS iii.11–12; iv.22; v.5–6; 1QM xvii.3; 1Q28b i.2; ii.25; CD iii.4). The group(s) behind the texts are the chosen who keep that pact in this present age of wickedness (1QS v.2; 9 [for Zadokite priests]; 1Q28a i.3; CD xx.17). God has remembered the covenant and renewed it with the community (e.g., 1Q34 3.ii.5–6; CD i.4; vi.2; xix.1; cf. 4Q501 2; 4Q504 v.9–11). In these texts several verbs appear frequently that refer to members of the group(s) and the covenant:

1. *bwʾ* ("enter"); 1QS ii.12, 18; v.8, 20; vi.15 [causative]; CD ii.2; iii.10; vi.11 [causative], 19; viii.1; ix.3; xiii.14; xv.5; xix.14; xx.25; 1QH xiii.23 [v.21]; xxi.9 [xviii.24; causative];
2. *ʿbr* ("cross over"); 1QS i.16, 18, 20, 24; ii.10; CD i.20 [causative]; xvi.12;
3. *ḥzq* ("hold fast to"); 1QS v.3; 1QH x.28 [ii.26]; xii.39 [iv.38]; xxiii.9 [xviii.8]; 1Q28b i.2; iii.23; cf. CD xx.27.

Those who have entered or crossed over into the covenant hold strongly to it by obeying its rules. The covenant is to be renewed annually, and the ceremony for renewal seems to have taken place in the third month, presumably on *Shavuʿot* as in *Jubilees*. The principal difference between the biblical covenant involving Israel and the one in the sectarian texts is that in the latter the covenantal community has shrunk: most Israelites—those who violated the laws of the covenant as the group understood them—are excluded. Only those who pledged to adhere to the covenant in sectarian terms were considered members.

The Damascus Document appears to have the structure of a covenantal text (Davies, 1983, pp. 50–53), and covenant is a central theme in it. It begins with a covenantal lawsuit. Israel had forsaken God who delivered them to the sword.

> However, when he remembered the covenant of the very first, he saved a remnant for Israel and did not deliver them up to destruction. . . . Three hundred and ninety years after having delivered them up into the hands of Nebuchadrezzar, king of Babylon, he visited them . . . (CD i.4–7)

Thus, the remnant is tied directly to the ancient covenant. The opponents of the Teacher of Righteousness, the leader of the group, are those on whom the curses of the covenant fall; these enemies are apparently fellow Jews (CD i.21–ii.1). The Damascus Document deals with the ways of those who are inside and outside the covenant (CD ii), referring to the patriarchs as eternal members of the covenant (CD iii.4). A key statement about the covenant and the points of dispute between the group and other Jews appears in the same column:

> But with those who remained steadfast in God's precepts, with those who were left from among them, God established his covenant with Israel for ever, revealing to them hidden matters in which all Israel had gone astray: his holy Sabbaths and his glorious feasts, his just stipulations and his truthful paths, and the wishes of his will which man must do in order to live by them. He disclosed (these matters) to them and they dug a well of plentiful water [= the Torah]; and whoever spurns them shall not live. (CD iii.12–17; see also vi.3–4)

The eternal covenant continued with God's new priestly and lay remnant, men of knowledge from Aaron and wise men from Israel (CD vi.2–3). The ones who had entered this pact were no longer to "enter the Temple to kindle his altar in vain" (CD vi.12).

The Damascus Document introduces the phrase "the new covenant in the land of Damascus" (CD vi.19; cf. viii.21; xix.33–34; xx.10–12), which apparently designates the renewed covenant that had been described previously. Whatever the precise meaning of "Damascus" may be, it is at least associated with the group's consciousness of having originated in a situation of exile. The renewed covenant required that those who entered it were to separate from the impure Temple cult and its wealth and from the apostates; they were also to refrain from mistreating the poor and were to differentiate between the clean and the unclean. The writer orders them to follow the exact interpretation of the law, including observing Sabbaths and festivals "according to what they had discovered, those who entered the new covenant in the land of Damascus" (CD vi.19; see also vi.11–vii.4). For those who obey the laws, the covenant guarantees life for one thousand generations (CD vii.5–6, xix.2), while those who renege after entering the agreement will be judged (CD viii.2–3; cf. xix.14, 16, 34–35). [*See* Festivals.]

The one who enters the covenant is enrolled with the oath of the covenant (CD xv.5–8; sons are also mentioned), and testing and approval by a superior are required:

> On the day when he talks to the Inspector of the Many, they shall enroll him with the covenant oath which Moses established with Israel, the covenant to re[vert to] the law of Moses with the whole heart [and with the whole] soul, to what has been discovered that has to be put into practice in all the a[ge of wickedness]. (CD xv.7–10)

No one with defects was permitted entry because the angels were present (CD xv.16–17). Relations with outsiders were severely circumscribed (e.g., CD xii.10–11, xiii.14–15), while disputes within the community were to be resolved without vengeance or resentment (CD ix.2–8). Judges in the group were to be learned in covenantal principles (CD x.6).

The fragmentary copies of the Damascus Document found in Cave 4 at Qumran not only preserve a number of the passages mentioned above but also add an important detail about covenant in the work. In a passage without parallel in the Cairo Genizah copies (but apparently following on CD xiv.8–21), one finds a series of penalties for violations, a ceremony for expelling those who despise the regulations of the Torah, and provision for recording their sentences: "The sons of Levi and the men of the camps will meet in the third month and will curse whoever tends to the right [or to the left of the] law" (4Q266 11.17–18 [4Q270 7.ii.11–12 in Baumgarten, 1996]; 4Q267, 18.v.16–18 [4Q270 11.ii.11–12 in García Martínez, 1996]). Mention of covenantal curses uttered by Levites (and other members) reminds one of *Deuteronomy* 27.14–26, where the covenant is being renewed, and also of the first columns of Rule of the Community (see below), which describe the annual covenantal ceremony. Hence, it is likely that the curses in the Cave 4 fragments of the Damascus Document are part of a covenantal ceremony that probably occurred on Shavuʿot.

The Rule of the Community in the form preserved in 1QS from Qumran Cave 1 (hereafter, 1QRule of the Community) contains several statements about covenant in the first column and details a covenantal ceremony in columns i–iii. Sections of these columns are attested in Rule of the Community[a–c] (4Q255–257) and Rule of the Community[h] (4Q262) (see also 5Q11), although they are not found in Rule of the Community[d] (4Q258), which may begin the text with what is column v in the Cave 1 copy. Among the tasks assigned to the *maskil* is to

> welcome into the covenant of kindness all those who freely volunteer to carry out God's decrees, so as to be united in the counsel of God and walk in perfection in his sight, complying with all revealed things concerning the regulated times of their stipulations; in order to love all the Sons of Light, each one according to his lot in God's plan, and to detest all the Sons of Darkness, each one in accordance with his blame in God's vindication. (1QS i.7–10)

The text emphasizes voluntary compliance by members to conduct themselves perfectly in God's revealed way (including the observance of correct festal dates according to their calendar), designates members as Sons of Light who are to love one another, and requires that they hate all others, all the Sons of Darkness. The covenant community does not include all Israel; it consists only of the Sons of Light, who do not attain their position by heredity. [*See* Calendars and Mishmarot.] The point is further elaborated:

> All those who enter the Rule of the Community shall establish a covenant before God in order to carry out all that he com-

mands and in order not to stray from following him for any fear, dread, or grief that might occur during the dominion of Belial. (1QS i.16–18; see also 4Q256 1)

The covenantal ceremony (1QS i.18–iii.12) involves priests, Levites, and individuals who are entering or reaffirming membership in the people of the pact. The priests recite the gracious acts of God, but the Levites detail Israel's sins during Belial's dominion. The entrants then offer their own confession and recognition of God's merciful behavior toward them (1QS i.24–ii.1). Next, the priests bless "the men of God's lot," that is, the entire covenantal community (1QS ii.1–4); their words are an expansion of the priestly blessing in *Numbers* 6.24–26. The Levites follow with curses on "all the men of the lot of Belial" (1QS ii.4–9). Their curses are a negative elaboration of the priestly blessing. Once those entering the covenant have responded to the blessings and curses with "Amen, Amen," the priests and Levites together curse any person who enters the covenant insincerely (1QS ii.11–17). Again, the entrants answer "Amen, Amen." The ceremony itself ends at this point, but the text goes on to supply more information about it. It is to be conducted annually (1QS ii.19), with the priests leading, the Levites second, and all who enter third (1QS ii.19–23). The writer describes the ideal atmosphere that was to prevail within the community (1QS ii.24–25), explains why the sinner is to remain outside it (1QS ii.25–iii.9), and exhorts such a person to walk perfectly in God's way. Should he become obedient, "he will be admitted by means of atonement pleasing to God, and for him it will be the covenant of an everlasting community" (1QS iii.11–12).

The Rule of the Community contains a few other references to covenant. For example, it speaks of "those of perfect behavior" who are "selected by God for an everlasting covenant and to them shall belong all the glory of Adam" (1QS iv.22–23, v.5–6 refers to them as the "community of the eternal covenant"). The Cave 1 copy requires that members accept the rule of the Zadokite priests, "who safeguard the covenant," and that of "the multitude of the men of the Community, those who persevere steadfastly in the covenant" (1QS v.2–3, see also 9). However, Rule of the Community[d] (4Q258 1.i.2–3) lacks the reference to the authority of the Sons of Zadok.

Józef Milik first suggested that Berakhot[a–e] (4Q286–290) constitute the text of the blessings that were pronounced during the annual covenantal ceremony (4Q287 4.1 refers to the annual recital). The wording of the Berakhot manuscripts differs from that of the Rule of the Community and reflects other biblical texts; nevertheless, they could preserve a later (the copies date from approximately 1 to 50 CE), expanded version of the script for the covenant renewal ceremony (Nitzan, 1994). Some phrases indicate the liturgical character of these texts, for example, "[the men of the] community council shall say, all together, Amen, Amen. And afterward, they shall damn Belial and all his guilty lot" (4Q286 7.ii.1–2).

Covenant in the New Testament and in Rabbinic Texts. While the New Testament contains references to the covenants of the Hebrew scriptures (e.g., *Acts* 7.8, *Rom.* 9.4) or to contemporary events as fulfillments of the ancient promises (*Lk.* 1.72), it also furnishes several instances of the phrase "a/the new covenant." In *Luke* 22.20, Jesus calls the wine at the Last Supper "the new covenant in my blood" (*Mt.* 26.28 and *Mk.* 14.24 lack "new" although many manuscripts add it). Paul uses the same word for the cup (*1 Cor.* 11.25) and calls himself and his associates "ministers of a new covenant, not of letter but of spirit" (*2 Cor.* 3.6; cf. 3.7–18). Also, the writer of *Hebrews* calls Jesus "the guarantee of a better covenant" than the old one and its priesthood (*Heb.* 7.22; see also 8.6–7 [*Jer.* 31.31–34 is quoted in *Heb.* 8.8–12], 8.13, 10.16–17). Christ is the mediator of "a new covenant" (*Heb.* 9.15, 12.24), and "the blood of the eternal covenant" is mentioned (*Heb.* 13.20).

In rabbinic literature, covenant, while not mentioned frequently, is everywhere presupposed. The covenant is made with the ancestors (in the Mishnah, especially the covenant of circumcision) and with the people of Israel at Mount Sinai. God had elected Abraham, Isaac, Jacob, and Israel and through his revealed law showed them the way to remain in proper communion with himself and one another. Israel's response to divine grace was to obey. Although there were certainly disputes about interpretation of laws, the scope of covenant in rabbinic literature is wider than at Qumran in that the covenant was viewed as one with all Israel, not just with one small group.

[*See also* Cairo Genizah; Damascus Document; Law and Lawgiving; *and* Rule of the Community.]

BIBLIOGRAPHY

Baumgarten, Joseph M. *Qumran Cave 4, XIII: The Damascus Document (4Q266–273)*. Discoveries in the Judaean Desert, 18. Oxford, 1996. Official edition of the Cave 4 copies of the Damascus Document.

Davies, Philip R. *The Damascus Covenant: An Interpretation of the "Damascus Document."* Journal for the Study of the Old Testament Supplement Series, 25. Sheffield, 1983. Detailed commentary on the Damascus Document and discussion of its covenantal structure.

García Martínez, Florentino. *The Dead Sea Scrolls. Translated.* 2d. ed. Leiden and Grand Rapids, Mich., 1996.

Jaubert, Annie. *La notion d'alliance dans le judaïsme aux abords de l'ère chrétienne*. Patristica Sorbonnesia, vol. 6. Paris, 1963. Comprehensive study of covenants in the Hebrew Bible, Second Temple Jewish texts, and the New Testament.

Milik, J. T. "Milkî-ṣedeq et Milkî-rešaʿ dans les anciens écrits juifs et chrétiens." *Journal of Jewish Studies* 23 (1972), 95–144.

Nitzan, Bilhah. "4Q Berakhot (4Q286–290): A Preliminary Report." In *New Qumran Texts and Studies: Proceedings of the First Meeting of the International Organization for Qumran Studies*, edited by

George J. Brooke with Florentino García Martínez, pp. 53–71. Studies on the Texts of the Desert of Judah, 15. Leiden and New York, 1994.

Schiffman, Lawrence H. "The Rabbinic Understanding of Covenant." *Review and Expositor* 84 (1987), 289–298. Summary and discussion of the references to covenant in classical rabbinic works.

Talmon, Shemaryahu. "The Community of the Renewed Covenant: Between Judaism and Christianity." In *The Community of the Renewed Covenant: The Notre Dame Symposium on the Dead Sea Scrolls*, edited by Eugene Ulrich and James VanderKam, pp. 3–24. Christianity and Judaism in Antiquity, 10. Notre Dame, Ind., 1994.

JAMES C. VANDERKAM

CREATION. According to the biblical doctrine of creation set forth in *Genesis* 1–3 and widely assumed in the Qumran writings, God (who is identified as the God of Israel) made the heavens and the earth, gave mankind stewardship over the earth, and despite mankind's sin continues to care for the created universe. For example, the Paraphrase of Genesis (4Q422 1.i.6–12) includes the final elements from the priestly account of *Genesis* 1.1–2.3 (the creation of the heavens and the earth, God's Sabbath rest) as well as material from *Genesis* 2.4–3.24 ("He set him in charge to eat the fruits . . . not to eat from the tree of the knowledge of good and evil"). Mankind's sin is traced to rebelliousness ("he rose up against [God]") and the "evil inclination." Another paraphrastic treatment of *Genesis* 1–3 appears in the Words of the Luminaries[a] (4Q504 8–9.4–9), which describes in terms of *Genesis* 1.26 and 2.7–8 the creation of the first human ("our father you formed in the likeness of [your] glory") and his subsequent rebellion and its consequences ("you obliged him not to turn aside . . . he is flesh, and to dust . . . ").

The Hymn to the Creator in Psalms[a] (11Q5 xxvi.9–15) stands in the biblical tradition (see *Prv*. 8 and *Sir*. 24) that attributes creation to the wisdom of God and is a pastiche of biblical phrases (see Ps. 89.5–7, 135.7; *Jer*. 10.12–13, 51.13, 51.15–16). It first describes the "great and holy" Lord in his majesty, with grace and truth around him, and with truth, justice, and righteousness as the foundations of his throne. Then it considers God's work in creation as "separating light from darkness" and establishing the dawn "by the knowledge of his heart." God's action in creation astounds the angels ("he showed them what they had not known"), and God provides food for every living thing. The hymn concludes with a blessing that highlights the role of God's wisdom in creation: "who establishes the world by his wisdom; by his understanding he stretched out the heavens."

In Hodayot[a] from Qumran Cave 1 (hereafter, 1QHodayot[a], 1QH[a]) there are frequent allusions to God as creator, and creation often provides the horizon against which other theological concerns are developed. The distinctive approach to creation in 1QHodayot[a] is expressed in this way: "And by your wisdom you established the eternal . . . and before you created them you knew all their works forever and ever. For apart from you nothing is done, and nothing is known without your good pleasure" (1QH[a] ix.7–8 [i.5–6]). Besides alluding to wisdom's role in creation, the text asserts the absolute sovereignty and foreknowledge of God. This affirmation in turn raises the theological questions of determinism or predestination and human freedom.

Goal of Creation. According to 1QHodayot[a], the goal or end of creation is the glory of God: "You have stretched out the heavens for your glory; all their host you have established for your good pleasure" (1QH[a] ix.9–10 [i.7–8]). Just as the heavenly bodies and the forces of nature follow the plan of God, so do the earth and the seas: "You have established them by your wisdom, and everything that is in them you have established for your good pleasure" (1QH[a] ix.14–15 [i.12–13]). Although mankind has been given dominion over the earth, humans too are subject to the sovereignty and foreknowledge of God: "By the wisdom of your knowledge you have established their course before they exist. According to your good pleasure everything happens, and apart from you nothing is done" (1QH[a] ix.19–20 [i.17–18]). While much clearly depends on biblical teachings (God's sovereignty, God's wisdom as the agent, God's glory as the goal), the emphasis on divine foreknowledge is distinctive.

The same basic doctrine of creation appears elsewhere in 1QHodayot[a] to express God and the fragile, sinful human race: "By the mysteries of your insight you have apportioned all [these] to make your glory known. But what is the spirit of flesh to understand your great and wondrous counsel?" (1QH[a] v.19–20 [xiii.13–14]). But if God is the creator of all and sovereign over all, God must then in some way be responsible for both the righteous and the wicked among human beings: "For you alone have created the righteous ones . . . and the wicked you have created for the time of your wrath" (1QH[a] vii.18–21 [xv.14–17]).

Doctrine of the Two Spirits. How these various theological elements regarding creation—God's sovereignty, God's foreknowledge, and the mixed character of mankind—fit together receives a full and systematic presentation in the "Treatise on the Two Spirits" in 1QRule of the Community (1QS iii.13–iv.25). The instruction was intended as a theological treatise for the community's spiritual director (the *maskil*) as he teaches the "Sons of Light." It begins with an affirmation of God's absolute sovereignty over creation: "From the God of knowledge is all that is and will be, and before they existed he established all their design; and when they come into being according to their course, it is in accord with his glorious design that they fulfill their task and without change" (1QS iii.15–16).

The questions of the mixed character of mankind and the existence of evil in God's creation are resolved by the doctrine of the two spirits. Receding for the present from direct involvement in human affairs, God has appointed "two spirits in which to walk until the time of his visitation" (1QS iii.18). These two spirits are identified as Truth and Falsehood. Under the leadership of the Prince of Light (Truth), the children of light do the deeds of light. And under the leadership of the Prince of Darkness (Falsehood), the children of darkness do the deeds of darkness. This will continue "until the determined end and the renewal" (1QS iv.25), the eschatological intervention that will result in the vindication of the righteous and the destruction of the wicked when God's sovereignty over creation will be fully manifest once more. Thus, the existence of sin and evil in God's creation is explained by a doctrine of modified dualism whereby the sovereign creator and Lord grants temporary control over human affairs to the two spirits. The text acknowledges the problem of determining to which spirit one belongs and gives a brief answer ("according to whether each one's inheritance be great or small," 1QS iv.16), without going deeply into the theological questions raised by such a solution.

Other Qumran texts reaffirm various aspects of the understanding of creation found in Hodayot and the Rule of the Community. The high priest's discourse in the War Scroll lists all the things in the heavens and on earth that God has created: "the dome of the sky, the host of luminaries, the tasks of the spirits and the dominion of the holy ones . . . beasts and birds, man's image . . . sacred seasons and the cycles of years and times everlasting" (1QM x.11–16). Having established reasons for trusting in the sovereignty of God and assuming that this sovereign God is on the side of the Sons of Light, the high priest proclaims: "The battle is yours!" (1QM xi.1).

Sovereignty of God. The theme of God's foreknowledge with regard to creation appears in other texts. According to the Ages of Creation, God established beforehand what would happen in each age: "Before he created them, he determined their works . . . age by age" (4Q180 1.2–3). According to the Damascus Document, God knew that wicked persons would turn aside from the way of righteousness: "For God did not choose them from the beginning of the world, and before they were established he knew their deeds" (CD ii.7–8). The contrast between the orderliness of creation as established by the sovereign creator and the ignorance and disobedience displayed by humans is developed in the Liturgical Prayers: " . . . the great light for [day-]time, [and the small one for night-time . . .] without breaking their laws . . . and their dominion is over all the world. But the seed of mankind has not understood all that you gave them to inherit, and they have not known you, to do your word" (1Q34 3.ii.1–3).

Several fragments from the large wisdom apocryphon known as Sapiential Work A (1Q26; 4Q415–418, 423) refer to God's action in creation as a framework or horizon for human understanding and wise activity. In Sapiential Work A[b] (4Q146 1, 7, 10, which may have been the beginning of the work), the instructor appeals both to the orderliness of God's creation ("and the host of the heavens he has established") and to the coming judgment ("in heaven he will pronounce judgment upon the work of wickedness, and all his faithful children will be accepted with favor by him"). In the context of God's judgment, the instructor in Sapiential Work A[a] affirms the omnipotence and omniscience of God the creator: "they do not come into being without his favor, and apart from his wisdom" (4Q418 126.ii.5).

A peculiar part of the instruction in Sapiential Work A[e] (4Q423 2.1–8) weaves together phrases from *Genesis*: "every fruit of produce and every tree pleasant and delightful to contemplate" (4Q423 2.9); "and over it he has set you in authority, to till it and to keep it" (4Q423 2.15); "thorn and thistle it will cause to sprout forth for you" (4Q423 3.18); and perhaps "she gave birth, and all the wombs of the pregnant ones . . . " (4Q423 3.16). Although the use of the creation story from *Genesis* 2–3 is obvious, its lesson is not.

Much of what the Qumran scrolls say about creation and God's sovereignty over creation stands squarely within the biblical tradition. As in *Ben Sira* and *1 Enoch*, there is a living interest in creation and God's creative activity as a horizon for ethical instruction. Further, the idea of the purpose of creation to glorify God also echoes biblical sentiments (see *Psalms* 19.1, 24.9–10, 29.3).

What is most interesting from a theological perspective is the insistence in several texts on God's predetermination and foreknowledge of every aspect of creation. As in the New Testament (see *Romans* 9–11), the theological emphasis is on the sovereignty of God and the divine grace offered to the elect. Nevertheless, such language does raise questions about the evil actions of humans and God's responsibility for them in the unfolding of creation.

The "Treatise on the Two Spirits" (1QS iii.13–iv.25) attempts to explain, if not resolve, those questions by asserting that God has freely ceded control over creation to the two spirits (Truth and Falsehood) who will remain locked in cosmic struggle until the final divine intervention or visitation. This framework of modified dualism, which affirms God's absolute and ultimate sovereignty while assigning the present incompleteness and sinfulness of creation to the permissive will or mysterious plan of God, seems to be the assumption of much Pauline (see *Romans* 1–8) and Johannine theology. The crucial difference is that for early Christians, God's decisive intervention through Jesus' death and resurrection had already broken the real power of sin, death, and the Law (Paul), and of darkness or the "world" (John), whereas the Qumran texts are more oriented to the future for such an intervention (though there are elements of "realized eschatology" in them).

These issues are glimpsed also in Josephus's contrasting descriptions of the Pharisees and Sadducees (*The Jewish War* 2.162–166; see also *Jewish Antiquities* 13.297–298, 18.12–15; *Acts* 23.6–10), though allowance must be made for his addressing non-Jewish readers in their own terminology (fate, immortality of the soul) and the shifting meaning of the term *Sadducee*. The Pharisees are said by Josephus to ascribe everything to fate and God, whereas the Sadducees deny fate and hold that God is so remote that he can neither commit sin nor even see it. For the Pharisees the decision to choose to do right or wrong rests mainly with human beings; nevertheless fate is at work in every action. But the Sadducees say that humans are entirely free to choose between good and evil, and each individual chooses his course of action without the influence of God or fate. The Pharisees are said to have believed in the immortality of the soul as well as in reward and punishment after death, whereas according to Josephus the Sadducees denied both. The rabbis generally followed the Pharisees's balanced combination of divine guidance and human freedom in choosing what one should do.

[*See also* Damascus Document; Hodayot; Mystery; Rule of the Community; *and* Wisdom Texts.]

BIBLIOGRAPHY

Elgvin, Torleif. "The Genesis Section of 4Q422 (4QParaGenExod)." *Dead Sea Discoveries* 1 (1994), 180–196.

Harrington, Daniel J. "Wisdom at Qumran." In *The Community of the Renewed Covenant: The Notre Dame Symposium on the Dead Sea Scrolls*, edited by Eugene Ulrich and James C. VanderKam, pp. 137–151. Notre Dame, Ind., 1994. Treatment of the role of creation in Sapiential Work A and *Ben Sira*.

Holm-Nielsen, Sven. *Hodayot: Psalms from Qumran*. Aarhus, 1960. Good treatment of biblical and theological aspects of the Hodayot.

Leaney, A. R. C. *The Rule of Qumran and Its Meaning*. Philadelphia, 1966. A literary and theological exposition of the 1QRule of the Community.

Ringgren, Helmer. *The Faith of Qumran: Theology of the Dead Sea Scrolls*. Expanded ed. New York, 1995. Contains a good treatment of creation (pp. 52–57).

DANIEL J. HARRINGTON

CROSS, FRANK MOORE, was born on 13 July 1921. He received a bachelor of divinity degree from McCormick Theological Seminary in 1946 and a doctor of philosophy, under William F. Albright, from Johns Hopkins University in 1950. He then taught at McCormick until he was appointed to the Hancock Professorship of Hebrew and Other Oriental Languages at Harvard University in 1957. He remained at Harvard until his retirement in 1992. During those years he supervised more than one hundred doctoral dissertations and was curator and then director of the Harvard Semitic Museum. He has been very active in learned societies such as the American Schools of Oriental Research and the Society of Biblical Literature, serving as president of both.

Cross's first essay on the Dead Sea Scrolls appeared in 1949, and in light of his training under Albright in epigraphy, paleography, and orthography, he was appointed in 1953 as the first member of the newly formed team of scholars to join Józef T. Milik in the sorting and editing of the innumerable fragments from Qumran Cave 4. He identified the many thousands of biblical fragments, forming copies of *Genesis* (13), *Exodus* (9), *Leviticus* (6), *Numbers* (1), *Deuteronomy* (18), *Joshua* (2), *Judges* (2), *Samuel* (3), *Kings* (1), *Jeremiah* (5), *Ezekiel* (3), *The Twelve Minor Prophets* (6), *Job* (2), *Ruth* (2), *Song of Songs* (3), *Ecclesiastes* (2), *Lamentations* (1), *Daniel* (5), *Ezra* (1), and *Chronicles* (1). He published preliminary editions of several of these manuscripts, and all have now been published in the Discoveries in the Judaean Desert series (vols. 12, 14–17), many of them by his students whose dissertations he had supervised.

Cross was a pioneer of many insights that have shaped Qumran studies. He expressed his views in his widely used introduction to the Dead Sea Scrolls, *The Ancient Library of Qumran and Modern Biblical Studies* (first edition, 1958; second edition, 1961; a third edition of the work appeared in 1995 under the shortened title *The Ancient Library of Qumran*).

He wrote a series of essays on the implications of the textual variants in the biblical manuscripts for the development of the texts of the Hebrew Bible. He argued that in the Second Temple period there were three local texts of the Pentateuchal books (the one represented now in the Masoretic Text, of Babylonian origin, the one in the Septuagint, of Egyptian origin, and the one in the Samaritan Pentateuch, of Palestinian origin) and that when the text was standardized after the fall of Jerusalem in 70 CE, one of these, the Masoretic Text, was chosen as the normative text. For other books in the Hebrew Bible there were two textual families and again just one was chosen after 70 CE. He was also able to clarify the history of the Greek text through use of the Qumran Hebrew texts and evidence from other Judean Desert sites.

In addition to his contributions to the study of the text of the Hebrew and Greek Bibles, Cross also produced

"The Development of the Jewish Scripts" (1961), which still remains four decades later the standard paleographical study of the scribal hands used in writing the Qumran manuscripts and other finds from the Judean Desert.

BIBLIOGRAPHY

Miller, Patrick D., Jr., Paul D. Hanson, and S. Dean McBride, eds. *Ancient Israelite Religion: Essays in Honor of Frank Moore Cross.* Philadelphia, 1987. Pages 645–656 contain a bibliography up to that date of Cross's more than two hundred publications.

EUGENE ULRICH

CRUCIFIXION. Extremely widespread as a method of execution even before Rome conquered the East, sources such as *Esther* (7.9–10), *Ezra* (6.11), and Herodotus (for example, *Hdt.* 1.128.2) suggest that crucifixion originated among the Persians. By the fourth century BCE at the latest, this mode of punishment had become familiar to the Greek-speaking world. Crucifixion is apparently attested in Ptolemaic papyri, and during the fourth and third centuries BCE, Alexander the Great and his successors, the Diadochi, especially the Ptolemies and the Seleucids, all employed it. Among the Seleucids, Antiochus III, who directly ruled the Jews beginning in 203 BCE, is particularly noteworthy for crucifying several individuals.

Crucifixion may have become a penalty for state crimes among the Jews as early as the Maccabean Revolt, and it remained as such under the early Hasmoneans. According to Josephus (*Jewish Antiquities* 12.256), Antiochus IV Epiphanes imposed the penalty on some Jewish loyalists who refused to abandon their ancestral traditions in 168/167 BCE: "They were scourged and their bodies mutilated. While still breathing and alive they were crucified. Their wives and children, whom they had circumcised in contravention of the king's orders, were strangled, then hung from the necks of the crucified fathers." [*See* Antiochus IV Epiphanes.] It should be noted, however, that some scholars doubt the reliability of Josephus on crucifixion during the Maccabean period. No mention of the penalty appears in *Maccabees*. During his reign the Jewish high priest Alcimus executed a large number of Hasideans who had deserted Judah the Maccabee to ally themselves with him. Although it is not certain, numerous scholars believe that these executions, dating to 162 or 161 BCE, were by crucifixion. [*See* Hasideans.] The *Testament of Moses* (8.1) contains a reference to either these crucifixions or other contemporary crucifixions (again, the historical reliability of this source is questionable, since it underwent some revision during the Roman period).

Not too many years later (perhaps in 77 BCE, if the colophon refers to Ptolemy XII), the *Book of Esther* was translated from Hebrew into Greek. The Greek version unquestionably understood Haman's execution as a crucifixion, for it rendered *Esther*'s Hebrew *talah* ("hang") by the Greek *stauroo* ("crucify"). Since the Jewish translator presumably interpreted the biblical events in light of his own contemporaries' use of *talah*, this version is crucial for understanding the apparent references to crucifixion found in the Dead Sea Scrolls. All these references use the verb *talah*. The *Esther* translation shows that this ambiguous term was the normal Hebrew word for the term *crucify* in the period of the scrolls.

In the Roman legal tradition, crucifixion represented the supreme penalty. This was true by the time of Cicero (*In Verrem* 2.5.168), and when the works of the jurist Julius Paulus were compiled in the *Sententiae* some four centuries later, *crux* ("the cross") still stood at the head of the list of "supreme penalties," followed by burning and decapitation. The *Sententiae* include as crimes properly punished by crucifixion desertion to the enemy, betraying of state secrets, inciting to rebellion, murder, prophecy regarding the health of rulers, magic, and aggravated falsification of wills.

In the areas of Roman rule, crucifixion was presumably a common punishment, generally inflicted on members of the lower classes. Presumably, for the elite there were less horrible alternatives because the literary and inscriptional evidence regarding crucifixion is limited; only a single Latin epigraph appears to refer to it, and mentions in literary contexts are sparse. Martin Hengel (1977, p. 38) has suggested that "the relative scarcity of references to crucifixions in antiquity, and their fortuitousness, are less a historical problem than an aesthetic one, connected with the sociology of literature. . . . The cultured literary world . . . as a rule kept quiet about it."

Two—perhaps three—passages in the Dead Sea Scrolls refer to crucifixion. As noted, in each case the verb *talah* is used. The word first appears in Temple Scroll[a] (11Q19 lxiv.6–9). This portion of the Temple Scroll is reacting to *Deuteronomy* 21.22–23, which reads in part: "If a man is guilty of a sin whose sentence is death, let him be put to death. Then you shall hang him on a tree." The biblical passage leaves many questions unanswered, but it clearly indicates that the guilty party is first executed, then hung on a tree. The object is not crucifixion, but rather exposure of the corpse. Temple Scroll[a] rewrites *Deuteronomy*:

> If a man is a traitor against his people and gives them up to a foreign nation, so doing evil to his people, you are to hang him on a tree until dead. On the testimony of two or three witnesses he will be put to death, and they themselves shall hang him on a tree. If a man is convicted of a capital crime and flees to the nations, cursing his people and the children of Israel, you are to hang him, also, upon a tree until dead.

Two points stand out in the scroll's treatment of the biblical text. First, the author (or an earlier source upon which he relies) has reversed the order of the biblical text's verbs for "put to death" and "hang." By this reversal the text is modified, requiring that the guilty party be hung on a tree while still alive, that is, crucified. Second, Temple Scroll[a] has specified the crimes for which crucifixion is the penalty. The two crimes are among those the Roman law punished by such means: betrayal of state secrets and desertion to the enemy. Presumably, therefore, the author of Temple Scroll[a] or his sources were familiar with aspects of Roman jurisprudence. A halakhic text (4Q524) also contains a form of the Temple Scroll's treatment. Whether this work represents a source used by the author of Temple Scroll[a] or whether it is a quote from the scroll remains to be determined.

A second text that mentions crucifixion is Pesher Nahum (4Q169 3–4.i.6–9). The author of the work interprets a passage from *Nahum* (*Na.* 2.12b–13a). He writes:

> "[He fills] his cave [with prey], his den with game." This refers to the lion of wrath [. . . ven]geance against the Seekers of Smooth Things, because he used to hang men alive, [as it was done] in Israel of old. For to anyone hanging alive on the tree [the verse ap]plies: "Behold, I am against [you, says the Lord of hosts."

Before the discovery of Temple Scroll[a], scholars had supposed that Pesher Nahum was against crucifixion; they had restored the crucial lacuna "alive, [which was never done] in Israel of old." It was Yigael Yadin, the editor of the Temple Scroll, who, on the basis of the Temple Scroll's laws, first proposed the restoration adopted here, which has since become the consensus.

Furthermore, scholars agree that the crucifixions described in Pesher Nahum are those noted by Josephus, who narrates the reign of Alexander Jannaeus. [*See* Alexander Jannaeus.] Alexander Jannaeus had been engaged in a civil war against the Pharisees and their supporters and eventually was able to quell the revolt. Alexander Jannaeus had leaders of the opposition, numbering some eight hundred men, crucified (*Antiquities* 13.380). This event probably occurred in 88 BCE. The particular crime for which these Pharisees were crucified was that of inviting Demetrius III Eukerus, the Seleucid king of Syria, to ally with them and invade Judea. [*See* Demetrius III Eukerus.] Thus, they were guilty of treason and suffered crucifixion in accordance with Temple Scroll[a]. Some scholars have argued that both Temple Scroll[a] and Pesher Nahum reflect events that occurred under Alexander Jannaeus, making it possible to arrive at a *terminus post quem* for the composition of the Temple Scroll. Since, however, abundant evidence exists for the use of crucifixion to punish crimes against the state as far back as the Maccabean period, this argument has failed to win a substantial following. A much more important result of the comparison of the Pesher Nahum passage with Josephus's description is that it makes possible the identification of the group designated in a number of scrolls as the "Seekers after Smooth Things": the Pharisees and their faction.

A third text in the Dead Sea Scrolls in which a reference to crucifixion has been found is Aaronic Text A = Aramic Levi[d]? (4Q541). In a very difficult portion of the manuscript (4Q541 24.4), Émile Puech read the Aramaic word *taliya'* and understood it as a noun, "hanging." Yet, there are fundamental objections to this understanding. First, the usual and therefore expected root in Aramaic for "crucifixion" is *ṣlb* (although *tl'* is not unknown; it exists in Syriac, for example). More telling is criticism of the reading itself. Several scholars have questioned the correctness of the first two letters of Puech's rendering, and various other suggestions have been made that would eliminate any reference here to crucifixion. If these scholars are correct, and this seems to be the growing consensus, the number of references to crucifixion in the scrolls is reduced from three to two—Temple Scroll[a] and Pesher Nahum.

BIBLIOGRAPHY

Allegro, John Marco. *Qumran Cave 4, I (4Q158–186).* Discoveries in the Judaean Desert, 5. Oxford, 1968. *Editio princeps* of Pesher Nahum (4Q169), including photographs, a transcription, and an English translation. Does not have crucial restoration.

Baumgarten, Joseph M. "Does *TLH* in the Temple Scroll Refer to Cruxifixion?" *Journal of Biblical Literature* 91 (1972), 472–481. Argues that Temple Scroll[a] does not refer to crucifixion, though Pesher Nahum, with its slightly different use of root, does.

Hengel, Martin. *Crucifixion in the Ancient World and the Folly of the Message of the Cross.* Translated by John Bowden. Philadelphia, 1977. A full discussion of all the evidence for crucifixion in classical sources, including Roman jurisprudence.

Puech, Émile. "Fragments d'un apocryphe de Lévi et le personnage eschatologique. 4QTestLévi[c–d](?) et 4QAJa." In *The Madrid Qumran Congress: Proceedings of the International Congress on the Dead Sea Scrolls, Madrid 18–21 March 1991,* edited by Julio Trebolle Barrera and Luis Vegas Montaner, vol. 2, pp. 448–501. Studies on the Texts of the Desert of Judah, 12. Leiden, 1992. *Editio princeps* of Aaronic Text A = Aramaic Levi[d]? (4Q541), with brief discussion of the difficult passage in fragment 24. Plate 21 at the end of the volume is a photograph of the portion.

Qimron, Elisha. *The Temple Scroll: A Critical Edition with Extensive Reconstructions.* Beersheba-Jerusalem, 1996. Presents the evidence of halakhic text 4Q524 as it pertains to column lxiv of Temple Scroll[a]. Page 124 is a photograph of the portions (mistakenly labeled 4Q542).

Yadin, Yigael. "Pesher Nahum (4QpNahum) Reconsidered." *Israel Exploration Journal* 21 (1971), 1–12. Classic article suggests how, on the basis of Temple Scroll[a], the Pesher Nahum passage on crucifixion ought to be restored.

Yadin, Yigael. *The Temple Scroll.* 3 vols. and supplementary plates. Jerusalem, 1983. The *editio maior* of the Temple Scroll, with extensive discussions of linguistic and interpretive issues, and photographs. Volume 2, pages 289–290 discusses linguistic elements of column lxiv and the reference to crucifixion; volume 1, pages 373–385 is a full analysis of the passage in light of rabbinic and other sources.

MICHAEL O. WISE

CYNICS were adherents of a philosophical sect that derives ultimately from Antisthenes (c.446–366 BCE), one of Socrates' students. He not only discounted the importance of a good general education as a prerequisite for philosophical study, but also rejected both logic and physics as indispensable aspects of philosophy. This same stance was adopted by Diogenes, often regarded as the second founder of Cynicism. Because they and their successors concentrated on ethics as the only necessary branch of philosophy, Cynicism was often depicted as a shortcut to virtue and happiness. This emphasis also led to the ancient debate as to whether Cynicism was truly a philosophy or simply a distinctive manner of life.

Cynics were famous for wearing a short cloak, carrying a begging bag, and using a staff. Many also wore long hair, went barefoot, and had a simple, day-to-day existence in which they drank water from fountains and springs, begged for bread, ate plants that grew by the road, and slept on the ground. As a result of their rugged way of life, they experienced numerous hardships and often had an unkempt appearance that critics found repulsive. Yet the Cynic's austere life was freely chosen and expressed his conviction that a simple life of self-control and virtue lived in accordance with nature was sufficient for happiness. His serene endurance of adversity demonstrated his virtue and proved that poverty was utterly insignificant. In addition, the Cynic's independent manner of life showed his freedom from the conventions and values of Greco-Roman aristocratic society, provided a model of self-sufficiency, and gave him the moral authority to speak boldly to all those whose lives he deemed deficient. Some Cynics did this harshly, whereas others used a more gentle approach. Such verbal "biting" and occasional "doggish" disregard for societal mores were in keeping with the fact that the term *Cynic* means "dog," and Cynics saw themselves as society's watchdogs.

Zeno of Citium, the founder of Stoicism, was the student of Crates, one of early Cynicism's most important and learned representatives. As a result, Stoicism inherited much from Cynicism, and this legacy meant that Cynic tenets, often in a modified form, influenced Greco-Roman society during the period of Stoicism's philosophical dominance. Indeed, imperial Stoics often presented Cynics as models of the ideal wise man. Furthermore, there was a revival of Cynicism during the early empire, so that Cynics once again became conspicuous during this period and produced pseudonymous letters in the names of the early Cynics and other ancient philosophers.

In recent years, A. J. Malherbe has convincingly demonstrated that Paul was well aware of Cynic traditions and adapted these to express his own self-understanding as well as to address debated issues in his churches (Malherbe, 1989). More controversial and less persuasive have been claims that Jesus and John the Baptist are depicted as Jewish Cynics in the gospel tradition's earliest layers. The Essenes were certainly not Cynics, yet they are sometimes described in terms congenial to Cynicism. Philo, for example, depicts them as rejecting both logic and physics (except for theology and creation) and devoting themselves exclusively to ethics, a subject in which they were trained to know what is truly good, evil, and neutral. Thus, like the Cynic sage, they were models of virtue, endurance, and self-control, totally free from the love of money and reputation (*Every Good Man Is Free* 80.83–84).

BIBLIOGRAPHY

Downing, F. G. *Cynics and Christian Origins*. Edinburgh, 1992. Analysis of the Cynic features of early Christianity, with comparison also made between Cynics and Essenes.

Dudley, Donald R. *A History of Cynicism from Diogenes to the 6th Century A.D.* London, 1937. Early comprehensive study of Cynicism.

Fitzgerald, John T. *Cracks in an Earthen Vessel: An Examination of the Catalogues of Hardships in the Corinthian Correspondence*. Society of Biblical Literature Dissertation Series, 99. Atlanta, 1988. Discussion of the use of lists of hardships by Cynics and other philosophers to depict the ideal wise man.

Hock, Ronald F. "Cynics." In *The Anchor Bible Dictionary*, edited by David Noel Freedman, vol. 1, pp. 1221–1226. New York, 1992. Excellent overview of the history and characteristics of Cynicism, with basic bibliography.

Malherbe, Abraham J. *The Cynic Epistles: A Study Edition*. Society of Biblical Literature Sources for Biblical Study, 12. Missoula, Mont., 1977. Text and translation of the Cynic epistles, with introductions.

Malherbe, Abraham J. *Paul and Popular Philosophers*. Minneapolis, 1989. Collection of superb studies on Cynicism and early Christianity. Includes a treatment of cynic self-definition that emphasizes the diversity within Cynicism as well as its distinction from stoicism.

JOHN T. FITZGERALD

D

DALIYEH, WADI ED-. [*This entry comprises two articles*: Archaeology *and* Written Material.]

Archaeology

Located about halfway between Jericho and Samaria in the central hill country, Wadi ed-Daliyeh is one of the depressions through which the winter rains tumble into the Jordan Valley. The hill country begins to descend about four miles east of the village of el-Mughâyir, where the ridge consists of rolling tableland farmed by the villagers, and the wadi makes a sharp gash into the eastern rim of the hill country, leaving steep cliffs sometimes of a hundred feet or more. It descends to the narrow plain five miles from Khirbet Fasâyil, which lies about fifteen miles north of Jericho in the Jordan Valley.

Caves honeycomb the sides of the wadi. Some are small; others contain thousands of feet of passageways. It was in one of these caves, Mugharet Abu Shinjeh, that the Wadi ed-Daliyeh, or Samaria papyri, were found.

On the south side of the wadi, Mughâret Abu Shinjeh ("Cave of the Father of the Dagger") was investigated by the Taʿamireh bedouin in the winter of 1962 when they were driven north of their usual encampments by drought. Since the original discovery of the Dead Sea Scrolls in 1947, they had been making systematic searches of the hill-country caves and recognized that dryness, and often the accumulation of layers of bat excrement and the sealing of a cave by collapsed limestone at its entrance, preserved ancient finds within. Their usual method of exploration was to dig test pits through the bat guano and to tap the rocky façade and cave walls for the hollow thud that would indicate accessible passages.

Their efforts in Mugharet Abu Shinjeh brought to light fragments of mats, human bones, a gold ring, ancient pots (which they broke in their search for gold or manuscripts), some stamped lumps of clay (bullae, or seals), and finally a few beads, coins, more seals, and some rolls and fragments of papyri. The papyri made their way through fellow Taʿamireh bedouin to Khalil Iskandar Shahin in Bethlehem and finally reached the scholarly community in Jerusalem in April 1962. [*See* Scrolls Research; *biography of Shahin.*] When a small papyrus fragment with Aramaic written on both sides came to the attention of Yusif Saad of the Palestine Archaeological Museum and Roland de Vaux of the École Biblique et Archéologique Française, then head of the Dead Sea Scroll team, they recognized their possible importance. They took some fragments to the American Schools of Oriental Research in Jerusalem where the director Paul Lapp, after a night of study, reported that the largest fragment was part of an official document in a script dating from about 375 BCE, in which the city of Samaria was clearly mentioned.

The collection offered for sale by the bedouin consisted of many small worm-eaten papyrus fragments, including a few rolls (none complete), several dozen bullae, and a few coins. First efforts concentrated on financing this purchase, and by November 1962 a fund had been established within the American Schools of Oriental Research. By the end of the month the purchase was made.

Besides the study of the documents and seals, it was important to examine the context in which they were found and, if possible, the circumstances under which they were deposited there. Through further negotiations, the Taʿamireh disclosed the cave of their explorations, and examination indicated the probability of their claim. The next step was scientific excavation to reveal any possible remaining evidence. This task fell to Lapp.

The first campaign took place early in 1963; the second in February 1964. Logistics always presented extreme difficulties. Tents for sleeping and working were pitched in the mouths of the caves on both sides of the wadi, and water as well as all food and excavation supplies had to be brought in by donkey along a circuitous, uphill, five-mile route. In the second campaign it was possible to bring in small generators by camel, which slightly improved excavation conditions. The staff consisted of ten to fifteen archaeologists, with about fifty additional workers for each campaign.

Excavation was first carried out in the Manuscript Area (the section of the cave from which it was believed the papyri had come) and in a meter-wide (about 1 yard) trench from the mouth of the cave back to the part of the cave designated the *Manuscript Area*. The trench would provide the occupational history of the cave and would reveal any other possible openings or passages the bedouin had not found.

The meter-wide trench stretched and turned about fifty

meters back to the Manuscript Area. The trench and small alcoves off the trench yielded pots and sherds (pottery fragments) from the latter part of the fourth century BCE covered by a thin scattering of early Roman sherds. By the end of the second campaign all the debris of the Manuscript Area had been excavated and sifted, producing pieces of pots (recently broken) and sherds from the second half of the fourth century BCE; bones and bone fragments; a few beads; a fibula (a pin for fastening clothing); two bullae; pieces of cloth, mats, pits, seeds; and bits of papyri with hints of a letter or two. One larger fragment, the only one the bedouin seemed to have missed, had six lines of text. Two other areas of the cave, called the *Bat Dome* and *Hot Room*, were excavated and produced similar material. A tiny silver coin was found in the passageway between the Manuscript Area and the Bat Dome, where the bedouin claimed to have found five silver coins (probably those offered for sale with the papyri).

The archaeological evidence on the whole supports the finds as reported by the bedouin: three hundred skeletons (however, archaeological evidence points to between thirty and fifty skeletons) covered by mats near which were the papyrus rolls and other finds. The explanation for their presence is suggested by the historians Josephus and Curtius Rufus, who wrote that the inhabitants of the city of Samaria had burned alive Andromachus, Alexander the Great's prefect in Syria, while Alexander was in Egypt; Alexander returned and destroyed the city. The Wadi ed-Daliyeh finds seem to indicate that leaders of Samaria who may have been implicated in the rebellion fled, probably down Wadi Farah into the wilderness to hide out in Wadi ed-Daliyeh. They took their food, pottery containers, jewelry and luxury items, and sealed legal documents with them. Their hiding place most likely was discovered by Alexander's Macedonian troops, and a fire built in the mouth of the cave probably suffocated the victims.

Excavations were conducted in a second cave, ʿArâq en-Naʿsâneh (Caverns of the Sleepy One), although the finds were not related to the Samaria papyri. ʿArâq en-Naʿsâneh was located slightly up and on the other side of the wadi from Mughâret Abu Shinjeh. This cave, though entered through a small hole, opened into a large room and many additional caverns, providing well-circulated air. Undisturbed finds indicated occupation during the Middle Bronze I period and the period of the Bar Kokhba Revolt. The latter occupation is paralleled by finds in the caves of Wadi Murabbaʿat and the Judean Desert.

BIBLIOGRAPHY

Cross, Frank M. "The Discovery of the Samaria Papyri." *Biblical Archaeologist* 6 (1963), 110–121. A prompt report of the discoveries and their historical context.

Damati, Emanuel, and Zeev Erlich. "A Hoard of Denarii and a Tridrachma from Wâdī ed-Dâliyeh." *Israel Numismatic Journal* 5 (1981), 33–37.

Gropp, Douglas M. "The Samaria Papyri from Wâdī ed-Dâliyeh: The Slave Sales." Ph.D. diss., Harvard University, 1986.

Lapp, Nancy L. "The Cave Clearances in the Wâdī ed-Dâliyeh." In *The Tale of the Tell: Archaeological Studies*, edited by Paul W. Lapp, pp. 66–76. Pittsburgh Theological Monograph Series, 5. Pittsburgh, 1975.

Lapp, Paul W. "The Samaria Papyri." *Archaeology* 16 (1963), 204–206.

Lapp, Paul W., and Nancy L., eds. *Discoveries in the Wâdī ed-Dâliyeh.* Annual of the American Schools of Oriental Research, 41. Cambridge, 1974.

Leith, M. J. W. *Greek and Persian Images in Pre-Alexandrine Samaria: Wâdī ed-Dâliyeh Seal Impressions.* Ann Arbor, 1991.

NANCY L. LAPP

Written Material

The written material from the Abu Shinjeh cave in the Wadi ed-Daliyeh, about 14 kilometers north of Jericho on the western rim of the Jordan rift, consists of fragmentary papyri and a few legible sealings and coins. Most of these were discovered in the early spring of 1962 by the Taʿamireh bedouin. Subsequent archaeological explorations in January 1963 and February 1964 contributed modestly to the initial find and put the written materials in a more definite context (cf. P. W. Lapp and N. L. Lapp, 1974). [*See* Daliyeh, Wadi ed-, *article on* Archaeology.]

The most significant of these written remains, the papyri, are quite fragmentary. Eighteen of the fragments are long enough, that is, complete enough in their vertical dimension, to be called "papyri." The largest papyrus, a deed of slave sale (WDSP 1), is no more than 45 percent extant. A few of these fragments are no more than a thin strip of papyrus; a couple of others are in tatters. Nine or ten further pieces are sizable enough to allow some assessment of their legal import. Nine other museum plates contain nearly 150 additional fragments of various shapes and sizes. All the plates are housed in the Rockefeller Museum in Jersusalem.

Despite the location in which they were found, the papyri are all legal documents originally drafted in Samaria in the fourth century BCE. The place where the documents were executed is given either in the first or last line of the document. In the eleven documents in which the place is preserved, it is named as the city or province of Samaria. The documents were also dated by the reign of the current Persian king in their first or last lines. Where the name of the king is preserved, it is usually Artaxerxes (at least five times). One document is dated to sometime between the thirtieth and thirty-ninth year, and therefore must come from the reign of Artaxerxes II (Mnemon), between 375 and 365 BCE. The date of WDSP 1 is fully preserved as 19 March 335 BCE, the second year of Darius

III (Codomannus; Cross, 1985). Most of the papyri were probably written during the reign of Artaxerxes III (Ochus; 358–337 BCE). The late pre-Alexandrine coins found in the cave strongly corroborate the internal indications of dating (Cross, 1974), the latest being of a Tyrian issue of 334 BCE. The script of the papyri is somewhat more advanced typologically than the script of the Aramaic corpora from the late fifth century and so fits well within this horizon.

The Samaria papyri provide a rich and varied paleographic resource, from a previously underrepresented period, for better understanding the development of the Aramaic script in the second half of the first millennium BCE. Since the Samaria papyri are dated, their scripts provide an invaluable guide to dating other papyri and ostraca from Egypt and Palestine in the same general period. They are also important for reassessing the scripts of the oldest manuscripts from Qumran (Cross, 1974). But aside from the importance of this resource for epigraphists, archaeologists, and historians, familiarity with these fourth-century Aramaic scripts is crucial to biblical text critics for assessing possible transcriptional errors in restoring the biblical text.

The language of the Samaria papyri is "Official Aramaic," the ideal standard language in which scribes of the Persian period (probably from Darius I to Darius III [522–333 BCE]) would draft documents of an official nature (Gropp, 1997). The language of the Samaria papyri is virtually identical to the language of the fifth-century Elephantine legal papyri and the Arsames correspondence. In fact, despite being chronologically later, the language of the Samaria papyri is even more consistently conservative in its conformity to the norm of Official Aramaic than the language of the other two corpora. In spite of its later provenance, it also reflects little or no Persian influence in contrast to the Elephantine papyri, but especially to the Arsames correspondence where Persian influence is more extensive. The Samaria papyri do show a greater proportion of specifically late Neo-Babylonian loanwords, but this is clearly related to the origins of its legal formularies (Gropp, 1990).

If it were not for some auspicious circumstances, which provide extraordinary possibilities for reconstructing the text of the papyri, their significance would have been greatly reduced. The possibilities of reconstruction correlate directly with the legal genres represented. The best represented type of deed is the slave sale. It has proved possible to propose full reconstructions for nine or ten of these deeds despite their fragmentary condition. The slave sale deeds seem to share a common formulary to such an extent that they provide us with partially overlapping bits and pieces of the same formulary. There is remarkably little variation in the verbal realization of each formula, and even less variation in the sequence of formulas within the sale formulary. The date, the names of the principals, the names of the slaves, the sale prices, and the amount of the penalty for contravention of the sale are basically the only elements that vary from deed to deed. Each papyrus contributes a little to our knowledge of that formulary. By constant comparison and rearranging of all the bits of writing serially, Frank Moore Cross and Douglas Gropp have been able to reconstruct the entire formulary. Proposed reconstructions have been tested against estimated line lengths for each papyrus. In addition to the constraints of space, we have been aided by legal parallels from Mesopotamia to Egypt. Circular reasoning, while not wholly escaped, can be reduced to a minimum. Now that this formulary for the deeds of slave sale is established, it can be applied as a kind of template for interpreting other deeds of conveyance. Such a procedure has been successful in reconstructing a deed of house sale, but only modestly helpful in interpreting texts of other genres.

Of the fragments sizable enough to allow some assessment of their legal genre, at least half are slave sales. Some of these represent the sale of a single slave (WDSP 1, 3, 4, 11 recto, 18, 19, and 26?), others of multiple slaves (WDSP 2, 5, 6, 7, 8, 9, and 20). But a variety of other legal genres are represented. There is a clear instance of a house sale (WDSP 15) and a conveyance of chambers in a public building (WDSP 14), in addition to several deeds of sale whose objects cannot be ascertained (WDSP 21, 22, 24, and 25). Two or more documents look like a pledge of a slave in exchange for a loan (WDSP 10, 12, 13 recto?, and 27?). It is impossible to be confident about the terms of these fragmentary contracts apart from some hermeneutical key provided by closer legal parallels. One conveys a vineyard, possibly as a pledge rather than as a sale (WDSP 16). Several documents may resolve some contingency, but in most cases the papyri are too fragmentary for confident interpretation. There is a receipt for the repayment of a loan involving a pledge (WDSP 17: a double document), the release of a pledged slave (WDSP 13 verso), the settlement (?) of a dispute over a slave (WDSP 11 verso), and possibly a judicial settlement by an oath (WDSP 23).

The Samaria papyri may ultimately prove most interesting for the light they shed on the history of law. They provide an especially promising occasion for the study of the contact between Aramaic and cuneiform traditions. Comparison of legal formularies provides one of the most controllable instances for the study of cultures in contact. The legal formulary of the slave sales is obviously dependent proximately or ultimately on cuneiform antecedents. But aside from a few important parallels, the extent to which the formularies of the Samaria papyri differ from the formularies of the Elephantine legal papyri is remarkable. On the other hand, the Samaria papyri share a large number of features with the later Murabbaʿat and Naḥal Ḥever deeds. The Samaria papyri thus provide some counterbalance to the understandably heavy reliance on the Elephantine legal papyri for reconstructing the early development of Jewish law.

To be more specific, the origin of the sale formulary of the Samaria papyri is threefold: (1) Aramaic scribes in Babylonia adopted the late Neo-Babylonian formulary for the sale of movables (from the time of Darius I on) as their basic model, (2) Aramaic scribes (still in Babylonia) creatively modified this model by drawing on formulas from other types of late Neo-Babylonian documents, and (3) Aramaic scribes (probably in Palestine) further modified the adopted formulary by partially assimilating it to their own native legal traditions.

Notwithstanding a great deal of functional equivalence between the formularies of the Elephantine deeds of conveyance and the Samarian deeds of sale, there is very little concrete phrasing in common. The two groups of legal papyri represent fundamentally different legal traditions. The Elephantine legal papyri stem from a somewhat provincial Neo-Assyrian tradition probably of the late ninth or early eighth centuries BCE (Muffs, 1969). Both formularies provide evidence of an extended symbiosis between Aramean and Akkadian scribes. But the two cases of symbiosis are parallel and analogous rather than homologous. The Elephantine legal papyri stem ultimately from an Assyro-Aramean symbiosis (Tadmor, 1982), whereas the Samaria papyri derive from a Babylonian-Aramean symbiosis (Greenfield, 1982). The agreement in language between the Elephantine papyri and the Samaria papyri thus offers a counterpoint to the divergence in legal traditions. The formularies of the deeds from Murabbaʿat and Naḥal Ḥever represent a later stage of this Babylonian-Aramean symbiosis more than a simple direct inheritance from the legalese of fourth-century Samaria. Nevertheless, they stand in the same general tradition. The evidence of the Samaria papyri both clarifies and expands our picture of the role of Aramaic scribes as creative intermediaries of cultural traditions throughout the ancient Near East.

Because the Samaria papyri are so formulaic, they offer the historian only limited evidence of the realities of life in fourth-century Samaria. They do, however, provide a few details about administration. The city of Samaria is variously designated as a "city" (*qiryata*ʾ) and as a "citadel" (*birta*ʾ) within the Persian province (*medinta*ʾ) of Samaria. The papyri name two types of officials, the chief being "the governor" (*paḥat shomrayin*), and the second being "the prefect" (*segana*ʾ). The fragmentary evidence of the papyri and of an inscribed bulla (WD 22) suggests that the governorship, if not also the prefecture, was kept within the Sanballatid family. [*See* Sanballat.]

A diversity of personal name types attested in the documents points to a diversity in the ethnic composition of the population of fourth-century Samaria. Hebrew names, most of which can be paralleled in biblical and epigraphic Hebrew, predominate. Many of these are Yahvistic. But other personal names can be identified as Aramaic, Edomite, Phoenician, Akkadian, Persian, and perhaps belong to other ethnic groups as well. It is certainly possible to make false inferences from personal names. For instance, the bearers of the Akkadian names may in fact be Arameans. Similarly, the hybrid name *yhvbgh* ("Yahu is God") cautions us from drawing too much from the impeccably Persian *bgbrt* ("by God lifted up, esteemed"). The slaves sold are as likely to bear Yahvistic names as either the sellers or the buyers. In one case, a woman becomes the new owner of a male and a female slave (WDSP 2).

The slaves are generally sold for life (contrary to the regulations of *Lv*. 25.39–47). [*See* Slavery.] It is not completely clear whether the loan contracts are constructed in such a way as to circumvent a ban on interest. Antichretic use of the pledged slave or vineyard may have stood in place of interest. Because the term for chambers in a public building (*nshkt*ʾ) in WDSP 14 is only rarely used outside of a sacral context, it has fueled the debate as to whether there was a temple in Samaria before the coming of Alexander (Eshel, 1996).

BIBLIOGRAPHY

Cross, Frank Moore. "The Discovery of the Samaria Papyri." *Biblical Archaeologist* 26 (1963), 110–121.

Cross, Frank Moore. "Aspects of Samaritan and Jewish History in Late Persian and Hellenistic Times." *Harvard Theological Review* 59 (1966), 201–211.

Cross, Frank Moore. "Papyri of the Fourth Century B.C. from Dâliyeh." In *New Directions in Biblical Archaeology*, edited by David Noel Freedman and Jonas C. Greenfield, pp. 41–62, figs. 34–39. Garden City, N.Y., 1969.

Cross, Frank Moore. "The Papyri and Their Historical Implications" and "Other Finds: Coins; Scarab." In *Discoveries in the Wâdi ed-Dâliyeh*, edited by Paul W. Lapp and Nancy L. Lapp, pp. 17–29, 57–60. Annual of the American Schools of Oriental Research, 41. Cambridge, Mass., 1974.

Cross, Frank Moore. "Samaria Papyrus 1: An Aramaic Slave Conveyance of 335 B.C.E." *Eretz-Israel* 18 (1985), 7*–17*, pl. 2. Preliminary publication of WDSP 1.

Cross, Frank Moore. "A Report on the Samaria Papyri." In *Congress Volume: Jerusalem, 1986*, edited by J. A. Emerton, pp. 17–26. Supplements to Vetus Testamentum, 40. Leiden, 1988. Includes a preliminary publication of WDSP 2.

Eshel, Hanan. "Wâdi ed-Dâliyeh Papyrus 14 and the Samaritan Temple" (in Hebrew). *Zion* 61 (1996), 359–365.

Greenfield, Jonas C. "Babylonian-Aramaic Relationship." In *XXI Rencontre Assyriologique Internationale, Berlin, July 3–7, 1978*, edited by Hans-Jörg Nissen and Johannes Renger, vol. 1, pt. 2, pp. 471–482. Berlin, 1982.

Gropp, Douglas M. "The Samaria Papyri from the Wâdi ed-Dâliyeh: The Slave Sales." Ph.D. diss., Harvard University, 1986.

Gropp, Douglas M. "The Language of the Samaria Papyri: A Preliminary Study." *Maarav* 5–6 (1990), 169–187.

Gropp, Douglas M. "The Origin and Development of the Aramaic *šallīṭ* Clause." *Journal of Near Eastern Studies* 52 (1993), 31–36.

Gropp, Douglas M. "Imperial Aramaic." *Encyclopedia of Near Eastern Archaeology* 3 (1997), 144–146.

Lapp, Paul W., and Nancy L. Lapp. *Discoveries in the Wâdi ed-Dâliyeh*. Annual of the American Schools of Oriental Research, 41. Cambridge, Mass., 1974.

Muffs, Yochanan. *Studies in the Aramaic Legal Papyri from Elephantine*. Leiden, 1969.

Tadmor, Hayim. "The Aramaization of Assyria: Aspects of Western Impact." In *XXI Rencontre Assyriologique Internationale, Berlin, July 3–7, 1978*, edited by Hans-Jörg Nissen and Johannes Renger, vol. 1, pt. 2, pp. 449–470. Berlin, 1982.

DOUGLAS M. GROPP

DAMASCUS. Located on the banks of the Barada River, Damascus is the capital of modern Syria. In ancient times abundant waters created fertile oases (Weber, 1989), whose most famous export was the wine of Helbon (*Ezek*. 27.18–19; Millard, 1962). The name *Damascus* may mean "wine pourer" (Gordon, 1952).

How long the city had existed before its mention in the victory list of Thutmose III (c.1482 BCE) is uncertain—archaeological work has been sporadic and unsystematic. After the Amarna Letters, which thrice mention Damascus, there is a long silence until *2 Samuel* 8.5–7 notes David's victory over the Aramaeans of Damascus. Rezon recaptured the city from Solomon and proclaimed himself king (*1 Kgs*. 11.23–25). Thereafter Damascus enjoyed great political power as the capital of Aram, which was the implacable enemy of the northern kingdom of Israel. In the late eighth century BCE the Assyrians reduced Damascus to the status of chief town of a province, a role it retained under the Babylonians in the sixth century.

Damascus recovered much of its former glory in the framework of the Persian empire (Strabo, *Geography* 16.2.20). The city changed hands repeatedly in the struggles between the Ptolemies and the Seleucids, and in the early first century BCE it was occupied by Aretas III of Nabatea and Tiganes of Armenia. In 63 BCE Pompey made Damascus part of the Roman province of Syria, whose capital, however, was Antioch-on-the-Orontes. The territory of Damascus extended to the frontier of Sidon (Josephus, *Jewish Antiquities* 18.153). It was considered a city of the Decapolis (Pliny, *Natural History* 5.16.74). The absence of coins of Caligula and Claudius confirms Paul's report (*2 Cor*. 11.32–33) that it came under Nabatean control, probably shortly after the death of Tiberius in 37 CE (Taylor, 1992). Roman coins begin again with Nero.

Herod the Great's donation of a gymnasium to Damascus (Josephus, *The Jewish War*, 1.422) probably attests a well-established Jewish community (Smallwood, 82), whose origins may go back several centuries. According to Josephus, the Jews in the city were numerous. This is all that can be deduced from his conflicting assertions that 10,500 (*The Jewish War* 1.599–61) or 18,000 (*The Jewish War* 7.368) were slaughtered at the beginning of the First Jewish Revolt.

The translation of *medinat darmeseq* (Genesis Apocryphon, 1QapGen xxii.5) as "the land of Damascus" (Maier, 1960, vol. 1, p. 164) is inadequate; the choice must be between the "province" or "city" of Damascus (Fitzmyer, 1971, p. 169). The same document in writing "as far as Helbon to the north of Damascus" (1QapGen xxii.10) substitutes the well-known *Helbon* for the unknown *Hobah* in *Genesis* 14.15. In these two texts there is no doubt that Damascus is to be understood geographically. Regretfully the same cannot be said of the other references, all of which occur in the medieval manuscripts of the Damascus Document. The sole preserved instance of *Damascus* in the Qumran fragments is in Damascus Document[b] (4Q267 3.iv.8 [= Damascus Document CD-A vii.19]). [*See* Damascus Document.]

All except two instances in CD-A contain the formula *be-ʾerets dameseq*, "in the land of Damascus." We are told of "the converts of Israel, who left the land of Judah and lived in the land of Damascus" (CD-A vi.5). "The new covenant" was enacted "in the land of Damascus" (CD-A vi.19, 8.21; CD-B xix.34, xx.12). The pattern is broken by the citation of *Amos* 5.26, in a form that does not agree with the Masoretic Text, "I will deport the Sikkut of your King and the Kiyyum of your images away from my tent to Damascus," in CD vii.15 (Rabin, 1954, p. 28; cf. Maier, 1960, vol. 1, p. 56), which is followed in the same context by "the star is the Interpreter of the Law who will come to Damascus" (vii.18–19).

When the Damascus Document was first published, its references to *Damascus* were understood in a straightforward geographical sense, and this meaning is still retained in various reconstructions of Essene history (Davies, 1982, p. 16; Stegemann, 1993, p. 207). Others, however, considered the real Damascus as inappropriate both politically and theologically and argued that *Damascus* was a symbolic name for Qumran (Jaubert, 1958). R. North made an effort to reconcile these two interpretations by emphasizing *land* rather than *Damascus*. He argued that the Nabateans controlled southern Syria and the northern end of the Dead Sea, and that their entire territory could be named after its most important city. Hence Qumran was in the land of Damascus. This hypothesis has neither archaeological nor textual support (de Vaux, 1973, p. 114). [*See* Nabatean.]

The Qumran interpretation is excluded by Damascus Document, CD-A vi.5, because Qumran is in "the land of

Judah." The Babylonian exile was the most significant exodus from Judah, and it is to this period that we are directed by the historical survey of CD-A ii.18–3.12. In this perspective *Damascus* would be an allegorical name for the place of captivity (Rabinowitz, 1954, p. 17, note 20b), that is, Babylon (Jaubert, 1958, p. 226; Davies, 1982, p. 122). No convincing objections have been raised against this hypothesis (Murphy-O'Connor, 1985, pp. 224–230). The destination of the Exodus and its coercive nature are confirmed by the way *Amos* 5.25–27 ("I will take you into exile beyond Damascus") is cited in CD-A vii.14–15, where "beyond Damascus" becomes simply "Damascus." The obvious hypothesis that *Damascus* here was intended to mean Babylon is supported by the way Luke cites the same prophetic text, "I will remove you beyond Babylon" (*Acts* 7.23).

If *Damascus* designated the original place of exile in which the Essene movement began, there is no difficulty in its subsequent transferral to Qumran, the place of self-imposed exile, and thus to the community that lived there (cf. *Zec.* 9.1). This is the sense of *Damascus* demanded by CD-A vii.18–19. The community expected eschatological figures to appear in its midst (Rule of the Congregation, 1Q28a ii.11–17); note the parallel with the Florilegium (4Q174 11–12), especially in the light of the identification of the community with Jerusalem. [*See* Florilegium; Jerusalem; *and* Rule of the Congregation.] The radically divergent interpretations of *Micah* 1.5–6 in Pesher Micah (1Q14 10.3–6) exclude any possible objection to *Damascus* having two different symbolic meanings.

[*See also* Geography in the Documents.]

BIBLIOGRAPHY

Davies, Philip R. *The Damascus Covenant. An Interpretation of the "Damascus Document."* Journal for the Study of the Old Testament. Supplement Series, 25. Sheffield, 1982.

Davies, Philip R. "The Birthplace of the Essenes: Where Is 'Damascus'?" *Revue de Qumrân* 14.56 (1990), 503–519.

de Vaux, Roland. *Archaeology and the Dead Sea Scrolls. The Schweich Lectures of the British Academy 1959.* London, 1973.

Fitzmyer, Joseph A. *The Genesis Apocryphon of Qumran Cave 1. A Commentary.* Biblica et Orientalia, 18A. 2nd ed. Rome, 1971.

Gordon, Cyrus H. "Damascus in Assyrian Sources." *Israel Exploration Journal* 2 (1952), 174–175.

Jaubert, Annie. "Le pays de Damas." *Revue biblique* 65 (1958), 214–248.

Maier, Johann. *Die Texte vom toten Meer.* 2 vols. Basel, 1960.

Millard, Alan R. "Ezekiel XXVII.19: The Wine Trade of Damascus." *Journal of Semitic Studies* 7 (1962), 201–203.

Murphy-O'Connor, Jerome. "The *Damascus Document* Revisited." *Revue biblique* 92 (1985), 223–246.

North, Robert. "The Damascus of Qumran Geography." *Palestine Exploration Quarterly* 86 (1955), 34–48.

Rabin, Chaim. *The Zadokite Documents. I. The Admonition. II. The Laws.* Oxford, 1954.

Rabinowitz, Isaac. "A Reconsideration of 'Damascus' and '390 Years' in the 'Damascus ('Zadokite') Fragments." *Journal of Biblical Literature* 73 (1954), 11–35.

Smallwood, S. Mary. *The Jews under Roman Rule from Pompey to Diocletian. A Study in Political Relations.* Studies in Judaism in Late Antiquity, 20. Leiden, 1976.

Stegemann, Hartmut. *Die Essener, Qumran, Johannes der Täufer und Jesus. Ein Sachbuch.* Freiburg, 1993.

Taylor, Justin J. "The Ethnarch of King Aretas at Damascus. A Note on 2 Cor 11.32–33." *Revue biblique* 99 (1992), 719–728.

Weber, Thomas. "DAMASKEA (in Greek). Landwirtschaftliche Produkte aus der Oase von Damaskus im Spiegel griechisher und lateinischer Schriftquellen." *Zeitschrift des Deutschen Palästina-Vereins* 105 (1989), 151–165.

JEROME MURPHY-O'CONNOR

DAMASCUS DOCUMENT. First published in 1910 by Solomon Schechter under the title *Fragments of a Zadokite Work*, the Cairo Damascus Document (CD), as it came to be known, has since the discovery of the Dead Sea Scrolls been recognized as one of the foundational works of the Qumran Community. Of the two medieval manuscripts from the Cairo Genizah, manuscript A (tenth century) has sixteen columns, while manuscript B (twelfth century) has two long columns. These still contain the largest continuous portions of the text. However, Qumran Cave 4 has yielded eight ancient manuscripts with not only substantial parallels to the Genizah texts, but major supplements, including the beginning and end of the work. The following is a list of the known Qumran manuscripts:

Eight manuscripts from Qumran Cave 4 have been identified by J. T. Milik:

- Damascus Document[a] (4Q266) is written in a semi-cursive Hasmonean hand of the first half of the first century BCE. The eleven plates of facsimiles embrace the opening and end of the work, as well as substantial additions to the corpus of laws.
- Damascus Document[b] (4Q267) is written in an early Herodian formal hand from about the end of the first century BCE. The two plates of photos include parallels to the parenetic as well as the organizational portions of CD.
- Damascus Document[c] (4Q268) is written in a calligraphic Herodian bookhand from the early first century CE. The single plate parallels the opening of the Genizah text.
- Damascus Document[d] (4Q269) is written in an early Herodian formal hand from the late first century BCE. The relatively small fragments extant contain rules of purity and communal discipline.
- Damascus Document[e] (4Q270) is written in a Herodian formal hand from the first century CE with guidelines.

The five plates include various Qumran legal norms, a list of the sins of transgressors apparently among contemporaries, as well as the end of the concluding column of the work.

- Damascus Document[f] (4Q271), written in an early Herodian bookhand, contains a variety of legal rulings, including substantial parallels to the Sabbath code of CD.
- Damascus Document[g] (4Q272), written in an early Herodian formal hand, deals with the biblical laws of skin disease and fluxes.
- Damascus Document[h] (4Q273), written on papyrus in a formal Herodian script, is very poorly preserved. Extant are halakhic rules, some with parallels in the other manuscripts.

Damascus Document (5Q12) is a small fragment from Cave 5, which corresponds to CD ix.7–10.

Damascus Document (6Q15) from Cave 6 consists of five fragments, four of which correspond to passages from the Admonition of CD, while one has a few words of laws concerning forbidden sexual relations found also in Damascus Document[e].

Summary of Contents. (Segments found only at Qumran are marked with an asterisk.)

The admonition

*1. The work begins with a teacher's first person call to the Sons of Light to separate from transgressors.
2. Based on the concept of preordained periods of wrath and redemption, a historical discourse on the emergence of a penitent remnant 390 years after the Babylonian destruction of the Temple.
3. A second discourse on the lessons of biblical history.
4. The Three Nets of Belial: fornication, wealth, pollution of the sanctuary. Fornication is exemplified by the sins of polygamy and uncle-niece marriages. The sanctuary is defiled by those who have intercourse with women during their menstrual impurity.
5. The Community of the Renewed Covenant and the future punishment of backsliders.

The laws. (The placement of some of the Qumran pericopes is tentative.)

*6. A catalogue of transgressors of various kinds ending with an appeal to those who know how to choose between the paths of life and perdition.
*7. The Zadokite priests and their communal role; rules about priestly disqualification.
*8. Diagnosis (by the priests) of skin diseases; menstruant and parturient women.
*9. Harvest laws: gleanings, fruits of the fourth year, measures, and tithes.
*10. Impurity of idolaters' metals; corpse impurity; disqualification of minors to sprinkle the purification water.
*11. The *Soṭah* (wife suspected of adultery) ordeal.
*12. Integrity in commercial dealings and arrangement of marriage.
13. The oath of those entering the covenant; exclusion of the mentally and physically incompetent.
14. Laws about oaths, vows, and bans.
15. Law about a "ban" of destruction against a person.
16. Laws about judicial procedures.
17. "Concerning purification in water."
18. "Concerning the Sabbath," an extended pericope of Sabbath rules.
19. The purity of the Temple and the Temple City.
20. Treatment of blasphemers and gentiles.
21. Dietary and purity rules. End of the rule for "cities of Israel."

Communal rules

22. Priests, Levites as legal deciders for communal cells.
23. The function of the Overseer.
*24. The penal code.
*25. Ritual for the expulsion of offenders at the annual renewal of the covenant. Conclusion of the work.

The Laws. It is apparent from the above outline that the corpus of laws, augmented by the now available Qumran fragments, constitutes the central body of the Damascus Document. This is indicated not merely by the preponderance of space allotted to the laws, but by the summation formula found at the end of the work: "This is the explanation of the laws to be followed during the entire period of visitation. . . . Behold it is all in accordance with the final interpretation of the Law" (Damascus Document[a] [4Q266] xi.18–21). Hartmut Stegemann (1993) suggests that *Final Interpretation of the Law* was the actual title of the Damascus Document. This term, however, occurs elsewhere within the legal corpus (4Q266 5.i.16) and may merely indicate that the explanation of the laws is in conformance with the latest insights granted to the sect's legists. In any case, it is noteworthy that the legal corpus, which some scholars were disinclined to consider as an integral part of the Damascus Document, now emerges as its central core. The Admonition on the other hand appears to serve primarily as a hortatory preface to the nomistic pronouncements of the Qumran teachers.

The laws themselves may be broadly divided into two categories: (a) interpretations of religious law and general *halakhah* and (b) communal regulations. Among the religious laws there are a number with similarities to rabbinic tradition, that which the Talmud later called Oral Law. Thus, in the Sabbath code the cessation from work on the eve of the Sabbath begins well before sundown, the limit (*teḥum*) of walking more than two thousand cubits outside the city is applied to pasturing animals, and the ban on handling working implements is strictly followed. Such similarities led Louis Ginzberg in 1922 to identify CD as a Pharisaic work, although he was able to maintain this conclusion only by dismissing the allusion in CD xvi.2–4 to the solar calendar of *Jubilees* as a later interpolation. He also had to recognize the prohibition of polygamy and uncle-niece marriages as departures from the norms of what became rabbinic *halakhah*. In the light of the Qumran findings Ginzberg's thesis can no longer be maintained.

The Cave 4 supplements to the legal corpus supply significant new illustrations of the sect's opposition to contemporary Pharisaic practices. Thus, in preparing the waters mixed with the ashes of the red cow and in sprinkling them for purification, it was customary in Temple times to use young boys who had never been ritually defiled, as recorded in *M. Para*. 3.2. The Qumran ruling, referred to above, that a minor below twenty is ineligible to perform the sprinkling, was ostensibly directed against this practice. Only mature priests were held eligible to do the rites of purification.

With regard to the fourth-year fruit of newly planted trees, which rabbinic *halakhah* treated like second tithe belonging to the farmer, the Qumran legists held it to be like firstfruits given to the priests. In the case of *ḥallah*, the priestly portion of the dough, which rabbinic practice required to be separated from every kneading, Qumran deemed it to be a like a first-fruit offering brought "once a year."

The Qumran view of fetal life differed from that prevailing in rabbinic *halakhah*. This view emerges from two transgressions listed in the catalog of sins found in Damascus Document[e]. The first is the slaughter of pregnant animals, which Qumran saw as violating the biblical ban on slaying the parent with the young (*Lv*. 22.28, *Dt*. 22.6). Implicitly, the fetal animal was regarded as a distinct creature. The second transgression, in accordance with a probable restoration, is intercourse with a pregnant woman. The reason given is somewhat obscure, "he causes blood to stir (?)" (*meqits dam*), which may refer to possible harm to the fetus or causing bleeding through coital pressure, thus making intercourse illicit. Normative talmudic *halakhah* did not forbid marital relations during pregnancy.

The wide range of biblical law treated in the legal corpus of Damascus Document thus comprises both similarities and contrasts with the Pharisaic-rabbinic system. Methodologically, it is noteworthy that some of the laws are accompanied by exegetical references, such as the biblical citations used to support the sectarian polemic against polygamy and uncle-niece marriages. However, the bulk of the rules found in Damascus Document[d] are formulated apodictically, without scriptural proof. This is likewise characteristic of the Mishnah. Of special interest are the topical rubrics used to introduce particular subjects: "Concerning one who is purifying himself in water" (CD x.10), "Concerning the Sabbath" (x.14), "Concerning the oath of a woman" (xvi.10). Here we have the first post-biblical collections of legal rulings by subject categories, a process which later in rabbinic tradition culminated in the six major orders of Rabbi Judah's Mishnah.

Since the study of scripture and the exposition of law were the perpetual activities to which the sect was devoted (Rule of the Community, 1QS vi.6), we may presume that some of the religious laws were academic in nature and do not necessarily reflect the community's own experience. The communal regulations, on the other hand, are indubitably the product of the sect's organizational development. The Damascus Document and the Community Rule have in common the references to one of the important communal institutions, the annual renewal of the covenant. In the former this is found at the end of the work after the description of the ritual for the expulsion of sinners: "All the inhabitants of the camps shall congregate in the third month and curse those who turn right or left from the Law." The date derives from *Exodus* 19.1, where the preparations for the Sinaitic covenant are detailed, and similarly lacks specification as to which day of the third month. Milik places the annual renewal of the covenant on Pentecost, the fifteenth of the month, but it may be that the ceremony was intended as preparatory for Pentecost.

Many scholars have pointed out the differences in communal lifestyle between the Rule of the Community and the Damascus Document. The Rule appears to stem from a community of men living in a close-knit order (*yaḥad*), sharing their goods and a discipline in accordance with a strict penal code. The Damascus Document, by contrast, presupposes men and women living a normal family life, with private property, and a discipline consisting primarily of adherence to the laws of the Torah. As far as the Genizah manuscripts are concerned, this depiction was adequate, although it failed to account for a vestige of the penal code (CD xvi.20–21) that deals with the offense of deliberately lying about property. The same offense is found in the Rule (1QS vi.24–25). We now have in the 4Q manuscripts an extensive pericope from the penal code that closely parallels that of the Rule in substance and in wording. However, the penalty of a reduction in the food ration (1QS vi.25) is absent in Damascus Document, which suggests that it was applicable only to men living together in the *yaḥad*. On the other hand, the penal code of Damascus Document includes offenses such as "fornication" with one's wife, apparently involving violation of some sexual ban, and murmuring against the Fathers and Mothers of the community. These offenses presuppose conventional family life. Another difference from the Rule is the consistent pattern of dual punishment in the penal code of Damascus Document, suspension of access to purities and another penalty, each for a specified period of time.

The plurality of social practices has also been inferred from CD vii.6–7, which distinguishes between members of the sect who walk in "holy perfection" and those who dwell in camps in the manner of the land, marrying and bearing children, while following the Torah. This may reflect a bifurcation in social patterns, celibate and family oriented, within the Covenant community, not unlike what Josephus records about the Essenes (*The Jewish War* 2.160–161).

Theology. The Damascus Document does not contain any explicit formulation of the sect's theological beliefs comparable with that found in the Rule. Yet, it is clear that its author/s shared the deterministic and dualistic Qumran view of the world and of man. Neophytes are ranked according to their "inheritance in the lot of light" (CD xiii.12). In the now available opening passage the sage addresses his instruction to the "Sons of Light," warning them about the "fixed time of visitation" against the "spirit of iniquity." This is elaborated in a characteristically predestinarian fashion, "for they can neither come before or after their appointed times."

This determinism is also applied to the contrasting destiny of Israel and the nations. The expulsion ceremony at the end of Damascus Document opens with a blessing, which acclaims the universal creator who "established peoples according to their families and tongues for their nations, but made them go astray in a trackless void," while "our ancestors you did choose and to their descendants you gave your truthful statutes" (Damascus Document[a] [4Q266 1.xi.1]). Here the nations are baldly depicted as being led astray by divine decree.

The messianic references in the Damascus Document to "the Messiah of Aaron and Israel" have been the subject of much debate between those who take them as designations for a single Messiah with priestly and royal functions, and those who interpret them in conformity with the Two Messiahs doctrine of the Community Rule. In CD xiv.19 the reference to the Messiah of Aaron and Israel is followed by the phrase "and he will atone their sin" (*wa-yekhapper ʿavonam*), which could be taken to mean that the Messiah has the power of forgiveness for sin. In *Mark* 2.7–10 the claim of such authority by Jesus is considered blasphemy in the eyes of the scribes.

History. One of the valuable aspects of the Damascus Document is the account of how the Qumran sect viewed its own history. According to the first historical discourse the community began with a nucleus of penitents who realized the errors of their ways "in the period of wrath," 390 years after the Babylonian conquest. After a twenty-year period of blind groping the Teacher of Righteousness became their guide. Among his antagonists was a figure called the Man of Mockery, whose followers "sought smooth things," a pejorative epithet applied elsewhere in Qumran writings to the Pharisees. This and other nicknames, such as "removers of the bounds" and "builders of the wall," are metaphors for religious laxity in matters of law. The Teacher of Righteousness and his faithful went into exile in "the land of Damascus" and entered into a "new covenant." The Damascus Document, in its present form, was composed after the death of the Teacher, whose "gathering in" is referred to in CD xx.14.

The utilization of this account for historical purposes is complicated by a number of factors. The number "three hundred and ninety" may be derived from *Ezekiel* 4.5. Moreover, we don't know whether the Qumran writers had any realistic knowledge of biblical chronology. "The land of Damascus" is ostensibly influenced by *Amos* 5.26–27, which refers to an exile "beyond Damascus." Many scholars have therefore argued that it does not refer to Syria, but to the sect's exile at Qumran. The author/s characteristic use of sobriquets for the protagonists in the sect's conflicts makes their individual identification little better than conjecture. Nevertheless, one can with greater confidence infer that the sect's image of its own history was that of a reformist group intent on disassociating itself from the religious and moral errors of its age. This would tend to support S. Talmon's characterization of the Covenanters as a millenarian movement with an anti-traditional, though hypernomistic posture.

Time and Sources. Of the Qumran manuscripts of the Damascus Document, the oldest copy is estimated to come from the beginning of the first century BCE. One may presume that the work in substantially its present form was in existence earlier. A *terminus post quem* is provided by the allusion to the death of the Teacher of Righteousness, which some scholars hypothesize occurred circa 110 BCE. However, these estimated parameters do not necessarily apply to each of the varied components that constitute the work. Thus, there are grounds for believing that the penal code of the Damascus Document represents an earlier system of penalties than that of the Rule, to which it is closely related.

Scholars have long attempted to apply source-critical techniques to the Admonition, but there has been little agreement in delimiting the literary segments and their chronological provenance. Murphy-O'Connor proposed four independent sources prior to the Essene occupation of Qumran: the missionary exhortation (ii.14–vi.1), the memorandum (vi.11–viii.3), the critiques of the princes of Judah (viii.3–18), and the call to faithfulness (xix.33–xx.34). P. R. Davies (1983) sees a different fourfold structure of the Admonition: a historical description of the community's origin (i.1–iv.12a), a demonstration of the validity of the sect's stringent laws (iv.12b–vii.9), a secondary midrashic expansion added to reinforce the sectarian claims (vii.5–viii.19), and a supplement stemming from the "new covenant" Qumran group led by the Teacher (xix.33–xx.34). Both of the aforementioned writers are inclined to accept S. Iwry's thesis that the sect originated from a nucleus of returnees (*shavei yisra'el*) from the Babylonian exile. However, most other proposed reconstructions of Qumran history are based on the premise of a Judean background for the community.

Influences. The importance of the Damascus Document in the Qumran library can be gauged by the number of manuscripts that are extant. The work is, as far as we know and as we would expect, nowhere referred to in rabbinic literature. However, it was very likely of great interest to the early Karaites as an ancient antecedent for their rejection of rabbinic tradition. Schechter already noted in his introduction to *Fragments of a Zadokite Work* that the tenth-century Karaite scholar Al-Qirqisani refers in his history of Jewish sects to Zadok, the reputed founder of the Zadokites, as "the first to expose the errors of the Rabbanites." He reports that Zadok produced no proof for anything that he claimed "except for one thing, namely, the prohibition of marrying one's niece, which he deduced from her being analogous to the paternal and maternal aunt." This fits very well with the exposition in CD v.8–11. Of the legal doctrines of the Zadokites, Al-Qirqisani records that they prohibit divorce, although it is permissible according to scripture. No explicit prohibition of divorce is found in the Damascus Document, although some have inferred this from the ban on "taking two wives in their lives" (CD iv.20–21). Concerning the Zadokite calendar, he states that "they make all months of thirty days; perhaps they rely in regard to this upon the story of Noah." Schechter suggested plausibly that this alludes to the 150 days (*Gn*. 8.3; cf. *Jub*. 5.27) reckoned for the five-month duration of the flood. Interestingly, the writer of a Qumran text (Commentary on Genesis A [4Q252]) tried to harmonize this with the solar calendar, in which the third month of each quarter has thirty-one days, by interpolating two additional days between the end of the flood and the coming to rest of the ark.

The possibility that the medieval manuscripts of the Damascus Document were copied by Karaite scribes from an ancient *Vorlage*, which perhaps became available through an earlier scroll discovery, seems worthy of further consideration. It would account for the surprisingly close textual correspondence between the portions of Damascus Document preserved in the Genizah manuscripts and their ancient counterparts from Qumran Cave 4, despite the chronological gap of over a millennium, which separates them.

BIBLIOGRAPHY

Baumgarten, J. *The Damascus Document, 4Q266–4Q273*. Discoveries in the Judaean Desert, 18. Oxford, 1996. Based on the transcriptions of J. T. Milik.

Baumgarten, J. M., and D. R. Schwartz. *The Dead Sea Scrolls*, vol. 2, *Damascus Document*, edited by J. M. Charlesworth. Tübingen, 1995.

Broshi, M., ed. *The Damascus Document Reconsidered*. Jerusalem, 1992. The best available facsimiles of the Genizah texts, with textual notes by E. Qimron, an essay on the laws by J. Baumgarten, and a bibliography of studies, 1970–1989, by F. García Martínez.

Davies, P. R. *The Damascus Document*. Sheffield, 1983. Valuable for literary-historical analyses of the Admonition, although the author largely ignored the legal corpus.

Ginzberg, L. *An Unknown Jewish Sect*. New York, 1976. Translation of Ginzberg's German commentary (1911–1914) with detailed evaluation of the laws from the perspective of rabbinic *halakhah*.

Rabin, C. *The Zadokite Documents*. Oxford, 1954. A widely used edition of the Hebrew text with concise, erudite commentary.

Schechter, Solomon. *Documents of Jewish Sectaries*, vol. 1 (Reprint, New York, 1970). With J. A. Fitzmyer's prolegomenon and bibliography.

Schiffman, L. H. *The Halakhah at Qumran*. Leiden, 1975. With a detailed commentary on the Sabbath code.

Schiffman, L. *Reclaiming the Dead Sea Scrolls*. Philadelphia, 1994. See Chapter 17, "The Law of the Sect."

Stegemann, H. *Die Essener, Qumran, Johannes der Täufer und Jesus*, p. 165. Freiburg, 1993.

JOSEPH M. BAUMGARTEN

DANIEL, BOOK OF. [*This entry comprises three articles:* Hebrew and Aramaic Text; Greek Additions; *and* Pseudo-Daniel.]

Hebrew and Aramaic Text

The figure of Daniel and the literary traditions surrounding him exercised a strong attraction for Judaism in the Second Temple period, and the community gathered at Qumran apparently shared this interest. Eight manuscripts of the *Book of Daniel* were discovered there, as were fragments of several other lost works related to Daniel.

Of the *Book of Daniel* fragments, two manuscripts were recovered from Cave 1, five from Cave 4, and one on papyrus from Cave 6, while seven sets of fragments from other related works were found in Cave 4:

Daniel[a] (1Q71)	Prayer of Nabonidus (4Q242)
Daniel[b] (1Q72)	Pseudo-Daniel[a] (4Q243)
Daniel[a] (4Q112)	Pseudo-Daniel[b] (4Q244)
Daniel[b] (4Q113)	Pseudo-Daniel[c] (4Q245)
Daniel[c] (4Q114)	Aramaic Apocalypse (4Q246)
Daniel[d] (4Q115)	Daniel-Susanna? (4Q551)
Daniel[e] (4Q116)	Four Kingdoms[a,b] (4Q552–553)
Daniel (6Q7)	

With those eight copies, the *Book of Daniel* ranks next after the Torah, *Psalms*, and *Isaiah* in popularity. Only those books of the ones in the present Hebrew Bible boast more copies at Qumran. In contrast with this small book, eight copies of the twelve Minor Prophets (treated as a single book in the scrolls) and only six of *Jeremiah* and six of *Ezekiel* were found at Qumran, even though those three books are three times larger than *Daniel*. For yet other large books, such as *Joshua, Judges, Samuel, Kings, Job,* and *Proverbs,* no more than four copies survive.

Date and Characteristics of the Scrolls. With regard to date, Daniel[c] and Daniel[e] are the oldest manuscripts of the book that are extant, dating paleographically from the early Hasmonean period (the late second or beginning of the first century BCE). Thus, they were copied only about a half century after the composition of the book. Though parts of the composite *Book of Daniel* date from the Persian period, the traditional twelve-chapter edition of the book as in the Masoretic Text dates between the persecution initiated by Antiochus IV Epiphanes in 168 BCE and the Maccabean victory in 164 BCE. For the Hebrew Bible, this half-century distance between original composition and extant manuscript parallels the New Testament papyrus of the *Gospel according to John* from the second century CE in the John Rylands Library in Manchester.

Daniel[c] is inscribed in an early semicursive script dated to "the late second century" BCE by Frank Moore Cross (1961, p. 43). In his comprehensive study of the development of Jewish scripts, Cross gives a description of the script and a paleographic chart ("The Development," pp. 181–188 plus 149, fig. 4, line 2; "Palaeography," pp. 395–401 plus plate 12, line 2). In these articles he assigned the date of the script to 100–50 BCE, but he has maintained his original date both through personal communication and in print (1974, p. 26), pointing to the evidence of the Daliyeh papyri as his basis for preferring the earlier date.

Daniel[e] is copied in a large semicursive script. Only five tiny fragments survive, with three complete and thirteen partial words, so firm conclusions are difficult to attain. It appears to have had only nine lines per column (assuming a text similar to that in the Masoretic Text). A rough calculation indicates that, if it had been a scroll of the entire *Book of Daniel,* about 120 columns would have been required. It is more likely that this scroll, with such an unusually small format, preserved only a portion of *Daniel,* perhaps just the prayer of 9.4–19. That would have required approximately ten columns, measuring slightly more than one meter in length. Other short, excerpted biblical texts, often prayers of liturgical passages, are known at Qumran (cf. 4QDeut[j,n,q] [4Q37, 4Q41, 4Q44], 4QPsalms[g,h] [4Q89 and 4Q90], and 5QPsalms [5Q5]). It is even conceivable, in view of the early date of this scroll, that it is a copy of an originally independent prayer that had been incorporated into the *Book of Daniel* because of its appropriateness. If this were to prove correct, Daniel[e] could, like the Prayer of Nabonidus, be considered as a source for the *Book of Daniel.*

Daniel[a] (4Q112; hereafter called 4QDaniel[a]) is written in an elegant formal hand from the late Hasmonean period or the transition into the Herodian period (from around the middle of the first century BCE). It attests parts of every chapter of the book except chapters 6, 9, and 12. In its sixty-six variants, it never agrees with the Masoretic Text in contrast to other scrolls or the Old Greek. One correction by the original scribe is interesting. The first verse of chapter 10 reads: "In the third year of King . . . , a word was revealed." When writing the first verse of chapter 8, the scribe wrote: "In the third year of King . . . , a word was revealed" (as in 10.1), then crossed out "a word was revealed" and wrote the correct reading, "a vision was seen."

Daniel[b] (1Q72; hereafter called 1QDaniel[b]) was also copied in the Hasmonean period, whereas Daniel[a] (1Q71; hereafter called 1QDaniel[a]) and Daniel (6Q7) were copied later in the Herodian period (the late first century BCE or first half of the first century CE). With regard to the dual-language traditional form of the book, 1QDaniel[a] shows the shift from Hebrew to Aramaic precisely at *Daniel* 2.4b as expected, and this shift is supported by 4QDaniel[a] as well, since it has chapter 1 in Hebrew and its next fragment at 2.9–11 in Aramaic. 4QDaniel[a] and Daniel[b] (4Q113, hereafter called 4QDaniel[b]) also document the shift from Aramaic back to Hebrew at 8.1.

Daniel[d] preserves only about a dozen small fragments that are identifiable. Its decipherment is especially difficult because apparently acid in the ink has badly corroded and eaten through the leather, so that often only the vague outlines of the letters remain. Since the script displays few exact features, dating is uncertain, but it appears to be from the late Hasmonean or early Herodian period (near the middle or latter part of the first century BCE). The text seems to be of the same general form as that in the other *Daniel* scrolls and the Masoretic Text, including 3.24 following directly after 3.23, without the *Prayer of Azariah* and *The Song of the Three Young Men*. But there are numerous orthographic, morphological, and textual differences, sometimes inferior, from the traditional text.

4QDaniel[b] is copied in a large, clear, stately hand described by Cross as a "developed Herodian formal script" from approximately 20–50 CE ("The Development," pp. 173–181 and 139, fig. 2, line 6; "Palaeography," plate 10, line 6). It is curious that, with regard to orthography, 4QDaniel[b] expands considerably beyond the spelling practices of 4QDaniel[a] and the Masoretic Text, which are generally similar, whereas the textual variants show a dramatically different arrangement. In the few places where their fragments overlap, 4QDaniel[a] and 4QDaniel[b] share two certain pluses and two probable pluses as variants against the Masoretic Text, with two of those four being shared by the Old Greek as well. In contrast, neither of the two Qumran scrolls ever agrees with the Masoretic Text in a textual variant against the other Qumran scroll. Though it cannot be proved, it is intriguing to question whether Daniel[b] may have been copied from 4QDaniel[a] while expanding its orthography.

Contents of the Scrolls. The eight manuscripts preserve the following passages:

1QDaniel[a]
- 1.10–17
- 2.2–6

1QDaniel[b]
- 3.22–30

4QDaniel[a]
- 1.16–20
- 2.9–11, 19–49
- 3.1–2
- 4.29–30
- 5.5–7, 12–14, 16–19
- 7.5–7, 25–28
- 8.1–5
- 10.16–20
- 11.13–16

4QDaniel[b]
- 5.10–12, 14–16, 19–22
- 6.8–22, 27–29
- 7.1–6, 11?, 26–28
- 8.1–8, 13–16

4QDaniel[c]
- 10.5–9, 11–16, 21
- 11.1–2, 13–17, 25–29

4QDaniel[d]
- 3.23–25
- 4.5–9, 12–16
- 7.15–23

4QDaniel[e]
- 9.12–17

6QDaniel
- 8.16–17?, 20–21?
- 10.8–16
- 11.33–36, 38

Although no fragments have been identified as containing the Greek "additions" to *Daniel*, all the chapters of the Hebrew-Aramaic book are represented except chapter 12. That chapter, however, was certainly known, since another manuscript, the Florilegium from Cave 4, quotes *Daniel* 12.10 with the formula for introducing citations from scripture: ". . . it is written in the book of the prophet Daniel . . ." (4Q174 1–3.ii.3–4). In considering Daniel a prophet, and thus the *Book of Daniel* among "the Law and the Prophets," the Qumran community shared the common Jewish view. The *Gospel according to Matthew* refers to Daniel as a prophet (*Mt.* 24.15; see also *Mk.* 13.14), as does Josephus (*Jewish Antiquities*, 10.249, 266–267). The Christian Bible kept *Daniel* among the Prophets, whereas the first evidence within Jewish tradition that places *Daniel* among the Writings as opposed to the Prophets is the fifth-century CE Babylonian Talmud (B.B. 14b). It is likely, however, that after the Roman destruction of Jerusalem and the threat of Christianity, the rabbis began to emphasize the wisdom aspects of the book in contrast to the prophetic or apocalyptic aspects. Melchizedek from Cave 11 (11Q13 2.18) also refers to *Daniel*, apparently intending *Daniel* 9.25.

Textual Form. All the identified fragments from Daniel at Qumran share the same general text tradition as that transmitted in the Masoretic Text (as opposed to the longer Greek edition), though there are numerous interesting variants. There are also some small fragments appearing to belong to those manuscripts that cannot be placed using only the Masoretic Text form of the text. It is also possible that there are unidentified Hebrew and Aramaic fragments that simply have text from *Daniel* beyond that known from the Masoretic Text, whether small variants or from Hebrew or Aramaic forms of "the additions" to *Daniel*. The fact that Proto-Theodotion includes "the additions" in his Greek recension, while he is thought to have revised the Old Greek translation back toward a Hebrew-Aramaic text of his day, suggests that he may have known a Semitic text of *Daniel* for those parts that otherwise survive only in the Greek.

Growth of the Traditions. The literary traditions centering around Daniel first appear to have gained prominence within the biblical tradition in the Aramaic chapters 2–6 of *Daniel* during the Persian period (fifth–fourth centuries BCE). There are, of course, brief indications of age-old admiration, broader in scope than Israel but including Israel, of an ancient sage revered for his wisdom. The Canaanite myth of Aqhat from the second millennium BCE discovered at Ugarit has King Dan'el ("El/God judges") as the father of Aqhat; as with Solomon, wisdom was associated with the royal leader. *Ezekiel* 14.14, 20 (cf. 28.3) also attests to the age-old figure alongside Noah and Job, singling out these three as models of righteousness. In the context of an oracle of judgment against a country that has sinned against the Lord and is then about to be punished, the message was that "even if these three, Noah, Dan'el, and Job, were within it, they could save (only) their own lives because of their righteousness" (*Ezek.* 14.14; cf. 14.20), whereas the rest of the population would be punished.

There does not seem to be any evidence warranting more than a general connection between the ancient figure of the wise Dan'el and the protagonist of *Daniel* in chapters 2–6. These stories probably circulated as wisdom stories in the Persian period, functioning as model stories for teaching the youth how to succeed in the foreign imperial court service while also remaining faithful to the Jewish God, religion, and people.

The Prayer of Nabonidus (4Q242), considered by many to be in some sense a source upon which chapter 4 of *Daniel* was built, also illuminates the growing traditions. Nabonidus (556–539 BCE) was the Babylonian king who is credited with losing that magnificent empire to Cyrus, founder of the Persian empire. The words of his prayer relate that he had been plagued for seven years with a virulent inflammation at God's command while he was in the desert oasis of Teima. He had, for those seven years, been praying to "the gods of silver and gold, [bronze and iron], wood, stone, and clay" (see *Dn*. 5.4), and "was changed" (presumably into some animal's mind; see *Dn*. 4.16). A Jewish exorcist suggested that he write down his account and give glory to God, who "forgave my sins" and presumably healed the king. *Daniel* (chap. 4) relates a similar story, now told about the more famous king Nebuchadnezzar, known more widely to Jews and all too well as the king who had sacked Jerusalem and taken the Jewish people into exile.

With the persecution of Antiochus IV Epiphanes (175–164 BCE), the apocalyptic sections, chapters 7–12, were added to the collection as visions from that ancient seer. The distant time of the ancient wisdom figure now became the exilic period, whereas to the exilic prophet Ezekiel, the distant time had been that of Noah and Job.

The twelve-chapter form of the collection, preserved in the Masoretic Text, thus assumed its present shape somewhere around 166 BCE, and the Hebrew-Aramaic manuscripts found at Qumran exhibit generally this form of the text tradition. Further traditions centered around *Daniel*—it is unknown whether these were composed in Hebrew/Aramaic or in Greek—continued to be collected in the textual form transmitted in the Greek, including *Bel and the Dragon*, *Susanna*, the *Prayer of Azariah*, and *The Song of the Three Young Men*.

Daniel's Impact on Qumran. The vocabulary, apocalyptic thought, angelology, and other aspects of the late parts of *Daniel* strongly impacted the thought and vocabulary of the closely contemporary group at Qumran (e.g., "*maskil*," "the many," and "the time of the end," *Dn*. 12.3–4). Even the characteristic method by which Qumran Covenanters interpreted the scriptures, clearly exemplified in the *pesharim*, is visible in *Daniel* 9.2, 24–27. Daniel studies "the books," in this case *Jeremiah*, to learn how long the devastation of Jerusalem brought on by Antiochus will last. In the "seventy years" that he read in *Jeremiah* 25.11–12 and 29.10, he found the clue to the revealed divine plan (*raz*). The author, removing the number from the historical context that Jeremiah was addressing, multiplies the number for Gabriel's revealed interpretation (*pesher*). The "seventy weeks of years" (*Dn*. 9.24) brings the time down to the general period of Antiochus and the time of the "end" (*Dn*. 9.26).

This method of understanding prophetic revelation, as seen in *Daniel* and at Qumran, was shared by other Jews who focused on prophecy, including the early Christians. Revelation was seen as the word of God spoken long ago through the prophets. Its main application was found, not in what the prophet had meant and in what his audience had understood by his words, but in the illumination that those words now provided for their own time (e.g., *Mt*. 1.22–23; 2.5–6, 15, 17–18; *Heb*. 1.5–13; 5.5–6).

BIBLIOGRAPHY

Baillet, Maurice, Jozef T. Milik, and Roland de Vaux. *Les 'Petites Grottes' de Qumrân*. Discoveries in the Judaean Desert, 3. Oxford, 1962. Critical edition of the 6QDaniel papyrus.

Barthélemy, Dominique and Józef T. Milik. *Qumran Cave 1*. Discoveries in the Judaean Desert, 1. Oxford, 1955. Critical edition (without photographs available) of the two Cave 1 *Daniel* scrolls; the photographs were published by John Trever.

Collins, John J. *Daniel*. Minneapolis, 1993. An excellent commentary on the *Book of Daniel* in the Hermeneia series.

Cross, Frank Moore. *The Ancient Library of Qumran*. Grand Rapids, Mich., 1961.

Cross, Frank Moore. "The Development of the Jewish Scripts." In *The Bible and the Ancient Near East*, edited by George Ernest Wright, 2d ed., pp. 133–202. Garden City, N.Y., 1961. Comprehensive treatment of the paleography of the scrolls, including specifically 4QDaniel[b]. See also "Palaeography and the Dead Sea Scrolls," in *The Dead Sea Scrolls after Fifty Years: A Comprehensive Assessment*, edited by P. W. Flint and J. C. VanderKam, vol. 1, pp. 379–402. Leiden, 1998.

Cross, Frank Moore. "The Papyri and Their Historical Implications." In *Discoveries in the Wâdī ed-Dâliyeh*, edited by Paul Lapp, p. 26. Cambridge, Mass., 1974.

Pace [Jeansonne], Sharon. "The Stratigraphy of the Text of Daniel and Question of Theological *Tendenz* in the Old Greek." *Bulletin of the International Organization for Septuagint and Cognate Studies* 17 (1984), 15–35. A good study of the development and interrelationships of the textual forms of the *Book of Daniel*.

Pfann, Stephen J. "4QDaniel[d] (4Q115): A Preliminary Edition with Critical Notes." *Revue de Qumrân* 17 (1996), 37–71.

Trever, John C. "Completion of the Publication of Some Fragments from Qumran Cave 1." *Revue de Qumrân* 5 (1964–1966), 323–344. Includes photographs of the two Cave 1 Daniel Scrolls.

Ulrich, Eugene. "Daniel Manuscripts from Qumran. Part 1: A Preliminary Edition of 4QDan[a]." *Bulletin of the American Schools of Oriental Research* 267 (1987), 17–37.

Ulrich, Eugene. "Daniel Manuscripts from Qumran. Part 2: Preliminary Editions of 4QDan[b] and 4QDan[c]." *Bulletin of the American Schools of Oriental Research* 274 (1989), 3–26.

Ulrich, Eugene. "Orthography and Text in 4QDan[a] and 4QDan[b] and in the Received Masoretic Text." In *Of Scribes and Scrolls: Studies on the Hebrew Bible, Intertestamental Judaism, and Christian Ori-*

gins Presented to John Strugnell on the Occasion of His Sixtieth Birthday, edited by Harold W. Attridge, John J. Collins, and Thomas H. Tobin, pp. 29–42. Lanham, Md., 1990. An analysis of the orthographic and textual interrelationships of the three texts.

Ulrich, Eugene, et al. *Qumran Cave 4, XI: Psalms to Chronicles*. Discoveries in the Judaean Desert, 16. Oxford, 2000. Critical editions of the five Cave 4 Daniel scrolls.

EUGENE ULRICH

Greek Additions

Sections of the *Book of Daniel* are contained in the Greek translation and its daughter versions, but not in the Masoretic Text. Although some or all of these sections may be older than parts of the Aramaic and Hebrew *Book of Daniel*, they are surely additions to the originally composed form of the book (167–164 BCE). Nonetheless, they are integral parts of the versions in which they are included and are canonical scripture for the Roman Catholic and Eastern Orthodox Churches.

The Greek version of *Daniel* has been preserved in two different text forms (Collins, 1993, pp. 3–11). The Old Greek version (OG, c.100 BCE) is extant in its entirety in only two manuscripts (88 [ninth to eleventh century] and the SyroHexapla [616–617 CE]), and parts of it are preserved in two fragmentary papyri (967, c.200 CE; 29255, fifth century CE). The translation ascribed to Theodotion (the turn of the era), which came to replace the Old Greek in Christian usage, is thought to be, alternatively, a revision of the Old Greek or an independent translation (Collins, 1993, pp. 9–11; McLay, 1996, favors the latter).

The Story of Susanna. According to this short story set in Babylon, Susanna, a devout and virtuous Jewish woman, is propositioned by two elders who are smitten by her beauty. When she refuses them, they accuse her of adultery. Susanna prays for deliverance, and God prompts the young Daniel to come to her defense. He interrogates the elders and finds contradictions in their testimony that show their charges to be false. Susanna is delivered from death, and her accusers are executed.

Aspects of the story are reminiscent of widespread folk motifs (Moore, 1977, pp. 88–89); however, its theme and plot line closely parallel the court tales in *Daniel* 3 and 6 and, to a degree, *Genesis* 37–45 and the *Book of Aḥiqar* (Nickelsburg, 1981, 1985). The protagonist is conspired against, condemned to death, rescued by God, and vindicated. Like the heroes in *Daniel* 3 and 6, Susanna's piety is the cause of the accusations against her. The story differs from other examples of the genre in that the protagonist is an ordinary person rather than a court official and a woman rather than a man. Certain details in the story, however, parallel the story of Joseph and Potiphar's wife (*Gn*. 39), with the male and female roles reversed. Although the story of *Susanna* is set in the Diaspora, it focuses on the situation in the Jewish community and encourages obedience to God in the midst of the temptations and pressures that could arise in the Israelite community. There is also a certain antiestablishment motif present, with the young charismatic Daniel set in opposition to the elders of the community, who abuse their judicial functions for their own selfish and sinful ends. Brüll's hypothesis that the story of *Susanna* was created as a Pharisaic polemic against the court procedures and theories of the Sadducees has not found wide acceptance.

Theodotion's version of *Susanna* presents a more elaborate form of the story than the Old Greek and is marked by a heightened focus on Susanna. It alone contains the episode about Susanna's bath that enhances the story's dramatic and erotic interest (Collins, 1993, p. 426) and plays a major role in artistic and musical interpretations of the story. In the Old Greek the story is placed at the end of the *Book of Daniel*, either before or after the tale of Bel and the Dragon. The story concludes by praising the single-minded, pious, and wise youths of Israel, of which Daniel is the epitome. This conclusion diverts the focus of the story from the virtuous conduct of the protagonist, Susanna, to the upright behavior of her deliverer, who is the main character in the book to which the story is attached. In the manuscript tradition of Theodotion, the story stands at the beginning of the *Book of Daniel*, and its last verse provides a transition to the stories in chapters 1–6 by explaining that the Susanna incident contributed to Daniel's rise to prominence.

The use of Greek wordplays in the text has led some critics to suppose that the story was composed in that language; however, old wordplays can always be recreated in a translation (see Milik, 1981, pp. 350–353, for suggestions in Aramaic). More persuasive is the evidence presented for mistranslations and alternative translations from a Semitic-language original (Moore, 1977, pp. 82–84; Collins, 1993, pp. 427–428). Milik suggests that Daniel-Susanna(?) (4Q551) preserves fragments of an Aramaic version of the story, but the fragments show remarkable verbal parallels to the *targum* of the biblical story of the Levite and his concubine (*Jgs*. 19.16–30) (Nickelsburg, 1997).

Bel and the Dragon. This triple narrative stands at the end of the Greek version of the *Book of Daniel*, where it serves as a final story depicting Daniel's interaction with the kings of Mesopotamia. (The reference to Cyrus in *Daniel* 10.1 has no counterpart in the narratives in chapters 1–6.) The first episode sets the living God and his servant Daniel in opposition to the god Bel and his servants, the priests, and King Cyrus (vv. 3–22). Daniel challenges the divine nature of the idol, while the king acclaims Bel. In the end Bel is shown to be only clay and brass, the priests are killed, and Bel is destroyed. In the second episode (vv. 23–30), the living God and Daniel oppose the dragon (or perhaps better, serpent) and Cyrus. With the king's permission, Daniel feeds the beast a lethal concoction that causes it to explode. The people claim that "the king has become a Jew" and demand that Daniel be handed over to them. This leads to the third episode (vv. 31–42), in which Daniel is thrown into a lions' den, from which he is rescued by the prophet Habakkuk. Now the king acknowledges the power and uniqueness of Daniel's God, and Daniel's enemies are destroyed.

This story has clear thematic and narrative parallels with the stories in *Daniel* 1–6. Daniel, the servant of the true God, is pitted against a Mesopotamian monarch and his idolatrous god. A life-threatening ordeal vindicates Daniel and results in the monarch's declaration of faith in God and the destruction of Daniel's enemies. The episode about the lions' den, in particular, is a version of the story preserved in *Daniel* 6. Some of its elements seem more developed than *Daniel* 6 (Nickelsburg, 1985, p. 40); but other considerations may indicate that the two versions developed independently of one another (Collins, 1993, pp. 411–412). The other two episodes may have originated as separate stories (Moore, 1977, pp. 121–125). In any case, the three parts of the story are presently bound together by a single plot that moves from the king's idolatrous worship of Bel and opposition to Daniel and his God to the king's acclamation of Daniel's God.

Its many parallels in *Daniel* 1–6 notwithstanding, *Bel and the Dragon* has its own peculiar emphasis: an explicit and repeated polemic against idolatry. A string of similarities between *Bel and the Dragon* and *Isaiah* 45–46 may indicate that the double stories about Bel and the dragon developed or were enhanced by an exegesis of these chapters of *Isaiah*. Other elements in the text reflect traditional motifs. The term "living God" frequently is found in Jewish polemics against idols. The sarcastic touches in the narrative stand in a long tradition of such polemics (*Is*. 44.9–20, *Wis*. 13–14, *Let. Jer*., Ap. Ab. 1–8; see Roth, 1975, pp. 42–43). Daniel's destruction of Bel's temple recalls similar incidents attributed to Abraham (*Jub*. 12.1–14) and Job (*Testament of Job* 2–5).

Although the language of the story's composition is uncertain, it may well have been composed in a Semitic language (Collins, pp. 410–411). The time and place of composition also are uncertain, but there is no compelling evidence that they were composed with a knowledge of the present book of *Daniel* or even chapters 1–6 (Collins, 1993, p. 412).

Prayer of Azariah and the Song of the Three Young Men. This section of text, inserted between *Daniel* 3.23 and 3.24 of the Aramaic text, comprises a prayer of confession ascribed to Azariah (Abednego) and a hymn of thanksgiving placed on the lips of the three young men. The addition of the liturgical compositions into a narrative context has a number of biblical models (e.g., *Ex*. 15, *Jgs*. 5, and *1 Sm*. 2).

Azariah's prayer is a confession of the nation's sins based on traditional covenantal theology, particularly as expressed in *Deuteronomy* 28. It has especially close parallels in *1 Baruch* 1.15–3.8, *Daniel* 9.4–19, and Words of the Luminaries. [*See* Words of the Luminaries.] The prayer seems to have been a previously extant composition inserted into the narrative according to a typical literary pattern (deliverance comes in response to prayer). Its contents fit the general circumstances of the Babylonian exile or the persecution under Antiochus IV Epiphanes rather than the specifics of the young men's predicament. The prayer may well have been composed during the Antiochan persecution, possibly in Hebrew (Collins, 1993, pp. 202–203).

A prose insertion following the prayer emphasizes the ferocity of the fire (thus heightening the miraculous rescue of the three young men) and provides a transition to the song of thanksgiving. This hymn divides into four sections: a doxology to the God who is enthroned in his temple (vv. 31–33), perhaps the heavenly temple (v. 34), and a threefold appeal for the whole creation to join in the praise of God (heaven and its inhabitants and elements, vv. 35–51; the earth and its inhabitants, vv. 52–60; and Israel, vv. 61–65). The hymn has been influenced by the language and style of the canonical *Book of Psalms*, particularly Psalms 136 and 148. Its lack of specific relevance to the particulars of its context suggests that it was an independent composition, written quite likely in Hebrew at some unknown date prior to the Greek translation of *Daniel* (Collins, 1993, p. 205).

The Qumran corpus contains several works that use Daniel's name or are reminiscent of the Daniel stories and visions. The Prayer of Nabonidus (4Q242) recalls the setting of *Daniel* 4, while Pseudo-Daniel[a–c] (4Q243–245) mentions him and apparently attributes to him a survey of biblical history and the last days. The Aramaic Apocalypse (4Q246) reminds one of *Daniel* 2 and 7. [*See* Aramaic Apocalypse.] None of these texts, however, seems to be connected with the additions found in the Greek forms of *Daniel*; this is further evidence for a wider cycle of Danielic works than had been recognized before. The Prayer of Nabonidus may provide a glimpse at a form of the story about Nebuchadnezzar's illness in *Daniel* 4 that is earlier than the one preserved in the canonical text. The Pseudo-Daniel texts from Qumran may parallel or elaborate on various parts of an existing text of *Daniel*.

Importance for the Hebrew Scriptures, Septuagint, and Early Jewish Literature. As is indicated by the parallel biblical passages cited above, each of the additions to *Daniel* attests the ongoing life of biblical traditions in

Jewish narrative and liturgy of the Hellenistic period. The inclusion of these additions in the Greek *Daniel* is evidence that its translators felt free to elaborate on a received biblical text (the Hebrew scriptures form of Daniel) that they did not yet consider to be fixed. The process has parallels in the development of the Hebrew scriptures (in *Jubilees*) and later in some of the *targumim*. The stories of *Susanna* and *Bel and the Dragon* are parts of literary corpora that provide evidence about the status of women in Hellenistic Judaism (Levine, 1995) and reflect the Jewish aversion to idolatry. The incorporation of the prayer and hymn into the story in *Daniel* 3 is a reminder that one should include the practice of liturgical piety in one's reconstruction of the history of Judaism, which is often dominated by a focus on religious ideas, that is, theology.

[*See also* Court Tales.]

BIBLIOGRAPHY

Collins, John J. *Daniel: A Commentary on the Book of Daniel*. Hermeneia. Minneapolis, 1993. Introduction, translation, and commentary.

Koch, Klaus. *Deuterokononische Zusätze zum Danielbuch: Entstehung und Textgeschichte*. 2 vols. Alter Orient und Altes Testament, 38 1.2. Neukirchen Vluyn, 1987. Introduction, translation, and commentary.

Levine, Amy-Jill. "'Hemmed in on Every Side': Jews and Women in the Book of Susanna." In *Reading from This Place*, edited by Fernando F. Segovia and Mary Ann Tolbert, pp. 175–190. Minneapolis, 1995. Feminist reading of the story of *Susanna*.

McLay, Tim. *The OG and The Versions of Daniel*. Septuagint and Cognate Studies, 43. Atlanta, 1996. History of the text of the Greek *Daniel*.

Milik, Józef T. "Daniel et Susanne à Qumrân." In *De la Tôrah au Messie*, edited by Maurice Carrez, Joseph Doré, and Pierre Grelot, pp. 337–359. Paris, 1981. Textual, literary, and historical aspects of *Susanna* and publication of fragments of Daniel-Susanna(?) 4Q551.

Moore, Carey A. *Daniel, Esther, and Jeremiah: The Additions*. The Anchor Bible, 44. Garden City, 1977. Introduction, translation, and commentary.

Nickelsburg, George W. E. *Jewish Literature between the Bible and the Mishnah*. Philadelphia, 1981.

Nickelsburg, George W. E. "Stories of Biblical and Early Post Biblical Times." In *Jewish Writings of the Second Temple Period*, edited by Michael E. Stone, pp. 33–87. Compendia Rerum Iudaicarum ad Novum Testamentum 2.2. Philadelphia, 1985.

Nickelsburg, George W. E. "4Q551: A Vorlage to the Story of Susanna or a Text Related to Judges 19." *Journal of Jewish Studies* 48 (1997), 349–351.

Roth, W. M. H. "For Life, He Appeals to Death (Wis. 13:18)." *Catholic Bible Quarterly* 37 (1975), 21–47.

Spolsky, Ellen, ed. *The Judgment of Susanna: Authority and Witness*. Early Judaism and Its Literature, 11. Atlanta, 1996. Multidisciplinary discussion of the story and its interpretation in the West.

GEORGE W. E. NICKELSBURG

Pseudo-Daniel

The name Daniel occurs in three manuscripts found at Qumran that are not part of the *Book of Daniel*, Pseudo-Daniel[a–c] (4Q243–245). In addition, there are four other manuscripts where a relationship to the *Book of Daniel* has been proposed.

Pseudo-Daniel[a–c]. The Pseudo-Daniel manuscripts were partially published by Józef T. Milik (1956). Pseudo-Daniel[a–b] overlap and clearly belong to the same manuscript. Milik tentatively proposed that Pseudo-Daniel[c] belonged to the same work, but this now seems doubtful. Pseudo-Daniel[a–b] present a speech by Daniel in a royal court. The speech is an overview of history, beginning with Noah and the flood and continuing down to the Hellenistic period. (The document contains several personal names. Only one, Balakros, is fully preserved. This name was borne by several figures in the early Hellenistic period.) Pseudo-Daniel[c] contains a long list of names. In part, this list gives the names of high priests from the patriarchal period (Qahath) down to the Hellenistic age (Onias, Simon). It then continues with a list of kings, including David, Solomon, and Ahaziah. It is difficult to see how these lists could be integrated into the document preserved in Pseudo-Daniel[a–b]. The latter document views Israel in the context of universal history and is concerned with the problem of foreign domination; Pseudo-Daniel[c] is focused on the internal history of Israel. The two documents may come from the same or related circles, but their relationship seems to be only complementary.

Forty fragments of Pseudo-Daniel[a] and fourteen fragments of Pseudo-Daniel[b] have been preserved. Both manuscripts are written in Herodian script (late first century BCE). Although Milik found affinities between this text and the *Book of Daniel* in allusions to seventy years and a four-kingdom schema, neither element is actually found in the fragments. The reconstruction of "seventy years" seems more plausible than any alternative in Pseudo-Daniel[a], fragment 16. The reference, however, might not necessarily refer to the Exile, as it does in *Daniel* 9; Pseudo-Moses[e] (4Q390) has two references to seventy years, neither of them in an exilic context. The four-kingdom schema is inferred from the fourth line of the same fragment, which reads *hi' malkhuta' qad*[] ("it is the . . . kingdom"). Milik restored *qad*[*mita'*] ("first"). This reconstruction is problematic on two counts (see Collins and Flint, 1996). First, two lines earlier in the same fragment we read that "he will save them." It seems unlikely that an act of salvation would be followed immediately by the inauguration of the first of a series of gentile kingdoms. Second, if Milik's interpretation were correct, this would be the only case in which the four-kingdom sequence (known from the *Book of Daniel* and the fourth *Sibylline Oracle*) is inaugurated after deliverance from the Exile. The first kingdom is always either Babylon or Assyria. Alternative reconstructions are possible. The phrase can be read as *malkhuta' qadishta'* ("holy kingdom"), and the passage may be located in the eschatological phase of the prophecy.

Pseudo-Daniel[c] survives in four fragments, one of which contains the list of names already noted. The second fragment contains a passage reminiscent of the Damascus Document (CD i), where some people are said to wander in blindness. There follows a statement that "these then will rise" (*yequmun*). Milik saw here a reference to resurrection and a parallel to *Daniel* 12, but the verb *qum* is not used in *Daniel* 12 and does not necessarily refer to resurrection at all. The following line says that some people "will return" (*yetuvun*). It seems then that these fragments may be largely independent of the *Book of Daniel* and derive from distinct pseudepigraphic compositions, which attributed new revelations to the biblical sage.

We can only guess at the provenance of these compositions. Even if Pseudo-Daniel[c] did not form a part of Pseudo-Daniel[a–b], these probably had an eschatological conclusion. Fragment 24 of Pseudo-Daniel[a] speaks of the gathering of the elect, and fragment 25 seems to imply an eschatological battle ("the land will be filled . . . with decayed carcasses"). Pseudo-Daniel[a–b] share several motifs with other quasi-prophetic pseudepigrapha of the time. Israel at large lives in error, owing to the influence of demonic spirits. Eschatological restoration is the destiny of an elect group, who walk in the way of truth, in contrast to the "error" of others. The eventual emergence of this elect group is surely one of the major themes of this work. In this respect it resembles such works as the "Animal Apocalypse" (*1 En.* 83–90), the "Apocalypse of Weeks" (*1 En.* 93.1–10, 91.11–17), the Damascus Document, and Pseudo-Moses[e]. While all these works resemble each other in describing the emergence of an elect group, there are too many differences between them for all to be attributed to the same circle of authors.

The best known "elect group" that emerged in the second century BCE was the Qumran sect. There are distinct parallels in Pseudo-Daniel to the Damascus Document in the account of the Exile as giving Israel into the hand of Nebuchadnezzar for the desolation of the land (see CD i.12; v.20). Yet there is no mention of a *yaḥad* sect, and no unambiguously sectarian language. Pseudo-Daniel's relation to the Dead Sea sect may be analogous to that of *Jubilees* or *1 Enoch*, which were evidently treasured at Qumran but which derived from separate, older movements.

Pseudo-Daniel[c] also envisages a group that wanders in blindness and another group that "returns." The key to the provenance of the document, however, lies in the list of names. The priestly names include *Ḥoniah* (Onias) and, in the following line, Shimʿon. The name preceding Shimʿon ends in *n*, and the trace of the preceding letter seems more like *tav* than *nun*. The possibility arises that the text is referring to Jonathan and Simon Maccabee. If this is so, Jonathan and Simon may be presented simply as the culmination of a series of high priests, or the fragmentary text may have regarded them as usurpers of the priesthood (see Collins and Flint, 1996). Since the following fragment speaks of people wandering in blindness and envisages some eschatological reversal, the latter possibility seems more likely. Nothing is certain, however, in view of the fragmentary state of the text.

Prayer of Nabonidus. Together with the Pseudo-Daniel fragments, Milik also published fragments of the Prayer of Nabonidus (4Q242), which is relevant to the interpretation of *Daniel* 4. While there are some problems of interpretation, the text is clearly presented as a proclamation of Nabonidus, the last king of Babylon, who says that he was afflicted with a disease during his sojourn at the oasis of Teima in Arabia and that he was instructed by a Jewish diviner to pray to the most high God. The historical Nabonidus was absent from Babylon and lived in Teima for ten years. The Qumran text gives the sojourn as seven years, the same length as Nebuchadnezzar's madness in *Daniel* 4. Long before the discovery of the prayer of Nabonidus, scholars had suspected that the legend in *Daniel* 4 had its origin in the prolonged absence of Nabonidus from Babylon. *Daniel* 4 also tells of a Babylonian king brought low by distress, who is directed to the true God by a Jewish exile. It is likely, then, that the prayer preserves some older aspects of the tradition that underlies *Daniel* 4.

Some scholars have restored the text of the prayer in ways that enhance the parallels with *Daniel* 4. Frank Moore Cross (1984) reconstructs line 3 of column i to read "I was like a beast" (cf. *Dn.* 5.21). Rudolf Meyer (1962) reconstructs a dream about a great tree in column ii. These reconstructions go beyond the available evidence (Collins, 1996). It is not necessary to suppose that *Daniel* 4 depended directly on the Prayer of Nabonidus, but the two texts draw on a common tradition.

Aramaic Apocalypse. A clear relationship to the *Book of Daniel* can also be seen in the Aramaic Apocalypse (4Q246), the so-called Son of God text, where there is a general similarity in setting. The Aramaic Apocalypse is the interpretation of a vision, apparently the vision of a king, by someone who falls before the throne in the opening verse. There are verbal parallels to *Daniel* (ii.5): "His kingdom is an everlasting kingdom" (cf. *Dn.* 4.3, 7.27), and "His sovereignty is an everlasting sovereignty" (ii.9; cf. *Dn.* 4.31, 7.14). Another possible allusion to Daniel is the use of the word "to trample" (*dush*) [ii.3]; (cf. *Dn.* 7.7). These parallels give rise to the suspicion that the Aramaic Apocalypse may be an adaptation of *Daniel* 7, although it is certainly not a systematic interpretation. Émile Puech

(1992), however, prefers to regard the text as a roughly contemporaneous parallel to *Daniel* that shares some language with the biblical book.

Two other vaguely Danielic writings may be noted more briefly. Milik (1956) referred to a text with four talking trees. The first is asked its name and responds "Babylon." The following line reads "[Y]ou are he who rules over Persia." The text is extremely fragmentary; it is identified as Four Kingdoms[a–b] (4Q552–553). Robert Eisenman and Michael Wise (1992) have translated the text and proposed some reconstructions. The motif of four kingdoms was known apart from the *Book of Daniel*; however, here a relationship with *Daniel* is suggested solely because Babylon is identified as the first kingdom (Assyria usually holds that position in texts other than *Daniel*, e.g., *Sibylline Oracle* 4). Milik has also tentatively suggested that Aramaic fragment Daniel-Susanna? (4Q551) belongs to the story of Susanna. The basis for the suggestion is that the fragment appears to deal with the selection of a judge, but this is hardly sufficient evidence to warrant an identification with Susanna. Finally, Magen Broshi and Esther Eshel have proposed that 4Q248 (= 4QHistorical Text) (Acts of a Greek King) was a source for the Book of Daniel. This fragment reports the activities of a king in Egypt and Israel, including "the city of the sanctuary," Jerusalem. Broshi and Eshel read lines 9 and 10 as [*u-kekhalot*] *nappēts yad ʿam ha-[qodesh*: "and when the shattering of the power of the holy people is complete." This would correspond to *Daniel* 12.7, except for the omission of a definite article in the biblical text. The parallel is exceptionally interesting, since most scholars have emended the text of Daniel to read "when the power of the oppressor of the holy people comes to an end," and the emendation would now seem unlikely. The actual reading of the key phrase, however, is very doubtful. The *nun* of *napets* has to be reconstructed, and other scholars read *b* (*bet*) instead of *p* (*pe*). If the reading *napets* is not correct, this text has no relationship to *Daniel*.

[*See also* Apocrypha and Pseudepigrapha; Court Tales.]

BIBLIOGRAPHY

Broshi, Magen, and Esther Eshel, "The Greek King in Antiochus IV (4Q Historical Text = 4Q248), *Journal of Jewish Studies* 48 (1997), 120–129.

Collins, John J. "The *'Son of God'* Text from Qumran." In *From Jesus to John: Essays on Jesus and New Testament Christology in Honour of Marinus de Jonge*, edited by Martinus de Boer, pp. 65–82. Journal for the Study of the New Testament, Supplement Series, 84. Sheffield, 1993. Analysis of the Aramaic Apocalypse.

Collins, John J. "Pseudo-Daniel Revisited." *Revue de Qumrân* 17 (1996), 111–135.

Collins, John J. "4Q242: Prayer of Nabonidus." *Qumran Cave 4: Parabiblical Texts, Part 3*, edited by George J. Brooke, John Collins, Torleif Elgvin, and Peter Flint. Discoveries in the Judaean Desert, 22. Oxford, 1996.

Collins, John J., and Peter W. Flint. "4Q243–245: Pseudo-Daniel." In *Qumran Cave 4: Parabiblical Texts, Part 3*, edited by Julio Trebolle Barrera, George J. Brooke, John Collins, Torleif Elgvin, and Peter Flint. Discoveries in the Judaean Desert, 22. Oxford, 1996.

Cross, Frank Moore. "Fragments of the Prayer of Nabonidus." *Israel Exploration Journal* 34 (1984), 260–264. Important essay on the reconstruction of the Prayer of Nabonidus.

Eisenman, Robert H., and Michael Wise. *The Dead Sea Scrolls Uncovered*. Rockport, Mass., 1992. Pages 71–74 present Four Kingdoms[a–b] (552–553 [Labeled 4Q547]).

García Martínez, Florentino. *Qumran and Apocalyptic*. Studies on the Texts of the Desert of Judah, vol. 9, Leiden, 1992. Contains essays on the Prayer of Nabonidus, Pseudo-Daniel, and the Aramaic Apocalypse.

Meyer, Rudolf. *Das Gebet des Nabonid*. Berlin, 1962. Monograph devoted to the Prayer of Nabonidus.

Milik, Józef T. "'Prière de Nabonide' et autres écrits d'un cycle de Daniel." *Revue biblique* 63 (1956), 407–415. The original publication of the Prayer of Nabonidus and the Pseudo-Daniel fragments.

Milik, Józef T. "Daniel et Susanne à Qumrân?" In *De La Tôrah au messie: Études d'exegèse et d'herméneutique bibliques offertes à Henri Cazelles*, edited by Maurice Carrez, Joseph Doré, and Pierre Grelot, pp. 337–359. Paris, 1981. Tentative (and dubious) identification of a fragment of Susanna in Aramaic.

Puech, Émile. "Fragment d'une apocalypse en araméen (4Q246 = pseudo-Dan[d]) et le 'Royaume de Dieu." *Revue biblique* 99 (1992), 98–131. Edition of the Aramaic Apocalypse with commentary.

Puech, Émile. *La croyance des esséniens en la vie future: immortalité, résurrection, vie éternelle*? 2 vols. Études bibliques, 21–22. Paris, 1993. Includes transcription of Pseudo-Daniel in vol. 1, pp. 568–570.

JOHN J. COLLINS

DARGAH, NAḤAL. *See* Murabbaʿat, Wadi.

DAVID. David's role and portrait in the Dead Sea Scrolls has much in common with what we find in the Hebrew Bible (where it occurs more than one thousand times), but has been further developed in significant ways. In the Hebrew Bible, David is an important theological symbol and a paradigmatic figure who features as: (a) Israel's greatest king and founder of Israel's foremost dynasty with whom God made a covenant; (b) the man after God's own heart who accomplished much despite his flaws; (c) the Psalmist par excellence; and (d) the inspiration for the messianic hopes of Jews and Christians.

The discussion below is confined to material found in the Qumran caves (and the Cairo Damascus Document), where references to David are conveniently grouped under four headings: (1) David as Psalmist, (2) David as Righteous Example, (3) David as a Wisdom or Prophetic Figure, and (4) David in Eschatological and Messianic Traditions. Some overlap between these categories will inevitably occur.

David as Psalmist. Any treatment of David at Qumran should include the *Psalms* scrolls, which contain material that differs markedly from our received book of 150 *Psalms*. A total of 40 *Psalms* scrolls were found in the Judean Desert (37 at Qumran), which makes the psalter by far the best represented book. Its prominence is reflected in the halakhic letter MMT[d] (4Q397 14–21; C.9–10): "the book of Moses and the books of the Prophets and David," which apparently denotes the emerging third division of the Hebrew Scriptures by the Psalter as the foremost Davidic book.

Although none of the *Psalms* scrolls is complete, it seems that Psalms 1–89 were generally in the form now preserved in the Masoretic Text. For Psalms 90 onward, however, the picture is markedly different. At least three *Psalms* scrolls (4Q87, 11Q5, and 11Q6) preserve the latter part of a distinctive Psalter, both in the presence of additional Psalms (e.g., the Apostrophe to Zion) and in the ordering of compositions (e.g., Psalms 141→133→144→155→142→143). The arrangement of such material, the inclusion of Davidic superscriptions in two Psalms (104 and 123) where these are lacking in the Masoretic Text, plus the final two autobiographical *Psalms* (*151A* and *151B*) give this "11Q5 Psalter" a far stronger Davidic character than the Masoretic Text 150 Psalter.

The statement in "David's Compositions" that David, son of Jesse, wrote 3,600 psalms and a total of 4,050 pieces (11Q5 xxvii.4–10) indicates that for its compiler David wrote many more psalms than those preserved in the Masoretic Text. These would include all or most of the "apocryphal" pieces found in Psalms[a] (11Q5, hereafter called 11QPsalms[a]) and the other *Psalms* scrolls, some of which contain Davidic superscriptions (notably *151A* and *151B* in 11QPsalms[a], and the final piece in Apocryphal Psalms[a] [11Q11]), as well as compositions found in some other scrolls (possibly Noncanonical Psalms A [4Q380] and Noncanonical Psalms B [4Q381]). "David's Compositions" also makes it clear that the number of psalms and songs written by David has some relationship to the solar calendar of 364 days. Since the calendar was related to the festivals where psalms were sung, it is not surprising to see David in a calendrical role. In *1 Chronicles* 24.1–19 he is described as the founder of the *mishmarot* or priestly shifts that feature so prominently in some calendrical texts found at Qumran. David's role in arranging the festivals and their times throughout the year is also specified in *Ben Sira* 47.10.

David as Righteous Example. Several scrolls refer to the historical David and events in his life, usually to illustrate his faithfulness to God or his virtues. Two interesting cases are *Psalms 151A* and *151B* in 11QPsalms[a], the only "Davidic" Psalms that are *unambiguously* autobiographical in terms of their content. For example, *151A* reads: "Smaller was I than my brothers, . . . so he made me shepherd of his flock. . . . He sent his prophet to anoint me, Samuel." *Psalm 151B* continues: "Then I [saw] a Philistine uttering defiances from the r[anks of the enemy]". David's triumph over Goliath is also celebrated in the War Scroll (1QM): "Indeed, Goliath the Gittite, a mighty man of valor, you delivered into the hand of David your servant, because he trusted in your great name and not in sword and spear. For the battle is yours" (1QM 11.1–2). Such passages portray David as faithful to God and as a model of piety and virtue. In a similar vein the Damascus Document states that "the deeds of David were all excellent" (CD v.5), while MMT[e] (4Q398) urges the reader to "remember David, he was a pious man" (4Q398 2.ii.1).

But David's failings are not simply ignored. The two passages quoted immediately above continue: "(were all excellent), except for the murder of Uriah, but God forgave him for that" (CD v.5–6); and "(a pious man), and indeed he was delivered from many troubles and forgiven" (4Q398 2.ii.1). As occurs earlier in the Chronicler's retelling of *Samuel* and *Kings*, several Qumran texts accentuate the positive in David and his virtues, playing down his failures and sins. Yet one more example is found in CD v (= 4Q273 frg. 5), which is critical of those who practice divorce and remarriage and quotes *Deuteronomy* 17.17 with respect to "the leader": "He shall not multiply wives to himself" (line 2). Since David had several wives and would thus be culpable, the passage proceeds to excuse David because he was unaware of this ruling: "David had not read the sealed book of the Law in the Ark; for it was not opened in Israel from the day of the death of Eleazar and Joshua and the elders who served the goddess Ashtoret. It lay buried (and was not) revealed until the appearance of Zadok."

David as a Wisdom or Prophetic Figure. David's connection with prophecy and wisdom is particularly evident in David's Compositions:

> And David, the son of Jesse, was wise, and a light like the light of the sun, and literate, and discerning and perfect in all his ways before God and men. And the Lord gave him a discerning and enlightened spirit. And he wrote . . . 4,050 (compositions). . . . All these he composed through prophecy which was given him from before the Most High. (xxvii.2–11)

The notion of David as a wisdom figure is rare in the scrolls, and is not a prominent component of his profile at Qumran. The above quotation is perhaps best viewed as serving a special function of claiming Davidic authorship and authority for the Psalter found in 11QPsalms[a] or of associating it with wisdom circles. Another relevant passage is *Pesher* Isaiah[a] (4Q161) quoting *Isaiah* 11.1–2: "[A rod will grow from] Jesse's stock, a sprout [will bloom] from his [roots]; upon him wi[ll rest] the spirit of [the Lord: a spirit of] wisdom and insight, a spirit of good coun[sel and strength], a spirit of true know[ledge and reverence for the Lord," which relates to messianism as well as wisdom (frgs. 8–10).

Although it has been claimed that David was regarded as a "prophet" at Qumran, caution seems advisable. 11QPsalms[a] tells us that he composed his works "through prophecy," but does not call him a prophet; compare *1 Samuel* 16.13, which says that the spirit of the Lord came upon David, and *2 Samuel* 23.1–7, which describes his last words as an "oracle" or "declaration." The evidence seems to suggest that at Qumran David was associated with prophecy, but falls short of identifying him as an actual prophet. Such caution seems justified in view of the apparent distinction between "the books of the Prophets" and "David" in MMT[e] (quoted above). The notion of David as prophet is evident in the New Testament (*Acts* 2.30–31), and is more fully articulated in rabbinic writings such as the Babylonian Talmud: "Who are the first prophets? Rabbi Huna said: 'They are David, Samuel, and Solomon'" (B.T., *Sot*. 48b).

David in Eschatological and Messianic Traditions. References to David in this section are of two main types, both of which are significant for messianic expectation in the Qumran scrolls. First, some texts refer to David's kingship or eschatological themes without overt reference to the Qumran *yaḥad* or its distinctive doctrines. One example is the Words of the Luminaries[a] (4Q504), which affirms God's covenant with David and the everlasting Davidic dynasty: "And you chose the tribe of Judah, and your covenant you established with David so that he would be like a shepherd, a prince over your people, and would sit on the throne of Israel in your presence for ever" (4Q504 frg. 4.5–8). Such imagery is often reminiscent of biblical texts, in this case Psalm 89.3–4 and *2 Chronicles* 21.1.

The second group of texts in this category are more closely associated with the Qumran covenanters or contain "sectarian" language or imagery characteristic of the *yaḥad*. One rather intricate example is CD vii.15–17 (= Damascus Document[d], 4Q269 frg. 5), which understands the "fallen tent of David" that will be set up again (*Am.* 9.11) as referring to the king or leader of the nation. The Florilegium (4Q174 frg. 3.10–13) affirms the "throne of his kingdom [for e]ver" (*2 Sm.* 7.13) and interprets the "son" of *2 Samuel* 7.14 as the "Shoot of David, who is to arise with the Interpreter of the Law, and who will [arise] in Zi[on in the La]st Days." Like CD vii, this text also quotes *Amos* 9.11, specifically stating that "this passage describes the fallen Branch of David, [w]hom He shall raise up to deliver Israel." Another relevant text is the Commentary on Genesis A (4Q252 1.v.1–6) on *Genesis* 49.10, which also affirms the everlasting Davidic dynasty ("[And] the one who sits on the throne of David [shall never] be cut off"), the coming of "the Righteous Messiah, the Branch of David," and the giving of "the covenant of the kingdom of his people to him and to his seed" for ever, because [this king] "has kept . . . the law together with the men of the *yaḥad*."

The *pesher* on Isaiah[a] quotes *Isaiah* 11.1–5 as referring to "[the Branch of] David, who will appear in the Las[t Days]." This passage offers several more characteristics of the coming Davidic messiah: for example, the spirit of the Lord will rest upon him, a spirit of wisdom and insight, of good counsel and strength, of true knowledge and reverence for the Lord, and he will delight in reverence for the Lord. But the War Rule (4Q285) tells us that this messiah will also judge and slay his enemies: "A shoot shall come out from the stump of Jesse [and a branch shall grow out of his roots (*Is*. 10.34–11.1). This is the] Branch of David. Then [all forces of Belial] shall be judged, [and the king of the *Kittim* shall stand for judgment] and the Leader of the nation—the Bra[nch of David]—will have him put to death. [Then all Israel shall come out with timbrel]s and dancers, and the [High] Priest shall order [them to cleanse their bodies from the guilty blood of the c]orpse[s of] the *Kittim*" (4Q285 frg. 5.2–6).

The references to David in the Qumran scrolls build on themes in the Hebrew Bible but also offer new emphases. Most prominent is the fuller and more extensive picture of David as Psalmist, and as a messianic figure whose throne and kingdom will last for ever and who will judge and slay his enemies.

[*See also* Messiahs; Psalms Scroll.]

BIBLIOGRAPHY

Evans, C. A. "David in the Dead Sea Scrolls." In *The Scrolls and the Scriptures*, edited by S. E. Porter and C. A. Evans, pp. 183–197. Roehampton Institute London Papers, 3; JSPSup, 26. Sheffield, England, 1997.

Fitzmyer, J. "David, Being Therefore a Prophet . . . ? (*Acts* 2.30)," *CBQ* 34 (1972), 332–339.

Fokkelman, J. P. "David." *Harpers Bible Commentary* (1985), 208–211.

Howard, D., Jr. "David." *Anchor Bible Dictionary* 2.41–49.

Petersen, D. L. "Portraits of David: Canonical and Otherwise." *Iliff Review* 42 (1985), 2–21.

Pomykala, K. *The Davidic Tradition in Early Judaism: Its History and Significance for Messianism*. SBLEJL, 7. Atlanta, 1995.

Roger, C. L., Jr. " The Promises to David in Early Judaism." *Bibliotheca Sacra* 150 (1993), 285–302.

Sanders, J. A. *The Psalms Scroll of Qumrân Cave 11 [11QPs[a]]*. Discoveries in the Judaean Desert, 4. Oxford, 1965.

Sanders, J. A. *The Dead Sea Psalms Scroll*. Ithaca, N.Y., 1967.

Wise, M., M. Abegg Jr., and E. Cook. *The Dead Sea Scrolls: A New Translation*. San Francisco, 1996.

PETER W. FLINT

DAVID, NAḤAL. *See* Sdeir, Wadi.

DEAD SEA. With its northern shore located about 20 kilometers (13 miles) due east of Jerusalem, the Dead Sea figures prominently in biblical, Jewish, and Christian literature. The name *Dead Sea* was first used by Pausanias (*Perigesis* 5.7, 4–5) in the second century CE. In the Hebrew scriptures, it is most frequently called "Salt Sea" (e.g., *Gn*. 14.3 and other texts in the Hexateuch), "Sea of Arabah" (e.g., *Dt*. 3.17), and "Eastern Sea" (in relation to Jerusalem, e.g., *Ezek*. 47.18). In *2 Esdras* 5.7, sometimes in Josephus, and in the Talmud, it is the "Sea of Sodom" (e.g., Josephus, *Jewish Antiquities* 5.1.22; B.T., *Shab*. 108b); Greek and Roman writers, including also at times Josephus, called it "Sea of Asphalt" (e.g., Pliny, *Natural History* 5.15.15); Arabic literature calls it "Sea of Sodom and Gomorrah," "Sea of Zoʿar," and, since medieval times, "Sea of Lot"; a few European travelers called it "The Devil's Sea." Early Greek writers who mention it include Aristotle (*Meteorology* 2.3, 39) and Strabo (5.2.42). The mineralogical importance of the region was known from very ancient times. Alexander the Great's generals Antigonus and Demetrius tried, but failed, to subdue the Nabateans of the region in order to get at the minerals (Diodorus 19.95–96). The southern end of the Dead Sea was known for its bitumen even in biblical times (*Gn*. 14.10).

Physical Properties. The Dead Sea is one of the most interesting geographical features of the earth. The area immediately around it is the lowest spot on the planet not covered with water, and the sea itself contains the highest proportion of salts of any major body of water. It is rapidly becoming a major tourist attraction for those wishing to float in its buoyant waters and others who fancy health and beauty advantages in its mineral-rich water and black mud.

The geological existence of the Dead Sea is the result of plate tectonics in which the Mediterranean plate, which includes Palestine, is pulling away from the Arabian plate, creating the Great Rift Valley. This is a deep graben, or trough-shaped, valley, stretching from southern Turkey to eastern Africa, a distance of about 6,000 kilometers (3,500 miles). It includes the Beqaʿ Valley of Lebanon, the Hulah-Galilee-Jordan-Dead Sea-Arabah Valleys of Palestine, the Red Sea, and the Olduvai Gorge of eastern Africa. This geological activity causes frequent earthquakes in the region as the continental plates pull apart in relatively small blocks of land between transverse faults.

About 100,000 years ago, the Red Sea stretched into the Great Rift Valley up to the Galilee basin. Over time, this long bay shrank to a large inland saline sea called Lake Lisan, named after the peninsula which divides the present Dead Sea into two parts (*lisan* means "tongue" in Arabic). It extended from the Galilee basin in the north to a point about 30 kilometers (18 miles) south of the present Dead Sea and was about 200 meters (700 feet) higher than today's level. Alluvial deposits built up in the lake as rivers flowed into it; they are preserved today as light-colored gravels known geologically as *Lisan marls*. Many ancient sites in the Jordan and Dead Sea Valleys, including Qumran, were built on ridges made up of this marl. They tend to reach out into the valley, providing excellent strategic locations, often with perennial streams flowing beside them, especially those on the eastern side of the valley.

The present Dead Sea is the remnant of Lake Lisan. Until recently, it extended about 80 kilometers (45 miles) in length and was an average of 14 kilometers (9 miles) wide. Now, because of intensive irrigation agriculture by both Israelis and Jordanians, the level of the Sea has fallen over 10 meters (33 feet) and the bay south of the Lisan Peninsula has largely disappeared. Indeed, except for a small canal built by Israeli chemical companies, there is dry ground from Masada in the west to the Lisan Peninsula. As a result, the Dead Sea is considerably smaller than it was thirty years ago. However, there is literary and archaeological evidence that the level of the Sea has oscillated significantly through time. A Roman road probably crossed on dry ground from the Lisan Peninsula toward Masada, indicating that the level of the sea was similar to that of today and making Masada, which was occupied at that time, less remote than its recent isolation would suggest. At an even earlier period, the story in *2 Chronicles* 20.2 would make more sense if the Ammonites and Moabites had crossed here as well.

After the recent drop in level, the Dead Sea shoreline today is slightly more than 400 meters (1,325 feet) below sea level; the bottom of the sea in the northeastern portion is another 400 meters deep. Mean monthly temperatures range from 13 to 32.5 degrees Celsius (55 to 90.5 degrees Fahrenheit) with a mean extreme monthly range from 10 to 45 degrees Celsius (40 to 113 Fahrenheit). Because of its depth and location in the rain shadow behind the Judean hills, the region gets very little rain, about 100 millimeters (2.5 inches) in the north and only 20 to 30 millimeters (1 inch) in the south. The high temperatures, long periods of solar radiation, and lack of rain cause a high rate of evaporation, estimated by some to be about 1.4 meters (55 inches) per year. This evaporation is an important part of the regional climate, especially for the areas to the east of the sea, which receive some of that evaporation as rain during the winter months and as dew during the summer. Both the Israelis and Jordanians use the resources of the sea for tourism and chemical exports. Both countries are likewise concerned with the drop in level. Two large-scale engineering projects have been proposed to solve the problem. The first, called the Med-

Dead solution, would construct a canal from the Mediterranean Sea, bringing water through a closed canal and tunnel system beneath the hill country and into the Dead Sea. The second, called Red-Dead solution, would see an open canal flowing through the Arabah from the Red Sea. Most solutions accept the need for continued usage of runoff for irrigation, meaning that very little rainwater will flow into the Dead Sea in the foreseeable future.

Because the sea has no outlet, the salts flushed into it by the rivers over thousands of years, made all the stronger by large concentrations of rock salt in the mountains along the southwestern coast, have raised the salt content of the Dead Sea almost 30 percent, almost ten times that of the oceans. The salts include chlorides of magnesium, sodium, calcium, and potassium, as well as magnesium bromide. Magnesium chloride constitutes the largest amount. The salt density allows swimmers to float nicely, but it also causes a strong burning sensation to open sores and causes pain to the eyes. The water appears "oily" to sight and touch, but this is more apparent than real: Rocks under the water are not slippery and fresh water easily washes off the thin sheen of salts. Moreover, no oil floats on the surface. Estimates suggest that there are about 135 cubic kilometers of water in the Dead Sea, containing approximately 44 billion tons of salts.

The heaviest concentration of salts is in the lowest level of the sea, below 40 meters (130 feet), in the northern part of the sea. This water layer seems to be "fossil" water; that is, it has been in its present state for millennia. The thick brine in the lower level has deposited extremely thick layers of salts at the bottom.

Settlement Patterns. In spite of the adverse climate during the long summer months and the impossibility of using Dead Sea water for any type of agriculture, the environs of the Dead Sea were almost never bereft of settlements. There are several reasons for this. The depth of the Great Rift Valley meant that significant springs gushed forth from a variety of locations, including that of ʿEin-Feshkha just south of Qumran. The winter rains in the eastern highlands provided several perennial streams which flowed into the sea and the Arabah just to its south. These could be irrigated into highly productive agricultural areas (*Gn.* 13.10) which can, when well managed, produce three or four crops a year, providing a boom economy for its inhabitants. In *Genesis* 13, Lot's choice of the Sodom area seems to reflect this type of situation. Certainly, except for a short time in the winter, this is not an enviable climate for a happy existence. The economic rewards need to be significant for occupation to flourish. Political stability was also necessary for sedentary occupation (nomads probably always came down to the valley during the winter, as the bedouin still do in Jordan today). Generally, settled activity was at its greatest when a strong political organization controlled the highlands on either side of the valley.

Settlement patterns fall into two geographic zones, divided by the major escarpments on both the west and east sides of the sea, roughly one third of the way from north to south. The escarpment on the east rises in a series of cliffs and terraces about 1,600 meters (about one mile) to the highlands above. The cliffs on the east are similar, but not quite so abrupt. Before the present drop in the level of the sea, cliffs descended directly into the sea on the east and nearly so on the west. There is very little evidence for ancient roads traversing the shoreline from north to south on either side. The Israelis built the present highway on the west only after the 1967 war, and the Jordanians completed a new highway on the east early in the 1990s. Construction crews for both highways needed to dynamite portions of the cliffs. This meant that, in ancient times, communication from the northern to the southern parts of the Dead Sea could occur only by roads ascending high into the hills surrounding the sea or by boat.

This difficulty of north-south communication seems to be represented in the settlement patterns. Many sites have been found by surveys on the broad plains and valleys bordering the southeastern shores of the sea, including every period from Paleolithic flint scatters (above the level of Lake Lisan which was present at the time) to modern times. Except for Stone Age settlements, when the climate was probably wetter and colder (at least during global glacial periods), most inhabitants probably desired the economic advantages of year-round irrigation agriculture. Especially significant were the many small settlements of almost every period around the perennial streams at Wadi Isal, Safi (Wadi Hasa) and Feifeh at the southeastern edge of the sea. These include everything from sherd scatters to fortresses to major towns. The most important excavated sites in this area include the Early Bronze Age (third millennium BCE) sites of Bab edh-Dhraʿ and Numeira; Deir ʿAin Abata was a Byzantine monastery dedicated to St. Lot. There are several important unexcavated sites from most other periods, including Iron II fortresses (the time of the Hebrew kings), Roman fortresses and towns, Byzantine monasteries and towns, Crusader anchorages, and medieval Arab settlements (sugar plantations).

Excavations on the western shore have exposed a Chalcolithic temple (fourth millennium BCE) as well as an Iron Age, Persian, and Hasmonean town at ʿEin-Gedi. Hellenistic (Hasmonean), Roman, and Byzantine settlements seem to have existed at ʿEin-Buqeq and, at least from the Roman and Byzantine periods, at Masada. Evidence for shipping on the sea comes from literary sources for the Roman period, when Vespasian pursued rebellious Jews by ship (Josephus, *The Jewish War* 3.9.522–531). The Madaba mosaic map from the Byzantine period depicts two sailboats on the sea, apparently shipping grain south and bitumen north. The Crusaders also supplied their castles at Kerak and Shobak by shipping across the sea.

The northern shores of the sea, where Qumran and the caves of the Dead Sea Scrolls are located, supported fewer settlements in virtually every period, probably because of the limited space between the sea and the cliffs and the lack of water resources. Although the oasis at Jericho is a bit removed from the sea, it contained one of the most important Neolithic (c.10,000 BCE) settlements in Palestine; arguably the most important Chalcolithic (5,000–3,500 BCE) site was at Tuleilat Ghassul, near the northeastern edge of the sea, but other sites also existed in caves of the Wadi Murabba'at and Tell Azeimeh, near Ghassul. Bronze Age sites (3,500–1,200 BCE) are rare—the most important was at Jericho.

Near the end of the Iron II period (seventh and sixth centuries BCE), small agricultural sites arose in the Buqei'a plateau above the cliffs to the west of Qumran, and small fortresses and settlements have been found by excavations and surveys at Qumran, 'Ein-Feshkha, and two other locations along the sea, south of Qumran. These were undoubtedly connected with the Kingdom of Judah from the time of Hezekiah to the Babylonian conquest. The Iron Age site at Tell Azeimeh may have been Ammonite.

With the extension of Hasmonean control across the valley to the highlands of Transjordan, including Heshbon, near Mount Nebo, other small settlements sprouted up: at Qumran, 'Ein-Feshkha, Khirbet Sweimeh, and Zara. The latter site, probably to be identified with Roman Callirhoë, had thirty-eight separate thermal springs ranging in temperature from 45 to 64 degrees Celsius (113–147 degrees Fahrenheit). Herod the Great frequented them during the winter (Josephus, *The Jewish War* 1.33.5). The site may have been on a road to Transjordan, which split north of the Dead Sea, one branch ascending to Machaerus (a fortress site on a prominent hill much like that of Herodium) in the south and the other to Amman (Philadelphia of the Decapolis), perhaps via Heshbon, in the north. These sites continued into the early Roman (or Herodian) period and were contemporary with Qumran. With a flourishing settlement pattern in the highlands on both sides of the Rift Valley, as well as royal Herodian palaces at Jericho and Machaerus, there must have been considerable traffic on a major road crossing the valley south of Jericho going from Jerusalem to the Amman area. Qumran was not far from this road, and we should probably not consider it to have been as isolated as is sometimes assumed. Although it does not seem to have been ideally suited as a way station on this road, the site was not difficult to access by travelers.

The region again saw activity (but not very much of the settled variety) in the late Roman period with the Bar Kokhba rebellion (caves in the Wadi Murabba'at and coins at 'Ein-Feshkha). In the Byzantine period a monastery was built at 'Ein-Feshkha, and surveys have shown other settlements at Khirbet Sweimeh and Tell Azeimeh. The Ayyubid/Mamluk period (thirteenth-fifteenth centuries CE) probably saw sugar plantations at the last two sites as well.

Very little human activity took place in the Dead Sea area during the Ottoman Empire. Two early European explorers met their demise while trying to navigate the sea: C. Costigan died in 1837 when a storm shipwrecked him on the Lisan Peninsula without food and water; T. Molyneux died in 1847 shortly after he returned to Beirut after going by boat from Galilee to the Dead Sea. The first potash and bromine works began in 1930 on the northwest coast of the Sea at Rabbat Ashlag.

LARRY G. HERR

DEATH. To a certain degree, ancient Israel shared the concepts of life and death that are common to the literatures of the Near East, well known for the abundance of elaborate rituals to ward off the malevolent action of divinities, demons, and spirits associated with death and the underworld. Some mythological accounts retell the efforts of heroes in search of immortality, such as Gilgamesh, who set out to seek the plant of life for his friend Enkidu. The figure of Gilgamesh is still attested in a few Aramaic fragments from Cave 4 (Book of Giants[b–c] 4Q530–531). [*See* Giants, Book of.] Also, to counter the destructive powers of illness and death, such as those of Resheph, the god of the plague (*Hb.* 3.5, *Jb.* 5.7, etc.), people developed incantations, invented various protective charms, and institutionalized certain practices. These practices, which initially arose out of polytheistic beliefs, did not totally vanish from the monotheistic religion of Israel. These included a belief in the power of insatiable Death, necromancy, a certain cult of the dead, and the use of all sorts of talismans. Apocryphal Psalms[a] (11Q11) bears witness to the use of psalms of exorcism attributed to David; Songs of the Sage[a–b] (4Q510–511) may also play a comparable role.

Death, the "return to dust," is seen as the normal end of life (*2 Sm.* 14.14) when a person dies in the fullness of days, leaving behind descendants (*Gn.* 25.8); but death poses a dilemma as an injustice when it occurs prematurely. Biblical etiology, then, suggests that death is the consequence of disobeying God. Along with suffering it is a punishment imposed on humanity, since God is the origin of life and death (*Dt.* 32.39). Thus biblical humanity praises God for his total mastery, and praise is a sign of life just as the inability to praise is a sign of death (Ps. 30.9–10; 6.6; 88.11–13; *Is.* 38.9–20; Qumran hymns and prayers). [*See* Psalms, Hymns, and Prayers.] For their part, the wisdom texts associate life with the path of justice, while the way of perversity leads to death (*Prv.* 12.28; 15.24, etc.). [*See* Wisdom Texts.] Therefore what matters is to follow Lady Wisdom and not Lady Folly. Every sensible man ought to flee the foreign woman (cf. Wiles of the Wicked Woman, 4Q184) who would lead him into sin and death. [*See* Wiles of the Wicked Woman.] In making life choices each one has a personal responsibility. The just are destined for the resurrection, to be awakened from the dust of the dead, while the wicked are doomed to punishments and everlasting disgrace (*Is.* 26, *Dn.* 12, Ages of Creation 4Q181, etc.).

This biblical conception is found again in the New Testament where Paul affirms that the "wages of sin" is death (*Rm.* 6.23), that death came through one man, and that all die in Adam (*1 Cor.* 15.21–22, *Rm.* 5.12–21). God alone is immortal (*1 Tm.* 6.16); every person is mortal (*Heb.* 9.27) except Enoch (*Gn.* 5.24, *Heb.* 11.5) and Elijah (*2 Kgs.* 2.11, *Sir.* 48.9, 48.12), who were taken up into heaven. But the gift of immortality is promised at the return to everyone who believes in Christ (*1 Cor.* 15.53). By his death and resurrection the second Adam has obtained justification that gives life (*Rm.* 5.10, 18). He has overthrown Death and Sin (*1 Cor.* 15.26, 56; *Heb.* 2.14; *Tim.* 1.10) Death could not keep in its power the Lord of the living and the dead (*Acts* 2.24, *Rm.* 14.9). Christ has received the keys of Death and Hades (*Rv.* 1.18). Seen in the light of the resurrection of Jesus, death is no longer any more than a break, not the end of human life; it is even a gain since "life is Christ" (*Phil.* 1.21), eternal life already experienced by the believer (*Jn.* 3.36) but lived in its fullness at the time of judgment in the transformation into glory (*1 Cor.* 15.50–53, *1 Thes.* 4.16–18). The New Testament attests the belief in a general resurrection, following *Daniel* 12 (Septuagint) and other Jewish writings, for rewards and punishments (*Rv.* 20), with the punishment of the Devil who was a murderer from the beginning (*Jn.* 8.44) and of the Beast in the fire, and the appearance of the heavenly Jerusalem, of a new heaven and a new earth (*Rv.* 21). But it is the Messiah Jesus, seated upon the throne of glory, who welcomes the just into the Kingdom and sends the damned away into everlasting fire (*Mt.* 25.31–46).

Somewhat at the pivotal point between the world of the Old Testament and that of the New Testament is where we find the Essene conceptions of death, life after death, the last judgment, the eternal punishments of the wicked (Jews and pagans) and of Belial and the evil angels, and in contrast the rewards of the just Essenes in the company of the angels. [*See* Angels; Eternal Life; Heaven; *and* Resurrection.] The vocabulary is nearly the same: *mwt*, ("die"); *ʾsp*, ("gather"); *hrg*, ("kill"); *ʾbd*, ("perish"); *nkh*, ("smite"); *ḥll*, ("pierce"); *tmm*, ("be complete") or metaphorically *shkb* ("sleep"), although it is even richer in the non-Essene texts with *yshn* ("sleep"), *lwn* ("lodge"). However, only the Qumran texts use *gpʾ* for the wicked who fall stone cold into Hell, and the image of the bridge (Messianic Apocalypse 4Q521 5.ii). These words have to be related to the noun *Death* as the "return to dust" of the creature made of clay, and to the abstract terms *Sheol*, *Abaddon*, *abyss*, *darkness*, *punishments*, *extermination*, (as opposed to *healing*, *life*, *length of days*, *light and eternal joys*, *peace*, *glory of Adam*, *delights*, *crown of glory*, *eternal rest*, *rewards*). This vocabulary, directly linked to individual eschatology, should be connected to the images of collective eschatology: resurrection, Visitation, eternal Judgment, universal conflagration, and renewal of creation, which follow upon the images of the Messianic kingdom and the eschatological war that seals the victory of the good over the evil. Sheol is no longer the place of no return where God would abandon the just.

This vocabulary and these images show that Essene eschatology inherited the prevalent Jewish and biblical conception but adapted it to its own conception of the sole elect remnant, the true Israel, for whom the Teacher of Righteousness was recipient of revelations of the divine mysteries. [*See* Teacher of Righteousness.] Thus, following upon the religious experience of a life of intimacy with God perceived by the biblical person, of the happiness of paradise lost and yet awaited in the life to come, the Qumran texts emphasize the election and the favors of which the members of the community are presently beneficiaries, until the fulfillment of the divine promises in the life to come. Of course this eschatological fulfillment depends on commitment and acting in the present, hence the experience of the faithful one who already lives in communion with God in the company of the angels. However, he awaits the prolongation of this communion in the eternity of the end of time, beyond death, according to a paradigm of altogether individual and collective eschatology, while strongly underscoring the personal identity of the beneficiary of the eternal rewards (Hodayot[a] from Cave 1 at Qumran [hereafter, 1QHodayot[a]], 1QH[a] xi [iii].)

Far from being a belief in reincarnation or reanimation of a corpse, the resurrection of the dead or the glorification of the living faithful is awaited as the entry into eternal life in the presence of God. Personal identity is emphasized by the resurrection of individual bodies as already found in Visions of Amram[f]? (4Q548 1.ii), but also in Pseudo-Ezekiel[a–d] (4Q385, 386–387, 388), Messianic Apocalypse (4Q521), *Ages of Creation*, necropolises of Khirbat Qumran and of ʿEin-el-Ghweir, and the *Elenchos* of Hippolytus concerning the belief of the Essenes. [*See* Amram; Ezekiel, Book of, *article on* Pseudo-Ezekiel; *and* Visions.] This conception is subsequently shared by the Pharisees, particularly the School of Shammai, and the New Testament, but rejected by the Sadducees. [*See* Pharisees; Sadducees.]

Visions of Amran[f]? (4Q548 1.ii.12–16) already links victory over death and the illumination of the just to the great judgment and to the resurrection along the lines of *Isaiah* 26, thus anticipating *Daniel* 12. Taking up the vision of *Ezekiel* 37, Pseudo-Ezekiel from Cave 4 at Qumran (which may be an Essene composition) places that victory in a context of the individual retribution of the just at the end of the time of distress, the resurrection of the faithful at the end of time being the reward for their present devotion. In an exhortation to the devout to persevere in their choice, the Messianic Apocalypse outlines the stages in the divine plan of salvation: first the blessings that God himself will accomplish upon the arrival of the messianic times that have been prepared by the return of Elijah: "He shall heal the wounded, the dead he shall raise up. . . ." (4Q521 i.ii–iii); then at the judgment at the end of time when God will act with power as in the first creation: "the damned shall be destined for death [when] the life-giver shall [rai]se the dead of his people," for in his justice "the Lord [has delivered] the son[s of dea]th and has opened" [next come the allusions to the "valley of death] . . . , and the bridge of the Abyss [. . . , the damned have petrified] . . . , and the heavens have welcomed [the just . . . and al]l the angels" (4Q521 5.ii, 7). [*See* Messianic Apocalypse.] These lines are the most explicit of all the Qumran texts for the description of the End of Days: the last judgment with the allusion to the punishments of the damned in Hell, where they fall rigid and frozen, while the Lord rewards the blessed by raising up the dead and delivering the living from death, which was the common lot of mankind. The just man does not have to fear death, because God will again bestow life on him, restoring to him the glory that was lost and welcoming him into the company of the angels. This text foreshadows *Matthew* 24.31–46, in particular, with its conception of the eternal rewards and punishments connected with the last judgment, although it had not yet, in the biblical rereadings of the synagogues (Septuagint, *targums*), gone as far as in favor of a belief in a general resurrection. It remains at the stage of resurrection and glorification for the just alone, the Essene faithful. But it also shows some extrabiblical influences, Zoroastrian to be more precise, that came from Persia (e.g., the *Bridge of the Abyss*).

This Essene belief in the resurrection as victory over death, which Josephus (*The Jewish War* 2.151–158) fairly well distorted when he attributed to Essenes neo-Pythagorean beliefs about the fall of immortal souls, which death frees from the prison of their bodies, was properly transmitted by the *Elenchos* of Hippolytus of Rome (9.27–29). He affirms the immortality of the soul, the intermediate state, the resurrection of the body for the just, the judgment, the universal conflagration, and the eternal punishments of the wicked. [*See* Hippolytus; Josephus Flavius.] The image of the conflagration can be read in several places including 1QHodayot[a] (1QH[a] xi.20–37 [= iii.19–36], xiv.38 [= vi.35], the Florilegium (4Q174 1–3.ii; see *1 Pt*. 4.12), and the image of the renewal of creation at the judgment in the Rule of the Community from Cave 1 at Qumran (1QS iv.25, cf. 1QH[a] xix.16–17 [= xi 13–14], 28–29 [= xiii.11–12]. [*See* Florilegium; Hodayot; Rule of the Community.] Thus, even though the later expression *teḥiyyat ha-metim* (Mishna *Sanhedrin* ["resurrection of the dead"] 10.1) is not used, the belief in the resurrection is present in the Essene texts, just as it is in the Hebrew scriptures or the apocryphal texts (see also 1QH[a] xiv.32–39 [= vi 29–36], 4Q181 1.ii.3–6, where "the just shall be destined for life" while "the wicked shall be for everlasting disgrace"; cf. 4Q521 7, "the damned shall be destined for death"). But this does not require their resurrection for judgment and damnation, as will later be the case in Pharisaic and Christian circles (second death).

As expected, this belief, which is rooted in the scriptures (*Isaiah* 26 and *Daniel* 12 are very frequently cited in the manuscripts) and is reflected in some of the apocryphal books (*1 Enoch*, Visions of Amram from Cave 4 at Qumran more particularly), influenced the funeral practice of the Qumran communities. [*See* Cemeteries.] The individual tombs and the cemeteries of Khirbet Qumran, which are aligned south-north, are clearly turned away from the Holy City and its temple administered by wicked hands in order to look toward the north where, according to *1 Enoch*, the paradise of righteousness, the divine throne, the reservoir of souls, the tree of life, and the New Jerusalem are found. Thus, upon being awakened, the deceased (man/Essene) will arise facing the north in order to enter into the paradise of the blessed. It is likely that, following *Deuteronomy* 32.43, the Essenes may have attributed to the land of Israel a power to purify the flesh of sin while they await the resurrection. This would explain the individual tombs directly in the ground without any disturbance of the bones during their eternal rest, in contrast to the *ossilegium* (common bone repository) of family tombs and even the use of ossuaries afterward. Victory over death, seen as the consequence of Adam's sin, is to restore the just Essene to the glory of Adam, an immortal being living once again in intimate relationship with God in a new world. Since death and the tomb were not seen as the end of an Essene's existence—in contrast to the view of the Sadducees, the resurrection of the body is not awaited as a reanimation of a corpse or a return to former life, but as a re-creation of the person in eternal glory in the company of the angels.

[*See also* Essenes; Religious Beliefs, Qumran Sect.]

BIBLIOGRAPHY

Cavallin, Hans C. C. *Life after Death. Paul's Argument for the Resurrection of the Dead in I Cor 15.* Part I. *An Enquiry into the Jewish Background.* Coniectanea biblica, New Testament Series, 7. Lund, 1974.

Nickelsburg, George W. E. *Resurrection, Immortality, and Eternal Life in Intertestamental Judaism.* Harvard Theological Studies, 26. Cambridge, 1972. Succinct presentation.

Puech, Émile. *La croyance des Esséniens en la vie future: immortalité, résurrection, vie éternelle? Histoire d'une croyance dans le Judaïsme ancien.* I—*La résurrection des morts et le contexte scripturaire.* II—*Les donnés qumraniennes et classiques.* Études bibliques 21–22. Paris, 1993. Exhaustive and detailed study of the context of Qumran and the Qumran texts.

ÉMILE PUECH

Translated from French by Robert E. Shillen

DEEDS OF SALE. The so-called Samaria papyri were discovered in 1962–1963 in a cave at Wadi ed-Daliyeh near Jericho, where wealthy people from Samaria hid their documents and themselves during the revolt against Alexander the Great (331 BCE). Twenty-seven documents survived, mostly slave conveyances, one sale of a house (WDSP 15), one sale of a vineyard (WDSP 16), and one receipt of payment (WDSP 17, the only "double document"). All were written in Samaria ("the city/citadel in Samaria the province"). The language is Imperial Aramaic, the legal tradition neo-Babylonian. The earliest document dates from 375 or 365 BCE and the latest from 335 BCE.

The formulary of a slave conveyance starts with the date (day, Babylonian-Jewish month, and the accession year of Artaxerxes II, Artaxerxes III, or Darius III) and the place of execution (Samaria). (Some documents conclude with the date and place of execution.) There follows a description of the sale (the object and its provenance; the description of the slave), the name of the seller and of the buyer, and the "exact and full price" *(shḥrtts dmyn gmyrn)*. Then follows the confirmation of payment and of taking possession of the object, along with the clause that confers upon the buyer and his sons the power of disposition of the object. Next is a long clause in which the seller guarantees his performance of the contract. This is made in the framework of an obligatory covenant (*'srh*) established between the parties. It contains the defension clause: in the case of litigation involving the object, the seller agrees to restore the object to its former purity (cleansing clause), and if the seller violates the covenant by denying the sale or the payment or by returning the payment made by the buyer, the seller remains liable and has to pay a penalty to the buyer without litigation (tenfold the amount of the purchase price; the penalty clause). This obligatory covenant ends with a clause that again confirms the buyer in his power of disposition of the object. The deed of sale ends with the validation of the document: executed before provincial officials (like "the governor of Samaria") and the following witnesses, whose seals are affixed.

The private legal documents found since 1951 in the caves near Khirbet Qumran, in Wadi Murabbaʿat, Khabra, and Naḥal Ṣe'elim, include twenty-nine deeds of sale: three in Hebrew, twenty in Aramaic, six (?) in Nabatean, and two in Greek.

Hebrew: deed of sale of land Mur 22, deed of sale Mur 29, deed of sale of plot Mur 30; outer text of contract (Kefar Baru) XḤev/Se 8.

Aramaic: sales of land 4Q345–346; deed of sale? Mur 23, deed of sale of land Mur 25, deeds of sale Mur 26–28 (Mur 26 is now together with deed of land sale XḤev/Se 49, now promissory note on parchment XḤev/Se 50), fragments of deeds of sale Mur 31; sale of donkey 5/6Ḥev 8 (not yet published), deed of sale of half of a garden I 5/6Ḥev 47a (not yet published), deed of sale of half of a garden II 5/6Ḥev 47b (not yet published); contract XḤev/Se 7, contract (Kefar Baru) XḤev/Se 8; contract (Kefar Bario?) XḤev/Se 8a; deed XḤev/Se 9, deed of sale XḤev/Se 21, unclassified document XḤev/Se 22, deed XḤev/Se 23, deed of land sale XḤev/Se 49 (now together with Mur 26 as XḤev/Se 50).

Nabatean (all unpublished): sales of property 5/6Ḥev 2–3, sale 5/6Ḥev 4, lease of land? 5/6Ḥev 6, quittance 5/6Ḥev 9; contract XḤev/Se Nab. 1.

Greek: purchase of a date crop 5/6Ḥev 21, sale of a date crop 5/6Ḥev 22.

The oldest documents are sales of land 4Q345 (Accelerator Mass Spectrometry date 373–171 BCE) and 4Q346 (late first century BCE), followed by the Nabatean sales of property 5/6Ḥev 2–3 and sale 5/6Ḥev 4 (99 CE), the sale of a donkey 5/6Ḥev 8 (122 CE), the Greek purchase and sale of a date crop 5/6Ḥev 21–22 (130 CE), and, from the time of the Bar Kokhba Revolt (c.132–135 CE), deed of sale of land Mur 22, deed of sale? Mur 23, and deed of sale Mur 29 (132 CE); promissory note on parchment XḤev/Se 50 (formerly XḤev/Se 49; 133 CE); deed of sale of land Mur 25 (134 CE); contracts XḤev/Se 7 and (Kefar Bario?) XḤev/Se 8a (134/35 CE); and contract (Kefar Baru) XḤev/

Se 8, deed of sale of plot Mur 30, and deeds of sale of half of a garden I and II 5/6Ḥev 47a–47b (135 CE). Documents whose dates are unclear but are before 135 CE are deeds of sale Mur 27–28, fragments of deeds of sale Mur 31, deed XḤev/Se 9, deed of sale XḤev/Se 21, unclassified document XḤev/Se 22, and deed XḤev/Se 23.

All documents are written on papyrus, with the Hebrew and Aramaic ones written in a more or less cursive script (a modification of the Jewish square script), the Nabataean ones in a Nabatean cursive script (a predecessor of the Arabic script), and the Greek ones in more or less a bookhand script. [*See* Paleography.]

The language of the Hebrew documents is proto-Mishnaic (with Aramaisms), and the Aramaic documents are in post-Achaemenid Imperial Aramaic (with Hasmonean characteristics and influenced by the spoken Judean Aramaic; Beyer, 1984). The Nabatean ones are in Nabatean Aramaic (influenced by the spoken Arabic; Beyer, 1984), and the Greek ones are in postclassical Koine Greek (with Semitisms; Lewis, 1989, pp. 13–16).

Except for the Aramaic sale of donkey 5/6Ḥev 8, contract (Kefar Bario?) XḤev/Se 8a (not clear Mur 27; 4Q346; XḤev/Se 23), Nabatean quittance 5/6Ḥev 9, and Greek purchase and sale of a date crop 5/6Ḥev 21–22, all documents are so-called double documents (cf. *Jer.* 32.10–15; *B.B.* X,1.2; T. *B.B.* XI,1; Koffmahn, 1968); that is, the text is written twice on one side. The upper one (the inner text) is mostly an abridged version written in a strongly cursive script, rolled and tied up and sealed for protection against forging. The one below (the outer text) is only folded, so that it could be read every time. The signatures of the parties and of the witnesses are written on the back of the outer text at a right angle to the script on the front. The inner and outer text are written upside down in deeds of sale of half of a garden I and II 5/6Ḥev 47a–b, and in contract (Kefar Baru) XḤev/Se 8, the languages differ (the inner text is Aramaic, the outer text Hebrew). So-called simple documents are sale of donkey 5/6Ḥev 8; contract (Kefar Bario?) XḤev/Se 8a; both Greek documents, purchase and sale of a date crop, 5/6Ḥev 21–22; and perhaps deed of sale Mur 27. The signatures stand under the text, which is written only once on the front side.

Under the Greek text of purchase of a date crop 5/6Ḥev 21 follow a summary and the signatures in Aramaic script and again a summary in Aramaic script on the back. The summary under the Greek text of sale of a date crop 5/6Ḥev 22 is Nabatean, and the signatures are in Aramaic script.

The Nabatean sales of property 5/6Ḥev 2–3, sale 5/6Ḥev 4, lease of land? 5/6Ḥev 6, and the Greek purchase and sale of a date crop 5/6Ḥev 21–22 belong to the archive of Babatha, a rich woman from Maoza in the district of Zoara. The documents in this archive offer information about the legal practices of the Roman province of Arabia (from the autumn of 106 CE). Legal authority of the Nabateans is vested in the council of the people of Petra (extract from council minutes 5/6Ḥev 12 15.27). The department for complaints regarding legal affairs is the court and the tribunal of the Roman governor (*hegemon*; 5/6Ḥev14.15.25), the Legatus pro Praetore (summons 5/6Ḥev 23 26) at Petra or in Rabbat Moab (summons, countersummons 5/6Ḥev 25). It seems that Judea exercised more or less autonomous jurisdiction in the years before and during the Bar Kokhba Revolt. The documents distinguish between Jewish and Greek law and customs (cf. marriage contracts 5/6Ḥev 10, 18, and 37; *n(w)mws/ś* and *nms*ʾ in marriage contract Mur 21 11; lease of land 5/6Ḥev 46 6; 17). The deeds of sale often use the term *as customary* (*kedi ḥazah*) to refer to existing Jewish law and custom (XḤev/Se 8 5.7; XḤev/Se 9 5.11; XḤev/Se 21 5; XḤev/Se 50 7).

Jerusalem and nearby towns are the places in which some of the documents written during the Bar Kokhba Revolt were executed. Deeds of sale of half of a garden I and II 5/6Ḥev 47a–b were written at ʿEin-Gedi, according to registration of land 5/6Ḥev 16 (127 CE): "a village of the district of Jericho in Judea." Most of the land at ʿEin-Gedi belonged to the crown from the time of the Hasmoneans Alexander Jannaeus and Shelamzion Alexandra.

All deeds of sale from the Judean desert as well as all Aramaic deeds of sale from outside Palestine are drawn up from the point of view of the seller (*ex latere venditoris*). The structure and language of the formulary are stereotyped, similar to the Aramaic legal style from Elephantine (fifth or fourth century BCE; cf. Cowley 13; Kraeling 1.12.13), which is in full correspondence with the Egyptian practice, while the formulation from the point of view of the buyer (as in deeds of purchase 5/6Ḥev 8 and the Greek 5/6Ḥev 21) conforms more with the old Babylonian and neo-Assyrian practice (Yaron, 1961, pp. 124f), although the Greek purchase and sale of a date crop 5/6Ḥev 21–22 point to the Roman concept of purchase and sale (*emptio venditio*; Lewis, 1989, p. 94). Obviously the legal formulary is related to the Greek, to the Roman, and also to the Talmudic legal language (cf. Yaron, 1989, pp. 99–128; Gulak, 1935, pp. 95–102).

The deeds of sale start with the date. The Hebrew and Aramaic documents begin with the day, the Babylonian-Jewish month, and the year of the era of the "freedom of Israel/Jerusalem" ("in the name/days of Simon, the son of Kosiba, the prince of Israel" or only "of Simon, the son of Kosiba"). The Nabatean documents open according to the Roman consulship, the year of the Roman Caesar, and the day, Babylonian-Jewish month, and year of the Nabatean era ("this *eparchia*" from the autumn of 106 CE or the year of the Nabatean king with the addition "who maintained life and brought deliverance to his people"). The Greek documents begin according to the accession year of the Roman Caesar and of both Roman consuls, the day and month of the Roman calendar, the year of the Nabatean era, and the day of the Macedonian month. Then follows the place of execution (Mur 29 and 30, Jerusalem; XḤev/Se 9, Yaqim; Mur 28, Harrimmona, all not far from Jerusalem; 5/6Ḥev 47a–b, ʿEin-Gedi; XḤev/Se 8–8a, Kafar Barrai(u); 5/6Ḥev 2.8, 21, 22, Mahoza). The deed of sale of plot Mur 30 adds the names of four notaries in Jerusalem *(ḥotmim)*. Next comes the statement of the transfer, always the sale, in 5/6Ḥev 8 and 21 (the purchase). Sometimes this statement is introduced by a greeting (5/6Ḥev 21 and 22) and by "he said: I acknowledge that I have sold/bought," and sometimes there follows a description of the condition, "of his own free will." After the transfer, the name and provenance of the transferor(s) are mentioned together with the object; what is transferred (real estate, house, land, garden, date crop, donkey) is described according to its measure. Then the price of the object is quoted ("silver zuz," "silver denar," "denar of Tyrian silver," together with the rate in "*selaʿ*") or the payment in natural produce. Then follows a detailed description of the object (its belongings and its borders according to the four cardinal points). Next follows the confirmation of payment ("the [full] price" [*damin* (*gemirin*)]; in XḤev/Se 8a already within the quotation of the price) or the confirmation of taking possession of the object and of the payment (5/6Ḥev 8).

Then begin the special clauses. First, the clause of confirmation of ownership: the buyer's power to dispose of the object (*shalliṭ* clause; with reservations in Mur 22 and XḤev/Se 8a). In the next clause the seller confirms his liability against his possessions to keep the sold object clean of someone's claim to the object by demurrer, and the seller confirms that he will perform the contract (cleansing clause, defension clause). Only sale of a date crop 5/6Ḥev 22 and sale of property 5/6Ḥev 2 mention the payment of a penalty in case of nonperformance of the contract. Deed of sale of plot Mur 30 has a benefit clause for the wife of the seller, but contract (Kefar Bario?) XḤev/Se 8a excludes it. Then follow clauses to the effect that only this document is valid, that restitution is to be paid from the possessions of the seller, and that the seller has to return the document when the buyer wants it (restitution clause). Deed of sale Mur 26, now promissory note on parchment XḤev/Se 50, confirms again that only the buyer has power over the object. In contract XḤev/Se 8a there follows a statement about the kind of document in question ("simple [*peshiṭ*] and signed inside [*wa-ḥatim be-gaveh*]"; cf. Hebrew XḤev/Se 49, now 50). The last section of the formulation brings the validation of the document: the signatures on the double documents on the back and on the simple documents on the front. The Greek documents purchase and sale of a date crop 5/6Ḥev 21 and 22 introduce this section with a brief summary of the contract in Aramaic and Nabatean. In the deeds of sale only the seller signs with his name and the phrase "for himself" (obligatory, *ʿal nafshaf*). If his wife is participating in the contract, she also signs, including this phrase. In the deeds of purchase (5/6Ḥev 8 and 21), the buyer signs without this phrase but with the words "has written it" (*ketubah;* 5/6Ḥev 21). If the seller (Mur 29; XḤev/Se 8a; XḤev/Se 49, now 50) or the buyer (5/6Ḥev 8) is illiterate, someone else writes the seller's or buyer's name together with his own name. After the signature of the seller or buyer, sometimes set off by spacing (Mur 29 and 30), come the signatures of the witnesses, only males, usually three but sometimes more, always with the addition "witness" (Hebrew: *ʿed;* Aramaic: *sahed*), sometimes interrupted by the signature of the scribe of the document (XḤev/Se 49, now 50; 5/6Ḥev 21 and 22). At times the respective place of residence of the seller, the scribe, and the witnesses is mentioned.

BIBLIOGRAPHY

Applebaum, Shimon. "Economic Life in Palestine." In *The Jewish People in the First Century*. Compendia Rerum Iudaicarum ad Novum Testamentum, section 1, vol. 2. Assen and Amsterdam, 1976. See pages 631–700.

Applebaum, Shimon. "Judaea as a Roman Province: The Countryside as a Political and Economic Factor." In *Aufstieg und Niedergang der Römischen Welt II*, vol. 8, edited by H. Temporini and W. Haase, pp. 355–396. Berlin, 1977.

Beyer, K. *Die Aramäischen Texte vom Toten Meer*. Göttingen, 1984. *Ergänzungsband*. Göttingen, 1994.

Broshi, Magen. "Agriculture and Economy in Roman Palestine: Seven Notes on the Babatha Archive." *Israel Exploration Journal* 42 (1992), 230–240.

Cotton, H., and Ada Yardeni. *Aramaic, Hebrew, and Greek Documentary Texts from Naḥal Ḥever and Other Sites, with an Appendix containing Alleged Qumran Texts (The Seiyâl Collection, vol. II)*. Discoveries in the Judaean Desert, 27. Oxford, 1997.

Cotton, H., W. Cockle, and F. Millar. "The Papyrology of the Roman Near East: A Survey." *Journal of Roman Studies* 85 (1995), 214–235.

Cross, F. M. "Samaria Papyrus 1: An Aramaic Slave Conveyance of 335 BCE Found in the Wâdi ed-Dâliyeh." *Eretz-Israel* 18 (1985), 7–17. See plate II.

Cross, F. M. "A Report on the Samaria Papyri." In *Congress Volume: Jerusalem, 1986*, edited by J. A. Emerton, pp. 17–26. Supplement to Vetus Testamentum, 40. Leiden, 1988.

Fitzmyer, Joseph A., ed. *An Aramaic Bibliography, Part I*. Baltimore, 1992.

Greenfield, J. C. "The Defension Clause in Some Documents from Naḥal Ḥever and Naḥal Ṣeʾelim." *Revue de Qumrân* 25 (1991-1992), 467–471.

Greenfield, J. C., B. Levine, Y. Yadin, and A. Yardeni, eds. *The Documents of the Bar Kokhba Period in the Cave of Letters II: Hebrew, Aramaic, and Nabataean Documents*. Jerusalem (forthcoming).

Gropp, D. M. "The Origin and Development of the Aramaic *Šalliṭ* Clause." *Journal of Near Eastern Studies* 52 (1993), 31–36.

Gulak, A. *Das Urkundenwesen im Talmud im Lichte der griechisch-ägyptischen Papyri und des griechischen und römischen Rechts*. Jerusalem, 1935.
Koffmahn, E. *Die Doppelurkunden aus der Wüste Juda*. Studies on the Texts of the Desert of Judah, 5. Leiden, 1968.
Lewis, Naphtali, ed. *The Documents from the Bar Kokhba Period in the Cave of Letters: Greek Papyri*. Jerusalem, 1989.
Milik, J. T., P. Benoit, and R. de Vaux, eds. *Les Grottes de Murabbaʿat*. Discoveries in the Judaean Desert, 2. Oxford, 1961.
Muffs, Yochanan. *Studies in the Aramaic Legal Papyri from Elephantine*. Studia et documenta ad jura Orientis antique pertinentia, 8. Leiden, 1969.
Porten, Bezalel, and Ada Yardeni. *Textbook of Aramaic Documents from Ancient Egypt*. Winona Lake, 1989.
Safrai, Z. *The Economy of Roman Palestine*. London and New York, 1994.
Tov, E., ed. *The Dead Sea Scrolls on Microfiche*. Leiden, 1993.
Yardeni, Ada. *Teʿudot Naḥal Ṣeʾelim*. Jerusalem, 1995.
Yaron, Reuven. "The Murabbaʿat Documents." *Journal of Jewish Studies* 11 (1960), 157–171.
Yaron, Reuven. *Introduction to the Law of the Aramaic Papyri*. Oxford, 1961.

G. WILHELM NEBE

DEMETRIUS III EUKERUS, among the last of the kings of the house of Seleucus [*See* Seleucids.] The son of Antiochus Grypus, Demetrius III (nicknamed Eukerus) ruled between 96 and 88 BCE. He was crowned in Damascus at the invitation of Ptolemy Lathyrus, king of Cyprus. Demetrius ruled part of Syria, and Philip, his brother, ruled another part of Syria.

In 88 BCE, the Pharisees invited Demetrius to invade Judea and to fight against the Hasmonean ruler Alexander Jannaeus. With the aid of the Pharisees, Demetrius gained a victory in a battle near Shechem. Soon after, six thousand Jews turned from Demetrius and instead supported Alexander Jannaeus. Demetrius returned to Syria. After Demetrius had retreated, Alexander Jannaeus captured eight hundred of the Jewish leaders who had rebelled against him and crucified them in Jerusalem. [*See* Alexander Jannaeus.]

Immediately after this, a war erupted between Demetrius and Philip II. Demetrius was taken prisoner and exiled to the court of Mithridates II of Pontus, where he died in captivity.

Pesher Nahum (4Q169) is unique among the Dead Sea Scrolls in that it mentions the names of Seleucid kings. [*See* Pesher Nahum.] An attempt was made in the *pesharim* not to mention historical figures (primarily rulers) by their true names but by nicknames that had been agreed upon (for instance, the Hasmonean leaders were nicknamed in the *pesharim* the Evil Priest, the Lion of Wrath, and the Man of Belial). In his interpretation of *Nahum* 2.1–14, the author of Pesher Nahum mentioned the names of gentile kings for whom there were no agreed-upon nicknames. Therefore, the author of the *pesher* called Antiochus and Demetrius III by their names.

Demetrius was called "king of Greece" by the author of Pesher Nahum; in this instance, *Greece* refers to the Seleucid kingdom. In Pesher Nahum it is explained that the Seekers after Smooth Things, who are the Pharisees, invited Demetrius to Jerusalem. [*See* Pharisees.] The author of Pesher Nahum wrote his composition following the Roman conquest in 63 BCE. The *pesher* dealt with Demetrius's invasion of Judea on account of the incident of the execution by hanging of the rebellious leaders by Alexander Jannaeus.

It appears that the events of 88 BCE were mentioned in Pesher Hosea[b] (4Q167) as well. [*See* Pesher Hosea.] In this composition, fragments of Pesher Hosea[b] were preserved:

> And Ephraim saw its illness and Judah its wound and Ephraim went to Assyria and sent for a rival king, but he will not be capable of curing you or removing your wound. For I will be like a lion to Ephraim and like a cub to the house of Judah. I shall prey and go away, and I shall carry away and there will be no savior. (4Q167 5.13–14)

The fragments of the *pesher* for these passages mentioned the Lion of Wrath, the usual nickname of Alexander Jannaeus. The Lion of Wrath set forth his hand to hurt Ephraim. Ephraim in the *pesharim* and other Qumran compositions is a nickname for the Pharisees. It seems that the author of Pesher Hosea[b] interpreted the words "And Ephraim went to Assyria and sent for an enemy king" in *Hosea* 5.13 as describing the events of 88 BCE and the invitation of Demetrius to Judea by the Pharisees. *Hosea* 14.5, which mentions that the lion will harm Ephraim and that the house of Judah will be without a savior, was understood by the author of Pesher Hosea as relating to the execution (by Alexander Jannaeus) of the rebels who had invited Demetrius to invade Judea.

[*See also* Hasmoneans.]

BIBLIOGRAPHY

Amusin, Joseph D. "The Reflection of Historical Events of the First Century B.C. in Qumran Commentaries (4Q161, 4Q169, 4Q166)." *Hebrew Union College Annual* 48 (1977), 123–152.
Stern, Menahem. "Judea and Her Neighbors in the Days of Alexander Jannaeus." *Jerusalem Cathedra 1* (1981), 22–46.

HANAN ESHEL
Translated from Hebrew by Daphna Krupp

DEMONS. Qumran writings mention demons and evil forces in several places. Nowhere is this demonology presented in a coherent fashion; it comprises different traditions that might be conceived as sometimes opposing views of the subject. Because of the dualistic views necessary for any demonology, such a belief puts the so-called Jewish monotheism of the biblical and postbiblical tradition seriously into question. It seems, therefore, that belief in demons could emerge and find expression only slowly. To what degree biblical tradition suppressed existing demonologies is open to question (see Psalm 91). However, the Persian and Hellenistic periods evince a growing interest not only in angelology but also in its negative counterpart, demonology (Baumgarten, 1991). [*See* Angels.] The Qumran writings combine what might be called demons with two major figures, namely Belial and Mastemah, who quite frequently are depicted as the cause of evil; hence, the discussion of beliefs in demons in the Dead Sea Scrolls includes discussion of the "evil one."

The Greek term *daimon* ("demon") and the modern equivalents (mostly dependent upon the specific meaning given to the term in the literature of the New Testament) have hardly any precise parallels in Biblical Hebrew (the usual rabbinic term *shed*, itself originally an Assyrian word, is used only twice in the Hebrew scriptures, in *Deuteronomy* 32.17 and *Psalms* 106.37; it occurs in the Aramaic version of *Tobit* [in Tobit[a–b], 4Q196–197, five times, always parallel to the Greek *daimon*]; in Songs of the Sage[a–b], 4Q510–511; and in Apocryphal Psalms[a], 11Q11 i.3).

Other Hebrew names denoting that specific kind of supernatural being were formed for the first time during this period. Here, too, the Qumran texts are part of the general Jewish developments of the time. The variety of names causes some trouble, since it is not self-evident that heavenly beings with negative effects on humans are necessarily opposed to God. They may just fulfill his will, and their deeds will then appear as punishing acts (e.g., Rule of the Community from Qumran Cave 1, hereafter, 1QRule of the Community 1QS, iv.12–13; cf. Davidson, 1992, pp. 157–158; Gammie, 1985; Mach, 1992, pp. 105–112). The Hebrew terminology for these beings is not yet systematized. Given this situation, one has to judge from text to text whether the beings involved are to be understood in modern terms as demons or else as God's ministers who happen to perform certain acts. The same terms may be used in each case, for example, the destroying angels, the angels of darkness, Belial's or Mastemah's angels, the spirits of bastards.

Despite the diffuse references to the demons, the Qumran belief is much more coherent than expected. For a better understanding, one has to include *1 Enoch* and *Jubilees*, which did not originate at Qumran but are present in several copies in the sect's library.

In Songs of the Sage[a–b], in combination with *1 Enoch* 6–16, the term *spirits of the bastards* discloses the origin of the demons: they are the illegal offspring of the sexual intercourse between the rebelling angels and women (following *Gn.* 6.1–4). One of the three nets of Belial (Damascus Document, CD iv.12) is accordingly fornication. The combination of illegal sexual behavior and idol worship is commonplace at several stages of Jewish tradition and seems to be implied by *1 Enoch* and the members of the Qumran community alike. Within this broader topic belongs the text Wiles of the Wicked Woman (4Q184). This has been interpreted convincingly by Joseph Baumgarten as depicting Lilith, a well-known Babylonian female demon who seduces young men and harms young women. Interestingly enough, Lilith is depicted in Wiles of the Wicked Woman with wings and perhaps with horns (though the latter are not certain; see Baumgarten, 1991, p. 140).

However, these spirits must be seen in a wider context. The famous division of humanity according to the Angel of Light and the Angel of Darkness (the "Treatise on the Two Spirits" in 1QRule of the Community, 1QS iii.13–iv.26) is reflected in many texts mentioning Belial (e.g., CD iv.12, v.18–19; War Scroll, 1QM xiii.10–12; Catena[a], 4Q177; Hodayot[a] from Qumran Cave 1, hereafter, 1QHodayot[a], 1QH[a] ii.22; cf. Davidson, 1992, pp. 162–165) and his rule over this world (e.g., 1QS i.16–18; CD vi.10, xvi.5; 1QM xiii.11). The community stands against all those who belong to the lot of Belial (e.g., 1QS ii.19) and curses Belial and his angels during the yearly renewal of the covenant (a rite that is to take place during all the time of Belial's reign [1QS i.16–18, ii.19; 1QM xiv.9–10; Berakhot[a–b], 4Q286–287 2–7] is problematic; see Kobelski, 1981, p. 43). Belial's reign is a reign of injustice (1QS iv.19–20; cf. Davidson, 1992, pp. 162–165), and he appears to be the "prince of the kingdom of wickedness" (1QM xvii.5–6). The destroying angels are placed under his dominion as are the people who do not belong to the community (cf. *Jub.* 14.31–33, 1QM xiii.10–13).

This latter element may be connected to the more elaborated story in *Jubilees*, where Mastemah is the prince of all the unclean spirits. According to that source (also well attested in Qumran), Mastemah begs God not to destroy all his spirits, since then he could not fulfill his duty to seduce humans (*Jub.* 10.8; cf. 11.5). He is granted a certain number of destroying angels. In the following story, Mastemah operates much as Satan does in other sources (so at the binding of Isaac [*Gn.* 22, *Jub.* 17] and during the Exodus out of Egypt [*Jub.* 47ff.]). The functional equivalence of Belial and Mastemah can be seen by comparing *Jubilees* 15.33 (Belial) with the Damascus Document (CD xvi.3–6; the angel of Mastemah).

The name Belial occurs several times in the Hebrew scriptures, yet its meaning is uncertain and debated. Without entering into the details of that discussion, one generally may say that Belial denotes either a negative attitude or a mythological figure. At least in some places in the Bible, Belial is connected with death and the underworld (*Ps.* 18.5, *2 Sm.* 22.5). The term appears at other times in connection with a critique of officials of the cult (*1 Sm.* 2.12) or as a designation for those who lead Israel astray from legitimate worship; these are "the men, sons of Belial" (*Dt.* 13.14). What remains in dispute mostly is the question of to what degree, if at all, the biblical term was related to a mythological figure, for example, the ruler of the underworld. (If taken as an abstract noun, *belial* often is translated as "worthlessness"; but even that meaning is disputed among scholars of the Hebrew scriptures.) The understanding of Belial and Mastemah as demonic beings best fits the context of the Qumran sect. It is noteworthy that the Hebrew term for "demon," namely, *shed*, is used in the biblical references in connection with idol worship (*Dt.* 32.17 and *Ps.* 106.37).

The principal question of whether Mastemah is used as a personal name or as an abstract noun in the Qumran literature as well as in *Jubilees* is debated. It seems that the noun is a derivative form of the Hebrew *stm*, a variation of *stn*, from which the name Satan was constructed. Scholars tend to understand Mastemah in the Dead Sea Scrolls more often as an abstract noun, meaning "hostility," than as a personal name. Belial occasionally is referred to as "Belial in his hostile scheme" (*Berakhot*).

Belial/Mastemah, who should be identified with the Angel of Darkness in the "Treatise on the Two Spirits," rules this world with his angels or spirits. Significantly, these are sometimes called "spirits of (ritual) uncleanness." Yet, these spirits and angels are not only the forces that stand against God; they may fulfill his punishment as, for example, in the Damascus Document (CD ii.5–7). This might be an accurate understanding of the "strong angel" in Apocryphal Psalms[a] (11Q11 3.5). The "Treatise on the Two Spirits" makes it abundantly clear that predetermination alone is not responsible for human deeds. The world outside the covenant is under Belial's rule; yet, even the covenanters might be afflicted by him. During his reign, Belial lies in wait extending three nets: those of unchasteness, wealth, and defiling the sanctuary (CD iv.12–18). It is evident that such warnings describe a group who fears these nets more than the demons or their leader.

However, being tempted by Belial is no excuse for human beings. Varying evaluations as to whether the spirits exercise the more neutral task of punishing or a demonic role are probably due to differing theological opinions of the various authors (and redactors) of the scrolls (see Davidson, 1992, pp. 157–158).

Even in their hostility toward humans and their own wickedness, these forces were created by God for that purpose, as explicitly stated by, for instance, the War Scroll (1QM xiii.10–15): "You have made Belial to corrupt, a hostile angel. . . . his counsel is aimed toward wickedness and guiltiness. All the spirits of his lot, angels of destruction, are behaving according to the statutes of darkness; toward it is their one [de]sire. . . . Who, be he an angel or a commander, is like the help of p[. . .]." Yadin has restored the last word as "your face" and takes it as an allusion to *Isaiah* 63.8–9.

One of the possibilities for escaping the influence of the evil one and his angels is to return to the "Torah of Moses," as clearly taught in the Damascus Document (CD xvi.4–5). Several texts point in the same direction: membership in the covenant and the yearly renewal are part of the community's protective devices against Belial (CD vii.2, xix.14; 1QS iv.11–12). Under certain conditions the angel of his [God's] truth stands helpfully at the covenanter's side against Belial and his angels (4Q177). According to *Jubilees* 1.20, Moses asked God not to allow Belial to do any harm to Israel.

Prayer is one of the means by which to guard against these demons. This becomes clear from the fact that Qumran prayers contain phrases like "do not allow Satan or any spirit of uncleanness to rule over me" (Psalms[a], 11Q5 19.15–16; cf. Nitzan, 1994). The formulation here is comparable to those in some traditional Jewish prayers used up to the present.

However, the same scroll includes "four songs to play for those stricken (by evil spirits)" (11Q5 27). At this point it becomes apparent that the members of the Qumran community did not only pray for deliverance from the evil spirits but also used special liturgies that were to be recited or performed in a manner defined as "magic" by modern commentators (see Baumgarten, 1991; Nitzan, 1994). An apocryphal psalm is most obviously an exorcisory ritual (11Q11 iii; see Puech, 1990) probably ascribing to David and Solomon the usage of divine names against the demons. Only in light of such exorcistic practices can a certain ordinance in the Damascus Document be understood more clearly: "anyone who is possessed by spirits of Belial and speaks apostasy is to be judged in accordance with the law of the necromancer and the familiar spirit" (CD xii.2–3). Songs of the Sage[a–b] are long exorcisory rituals, referring to the female demon Lilith (Nitzan, 1994). Baumgarten (1991) rightly adds to this list the Hymn from Qumran Cave 8 (8Q5; Baillet, 1962, p. 161).

Within such a framework the belief in demons easily could be introduced into scriptural exegesis. The statement that the Prince of Light installed Moses and Aaron, whereas Jannes and his brother were installed by Belial (CD v.17–19), alludes to the whole set of traditions concerning Jannes and Jambres, the two Egyptian sorcerers who allegedly assisted Pharaoh against Israel.

Yet, the war at the End of Days will bring about the destruction of all the evil forces. The War Scroll includes this statement within the high priest's speech before the last battle (1QM xvii.5–8). Words of the Luminaries[a] (4Q504) describes the future salvation as a time without any Satan. The Florilegium interprets the repose granted to David in this light (4Q174 7–9), and another fragmentary narrative text (4Q463) seems to imply an eschatological salvation from Belial.

The world is now under the reign of the leader of these denomic forces who constantly try to lead the righteous away from God's ordinances, who will perform the judgment of the sinners, and, not really fitting the picture, who will be punished for their deeds at the end of time. These forces are to be feared (and certain protective means are available); however, they indeed rule the wicked. They are organized under the rule of their leader Belial/Mastemah.

BIBLIOGRAPHY

Baillet, Maurice, Józef T. Milik, and Roland de Vaux, eds. *Les 'Petites Grottes' de Qumran*. Discoveries in the Judaean Desert, 3. Oxford, 1962.

Baumgarten, Joseph M. "On the Nature of the Seductress in 4Q184." *Revue de Qumrân* 15 (1991), 133–143. In his discussion of Wiles of the Wicked Woman in particular, the author presents an overview of Qumran demonology, especially important for its link to ancient Near Eastern beliefs.

Davidson, Maxwell J. *Angels at Qumran: A Comparative Study of 1 Enoch 1–36, 72–108 and Sectarian Writings from Qumran*. Journal of the Study of the Pseudepigrapha Supplement Series, 11. Sheffield, 1992.

Gammie, John G. "The Angelology and Demonology in the Septuagint of the Book of Job." *Hebrew Union College Annual* 56 (1985), 1–19.

Kobelski, Paul J. *Melchizedek and Melchireša*ʿ. Catholic Biblical Quarterly Monograph Series, 10. Washington, D.C., 1981. Of special interest is the chapter about the heavenly opponents (pp. 75–83).

Lange, Armin. "The Essene Position on Magic and Divination." In *Legal Texts and Legal Issues: Proceedings of the Second Meeting of the International Organization for Qumran Studies*, edited by Joseph M. Baumgarten, F. García Martínez, and J. Kampen. Studies on the Texts of the Desert of Judah, 23, pp. 377–435. Leiden, New York, and Cologne, 1997.

Mach, Michael, *Entwicklungsstadien des jüdischen Engelglaubens in vorrabbinischer Zeit*. Texte und Studien zum Antiken Judentum, 34. Tübingen, 1992. General overview of developments in angelology from the Hebrew scriptures to the end of the second century CE. Bibliography up to the end of 1991.

Nitzan, Bilhah. *Qumran Prayer and Religious Poetry*. Translated by Jonathan Chipman. Studies on the Texts of the Desert of Judah, 12. Leiden, New York, and Cologne, 1994. For magical poetry see pages 227–272; discusses the important Songs of the Sage in detail. For an earlier version, see her "Songs of Praise to Scare and Terrify Bad Spirits: 4Q 510 and 4Q 511" (in Hebrew with English summary), *Tarbiz* 55 (1986), pp. 19–46, and the reactions following her article.

Otzen, Benedict. "Beliyyaʿal." *Theological Dictionary of the Old Testament*, edited by G. J. Botterweck and H. Ringgren, vol. 2, pp. 131–136. Grand Rapids, Mich., 1975.

Penney, Douglas L., and Michael O. Wise. "By the Power of Beelzebub: An Aramaic Incantation from Qumran (4Q560)." *Journal of Biblical Literature* 113 (1994), 627–650.

Puech, Émile. "11QPsAp[a]: Un rituel d'exorcismes; Essai de reconstruction." *Revue de Qumrân* 14/15 (1990), pp. 377–408.

Sekki, Arthur E. *The Meaning of* Ruaḥ *at Qumran*. Atlanta, 1989. See pages 145–171 for *ruaḥ* as "angel/demon."

MICHAEL MACH

DEPARTMENT OF ANTIQUITIES OF JORDAN.

As the primary body of government charged with preserving the archaeological remains and monuments of the Hashemite Kingdom of Jordan, the Department of Antiquities of Jordan played a central role in the initial attempts at recovery and preservation of the Judean Desert manuscripts. From 1948 to 1967, during the period of Jordanian control over the northwest shore of the Dead Sea and the northern Judean Desert region, officers of the Jordanian Department of Antiquities coordinated the activities of foreign institutions in the study and publication of the manuscripts finds. They also participated in the excavation and preservation of Khirbet Qumran and other archaeological sites in the region. Since the 1967 Arab-Israeli War, the Department of Antiquities of Jordan has retained custody of the Copper Scroll (3Q15) and has underwritten intensive efforts to record its contents and ensure its physical preservation.

At the time of the initial discovery of the Judean Desert manuscripts in the winter of 1946–1947, the Department of Antiquities of the British Mandatory government was gradually losing its effectiveness. In fact, it was not until after the Israeli-Jordanian cease-fire concluding the 1948 war, in which Qumran and the surrounding area came under Jordanian control, that efforts could be made to locate the site of the find. In January 1949, Captain Philippe Lippens, an officer of the United Nations cease-fire observer force, assisted by Captain Akkash el-Zebn of the Arab Legion, located the site of Cave 1 and alerted the director of the Jordanian Department of Antiquities, Gerald Lankester Harding. In February and March, Harding joined forces with Roland Guérin de Vaux of the École Biblique et Archéologique Française in Jerusalem to excavate the cave, document its location and inner dimensions, and recover fragments of about seventy scrolls and shards from dozens of scroll jars. [*See* École Biblique et Archéologique Française.] In the following months the Jordanian Department of Antiquities also began to purchase scroll fragments that had been illegally excavated by the Taʿamireh bedouin.

In October 1951, soon after the Taʿamireh made another important discovery of manuscript materials in Wadi Murabbaʿat, Inspector Awni Dajani of the Jordanian Department of Antiquities, alerted to the unauthorized looting, directed a salvage excavation in which additional texts of the Bar Kokhba Revolt were retrieved. [*See*

Murabbaʿat, Wadi.] In November and December, large-scale excavations at Khirbet Qumran were begun under the sponsorship of the Jordanian Department of Antiquities and the École Biblique. This project continued for five excavation seasons between 1953 and 1958, during which the nearby site of ʿEin-Feshkha was also explored. [*See* ʿEin-Feshkha.] In February 1952, the Jordanian Department of Antiquities coordinated the efforts of French and American teams in an intensive survey of caves in the vicinity of Qumran.

With the news of the discovery of the enormous cache of texts in Cave 4 at Qumran by the Taʿamireh in September 1952, the involvement of the Jordanian Department of Antiquities intensified. After organizing a salvage excavation in Cave 4 to retrieve the remaining manuscript finds, Harding worked closely with the trustees of the Palestine Archaeological Museum to mount an international effort to raise funds for the purchase of the illegally excavated texts that remained in private hands. [*See* Palestine Archaeological Museum.] Yet the purchase of the scroll fragments was only the initial challenge. Although the government of Jordan guaranteed a sum of fifteen thousand Jordanian dinars to recover the texts, an international team of scholars had to be recruited to study and publish them. Therefore, in the summer of 1953, the trustees of the Palestine Archaeological Museum, working closely with Harding, assembled a small group of scholars from England, France, Germany, Poland, and the United States to oversee the transcription and publication of the Cave 4 texts from Qumran.

The Suez Crisis of 1956 and the rise of Arab nationalist sentiment within Jordan eventually affected the workings of the Jordanian Department of Antiquities and the ongoing study of the Dead Sea Scrolls. The conspicuous involvement of foreign institutions in the efforts to purchase scroll fragments (on the basis of agreements that promised certain texts to the contributing institutions after the completion of their initial study and publication in Jordan) aroused protest in the Jordanian press. With the government decision to replace all non-Jordanians serving in high administrative posts in the kingdom, Harding was succeeded on 1 October 1956 as director of the Jordanian Department of Antiquities by Dr. Abdul Karim al-Gharaybeh. During his tenure, additional policy decisions were taken by the Ministry of Education to make it clear that all the Judean Desert manuscripts were the property of the Hashemite Kingdom of Jordan and that no fragments or original photographs would be transferred abroad. On 25 February 1957 Education Minister Shafiq Rusheidat established a new committee to oversee the study and publication of the scrolls consisting of the mayor of Jerusalem, the director of antiquities, the director of the American Schools of Oriental Research, and the director of the École Biblique. On 27 July 1960 the Council of Ministers further ruled that the Dead Sea Scrolls were not to be taken out of the country, and all sums contributed by foreign institutions for their purchase from the Taʿamireh and their agents were to be reimbursed.

With the appointment of Dr. Awni Dajani as director of the Jordanian Department of Antiquities in 1960, excavation projects in the Qumran region resumed. An expedition headed by John Allegro was unsuccessful in its search for treasures mentioned in the Copper Scroll at Qumran and nearby sites along the northwestern shore of the Dead Sea. Yet, as a close confidant and colleague of Dajani, Allegro was appointed Scroll Advisor to His Majesty's Government in 1961.

A final administrative decision by the Council of Ministers in November 1966 resulted in the nationalization of the Palestine Archaeological Museum. On 28 November 1966 the museum and its collections, including the scrolls, came under the supervision of former Jerusalem mayor Aref al-Aref, who was named director general of the museum. Together with Dajani of the Jordanian Department of Antiquities, al-Aref began a long-term reassessment of the state of scroll study and preservation. Before any changes could be made, however, the 1967 Arab-Israeli War intervened, and the oversight of Qumran, the Palestine Archaeological Museum, and the manuscripts that were stored there passed to the Israel Department of Antiquities.

With only a few manuscript fragments and the Copper Scroll remaining in the custody of the Department of Antiquities of Jordan in Amman, where they had been on exhibit when the 1967 Arab-Israeli War broke out, the Judean Desert manuscripts subsequently became only a minor part of the department's responsibilities. [*See* Copper Scroll.] Yet over the years, interest in the Dead Sea Scrolls in Jordan continued. In the 1980s, the recognition of the seriously deteriorating physical condition of the Copper Scroll led the Department of Antiquities of Jordan to undertake an ambitious project of photographic documentation and physical preservation. In 1993, the scroll was transferred to Paris under the auspices of the Department of Antiquities of Jordan and the French Institute of Archaeology of the Middle East (Institut Française d'Archéologie du Proche Orient), where it was cleaned and remounted by the technical staff of the Valectra Laboratories of Electricité de France (EDF). In addition to the physical preservation work, the restoration team performed a digital scan of the scroll's surface to prepare highly accurate, three-dimensional reproductions of the text for the use of scholars around the world. In 1997, at the conclusion of the restoration project, the Copper Scroll was returned to the National Museum in Amman.

[*See also* Amman Museum; Discovery and Purchase; Museums and Collections; *and* Scrolls Research.]

BIBLIOGRAPHY

Allegro, John M. *Search in the Desert.* Garden City, N.Y., 1964. Allegro's first-person account of his relations with the Jordanian authorities and his search for the treasure of the Copper Scroll.

Harding, G. Lankester. *The Antiquities of Jordan.* London, 1959. Harding's personal résumé and experience with the antiquities of Jordan. The scrolls and Qumran play a significant role.

Sauer, James A., and Lloyd A. Willis. "Archaeology in Jordan." In *The Oxford Encyclopedia of Archaeology in the Near East,* vol. 3, edited by Eric M. Meyers, pp. 51–56. New York, 1997.

Silberman, Neil Asher. *The Hidden Scrolls: Christianity, Judaism, and the War for the Dead Sea Scrolls.* New York, 1994. An account of the political context of the discovery and study of the scrolls.

Trever, John C. *The Untold Story of Qumran.* Westwood, N.J., 1965. The most detailed chronology and events of the discovery of the scrolls, by one of the participants.

NEIL ASHER SILBERMAN

DETERMINISM, as a philosophical concept, is the view that "given certain initial conditions, everything that ensues is bound to happen as it does and in no other way" (Marcoulesco, 1987). A closely related notion is that of predestination, which is the determination, by a conscious and voluntary act of a deity, of the destiny of individuals or groups as salvation or damnation (double predestination). Free will, on the contrary, is the conviction that human beings have a capacity to make deliberate choices, especially between moral alternatives, and therefore bear full responsibility for the ultimate consequences of their actions. A middle position, compatibilism, considers that even if a certain amount of causality does exist, either in natural laws or as the result of a divine decision, there is nevertheless room for personal options.

Josephus summarizes the divergent opinions of the Pharisees, Sadducees, and the Essenes about fate. The Essenes maintain, he says, "that fate is ruler of all things, and that nothing happens to people except it be according to its decree" (*Jewish Antiquities*, 13.172), whereas for the Pharisees "only some things are the work of fate" and none according to the Sadducees. Later on, Josephus adds another short statement about the Essenes' position: "The doctrine of the Essenes is that they like to leave all things to God" (*Antiquities*, 18.18). The same deterministic beliefs show up in the Qumran literature, and this fact is regularly used to support the identification of the Qumranites as a group of Essenes (see Beall). Scholars are divided, however, about the exact meaning of texts which contain statements about determination or predestination, particularly when the same texts apparently claim also some form of human freedom. Various solutions have been proposed to this riddle. Questions have also been raised about the sources of Qumran determinism and its influence on later Jewish and Christian literature.

Determinism and Predestination in the Dead Sea Scrolls. In the Dead Sea Scrolls, a group of nonsectarian wisdom texts express the idea of a preexistent, hidden order of the world; Armin Lange has scrutinized these texts and demonstrated how the sectarians took over and modified this concept. In 4Q Sapiential Work A^{c} (4Q417 2.i.1–18), a sage is admonished to recognize, among other things, the "mystery of becoming" (*raz nihyeh*), that is the dualistic plan of the creation, through which God has separated good from evil as well as the ways of mankind and their sanction (*pequdah*) for all times, including the *eschaton*. This sapiential order, engraved on heavenly tablets, was revealed through both the Torah and a "vision of explanation" received by Enosh, the son of Seth. The eschatological realization of the "mystery of becoming" is emphasized in the Mysteries (1Q27 1.i.1–12): rejecting mantic means of gaining knowledge about the preexistent order of the world, the text states, in a prophetic form, that it will be fully revealed only at the end, when evil and folly will disappear forever while justice and knowledge will stand. Another allegedly non-Essene text, the Instruction on the Two Spirits (1QS iii.13–iv.26), teaches that, before creating them, the God of knowledge has designed the "plans" (*maḥsahvah*) of all beings according to a dualistic order which unfolds without a single change and is manifested at various levels, cosmic and anthropological (conflict between light and darkness within the universe and the human heart), ethical (virtues and vices), and eschatological (salvation versus destruction). The *yaḥad* later stressed the dualistic character of the Instruction in order to sustain its claim to be the only legitimate heir to the covenant between God and his people. [*See* Dualism.] The Fifth Song of the Sabbath Sacrifice (4Q402 4.1–15) hints that all epochs of history, starting with the distribution of knowledge at creation and culminating with the eschatological war, are affected by the preexistent order of the world. This view would have been developed in sapiential circles to answer the crisis faced by the experiential denial of the traditional postulate of retribution; prophetic and apocalyptic tones were added by the integration of eschatology and history into its original cosmological and ethical perspective.

Among the texts displaying sectarian features, a hymn praises God for having created the heavens, the earth, and humanity according to his wisdom, knowing all their deeds in advance (1QH^{a} ix.1–x.4). In the same way as he set the course of stars or separated the earth from the seas, God has, for human beings, divided (*pileig*) "their tasks in all their generations" for all periods of history and "ordered (*hekhin*) their [w]ays" along with the sanction which brings them either fulfillment or affliction. The section ends with the statement that "in the wisdom of your knowledge, you have ordered their destiny (*te'udah*) before they existed, and everything happens according to [your] wi[ll], and nothing is done without you" (ix.17–22). The Damascus Document (ii.2–13), addressed to those entering the covenant, declares that God did not choose the wicked at the beginning of the world and that he knew their deeds already, hated them, and caused them to stray; on the other hand, he raised up those called to become a remnant and revealed to his prophets the (celestial) record of their names. A fragmentary thematic *pesher* from Qumran (4Q180.1.1–10) details the ages of history. If read correctly, the introduction (frg. 1 1–3) refers to a period, prior to the creation, for God "to comple[te all that was] and is to be," to order their deeds for the present time until the *eschaton*, and to write this down on (heavenly) tablets; hence, for the *pesher* as for some apocalypses, the preexistent order of beings includes the course of history. The Pesher Habakkuk shares this conviction and urges the truthful not to abandon their service in spite of the delay of the *eschaton*, "for all periods of God will come according to their order, as he inscribed it for them in the mysteries of his wisdom" (vii.5–14). By taking over the deterministic notion of a preexistent order of beings, stressing its historical dimension, and spelling out the predestinations of individuals which it implies, the sect could make sense of a reality that apparently disproved its claims and hopes.

In addition to the concept of a preexistent order of the world, attention has also been drawn to related texts that suggest a belief in determinism or in the predestination of individuals (Hengel, Lichtenberger, Merrill, etc.). Similar ideas are found in 1QHodayot[a] vii.16–26, where God is said to have fashioned every spirit and established its plan (?) before he created it. He made both the just and the wicked, and has determined for the former a period of approval and for the latter the day of annihilation, as witnesses to his own glory and might. The human, who is but flesh and dust, cannot understand God's design unless he is given inspired knowledge of it, and he is unable to change anything in it. The last section of the hymn concluding 1Q Rule of the Community (xi.9–22) stresses even more the nothingness of a human being, who is unable to establish his own step. Only God, who has ordered everything according to his plan, can do so by remitting all sins and by cleansing the one shaped from dust and fashioned with clay.

Such texts have completely evacuated the biblical notion that humankind is made in the image of God, as does also the "Treatise on the Two Spirits" (Maier). But one still finds in the Qumran literature the idea that God could take the initiative of electing Israel or a group within it, Jerusalem as the holy city, or an individual (see, for example, 1QM x.9; 4Q504 iii.9, iv.3–8; 4Q266 x.11; 4Q534), while rejecting others, such as sinners of the past (1Q34 3.ii.4), or leading them astray as in the case of foreign nations (4Q260 xi.9–11; cf. 1Q27 1.i.9–12). This concept has been appropriated by those who have joined the community: they express their conviction to be "those that God has chosen" (*baḥar*), "cast in the lot (*goral*) of light" (as opposed to the lot of Belial) to become an "everlasting people," and to "inherit the lot of the holy ones" (see, for example, 1QS ii.1–18, iv.22, ix.7–8.16; 1Q28b i.1–2; 1QM xiii.9–10; 1QH[a] xix.10–14).

It is to be noticed, however, that even within this community of the elect, individuals themselves are variously gifted and are to be differentiated according to their specific "inheritance" (*naḥalah*) in the spirits of light and darkness (1QS iv.24; see CD xiii.12 and 4Q267 9.iv.9), perhaps in relation to the time of their conception or birth (4Q186). When someone enters the community, the sons of Aaron are to test his "spirits," to assess his insight and his deeds in law, and to rank him in the proper place among his fellows. This classification, strictly observed during the communal gatherings, is to be reviewed yearly (1QS ii.23, v.19–25). In another section of 1Q Rule of the Community (ix.12–16) a similar role of discrimination is played by the instructor who "should separate and weigh all the sons of Zadok according to their spirits," promote or demote them on the basis of their intelligence and behavior, and consequently love or hate them (see also 1QH[a] vi.19).

Free Will. These observations do not leave much room for chance, and there is indeed no real hint in the Qumran literature that nature or history could escape God's determination or that God's plan could be changed substantially. As far as human beings are concerned, however, things seem to be different, since voluntary actions are referred to in many instances, strongly suggesting some form of free will. In the first place, entrance in and belonging to the community is the result of a deliberate individual decision: The men of the community are people "who freely volunteer (*mitnadvim*) to convert from all evil and to keep themselves steadfast in all he [= God] prescribes in compliance with his will" (1QS v.1; cf. 1.7.11, v.6.8.10.21–22, vi.13; 1Q14 x.7). This decision is expressed in the form of a "binding oath to return to the Law of Moses . . . with all heart and with all soul" (1QS v.8–9). When living in the community, the member aims at loving God "freely," with his whole heart (1QH[a] vi.26), and "freely delights" in all that happens to him, probably understood as sent by God (1QS ix.24). In liturgical terms, his perfection of way is compared to a "pleasant free will offering" (*ke-nidvat minḥat ratson* 1QS ix.5). In military terms, it could be understood as a "wholehearted" enrollment for the eschatological war against darkness (War Rule, 4Q285 vii.5, ix.5).

But among those entering the covenant there might be a false convert, who is ritually cursed for "leaving his guilty obstacle in front of himself to backslide (*le-hissog*) over it" (1QS ii.11–12). Sometimes, members were assaulted by Belial and the spirit of his lot, who were to make them stumble (*le-hakhshil*) (1QS iii.24) and eventually they could not stand the purifying test of the crucible (see, for example, 1QM vii.15, xvii.1.9). On such occasions, those who were not living up to their commitment were rebuked by the overseer of the community (as witnessed by 4Q477) or punished according to the gravity of their offense on the basis of elaborated penal codes (1QS vi.24–vii.25; CD xiv.20–22; 4Q266 10.ii, 4Q267 9.vi, 4Q269 11 i–ii, 4Q270 7 i). Ultimately those whose behavior did not improve were not to be "reckoned among all the sons of his truth" and were to be expelled (4Q266 11). This implies that each individual was held at least partly accountable for his misconduct and was conceived of as usually having the possibility of rectifying it if he was determined to do so. Up to a certain point, then, even his eschatological fate rested in his own hands.

Accounting for the Tension. Various attempts have been made to explain the apparent tension between determinism or predestination on the one hand and human free will on the other. Beside attempts to stress one of these two dimensions or to put them in an evolutionary perspective, scholars integrate both in different forms of compatibilism. Gerhard Maier and Martin Hengel see the Qumranites as being in continuity with Ben Sira, but much more pessimistic than the latter (*Sir.* 15.11–20, 33[36].7–15) in viewing the human as transitory, weak, sinful, impure, and unable to understand divine mysteries. In their view, this anthropology led the Essenes to formulate, in the "Treatise on the Two Spirits," the strongest teaching on predestination ever found in Judaism. Other scholars see the determinism as dominant. The only freedom that one is given, in Devorah Dimant's words, "is not to choose where to go but to discover where he is," which is fully realized for the elect only through the divine gift of knowledge (cf. Lichtenberger). In Nötscher's opinion, things are less one-sided: The Qumranites were certainly conscious of being dependent on God and having physical as well as moral deficiencies, but they were just as convinced of having duties and responsibilities without which their communal religious life would have been impossible. As Alfred Marx reads them, the Qumran texts teach that the individual is responsible for his conversion, even if he always needs divine grace for it. There is no predestination as such in texts like the "Treatise on the Two Spirits," but only God's eternal decision to reward those who walk in the spirit of truth and to punish others.

Roland Bergmeier explains the conflicting statements about predestination and free will by their different origin. Free will is not in tension with the original determinism found in the earlier Qumran literature, but only with predestination, found in texts which came later or from other sources. The hymns attributed to the most influential leader of the community, the Teacher of Righteousness (see, for example, 1QH[a] x.1–19, xii.5–xiii.4, xiii.20–xv.5), display deterministic and antithetic structures common to wisdom creation theology, but leave room for free choice. The Teacher had indeed urged the righteous among the Israelites to accept the interpretation of the Torah revealed to him, to separate from the wicked, and to join the community of the covenant. This view was modified afterward in the communal hymns of 1QRule of the Community (xi.10–11) and 1QHodayot[a] (iv.17–25, vi.8–22, vii.15–26; xxiii–xxv) which praise the creator for predestining his creatures rather than simply determining the structure of the world. Under such conditions, one is no more in a position to achieve salvation through personal decision. This new interpretation of deterministic thinking is deepened further in dualistic texts from other sources such as the Damascus Document (ii.3–13) or the "Treatise on the Two Spirits" (cf. Baudry).

A few authors have articulated more clearly what could have been the compatibilist understanding of the Qumranites. Since one encounters in 1QHodayot[a] texts "which unquestionably teach predestination" as well as affirmations of free will, Eugene H. Merrill concludes that "the Qumran sectarians found it possible to hold for the need for individual, voluntary response to divine promptings within the framework of a rigid predestinarianism": God had a foreknowledge of how human beings would respond to his "gracious overtures" and, on that basis, had assigned their destinies before their creation (cf. with variations, E. P. Sanders, Hopkins, Röhser).

Origins and Further Developments. The origins of the determinism of the Dead Sea Scrolls have been searched for in similar ideas, such as the sapiential conception of the world, the apocalyptic theology of history, and the teachings of foreign philosophic or religious systems. The representation of a preexistent order of the world, identified as wisdom, is already found in sapiential works from the Second Temple period (*Job*, *Proverbs* 1–9, *Ecclesiastes*, *Ben Sira*; *1 Baruch* 3–4). It is characterized as cosmological and ethical and is even personified (Hengel, Lange, von Rad). As observed by von Rad, *Ben Sira* (33.12) suggests that the control of history is also subject to the divine determination. For prophetic traditions, God's interventions are usually the result of decisions made during the course of time. Later didactic and apocalyptic writings interpret them rather as the unfolding of an irrevocable divine plan engraved on heavenly tablets and encompassing all epochs of history. The heavenly tablets (a motif also known in Mesopotamian and Greco-Roman literature) were read by patriarchs like Asher, who learned from them that his children were to disobey God and not to pay attention to his law (*Testament of Asher* 7.5, cf. also *Testament of Levi* 5.4; *1 En.* 106.19–107.3). According to the book of the *Jubilees*, their contents, that is, "the first things and the last things that shall come to pass in all the divisions of the days . . ." (*Jub.* 1.4, 1.26–29), were revealed to Moses by an angel on Mount Sinai. The setting of history in predetermined periods is already evident in the depiction, found in *Daniel* 2 and 7, of the four successive kingdoms (Babylonian, Median, Persian, and Hellenistic) which are to be superseded soon by the kingdom of God. In *1 Enoch*, an even sharper periodization takes two different forms. The "Animal Vision" (*1 En.* 85–90) offers a zoomorphic representation of nations and persons in history, down to the Maccabees. In the "Apocalypse of Weeks" (*1 En.* 93.1–10, 91.12–17), Enoch is shown, on heavenly tablets, the course of all of history, which appears as a succession of ten separate units, with a turning point at the end of the seventh. The righteous are then chosen to initiate over the wrongdoers the final judgment, which culminates in the tenth, final period. Fragments of these or of similar works (*Daniel*; Pseudo-Daniel; *Jubilees*; Enoch; Apocalypse of Weeks?), as well as other documents, like the Ages of Creation (4Q180 and 181) and the Pesher Habakkuk, confirm that these deterministic ideas were known at Qumran, but the more sectarian material has a sharper dualistic tone and often lacks the usual apocalyptic tropes. There is no heavenly journey, no revelatory angel, no images to symbolize various epochs or historical characters, and so forth. This suggests that the Qumranites and their forerunners, though they share a similar view of history, have elaborated different variations of it.

Scholars have also discussed possible foreign influences, especially from Iran or Greece, on the deterministic thought of the Scrolls (Hengel, Martone, Rösher). Attention has been drawn particularly to the schematization of world history in the Iranian conception of eschatology reported by Theopompus (fourth century BCE). According to him, the Iranians envisioned history as a succession of several periods of three thousand years dominated alternatively by two opposite heavenly figures, Oromazes and Ahriman. These were to be followed by a period of conflict between the two which would eventually result in the victory of Oromazes, thereby opening an era of well-being for humanity. The correspondence with the general model of eschatology attested, for example, in the "Treatise on the Two Spirits" or in the War Scroll is striking, but a direct connection is hard to demonstrate, since these and other Iranian ideas were known elsewhere in the Hellenistic world. On the other hand, the strict determination of the cosmos as well as of human action is characteristic of the Stoic philosophy, which was also quite widespread. In Chrysippus' teaching, fate (*heimarmene*) is the precise ordering, rooted in nature itself, of everything that occurs in the universe as well as in the life of each individual; the true sage is the one who fits himself within this order. The determinism of the Qumran texts, including those displaying astronomical and astrological interest, is arranged on a similar pattern, but is at variance on a fundamental point: It is based on a "nontraditional revelation" rather than on a "rational ground" (Martone). Determinism is not attributed to an impersonal fate but to God's plan, "as the free disposition of his personal transcendant power" (Hengel).

The teachings of the Dead Sea Scrolls about determinism have echoes in other Jewish texts from the period which they could have influenced directly or indirectly, particularly if the Qumranites are to be identified as a group of Essenes. Dualistic and deterministic features appear in additions or variations in the Hebrew text of *Ben Sira* (11.16, 15.14, 16.15–16, 33.14); this may be the result of an Essene recension of the book by or after the middle of the first century BCE. Later, rabbinism usually allowed for both "God's foresight and providence directing all things and human freedom of choice with respect with doing good or evil" (Wallace).

The problem of the divine determination of the course of history and of the destiny of individuals was a matter of reflection in Gnosticism (Bergmeier) and in early Christianity (Bergmeier, Maier, Röhser), as witnessed particularly by the writings of John (*Jn.* 6.37–45, 6.65, 8.47, 10.1–30, 12.39–40, 17.12, 18.37) and Paul (*Rom.* 8.24–30, 9–11, *Eph.* 1.3–14, *Phil.* 2.12–13, *2 Thes.* 2.13). Many of these concepts have significant parallels in deterministic sections of the Dead Sea Scrolls (cf. 1QS i.3–4, iii.13–iv.26, xi.7–13; CD ii.9–13, viii.14–15, 1QH[a] iv.24, vi.8–12, ix.5–27, xii.29–32). On the basis of these similarities, Maier has concluded that even if Paul has conceived his view of predestination after *Ben Sira* 33, he is much closer to the Essenism of Qumran and is probably arguing against Pharisaic views (perhaps consciously against *Odes of Solomon* 9.4).

The sapiential and sectarian groups mirrored in the Dead Sea Scrolls have elaborated, through deterministic teachings, an understanding of the ordering of the cosmos, history, and individuals according to God's hidden plan. As part of the "social symbolics of knowledge," these provided powerful means "to resolve the ideological and historical contradictions created by the political domination of international empires" (Newsom) and to overcome a seemingly hopeless situation of marginalization and oppression (Hengel). These texts tend to support Josephus' statements about the Essenes' beliefs, but the ambiguity around their origins cannot be dissipated completely, since their interpretation is still open to debate.

BIBLIOGRAPHY

Baudry, Gérard-Henry. "Le péché originel dans les écrits de Qumrân." *Mélanges de sciences religieuses* 50 (1993), 7–23. An exploration of the relationship between the teachings of Qumran on predestination and the Christian doctrine of hereditary sin.

Beall, Todd S. *Josephus' Description of the Essenes Illustrated by the Dead Sea Scrolls*. Society for New Testament Studies Monograph Series, 58. Cambridge, 1988. A thorough comparison between what Josephus reports on the Essenes and what is found in the Dead Sea Scrolls.

Bergmeier, Roland. *Glaube als Gabe nach Johannes*, Beiträge zur Wissenschaft vom Alten und Neuen Testament, 112. Stuttgart, 1980. See pages 48–116. Studies on the notions of determinism, predestination, and dualism in ancient Judaism (specially Qumran) and gnosticism as a step toward a better understanding of faith in the Johannine writings.

Dimant, Devorah. "Qumran Sectarian Literature." In *The Literature of the Jewish People in the Period of the Second Temple and the Talmud*, vol. 2, edited by Michael E. Stone, pp. 483–550. Philadelphia, 1984. A general introduction to the texts of Qumran, with special attention to the religious thought of the sect.

Dombrowski Hopkins, Denise. "The Qumran Community and 1Q Hodayot: A Reassessment." *Revue de Qumrân* 10 (1981), 323–364. Studies dualism and determinism in 1QHodayot[a] to clarify what this particular document reveals about the attitude of the sectarians toward the rest of the world.

Hengel, Martin. *Judaism and Hellenism*, vol. I, pp. 107–254. Philadelphia, 1981. Particularly important on the determinism of the Dead Sea Scrolls and its background: the Hebrew Bible, Palestinian Judaism, early Apocalyptic, and the Hellenistic environment.

Lange, Armin. *Weisheit und Prädestination*. Studies on the Texts of the Desert of Judah, 18. Leiden, 1995. A fundamental study on the notion of a preexistent order of the world in the Dead Sea Scrolls. A short summary of this book is found in Armin Lange, "Wisdom and Predestination in the Dead Sea Scrolls." *Dead Sea Discoveries* 2 (1995), 340-354.

Lichtenberger, Hermann. *Studien zum Menschenbild in Texten der Qumrangemeinde*. Studien zur Umwelt des Neuen Testaments, 15. Göttingen, 1980. Studies determinism and predestination as part of the structure of the anthropology of the Qumran community.

Maier, Gerhard. *Mensch und freier Wille*. Wissenschaftliche Untersuchungen zum Neuen Testament, 12. Tübingen, 1971. An attempt to verify Josephus' description of the respective positions of the Pharisees, Sadducees, and Essenes on determinism and their relation to *Romans* 9–11.

Marcoulesco, Ileana. "Free will and determinism," in *Encyclopedia of Religions*, edited by Mircea Eliade, vol. 5, pp. 419–421. New York, 1987. A general treatment of the two notions from a philosophical and historical point of view.

Martone, Corrado. "Qumran and Stoicism." The collected papers of the Jerusalem Congress celebrating the 50th anniversary of the Qumran discoveries (1997). Forthcoming. Compares Qumran and Stoic determinism.

Marx, Alfred. "Y a-t-il une prédestination à Qumrân?" *Revue de Qumrân* 6 (1967), 163–182. Argues that there is "grace," rather than predestination, at Qumran.

Merril, Eugene H. *Qumran and Predestination*. Leiden, 1975. A careful study of the doctrine of predestination in 1Q Hodayot[a].

Newsom, Carol. "Knowing as Doing: The Social Symbolics of Knowledge at Qumran." *Semeia* 59 (1992), 139–153. Suggests that the deterministic doctrine of the Qumranites helped them to overcome symbolically their lack of power in the society.

Nötscher, Friedrich. "Schicksalsglauben in Qumran und Umwelt." *Biblische Zeitschrift* 3 (1959), 204–234; 4 (1960), 98–121. Describes the evolution of deterministic beliefs in Mesopotamia, Egypt, Ugarit, Qumran, later Judaism, Arabian traditions, and Islam.

Prigent, Pierre. "Psaumes de Salomon." In *La Bible. Écrits intertestamentaires*, edited by André Dupont-Sommer and Marc Philonenko, pp. 945–992. Paris, 1987. An annotated French translation of the Psalms of Solomon that reads them as an Essene composition.

Rad, Gerhard von. *Wisdom in Israel*. London, 1972. Seeks in the wisdom traditions the roots of the apocalyptic view that history has been determined by God before the creation.

Röhser, Günter. *Prädestination und Verstockung*. Texte und Arbeiten zum neutestamentlichen Zeitalter, 14. Tübingen, 1994. Uses an "interactive model" to understand predestination and hardening of the heart of human beings by God in the Hebrew Bible, early Judaism, and Pauline and Johannine writings.

Sanders, E. P. "The Dead Sea Scrolls." *Paul and Palestinian Judaism*, pp. 233–328. Philadelphia, 1977. Analyzes election and predestination as an element of the soteriological pattern of the Qumran documents.

Vermes, Geza, and Martin D. Goodman. *The Essenes according to the Classical Sources*. Oxford Centre Textbooks, 1. Sheffield, 1989. An English translation, with a short introduction, of the most important Greek or Latin texts relating to the Essenes.

Wallace D. Dewey Jr. "Free Will and Predestination. An Overview," in *Encyclopedia of Religions*, edited by Mircea Eliade, vol. 5, pp. 422–426. New York, 1987. A general treatment of the two notions as they appear in the history of religions.

JEAN DUHAIME

DEUTERONOMY, BOOK OF. Manuscripts recovered from Qumran and other major sites in the Judean Desert provide ample testimony to the importance of the *Book of Deuteronomy* in ancient Judaism. The fifth book of the Pentateuch is widely represented, in copies of the biblical book, in texts used for prayer and study, and in sectarian and other nonbiblical compositions. In this article these witnesses will be examined under four categories: biblical manuscripts; phylacteries and *mezuzot*; excerpted texts; and nonbiblical compositions.

Biblical Manuscripts. Among the biblical scrolls coming from the Judean Desert, twenty-nine manuscripts of *Deuteronomy* have been identified. Three of these are manuscript fragments discovered at Wadi Murabbaʿat (Mur 2; hereafter, MurDeuteronomy), Masada (Maslc; hereafter, MasDeuteronomy), and at Naḥal Ḥever (XḤev/Se3, hereafter XḤev/SeDeuteronomy; see Greenfield, 1992). [*See* Ḥever, Naḥal, *article on* Written Material; Masada, *article on* Written Material; Murabbaʿat, Wadi, *article on* Written Material; *and* Ṣeʾelim, Naḥal, *article on* Written Material.] The other twenty-six all have come from the caves near the western shore of the Dead Sea at Khirbet Qumran. The number of copies confirms that *Deuteronomy* was a popular book at Qumran, rivaled only by the *Psalms* (found in thirty-six copies). The other four books of the Pentateuch are represented in significantly lower numbers (*Genesis*, in nineteen; *Exodus*, in seventeen; *Leviticus*, in twelve; and *Numbers*, in six).

All the manuscripts found thus far were written in Hebrew, with the exception of one fragmentary Cave 4 scroll written in Greek (Septuagint Deuteronomy [4Q122]). The various *Deuteronomy* manuscripts were copied over a span of roughly three centuries (with the date being established on paleographical grounds). [*See* Paleography.] The oldest witness to *Deuteronomy* is paleo-Deuteronomy[s] (4Q46), a scroll consisting of one small fragment containing *Deuteronomy* 26.14–15, dated to the second half of the third century BCE. The oldest copy of *Deuteronomy* in the square script sequence is from Cave 5 at Qumran (5Q1; hereafter 5QDeuteronomy); it contains portions of chapters 7, 8, and the beginning of 9 and was written around the first quarter of the second century BCE. Late copies of the book are seen in the manuscripts from Masada and Murabbaʿat, and in Deuteronomy[j] from Cave 4 at Qumran (4Q37; about the first century CE). All the scrolls are inscribed on leather, with one possible exception from Cave 6, a small piece of papyrus that contains a few letters uncertainly identified as *Deuteronomy* 26.19 (Deuteronomy? [6Q3]).

Despite the abundance of manuscripts, textual evidence for the form of *Deuteronomy* at Qumran remains slim, since the majority of these manuscripts are relatively fragmentary (there is no manuscript that even approaches the completeness of the great Isaiah scroll from Cave 1, Isaiah[a] [1QIsa[a]]). In fact, fifteen of the twenty-nine scrolls preserve ten verses or fewer of the book. The largest *Deuteronomy* manuscript from the Judean Desert is Deuteronomy[c] from Cave 4 at Qumran (4Q30), which contains one hundred twenty verses from nineteen chapters. Deuteronomy[f] (4Q33) and paleo-Deuteronomy[r] (4Q45) are next, having ninety-two verses each. In all these cases as well, however, material is more often than not fragmentarily preserved.

Because of their fragmentary state, the affiliations of the various manuscripts with the three major traditions—the Masoretic Text, the Septuagint, and the Samaritan Pentateuch—cannot be established in most cases. In a few instances, however, an alignment with one of the three may be discerned: Deuteronomy[g] (4Q34) is virtually identical to the tradition underlying the Masoretic Text in spelling practices, paragraph divisions, and content. Deuteronomy[b] (4Q29) shows affinities with the Hebrew text behind the Septuagint in that it concurs uniquely with it in a few distinctive errors. In addition to this biblical text, excerpted manuscript Deuteronomy[q] (4Q44), which preserves the end of the Song of Moses from chapter 32 (vv. 37–43), agrees with the Hebrew forerunner of the Greek text in additional lines of text that are not found in the other traditions (see Skehan, 1954). No biblical manuscripts of *Deuteronomy* show an affinity with the Samaritan Pentateuch; however, three excerpted texts, Deuteronomy[j], Deuteronomy[kl], and Deuteronomy[n] (4Q37, 38, 41), show certain typological similarities with it, attesting the kinds of expansions, minor explications, and harmonizations that are the hallmark of that tradition (on the textual character of these three manuscripts see Duncan, 1997). Deuteronomy[n], also referred to as the "All Souls Deuteronomy," exhibits the most striking example of a harmonization akin to the sort found in the Samaritan tradition, containing an addition to the Decalogue that harmonizes the passage with its *Exodus* form. In the Sabbath command, the motive clause of *Deuteronomy* 5.15, which cites Israel's servitude in Egypt and the Exodus, is augmented with the version of the motivation from *Exodus* 20.11: "For on the sixth day, the Lord made the heavens and the earth, the sea, and all that is in them, and he rested on the seventh day." In this way two divergent traditions for the sanctity of the Sabbath are blended into one text.

With respect to the overall textual character of these scrolls, it may be observed that they not infrequently attest slightly expanded variant readings—minor explications or readings influenced by closely parallel phrases. Though these textual phenomena mark, to varying degrees, the transmission process of any biblical book, they are particularly prevalent in the witnesses to *Deuteronomy*, owing to the distinctive style of the book. *Deuteronomy* is characterized by repetition—replete with formulaic phrases echoing one another closely—and, in the legal portions, by an elaborative and redundant style. In the Dead Sea manuscripts these (mostly minor) expansionistic textual traits are exhibited not only in the later texts but in some of the more primitive manuscripts as well (for instance 5QDeuteronomy [c.200–175 BCE], Deuteronomy[c] [c.150–100 BCE], and paleo-Deuteronomy[r] [c.100–50 BCE]), thus demonstrating that this textual phenomenon entered the transmission process early on (see Wevers, 1978, who has documented this trait in the Greek witnesses). This particular category of variants, arising from the singular style of the book, accounts for more than a quarter of all the variants attested in the *Deuteronomy* material from the Judean Desert. A comparison of the major witnesses in such variants shows that the tradition that appears to have escaped this sort of expansionistic tendency most consistently is the (proto-) Masoretic. The Samaritan Pentateuch is next after it. By contrast, the Dead Sea Scrolls and the Greek are the most heavily influenced in this direction (the Greek tradition slightly more so than the scrolls). The relative relationship of the witnesses seen in this comparison is, on the whole, the same in a more comprehensive analysis of all extant variants. A total of 208 variants are preserved in the 28 texts from the Judean Desert (the Masada text of *Deuteronomy* is not included in this assessment; for a preliminary treatment see Talmon, 1998). Of these a preferable reading can be determined with reasonable certainty in 153 cases (the Greek can be assessed in 123 of these). The Masoretic Text carries the preferable reading in 74 percent of these instances. The scrolls attest the preferable reading in only 50 percent, followed closely by the Septuagint with 47 percent. The Samaritan Pentateuch, with 60 percent preferable readings, falls between the Masoretic Text on the one hand and the latter two witnesses on the other.

Some of the *Deuteronomy* texts from Qumran in particular have helped to shed further light on the nature of the Septuagint as translation. Especially striking are some readings from ancient poetry, where variants from Qumran have substantiated a Hebrew *Vorlage* for the Greek where none previously was known. One such variant is found in *Deuteronomy* 32.8 in the Song of Moses. The Masoretic and Samaritan traditions read here:

> When Elyon apportioned the nations,
> When he distributed humankind,
> He established the boundaries of the peoples
> According to the number of the *sons of Israel.*

In place of the reference to the "sons of Israel" the Greek witnesses read "angels of God" or "sons of God" (the latter is found in the most ancient tradition), a reading presupposed in several early sources and referred to as late as the medieval period (see Fishbane, 1985, p. 69). The *Vorlage* of the Greek is now confirmed by Deuteronomy^{j}, which preserves the phrase "sons of Elohim" (cf. Psalm 82.1 for a similar reference to divine beings). This is in all likelihood the original reading, as it is more probable that a reference to divine beings was later suppressed for theological reasons than that it was substituted for the reading "sons of Israel." Another noteworthy variant from Qumran supporting the Greek occurs in the poem of *Deuteronomy* 33, known as the Blessing of Moses. In the blessing of Benjamin (v. 12) the Masoretic text reads: "The beloved of the Lord will dwell securely upon him" with the parallel line reading: "(He) encompasses him all day long." The text is problematic since the logical end of the first phrase appears to be at the word *securely* (in fact the Samaritan tradition omits "upon him"); moreover the subject of the following line is unclear. Prior to the Qumran finds it was suggested that "upon him" should instead be read as the divine name ʿEli, meaning "(Most) High One," and said to be a variant form of ʿElyon (the consonantal text is very close to this epithet). This conjecture finds some support in the Greek, which reads "God" (Theos), and also clarifies this point as the beginning of a new phrase by placing a conjunction before the proper name. A reading preserved by a Cave 4 manuscript, Deuteronomy^{h} (4Q35), now provides further support for this proposal, though the specific form of the divine name attested is the more common El rather than ʿEli. In addition to this example, Deuteronomy^{h} preserves a few other readings that agree with the *Vorlage* of the Greek (most of them from the blessing of Levi; see Duncan, 1995). Deuteronomy^{h} is of additional interest for its special relationship to a nonbiblical text, Testimonia (4Q175).

Phylacteries and Mezuzot. Select portions of *Deuteronomy* are attested in the nine *mezuzot* and thirty-three phylacteries found among the Judean Desert documents. [*See* Phylacteries and Mezuzot.] The phylacteries include segments from *Deuteronomy* 5.1–6.9 (the Decalogue and the Shemaʿ, that is, the passage introduced by "Hear, O Israel"), and/or *Deuteronomy* 10.12–11.21, and/or passages from *Exodus* 12.43–13.16. In one instance, verses from *Deuteronomy* 32 (the Song of Moses) are preserved. Both the range of passages and their delimitations are noteworthy, since the selection prescribed by the rabbis is restricted to *Deuteronomy* 6.4–9 and 11.13–21 and *Exodus* 13.1–16 (see B.T., *Men.* 34a–37b and 42b–43b; Massekhet Tefillin 9). Especially significant is the inclusion of the Decalogue, which is found in the Qumran material only. Mishnaic evidence suggests that the Qumran texts may, in fact, reflect general practice prior to the promulgation of rabbinic legislation (see Vermes, 1959). According to *Tamid* 5.1, in the Second Temple period recital of the Decalogue (along with the Shemaʿ and *Dt.* 11.13–21) was a part of the morning Temple prayer service (see Habermann, 1954). A statement in the Jerusalem Talmud implies, moreover, that these texts also were recited outside the precincts of the Temple (J.T., *Ber.* 3c). Direct evidence for such a liturgical use of the Decalogue outside of Jerusalem is seen in the Nash Papyrus from Egypt (second century BCE), which contains the Decalogue and the Shemaʿ on a single leaf and appears to have been a type of lectionary (see Mann, 1927, p. 288). It is significant that phylacteries found at two sites occupied by refugees at the time of the Bar Kokhba Revolt (c.132–135 CE)—Naḥal Ṣeʾelim and Murabbaʿat—do not include the Decalogue (and moreover attest only the restricted corpus for the other sections), thus indicating that the Mishnaic practice had obtained by at least the early second century CE.

Two of the eight *mezuzot* found at Qumran attest portions of the Decalogue. Other passages included in these texts are the Shemaʿ and portions from *Deuteronomy* 10–11 (the *mezuzah* from Cave 8 [8Q4] clearly once contained *Deuteronomy* 10.12–11.21 in its entirety), along with *Exodus* 13. The single *mezuzah* from Murabbaʿat is no longer readable.

Excerpted Texts. A few *Deuteronomy* texts (from Cave 4), originally thought to be biblical manuscripts, have now been identified as special selections excerpted from various parts of the book: Deuteronomy[j], Deuteronomy[kl], Deuteronomy[n], and Deuteronomy[q] (see Duncan, 1997; (Crawford) White, "4QDt[n]," 1990; Stegemann, 1967). These texts, all dating from the Herodian period (30 BCE–68 CE), include portions from one or more of the following passages: *Deuteronomy* 5.1–6.3, 8.5–10, 11, and 32. Deuteronomy[j] is of special interest as it also includes passages from *Exodus* 12.43–51 and 13.1–5. (The Exodus fragments originally were classified with Deuteronomy[j] on the working assumption that this was a biblical scroll containing interpolations from *Exodus*. It was clear, in any case, that both derived from the same scribal hand.) Since all the *Deuteronomy* manuscripts are fragmentary, it was some time before the specific nature of these scrolls as selections (versus fragmentary remains) could be substantiated. It is, in particular, the emergence of the Qumran phylacteries and *mezuzot* with their broader repertoire of passages that has facilitated the identification of these four scrolls as special-use texts. In fact, with the exception of *Deuteronomy* 8 portions of all the passages found in these four scrolls are attested in the Qumran phylactery and *mezuzot* texts. Corroborating evidence has been provided by material aspects of the scrolls themselves. For instance in Deuteronomy[q], which preserves the final verses of *Deuteronomy* 32, a very wide margin, without stitching, follows the end of the poem, clear indication that the passage was not followed by *Deuteronomy* 33 and 34. In Deuteronomy[j] material evidence is more tenuous; however, it appears that *Exodus* 12.43 (the beginning of a paragraph) is preceded by verse 21 of *Deuteronomy* 11 (in any case the preceding word that is preserved could not have come from *Exodus* 12.42, whereas reconstruction indicates it might well be from *Deuteronomy* 11.21 [see Duncan, Discoveries in the Judaean Desert, 14, 1995, p. 88]). Deuteronomy[n], the best preserved of the four scrolls, contains the most dramatic material evidence. Here a column consisting of *Deuteronomy* 8.5–10 clearly *precedes* the Decalogue of *Deuteronomy* 5 (see (Crawford) White, "4QDt[n]," 1990). In fact, chapter 8 of *Deuteronomy* appears also in Deuteronomy[j], which preserves precisely the same section (here, too, as in Deuteronomy[n], a discrete column appears to have been reserved for it). (On the status of *Dt*. 8.5–10 as a special text, see Stegemann, 1967, who notes that it is distinguished as a separate paragraph in the Samaritan Pentateuch, and Weinfeld, 1992, who observes that in rabbinic tradition *Dt*. 8.5–10 is the basis for the duty of the blessing after meals, B.T., *Ber*. 44a.)

A material feature that unites all these manuscripts is the small proportions of their columns (shorter by almost half than the columns in most biblical manuscripts), further indication that these scrolls contained less material than full-scale biblical manuscripts. Though the *Sitz im Leben* and precise function of these texts are debatable, it seems most likely that the greater part of them would have had a liturgical or devotional function, especially given the fact that they so clearly duplicate the corpus of the phylacteries. One might stress, however, an important distinction between these two kinds of texts. In the phylacteries it was not considered necessary to write passages out in their entirety, whereas in the excerpted texts it is apparent, despite their fragmentary state, that the selections were written out fully and continuously (witness the Decalogue in Deuteronomy[j] and Deuteronomy[n]). This difference probably reflects the more symbolic function of the phylacteries, as opposed to some more practical function of the excerpted scrolls as texts for study and/or for prayer services.

Deuteronomy in Major Nonbiblical Compositions. In addition to the biblical manuscripts and the prayer and study texts of *Deuteronomy*, the book is quoted, alluded to, or paraphrased in several of the major Judean Desert texts. Use of it indicates that the book was of central importance and was considered authoritative (it is probably cited as such more than any other book of the Torah; see VanderKam, 1994, pp. 149–153). Among the legal texts it is found notably in Temple Scroll[a] from Cave 11 (11Q19). The latter sections of this lengthy composition contain legal material largely drawn from *Deuteronomy*, written, however, in the voice of the first person (thus the contents are presented as the direct address of God). *Deuteronomy* also is cited (eight times) in the fragments of the Damascus Document from Qumran (4Q266–273, 5Q12, 6Q15). Citations from *Deuteronomy* occur in three thematic commentaries from Qumran (compositions made up of various passages from scripture focusing on one or a few themes). Melchizedek (11Q13), a very fragmentary manuscript containing biblical interpretation around the figure of Melchizedek from *Genesis* 14, cites *Deuteronomy* 15.2 (at least). Testimonia (4Q175), an anthology of passages having in common a messianic motif, and Florilegium (4Q174), which takes as its focus *2 Samuel* 7 (the promise of an eternal dynasty for David) and *Psalms* 1 and 2, also cite *Deuteronomy*. Notably, both compositions include the same section from the ancient poem of *Deuteronomy* 33—the blessing of Levi (vv. 8–11)—though it is only very fragmentarily preserved in the Florilegium. The latter also contains a portion from the blessings of Zebulun and Gad (vv. 19–21), again in a very fragmentary state. Testimonia also cites *Deuteronomy* 5.28–29 and 18.18–19 (the latter speaks of a prophet like Moses). A special feature of interest in the blessing of Levi in Testimonia is the striking similarity between its text and that of biblical manuscript Deuteronomy^{h}, discussed above. A few textual features are shared exclusively by these two scrolls, suggesting that this quotation in Testimonia is dependent on a textual tradition like Deuteronomy^{h} (see Duncan, "New Readings," 1995). The *Book of Deuteronomy* also is the primary influence in the poetic work of the Apocryphon of Joshua (4Q378–379). In the extensive but fragmentary Reworked Pentateuch (4Q158, 364–365, 366–367), a biblical paraphrase, *Deuteronomy* is covered through chapter 19.

BIBLIOGRAPHY

PRIMARY SOURCES

Baillet, Maurice, J. T. Milik, and Roland de Vaux, eds. *Les "Petites Grottes" de Qumran (Textes)*. Discoveries in the Judaean Desert, 3. Oxford, 1962. See pages 106–107.

Barthélemy, Dominique. "1QDeut^{ab}." In *Qumran Cave 1*, edited by D. Barthélemy and J. T. Milik, pp. 54–62 and 72–76. Discoveries in the Judaean Desert, 1. Oxford, 1955.

(Crawford) White, Sidnie. "4QDeut$^{a,c,d,f,g,i,n\text{-}p}$." In *Qumran Cave 4, IX: Deuteronomy, Joshua, Judges, Kings*, edited by Eugene Ulrich and Frank Moore Cross, pp. 7–8, 15–38, 45–59, 71–74, 117–136. Discoveries in the Judaean Desert, 14. Oxford, 1995.

Duncan, Julie A. "4QDeut^{b,e,h,j,k,l,k2,k3,l,m}." In *Qumran Cave 4, IX: Deuteronomy, Joshua, Judges, Kings*, edited by Eugene Ulrich and Frank Moore Cross, pp. 9–14, 39–44, 61–70, 75–116. Discoveries in the Judaean Desert, 14. Oxford, 1995.

Milik, Józef T. "murDeut." In *Les Grottes de Murabbaʿât (Textes)*, edited by P. Benoit, J. T. Milik, and Roland de Vaux, pp. 78–79. Discoveries in the Judaean Desert, 2. Oxford, 1961.

Milik, Józef T. "murPhyl." In *Les Grottes de Murabbaʿât (Textes)*, edited by P. Benoit, J. T. Milik, and Roland de Vaux, pp. 180–185. Discoveries in the Judaean Desert, 2. Oxford, 1961.

Milik, Józef T. "5QDeuteronomy." In *Les "Petites Grottes" de Qumrân (Textes)*, edited by Maurice Baillet, J. T. Milik, and Roland de Vaux, pp. 169–171. Discoveries in the Judaean Desert, 3. Oxford, 1962.

Milik, Józef T. "Tefillin, Mezuzot et Targums (4Q128–4Q157)." In *Qumrân Grotte 4: 4Q128–4Q157*, edited by Roland de Vaux and J. T. Milik, pp. 33–90. Discoveries in the Judaean Desert, 6. Oxford, 1977.

Ploeg, J. van der. "Les manuscrits de la grotte XI de Qumran." *Revue de Qumrân* 12.45 (1985), 3–15. Transcription of most of Deuteronomy from Cave 11 at Qumran (11Q3) on page 10.

Ulrich, Eugene. "4QpaleoDeut$^{r\text{-}s}$." In *Qumran Cave 4: Palaeo-Hebrew and Greek Biblical Manuscripts*, edited by Patrick W. Skehan, Eugene Ulrich, and Judith E. Sanderson, pp. 131–154. Discoveries in the Judaean Desert, 9. Oxford, 1992.

Ulrich, Eugene, and Patrick W. Skehan. "4QDeut^{q}." In *Qumran Cave 4, IX: Deuteronomy, Joshua, Judges, Kings*, edited by Eugene Ulrich et al., pp. 137–142. Discoveries in the Judaean Desert, 14. Oxford, 1995.

SECONDARY SOURCES

(Crawford) White, Sidnie. "4QDt^{n}: Biblical Manuscript or Excerpted Text?" In *Of Scribes and Scrolls: Studies on the Hebrew Bible, Intertestamental Judaism, and Christian Origins Presented to John Strugnell*, edited by H. W. Attridge, J. J. Collins, and T. H. Tobin, pp. 13–20. College Theology Society Resources in Religion, 5. Lanham, Md., 1990.

(Crawford) White, Sidnie. "The All Souls Deuteronomy and the Decalogue." *Journal of Biblical Literature* 109 (1990), 193–206.

(Crawford) White, Sidnie. "Special Features of Four Biblical Manuscripts from Cave IV, Qumran: 4QDt^{a}, 4QDt^{c}, 4QDt^{d}, and 4QDt^{g}." *Revue de Qumrân* 15 (1991), 157–167.

(Crawford) White, Sidnie. "Three Deuteronomy Manuscripts from Cave 4, Qumran." *Journal of Biblical Literature* 112 (1993), 23–42.

Duncan, Julie Ann. "Considerations of 4QDt^{j} in Light of 'All Souls Deuteronomy' and Cave 4 Phylactery Texts." In *The Madrid Qumran Congress: Proceedings of the International Congress on the Dead Sea Scrolls, Madrid, 18–21 March 1991*, vol. 1, edited by Julio Trebolle Barrera and Louis Vegas Montaner, pp. 199–215. Studies on the Texts of the Desert of Judah, 11.1. Leiden, 1992.

Duncan, Julie Ann. "New Readings for the 'Blessing of Moses' from Qumran." *Journal of Biblical Literature* 114 (1995), 273–290.

Duncan, Julie Ann. "Excerpted Texts of Deuteronomy at Qumran." *Revue de Qumrân* 18 (1997), 43–62.

Fishbane, Michael. *Biblical Interpretation in Ancient Israel*. Oxford, 1985.

Greenfield, Jonas C. "The Texts from Naḥal Ṣe'elim (Wadi Seiyal)." In *The Madrid Qumran Congress: Proceedings of the International Congress on the Dead Sea Scrolls, Madrid, 18–21 March 1991*, vol. 2, edited by Julio Trebolle Barrera and Luis Vegas Montaner, pp. 661–665. Studies on the Texts of the Desert of Judah 11.2. Leiden, 1992.

Habermann, A. M. "The Phylacteries in Antiquity" (in Hebrew). *Eretz Israel* 3 (1954), 174–177.

Mann, Jacob. "Changes in the Divine Service of the Synagogue due to Religious Persecutions." *Hebrew Union College Annual* 4 (1927), 241–310. See especially pages 288–299.

Skehan, Patrick. "A Fragment of the 'Song of Moses' (Deut 32) from Qumran." *Bulletin of the American Schools of Oriental Research* 136 (1954), 12–15.

Stegemann, Hartmut. "Weitere Stücke von 4QpPsalm 37, von 4QPatriarchal Blessings und Hinweis auf eine unedierte Handschrift aus Höhle 4Q mit Exzerpten aus dem Deuteronomium." *Revue de Qumrân* 6 (1967), 193–227. See especially pages 217–227. Earliest discussion of excerpted text Deuteronomy^{n}.

Talmon, Shemaryahu. "Fragments of a Deuteronomy Scroll from Masada: Deuteronomy 33.17–34.6 (1043/A-D)." In *Boundaries of the Ancient Near Eastern World: A Tribute to Cyrus Gordon*, edited by Meir Lubetski, Claire Gottlieb, and Sharon Keller, pp. 150–161. Journal for the Study of the Old Testament Supplement Series, 273. Sheffield, 1998.

VanderKam, James C. *The Dead Sea Scrolls Today*. Grand Rapids, Mich., 1994.

Vermes, Geza. "Pre-Mishnaic Jewish Worship and the Phylacteries from the Dead Sea." *Vetus Testamentum* 9 (1959), 65–72.

Weinfeld, Moshe. "Grace after Meals in Qumran." *Journal of Biblical Literature* 111 (1992), 427–440. Includes a citation of evidence of liturgical use of *Deuteronomy* 8.5–10 and *Deuteronomy* 32.

Wevers, John W. *Text History of Greek Deuteronomy*. Abhandlung der Akademie der Wissenschaften in Göttingen, Philologisch-Historische Klasse, Dritte Folge 106; Mitteilungen des Septuaginta-Unternehmens, 13. Göttingen, 1978. See especially pp. 86–99.

JULIE A. DUNCAN

DE VAUX, ROLAND (1903–1970), French archaeologist, was born in Paris on 17 December 1903. He was ordained a priest in 1929, and he entered the Dominican order the same year. He left for Jerusalem in 1933 and, from 1934 until his death on 10 September 1970, he taught at the École Biblique. De Vaux was editor of the *Revue biblique* from 1938 to 1953. He was director of the École Biblique from 1945 to 1965. It was both as director of the École Biblique and as an archaeologist that he became closely involved in the finding of the manuscripts at Qumran and in the excavation of the site.

The archaeological activities of de Vaux were certainly very important: a Byzantine mosaic at Mâʿin starting in 1937; a caravansary at Qaryet el-ʿEnab/Abu Gôsh in 1944; and Tell el-Farʿah near Naplouse between 1946 and 1960 (nine campaigns). He began excavations at Khirbet Qumran and the surrounding area in 1949, and they lasted until 1958.

With the end of the Arab-Israeli War in 1948, it became possible to excavate the cave where the Dead Sea Scrolls, which Archbishop Athanasius Yeshua Samuel and Professor Eleazar L. Sukenik had bought, had been found. This cave (Qumran Cave 1) was reopened at the end of January 1949. G. Lankester Harding, director of the Antiquities Department of Jordan, asked de Vaux to carry out the excavation of this cave (15 February–15 March) with the assistance of the Antiquities Department and the Palestine Archaeological Museum. In addition to a large quantity of pottery (cf. Discoveries in the Judaean Desert, 1, 1955, pp. 8–17), many fragments of written documents were found during the excavation, and, in some cases, they allowed a link to be made to manuscripts held by the Hebrew University in Jerusalem (see 1QIsaiah^b [1Q833.35] and Discoveries in the Judaean Desert, 1, 1955, pp. 66, 135–136).

After 1949, archaeological excavations continued first of all on the site of Khirbet Qumran, but also in other caves as they were gradually discovered. The first caves to be excavated were those of Murabbaʿat (21 January–3 March 1952), and the archaeological results were published in 1962 (cf. Discoveries in the Judaean Desert, 2, 1961, pp. 3–50). The importance of the texts from the period of the Roman occupation became clear, especially from the time of the Bar Kokhba Revolt (132–135 CE), because the caves served as a hiding place for those who were fighting against the Romans. In 1952, Qumran Caves 2 and 3 were excavated (10 March–29 March). In September of the same year, Caves 4 through 6 were found in the marl plateau around Khirbet Qumran. In 1955 (7 February–15 March), Caves 7 through 10 were excavated and, in 1956, Cave 11 was excavated. The results of the excavation of these caves, except Qumran Cave 11, were published by de Vaux (Discoveries in the Judaean Desert, 3, 1962, pp. 3–36 and, in the case of Cave 4, Discoveries in the Judaean Desert, 6, 1977, pp. 3–22). [*See* Discoveries in the Judaean Desert.]

In 1951, the first campaign of excavations began on the site of Khirbet Qumran; although interrupted by the work in the caves, the excavations were resumed from 1953 to 1955. In 1958 (25 January–21 March), de Vaux directed excavations at ʿEin-Feshkha, a site 3 kilometers to the south of Qumran.

In 1961, de Vaux presented the main historical conclusions of the excavations carried out at Khirbet Qumran. Leaving aside the remains from Iron Age II, the occupation of the site divides into three periods: Period I (subdivided into Ia and Ib), which began shortly before John Hyrcanus (135–104 BCE) and extended to 31 BCE, when an earthquake shook the region; Period II, which extends from the reign of Herod Archelaus (4 BCE–6 CE) until 68 CE, when the site was destroyed by the Roman army; and Period III, which is represented by a military post occupied by the Romans from 68 to 73 CE. Subsequently, the abandoned buildings were used as a shelter during the Second Jewish Revolt (132–135 CE), but only briefly.

These results are open to discussion, but the absence of a final report means that we have to keep them in abeyance while we wait until such time as a much more detailed account of the excavations is published, an account that de Vaux was unable to produce himself. However, in 1994 this account began with a first volume edited by Jean-Baptiste Humbert and Alain Chambon (Humbert and Chambon, 1994) and presenting 538 photographs and a synthesis of the field notes of de Vaux. Four other volumes are expected.

Before 1947, de Vaux was also chairman of the Board of Trustees of the Palestine Archaeological Museum (sponsored by the Rockefeller Foundation), alternatively directed by the American, British, and French Schools of Archaeology at Jerusalem. [*See* Palestine Archaeological Museum.] For this reason he played an important part in the purchase of fragments owned by bedouin and in the search for funds for the publication.

De Vaux was not himself an epigraphist, but he published three fragments from Qumran Cave 1 (de Vaux, 1949). However, in 1954 he became editor in chief for the publication of manuscripts, and he retained this position until his death in 1970.

BIBLIOGRAPHY

de Vaux, Roland. "La grotte des manuscrits hébreux." *Revue biblique* 56 (1949), 586–609.

de Vaux, Roland. "Fouilles au Khirbet Qumrân: Rapport préliminaire." *Revue biblique* 60 (1953), 83–106. First campaign at Khirbet Qumran.

de Vaux, Roland. "Exploration de la région de Qumrân." *Revue biblique* 60 (1953), 540–561.

de Vaux, Roland. "Fouilles au Khirbet Qumrân: Rapport préliminaire sur la deuxième campagne." *Revue biblique* 61 (1954), 206–236.

de Vaux, Roland. "Fouilles de Khirbet Qumrân: Rapport préliminaire sur les troisième, quatrième, et cinquième campagnes." *Revue biblique* 63 (1956), 533–577.

de Vaux, Roland. "Fouilles de Feshkha: Rapport préliminaire." *Revue biblique* 66 (1959), 225–255.

de Vaux, Roland. *Archaeology and the Dead Sea Scrolls: The Schweich Lectures of the British Academy, 1959*. Revised edition in an English translation. London, 1973. Published in French in 1961. Synthesis of the excavations at Qumran and ʿEin-Feshkha.

Humbert, Jean-Baptiste, and Alain Chambon. *Fouilles de Khirbet Qumrân et de ʿAin Feshkha, I: Album de photographies, répertoire du fonds photographique, synthèse des notes de chantier du Père Roland de Vaux*. Novum Testamentum et Orbis Antiquus, Series Archaeologica, 1. Fribourg-Göttingen, 1994.

JACQUES BRIEND

DIDACHE, or "Church order," is a collection of ethical instructions and guidelines for rituals and organization of an early Christian community. The Greek text survives in one eleventh-century manuscript, complete but for the final lines, which was discovered by Theophilus Bryennios in 1873 in Constantinople and first published in 1883. A fragmentary Greek papyrus of the late fourth century (P.Oxy. 1782) contains a portion of the text. There exist also a Coptic fragment (*Br. Mus. Or. 9271* [*Copt.*]) and evidence of Ethiopic and Georgian translations. The fourth-century *Apostolic Constitutions* paraphrased the whole *Didache* (*Ap. Const*. 7.1.2–32.4). Other ecclesiastical sources through the Middle Ages indicate knowledge of the text or of its sources.

The collection begins with ethical instruction, apparently to be used in baptismal catechesis (1.1–6.3). Ritual instructions follow, treating baptism (7.1–4), fasting and prayer (8.1–3), and the Eucharist (9.1–110.7). A section on ecclesiastical discipline deals with itinerant prophets and apostles (11.1–12), other obligations of hospitality (12.1–5), prophets and teachers who wish to remain in a community (13.1–7), confession and reconciliation (12.1–3), and the election of bishops and deacons (15.1–4). The incomplete concluding chapter offers parenesis in the context of an eschatological scenario (16.1–8). The text was probably composed in the late first or early second century CE in a Jewish-Christian environment in Syria or Palestine.

There is a broad generic similarity between the Rule of the Community (1QS) and the *Didache*, since both have homiletic elements and are concerned with questions of community order. Of particular interest is the initial section of the *Didache*, the "Two Ways" Tractate, which parallels the Rule of the Community (1QS iii.18–iv.26).

The *Didache* has probably used a source document, likely to be of Jewish origin, to which the author, or perhaps a subsequent redactor, added a series of specifically Christian precepts (1.3b–2.1). Some (e.g., 1.4: "turn the other cheek") are reminiscent of the Sermon on the Mount; others (e.g., 1.6: "let your alms sweat in your hands until you know to whom you are giving it") are later developments. Whether this section was developed directly from the Synoptic Gospels or from parallel early Christian oral tradition remains debated.

The rest of the Way of Life (1.1–3a, 2.2–4.14) contains admonitions based on the Ten Commandments (2.2–3), expanded to condemn such evils as magic and abortion; proverbial directives to the "child" to avoid the sources of evil acts (3.1–6); encouragement to meekness and humility (3.7–10); rules for social behavior (4.1–10); and a concluding exhortation to pursue this Way of Life (4.11–14). The Way of Death (5.1–2) consists of a brief list of vices to be avoided, followed by a general conclusion (6.1–2).

Material similar to the "Two Ways" tradition used by the *Didache* enjoyed considerable popularity in early Christian circles. A close parallel, without the New Testament material of *Didache* 1.3b–2.1, appears in the second-century *Epistle of Barnabas* (18.1–20.2). Later patristic works also transmit modified forms of the "Two Ways" teaching. These include the Latin *Doctrina apostolorum*, probably composed in antiquity but preserved in an eleventh-century manuscript, and the fourth-century Greek *Apostolic Church Order* or *Canons of the Holy Apostles* and its *Epitome*. Other works, such as Ps.-Athanasius *Syntagma doctrinae*, *Fides CCCXVIII patrum*, the Arabic *Life of Shenoute*, and the *Rule of Benedict*, show traces of the "Two Ways" schema.

The *Didache* and Rule of the Community represent different versions of the venerable motif. Biblical and postbiblical Jewish literature frequently used the contrast of two ways, often combining them with value-laden dichotomies, for example, Psalm 1.1–6; *Proverbs* 4.18–19 ("light" and "darkness"); 12.28 ("life" and "death"); *Jeremiah* 21.8 ("life" and "death"); *1 Enoch* 94.1–5; *2 Enoch* 30.15 [long recension] ("light" and "darkness"); *T. Ash*. 3.1–5 ("two spirits"); *Sibylline Oracles* 8.399–401 ("two spirits"); cf. M. *Avot* 2.9. The version of the treatment in the Rule of the Community (1QS iii.18–iv.26), unlike the *Didache*, uses the notion of two cosmic spirits to frame balanced lists of virtues ("meekness, patience, compassion, etc.," 1QS iv.3) and vices ("greed . . . irreverence, deceit, pride, etc.," 1QS iv.9); each set is followed by a discussion of the appropriate reward or punishment. The *Didache*, using the contrast of life and death, absent from Rule of the Community, displays more formal diversity in the material in the Way of Life, which receives greater emphasis than its negative counterpart. Both texts share a concern with virtues of the "meek" (1QS iv.3; *Did*. 3.7–10).

Other parallels are few. In comparison with the scrolls' fragmentary Baptismal Liturgy (4Q414), the *Didache*'s instructions for baptism offer no responsory prayer. They focus on the action of the officiant, the type of water to be used, and the requirement to fast. A trinitarian formula indicates the ritual's Christian character in the *Didache*.

The *Didache*'s instructions for the the community meal prescribe recitation of "eucharistic" or thanksgiving prayers before (9.1–5) and after (10.1–7) the meal. The *Didache*, like CD vi.16–17 and 20–21, excludes novices, for the *Didache* the unbaptized, from the sacred meal. The prayer after the meal (10.1–7) resembles the *Birkat Ha-Mazon* (Grace after Meals), now paralleled in Grace After Meals? (4Q434a). Both bless the Lord's name, the *Didache* for the knowledge made known through Jesus (10.2), the scroll for the Law.

BIBLIOGRAPHY

Audet, Jean-Paul. "Affinités littéraires et doctinrales du 'Manuel de discipline.'" *Revue biblique* 59 (1952), 219–238.

Braun, Herbert. *Qumran und das Neue Testament*. 2 vols., pp. 2.185–189. Tübingen, 1966.

Niederwimmer, Kurt. *The Didache*. Minneapolis, Minn., 1998.

Suggs, M. Jack. "The Christian Two Ways Tradition: Its Antiquity, Form, and Function." In *Studies in New Testament and Early Christian Literature: Essays in Honor of Allen P. Wikgren*, edited by David E. Aune, pp. 60–74. Leiden, 1972.

HAROLD W. ATTRIDGE

DISCOVERIES IN THE JUDAEAN DESERT. The international team whose task it has been since 1953 to publish the scrolls found in the Judean Desert created a series, Discoveries in the Judaean Desert (of Jordan), in which these texts would be published. The editor in chief of the international team served at the same time as the general editor of this series: Roland de Vaux (vols. 1–5), Pierre Benoit (vols. 6–7), John Strugnell (vol. 8), and Emanuel Tov (vols. 9–). The volumes are produced by Oxford University Press, under the (often joint) auspices of the Jordan Department of Antiquities (vols. 1–3), École Biblique et Archéologique Française (vols. 1–3, 5), Palestine Archaeological Museum (vols. 1–5), and the American Schools of Oriental Research (vols. 3–4). No such auspices are listed for volume 6 (1977) and subsequent volumes. Volume 8 and all subsequent volumes were and are published under the auspices of the Israel Antiquities Authority, which has been actively involved in the publication effort since 1990. Throughout, the series has been named Discoveries in the Judaean Desert, with an interlude (1962–1968) during which volumes 3–5 were named Discoveries in the Judaean Desert of Jordan.

All the fragments and artifacts found in the Judean Desert from 1947 to 1956 by archaeologists or purchased from bedouin are scheduled to be published in the Discoveries in the Judaean Desert series, as well as the archaeological background of the sites. These volumes thus cover texts and artifacts found within the boundaries of Mandatory Palestine (Cave 1, 1947) and of the Hashemite Kingdom of Jordan during those years, with the exception of material from Naḥal Ḥever in Israel, brought to Jordan and incorrectly labeled as being from Seiyal (note, for example, the small fragments of the Greek Minor Prophets scroll found at Naḥal Ḥever after the large scroll had become known as "Seiyal"—see vol. 8, p. 1). In his preface to volume 1, G. Lankester Harding, Director of the Department of Antiquities of the Hashemite Kingdom of Jordan, describes the area covered by the Discoveries in the Judaean Desert series as "the area of the Judaean desert between, roughly, Jericho and Wady Murabbaʿat." The following sites are thus covered, from north to south: Wadi ed-Daliyeh, Khirbet Qumran and the caves of Qumran, Khirbet Mird, ʿEin-Feshkha, Wadi Murabbaʿat, Seiyal = Naḥal Ṣeʾelim (although most documents from Seiyal actually derived from Naḥal Ḥever).

The scholars involved in the publication of the texts in the first seven volumes of Discoveries in the Judaean Desert were the members of the initial international team, which consisted of the following eight scholars (in alphabetical order): John M. Allegro, Frank M. Cross, C.-H. Hunzinger (subsequently replaced by Maurice Baillet), Józef T. Milik, Patrick W. Skehan, Jean Starcky, John Strugnell, and Roland de Vaux. The work of these scholars (as well as that of Pierre Benoit and Dominique Barthélemy) was supplemented by a few technical appendixes such as on linen textiles from Cave 1 (vol. 1, pp. 18–38), and by the publication of Psalms[a] from Qumran Cave 11 (11Q5) by James A. Sanders in volume 4. The work of Skehan was published posthumously, in conjunction with Eugene Ulrich and Judith E. Sanderson (vol. 9).

It was the intention of the original team that the Discoveries in the Judaean Desert series would contain the official publication of the texts in conjunction with a commentary, but not in all cases was this the *editio princeps*. A concise publication of some texts was presented elsewhere in individual instances, sometimes involving mere transcriptions without photographs, and in other cases only photographs without transcriptions. Over the years the number of such preliminary editions increased, often constituting a full-fledged edition of the text, of which a revised version appeared later in Discoveries in the Judaean Desert.

The basic format of the series, as determined in volume 1, contains the following components:

1. a general introduction to each document describing its physical condition, color, orthography, paleography, and textual character;
2. a transcription of the text(s), with or without reconstructions, approaching as closely as possible the layout and content of the fragments;
3. a translation of the nonbiblical fragments or sections;

4. short notes on the readings, sometimes suggesting alternative readings;
5. a commentary on the contents of the fragments, in the biblical fragments involving comparisons with the other textual witnesses;
6. plates and figures documenting all the fragments published in the volume (with or without scale indicators), accompanied by drawings in the case of the Copper Scroll (3Q15) from Qumran Cave 3 in volume 3. These plates are usually based on the latest arrangement of the fragments recorded in the Palestine Archaeological Museum photos of the forty-three series taken in 1959–1961, sometimes accompanied by earlier photographs, or by more recent photographs of the Israel Antiquities Authority.

In these text editions the presentation of the text (transcription) is often the most important element. For many nonbiblical texts that were previously unknown and for which there are no parallel texts, the identification of the text and the presumed sequence of the fragments is very uncertain (cf. the introduction to vol. 1, pp. 43–45). Upon their publication, several texts were identified differently. The most well-known example is probably that of the Greek fragments from Qumran Cave 7 (7Q3–18) published as "fragments non identifiés," but tentatively identified by J. O'Callaghan and C. P. Thiede as reflecting segments of the New Testament and by others as reflecting parts of the Septuagint and other works. In other cases, different manuscripts of the same composition given to different scholars and published with different names were subsequently combined. For example, text 4Q158 was published by John M. Allegro in volume 5 as Biblical Paraphrase and then was renamed Reworked Pentateuch[a] by Emanuel Tov in volume 13 in conjunction with the publication of other manuscripts of that composition as Reworked Pentateuch[b–e] (4Q364–367).

The general philosophy behind the Discoveries in the Judaean Desert editions is to provide the scholarly public with a workable edition of the text, which, though presenting the best possible edition according to its editor, is likely to be improved upon by subsequent generations of scholars. In accordance with this philosophy, most scholars provided a minimal commentary (especially John M. Allegro in vol. 5), to be improved upon and augmented subsequently by others or by themselves.

The first volume of Discoveries in the Judaean Desert introduced a system of presentation of the texts that attempts to represent in the transcription all the elements of the text as precisely as possible, including the exact position of the letters in the columns and fragments and the spaces between them, corrections, crossing out with a line, erasures, supralinear additions, the existence of margins, marginal notes, dots between words in the paleo-Hebrew script, letters or words in the paleo-Hebrew script, numbers, and so on (see the detailed description in vol. 1, pp. 44–48: "Table des sigles"). According to this system, partially preserved letters are indicated with a supralinear dot or circle in accordance with the different degrees of certainty regarding the preserved part of the letter, and undetermined remnants of letters are indicated with midline circlets. This system has been used from volume 1 onward, and, although there are necessarily different conceptions of the certainty of the preserved parts of letters, basically the system has been used consistently. At the same time, differences exist between scholars over the amount of reconstruction they allow themselves for the segments that have not been preserved. Also, some scholars will make more suggestions than others regarding the column structure of the scroll on the basis of the preserved fragments, and even on the length and height of the column.

The "Table de sigles" in volume 1 also presents the system used in Discoveries in the Judaean Desert for designating the fragments found in the Judean Desert, a system that is more or less followed throughout for newly discovered or identified fragments. When devising the system of presentation of the partially preserved texts, the members of the international team found little guidance in the scholarly literature of Semitic texts in the beginning of the 1950s, while in many ways their system resembles that of the Greek papyrological conventions. At the same time, some conventions developed only later. For example, the designation *Paleo* for the texts written in the Paleo-Hebrew script was not yet used, thus paleo-Leviticus from Qumran Cave 1 (1Q3) was described in Discoveries in the Judaean Desert as "Lévitique et autres fragments en écriture 'Phénicienne.'" The term *Paleo* appears for the first time in volume 3, page 104, with regard to text 6Q1 ("Genèse en écriture paléo-hebraïque"), now entitled 6Qpaleo-Genesis. Likewise, only at a later stage did "pap(yrus)" become an integral part of the name of compositions.

Most volumes are published or scheduled to be published in English, while a smaller number were published in French (vols. 1, 2, 3, 6, 7). The sequence of publication is not determined by the manuscript numbers (which follows a basic biblical and nonbiblical arrangement). Rather, as often occurs in the publication of a series, the volumes are not released according to a specific sequence. Thus, the first volume of material from Qumran Cave 4 (vol. 5) covered texts 4Q158–4Q186, although many may have expected to see the publication of Genesis-Exodus[a] (4Q1) and the following biblical texts first (see the foreword of de Vaux to vol. 5). Since 1991, a general timetable has been established expanding the complete series to thirty-nine volumes (of which twenty-eight are devoted to Qumran) and grouping the material, for the most part, on the basis of literary genre.

The contents of the volumes as recorded in the aforementioned list reflect in the first place the different places of origin (Murabbaʿat, Naḥal Ḥever, Qumran, Wadi ed-Daliyeh), and in the second place the different caves. Thus, volume 1 is devoted to all the texts found in Qumran Cave 1 (except for the Pesher Habakkuk, 1QpHab; Isaiah[a], 1QIsa[a] and 1Q8; the Rule of the Community, 1QS; the War Scroll, 1QM; the Genesis Apocryphon, 1QapGen and 1Q20; and Hodayot[a], 1QH[a]), volume 2 is devoted to Murabbaʿat, and so on. The first ten volumes are mainly the work of individuals or combinations of one, two, or three scholars. By far the greatest number of volumes is devoted to Qumran Cave 4, for which no fewer than twenty-seven volumes are ultimately scheduled to appear. Within all these volumes the material is further subdivided according to a binary division of biblical and nonbiblical texts, in which the appellation *biblical* refers to the canonical texts of the Hebrew scriptures.

The nonbiblical texts further reflect a subdivision into literary genres. Thus, the nonbiblical texts of volume 1 are subdivided into "commentaires, livres apocryphes, textes juridiques et liturgiques, recueils hymniques, groupes non caractérisés." Likewise, the nonbiblical texts from Qumran Cave 4 in volume 13 reflect single literary genres, for example, parabiblical texts (vols. 13, 19, 22). That is, while it was the original intention of the international team that the published volumes should reflect the different allotments to the individual scholars, which in themselves often reflected different literary genres, subsequently this arrangement was changed. With the reorganization of the team in 1990, a different procedure was started for the Qumran Cave 4 material, resulting in the publication of the texts in the first place according to their literary character.

While most volumes contain publications of texts, several volumes (1, 2, 3, 6, 8, 9, 38) also publish archaeological data on the caves in which the scrolls or artifacts were found, on the artifacts themselves, and on the archaeological missions. These descriptions comprise the following topics: the pottery found in Qumran Cave 1 (vol. 1, pp. 8–17), in the "Minor Caves" (vol. 3, pp. 13–41), and in Qumran Cave 4 (vol. 6, pp. 15–20), as well as at Murabbaʿat (vol. 2, pp. 14–15, 26–34); the linen textiles of Qumran Cave 1 (vol. 1, pp. 18–38) and of Murabbaʿat (vol. 2, pp. 51–63); and the fastenings on the Qumran manuscripts (vol. 6, pp. 23–28). The volumes also include an archaeological description of Qumran Cave 1 (vol. 1, pp. 3–7), of the "Minor Caves" (vol. 3, pp. 3–13), and of Qumran Cave 4 (vol. 6, pp. 9–22), as well as a very detailed description of the different caves of Murabbaʿat (vol. 2, pp. 1–63). A similar description is planned for Cave 11 (vol. 27). All these descriptions are accompanied by plates.

Volumes 1–8 contain indexes (single words) of the Hebrew, Aramaic (vols. 1, 2), Greek (vol. 2, 3, 8, 9), Latin (vol. 2), and Arabic (vol. 2) words of the nonbiblical texts or sections as well as signs (vol. 7). These indexes refer to all the texts included in a volume, while volume 3 lists the words of the Copper Scroll (3Q15) separately. Using a different system, volumes 10 on contain concordances (keyword in context) of all the words in the nonbiblical texts or sections, listed separately for the different texts. In addition, the volumes recording the biblical texts from Qumran Cave 1 (vol. 1), the "Minor Caves" (vol. 3), and Qumran Cave 4 (vols. 6, 9, 12, 14, 15) list the exact biblical passages recorded in the volume (vols. 16–17 are scheduled to contain similar indexes). Volume 10 also contains a reverse index to the Hebrew words. As a rule, the analysis and commentary in the first volumes of Discoveries in the Judaean Desert are shorter than those in volumes 8 on. Also in these later volumes the description of the orthography, physical appearance, and paleography is usually more extensive than in the earlier volumes.

BIBLIOGRAPHY

Alexander, P., and G. Vermes. *Qumran Cave 4, XIX: 4QSerekh Ha-Yaḥad and Two Related Texts.* Discoveries in the Judaean Desert, 26. Oxford, 1998.

Allegro, John M. *Qumran Cave 4, I (4Q1588–4Q186).* Discoveries in the Judaean Desert, 5. Oxford, 1968.

Attridge, Harold, et al., in consultation with James VanderKam. *Qumran Cave 4, VIII: Parabiblical Texts, Part 1.* Discoveries in the Judaean Desert, 13. Oxford, 1994.

Baillet, Maurice, *Qumrân grotte 4, III (4Q482–4Q520).* Discoveries in the Judaean Desert, 7. Oxford, 1982.

Baillet, Maurice, Józef T. Milik, and Roland de Vaux. *Les 'Petites Grottes' de Qumrân.* Discoveries in the Judaean Desert, 3. Oxford, 1962.

Barthélemy, Dominique, and Józef T. Milik. *Qumran Cave 1.* Discoveries in the Judaean Desert, 1. Oxford, 1955.

Baumgarten, J. M. *Qumran Cave 4, XIII: The Damascus Document (4Q266–273).* Discoveries in the Judaean Desert, 28. Oxford, 1996.

Baumgarten, J., et al. *Qumran Cave 4, XXV: Halakhic Texts.* Discoveries in the Judaean Desert, 35. Oxford, 1999.

Benoit, Pierre, Józef T. Milik, and Roland de Vaux. *Les grottes de Murabbaʿat.* Discoveries in the Judaean Desert, 2. Oxford, 1961.

Brooke, G., et al. *Qumran Cave 4, XVII: Parabiblical Texts, Part 3.* Discoveries in the Judaean Desert, 22. Oxford, 1996.

Broshi, Magen, et al., in consultation with James VanderKam. *Qumran Cave 4, XIV: Parabiblical Texts, Part 2.* Discoveries in the Judaean Desert, 19. Oxford, 1995.

Chazon, E., et al. *Qumran Cave 4, XX: Poetical and Liturgical Texts, Part 2.* Discoveries in the Judaean Desert, 29. Oxford, 1999.

Cotton, H. M., and A. Yardeni. *Aramaic, Hebrew, and Greek Documentary Texts from Naḥal Ḥever and Other Sites with an Appendix Containing Alleged Qumran Texts (The Seiyâl Collection II).* Discoveries in the Judaean Desert, 27. Oxford, 1997.

Cross, F. M. *Qumran Cave 4, XII: Samuel.* Discoveries in the Judaean Desert, 17. Oxford, forthcoming.

de Vaux, Roland, and Józef T. Milik. *Qumrân grotte 4, II, I. Archéolo-*

gie, II. Tefillin, Mezuzot et Targums (4Q128–4Q157)*. Discoveries in the Judaean Desert, 6. Oxford, 1977.

Dimant, D. *Qumran Cave 4.XXI: Parabiblical Texts, Part 4.* Discoveries in the Judaean Desert, 30. Oxford, forthcoming.

Elgvin, T., et al. *Qumran Cave 4.XV: Sapiential Texts, Part 1.* Discoveries in the Judaean Desert, 20. Oxford, 1997.

Eshel, E., et al. *Qumran Cave 4.VI: Poetical and Liturgical Texts, Part 1.* Discoveries in the Judaean Desert, 11. Oxford, 1998.

García Martínez, F., E. J. C. Tigchelaar, and A. S. van der Woude. *Qumran Cave 11.II: 11Q2–18, 11Q20–30.* Discoveries in the Judaean Desert, 23. Oxford, 1998.

Glessmer, U., S. Pfann, and S. Talmon. *Qumran Cave 4.XVI: Calendrical Texts.* Discoveries in the Judaean Desert, 21. Oxford, forthcoming.

Gropp, D. *Wadi Daliyeh II: The Samaria Papyri from Wadi Daliyeh.* Discoveries in the Judaean Desert, 28. Oxford, forthcoming.

Leith, M. J. W. *Wadi Daliyeh I: The Wadi Daliyeh Seal Impressions.* Discoveries in the Judaean Desert, 24. Oxford, 1997.

Puech, É. *Qumran Cave 4.XVIII: Textes Hébreux (4Q521–4Q528, 4Q576–4Q579).* Discoveries in the Judaean Desert, 25. Oxford, 1998.

Puech, É. *Qumran Cave 4.XXII: Textes en Araméen, tome 1: 4Q529–549.* Discoveries in the Judaean Desert, 31. Oxford, forthcoming.

Qimron, Elisha, and John Strugnell. *Qumran Cave 4, V. Miqṣat Maʿase ha-Torah.* Discoveries in the Judaean Desert, 10. Oxford, 1994.

Sanders, James A. *The Psalms Scroll of Qumrân Cave 11 (11QPs[a]).* Discoveries in the Judaean Desert, 4. Oxford, 1965.

Skehan, Patrick W., Eugene Ulrich, and Judith E. Sanderson. *Qumran Cave 4, IV, Palaeo-Hebrew and Greek Biblical Manuscripts.* Discoveries in the Judaean Desert, 9. Oxford, 1992; repr. 1995.

Strugnell, J., D. J. Harrington, S.J., and T. Elgvin. *Qumran Cave 4.XXIV: 4QInstruction (Musar le-Mevin): 4Q415 ff.* Discoveries in the Judaean Desert, 34. Oxford, 1999.

Tov, Emanuel, with the collaboration of Robert A. Kraft. *The Greek Minor Prophets Scroll from Naḥal Ḥever (8ḤevXIIgr).* Discoveries in the Judaean Desert, 8. Oxford, 1990; repr. 1995.

Ulrich, E., ed. *Qumran Cave 4, X: The Prophets.* Discoveries in the Judaean Desert, 15. Oxford, 1997.

Ulrich, E., ed. *Qumran Cave 4, XI: Psalms to Chronicles.* Discoveries in the Judaean Desert, 16. Oxford, 1999.

Ulrich, Eugene, and Frank M. Cross, eds. *Qumran Cave 4, VII: Genesis to Numbers.* Discoveries in the Judaean Desert, 12. Oxford, 1994.

Ulrich, Eugene, and Frank M. Cross, eds. *Qumran Cave 4, IX: Deuteronomy, Joshua, Judges, Kings.* Discoveries in the Judaean Desert, 14. Oxford, 1995.

Ulrich, E., P. Flint, and M. Abegg. *Qumran Cave 1, II: The Isaiah Texts.* Discoveries in the Judaean Desert, 32. Oxford, forthcoming.

EMANUEL TOV

DISCOVERY AND PURCHASE. The earliest manuscript finds in the Judean Desert are reported by Origen, who in his hexapla used a Greek translation that was discovered "together with other Hebrew and Greek books in a jar near Jericho," probably about 217 CE, discoveries later referred to by Eusebius (*Ecclesiastical History* VI xvi I).

In about 800 CE, Timotheus I, Nestorian patriarch of Seleucia, mentioned manuscripts found in a cave near Jericho, manuscripts later related to the Karaites. Several medieval Arab authors refer to "scriptures" used by "cavemen" in the area of Jericho, probably a reference to ancient recollections of the Qumran community.

Modern Discoveries. The first scrolls discovered in the Judean Desert in modern times came from Qumran. A number of scrolls were discovered at other sites in the Judean Desert as well.

Qumran. Published accounts of the discoveries of the scrolls near Qumran have contained contradictory details from the beginning. The main points, however, seem to be established. Sometime between November 1946 and February 1947 (possibly one or two years earlier), at least three Taʿamireh bedouin, Muhammed edh-Dhib Hasan (Muhammed Ahmed el-Hamed, possibly to be identified with Abu-Daoud, who died in Bethlehem in January 1998, or with another bedouin who died in Jordan in 1997), Jumʿa Muhammed (reported to be alive in Bethlehem as late as 1994), and Khalil Musa, accidentally discovered a cave near Qumran while shepherding sheep and/or goats. Either as a result of a game to see who could hit an opening in the mountainside, or the sighting of an opening during a search for a lost goat, a rock was tossed into this hole, and the sound of breaking pottery was heard. Thinking that something valuable might be contained in the pots, edh-Dhib and at least one other companion investigated, probably the next day after securing candles and a rope. Upon entering the cave, the men discovered several large clay jars (at least ten, perhaps as many as fifty), all with lids, some or all sealed to the jars with clay. Breaking open the jars, expecting perhaps to find gold or other treasure, the bedouin discovered only seeds (or "red dirt" or something resembling "dead bugs"), except in one jar, which contained three (or four) bundles wrapped in linen coverings that had a "green" color.

Taking them back to the camp, the bundles were hung in a bag on a corner tent pole for some months (early accounts say as long as two years), and one is reported to have been destroyed by children playing with it (a fourth original scroll?).

In March 1947, Jumʿa and Khalil offered three scrolls to Ibrahim ʿIjha, a carpenter and antiquities dealer in Bethlehem, who showed them to another antiquities dealer, Faidi Salahi. ʿIjha kept them for several weeks but then returned the bundles, fearing they were stolen goods. These were the complete Isaiah scroll from Cave 1 at Qumran, Isaiah[a] (hereafter, 1QIsaiah[a]; 1QIsa[a]), Pesher Habakkuk (1QpHab), and the Rule of the Community (hereafter, 1QRule of the Community; 1QS).

Jumʿa next showed the scrolls to George Ishaʿya (Shamoun), a Bethlehem peddler, but he did not entrust George with the scrolls. Then Jumʿa showed the scrolls to Sheikh ʿAli Subh, chief of the Taʿamireh, who suggested they bring them to Khalil Iskander (Kando Shahin), a Syrian Orthodox merchant in Bethlehem.

During Holy Week of (April) 1947, George mentioned the manuscripts to the Syrian Orthodox metropolitan Athanasius Yeshue Samuel at Saint Mark's Monastery in Jerusalem's Old City. Kando and George brought one manuscript, 1QRule of the Community, to Metropolitan Samuel within about a week's time. Samuel realized that it was written in Hebrew and offered to buy it or any other similar manuscripts. Kando left with the scroll, not contacting the metropolitan again for about ten weeks.

Some months after the original discovery, probably in May or June 1947, Jumʿa returned to the cave (or perhaps another cave) with George and removed four more scrolls. Three of these they sold to Faidi Salahi, the Bethlehem antiquities dealer who had seen the first three. These three were later bought by Professor Eleazar L. Sukenik: Isaiah[b] (hereafter, 1QIsaiah[b]; 1Q8), the War Scroll (1QM), and Hodayot[b] (1Q35). The fourth, Genesis Apocryphon (1QapGen), was kept by Kando.

About 5 July 1947, Kando sent Jumʿa Muhammed, George Ishaʿya, and Khalil Musa to the monastery in Jerusalem, where they were rudely turned away at the door by one of the monks, Bulos Gilf, who had not been informed about Kando's previous offer. The bedouin and Kando were deeply offended, but two weeks later Kando returned, this time with five scrolls (1QIsa[a], 1QpHab, 1QS in two halves, and 1QapGen). On 19 July 1947, Kando took the scrolls on consignment from the bedouin for one-third of whatever he could obtain for them. He sold these to Metropolitan Samuel shortly afterward for £P (Palestine pounds) 24 ($97.20), of which he gave £P16 ($64.80) to the bedouin according to the agreement.

During the next few days Metropolitan Samuel consulted Stephan Hanna Stephan, a Syrian Christian employed by the Palestine Department of Antiquities, and Fathers Marmardji and van der Ploeg, all of whom examined the scrolls but considered them late (medieval) and therefore of no great value.

During August 1947, the metropolitan sent another of Saint Mark's priests, Father Yusef, with George Ishaʿya to check the cave for further details, at least the second trip back by the bedouin or others after the discovery.

In September 1947, Anton Kiraz traveled with Metropolitan Samuel to Homs, Syria, where the scrolls were shown to the Syrian Orthodox patriarch of Antioch, who also doubted their antiquity. Metropolitan Samuel next traveled to Beirut to show them to the Professor of Hebrew at the American University, only to find that he was on vacation. On September 26, the metropolitan returned to Jerusalem, still confident that the scrolls were ancient but without any support for his views on their antiquity.

During the first week of October, Anton Kiraz and Metropolitan Samuel became partners in the scrolls in return for Kiraz's financial support. The metropolitan again asked for help from Stephan Hanna Stephan, who brought along a Jewish expert and specialist in antiquities, but both steadfastly identified the scrolls as late. In October 1947, the metropolitan asked Dr. Maurice Brown for assistance. Dr. Brown contacted Dr. Judah L. Magnes, president of Hebrew University of Jerusalem on Mount Scopus. Magnes sent two librarians, who examined the scrolls but never returned to see them again, despite the metropolitan's agreement that they might photograph some of the columns. Another Jewish antiquities dealer, Mr. Sassun, suggested sending the scrolls to experts in Europe, but the metropolitan declined.

In early February 1948, Reverend Butros Sowmy, assistant to Metropolitan Samuel, recalled having visited the American Schools of Oriental Research (now the Albright Institute of Archaeological Research), where he had been given a cordial welcome some ten years before. He suggested to Metropolitan Samuel that he might obtain information there about the antiquity of the scrolls. On February 18, Sowmy telephoned the school, only to discover that the director, Millar Burrows, was in Iraq. Dr. John C. Trever, acting director in Burrows's absence, invited Sowmy to come to the school on the following day. In a few weeks' time, Trever, with the help of William H. Brownlee, was able to photograph 1QIsaiah[a], Pesher Habakkuk, and 1QRule of the Community. He later sent copies of the photographs to William F. Albright, who dated the scrolls paleographically to about 100 BCE.

Meanwhile, in West Jerusalem, on 23 November 1947, an Armenian antiquities dealer had contacted Sukenik. Sukenik subsequently met with the Armenian (identified only as Mister X in published accounts) across a barbed wire fence at the gateway to Military Zone B in Jerusalem. Sukenik was shown a scrap of leather with Hebrew script written on it. He was told that bedouin had brought several parchment scrolls from the Dead Sea region to a mutual friend, an old antiquities dealer in Bethlehem (Faidi Salahi), who wished to offer the scrolls to the Museum of Jewish Antiquities of the Hebrew University. Sukenik recognized the script of the fragment as similar to that on some coffins and ossuaries from before the Roman destruction of Jerusalem (which he previously had excavated on Anton Kiraz's property) and requested that the Armenian dealer proceed to Bethlehem to obtain more samples.

On 27 November the Armenian telephoned Sukenik to say that he had additional fragments, and they met at the Armenian's shop in the Old City. Sukenik and Mister X decided to go to Bethlehem to arrange a purchase of the bundles from Salahi, who had two jars in which bundles had been found, removed by the bedouin at the time of the original discovery. After reading one of the scrolls, written in Biblical Hebrew, the text of which was unfamiliar to him, Sukenik took the scrolls for inspection and returned to Jerusalem.

Back in Jerusalem Sukenik continued to read the scrolls and later informed Salahi, through his Armenian friend, that he would purchase them. Sukenik bought the War Scroll and Hodayot[a] (hereafter, 1QHodayot[a]; 1QH[a]) from Salahi on November 29. Later that night the United Nations voted to partition Palestine, the first step in the establishment of the modern State of Israel. Sukenik purchased an Isaiah[b] fragment on 22 December 1947 and possibly some Daniel fragments as well.

Not long afterward, Sukenik received a telephone call from Mister X saying that he hoped to get more scrolls from the same source in Bethlehem. Now Sukenik began to seek a personal loan from the bank in order to buy the scrolls.

He visited Mister X several times in the Old City, asking him to encourage the Arab dealer to obtain whatever else he could from the bedouin. At the end of January 1948, Sukenik received a letter from Anton Kiraz, offering to show Sukenik ancient Hebrew scrolls. Sukenik met Kiraz at the YMCA building in Jerusalem and was shown several scrolls, including one of the entire book of Isaiah (1QIsa[a]). Sukenik believed these scrolls to be of the same origin as those he had obtained from the Bethlehem dealer and established that his friend had bought these from Taʿamireh bedouin, the same tribe that had brought scrolls to the Bethlehem dealer Salahi. Kiraz said that these scrolls now belonged to him and the metropolitan (though Metropolitan Samuel later denied consenting to this meeting). Sukenik took these scrolls home for examination and made partial transcriptions and copies of some of the texts.

Sukenik's bank refused his loan request, and he was unable to contact officials at the Jewish Agency and Bialik Foundation for funding. On 6 February, Sukenik returned the second set of scrolls to Kiraz at the YMCA in West Jerusalem. Although they negotiated, they were unable to agree on a price. A few days later Sukenik received word from the Jewish Agency that it would fund the purchase of the scrolls, but it was too late.

Weeks passed, and finally Sukenik received a letter from Kiraz and Metropolitan Samuel informing him that they had decided not to sell. Sukenik later discovered that two weeks after he returned the scrolls, Sowmy had gone to the American Schools of Oriental Research, resulting in Trever's photographs and eventual publication by the school of 1QIsaiah[a] and Pesher Habakkuk (1950) and 1QRule of the Community (1951).

With war impending, Father Sowmy took the scrolls to Beirut for safekeeping on 25 March 1948. Trever left Jerusalem on 5 April, and the British Mandate ended on 15 May, precipitating the Israeli War of Independence.

Probably in August 1948, George Ishaʿya visited the cave again and secured some Daniel and Prayer Scroll fragments, as well as a few others, which he turned over to Saint Mark's. In November, Ishaʿya, Kando, and others excavated the cave and secured many more fragments.

In January 1949, O. R. Sellers and Yusef Saad, secretary of the Palestine Archaeological Museum, attempted to locate the cave, but George Ishaʿya demanded payment to guide them, and negotiations ceased. On 24 January, Captain Philippe Lippens asked for help from the Arab Legion to locate the cave, which was accomplished on 28 January.

On 29 January 1949, Metropolitan Samuel arrived in the United States with four scrolls and various fragments. Six days later, on 4 February, Trever met the metropolitan in New Jersey to begin arrangements for unrolling the "fourth scroll," the Genesis Apocryphon.

Additional scroll discoveries, for the most part by the bedouin, soon followed. Cave 1 at Qumran was excavated between 15 February and 5 March 1949 under the direction of G. Lankester Harding (Palestine Archaeological Museum) and Roland de Vaux (École Biblique et Archéologique Française), with fragments of about seventy scrolls and pieces of fifty pottery jars and covers recovered.

From 7 to 9 April 1949 the Saint Mark's fragments in the United States were separated, mounted, photographed, and identified as parts of Daniel[a–b] and later as Liturgical Prayers.

On 10 April a large fragment of the fourth scroll was separated from the roll and tentatively identified as the Lamech Document, later named the Genesis Apocryphon. Four days later it was taken to Harvard's Fogg Art Museum to be prepared for complete opening, but it was completely unrolled only in 1956 by Yigael Yadin and Bieberkraut after its arrival in Israel. That summer, 1QIsaiah[b] was opened at Hebrew University.

Yusef Saad finally succeeded in purchasing the remainder of the Cave 1 fragments from Kando in the spring of 1950: the Rule of the Congregation (1Q28a) and the Rule of the Blessings (1Q28b).

For six years the metropolitan tried to sell the four scrolls in his possession in the United States. Trever repeatedly but unsuccessfully tried to raise money to buy them. Just when he thought he had succeeded, Yadin (son of Sukenik, who had died in 1953) announced their purchase for Israel. During June 1954, Morty Jacobs of New York had called Yadin to inform him that the scrolls were advertised for sale in the *Wall Street Journal*. The next day a banker, acting as an intermediary for Yadin, replied to the advertisement. On 11 June 1954 an agreement was reached to purchase the four scrolls for $250,000, through the assistance in various ways of Avraham Harman, Isak Norman, Samuel Rubin, and Teddy Kollek. Later that month, Professor Harry Orlinsky of the Hebrew Union College–Jewish Institute of Religion in New York, posing as a Mr. Green, authenticated the scrolls, and after the conclusion of the agreement and transfer of the scrolls, Samuel Gottesman donated the money to cover loans made for their purchase. The scrolls were shipped back to Israel separately, and on 13 February 1955 Yadin announced to the world that the scrolls were now in Israel and had been reunited with those purchased by his father some years before.

Between 24 November and 12 December 1951, de Vaux and Harding made soundings at Khirbet Qumran, confirming the site's connection with the scroll cave through pottery and establishing an approximate date through coins. Cave 2 was discovered close to Cave 1 in February 1952. From 10 to 20 March 1952 a team led by de Vaux and William Reed, director of the American Schools of Oriental Research, explored about 225 caves in the Qumran region, discovering Cave 3 with the Copper Scroll (3Q15) together with several dozen fragments from other scrolls.

Cave 4 was discovered adjacent to Khirbet Qumran by bedouin in August 1952. According to Abu-Daoud (possibly to be identified with Muhammed edh-Dhib Hasan), he and his friends heaped as many fragments as possible in their kaffiyehs and carried them off. They also found "pieces of wood" (shelves?), which they threw out of the cave into the wadi.

Fragments from Cave 4 were purchased by the Palestine Archaeological Museum from bedouin over a period of three years, mostly through Kando as intermediary. For example, on 20 September 1952 the Palestine Archaeological Museum was offered a group of approximately fifteen thousand fragments, for which the Jordanian government paid 15,000 dinars ($42,000) in early 1953. A second large purchase was made in February 1954 and a third in July 1958. Funds for Cave 4 purchases came, among others, from the All Souls Church (New York); the federal government of Bonn and the government of Baden-Württemberg on behalf of the University of Heidelberg through K. G. Kuhn; the Jordanian Government; Manchester University and one of its donors; McCormick Theological Seminary; McGill University; an unnamed widow; the endowment of the Palestine Archaeological Museum; and the Vatican Library.

From 22 to 29 September 1952, de Vaux and his team excavated Cave 4, recovering fragments from about one hundred manuscripts. More than forty thousand fragments later were identified as having come from nearly six hundred manuscripts in Cave 4, of which at least one hundred were biblical.

Cave 5, discovered a short distance north of Cave 4 in September 1952, was excavated by Józef T. Milik, and nearly at the same time Cave 6 was discovered by bedouin in a cliff of Wadi Qumran. Caves 7, 8, 9, and 10 were discovered between February and April 1955 in the terraces around Qumran. All these caves yielded relatively small numbers of fragments.

The eleventh and final Qumran cave was discovered by bedouin in February 1956. Fragments were secured partly through donations from Kenneth and Elizabeth Hay Bechtel and the Royal Academy of Sciences of the Netherlands. On 1 March 1956 the Palestine Archaeological Museum paid JD (Jordanian dinars) 16,000 ($44,800) to Kando for "eight cardboard boxes and one package of fragments" from Cave 11 and, on 17 July of the same year, JD14,000 ($39,200) for New Jerusalem from Qumran Cave 11 (hereafter, 11QNew Jerusalem; 11Q18) and Targum of Job (hereafter, 11QTargum of Job; 11Q10) bought in 1961 by the Royal Academy of Sciences of the Netherlands. Temple Scroll[a] (11Q19) was not recovered by scholars until 1967 when Yadin seized it from Kando immediately after the capture of Bethlehem during the 1967 Arab-Israeli War (the Israel Department of Antiquities and Museums later paid Kando more than $100,000).

Wadi Murabbaʿat. In October 1951 Taʿamireh bedouin made another discovery, this time in the caves of Wadi Murabbaʿat, south of Qumran. Two fragments of inscribed leather were offered for sale, first in Jerusalem, and from November 1951 through January 1952, Kando offered many other fragments to the École Biblique et Archéologique Française. From 21 January to 3 March 1952, Harding and de Vaux interrupted their excavations at Qumran to search caves at Murabbaʿat. In March 1955 a Hebrew scroll of the Minor Prophets (Mur 88) was discovered by bedouin in a fifth Murabbaʿat cave. The last fragments from Murabbaʿat were purchased in 1958 by the Palestine Archaeological Museum and the École Biblique et Archéologique Française.

Khirbet Mird. In July 1952, bedouin also discovered Byzantine and early Arabic manuscripts, including some Greek New Testament manuscripts, all from about the sixth through seventh centuries CE at Khirbet Mird (Horqaniah), the ruins of a monastery about 5 miles from Qumran. This site was excavated by R. de Langhe of the University of Louvain-la-Neuve between February and April 1953.

Wadi ed-Daliyeh. In February 1962, bedouin discovered about forty Samaritan papyrus documents in a large cave (Abu Shinjeh Cave, Cave of the Papyri) in Wadi ed-

Daliyeh, about 9 miles north of Jericho. First offered to the Palestine Archaeological Museum by Kando, they were brought by the American Schools of Oriental Research through Bechtels. These documents, left behind by Samaritans, date to the fourth century BCE.

Masada. Between 18 and 29 March 1955 an Israeli expedition found one papyrus fragment. A further survey between 7 and 17 March 1956 turned up no other fragments, but excavators working under Yigael Yadin at Masada from October 1963 to April 1964 and December 1964 to March 1965 discovered fragments of many manuscripts, including parts of *Leviticus, Deuteronomy, Ezekiel, Psalms*, and *Ben Sira* (Mas1a–1h), Songs of the Sabbath Sacrifice (Mas1k), and other Hebrew and Aramaic documents, as well as a large number of Latin and Greek documents.

Naḥal Ḥever. Between July and August 1952, bedouin brought to Jerusalem manuscripts from a cave, probably Naḥal Ḥever, which included a Greek text of the Minor Prophets. Taking the lead from recent bedouin discoveries in the area, an Israeli expedition surveyed the ʿEin-Gedi region from 23 March to 6 April 1958 and found a cave in Naḥal Ḥever with fragments from *Psalms* and fifteen papyrus letters in Hebrew, Aramaic, and Greek. The following March, Naḥal Ḥever was further excavated, and about forty papyrus business documents in Hebrew, Aramaic, Nabatean, and Greek dating from about 88 CE to 132 CE were recovered.

The Cave of the Letters (Cave 5/6) in Naḥal Ḥever was excavated by Yadin from 23 March to 6 April 1960, during which he discovered the Bar Kokhba letters. Another expedition, from 14 to 27 March 1961, discovered the Babatha archive and land contracts originally from ʿEin-Gedi.

Also between 14 and 17 March 1961, Yohanan Aharoni excavated the Cave of Horror (Cave 8), discovering the very important Greek Minor Prophets.

Naḥal Ṣeʾelim (Seiyal). By early 1960, rumors that many fragments brought to Jerusalem by bedouin had come from Naḥal Ṣeʾelim resulted in a survey of the valley by Aharoni. In an excavation of several caves in 1960, documentary fragments were found only in Cave 34.

Wadi el-Mafjar. Hanan Eshel excavated Wadi el-Mafjar between April and May 1986 and 22 to 23 June 1986. Fragments discovered there included an Aramaic list of names, fourth-century BCE Aramaic legal documents, and second-century BCE nonliterary documents in Greek.

Wadi en-Nar and Wadi Ghweir. Neither location is precisely known. According to bedouin accounts, Greek and Hebrew/Aramaic documents on papyrus and skin were discovered in these regions.

Wadi Sdeir. Bedouin sold fragments from a Genesis scroll (Sdeir 1) and at least two Greek documents found here.

Ketef Jericho. The latest discovery of scrolls occurred in November 1993, when Hanan Eshel discovered Aramaic and Greek commercial/nonliterary documents from the Bar Kokhba period on an upper shelf of a cave in Ketef Jericho, near Jericho.

BIBLIOGRAPHY

Abu-Daoud (Muhammed edh-Dhib Hasan?), interviews and conversations conducted by Weston W. Fields, 1993–1997, regarding Jerusalem, Bethlehem, Qumran, Wadi Murabbaʿat, and Wadi ed-Daliyeh. David Bar-Levav, translator.

Allegro, John M. *The Dead Sea Scrolls.* Baltimore, 1956.

Allegro, John M. *The People of the Dead Sea Scrolls.* London, 1959.

Brownlee, William H. "Muhammad Ed-Deeb's Own Story of His Scroll Discovery." *Journal of Near Eastern Studies* 16.4 (1957), 236–239.

Brownlee, William H. "Edh-Dhib's Story of His Scroll Discovery." *Revue de Qumrân* 3.4 (1962), 483–494.

Brownlee, William H. "Some New Facts concerning the Discovery of the Scrolls of 1Q." *Revue de Qumrân* 4.3 (1963), 417–420.

Burrows, Millar. *The Dead Sea Scrolls.* New York, 1955.

Cross, Frank M., Jr. *The Ancient Library at Qumran*, 3d ed. Sheffield, 1995.

Driver, G. R. *The Judaean Scrolls.* Oxford, 1965.

Dupont-Sommer, A. *The Dead Sea Scrolls.* Translated by E. Margaret Rowley. Oxford, 1952.

Pfann, Stephen J. "History of the Judaean Desert Discoveries." *The Dead Sea Scrolls on Microfiche, Companion Volume*, pp. 97–108. Leiden, 1993.

Pfann, Stephen J. "Sites in the Judean Desert Where Texts Have Been Found." *The Dead Sea Scrolls on Microfiche, Companion Volume*, pp. 109–119. Leiden, 1993.

Samuel, Mar Athanasius Y. "The Purchase of the Jerusalem Scrolls." *Biblical Archaeologist* 12 (1949), 26–31.

Trever, John C. "The Discovery of the Scrolls." *Biblical Archaeologist* 11 (1948), 46–68.

Trever, John C. "When Was Qumran Cave 1 Discovered?" *Revue de Qumrân* 3.1 (1962), 135–141.

Trever, John C. *The Untold Story of Qumran.* London, 1965.

Wright, G. E. "Archaeological News and Views." *Biblical Archaeologist* 12 (1949), 32–36.

Yadin, Yigael. *The Message of the Scrolls.* London, 1957.

WESTON W. FIELDS

DIVREI HA-MEʾOROT. *See* Words of the Luminaries.

DOCUMENTARY TEXTS. Reflecting daily, normal life in the place and time in which they were written, documentary texts give us insight into various aspects of society: social, economic, legal, administrative, and linguistic. Documentary texts are to be contrasted with literary and pseudoliterary texts, and, in the case of the documents from the Judean Desert, with biblical, parabiblical, sectarian, and Christian texts. The documents surveyed here were written on leather, papyrus, sherds (ostraca), and jars (*tituli picti*). Inscriptions (on stone and metal) and graffiti are excluded. The more substantial documents preserved are legal deeds. [*See* Legal Works.] A great part of the documents from the Judean Desert has remained unpublished to this day or has been only preliminarily published. The emphasis in the following survey naturally will be on the published material.

Chronologically four main groups of documentary texts can be discerned (a few single documents from other periods are ignored).

Samaritan Papyri. In the Aramaic language, from the fourth century BCE (375–335 BCE), the Samaritan papyri were found in Wadi ed-Daliyeh. [*See* Daliyeh, Wadi ed-, *article on* Written Material.] Only deed of slave sale WDSP 1, a slave conveyance from 335 BCE, has been published to date (Cross, 1985). The majority of the other documents are also slave conveyances. The papyri belong to wealthy slave owners from Samaria who seem likely to have hidden in the cave in Wadi ed-Daliyeh in the wake of the revolt of Samaria against Alexander the Great in 331 BCE (Curtius Rufus: *De rebus gestis Alexandri magni*, 4.8–9–11). The legal formulas in the Samaritan documents are familiar from the Elephantine papyri of the fifth century BCE. Some other Aramaic fragments from the same period were found in the Cave of Avi'or in Ketef Jericho (Eshel and Misgav, 1988). [*See* Deeds of Sale; Elephantine Texts; *and* Mafjar, Wadi el-.]

The Aramaic ostraca from Idumea from the fourth century BCE, although not strictly from the Judean Desert, should be mentioned here. Their precise provenance is unknown since they were not found in the course of controlled excavations. They were written during the last thirty years of Persian rule and the beginning of the Hellenistic period (360–311 BCE). They shed some light on demographic and economic aspects of Idumea at the time. The *Onomasticon* reveals the mixture of Edomite and Arabic names in the area with which we are acquainted from later sources. Of the many hundreds of these ostraca, some two hundred were published recently (Lemaine, 1996; Lozachmeur and Lemaire, 1996). We must see these ostraca in the contexts of the Arad ostraca of the fifth century BCE, the Beersheba ostraca of the fourth century BCE, and other contemporary Aramaic ostraca discovered in other sites in southern Palestine.

Masada. The material from Masada is dated to the period before the fall of the fortress in spring of 73 (or 74) CE. It falls into three groups.

The majority of *tituli picti* in Jewish script (Mas 462–553), Latin (Mas 795–852), and Greek (Mas 854–914) on local and imported storage jars are likely to belong to the Herodian period at Masada (37–4 BCE), reflecting the economic activity stimulated by the setting up of Herod's stores (Josephus, *The Jewish War* 7.295–296). Some of the imported jars contained luxury products—choice wines, fish sauce, and apples—and carried Herodian dates. *Tituli picti*, both dated and undated, advertising the contents of the jars and/or their owner's names, are known from other parts of the Roman world; they are collected in the volumes of the *Corpus inscriptionum Latinarum* under *instrumentum domesticum*. For comparison with the Masada texts, see the collections from Rome and Pompeii in *Corpus inscriptionum Latinarum*, volumes 15 and 4, respectively.

The ostraca in Jewish script (Mas 1–461) and in Greek (Mas 772–792) as well as the Greek papyri (Mas 739–747) belong to Jews, and probably to the Sicarii who occupied Masada between 66 and 73/74 CE. The majority bear witness to the food-rationing system adopted by the Sicarii (Mas 1–428, 739–747, 772–792); others testify to the Sicarii's strict observance of ritual laws concerning tithes and dietary laws (Mas 441–461). [*See* Sicarii.]

The Latin papyri and ostraca, to be dated from approximately 72 to 73/74 CE, belong to soldiers of the Tenth Legion, the legionary garrison of the province of Judea, which together with auxiliary forces, besieged and conquered Masada in 73/74 CE (*The Jewish War* 7.252–407). The papyri constitute a random and mostly fragmentary collection of discarded texts. The most important items are a line from Virgil's *Aeneid* (4.9: Mas 721), a legionary pay record of a cavalry man from 72 CE (Mas 722), and a list of hospital supplies (Mas 723). Not much can be gleaned from our material to add to what is already known about the Tenth Legion in Palestine. It is of paramount importance, though, that all Latin documents found at Masada have a precise historical context and date. This is crucial not only for students of Latin paleography but also for military historians, who now have more dated information about the bureaucratic development of the Roman army. The evidence from Masada can now be added to that derived from Egypt and Dura Europos in Syria.

The entirety of the documentary material discovered at Masada in 1963–1964 and 1964–1965 has been published. Renewed excavations at Masada in 1995–1996 and 1996–1997 uncovered more material that has not yet been published. [*See* Ḥever, Naḥal, *article on* Written Documents; Ṣe'elim, Naḥal, *article on* Written Material.]

Documents from Wadi Murabbaʿat, Naḥal Ḥever, Naḥal Ṣeʾelim, and Other Sites. Most of this corpus owes its preservation to the upheaval caused by the Bar Kokhba Revolt (132–135 CE). [*See* Bar Kokhba Revolt.] Most of it is thus limited in time to the years immediately preceding the Bar Kokhba Revolt and those of the revolt itself (although some documents are much earlier; for example, debt acknowledgment, Mur 18, written in Aramaic, from 55 or 56 CE, contract XḤev/Se Nab. 1, from 60 CE, Mur 29 and 30 from before the First Revolt [Cotton, 1999]). On the other hand, people attested in the documents come from villages as scattered as Mazra'a and Maḥoza/Maḥoz 'Eglatain in the Dead Sea area in the province of Arabia: Sophathe in the Perea in Transjordan, which belonged to the province of Judea: 'Ein-Gedi on the western shore of the Dead Sea; Kesalon and Ḥardona in the vicinity of Jerusalem; Kaphar Barucha, Yaqim (or Yaqum); and Aristoboulias in the area southeast of Hebron; Bethbassi near Herodium; Galoda in eastern Samaria, and Betharda in southern Samaria. The great majority of the documents, whether letters or legal deeds, were written by, or at least involve, Jews, thus giving a glimpse of Jewish village society in the Roman provinces of Arabia and Judea at the time that they were written.

Four private archives (i.e., a collection of documents belonging to a person or a family) were found among the documents: those of Babatha, Salome Komaïse daughter of Levi, Jonathan son of Baianos, and Yeshu'a son of Galgula. The Babatha archive, P.Yadin 1–35, was discovered in the Cave of the Letters in Naḥal Ḥever. [*See* Babatha.] It begins on 11 August 94 CE and ends on 19 August 132 CE. Only the Greek part (P.Yadin 5, 11–35) of the Babatha archive has so far been published (Lewis, 1989). The archive of Salome Komaïse daughter of Levi (XḤev/Se 12, XḤev/Se 60–65) also is from the Cave of the Letters in Naḥal Ḥever. This archive begins on 29 January 125 and ends on 7 August 131 CE. The Nabatean contracts XḤev/Se Nab. 1–5 are likely to belong to one of these archives or to both. The documents designated *XḤev/Se* belong to the so-called Seiyâl (Naḥal Ṣe'elim) collection, the majority of which come from Naḥal Ḥever. The Aramaic, Hebrew, and Greek documents that belong to this collection (but not the Nabatean documents) were published by Hannah M. Cotton and Ada Yardeni (1997).

The two archives revolve around the legal affairs of Jewish families in Maḥoza/Maḥoz 'Eglatain, a village on the southern shore of the Dead Sea, in what used to be the Nabatean kingdom and in 106 CE became the Roman province of Arabia. They contain legal documents in Nabatean, Aramaic, and Greek: receipts, hypothecary loans, land declarations, renunciations of claims, summonses to the Roman governor's court, marriage contracts, deeds of gift, promissory notes, deeds of purchase and sale, minutes of a city council, and copies of legal formulas. The documents demonstrate the successful integration of the Jews into the Nabatean environment: Jews own houses and orchards in Maḥoza/Maḥoz 'Eglatain; their Nabatean neighbors serve as witnesses and subscribers to their documents and as guardians of their children. The frequent appeals in the Babatha archive to the Roman governor of Arabia and the latter's accessibility and involvement in legal affairs between Jews reveal an aspect of Roman-Jewish relations not often in evidence.

The two archives belong to two of Bar Kokhba's administrators. The archive of Jonathan son of Baianos from 'Ein-Gedi (P.Yadin 49–56, 58–60, unpublished), contains letters in Aramaic and Greek from Bar Kokhba to Jonathan and sometimes to Jonathan together with Masabalah son of Shim'on. It was also found in the Cave of the Letters in Naḥal Ḥever. The archive of Yeshu'a son of Galgula (Mur 42–44) contains three letters addressed to him in Hebrew: two letters from Bar Kokhba and one from the *parnasim* ("administrators") of Beit-Mahiko. The archive was found in Wadi Murabba'at. It is possible that these archives, like the ones just discussed, were brought to the caves by women of the family: Miriam daughter of Baianos (of P.Yadin 26), Babatha's second husband's first wife, might be the sister of Jonathan son of Baianos; and Salome daughter of Iohannes Galgula, the wife in the Greek remarriage contract from Wadi Murabba'at (Mur 115 of 124 CE), might be the sister or niece of Yeshu'a son of Galgula.

The Babatha archive reveals the existence of intimate ties between families in 'Ein-Gedi in the province of Judea and those in Maḥoza/Maḥoz 'Eglatain in the province of Arabia: people described in the documents as from 'Ein-Gedi reside in Maḥoza, own property there, and intermarry with the Jews of Maḥoza. These ties may well go back to the time of the First Jewish Revolt when 'Ein-Gedi, raided by the Sicarii from Masada in 68 CE (*The Jewish War* 4.402) and later by the Romans, must have been practically abandoned, at least for a while (Pliny, *Natural History* 5.73). Part of its population may have settled in Maḥoza/Maḥoz 'Eglatain, a place with similar climatic conditions, similar types of cultivation, and a similar watering system (P.Yadin 7, XḤev/Se 64, and the unpublished P.Yadin 42). The Bar Kokhba Revolt reunited the families: notwithstanding their relations with their neighbors, the Nabateans, the well-off Jews of Arabia left their property behind and crossed over to Judea to take part in the Bar Kokhba Revolt. Only this can explain the presence of their documents in the same caves where documents from 'Ein-Gedi are found.

Another group of documents includes leases and subleases of land in Ir ha-Naḥash (in the region of Beth Guvrin? Mur 24A–L, 134 CE) and in 'Ein-Gedi (P.Yadin 42–43, 132 CE, and P.Yadin 44–46, 134 CE, unpublished). They were written in Hebrew and Aramaic by the Bar Kokhba administration. 'Ein-Gedi is attested in 124 CE as "a village of our Lord Caesar" (P.Yadin 11 and XḤev/Se gr 67). The leases and subleases attested in the documents from Wadi Murabba'at and Naḥal Ḥever, as well as some of Bar Kokhba's letters to his administrators in 'Ein-Gedi, imply that Bar Kokhba laid his hands on parts of the imperial domain and especially on the precious balsam grove in 'Ein-Gedi.

Finally, many private documents belonging to single

people and including letters, legal deeds, lists of names, and accounts in Aramaic, Hebrew, and Greek (small fragments and scraps are excluded here) come from Wadi Murabbaʿat (Mur 18–23, 25–33, 89–97, 113–116) and Naḥal Ḥever (XḤev/Se 7–13, 49–50 [mostly Aramaic], 66–73 [Greek]). More than a dozen documents allegedly from Cave 4 at Qumran are published with the Seiyal collection. A few other documents in Greek and Aramaic come from the Cave of Horror in Naḥal Ḥever, Naḥal Ṣe'elim, Ketef Jericho, Naḥal Mishmar, and Wadi Sdeir. [*See* Mishmar, Nahal, *article on* Roman period.] None of them has been published.

The double document, which fell into desuetude in Egypt in the first century BCE (with the exception of documents submitted by Roman citizens), is very typical of the legal texts in all three languages from the Judean Desert, as it is of legal documents from other parts of the Roman Near East. Roman influence is detectable in the dating formulas of private documents from Arabia and Judea, like those from Syria and Mesopotamia, and in contrast to those from Egypt, use consular dates and Roman months, often in addition to regnal years of the Roman emperor and the provincial era. The exceptions are the documents that are dated by the years of the Bar Kokhba Revolt.

It is especially in the case of legal documents written in Greek (almost all of which are now published) that one is struck by the absence of anything that might mark them as "Jewish" apart from the identity of the parties as disclosed by their names. Thus we find deeds of sale, renunciations of claims, land registrations, receipts, mortgages, promissory notes, deeds of gift, and even marriage contracts bearing a striking resemblance to their Egyptian and other Near Eastern counterparts, thereby revealing the remarkable degree of integration of Jewish society into its environment, which may upset some deeply entrenched views about the contrast between Jews and non-Jews in the Greco-Roman world. However, as demonstrated by their Aramaic subscriptions and signatures, and sometimes by the faulty Greek they use, these are not Hellenized Jews. To say that Jews are writing "non-Jewish" contracts is merely to say that the legal usage current in these contracts is not always in harmony with what eventually came to be normative Jewish law. The diversity and fluidity manifested in the documents from the Judean Desert, and the incursion of different legal systems sometimes, but not always, overlapping with what came to be halakhic law, are the best evidence we have for the state of Jewish law and the authority exercised by the rabbis at the time.

Arabic, Greek, and Syriac Documents from Khirbet Mird. The one hundred Arabic texts (out of one hundred fifty) of the eighth and ninth centuries published so far are extremely fragmentary and yield little information about the period of the Umayyad dynasty in Palestine. The documents include protocols (i.e., the manufacturer's label on the first sheet of the papyrus roll), legal texts, lists, and official and private letters. Of the two hundred Greek texts, presently stored mainly at the University Library of Leuven with some at the University of Chicago, only five have so far been published; two of them are letters. Of more than ten texts in Syriac, one letter was published. The editors suggest that the Syriac and Greek texts are connected with the monks of the monastery of Kastellion founded by Saint Sabas. It seems unlikely that the Greek texts from Khirbet Mird, fragmentary as they are, will yield anything to compare with the archive of Petra and Nessana.

BIBLIOGRAPHY

Cotton, Hannah M. "Introduction to the Greek Documentary Texts." In *Aramaic, Hebrew and Greek Texts from Nahal Hever and Other Sites with an Appendix containing Alleged Qumran Texts (The Seiyal Collection, vol. II)*, edited by H. M. Cotton and A. Yardeni, pp. 1–5. Discoveries in the Judaean Desert, 27. Oxford, 1997. A discussion of the so-called Seiyal collection.

Cotton, Hannah M. "Ein-Gedi between the Two Revolts in the Light of the Documents from the Judean Desert." *Scripta Classica Israelica* 17 (1998), forthcoming.

Cotton, Hannah M. "The Rabbis and the Documents." In *The Jews in the Graeco-Roman World*, edited by M. Goodman. Oxford, forthcoming. Discussion of the relationship between the *halakha* and the documents.

Cotton, H. M. "Die Papyrusdokumente aus den judäischen Wüste und ihr Beitrag zur Erforschung der jüdischen Geschichte des 1. und 2. Th. n. Chr." *Zeitschrift des Deutschen Palästina-Vereins* 115 (1999).

Cross, F. M. "A Report on the Samaria Papyri." In *Congress Volume: Jerusalem 1986*. Supplements to Vetus Testamentum, vol. 40, edited by J. A. Emerton, pp. 17–26. Leiden, 1988.

Lemaire, A. "Nouvelles inscriptions araméénnes d'Idumée au Musée d'Israël." Supplément no. 3 à Transeuphratène. Paris, 1996.

Lozachmeur, H., and A. Lemaire. "Nouveaux ostraca araméenes d'Idumée." Collection Sh. Moussaïeff, *Semitica* 46 (1996), 123–142.

Tov, E., with the collaboration of S. J. Pfann. *The Dead Sea Scrolls on Microfiche, Companion Volume*. Rev. ed. Leiden, 1995.

Wasserstein, Abraham. "Non-Hellenized Jews in the Semi-Hellenized East." *Scripta Classica Israelica* 14 (1995), 111–137.

Yardeni, Ada. "Introduction to the Aramaic and Hebrew Documentary Texts." In *Aramaic, Hebrew and Greek Texts from Nahal Hever and Other Sites with an Appendix containing Alleged Qurman Texts (The Seiyal Collection, vol. II)*, edited by H. M. Cotton and A. Yardeni, pp. 9–17. Discoveries in the Judaean Desert, 27. Oxford, 1997.

HANNAH M. COTTON

DUALISM, as opposed to monism, is defined by Ugo Bianchi as the doctrine of a religion or a worldview that postulates two irreductible principles as the cause of the constitutive elements of all that which does or seems to exist in the world. It is more than dichotomy, polarity, or duality: Dualism properly exists only when pairs of opposites are understood as "the principles responsible for bringing the world and man into existence," that is, when cosmogony or anthropogony is involved. Mircea Eliade adds an ethical dimension to the concept: True dualism means that the negative aspects of life, "until then accepted as constitutive and unexceptionable parts of the cosmic totality, lost their initial function and began to be interpreted as various manifestations of *evil*."

In the Dead Sea Scrolls, there is no radical dualism in the narrow sense defined by Bianchi, since God's transcendence and authority are never questioned. But, using somewhat broader definitions and typologies, scholars have identified various forms of an attenuated dualism (a dualism "under God") in many documents from the Qumran literature and, above all, within the "Treatise on the Two Spirits" and related sectarian texts. The scope of the corpus to be considered is a debated issue, as are problems concerning the origin, development, and coherence of Qumran dualistic teachings.

"The Treatise of the Two Spirits" is found in its full form in columns iii and iv of the Cave 1 copy of the Rule of the Community (1QS iii.13–iv.26), dated paleographically from 100 to 75 BCE; remnants of a few lines are also preserved in a fragment of a contemporary copy of the same Rule found in Cave 4 (4QS^{c} frg. 2). In 1QRule of the Community, the beginning of the Treatise (iii) is marked graphically by a blank and a marginal tick; similar devices signal five sections within the Treatise itself.

The opening lines (iii.13–15a) describe what follows as the doctrine to be taught by a master, the *maskil*, to disciples identified as "Sons of Light." It is therefore a catechesis for people who stand on one side, light, as opposed to darkness. It claims to make them understand the "nature (*toledot*) of all human beings according to their types of spirits," as well as the particular characteristics of their actions and of their consequent destiny. The introductory section then grounds the whole teaching within the framework of an exclusive monotheism and a strong determinism (iii.15b–18a). God is characterized as the knowing one who has masterminded every element of Creation beforehand, the God whose design is unfailingly realized at appointed times, and the ruler who takes care that the prescriptions pertaining to his creatures be applied in every matter. Without detailing these, the text focuses directly on its specific topic, the ancillary role of the two spirits for the mission of humankind: "He created humankind for the domination of the world and he has provided it with two spirits according to which to behave (*le-hithalekh*) until the fixed time of his visitation."

The two spirits are identified ethically as the spirit of truth (*emet*) and deceit (*ʿavel*), but, also, from a cosmic standpoint, as the spirit of light (*or*) and the spirit of darkness (*ḥoshekh*). Their origin, leadership, and fellowship are briefly considered, side by side (iii.18b–iv.1): Having their origin (*toledot*), respectively, in light and darkness, truth and deceit are under the dominion of supernatural powers, a Prince of lights and an Angel of darkness who in turn influence two separate groups of human beings, the "sons" of righteousness, who walk in light, and the "sons" of deceit, who walk in darkness. There is conflict and hostility between the two parties. The righteous, who are harassed by the Angel of Darkness and his spirits, resulting in sin and guilt, are granted the help of the God of Israel and his Angel of Truth. No explanation is provided for such a negative pressure, except that it is mysteriously allowed by God for a limited time. Being ultimately responsible for the situation, since he has created the two spirits and established upon both the course and judgment of every deed, God nevertheless everlastingly prefers the ways of the spirit of light over those of the spirit of darkness.

The ways of the spirits "in the world," along with their rewards, are listed in two separate sections introduced by a single heading. The key words "light" and "truth" frame the list of virtues (iv.2–6a), as the words "deceit" and "darkness" frame the list of vices (iv.9–11a); each begins with a general statement, followed by short series of related terms arranged in larger units; each section ends with the proper rewards.

The last section (iv.15–26) specifies that God has set a sharp division (*miflagah*) between these spirits and has made them hostile to one another from the beginning until the end time. All human beings inherit various portions of them and act accordingly, generation after generation, in a world dominated by deceit. At the end time, however, a dramatic shift will take place. Deceit will be destroyed altogether by God, and truth will rise up forever in the world. Those persons who behave properly will have the spirit of deceit removed from the innermost part of their flesh and the spirit of truth sprinkled upon them as purifying waters. Being restored in the initial glory of Adam and made partners of God for an eternal covenant, they will share some of the divine understanding, as wise angels do. But until then, the spirits of truth and deceit allotted to a person struggle within his heart. They prompt his love or his hate for them, provide him with a knowledge of good and evil, and lead him to wise or foolish conduct.

The dualism found in the Treatise is multiform. It is cosmic and mythological in that the fundamental structure of the world, as planned and created by God, consists in the division between light and darkness as two separate domains under the power of antagonistic supernatural leaders. As spirits, they rule over human beings as well and influence their behavior, by which they are qualified ethically as sons of righteousness or sons of deceit. This dualistic teaching also has anthropological and psychological dimensions, for each individual inherits and internalizes various proportions of both spirits. Finally, the whole system is set in an eschatological framework. The two spirits, their heads, and those under their command are thought of as being hostile to one another and maintaining an antagonistic relationship from the very beginning to the very end of history. At the appointed time, deceit will be eradicated forever and human beings will be given their proper reward—a few of them selected by God to be purified and granted knowledge and glory.

Other Documents from Qumran preserve only fragmentary descriptions of the cosmological speculations of the sectarians or their forerunners (e.g. 4QJubilees 1 vi = *Jubilees* 2.1–4). Such speculations are probably at the basis of the complex calendar systems of these groups (cf. 4QPhases of the Moon, 4QZodiology and Brontology; 4QCalendrical Documents) and are reflected especially in the attempt to synchronize the daily prayers with the "decree recorded forever" in the daily alternation of light and darkness, together with the movement of the sun, the moon, and the stars (1QRule of the Community ix.1–8, 1QHodayot[a] xx.4–11, 4QDaily Prayers). The regular disappearance of darkness before the light is also seen as pointing to the vanishing of evil before justice (1QMysteries 1.i.5).

Under various names, such as Michael, the majestic angel, or Melchizedek, on the one hand, and Belial, Mastemah, the Prince of dominion of evil, or Melchirescha', on the other hand, the supernatural leaders of light and darkness appear in texts which insist less on the physical extent of their respective dominions than on their actual power over human beings and their rival action in history and eschatology (1QRule of the Community i–ii; Damascus Document v.17–18; War Scroll i, xiii–xix; 4QVisions of Amram; 11Q Apocryphal Psalms[a]; 11QMelchizedek; etc.; see Kobelski, 1981). They do not always stand side by side in the same text, however. Belial (Mastemah, etc.) is sometimes mentioned alone (e.g. Damascus Document iv.12–vi.1, viii.1, xii.2, xvi.5; 4QMMT c28–30) or countered directly by God himself rather than by the angel who represents his mighty hand (1QRule of the Community i–ii, 1QHodayot[a] xii.12–14, War Scroll xiii.1–6, 4QBerakhot[a] 7.ii, 4QBerakhot[f], etc.). The prayer of the sage offers another means of stopping the influence of ravaging angels, bastard spirits, and demons who "lead astray the spirit of knowledge . . . in the era of the rule of wickedness and in the periods of humiliation of the Sons of Light" (4QSongs of the Sage[a] 1 5–7).

The most recurrent form of dualism in the Qumran literature is the ethical one. A general expression of it is found, for instance, in the patriarch Levi's exhortation to his sons that they act in truth and justice, sow goodness, and harvest the good (4QAramaic Levi[a] 5 i–8, cf. 4QTestament of Qahat i.7–13); similarly, the sage's disciple is invited to "consider all the paths of truth and examine all the roots of evil" (4QSapiential Work A[b] 2.iii.13). According to the sectarians, the present era is under the dominion of Belial (1QRule of the Community i.18, i.24, ii.19; War Rule xiv.9; etc.), who leads astray the children of Israel through the three nets of fornication, wealth, and defilement of the Temple (Damascus Document iv.15–17; cf. 4QWiles of the Wicked Woman). Those who enter the community repent from sin and are willing to "walk unblemished" in God's paths, while the "men of the lot of Belial" continue to perform "wicked, blameworthy deeds" (1QRule of the Community i.21, ii.10); they are to "do what is good and just" in the presence of God and "to love everything that he selects and to hate everything that he rejects," to "love all the Sons of Light (. . .) and to detest all the Sons of Darkness" (1QRule of the Community i.2–8; cf. Damascus Document ii.14–16; War Scroll i, xv.9; 4QCatena[a]; 4QFlorilegium 1–3.i.7–9; 11QMelchizedek, and so forth). The will of God is known through the Law of Moses, and its true interpretation has been revealed to the sons of Zadok who lead the community (1QRule of the Community v.8–9; cf. Damascus Document xv.8–9). The halakhic letter 4QMMT suggests that such a claim could have motivated the Qumran community's split from the larger society, whereas the conviction that God had "revealed the paths of truth and the deeds of evil, wisdom and folly" and freed the faithful "from the zeal of the sowers of deceit, from the congregation of the interpreters of flattering things" is expressed in the hymns (1QHodayot[a] v.9–10; x.31–32). Law and wisdom are closely related, as in *Ben Sira* (cf. 4QWisdom Text with Beatitudes 2.ii.3–4, 4.9–14).

The sharp division between truth and deceit is never to be taken for granted once and for all. The Pesher Habakkuk describes not only the external conflict of the Teacher of Righteousness with the Wicked Priest or other opponents, but also his internal fight with the Man of Lies who challenged his authority and "rejected the Law in the midst of their whole comm[unity]" (1QPesher Habakkuk v.10–12; cf. 4QPesher Psalms[a] i.26–27, 1QHodayot[a] xiii.23–25). Among themselves, the covenanters regularly deal with false converts who still regard "darkness as paths to light" (1QRule of the Community iii.3), "plot intrigues of Belial," look for God "with a double heart" and "are not firmly based" in his truth (1QHodayot[a] xii.13–14; cf. xiii.23–25, xiv.19–22). A document from Cave 4 preserves the rebukes of an overseer against members of the community who do evil, are short-tempered, haughty in spirit, choose a good life, and so forth (4QRebukes of the Overseer; cf. 1QRule of the Community iv.9–11a). If their conduct does not change, such members are to be expelled (1QRule of the Community vi.24–vii.27; cf. Damascus Document xx.1–13, 4QDamascus Document[a] 11.5–14).

The ambiguity of human behavior may be explained by one's lot in God's plan and by the war which the spirits of light and darkness are waging within one's heart (1QRule of the Community vii.20–21, x.21; Damascus Document viii 1–2; 1QHodayot[a] xiv 19–22; 4QBerakhot[f]). The basic anthropology behind this view is that God, who has created every spirit (1QRule of the Community i.10; 1QHodayot[a] vi.16b–32, ix.7–9), has allotted to each human being various parts of light and darkness (1QRule of the Community i.10, ii.20; 1QRule of the Congregation i.17–18; 1QHodayot[a] vi.8–16; cf. 4QHodayot[b] 7; 4QSapiential Work A[a] 81). According to a horoscopic document from Cave 4 (4Q186), one's condition may be deduced from the position of stars and planets at the time of conception or birth. Whoever has a substantial part in light and enters the community swears with a binding oath "to revert to the Law of Moses with all its decrees, with whole heart and whole soul" (1QRule of the Community v.8–9; cf. v.4–5; Damascus Document xv.4–5). His spirits are to be tested, and his rank among his fellows is to be reviewed regularly "according to his insight and his deeds . . . in order to upgrade each one to the extent of his insight and the perfection of his path, or to demote him according to his failings . . . " (1QRule of the Community v.21–24; cf. vi.17; Damascus Document xiii.11–12; 1QHodayot[a] vi.17–22, xvii.15–16, xviii.27–29). The instructor (*maskil*) plays an important role in the process, particularly among neophytes (1QRule of the Community ix.14–16), but one is also educated through God's wisdom (4QBeatitudes 2). The convert is purified by means of suffering and testing, like pure gold refined in a crucible (Damascus Document xx.2–3; War Rule xvi.15, xvii.1, xvii.9; 4QFlorilegium 1–3.ii.3; 4QCatena[a] ii.9–11; 4Q183 3–7; 1QHodayot[a] x.14–19, xiv.6–8). Everyone needs such purification, since the human being is nothing but dust and wicked flesh strongly inclined toward evil (1QRule of the Community xi.9–20; 1QHodayot[a] iv.25, v.20–21, ix.21–33, xii.29–35, xiii.16, xiv.32, xviii.3–12, xx.24–27, etc.). God, however, supports those who acknowledge their condition and beg for his mercy (1QHodayot[a] vi.23–27, viii.12–26, xvii.6–18, xvii.23–26), so that they may be cleansed and enabled to stand in his presence, united with the assembly of heaven (1QHodayot[a] xi.21–22, xv.26–32, xix.3–14).

The eschatological character of Qumran dualism surfaces in numerous documents. The present period is experienced as an age of wickedness (Damascus Document vi.14, xii.22–23, xv.6–7; 4QDamascus Document[f] 2.12; 4QSongs of the Sage[a] 1.6; 4QSongs of the Sage[b] 10.3), during which the world is under the dominion of Belial (1QRule of the Community 1.16, i.23–24, ii.19; Damascus Document iv.12–14; War Scroll xiv.9). The situation is about to change radically with the coming of the end of days, depicted as a time of visitation, judgment, and retribution (4QMMT[c] 11–13.4, 14–17.ii.6; War Scroll; 4QFlorilegium; 11QMelchizedek; 4QPesher Isaiah[a–c]; 1QPesher Micah; 4QPesher Nahum; 1QPesher Habakkuk; 4QCatena[a]; 4QAges of Creation). In the War Scroll, it is viewed as "a time of salvation for the people of God and . . . of everlasting destruction for all the lot of Belial . . . with no remnant remaining . . . [for the So]ns of Darkness" (War Scroll i.5–6). A fierce battle is expected between the Sons of Light and the Sons of Darkness, wherein angels and their leaders side with both camps; this fight will culminate in God's final destruction of Belial, all the angels of his dominion, and all the men of his lot (i.14–15). Those promised salvation will escape this age of visitation (Damascus Document xix.10) and be freed from the hand of Belial (11QMelchizedek ii.13, ii.25). God or his Messiah will indeed perform marvelous acts for them (4QMessianic Apocalypse); they will be granted peace, knowledge, joy, glory, and eternal life among the angels (1QRule of the Community ii.1–4a; Damascus Document iii.20, vii.4, xix.1; War Scroll i.9; 1QHodayot[a] iv.15; 4QSapiential Work A[a] 69 12; 1QRule of the Blessings iv.25–26; etc.). The followers of Belial will be destroyed forever either by God's sword or through various mediations, such as that of "the sons of his truth," the Messiah of Aaron and Israel, or even Belial himself. In any case, they are doomed to complete annihilation, as are Belial and his spirits (1QRule of the Community ii.4b–18, v.12–13; Damascus Document viii.1–2, xix.5–11; 11QMelchizedek iii.7; 1QHodayot[a] xiv.29–33; 4QSapiential Work A[a] 69 8; 4QBerakhot[f]; 4QBerakhot[a] 7.ii.4–6).

Debated Issues about Qumran dualism are numerous. The role and importance of the "Treatise of the Two Spirits" within the Qumran community has usually been taken for granted among Qumran scholars. Generally considered the authoritative expression of the sectarian dualistic doctrine, it is believed to have had a huge and lasting influence on the members of this group (Besch, Collins, Huppenbauer, etc.). However, on the basis of the differences between this text and other sectarian documents, such as the final form of the War Rule, the Hodayot from Cave 1, and the astrological document from Cave 4 (4Q 186), Harmut Stegemann has suggested that the Treatise could mirror the particular teaching of a specific member of the community or even be an external composition preserved in the group without representing an essential aspect of its theology. He even doubts that dualism is the primary concern of this text.

The scope of the corpus to be considered in the study

of Qumran dualism is a critical question as well. In his 1959 work, Hans W. Huppenbauer made use of the Damascus Document and of all relevant manuscripts from Cave 1 available at the time. Since then, the release of many other texts from Qumran displaying dualistic elements has raised the question of whether all these documents are of sectarian origin. The problem needs to be addressed if one wishes to understand the specific character of the dualistic view of this particular community and to assess correctly its relationship with the ideas of antecedent or related groups. In his study of the anthropology of the Qumran community, Hermann Lichtenberger has analyzed only texts possibly belonging to the community established by the Teacher of Righteousness. Bernt Besch has selected for his dissertation on Qumran dualism only a core group of texts limited to 1QRule of the Community, the Damascus Document, War Rule, 1QHodayot[a], 4QFlorilegium, 4QPesher Psalms[a], 11QMelchizedek, 4QPurification Rules, 4QBerakhot, and the Songs of the Sabbath Sacrifice (4Q400–407, 11Q17, Mas 1k). Further study must be made in that direction.

Scholars are divided on the subject of the historical origin of Qumran dualism. As early as 1952, the dualism found in the "Treatise of the Two Spirits" was related to similar Iranian ideas expressed in the old Gathas attributed to Zoroaster (*Yasna* 30, 45) and in the later Zurvanite myth reported by Plutarch in his *De Iside et Osiride* (Hengel, Philonenko, Shaked, Winston). This view is still maintained, but is also regularly disputed by opponents who argue that a clear relationship with Iranian thought is far from demonstrated and that Qumran dualism may be an inner development of the biblical and Jewish traditions as well (Barr, Besch, Duhaime, Osten-Sacken, etc.). Other concepts that might have contributed to the development of Qumran dualism include the symbolic meaning of light and darkness (*Gn.* 1.4, *Is.* 5.20, 45.7), the evocation of a good or an evil spirit (*Jgs.* 9.23, *1 Sm.* 16.14–16, *1 Kgs.* 22.13–28), the rivalry between two angels (*Zech.* 3, *Dan.* 10), the doctrine of the two ways (Ps. 1), the blessings and curses attached to God's covenant with Israel (*Dt.* 27–28, 30.15–20), the opposition between the just and the wicked (Ps. 37, *Prov.*, etc.), the victory of God over the powers of chaos (Ps. 74.12–14), the traditions of holy war (*Num.* 10, *Josh.* 6, *Jgs.* 4–5, *1 Sam.* 4–5, etc.), the expectation of the Day of the Lord (*Is.* 2.9–22, 13, 34; *Am.* 5.18–20, etc.), and the judgment against Gog (*Ezek.* 38–39). The historical context of the Maccabean revolt also would have been fertile ground from which Qumran dualism could sprout.

Questions have been raised about the development and coherence of Qumran dualism. According to Peter von der Osten-Sacken, the oldest form of dualism is preserved in the first column of War Rule and consists in the anticipation of an eschatological conflict between Israel and the nations; it is pre-Qumranian and mirrors the tensions of the Maccabean era. It shows clear connections with the book of *Daniel* and with traditions about the Day of the Lord and holy war. The other dimensions of Qumran dualism would be secondary developments in the direction of ethics, anthropology, history, and cosmology. Data not available to Osten-Sacken, such as the Visions of Amram (4Q543–548), suggest, however, that the ethical dualism is at least as ancient as the eschatological one and may be pre-Qumranian as well (Duhaime). Jörg Frey proposes that two patterns of dualism with different origins were conflated and developed in Qumran literature: the "Treatise of the Two Spirits" witnesses to a multidimensional, ethically oriented, cosmic dualism with a sapiential background, whereas a priestly type of sheer cosmic dualism is found in War Rule, 4QVisions of Amram, and 11QApocryphal Psalms[a]. Osten-Sacken's thesis also seems to deny the possibility that the various forms of dualism found in the sectarian texts themselves could have worked as a relatively coherent multidimensional system, as Besch, Collins, and others maintain.

The similarities and influences of Qumran dualism have been widely explored. It is claimed that its theology of the two ways could have inspired Jewish works as various as the *Testaments of the Twelve Patriarchs* or Philo's commentary on Exodus (*Quaest. in Exod.* i:23, etc.); the ethical dualism of Qumran also has remote similarities with the idea that a person is attracted by both a good and an evil inclination (*yetser*; cf. *Ben Sira* 15.14, B.T., *Ber.* 61a, etc.). In the New Testament, the Gospel and Epistle of John display a similar sharp division between light and darkness, truth and perversion, the spirit of truth and the spirit of error, and the victory of Christ over Satan (Bergmeier, Charlesworth). In later Christian literature, different dualistic views are found in works such as *Didache*, the *Epistle of Barnabas*, the *Shepherd of Hermas*, the *Pseudo-Clementine Homilies*, Lactantius's *Institutiones* and *De opificio*, and also in various forms of gnosticism (Couliano, Philonenko).

Dualism, with its various forms and its complex development, seems to have been a key theological feature of the Qumran community. Grounded in biblical teachings, but probably integrating Iranian components as well, it displays a strong concern for understanding the nature and role of the human being within the basic structure of the universe, establishing its relationship to God and other supernatural powers, and clarifying the ambiguity of its behavior and its corresponding fate. In a critical period of Jewish history, it provided this sectarian group, as well as related ones, with the theological and ideological legitimation for its separation from the larger community. It helped to shape its radical interpretation of the

Law, to set and maintain very high ethical standards for its members, and to support their commitment until the final vindication, triumph, and exaltation promised to them.

BIBLIOGRAPHY

Barr, James. "The Question of Religious Influence: The Case of Zoroastrianism, Judaism, and Christianity." *Journal of the American Academy of Religion* 53 (1985), 201–235. Argues that Iranian influence behind Jewish notions, and Qumran theology in particular, "though entirely conceivable and possible, remains intangible and undemonstrable."

Bergmeier, Roland. *Glaube als Gabe nach Johannes*, pp. 48–116. Beiträge zur Wissenschaft vom Alten und Neuen Testament, vol. 112. Stuttgart, 1980. Explores the notions of determinism, predestination, and dualism in Ancient Judaism and especially in the Qumran literature.

Besch, Bernt. "Der Dualismus in den Kernschriften von Qumran." Ph.D. Diss., Pont. Univ. S. Thomae in Urbe. Rome, 1996. Addresses all essential issues on the topic but needs to be used cautiously.

Bianchi, Ugo. "Dualism." In *Encyclopedia of Religion*, edited by Mircea Eliade, vol. 1, pp. 506–512. New York, 1987. A basic general treatment of the notion of dualism from the broad perspective of history of religion.

Charlesworth, James H. "A Critical Comparison of the Dualism in 1QS 3:13–4:26 and the "Dualism Contained in the Gospel of John." In *John and the Dead Sea Scrolls*, edited by James H. Charlesworth, pp. 76–106. New York, 1990. Argues for a possible influence of the Instruction on the Two Spirits on Johannine terminology and mythology.

Collins, John J. *The Apocalyptic Imagination*, pp. 115–141. New York, 1984. Presents the various dimensions of Qumran dualism as part of a coherent apocalyptic worldview.

Couliano, Ioan P. *Les gnoses dualistes d'Occident*. Paris, 1990. A comparative analysis of Western dualistic myths and an attempt to uncover their basic structure.

Davies, Philip. *1QM, The War Scroll from Qumran*. Biblica et Orientalia, n.32. Rome, 1977. An original exploration of the disputed question of the redactional history of one of the major documents for the study of Qumran dualism.

Duhaime, Jean. "Dualistic Reworking in the Scrolls from Qumran." *Catholic Biblical Quarterly* 49 (1987), 32–56. Argues that some of the key dualistic texts from Qumran contain secondary material.

Duhaime, Jean. "Le dualisme de Qumrân et la littérature de sagesse vétérotestamentaire." *Eglise et Théologie* 19 (1988), 401–422. A survey of the various types of dualism found in the Qumran literature and their precedent in biblical wisdom texts.

Eliade, Mircea. "Prolegomenon to Religious Dualism." In *The Quest: History and Meaning in Religion*, pp. 127–175. Chicago, 1969. Distinguishes between systems involving groups of polarities and dualism *per se*.

Hengel, Martin. *Judaism and Hellenism*, vol. 1, pp. 218–247. Philadelphia, 1981. Sets Qumran dualism against the background of the Hellenistic reform and of alien influences on Palestinian Judaism.

Kobelski, Paul J. *Melchizedek and Melchirešac*. Catholic Biblical Quarterly Monograph Series, 10. Washington, D.C., 1981. An investigation of the Heavenly Opponent Figures of the Qumran documents and their New Testament similarities.

Huppenbauer, Hans W. *Der Mensch zwischen zwei Welten*. Abhandlungen zur Theologie des Alten and Neuen Testaments, 34. Zürich, 1959. The first extensive monograph on Qumran dualism; still worth reading.

Lichtenberger, Hermann. *Studien zum Menschenbild in Texten der Qumrangemeinde*. Studien zur Umwelt des Neuen Testaments, 15. Göttingen, 1980. Studies dualism as part of the structure of the anthropology of the Qumran community, along with determinism, predestination, etc.

Osten-Sacken, Peter von der. *Gott und Belial. Traditionsgeschichtliche Untersuchungen zum Dualismus in den Texten aus Qumran*. Studien zur Umwelt des Neuen Testaments, 6. Göttingen, 1969. A detailed attempt, although not totally convincing, to reconstruct the origin and development of dualism in the Qumran literature.

Philonenko, Marc. "La doctrine qoumrânienne des deux esprits. Ses origines iraniennes et ses prolongements dans le judaïsme essénien et le christianisme antique." In *Apocalyptique iranienne et dualisme qoumrânien* by Geo Widengren, Anders Hultgård, and Marc Philonenko, pp. 163–211. Recherches Intertestamentaires, 2. Paris, 1995. A strong claim for the Iranian origin of Qumran dualism and for its survival in later Jewish and Christian literature.

Shaked, Shaul. "Qumran and Iran: Further Considerations." *Israel Oriental Studies* 2 (1972), 433–446. Holds that contacts between Jews and Iranians helped in formulating the dualism found at Qumran.

Stegemann, Hartmut. "Zu Textbestand und Grundgedanken von *IQS* III,13–IV,26." *Revue de Qumrân* 13 (1988), 95–131. Sees the Instruction on the Two Spirits as a particular teaching not as authoritative and influential in the Qumran community as usually believed.

Winston, David. "The Iranian Component in the Bible, Apocrypha, and Qumran: A Review of the Evidence." *History of Religion* 5 (1965–1966), 183–216. Argues that cumulative evidence suggests the probability of an Iranian penetration into Qumran.

JEAN DUHAIME

DUPONT-SOMMER, ANDRÉ (1900–1983), was a French epigraphist and historian. He was born on 23 December 1900 at Marnes-la-Coquette in France. After leaving secondary school, his interest in the history of the peoples of the ancient Near East led him to study at the Sorbonne, where he obtained a *Licence-ès-Lettres* in 1924. He stayed in Jerusalem at the École Biblique et Archéologique Française and took part in archaeological digs (Ramat el-Khalil, Byblos). Upon his return to France, he taught at the École Pratique des Hautes Études (1938–1971) and also at the Faculté des Lettres de Paris (1949–1953). Later he became a professor at the Collège de France (1963–1971), where he held the chair of Hebrew and Aramaic. He was elected as a member of the Académie des Inscriptions et Belles-Lettres in 1961; he became general secretary in 1968.

Dupont-Sommer was interested in many areas, as demonstrated by his work in Phoenician, Aramaic, and Hebrew epigraphy and the archaeology and the history of the ancient Near East. He developed a passionate interest in the Hebrew and Aramaic manuscripts discovered in the caves near the Dead Sea, because he saw in these documents the means of deepening knowledge of Jewish life just before Christianity was established. His first article dates back to 1949, and his first published synthesis, *Aperçus préliminaires sur les manuscrits de la Mer Morte*, came out the following year; it was translated into English in 1952. He quickly published a translation of the known Qumran texts (the first edition appeared in 1959), which was reprinted in *La Bible, Ecrits intertestamentaires* (1987). This work has been translated into German (*Die essenische Schriften vom Toten Meer*, 1960) and into English (*The Essene Writings from Qumran*, 1961). In this book Dupont-Sommer defends the idea of an Essene origin for Christianity, an idea carried forward by Edmund Wilson (*The Scrolls from the Dead Sea*, London, 1955).

The first publications dealing with the Qumran texts reveal Dupont-Sommer's ability to discover in the published texts their relationship with the Essene community mentioned by Pliny the Elder, his interest in the Teacher of Righteousness and his actions, and finally, his concern to establish a link between the texts and early Christianity. If his conclusions sometimes have been criticized, his publications nonetheless have contributed to understanding the historical importance for Judaism as well as for Christianity of the documents that have been discovered.

BIBLIOGRAPHY

Dupont-Sommer, André. *The Dead Sea Scrolls: A Preliminary Survey*. Oxford, 1952.

Dupont-Sommer, André. *The Jewish Sect of Qumran and the Essenes*. London and New York, 1954.

Lozachmeur, Hélène. "Publications de Monsieur André Dupont-Sommer." In *Hommages à André Dupont-Sommer*, pp. 547–553. Paris, 1971.

Sznycer, Maurice. "André Dupont-Sommer, 1900–1983." *Journal Asiatique* 272 (1984), 1–13. See bibliography by Hélène Lozachmeur, pages 10–13.

JACQUES BRIEND

DYE. *See* Textiles.

E

EARLY CHRISTIAN WRITINGS. The Qumran scrolls and early Christian writings have been particularly susceptible to parallelomania. Sometimes similarities between the scrolls and early Christian practices and texts have been mistakenly thought to indicate identity or a genetic relationship between the groups represented by them. While in most cases scholars have not been convinced of direct connections and contacts between the earliest Jesus movement and the Qumran community, it is clear that the scrolls provide what Joseph Fitzmyer (1974) has called "an intelligible Palestinian matrix for many of the practices and tenets of the early Church." The relationship between the scrolls and non- and post-New Testament Christian literature, however, has been much less studied than that between the scrolls and the New Testament.

Early Christian Fathers and the Greek Prophets Scroll. Dominique Barthélemy's study of the Greek Minor Prophets Scroll discovered at Naḥal Ḥever (8ḤHev 1) demonstrated that this translation, designated *kaige* for the unique manner in which the word *ve-gam* ("and also") was rendered, attempts to bring the Greek into closer agreement with the developing Hebrew text of the scriptures. [*See* Minor Prophets.] Several Christian writers knew and used this translation. Justin Martyr's citations of the Minor Prophets, most prominently a quote of *Micah* 4.3–7 in *Dialogue with Trypho* 109, agree with the text of the Greek Minor Prophets scroll. Origen's Quinta text of the Minor Prophets, Jerome's citations in his commentaries on these prophets, the "hébraïsmes" of Codex Washingtonensis and the Coptic versions of the Minor Prophets all reflect this textual tradition. [*See* Origen.]

Parallel Ideas in Early Christian Writings and the Judean Desert Corpus. One must distinguish between those places where early Christian literature shows contact with the Qumran scrolls and those where the scrolls and early Christian texts simply demonstrate parallel ideas. Evidence suggesting the former is scarce before approximately 800 CE when a Christian bishop named Timotheos writes about manuscript discoveries made near the Dead Sea. The parallels between the scrolls and early Christian literature, however, help to elucidate Christian practices and ideas, and they most likely represent religious impulses or options in Judaism that early Christians and the Qumran sectarians independently exercised.

Many of these common ideas and practices, such as eschatological expectation, attitudes toward the Temple, a communal meal, the place of Jesus as compared with the Teacher of Righteousness, and theological dualism, pervade earliest Christianity and indicate the continuity of the earliest followers of Jesus with Judaism. In the second century CE and following, Ebionite Jewish-Christian writings evidence some of the closest parallels to practices found in the Judean Desert corpus, so close in fact that J. L. Teicher (1951) identified the two, and Oscar Cullmann (1954) proposed that the Qumran sectarians joined the Ebionites after the First Jewish Revolt. [*See* Ebionites; Jewish Christians.] Fitzmyer concludes that although some similarities do exist, the differences between the Ebionites and the Qumran sectarians make Teicher's and Cullmann's positions untenable. The Ebionite criticism of the Hebrew scriptures noted by Epiphanius (*Panarion* 30.18) and the Ebionite rejection of animal sacrifice are especially noteworthy in this regard. The Pseudo-Clementine literature contains the closest similarities to the Qumran scrolls, but other Christian texts, like the *Apostolic Constitutions,* that use Jewish sources may also bear examination. [*See* Apostolic Constitutions; Pseudo-Clementine Literature.] Some of the most important points of possible contact are:

Baptism. For the Qumran community, lustrations, which were performed frequently, served the purposes of spiritual regeneration (Rule of the Community from Cave 1 at Qumran [hereafter, 1QRule of the Community] 1QS iii.9) and purification (1QS iii.4–5, 9, iv.20–21). The Pseudo-Clementine literature is also evidence of repeated lustrations. In *Homilies* 11.27–30 (from the *Kerygmata Petrou,* a basic Jewish-Christian source of the Pseudo-Clementine literature), an initiatory baptism is followed by repeated washings that remove ritual uncleanness, like that contracted through sexual intercourse.

Communal meal. The Qumran sectarians observed a communal meal restricted to members only (1QS vi.3–6), which is given eschatological importance in that the Messiah of Israel will celebrate the meal with the community (Rule of the Congregation 1Q28a ii.11–22). The Pseudo-Clementine literature prohibits eating with unbaptized nonmembers (*Homilies* 3.4; *Recognitions* 2.71) and indicates the practice of a communal meal, which is apparently not the Eucharist and at which people are seated according to rank (*Recognitions* 4:37). It is not, however, given an eschatological interpretation. The messianic meal mentioned in *Recognitions* 4.35 is not the same as the communal meal and reflects the eschatological banquet that appears in several New Testament books.

Dualism/two ways. There is at least a surface similarity between the dualism evident in Qumran texts like 1QRule of the Community, the War Scroll (1QM), and Hodayot[a] (hereafter, 1QHodayot[a]; 1QH[a]) from Cave 1 at Qumran, and the Pseudo-Clementine literature. [*See* Hodayot; Rule of the Community; War of the Sons of Light against the Sons of Darkness.] The idea in *Homilies* 7.6–7 of the two paths governed by belief and unbelief compares with the two spirits of truth and perversity in 1QRule of the Community (1QS iii.18–26). The doctrine of the syzygies (that created things exist in paired opposites) found in Pseudo-Clementine literature, however, has a physical aspect grounded in the created order not found in the Qumran texts. The two paths/two spirits idea also finds a clear parallel in *The Shepherd of Hermas* 36, *Epistle of Barnabas* 18–21, and the *Didache* 1–6. [*See* Didache; Dualism.]

Biblical interpretation and eschatology. Much has been written about the common aspects of interpretation of the Hebrew scriptures at Qumran and the New Testament, especially as it pertains to the *pesher* method. Both Qumran exegesis and some early Christian texts regard the biblical texts as a code that must be cracked to reveal the mysteries of the *eschaton,* which for the Qumran community and some early Christians was their own generation, but for many Christians still remained in the future. God revealed to the prophets secrets whose unraveling could only be done in the "present" time. The most prominent example at Qumran is Pesher Habakkuk (1QpHab) vi.15–7.5 in which the claim is made that it was only to the Teacher of Righteousness that God revealed the "mysteries of the words of his servants the prophets." [*See* Pesher Habakkuk.] Irenaeus of Lyons (*Against the Heresies* 5.34.2), to cite one Christian example, evidences a similar attitude in a comment about *Daniel* 7.27: "And lest the promise named should be understood as referring to this time [i.e., the time of Daniel], it was declared by the prophet, 'Come and stand in your lot at the consummation of the days,'" a clear reference to the prophecy's expected fulfillment in Irenaeus's own day. In this vein also see *Barnabas* 4.3–6, a section that cites the book of Enoch and *Daniel* and that begins, "The final scandal is at hand concerning which it has been written."

Prayer and liturgy. Book 7 of the *Apostolic Constitutions* contains a form of the Seven Benedictions, probably adapted from Jewish synagogue prayers (Fiensy, 1985). 1QRule of the Community x.16, part of the "order of benedictions" identified by Shemaryahu Talmon (1959–1960), may represent an early form of the benediction in the *Apostolic Constitutions* 7.33–38. Research into the Qumran prayers and liturgical texts and early Christian literature would appear to be an area of great promise.

Christian Use of Jewish Texts Found at Qumran. Though clear similarities exist between some ideas in early Christian texts and the Qumran scrolls, early Christian writings contain no clear example of citation from any of the Qumran sectarian texts (i.e., 1QRule of the Community, the War Scroll, the *pesharim*), and it is unclear whether early Christian writers knew any of them. The "two ways" material in the *Didache, Shepherd of Hermas*, and *Epistle of Barnabas,* however, may bear examination in this regard. Scholarly understanding of some Jewish apocrypha and pseudepigrapha known primarily through Christian transmission (like *1 Enoch, Jubilees, Testaments of the Twelve Patriarchs*) has been enhanced by their discovery among the Qumran scrolls. One of the more prominent examples is the Book of the Luminaries (*1 En.* 72–82) whose Qumran version is longer and more detailed than the version transmitted in Ethiopic Christianity, where *1 Enoch* is part of the biblical canon. [*See* Enoch, Books of.]

Church fathers, however, knew and used nonsectarian Jewish apocrypha and pseudepigrapha, the existence of which was otherwise unknown until the Judean Desert discoveries. For instance, among the Cave 4 finds were several copies of a previously known Jewish pseudepigraphal work, Pseudo-Ezekiel[a–e]? (4Q385, 386–387, 388, 391). [*See* Ezekiel, Book of.] This work, framed as a dialogue between Ezekiel and God and based largely on the biblical book of *Ezekiel,* was known to the author of *Barnabas* (Kister, 1990) and the *Apocalypse of Peter* (Bauckham, 1992). It may perhaps have some relationship to the Greek *Apocryphon of Ezekiel* cited by several church fathers (Mueller and Robinson, 1983). In another case, Yiphtah Zur (1993) has posited a relationship between the Syriac *Acts of Thomas* 6–7, the "Hymn of the Bride," and the Wiles of the Wicked Woman (4Q184).

It may be as well that some citations in the works of Christian authors whose source is unknown originated in texts found at Qumran. One citation in *1 Clement* 50.4 may reflect the text of Pseudo-Ezekiel[a] (4Q385 12; Wright, 1997). Possible relationships between anonymous citations in Christian literature and the Judean Desert corpus constitute another potentially fruitful avenue for research.

Christian Gnosticism. Birger Pearson (1984) has shown the extensive use of Jewish traditions by Christian Gnostics, several of which are parallel to material found in the Qumran scrolls. For example, the *Apocryphon of John* (*NH* II.26.15–22) contains a discussion of the Spirit of Life and the "opposing spirit" that resembles closely the two spirits of 1QRule of the Community. Also Melchizedek, an important figure at Qumran (Kobelski, 1981), is the subject of a fragmentary Nag Hammadi Codex tractate that shows the use of "pre-Christian Jewish Melchizedek material" (Pearson). [*See* Melchizedek.] The Enochic Book of Giants now known from Aramaic fragments at Qumran was used as a source by Mani for his *Book of Giants* (Pearson; Milik, 1976). [*See* Giants, Book of; Gnosticism.]

BIBLIOGRAPHY

Bauckham, Richard. "A Quotation from *4Q Second Ezekiel in the Apocalypse of Peter.*" *Revue de Qumrân* 15 (1992), 437–445. Argues that the reference to the dry bones vision in *Apocalypse of Peter* 4.7–9 is a citation of Pseudo-Ezekiel from Cave 4 at Qumran not the biblical *Ezekiel.*

Barthélemy, Dominique. *Les Devanciers d'Aquila.* Leiden, 1963.

Cullmann, Oscar. "Die neuentdeckten Qumrantexte und das Judenchristentum der Pseudoklementinin." *Beihefte zur Zeitschrift für die neutestamentliche Wissenschaft* 21 (1954), 35–51.

Daniélou, Jean. *The Dead Sea Scrolls and Primitive Christianity.* Baltimore, 1958. The text of three lectures by Daniélou that explore the possible relationships between the Qumran scrolls, the Essene sect, and early Christianity. He argues, for instance, that Dositheos, a Christian Gnostic, was an Essene and that the author of the *Shepherd of Hermas* was a converted Essene.

Daniélou, Jean. *The Theology of Jewish Christianity.* The Development of Christian Doctrine before the Council of Nicaea, 1. Chicago, 1964. Daniélou's *magnum opus* on Jewish Christianity in which he frequently draws parallels between his understanding of Jewish-Christian theology and the Qumran scrolls.

Fiensy, David A. *Prayers Alleged to Be Jewish: An Examination of the Constitutiones Apostolorum.* Brown Judaic Studies, 65. Chico, Calif., 1985. A study of the prayers in *Apostolic Constitutions* 7 and 8 and their presumed Jewish derivation.

Fitzmyer, Joseph. "The Qumran Scrolls, the Ebionites and Their Literature." *Essays on the Semitic Background of the New Testament.* Missoula, Mont., 1974.

Kister, Menahem. "Barnabas 12.1–3 and 4QSecond Ezekiel." *Revue de Qumrân* 13 (1990), 63–67. Argues that these two passages in *Barnabas* are citations of Pseudo-Ezekiel from Cave 4 at Qumran. The text in *Barnabas* 12.1 is more likely to be from the Qumran pseudepigraphal text than that in 4.3.

Kobelski, Paul J. *Melchizedek and Melchireša*[c]. Catholic Biblical Quarterly Monograph Series, 10. Washington, D.C., 1981. Examines the texts from Qumran that treat Melchizedek and Melchiresha[c] and looks at the roles attached to these figures in Judaism.

Kraft, Robert. "Review of Dominique Barthélemy, *Les Devanciers d'Aquila.*" *Gnomon* 37 (1965), 474–483. Detailed review of Barthélemy's work on 8ḤevXIIgr the Greek Minor Prophets (8Ḥev 1) and its implications for the study of the Jewish-Greek scriptures.

Milik, J. T. *The Books of Enoch: Aramaic Fragments of Qumrân Cave 4.* Oxford, 1976. Study of the Enoch fragments from Qumran that includes the Book of Giants. Milik's arguments for the existence of an Enochic Pentateuch at Qumran have not been generally accepted.

Mueller, James R., and William Robinson. "The Apocryphon of Ezekiel." In *The Old Testament Pseudepigrapha,* vol. 1, edited by James H. Charlesworth, pp. 487–495. Garden City, N.Y., 1983. Gives an English translation of the Greek *Apocryphon of Ezekiel* that may be related to Pseudo-Ezekiel from Cave 4 at Qumran. The translation appeared before the publication of any of the Qumran fragments.

Pearson, Birger. "Jewish Sources in Gnostic Literature." In *Jewish Writings of the Second Temple Period,* edited by Michael E. Stone. Compendia rerum Iudaicarum ad novum Testamentum, 2.2. Philadelphia, 1984.

Talmon, Shemaryahu. "The 'Manual of Benedictions' of the Sect of the Judaean Desert." *Revue de Qumrân* 2 (1959–1960), 474–500.

Teicher, J. L. "The Dead Sea Scrolls: Documents of a Jewish Christian Sect of Ebionites." *Journal of Jewish Studies* 2 (1951), 67–99.

Wright, Benjamin. "Qumran Pseudepigrapha in Early Christianity: Is *1 Clement* 50:4 a Citation of 4QPseudo-Ezekiel?" Paper presented to the Orion Center Symposium on Pseudepigrapha and the Dead Sea Scrolls. Jerusalem, January 12–14, 1997. Argues that *1 Clement* contains a citation of the Jewish work Pseudo-Ezekiel[a] 12.

Zur, Yiphtah. "Parallels between Acts of Thomas 6–7 and 4Q184." *Revue de Qumrân* 16 (1993), 103–107.

BENJAMIN G. WRIGHT III

EBIONITES. The Judeo-Christian sect of Ebionites (Gr. *Ebionaioi* or *Ebionitai*; Lat. *Ebionaei* or *Ebionitae*) took its name from the Hebrew word *ʾevyonim* meaning "poor ones." The designation may have been adopted by them from the phrase "Blessed are the poor in spirit" in *Matthew* 5:3//*Luke* 6:20. Eusebius (c.263–339 CE) wrote that the name Ebionite indicated the poverty of their intelligence (*Ecclesiastical History* 3.27.6). However, it may have reflected, besides their spiritual humility, their low social status and actual poverty (cf. e.g. *Js.* 2:1–7). The Ebionites were considered heretics by both Jews and Christians. They accepted some of the principal Jewish laws such as circumcision and sabbath observance, but Epiphanius says that they rejected certain parts of the Pentateuch (*Panarion* 30.18.7). Eusebius adds that for them Jesus was an ordinary man who became righteous through improving his character and who was born in a natural way from Mary and her husband (*Ecclesiastical History* 3.27.2). According to *Panarion* 30.16.3, they believed that Jesus was elected and named God's Son after the descent of the Christ from above in the form of a dove. The so-called *Gospel of the Ebionites* speaks of the dove descending and entering Jesus in the baptismal scene (see *Panarion* 30.13.7; cf. *Lk.* 3:21–22; Ps. 2:7; *Hb.* 1:5; 5:5). Hippolytus, too, indicates that for them Jesus' justification and his being named *Christ* came about because he obeyed the law; the Ebionites were therefore also to obey the law so that they could become christs (*Refutatio* 7.22). Eusebius does say that there was a group of them who accepted the virgin birth but even these did not acknowledge his divine pre-existence as Logos and Wisdom (*Ecclesiastical History* 3.27.3).

Their views about the prophets are not clear. Irenaeus says they had an unusual way of interpreting prophecies (*Hereses* 1.26.2), but Epiphanius gives the impression that they rejected the prophets and psalms (*Panarion* 30.15.2). The Ebionites also rejected the letters of Paul who was regarded as an apostate from the law. They were vegetarians and, after their baptism, engaged in daily baptisms according to Epiphanius (*Panarion* 30.153–16.1).

It seems that the Ebionites were among the Christians who fled from Jerusalem (before it was destroyed in 70 CE) to the town of Pella (*Panarion* 30.2.7; cf. *Rm.* 15:26; *Gal.* 2:10 where Paul calls some Jerusalem Christians "the poor"). Symmachus, who translated the Hebrew Bible into Greek, was an Ebionite (so Eusebius, *Ecclesiastical History* 5.8; 6.17). B.T., *Shabbat* 116a makes mention of the "house of the Ebionites" along with the "house of the Nazarenes."

The sources indicate that the Ebionites used only the *Gospel of Matthew* which they called the *Gospel according to the Hebrews*. However, the contents of the quotations from their gospel in *Panarion* 30.3.13–14, 16.21 lead one to think that it was composed on the basis of all three synoptic gospels. Epiphanius thought that their gospel was a distorted version of *Matthew* written in Hebrew (that is, in Aramaic). Some scholars believe that the *Gospel of the Ebionites* is to be identified with the *Gospel of the Twelve* (that is, the *Gospel according to the Apostles* mentioned by Origen [*Homily I on Luke*] and Jerome [in *In. Matt.* Prologue and *Dialogi Contra Pelagianos* 3.2]) on the grounds that in the fragments found in the *Panarion* the apostles are the narrators, but others have opposed this conclusion.

From the earliest days of Qumran studies, the use of the term *ʾevyonim*, "poor ones," in the Dead Sea Scrolls has been compared with the designation for this Jewish Christian group. In Pesher Psalms[a] (4Q171) 1–10.ii.10 and iii.10 the Qumran community is called "the congregation of the poor ones" (*ʿadat ha-ʾevyonim*; cf. War Scroll[a] [4Q491] frg. 11.i.11 which refers to the "council of the poor ones" [*ʿatsat ha-ʾevyonim*]). Several times the sectarians are called simply "poor ones" (*ʾevyonim*; for examples, see 1QpHab xii.3, 6, 10; 1QM xi.9, 13; xiii.13–14; cf. also 1QH[a] ii.32; iii.25; v.16, 18, 22; frg. 16.3). The Qumranites also referred to themselves as "oppressed ones/humble ones" (*ʿaniyyim*) and "simple ones" (*petaʾyim*), as if contrasting themselves with the Pharisaic "sages" (*ḥakhamim*) and "pupils of the sages" (*talmidei ḥakhamim*). In the War Scroll (1QM xiv.7) we meet the expression "poor in spirit" (*ʿaniyyei ruaḥ*; an alternate reading is *ʿanwei ruaḥ* "humble in spirit"). In light of Hippolytus's comment that the Ebionites' main goal was to fulfill the law, it is worth noting that the Qumranites designated themselves *ʿosei ha-torah* "the doers of (that is, those who fulfill, observe) the law" (e.g. 1QpHab vii.11; viii.1; xii.4–5; 4QpPs[a] 1–10.ii. 15, 23; cf. *1 Mc.* 2:67; 13:48; *John* 7:19; *Js.* 4:11; *Rm.* 2:13). In connection with the baptismal scene in the *Gospel of the Ebionites*, one should also mention 1QSa ii.11ff, which describes the coming (begetting) of a lay messiah, with an obvious allusion to Ps. 2:7. 4Q534 i.10, in connection with "the elect one of God" refers to his birth and apparently calls him "the breath of his spirit." In 4Q246 the lay messiah is called the "son of God (Most High)."

J. L. Teicher proposed that the Qumran texts were composed by the Ebionites and identified the Teacher of Righteousness, the charismatic leader of the Qumran congregation [*see* Teacher of Righteousness], with Jesus Christ and his antagonist and oppressor, the Wicked Priest [*see* Wicked Priest], with the Apostle Paul. His proposal has not received much support, however.

BIBLIOGRAPHY

Bertrand, D. A. "L'Évangile des Ébionites: Une harmonie évangelique anterieure au Diatessaron." *New Testament Studies* 26 (1980), 548–563.

Boismard, M.-É. "Évangile des Ébionites et problème synoptique." *Revue biblique* 73 (1964), 321–352.

Elliott, J. K. *The Apocryphal New Testament: A Collection of Apocryphal Christian Literature in an English Translation.* Oxford, 1993.

Fitzmyer, J. A. "The Qumran Scrolls, the Ebionites and Their Literature." *Theological Studies* 16 (1955), 335–372.

Keck, L. "The Poor among the Saints in Jewish Christianity and Qumran." *Zeitschrift für die Neutestamentliche Wissenschaft und die Älteren Kirche* 57 (1966), 54–78.

Klijn, A. F. J., and G. J. Reinink. *Patristic Evidence for Jewish-Christian Sects.* Novum Testamentum Supplement, 36. Leiden, 1973.

Schoeps, H.-J. *Jewish Christianity: Factional Disputes in the Early Church.* Translated by D. Hare. Philadelphia, 1969.

Teicher, J. L. "The Dead Sea Scrolls—Documents of the Jewish Christian Sect of Ebionites." *Journal of Jewish Studies* 2 (1951), 67–99.

Teicher, J. L. "The Teaching of the Pre-Pauline Church in the Dead Sea Scrolls." *Journal of Jewish Studies* 3 (1952), 111–118, 139–150; 4 (1953), 1–13, 49–58, 93–103, 139–153.

IGOR R. TANTLEVSKIJ

ECCLESIASTES, BOOK OF. *See* Five Scrolls.

ÉCOLE BIBLIQUE ET ARCHÉOLOGIQUE FRANÇAISE. The École Pratique d'Études was founded on 15 November 1890 by Father Marie-Joseph Lagrange (1855–1938), on the premises of the Dominican Monastery of Saint Stephen in Jerusalem. Its location in the Holy Land permitted the École to undertake wide-ranging exploratory journeys that enabled it to study the Bible in the physical and cultural context in which it had been written. The results were published in the periodical *Revue biblique* (1882–) and in the monograph series *Études bibliques* (1903–). The original name of the school was modified in 1920 when the Académie des Inscriptions et Belles-Lettres in Paris recognized its achievements and designated it the École Biblique et Archéologique Française. It has developed a comprehensive teaching program and is the only foreign national school of archaeology in Jerusalem to award doctorates in biblical studies. Its celebrated library is known particularly for its detailed subject catalog.

The faculty of the École and scholars-in-residence had contact with the Dead Sea Scrolls, almost from the time of their discovery. For example, J. van der Ploeg, a Dutch biblical scholar who was staying at the École in 1947, was shown the scrolls then in the possession of Archbishop Athanasius Yeshue Samuel and was apparently the first to recognize one of them as a copy of the *Book of Isaiah.* He concluded, however, that the scrolls were medieval. Like many others, the faculty of the École had serious doubts regarding the authenticity of the original Dead Sea Scrolls when knowledge of their existence first became available. That attitude did not last long. At the invitation of Gerald Lankester Harding, Director of Antiquities of Jordan, Roland de Vaux, then director of the École, participated in the excavation of Cave 1 at Qumran (15 February–5 March 1949). In October 1951 significant new scroll fragments came on the market, and soundings at Khirbet Qumran brought to light pottery identical with that found in Cave 1. Harding invited de Vaux to participate in the excavation of the Qumran site. A short exploratory dig in late 1951 was followed by four full seasons (1953–1956). De Vaux also spent one season in the caves of Wadi Murabba'at (1952; he had contacts in Jerusalem with the bedouin responsible for finding written materials there) and one season at 'Ein-Feshkha (1958). Between 10 and 29 March 1952, in association with the Palestine Archaeological Museum and the American Schools of Oriental Research in Jerusalem, the École was involved in conducting a systematic search of the cliffs for 4 kilometers (2.48 miles) on either side of Qumran. Two hundred sixty-seven caves were investigated.

De Vaux published annual reports on the excavations in the *Revue biblique* and offered a synthetic overview in his 1959 Schweich Lectures of the British Academy, which he brought fully up-to-date for its English translation *Archaeology and the Dead Sea Scrolls* (1973). The first volume of the final report has been published by Jean-Baptiste Humbert, professor of archaeology at the École, and Alain Chambon (1994). The succeeding volumes are the responsibility of Professor Robert Donceel of the University of Louvain-la-Neuve in Belgium, who was appointed in 1987 to publish the archaeological material from Qumran.

The École became responsible for the publication of the first scrolls by default. The fledgling Jordan Department of Antiquities had no textual expert, and the political situation before 1967 excluded Jewish cooperation. The task of publication fell to the youngest professor, Dominique Barthélemy, and Josef Milik, a Polish priest studying at the École. They co-opted Father Maurice Baillet when he arrived as a student at the École in 1952. With the growing number of fragments, de Vaux recognized that more scholars had to be recruited if the material was to be published quickly.

De Vaux won the consent of the Jordanian government to the formation of an international and interconfessional team, of which he became the coordinator. Barthélemy and Pierre Benoit were the only professors of the École to whom manuscripts were assigned. From 1974 Emile Puech, who later became a member of the faculty of the École, worked with Jean Starcky, and upon Starcky's death in 1988, Puech assumed full responsibility for his material. In 1986 Puech succeeded Jean Carmignac to become editor of the *Revue de Qumrân*.

The first five volumes of *Discoveries in the Judaean Desert* appeared under the general editorship of de Vaux. He also contributed several articles of his own, including one devoted to the texts from Wadi Murabba'at and an introduction to the edition of the Copper Scroll. By the time he died (10 September 1971) the chairman of the editorial team had only two functions: to encourage the members to publish quickly and to make arrangements with the publisher. The team chose Benoit, then director of the École, as the new chairman. The slowness of publication was becoming a scandal as scholars denied access to the unpublished scroll fragments became more vociferous in their complaints. Convinced of the justice of their case, Benoit did his best to exert pressure on tardy editors, but only two more volumes of *Discoveries in the Judaean Desert*—volume 6 (1977) and volume 7 (1982)—had appeared before his death on 23 April 1987. John Strugnell, who, like many other scrolls scholars, often resided at the École but had no official connection with it, was then chosen to be the new chairman.

That the first two chairmen of the editorial team were members of the Dominicans, a Roman Catholic religious order once associated with the Spanish Inquisition, became the basis of a popular conspiracy theory. Michael Baigent and Richard Leigh claimed that the Vatican, fearing that revelations in the Dead Sea Scrolls would be damaging to Christianity, had placed de Vaux and Benoit at the École to subvert the editorial process.

This accusation provoked an outburst of media hostility despite the real situation as to access to the scolls: no important manuscripts were confided to Dominicans, and de Vaux and Benoit had no authority to permit manuscripts to be seen by anyone else, once they had been assigned to members of the team and no authority to forbid the team members to show them to outsiders. Only when the publication of all the photographs of the scrolls confirmed that nothing in the scrolls posed the slightest danger to Christianity did the shadow of scandal subside.

[*See also* American Schools of Oriental Research; Palestine Archaeological Museum; *and the biographies of Barthélemy, de Vaux, Milik, and Starcky.*]

BIBLIOGRAPHY

Benoit, Pierre, O. P. "Activités archéologiques de l'École Biblique et Archéologique Française à Jérusalem depuis 1890." *Revue biblique* 94 (1987), 397–424. Reprinted as "French Archaeologists," in *Benchmarks in Time and Culture: Essays in Honor of Joseph A. Callaway,* edited by J. F. Drinkard et al., pp. 63–86 (Atlanta, 1988). Contains full bibliographical references for all the archaeological work of the École Biblique to 1986.

Betz, Otto, and Rainer Riesner. *Jesus, Qumran and the Vatican: Clarifications.* New York, 1994.

Humbert, Jean-Baptiste, and Alain Chambon. *Khirbet Qumran et Ain Feshkha. La fouilles de l'École Biblique et Archéologique Française de Jérusalem,* vol. 1, *Album de photographies Répertoire du fonds photographique, Synthèse de notes de chantier de Roland de Vaux.* Fribourg, 1994.

Murphy-O'Connor, Jerome, with a contribution by Justin Taylor. *The École Biblique and the New Testament: A Century of Scholarship, 1890–1990.* Novum Testamentum et Orbis Antiquus Series, 13. Fribourg and Göttingen, 1990. Profiles of the seven New Testament professors with full bibliographies.

Vesco, Jean Luc., ed. *L'Ancien Testament. Cent ans d'exégèse à l'École Biblique.* Cahiers de la *Revue biblique* Series, 28. Paris, 1990. Surveys and evaluation of the contribution of the École Biblique to biblical, intertestamental, and Oriental studies.

Viviano, Benedict T. "École Biblique et Archéologique Française de Jérusalem." *Biblical Archaeologist* 54 (1991), 160–167. Presentation of the current faculty and situation of the École Biblique.

JEROME MURPHY-O'CONNOR

ECONOMIC LIFE. According to Josephus and Philo, wherever the Essenes lived, they were organized in cooperative fellowships, which to some extent were closed economic units. [*See* Judea, *article on* Economy.] The literary testimonies (descriptions by sectarian and nonsectarian writers), the archaeological finds from Khirbet Qumran and the surrounding area, and the background of the ecological conditions at the Dead Sea coast allow us to draw a number of conclusions concerning the economic structure and way of life of the Essene sect.

Khirbet Qumran was not the only Essene center along the northern bank of the Dead Sea. A second sectarian center was discovered to the south of Qumran at Wadi Ghweir. At this site, located about 18 kilometers (11 miles) to the south of Qumran, P. Bar-Adon excavated a large structure (19.5 by 43 meters [64 by 141 feet]) which was in use during the same time period as the Khirbet Qumran site, from the late Hellenistic period to 68 CE. [*See* Ghweir, Wadi.] In addition, tombs of the type existing at Qumran were uncovered near Jericho, and at Ḥiam el-Saʿaha (north of Murabbaʿat) and el-Buqeia. An additional cemetery of this type was discovered in Jerusalem. Philo and Josephus write that there were more than four thousand Essenes. [*See* Essenes.] The sites found in the Judean Desert could have supported only a small portion of this number, which is no more than a general estimate. [*See* Archaeological Surveys; Archaeology.]

Khirbet Qumran was not a residential site, but rather a communal center used for common meals, immersion, study, and workshops. Most of the members slept in the marl caves. These dwellings were rock-cut and established at a distance from the site not exceeding the Sabbath bounds (1.2 kilometers [0.75 miles] in each direction). The network of paths that connected the caves with the site bears signs of intensive use (sandal nails, pottery vessels, and coins). Additional structures discovered near ʿEin-Feshkha apparently were used by the inhabitants of Qumran. The number of members using the Qumran site was not large. B. Wood attempted to estimate the number of users on the basis of the quantity of water that accumulated in the ruins. The quantity of water required by the community, however, was flexible and cannot be estimated, as was proved by G. Stephens, especially as a large part of the drinking water was brought from the ʿEin-Feshkha springs. According to Magen Broshi's calculations, the dining room could have held at most 150 diners with modern-day seating arrangements. If they reclined as was common in Hellenistic society, and during festive meals in Jewish society, it could have accommodated only half as many diners. The quantity of serving utensils found near the dining room attests to a maximum participation by two hundred people in the common meals.

The climatic conditions of the Dead Sea area severely hinder any agricultural activity based on rainwater, and only those areas that are watered from springs are cultivatable. The soil in the Dead Sea region is salty and can be prepared for agriculture only with great effort. Arable areas are to be found near ʿEin-Feshkha and in the vicinity of ʿEin-el-Ghweir. Floodwaters are an additional source of water, but considerable effort is required to utilize this source. There is a limited number of floods, only two to three annually, and each carries along a tremendous quantity of water. Therefore, even if the water was diverted from the streambeds by aqueducts, a large number of reservoirs would have had to have been built in order to hold the great quantity of water that sporadically flowed through.

The Late Second Temple Period Settlement in the Dead Sea Area. To the north of Qumran was Jericho, which was a flourishing town and governmental center at the time. A government estate in which balsam, dates, and other crops were cultivated was constructed near Jericho. The winter palaces of the Hasmonean dynasty and King Herod were constructed in the center of this estate. At ʿEin-Gedi, an oasis surrounded by several perennial springs on the western shore of the Dead Sea to the south of Qumran, was another settlement. Its economy was based on the production of balsam, dates, grapes, and additional crops. [*See* ʿEin-Gedi.] Pliny writes that the flourishing settlement was second only to Jerusalem in agricultural quality (*Natural History* 5.73), although some scholars feel that in this instance Pliny is mistaking ʿEin-Gedi for Jericho. There was a royal palace on top of the desert fortress of Masada, south of ʿEin-Gedi on the western shore of the Dead Sea. In the time of Herod, the fortress was an economic center and an important consumer of services. Additional sites were located to the south of the fortress. At ʿEin-Buqeq, M. Gichon excavated a workshop that may have been used to produce balsam. The survey conducted by Bar-Adon uncovered seven structures constructed along the western shore of the Dead Sea, as well as two small villages. On the northeast shore of the Dead Sea, opposite Qumran, was Callirrhoe, with its medicinal baths that were used by King Herod and others. A bit to the south of this site are the medicinal hot baths of Baʿara.

Living conditions in the Dead Sea region are difficult. Nonetheless, the area flourished in the late Second Temple period, probably due to the cultivation of balsam in the oases of Jericho, ʿEin-Gedi, ʿEin-Buqeq, and probably ʿEin-Zohar. The high price of the spice derived from this tree justified the tremendous effort required of those engaging in agriculture in the Dead Sea region. Another item produced in the region was salt, an essential and costly commodity in the Roman period. The production of and trade in this commodity was a natural resource of the area. Bitumen is another mineral present in the Dead Sea area; its economic significance has not been determined. As a consequence of these unique natural resources, the region became the site of a trade route as well as a source of livelihood. In order to accommodate the increased commercial activity, a number of ports were built along the Dead Sea, such as Maoza, the port of Zoara. A ship at ʿEin-Gedi is mentioned in one of the Bar Kokhba letters, and several ships' anchors were discovered at the site. A large pier leading to a structure constructed in the Hasmonean period was discovered at Rujm el-Bahr, on the northern coast of the Dead Sea to the south of ʿEin-Feshkha. The Dead Sea area thrived and was the center of an open and specialized economy in the late Second Temple period. The inhabitants of the region produced special goods, the proceeds from which enabled them to purchase essential commodities. At least a portion of the area's inhabitants were wealthy, and the entire population was quite well established. There were governmental interests in the Dead Sea region; consequently, if the inhabitants of Khirbet Qumran were desirous of evading the watchful eye of the authorities, then their choice of the Dead Sea shore was ill advised.

The Socioeconomic Ideology of the Sect Members. The rabbinic literature mentions a sect known as the Sons of Rekhab. The tannaitic traditions collected by Z. Safrai regarding this sect indicate that it was an organized group whose members left their homes and went into the wilderness to study Torah. They are described as "water drinkers," that is, they abstained from wine. The members of the Sons of Rekhab community generally did not visit the Temple. On one occasion, one of their number came to the Temple, and his offering was accepted only after much deliberation. The sect members did not live in houses, but in booths and tents, and did not anoint themselves with oil. A certain degree of divine inspiration and Torah scholarship was attributed to them. Their migration to the wilderness apparently ensued from their desire to engage in Torah study, asceticism, and also because they heralded the advent of the Messiah, similar to other heralds such as Elijah and Melchizedek. All these characteristics are suitable to a general description of the Essene sect. These *midrashim* regarding the Sons of Rekhab may preserve the memory of the *yaḥad* ("community"), as it was recalled a generation or two after the Essenes ceased to continue to be a tangible threat to the rabbis. These testimonies regarding the Sons of Rekhab are consistent with the economic character of the group residing at Qumran.

The historical descriptions portraying the Essenes and the scrolls found in Qumran enable us to reconstruct the ideology of the group resident in the area. [*See* Essenes.] It should be noted, however, that life there was difficult and many groups throughout history that possessed a religious economic policy were often forced to compromise some of their principles when everyday needs undercut the realization of their economic ideals. The authors describing the Essenes stress the ascetic orientation of these groups. Philo states that the Essenes do not amass property, are not interested in large estates, and despise a life of luxury. Josephus also emphasizes that they reject a life of riches (*The Jewish War* 2.122–127). The sexual abstinence prevalent in some of these groups also harmonizes with this tendency, albeit with additional reasons for such conduct. The element of abstinence is not stated outright in the sectarian writings, but allusions to that effect do appear in one of the wisdom writings, namely, Sapiential work A^{b} (4Q416). In this composition, poverty is a fact and not an ideological goal. Other works express opposition to unjust riches, such as Rule of the Community from Qumran Cave 1 (1QS xi.2, xxii.9) and Hodayot^{a} from Qumran Cave 1 (1QH^{a} x.22–25). Their opposition, however, is directed against wrongful riches, and not against the accumulation of property per se.

Going forth to the wilderness was a central component of the sectarian experience even though there were Essenes who did not live in these barren areas. They believed that the messianic era would be revealed in the wilderness, as the prophet states, "A voice rings out: 'Clear in the desert a road for the Lord!' " (*Is.* 40.4). Their time was the proper time to clear a road (or "turn") to the desert (1QS viii.15). Additionally, the wilderness facilitated a socioeconomic separation from the Jewish environment. The desire for an ascetic life also played a part in the decision to move to the wilderness. Going forth to the wilderness, however, did not constitute an attempt to flee from the authorities.

A central motivating force in the life of the sectarians was the desire to limit their economic ties with anyone not belonging to the group. While the nonsectarian sources such as Josephus, Philo, Pliny, and the rabbinic literature do not emphasize this aspect, the sectarian scrolls found at Qumran do indeed make explicit mention of the subject. However, the economy of the sectarians was based on commercial relations with the surrounding nonsectarian environment, and, consequently, it would seem that no prohibition was imposed on the sale of agricultural produce to people who were not members of the community.

Josephus and Philo relate that the Essenes maintained a communal system of property ownership. Work was done jointly, with all profits given over to the treasurer (1QS vi.2, with many additional testimonies in other scrolls found at Qumran). According to Josephus and the Rule of the Community, any new member had to transfer his possessions (Greek: *tagmata*, Hebrew: *hon*) to the community (1QS vi.20, vi.23; 11Q19 lvii.21). An ostracon discovered at Qumran in 1996 contains a writ documenting the transferal of a house, vineyard, figs trees, olive trees, and a slave (apparently from Transjordan) by a new sectarian member to the community. The number of those joining the sect was most likely substantial. Some of the Essene fellowships opposed marital life, and the continued existence of these groups was made possible only by sufficient numbers of new members. Philo and Pliny say that many joined the sect. Even if these reports are somewhat exaggerated, there were significant numbers of new recruits whose entrance into the sect allowed for a steady flow of property into the public treasury. It is not inconceivable, however, that the members of the community retained some private possessions. Most of those transgressing the laws of the sect were punished by partial excommunication. The lack of economic sanctions attests to the absence of private property held by individual members. Nonetheless, the individual who caused loss to the property of the community had to pay (1QS vii.7), and was presumably capable of doing so.

Josephus and Philo presented sectarian economic cooperation as a continuation and consequence of the ascetic worldview. The literature of the sect, however, provides an alternative explanation: "They shall bring all their knowledge and their powers and their wealth into the community of God . . . according to the perfection of his ways and all their wealth by the counsel of his righteousness" (1QS i.12–13). This is an application of the biblical commandment: "You shall love the Lord your God with all your heart and with all your soul and with all your might (*me'odekha*)" (*Dt*. 6.5). The rabbis understood *me'odekha* to mean money, which is the precise interpretation of the biblical and sectarian term *hon*. Consequently, *hon* had to be an instrument for the service of the Lord, and obviously could not be used for nonsacred purposes. The shared nature of property was therefore part of the totality of requirements imposed upon the sect members, a demand intended to bring about absolute devotion to the worship of the Lord, and was not a goal unto itself. Beyond the communal ownership of property, it is noteworthy that the productive labor of the sect's members was done on a cooperative basis, under the direction of the community's leaders. Consumption also was on a common basis. Josephus speaks of excess property that was given to charity, and to aid the elderly and sick members of the sect. He makes no allusion, however, to any help extended to individuals not belonging to the community.

Economic Livelihood of the Qumran Sect. 'Ein-Feshkha is a significant and consistent source of water; however, some of the water is saline to different degrees. Moreover, the level of the Dead Sea changes, and every variation either reveals or covers many springs and alters the salinity level of the water. At any rate, 'Ein-Feshkha is larger than the 'Ein-Gedi springs. [*See* 'Ein-Gedi.] The area of land that can be cultivated in the 'Ein-Feshkha region is 1.5–2.0 square kilometers, and water of only an intermediate quality or better sufficed to utilize this area (a dunam of plantations requires 150–200 cubic meters annually). Terraces and remains of aqueducts were discovered in a survey of the area between Qumran and 'Ein-Feshkha, and it may be assumed that the water and land were used in the late Second Temple period to grow dates, the only crop not affected by the salinity level of the water. [*See* Cisterns and Reservoirs; Water Systems.] The water supplied by the springs in 'Ein-el-Ghweir is estimated at 5,000,000–15,000,000 cubic meters annually, but the salinity level varies from one spring to another, and, again, only some of this water is suitable for agrarian purposes. The arable area at 'Ein-el-Ghweir is about 300 dunams, and this area was fully utilized for the cultivation of dates.

Our sources do not mention the cultivation of balsam at 'Ein-Feshkha or 'Ein-el-Ghweir. The water at 'Ein-Feshkha and 'Ein-el-Ghweir was most likely too salty for the cultivation of balsam, and was used to grow dates instead. The rabbinic *midrashim* mentioning the Sons of Rekhab state that they earned their livelihood, among other ways, as planters, a possible reference to the dates that provided an economic livelihood for the members of the sect who prohibited anointing with oil, and probably also frowned upon the use of an expensive spice such as balsam. Fish are to be found to this day in the pools at ʿEin-Feshkha, thus raising the possibility that the inhabitants of Qumran may have pursued the raising of fish in these ponds as an additional source of food or income for the sect.

An additional occupation that provided a living for the inhabitants of Qumran was sheep raising. Two sheepfolds were built between Caves 11 and 1, and a large portion of the scrolls were written on sheep parchment. De Vaux conjectured that various installations unearthed at ʿEin-Feshkha were workshops for the production of parchment from hides. (DNA tests of the scrolls, currently in progress, seek to determine if there is any genetic relationship between the physical remains of sheep and goats in the area and the hides on which the scrolls were written; if such a relationship exists, then the hides came from the same flock.) In the desert region, a sheep requires about 16 dunams of natural pasture. The plateau around Qumran in which the sect members lived totals about 5 square kilometers (1,236 acres), only about half of which is suitable for grazing, the rest consisting of steep cliffs. Only 150–200 sheep can be raised in this area. Assuming, therefore, that all the inhabitants of Qumran did not distance themselves from the site and that all were careful to participate daily in the prayers and the common meals, then sheep herding was no more than an ancillary economic branch that provided the Qumran inhabitants with some meat, milk, and wool. [*See* Agriculture.] If, however, it may be assumed that some members of the sect or the candidates were not required to physically participate in the religious ceremonies at Qumran, or that they entrusted their flocks to professional shepherds who were not members of the community, then they may very well have possessed larger flocks that wandered throughout the Judean Desert. One of the jars discovered at Qumran attests to the practice of dyeing wool red at the site. The jar, which had two rims, was found resting on a stone basin in the central courtyard of the eastern structure at Qumran. One member used the dye in the jar to write his name (Yoḥanan Haṭla) on the vessel itself. To the best of our knowledge, the members of the Qumran sect wore white garments, but they most likely also used red wool threads. The burnt sheep bones unearthed in the Khirbet Qumran excavations indicate that meat was eaten at the common meals. A structure composed of stables was discovered on the western side of Khirbet Qumran, but these were probably for donkeys.

To the west of Khirbet Qumran is el-Buqeiʿa, a mountainous plateau with moderate topographical features. The entire region is arid, and on average about 150 millimeters of rain falls annually in el-Buqeia. Notwithstanding this meager precipitation, the people of Qumran apparently attempted to grow barley in this region, which required those involved in this work to be absent from the communal ceremonies for a few days. The descent from el-Buqeiʿa to Qumran takes about three hours, while the ascent to the plateau takes more time, and it would thus seem that it was not possible to go to el-Buqeiʿa and return to Qumran on the same day. At the beginning of winter a group of sect members would most probably go out to plant barley in el-Buqeiʿa, and if the crop proved to be successful, they would go out after the Passover holiday to harvest the grain. The discovery of Qumran-type tombs in el-Buqeiʿa tends to confirm the hypothesis of sectarian involvement at the site.

In his description of the Essenes, Josephus emphasizes their employment in various crafts, and Philo mentions their work both as farmers and in different crafts. These descriptions reflect life in the Essene centers outside Qumran. In Qumran itself, agriculture was the primary form of occupation, although the inhabitants of this center also engaged in a number of branches of labor. Khirbet Qumran itself did not contain dwellings, but rather functioned as a communal center. Traces of a number of installations were found at the site, such as a pottery kiln. The members of all the sects of the late Second Temple period were meticulous in their observance of purity, in excess of the demands of the *halakhah*. Under these conditions, during periods of respite in the intersectarian struggles, some sectarians likely preferred to purchase pottery vessels that had been produced by potters whose observance of purity practices was impeccable. The marl on which Khirbet Qumran was built assured the potters in Qumran of a sufficient supply of raw material for the production of pottery vessels.

Room 30 at Khirbet Qumran contained a number of tables and inkstands, leading scholars to conclude that some of the scrolls were copied there. The Qumran library contained hundreds of scrolls, and copying most probably became an important economic activity providing a livelihood for sect members. The last two assumptions regarding the production of pottery and the copying of texts have not been proved, but the *midrashim* describe the Sons of Rekhab, "whose livelihood came from [the production] of pottery vessels." They are also described as "the families of the 'scribes' [*soferim*]" (*Midrash ha-Gadol* on *Exodus* 18.27, p. 371; Safrai, 1979 *A.R.N.*, version A, chap. 35, p. 53).

Thousands of date pits and presses were found in the south part of Khirbet Qumran. Date honey was probably produced here. As was noted, the inhabitants of Qumran raised dates in areas irrigated by the ʿEin-Feshkha springs, and the crop was most likely processed in a workshop producing honey that was sold outside Qumran. The *midrash* refers to the Sons of Rekhab, as those "who dwelt at *Neṭaʿim*," thus attesting to their livelihood from plantations (*meṭṭaʿim*).

In 1992, V. Jones excavated a cave containing an accumulation of organic material. The excavator claimed, without any specific basis or historical probability, that these were remnants of the components of incense. This find is most likely a store of *borit* ("lye"), a sort of soap, which was a mixture of Dead Sea salts and various forms of desert vegetation. This, therefore, attests to an additional industrial activity that provided a livelihood for the inhabitants of Qumran.

Only a small portion of the sectarian halakhic material was concerned with the economic world. A copy of the Cairo Damascus Document from Qumran Cave 4 contains agrarian *halakhot*. Of special interest is the obligation to give the priest only 1 percent of what is obtained by trapping or fishing (11Q19 lx.8–10), which constituted part of the livelihood of the sect members. The connection between the Temple Scroll and the economic conditions prevailing at Qumran is likely to be wholly incidental. Halakhah[a] (4Q251) is concerned with the use of animal hides and the prohibition of carrying items outside a tent enclosure on the Sabbath. Other *halakhot* are of a more commercial nature, such as the prohibition in Miqtsat Maʿasei ha-Torah (4Q394–399) of the use of metal vessels and the grain of gentiles.

The Standard of Living of the Qumran Sectarians. The authors who describe the Essenes portrayed them as opposing wealth, but not as being poor. The inhabitants of Qumran lived a simple life, they lived in marl caves in the desert, but conclusions should not be drawn from this regarding the communal standard of living. The high standard of living of the Qumran community may be inferred from several kinds of evidence.

1. Hundreds of silver and bronze coins were unearthed at Qumran. These coins, which were published by de Vaux, Sharabani, and Arif, attest to the dimensions of the commercial activity and the open nature of the Qumran economy. As was noted, the open economy of the Dead Sea region was exceptional.
2. Great quantities of water were accumulated at Qumran (Wood, 1984) relative to the number of people at the site (Broshi, 1992).
3. The aqueduct bringing water to the site is short but highly sophisticated, and required the use of Roman measuring instruments and technology.
4. Many utensils were unearthed next to the dining room, some of which were serving utensils used to bring food to the tables. The majority were individual utensils for dining: 210 plates, 708 bowls, and 75 beakers. The numbers of utensils in the dining-room storeroom probably corresponded to the approximate number of sectarians partaking of meals in the dining room. The presence of a pottery workshop at Qumran undoubtedly facilitated the supply of vessels. The two hundred plates found in the storeroom were probably more than sufficient, since the dining room could not accommodate a greater number of diners, leading us to conclude that fewer than two hundred people inhabited the site. The seven hundred bowls found in the storeroom (even if some were surplus) attest to tables set with several dishes served at the communal meals, which therefore differed from the simple meals depicted by Josephus. The quantity of burnt bones found at the site shows that meat was served in the dining room. Meat was expensive in Judea, and slightly less costly in the desert, with its expansive pasture lands, but the consumption of meat on a daily basis is not consistent with poverty. D. Flusser noted that the *pesharim* scrolls mention that people joined the community when a famine was raging in Judea, thus indicating that the community resident at Qumran succeeded in maintaining itself and providing living conditions that attracted people from Judea during times of crisis.
5. The structure at Qumran and the meager finds unearthed there also show that the people of Qumran were not poverty-stricken. The *midrashim* preserve the memory of the Sons of Rekhab as a group that emerged from the wealthy class in Judea (Safrai, 1979, p. 46). Another *aggadah* describing the secession of the Sadducees and the Boethusians stresses that the dissidents "used silver vessels and gold vessels." (*A.R.N.*, version A, chap. 5; version B, chap. 10.) This obviously is nothing more than an aggadic portrayal, but it nevertheless gives expression to a dim memory that the members of the groups that broke away from Jerusalem were wealthy individuals. Those who joined the sect came primarily from the elite strata of Judean society, and when they joined the Qumran community, they brought with them considerable funds and means of production. The aforementioned ostracon discovered in Qumran in 1996 attests to a propertied new member who gave over his possessions to the community. The supposition that those joining an ascetic community came from the ranks of the wealthy may be surprising. Throughout history, however, members of the elite strata have been the ones to initiate many social revolutions, from the monastic movement to the Communist movement in Europe. This assumption explains the halakhic proximity between the Sadducees and the Essenes, and the tension and rivalries between the two movements, which emerged from a similar social context.

BIBLIOGRAPHY

Amar, Z. "The Ash and the Red Material from Qumran." *Dead Sea Discoveries* 5 (1998), 1–15.

Arif, A. S. *A Treasury of Classical and Islamic Coins: The Collection of the Amman Museum*, pp. 15–21. London, 1986.

Bar-Adon, P. "The Judean Desert and Plain of Jericho." In *Judea, Samaria and the Golan: Archaeological Survey 1967–1968* (in Hebrew), edited by M. Kochavi, pp. 92–149.

Bar-Adon, P. "Another Settlement of the Judean Desert Sect at ʿEn el-Ghuweir on the Shores of the Dead Sea." *Bulletin of the American Schools of Oriental Research* 227 (1977), 1–25.

Bar-Adon, P. *Excavations in the Judean Desert.* *ʿAtiqot* (Hebrew series) 9 (1989).

Baumgarten, J. M. "A Qumran Text with Agrarian Halakhah." *Jewish Quarterly Review* 86 (1995), 1–8.

Berquist, B. "Sympotic Space: A Functional Aspect of Greek Dining Rooms." In *A Symposium on the Symposium*, edited by D. Murray, pp. 37–65. Oxford, 1990.

Blackborn, M. "What Factors Govern the Number of Coins Found on an Archaeological Site?" In *Medieval Archaeology Group*, edited by H. Clarke and E. Schia, pp. 15–24. British Archaeological Reports, 556. Oxford, 1989.

Broshi, M. "The Archaeology of Qumran—A Reconsideration." In *The Dead Sea Scrolls: Forty Years of Research*, edited by D. Dimant and U. Rappaport, pp. 103–115. Jerusalem and Leiden, 1992.

Cross, F. M., and E. Eshel. "Ostraca from Khirbet Qumran." *Israel Exploration Journal* 47 (1997), 17–28.

de Vaux, R. *Archaeology and the Dead Sea Scrolls*. London, 1973.

Feliks, Y. "The Incense of the Tabernacle." In *Pomegranates and Golden Bells: Studies in Biblical, Jewish, and Near Eastern Ritual, Law, and Literature in Honor of Jacob Milgrom*, edited by D. P. Wright, D. N. Freedman, and A. Hurvitz, pp. 125–149. Winona Lake, Ind., 1995.

Flusser, D. "Qumran and the Famine during the Reign of Herod." *Israel Museum Journal* 6 (1987), 7–16.

Flusser, D. "The Social Message from Qumran." In *Judaism and the Origins of Christianity*, pp. 193–201. Jerusalem, 1988.

Gichon, M. *En Boqeq: Ausgrabungen in einer Oase am Toten Meer*. Mainz am Rhein, 1993.

Hadas, G. "Stone Anchors from the Dead Sea." *ʿAtiqot* 21 (1992), 55–57.

Laperrousaz, E. M. *Qumrân, l'éstablissement essénien des bord des la Mer Morte: Histoire et Archeologie du site*. Paris, 1976.

Safrai, Z. "The Sons of Yehonadav Ben Rekhav and the Essenes" (in Hebrew). *Bar-Ilan* 16–17 (1979), 37–58.

Safrai, Z. *The Jewish Community in the Talmudic Period* (in Hebrew). Jerusalem, 1995.

Sharabani, M. "Monnaies de Qumrân au Musée Rockefeller de Jerusalem." *Revue biblique* 87 (1980), 274–284.

Stephens, G. R. "Aqueduct Delivery and Water Consumption in Roman Britain." *Institute of Archaeology Bulletin* 21 (1984–1985), 111–118.

Wood, B. G. "To Dip or Sprinkle? The Qumran Cisterns in Perspective." *Bulletin of the American Schools of Oriental Research* 256 (1984), 45–60.

Woodward, S. R., et al. "Analysis of Parchment Fragments from the Judean Desert Using DNA Techniques." In *Current Research and Technological Developments on the Dead Sea Scrolls*, edited by D. W. Parry and S. D. Ricks, pp. 215–238. Leiden, New York, and Cologne, 1996.

ZE'EV SAFRAI
HANAN ESHEL

EGYPT, the Nile Delta and the narrow strip of land stretching along the Nile up to the First Cataract, has always been characterized by two unique qualities. First, the fact that it was surrounded by large deserts, and afforded only a few, and easily defensible, approaches, assured it relative security against foreign invaders. Second, its dependence on the Nile's yearly flooding, rather than on rain, for agricultural production, assured it a greater degree of immunity to famine than most other countries in the ancient world. These two factors determined Egypt's major role in the regional politics of the Eastern Mediterranean basin and the Fertile Crescent. From a Jewish perspective, Egypt's unique position entailed both a fear of Egyptian power and the allure of emigrating there in times of economic or political hardship. Thus, one finds in the Hebrew scriptures several references to Egyptian campaigns in Palestine, and numerous references to its economic appeal for Palestine's inhabitants. By far the most enduring biblical image of Egypt, however, is that connected with the Jews' enslavement following the emigration there of Jacob's sons, and the subsequent Exodus, described and alluded to in innumerable biblical passages. Moreover, while some of the biblical references to Egypt evince little interest in the land or its people, other passages—such as the Joseph cycle of *Genesis*, or the prophets' railings against Egyptian idolatry—demonstrate an intimate familiarity on the part of many Jews with the geographical, social, and cultural *realia* of Egyptian life.

Egypt's importance in Jewish eyes is amply reflected in the literature of the Second Temple period as well. Numerous narratives recount and embellish the events connected with the Jews' exile in Egypt and the Exodus. Naturally, texts written by Egypt's Jews (e.g., *Joseph and Asenath*, Ezekiel's *Exagoge*, and the works of Artapanus and Aristobulus) display a greater familiarity with Egypt than those written in Palestine (e.g., *Jubilees*, Pseudo-Philo's *Biblical Antiquities*), but even the latter are not uninterested in the land of the Nile, its people, its gods, and its Jewish inhabitants. Other writings of Egypt's Jews—such as the *Letter of Aristeas*, the *Sibylline Oracles*, and *3 Maccabees*—focus not on Egypt's biblical past but on its Jews' more recent history and on their hopes for the future.

In comparison with the references to Egypt in the Hebrew scriptures and later Jewish literature, the references to that land in the scrolls—excluding the biblical manuscripts and those of the Apocrypha and pseudepigrapha (such as *Jubilees*)—are quite disappointing. As often is the case, many references to Egypt appear in fragments too small to allow any appraisal of their nature and meaning (e.g., 4QPesher Hosea[b] 17 1, 1; 4QPesher Isaiah[c] 28 1, 1; 3Q14 17 1, 2; 4Q225 1.5; 4Q226 1.3; 4Q391 1.2,

5.4, 48.2, 70.2). Moreover, many of the better-preserved passages that mention Egypt consist of common stock phrases such as "the Lord who brought you out of Egypt," or general allusions to the Exodus (e.g., 1QDM 1, 1; 4QOrdinances 2–4.i.3; 4Q379 12 1, 5; 11QTemple Scroll[a] liv.16, lxi.14). Other passages merely repeat, or allude to, biblical references to Egypt, such as the injunction upon the king not to make the people go back to Egypt (11QTemple Scroll[a] lvi.16; cf. *Dt.* 17.16), or the admonition in the sapiential work 4Q185 1–2.i.15 to remember the miracles that God had performed in Egypt.

In addition to such references, several Qumran texts display amplifications or modifications of biblical scenes connected with Egypt. In the Damascus Document iii.5, a reference to the Jews' sins in Egypt adds an element not found in the book of *Exodus*. In the Genesis Apocryphon, the biblical account of Abraham and Sarah's sojourn in Egypt and their brush with the Egyptian king is greatly expanded (cf. Genesis Apocryphon col. xixff. with *Gn.* 12.10–20). Numerous details are added to the biblical account—including such data as the name of one of Pharaoh's princes (*Ḥrqnvsh*)—but no attempt is made to add an authentic Egyptian coloring to the story. In both texts, Egypt itself did not attract the authors' attention.

Finally, a small number of texts refer to Egypt in ways that seem not to depend on existing biblical models. Unfortunately, here too the texts' poor preservation hinders our understanding of their context or significance. In one unidentified narrative (4Q462), a description of the Jews' plight in Egypt and their appeals for God's help—and, presumably, the Exodus itself—is followed by the statement that "they were delivered up to Egypt for a second time at the end of the kingdom . . . to the dwellers of Philistia and Egypt for despoliation and destruction, and they shall raise it . . . " Unfortunately, it is not clear from the text whether the reference to a second exile in Egypt relates to the events following Gedaliah's murder (cf. *Jer.* 42ff.), or to events of the Persian or Hellenistic periods. In the War Scroll, on the other hand, the context of the two references to Egypt is somewhat clearer: in the first (1QM i.4), the forces of the *Kittim* (i.e., Romans) in Egypt are mentioned in the scenario for the great eschatological war. In the second (1QM xiv.1), God's destruction of the Sons of Darkness is compared to his destruction of the idols of Egypt (cf. *Ex.* 12.12, *Is.* 19.1, etc.). Here, too, however, there is little evidence that the authors of the Dead Sea Scrolls had any specific interest in, or knowledge of, Egypt.

BIBLIOGRAPHY

Redford, D. B. *Egypt, Canaan, and Israel in Ancient Times*. Princeton, 1992.

Charlesworth, J. H. *Graphic Concordance to the Dead Sea Scrolls*. Tübingen, 1991.

GIDEON BOHAK

EGYPTIAN RELIGION. The most conspicuous aspects of the Egyptian religion in the Greco-Roman world were its specialized caste of priests, its numerous temples, its strong emphasis on the soul's life after death and, above all, its worship of animal deities. This zoolatrous tendency, and the abundance and polyform iconography of the Egyptian gods, constituted the greatest difference between that religion and anything known among Greco-Roman Jews. Beyond these major differences, however, there were many traits of Egyptian religion that find interesting parallels in the Jewish world, including that of Qumran.

Unlike the practice among Greeks and Romans, where priesthood commonly was taken up by nonspecialized men and women for set periods of time, in Egypt religious and cultic functions were the domain of a hereditary class of male priests who served in the temples for life. These priests were not only responsible for conducting the temple rituals, they also were in charge of all sacred knowledge, including writing, and were expected, and obliged, to adhere to purity laws and taboos far stricter than those of ordinary Egyptians. Moreover, the complexity of the Egyptian writing systems, and the lack of any one body of core religious texts, ensured that the process that took place among Greco-Roman Jews—the rise of nonpriestly groups of religious experts—was virtually impossible in Egypt prior to the rise of Christianity. As among the Jews, the Egyptian priests' high social status, and the economic benefits that accrued to them, facilitated rapid Hellenization among them. On the other hand, the available evidence for anti-Greek sentiments in Ptolemaic Egypt—and especially the so-called Potter's Oracle—also seems to stem from Egyptian priestly circles, and it is clear that the foreign presence in Egypt was interpreted by at least some priests in line with the myth of the struggle between the good god Horus and his wicked brother Seth, the god of all evil foreigners. But Egypt's great size and regional diversity, its numerous temples, and the Ptolemies' active support of these temples, all prevented the emergence of any major rift between different groups of priests on the question of Hellenization, similar to the one that emerged in Jerusalem around the time of the Maccabean Revolt.

As noted above, Egyptian priests observed an elaborate set of rules of ritual purity. These included not only circumcision and the avoidance of certain foods, but also the wearing of linen garments and the removal of all bodily hair, practices that made the priests visibly different from all other Egyptians. Ordinary Egyptians also observed certain taboos, especially in matters of diet, and these often differed from one region to the next, according to the different animals held most sacred by each region. Such divergence—the refusal of the residents of one region to eat certain fish, while those of another avoided harming dogs, and so forth—could also lead to violent local disputes, and, together with Egyptian zoolatry in general, was a cause of great amazement to Greek and Roman observers.

The Egyptian religious literature of the Greco-Roman period was abundant and multifarious, consisting both of older texts and of contemporary compositions, including works of Egyptian religiosity translated into Greek or composed in the Greek language itself. Hymns, prayers, lamentations, funerary texts, and mythological texts were all common, as were collections of spells and rituals for success in this life and the next, and treatises of an astrological or mystical nature. Religious speculation focused on the different gods and their manifestations, as well as the soul's travels and trials in the underworld. The strong belief in an afterlife was the motivating force behind the widespread Egyptian practice of mummification; it also entailed a strong exhortation to live a life of justice in this world, so as not to be punished in the next.

The Egyptian calendar was solar, comprising twelve months of thirty days each, to which five epagomenal ("additional") days were added at the end of the year. Several attempts to amend the calendar, and make it conform fully to the true solar year—about three hundred and sixty-five and a quarter days—did not prove successful, and the Egyptian year, with all its festivals, slowly moved backward with respect to the natural seasons. The worship of the Egyptian gods was not limited to the native Egyptians, but encompassed many of the foreigners who settled in Ptolemaic and Roman Egypt. The Egyptians themselves, in turn, were not averse to worshiping the newcomers' gods as well, and only rarely did the Egyptian gods, or their adherents, display clear signs of any religious exclusivity. Moreover, several Egyptian gods, and especially Isis and Sarapis, won great popularity outside Egypt as well. Both the Judeo-Greek literature and the Rabbinic writings display some familiarity with the Egyptian gods and their myths, and especially with Isis, Osiris, and Sarapis. But, as among the Greeks and Romans, it was especially the Egyptians' zoolatry that the Jews found so fascinating—and repulsive. From the *Letter of Aristeas* and the *Third Sibylline Oracle* in the second century BCE, to Philo's writings and the *Wisdom of Solomon* in the first century CE, Judeo-Greek writers railed against the worship of "dumb and senseless animals." Only rarely does one find a positive Jewish attitude toward the Egyptian gods, such as Artapanus' claim (second century BCE?) that it had been Moses himself who instituted Egyptian zoolatry. In the Qumran writings, on the other hand, there is little evidence of any interest, even polemical, in Egyptian religion. Of course, the members of the Qumran community were well aware of the biblical condemnations of Egypt, such as Ezekiel's mocking references to the divinization of the Pharaoh (*Ezekiel* 29). They may even have been aware of some of the Judeo-Greek references to Egyptian religion, as fragments of Judeo-Greek works were found among the fragments from Cave 7. And yet, the Hebrew and Aramaic texts from Qumran show little interest in this topic, even on such occasions when references to Egyptian religion might have been inserted (e.g., in the Genesis Apocryphon's description of Abraham in Egypt, or in the apocryphal Jeremiah materials).

In noting the Qumranians' disinterest in Egyptian religion, some signs of possible connections between the Qumran community and the Jews of Egypt should also be noted. Several Judeo-Greek texts may display Essene influences (e.g., the *Testament of Job*), and the Jewish community of the Therapeutai, known to us solely through one Philonic treatise, seems to have shared certain practices with the Essenes. Moreover, the flight to Egypt of Onias IV and his followers and the establishment there of a second Jewish temple raise the possibility of some connection between these Jewish priests and the other priestly groups who challenged the authority of the Hasmonean high priests. The Dead Sea Scrolls, however, provide no firm evidence to support such links, nor are such links clearly attested in any other source.

BIBLIOGRAPHY

Bagnall, R. S. *Egypt in Late Antiquity*. Princeton, 1993.

Bowman, A. K. *Egypt after the Pharaohs: 332 BC–AD 642*. Berkeley, 1986.

Griffiths, J. G. *The Divine Verdict: A Study of Divine Judgment in the Ancient Religions*. Leiden, 1991.

Hornung, E. *Conceptions of God in Ancient Egypt: The One and the Many*, trans. John Baines. Ithaca, 1982.

Pinch, G. *Magic in Ancient Egypt*. Austin, 1994.

Quirke, S. *Ancient Egyptian Religion*. London, 1992.

Smelik, K. A. D., and E. A. Hemelrijk. "Who Knows Not What Monsters Demented Egypt Worships?: Opinions on Egyptian Animal Worship in Antiquity as Part of the Ancient Conception of Egypt." *Aufstieg und Niedergang der Römischen Welt* 2.17.4 (1984), 1852–2000.

GIDEON BOHAK

'EIN-EL-GHWEIR. *See* Ghweir, Wadi.

'EIN-EL-TURABEH. Along the shore of the Dead Sea, south of 'Ein-el-Ghweir, near the springs that in Arabic are called *Al el-Turbeh* lies 'Ein-el-Turabeh (Ar., *Katser el-Tarbi*). It appears that this site should be identified with the Nibshan mentioned in *Joshua* 15.62. Explored and excavated by Ian Blake in 1966, the site is divided into two parts: a nearly square structure, 15 by 13 meters (49 by 42 feet), and a courtyard, 19 by 20 meters (62 by 66 feet), which adjoins the structure's northern side. The entrance to the courtyard was also on the northern side, and guard rooms were erected adjacent to the courtyard gate. On the northern side of the courtyard and on the southern side, rows of pillar foundations that parallel the walls of the courtyard were discovered. The pillars were made of wood and are well preserved.

The entrance to the square structure was from within the courtyard. A ramp through which one entered the square structure was built parallel to the southern wall of the courtyard. The ramp led from the square structure to another room (6 meters by 3.2 meters [20 feet by 10.5 feet]) surrounded by seven smaller rooms. Outside of the square structure's western and southern sides is an inclined wall: its thickness is approximately 2 meters (6.6 feet), while the southern wall is approximately 2.5 meters (8.2 feet) thick. Blake reported that much brick material was found around the walls. The structure had a stone foundation while the building above it was made of brick.

The pottery at the site is primarily from the eighth and seventh centuries BCE. It appears that the structure was already abandoned during the course of the First Temple period. A small amount of pottery from the Hellenistic and Roman periods was also discovered in the structure. Hence one can assume that the structure was used again in the latter days of the Second Temple period. From this period an assemblage of three cooking pots and three pitchers was discovered. A similarity does indeed exist between the inclined wall discovered at ʿEin-el-Turabeh and the inclined wall adjacent to the tower in the ruins of Qumran; but the square structure at ʿEin-el-Turabeh is from the Iron Age while the tower at Qumran is from the Hellenistic period. [*See* Qumran, *article on* Archaeology.]

[*See also* Archaeology.]

BIBLIOGRAPHY

Bar-Adon, Pessah. *Excavations in the Judean Desert*. ʿAtiqot, Hebrew Series, 9. Jerusalem, 1989. See pages 41–49.

Blake, Ian. "Dead Sea Sites of the 'Utter Wilderness.'" *Illustrated London News* (4 March 1967). See pages 27–29.

Eshel, Hanan. "A note on Joshua 15: 61–62 and the Identification of the City of Salt." *Israel Exploration Journal* 45 (1995), 37–40.

HANAN ESHEL

Translated from Hebrew by Daphna Krupp

ʿEIN-FARA, located approximately 8 kilometers northeast of Jerusalem, is the westernmost of the three perennial springs of Wadi Qilt and the most abundant one. In this area the wadi has cut a deep canyon, approximately 1.5 kilometers long, and many caves are located in the steep cliffs. This section of the wadi is identified with "the valley known as Pheretae," the location of the cave encampment of Simeon son of Gioras mentioned by Josephus Flavius (*The Jewish War* 6.511–513) in his account of the civil war in Judea in 68–69 CE, when the pressure of the Roman army on the rebels was temporarily lifted. This may also be the ravine of Beth Tamar mentioned in the Copper Scroll (3Q15 xi.14–15, ed. Milik), unless the reference is to the cliff of Wadi Suweinit. [*See* Naḥal Michmash.] At the beginning of the fourth century CE, the monk Chariton, the founder of monasticism in the Judean Desert, established near the spring the first laura in the Judean Desert, which was called Pharan. [*See* Monasteries.] The church of the laura was consecrated in a cave where Chariton had been kept captive by bandits, from whom he was saved by a miracle. This large artificial cave (no. 7), consisting of a spacious rectangular hall (8.3 by 6.3 meters), with three rooms annexed to its eastern end, was presumably first cut into the rock by the men of Simeon son of Gioras, and served as his headquarters.

Nineteen rock-cut caves were discovered and explored in 1983–1984, during the Archaeological Survey of the Judean Desert Caves carried out on behalf of the Institute of Archaeology at the Hebrew University of Jerusalem and directed by J. Patrich. Most caves were located high in the southern cliff. Their locations and configurations indicate that they were originally cut to serve as hideouts. The natural crevice-like appearance of their mouths was not touched, thus concealing the existence of a large chamber hollowed out of the rock beyond. On the basis of size and shape the caves were classified into several types: small cells (6–10 square meters in area) cut in the perpendicular bank or high in the inner wall of a large, natural cave; cells in several levels along a narrow natural crevice; and caves with a large inner chamber. Storage cells were cut in the walls of some caves, and some caves had built-in cisterns.

A peculiar feature, common to some types of caves (no. 2 and no. 7), is a vertical rock-cut entrance shaft, cut in the floor of the cave; the cross section of the shaft is generally 1 meter square, and its depth is generally 2 to 5 meters. Projections and depressions in the shaft's vertical walls facilitate climbing, and in the bottom there is a well-cut entrance. Such entrance shafts were also common in the contemporary hideouts at Naḥal Michmash, a northern tributary of Wadi Qilt. [*See* Michmash, Naḥal.] A stable (no. 18), consisting of a series of eight niches cut side by side in the wall with holes in their floors to tether animals, is located at the western end of the site.

Shards and stone vessels dating to the end of the first and the beginning of the second centuries were found on the surface of many of the caves, indicating that they were cut in the Second Temple period and then reused as hideouts during the Bar Kokhba Revolt. Some caves also contained pottery from the Byzantine period, when they were used by monks. Cave 13 contained a heap of ropes made of palm fibers, as well as a braid of human hair. There were no inscribed finds. Some natural caves in the canyon, which are lower and more readily accessible, contained quantities of shards from the Early Bronze Age and human bones.

Hermitages of the Byzantine laura extend along an approximately 3-kilometer section of its course. Some were reusing the earlier hideouts, and others were built of masonry. The laura core, including two chapels, one in the cave and another built of masonry, was adjacent to the spring. A secondary center to the east, which seems to be associated with the laura, is comprised of four ruined buildings, including a chapel with a colorful mosaic floor, cisterns, pools, and many tombs. It is located at Jurat Musa, approximately 1 kilometer to the east of the spring, near the confluence of Wadi en-Nimr to Wadi Fara. It got its water from the spring by means of two aqueducts.

BIBLIOGRAPHY

Dinur, U., and N. Feig. "Qal'at Musa." *Excavations and Surveys in Israel* 5 (1986), 86–88.

Finkelstein, I., ed. *Archaeological Survey of the Hill Country of Benjamin* (sites no. 511, 527, 539). Jerusalem, 1993.

Hirschfeld, Y. "List of Byzantine Monasteries in the Judean Desert." In *Christian Archaeology in the Holy Land: New Discoveries* [*Archaeological Essays in Honour of Virgilio C. Corbo ofm*], edited by G. C. Bottini, L. DiSegni, and E. Alliata, pp. 6–7. Jerusalem, 1990.

Patrich, J. "Dissidents in the Desert: The Cave Encampment of Simeon Son of Gioras." *Eretz Magazine* (Autumn 1985), pp. 50–61.

Patrich, J. "The Caves Encampment of Simon Son of Gioras in the Ravine Called 'Pheretae'" (in Hebrew). In *Ninth World Congress of Jewish Studies*, B.1, pp. 21–26. Jerusalem, 1986.

Patrich, J. "Hideouts in the Judean Wilderness." *Biblical Archaeology Review* 15.5 (1989), 32–42.

JOSEPH PATRICH

ʿEIN-FESHKHA. Located by brackish springs on the northwest shore of the Dead Sea, ʿEin-Feshkha lies 3 kilometers (2 miles) south of Khirbet Qumran. The site was excavated in 1958 by Roland de Vaux of the École Biblique et Archéologique Française in Jerusalem. De Vaux uncovered the remains of a building complex contemporary with the settlement at Qumran, which he believed was inhabited by the same community.

Main Building. The complex at ʿEin-Feshkha consists of a main building with an industrial area to the north and an enclosure with a porch or shed to the southwest. The main building is a large rectangle measuring 24 by 18 meters (76.8 by 57.6 feet): it had an open courtyard in the center surrounded by rooms on four sides. Two side-by-side doorways on the eastern facade provided access into the building. De Vaux suggested that the northern passage (L9; L = locus [findspot]) provided access to the northern suite of rooms (L21–22), while the southern passage (L11A) led into the central courtyard.

The rooms along the northern side of the courtyard (L21, L22, and L22bis) were entered through a single doorway and were separated from each other by low, narrow walls. De Vaux suggested that these rooms and those on the southern side of the courtyard (L7, L10) were storerooms; the last two were separated by a poorly constructed wall and were paved with small stones. Thirty-two coins were found in a room in the southeast corner of the building (L11B) that had a drain running diagonally through it to carry water away from the courtyard. Perhaps it and rooms on the western side of the building (L3 and L5) served as residential quarters or offices. One of the western rooms (L3) was paved with small stones, while the other (L5) had a semicircular paved area against the east wall. A cut column drum was found in the debris in this room. A staircase on the southeastern side of the building led up to a roof terrace above the rooms on the northern and southern sides of the courtyard and to a second story of rooms on the western side (above L3 and L5). A square pier in front of the rooms on the western side of the courtyard (L3 and L5) originally supported a balcony in front of the rooms above.

Industrial Area. Excavations in the eastern half of the enclosed area to the north of the main building revealed a system of basins and water channels. Water flowed through a sluice in the northern enclosure wall (L29) to a small rectangular tank (L23). One channel running south from the rectangular tank fed a large, square, plastered basin (L24), the bottom of which was covered with a whitish deposit. An opening at the base of the southeast wall of this basin led to a trough and a plastered pit on the other (south) side (L25). Another branch of the channel that fed the plastered basin encircled it on the west and terminated at a second plastered basin (L27). A second channel ran southeast from the rectangular tank, leading to a rectangular basin (L26). The area between the plastered basins (L24 and L27), the plastered pit (L25), and the channel that fed the rectangular basin (L26) was paved with large stone slabs. An intact jar and two large oblong stones were found lying in this area; a third stone lay at the bottom of the large, square, plastered basin (L24). De Vaux pointed out that the shallowness of these basins indicates that they were not cisterns, while the absence of steps rules out their use as baths. This must have been an industrial installation in which water played a major role. However, the nature of the industry is unknown. De Vaux suggested that it was a tannery. He believed that the absence of tannin in the deposits could be explained if production of parchment instead of leather had occurred here. In this case, some of the parchment used for the Dead Sea Scrolls might have originated in the workshop at ʿEin-Feshkha. Frederick Eberhard Zeuner, noting the absence of animal hairs in the deposits, suggested instead that fish were raised in the basins. De Vaux objected to this because of the small size of the basins and the presence of plaster on the basin walls.

Enclosure. To the southwest of the main building lay an enclosed area measuring over 40 meters on each side. The only structure found within it was a row of square piers running parallel to the northern wall of the enclosure, which created a porch or shed that was open to the south. A pavement of small stones covered much of the floor of the porch, ending neatly to the south of the row of piers, at the point where the roof would have terminated. Rooms or enclosed areas at either end of the porch (L20 and L19) could have been used as living quarters. The rest might have provided temporary shelter for people or animals, or, as de Vaux suggested, might have been used as a drying shed for dates (which may have been cultivated in the brackish water of the springs).

Chronology of ʿEin-Feshkha. The main phase of occupation distinguished by de Vaux at ʿEin-Feshkha is contemporary with Period II at Qumran (c.4/1 BCE–68 CE). Most of the pottery recovered in the excavations belongs to this phase, and the dating is supported by the numismatic evidence. As at Qumran, Period II at ʿEin-Feshkha ended with destruction by fire. De Vaux also found traces of an earlier phase of occupation, Period I. The architectural evidence for this phase is scanty, consisting mostly of an earlier level in a small room in the northwestern corner of the courtyard in the main building (L6) and in the rooms along the northern side of the courtyard (L21 and 22). Most of the pottery associated with Period I is fragmentary, and much of it comes from piles of rubbish that were cleared out of the main building and discarded outside its northern wall when the site was reoccupied at the beginning of Period II. Neat piles of square white limestone tiles found outside the northern wall of the main building (L28) and white limestone and dark bituminous square and triangular tiles (recovered in the fill of L11A-B) may have belonged to *opus sectile* ("tile") floors of Period I. Though he equated it with Period Ib at Qumran (c.100–31 BCE), de Vaux noted that there is no evidence that Period I at ʿEin-Feshkha ended with violent destruction, either an earthquake or fire. However, the fact that the building was cleared out suggests that it was abandoned for some time.

The pottery and coins published from Period I contexts at ʿEin-Feshkha point to a date no earlier than the reign of Herod the Great for this phase. De Vaux was, however, puzzled by the fact that there was no evidence for the earthquake of 31 BCE at ʿEin-Feshkha, which is just 3 kilometers (2 miles) from Qumran. In view of this, a post–31 BCE date for the initial phase of occupation at ʿEin-Feshkha would account for the absence of earthquake destruction at the site. Because of the limited nature of the published ceramic material, it is difficult to determine whether the end of Period I at ʿEin-Feshkha is contemporary with the end of Herodian Period Ib at Qumran, that is c.9/8 BCE or some time thereafter. At any rate, the ceramic evidence does not contradict the possibility that ʿEin-Feshkha was abandoned (but not destroyed) at the same time as Qumran.

De Vaux also distinguished a third phase of occupation (Period III), which was attested only in the rooms along the northern side of the main building (L21 and L22). On the basis of the ceramic and numismatic evidence, he attributed this phase to a small unknown group in the late first century CE or to Jewish rebels at the time of the Bar Kokhba Revolt (c.132–135). Finally, de Vaux dated the rebuilding of the room at the eastern end of the porch or shed (L20) to the Byzantine era, when he suggested that a garden was cultivated by monks from nearby Khirbet Mird.

The settlement at ʿEin-Feshkha was apparently established after 31 BCE. The main phase of occupation lasted until 68 CE, when it suffered a violent destruction. Despite its physical proximity and contemporaneity, the absence of scrolls and scroll jars from ʿEin-Feshkha leaves open the question of whether it was occupied by the same community as at Qumran.

[*See also* Mird, Khirbet; Qumran, *article on* Archaeology.]

BIBLIOGRAPHY

de Vaux, Roland. "Fouilles de Feshka, Rapport preliminaire." *Revue biblique* 66 (1959), 225–255. De Vaux's preliminary report on his excavations at ʿEin-Feshkha.

de Vaux, Roland. *Archaeology and the Dead Sea Scrolls*. London, 1973. The best English-language summary of de Vaux's excavations at Qumran and ʿEin-Feshkha.

Humbert, Jean-Baptiste, and Alain Chambon. *Fouilles de Khirbet Qumran et de Ain Feshka I*. Göttingen, 1994. The first volume of the final report on de Vaux's excavations.

Magness, Jodi. "The Chronology of the Settlement at Qumran in the Herodian Period." *Dead Sea Discoveries* 2 (1995), 58–65. A reevaluation of de Vaux's chronology, suggesting that there was no gap in occupation at Qumran after 31 BCE.

JODI MAGNESS

ʿEIN-GEDI. The largest oasis on the western shore of the Dead Sea, ʿEin-Gedi lies 38 kilometers (24 miles) southeast of Jerusalem, and comprises an area of about 1.4 square kilometers (0.5 square miles). ʿEin-Gedi, which means "spring of the young goat," is the Hebrew name of a perennial spring flowing from the rocks about 200 meters (656 feet) above the Dead Sea, in the northwest section of the oasis. In Greek and Latin sources, it is referred to as *Engadi, Engade, Engedene, Engedon*, and *Engadenos* and similar versions. Its Arabic name—*ʿEin Jidi*—led to its identification with the ancient ʿEin-Gedi by Edward Robinson in 1841.

The "wilderness of 'Ein-Gedi" and the "strongholds of 'Ein-Gedi" appear in the stories of David's flight from Saul (*1 Sm.* 23.29, 24.1). 'Ein-Gedi is mentioned in the list of the cities of Judah among those in the wilderness (*Jos.* 15.62) and is identified, rather arbitrarily, with Hazazon-Tamar in a record of an Ammonite-Moabite invasion of Judah during the reign of Jehoshaphat (*2 Chr.* 20.2). It is also mentioned in a prophecy of Ezekiel (*Ezek.* 47.10), and its vineyards are mentioned in the *Song of Solomon* (1.14).

Historical References. The first permanent settlement was founded at Tell Goren, in the southwest of the oasis, toward the end of Iron Age II period in the seventh century BCE (or perhaps slightly earlier?), probably in connection with the cultivation of balsam (G., *opobalsamon*), apparently under royal auspices. The settlement was destroyed early in the sixth century BCE, perhaps by the Edomites in 582/81 BCE. Its importance as a center for growing and producing balsam remained its economic mainstay until the sixth century CE, however. It was thus rebuilt in the postexilic period (fifth century BCE) and may have been destroyed during the Tennes rebellion (c.345 BCE). It was settled during the Hellenistic period and came under Hasmonean control during the reign of John Hyrcanus (c.112/111 BCE). It is not known whether the oasis was entirely or partly abandoned between the late first century BCE and the early first century CE owing to a change in the level of the Dead Sea. Josephus mentions it as one of the eleven districts (toparchies) of Judea before the First Jewish Revolt (*The Jewish War* 3.55). The Sicarii of Masada raided it during Passover in 68 CE, killing more than seven hundred women and children and rifling the provisions (*The Jewish War* 4.402–404). In the period between the First Jewish Revolt and the Bar Kokhba Revolt (70–132) it was garrisoned by a Roman auxiliary force. In a legal document from the Cave of the Letters, it is referred to as "'Ein-Gedi village of lord Caesar." It seems likely that 'Ein-Gedi was crown property from its earliest days to its end during the Byzantine period.

During the Bar Kokhba Revolt (c.132–135) 'Ein-Gedi was of special importance for the insurgents, its port serving to receive badly needed supplies. [*See* Bar Kokhba Revolt.] From the third century to the sixth century CE, 'Ein-Gedi flourished and is described in the *Onomasticon* by Eusebius (early fourth century CE) as "a very large Jewish village" (Klostermann, ed., p. 86, 1.18). Besides balsam, 'Ein-Gedi was famous for its date groves, sacramental wine, and baskets and mats plaited from date branches. Jewish 'Ein-Gedi was destroyed early in the reign of Justinian I (c.531 CE). It was settled sporadically during medieval times as a place where its inhabitants were safe from nomadic raids.

Archaeology. The first archaeological survey of 'Ein-Gedi was carried out by Avraham Reifenburg and Benjamin Mazar in 1949 for the Hebrew University of Jerusalem; surveys of the oasis and its agricultural terraces and irrigation installations have been undertaken since 1956. Extensive excavations followed in 1961–1962 and 1964–1965 at numerous sites in the oasis conducted by Mazar, Immanuel Dunayevsky, and Trude Dothan. The synagogue, which dates from the third through the sixth century CE, was excavated in 1970–1972 by Dan Barag and Yosef Porath. Work was resumed near the site of the synagogue by Gideon Hadas in 1995 and Y. Hirschfeld in 1996. A cemetery from the Hasmonean period was excavated by Nahman Avigad in the Naḥal David wadi, on the northern borders of the oasis, and nine similar tombs were cleared by Hadas in the oasis between 1984 and 1989. [*See* Cemeteries.]

On the cliffs 150 meters (492 feet) above the 'Ein-Gedi spring are the remains of a temple enclosure from the Chalcolithic-Ghassulian culture, dating from the fourth millennium BCE, which were excavated in 1962 and 1964. The temple probably served as a cult center and was abandoned after a relatively short period. It stands to reason that the spectacular treasure of 416 ritual copper objects, such as mace heads (and a small group of objects made of ivory and hematite), discovered by Pessah Bar-Adon in the Cave of the Treasure in Naḥal Mishmar in 1961, was among the temple furniture of this important sanctuary. [*See* Mishmar, Naḥal.]

The remains of the ancient site of 'Ein-Gedi were discovered on the narrow and steep hillock of Tell Goren and excavated in 1961–1962 and 1964–1965. In Stratum V (late eighth–early sixth century BCE) traces of numerous houses on the slopes of the hill were discovered. Ovens and vats, apparently belonging to industrial installations connected with the production of perfumes from the balsam plants, were uncovered along a street. Finds include two Hebrew stone seals, one of Uriyahu [son of] 'Azaryahu and another of Tobshalem, as well as a hoard of silver ingots probably used as currency. Most of the many pottery vessels date from c.630–582/81 BCE, except for a handle stamped with the royal four-winged Judean seal of the city of Ziph and an unusual royal two-winged seal impression.

The Persian period settlement of Stratum IV (fifth–mid-fourth century BCE) extended over a larger area than that of Stratum V. On the northern slope a stone building of twenty-three rooms was cleared along with the remains of other houses in its vicinity. Among the finds are stamped pottery handles bearing the seals of the Persian province of Yehud (Judah) and potsherds of imported Attic vessels. This settlement was destroyed c.400 BCE and again in the mid-fourth century BCE. A citadel occupied the summit of the site during Stratum III, dating from the Hellenistic period, and served garrisons of Ptolemies and Seleucids (third century–second century BCE) and Hasmoneans (c.112/111–37 BCE). Wooden coffins, wooden vessels, pottery, mats, shoes, and bronze wine ladles with duck-head handles were discovered in the multiple burial caves of the first century BCE at Naḥal David and other locations in the oasis. [*See* Sdeir, Wadi.] The finds differ from regular Jewish tombs of that period and may belong to Idumeans converted to Judaism by John Hyrcanus. To Stratum II (first century CE) belongs a tower added to the citadel and a house on the northern slopes that yielded a hoard of 139 bronze coins dating from 42/43 to 67 CE. It was destroyed in 68 CE. During the Roman and Byzantine periods Tell Goren became an area of cultivated terraces.

The built-up area of that period was northeast of Tell Goren; a bathhouse from the period 70–132 CE was excavated there. It included the typical elements of a Roman bath set in a row: a frigidarium (cold room), a tepidarium (warm room), a caldarium (hot room), and a furnace, as well as numerous pools. A synagogue was excavated some 300 meters (984 feet) northeast of Tell Goren. [*See* Synagogues.] In Stratum III B (third century CE) it was a simple prayer hall with two entrances in the northern wall oriented toward Jerusalem. Its black and white mosaic pavement included a panel with a swastika. In Stratum III A (fourth century CE) the central northern entrance was blocked and turned into a niche for a Torah ark; a "seat of Moses" was constructed on its eastern side. The building was divided into a nave and eastern and southern aisles. Three entrances were constructed on its western side, and a porch with three columns was added. In Stratum II (mid-fifth century–c.531 CE) a large Torah ark with an apse and a small rectangular area enclosed by a chancel-screen (*bimah*) in front replaced the earlier niche and ark; a new mosaic pavement with birds and three seven-branched menorahs was also added. A narthex was built on the western side of the building.

In the new western aisle (the former porch) there are five mosaic inscriptions in Hebrew and Aramaic. The first quotes *1 Chronicles* 1.1–4. The second lists the names of the twelve signs of the zodiac, the twelve months of the year, the three patriarchs, and the three companions of Daniel. The third inscription, in Aramaic, blesses three donors and warns against those who cause dissension in the community, pass malicious information to the gentiles, or reveal the secrets of the town. (The latter may be secrets connected with the cultivation of the balsam.) The fourth inscription, in Aramaic, refers to two of the three donors of the third inscription, and the fifth inscription, in Aramaic, blesses all the people of the town who renovated the synagogue. The synagogue was destroyed by fire c.531 CE. A short-lived attempt to reconstruct it may have been made in the early seventh century during the Sassanian occupation (611–629 CE). A very remarkable find from Stratum II is a cast bronze menorah about 22 centimeters (9 inches) wide that served as a decoration.

Relation to the Dead Sea Scrolls. Property in ʿEin-Gedi belonging to Babatha, daughter of Simon, is mentioned in ten of the thirty-seven legal documents that date from 93/94–132 CE, and that were discovered by Y. Yadin in the Cave of the Letters. [*See* Babatha; Ḥever, Naḥal.] The marketplace and a synagogue at ʿEin-Gedi (both unidentified) are also mentioned. Yadin's explorations in the Cave of the Letters yielded twenty-one documents in Aramaic, Hebrew, and Greek from the time of the Bar Kokhba Revolt (c.132–135 CE). Six documents belong to Bar Kokhba's administration at ʿEin-Gedi, concerning, for example, the leasing of state-owned land. A group of fifteen letters includes thirteen written in the name of Bar Kokhba to his two officers at ʿEin-Gedi. These documents furnish very important information about Bar Kokhba's administration, legal and economic matters, and topographical issues and are reminiscent of the Bar Kokhba documents from Wadi Murabbaʿat. [*See* Murabbaʿat, Wadi, *article on* Written Material.]

[*See also* Qumran, *article on* Archaeology.]

BIBLIOGRAPHY

Avigad, Nahman. "The Nahal David Caves," in *The New Encyclopedia of Archaeological Excavations in the Holy Land*, edited by Ephraim Stern, pp. 832–833. Jerusalem, 1993.

Hadas, Gideon. "Nine Tombs of the Second Temple Period at ʿEn Gedi." *ʿAtiqot* 24 (1994).

Lewis, Naphtali. *The Documents from the Bar Kokhba Period in the Cave of Letters.* Jerusalem, 1989.

Mazar, Benjamin, Trude Dothan, and Immanuel Dunayevsky. "En Gedi, The First and Second Seasons of Excavations, 1961–1962." *ʿAtiqot, English Series* 5 (1966).

Mazar, Benjamin, and Dan Barag. "ʿEn Gedi." In *The New Encyclopedia of Archaeological Excavations in the Holy Land*, edited by Ephraim Stern, pp. 399–409. Jerusalem, 1993.

Ussishkin, David Yigael. "The Ghassulian Shrine at ʿEn Gedi." *Tel Aviv* 7 (1980), 1–44.

Yadin, Yigael. "Cave of Letters." In *The New Encyclopedia of Archaeological Excavations in the Holy Land*, edited by Ephraim Stern, pp. 826–832.

DAN BARAG

ELECT OF GOD. Some fragments of a somewhat poorly preserved Aramaic manuscript (Elect of God [4Q534]), the copy of which is dated from the early Herodian period (second half of the first century BCE), were at first understood in a messianic sense. In a preliminary edition, Jean Starcky proposed attributing to a unique and very characteristic expression in this manuscript, *beḥir ʾelahaʾ* ("Elect of God"), the full-blown meaning it is given in the "Book of Parables" in *1 Enoch* and the New

Testament reference to a messianic figure (*Jn.* 1.34). However, in the few fairly well preserved lines of the text, nothing warrants such a clear-cut conclusion:

> [And] he shall know the mysteries of mankind and his wisdom shall go to all the peoples and he shall know the mysteries of all the living. [And] all their calculations according to him shall be fulfilled and the number / the opposition of all the living shall be great [. . . according to] to his calculations because he is the Elect of God. His progeny and the spirit of his vital breath [. . . , therefore] his calculations shall be for eternity.

The presentation of this personage in this manuscript emphasizes his conception and his life as being in accordance with the tripartite divisions of zodiac signs and with certain features of his body, the significance of which is described in physiognomic texts (see fragment 1.i.1–3, 9–10; compare a Qumran Cave 4 horoscope work, 4Q186). From a very young age, this individual is to acquire the knowledge of the three books in order then to gain "prudence and knowledge [. . . and the language (?)] of visions in order to depart above the higher (sphere) and with his father and his ancestors [. . . life] and old age, with him shall be counsel and prudence" (frg. 1.i.1–7). Such a description better fits the mystic initiation of Noah, which takes up again the dream experiences of Enoch, than it does the Messiah, Elect of God—and even more so since it does not involve kingship or priesthood. [*See* Messiahs.] It is significant that one medieval Samaritan tradition recounts: "At the age of seven (Noah) learned the three books of creation: the Book of Signs, the Book of the Stars and the Book of Wars, that is to say, the Book of the Generations of Adam" (see Milik, "Écrits esséniens de Qumrân: d'Hénoch à Amram," in *Qumrân. Sa piété, sa théologie, et son milieu*, by M. Delcor, Paris, 1978, p. 94).

This identification, proposed by Joseph A. Fitzmyer (1965) and Pierre Grelot (1975) based on other factors, was accepted by Starcky (*Le Monde de la Bible* 4 [1978], 56) and was defended at length by F. García Martínez (1992), and even more since the mention of the "waters" in fragment 2.14 seems to lend weight to this solution. Others proposed identifying this individual with other figures: "Melchizedek" (J. C. Greenfield) or the "Elect" of the "Book of Parables," "Enoch *redivivus* (who has come back to life)" (A. Dupont-Sommer and A. Caquot, in Caquot 1991, p. 155). But since Enoch was the first one who wrote books (see *Jub.* 4.17–22), it would therefore seem impossible for him to learn from the "three books"; furthermore, these books were passed down by inheritance (*1 En.* 82.1, etc.). Noah, the only one who survived the Flood, was then able to hand down his wisdom to all the peoples (see *Wis.* 10.4).

The main fragment is placed after the birth of the hero, describing the physical marks of divine election that destine him for the particular role he is to play after his training in the ancestral books of wisdom and his learning the knowledge of the mysteries of mankind.

BIBLIOGRAPHY

Caquot, André. "4QMess Ar 1 i 8–11" in *Mémorial Jean Starcky, Textes et études qumraniens -I*, under the direction of émile Puech and F. García Martínez, *Revue de Qumrân* 15 (1991), 145–155.

Fitzmyer, Joseph A. "The Aramaic Elect of God Text from Qumran Cave 4." *Catholic Biblical Quarterly* 27 (1965), 349–372.

García Martínez, Florentino. "4QMess Ar and the Book of Noah." In F. García Martínez, *Qumran and Apocalyptic, Studies on the Aramaic Texts from Qumran*, pp. 1–44. Leiden and New York, 1992.

Grelot, Pierre. "Hénoch et ses écritures." *Revue biblique* 82 (1975), 481–500.

Starcky, Jean. "Un texte messianique araméen de la grotte 4 de Qumrân." In *Mémorial du Cinquantenaire de l'École de Langues Orientales Anciennes de l'Institut Catholique de Paris*, pp. 51–66. Paris, 1964.

ÉMILE PUECH

Translated from French by Robert E. Shillenn

ELEPHANTINE TEXTS. Aramaic papyri from Elephantine Island were acquired on the antiquities market by Charles Edwin Wilbour in Aswan in 1893 and are now housed in Brooklyn. Ostraca and papyri excavated on Elephantine Island between 1906 and 1909 by Otto Rubensohn and Friedrich Zucker of Germany are now located in Berlin and Cairo, and Charles Clermont-Ganneau, Jean Clédat, and Joseph-Étienne Gautier of France brought papyri to Paris. Individual ostraca were acquired as early as the 1870s and excavated as recently at 1988 and are scattered in ten museums and libraries (Oxford, Cambridge, London, Munich, Berlin, Vienna, Moscow, Cairo, Elephantine, Jerusalem). For a long time Arthur E. Cowley was synonymous with Aramaic papyri. His work later was supplemented by the publications of Emil G. Kraeling (1953), Edda Bresciani, and Murad Kamil (1960, 1966). A multivolume collation of all Egyptian Aramaic texts has been published by Bezalel Porten and Ada Yardeni (*Textbook of Aramaic Documents from Ancient Egypt* [*TAD* A-D]). Fifty-two of these texts have been supplied with updated commentary in *The Elephantine Papyri in English* by Porten (1996 [*EPE* B1–52]). Documentary papyri in Hebrew, Aramaic, Nabatean, and Greek were uncovered by bedouin and in the Judean Desert in excavations at Wadi Murabba'at and apparently at Naḥal Ḥever (including those excavated by Yigael Yadin). The Murabba'at texts were published by J. T. Milik (1961) and the Naḥal Ḥever texts by Naphtali Lewis (1989), Ada Yardeni (1995), and Hannah Cotton and Yardeni (1997). The remaining Aramaic and Nabatean texts will be published by Ada Yardeni and Baruch Levine. Their external features are discussed here for purposes of comparison.

Letters. The Aramaic letters on papyri number thirty-six. Not all are fully intact, and many are fragmentary. Twenty-eight belong to Elephantine (*TAD* A3.1–10, 4.1–10, 5.2, 5.5, 6.1–2) or Syene (*TAD* A2.1–4), written in the fifth century BCE. Unlike contracts, letters were usually written on both sides of the papyrus (except *TAD* A3.4, 3.9, 4.4, 5.2), beginning on the side perpendicular to the fibers. The bottoms were then turned up and the letters were concluded on the side parallel to the fibers. Occasionally, the piece was turned sideways (*TAD* A3.9). There were two standard sheet widths: scroll height approximately 32 centimeters (*TAD* A3.4–10, 4.2–4, 4.7–8, 5.2, 6.1–2) and 27–28 centimeters (*TAD* A2.1–7, 3.11, 4.1). Unlike contracts, which were rolled up and folded in thirds, letters were rolled up and folded in half, addressed on one of the exposed bands with the name of the sender and the recipient (and sometimes the destination [*TAD* A2.1–7]), and then tied and sealed just like the contracts. Two official letters have a second entry on the other exposed band recording scribe and date (*TAD* A6.1–2). Contracts were meant to be stored for extended periods of time, so top sheets were left blank as insurance against external damage obliterating any part of the opening lines. Since letters were meant to be opened and read immediately, there was no need for a top blank sheet. Letters were shorter than contracts, usually running between five (*TAD* A2.7, 3.11) and fifteen lines (*TAD* A2.1–4, 3.2, 3.3, 3.8, 4.2), with the average length being ten lines (*TAD* A2.5, 2.6, 3.5, 3.9, 3.10, 4.1, 4.3, 4.4). Official letters dealing with matters of great importance (*TAD* A4.7–8) or requiring detailed enumeration (*TAD* A6.2) run as much as twenty-three or twenty-nine and thirty lines.

Letters may be classified according to four categories—private, communal, official, satrapal. At least eighteen letters may be assigned to the first category (*TAD* A2.1–7, 3.1–11). They were dispatched by peripatetic correspondents, Aramaean and Jewish soldiers in government employ (*peras* ["salary"; *TAD* A2.3:8, 3.3:3; B4.2:6]) traveling between Migdol and Syene (*TAD* A2.5–7, 3.3; cf. *Ezek.* 29.10, 30.6). One parcel of six Aramaean family letters (*TAD* A2.1–6) was written for the stepbrothers Nabushezib and Makkibanit by the same scribe, probably one after the other on the same papyrus roll, sealed with the same Egyptian seal, and addressed to different women all designated as "sister" and to Psami, designated by Makkibanit alternately as "my lord" and "my father" (*TAD* A2.3, 2.4). The letters communicate matters of concern and issue instructions about the management of affairs: they request the dispatch of certain items (e.g. castor oil, containers, and garments), and report on the purchase of other items (oil and cloth), awaiting a reliable traveler for dispatch. The letters are particularly fulsome in sending greetings and expressing interest in the personal welfare of others. Economic activity is featured in a letter from the Jew Hosea, who instructs Ḥaggus to raise money either by taking an interest-bearing loan or selling real estate (*TAD* A3.8). Persians and Egyptians also wrote to each other in Aramaic (*TAD* A3.10).

The ten papyri in the communal archive of leader and perhaps high priest Jedaniah bar Gemariah are historically the most significant of the Elephantine texts (*TAD* A4.1–10). The fragmentary Passover letter sent to him in 419/18 BCE by one Ḥananiah instructs the Jewish garrison in the proper observance of the two festivals of Passover and of Unleavened Bread (*TAD* A4.1). Three letters attest to the tension between the Jews and the priests of Khnub, triggered by the arrival of one Ḥananiah (*TAD* A.4.2–4) and culminating in the destruction of the Jewish temple by the priests of Khnum during the summer of 410 BCE, in connivance with the Persian governor Vidranga. Reports of the destruction, petitions for restoration, and follow-up responses fill five letters and one memorandum (*TAD* A4.5–10). The Elephantine Jews appealed to the authorities in Jerusalem and Samaria to intercede and were prepared to accept restoration of a cult limited to meal and incense and excluding animal sacrifices. It is from the last contract of the Anani archive, dated 13 December, 402 BCE (12 Thoth, 4 Actaxenxes [II]), that we learned of the continued presence of the temple of YHW (*TAD* B3.12:18–19), indicating that if it had not yet been rebuilt, its place had not been taken by another structure.

Four letters may be classified as official, two concerning a hereditary land lease (*TAD* A5.2, 5.5) and two involving the satrap Arsames. One is addressed to him by a panoply of Persian and Egyptian officials involving the disposition of a *menat* ("share") of land (*TAD* A6.1); the other, sent by him through his Jewish chancellor and scribe Anani, illustrates the bureaucratic procedure necessary to repair a boat held in hereditary lease by two Egyptian "boatholders of the Carians" (*TAD* A6.2).

Letters discovered from the Dead Sea region were all official. Seven Hebrew items and many fragments were found in Wadi Murabbaʿat (Mur 42–48, 49–52), three addressed to Jeshuaʿ ben Galgoula (Mur 42–44) and one to Joseh (Mur 46). More than a dozen letters, (two Greek; four Hebrew [P.Yadin 49, 51, 61; also XḤev/Ṣe 30] and eight Aramaic [P.Yadin 50, 53, 54 (wood), 55–58, 63] were discovered by Yigael Yadin in a cave in Naḥal Ḥever, carefully tied in a bundle and deposited in a water skin alongside a woman's personal possessions. Fleeing from ʿEin-Gedi, she took with her letters addressed to her husband(?) Jonathan ben Beaya, and his colleague, Masabala ben Simeon. Written in the name of Simeon son of

Kosiba (*Khosiba* in Greek) by different scribes (132–135 BCE), these letters followed no clear tradition regarding the size and shape of the writing material. The papyrus sheets were of varying widths, as narrow as 7 centimeters and as wide as 22, with a median width of 9.5–11.5 centimeters. Some were palimpsests (5/6Ḥev 63) or cut from the lower edge of a previous document (5/6Ḥev 57). They contained between four (5/6Ḥev 58) and fifteen lines (5/6Ḥev 50), the mean being eight to ten lines (P. Mur. 43–44; 5/6Ḥev 55–56, 61, 63; XḤev/Se 9), usually written parallel to the fibers (exceptions are 5/6Ḥev 53, 57–58) and therefore folded sideways. One letter was written in two columns, of six–eight lines each (5/6Ḥev 49; cf. *TAD* A4.5). The height of a horizontally written piece was usually the height of the original scroll, but these pieces varied in size from 6.6 centimeters (5/6Ḥev 57) to 26.2 centimeters (5/6Ḥev 51). Some had little or no lower margin (P. Mur. 46; 5/6Ḥev 49, 53, 57), while others left 11–14 centimeters blank at the bottom (5/6Ḥev 51, 55–56). There is no evidence of an external address on the Hebrew and Aramaic letters, but two Greco-Roman bullae (originally attached to the Greek letters?) were found in the cache. Most of the letters are stern in tone and thus reminiscent of the rebukes and reprimands of the satrap Arsames and his aristocratic peers (*TAD* A6.8, 10, 13–15). [*See* Letters.]

Legal Documents. Elephantine has yielded forty-three contracts, most intact, and numerous fragments written between 495 and 400 BCE. They are usually written on only one side of the papyrus (*TAD* B1.1, 2.3–4, 3.3, 4.4 are exceptions), perpendicular to the fibers and parallel to the joins. The width of the papyrus sheet (height of the scroll) in the first half of the fifth century measured between 25.5 and 28.5 centimeters (*TAD* B1.1, 2.1–6, 3.1–2, 4.2–4) and between 28.5 and 34 centimeters in the second half of the century (*TAD* B2.7–11, 3.3–13, 6.1, 6.4). A small-sized document of fourteen to fifteen lines with no blank space at the top or bottom would measure between 27.5 (*TAD* B3.3) and 32.7 centimeters (*TAD* B3.2), while a long document of forty-five lines with blank space at the top and bottom would be almost a meter tall (*TAD* B3.8). Upon completion, a scribe usually rolled his document up from the bottom to just below the top, turned down a fold or two, wrote a one-line summary on the exposed band (endorsement), folded the roll in thirds, tied and sealed it. The few preserved anepigraphic bullae are Egyptian or Persian. Four pieces from the end of the century were written parallel to the fibers and perpendicular to the join (*TAD* B4.6, 7.1–3). These were folded from left to right and no endorsement has been preserved. During the course of the fifth century, there appears to have been an increase in the size of the rolls, from 25.5–28.5 centimeters with a mean width of the individual sheets at approximately 10 centimeters (*TAD* B1.1, 2.1–6, 3.1–2, 4.2–4) to a height of 28.5–34 centimeters with the mean width of the individual sheets rising to approximately 14 centimeters (*TAD* B2.7–11, 3.3–13, 6.1, 4).

Some fifty Hebrew (Mur 22, 24, 29–30; 5/6Ḥev 44–46), Aramaic (Mur 18–21, 23, 25–28, 32–33; 5/6Ḥev 7–8, 10, 42–43), and Nabatean (5/6Ḥev 1–4, 6, 9, 36+P. Starcky; XḤev/Se 2) contracts were discovered in the caves near the Dead Sea (c.54/55–135 CE). One or two were written on leather (XḤev/Se 7; P. Naḥ Se 49) and the rest on papyrus. With a few exceptions, they were double documents (tied documents [*Bab. Bath* 10.1]), probably like the one drawn up by the prophet Jeremiah (*Jer.* 32.1–14; 587 BCE) and as evidenced by the earliest Elephantine Greek papyri (*P. Eleph*. 1–4 = *EPE* D2–5). The document was written perpendicular to the fibers, sometimes with blank space at the top, and turned bottoms-up when completed. A second version, usually in a smaller, more cursive script, was sometimes begun at the bottom of the verso and continued in the blank space at the top of the recto; at other times it began on the recto. The top of the document was then folded down to the end of the inner text and tie-stitched some five or seven times. The document was turned back to the verso, tilted ninety degrees, and signed by the witnesses next to the stitch holes. Returned to the recto, the outer document was then rolled up to meet the inner document, and the piece, sometimes folded in half, was tied with cord and perhaps protected by some wrapping. No seals were applied, and only once, in a marriage document, was there an outside endorsement (5/6Hev 10). Nor does there appear to have been any standard size width. The Murabbaʿat rolls ranged from 11 to 12 centimeters (Mur 19, 56), to 13–14 centimeters (Mur. 18, 29, 32), to 15 or 16 centimeters (Mur 21–22). The Hebrew and Aramaic rolls from Naḥal Ḥever and Naḥal Ṣeʾelim were wider, between 14–16 centimeters (5/6Ḥev 7–8, 46; XḤev/Se 50), 18–19 centimeters (5/6Ḥev 10, 42; XḤev/Se 21), and 23–27 centimeters (5/6Ḥev 47; XḤev/Se 8, 9). The Nabatean documents from Naḥal Ḥever were written on smaller scrolls, 12.8 to 18 centimeters tall (document width). Only some of the Greek texts measured approximately 31 centimeters (5/6Ḥev 15, 28–30), like the Elephantine papyri. The height, of course, varied with the number of lines. A marriage contract with five lines of inner text (upper) and fifteen lines of outer text (lower) measured 27 centimeters tall (Mur 21) while a Nabatean conveyance with ten upper lines and forty-nine lower measured 81 centimeters (5/6Ḥev 1). The longest text totaled twenty-nine lines of inner text (ten of which were on the back) and forty-three of outer text, though it measured only 43.9 centimeters tall (5/6Ḥev 7). For leases, the sale of a donkey or of a house to a neighbor, or a quitclaim, a "simple document" sufficed; the writing was parallel to the fibers and witnesses signed below. These documents ranged between eleven and thirty-four lines and stood 10.9 to 26.8 centimeters tall (5/6Ḥev 8, 42, 44–46; XḤev/Se 8a, 13).

The most intact of all the Elephantine papyri were those acquired by purchase on the antiquities market. These constitute two family archives. The other legal documents (loosely referred to as "contracts") may be divided into five categories: deeds of obligation (*TAD* B4.1–6), conveyances (*TAD* B5.1–5), documents of wifehood (*TAD* B6.1–4), judicial oaths (*TAD* B7.1–4), and court records (*TAD* B8.1–12 [only Saqqarah]). Representative documents from the first three categories also appear in the family archives. Except for Egyptians, the parties regularly were identified by ethnicon, occupation, and residence, witnesses and neighbors less regularly. The alienor was presented as speaking to the alienee. The documents were drawn up by a scribe skilled in legal terminology "upon/at the instruction of" the alienor and occasionally of the alienee, when (s)he was one of the speakers (*TAD* B3.8, 6.3–4). There were thirteen known scribes at Elephantine, six with Hebrew names and seven with non-Hebrew ("Aramaean") names. Jewish scribes, with but one exception (*TAD* B7.1), drew up their documents at Elephantine (*TAD* B2.9–10, 3.6, 3.8, 3.10–12), while Aramaean scribes, with but one exception (*TAD* B2.11), drew up theirs at Syene (*TAD* B2.2–4, 3.9, 3.13).

The Mibtaḥiah archive contains eleven documents and spans three generations (471–410 BCE) of one of Elephantine's leading Jewish families. The first four documents constitute a miniarchive concerning a house plot bequeathed by the hereditary property holder Maḥseiah to his daughter Mibtaḥiah (*TAD* B2.1–4). The second set of four documents introduces Mibtaḥiah's spouse(s), presents her Egyptian connection, and shows her property expanded (*TAD* B2.5–8). The last three documents in the archive cover the decade 420–410 BCE and deal with problems arising out of the estate of the deceased parents (*TAD* B2.9–11).

The Anani(ah) archive contains thirteen documents (*TAD* B3.1–13), touches upon two interrelated families, and spans two generations (456–402 BCE). A minor temple official married an Egyptian handmaiden, Tamet (*TAD* B3.3), acquired a piece of abandoned property from a Caspian couple (*TAD* B3.4), and parceled it out over the years, first to his wife (*TAD* B3.5), then to his daughter Jehoishma (*TAD* B3.7, 10–11), and finally to his son-in-law Anani (*TAD* B3.13). Tamet, who had virtually no dowry upon marriage, was eventually emancipated (*TAD* B3.6) and handsomely endowed by her adoptive brother Zaccur, son of their former master, Meshullam bar Zaccur (*TAD* B3.8).

Accounts and Lists. The most significant account, religiously and onomastically, is the eight-column Collection Account from Elephantine, probably of 400 BCE (*TAD* C3.15), which lists one hundred twenty-eight Jewish contributors of two shekels each, initially designated for Yahveh but in the end divided up between him and the deities Eshembethel and Anathbethel. The scribe of this list was probably the one who drew up in the same year what is now a fragmentary account (parts of three columns have been preserved) of the disbursement of barley to the Aramaean garrison at Syene (*TAD* C3.14). On the back of the Bisitun inscription and following immediately upon its conclusion is a multicolumn record of memoranda of the transfer of vessels from one person to another (*TAD* C3.13). Ethnically, the five lists display the cosmopolitan nature of society in the Persian period: three consist essentially of Jews, with a sprinkling of Aramaean and Egyptian names (*TAD* C4.4:2, 7, 9; 4.5:9; 4.6:3, 5, 8, 9); one of Persians only (*TAD* C4.7); and one of mixed Egyptian and Aramaean names, with a sprinkling of Jewish and Babylonian names (*TAD* C4.8:1, 3, 8, 9). Lacking or missing titles, the lists conceal their intent. They may have constituted military units, collection lists (cf. *TAD* C3.15), or ration lists (cf. *TAD* C3.14, 3.27). The list of Persians (*TAD* C4.7) may be one of officers or officials.

Literary and Historical Texts. In addition to the letters and contracts are one literary text "the Words of Aḥiqar" (*TAD* C1.1); one historical text—a fragmentary version of the Bisitun inscription of Darius (*TAD* C2.1); some eight accounts (*TAD* C3.3–4, 9–10, 13–16); and five lists (*TAD* C4.4–8). The distinctive characteristic of these texts is the mode of their inscription. Written in columns parallel to the fibers and perpendicular to the join, the scrolls were rolled from left to right rather than from bottom to top.

Eleven sheets containing fourteen columns of the Aḥiqar text are preserved (TAD C1.1). The first five columns relate the story of the "wise and skillful scribe . . . counselor of all Assyria and [be]arer of the seal" for King Sennacherib and his son King Esarhaddon; the last nine columns contains some one hundred twenty proverbs, mostly pithy one-liners. (For example, "[My] son, do not d[a]mn the day until you see [nig]ht" [line 80].) Extensive papyrological and textual work has restored seventy-nine lines of the approximately one-hundred ninety lines of the Bisitun text, copied around 420 BCE, perhaps to commemorate the one-hundredth anniversary of the victory of Darius I over nineteen rebels in one year.

The nine preserved paragraphs correspond to eight campaigns, with separate paragraphs for individual battles in the two Armenian campaigns. The tenth and final paragraph is a composite piece, which corresponds to the last paragraph of the Naqshi-Rustam inscription of Darius.

Fragments. Among the numerous document fragments, thirty may be classified as letters (*TAD* D1.1–14, 1.18–31, 33–34), almost thirty as contracts (*TAD* D2.1–28), and over twenty-five as accounts and lists (*TAD* D3.1–26). In addition, more than seventy fragments do not permit classification (*TAD* D4.1–33, 5.1–41).

Ostraca and Jar Inscriptions. Some three hundred eighty Aramaic ostraca have been discovered, almost all from Elephantine and most from excavations (twenty-six by the Germans and almost three hundred by the French). Almost all the ostraca unearthed by the Germans have been published, but ninety years after their discovery only a handful of the pieces discovered by the French have been published. The ostraca may be divided into four groups: letters (*TAD* D7.1–54), the most numerous; accounts (*TAD* D8.2); lists (*TAD* D9.1–14); and abecedaries (*TAD* D10.1). Most letters were written by a single scribe in the first quarter of the fifth century BCE, who took dictation at Syene from soldiers needing to communicate with their families and friends in Elephantine. The letters were written on randomly shaped sherds that measured roughly 7 by 10 centimeters, beginning regularly on the concave side and continuing on the convex, and averaging a dozen lines. They contained reports, requests, instructions, and occasionally matters of religious import and were sent by the regular ferry service that ran, then as now, between the mainland and the island.

Only about half of the thirty-five jar inscriptions from Elephantine have been published (*TAD* D11.2–20). These include Aramaic and Phoenician names and the notations *le'malka'* ("for the king") followed by a ṭeit-like sign, written, incised, or inked on the jar, usually at the top, at the time of its manufacture, transport, or storage: in this case, two scribes were responsible for eighty-four jar inscriptions apiece (*TAD* D1.4–7, 8–11). Finally, there are a handful of inscriptions on leather, wood, and stone: an indecipherable text (completely legible but the language is uncertain [*TAD* D6.2]), two lists of names (*TAD* D12.1, 13.3), a palette (*TAD* D13.1) and part thereof (*TAD* D13.4), a stamp(?) (*TAD* D13.5), a mummy label (*TAD* D19.7), and a limestone dedicatory inscription (*TAD* D17.1).

[*See also* Documentary Texts; Ḥever, Naḥal, *article on* Written Material; Murabbaʿat, Wadi, *article on* Written Material; *and* Ṣe'elim, Naḥal, *article on* Written Material.]

BIBLIOGRAPHY

Benoit, P., J. T. Milik, and R. de Vaux. *Les Grottes de Murabbaʿat*. Discoveries in the Judaean Desert, 2. Oxford, 1961. Aramaic and Hebrew contracts and letters with excellent commentary and plates.

Bresciani, Edda, and M. Kamil. "Le lettere aramaiche di Hermopoli." *Atti della accademia Nazionale dei Lincei, Classe di Scienze Morale, Memorie*, Ser. 7, 12 (1966), 357–428. Eight intact letters addressed to Luxor and Syene but deposited in an ibis jar in Hermopolis. Excellent commentary and plates.

Cotton, Hannah, and Ada Yardeni. *Aramaic, Hebrew and Greek Documentary Texts from Naḥal Ḥever and other Sites*. Discoveries in the Judaean Desert, 27. Oxford, 1997.

Cowley, Arthur E. *Aramaic Papyri of the Fifth Century* BC. Oxford, 1923. The most convenient collection of all papyri published until that date. Readings must be checked against later publications.

Driver, Godfrey R. *Aramaic Documents of the Fifth Century* BC. Oxford, 1954. Superb publication of parchment letters sent from outside Egypt to satrapal officials. Excellent full-size plates. Abridged and revised (without plates) in 1957.

Fitzmyer, Joseph A., and Stephen A. Kaufman. *An Aramaic Bibliography. Part I. Old, Official, and Biblical Aramaic*. Baltimore, 1992. Complete listing of all texts and extensive bibliography for each. Classification according to *TAD* sigla where available; otherwise classification is cumbersome.

Greenfield, Jonas C., and Bezalel Porten. *The Bisitun Inscription of Darius the Great: Aramaic Version*. London, 1982. New edition with restored text; comparison to Akkadian version; papyrological treatment. Minor revisions in *TAD* C2.1

Kraeling, Emil G. *Brooklyn Museum Aramaic Papyri: New Documents of the Fifth Century B.C. from the Jewish Colony at Elephantine*. New Haven, 1953. Publication of Anani family archive discovered in 1893 by Wilbour. Comprehensive introduction. Readings must be checked against later publications.

Lewis, Naphtali. *The Documents from the Bar Kokhba Period in the Cave of Letters Greek Papyri*. Judean Desert Studies. Jerusalem, 1989. The texts discovered by Yigael Yadin.

Naveh, J. *The Development of the Aramaic Script*. Proceedings of the Israel Academy of Sciences and Humanities, 5.1. Jerusalem, 1970. Basic work for paleographical dating of all Aramaic texts.

Pardee, Dennis. *Handbook of Ancient Hebrew Letters*. Chico, Calif., 1982. Excellent translation of and commentary on a dozen letters from the Judean desert.

Porten, Bezalel. *Archives from Elephantine: The Life of an Ancient Jewish Military Colony*. Berkeley, 1968. Most comprehensive synthesis of the material. Treatment of legal topics updated by joint studies of Porten and Szubin.

Porten, Bezalel. "The Calendar of Aramaic Texts from Achaemenid and Ptolemaic Egypt." In *Irano-Judaica II*, edited by Shaul Shaked and A. Netzer, pp. 13–32. Jerusalem, 1990. Detailed examination of every date. Discussion of dating patterns in contracts, letters, and accounts; synchronous Babylonian-Egyptian dates.

Porten, Bezalel. "The Jews in Egypt." In *The Cambridge History of Judaism*, edited by W. D. Davies and Louis Finkelstein, vol 1., pp. 372–400. 3 vols. Cambridge, 1984. Update of Porten, *Archives from Elephantine* with basic bibliography.

Porten, Bezalel. "Elephantine Papyri." In *The Anchor Bible Dictionary*, edited by David Noel Freedman, vol, 2, pp. 445–455. New York, 1992. Detailed survey of discovery and contents of all Elephantine papyri; elaborate bibliography.

Porten, Bezalel. *The Elephantine Papyri in English: Three Millennia of Cross-Cultural Continuity and Change* Leiden, 1996. Translation of and commentary on 175 documents, including 52 Aramaic.

Porten, Bezalel, and Ada Yardeni. *Textbook of Aramaic Documents from Ancient Egypt, Newly Copied, Edited, and Translated into Hebrew and English*. 3 vols. (= *TAD* A–C). Jerusalem/Winona Lake, Ind., 1986–1993. Most up-to-date collection of Egyptian Aramaic papyri and parchments, includes letters, contracts, literature, accounts, and lists. Each text newly collated at source and reproduced in hand copy. Detailed excurses. *TAD* D has just appeared; it includes papyrus fragments and inscriptions on material other than papyrus.

Sachau, Eduard. *Aramäische Papyrus und Ostraka aus einer jüdischen*

Militärkolonie zu Elephantine. Leipzig, 1911. Publication of seventy-five papyrus items and numerous inscriptions on sherds, jars, wood, stone, and leather, mostly from the 1906–1908 Elephantine excavations by Rubensohn and Zucker. Plates are indispensable.

Sayce, Archibald H., and Arthur E. Cowley. *Aramaic Papyri Discovered at Assuan*. London, 1906. Mibtaḥiah archive plus several ostraca. Full-size plates. Excellent bibliography of all Aramaic texts to date by Seymour de Ricci. Readings must be checked against later publications.

Yadin, Yigael. *Bar-Kokhba. The Rediscovery of the Legendary Hero of the Second Jewish Revolt against Rome*. New York, 1971. Discovery and preliminary presentation of the Bar Kokhba letters and the Babatha archive from the Cave of Letters in Naḥal Ḥever.

Yardeni, Ada. *'Naḥal Ṣe'elim' Documents*. Jerusalem, 1995 (Hebrew). Judean Desert Studies.

BEZALEL PORTEN

ELIJAH, ninth century BCE prophet in the northern kingdom of Israel. Elijah's zealous loyalty to the Lord, his role as prophet and teacher, his struggle against the Baalim (Canaanite and Phoenician gods), his going up to heaven in the fiery chariot, and his expected return are biblical motifs (*1 Kgs*. 17–21; *2 Kgs*. 1–2; *Mal.* 3.1.23) that were further developed in the Jewish and Christian traditions.

Elijah's command of the heavens is referred to in *Ben Sira* 48.3: "he shut up the heavens and . . . brought down fire." In *Revelation* 11.4–7, Elijah is one of the "two olive trees," usually identified as Elijah and Moses, who has authority "to shut the sky . . . and to turn water into blood." Among the Dead Sea Scrolls, the expectation of Elijah as precursor to the Messiah is attested in a fragmentary Aramaic text called Vision B (4Q558). Line 4 reads "therefore I will send Elijah be[fore . . .]." In the messianic Apocalypse (4Q521 2.ii.1 ". . . heaven and earth will obey his messiah"), there is an allusion to an anointed prophet who speaks of the End of Days, either Elijah or a prophet like Elijah. The lines "for he will heal the wounded, give life to the dead . . ." (4Q521 2.ii.12) and "I will free them" (4Q521 2.iii.1) seem to refer to Elijah or an Elijah-like figure, in whose time the sick are healed and the dead are raised. The most surprising parallel comes from *Matthew* 11.2–5, and *Luke* 7.22; which identify John the Baptist with the messenger sent to prepare the way (*Mal*. 3.1). The signs alluded to in these passages could suggest that Jesus was Elijah *redivivus*, an identification envisaged also in *Mark* 6.14–15 and 8.28. In *John* 1.19–21, John the Baptist denies that he is either the Messiah, Elijah, or "the Prophet."

The Interpreter of the Law, "he who teaches justice at the End of Days" (Damascus Document CD vi.11; cf. Florilegium 4Q174 1–3.i.11) could be identified with Elijah. Later rabbinic tradition applied *Hosea* 10.12, "until he comes and teaches righteousness for you," to Elijah and assigned to him, as precursor of the Messiah, the role of settling the unresolved controversies in Jewish law.

The translation of Elijah to the heavens together with the accounts of Moses' shining face may be the models for the transfiguration and ascent to heaven motifs in some texts (cf. Aaronic Text A = Aramaic Levi[d] 4Q541).

Elijah's return was a classical motif in Jewish apocalypses that was rooted in *Malachi* 3.23, "I will send you the prophet Elijah before the great and terrible day of the Lord comes." A traditional view based mostly on the New Testament (*Mk.* 9.11) takes for granted that in the first century BCE it was generally believed that Elijah would return before the coming of the Messiah. Elijah has an eschatological role in *Ben Sira* 40.10, but the concept of Elijah as forerunner of the Messiah is not widely attested in the Pseudepigrapha (*4 Ez.* 6.26, *Sib. Or.* 2.187–189, the Coptic *Apocalypse of Elijah*, and the Hebrew *Apocalypse of Elijah*).

In later Jewish tradition Elijah, of Aaron's tribe (*Lives of Prophets* 21), was often regarded as a priest or high priest, through an association with Phineas and their shared motif of zeal (Pseudo-Philo's *Biblical Antiquities* 48; *Pirqei de-Rabbi Eli'ezer* 47.3). Elijah would anoint the Messiah (Justin, *Dialogue with Trypho* 49) and destroy the Antichrist (*Apocalypse of Elijah* 5.32; *Apocalypse of Daniel* 14). He is considered by some one of the righteous men of old (*Apocalypse of Zephaniah* 9). The tradition of his martyrdom is found in *Apocalypse of Elijah* 4.7–19.

In the Samaritan tradition, the eschatological role of messianic restorer (*taheb*) is related to Elijah; the same may be true of Taxo (*Testament of Moses* 9.1).

[*See also* Apocalyptic Texts; Eschatology; Messiahs; *and* Prophecy.]

BIBLIOGRAPHY

Allison, Dale C. "Elijah Must Come First." *Journal of Biblical Literature* 103 (1984), 256–258.

Collins, John J. *The Scepter and the Star: The Messiahs of the Dead Sea Scrolls and Other Ancient Literature*. The Anchor Bible Reference Library. New York, 1995.

Feierstein, Morris M. "Why Do the Scribes Say that Elijah Must Come First?" *Journal of Biblical Literature* 100 (1981), 75–86.

Fitzmyer, Joseph A. "More About Elijah Coming First." *Journal of Biblical Literature* 104 (1985), 295–296.

Puech, Émile. *La croyance des esséniens en la vie future: immortalité, résurrection, vie éternelle?* 2 vols. Paris, 1993.

Stone, Michael E., and John Strugnell. *The Books of Elijah: Parts 1–2*. Missoula, Minn., 1979.

van der Woude, Adam S. *Die messianische Vorstellung der Gemeinde von Qumrân*. Assen, 1957.

JULIO TREBOLLE BARRERA

ELISHA (ninth century BCE), like Elijah, a prophet in the northern kingdom of Israel. The Elijah-Elisha biblical tradition (*1 Kgs*. 19.16, 21.29; *2 Kgs*. 2–13) combined visionary prophecy and thaumaturgy (the performance of miracles). The later Jewish traditions developed the master-disciple relationship and Elisha's thaumaturgical character, zeal, and holiness.

There are a number of texts in the Dead Sea Scrolls that mention Elisha. The Damascus Document's statement, "This is the word that . . . Elisha [spoke] to Gehazi his servant. . . ." (CD viii.20–21, A text) seems to apply the lesson of Gehazi's punishment for betraying his master from *2 Kings* 5.26–27 to the punishment of those who abandon the teachings of their master. The citation could be related to a lost pseudepigraphic work.

The fragmentary text mentioning Elisha (4Q481a) is a manuscript from the late Hasmonean period preserved in three fragments. The text of fragment 2, lines 3–6, seems to correspond to *2 Kings* 2.14–16. Lines 1–2 of fragment 2, as well as fragments 1 and 3, probably belong to a paraphrastic work on the Elisha story. The word *qinah* in fragment 3, line 3, suggests a text of "lamentation" following "and he said." The words *ra]v* or *ʾa]v wa-ʾadon* ("chief [teacher] and master" or "father and master") seem to imply a master-disciple relationship (cf. *2 Kgs.* 2.12, MT *ʾby*, targum *rby*).

Paraphrase of Kings et al. (4Q382 9;11) also quotes *2 Kings* 2.3–4 adding parabiblical material. Fragments 1–5, 9–11, 30, and possibly 40 seem to be a paraphrase or a rewriting of the stories of Elijah and Elisha.

Further mention of Elisha occurs in *Ben Sira* 46.12, which seems to allude to the story of Elisha's bones (*2 Kgs.* 13.20–21), while *Ben Sira* 49.9 refers to Elisha's anointing by Elijah (*1 Kgs.* 19.16) and 48.12 to his double portion of Elijah's spirit (*2 Kgs.* 2.9–10). Elisha's fearlessness is praised in *Ben Sira* 48.12–14.

In *Lives of Prophets* (22.2) Elisha is a prophet born to destroy the idols in Israel. Josephus is more interested in the prophet's public miracles such as the deliverance from the Syrian army, characterized as an epiphany of the Israelite God (*Jewish Antiquities*, 9.4.4). In *The Jewish War* (4.8.3) Josephus rewrites *2 Kings* 2.19–21, making Elisha a Greco-Roman "divine man."

In the New Testament, *Luke* 4.26–27 uses the Elijah-Elisha stories as a typology of the prophet rejected by Israel or as a prefigurement of the mission to the Gentiles. In *Acts* 9.36–42, Luke makes an implicit comparison between Elisha and Peter as a counterpart to Jesus and Elijah in his gospel (7.11–17).

In *Gospel of John*, Jesus is perhaps presented as the new Elisha who accomplishes seven of the prophet's miracles: transformation, healing of a sick boy, multiplication of food, healing of a sick man, levitation, healing of a blind man, and raising of the dead. The story of Naaman (*2 Kgs.* 5.1–14) has influenced *John* 5.1–11, and the account of the multiplication of food for the crowd (*Jn.* 6.1–14) is influenced by *2 Kings* 4.42–44.

The rabbinic literature praises Elisha's holiness discerned by the Shunammite woman (*2 Kgs.* 4.9) because of the pleasant fragrance surrounding him. Elisha did not refuse her hospitality because a sage may benefit from the generosity of his followers (B.T., *Ber.* 10b). He revived two dead persons, one more than his master, the leper Naaman being considered a dead man (B.T., *Hul.* 7b). Elisha sanctified God's name when he refused to accept any recompense from Naaman (*Nm.* Rab. 7.5).

[*See also* Elijah.]

BIBLIOGRAPHY

Betz, Otto. "Das Problem des Wunders bei Flavius Josephus im Vergleich zum Wunderproblem bei den Rabbinen und im Johannesevangelium." In *Josephus-Studien. Untersuchungen zu Josephus, dem antiken Judentum und dem Neuen Testament,* edited by Otto Betz, Klaus Haecker, and Martin Hengel, pp. 23–44. Göttingen, 1974.

Betz, Otto. "Miracles in the Writings of Flavius Josephus." In *Josephus, Judaism, and Christianity,* edited by Louis H. Feldman and Gohei Hata, pp. 212–235. Leiden and Detroit, 1987.

Bostock, D. Gerald. "Jesus as the New Elisha." *Expository Times* 92 (1980), 39–41.

Olyan, Saul. "4Qpap paraKings et al." In *Qumran Cave 4: Parabiblical Texts, Parts 1,* edited by Harold Attridge, et al. Discoveries in the Judaean Desert, 13. Oxford, 1994.

Smith, Morton. "The Occult in Josephus." In *Josephus, Judaism, and Christianity,* edited by Louis H. Feldman and Gohei Hata, pp. 236–256. Leiden and Detroit, 1987.

Trebolle Barrera, Julio. "Histoire du texte des livres historiques et histoire de la composition et de la rédaction deutéronomistes avec une publication préliminaire de 4Q481a, 'Apocryphe d'Élisée.'" In *Congress Volume: Paris, 1992,* edited by J. A. Emerton, pp. 327–342. Supplements to Vetus Testamentrum, 61. Leiden and New York, 1995.

JULIO TREBOLLE BARRERA

ELKESAITES. Also known as Elchasaites, the Elkesaites were Jewish Christians in the second to the third centuries CE. [*See* Jewish Christians.] One of their missionary leaders, a certain Alcibiades, came from Apamea in Syria and was active in Rome (c.220). Elkesaites were also active in Palestine in the third century and seem to have originated in Transjordan at the beginning of the second century, during the reign of the emperor Trajan (98–117 CE). Their name stems from their sacred writing, the "Book of Elkesai," containing a revelation from an enormous angel and originally written in Aramaic. Elkesai (or Elchasai) was probably the name of this angel rather than of the author.

The sources for our knowledge of the Elkesaites (and their book) are Hippolytus (c.170–236 CE; *Refutation of All Heresies* 9.13–17, 10.29), Origen (c.185–254 CE) in a sermon quoted by Eusebius (c.260–340 CE; *Ecclesiastical History* 6.38) and Epiphanius (c.315–403 CE; *Panarion* 19.1–4, 30.17, 53.1). [*See* Epiphanius; Hippolytus; *and*

Origen.] Origen and Eusebius call these Jewish Christians "Helkesaites." The form used by Epiphanius is "Elxai," which he derives from an Aramaic term meaning "hidden power." "Elchasai" is the form of the name used by Hippolytus.

The information provided by these church fathers about the beliefs and practices of the Elkesaites is very limited and of uncertain value. The Aramaic original of the "Book of Elkesai" is lost, and we must rely on the fragmentary and tendentious accounts of the church fathers (who wrote in Greek) for its contents and for an account of Elkesaite beliefs and practices. The Elkesaites apparently rejected the letters of Paul (so Origen), while Alcibiades required that Christians practice circumcision and observe the Mosaic law (so Hippolytus). The Elkesaites prayed facing Jerusalem though they rejected sacrifices and priestly rites (Epiphanius). Both Origen and Hippolytus report that the Elkesaites promised forgiveness of sins to all those who heeded their "Book of Elkesai."

In at least two respects, the beliefs and practices of the Elkesaites have notable similarities to the community of Qumran, its literature, and its ideology.

First, the "Book of Elkesai" apparently contained elements of an apocalyptic prophecy concerning an imminent eschatological, angelic war: "when three years of the emperor Trajan are complete, from the time when he subjected the Parthians to his own authority, when these three years are fulfilled, the war between the godless angels of the north will break out" (Hippolytus 9.16.4, 9.15.1, 9.16.1; cf. War Scroll [1QM]).

Second are the instructions to be baptized "a second time" for gross sexual sins (bestiality, homosexuality, incest, adultery, fornication [cf. CD iv.15–19], but also false prophecy [cf. 4Q339]) and to undertake repeated immersions for sickness and demon possession: "The consumptive are also to baptize themselves in cold water forty times in seven days, and likewise also those possessed by demons" (Hippolytus). The Elkesaites thus seem to have combined an initiatory rite of baptism with the practice of repeated washings, as did (in their own way) the community of Qumran (see Rule of the Community from Cave 1 at Qumran [1QS] and the Damascus Document [CD]). According to Josephus, the Essenes bathed themselves daily and did so "in cold water" (*The Jewish War* 2.129). [*See* Josephus Flavius.]

[*See also* Pseudo-Clementine Literature.]

BIBLIOGRAPHY

Irmscher, Johannes. "The Book of Elchasai." In *New Testament Apocrypha*, vol. 2, edited by E. Hennecke, W. Schneemelcher, and R. McL. Wilson, pp. 745–750. Philadelphia, 1965; rev. ed. Louisville, 1992, pp. 685–690. Translation and discussion of "The Book of Elkesai."

Klijn, A. F. J., and G. J. Reinink. *Patristic Evidence for Jewish-Christian Sects. Supplements to Novum Testamentum*, 36. Leiden, 1973. The standard sourcebook of patristic texts on Jewish-Christian groups. See pages, 54–73 for the Elkesaites.

Luttikhuizen, G. P. *The Revelation of Elchesai. Investigations into the Evidence for a Mesopotamian Jewish Apocalypse of the Second Century and its Reception by Judeo-Christian Propagandists.* Texte und Studien zum Antiken Judentum, 8. Tübingen, 1985.

MARTINUS C. DE BOER

ENCRATITES were early Christian ascetics. The name *Encratites* is derived from a Greek word (*enkrateia*) meaning self-control, which was a virtue extolled by Plato and Aristotle and highly regarded by the Stoics. The ideal of self-control found its way into Judaism in the Hellenistic period (cf. *Sir.* 18.30–19.3, *4 Mc.* 5.34, the Alexandrian Jewish philosopher Philo) and into Christianity via Paul, who lists it alongside love, joy, peace, and so forth, as a fruit of the Spirit (*Gal.* 5.23; cf. *1 Cor.* 7.9, 9.25; *Ti.* 1.8; *Acts* 24.25; *2 Pt.* 1.6). In *1 Corinthians* 7.9, as a concession, Paul recommends marriage for Christians who cannot exercise sexual "self-control" as he does.

In the second and third centuries, the church fathers Irenaeus (c.130–200 CE), Clement of Alexandria (c. 150–215 CE), and Hippolytus (c.170–236 CE) applied the name Encratites to a diverse array of early Christian groups adopting ascetic practices such as celibacy, abstinence from wine, and vegetarianism. Particularly important is an organized Jewish-Christian community that, according to Irenaeus (*Adversus omnes Haereses* 1.28), was founded in the latter part of the second century in Mesopotamia by Tatian. [*See* Jewish Christians.] Tatian was a pupil of Justin Martyr (c.100–165 CE) and author of the *Diatessaron* (a famous harmony of the four canonical Gospels). Mesopotamia was Tatian's homeland, and he apparently returned there after Justin's death. Almost nothing, however, is known about the Encratite community supposedly founded by Tatian. Irenaeus claims that they rejected marriage, abstained from meat, and denied the salvation of Adam (*Adversus omnes Haereses* 1.28). To what extent the asceticism associated with Qumran influenced the practices of these Encratites (and other Christian groups to whom the label was somewhat loosely applied) remains unclear. Although the men who lived at Qumran were in the opinion of most scholars Essenes who were apparently celibate, they were not vegetarians, nor did they abstain from wine.

[*See also* Essenes.]

BIBLIOGRAPHY

Bolgiani, F. "La tradizione eresiologica sull'encratismo: 1, le notizie di Ireneo." *Atti della Accademia delle Scienze di Torino* 91 (1956–1957), 1–77.

Edwards, O. C., Jr. "Encratism." *The Anchor Bible Dictionary*. Vol. 2. New York, 1992. See pages 506–507.
Grant, R. M. "The Heresy of Tatian." *Journal of Theological Studies*, n.s. 5 (1954), 62–68.

MARTINUS C. DE BOER

ENOCH, the seventh antediluvian forefather according to the genealogy in *Genesis* 5. The terse account of Enoch's life (*Gn.* 5.21–24) diverges from the other biographical summaries provided in *Genesis* in three ways: his life span is significantly shorter (a mere 365 years); his piety is noted "and Enoch walked with God" (*Gn.* 5.22); and no mention is made of his death. Instead, the text states "then he was no more, because God took him" (*Gn.* 5.24).

This passage provides the background for the much richer portraits of Enoch produced in Second Temple Jewish pseudepigraphal literature. Enoch's sudden disappearance from human society encodes an ascent experience, whereby Enoch is granted access to all manner of heavenly mysteries regarding the governance of the cosmos and the progression of terrestrial history. His exemplary righteousness qualifies him for permanent residence with the angels, a reward that eventually is heightened in later literature by his transformation into the angel Metatron. Finally, his association with the number 365 connects him with the reckoning of the solar year, and hence Enoch is credited with the invention of astronomical science, chronological sequencing, and the means by which these discoveries can be transmitted to future generations—the art of writing. Enoch thus enjoyed renown as an authoritative author and scribe. Two pseudepigraphal books of Enoch were preserved among certain Christian scribal circles, and they are conventionally designated *1 Enoch* (the only complete version is in Ethiopic) and *2 Enoch* (the two recensions are in Old Slavonic).

Interest in the figure of Enoch and his alleged literary productions is evident from the Dead Sea Scrolls, doubtless due to sectarian concern about issues pertaining to revelatory authority, calendrical computation, scribal wisdom, and eschatological events. Eleven Aramaic manuscripts, all recovered from Cave 4 at Qumran, preserve parts of four early Enoch texts: they are the oldest extant specimens of Enochic literature.

In addition to material allegedly authored by Enoch, the Dead Sea Scrolls also include examples of literature in which Enoch figures prominently. One such work is the *Book of Giants*, an elaborate Aramaic expansion of the brief story about what was understood to be the birth of the Giants in *Genesis* 6.1–4. According to the extrabiblical elaboration of this narrative, two of the Giants experience troubling dreams. To secure an authoritative interpretation, they dispatch an emissary to the habitation of Enoch, a place situated "beyond the wastelands, the great desert . . ." (4Q530 3.5). The need for such a journey clearly alludes to the tradition about Enoch's removal from the customary haunts of humankind (*Gn.* 5.24), as does the distinctive epithet used with his name in the Enoch Giants[a] "the scribe (who is) set apart" (4Q203 8.4, 4Q530 2.14). Enoch presents the messenger with two tablets expounding the ominous dreams, an illustration of his supernaturally acquired prophetic prowess.

Similarly, the Genesis Apocryphon from Cave 1 (1QapGen) mentions a lengthy journey undertaken by Methuselah, son of Enoch, to the dwelling place of his father in order to learn whether the infant prodigy Noah was truly of human parentage (ii.19–26). The account of this interview, portions of which parallel the story in *1 Enoch* 106–107, once occupied the bulk of fragmentary columns iii–v of the Genesis Apocryphon. Enoch eventually reassures his nervous interrogator of Noah's legitimate status (v.4). The same composition later portrays Abram instructing three visitors from the Egyptian royal court in "wisdom and truth," employing for this purpose what scholars have plausibly reconstructed as "a [book] of the words of [En]och" (xix.25; see also *Pseudo-Eupolemus*). Finally, Pseudo-Jubilees[c] (4Q227) mentions Enoch's educational sojourn among the angels and his production of writings about "the heavens and the courses of their hosts . . . ," an attribution reminiscent of *Jubilees* 4.17–24. The copy of *Ben Sira* found at Masada (Mas1h) shows that Enoch was mentioned only in 49.14 and not in 44.16.

[*See also* Enoch, Books of; Genesis Apocryphon.]

BIBLIOGRAPHY

Milik, J. T. *The Books of Enoch: Aramaic Fragments of Qumrân Cave 4*. Oxford, 1976. The standard edition of the Aramaic fragments of *1 Enoch*.
VanderKam, James C. *Enoch and the Growth of an Apocalyptic Tradition*. Catholic Biblical Quarterly Monograph Series, 16. Washington, D.C., 1984. A pioneering investigation of the development of the figure of Enoch in Second Temple literature.
VanderKam, James C. *Enoch: A Man for All Generations*. Studies on Personalities of the Old Testament. Columbia, S.C., 1995. An overview of Enoch and the Enochic traditions.

JOHN C. REEVES

ENOCH, BOOKS OF. A group of revelatory writings composed in the name of the patriarch mentioned in *Genesis* 5.18–24, the term designates three related literary corpora. The first, usually known as *1 Enoch*, or the Ethiopic *Apocalypse of Enoch*, is the focus of this article. Its component parts were composed in Aramaic between approximately 400 BCE and the turn of the era and were translated into Greek and from Greek into classical Ethiopic (Geʿez), in which version alone the full collection is preserved. The Greek version of *1 Enoch*, or a similar corpus, was the basis for *2 Enoch*, an Egyptian text of uncertain date that is preserved in a Church Slavonic translation of its Greek original. The Hebrew *Apocalypse of Enoch*, also known as *3 Enoch*, is a collection of Jewish mystical traditions, written in Hebrew over a long period of time and edited into their present form probably in the fifth or sixth century CE.

Content. The book *1 Enoch* is divided into five major sections, to which two appendices have been added. The core of the first book, the "Book of Watchers" (chaps. 1–36), is a set of mythic narratives about the origins and ultimate obliteration of sin and evil (chaps. 6–11). Based on *Genesis* 6.1–4 and non-Israelite myths about the mating of gods and mortals and the rebellion of Prometheus or a similar figure, these traditions ascribe the presence of violence and sexual promiscuity to a primordial rebellion by the angels ("watchers"). They mate with women, who give birth to a race of giants who devastate the earth, and they reveal secrets about metallurgy and mining, magic, and astrology. These myths of ancient rebellion and its punishment in the Flood depict a prototype for the evils of the authors' own times, which they expect to be eradicated in coming judgment that will usher in a new, final age of divine blessing. The myths, which were composed possibly as part of a cycle of stories about Noah, are elaborated in a set of narratives about Enoch, who ascends to heaven to be commissioned as a prophet of doom to the watchers (chaps. 12–16) and then travels across the earth in the company of angels to view the places of eternal reward and punishment (chaps. 17–36). The final editor of the "Book of Watchers" (c.250–200 BCE) prefaced this material with an oracle of judgment that identifies Enoch as the first prophet and the source of a wide-ranging revelatory tradition (chaps. 1–5). A scrap of tradition in *1 Enoch* 81.1–82.3 indicates that the "Book of Watchers" ended with Enoch's viewing the heavenly record of human deeds and returning to earth to write down his revelations, so that his son Methuselah could preserve them as Enoch's testament and testimony for future generations.

The Enochic "Book of Parables" (chaps. 37–71) dates from the turn of the era. Explicating traditions from the "Book of Watchers," it recounts Enoch's ascent to heaven, his cosmological and eschatological visions, and his final translation to Paradise. Traditional Enochic material includes references to the angelic rebellion and revelation of forbidden secrets to mankind. Enoch's viewing of celestial phenomena (see below on chaps. 72–82), and his journeys to the places of punishment. To these are added traditions about Noah and the Flood. The book's special character lies in a set of heavenly tableaux about the coming judgment and the events associated with it. The central figure in these scenes is an enthroned heavenly figure, who combines features drawn from biblical texts about the Davidic king, oracles about the servant of the Lord in *Isaiah* 40–55, and the vision in *Daniel* 7. The author designates the protagonist as "the anointed one," "the chosen one" and the "righteous one," and the "son of man." The champion of God's chosen and righteous ones, he will judge their persecutors, "the kings and the mighty," a designation for the Romans and Herod the Great. In its present form, the "Book of Parables" ends as Enoch's final translation is interpreted as his transformation into the Son of Man who had dominated the scenes he had witnessed.

The "Book of Parables" is followed in the present form of *1 Enoch* by the "Book of Luminaries" (chaps. 72–82), which recounts Enoch's journeys through the heavens in the company of the angel Uriel, who explains the celestial and cosmic phenomena that validate a 364-day solar calendar as the basis for religious observance. It is perhaps the oldest stratum in the Enochic corpus, dating back to the fourth century BCE. [*See* Calendars and Mishmarot.]

The fourth book of *1 Enoch,* the "Book of Dreams," recounts two Dream Visions. In the first the child Enoch foresees the Flood (chaps. 83–84). The second, which Enoch dreamed as a young man, is an extended allegorical account of the history of humanity from creation to the end time (chaps. 85–90, known as the "Animal Apocalypse"). It was written in 164 BCE, shortly after its last recorded historical event—Judah the Maccabee's battle at Beth Zur.

The Dream Visions are followed by a testamentary scene (chap. 91, which is related to 81.1–82.3), in which Enoch asks Methuselah to gather Enoch's children, so that they can hear his revelations about the future. This leads to the last major section of the corpus, the "Epistle" (chaps. 92–105), which Enoch wrote for the benefit of his "children" in future generations. It consists mainly of alternating strings of woe oracles against sinners and admonitions encouraging the righteous to have faith and hope and not to fear. Its Enochic character is indicated by its superscription (92.1) and by the "Apocalypse of Weeks" (93.1–10, 91.11–17), in which Enoch summarizes the history of humanity as he saw it recorded on the heavenly tablets (cf. 81.1–4). The "Epistle" is laced with references and allusions to events and phenomena that had been revealed to Enoch in heaven and in the hidden places of the earth according to the "Book of Watchers" and the "Animal Apocalypse." The "Epistle" was composed either at the beginning or toward the end of the second century BCE and reflects serious concern about the rich oppressing the poor and false teachers "leading many astray" and "perverting the eternal covenant."

To the "Epistle" is appended a narrative about Noah's

birth (chaps. 106–107) that depicts Noah as a savior figure who will renew the earth. Chapter 108 concludes the corpus with a reprise of earlier Enochic visions about the judgment and its consequences.

Manuscripts and Texts. Fragments of eleven Aramaic manuscripts from Cave 4 attest the presence at Qumran of all major parts of the corpus except the "Book of Parables" and chapter 108. These manuscripts, the fragments of which preserve only bits and pieces of the relevant sections, are the following (dates are those of their editor, J. T. Milik, 1976): Enoch[a] ("Book of Watchers," 200–150 BCE), Enoch[b] ("Book of Watchers," c.150 BCE); Enoch[c] ("Book of Watchers," "Animal Apocalypse," "Epistle [104]," "Noah's Birth," 30–1 BCE); Enoch[d] ("Book of Watchers," "Animal Apocalypse," 30–1 BCE); Enoch[e] ("Book of Watchers," "Animal Apocalypse," 100–50 BCE); Enoch[f] ("Animal Vision," 150–125 BCE); Enoch[g] (chapter 91 + "Epistle," c.50 BCE); and on separate manuscripts, portions of the "Book of Luminaries" and related material: Astronomical Enoch[a] (4Q208, c.200 BCE); Astronomical Enoch[b] (4Q209, early first century CE); Astronomical Enoch[c] (4Q210, c.50 BCE); Astronomical Enoch[d] (4Q211, 50–1 BCE).

The Greek translation of *1 Enoch* was completed by the end of the first century CE since it is attested by citations in the *Letter of Jude* and the *Epistle of Barnabas*. Parts of the Greek text are preserved in three manuscripts: the Chester Beatty papyrus (97.6–107.3, fourth century CE); Codex Panopolitanus (1.1–32.6, fifth or sixth century CE); Oxyrhynchus papyrus fragment 2069 (77.7–78.1, 78.8, 85.10–86.2, 87.1–3, fourth century CE), and knowledge of it, or its contents, is widely attested in the Greek and Latin church fathers of the second to fourth centuries. Part of the "Book of Watchers" is also preserved in the Chronography of George Syncellus (6.1–11.2, 15.8–16.1, ninth century), who draws on chronographers of the fourth century. The Ge'ez translation of *1 Enoch* was made in the fifth or sixth century and is included in the manuscripts of the Ethiopic Bible. Other textual witnesses to *1 Enoch* include a fragment of the Apocalypse of Weeks (93.3–8) from a sixth- or seventh-century Coptic manuscript and an abridged Latin version of *1 Enoch* 106.1–18 in an eighth-century manuscript.

Original Language. The Qumran Aramaic manuscript tradition resolves earlier debates about the language of composition, making it virtually certain that the "Book of Watchers," the "Book of Luminaries," the "Book of Dreams," the "Epistle," and the narrative about Noah's birth were composed in Aramaic. The wordplay on the verb *yarad* ("descend") in *1 Enoch* 6.5, which is impossible in Aramaic, may be a remnant of Hebrew tradition, but it scarcely indicates that any substantial part of chapters 6–11 was composed in Hebrew. The language of composition for the "Book of Parables" is generally thought to have been either Hebrew or Aramaic.

Worldview and Religious Thought. Blending the idioms and literary forms of Israelite prophecy and sapiential tradition, the Enochic authors presented an apocalyptic worldview that mediated spatial and temporal dualities by means of a revelation that had the power to save the chosen who lived in the last times and trusted in its message. In contrast to the present evil time and the troubling world of experience, the revelation transmitted knowledge about the future judgment and the hidden places of the universe where God and the angels lived and presided over the mechanisms of reward and punishment. The book *1 Enoch* makes scant reference to the Mosaic covenant and Torah and ties its authority to revelations that Enoch received when he penetrated the hidden spaces and obscure future long before the birth of Moses. Although the corpus of *Enoch* uses material from most of the books of the Hebrew scriptures, it never refers to them. Instead, it claims to be scripture itself, the written deposit of the wisdom that constitutes the eschatological community of the chosen.

Provenance and Relation to Qumran. Texts like *1 Enoch* 90.6–7 and 93.9–10 suggest that the Enochic authors were leaders in one segment of a broader reform movement that appealed for a return to righteous behavior based on revealed wisdom. *Jubilees* 23.17–31 and the *Testament of Moses* provide further evidence for the history of such a movement, though they identify revealed wisdom with the Mosaic Torah. The presence of *Enoch* manuscripts at Qumran and the similarity between *1 Enoch* 90.6–7 and 93.9–10, the Damascus Document (CD i), and the Rule of the Community from Cave 1 (1QS) viii.1–16 indicate that at least some members of the Qumran Community stood in historical continuity with the authors of the Enochic corpus. The large number of *Jubilees* manuscripts at Qumran and the community's emphasis on the revealed interpretation of the Mosaic Torah, however, complicate an attempt to reconstruct this historical continuity.

It is uncertain to what degree and when the Enochic corpus may have been considered scripture by the Qumran community. The "Book of Luminaries" informed calendrical calculation in Qumran, and other Enochic texts supported the eschatological convictions and apocalyptic worldview of the Qumran community, speaking to their anti-Temple attitudes and their self-understanding as the persecuted righteous. The dating of the manuscripts suggests that at the turn of the era, the "Book of the Luminaries" continued to be used, but that the popularity of the other works was waning, perhaps because of the community's emphasis on Mosaic Torah and its tying of its eschatology to an exegesis of the canonical prophets.

Related Texts. The influence of the Enochic tradition is attested by a range of other texts found at Qumran, but for the most part not composed there. The *Book of Giants,* (1Q23, 1Q24, 2Q26, 4Q203, 4Q530–533, 6Q8) continues the narrative tradition about the watchers and their progeny. A Noah fragment (1Q19) written in Hebrew is closely related to *1 Enoch* 9–10. *Jubilees* interpolates into its retelling of *Genesis* 1-*Exodus* 12 substantial pieces of the narrative in *1 Enoch* 6–11 and celebrates Enoch as "the first one to write a testimony." [See Jubilees, Book of.] The Genesis Apocryphon (1QapGen, 1Q20) elaborates the story of Noah's birth in *1 Enoch* 106–107. The Ages of Creation (4Q180–181), which may have been composed at Qumran, is an interpretation of the "Apocalypse of Weeks." The presence of these texts at Qumran indicates an interest in the concerns of the Enochic authors, while at the same time the non-Qumranic origin of these texts attests the influence of the Enochic writings outside of Qumran.

The "Book of Parables" is a special case. Noting that the Book of Parables is not represented at Qumran, J. T. Milik (1976, pp. 89–98) has argued that it is a Christian composition written in Greek from the third century CE. Most scholars, however, see the Book of Parables as a Jewish composition of the late first century BCE or the first century CE. Thus, the book reflects the ongoing life of the Enoch tradition, which had begun prior to the formation of the Qumran community and which was transmitted in Jewish circles outside of Qumran.

Value for the Study of Judaism and Christianity. The Enochic writings bear witness to the richness and complexity of Judaism in the Greco-Roman period and complement evidence from the late books of the Hebrew scriptures, the Apocrypha, the Qumran sectarian documents, the writings of Philo and Josephus, and later rabbinic texts. *1 Enoch*'s fusion of prophetic and sapiential traditions and its lack of interest in the Mosaic Torah attest a significant aspect of the religious development in Judaism of the Hellenistic period. Its combination of astronomy, cosmology, and eschatology presents a form of apocalypticism that is earlier and more variegated than that of *Daniel.* It also provides a context for the rise of the Qumran community.

The Enochic writings are crucial for an understanding of the history of early Christianity. Speculation about Jesus as the Son of Man derives from the interpretation of *Daniel* 7 found in *1 Enoch*'s "Book of Parables." The "Book of Watchers" and its explanation of the origins of evil and the demonic realm influenced major orthodox writers from the second to the fourth centuries and played an important role in Gnostic and Manichaean speculation.

Eventually the Enochic writings fell into disrepute in Mediterranean Christianity, probably because they were used by the heretics and because their mix of primordial myth and apocalypticism did not suit the philosophical interests of the orthodox fathers. But before this process of rejection was complete, Egyptian or Syrian missionaries brought the Enochic writings to Ethiopia, where they fit well with the worldview of these new Christians and were accepted into their Bible. In Ethiopia they are still cited in theological discourse, and thanks to the ancient biblical manuscripts preserved in Ethiopian libraries, they have shed light on the history of the communities that created, used, and then disavowed the Enochic texts.

[*See also* Apocalyptic Texts; Apocrypha and Pseudepigrapha; Enoch; *and* Giants, Book of.]

BIBLIOGRAPHY

Alexander, Philip. "3 (Hebrew Apocalypse of) Enoch." In *The Old Testament Pseudepigrapha,* edited by James H. Charlesworth, vol. 1, pp. 223–315. Garden City, N.Y. 1983.

Andersen, Francis I. "2 (Slavonic Apocalypse of) Enoch." In *The Old Testament Pseudepigrapha,* edited by James H. Charlesworth, vol. 1, pp. 91–221. Garden City, N.Y. 1983.

Argall, Randal A. *1 Enoch and Sirach: A Comparative Literary and Conceptual Analysis of the Themes of Revelation, Creation, and Judgment.* Society of Biblical Literature, Early Judaism and Its Literature, vol. 8. Atlanta, 1995. Focuses on issues that tie *1 Enoch* to a classical Jewish sapiential text and on nuances that distinguish the two.

Berger, Klaus. "Henoch." In *Reallexikon für Antike und Christentum,* edited by Ernst Dassmann, vol. 14, cols. 473–545. Stuttgart, 1988. Excellent and exhaustive encyclopedia article.

Black, Matthew. *The Book of Enoch or 1 Enoch: A New English Edition with Commentary and Textual Notes.* Studia in Veteris Testamenti Pseudepigrapha, vol. 7. Leiden, 1985. Only English translation that incorporates evidence from Ethiopic and Greek texts and Aramaic fragments.

Charles, R. H. *The Book of Enoch or 1 Enoch.* Oxford, 1912. Formerly the standard English translation. Though out of print and outdated by the publication of the Greek text of the Epistle and the Qumran fragments, and the appearance of new methods, its detailed introduction and learned notes are still instructive.

Isaac, Ephraim. "1 (Ethiopic Apocalypse of) Enoch." In *The Old Testament Pseudepigrapha,* edited by James H. Charlesworth, vol. 1, pp. 5–89. Garden City, N.Y. 1983. Sometimes idiosyncratic translation of one Ethiopic manuscript. Notes are text-critical and explanatory of translation. Only edition to take account of book's content in Ethiopian Christianity.

Knibb, Michael A. *The Ethiopic Book of Enoch: A New Edition in the Light of the Aramaic Dead Sea Fragments.* 2 vols. Oxford, 1978. Text of one Ethiopic manuscript with apparatus of variants from many others. Translation of that text with notes mainly about philological matters and Qumran fragments. Excellent introduction focused on texts and version. Translation also published in H. F. D. Sparks, ed. *The Apocryphal Old Testament.* Oxford, 1984.

Milik, J. T. *The Books of Enoch: Aramaic Fragments of Qumrân Cave 4.* Oxford, 1976. Masterful edition of Aramaic fragments with translation. Lengthy and learned discussion of issues related to the fragments and the Greek and Ethiopic versions. Transcriptions and translations, with lengthy restorations of lacunae, can give the impression that more text is preserved than is the case. Some historical conclusions are dubious.

Nickelsburg, George W. E. *Jewish Literature between the Bible and the Mishnah.* Philadelphia, 1981. Discussion of various parts of *1 Enoch* on pp. 46–55, 90–94, 145–151, 214–223. Notes and bibliographies reference vast literature on *1 Enoch.*

Nickelsburg, George W. E. "The Apocalyptic Construction of Reality in 1 Enoch." In *Mysteries and Revelations: Apocalyptic Studies since the Uppsala Colloquium,* edited by John J. Collins and James H. Charlesworth, pp. 51–64. Journal for the Study of the Pseudepigrapha, Supplement Series, vol. 9. Sheffield, 1991.

Nickelsburg, George W. E. "Son of Man." In *The Anchor Bible Dictionary,* edited by David Noel Freedman, vol. 6, pp. 137–150. New York, 1992. Use and connotations of the term in the Old Testament, Jewish literature, and the New Testament.

Tiller, Patrick A. *A Commentary on the Animal Apocalypse of 1 Enoch.* Society of Biblical Literature, Early Judaism, and Its Literature, vol. 4. Atlanta, 1993. Text, translation, and illuminating commentary on a difficult text.

VanderKam, James C. *Enoch and the Growth of an Apocalyptic Tradition.* Catholic Biblical Quarterly, Monograph Series, 16. Washington, D.C., 1984. Biblical and early Jewish texts in their ancient Near Eastern context.

VanderKam, James C. *Enoch: A Man for All Generations.* Columbia, S.C., 1996. Figure of Enoch in Old Testament, Jewish literature, New Testament, and second- to third-century Christian writings.

VanderKam, James C. "1 Enoch, Enochic Motifs, and Enoch in Early Christian Literature." *The Jewish Apocalyptic Heritage in Early Christianity,* edited by James C. VanderKam and William Adler, pp. 32–100. Compendia Rerum Iudaicarum ad Novum Testamentum, section 3, vol. 4. Minneapolis, 1996.

GEORGE W. E. NICKELSBURG

EPHRAIM AND MANASSEH. A number of sectarian texts use the terms *Ephraim and Manesseh,* evolving contemporizing exegesis of biblical verses. This type of exegesis exists in the *pesharim* and in a number of similar texts, for example in segments of the Damascus Document and in one of the paragraphs of Testimonia (4Q175). The terms *Ephraim* and *Manasseh* were chosen to designate the sects that were active at the end of the Second Temple period, because the sectarian authors knew many biblical verses mentioning the tension between Ephraim and Manasseh and Judah. The authors of the *pesharim* identified with the tribe of Judah and saw the sect to which they belonged as representing the Kingdom of Judah. The term *Ephraim* was used in their writings to designate the Pharisees, while the term *Manasseh* was used to designate the Saduccees.

From Pesher Nahum (4Q169) it is clear that Ephraim designates the Seekers after Smooth Things as the Pharisees. In this composition a *pesher* to *Nahum* 3.1 appears in which the author of the *pesher* identified Nineveh, the city against which the prophet Nahum prophesied, as the city of Ephraim, which is led by the Seekers after Smooth Things, who will go in the path of robbery and lies. In an interpretation of *Nahum* 3.4, the author of the *pesher* explained that Nineveh, meaning Ephraim, entices nations and families. Following this he specifies the nations and families enslaved by the people of Ephraim in whose "instruction [*Talmud*] is their falsehood." The use of the term *talmud* regarding the people of Ephraim, the Pharisees, already in the days of the Second Temple is more intriguing, even though it is possible to explain it not as a technical term but as denoting a method of instruction. In the *pesher* to *Nahum* 3.6–7 the author called the people who followed Ephraim the "simple of Ephraim." Likewise, he noted that when the honor of Judah is revealed (in this instance Judah is a phrase denoting the name of the sect to which the author of the *pesher* belonged), the simple ones who were fooled and followed Ephraim will return to the correct path and will join Judah. In the continuation, the author of the *pesher* revealed his opinion that he and his group are the "true Israel." [*See* Pesher Nahum; Pharisees; Seekers after Smooth Things.]

As noted, the author of Pesher Nahum identified Nineveh as the city of Ephraim, while he identified Thebes (No amon) as Manasseh. In the *pesher* to *Nahum* 3.8 we see that Manasseh had leaders and, if the restoration is correct, the heads of the city strengthened Manasseh. From an interpretation of *Nahum* 3.9 and 10 we see that the reign was that of Manasseh and that this kingdom will be disgraced in the final age. This is an additional indication that Pesher Nahum was composed after the conquest of Pompey (63 BCE). Definite evidence of this exists in the first column of this text, where it is noted that the rulers of the *Kittim*, meaning the Romans, will conquer Jerusalem.

In Pesher Psalms[a] (4Q171) there appears an interpretation of Psalm 37.15–16 in which the author of the *pesher* identified the poor and the destitute with the Teacher of Righteousness, while identifying the wicked who tried to harm the Teacher with the wicked of Ephraim and Manasseh. It cannot be determined from this paragraph that there was a difference between the wicked of Ephraim and the wicked of Manasseh; however, this distinction exists in Pesher Nahum and it is reasonable to assume that the author of the *pesher* to Psalm 35 utilized it as well. Pesher Psalms was composed after 63 BCE, because the author of the *pesher* explained that verse 16 established that the wicked of Ephraim and Manasseh were given into the hands of the nations; this most likely alludes to the conquest of Pompey. [*See* Pesher Psalms.]

In the first column of Pesher Nahum the author of the *pesher* explained that *Nahum* 2.12–13 addresses the events of the year 88 BCE. In this year the Seekers after Smooth Things invited Demetrius III Eukerus to conquer Judea. After Demetrius retreated from Judea, the Lion of Wrath, who clearly is Alexander Jannaeus (103–76 BCE), punished the Seekers after Smooth Things and hanged them alive upon a tree. Likewise, in Pesher Hosea[b] (4Q167) there is an interpretation of *Hosea* 5.14 that apparently speaks of the events of 88 BCE. Alexander Jannaeus is called the last priest in this *pesher*, and he punishes the Pharisees who had invited Demetrius to Judea. [*See* Alexander Janneus; Demetrius III Eukerus.]

In the Damascus Document (CD vii.9–14) as well there is a passage in which Ephraim's departure from Judah is emphasized; that is to say, the Pharisees are portrayed as the ones who secluded themselves from Judah. The term *Judah* designates in this instance the sectarians.

At the end of page thirteen and the beginning of page fourteen of the Damascus Document an additional interpretation is brought to *Isaiah* 7.17. In this *pesher* it is noted that very hard times arrived when the people of Ephraim departed from Judah; however, these hard times would not befall those faithful people who kept the oath and were loyal to the Lord, meaning the sectarians, but would only affect the simple who deviated from the path of the righteous.

It appears that in Testimonia as well the term *Ephraim* is utilized to mean Pharisees. In a pesher to *Joshua* 6.26 the author described the evil of Hyrcanus's sons, whom Hyrcanus appointed as rulers of Judea. The author of the *pesher* alluded to Aristobulus and Antigonus, the sons of John Hyrcanus, as harming the Pharisees and Judah, which most likely in this instance also designates the members of the sect of Qumran.

BIBLIOGRAPHY

Amousine, S. "Ephraïm et Manassé dans le Péshér de Nahum." *Revue de Qumrân* 4 (1963), 389–396.

Dupont-Sommer, A. "Lumières nouvelles sur l'arrière-plan historique des écrits de Qumran." *Eretz-Israel* 8 (1967), 27–28.

Eshel, H. "The Historical Background of the Pesher Interpreting Joshua's Curse on the Rebuilder of Jericho." *Revue de Qumrân* 15 (1992), 409–420.

Flusser, D. "Pharisäer, Sadduzäer und Essener im Pescher Nahum." In *Qumran: Wege der Forschung*, edited by Grözinger et al., pp. 121–166. Darmstadt, 1981.

Kister, M. "Biblical Phrases and Hidden Biblical Interpretations and *Pesharim*." In *The Dead Sea Scrolls: Forty Years of Research*, edited by D. Dinant and U. Rappaport, pp. 27–39. Leiden, 1992.

Schwartz, D. R. "To Join Oneself to the House of Judah." *Revue de Qumrân* 10 (1981), 257–266.

Yadin, Y. "Pesher Nahum (4Q pNahum) Reconsidered." *Israel Exploration Journal* 21 (1971), 1–12.

HANAN ESHEL

Translated from Hebrew by Daphna Krupp

EPICUREANS. Adherents of a philosophical school established by Epicurus (341–270 BCE) were fiercely loyal to their founders and fittingly called *Epicureans*. Epicurus, a native of Samos who was greatly influenced by the atomistic philosophy of Democritus, moved to Athens in 307/6 and purchased a house with a garden where he lived together with his followers. Because of this setting, his school became known in antiquity as "the Garden." Epicurus was a prolific author who wrote about three hundred works on papyrus rolls; unfortunately, only the following documents survive: a *Letter to Herodotus* (an epitome of his physics), a *Letter to Pythocles* (on astronomy and meteorology), a *Letter to Menoeceus* (an elementary summary of his ethics), a collection of forty moral maxims known as the *Kyriai doxai* or *Ratae sententiae* (*Principal Doctrines*), a similar collection of eighty-one short sayings known as the *Vatican Sayings*, and fragments of his *magnum opus, On Nature*.

Because so few of Epicurus's own writings survive, the works of three later Epicureans have received great attention. The first of these is the Latin poet Lucretius (c.94–55 BCE), who wrote a philosophical poem *On the Nature of Things* in six books. The second is Philodemus (c.110–c.40 BCE), a native of Gadara who was active at Herculaneum in southern Italy. A number of his works were discovered there among the carbonized papyrus scrolls found in the library of the Villa of the Papyri at Herculaneum and are slowly in the process of being (re)edited and translated. They include works on the history of philosophy, scientific method, aesthetics, rhetoric, theology (*On Piety* and *On the Gods*), and ethics. The third is Diogenes of Oenoanda, who erected a massive Greek inscription that contains the basic tenets of Epicureanism.

Accepting *ataraxia* ("imperturbability") as their ideal, Epicurus and his followers argued that the tranquillity of human life was disturbed by the irrational fear of the gods, of pain, and of death. To remove these fears they applied the *tetrapharmakos*, or "fourfold remedy," necessary for happiness. Succinctly stated, this remedy consists of the knowledge that "god presents no fears" (for the gods do not intervene in human affairs either to reward or to punish); "death occasions no worries" (for the soul, which is not immortal, disintegrates upon death and thus feels no sensation); "the good can be easily attained" (by adopting an Epicurean understanding of the nature of reality); and "pain can be readily endured" (for extreme pain is experienced only briefly, whereas chronic pain can be offset through carefully chosen pleasures). Furthermore, since involvement in political affairs is not conducive to living an undisturbed life, the Epicureans tended to withdraw from public life and pursue the goal of pleasure by living simple lives in the company of friends. The Epicureans were famous for their practice of friendship, which involved the ethical responsibility of admonishing fellow members who failed to live by the tenets of the group.

Josephus (*The Jewish War* 2.164–165; *Jewish Antiquities* 13.173, 18.16) depicts the Sadducees as Jewish Epicureans, denying the power of fate, the immortality of the soul, and all postmortem rewards and punishments. [*See* Josephus Flavius; Sadducees.] Although such beliefs do not coincide with those articulated in the Dead Sea

Scrolls, there are some points of comparison between the Epicureans and the community at Qumran. These include a withdrawal from society at large and entry into a close-knit alternative community that lived simply, carefully studying and transmitting the teachings of the founder as well as admonishing and punishing those members who failed to abide by the community's standards. Finally, the Epicureans' cultivation of friendship recalls Josephus's statement that the Essenes had the closest bonds of affection of any Jewish sect (*The Jewish War* 2.119).

BIBLIOGRAPHY

Arrighetti, G., ed./trans. *Epicuro. Opere*. 2nd ed. Biblioteca di cultura filosofica, vol. 41. Torino, 1973. Text of Epicurus's extant works, including the papyrus fragments of *On Nature*.

Asmis, Elizabeth. *Epicurus' Scientific Method*. Cornell University Studies in Classical Philosophy, vol. 92. Ithaca, 1984. The fundamental work on Epicurean scientific methodology.

Bailey, Cyril., ed./trans. *Epicurus: The Extant Remains*. Oxford, 1926. Text and translation, with commentary, of Epicurus's works, excluding the fragments.

Festugière, A. J. *Epicurus and His Gods*. Oxford, 1955. Classic introduction to Epicurean friendship and religion.

Frischer, Bernard. *The Sculpted Word: Epicureanism and Philosophical Recruitment in Ancient Greece*. Berkeley, 1982. Depiction of the Epicureans as an alternative community, with suggestions as to how they combined retreat from the dominant culture with recruitment strategies to win new converts.

Hengel, Martin. "Qumran and der Hellenismus." In *Judaica et Hellenistica: Kleine Schriften I*. pp. 258–294. Wissenschaftliche Untersuchungen zum Neuen Testament, 90. Tübingen, 1996. Careful comparison of the Qumran community with Hellenism, including the Epicureans.

Long, A. A. "Epicureans and Stoics." In *Classical Mediterranean Spirituality: Egyptian, Greek, Roman*, edited by A. H. Armstrong, pp. 135–153. World Spirituality, 15. New York, 1989. Basic comparison of Epicureans and Stoic theology.

Mitsis, Phillip. *Epicurus' Ethical Theory: The Pleasures of Invulnerability*. Cornell Studies in Classical Philosophy, vol. 48. Ithaca, 1988. Important treatment of Epicurean ethics.

Rist, J. M. *Epicurus: An Introduction*. Cambridge, 1972. An advanced introduction to Epicurean thought.

Usener, H., ed. *Epicurea*. Leipzig, 1887. Classic edition of texts and fragments, excluding the papyri.

JOHN T. FITZGERALD

EPIPHANIUS (c.315–403), bishop of Salamis. Born in Palestine, Epiphanius was trained by monks from an early age to uphold Nicene Christianity. When he was twenty years old, he founded a monastery at Eleutheropolis (Beth Guvrin) in Judea. Appointed bishop of Salamis in Cyprus in approximately 367 CE, he was strongly against any teachings other than Nicene Christianity, especially the teachings of Origen.

Epiphanius's major literary work, written in less than three years (between 374 and 377), is the *Panarion* ("Medicine Chest"). It is a massive fifteen-hundred-page treatment of eighty sects from ancient times to Epiphanius's own time. Since Epiphanius viewed these sects as wild beasts or serpents, he regarded his *Panarion* as the medicine chest that would provide the antidote for those who might be bitten (*Panarion* Proem I 1.2).

The first twenty sects discussed by Epiphanius are pre-Christian. These are divided into five main groups: Barbarism, Scythianism, Hellenism, Judaism, and Samaritanism. Judaism is further divided into seven sects (Scribes, Pharisees, Sadducees, Hemerobaptists, Ossaeans, Nasaraeans, and Herodians), while Samaritanism has four offshoots: Gorothenes, Sebuaeans, Essenes, and Dositheans (*Panarion* Proem I 3.1–5). For Epiphanius, then, the Essenes are a sect of the Samaritans, not of the Jews.

Epiphanius's treatment of the Essenes is very brief. He states that they agree with the other Samaritan sects in matters of circumcision, the Sabbath, and other points of the Law. The Sebuaeans, however, changed the dates of the feasts (Unleavened Bread, Passover, Shavu'ot, and Sukkot), but the Gorothenes did not. The Essenes who lived near the Sebuaeans went along with them, but Essenes elsewhere observed the normal feast days. Epiphanius also notes that the Essenes "kept to their primitive way of life without transgressing it in anything" (*Panarion* 10.1.1–12.1.2). As to the current state of the Essenes, Epiphanius writes that "there are no Essenes at all; it is as though they have been buried in darkness" (*Panarion* 20.3.4).

Epiphanius also mentions the Ossaeans, a sect of Judaism that originally came from the Transjordan region. He translates their name as "sturdy people" and describes them as hypocrites and skillful in their inventiveness (*Panarion* 19.1.1–3). He notes that they observe the Sabbath, circumcision, and keeping the whole Law, while forbidding the books of Moses (*Panarion* 19.5.1). Most of his description of the group is taken up with an unflattering portrait of Elxai, a man who joined the group later on, during the reign of the Roman Emperor Trajan (98–117). Epiphanius notes that there exists in his day a remnant of Ossaeans who no longer practice Judaism but have joined with a sect called the Sampsites (*Panarion* 20.3.2–4).

Evaluation of Epiphanius's description of the Essenes and the Ossaeans is difficult. Much of his information is derived from earlier sources (including Irenaeus, Hippolytus, Hegesippus, and Eusebius), and scholars agree that his descriptions of sects closer to his own time are far more reliable than the others, especially the pre-Christian sects. [*See* Hippolytus.] It is strange that he does not mention the Judean Essenes known by other ancient writers, and instead links the Essenes with the Samaritans. Josephus, however, states that the Essenes "have no one city, but many settle in each city" (*The Jewish War* 2.8.4).

[*See* Josephus Flavius.] Further, some biblical manuscripts from Qumran reflect the Samaritan recension (for example, paleo-Exodus^{m} [4Q22]) though without the explicitly Samaritan sectarian variants. In light of our limited knowledge of the history and scope of the Essenes, it would perhaps be wisest to defer judgment on the existence of a Samaritan branch of Essenes at some point in their history. [*See* Samaritans.]

As for the Ossaeans, some scholars have suggested that they were the original group of Essenes at Qumran, who then migrated to the Transjordan region after the destruction of Qumran by the Romans in 70 CE. There is, however, little corroborating evidence outside of Epiphanius for this hypothesis.

[*See also* Essenes.]

BIBLIOGRAPHY

Adam, Alfred. *Antike Berichte über die Essener.* 2d ed. Berlin, 1972. Greek text and brief commentary on all the ancient accounts of the Essenes.

Amidon, Philip R. *The Panarion of St. Epiphanius, Bishop of Salamis: Selected Passages.* Oxford, 1990. Most recent English translation of selected passages of the *Panarion.*

Black, Matthew. *The Scrolls and Christian Origins: Studies in the Jewish Background of the New Testament.* 1961; reprint, Chico, Calif., 1983. Though dated, Black's treatment of the reliability of Epiphanius's account of the Essenes and Ossaeans is still valuable.

Holl, Karl. *Epiphanius.* Erster Band. Griechischen christlichen Schriftsteller der ersten Jahrhunderte, Bd. 25. Leipzig, 1915. The standard Greek edition of Epiphanius's *Panarion,* currently under revision by Jürgen Dummer.

Quasten, Johannes. "Epiphanius of Salamis." In *Patrology* by Johannes Quasten, vol. 3, pp. 384–396. Westminster, Md., 1950–1960; reprint, 1983. Brief biography of Epiphanius and discussion of his writings.

Williams, Frank. *The Panarion of Epiphanius of Salamis.* Nag Hammadi and Manichaean Studies, 36. Leiden, 1987. Good introduction and English translation of Book I of the *Panarion.*

TODD S. BEALL

ESCHATOLOGICAL MIDRASHIM. *See* Catena; Florilegium.

ESCHATOLOGICAL PRIEST. *See* Messiahs.

ESCHATOLOGICAL PROPHET. *See* Messiahs.

ESCHATOLOGY, or the doctrine of "last things," embraces several complexes of motifs in the context of biblical studies, many of which deal with the future of Israel and the expectation of divine intervention for judgment and salvation. One strand of tradition emphasizes the cosmic character of this intervention and describes it in mythological language; another allows more room for human agency and envisages the restoration of Israel in more realistic terms. In the Hellenistic period, and especially in the apocalyptic literature, there arises the expectation of the judgment of individuals after death, resulting in everlasting salvation or damnation. This judgment may or may not entail bodily resurrection. The apocalyptic books (e.g., *Daniel, 1 Enoch*) frequently contain panoramic overviews of history, dividing it into a set number of periods (seventy weeks of years, four kingdoms, etc.) and culminating in a catastrophic judgment that entails the end of this world. All these motifs and ideas play a part in the Dead Sea Scrolls.

The End of Days in the Bible. It will be useful at the outset to highlight two biblical motifs that establish a context for eschatological expectations. The first is the "End of Days" (*aḥarit ha-yamim*). The second is the "end" (*qets*) as in the day of judgment or the day of the Lord.

The phrase *aḥarit ha-yamim* probably originally meant "in the course of time," or "in future days." A cognate expression with this sense is found in Akkadian. The phrase appears in the Pentateuch in *Genesis* 49.1 (the blessing of Jacob) and *Numbers* 24.14 (Balaam's oracle). Both passages contain archaic prophetic texts, which originally referred to the future in an unspecified but limited sense, but were interpreted in the postexilic period so that they were now understood to refer to a final, definitive phase of history. In the Prophets, the "End of Days" implies a definitive transformation of Israel in the distant future. Usually, the reference is to the time of salvation (e.g., *Is.* 2, *Mi.* 4), but in *Ezekiel* and *Daniel* the concept was broadened to include not only the age of salvation but also the drama that leads up to it. This broader usage is continued in the Dead Sea Scrolls.

The expectation of an end is also found in the Prophets, however, with reference to a more specific, decisive event, the day of judgment. When the prophet Amos proclaims that "the end has come upon my people Israel" (*Am.* 8.2), he speaks of the end of Israel as an independent kingdom, not of the end of the world. He also speaks of this event as "the day of the Lord," which would be darkness and not light (*Am.* 5.18–20). Other prophets expanded this concept into a day of cosmic judgment (*Is.* 2.10–22, 13.9–13; *Zep.* 1.14–16). The motif of the day of the Lord usually places the emphasis on destruction, but it also entailed the exaltation of the Lord and deliverance for the faithful. The double aspect of the day of judgment is clear in *Daniel* 12.1, which promises both a time of anguish and deliverance for "your people." Deliverance in *Daniel* entails resurrection of the dead.

There was another development in the *Book of Daniel* of momentous importance for later tradition. Here, for the first time, we find an attempt to calculate the time of the end, grounded in an elaborate schema that is spelled out in *Daniel* 9, where Jeremiah's prophecy that Jerusalem would lie desolate for 70 years is reinterpreted as 70 weeks of years, or 490 years. This period could also be interpreted as ten jubilees. (For the notion of jubilee, see *Leviticus* 25.) The last week of years, or seven-year period, was initiated by the murder of the high priest Onias, and the midpoint of the last week was marked by the "installation that makes desolate" in the Temple, an event that is usually dated to December 167 BCE (*Dn.* 9.26–27). The conclusion to be drawn from Daniel's prophecy, then, is that the end would come three and a half years after the profanation of the Temple, some time in the summer of 163 BCE. The same chronology is implied in *Daniel* 7.25, which gives the length of the persecution as "a time and times and half a time." Daniel makes more specific attempts to calculate the precise number of days until the end in *Daniel* 8.14 and 12.11–12.

One other development in apocalyptic eschatology should be noted before turning to the Dead Sea Scrolls. The "Apocalypse of Weeks" (*1 Enoch* 91.11–17, 93.1–10) is a revelation in the name of Enoch, written about the time of the Maccabean Revolt. Here, as in *Daniel*, history is divided into weeks, presumably weeks of years. At the end of the seventh week, "the chosen righteous from the eternal plant of righteousness will be chosen," but history does not come to an end. In the eighth week a sword is given to the righteous, to execute judgment. In the ninth, "the righteous judgment will be revealed to the whole world . . . and the world will be written down for destruction." Finally, in the tenth week, there will be a great judgment, the old heaven will be taken away, and a new heaven revealed. Thereafter, "there will be many weeks without number." Even though this apocalypse envisages the end of this world, the end is not exactly a fixed point. Rather, we have an eschatological scenario in which there is a series of ends as the old order passes away and is replaced by the new.

The End of Days in the Dead Sea Scrolls. Each of the traditions we have considered so far plays an important part in the eschatology of the Dead Sea sect. The expression *aḥarit ha-yamim* occurs more than thirty times in the Dead Sea Scrolls (Steudel, 1993). The Miqtsat Maʿasei ha-Torah (MMT; 4Q394–399) declares that "this is the End of Days," and the Rule of the Congregation (1Q28a), one of the supplements to the Rule of the Community from Qumran Cave 1, is introduced as "the rule for all the congregation of Israel in the End of Days." There are two references in the Damascus Document. The great majority of the occurrences, however, are found in exegetical literature, in the *pesharim*, and in midrashic texts such as the Melchizedek scroll (11Q13) and especially the so-called eschatological midrash (the Florilegium, 4Q174; the Catena[a], 4Q177), which contains approximately one-third of the references. Surprisingly, the phrase does not occur in the Rule of the Community, Hodayot, or the War Scroll, a manuscript of the War Rule.

The End of Days in the scrolls has two aspects. It is a time of testing, and it is a time of at least incipient salvation. The time of testing is explicit in the Florilegium: "it is a time of refining that co[mes . . .] . . . as is written in the *Book of Daniel*, the prophet . . . " In the context of *Daniel*, the time of refining is the period immediately before Michael rises in victory, although arguably it may continue into the time of distress that follows Michael's rise in *Daniel* 12.1. Several other passages corroborate the view of the End of Days as a time of testing. Catena[a], which may be part of the same document, speaks of testing and refining the men of the community at the End of Days. Pesher Habakkuk refers to traitors and ruthless ones at the End of Days (1QpHab ii.5–6; cf. 4Q169 3–4.ii.2). But the Florilegium also refers to the temple that the Lord will establish with his hands at the End of Days, in contrast to the "temple of men" (which serves in the interim) and to the Branch of David who will arise with the Interpreter of the Law at the End of Days.

The positive aspects of the End of Days are clearly still in the future from the perspective of the authors of the scrolls. There is no suggestion anywhere that the Messiahs have already come. Many scholars hold, however, that the time of testing was already being experienced by the sect (Brooke, Steudel). The language of the scrolls is often ambiguous; for example, the phrase "a time of refining that co[mes . . .]" can mean grammatically either that the time has come or that it is coming. Annette Steudel has argued that it must mean that the time has already come. Pesher Psalms[a–b] (4Q171, 4Q173, respectively), speak of attempts to lay hands on the Teacher of Righteousness at the time of refining, and Steudel assumes that the Teacher was already dead when the *pesher* was written. If she is right, we must assume that the End of Days entails two phases, the time of testing and the coming of the Messiahs, and that the first phase had already begun.

Only one text in the Qumran corpus says explicitly that the End of Days has already begun. This is the Miqtsat Maʿasei ha-Torah (4Q394–399), but its presentation of the End of Days is exceptional in a number of respects. Miqtsat Maʿasei ha-Torah from Qumran Cave 4 C 13–15 cites *Deuteronomy* 30.1–3: "And it is written 'and it shall come to pass, when all these things [be]fall you,' at the End of Days, the blessings and the curses, ['then you will take] it to hea[rt] and you will return unto Him with all your heart and with all your soul,' at the end. . . . " The text goes on to say that "we know that some of the blessings and the curses have [already] been fulfilled as it is written in the book of Moses," but the reference is apparently to the blessings experienced under David and Solomon and the curses experienced from the time of Jeroboam to the Babylonian Exile. The fulfillment of these curses and blessings, then, is not itself part of the End of Days and is hardly proof that the End of Days is at hand. Nonetheless, the Miqtsat Maʿasei ha-Torah continues: "And this is the End of Days when they will return to Isra[el]." Thus, the point is not that signs of the End of Days have recently begun to appear, but that the time of decision is now. The Miqtsat Maʿasei ha-Torah is exceptional among the Dead Sea Scrolls insofar as it is addressed to someone outside the sectarian community. Consequently, it makes no attempt to argue from the experience of the sect that prophecy is being fulfilled, since the recipient of the document could not be expected to accept such an argument.

The precise limits of the End of Days are never clearly defined in the scrolls. The ambiguity of the situation may be illustrated with reference to the opening column of the Damascus Document. There we are told that at the time of the Babylonian Exile, God saved a remnant from Israel. Then, "in the age of wrath, 390 years after having delivered them up into the hands of Nebuchadnezzar, king of Babylon, he visited them, and caused a plant root to spring from Israel and from Aaron." It is not clear, however, whether the whole 390 years qualify as "the age of wrath" or whether that age begins only after 390 years. The phrase "age of wrath" (*qets ḥaron*) involves a wordplay on "the last age" (*qets ha-ʾaḥaron*), a phrase from the *pesharim*, which can scarcely be distinguished from the "End of Days" and must also be related to the "last generation" (*dor ha-ʾaḥaron*) of the Damascus Document (CD i.12). This is the period when "Belial is loosed against Israel" (CD iii.13). It is hardly possible that the End of Days was thought to have begun as early as the Babylonian Exile, but its beginning could well have coincided with the emergence of the sect. As I have noted already, the period extends to the coming of the Messiahs, which clearly remains in the future according to all the Dead Sea Scrolls. The Rule of the Congregation (1Q28a) assumes that the conditions of human existence are not greatly altered by the coming of the Messiahs (Schiffman, 1989). Provision must still be made for the education of children and for community meals and regulations. One of the tasks of the princely Messiah, however, was to wage war on the *Kittim*, the gentile enemies of Israel (Collins, 1995, pp. 49–73). This war is included in the End of Days in Pesher Isaiah (4Q161). The phrase is never applied, however, to the conditions that ensue after the eschatological war. We should perhaps allow for some variation in the way the motif is used, but in general we may agree with Steudel (1993, p. 231) that the End of Days is "the last period of time, directly before the time of salvation." [*See* Kittim.]

There are also indications in the scrolls, however, that the Dead Sea sect envisaged a more specific end point (cf. 1QS iv.18–19). This end was not in the vague and distant future but was expected at a particular time in the sect's history. There are primarily two pieces of evidence that point to such a specific expectation, one passage in Pesher Habakkuk and another at the end of the Damascus Document.

Pesher Habakkuk comments on *Habakkuk* 2.3 as follows:

> For there is yet a vision concerning the appointed time. It testifies to the end time [*qets*], and it will not deceive. The interpretation of it is that the last end time [*qets ha-ʾaḥaron*] will be prolonged, and it will be greater than anything of which the prophets spoke, for the mysteries of God are awesome. If it tarries, wait for it, for it will surely come, and it will not be late. The interpretation of it concerns the men of truth, those who observe the Law, whose hands do not grow slack in the service of the truth, when the last end time is drawn out for them, for all of God's end times will come according to their fixed order. (1QpHab vii.6–13)

(This passage from Habakkuk is also cited several times in *Daniel* [*Dn*. 8.17, 10.14b, 11.27, 11.35, 12.12] to make the point that the vision will only be fulfilled at its appointed time.)

The prolongation of the end time is not merely a theoretical possibility; it is the experience of the community, for which the author seeks an explanation in the prophetic text. It is reasonable to infer, then, that the end was expected shortly before the *pesher* was written. While we do not know the exact date of the *pesher*, all indicators point to the middle of the first century BCE. The manuscript is dated on paleographic grounds to the Herodian period (F. M. Cross, *The Ancient Library of Qumran and Modern Biblical Studies*, Garden City, N.Y., 1961, p. 120, n.20), but it is not an autograph, and it contains copyist errors. The *Kittim* in this document are clearly the Romans, who "sacrifice to their standards" (1QpHab vi.3–4). The prediction that the wealth and booty of the "last priests of Jerusalem will be given into the hand of the army of the *Kittim*" (ix.6–7) suggests that the conquest of Jerusalem by the Romans (63 BCE) either was imminent or had already taken place. Pesher Nahum (4Q169) refers to events in the early first century BCE, down to the time of Hyrcanus II (63–40 BCE) and Aristobulus II (67–63 BCE). If we assume that these *pesharim* were written at about the same time, a date around the middle of the century is plausible.

The other witness to the expectation of an end at a specific time, the Damascus Document, also points to a date toward the middle of the first century BCE. In the Damascus Document (CD xx.14) we are told that "from the day of the ingathering of the Unique Teacher until the destruction of all the men of war who turned back with the Man of Lies there shall be about forty years." This calculation is evidently related to the figures found in column i of the same document. The time from the Babylonian Exile to the emergence of the sect is 390 years. Then the first members wander in blindness for 20 years until the arrival of the Teacher of Righteousness. If we allow the conventional figure of 40 years for the Teacher's career, this brings us to 450 years. Forty years after his death would then bring us to 490 years, the time stipulated in the *Book of Daniel*. That this figure was important for the eschatology of the sect is clear from the Melchizedek scroll (11Q13): "Now the D[ay of Expia]tion i[s the en]d of the tenth [ju]bilee, when expiation (will be made) for all the sons of [light and] for the m[e]n of the lot of Mel[chi]zedek." The end of the tenth jubilee is of course the culmination of 70 weeks of years, or 490 years.

It appears then that the Dead Sea sect expected the fulfillment of Daniel's prophecy about forty years after the death of the Teacher of Righteousness. Unfortunately, we do not know when this took place. A date around the end of the second century BCE seems likely, but we must allow a generous margin of error. If the Teacher died about 100 BCE, this would point to an end about 60 BCE, which would be highly compatible with the evidence of Pesher Habakkuk.

Some scholars believe they can reconstruct the date at which the end was expected with greater specificity (Steudel, 1993, pp. 233–240). Fundamental to any such attempt is the assumption that the figure of 390 years in the Damascus Document, for the period from the Babylonian Exile to the rise of the sect, is reliable chronological information. Two possible calculations have been proposed. Assuming the modern chronology of the exile and postexilic period, we arrive at the year 197/196 BCE for the emergence of the plant root from Aaron and Israel and 177/176 BCE for the advent of the Teacher of Righteousness. It has been pointed out, however, that some ancient Jewish authors calculated a later date for the exile and a shorter postexilic period. The Jewish chronographer Demetrius, who wrote in Egypt in the late third century BCE, calculated that there were 338 years between the Babylonian Exile of Judah (587/586 BCE) and Ptolemy IV (222 BCE) rather than 364 or 365 years as modern historians reckon (Antti Laato, "The Chronology in the Damascus Document of Qumran," *Revue de Qumrân* 15 [1992], 605–607). This adjustment of twenty-six years, would make possible the emergence of the Teacher of Righteousness at about 150 BCE, shortly after the usurpation of the high priesthood by Jonathan (Hasmonean), which many scholars have supposed to be the occasion for the secession of the Qumran sect. If we then allow forty years for the career of the Teacher and a further interval of forty years following his death, we conclude that the end was expected about 70 BCE.

These suggestions are intriguing and are not impossible; however, they are unreliable. While there is evidence for speculation on biblical chronology, such as we find in Demetrius, in such document as *Jubilees* and the Aramaic Apocryphon of Levi, there is no actual evidence that the Damascus Document used the chronology of Demetrius. The argument is simply that this chronology would support a popular hypothesis about the origin of the Dead Sea set—a hypothesis far from established fact. Besides, the chronological data attributed to Demetrius are confused and contradictory. The figure of forty years for the career of the Teacher of Righteousness is only a round number. The same must be said for the 390 years of the Damascus Document, which is a symbolic number for the duration of the desolation, derived from *Ezekiel* 4.5. The attempt to derive chronological information from it rests on a shaky foundation. It is no more likely to be accurate than the 490 years in *Daniel* 9.

This is not to deny that the sectarians of Qumran had a specific time in mind for the coming of the eschaton. In order to arrive at that date, however, they did not need to verify every stage of the chronology. It was sufficient that they remember how much time had passed since the death of the Teacher of Righteousness. Even the Damascus Document did not claim that divine intervention would come exactly forty years after that event, but an approximate number was enough to fuel lively expectation. There is no evidence that anyone at Qumran ever counted the days, in the manner of the *Book of Daniel*, or that their expectation ever focused on a specific day or year. Nonetheless, as the years passed, they were aware that the end time was prolonged. "About forty years" could not be extended indefinitely. The lack of a specific date, however, mitigated the disappointment, and made it easier for the community to adapt to the postponement of their expectations.

The Nature of the End. The texts are not as explicit as we might wish about what was to happen forty years after the death of the Teacher of Righteousness. The Damascus Document still expected the coming of the Messiahs, so this is one obvious possibility. Their coming is described as "the age of visitation" when the unfaithful will be put to the sword (CD xix.10). The Damascus Document speaks explicitly of the destruction of the men of war who turned back with the Men of the Lie. The Damascus Document does not indicate, however, how long the judgment would take. The Rule of the Community from Qumran Cave 1 speaks of "an end to the existence of injustice" (1QS iv.18). The Melchizedek scroll says that after the tenth jubilee is the time for "Melchizedek's year of favor" when he will exact "the ven[geance] of E[l's] judgments" (11Q13 ii.13). It is also "the day [of salvation about w]hich [God] spoke [through the mouth of Isa]iah the prophet" (11Q13 ii.15). From these passages it is clear that the community expected a day of judgment, as foretold by the prophets. Other passages, however, indicate that a lengthier process was envisaged. The day of salvation in the Melchizedek scroll is the occasion of the arrival of the herald, the "anointed of the spirit" or eschatological prophet. We might expect that he would be followed by the messiahs of Aaron and Israel (cf. 1QS ix.11) and then by the eschatological war, which takes forty years according to the War Scroll.

It is not apparent, however, that all these texts were ever synthesized into a coherent system. The Melchizedek scroll does not speak of messiahs (except the "anointed of the spirit"), and the Rule of the Community from Qumran Cave 1 does not mention the tenth jubilee. Different texts provided different models for the end time or highlighted different aspects of it. Some of these, such as the expectation of messiahs, envision the restoration of a utopian Israel on earth. Other aspects, such as the dualistic conflict between the archangel Michael and Belial, have a cosmic and supernatural character. These different emphases cannot be clearly separated in the Qumran documents. The major rule books (Rule of the Community, Damascus Document, War Rule) all allude both to messianic figures and to the conflict with Belial. Presumably, these different aspects were regarded as complementary, but there is no evidence that they were ever synthesized into a consistent doctrine.

While the various models of eschatology found in the scrolls do not yield a fully coherent system, some ideas may be characterized as typical of the sect. One such idea is the expectation of an eschatological war. This is described elaborately in the War Rule, although even the War Scroll found in Qumran Cave 1 (1QM) combines traditions that are in some tension, if not contradictory. But the final war is also alluded to in the *pesharim*, Hodayot, the Rule of the Community, and other texts. A messianic prince would play an important role in this war (4Q285, 4Q161). There was also place for an angelic deliverer, variously identified as Michael, Melchizedek, or the Prince of Light. These deliverers might be accented differently in different documents; the crucial affirmation was that God would put an end to wickedness.

There are surprisingly few descriptions of the state that was to follow the eschatological war. The War Scroll mentions the rule of Michael among the angels and the kingdom of Israel on earth (1QM xvii.7–8), and this is in accordance with the *Book of Daniel*. There are frequent references to the blessed state of the elect after death, but references to resurrection are remarkably rare, and the few clear texts are of uncertain provenance.

Eschatology of the Essenes. It is interesting in this regard to compare what we find in the scrolls with the descriptions of the eschatology of the Essenes, with whom the Dead Sea sect is most frequently identified. We have, in fact, two sharply different accounts of Essene eschatology. According to Josephus, "It is a firm belief among them that although bodies are corruptible, and their matter unstable, souls are immortal and endure forever" (*The Jewish War* 2.154–158). He goes on to compare the ideas of the Essenes to those of the Greeks with respect to reward and punishment after death, comparing the abode of the righteous dead with the Islands of the Blessed. He says nothing about any transformation of this world. Hippolytus of Rome, in contrast, writing more than a century later, claims that "the doctrine of the resurrection has also derived support among them, for they acknowledge both that the flesh will rise again, and that it will be immortal, in the same manner as the soul is already imperishable." He goes on to compare Essene and Greek concepts of eschatology in terms very similar to those used by Josephus, including the comparison with the Islands of the Blessed. In addition to the postmortem rewards and punishments, however, Hippolytus allows for "both a judgement and a conflagration of the universe" (*Refutation of All Heresies* 27).

There is good evidence that Josephus and Hippolytus used a common source; Hippolytus was not dependent on Josephus for his information. Some of the statements that are peculiar to Hippolytus seem to be due to confusion; he says that the Essenes are also called Zealots and Sicarii (*Refutation of All Heresies* 26). He may preserve some information that was omitted by Josephus. The idea of a conflagration of the universe finds striking support in a passage in Hodayot[b] (1Q35 xi.29–32; formerly iii.29–32). This is, however, the only passage in the scrolls that attests to such a belief, so it does not appear to have played any central role in the expectations of the sect.

Hippolytus's claim that the Essenes affirmed bodily resurrection receives little support from the Dead Sea Scrolls. While the belief in resurrection is prominent in the apocalypses of Enoch and Daniel, which were also found at Qumran, only two of the previously unknown texts clearly affirm such a belief. These are the Messianic Apocalypse ("He will . . . revive the dead"; 4Q521 2.ii.12) and Pseudo-Ezekiel[a] and Pseudo-Ezekiel[b] (4Q385, 4Q386). Neither can be identified unambiguously as a product of the Dead Sea sect. Even if they are sectarian compositions, the evidence suggests that resurrection was only a minority belief at Qumran and was not typical of the eschatology of the sect. The sectarians hoped for fellowship with the angels and for "eternal joy in life without end," while they condemned the wicked to "destruction by the fire of the dark regions" (1QS iv). The resurrection of the body did not figure prominently in their hopes. Josephus's account, although admittedly cast in Hellenistic terms, corresponds more closely to the typical expectations of the scrolls.

It must be admitted, however, that neither Josephus's nor Hippolytus's account of the Essenes corresponds completely with what is found in the scrolls. No ancient account of the Essenes mentions the expectation of messiahs nor the prospect of an eschatological war. This discrepancy is not fatal to the view that the Dead Sea sect was Essene. The source on which Josephus and Hippolytus drew was evidently composed for a Hellenistic audience, and the author may have judged that some aspects of Essene belief were better ignored. But if the scrolls contain firsthand evidence of Essene views, then the accounts of the Greek authors (Philo, Josephus, and Hippolytus) are less than fully reliable.

[*See also* Apocalyptic Texts; Catena; Damascus Document; Essenes; Florilegium; Hodayot; Messiahs; Miqtsat Ma'asei ha-Torah; Pesher Habakkuk; Resurrection; Rule of the Community; Rule of the Congregation; Teacher of Righteousness; *and* War of the Sons of Light against the Sons of Darkness.]

BIBLIOGRAPHY

Brooke, George J. *Exegesis at Qumran: 4QFlorilegium in Its Jewish Context*. Journal for the Study of the Old Testament Supplement Series, 29. Sheffield, 1985. Analysis of the Florilegium (4Q174).

Collins, John J. *The Apocalyptic Imagination*. New York, 1984. Overview of Jewish apocalyptic literature, with a chapter on the eschatology of the Qumran sect.

Collins, John J. *Daniel*. Hermeneia. Minneapolis, 1993. Detailed commentary on a book that exercised profound influence at Qumran, with extensive use of Qumran material.

Collins, John J. *The Scepter and the Star*. Anchor Bible Reference Library. New York, 1995. Analysis of the messianic texts from Qumran.

Collins, John J. *Apocalypticism in the Dead Sea Scrolls*. London, 1997.

Kobelski, Paul J. *Melchizedek and Milchireša'*. Catholic Biblical Quarterly Monograph Series, 10. Washington, D.C., 1981. Edition of Melchizedek and related texts with commentary.

Puech, Émile. *La croyance des Esséniens en la vie future: Immortalité, résurrection, vie éternelle?* 2 vols. Études bibliques, 21–22. Paris, 1993. Comprehensive study of all possible references to life after death, not only in the scrolls but also in the Bible and pseudepigrapha.

Schiffman, Lawrence H. *The Eschatological Community of the Dead Sea Scrolls*. Society of Biblical Literature Monograph Series, 38. Atlanta, 1989. Analysis of the Rule of the Congregation (1Q28a).

Steudel, Annette. " 'End of Days' in the Texts from Qumran." *Revue de Qumrân* 16 (1993), 225–246. Comprehensive study of the expression "End of Days."

Steudel, Annette. *Der Midrasch zur Eschatologie aus der Qumrangemeinde (4QMidrEschat^{a-b})*. Studies on the Texts of the Desert of Judah, 13. Leiden, 1994. Analysis of the Florilegium (4Q174) and Catena^{a} (4Q177), which she takes to be one work.

Wacholder, Ben Zion. "Chronomessianism: The Timing of Messianic Movements and the Calendar of Sabbatical Cycles." *Hebrew Union College Annual* 46 (1975), 201–218. A study of chronological systems on which attempts to calculate the end were based.

Wise, Michael O. "The Eschatological Vision of the Temple Scroll." *Journal of Near Eastern Studies* 49 (1990), 155–172. A provocative thesis about the foundational impulses of the Dead Sea sect.

JOHN J. COLLINS

ESSENE GATE. In the description of the walls of Jerusalem prior to the city's fall in 70 CE, Josephus also tells about the western and southern sections of the First Wall (*The Jewish War* 5.145); starting from the Hippicus tower (the approximate site of the present-day citadel), the First Wall passed by a place called Bethso (q.v.) to the Essene Gate.

The likeliest candidate for this gate is the one excavated in 1894–1895 by F. J. Bliss and A. C. Dickie and reexcavated with its surroundings between 1977 and 1988 by Bargil Pixner, Doron Chen and Shlomo Margalit. The gate, built with well-cut ashlar stones, is 2.66 meters (9 feet) wide and lies close to the southwestern corner of the city. Its earliest stage (out of three) is to be dated to the Herodian period, an intrusion into the Hasmonean wall.

A gate in the Western Wall unearthed between 1973 and 1978 by Magen Broshi and Shimon Gibson was identified by Yigael Yadin as the Essene Gate. Yadin's suggestion is hard to accept since this seems to have been a private entrance to Herod's palace and not a public thoroughfare.

It is highly plausible that the Essene Gate got its name from a nearby Essene neighborhood. However, no archaeological remains were unearthed in the vicinity of the gate that would show that this area was settled by sectarians (but it is doubtful that nonmonastic Essene residences differed from those of other Jews). The existence of an Essene community in or near Jerusalem was proven recently by the discovery of a large cemetery, the tombs of which are very similar to those of Qumran. In this cemetery, 4.5 kilometers (3.8 miles) to the southwest of the Essene Gate in the southwestern corner, B. Zissu excavated in 1996 over forty shaft graves totally different from the normal Second Commonwealth burials but of great similarity to those dug at Qumran. [*See* Cemeteries.]

[*See also* Archaeology; Qumran, *article on* Archaeology.]

BIBLIOGRAPHY

Broshi, Magen, and Shimon Gibson. "Excavations along the Western and Southern Walls of the Old City of Jerusalem." In *Ancient Jerusalem Revealed*, edited by Geva Hillel, pp. 147–155. Jerusalem, 1994.

Pixner, Bargil. "The History of the 'Essene Gate' Area." *ZDPV* 105 (1989), 96–104. Includes comprehensive bibliography.

Pixner, Bargil, Doron Chen, and Shlomo Margalit. "Mount Zion: The Gate of the Essenes Re-excavated." *Zeitschrift des Deutschen Palaestina-Vereins* 105 (1989), 85–95.

Riesner, Rainer. "Josephus' 'Gate of the Essenes' in Modern Discussion." *Zeitschrift des Deutschen Palaestina-Vereins* 105 (1989), 105–109. Includes comprehensive bibliography.

Yadin, Yigael. *The Temple Scroll: The Hidden Law of the Dead Sea Sect*. London, 1985. See pages 180–185. Includes comprehensive bibliography.

Zissu, B. "Field Graves at Beit Zafafa: Archaeological Evidence for the Essene Community" (in Hebrew). In *New Studies on Jerusalem, Proceedings of the Second Conference*, edited by A. Faust, pp. 32–40. Ramat Gan, 1996.

MAGEN BROSHI

ESSENES were members of a Jewish sect existing from the second century BCE to the end of the first century CE. This sect is described by various Greek and Latin writers, the most important of whom are Philo, Josephus, and Pliny. These ancient testimonies provide an enlightening and sometimes contradictory account of the customs and beliefs of the Essenes. Following the discovery of the Dead Sea Scrolls in 1947, most scholars have identified the community responsible for the scrolls as Essene. If that identification is correct, then the sectarian texts of the Dead Sea Scrolls provide much additional information about the Essenes at Qumran and elsewhere.

Etymology. The name of the sect is given variously in the classical sources. In Greek the group is called *Essenoi* (by Josephus [fourteen times], Dio, Hippolytus, and Epiphanius) or *Essaioi* (by Philo, Hegesippus, and Josephus [six times]); in Latin it is called *Esseni* (by Pliny). Epiphanius also mentions a group he called the *Ossenoi*, but the relationship of this group to the Essenes is unclear, especially because Epiphanius also mentions a different group he calls the *Essenoi*. [*See* Epiphanius.]

The etymology of the name remains difficult, although there have been many proposals. Philo himself suggests that it may be related to the similar-sounding Greek word *hosiotes*, "holiness," and later calls the group *hosioi*, "holy ones" (*Every Good Man Is Free* 12.75; 13.91). But it is more likely that the name had a Semitic origin. Others (for example, Cross, 1995) regard the name as derived from the Aramaic *ḥasayya'*, the equivalent of Hebrew *ḥasidim*, "pious ones." If this identification is correct, it might indicate that the Essenes are related to the Hasideans (*ḥasidim*; Greek *asidaioi*) mentioned in *1 Maccabees* 2.42, 7.13, and *2 Maccabees* 14.6. One problem with this proposal is that the root *ḥsy* does not generally mean "pious" in the Palestinian dialect (although a passage in the Aramaic Levi^{b} [4Q213a] does contain the word with this sense). [*See* Hasideans.]

Many suggestions for the etymology of "Essene" have been proffered in light of the Qumran material. Although none is without difficulties, three of the more possible are as follows:

1. It has been derived from the Hebrew word *'etsah* meaning "council" or "party" in Qumran literature. The Essenes would thus be "Men of the Council" (so Dupont-Sommer). But the linguistic derivation is problematic, and it seems more likely that the sect would rather have chosen *yaḥad* ("community").
2. It has been linked to the common Hebrew verb *'asah*, meaning "to do, bear, bring forth," with the idea that the Essenes are the "doers" of the Law (e.g., Pesher Habakkuk [1QpHab vii.11]) who will "bring forth" redemption (Goranson). Though ingenious, there is no explicit evidence for this linkage.
3. Others have suggested that the term is derived from the Aramaic *asayya'*, "healers" (so Vermes, 1978), which would fit with Josephus's statement that the Essenes sought out medicinal roots and stones for healing diseases (*The Jewish War* 2.136). This might also tie in nicely with Philo's description of the Therapeutae (lit., healers) and his statement that the Essenes are especially devout in the *therapeutai* of God (*Every Good Man Is Free* 12.75). But in the context *therapeutai* probably means "service" rather than "healers," and as mentioned above, Philo himself gives a quite different explanation of the meaning of "Essene." Furthermore, healing does not appear to be so characteristic of the group that it would provide the basis for its name. [*See* Therapeutae.]

Sources. Unlike the Pharisees and Sadducees, the Essenes are not mentioned in the New Testament or in Talmudic literature. Information concerning the group is limited to the classical sources, possibly supplemented by the Dead Sea Scroll material if the Qumran community was, in fact, Essene. Since this identification is not accepted by all scholars, it is best to consider first the information about the Essenes from the classical sources and then to compare that with the data from Qumran.

The earliest mention of the Essenes comes from Philo, an Alexandrian Jew, in two works written prior to 40 CE: *Every Good Man Is Free* (12–13.75–91) and *Hypothetica* (11.1–18, preserved in Eusebius, *Praeparatio evangelica*). [*See* Philo Judaeus.] Philo does not appear to have firsthand knowledge of the group, and he presents a somewhat idealized picture of the Essenes with frequent favorable comparisons to Greek thought and practice. Philo also speaks in a third work (*The Contemplative Life*) of a group in Egypt called the Therapeutae, who are similar to the Essenes, but live a more contemplative life.

A second important early reference to the Essenes comes from the Roman writer Pliny. In a section of his *Natural History*, completed in 77 CE, Pliny describes the topography of Judea (5.15.73). He speaks of the Essenes to the west of the Dead Sea, then ʿEin-Gedi below the Essenes, and Masada south of ʿEin-Gedi. The location of the Essenes in the same area as Qumran is most intriguing.

In a brief testimony, Dio Chrysostom (c.40–112 CE), a Greek orator and philosopher, also locates the Essenes by the Dead Sea. In words similar to Pliny, Dio's biographer Synesius (c.370–413 CE) speaks of Dio's praise for the Essenes, "who form an entire and prosperous city near the Dead Sea, in the center of Palestine, not far from Sodom" (*Dio* 3.2).

The most detailed ancient description of the Essenes comes from the Jewish historian Josephus (ca. 37–100 CE). Josephus mentions the Essenes thirteen times in his works, including two major passages: one in *The Jewish War*, written circa 73 CE (*The Jewish War* 2.119–161) and one in *Jewish Antiquities*, completed in 94 CE (*Jewish Antiquities* 18.11, 18–22). Josephus claims to have spent time with the Essenes when he was sixteen, but from the chronology he presents of his life he probably spent no more than six months with them (*Life* 1.10–12). Still, the fact that Josephus was a Palestinian Jew who probably had some direct contact with the group makes his detailed accounts of unique importance among the classical sources. As with Philo, however, Josephus's apologetic purpose to explain Judaism in a favorable light to a Greek-speaking world undoubtedly resulted in some idealization and accommodation to Greek thought in his depiction of the Essenes. [*See* Josephus Flavius.]

Brief mention of the Essenes is also made by Hegesippus, a second-century Christian historian, fragments of whose work is preserved in Eusebius. Hegesippus lists the Essenes in a group of seven Jewish sects.

The Roman bishop Hippolytus (c.170–236 CE) provides a description of the Essenes in his *Refutatio Omnium Haeresium* (9.18–28). This account is similar to Josephus (*The Jewish War* 2.119–161), and may be dependent upon him or derived from a common source. One interesting difference is that Hippolytus describes the Essenes as believing in a bodily resurrection. Hippolytus is the first of many later Christian writers to view the Essenes as a heretical Jewish sect (*Refutatio* 9.17) rather than simply as one of several mainstream Jewish sects.

As noted above, Epiphanius (c.315–403 CE) mentions both the Essenes (as a sect of the Samaritans) and the Ossaeans (a sect of Judaism that denies the Mosaic Law), but gives little information about either group. [*See* Epiphanius.] The later Christian writers provide no new information about the Essenes.

Customs and Beliefs of the Essenes According to the Classical Sources. The following brief summary of the major customs and beliefs of the Essenes is derived largely from the writings of Philo, Pliny, and Josephus.

Location. Philo and Josephus both agree that the total number of Essenes was over four thousand, and that they lived in many cities in Palestine (*The Jewish War* 2.124; *Hypothetica* 11.1). Elsewhere, however, Philo contradicts himself by saying that they lived in villages and avoided the cities (*Every Good Man Is Free* 12.76). Pliny puts them by the Dead Sea. Thus there appears to have been a major settlement in the Dead Sea region with other, smaller groups elsewhere in Palestine.

Admission. Josephus describes a three-year initiation period. During the first year, while the novice remained outside, he was required to follow the sect's way of life. In the second and third years, he was permitted to join in their purificatory baths, but could not partake of the common meal. Finally, after taking "awesome oaths," he was admitted as a full member into the community (*The Jewish War* 2.137–42).

Organization and authority. The sect was highly organized. Josephus states that nothing was done "except by the order of their overseers" (*The Jewish War* 2.134). One of the oaths of the initiate was trustworthiness to all, especially to those in authority (*The Jewish War* 2.140). In addition, the teachings of the sect were to be kept secret from nonmembers (*The Jewish War* 2.142). Obedience to the elders was stressed (*The Jewish War* 2.146), and in the case of disobedience or other matters of justice, at least one hundred members constituted the court. Severe offenses resulted in expulsion from the order (*The Jewish War* 2.143–145).

Communal property. All three first-century sources stress that a major tenet of the Essenes was communal property. Those entering the sect transferred their property to the order, so that no one was richer than another (*The Jewish War* 2.122; *Jewish Antiquities* 18.20; *Hypothetica* 10.4; *Every Good Man Is Free* 12.77; *Natural History* 5.15.73). Even food and clothing were held in common (*Hypothetica* 11.12). Hatred of riches is stressed by both Josephus and Philo (*The Jewish War* 2.122; *Hypothetica* 11.11). Josephus reports that, as a result of their frugality, the Essenes did not replace clothing or sandals until they were completely worn out (*The Jewish War* 2.126). Overseers of the common property were elected by the members (*The Jewish War* 2.123; *Hypothetica* 11.10).

Celibacy. Pliny states that the Essenes renounced love entirely and were without women (*Natural History* 5.15.73). Philo likewise states that "no Essene takes a wife" (*Hypothetica* 11.14–17). Josephus also notes the Essenes did not marry because wives caused factions. They did, however, adopt other peoples' children at an early age (*Jewish Antiquities* 18.21; *The Jewish War* 2.120). In contrast, Josephus later mentions another order of Essenes who *did* marry.

Daily work. Josephus states that Essenes worked entirely in agriculture (*Jewish Antiquities* 1.19), while Philo adds that they were also shepherds, beekeepers, and craftsmen in different trades (*Hypothetica* 11.8). Commerce was forbidden because it led to greed. They did not make any implements of war, nor did they own any slaves (*Every Good Man Is Free* 12.78–79). However, Josephus depicts John the Essene as leading in war at Ascalon (*The Jewish War* 3.9–12).

The daily routine consisted of prayer before sunrise, work until midday, participation in a purificatory bath and a common meal, work until evening, and a second common meal (*The Jewish War* 2.128–132).

Rituals. The Essenes were very concerned with ritual purity. Philo states that they demonstrated their love for God by their continual purity (*Every Good Man Is Free* 12.84). Josephus speaks of a daily purificatory bath taken by all Essenes except novices prior to the midday meal (*The Jewish War* 2.129). He also mentions that senior Essenes touched by juniors "must wash as if they had been in contact with a stranger" (*The Jewish War* 2.150). They were always dressed in white clothing (*The Jewish War* 2.123).

Both Philo and Josephus mention the Essene common meal, Josephus saying that they went into the dining room "even as into some holy shrine." The priest would pray before and after the meal, which was eaten in relative silence (*The Jewish War* 2.129–133).

The Essene attitude toward sacrifice is unclear. Philo states that the Essenes "have shown themselves especially devout in the service of God, not by offering sacrifices of animals, but by resolving to sanctify their minds" (*Every Good Man Is Free* 12.75). This statement may mean that the Essenes did not sacrifice at all, but it also might simply mean that sacrifice was not the focal point of their worship. The Epitome and Latin versions of Josephus state that the Essenes did *not* offer sacrifices, but the Greek text (probably to be preferred on the basis of slightly superior external evidence) omits the negative. According to the Greek text, Josephus says that while the Essenes offered sacrifices, they were excluded from the common court of the Temple because of a difference in their purification rites, and thus offered sacrifices by themselves (*Jewish Antiquities* 18.19).

Josephus describes the ritual morning prayers of the Essenes: before the rising of the sun they "direct certain ancestral prayers towards it, as if entreating it to rise" (*The Jewish War* 2.128). The reference is probably to the direction the Essenes faced as they prayed (i.e., eastward), rather than to worship of the sun.

The Essenes were devoted to the law and thus were strict observers of the Sabbath. Josephus says that they held Moses in greatest reverence (after God; *The Jewish War* 2.145), and he writes that "they were stricter than all Jews in not undertaking work on the seventh day" in that they did not cook, move a vessel, or even relieve themselves (since to do so they would need to dig a pit; *The Jewish War* 2.147; so also Philo, *Every Good Man Is Free* 12.81–82).

Other beliefs. The Essenes were deterministic in their outlook. Josephus states that they "like to leave all things to God" and believe that "fate is the ruler of all things" (*Jewish Antiquities* 18.18; 13.171–172).

The Essenes were also very interested in the study of "holy books" and "the writings of the ancients" (*The Jewish War* 2.136; 2.159; see also Philo, *Every Good Man Is Free* 12.80–82). Certainly this would include the biblical books, but might encompass other books as well, because Josephus states further that the Essenes used these writings to "search out medicinal roots and the properties of stones" to heal diseases (*The Jewish War* 2.136).

Also important to the Essenes were angels. The person joining the community had to swear to preserve "the books of their sect and the names of the angels" (*The Jewish War* 2.142).

Josephus also mentions that some Essenes professed to foresee the future. He adds that "rarely, if ever, do they err in their predictions" (*The Jewish War* 2.159). Elsewhere Josephus gives three examples of Essene prophecy. One involves an Essene named Judas in the time of Aristobulus I, who "never erred in his predictions" (*The Jewish War* 1.78–80; *Jewish Antiquities* 13.311–313); in another case Simon interpreted the dream of Archelaus correctly (*The Jewish War* 2.111–113; *Jewish Antiquities* 17.346–348); and in the third example Menahem made several accurate predictions concerning Herod. Josephus notes that it is because of the virtue of Menahem in particular and the Essenes in general that they were "thought worthy of this acquaintance with divine things" (*Jewish Antiquities* 15.371–379).

Finally, Josephus speaks at length on the Essene teaching of the immortality of the soul. The body was regarded as a prison house of the soul, but once the body died the soul was set free. Good souls went to a refreshing place "beyond the ocean," while evil souls went to a gloomy place "filled with incessant punishments" (*The Jewish

War 2.154–158). Josephus mentions that this doctrine is similar to that of the Greeks. One wonders how much of the Greek flavoring of this Essene teaching is the author's own invention. Similarly, when treating the Pharisees, Josephus speaks of their doctrine of the immortality of the soul, but does not mention their belief in a bodily resurrection (*Jewish Antiquities* 18.14; *The Jewish War* 2.163). Hippolytus goes beyond Josephus at this point and states that the Essenes believed in a bodily resurrection (*Refutatio* 9.27). It is uncertain whether Hippolytus is simply adding a Christian slant to the Essenes' beliefs, or whether his account here is more trustworthy than that of Josephus.

Relationship of the Essenes to the Dead Sea Scroll Community. Ever since the discovery of the Dead Sea Scrolls, many scholars have identified the Dead Sea Scroll community as Essene. It is still the most widely held view among scholars today. Since a full description of the Qumran community and alternative identifications of the community are treated elsewhere, the focus in this section will be the evidence for the identification of the Qumran community as Essene.

Chronology. Chronologically, Josephus's first mention of the Essenes is in connection with Jonathan Maccabee in the mid-second century BCE (*Jewish Antiquities* 13.171). In addition, he attests to the presence of Essenes during his lifetime (*Life* 1.10–12). This fits with the archaeological and paleographic data, which confirm the existence of the Qumran community from the mid-second century BCE to 68 CE.

Location. The geographical reference by Pliny makes the identification of the Qumran community with the Essenes somewhat compelling. In describing the western side of the Dead Sea, Pliny speaks of the Essenes to the west of the Dead Sea, then ʿEin-Gedi below them (*infra hos Engada*), and then Masada further south. Although some have objected that Pliny (writing in 77 CE) could not be talking about Qumran in the present tense because it was destroyed in 68 CE, it is probable that he used earlier source material. Pliny also notes that the Essenes live among palm trees, which would fit the region between Khirbet Qumran and ʿEin-Feshkha, the spring just south of their farm area.

Communal life and practice. There are many similarities between the practices of the Essenes as described by the ancient sources and those presented in the Dead Sea Scrolls, particularly the Rule of the Community (1QS) and the Damascus Document (CD). While there are other fragmentary copies of both works from the Qumran caves, the most complete copies, 1QS and CD, will be referenced here.

Admission. Admission into the sect is described in a lengthy section in the Rule of the Community (1QS vi.13–23), which is quite similar to that described by Josephus. While there is some difference in details, both sources agree on the following: a period of time spent outside the sect; a two-year period of initiation within the community itself; participation in the common meal denied to the novice; and a solemn oath made prior to full acceptance into the community. We know of no other group in ancient Judaism that had such an elaborate multi-year process of admission.

Organization and obedience to authority. As in Josephus's account of the Essenes, order within the community and obedience to authority were stressed in Qumran. Those who joined the community had to submit to the authority of the leaders (1QS v.2–3), obey those of higher rank (1QS v.23, vi.2, 25–26), and respect the authority of the community (1QS vii.17).

Communal property. Sharing of property is also evident in Qumranian literature. New members transferred their property to the community, and the full member mingled his property with that of the community (1QS i.11–12, v.1–2; vi.17–22). But in 1QS vii.8–9 the requirements for a person to reimburse the community for damage to communal property imply that some members had personal property. In the Damascus Document property could be lost or stolen from its owner (CD ix.10–16; see also CD xiv.12–13). The archaeology of Qumran confirms pooled possessions: hundreds of coins were found in the administration building, but not a single coin in the living quarters. Also an ostracon found by excavators in 1996 at the base of the eastern perimeter wall may record the gift of a man's property, including a slave, to the community. If the Cross/Eshel reconstruction (disputed by A. Yardeni) is correct, it would provide further evidence from archaeology of a new member's transfer of his property to the community.

Celibacy. The Dead Sea Scrolls do not speak of a prohibition of marriage (as Philo and Josephus do), although the Rule of the Community is silent on the subject, not mentioning women at all. But the Damascus Document does speak of marriage (in a prohibition of polygamy, CD iv.19–v.2; in other contexts, CD v.6–7, vii.6–7, xii.1–2, xvi.10–12), as does the Rule of the Congregation, where a young man was prohibited from sexual relations with a woman until he was twenty (1Q28a i.9–12).

The archaeology of Qumran may shed light on this important question, as all the skeletons excavated in the main, planned part of the cemetery were male, while skeletons of women and children were found only on the outskirts. This may indicate that there was both a celibate group as well as a married group (who lived elsewhere?) among the sectarians, which would fit well with Josephus's statement that there was both a celibate group of Essenes and another group of Essenes who married.

Daily work. Archaeology of the Qumran area indicates that the inhabitants were occupied in both agriculture and craft work. This fits well with the statements of Josephus and Philo concerning the Essenes.

Rituals. Purificatory washings, mentioned by Josephus, were apparently practiced at Qumran. Archaeologists have found seven large cisterns with steps that might have been used for this purpose. Both the Rule of the Community (e.g., 1QS v.13–14) and the Damascus Document refer to purificatory washing (CD xi.21–22), although neither refers to the daily washings mentioned by Josephus.

Josephus notes that the Essenes avoid oil because it is a defilement (*The Jewish War* 2.123), and the Damascus Document says that substances with oil are impure (CD xii.15–17). In 4QMMT (4Q394–4Q399) the reason for the impurity of oil is that liquids transmitted ritual impurity from one item to the next.

Avoidance of spitting is also mentioned by Josephus as a practice of the Essenes (*The Jewish War* 2.147). The Rule of the Community contains a similar prohibition (1QS vii.13).

The common meal spoken of by Josephus is well attested at Qumran, both by the archaeological evidence (with a pantry containing more than one thousand vessels for eating adjacent to a large room) and direct statements in the scrolls. The Rule of the Community states that "they shall eat together and they shall bless together" (1QS vi.2–3) and goes on to describe the common meal (1QS vi.4–5; cf. 1QS v.13, vi.16–17, 22, 24–25, vii.19–20 and viii.16–18).

The evidence concerning sacrifice in the Dead Sea Scrolls is not much clearer than Josephus's testimony on the same subject. Although the evidence, notably CD vi.11–14 and xi.17–22, could be interpreted in different ways, it is probable that both Josephus and some Qumranian literature permitted Temple sacrifices, but with a great concern for ritual purity in the process.

Devotion to the law and strict observance of the Sabbath, both emphasized by Josephus, are likewise mentioned often in the scrolls (1QS viii.22; cf. 1QS i.1–3, v.8; CD xv.8–9, 12–13, xvi.2). With respect to the Sabbath, the Damascus Document contains a long list of activities prohibited on the Sabbath; this list is sometimes even more strict than rabbinic law (CD x.14–xi.18; so also CD iii.14, vi.18, xii.3–6).

Other beliefs. The deterministic outlook mentioned by Josephus as characteristic of the Essenes is also evident throughout the scrolls. For example, the Hodayot states that "before You created them You knew all their deeds forever and ever. [Without You no]thing is done, and apart from Your will nothing ever can be known" (1QH[a] i.7–8; so also 1QH[a] vii.31–32, xv.12–15, 17; 1QS iii.15–16, ix.23–24; the War Scroll [1QM] xvii.5).

The Essene interest in the study and use of books, as mentioned by Josephus, is overwhelmingly evident at Qumran. Biblical, deuterocanonical, and pseudepigraphical books are well attested, as are many sectarian works. Interest in healing may also be seen in the Genesis Apocryphon (1QapGen xx.19–20) as well as in the numerous copies of Jubilees and Enoch, both of which speak of healing.

Interest in angels is another point of agreement between Josephus's testimony about the Essenes and Qumran. Not only are angels abundantly mentioned in Enoch, but they are likewise referenced in the rule books, the Hodayot, the War Scroll (see especially 1QM ix.14–17, xii.1–5), and the Songs of the Sabbath Sacrifice.

Josephus's statement concerning Essene interest in the prophets and in prophecy is seen in the Qumran texts. There are direct statements concerning the importance of the prophets in the Rule of the Community and the Damascus Document (1QS i.2–3, ix.11; CD vii.17–18), as well as numerous copies of the biblical prophetic books and a large number of citations from these books in the rest of Qumranian literature. Furthermore, the *pesharim* ("commentaries" on biblical passages) found at Qumran contain reinterpretations of prophetic texts in which the fulfillment is found in the contemporary situation of the community (see, e.g., Pesher Habakkuk [1QpHab]).

Finally, concerning the afterlife, there is mention of everlasting life (1QS iv.6–8; CD iii.20; see also Rule of the Blessings [1Q28b] iv.24–26), and several passages may speak of bodily resurrection, although the evidence is not clear (see 1QH[a] iii.10–22, iv.34 ["they that lie in the dust raise the banner and the worms of the dead raise the standard"]; xi.12; 1QM xii.1–4; and especially Messianic Apocalypse [4Q521]). The ancient sources on the Essenes and the scrolls agree on eternal life for the soul, but the sources disagree on the Essene view of the fate of the body (Hippolytus asserts resurrection of the body, but not Josephus), with the data from the sectarian scrolls inconclusive.

Possible discrepancies. Aside from the areas where either our sources concerning the Essenes or the Qumranian documents contain internal disagreements within themselves (for example, Philo's assertion of celibacy versus Josephus's statement that there is a marrying group of Essenes), there are surprisingly few disagreements between the Dead Sea Scrolls and the accounts of the Essenes. There are small differences in entrance procedure and oaths, but overall there is more similarity in the two descriptions. In some cases, both the Essene accounts and the scrolls are unclear (for example, the issue of sacrifice or the belief in a bodily resurrection).

While some correspondences between the Essenes and the scrolls could characterize any Jewish group, many agreements, even in minutia such as avoidance of spitting, or the priestly praying before the common meal, are impressive.

Still, there are some areas where the scrolls do not appear to line up with the Essene identification. The scrolls speak of the importance of priests and of prominent figures such as the Teacher of Righteousness and the Wicked Priest. In addition, the scrolls highlight the group's messianic expectation (with dual messianic figures) and their unusual solar calendar. Yet, with the exception of a brief mention of priests in Josephus, none of these areas is discussed in the classical descriptions of the Essenes.

With the recent publication of Miqtsat Maʿasei ha-Torah (4Q394–4Q399), some scholars have revived an earlier proposal that the Qumran community originated as a group of Sadducees. Miqtsat Maʿasei ha-Torah contains some agreements in a few legal matters with the Sadducees over against the Pharisees. One of these is the view that a stream of liquid conveys impurity from one item to the next. But this document supports Josephus's statement about the Essene avoidance of oil, and contains no inherent contradiction with any known Essene position. Furthermore, it is highly unlikely that the Qumran sect was Sadducean, since the scrolls teach the non-Sadducean doctrines of the existence of angels and the importance of fate.

In any discussion of the identification of the Qumran group or the movement of which it was a part, it is important to remember that works such as the Rule of the Community and the Damascus Document may represent different stages in the community's development, and this may well account for some of the discrepancies between the Qumran documents as well as between these documents and Josephus. Overall, Josephus's description of the Essenes more closely parallels the Rule of the Community than the Damascus Document. With respect to matters that are reflected in the scrolls but not mentioned by the ancient sources, Josephus and Philo may have thought that these matters (messianic expectation, solar calendar) were not important or relevant to their purpose—making this Jewish sect appealing to the Greek mind. While there is still much that is not known about either the Essenes or the writers of the scrolls, on balance it is still likely that the identification of the Qumran community as Essene in some form is correct.

History of the Group. The ancient sources say little about the history of the Essenes. Josephus notes that the three philosophies among the Jews were "inherited from the most ancient times" (*Jewish Antiquities* 18.11) and Pliny states that "for thousands of centuries a race has existed which is eternal" (*Natural History* 5.15.73). Neither statement helps identify the beginning of the Essenes.

Josephus first speaks of the Essenes during the rule of Jonathan Maccabee (160–43 BCE) (*Jewish Antiquities* 13.171). He mentions three Essene prophets by name: Judas, during the reign of Aristobulus I (104–103 BCE) (*The Jewish War* 1.78–80; *Jewish Antiquities* 13.311–313); Menahem, who made two predictions concerning Herod the Great (ruled 37–4 BCE) (*Jewish Antiquities* 15.371–379); and Simon, who in 4 BCE interpreted a dream of Archelaus, ethnarch of Judea (4 BCE–6 CE), to mean that his reign would last for ten more years (*The Jewish War* 2.111–113; *Jewish Antiquities* 17.346–348). In his autobiography, Josephus mentions spending some time with the Essenes when he was about sixteen years old (ca. 53–54 CE).

Finally, Josephus speaks of the Essenes during the time of the first Jewish Revolt against the Romans (66–70 CE). In particular he mentions John the Essene, one of three generals who led an abortive attempt to take Ascalon in 67 CE (*The Jewish War* 2.566–568; *The Jewish War* 3.9–21).

Josephus records the Essene fearlessness in the war with the Romans in a remarkable passage in the *The Jewish War*. He says that this war "tested their souls in every way." Although tortured horribly, they did not "blaspheme the lawgiver or eat something forbidden"; instead, "they gave up their souls cheerfully, confident that they would get them back again" (*The Jewish War* 2.152–153). That is the last historical reference to the Essenes in Josephus.

Thus, from our ancient sources we have verification of the Essenes from c.150 BCE to the war against the Romans in 66–70 CE.

If, as was argued above, the Qumran community is Essene, then there is further information both from the archaeology of the Qumran site and from the scrolls themselves that may assist in establishing an outline of the history of the Essenes. Unfortunately, the scroll data are cryptic, and scholars do not even agree as to which of the scrolls were written by the sect. And once again various documents may have been written at different stages of the community's existence. All of this complicates the attempt to come up with a history of the Essenes and the Dead Sea Scroll sect. Several hypotheses are discussed briefly below.

One theory of the origin of the Essenes (held by Vermes, 1978; Cross, 1995; and many others) sees the group as springing from within Palestine, possibly from the Hasideans, in the mid-second-century BCE during the Maccabean period. *1 Maccabees* states that the Hasideans first supported the Maccabean revolt, but later broke with them (*1 Mc.* 2.42; 7.13–14). Some of these Hasideans may have become the Essenes (note the possible etymological link between the two names discussed earlier). The Damascus Document speaks of a period of twenty years of blind groping (CD i.9–10), which may be the period of support for the Maccabees. There arose a man called in the scrolls the Wicked Priest, who as a non-Zadokite usurped the high priesthood (see Pesher Habakkuk [1QpHab] viii.8–13, ix.9–12, xi.4–6, xii.7–9). The Wicked Priest has been identified as either Jonathan, when he was appointed High Priest in 152 BCE, or (less likely) Simon, when he and his house were given the high priesthood by decree in 140 BCE. It is noteworthy that Josephus's first mention of the Essenes is during the rule of Jonathan. The Wicked Priest was opposed by the Teacher of Righteousness (the leader of the group, and a priest himself according to Pesher Psalms[a], 4Q171 1, 3–4.iii.15), who led his group to the desert of Qumran.

A second theory of Essene origins (championed by Murphy-O'Connor, 1974) traces the beginning of the sect to Jews deported to Babylon in 586 BCE. The idea is that some of these Jews returned to Palestine after Judas Maccabee's victory, which created an independent Jewish state. But they became quickly disillusioned with Hellenistic tendencies they found there, so as a result a group of Essenes retreated to the desert of Qumran. Support for this theory comes from the beginning of the Damascus Document, which speaks of God causing a root of planting to spring up "390 years after He delivered them into the hands of Nebuchadrezzar king of Babylon" (CD i.5–8). In addition, the Damascus Document speaks of "the returnees of Israel who went out from the land of Judah and were exiled in the land of Damascus" (CD vi.5). Damascus may be symbolic for Babylon (another place of exile; see *Am.* 5.27, cited in CD vii.15; cf. *Acts* 7.23), although others see it as referring to Qumran or to Damascus itself.

A third theory (called the Groningen Hypothesis) has emerged recently from Florentino García Martínez and A. S. van der Woude. They argue that the Essene sect is Palestinian with ideological roots in the apocalyptic tradition of the late third century or early second century BCE. According to this view, there was a rift in the Essene movement dealing with calendar issues (and the corresponding cycle of feasts), temple worship, and purity. When other Essenes resisted the Teacher of Righteousness's attempt to push these issues, he led a break-off group to the desert retreat of Qumran in the days of John Hyrcanus (134–104 BCE). According to this theory, the Wicked Priest refers to a succession of high priests from Judas Maccabee (164–160 BCE) to Alexander Jannaeus (103–76 BCE).

Whatever the precise origin of the Essenes, it is clear from our ancient sources that they existed in numerous places other than Qumran. Josephus speaks of Judas as living in Jerusalem (*Jewish Antiquities* 13.311). He also refers to a "Gate of the Essenes" in Jerusalem (*The Jewish War* 5.145), which has apparently now been excavated (Pixner, 1997). [*See* Essene Gate.]

The history of the Essene (?) settlement at Qumran is described elsewhere. [*See* Qumran.] The site was occupied until 68 CE when the Romans conquered it. Some believe that the Zealots joined the group during this last phase of occupation prior to Roman conquest.

What happened to the Essenes after 68 CE is not known. Although the destruction of the Qumran site itself did not extinguish the Essenes who lived elsewhere, the effect of the war and the Roman occupation probably caused the Essenes to dissolve as an independent sect. Some Essenes may have joined the resistance at Masada until its capture in 74 CE (a copy of the Songs of the Sabbath Sacrifice was found there). There is no solid evidence of their existence after this time.

BIBLIOGRAPHY

Adam, A. *Antike Berichte über die Essener.* 2nd ed. Berlin, 1972. Greek text and brief commentary for all the ancient accounts of the Essenes.

Beall, T. *Josephus' Description of the Essenes Illustrated by the Dead Sea Scrolls. SNTSMS,* 58. Cambridge, 1988. Provides Greek text, English translation, and discussion of the Essene passages in Josephus and their relationship to the Dead Sea Scrolls.

Black, Matthew. *The Scrolls and Christian Origins: Studies in the Jewish Background of the New Testament.* Chico, Calif., 1983. Good general discussion of the ancient accounts of the Essenes.

Callaway, Phillip. *The History of the Qumran Community.* Sheffield, 1988. Good discussion of the history of the Qumran community; cautiously critical of the identification of the Qumran community as Essene.

Campbell, Jonathan. "Essene-Qumran Origins in the Exile: A Scriptural Basis?" *Journal of Jewish Studies* 46 (1995), 143–156. Contains a good survey of the various hypotheses of Essene and Qumran origins.

Cross, Frank Moore. *The Ancient Library of Qumran.* 3d ed. Minneapolis, 1995. Discussion of the Essenes as the sect responsible for the Dead Sea Scrolls.

Davies, Philip R. "Was There Really a Qumran Community?" *Currents in Research: Biblical Studies* 3 (1995), 9–35. A provocative analysis of recent works on the identity of the Qumran community.

Feldman, L. *Josephus and Modern Scholarship (1937–1980).* Berlin, 1984. Contains an extensive annotated bibliography on Josephus and the Essenes, including Josephus's account of the Essenes, etymology of "Essenes," origin of the Essenes, and beliefs and practices of the Essenes.

García Martínez, F., and Julio Trebolle Barrera. *The People of the Dead Sea Scrolls.* Translated from the Spanish by Wilfred G. E. Watson. Discusses the "Essenes of Qumran" and the Groningen hypothesis of the origin of the Qumran community.

Murphy-O'Connor, Jerome. "The Essenes and Their History." *Revue biblique* 81 (1974), 215–244. Proposes Babylonian hypothesis of the origin of the Essenes.

Pixner, B. "Jerusalem's Essene Gateway." *Biblical Archaeology Review* 23 (May/June 1997), 22–31, 64–67.

Schiffman, Lawrence. "The Sadducean Origins of the Dead Sea

Scroll Sect." In *Understanding the Dead Sea Scrolls,* edited by Hershel Shanks, pp. 35–49. New York, 1992. Argues that the Qumran community was originally Sadducean.

Stemberger, Günter. *Jewish Contemporaries of Jesus: Pharisees, Sadducees, Essenes.* Translated from the German by Allan Mahnke. Minneapolis, 1995. Good general discussion of the sources, history, and teaching of these three groups.

VanderKam, James. *The Dead Sea Scrolls Today.* Grand Rapids, Mich., 1994. Contains an up-to-date discussion of the identification and history of the Qumran community. Supports Essene identification.

VanderKam, James. "The People of the Dead Sea Scrolls: Essenes or Sadducees?" In *Understanding the Dead Sea Scrolls,* edited by Hershel Shanks, pp. 50–62. New York, 1992. Argues against Schiffman's view that the Qumran community was originally Sadducean.

Vermes, Geza. *The Dead Sea Scrolls: Qumran in Perspective.* Cleveland, Ohio, 1978. Discusses the identification of the Qumran community and the history of the sect. Supports Essene identification.

Vermes, Geza, and Martin Goodman. *The Essenes according to the Classical Sources.* Sheffield, 1989. Provides Greek/Latin text, English translation, and brief introduction for the major classical sources describing the Essenes.

Yardeni, Ada. "A Draft of a Deed on an Ostracon from Khirbet Qumrân." *Israel Exploration Journal* 47 (1997), 17–28, 233–237.

TODD S. BEALL

ESTHER, BOOK OF. As is well known, only two of the books of the Hebrew scriptures as it now stands were not found among the fragments of the Judean Desert corpus, the books of *Esther* and *Nehemiah*. However, since the books of *Ezra* and *Nehemiah* are often found together on one scroll, and fragments of the *Book of Ezra* are found in one manuscript from Qumran, Cave 4, it is considered that *Nehemiah* was most likely present at Qumran as well. *Esther,* therefore, is unique as the only biblical book not found among the Dead Sea Scrolls. Several reasons have been advanced for this anomaly: First, since the book is short, it is merely an accident or chance that no fragments have been preserved (after all, the book of Chronicles survived in only one fragment). Second, the all-male community at Qumran did not wish to possess a book in which a female was the heroine. Since the notion of an all-male, celibate community at Qumran has been seriously challenged, this argument appears to be groundless. Third, the community at Qumran, with its stringent rules concerning purity, was opposed to Esther, in which the Jews mingled freely with gentiles and did not observe the dietary laws. Fourth, the *Book of Esther,* written in the Diaspora, was not known in Palestine prior to the destruction of the Second Temple, and its festival, Purim (which would have been celebrated on a Sabbath in the 364-day calendar), was not celebrated there. Fifth, some scholars date the Hebrew version of Esther as late as the second century CE, making it too late for inclusion in the Judean Desert corpus. The first and fourth explanations appear to be most likely, depending upon one's dating of the book.

However, there is one text among the Dead Sea Scrolls that resembles the *Book of Esther* in style and setting. This text, Proto-Esther[a–f] 4Q550, was published by J. T. Milik in 1992 and entitled by him "4QprotoAramaic-Esther," although subsequent commentators have suggested that the title "Tales from the Persian Court" would be more apt. The manuscript, which is written in Aramaic (a language closely related to Hebrew), consists of six fragments which date approximately to the second half of the first century BCE. Although very small, they seem to recount the adventures of a group of Jews in the court of the Persian kings Darius and Xerxes. In general setting, the parallel to *Esther* is clear. However, the parallels are more particular than simply the setting. Fragments a–c describe the possible rivalry between a high functionary of the Persian court and a minor servant of the royal wardrobe. Within the fragments, the Persian king, identified as the son of Darius and thus Xerxes, has the royal annals read aloud to him, as in *Esther* 6.1. However, there are also clear differences: The protagonists are not clearly Jewish, and there is little evidence of a court conflict as is seen between Mordecai and Haman in the Esther story.

In addition to parallels to the Hebrew *Book of Esther,* fragment d of Tales of the Persian Court contains parallels to the Greek Additions C and D found in the Septuagint version of *Esther*. These Septuagint Additions are particularly important for their inclusion of religious elements, such as the prayer missing in the Hebrew version of Esther. The fragment opens with a prayer of a Jew to God, which has certain similarities to Esther's prayer in the Septuagint, Addition C. Other parallels to the *Book of Esther* follow: There is evidently a power struggle between a non-Jew and a Jew, in which the Jew emerges victorious; there is a dialogue between the Persian king and a female protagonist, and at the end of the fragment the king makes a proclamation praising God, as in the Septuagint, Addition E. However, there are also important differences (for example, the protagonist's name is Bagasraw, and his presumed enemy is Bagoshe) which make it impossible to posit a direct relationship between these Aramaic fragments and the Hebrew or Greek versions of the *Book of Esther*. Fragments e and f of Tales of the Persian Court are small and do not give much information, although fragment f contains a quotation of *Isaiah* 14.31–32, again a startling difference from the Esther corpus, which shows no awareness of other biblical texts. The conclusion that must be drawn concerning Tales of the Persian Court, therefore, is that it is not directly related to the Esther corpus as it has been preserved. However, it is possible that these fragments formed part of a cycle of tales concerning Jewish protagonists in the Persian Court, and this hypothetical cycle of tales may have served as a source for the Hebrew and Greek versions and their daughter versions of *Esther*.

Another small manuscript that may bear some relation to the biblical book of Esther is the so-called Apocryphon of Esther from Masada (Mas1m), so named by Yigael Yadin because of certain similarities of phrasing to the book of Esther, for example, "they hanged" (cf. *Est*., 7.10) and "favor in his eyes" (cf. *Est*. 5.8, 7.3). This small Hebrew manuscript, which dates to the Herodian period, survives in fifteen fragments reassembled into two columns. Unfortunately, the manuscript is so fragmentary that it is difficult to make sense of it, but there does not seem to be much in content that connects it with the *Book of Esther*.

BIBLIOGRAPHY

Collins, John J., and Deborah A. Green. "The Tales from the Persian Court (4Q550[a–e]) in *Antikes Judentum und Frühes Christentum*, pp. 39–50. Berlin, 1999.

Crawford, Sidnie White. "Has Esther Been Found at Qumran? 4Qproto-Esther and the Esther Corpus." *Revue de Qumrân* 17 (1996), 307–325.

Milik, J. T. "Les modèles araméens du livre d'Esther dans la grotte 4 de Qumrân." *Revue de Qumrân* 15 (1992), 321–399.

Talmon, Shemaryahu. "Fragments of Scrolls from Masada." *Eretz Israel* 20 (1989), 280. The preliminary publication of Mas1m.

SIDNIE WHITE CRAWFORD

ETERNAL LIFE. Granted by God as a reward to the righteous, eternal life is life that overcomes death. Sometimes eternal life is a consequence of resurrection. *Daniel* 12.2 employs the expression *ḥayyei ʿolam*, which is usually translated as "eternal life" or "everlasting life." The verse apparently alludes to the scenario in *Isaiah* 65.17–25, which says that after God re-creates the heavens and the earth, the righteous will live very long lives in the new Jerusalem. A parallel pàssage in *1 Enoch* (25.3–6) likens this to the fabulously long lives of the patriarchs. [*See* Resurrection.] However, even if *Daniel* 12.2 envisions a bodily life on earth, verse 3 states that the wise teachers "who brought many to righteousness" will receive special glory. Evidently exalted to the heavenly realm, they will "shine like the firmament" and "like the stars forever and ever." This notion of heavenly ascent and everlasting life is broadened in *1 Enoch* 102.4–104.8: the spirits or souls of all the righteous will be brought from Sheol to heaven, where they will shine like the luminaries and share the joyous company of the angels. The *Second Book of the Maccabees* 7 combines belief in a bodily resurrection with language about eternal life. The seven martyred brothers and their mother expect that God "will raise us to an eternal revivification of life" (*eis aionon anabiosin zoes hemas anastesei*; verse 9). Verse 36 seems to state (the text is uncertain), however, that the dead brothers are already drinking from the fountain of "ever-flowing life."

Immortality of the Soul and Eternal Life Apart from the Body. Although it has been argued that the Hebrew belief in resurrection of the body stands in contrast to Greek ideas of the immortality of the soul (Cullman, 1965), the distinction cannot be sustained for three reasons. First, an eternal life apart from the body need not imply or be stated in terms of a Greek notion of immortality of the soul. Second, a Hebrew/Greek antithesis contradicts the historical fact that Judaism in the Greco-Roman period was substantially Hellenized in many ways. Third, a number of Jewish texts do, in fact, posit a bodiless, heavenly existence, which on occasion is described as "immortality" or "incorruption."

Three texts in the Hebrew scriptures may already imply a postmortem life in the presence of God (Ps. 16.10–11, 49.15, 73.23–25; Martin-Achard, 1960, pp. 158–165). If such an idea is present, it should be interpreted not as immortality of the soul, but as a function of God's power to transcend death—conceived without specificity as to how or in what form this happens. Perhaps the earliest Jewish text that clearly refers to a life in God's presence apart from the body is *Jubilees* 23.31, which promises the righteous that "their bones will rest in the earth, but their spirits will have much joy." The idea parallels *1 Enoch* 103.4 and 104.4, which may be roughly contemporary with *Jubilees*, but *Jubilees* gives no indication that joy in God's presence will be preceded by a resurrection or, indeed, that a future resurrection will rejoin spirit and body.

Translation to a state of bliss immediately upon death is explicit in the *Wisdom of Solomon* 2–5, a heavily Hellenized work that clothes the idea of the soul's immortality in the Greek language. According to the *Wisdom of Solomon* 3.1–4, the righteous only seem to die. In fact, they are at peace, and they will live forever in God's presence (*Wis*. 5.15). An important aspect of this work's theology is the notion that death, on the one hand, and immortality and eternal life, on the other, are characteristic of the present existence of the wicked and righteous. The wicked have already made a covenant with death, while the righteous participate in the life whose consummation they will enjoy after they draw their last breath.

A similar belief in immortality, incorruptibility, and eternal life appears in *4 Maccabees* 7.3, 9.22, 14.5–6, 15.3, 16.13, 17.12, a Jewish philosophical treatise that recasts the story in *2 Maccabees* 7. Here, the moment of death is the transition from earthly life to immortality and eternal life in the presence of Abraham, Isaac, and Jacob (*4 Mc*. 9.22, 13.17, 16.25, 17.18–19). There is no hint that this author expects the bodily resurrection that is so central to *2 Maccabees* 7.

Belief in immortality of the soul also characterizes the contemporary writings of Philo (Wolfson, 1968). The *Wisdom of Solomon*, *Maccabees*, and the writings of Philo differ from typical Greek notions of immortality in that they conceive of immortality not as an inherent property of the soul, but as God's gift to the righteous.

Eternal Life in the Qumran Scrolls. That the authors of the Qumran scrolls believed in some form of substantial afterlife is a scholarly consensus. Evidence for such belief appears in the Rule of the Community (1QS iv.6–8) and Hodayot[a] (1QH[a] xi.19–23 [iii.18–22] and xix.10–14 [xi.7–11]). With respect to the texts in Hodayot, scholars debate whether they refer to a future resurrection of the body or whether they infer entrance into the community as the passage from death to life. The latter seems more feasible: the authors of these hymns believe that they are already participating in the blessings of eternal life, which will be consummated when they have taken their last breath. This viewpoint would parallel that of the *Wisdom of Solomon* and *4 Maccabees*, even though the scrolls do not use words that can be translated as "immortality" and "incorruptibility."

The Rule of the Community (1QS iii.15–iv.26) is a piece of ethical instruction that describes good and evil human actions as walking on two paths in the company of a good or evil angel (Nickelsburg, 1972, pp. 156–159). Catalogs of righteous and wicked deeds, which constitute the ways of light and darkness, are followed by lists of their consequences, which are the eternal postmortem blessings of the righteous (1QS iv.6–8) and the eternal punishments of the wicked (1QS iv.11–14). It is not clear, however, when these rewards and punishments occur. According to the Rule of the Community (1QS iv.18–26), there will be a final consummation, not unlike the scenarios described in Jewish apocalyptic writings (e.g., *1 En.* 10.16–11.2). The Rule of the Community does not state explicitly whether the blessings and curses will be effected at this future time or whether the righteous and wicked will receive their recompense at the time of their death. The interpretation of Hodayot favored above fits best with the latter notion. The righteous already participate in the blessings of eternal life, and their physical death is a transition to the consummation of these blessings in the presence of God. This viewpoint is also compatible with Two Ways theology; as one walks in the way that will issue in life, one already participates in that life.

Immortality and Eternal Life in Later Texts. Although belief in the resurrection of the dead is central to New Testament Christianity, a number of New Testament texts reflect the views of eternal life found in the scrolls. Especially noteworthy is the *Gospel of John*, where belief in Jesus entails experience of eternal life already in the present time (Nickelsburg, 1992, p. 690). Somewhat related ideas occur in *Romans* 6–11, where Paul uses a Two Ways theology, albeit with caution (Nickelsburg, 1992, pp. 688–689).

A belief in eternal life or immortality apart from the body and without a resurrection appears in four texts, which have been preserved only in Christian manuscripts, but which may well be Jewish in origin (Nickelsburg, 1981, pp. 244, 248–253, 260–261). The *Testament of Abraham* presents a detailed description of a postmortem judgment of the souls of the righteous and the wicked, which takes place immediately after death. For the author of the *Testament of Job*, the suffering patriarch finds hope in the knowledge that he has an immortal throne in heaven. In *Joseph and Aseneth*, when Joseph's Egyptian bride is converted from idolatry to the worship of the true God, she is transformed from death to immortality. The *Testament of Asher* in the *Testaments of the Twelve Patriarchs* interprets Psalms 73–74 in terms of Two Ways theology. The angel who leads one on the right or wrong path during life also escorts one to one's eternal destiny at the moment of death (Nickelsburg, 1972, pp. 161–162). According to rabbinic tradition, eternal life can be achieved only after the resurrection of the dead, which takes place after the coming of the messianic era.

[*See also* Eschatology; Essenes; Hodayot; Resurrection; Retribution; *and* Rule of the Community.]

BIBLIOGRAPHY

Cavallin, H. C. C. *Life after Death.* Coniectanea Biblica NT Series, 7.1. Lund, 1974. Discusses a wide range of Jewish texts, including the rabbinic corpus, and concludes that they express a variety of beliefs in resurrection, immortality, and eternal life.

Cullman, Oscar. "Immortality of the Soul or Resurrection of the Body: The Witness of the New Testament." In *Immortality and Resurrection*, edited by Krister Stendahl, pp. 9–53 (1958). Reprint, New York, 1965. Classical exposition of the claim that the Hebrew view of bodily resurrection stands in contrast to the Greek view of the immortality of the soul.

Fischer, Ulrich. *Eschatologie und Jenseitserwartung im Hellenistischen Diasporajudentum.* Beiheft zur Zeitschrift für die neutestamentliche Wissenschaft, 44. Berlin, 1978. Especially valuable for its treatment of the inscriptional material.

Martin-Achard, Robert. *From Death to Life: A Study of the Development of the Doctrine of Resurrection in the Old Testament.* Edinburgh, 1960. Still a useful exposition of relevant biblical texts.

Nickelsburg, George W. E. *Resurrection, Immortality, and Eternal Life in Intertestamental Judaism.* Harvard Theological Studies, 26. Cambridge, 1972. Study of texts in *Daniel*, the Apocrypha, pseudepigrapha, and Dead Sea Scrolls, which emphasizes the variety in these texts. Focuses on traditions and is less comprehensive than the work of Cavallin.

Nickelsburg, George W. E. *Jewish Literature between the Bible and the Mishnah: A Historical and Literary Introduction.* Philadelphia, 1981.

Nickelsburg, George W. E. "Resurrection: Early Judaism and Christianity." In *Anchor Bible Dictionary*, 6 vols., edited by Noel David Freedman, vol. 5, pp. 684–691. New York, 1992. Summarizes *Resurrection, Immortality, and Eternal Life in Intertestamental Judaism* and supplements it with a discussion of additional Jewish texts and a wide range of New Testament texts.

Puech, Émile. *La croyance des Esséniens en la vie future: Immortalité, résurrection, vie éternelle?* 2 vols. Études bibliques, 21–22. Paris, 1993. Comprehensive discussion of early Jewish texts, with special attention to the Qumran corpus. Finds a widespread belief in resurrection of the body, not least in the scrolls.

Wolfson, Harry Austryn. *Philo: Foundations of Religious Philosophy in Judaism, Christianity, and Islam.* 4th printing, rev. ed. Cambridge, 1968.

George W. E. Nickelsburg

ETERNAL PLANTING. The expression *eternal planting* is used in several texts composed during the period of the Second Temple to explain a biblical tradition that describes the restored people of Israel as a plant, established by God in the land and lovingly tended so that it produces righteous deeds, glory to God, and future growth (see *Is.* 60.21 and 61.3). The metaphor is expressed as *maṭṭa*ʿ (Hebrew) or *nitsbah* (Aramaic; "plant" or "planting") with the following modifiers: "eternal" (Rule of the Community from Qumran Cave 1, hereafter, 1QRule of the Community, 1QS, and Hodayot[a] from Qumran Cave 1, hereafter, 1QHodayot[a], 1QH[a]), "righteous" (*Jub.*), or "truthful" (*1 En.*). There appears to be no significant connection between the eternal planting and the tree of life or the biblical metaphor of the world tree (*Dn.* 4.9–12, *Ezek.* 31.2–14), except for one or two cases where the metaphors are mixed. Eternal planting seems to be a relatively fixed metaphor, and therefore we must assume a common cultural matrix in which *Jubilees, 1 Enoch,* 1QRule of the Community, and 1QHodayot[a] were first composed and transmitted. No specific literary dependence or common community origin need be assumed.

There are two interpretive directions in which the metaphor is taken. Some texts use it to describe the future, restored people of God, established on a restored earth (*1 En.* 10.16; *Jub.* 1.16). The Ethiopic *Apocalypse of Enoch* 10.3 interprets this to designate the future (from Enoch's point of view) of righteous individuals living at the time of Noah, those who will survive the eschatological judgment (see also *1 En.* 84.6). Other texts use the metaphor to describe non-eschatological Israel (*1 En.* 93.2, 5, 10; *Jub.* 16.26, 21.24, 36.6). In 1QRule of the Community (1QS viii.5; xi.8) and 1QHodayot[a] (1QH[a] xiv.19 [vi.15]; xvi.7 [viii.6]) both interpretations are combined, and the referent of the metaphor is significantly narrowed to apply only to the community itself or its immediate predecessors, and not to all Israel. The metaphor is often thought to be a sectarian self-designation indicating election; however, although it is used of the community, it does not imply that only the members of the community are elect.

1QHodayot[a] (1QH[a] xiv.19 [vi.15]) elaborates on the meaning of the metaphor. A shoot that will grow into a plant with branches big enough to cover the world and reach to the skies and with roots deep enough to reach down to the abyss represents the remnant of God's people who will be purified, pardoned, instructed, and established in a council where they will recount God's mighty deeds in company with the angels.

Jubilees 1.16, hinting at what will become in other works a regular association of the plant with the heavenly temple, refers to the "righteous plant" immediately before proclaiming "I will build my temple among them and will live with them." In *Jubilees* the metaphor itself does not imply an association with the heavenly temple, nor is the plant a present reality. In the pre-Qumranic wisdom text Sapiential Work A[a] (4Q418) however, it is likely that the addressee, an "understanding one" (line 15), is part of the "eternal planting" (4Q418 81.i.13). There is, however, no indication that the addressees constitute a distinct social group. Since the addressee is called a "most holy one" (line 4) and is told to "bless the holy ones" (line 1) and to "open a fountain (?) for the holy ones" (line 12), the students of this teacher of wisdom were probably expected to have some association with angels. Accordingly, the sectarian documents (1QRule of the Community and 1QHodayot[a]) regularly juxtapose "eternal planting" with indications of the heavenly status of the community. This juxtaposition probably indicates that the communities of these texts are the righteous remnant that already enjoys certain eschatological blessings. The Damascus Document (CD i.7) mixes the metaphor of planting with that of a root that represents a tiny remnant of the righteous ("root of planting").

BIBLIOGRAPHY

Dexinger, Ferdinand. *Henochs Zehnwochenapokalypse und offene Probleme der Apokalyptikforschung.* Studia Post-Biblica, 29. Leiden, 1977. See pages 164–170 for a careful review of the metaphor in the Qumran texts.

Tiller, Patrick. "'The Eternal Planting' in the Dead Sea Scrolls." *Dead Sea Discoveries* 4 (1997).

Patrick A. Tiller

ETHICS. The manner in which people should live was a major concern of Jews who were dispersed throughout the Greco-Roman world during the Second Temple era. This issue was viewed as important among both those Jews who had access to a Greco-Roman intellectual and literary education and those who relied on a Semitic tradition of study and interpretation. In order to describe Jewish ethics in the Second Temple period, we cannot presume the relatively modern distinction between religion and morality. Rather, we must presuppose that the stipulations of particular practices pertaining to both the conduct of human affairs and the relationship with the divine actions required justification, the rationale for which is related to issues of religious identity and perspective. Differing opinions within Second Temple Judaism regarding religious practice were most commonly rooted in interpretations of the Hebrew scriptures, the central religious document for Jews in the Greco-Roman period. The authors of the documents attributed to Qumran as well as the other inhabitants of the sectarian communities are part of this ethical tradition.

An attempt to describe the ethics of the sectarian authors and their communities must rely primarily on their literary legacy, most particularly on the literature attributed to the site of Qumran; secondarily, on descriptions of their lifestyle and ideology from outside observers from the Second Temple era and immediately thereafter; and, finally, on data collected as the result of archeological excavation and research. With such a diversity of sources, generalizations regarding a common ethical stance cannot simply be presumed. Connections between various sources must be carefully evaluated when attempting to describe their ethics.

Dualistic Worldview. The most dramatic ethic in this literature is the one described in the so-called sectarian texts, where it is rooted in a viewpoint characterized by dualism and determinism. New adherents who voluntarily chose to accept the Rule of the Community from Qumran Cave 1 (hereafter, 1QRule of the Community) were to "bring all their knowledge, powers, and possessions into the community of God" (1QS i.11–12). Purity was at the heart of this communitarian ethic, which sanctioned its distinctiveness within the Jewish communities of the time on the basis of a rigorous, well-defined interpretation of the commandments of God and an exclusive festal calendar. The worldview that sustained the mandated lifestyle was dualistic: in 1QRule of the Community (1QS iii.13–iv.26) all human beings are either children of righteousness who are ruled by the Prince of Light and walk in the ways of light or children of iniquity who are ruled by the Angel of Darkness and walk in the ways of darkness. Those who enter the covenant are to love all the children of light and hate all the children of darkness. The children of light are said to possess a spirit characterized by attributes such as humility, patience, abundant compassion, constant goodness, zeal for the statutes of righteousness, and a glorious purity that detests all unclean idols and the concealment of the truth about the mysteries of knowledge. Those outside the Rule of the Community are characterized by a spirit of iniquity, greed, falsehood, pride, slackness in the execution of righteousness, and insolent zeal for abominable deeds in a spirit of fornication and for defiled paths in the service of uncleanness (1QS iv.2–14). While those who are admitted into the community are equated with the children of light, there is a recognition that all human beings are ruled by both spirits and walk on both paths. This division between and within mankind will be brought to an end only in the final age when God will purify every deed of man with his truth.

This dualistic viewpoint undergirds a sectarian ethic emphasizing the common life of the group, including a regimen of work and study regulated by a ranked hierarchy. Money and property are turned over to the group. The Rule of the Community emphasizes the fraternal obligations and respect that should characterize the life of all its adherents. This fraternal emphasis includes almost no ethical obligations to those Israelites and gentiles outside the sect and in fact includes injunctions about hiding the knowledge to which members are privy from the remainder of the population. This ethic is supported by a determinism that sees world history bound up with the fate of the sect and the lives of the individual members whose lot is determined by God. The corresponding view of the low worth of individual human beings is reinforced in other sectarian texts, particularly in the Hodayot from Qumran Cave 1 (1QH[a,b]). Such determinism inspires the final sequence of events of world history spelled out in compositions such as the War Scroll (1QM, 4Q471, 4Q491–497), the Melchizedek text (11Q13), the Aramaic Apocalypse (Son of God text; 4Q246), and the Messianic Apocalypse (4Q521), thereby supporting the sectarian ethic identified in the Rule of the Community and the copies of the Damascus Document. [*See* Secrecy.]

Purity Laws. The stipulations spelled out in the Damascus Document (CD, 4Q266–273, 5Q12, 6Q15) for the adherents of the new covenant at certain points overlap with the legislation of the Rule of the Community (1QS, 4Q255–264a, 5Q11) but are placed within the context of the group's self-understanding of its historical development. Here, ethical injunctions such as the prohibition of polygamy, divorce, incest (including the marriage of an uncle to his niece), and "unlawful intercourse," (probably referring to sexual relations during the woman's menstrual period) are described in terms of purity and righteousness. These injunctions, stipulated for the adherents of the "new covenant in the land of Damascus," constitute a critique of the remainder of Judaism. Since they are found primarily in the Damascus Document (CD iv–vi; 4Q266 3.i–ii; 4Q269 3–4.i; 4Q270 1.ii.b), they are well integrated into the ideological and historical justification for the development of this "new covenant" within Judaism. After those particular features of this ethic are described and justified, we find more attention to those ordinances that sustain the common life of this branch of Judaism. While the detailed fraternal obligations in 1QRule of the Community are not present in the Damascus Document, the obligation to reprove erring sect members is present and given an exegetical justification on the basis of *Leviticus* 19.15–18 in the Damascus Document (CD vi.20–vii.3 and developed in CD ix.2–x.3, 4Q266 8.ii.10, 4Q267 9.i,

4Q270 6.iii.17–19). The command in the Damascus Document, "A man should seek the welfare of his brother" (CD vi.21) is followed by the injunction, "A man should reprove his brother according to the commandment and not bear a grudge from day to day" (CD vii.2–3). Detailed prescriptions similar to those in the Rule of the Community can be found in other manuscripts of the Damascus Document such as Damascus Document[a,b,e] (4Q266 18.iii–iv, 4Q267 12, 4Q270 11.i) and related material in Serekh Damascus (4Q265 1). [*See* Marriage and Divorce.]

The emphasis on purity that undergirds the ethical injunctions found in the Damascus Document differentiates the adherents of the new covenant from the rest of Judaism by distinguishing between the clean and unclean, and the holy and the profane (CD vi.17–18, xii.19–20; 4Q266 3.ii.23, 9.ii.6–7). These prescriptions enjoined them to be separate from all manner of uncleanness in accordance with the commandment (CD vii.3). We can see in the Damascus Document (CD v.6) the manner in which they understood these prescriptions to be anchored in the purity associated with the Temple: "Also they defile the sanctuary in that they do not separate according to the Torah." Intercourse with a menstruating woman and the marriage of an uncle and a niece are then cited as examples. The ethical stance for those who enter into the new covenant is to model the purity of those in the Temple, the congregation of men of perfect holiness, who have the holy angels in their midst (4Q266 17.i.8–9). In addition to repeating and/or developing material found in the Damascus Document (CD i–viii) and some of the Qumran Cave 4 manuscripts, the latter portion of the Cairo Genizah text of the Damascus Document also contains additional material. Notable here is the description of the exclusive binding oaths sworn by the adherents (CD xv–xvi, 4Q266 8.i, 4Q270 6.i.21–ii.9, 4Q271 4.i.10–ii.4) and the very strict Sabbath laws advocated by this group (CD x.14–xii.6, 4Q266 9.i, 4Q267 9.ii, 4Q270 6, 4Q271 5.i). These texts emphasize the divergent calendar that marked the members of the new covenant (cf. CD iii.12–16, vi.18–19). A rigid regulation of relationships with gentiles also characterizes this legislation (CD xii.6–11, 4Q266 9.i.16–17, 4Q267 9.iii, 4Q271 5.ii.2–9).

The composition from the Cave 4 fragments with an implied ethic most similar to that of the Damascus Document is Miqtsat Maʿasei ha-Torah (MMT[a–f], 4Q394–399). In the available fragments the author notes that "we have separated from the remainder of the people" (4Q396 7; 4Q397 14–21.7). The substantive part of this composition is a legal section that lists practices by which this group distinguished itself from the remainder of Judaism. Relations with gentiles, purity laws with regard to the Temple and its sacrifices, other purity laws such as the uncleanness conveyed by the pouring of liquids, and marriage laws form part of this legislation that would have helped the group's adherents form a unique and identifiable body within Second Temple Judaism, thereby providing a basis for the ethical stances that governed its daily life.

Absent from Miqtsat Maʿasei ha-Torah is any hint of the cosmological dualism undergirding the ethic of the Rule of the Community. While the texts of the Damascus Document contain hints of such dualism (for example, figures such as Belial are mentioned), they share with Miqtsat Maʿasei ha-Torah a critique based on a particular religious interpretation and an emphasis on cleanliness that form the basis for a social separation from the rest of Jewish society. An ethic based on this critique will have been shared by the adherents of the "new covenant in the land of Damascus" and those who lived by the legislation listed in the Miqtsat Maʿasei ha-Torah scrolls. This same social separation is justified by the cosmic dualism of 1QRule of the Community, which presumably provided the basis for the more extreme sectarian ethic characteristic of those persons who actually inhabited a remote site such as the one at Qumran.

A stringent interpretation of the separation between clean and unclean also characterizes the radical reworking and expansion of Pentateuchal legislation that comprises the Temple Scroll (11Q19–20). The unique festal calendar and the very particular purity laws of this composition would have provided an exegetical basis and hence ideological support for the distinctive ethical viewpoint and issues developed in the literature already discussed.

Practical Ethics. Biblical scholars have often related practical ethics to the wisdom literature of the Hebrew scriptures. Also noted has been the manner in which this practical wisdom becomes integrated with the Torah in *Ben Sira*. This correlation is also present in wisdom texts from Qumran, most notably in the sapiential work labeled 4Q185 and in the Wisdom Text with Beatitudes (4Q525 2.ii). The manuscripts of both Sapiential Work A and B (4Q415–419, 4Q423) and Mysteries (1Q27, 4Q299–300) contain repeated references to *mishpaṭ* ("judgment"), *mishpaṭim* ("laws" or "judgments") and *ḥuqqim* ("statutes"), pointing to the manner in which practical ethical instruction is rooted in the legal tradition of scripture in these texts. "Righteousness" and "the righteous" also receive prominent attention, a feature these works share with the versions of the Damascus Document. These texts also make frequent mention of the *raz nihyeh* ("mystery that is to be/come"), thereby pointing to the important role of eschatology in providing the rationale for the ethical injunctions that comprise these texts. While these compositions do not contain the sectarian injunctions characteristic of 1QRule of the Community and 1QHodayot, the use of the term *mystery* appears in similar dualistic contexts in both types of texts. [*See* Sapiential Work.]

Ethics of Essenes. The descriptions of the Essenes in the Greek and Latin texts also demand our attention. The rigorous ethic attributed to this "philosophy" is described most extensively in Josephus's *The Jewish War* 2.119–161, an account that finds some remarkable parallels in Hippolytus, *Refutation of All Heresies* 9.18–28. The descriptions in Philo, *Quod omnis probus liber sit* 75–91 and *Hypothetica* 11.1–18, resemble the account of Josephus in many of the essential characteristics with regard to lifestyle. While both authors stress the Essenes' dispersal throughout Judea, Philo describes them as eschewing city life and living only in rural villages (*Quod omnis probus liber sit* 76). As noted also in 1QRule of the Community, the property of persons admitted to full membership is turned over to the group (*The Jewish War* 2.122). This stipulation provides an example that illustrates the similarities between the ethic ascribed to the Essenes by Josephus and that developed in 1QRule of the Community and various texts of the Damascus Document (CD, 4Q266–273; and Serekh Damascus, 4Q265).

The account of Josephus similarly emphasizes the obligations of the sectarian members to one another, noting that "They neither buy nor sell anything among themselves; each man gives what he has to whoever needs it, and receives in return whatever he himself requires" (*The Jewish War* 2.127). The member also "swears to conceal nothing from the members of the sect, and to reveal nothing to outsiders, even though violence unto death be used against him" (*The Jewish War* 2.141). The strong code of conduct backed by a distinct hierarchical system of teaching and discipline is also described.

Purity laws are emphasized with regard to issues such as frugal meals, the use of white garments that are worn until torn or completely worn out, the Sabbath, defecation, and the avoidance of the use of oil on their bodies. While some of the practices mentioned differ between this account and the Hebrew texts just listed, the basic characteristics of the ethic described in both literatures are remarkably similar. The ideological justification, however, for the ethical system differs. While the Hebrew texts listed have their basis in a cosmological and ethical dualism, Josephus justifies the Essene ethic on the basis of the renunciation of pleasure and the virtue of resistance to control by the passions (*The Jewish War* 2.120). The basis of this disparity may be the different contexts of the respective writers and their intended audience. Josephus's emphasis, for example, on the importance of fate for the Essenes is probably a reference to the determinism noted above (*Jewish Antiquities* 13.172).

Two particular features of Essene ethics deserve comment. Both Philo and Josephus attribute the rejection of marriage to the Essenes (*Hypothetica* 11.14–17; *The Jewish War* 2.120–121; *Jewish Antiquities* 18.21). No such prohibition is to be found in the Hebrew texts of the Dead Sea Scrolls and, as noted above, both the Damascus Document and the Temple Scroll contain legislation regarding marital life. The concerns of purity rather than of celibacy are addressed in the latter works. Josephus does describe a group of Essenes who marry as an exception to his general description (*The Jewish War* 2.160–161). Graves containing the bones of women and children have been excavated at the Qumran site. [*See* Essenes; Josephus Flavius; *and* Women.]

Also noteworthy is the Essene prohibition of owning slaves (*Quod omnis probus liber sit* 79; *Antiquities* 18.21), justified on the basis of an appeal to freedom and equality. The Damascus Document (CD xii.11), however, does contain legislation concerning slaves and Temple Scroll[a] (11Q19 lxii.8) speaks of forced labor for those from an opposing city who surrender. The extent to which these texts are repeating biblical statements rather than representing an ethical viewpoint held by this sect in the second or first centuries BCE is very hard to determine.

[*See also* Covenant; Damascus Document; Dualism; Law and Lawgiving; Miqtsat Maʿasei ha-Torah; Purity; *and* Rule of the Community.]

BIBLIOGRAPHY

Baumgarten, Joseph M. "The Cave 4 Versions of the Qumran Penal Code." *Journal of Jewish Studies* 43 (1992), 268–276. A hypothesis on the development of this material in the Qumran literature.

Harrington, Daniel J. "Wisdom at Qumran." In *The Community of the Renewed Covenant: The Notre Dame Symposium on the Dead Sea Scrolls*, edited by Eugene Ulrich and James VanderKam, pp. 137–152. Notre Dame, Ind., 1994. A summary of relevant material at Qumran with particular attention to Sapiential Work A (4Q416–418).

Harrington, Daniel J. *Wisdom Texts from Qumran*. London, 1996.

Hempel, C. "The Penal Code Reconsidered." In *Legal Texts and Legal Issues: Proceedings of the Second Meetings of the International Organization for Qumran Studies, Cambridge, 1995, published in Honour of Joseph M. Baumgarten*, edited by M. Bernstein, F. García Martínez, and J. Kampen, pp. 337–348. Leiden, 1997. An alternative hypothesis to Baumgarten concerning the development of this literature.

Kimbrough, S. T., Jr. "The Ethic of the Qumran Community." *Revue de Qumrân* 6 (1969), 483–498. A brief discussion arguing that the ethic of Qumran was neither completely open nor completely closed, but one of limited flexibility.

Ringgren, Helmer. *The Faith of Qumran: Theology of the Dead Sea Scrolls*, translated by Emilie T. Sander and edited, with a new introduction, by James H. Charlesworth. Expanded ed. New York, 1995. Provides a comprehensive theological description of the viewpoints represented in the scrolls.

Schiffman, Lawrence H. *Sectarian Law in the Dead Sea Scrolls: Courts, Testimony, and the Penal Code*. Brown Judaic Studies, 33. Chico, Calif., 1983.

Weinfeld, Moshe. *The Organizational Pattern and the Penal Code of the Qumran Sect: A Comparison with Guilds and Religious Associa-*

tions of the Hellenistic Roman Period. Göttingen, 1986. A detailed comparative investigation of the rules and legal structures of the Qumran community with those of the cultic associations of the Hellenistic and Roman worlds.

JOHN I. KAMPEN

EUSEBIUS. *See* Hippolytus.

EXEGESIS. *See* Interpretation of Scriptures.

EXILE. The existence of the kingdoms of Israel and Judah was in each case brought to an end by the exile of the population (*2 Kgs.* 17.1–6, 25.1–21). Although the inhabitants of the northern kingdom were believed to have remained in exile in Assyria (*2 Kgs.* 17.23), the exile of Judah to Babylon is conventionally understood to have been brought to an end by the decree of Cyrus permitting the rebuilding of the Temple (*Ezr.* 6.3–5) and—according to the versions of the decree recorded in *Ezra* 1.2–4 and *2 Chronicles* 36.23—the return of the exiles to Jerusalem. In line with this, the books of *Ezra* and *Nehemiah* preserve a number of traditions, albeit at times confused and contradictory, concerning the return of the exiles, the rebuilding of the Temple, and events in the postexilic period. However, a very different understanding of the period of exile and its aftermath is reflected in a series of traditions in the Damascus Document concerning the origins of the group, assumed here to be the Essenes, responsible for this work.

According to the Damascus Document, the origins of the Essenes are to be traced directly back to the time of the exile. Thus in the Damascus Document (CD i.1–ii.1), reference to the events of the exile is followed immediately by the statement: "And in the time of wrath, 390 years after he [God] had given them into the hand of Nebuchadnezzar, king of Babylon, he visited them and caused a plant root [cf. *1 En.* 93.10; *Jub.* 1.16] to spring from Israel and Aaron, to possess his land, and to grow fat on the good things of his ground" (CD i.5–8). The passage goes on to refer to the raising up by God of the Teacher of Righteousness after a further period of twenty years.

It is significant in the above passage that no reference is made to the return from exile or to the events of the postexilic period. The emergence of the plant root—a symbolic term for the Essenes or for the group from which the Essenes emerged—is presented as the first event to have occurred since the start of the exile. The implication of this is that Israel remained in a state of exile long after their return at the end of the sixth century and that this state of exile was only brought to an end by God's bringing into existence the plant root. This essentially theological understanding of the exilic and postexilic period is underlined by the reference to the 390 years. The figure has been taken from *Ezekiel* 4.5 and serves in the Damascus Document to mark the length of Israel's period of punishment. It has been argued that the references to the 390 years and the twenty years (CD i) are secondary, but if so, they came into the text at a very early stage because they appear in Damascus Document[a], from Cave 4 at Qumran, which dates from the first half of the first century BCE.

The same theological interpretation of the exilic and postexilic periods is found in two other passages in the Damascus Document concerned with Essene origins (CD iii.9–20: v.20–vi.2). The first forms the climax of a survey of Israel's history in which a summary description of the exile (iii.9–12a) is followed immediately by the statement that it was with a faithful remnant that survived the exile that God made his covenant and to which he granted a special revelation (iii.12b–20). The second passage uses the symbolism of the well as the law (based on *Numbers* 21.18) to describe God's bringing into existence a group devoted to the interpretation of the law as the next event after the desolation of the land at the time of the exile.

The evidence of the Damascus Document led Jerome Murphy-O'Connor and Philip Davies to argue that the origins of the Essenes go back historically to the Babylonian exile. This view is, however, quite unlikely and, apart from other considerations, takes no account of the fact that the theological presentation of the exilic and postexilic periods that is found in the Damascus Document is also found in biblical and pseudepigraphal writings from the same period, particularly *Daniel* 9.24–27, *1 Enoch* 93.8–10, and *Jubilees* 1.13–18. The theological pattern in these writings differs slightly from that of the Damascus Document, which does not refer explicitly to the postexilic period: *Daniel* 9.25 does allude to the rebuilding of Jerusalem and the return at the end of the sixth century, describing the postexilic period as a troubled time, and all three writings describe the exilic and postexilic periods as a time of apostasy (*Dn.* 9.24, *1 En.* 93.9, *Jub.* 1.14). But all three writings, like the Damascus Document, present the exilic and postexilic periods as a unity, a state of exile, which was only brought to an end long after the return in the sixth century—in *Daniel* 9 in the events of the time of Antiochus IV Epiphanes; in the Damascus Document, *1 Enoch*, and *Jubilees*, which are probably all concerned with the origins of the same group, by God's bringing into existence a chosen group, the Essenes or their immediate predecessors.

Although the Damascus Document does not refer explicitly to the postexilic period, a concern with this period is to be found in other texts from Qumran, where it is presented both as a time of suffering and oppression (Apocryphon of Joseph[b], 4Q372 i.10–15) and as a time of apostasy (Pseudo-Moses[e], 4Q390, where the first generation of returnees is, exceptionally, exempted from blame).

The texts discussed above all offer a theological interpretation of the exile of Israel. But the concept of exile is also used in a quite different way to refer to the history of the community (or communities) responsible for the Qumran Scrolls. For example, a prophecy of judgment concerning exile "beyond Damascus" in *Amos* 5.27a is quoted in a revised form in the Damascus Document (CD vii.14–19) and interpreted to refer to the establishment at "Damascus" of a community devoted to the study of the law. In Pesher Habakkuk (1QpHab) xi.4–8 the Wicked Priest is said to have pursued the Teacher of Righteousness to "his place of exile"; however, although it is often assumed that this place was Qumran, this can only be a theory. The author of Hodayot[a] (1QH, xii.8–9), who is often thought to have been the Teacher of Righteousness, describes himself as being driven from his land "like a bird from its nest," and the same imagery is also used, apparently in reference to the men of the community, in Catena[a] (4Q177 i.8–9). In the latter case the passage is fragmentary, but the verb meaning "to go into exile" appears.

[*See also* Cairo Genizah; Damascus; Damascus Document; *and* Essenes.]

BIBLIOGRAPHY

Collins, John J. "The Origin of the Qumran Community: A Review of the Evidence." In *To Touch the Text: Biblical and Related Studies in Honor of Joseph A. Fitzmyer, S.J.*, edited by Maurya P. Horgan and Paul J. Kobelski, pp. 159–178. New York, 1989.

Davies, Philip R. *The Damascus Covenant: An Interpretation of the "Damascus Document."* Journal for the Study of the Old Testament, Supplement Series, 25. Sheffield, 1983. Gives the view that the origins of the Essenes are to be traced back to the exiles in Babylon.

Knibb, Michael A. "The Exile in the Literature of the Intertestamental Period." *Heythrop Journal* 17 (1976), 253–272.

Knibb, Michael A. "Exile in the Damascus Document." *Journal for the Study of the Old Testament* 25 (1983), 99–117.

Knibb, Michael A. *Jubilees and the Origins of the Qumran Community.* An Inaugural Lecture delivered on Tuesday, 17 January 1989 at King's College London. London, 1989.

Murphy-O'Connor, Jerome. "The Essenes and Their History." *Revue biblique* 81 (1974), 215–244. Gives the view that the origins of the Essenes are to be traced back to the exiles in Babylon.

Murphy-O'Connor, Jerome. "The Damascus Document Revisited." *Revue biblique* 92 (1985), 223–246.

MICHAEL A. KNIBB

EXODUS, BOOK OF. Before the discovery of manuscripts at Qumran there were three major sources for the text of *Exodus*. The first, the Masoretic Text, is the Hebrew text passed down in Jewish circles in an unbroken manuscript tradition from antiquity to the present, and is, overall, quite a good text that often (but by no means always) preserves the original reading. The second, the Septuagint, is an idiomatic, but accurate, translation into Greek made in the third century BCE. It has numerous small differences from the Masoretic Text, many of which seem to have been present in its Hebrew *Vorlage*. Finally, the Samaritan Pentateuch tends to expand the text by frequently inserting parallel material from other places in the Pentateuch.

Frank Moore Cross, following William Foxwell Albright, has argued that these three sources developed through long transmission in three different locations—Babylon, Egypt, and Palestine, respectively—and should be considered three distinct text-types. This theory has been widely challenged, especially by Emanuel Tov, and few, if any, scholars now accept the suggested geographical origins. I have argued that Cross is correct in essence, but that we should speak of two text-types—the Masoretic Text and the Septuagint—and one deliberate revision or recension, the Samaritan Pentateuch, based on the proto-Masoretic Text.

The textual basis of *Exodus* outlined above has been widened considerably by the recovery of at least sixteen fragmentary manuscripts of the book from Qumran: Exodus (1Q2), Exodus[a–c] (2Q2–4, hereafter called 2QExodus[a–c]), Genesis-Exodus[a] (4Q1), paleo-Genesis-Exodus[l] (4Q11), Exodus[b–e] (4Q13–16, hereafter called 4QExodus[b–e]), Exodus-Leviticus[f] (4Q17), Exodus[g–h,j–k] (4Q18–21), and paleo-Exodus[m] (4Q22). Another scroll containing *Exodus* (as well as *Genesis*, *Numbers*, and perhaps the entire Pentateuch) was found in the Wadi Murabbaʿat (Mur 1.4–5). Some of these manuscripts (Exodus, 2QExodus[c], Exodus[e], Exodus[g], Exodus[h], and Exodus[k]) are too fragmentary to give us much useful information on their contents and textual alignments.

The text of Genesis-Exodus[a] (which preserves parts of *Exodus* 1–8 or 9) is closely related to the Masoretic Text for the most part. Paleo-Genesis-Exodus[l] (containing material from *Exodus* 1–3, 8–12, 14, 16–20, 22–23, 25–28, 36, and 40[?]) appears, mostly on the basis of reconstruction, to lack the typographical expansions characteristic of the Samaritan Pentateuch and paleo-Exodus[m] (see below), but is not obviously tied closely to any of the previously known textual traditions in its shorter variants. Reconstruction indicates that 4QExodus[c] (with text from chapters 7–15 and 17–18) probably lacked the typological features of the Samaritan tradition and paleo-Exodus[m], but otherwise it does not show a clear filiation with any previously known textual tradition. It also has frequent cases of parablepsis—the inadvertant skipping of a word or phrase during copying of a manuscript. The text of the small fragments of the Murabbaʿat manuscript are identical to the Masoretic Text.

Paleo-Exodus[m] (an exceptionally well-preserved manuscript containing fragments of chapters 6–37) is very closely related to the Samaritan Pentateuch. It shares many of the typological expansions of that tradition, but apparently lacks the sectarian Samaritan alterations of the text. The Samaritan Pentateuch expands the Ten Commandments in *Exodus* 19 in three places, and reconstruction indicates that two of these additions were probably also present in paleo-Exodus[m]. However, the sectarian addition after 19.17 was missing. This expansion added *Deuteronomy* 11.29–30 and an altered version of *Deuteronomy* 27.2–7, making worship at Mount Gerizim (a Samaritan doctrine) the tenth commandment. The fact that this addition was not present in paleo-Exodus[m] seems to indicate that the textual tradition involving typological expansions of the Pentateuch predated the Samaritan schism, but also that this recension was adopted by the Samaritans and further altered for their own purposes. Exodus-Leviticus[f], one of the earliest manuscripts from Qumran, dating to the third century BCE and preserving material from *Exodus* 38–40, is also related to the Samaritan tradition. This manuscript confirms that the expansionistic textual tradition of the Samaritan Pentateuch was present in Palestine in the Second Temple period outside and independent of the Samaritan community. It is probable that the scant fragments of Exodus[j] should also be reconstructed according to this expansionistic tradition.

4QExodus[b], which contains fragments of chapters 1–5, has a close textual relationship to the Septuagint. It contains numerous readings that demonstrate that often, apparent variants in the Greek translation reflect a variant Hebrew *Vorlage* (e.g., in 1.1, 1.5, 1.19, 2.11, 2.14, 3.16, 3.19; and see below). 2QExodus[a] (with material from chapters 1, 7, 9, 11, 12, 21, 30, and 32) also has a number of variants in common with the Greek tradition (e.g., in 1.12).

Two manuscripts are of special interest because their texts are radically different from all other textual traditions of *Exodus*. One fragment of 2QExodus[b] contains *Exodus* 19.9 followed by a blank line, after which comes 34.10. It would appear that the text skipped from the middle of the introduction to the events on Mount Sinai to the later renewal of the covenant, omitting the Book of the Covenant (*Ex*. 20–23), the covenant ceremony and the ascent of the elders and Moses (*Ex*. 24), the account of the Tabernacle (*Ex*. 25–31), and the story of the Golden Calf and its aftermath (*Ex*. 32–34.9). Nonetheless, other fragments of the same manuscript contain material from chapters 21–22, 27, and 31 (as well as 4, 12 [?], 18), which seems to imply that the text was presented in an order unfamiliar to us. Likewise, the small fragment 4QExodus[d] contains *Exodus* 13.15–16 followed directly by 15.1, perhaps with half a blank line to be restored between them. It may be that *Exodus* 13.17–14.31 was omitted entirely or the text of the book may have been given in a different order. Perhaps both of these manuscripts were excerpted (liturgical?) texts rather than copies of *Exodus* strictly speaking. The Nash Papyrus is such an excerpted manuscript: this fragment from first or second century BCE Egypt contains the Ten Commandments according to a composite text of *Exodus* and *Deuteronomy*, along with the *Shema*ʿ passage from *Deuteronomy* 6.4–5. Deuteronomy[j] (4Q37) likewise combines texts from *Deuteronomy* 5–6, 8, 11, and 32 with a passage from *Exodus* 12–13. The phylacteries from Qumran contain a similar range of material. One or two other Deuteronomy manuscripts (Deuteronomy[n] [4Q41] and perhaps Deuteronomy[k1] [4Q38]) are also excerpted; the fourth commandment of the Ten Commandments in the former is influenced by the parallel text in *Exodus*.

A number of readings in the *Exodus* manuscripts are of interest in themselves and a few will be discussed here. The Masoretic Text of *Exodus* 1.5 reports that Jacob's offspring numbered seventy persons—a typically biblical round number. The Septuagint, however, reads seventy-five. The latter calculation is based on a different enumeration of Jacob's descendants in the Septuagint of *Genesis* 46.20 and 27, wherein five additional sons and grandsons of Manasseh and Ephraim are named (cf. *Acts* 7.14). The reading "seventy-five" is also found in *Exodus* 1.5 of Genesis-Exodus[a] and 4QExodus[b], confirming that both calculations go back to Hebrew *Vorlagen*. However, it is interesting to note that the readings in the two Qumran manuscripts are slightly different. The text of Genesis-Exodus[a] gives the number as "[seventy] and five," whereas the order in 4QExodus[b] (and the Septuagint) is "five and seventy." Perhaps the manuscript tradition behind Genesis-Exodus[a] originally read "seventy," but was altered to reflect the general tradition of a larger number entering Egypt, although not the exact variant text behind the tradition.

Frank Cross and David Noel Freedman have argued on the basis of linguistic and orthographic criteria that the poem in *Exodus* 15.2–18 is exceedingly ancient—probably written before the founding of the Israelite monarchy in approximately 1000 BCE. Part of this poem is preserved in 4QExodus[c] (15.12–18) and it is interesting to note that a number of the unusual and perhaps archaic features found in the Masoretic Text are not present in this manuscript. The nunnation on the third person plural imperfect form of the verb *rgz*, "to tremble," is missing in verse 14. The unusual form *ʾeymatah*, "terror," in verse 16 is read as *ʾeymah* as with the Samaritan Pentateuch. The archaic third masculine plural pronominal suffix *-mo* is read as the normal form *-m* twice in verse 17. These minor variants seem to show the distinctive language of the poem being homogenized into normal classical Hebrew.

Besides the systematically reworked redactions of the *Book of Exodus*, best exemplified by paleo-Exodus^m, there are documents that are inspired by *Exodus* (or by the Pentateuch overall) and that paraphrase it, sometimes closely. The text known as the Reworked Pentateuch (4Q158, 4Q364–365, 4Q366–367) is based on the Pentateuch but heavily rewrites, reorders, and supplements the material in it. For example, the poem in *Exodus* 15 is augmented by additional poetic material. The Hebrew text of *Jubilees* is preserved in fragments (1Q17–18, 2Q19–20, 3Q5, 4Q216–224, 11Q12). This book, presented as a revelation to Moses on Mount Sinai, rewrites *Genesis* and summarizes much of *Exodus*, paraphrasing much more freely than the Reworked Pentateuch. The scattered fragments of Pseudo-Jubilees (4Q225–227) also allude to events in *Genesis* and *Exodus*. Paraphrase of Genesis-Exodus (4Q422) paraphrases the Creation, Fall, and Flood narratives of *Genesis*, along with the story of the Egyptian oppression of the Israelites and the ten plagues from *Exodus*. A number of copies of a Moses pseudepigraphon (4Q385a, 4Q387a, 4Q388a, 4Q389, and 4Q390) show interesting parallels to material in the Old Testament pseudepigrapha preserved outside Qumran (including *Jubilees*, the "Animal Apocalypse," the *Testament of Levi*, and the *Testament of Moses*), as well as to the Qumran sectarian literature, especially the Damascus Document. Other manuscripts mentioning Moses include Words of Moses (1Q22), Liturgy of Three Tongues of Fire (1Q29), Discourse on the Exodus/Conquest Tradition (4Q374), and Apocryphon of Moses B$^{a–b}$ (4Q375–376), which may or may not be connected to the Moses pseudepigraphon. The Visions of Amram (4Q543–548) involves Amram (*Ex.* 7.20), the father of Moses, Aaron, and Miriam (her name also appears). Another text (4Q549) refers to Hur (mentioned several times in *Exodus*) and Miriam. One poorly preserved document, Biblical Chronology (4Q559), gives a schematic chronology of at least the period between Abraham and the Judges, and the names Amram and Aaron are found in it. An exceedingly fragmentary Greek manuscript (pap4QParaExod gr) mentions Moses, Pharaoh, Egypt, angels, and sins, and may refer to Aaron and Miriam. It clearly paraphrases elements of *Exodus*, but nothing of the story line can now be reconstructed.

The large number of copies of *Exodus* recovered from Qumran, as well as its wide influence on Second Temple texts also found there, indicate that this book was a very important work to the compilers of the Qumran library and to Second Temple Judaism in general.

BIBLIOGRAPHY

Most of the Exodus manuscripts from Qumran Cave 4 were published in Discoveries in the Judaean Desert 9 and 12. Most of the Hebrew manuscripts of *Jubilees* and some of the other paraphrases were published in Discoveries in the Judaean Desert 13. These are extremely technical studies of the original texts and are meant for the specialist.

Albright, W. F. "A Biblical Fragment from the Maccabaean Age: The Nash Papyrus." *Journal of Biblical Literature* 56 (1937), 145–176.

Cross, Frank Moore, and David Noel Freedman. *Studies in Ancient Yahwistic Poetry*. Missoula, Mont., 1975.

Cross, Frank Moore, and Shemaryahu Talmon, eds. *Qumran and the History of the Biblical Text*. Cambridge, Mass., 1975. A collection of important articles on this topic published between 1953 and 1975. Includes essays by Albright (pp. 140–146) and Cross (pp. 177–195, 278–292, 306–320) on the theory of local text-types in the Hebrew Bible.

Davila, James R. "Text-Type and Terminology: Genesis and Exodus as Test Cases." *Revue de Qumrân* 16/61 (1993), 3–37.

Dimant, Devorah. "New Light from Qumran on the Jewish Pseudepigrapha—4Q390. In *The Madrid Qumran Congress: Proceedings of the International Congress on the Dead Sea Scrolls, Madrid, 18–21 March 1991*, edited by Julio Trebolle Barrera and Luis Vegas Montaner, vol. 2, pp. 405–448 and pls. 24–25. 2 vols. Leiden, 1992. A technical treatment of Pseudo-Moses^e (4Q390), but some of the general discussion is also of interest to the nonspecialist.

Duncan, Julie A. "Considerations of 4QDt^j in Light of the 'All Souls Deuteronomy' and Cave 4 Phylactery Texts." In *The Madrid Qumran Congress: Proceedings of the International Congress on the Dead Sea Scrolls, Madrid, 18–21 March 1991*, edited by Julio Trebolle Barrera and Luis Vegas Montaner, vol. 1, pp. 199–215 and pls. 2–7. 2 vols. Leiden, 1992.

Sanderson, Judith E. *An Exodus Scroll from Qumran: paleo-Exod^m and the Samaritan Tradition*. Atlanta, 1986. A comprehensive technical study of the textual characteristics of paleo-Exod^m.

Sanderson, Judith E. "The Contributions of *4QPaleoExod^m* to Textual Criticism." *Revue de Qumrân* 13/49–52 (1988), 547–560. A convenient summary of the highlights of the preceding volume.

Skehan, Patrick W. "Exodus in the Samaritan Recension from Qumran." *Journal of Biblical Literature* 74 (1955), 182–187. The first preliminary publication of a column of paleo-Exod^m.

Tov, Emanuel. "A Modern Textual Outlook Based on the Qumran Scrolls." *Hebrew Union College Annual* 53 (1982), 11–27. An important article in which Tov criticizes Albright's and Cross's theory of text-types.

White, Sidnie Ann. "The All Souls Deuteronomy and the Decalogue." *Journal of Biblical Literature* 109 (1990), 193–206.

JAMES R. DAVILA

EXORCISM. *See* Magic and Magical Texts.

EZEKIEL, BOOK OF.

[*This entry consists of two parts:* Biblical Text *and* Pseudo-Ezekiel.]

Biblical Text

The biblical book that bears the name of Ezekiel son of Buzi, priest and prophet contains a diverse collection of oracles and visions believed to have been received by Ezekiel himself as well as elements that have been incorporated by later tradents and editors, some of whom may have belonged to his immediate circle of associates (that is, members of his prophetic guild). Most of the book's contents are dated to roughly the sixth century BCE. Following a brief introduction (1.1–3), the book consists of a large block of material that contains an account of Ezekiel's commission and a number of vision reports (1.4–24.25), oracles against foreign nations (25.1–32.32), an initial set of oracles concerning Israel's judgment and restoration (33.1–34.31), an oracle against Mount Seir and Edom (35.1–15), a second group of oracles describing the restoration of Israel (36.1–39.29), and a vision of the new Israel, Jerusalem, and Temple (40.1–48.35).

Of the book's many themes, some of the more important include: the prophet as moral sentinel (3.16–21), theological justification for the impending siege of Jerusalem (5.1–17), the dispersion of those who survive Israel's destruction (6.8–10), the departure of Yahweh's glory from the temple (10.18–22, 11.22–23), the persistence of the divine presence with those in exile (11.16), individual responsibility for sin (18.19–20), Yahweh's judgment against Ammon, Moab, Edom, Philistia, Tyre, and Sidon (25.1–32.32), and the future restoration of Israel (37.1–14, 40.1–48.35).

The Judean Desert has yielded only modest textual remains of *Ezekiel*. Six manuscripts have been found in four caves at Qumran (1Q9 [hereafter 1QEzekiel], 3Q1 [hereafter 3QEzekiel], 4Q73 [hereafter Ezekiel[a]], 4Q74 [hereafter Ezekiel[b]], 4Q75 [hereafter Ezekiel[c]], and 11Q4 [hereafter 11QEzekiel]) and one from Masada (Mas1d [hereafter MasEzekiel]). In all (excluding the material from Masada, which has just been published), these provide partial witnesses for some seventy-six verses of the book. This raises some questions about the relative importance of the book to those responsible for the textual assemblages at Qumran and elsewhere in the Judean Desert. It also makes drawing any far-reaching conclusions about the textual character of these remains problematic.

1QEzekiel is made up of two fragments. The first contains a portion of 4.16–5.1. Dominique Barthélemy and J. T. Milik (1955, pp. 68–69) have described the paleography as "assez classique" and have also suggested the possibility that this is a citation from *Ezekiel* rather than a manuscript fragment. The extant reading is identical to that of the Masoretic Text. Its orthography appears to conform with Masoretic conventions as well. The content and context of the second fragment are difficult to establish because so few letters remain.

3QEzekiel contains a single fragment preserving part of *Ezekiel* 16.31–33. M. Baillet (1962) has described its script as a careful Herodian hand that leans slightly to the left. There is little evidence upon which to make a thorough assessment of the manuscript's orthographic conventions. The portion of the text that is legible preserves a reading identical to that of the Masoretic Text. The *hapax legomenon* (that is, a word used only once in the entire Hebrew scriptures)—*le-qalles*—was a strong indicator to the original editors that the fragment was from *Ezekiel*.

Ezekiel[a] is made up of five fragments. The first two, which represent the bottom and top of contiguous columns, contain text from *Ezekiel* 10.6–11.11. The third preserves parts of 23.14–15, 23.17–18, 23.44–47. The fourth and fifth have text from 41.3–6. In terms of paleography, Sanderson (Ulrich, 1997) has described the script as Hasmonean with early semiformal Herodian tendencies and has dated it to the mid–first century BCE. She has noted that the orthography is similar to that of the Masoretic Text and that the manuscript contains only six minor variants from that text and is, thus, quite similar to it.

Ezekiel[b] contains six fragments representing three contiguous columns. They preserve text from 1.10–11 (frg. 1), 1.10–11 (frg. 2), 1.11–12 (frg. 3), 1.13 (frg. 4), 1.16–17 (frg. 5), 1.19 (frg. 6i), and 1.20–24 (frg. 6.ii). The hand has been described by J. Sanderson (Ulrich, 1997) as an early first century CE Herodian script. She has also noted that the orthography of the manuscript disagrees with the Masoretic Text in only two instances and that the text itself preserves two errors. The first, *ya'amodu* in 1.21, has a supralineal correction (the *dalet*). The second, *u-demutam*, is not corrected (cf., *u-demot* in the Masoretic and Old Greek Texts). In addition to these errors, Sanderson has indicated that the manuscript preserves only two other minor variants and is, thus, similar to the Masoretic Text.

Ezekiel[c] consists of a single fragment preserving five complete words and six individual letters from *Ezekiel* 24.2–3. Sanderson (Ulrich, 1997) has classified its script as Hasmonean and has dated it to the first century BCE (early to middle). These fragmentary remains preserve a reading identical to the Masoretic Text.

A preliminary edition of 11QEzekiel was prepared by W. H. Brownlee (1963–1964). He has noted that the scroll was found in a very poor state of preservation, only a small portion of it was capable of being salvaged and read, and the remainder was thought to be of sufficient size to contain most of the entire book. Unfortunately, the parchment scroll had solidified over time into a single mass from which only five fragments could be recovered. These fragments preserve parts of 44.3–5 (frg. A), 5.11–17 (frgs. B and C), 7.9–12 (frg. D), and 10.11 (frg. E). The text of fragment A agrees with the Masoretic Text.

Brownlee has commented that when read together, fragments B and C preserve two minor orthographic differences and one insubstantial textual variant that agrees with the Old Greek against the Masoretic Text. The text of fragment D is identical to the Masoretic Text as is that of fragment E. The paleography of the scroll is, according to Brownlee, either late pre-Herodian or early Herodian, and he has offered an approximate date range of 55–22 BCE. He has concluded that its text is quite similar to that of the Masoretic Text.

The *Ezekiel* material from Masada (MasEzekiel) has just been published. Ulrich (1995) has indicated that it consists of fragments from *Ezekiel* 31.11–37.15. Thus, an assessment of paleographic, orthographic, and other conventions employed in these texts cannot be offered at present.

As for other major witnesses to the text of *Ezekiel*, Emanuel Tov's (1992: 282–284, 333–334) comments are most illuminating. He has estimated that the Masoretic Text represents a longer text (by roughly 4 to 5 percent) than the supposed Hebrew *Vorlage* (underlying version) of the Old Greek version and has suggested that a "literary layer" (283, 334) consisting of "explicative-exegetical, harmonizing," (333) and other types of expansions was added to this older text to form the Masoretic Text. He has also noted that this Hebrew *Vorlage* contained a single recensional anomaly at 7.3–9 where verse order and content are at variance with the Masoretic witness. Otherwise, the Old Greek version offers what he has termed a "relatively literal" (333) translation. P. K. McCarter Jr. (1986: 91) has suggested that the Old Greek of *Ezekiel* is represented by LXX^{b} (Codex Vaticanus, a Septuagint manuscript from the fourth century), in chapters 1–27 and 40–48, but not in chapters 28–39, where witnesses to the Lucianic recension are crucial in reconstructing the Old Greek.

The Pseudo-Ezekiel (or Second Ezekiel) materials at Qumran (4Q385–4Q388, 4Q391) present their own unique set of hermeneutical difficulties (cf., Strugnell, 1988; Dimant, 1989; 1992; 1994). Devorah Dimant has offered the following general observations about Pseudo-Ezekiel: (1) that it consists of visions and divine explanations set within an autobiographical context in which the prophet Ezekiel functions as narrator, (2) that it includes visions from the biblical book of *Ezekiel*—for example, that of both the *Merkavah* and Dry Bones—along with others, and (3) that it contains a recapitulation of history that bears stylistic similarities to historical apocalypses such as *2 Baruch*, *4 Ezra*, and others (Strugnell, 1988: 46, 48; Dimant, 1992: 409). She has also pointed out that, in terms of lexical inventory and style, the authors of Pseudo-Ezekiel employed the biblical book of *Ezekiel* as a model, and that in those instances where Pseudo-Ezekiel contains a citation from its biblical counterpart, the Masoretic Text is quoted almost exactly.

Several other sources appropriate and/or interpret parts of *Ezekiel* as well. Those noted in the pertinent secondary literature (cf., Lust, 1986: 92–93; Strugnell, 1988: 47, esp. note 6; Dimant, 1990: 332, esp. note 3) include the Florilegium (4Q174), the Damascus Document (eight fragmentary copies of which were found in Qumran Cave 4—4Q266–273), Temple Scroll^{a-b} (11Q19–20), Songs of the Sabbath Sacrifice^{a-b} (4Q400–4Q407), Songs of the Sabbath Sacrifice (11Q17), and the Masada Songs of the Sabbath Sacrifice (Mas1k). The presence of such interpretive works is a strong indicator that the book was in fact a viable part of the ongoing intellectual life of the Qumran community. Moreover, it would appear that the vision of the *Merkavah* and the vision of the Temple garnered particular attention (on these interpretive texts, see especially Allegro, 1968; Yadin, 1983; Brooke, 1985; Newsom, 1985; Broshi, 1992; Baumgarten, 1996). It is also possible that Ezekiel's vision of the stream that would flow from the Temple to the Dead Sea near 'Ein-Gedi (chapter 47) influenced the original Qumran group to choose Khirbet Qumran as its place of residence. Unfortunately, it is difficult to say much more than this at present.

As stated above, the paucity of evidence from the Judean wilderness makes it especially difficult either to say much about the general character of *Ezekiel* manuscripts or to offer an in-depth analysis of the book's textual history. At most, one can offer a single rather modest conclusion—that taken together, the *Ezekiel* manuscripts found in the caves of Qumran are quite similar to the Masoretic Text and may be tentatively classified as pre-Masoretic in character.

BIBLIOGRAPHY

Allegro, J. M., ed. *Qumran Cave 4, I.* Discoveries in the Judaean Desert, 5. Oxford, 1968. This publication contains the critical edition of 4Q174 (Florilegium).

Baillet, M., J. T. Milik, and R. de Vaux., eds. *Les 'petites grottes' de Qumrân.* Discoveries in the Judaean Desert, 3. Oxford, 1962. This publication contains the critical edition of 3Q1 (3QEzekiel).

Barthélemy, D., and J. T. Milik, eds. *Qumran Cave 1.* Discoveries in the Judaean Desert, 1. Oxford, 1955. This publication contains the critical edition of 1Q9 (1QEzekiel).

Baumgarten, J. M., ed. *Qumran Cave 4, XIII: The Damascus Document (4Q266–273).* Discoveries in the Judaean Desert, 18. Oxford, 1996. This publication contains the critical edition of 4Q266–4Q273 (Damascus Document^{a-h}).

Brooke, G. J. *Exegesis at Qumran: 4QFlorilegium in Its Jewish Context.* Sheffield, 1985. This monograph explores exegetical praxis in late Second Temple Judaism generally and in the literature of the Qumran community specifically, with particular attention being given to 4Q174 (Florilegium).

Broshi, M., ed. *The Damascus Document Reconsidered.* Jerusalem,

1992. This publication contains a new critical edition of CDC (the Damascus Document)—prepared by E. Qimron, which includes an apparatus that cites many of the variant readings from manuscripts found at Qumran—and a reassessment of the text.

Brownlee, W. H. "The Scroll of Ezekiel from the Eleventh Qumran Cave." *Revue de Qumrân* 4 (1963–1964), 11–18. This article contains a preliminary edition of 11Q4 (11QEzekiel); an account of early efforts to open and read the scroll; and an analysis of its text, paleography, and orthography.

Dimant, D. "New Light from Qumran on the Jewish Pseudepigrapha—4Q390." In *Proceedings of the International Congress on the Dead Sea Scrolls—Madrid 18–21 March 1991*, pp. 205–448. Leiden, 1992. In addition to her examination of 4Q390 (Pseudo-Moses[e]), the author offers a brief assessment of the Pseudo-Ezekiel materials found at Qumran.

Dimant, D. "An Apocryphon of Jeremiah from Cave 4 (4Q385[b]=4Q385 16)." In *New Qumran Texts and Studies: Proceedings of the First Meeting of the International Organization for Qumran Studies, Paris 1992*, pp. 11–30. Leiden 1994. The author presents an examination of 4Q385[b] (Apocryphon of Jeremiah C).

Dimant, D., and John Strugnell. "The Merkabah Vision in Second Ezekiel." *Revue de Qumrân* 14 (1989), 331–348. This article contains partial publication of 4Q385 4 (4QPseudo-Ezekiel[a], frg. 4) and an analysis of its content.

García Martínez, F., and E. J. C. Tigchelaar, eds. *Qumran Cave 11. II. 11Q2–18, 11Q20–31.* Discoveries in the Judaean Desert, 23. Oxford, 1998. See pages 15–28.

Lust, J. "Ezekiel Manuscripts from Qumran: Preliminary Edition of 4QEza and b." In *Ezekiel and His Book: Textual and Literary Criticism and Their Interrelation*, pp. 90–100. Louvain, 1986. This article offers a brief survey of Ezekiel material from Qumran published through 1986 and a preliminary edition of 4Q73–4Q74 (4QEzekiel[a]–4QEzekiel[b]). Special attention should be given to the list of Qumran texts that quote Ezekiel on pages 92–93.

McCarter, P. K., Jr. *Textual Criticism: Recovering the Text of the Hebrew Bible*. Minneapolis, 1986. This monograph presents an introduction to the principles and objectives of textual criticism in Hebrew Bible research.

Newsom, C., ed. *Songs of the Sabbath Sacrifice: A Critical Edition*. Harvard Semitic Studies. Atlanta, 1985. This volume contains a critical edition of 4Q400–4Q407, 11Q17, and Mas1k (4QSongs of the Sabbath Sacrifice[a–h], 11QSongs of the Sabbath Sacrifice, and MasSongs of the Sabbath Sacrifice).

Strugnell, J., and D. Dimant. "4QSecond Ezekiel." *Revue de Qumrân* 13 (1988), 45–58. This article presents the authors' initial assessment of what was then held to be a complete corpus of Pseudo-Ezekiel manuscripts consisting of 4Q385–4Q390 along with partial publication of 4Q385. See the subsequent articles by Dimant for modifications of conclusions reached in this study.

Tov, E. *Textual Criticism of the Hebrew Bible*. Minneapolis, 1992. In this monograph, the author presents a comprehensive introduction to the art and science of Hebrew Bible textual criticism.

Ulrich, E. "An Index of the Passages in the Biblical Manuscripts from the Judean Desert (Part 2: Isaiah—Chronicles)." *Dead Sea Discoveries* 2 (1995), 86–107. This article contains an index of all Ezekiel manuscripts found at Qumran and Masada with a corresponding list of the chapters and verses from the biblical book contained in these texts.

Ulrich, E. et al., eds. *Qumran Cave 4, X: The Prophets.* Discoveries in the Judaean Desert, 15. Oxford, 1997. This volume contains J. Sanderson's critical edition of 4Q73 (Ezekiel[a]), 4Q74 (Ezekiel[b]), and 4Q75 (Ezekiel[c]).

Yadin, Y., ed. *The Temple Scroll, Vols. 1–3 and Supplement*. Jerusalem, 1983. This four-volume collection contains the critical edition of 11Q19–11Q20 (11QTemple Scroll[a–b]).

HUGH ROWLAND PAGE, JR.

Pseudo-Ezekiel

The Hebrew work now entitled Pseudo-Ezekiel (or sometimes, Second Ezekiel) was originally identified by John Strugnell. He assigned to it six copies, the ones enumerated below together with Pseudo-Ezekiel[c] (4Q387), Pseudo-Moses[c] (4Q389), and Pseudo-Moses[e] (4Q390). I split the collection into two different groups, representing two works: Pseudo-Ezekiel and the Apocryphon of Jeremiah. Each has a distinct style, themes, and vocabulary. According to my division, Pseudo-Ezekiel has survived in five fragmentary copies. Most of them date to around 50 BCE.

Description of Copies. Pseudo-Ezekiel[a] (4Q385) dates to 50–25 BCE. Fragments 1–6 and 12 can be assigned with certainty to Pseudo-Ezekiel. Fragment 12 is to be joined to the lower part of the column preserved in fragment 2. Pseudo-Ezekiel[b] (4Q386; 50–1 BCE) is a single large fragment preserving remains of three columns. Two additional tiny fragments have survived. Pseudo-Ezekiel[c] (4Q387) consists of eight fragments (earlier numbered as 6, 19, 24, 24–27, 30, 38). Fragment 1 (earlier numbered as 4Q385 24) comes clearly from Pseudo-Ezekiel, since the name of the prophet is explicitly mentioned. Pseudo-Ezekiel[d] (4Q388) consists of fragments 1–7 (earlier numbered as 7–14) and dates from around 50 BCE. Fragment 7 (earlier numbered as 8) overlaps Pseudo-Ezekiel[a] (4Q385 2 1–5). Pseudo-Ezekiel[e]? (4Q391) is a papyrus manuscript, and is the oldest copy of Pseudo-Ezekiel. It is dated to the second half of the second century BCE. There is no actual overlapping between this manuscript and the other copies of Pseudo-Ezekiel. Also, this manuscript displays some unique features, such as narrative sections and the mention of the activities of Ezekiel (e.g. 4Q391 9, 36, and 55) told in the first person. However, the obvious drawing upon canonical *Ezekiel* makes it extremely likely that it is another copy of the same work, which has preserved sections not preserved in other copies.

Content and Structure. It can be inferred from the text that the work has to do with the prophet Ezekiel, who speaks in the first person, but is not identical with the canonical *Book of Ezekiel*. The Qumranic text attaches itself to *Ezekiel* by quoting, rewriting, and expanding scriptural prophecies. The fragments belonging to Pseudo-Ezekiel can be identified with certainty by the mention of the name *Ezekiel* (4Q385 4 [earlier numbered as 3] 4; 6 [earlier numbered as 4] 5; 4Q385b 1 [earlier numbered as 24] 1), by drawing on the canonical theme, and by imitation of the style of the biblical prophet. For instance, God addresses Ezekiel with the title "son of man" (4Q385 2.5; 3 [earlier numbered as 12] 4; 4Q386 3 [earlier numbered as 1] ii.2). The surviving fragments preserve several visions revealed to the prophet and the nonbiblical explanations of them given by God following the queries of the prophet. In one of the fragments the Vision of the Dry Bones related in *Ezekiel* 37 is presented (4Q385 2; 4Q386 1.i; 4Q388 7 [earlier numbered as 8]). In another fragment the Merkabah Vision of Ezekiel 1 is preserved (4Q385 6 [earlier numbered as 4]). A third vision regarding Egypt and Babylon has no biblical counterpart, although it is obviously modeled on *Ezekiel* 29–32 (4Q385 1.ii–iii). Apparently, additional noncanonical visions were included in the compositions (e.g., 4Q385b 6 [earlier numbered as 9]), but due to the fragmentary state of the text it is difficult to make out the vision's content or context. The biblical visions are introduced by condensed and slightly altered quotations, omitting repetitions and redundancies. Occasionally such quotations are supplemented by small nonbiblical details. The meaning given to these visions by the author of Pseudo-Ezekiel is presented as divine responses granted to queries made by Ezekiel. Presumably such queries and answers were originally included for both the Vision of the Dry Bones and the Merkavah Vision, but only those pertaining to the first vision have survived. For the Merkavah Vision only the quotation itself is preserved.

According to Pseudo-Ezekiel the Vision of the Dry Bones is shown to the prophet as an answer to his query about the future recompense of the righteous. The author of this work found at Qumran understood, then, the biblical vision as referring to such future recompense. However, the true meaning of this vision for the author is conveyed by a nonbiblical detail added to the biblical description: according to it the resurrected people stood up and blessed God who had raised them (4Q385 2.8–9 and probably 4Q385 3 [earlier numbered as 12]), which describes the blessing uttered by a crowd of people, and therefore seems to fit the same context). Such a detail can hardly be interpreted in a metaphorical way, for it makes no sense in a metaphorical context. It shows rather that the author meant it literally, thus indicating that he understood the vision as referring to a real resurrection of the righteous in the eschatological future. Pseudo-Ezekiel, then, constitutes the earliest witness for such an understanding of *Ezekiel* 37.1–14, an understanding which later became widespread among Jews and Christians. In attesting the early existence of the belief in the resurrection of the righteous, Pseudo-Ezekiel joins *Daniel* 12.2, which must be roughly its contemporary in the first half of the second century BCE. Moreover, the blessing after resurrection seems to be based on *Isaiah* 26.19, which reads: "awake and sing (Septuagint: "they awoke and sang"), you (Septuagint: "those") who lie in the dust." Indeed, later interpreters took the *Isaiah* verse to refer to the resurrection, and to the following blessing (e.g., Aquila to *Is*. 26.19; in *B.T., San*. 92b the blessing is attributed to the resurrected of *Ezekiel* 37). Pseudo-Ezekiel seems to have the same understanding two centuries earlier. In fact, in speaking of resurrection in *Daniel* 12.2, it also refers to *Isaiah* 26.19. Both *Daniel* and Pseudo-Ezekiel show that already during the second century BCE *Isaiah* 26.19 was read as referring to resurrection. On the basis of *Daniel* 12.2 and *2 Maccabees* 7 the belief in the resurrection of the righteous was explained as devised to comfort martyrs during the Antiochene crisis. The fact that in Pseudo-Ezekiel the idea of resurrection is introduced without any connection to martyrdom suggests its independent, and perhaps more ancient, origin.

In another fragment, Pseudo-Ezekiel[a] (4Q385 4 earlier numbered as 3), God consents to grant Ezekiel's request to hasten the days in order to speed up the redemption of Israel. Although materially the fragment is not joined to fragment Pseudo-Ezekiel, 4Q385 2, containing the Vision of the Dry Bones, it is connected to the Vision through the underlying thematic development and exegetical links. The connection between the awaited eschatological resurrection and the hastening of time is expressed explicitly by Pseudo-Philo's *Biblical Antiquities* 19.13, and by *1 Clement* 50.3. It seems that such a link underlies the fragments of Pseudo-Ezekiel. Together with the passage on the Vision of the Dry Bones, Pseudo-Ezekiel[a] (4Q385 4 earlier numbered as 3) attests to the interest of the author in things to come at the final stages of history.

The same concern is apparent in the interpretation of a third vision, found in Pseudo-Ezekiel[b] (4Q386 1 ii–iii), which is not biblical. Ezekiel beholds the land of Israel lying desolate (inspired by *Ezek*. 36.35, 38; *Jer*. 36.10, 12?) and asks when the gathering of Israel from the Diaspora will come about. The divine response is given in the form of a forecast, relating events to take place in an unspecified time. The forecast speaks of events in Egypt (col. ii) and events in Babylon (col. iii). Perhaps the designations Egypt and Babylon are intended to refer to the kingdoms that occupied the same territories at the time of the author, namely to the Ptolemies in Egypt and the Seleucids in Syria-Mesopotamia. The events alluded to in connection with Egypt remain enigmatic. The apocalypse mentions "a Son of Belial" who planned to persecute Israel but was killed by divine intervention. The Israelites are to be rescued from Egypt. The identification of this figure and the events connected with it are uncertain, but the episode is obviously modeled on the Exodus story. Column iii has preserved a few words, perhaps alluding to a battle in Babylon.

Yet another fragment (4Q385b 1 earlier numbered as 24) rewrites one of Ezekiel's prophecies against the nations and especially Egypt (*Ezek.* 30.1–6), but it differs from treatments of the same theme in Pseudo-Ezekiel[b] 4Q386 1 ii) and in a copy of the Apocryphon of Jeremiah, 4Q385b 17 (earlier numbered as 6) ii.3–9. Coming from a different composition, this column (4Q385a 17.ii) quotes Nahum's prophecy on Egypt (*Na.* 3.8–10) rather than the one from *Ezekiel*.

Pseudo-Ezekiel does not contain any of the terminology and ideas distinctive of the Qumran community. Nor do the copies use the Qumranic scribal system. The affinities Pseudo-Ezekiel displays are with non-Qumranic apocalyptic visions, which foretell eschatological events. Pseudo-Ezekiel shows special affinity with two second-century CE pseudepigraphic apocalypses, *4 Ezra* and *2 Baruch*, both preserved only in translation. It is therefore of interest that the apocalyptic traditions embodied in these two writings are now extant in a much earlier Hebrew form. The meager remains of the work do not permit us to say anything on the origin and currency of this work. It seems to have been authored outside the Qumran community no later than the second century BCE. It is impossible to say whether Pseudo-Ezekiel is identical with one of the two books attributed by Josephus (*Jewish Antiquities* 10.80) to the prophet Ezekiel. Also the church fathers quote from an apocryphon of Ezekiel (e.g., Epiphanius, *Against Heresies* 64–70, 5–17), but apart from the general similarity of theme, that of resurrection, no quotation overlaps the extant fragments from Qumran.

It has, however, been suggested that the work was quoted by two early Christian writings: the *Epistle of Barnabas* 12.1 quotes Pseudo-Ezekiel[a] (4Q385 2.9–10), referring to "a tree which will bend and will stand erect" (Kister, 1990). The *Apocalypse of Peter* 4.7–8 quotes 4Q385 2.5–6. Both quotations add similar nonbiblical details to the Vision of the Dry Bones (Bauckham, 1992). In both cases it can be argued that the similarity which has led some scholars to identify these as quotations may be explained as common earlier traditions. It should be noted that the two alleged quotations are taken from the same passage on the Dry Bones and resurrection, a subject and a prooftext popular among Jewish as well as early Christian writers.

BIBLIOGRAPHY

EDITIONS

Dimant, Devorah. "New Light on the Jewish Pseudepigrapha—4Q390." *The Madrid Qumran Congress*, edited by Julio Trebolle Barrera and Luis Vegas Montaner, vol. 2, pp 405–448. Studies on the Texts of the Desert of Judah, 11. Leiden, 1992.

Dimant, Devorah. "A Quotation from Nahum 3:8–10 in 4Q385–6." In *The Bible in the Light of Its Interpreters: Sarah Kamin Memorial Volume* (in Hebrew), edited by S. Japhet, pp. 31–37. Jerusalem, 1994. Publication of 4Q385 6.

Dimant, Devorah, and John Strugnell. "The Merkabah Vision in Second Ezekiel." *Revue de Qumrân* 14 (1990), 341–348. Publication of 4Q385 6 (earlier numbered as 4).

Puech, Émile. *La croyance des Esséniens en la vie future: Immortalité, résurrection, vie éternelle?* Paris, 1993. See volume 2, 605–616.

Smith, M. "4Q391: 4QpapPseudo-Ezekiel[e]." In *Qumran Cave 4, XIV: Parabiblical Texts Pt.* 2, pp. 153–193. Discoveries in the Judaean Desert, 19. Oxford, 1995. Publication of 4Q391.

Strugnell, John, and Devorah Dimant. "Second Ezekiel." *Revue de Qumrân* 13 (1988), 45–56. Publication of 4Q385 2, 4.

Wacholder, B. Z., and M. Abegg. *A Preliminary Edition of the Unpublished Dead Sea Scrolls*, vol. 3, pp. 228–263. Washington, 1995. Based on the original transcriptions and edition of John Strugnell.

DISCUSSIONS

Bauckham, R. "A Quotation from 4Q Second Ezekiel in the Apocalypse of Peter." *Revue de Qumrân* 15 (1992), 437–445.

Kister, M. "Barnabas 12:1; 4:3 and 4Q Second Ezekiel." *Revue biblique* 97 (1990), 63–67.

Puech, Émile. "L'image de l'arbre en 4QDeutéro-Ezékiel (4Q385 2 9–10)." *Revue de Qumrân* 16 (1994), 429–440.

Qimron, E., and M. Kister. "Observations on 4QSecond Ezekiel." *Revue de Qûmrân* 15 (1992), 595–602.

DEVORAH DIMANT

EZRA AND NEHEMIAH, BOOKS OF. Only three fragments from *Ezra* have been recovered from the Judean wilderness (4Q117) and none from *Nehemiah*. The fragments correspond to *Ezra* 4.2–6 (parallel to *1 Esd.* 5.66–71), 4.9–11 (cf. *1 Esd.* 2.17), and 5.17–6.5 (cf. *1 Esd.* 6.21–26), the first Hebrew, the second and third Aramaic. In all, seventeen lines or about fifty words, fragmentary or entire, are legible. With only minor variations (*u-vaqqar* for the Masoretic Text *u-raqqaru*, *Ezr.* 6.1; *ve-hevelu* for the Masoretic Text *ve-hevel*, *Ezr.* 6.5), the text from Qumran is identical with the Masoretic Text and diverges significantly from the assumed *Vorlage* (underlying text) of *1 Esdras*. Frank Moore Cross (1975) aligned the Masoretic Text of *Ezra* and Ezra from Cave 4 at Qumran with his conflate and expansionist Palestinian text family as against the Egyptian-Alexandrian text type represented by *1 Esdras*. According to this view, the Hebrew-Aramaic *Vorlage* of *1 Esdras* represented a shorter and more pristine text than the Masoretic Text, which, together with *1 Chronicles* 10–*2 Chronicles* 34, comprised an older edition of the Chronistic work dating to the time of Ezra. However, the Qumran fragments are too meager to affect the debate on the relation between canonical *Ezra* and *1 Esdras*, begun by H. H. Howorth in the late nineteenth century, quite apart from the objections that have been raised against this theory of geographically distinct text families. It seems more likely that *1 Esdras*, composed in the late second or early first century BCE, drew either on a no longer extant Greek version of *Ezra-Nehemiah* or directly on the canonical Hebrew-Aramaic text. It gives the appearance of being a well-structured work dealing with the restoration of cult successively under Josiah, Zerubbabel, and Ezra, rather than an excerpt from an earlier edition of the Chronistic work, and its omission of *Nehemiah* appears to be deliberate. *1 Esdras* agrees with the Old Greek version (*Esdras* B) against the Masoretic Text in only one instance (*1 Esd.* 2.25, *meth' hippou*; *2 Esd.* 4.23, *en hippois* [with a horse]) and, in general, is quite different in character.

The Hebrew and Aramaic text of the Masoretic Text of *Ezra-Nehemiah* has been well transmitted on the whole. The very literal Old Greek version has a few superior readings, listed by Wilhelm Rudolph (1949, p. xx), as does the Syriac version, not originally part of the Peshitta, which follows the Masoretic Text quite closely. Apart from *Daniel*, *Ezra-Nehemiah* is the only biblical book without a Targum.

BIBLIOGRAPHY

Blenkinsopp, Joseph. *Ezra-Nehemiah. A Commentary*. The Old Testament Library. Philadelphia, 1988. See pages 70–72.

Cross, Frank Moore. "A Reconstruction of the Judean Restoration." *Journal of Biblical Literature* 94 (1975), 4–18.

Rudolph, Wilhelm. *Esra und Nehemia samt 3. Esra*. Tübingen, 1949. See pages x–xxi.

Ulrich, Eugene. "Ezra and Qoheleth Manuscripts from Qumran (4QEzra, 4QQoh^{a,b})." In *Priests, Prophets, and Scribes: Essays on the Formation and Heritage of Second Temple Judaism in Honour of Joseph Blenkinsopp*, edited by Eugene Ulrich, et al., pp. 139–157. Journal for the Study of the Old Testament Supplement Series, 149. Sheffield, 1992.

JOSEPH BLENKINSOPP

F

FALSEHOOD. *See* Truth.

FAMILY LIFE. Discoveries in the region of the Dead Sea shed light on family life in ancient Judea in two areas: (1) evidence from Qumran relating to marriage and families in sectarian circles and (2) documentary evidence from Naḥal Ḥever relating to family life in the time of Bar Kokhba (d.135 CE). Copies of *Ben Sira* and *Tobit*, which are greatly concerned with family life, have also been found at Qumran but do not alter the understanding of family life to be found in these books. [*See* Ben Sira, Book of; Tobit, Book of.]

Evidence from Qumran. There is very little discussion of family life in the major sectarian texts, but the fact that there are any references at all has attracted attention because of the hypothesis that Qumran was a settlement of celibate Essenes. A key text is found in the Damascus Document (CD vii.6–9): "And if they dwell in camps in accordance with the rule of the land, and take wives and beget children, they shall walk in accordance with the Torah and according to the commandment of the teachings, according to the rule of the Torah that says 'between a man and his wife, and between a father and his son.'"

This passage probably implies that not all members of the new covenant married and had children but that marriage was an option. There is an implicit contrast with "those who walk in perfect holiness," for whom God's covenant is a guarantee that they will live a thousand generations (CD vii.5–6). The Rule of the Community, in contrast, says nothing about family life, and consequently is often thought to be the rule for a celibate community (of "the men of perfect holiness"). The phrase "between a man and his wife" is an allusion to *Numbers* 30.17, but the reference is not very illuminating. *Numbers* refers to "a father and his daughter," and the context concerns the vows of women. The implication in the Damascus Document is that family life should be governed by the laws of the Torah and is not subject to special regulation. The Damascus Document had its own understanding of how the Torah should be interpreted, as can be seen especially in its stipulations about sex and marriage (CD v). But it does not have laws for the members of the new covenant that differ from those that apply to the rest of Israel. The Damascus Document also affirms the right of fathers and husbands to annul the oaths of their wives and daughters, but only if they know that they should be annulled (CD xvi.10–13). It provides for a common fund to support the needy, including orphans and unmarried women who have no relatives. Surprisingly, widows are not included in this list, despite the restrictive position taken on divorce in the document CD v. Another passage warns against the widow who has intercourse after she is widowed (4Q269 9.5; 4Q270 5.19; 4Q271 3.12). The following passage speaks of a girl who acquires a bad name while in her father's house. The danger of such an occurrence was a matter of great concern in ancient Judaism and inspires a notorious outburst on the subject of daughters by Ben Sira (*Sir.* 42.9–14).

The Rule of the Congregation (1Q28a) in the End of Days legislates for all who rally to the covenant, including women and children. It is clear that those who join the covenant in the End of Days are expected to continue to have families. The text stipulates how the children should be brought up. They are to be instructed in the Book of Hagu, according to their level of understanding. At the age of twenty they may join the holy congregation, together with their families. The Damascus Document (CD xv.5–6) also stipulates that the sons (*banim*; it is possible that daughters are included) of those who join the covenant should take an oath when they come of age. Young men are not allowed to have sexual intercourse until they reach the age of twenty. (In Talmudic law, twenty is the *terminus ante quem* for marriage, B.T., *Qid.* 29b.) It is not clear then what is meant by their families in the Rule of the Congregation. It may mean that young men are allowed to join their parents and older siblings in the sacred congregation when they reach the age of twenty. Alternatively, it may mean that their future wives and children are granted automatic membership, but this seems less likely.

Celibacy and restrictions. The clear provision for marriage in these texts is often raised as an objection to the identification of the Dead Sea sect with the Essenes. Josephus, Philo, and Pliny all emphasize the celibacy of the Essenes. According to Josephus, the Essenes

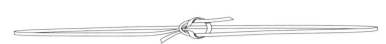

> regard marriage with contempt, but in adopting other people's children who are still pliable for learning, they consider them as their own kin and mold them according to their customs. They do not reject marriage and the propagation that

> comes from it, but they guard themselves against the licentious allurements of women and are persuaded that not one of them keeps her pledge to one man.
>
> (*The Jewish War* 2.120–121)

Josephus also grants, however, that "there is another order of Essenes, who have the same views as the rest in their way of life, customs, and laws, but are at variance in their opinion of marriage" (*The Jewish War* 2.160–161). These Essenes, however, test their wives for the ability to bear children and do not have intercourse during pregnancy, "demonstrating that they do not marry for self-gratification, but for the necessity of children."

Josephus, Philo, and Pliny all relied on other sources for their knowledge of the Essenes (despite Josephus's claim that he had tried out all the Jewish sects). Their accounts assimilate the Essenes to Greek models. Those who defend the identification of the Dead Sea sect with the Essenes argue that the Greek and Latin accounts distort their subject. The marrying Essenes were probably the norm, and the celibate ones the exception. I have noted above that the Damascus Document (CD vii) seems to imply that not all members of the sect married and had children. The Rule of the Congregation is concerned with the End of Days, when all Israel is expected to join the covenant. While the stipulations mentioned are presumably derived from sectarian practice in the present, the Rule of the Congregation does not require that all members of the covenant have families. The War Scroll also takes note of the existence of women and children at the time of the eschatological war but is mainly concerned with their removal from the camp in the time of active warfare (1QM vii.2–4). [*See* Josephus Flavius; Philo Judaeus.]

While the Damascus Document and the Rule of the Congregation allow for marriage, they take a restrictive approach to sex. The Damascus Document and the Temple Scroll both prohibit sex in "the city of the sanctuary" (11Q19 xlv.11; CD xii.1–2). The laws of the Damascus Document include a provision that apparently forbids intercourse during pregnancy (as reported by Josephus on the marrying Essenes), and one fragment (4Q270 7.i.13) prescribes a penalty for the man who "approaches to fornicate with his wife in violation of the law." Such a person must depart and return no more. The nature of the offense is unclear. It may refer to relations during menses, which are specifically denounced in the Damascus Document (CD v.6–7). Alternatively, the code may presuppose a rule of temporary abstinence for married members of the sect.

The presence of women and children in a community is not necessarily incompatible with celibacy. Philo describes the Therapeutae as a celibate community, which is in many ways a surrogate family. The young men who serve the meal behave "like sons to their real fathers and mothers" (*De vita contemplativa* 72). It has been suggested that the Ritual of Marriage (4Q502) may be related to a similar celebration. This text describes a ritual that pairs male and female, sons and daughters, old men and old women, boys and girls, but it is extremely fragmentary, and the context is far from clear. The Damascus Document[e] (4Q270 7.i.14) prescribes penalties for those who murmur against the Fathers and the Mothers, although the penalty is less for those who murmur against the Mothers. "Fathers" and "Mothers" appear to be honorific titles here, whether the people in question were actually fathers and mothers or not. [*See* Ritual of Marriage.]

Instructions. The most practical instructions relating to family life in the Dead Sea Scrolls are found in Sapiential Work A[b], Sapiential Work A[c], and Sapiential Work A[a] (4Q416–418). This text reiterates the injunction to honor parents, which is commonplace in Jewish wisdom literature from the Hellenistic era (e.g., *Ben Sira,* 3.1–16; *Pseudo-Phocylides* 8; Josephus, *Against Apion* 2.206). Like *Ben Sira,* this text promises length of days to those who honor their parents and reminds the children that their own honor is also at stake. A distinctive note is sounded in the recommendation to "honor your father in your poverty and your mother in your low estate." It is unclear whether the poverty in question is economic or spiritual. The Qumran text, however, provides one formulation of the honor due to parents that is without parallel in other Jewish literature of the time: "For as God is to a man, so is his father, and as a master is to a fellow, so is his mother." ("God" here is an emendation. The text reads "for as a father is to a man, so is his father," which is tautological. *See* Harrington, 1994, p. 44) The parity of esteem for father and mother is not unusual and is also found in *Ben Sira* 3.1–16. [*See* Sapiential Work.]

The Qumran wisdom text relates marriage to *Genesis* 2.24: "Walk together with the help-meet of your flesh according to the statute engraved by God that a man should leave his father and his mother . . . and that they should become one flesh" (4Q416 2.iii.21–iv.1). The motif of the help-meet is also paralleled in *Ben Sira* 36.29–30. Like *Ben Sira,* the Qumran text insists on the authority of the husband over the wife. If any other man claims authority over her, he "has displaced the frontier marker of his life" (4Q416 iv.6). The text goes on to reaffirm the authority of the husband to annul the vows of the wife, in accordance with *Numbers* 30. The Qumran text, however, lacks the derogatory, even misogynistic, remarks that characterize *Ben Sira*'s view of women. Indeed, the only derogatory picture of women in the Qumran scrolls is found in Wiles of the Wicked Woman (4Q184), and that text uses a particular kind of woman as a symbol of evil. [*See* Wiles of the Wicked Woman; Wisdom Texts.]

It is clear, primarily from the Damascus Document, that marriage and family life were permitted in the "new covenant." Nonetheless, the paucity of interest in family matters in the scrolls is striking. Where issues of marriage and family are discussed in the sectarian compositions, the discussion is often dominated by concern for purity.

Murabba'at and Naḥal Ḥever. The Qumran scrolls are conspicuously lacking in marriage contracts and personal archives. Precisely these kinds of documents have been found at Murabba'at and Naḥal Ḥever, dating from the early second century CE. Four marriage contracts have been found at Murabba'at, two in Aramaic and two in Greek, and also a bill of divorce in Aramaic. Four marriage deeds were found at Naḥal Ḥever, one in Aramaic and one in Greek, and also another document relating to a divorce.

Three of the contracts from Naḥal Ḥever belong to the archive of the woman Babatha, including the contract relating to her own second marriage. The Aramaic contracts are very similar in form to the later Jewish marriage document, the *ketubbah*. The husband promises to support his wife and records the amount of the *mohar* (bride price) due to the woman. (Since this was a paper figure, and was paid only in the event of divorce or widowhood, it is often referred to simply as the *ketubbah*.) None of these marriage contracts refers to divorce, although the practice of divorce is referred to in other documents. (J. T. Milik erroneously restored references to divorce in his edition of marriage contracts [Mur 20 and 21] in P. Benoit, J. T. Milik, and R. de Vaux, *Les Grottes de Murabba'at,* Discoveries in the Judaean Desert, 2, pp. 109–117. Oxford, 1961.)

Provisions of the marriage contract. Babatha's contract specifies that if she is taken captive her husband must redeem her and may not deduct the cost from her *ketubbah* money. This is in accordance with a provision in the Mishnah (*Ket.* 4.9). The contracts go on to make provision for male and female children and for the wife in the event of widowhood, again in accordance with the Mishnah. Sons inherit the money owed to the mother. Daughters are to be supported at home until marriage. The provision for widowhood in Babatha's contract reads as follows: "If I go to my eternal home before you, you will dwell in my house and be provided for from my house and from my estate until the time that my heirs wish to give you your *ketubbah* money." According to the Mishnah, the people of Jerusalem and Galilee used to write that the wife could remain in the house as long as she remained a widow, but the people of Judea gave the heirs the right to evict her if they paid her *ketubbah* money (*Ket.* 4.12). Babatha's contract conforms to Judean practice. The Greek contracts differ from the Aramaic insofar as they make no reference to "the Law of Moses and the Jews," and they are acknowledgments of the dowry brought by the wife rather than records of the *mohar* owed by the husband.

Polygamy and division of property. The Babatha archive throws interesting light on family life in Judea in the Roman era in two respects: it provides evidence of polygamy, and it illustrates the problems that arose in the administration of the estate of a deceased father and husband.

Babatha came from the town of Maoza, at the southern end of the Dead Sea. Her father gave all his possessions to her mother before his death, and Babatha inherited them. Her first husband, Yeshua ben Yosef, died and left a son, also named Yeshua. Babatha then married one Yehudah Khthousion from 'Ein-Gedi. Yehudah was already married to a woman named Miriam, whose brother was a lieutenant of Bar Kokhba. When Yehudah died, Babatha became involved in litigation over his property. One document records a summons she had issued to Miriam for her to appear before the Roman governor, "since you [Miriam] plundered everything in the house of Yehudah son of Eleazar Khthousion, my and your husband. . . ." Miriam replied: "I warned you not to approach the property of my husband . . . you have no claim against the said Yehudah, my husband, regarding the property." Ranon Katzoff has argued that Yehudah may have divorced Miriam, and that the rival claims may have derived from separate contracts that he had made with each in turn. The situation, then, would be serial monogamy rather than polygamy (Katzoff, 1995, pp. 128–32). But if Miriam had been divorced, Babatha would most certainly have pointed this out and not referred to "my and your husband" (Lewis, 1997, p. 152). We have here, then, clear evidence of bigamy, in a fairly remote rural area, among people of moderate means. While Babatha was not a poor woman, she was illiterate. Predictably, the rival wives were involved in bitter dispute over property after Yehudah's death.

When Babatha's first husband died, the town council of Petra appointed two men to be guardians of the orphan boy, who had been left a trust fund of four hundred denarii by his father. Almost immediately Babatha began to complain that the monthly allowance was inadequate. After she remarried, she summoned the guardians to the governor's court and offered to take full responsibility for her son if the trust funds were put at her disposal. Babatha offered to pay interest on the money and to put up her property as collateral. She was apparently unsuccessful, as she was still accepting the original monthly allowance seven years later. The incident underlines the dependent position of women under the law. Even a capable woman of means, who had herself enjoyed the right of inheritance, still had to accept male guardians of her own son after the death of his father.

One other aspect of the Babatha archive deserves notice here. Babatha's archive was found in the Cave of the Letters, where a number of Jews perished during the Bar Kokhba Revolt. The archive included the marriage contract of Babatha's stepdaughter Shelamzion, the daughter of Yehudah and Miriam. This fact suggests a close relationship between these two women, despite the litigation between Babatha and Miriam. It has been suggested that Babatha may have provided Shelamzion's dowry. This would explain why the younger woman's marriage contract was found in Babatha's archive. It is reasonable to infer that there were some bonds of affection involved, but the fact that Babatha kept the record of the dowry suggests that the money may have been a loan rather than an outright gift. [*See* Babatha.]

The documents from Naḥal Ḥever and Murabbaʿat are dominated by concerns arising from divorce, remarriage, and property rights. The prominence of these features here directs our attention to their absence from the Qumran scrolls, where divorce was most probably forbidden and property was shared, to varying degrees. The papyri from Naḥal Ḥever and Murabbaʿat stand in a well-established tradition. The same concerns are found in Elephantine papyri from the fifth century BCE, and to some extent also in the wisdom literature. Quite apart from the disputed issue of celibacy, the literature preserved in the Qumran scrolls is atypical of Second Temple Judaism where family life is concerned, because of its great concern for purity and its strict views on such issues as sex and divorce.

[*See also* Celibacy; Damascus Document; Ḥever, Naḥal, *article on* Written Material; Marriage and Divorce; *and* Murabbaʿat, Wadi, *article on* Written Material.]

BIBLIOGRAPHY

Baumgarten, Joseph M. "The Laws of the Damascus Document in Current Research." In *The Damascus Document Reconsidered,* edited by Magen Broshi, pp. 51–62. Jerusalem, 1992.

Baumgarten, Joseph M. *Qumran Cave 4.XIII: The Damascus Document (4Q266–273).* Discoveries in the Judaean Desert, 18. Oxford, 1996.

Collins, John J. "Marriage, Divorce and Family in Second Temple Judaism." In *Marriage and Family in Ancient Israel and Judah,* edited by Leo Perdue, pp. 104–62. Louisville, Ky., 1997. Survey of material pertaining to marriage and family in the entire Second Temple period.

Harrington, Daniel J. "Wisdom at Qumran." In *The Community of the Renewed Covenant,* edited by Eugene C. Ulrich and James C. VanderKam, pp. 137–152. Notre Dame, 1994. Lucid presentation of new wisdom material from Qumran.

Katzoff, Ramon. "Polygamy in P. Yadin?" *Zeitschrift für Papyrologie und Epigraphik* 109 (1995), 128–132.

Lewis, Naphtali, Yigael Yadin, and Jonas C. Greenfield, eds. *The Documents from the Bar Kokhba Period in the Cave of Letters.* Jerusalem, 1989. Includes documents from the Babatha archive.

Lewis, Naphtali. "Judah's Bigamy." *Zeitschrift für Papyrologie und Epigraphik* 116 (1997), 152.

Schiffman, Lawrence H. *The Eschatological Community of the Dead Sea Scrolls.* Society of Biblical Literature, Monograph Series, 38. Atlanta, Ga., 1989. Analysis of the Rule of the Congregation (1Q28a); pp. 11–27 deal with family issues.

Yadin, Yigael, Jonas C. Greenfield, and Ada Yardeni. "Babatha's Ketubba." *Israel Exploration Journal* 44 (1994), 75–101.

JOHN J. COLLINS

FESTIVALS. The Hebrew scriptures yield a list of festivals, some recalling great events of sacred history, and often elaborate on when, how, where, and why they were to be celebrated. The most detailed information about holidays appears in *Leviticus* 23 and *Numbers* 28–29.

Passover, a ritual meal on the fourteenth day of the first month, signified the remembrance of the Egyptian bondage and Exodus. It was to be celebrated in the home or, during some periods (*2 Kgs.* 22–23), at the central sanctuary. For those who were unable to observe Passover at the regular time, the Second Passover fell on the fourteenth day of the second month. [*See* Passover.]

The Festival of Unleavened Bread was observed from the fifteenth day to the twenty-first day of the first month. No leaven was to be consumed, recalling the hasty departure from Egypt. Around the time of Passover and the Festival of Unleavened Bread, on the "day after the Sabbath" (*Lv.* 23.11, 15) the Waving of the ʿOmer (*ʿomer,* "sheaf of new barley") was celebrated, when the first fruits of the barley harvest were to be presented before the Lord. Shavuʿot (Feast of Weeks) was celebrated on the fiftieth day after the Waving of the ʿOmer. At this time, the first fruits of the new wheat crop were presented before the Lord. [*See* Shavuʿot.]

The first day of the seventh month was a day of complete rest. It was observed with trumpet blasts.

On the tenth day of the seventh month, Yom Kippur (the Day of Atonement) was observed. Ceremonies were conducted to remove the guilt of Israel's sins for the past year. [*See* Yom Kippur.]

From the fifteenth day to the twenty-first day of the seventh month, Sukkot (Feast of Tabernacles) was celebrated to recall Israel's wandering in the wilderness, where they lived in booths. It marked the end of the harvest season. [*See* Sukkot.]

Purim, observed on the fourteenth and fifteenth days of the twelfth month, commemorated the saving of the Jews from destruction in the time of Queen Esther.

The Greek translation of the Bible adds one more festival to the list (*1 Mc.* 4.52–59). Ḥanukkah was observed for eight days, beginning on the twenty-fifth day of the ninth month, to celebrate the dedication of the Temple after it had been desecrated in the early Maccabean period.

These holidays became the standard Jewish festivals in rabbinic times. The Judean Desert documents mention all the rabbinic festivals except Purim and Ḥanukkah; some of the texts add several new holidays. *Jubilees*, many copies of which were found at Qumran and which influenced Qumran thought and practice, indicates that Shavuʿot took place on the fifteenth day of the third month and was a time for annual covenantal renewal (*Jub*. 6.17, 15.1); it also suggests that the festivals of the first fruits marked the points after which the old crops were no longer to be eaten (*Jub*. 32.11–14). The Temple Scroll offers the lengthiest enumeration of festivals, their dates, and the sacrifices that were to be offered on those days, while the calendrical documents allow one to infer the dates for most of the festivals. The Qumran texts contain a system based on a 364-day solar calendar in which a series of four first-fruits festivals (Waving of the ʿOmer, Shavuʿot, Festival of the New Wine, and Festival of the New Oil) are each separated by fifty days. The expanded list of festivals from the Dead Sea Scrolls is as follows.

In a fragmentary column of Temple Scroll[a] the first day of each month (11Q19 xiv.7–8) is mentioned. A possible Festival of the New Year might be designated for the first day of the first month (11Q19 xiv.9–18) when a prohibition against labor and specifications for sacrifices are given. Apparently starting after the Festival of the New Year, a consecration festival inducting priests and high priests is referred to in damaged columns of Temple Scroll[a] (11Q19 xv.3). This consecration festival lasted seven days (11Q19 xv.14).

Passover is mentioned in Temple Scroll[a] (11Q19 xvii.6–9) and in some of the calendrical documents, where it is designated as the fourteenth day of the first month as in the Bible. According to Temple Scroll[a], the Passover sacrifice was to be offered before the evening sacrifice and eaten in the Temple courtyards. (See also Calendrical Document A, 4Q320 4.iii.2, 12; 4.iv.7; 4.v.1, 10; 4.vi.5; Calendrical Document B[a], 4Q321 2.ii.4, 9; 2.iii.3, 7; cf. Calendrical Document G, 4Q329a 1.4–5; Rule of the Community[e], 4Q259 8.3; Serekh Damascus, 4Q265 4.3.)

Temple Scroll[a] (11Q19 xvii.10–16 [cf. xi.10]) specifies the fifteenth day of the first month as the beginning of the Festival of Unleavened Bread, a seven-day holiday, and stipulates the sacrifices. The festival is rarely mentioned in the calendrical texts (Calendrical Document E[a], 4Q326 1.3; Temple Scroll?, 4Q365a 1.2).

The Waving of the ʿOmer is explicitly dated in the Qumran texts to the twenty-sixth day of the first month (the date implied in *Jubilees*). The Qumran community understood "the day after the Sabbath" to mean the day after the weekly Sabbath (the twenty-fifth day of the first month), which occurred after the seven days of the Festival of Unleavened Bread. Temple Scroll[a] (11Q19 xviii.?–10) describes the sacrifices for it, but the date comes from Calendrical Document A (4Q320 4.iii.3, 13; it can be calculated because the number of the day in the week of service of the priestly course Yedaiah is given [4Q320 4.iv.8; 4.v.2, 11; 4.vi.6; 4Q321 2.ii.4, 9; 2.ii.3, 7; 4Q326 1.4]). In this last passage, the holiday is dated to the twenty-sixth day of the first month and is called the Festival of the New Barley since the first of the barley harvest was presented to the Lord on that day. Hence, the Waving of the ʿOmer became a first-fruits festival.

Although Temple Scroll[a] does not mention the Second Passover, it does appear several times in the calendrical texts (4Q320 4.iii.4; 4.iv.9; 4.v.3, 12; 4.vi.7; 4Q321 2.ii.5, 9; 2.iii.8). The system of priestly rotation of duty allows one to calculate the date as the fourteenth day of the second month.

Although Shavuʿot is not tied to a specific date in the Bible, the Qumran texts, with *Jubilees*, place it on the fifteenth day of the third month. Temple Scroll[a] (11Q19 xviii.10–xix.9 [cf. xi.10]) deals with the method for counting the fifty days between the Waving of the ʿOmer and Shavuʿot (*Pentecost* in Greek). It is also a first-fruits festival, when the first of the wheat is to be presented (11Q19 xviii.14, xix.9), just as in *Jubilees*. Temple Scroll[a] (xliii.3, 6–7) indicates that old wheat must be consumed by the time of the festival the following year. It is also mentioned in Calendrical Document A (4Q320 4.iii.5; 4.iv.1; 4.v.4, 13; 4.vi.8), Calendrical Document B[a] (4Q320 2.ii.1, 5; 2.iii.4, 8), and Rule of the Community[e] (4Q259 7.1). Shavuʿot appears to be the time when the covenant renewal ceremony took place (see Damascus Document[a], 4Q266 11.17–18 = Damascus Document[e], 4Q270 7.ii.11–12).

Temple Scroll[a] treats the Festival of the New Wine, an extrabiblical holiday (11Q19 xix.11–xxi.10). It prescribes that one is to count fifty days from Shavuʿot and to offer new wine as a drink offering on that date (the third day of the fifth month). Temple Scroll[a] (11Q19 xliii.3, 7–8) describes wine as subject to the standard first-fruits law; that is, it must be consumed before the festival comes around in the following year. The wine festival is never mentioned in the preserved sections of the calendrical texts.

The Festival of the First Fruits of the Oil, according to Temple Scroll[a], was to be observed fifty days after the previous first-fruits festival, that is, on the twenty-second day of the sixth month (11Q19 xxi.12–xxiii.9). The scroll stipulates that the oil is to be used before the festival occurs the following year (11Q19 xliii.3, 9–10). An occasion that is probably the same festival (although a different word for oil is used) is mentioned in Calendrical Document E[b] (4Q327 1.ii.4–7; there the twenty-second day of what seems to be the sixth month is given as its date [4Q327 2.ii.6–8]). The addition to *Leviticus* 23.42–24.2 in the Reworked Pentatench[c] found in Cave 4 at Qumran (4Q365 23.4–11) includes a reference to the Festival of the New Oil (23.9) followed immediately by a reference to bringing wood (see below).

Temple Scroll[a] (11Q19 xxiii.?–xxv.2) deals with the times when wood was to be brought to the Temple for burning sacrifices. This practice, known as the Festival of the Wood, is attested elsewhere; however, Temple Scroll[a] alone seems to date the activity to six days (two of the twelve tribes offering wood on each day) following the Festival of the New Oil. Since the next holiday mentioned is on the first day of the seventh month, Yigael Yadin suggested that the Festival of the Wood should be dated to the twenty-third through the twenty-ninth day of the sixth month. The festival is not mentioned in the calendrical documents, but Calendrical Document E[b] (4Q327 1.ii.10–11) may preserve part of the reference to it (cf. 4Q365 23.9–11).

Temple Scroll[a] (11Q19 xxv.2–10, which is very fragmentary) probably deals with the first day of the seventh month, called the "Day of Remembrance" elsewhere in the Qumran texts and the "New Year" in the rabbinic texts. It figures in Calendrical Document A (4Q320 4.iii.6; 4.iv.2; 4.v.5), Calendrical Document B[a] (4Q320 2.ii.2, 6; 2.iii.9), and Rule of the Community[e] (4Q259 8.4).

Yom Kippur is mentioned in Temple Scroll[a] (11Q19 xxv.10–xvii.10), which prescribes offerings for the Day of Atonement, and was to be observed on the tenth day of the seventh month. The day is also mentioned in Pesher Habukkuk (1QpHab xi.4–9), where it is also called "the day of fasting, the Sabbath of their rest" (1QpHab xi.9). It was the time when the Wicked Priest attacked the Teacher of Righteousness and his followers. [*See* Teacher of Righteousness *and* Wicked Priest.] It is possible that the Damascus Document (CD vi.19) and Pesher Psalms[a] (4Q171 1–10.ii.10; 1–10.iii.3) also refer to Yom Kippur as the Day or Festival of Fasting. Yom Kippur is mentioned in the calendrical texts in Calendrical Document A (4Q320 4.iii.7, 4.iv.3, 4.v.6, 4.vi.1), Calendrical Document B[a] (4Q321 2.ii.2, 6); Rule of the Community[e] (4Q259 7.2), and Rule (5Q13 4.2).

Sukkot is mentioned in Temple Scroll[a] (11Q19 xxvii.10–xxix.2 [or 3]). The section in which it is mentioned dates the first day of the holiday to the fifteenth day of the seventh month; the incomplete listing of days reaches the fourth day before breaking off (cf. 11Q19 xi.13). The author of Temple Scroll[a] (11Q19 xlii.10–17) commands that booths be built on the roof of the third story of the Temple; various groups are to sit there during the offerings for the festival. Sukkot appears frequently in the calendrical texts: Calendrical Document A (4Q320 4.ii.9, 4.iv.4, 4.v.7, 4.vi.2), Calendrical Document B[a] (4Q320 2.ii.2, 7; 2.iii.2, 6, 9), and Rule of the Community[e] (4Q259 4.3[?]; cf. 4Q365 23.1–2; *Lv.* 23.42–43). The festival also appears in the Bar Kokhba documents: Simon gives orders to bring the "four kinds" (*Lv.* 23.40) that were used in the celebration of Sukkot (5/6Ḥev 15—an Aramaic document). In the Greek letter 5/6Ḥev 3, Soumaios (apparently a Greek form of Simon's name) writes about transport of citrons by someone named Agrippa. He indicates that the items are needed soon for the festival.

[*See also* Calendars and Mishmarot; Psalms, Hymns, and Prayers; Sacrifice; Temple Scroll; *and* Worship, Qumran Sect.]

BIBLIOGRAPHY

Wacholder, Ben Zion, and Martin G. Abegg. *A Preliminary Edition of the Unpublished Dead Sea Scrolls: The Hebrew and Aramaic Texts from Cave Four,* fasc. 1, pp. 60–101. Washington, D.C., 1991. Hebrew texts of many of the calendrical documents.

Wise, Michael O. "Bar Kokhba Letters." In *The Anchor Bible Dictionary,* vol. 1, edited by David Noel Freedman, pp. 601–606. New York, 1992. Translation of 5/6Ḥev 3 and 15 on page 604.

Yadin, Yigael. *The Temple Scroll,* 3 vols. Jerusalem, 1983. First English edition of the Temple Scroll with full commentary and photographic plates.

JAMES C. VANDERKAM

FIRST JEWISH REVOLT. The war that broke out in Judea in 66 CE was preceded by 130 years of active resistance against the Roman administration (beginning with Pompey's conquest of Jerusalem in 63 BCE) and internal violence within the Jewish population. The Romans introduced direct rule in 6 CE after Herod's son Archelaus, the ethnarch, proved unable to handle constant insurrection. Every Roman prefect and procurator who is more than a name in the sources had to deal with Jewish rebellion in some form. After the death of the Jewish king Agrippa I, whose brief reign (41–44 CE) provided a peaceful interlude in direct Roman rule, the situation steadily deteriorated as Jewish revolutionary movements spread and the Roman procurators became more deliberately provocative. Ventidius Cumanus (48–52 CE) was recalled for mishandling four violent incidents, Antonius Felix (52–60? BCE) "practiced every kind of cruelty and lust" (Tacitus *Histories* 5.9.3), Porcius Festus (60–62 BCE) was plagued by Sicarii and "false prophets," and Lucceius Albinus (62–64 BCE) was notorious for theft, venality, and corruption. Finally, "the Jews' patience lasted until Gessius Florus became procurator" (Tac. *Hist.* 5.10.1). Josephus felt that Florus "made Albinus seem a paragon of virtue by comparison" (*The Jewish War* 2.277). His mishandling of the Jewish-Greek conflict in Caesarea, his removal of seventeen talents from the Temple treasuries, and his attack on Jews demonstrating good-will in Jerusalem provided fuel for the more extreme revolutionary elements, and in 66 CE they committed the nation irrevocably to war by stopping the regular sacrifices in the Temple on behalf of the Roman emperor and massacring the Roman garrison in Jerusalem.

Jewish Resistance Groups. The Jewish population was not united in its resistance to Roman rule. Revolutionary movements of all kinds proliferated in the decades before the war, not only inciting insurrection against Rome but competing with each other, often violently. Some, but certainly not all, were messianic, either heralding their own charismatic leader as the anointed king or anticipating his imminent arrival. The diversity of eschatological visions may be witnessed in the apocalyptic texts surviving from the period, including some of the scrolls from the Judean Desert. Apocalyptic fervor increasingly translated into political action in this period (apparently unlike the sect at Qumran), as many viewed war with Rome and with Jewish rivals as a cosmic battle heralding a new age. Yet, despite their common theme and purpose, the various apocalyptic texts show little unity in doctrine or details, and, more importantly, the various eschatologically motivated rebel groups, as well as those without such visions, showed little inclination to unify or cooperate, but were quite intolerant of each other.

Most rebel groups remain nameless. Individual Sadducees, Pharisees, and Essenes are known to have fought in the war, but there is no reason to believe that these sects participated as a whole. The two rebel organizations that are best known, because, unlike others, they survived to 66 CE and took an active part in the war, are the Zealots and the Sicarii. The former was a priestly group professing "zeal in their devotion to good deeds" (*The Jewish War* 4.161), led by Eleazar ben Simon, who became a major player in wartime Jerusalem. The Sicarii ("knife-men") were a dynastic group with messianic overtones, founded by Judah the Galilean in 6 CE, in response to the Roman census. This group is probably to be associated with the Fourth Philosophy, also founded by Judah, adhering to Pharisaic teachings in all matters except for "an almost inconquerable love of freedom" and refusal to submit to any master but God (*Jewish Antiquities* 18.23). Judah and his heirs kept up their militant defense of Jewish "freedom" for sixty years, apparently claiming more Jewish victims than Roman, for they did not shrink from "vengeance against relatives and friends" who did not share their passions (*Jewish Antiquities* 18.23). As the most successful and violent of the groups, their part in bringing on full-scale rebellion was considerable. Yet Judah's grandson Menahem, who led the Sicarii's bid to gain control of the rebellion in Jerusalem in 66 CE, was murdered by rival revolutionary factions, after which the Sicarii retreated to Masada where, under the leadership of Eleazar ben Yair (probably a great-grandson of Judah), they contented themselves with local raids and sat out the siege of Jerusalem.

Jews against Jews. Economic hardship contributed to the increasingly extreme and violent political expressions and aspirations. There is some evidence from the first century of demographic pressures, dislocations, shortages of cultivatable land, and heavier tax burdens (both Jewish and Roman), which caused prominent Jewish figures to be targeted along with the Roman administration. Banditry is mentioned as a growing problem, although the distinction between professional robbers and political revolutionaries is hard to see in the sources, as it must have been in the field; it depended on the subjective judgment of the observer, and the main sources reflect the Roman view. Yet, economic factors may be overemphasized (and have been in recent scholarship): well-off and aristocratic Jews associated themselves with anti-Roman ideas and actions as the political situation deteriorated, and inter-Jewish battles were as likely to be motivated by ideological as by economic differences. The Jewish War was at once a rebellion against Rome and a civil war, but the population did not split along class lines (an anachronistic notion in any case) and there were many more than two sides.

Campaigns. The uprising in Jerusalem sparked particularly gruesome anti-Jewish violence in Judea, Galilee and Perea, Syria, and Egypt. The Roman authorities concentrated on quickly crushing the revolt. The Syrian governor Cestius Gallus swept through Galilee and Judea, but inexplicably had to raise his siege of Jerusalem and hastily retreat, during which his troops were cut to pieces in the pass at Beth Horon. Cestius's humiliation made suppression of the revolt a matter of utmost importance for the Romans, not only to restore order in the area but to maintain peace throughout the empire. The emperor Nero assigned the task to his experienced general, Vespasian, who assembled a force of three legions (V, X, and XV) and many auxiliaries totaling perhaps sixty thousand. He launched his offensive in the spring of 67 CE.

After Cestius's defeat, the Jews formed a government in Jerusalem. At its head stood some of the leading aristocrats of that time, including high priests, noble priests, and wealthy lay nobility. This government saw to the war preparations, most importantly provisioning the capital and planning a strategy. The country was divided into administrative-military districts, and armed rebel groups were transformed into a kind of army, which, however, remained inactive after a failed attack on Ascalon in 66 CE. The historian Josephus, son of a distinguished Jerusalem priestly family, was dispatched to organize the defense of Galilee. The government also started minting coins both to fulfill propagandistic purposes and to meet its financial obligations: a brilliant silver shekel bearing the legend "Jerusalem the Holy" and a parallel bronze series with the legend "The Freedom of Zion," later modified to "The Redemption of Zion."

Vespasian's simple and obvious strategy was systematically to conquer the country from the periphery inward, drawing an ever-tightening circle around Jerusalem. The Roman army first conquered Galilee in a swift and effective campaign, abetted by the Jews' lack of cohesion. Many places fell with little struggle, and long sieges were required at only two places, Jotapata (where Josephus was captured) and Gamala. The revolutionary John of Gischala escaped to Jerusalem when Titus attacked his city. All of the north was in Roman hands by the autumn of 67 CE.

In the spring and summer of 68 CE, Vespasian subdued Perea, Samaria, Judea, and Idumea. It was probably during these campaigns that Qumran was destroyed, not without resistance, judging from the Roman arrowheads discovered there and the fact that the place was burned to the ground. No literary source records the event, and the archaeological evidence is not sufficient to determine the identity of the defenders: they could have been the inhabitants of the place, or the Sicarii from Masada (or elsewhere), or both. (The discovery of some of the same texts at Qumran and Masada is not conclusive either way.) Nero's suicide in June 68 CE plunged Rome into a year of civil war, causing Vespasian to postpone the attack on Jerusalem; he had to content himself the following year with limited operations in the south, expelling the revolutionary leader Simon bar Giora, who took his large army to Jerusalem. Late in 69 CE, Vespasian went to Egypt and then Italy to make himself emperor, leaving his son Titus to finish the war.

Roman delays were not exploited by the Jews, who were distracted by their own internal struggles. Sometime in the winter of 67/68 CE, after the fall of Galilee, the armed rebel factions in Jerusalem, apparently led by the Zealots, seized control of the Temple Mount, murdered the government leaders, and established themselves in power, legitimizing their actions by appointing their own high priest (a certain Pinchas, also mentioned in rabbinic sources). John of Gischala, who had drawn close to the first regime, betrayed his friends and emerged as one of the leaders of the second regime. Once the militants gained power, they started quarreling among themselves; John was not a Zealot and for the rest of the war had unstable relations with this group. Internecine struggles became much more violent and destructive once Simon bar Giora, who had amassed a sizable army in Idumea, was admitted into the capital in the summer of 69 CE through the connivance of high priests who were probably survivors from the first regime. Turf wars occupied the rest of that year, during which many people were killed and the considerable food supplies burnt. The destruction of the food supplies—recorded by Josephus, Tacitus, and the rabbis—was particularly unfortunate since Jerusalem's population had been swollen by the refugees arriving from all parts of the country conquered by the Romans.

The people of Jerusalem were divided and starving by the time Titus arrived in the spring of 70 CE with four legions (Leg. XII had been added to the force he received from his father) and numerous auxiliaries to begin the siege. The city was protected by three walls on the north, its only vulnerable side. The outer wall fell after three weeks of intense fighting, and the second wall nine days after that. The determination of the Jewish fighters, and their frequent successes in hand-to-hand combat, impressed even outside observers. Yet the Jews' defense of the city was hampered by almost continuous fighting within the walls as well as by spreading famine. Both Josephus and the rabbis tell awful tales of starvation. The suffering increased when the Romans, in response to the loss of quite extensive earthworks to Jewish counteroffensive measures at the innermost wall, surrounded the entire city with a siege wall, which blocked both escape from the city and the smuggling of food inside. Unburied corpses began to accumulate inside the city, and bloody purges took place as the ruling coalitions began to crack under the pressure.

Despite the effects of the siege wall, the Jewish defense did not completely collapse for another three months. Construction of new siege works took another three weeks, and the struggle for the Temple Mount—during which the two main Jewish factions abandoned turf wars to defend the Temple—was long, desperate, and costly for both sides. During six weeks of almost daily battles, the Romans slowly but systematically took possession of the Antonia fortress and surrounding porticoes. In the midst of the struggle, on 17 Panemos, according to the Macedonian calendar (= 17 Tammuz), the daily sacrifices stopped in the Temple because of the lack of sacrificial animals. Finally, on 10 Loos (= 10 Av, one day later than the traditional Jewish date commemorating the destruction), the Romans set fire to the Temple, which burned for days. The remnants of the rebel factions fled to the Upper City, where they were able to resist for about another month. After their final defeat, the Romans completed their systematic destruction of the city. Titus took Temple spoils and thousands of Jewish prisoners back to Rome, where they were displayed in the triumph, and Simon bar Giora was executed according to custom.

The war did not end with the destruction of Jerusalem, for the three fortresses—Herodium, Machaerus, and Masada—were still held by rebel forces. The governor, Lucilius Bassus, subdued the first two with little effort, and in 74 CE his successor, Flavius Silva, took Masada after a difficult siege, during which the Sicarii killed themselves to avoid falling into Roman hands.

Even the most skeptical or patriotic reader knows that most information about the First Jewish Revolt, and to a large extent how it is conceived and understood, depends on Josephus. Other sources—Greek and Latin literature, coins and archaeological finds, rabbinic literature—are comprehensible only by comparison to Josephus. The documents from the Judean Desert, given their nature, contain no clear direct reference to the struggle against Rome or the specific conflicts within the Jewish population attending the First Revolt. The allusions to Rome (*Kittim*) and visions of a monumental conflict at the end of time in the Qumran texts are general, schematic, and idealized, and merely help to clarify the factors that led to the massively destructive struggle.

BIBLIOGRAPHY

Avigad, Nahman. *Discovering Jerusalem*. Jerusalem, 1980.

Cohen, Shaye J. D. *Josephus in Galilee and Rome. His Vita and Development as a Historian*. Leiden, 1979.

Goodman, Martin. *The Ruling Class of Judaea: The Origins of the Jewish Revolt against Rome A. D. 66–70*. Cambridge, 1987.

Hengel, Martin. *The Zealots. Investigations into the Jewish Freedom Movement in the Period from Herod I until 70 A.D.* Translated by D. Smith. Edinburgh, 1989.

Josephus. *The Jewish War*. Translated by H. St. J. Thackeray, Loeb Classical Library: *Josephus* II–III. London, 1927; repr. Cambridge, Mass., 1976.

Price, Jonathan J. *Jerusalem under Siege: The Collapse of the Jewish State 66–70 CE*. Leiden, 1992.

Rhoads, David M. *Israel in Revolution: 6–74 CE*. Philadelphia, 1976.

Schürer, Emil. *The History of the Jewish People in the Age of Jesus Christ (175 B.C.–A.D. 135)* I–III. Edited and revised by Geza Vermes, Fergus Millar, Matthew Black, and Martin Goodman. Edinburgh, 1973–1987.

Stern, Menahem. "Zealots." In *Encyclopaedia Judaica Yearbook 1973*, pp. 135–152. Jerusalem, 1974.

JONATHAN J. PRICE

FIVE SCROLLS. The *Megillot*, or Five Scrolls, are five books belonging to the *Ketuvim*, or Writings, division of the Hebrew scriptures: *Song of Songs, Ruth, Lamentations, Ecclesiastes*, and *Esther*. These books were grouped together rather late in rabbinical tradition, and each is associated with a particular Jewish festival, during which it is read in its entirety: *Song of Songs* with Passover, *Ruth* with Shavu'ot, *Lamentations* with the Ninth of Av (the commemoration of the destruction of the First and Second Temples), *Ecclesiastes* with Sukkot, and *Esther* with Purim. All of the books, with the exception of *Esther*, appear in several copies in the Judean Desert corpus. They do not appear there as a group, but as separate scrolls. In addition, three of the books, *Song of Songs, Ecclesiastes*, and *Esther*, share the distinction that their place in the canon has been questioned at different times. Although it is difficult to determine the extent of the canon in the period of the Second Temple beyond the Torah, Prophets, and Psalms, the presence of *Song of Songs* and *Ecclesiastes* at Qumran would at least indicate their acceptability as reading matter during the Second Temple period.

The *Song of Songs* is a love song between a man and a woman, which was interpreted by the rabbis as a metaphor of God's relationship with Israel, and by Christians as a metaphor concerning Christ and the Church. Its composition is difficult to date, although tradition ascribes it to King Solomon, famous for his many wives. Its *terminus ante quem* (the latest date), however, is the dates of the four copies of *Song of Songs* which appear at Qumran. Three manuscripts from Cave 4 preserve fragments of the *Song of Songs*. 4QCanticles[a], dated paleographically to the early Herodian period, contains portions of chapters 3.7–11, 4.1–7, 6.11?–12, and 7.1–7. 4QCanticles[b], dated to the end of the first century BCE, contains portions of chapters 2.9–17, 3.1–2, 3.5, 3.9–10, 4.1–3, 4.8–11, 4.14–16, and 5.1. 4QCanticles[c], also dated to the end of the first century BCE, contains 3.7–8. 4QCanticles[a] and 4QCanticles[b] are what their editor, E. Tov, calls "short texts" of the *Song of Songs*. That is, sections of the *Song of Songs* are deliberately omitted from these manuscripts, leading one to the conclusion that these are excerpted texts, rather than straight biblical manuscripts. For example, 4QCanticles[a] omits the material in the *Song of Songs* from 4.8 to 6.11, while 4QCanticles[b] omits the material between 3.5 and 3.9. The fact that these omissions are not the same indicate that the whole text of the *Song of Songs* was known, and that these manuscripts are shortened copies of it. The reason for the abbreviations is unclear. It is possible that they were liturgical texts. In addition, 4QCanticles[b] contains scribal markings which resemble either Paleo-Hebrew or Cryptic A script; the purpose of these markings is uncertain. 4QCanticles[b] also shows Aramaic influence in its grammar and morphology; this seems to be a scribal peculiarity and is not an indication of an Aramaic *Vorlage*. One manuscript from Cave 6 survives: 6QCanticles, which contains 1.1–7 and which M. Baillet dated to c.50 CE. This manuscript deviates in small details from the Masoretic Text of the *Song of Songs*, but too little material survives to make a definitive judgment. The *Song of Songs* has not yet been shown to have been used elsewhere in the literature of the Dead Sea Scrolls.

The book of *Ruth*, a charming novella telling the tale of

Ruth, a Moabite who becomes the ancestress of King David, is, in the Greek biblical tradition, grouped with the histories, where it appears in chronological order, after *Judges* and before *1 Samuel*. Its date is not easily determined, although a postexilic date seems preferable. *Ruth* occurs in four manuscripts from Qumran, two from Cave 2 and two from Cave 4. 2QRuth[a], which is dated paleographically to the first century CE, contains 2.13–23, 3.1–8, and 4.3–4, and differs little from the received text of *Ruth*. 2QRuth[b] dates to c.50 BCE and contains 3.13–18. It displays, according to its editor, M. Baillet, a "certain independence" in its text, although there does not seem to be enough material remaining to determine its textual nature. 4QRuth[a] contains 1.1–12, and 4QRuth[b] contains 1.1–6, 1.12–15, not enough material to make any kind of textual statement. *Ruth* has not yet been shown to have been used elsewhere in the Judean Desert corpus.

The book of *Lamentations* is a collection of five poems, written in *qinah* meter, lamenting the destruction of Jerusalem by the Babylonians in 587 BCE. *Lamentations* was probably written shortly after that destruction in 587, and its author is unknown, although it is traditionally ascribed to the prophet Jeremiah. In fact, in the Greek tradition *Lamentations* is placed directly after the book of *Jeremiah*, and Josephus seems to group *Jeremiah* and *Lamentations* together as one book (*Against Apion* 1.8).

Lamentations occurs in four copies at Qumran, one from Cave 3, one from Cave 4, and two from Cave 5. 3QLamentations, a Herodian manuscript, contains 1.10–12 and 3.53–62. In it, the divine name *Yahveh* is written in Paleo-Hebrew script, but the remains are too small to make a judgment about the character of the text. 4QLamentations, written in a Herodian vulgar semiformal script, contains three columns comprising 1.1–18, and a small scrap containing 2.5. According to its editor, F. M. Cross, it occasionally presents better readings than the received text. 5QLamentations[a], dated to the first century CE, contains 4.5–8, 4.11–16, 4.19–22, 5.1–13, and 5.16–17. According to its editor, J. T. Milik, "the relationship of 5QLam[a] to other recensions of the same book [i.e., Masoretic Text, Septuagint] is not clear" (Milik, 1962, p. 175). 5QLamentations[b] also dates to the first century CE, but is written in a different hand than 5QLamentations[a]. It contains 4.17–20, which is not enough material to make a textual statement. *Lamentations* is not quoted or alluded to in other texts of the Dead Sea Scrolls.

The book of *Ecclesiastes* (or, in Hebrew, *Qohelet*) is part of the Wisdom corpus of the Hebrew scriptures (the other texts being *Proverbs*, *Job*, and certain of the *Psalms*), and dates probably to the fourth or third century BCE, although it is traditionally ascribed to Solomon, the legendary wise king. Ecclesiastes had trouble gaining canonical status because of the distinct antireligious tone adopted throughout the book; it was saved only by the pious coda (12.13–14), probably not the work of the original author.

Ecclesiastes exists in two manuscripts from Cave 4, Qumran, 4QQoheleth[a] and 4QQoheleth[b]. 4QQoheleth[a] is dated paleographically to 175–150 BCE, which makes it certain that the manuscript was not copied at Qumran, but was brought there from elsewhere, since the archaeological evidence places the founding of the settlement no earlier than circa 150 BCE. It contains 5.13–17, 6.1, 6.3–8, 6.12, 7.1–10, and 7.19–20. 4QQoheleth[b], dated to c.50 BCE, contains 1.10–14 (15?). Both manuscripts show only minor variants from the received text. *Ecclesiastes* is not cited or alluded to in other literature of the Dead Sea Scrolls.

The book of *Esther* is the only book of the Hebrew scriptures not preserved among the Dead Sea Scrolls (no trace of *Nehemiah* is found either, but scholars assume in its case that since it was often copied on the same scroll as *Ezra*, and *Ezra* is found at Qumran, *Nehemiah* was there as well). Several reasons have been advanced for the absence of *Esther*, but the more likely explanations are:

1. It is mere accident or chance that no fragments have survived.
2. The book, written in the Diaspora, was relatively unknown in Palestine at this time and its festival of Purim was not celebrated.
3. Some scholars date the Hebrew version of *Esther* as late as the second century CE; therefore it could not fall within the dates of the Judean Desert corpus, all prior to 135 CE.

While *Esther* itself does not appear among the Dead Sea Scrolls, there is an Aramaic text from Cave 4, 4Q550 or "Tales from the Persian Court," which resembles the book of *Esther* in style and setting. 4Q550 contains stories concerning Jewish protagonists in the Persian Court, and gives rise to the theory that there existed a cycle of tales concerning Jews in the Persian Court from which the book of *Esther* was derived, in much the same way as the book of *Daniel* was derived from a cycle of Daniel tales.

Although these five books do not appear as a group among the Dead Sea Scrolls, they do have certain characteristics in common. The four which are preserved at Qumran appear only in Cave 4 (the major storage cave) or in the minor caves. They are preserved in only a few copies, at most four, and these are all fragmentary. None of them is cited or alluded to in other literature of the Dead Sea Scrolls. While no conclusion can be drawn from this evidence concerning these five books' canonical status, it is possible to surmise that these texts were peripheral to the main currents of thought in the Qumran corpus, and occupied a less important place than other books that were not later canonized, such as *1 Enoch* and *Jubilees*.

BIBLIOGRAPHY

Baillet, M. "Textes des Grottes 2Q, 3Q, 6Q, 7Q à 10Q." In *Les 'petites grottes' de Qumrân*. Discoveries in the Judaean Desert, 3. Oxford, 1962.

Crawford, Sidnie White. "Has the Book of Esther Been Found at Qumran? 4QprotoEsther and the Esther Corpus." *Revue de Qumrân* 17 (1996), 307–325.

Cross, Frank Moore. "Studies in the Structure of Hebrew Verse: The Prosody of Lamentations 1:1–22." In *The Word of the Lord Shall Go Forth: Essays in Honor of David Noel Freedmen in Celebration of His 60th Birthday*, edited by Carol L. Meyers and M. O'Connor. 1983. The original publication of 4QLamentations.

Milik, J. T. "Les modèles araméens du livre d'Esther dans la grotte 4 de Qumrân." *Revue de Qumrân* 15 (1992), 321–399. The original publication of 4Q550.

Milik, J. T. "Textes des Grotte 5Q." In *Les 'petites grottes' de Qumrân*. Discoveries in the Judaean Desert, 3. Oxford 1962.

Tov, Emanuel. "Three Manuscripts (Abbreviated Texts?) of Canticles from Qumran Cave 4." *Journal for Jewish Studies* 46 (1995), 88–111.

Ulrich, Eugene. "Ezra and Qohelet Manuscripts from Qumran." In *Priests, Prophets and Scribes: Essays on the Formation and Heritage of Second Temple Judaism in Honor of Joseph Blenkinsopp*, edited by E. Ulrich et al., pp. 139–157. Sheffield, 1992.

Ulrich, Eugene. "An Index of the Passages in the Biblical Manuscripts from the Judean Desert (Part 2: Isaiah-Chronicles)." *Dead Sea Discoveries* 2 (1995), 36–108.

SIDNIE WHITE CRAWFORD

FLORILEGIUM. The text in 4QFlorilegium (4Q174) is not strictly a florilegium (anthology), but a thematic interpretation of various passages of scripture, notably parts of *Deuteronomy* 33, *2 Samuel* 7, and Psalms 1, 2, and 5. The term "the last days" occurs several times and has resulted in several scholars' designating the composition "Eschatological Midrash" (Allegro 1958:350–351; Steudel 1994). The composition shares many aspects of its formal presentation and vocabulary with the 4Q Catena[a] (4Q177), but there is no textual overlap between the two manuscripts, so they should be considered separate compositions for the time being (as also 4Q178, 4Q182, 4Q183).

Twenty-six fragments from Qumran Cave 4 in an early Herodian formal script with some rustic semiformal elements (Strugnell 1969–1970:177) have been assigned to this manuscript, which can be dated to the second half of the first century BCE. The orthography is generally full.

The editions of Allegro (1968) and Brooke (1985) analyzed the fragments largely independently of one another. In a more detailed study, Steudel (1994) has arranged the extant fragments according to their damage patterns. She has suggestively proposed that eighteen fragments can be assigned to six different columns belonging to two different sheets of parchment. The principal scriptural passages being interpreted are thus coincidentally in canonical order: *Deuteronomy, Samuel, Psalms* (Puech 1993:573; cf. *Sir.* 1.24–25). Steudel's column numbers are used in this article.

The extant part of column i (frgs. 6, 7, 8, 9) contains quotations of *Deuteronomy* 33.8–11 and 33.12, the blessings of Levi (cf. the Testimonia in 4Q175 14–20) with a small amount of interpretation between them. The remains of column ii (frgs. 4, 9, 10, 11) contain a quotation from *Deuteronomy* 33.20–21 with interpretation; fragment 4 has hints of a discussion of the rule of Belial and may have contained a secondary quotation of *Isaiah* 24.17–18 (Steudel 1994, 40; cf. CD iv.10–14) before leading into *2 Samuel* 7.10 (Puech 1993, 573).

Column iii (frgs. 1, 2, 21) preserves top and bottom margins, showing that there were nineteen lines per column in this manuscript. The column begins with a continuation of the quotation of *2 Samuel* 7.10–11, which is then interpreted through the secondary use of *Exodus* 15.17–18 stressing the sovereignty of God. The "place" (*maqom*) of *2 Samuel* 7.10 is interpreted as referring to the eschatological Temple, to which there will be limited access (cf. *Deut.* 23.2; 4Q396 1–2.i.5). This eschatological Temple, probably the Temple that God himself will make (cf. 11Q Temple Scroll[a] xxix.9), is proleptically anticipated by the community, which is described as a "sanctuary of men" (*miqdash adam*) (Dimant 1986), a phrase some have understood as "sanctuary amongst men" and others as "sanctuary of Adam" (Wise 1994). Quotation of part of *2 Samuel* 7.11 allows the commentator to argue that eschatological rest will be given to the sons of light, and the sons of Belial will stop all their devious scheming. *2 Samuel* 7.11–14 is then cited in a carefully abbreviated form and interpreted through the secondary quotation of *Amos* 9.11 (cf. CD vii.16; *Acts* 15.16). It is explained that the "Branch of David" (cf. *Jer.* 23.5, 33.15; 4Q161 7–10 iii.22; 4Q252 v.3–4; 4Q285 v.3–4) will arise with the Interpreter of the Law (cf. CD vi.7, vii.18) in the last days. The Interpreter of the Law is best understood as the anointed priestly counterpart to the Davidic messiah. Perhaps the earlier use of *Deuteronomy* 33.8–11 was interpreted to refer to this priestly messiah. The two figures together reflect the common community expectation of two messiahs. The Davidic messiah will arise in Zion to save Israel.

The whole passage (iii.1–13) is a delightful play on the full range of meanings of "place," "house," and "sanctuary"; reference is made to the Temple, past (iii.5–6), present (iii.6), and future (iii.3–4), to the community as sanctuary (iii.6; cf. The Rule of the Community, 1QS viii.5–9), and to the house of the Davidic messiah (iii.10–13). The sanctuary of men is described as a place where offerings will be made to God. These offerings are described as "works of thanksgiving" (*maʿasei todah*), probably a subtle play on the phrase "works of the Law (*maʿasei ha-torah*)" (4Q398 2.ii.3; cf. 1QpHab viii.1, xii.4; 4Q270 9.ii.19; 4Q398 18; CD iv.18, vi.14). The sanctuary of men may also be Adamic, inasmuch as it anticipates the time when the paradisiacal sanctuary (cf. 4Q265 2.ii.1–17; *Jub.* 1:17) will be restored and the community will share in "all the glory of Adam" (CD iii.20).

In a new paragraph introduced with the phrase "Midrash of" (*midrash min*), Psalm 1.1 is cited and then interpreted through the secondary use of *Isaiah* 8.11 (cf. CD vii.16) and *Ezek.* 37.23. There follows a citation of Psalm 2.1. Those who meditate on the Law are those who turn aside from the way of the wicked and are no longer defiled with idolatry. The interpretation of the Psalm runs into the top of column iv (frgs. 1, 3, 5, 12, 24) and includes the secondary quotation (some of it supralinear) of *Daniel* 11.32, 11.35, and 12:10. There is a detailed description of the community as the elect ones who will endure suffering and thus be like the righteous ones of *Daniel* 11.32. The community is also called the Sons of Zadok (cf. CD iv.3–4), and probably the House of Judah (4Q174 ii.15, iv.1; cf. CD iv.11, vii.12–13; 1QpHab viii.1).

To column v Steudel has assigned fragments 13 and 14, which contain part of Psalm 5.3 with interpretation. Fragments 15 and 19 (col. vi) probably contained a secondary quotation of *Isaiah* 65.22–23 and its interpretation.

Overall, this sectarian composition is concerned with the way various unfulfilled blessings and prophecies are being and will be fulfilled in the experiences of the community. The exegetical methodology of the interpreter is clear: secondary supportive proof texts are joined to the passage they interpret through catchwords (as in the rabbinic *gezerah shavah*). For example, *Exodus* 15.17–18 is joined to *2 Samuel* 7.10 through their common use of "to plant" (*nṭʿ*). As in 4QCatena[a], only the *Psalms* quotations have interpretation introduced with a formula using the technical term *pesher*. The use of the term *midrash* in iii.14 seems to be technical, not referring to a literary genre (as the later rabbinic *midrashim*), but identifying a method of scriptural exposition.

The principal fragments are primarily concerned with the sovereignty of God himself and with the character of the community as the eschatological Temple in anticipation and as the elect of Israel who are enduring a time of trials. There is also some interest in the Davidic messiah, though "his messiah" of Psalm 2:2 is interpreted to refer to "the elect ones of Israel," the community itself, rather than the Davidic messiah.

2 Samuel 7 and Psalm 2 are also treated together in *Acts* 13.33–37 and *Hebrews* 1.5. Several of the concerns of the Florilegium are also to be found in *2 Corinthians* 6.14–7.1, commonly thought to be an interpolation.

BIBLIOGRAPHY

Allegro, John M. "Further Messianic References in Qumran Literature." *Journal of Biblical Literature* 75 (1956), 174–187. The first publication of part of the scroll, drawing attention to its messianism.

Allegro, John M. "Fragments of a Qumran Scroll of Eschatological *Midrašim.*" *Journal of Biblical Literature* 77 (1958), 350–354. The first publication and preliminary notes on most of column iii.

Allegro, John M., with the collaboration of Arnold A. Anderson. *Qumrân Cave 4.I (4Q158–4Q186).* Discoveries in the Judaean Desert, 5. Oxford, 1968. The official edition of the scroll is presented on pp. 53–57; this will eventually be revised by M. Bernstein, G. J. Brooke, and F. H. Cryer.

Brooke, George J. *Exegesis at Qumran: 4QFlorilegium in Its Jewish Context*. Journal for the Study of the Old Testament Supplement, 29. Sheffield, 1985. The most extensive discussion of the exegetical methods and content of the manuscript.

Dimant, Devorah. "*4QFlorilegium* and the Idea of the Community as Temple." In *Hellenica et Judaica: Hommage à Valentin Nikiprowetzky*, edited by A. Caquot, M. Hadas-Lebel, and J. Riaud, pp. 165–189. Leuven-Paris, 1986. Argues for the idea of the community as temple.

Juel, Donald. *Messianic Exegesis: Christological Interpretation of the Old Testament in Early Christianity*. Philadelphia, 1988. A detailed consideration of several messianic passages in the scrolls in relation to the New Testament.

Puech, Émile. *La croyance des Esséniens en la vie future: immortalité, résurrection, vie éternelle? Histoire d'une croyance dans le judaïsme ancien*. Etudes Bibliques, 22. Paris, 1993. Pages 572–587 contain what amounts to an edition of 4Q174 ii:12–iv:11, together with some detailed commentary.

Steudel, Annette. *Der Midrasch zur Eschatologie aus der Qumrangemeinde (4QMidrEschat[a,b]): Materielle Rekonstruktion, Textbestand, Gattung und Traditionsgeschichtliche Einordnung des durch 4Q174 ("Florilegium") und 4Q177 ("Catena[a]") repräsentierten Werkes aus den Qumranfunden.* Studies on the Texts of the Desert of Judah, 13. Leiden, 1994. The most comprehensive analysis concerning the reading and positioning of the fragments.

Strugnell, J. "Notes en marge du Volume V des «Discoveries in the Judean Desert of Jordan»." *Revue de Qumrân* 7 (1969–70), 163–276. Assorted significant notes on fragments 1–12, 15, 16, 18, 19, and 21.

Wise, Michael O. *Thunder in Gemini and Other Essays on the History, Language and Literature of Second Temple Palestine.* Journal for the Study of the Pseudepigrapha Supplement Series 15. Sheffield, 1994. Chapter 4 argues for Adam to be read in 4Q174 iii:6.

GEORGE J. BROOKE

G

GENESIS, BOOK OF. Before the discovery of manuscripts at Qumran, there were three major sources for the text of *Genesis*. The Masoretic Text (MT), the Hebrew text passed down in Jewish circles in an unbroken manuscript tradition from antiquity to the present, is overall quite a good text and often (but by no means always) preserves the original reading. The Septuagint is an idiomatic but accurate translation into Greek made in the third century BCE. It has numerous small differences from the Masoretic Text, many of which seem to have been present in its Hebrew base text. The Samaritan Pentateuch tends to expand the text by frequently inserting parallel material from other places in the Pentateuch. These expansions are relatively rare in *Genesis*, however.

Frank Moore Cross, following William Foxwell Albright, has argued that these three sources of the Pentateuch—the Masoretic Text, the Septuagint, and the Samaritan Pentateuch—developed through long transmission in three different locations (Babylon, Egypt, and Palestine, respectively) and should be considered three distinct text types. This theory has been widely challenged, especially by Emanuel Tov, and few, if any, scholars now accept the suggested geographical origins. My contention is that Cross is correct in essence, but that we should speak of two text types (the Masoretic Text and Septuagint) and one deliberate revision or recension (the Samaritan Pentateuch) based on the proto–Masoretic Text (see Davila, 1993, 3–37; "Text-Type and Terminology: Genesis and Exodus as Test Cases" (*Revue de Qumrân* 16/61 [1993] 3–37).

The textual basis of *Genesis* outlined above has been widened considerably by the recovery of at least nineteen fragmentary manuscripts of the book from Qumran: 1QGenesis (1Q1), 2QGenesis (2Q1), 4QGenesis-Exodus^{a} (4Q1), 4QGenesis^{b-g} (4Q2–7), 4QGenesis^{h1} (4Q8), 4QGenesis^{h2} (4Q8a), 4QGenesis$^{h\text{-}title}$ (4Q8c), 4QGenesis^{j-k} (4Q9–10), 4QPaleo-Genesis-Exodus^{l} (4Q11), 4QPaleo-Genesis^{m} (4Q12), 4QGen^{n} (no inventory number), Genesis or Jubilees? (4Q483), 6QPaleo-Genesis (6Q1), and 8QGenesis (8Q1). (4QGenesis$^{h\text{-}title}$ contains only the title of the book—misspelled!) Several other manuscripts of *Genesis* have been found elsewhere in the Judean Desert: MasGen?, Mur 1:1–3, Mur?Genesis, and Sdeir 1. Some of these manuscripts (especially 4QGenesis^{h1}, 4QGenesis^{h2}, 4QPaleo-Genesis^{l}, and 4QGen^{n}) preserve only a few words or letters of the book. None of the Genesis manuscripts from anywhere in the Judean Desert is well preserved. All the Qumran manuscripts that contain enough material for analysis belong to the same text type as the Masoretic Text (4QGen^{b} is virtually identical), but most have some orthographic differences from it and contain minor textual variations. The fragments of *Genesis* from other sites in the Judean Desert are even closer to the Masoretic Text, with very few textual or orthographic variants. The variants in the Genesis manuscripts from the Judean Desert, including Qumran, all involve orthography or individual readings. There are no variant redactions like those found for *Exodus*, *Numbers*, and *Jeremiah*.

Some of the readings are of interest in themselves. For example, the text of *Genesis* 1.9 in the Septuagint has two significant variants from the Masoretic Text, both of which are attested in Hebrew at Qumran. Instead of "place" (*maqom*), the small scrap that constitutes 4QGenesis^{h1} reads "gathering-place" (*miqveh*). A fragment of 4QGenesis^{k} adds the phrase "[and the waters were gathered beneath the heavens to their gathering-places] and the dry la[nd] appeared" to the end of the verse, filling it out according to the normal structure of the acts of creation in the chapter. This longer reading is supported by the Septuagint and seems to be original. A smattering of readings in the manuscripts demonstrates that there were Hebrew base texts for a number of other variants in the Septuagint, confirming that at least some of the differences from the Masoretic Text found in the Septuagint were due to a different Hebrew base text rather than creative exegesis by the translator. This at least partial vindication of the Septuagint as a translation is probably the most important new datum provided by the *Genesis* manuscripts.

A particularly striking individual variant in *Genesis* 22.14 is found in a small fragment of 4QGenesis-Exodus^{a} and appears in no other text, with the possible exception of a Sahidic Coptic manuscript. In the other textual witnesses to this verse, Abraham names the place where his son Isaac was nearly sacrificed *Yahveh yirʾeh*, "Yahweh sees." But in 4QGenesis-Exodus^{a} the name is given as [*ʿE*]*lo*[*h*]*im yirʾeh*, "God sees." This difference is significant because many scholars have argued that the narrative in *Genesis* 22.1–4 was derived from the E (Elohistic) source, a source that is reconstructed to have used no divine name but *ʿElohim*, "God." The presence of the name

Yahveh in 22.14 has always been a difficulty, and it is my contention that it is secondary and that the original reading has been preserved by 4QGenesis-Exodus[a]. Thus the Qumran manuscripts of *Genesis* are relevant for source criticism of the Pentateuch as well as textual criticism.

Although there are no systematically reworked redactions of *Genesis* at Qumran, there are documents that are inspired by it (or by the Pentateuch overall) and that paraphrase it, sometimes closely. The text known as the Reworked Pentateuch[a–e] (4Q158, 4Q364–365, 4Q366–367) is based on the Pentateuch but heavily rewrites, reorders, and supplements the material in it. There are also fragments of Pesher-type commentaries on *Genesis* (4Q252–254a). The Hebrew fragments of the book of *Jubilees* (1Q17–18; 2Q19–20, 3Q5, 4Q216–224, 11Q12), a work known as Pseudo-Jubilees[a–c] (4Q225–227), and 4QExposition on the Patriarchs (4Q464), as well as the Aramaic Genesis Apocryphon (1QapGen, 1Q20) and so forth, follow the story line of Genesis but rewrite it and expand it more freely than the Reworked Pentateuch. 4Q422, entitled Paraphrase of Genesis-Exodus, also paraphrases the creation, fall, and flood narratives of Genesis, along with the story of the Egyptian oppression of the Israelites and the ten plagues. It is possible, although quite unlikely, that 6QGenesis? (6Q19) is an Aramaic translation or paraphrase of Genesis. Other texts, such as the Enoch literature (4Q201–202, 4Q204–212, etc.) and the Book of Giants (1Q23–24, 2Q26, 4Q203, 4Q530–532, 4Q533?, 6Q8), draw on the subject matter of *Genesis* without adhering to the wording or story line to any significant degree.

The large number of copies of the work recovered from Qumran, as well as its wide influence on Second Temple texts also found there, indicate that *Genesis* was a very important work to the compilers of the Qumran library and to Second Temple Judaism in general.

BIBLIOGRAPHY

Cross, Frank Moore, and Shemaryahu Talmon, eds. *Qumran and the History of the Biblical Text*. Cambridge, Mass., 1975. A collection of important articles on this topic published between 1953 and 1975. Includes essays by Albright (pp. 140–146) and Cross (pp. 177–195, 278–292, 306–320) on the theory of local text types in the Hebrew scriptures.

Davila, James R. "New Qumran Readings for Genesis One." In *Of Scribes and Scrolls: Studies on the Hebrew Bible, Intertestamental Judaism, and Christian Origins Presented to John Strugnell on the Occasion of His Sixtieth Birthday*, edited by Harold W. Attridge et al., pp. 3–11. Lanham, Md., 1990. A study of the variants in *Genesis* 1 found in the Qumran MSS.

Davila, James R. "The Name of God at Moriah: An Unpublished Fragment from 4QGenExod[a]." *Journal of Biblical Literature* 110 (1991), 577–582. A study of the variant in *Gen* 22:14 discussed above.

Davila, James R. "New Qumran Readings for the Joseph Story (Genesis 37–50)." In *The Madrid Qumran Congress: Proceedings of the International Congress on the Dead Sea Scrolls, Madrid, 18–21 March 1991*, edited by Julio Trebolle Barrera and Luis Vegas Montaner, pp. 167–175. 2 vols. Studies on the Texts of the Desert of Judah, 11. Leiden, 1992. A study of the variants in the Joseph story found in the Qumran MSS.

Hendel, Ronald S. *The Text of Genesis 1–11: Textual Studies and Critical Edition*. New York and Oxford, 1998.

Tov, Emanuel. "A Modern Textual Outlook Based on the Qumran Scrolls." *Hebrew Union College Annual* 53 (1982), 11–27. An important article in which Tov criticizes Albright's and Cross's theory of text types.

JAMES R. DAVILA

GENESIS, COMMENTARY ON. Four fragmentary manuscripts from Cave 4 (4Q252, 4Q253, 4Q254, 4Q254a) contain implicit and explicit commentary on the *Book of Genesis*, or selected passages thereof.

The most extensive of these is 4Q Commentary on Genesis A (4Q252; formerly 4QpGen[a]). Originally, two fragments containing quotation and interpretation of parts of *Genesis* 49 were allotted to J. M. Allegro, who published one of them as 4Q Patriarchal Blessings. As the remaining fragments from Cave 4 were sorted, J. T. Milik realized that those two fragments belonged with others as part of a single composition. Altogether, six fragments in an early Herodian hand have been assigned to this manuscript.

Based on various physical features, it can be determined that the scroll almost certainly consisted of a single sheet of parchment about 60 centimeters long with six columns of writing. The first four columns (7–9 cm) are wider than the last two (6.5 cm). The commentary covers various texts from *Genesis* 6–49. In those places where non-Masoretic variants are attested in the cited biblical text, these tend to reflect the type of text known from manuscripts of the Septuagint, an intriguing matter, since nearly all the manuscripts of *Genesis* from Qumran predominantly anticipate the Masoretic Text.

The contents of the scroll are especially significant because of the variety of types of biblical interpretation that are represented, including rewritten Bible, halakhic exegesis, and *pesher*. The opening (4Q252 i.1–ii.5) is a rewritten form of the flood narrative. Calendrical matters in the account are highlighted, and the chronology of the flood is shown to fit precisely with a 364-day year (cf. 11QPsalms[a] xxvii.6–7) in which dates are given according to the days of the week (first, second, etc.) as well as the days of the month. The 364-day calendar also lies behind the festival calendar of the Temple Scroll. Nothing in the flood narrative takes place on a Sabbath.

The commentary then explains (ii.5–8) why Canaan was cursed rather than Ham: in a poetic style which uses the phrasing of *Genesis* 9.1, 9.27 and *2 Chronicles* 20.7, the descendants of Ham and Japheth are excluded from divine favor. It is likely that this reflects a political wish at the time the commentary was composed for the exclusion of foreigners from the land of Israel (cf. 1QM i.6, xviii.2). A second section with chronological concerns treats the entry of Abram into the Land; ii.8–10 attempts to solve the textual problems of *Genesis* 11–12 by rewriting the narrative of *Genesis* 11.31 with a precise dating system. The commentary is thus interested in both annual calendars and also longer periods of years.

Several very fragmentary sections concerning Abraham, about which little can be said, follow: They appear to be concerned with the Covenant of the Pieces (*Gn.* 15.9, 15.17; 4Q252 ii.11–13); the twelve princes (*Gn.* 17.20; 4Q252 iii.1–2); the destruction of Sodom and Gomorrah (*Gn.* 18.31–32; 4Q252 iii.2–6), in which there is halakhic interpretation using phrases from *Deuteronomy* 13.16–17, 20.11, and 20.14; and the binding of Isaac (*Gn.* 22.10–12; 4Q252 iii.6–10). Then there seems to be reference to the blessing of Jacob (*Gn.* 28.3–4; 4Q252 iii.11–14). Discussion of the destruction of Amalek follows (*Gn.* 36.12 with *Dt.* 25.19; 4Q252 iv.1–3). Because Saul spared Agag and took the booty, his dynastic aspirations were forfeited; the exegesis shows that the destruction which Saul failed to carry out will be fulfilled in the eschatological period. Thus *Genesis* 36 becomes a kind of unfulfilled prophetic text. Other contemporary texts discuss the destruction of Amalek (*T. Sim.* 5.4–6.5; Pseudo-Philo, *Biblical Antiquities*, on *Judges* 19); Amalek is commonly associated with promiscuity and sexual misdemeanors.

From iv.3 to the end the text is a commentary on the blessings of the sons of Jacob. Parts of those for Reuben (*Gn.* 49.3–4), Judah (*Gn.* 49.10), as well as Asher and Naphtali (*Gn.* 49.20–21) survive. In this section the commentary takes the form of the explicit quotation of the biblical text followed by commentary formulaically introduced by the term *pesher*. The blessing of Reuben is completely represented. Its interpretation states that Jacob reproved Reuben for sleeping with his concubine Bilhah (*Gn.* 35.22). The blessing of Judah is interpreted with the language of *Jeremiah* 33.17 and understood to speak of the branch of David (cf. *Jer.* 23.5, 33.15; 4Q161 7–10.iii.22, 4Q174 1.i.11, 4Q284 5.3, 5.4), the royal Messiah. At this point the interpretation is clearly sectarian with mention of the "men of the community" (cf. 1QS vi.21, vii.20, viii.11).

It is difficult to discern how the commentator went about his task. Many of the interpretations explain problems in the plain meaning of the text of *Genesis*, but others are eschatological and sectarian. It seems that the commentator worked from a collection of sources which were written in different styles. This helps to explain the abrupt shift between the various pericopae and also the great variety of genres of interpretation in the six extant columns. The whole is organized according to the order of *Genesis* itself, but because only a selection of passages is discussed, it is not a continuous, running commentary (like the Pesher Habakkuk). The overall compilation can be read as a kind of exhortatory historical exegesis, setting right the chronologies of the past and indicating how the unfulfilled blessings and curses of *Genesis* are to be fulfilled. Alternatively, the commentary may have functioned as a quasi-legal document in which the commentator makes a claim to the Land (no sections of *Genesis* dealing with Abraham or Joseph outside of the Land are included) and makes a particular plea for how the true heirs to the Land should lead lives of calendrical and sexual propriety.

To 4QCommentary on Genesis B are assigned three fragments in a late Hasmonean or early Herodian hand. There are no overlaps with the Commentary on Genesis A. Fragment 1 mentions the Ark of the Covenant. Fragment 2 may be associated with Jacob and his cultic activities. Fragment 3 speaks of Belial, but cannot be placed in relation to the text of *Genesis*.

4QCommentary on Genesis C survives in seventeen small fragments written in an early Herodian formal hand. None of the fragments is extensive, but, like the Commentary on Genesis A, this text seems to offer interpretations of blessings and curses: the curse of Canaan (*Gn.* 9.24–25), the events leading up to the binding of Isaac (*Gn.* 22.5–17), as well as the blessings of Judah (*Gn.* 49.8–12), containing an allusion to the "two sons of oil" of *Zechariah* 4.14, of Issachar (*Gn.* 49.14–15), of Dan (*Gn.* 49.16–17), and of Joseph (*Gn.* 49.22–25).

The fourth manuscript in this group, 4QCommentary on Genesis D, is extant in three fragments in a developed Herodian formal hand. In fragments 1–2 there is a description of the measurements of Noah's ark, partly citing *Genesis* 6.15. Fragment 3 is concerned with Noah's disembarkation (cf. 4Q252 ii.1–5) and something that the raven makes known to the latter generations.

BIBLIOGRAPHY

Allegro, John M. "Further Messianic References in Qumran Literature." *Journal of Biblical Literature* 75 (1956), 174–175. The first publication of 4Q252, column v.

Bernstein, Moshe J. "4Q252: From Re-Written Bible to Biblical Commentary." *Journal of Jewish Studies* 45 (1994), 1–27. An important study highlighting the problems in the plain meaning of the text of Genesis which 4Q252 attempts to address.

Bernstein, Moshe J. "4Q252: Method and Context, Genre and Sources." *Jewish Quarterly Review* 85 (1994–1995), 61–79. Argues against reading 4Q252 in a thematic way.

Brooke, George J. "The Thematic Content of 4Q252." *Jewish Quarterly Review* 85 (1994–1995), 33–59. Argues for a thematic reading of 4Q252 in terms of unfulfilled blessings and curses, especially those concerning sexual misconduct.

Brooke, George J. "The Genre of 4Q252: From Poetry to Pesher." *Dead Sea Discoveries* 1 (1994), 160–179. Proposes that despite the variety of genres in 4Q252, the work has an overall structure.

Brooke, George J. *"4Q252 as Early Jewish Commentary."* *Revue de Qumrân* 17 (1996), 385–401. Argues that 4Q252 is a key to understanding the transition in Jewish interpretation from implicit to explicit exegesis.

Brooke, George J. "Commentaries on Genesis and Malachi." In *Qumran Cave 4.XVII: Parabiblical Texts, Part 3*, edited by George J. Brooke et al., pp. 185–236. Discoveries in the Judaean Desert, 22. Oxford, 1996. The principal edition of the four Genesis commentaries.

Glessmer, Uwe. "Antike und moderne Auslegungen des Sintflutberichtes Gen 6–8 und der Qumran-Pesher 4Q252." *Theologische Fakultät Leipzig: Forschungsstelle Judentum; Mitteilungen und Beiträge* 6 (1993), 2–81. A very detailed analysis of the calendrical information in 4Q252, columns i–iii.

Lim, Timothy H. "The Chronology of the Flood Story in a Qumran Text (4Q252)." *Journal of Jewish Studies* 43 (1992), 288–298. The first publication to draw attention to 4Q252, columns i–ii.

Stegemann, Hartmut. "Weitere Stücke von 4QpPsalm 37, von 4QPatriarchal Blessings, und Hinweis auf eine unedierte Handschrift aus Höhle 4Q mit Exzerpten aus dem Deuteronomium." *Revue de Qumrân* 6 (1967–1969), 211–217. Some important suggestions for the better understanding of 4Q252, column v.

GEORGE J. BROOKE

GENESIS APOCRYPHON. This fragmentary text 1QapGen, discovered in 1947 among the seven major scrolls from Cave 1 at Qumran, contains parts of twenty-three columns of an Aramaic paraphrase of stories in the *Book of Genesis*. Only three columns (1QapGen xx–xxii) are more or less completely preserved; three others (1QapGen ii, xii, xix) have a substantial part that is legible; and other columns (1QapGen i, iii, v–vii, x–xi, xvi–xvii) have preserved a few words or a few lines. To this text also belongs 1Q20 ("Apocalypse de Lamech"), which in a recent identification by Bruce Zuckerman and Michael O. Wise has been shown to be part of column 0, as well as the seven-line so-called Trever fragment, now lost, which still awaits official publication.

Written in a late Herodian script, this copy is dated paleographically to 25 BCE through 50 CE (plus or minus twenty-five years). It has not been subjected to radiocarbon dating. [*See* Carbon-14 Dating.] That date may also serve as the time of composition of the Genesis Apocryphon (1QapGen), because this copy may be the autograph; no other copy has been found. If it is not the autograph, then the date of composition might be pushed back to the early first century BCE because of its literary dependence on *Jubilees* and *1 Enoch*. L. F. Hartman (*Catholic Biblical Quarterly* 28, 1966, 497–498) has shown that the chronology of Abram's life is a development of *Genesis* 16.3 but closely tied to the "weeks" chronology of *Jubilees*. The text was composed in the Palestinian form of Middle Aramaic now known from other Qumran texts, which is transitional between the Aramaic of Daniel and that of the earliest of the classical Targums (Onkelos and Jonathan; Kutscher, 1958, p. 22).

The conventional title, Genesis Apocryphon, assigned by the original editors, is a misnomer; it says nothing about the literary form of the writing. Although the Aramaic at times translates literally the Hebrew text of *Genesis* (e.g., *Gn.* 14.1–24 in 1QapGen xxi.23–xxii.24), it more frequently renders the biblical text freely. Phrases literally translated then become part of an expanded paraphrase. Hence, the Genesis Apocryphon (1QapGen) is scarcely a Targum, not even one like the later paraphrastic Targums. Some of its expansions resemble elements found at times in classical *midrashim* of the later rabbinic period, but as a whole the text is not a *midrash* on *Genesis*. It is a form of parabiblical literature, resembling *Jubilees* (on which it depends); part of *1 Enoch*, and Pseudo-Philo's *Biblical Antiquities*. A more appropriate title was suggested by B. Mazar, "The Book of the Patriarchs," which in Aramaic would be *Ketav Avahata*.

The Genesis Apocryphon (1QapGen) narrates in expanded form the story of two biblical patriarchs: Noah (0–xvii?) and Abram (xviii?–xxii). [*See* Abraham; Noah.] The first well-preserved part recounts Lamech's anxiety about the conception of the remarkable child, Noah, born to his wife Bitenosh, and his consultation of his father Methuselah and of Enoch (i.?–iii.?). It then tells of Noah's family and God's message about the Deluge, Noah and his family's entrance into the ark and eventual sacrifices (vi.?–x.?), God's covenant with Noah, the children born to him after the Deluge and the planting of a vineyard on Mount Lubar (xi.?–xii.30), Noah's vision of trees and heavenly effects on them (xiii.?–xv.?), and finally Noah's division of the earth among his sons and his descendants (xvi.?–xvii.?).

The better preserved second part paraphrases the story of Abram in six sections:

- Abram in Ur and Haran (xviii.?–?)
- Abram in Canaan (xviii.?–xix.10a)
  - Journey to Bethel (xix.?–6)
  - Journey from Bethel to Hebron (xix.7–10a)
- Abram in Egypt (xix.10b–xx.33a)
  - His descent into Egypt because of the famine in Canaan (xix.10b–13)
  - His dream about the cedar and date palm on entering Egypt (xix.14–23a)
  - The visit to Abram by three Egyptian courtiers (xix.23b–27)
  - Sarai's beauty described to Pharaoh by the courtiers (xx.2–8a)
  - Sarai's abduction to Pharaoh and Abram's grief (xx.8b–11)
  - Abram's prayer that Sarai not be defiled (xx.12–16a)
  - A plague strikes Pharaoh and his household (xx.16b–21a)

- Pharaoh's cure by Abram's prayer and exorcism (xx.21b–31a)
- Pharaoh sends Sarai and Abram out of Egypt (xx.31b–33a)

• Abram in the Promised Land (xx.33b–xxi.22)
- Abram's return with Lot to Bethel (xx.33b–xxi.4)
- Lot's departure from Abram and settlement in Sodom (xx.5–7)
- Abram's dream about the Promised Land (xxi.8–14)
- Abram's exploration of the extent of the Promised Land (xxi.15–22)

• Abram's defeat of the four invading kings (xxi.23–xxii.26)
- The war of the four kings against the five Canaanite kings (xxi.23–34a)
- Lot is taken captive (xxi.34b–xxii.1a)
- Abram learns of Lot's capture and his pursuit of the four kings (xxii.1b–12a)
- The kings of Sodom and Salem meet Abram on his return from the defeat of the kings (xxii.12b–17)
- Abram's refusal to retain any of the booty of the king of Sodom (xxii.18–26)

• Abram's vision of God, who promises him an heir (xxii.27–?)
- Eliezer will not inherit him (xxii.27–34) [lost]

Despite claims to the contrary, the Genesis Apocryphon (1QapGen) is not a sectarian composition; it contains nothing related to the tenets or the dualistic theology of the Qumran community such as are expressed in its sectarian writings (rule books, hymnbooks, the War Scroll, [1QM] or the *pesharim*). Moreover, this text is composed in Aramaic, whereas the Qumran sectarian writings were composed in a form of postbiblical Hebrew. The Genesis Apocryphon represents, then, a text composed by Jews, which was found acceptable for reading and study in the Qumran community. Although it does show some relation to *Jubilees* and part of *1 Enoch,* that relationship explains only why it would have appealed to the members of the Qumran community. As do those writings, the Genesis Apocryphon reveals a way that biblical writings themselves were being interpreted among Palestinian Jews of the pre-Christian era. The text paraphrases the biblical story of two paragons of righteousness: Noah (*ish tsaddiq, Gn.* 6.9) and Abram (*va-yaḥsheveha lo tsedaqah, Gn.* 15.6).

Two elements of the Genesis Apocryphon are noteworthy: the insert into the *Genesis* story about Sarai's beauty (1QapGen xx.2–8a) and the insert about Abram's exploration of the Promised Land (1QapGen xxi.15–22). The first insert enables Egyptian courtiers who have visited Abram to laud Sarai's extraordinary beauty before the Pharaoh so that he abducts Sarai to be his wife. The poetic account of her beauty has been related to the literary genre known in Arabic literature as *watsf,* "description," which extols the personal charms of a loved one. Outside of the *Song of Songs,* this may be the only instance of such a form in Jewish writings. It is far more extensive than any of the statements about Sarai's beauty in later rabbinic literature (B.T., *Sanhedrin* 8.69b; *Tanḥuma,* Lekh 5; *Genesis Rabbah* 58.1).

The second insert tells how Abram went from Bethel, where he was living, to explore the land that God in a dream promised to give him and his posterity. God had instructed Abram to climb up to Ramath-Hazor, north of Bethel, to the highest spot in the Judean mountains, from which he would gaze to the east, south, west, and north. Abram did that on the day following his dream and gazed from the River of Egypt (the Nile) to Mount Lebanon and Senir (Mount Hermon), from the Great Sea (the Mediterranean) to Hauran (the plateau between the Pharpar and Yarmuk Rivers), at all the land of Gebal (Seir) as far as Kadesh, and at all the Great Desert (Syrian Desert) to the east of the Hauran as far as the Euphrates. God told Abram to travel through this area, which he proceeded to do. The insert itself (1QapGen xxi.15–22) tells how Abram started at the Gihon River (part of the Nile), moved along the (Mediterranean) Sea to the Mount of the Ox (Taurus mountain range), then from the Great Sea to the Euphrates River, then down along the Euphrates to the Red Sea (Persian Gulf and Indian Ocean), then along the Red Sea to the tongue of the Reed Sea (tongue-shaped Gulf of Suez), then back to the Gihon River, whence he started. Then he returned to Hebron, where he feasted with his Amorite friends. What is noteworthy in this description of Abram's travels is the distinction of *yamma simmoqa,* "Red Sea," from the *lissan yam suf,* "the tongue of the Reed Sea." Josephus (*Jewish Antiquities* 1.39) also knows that the Tigris and the Euphrates empty into the Red Sea (*Erythran thalassan*), as do other ancient writers. Also remarkable is the geographical extent of what the Promised Land was to be.

Likewise important is the treatment of the king of Sodom and Melchizedek in the Genesis Apocryphon (1QapGen) xxii.12–23, which purports to be a rendering of *Genesis* 14.17–24. First, it tells of the king of Sodom coming to "Salem, that is Jerusalem" (1QapGen xxii.13). This equation stands in contrast to *Hebrews* 7.1–2, where Melchizedek himself is called "the king of Salem," which is said to mean "king of peace," a popular etymology current in the first century CE. The identification of "Salem" with "Jerusalem" is to be traced to the tradition preserved in *Psalms* 76.2, where Salem stands in parallelism to Zion (cf. Josephus, *Jewish Antiquities* 1.180). It stands in conflict, however, with the opinion of some modern scholars (Hermann Gunkel, W. F. Albright), who maintained that

Genesis 14.18–20 originally had nothing to do with Jerusalem. In the Genesis Apocryphon (1QapGen) xxii.14–15, Melchizedek is said to have brought out "food and drink for Abram and all the men who were with him"; so the "bread and wine" of *Genesis* 14.18 are interpreted. This agrees with the paraphrase of this *Genesis* text in Josephus's *Jewish Antiquities* 1.181 but differs from the sacrificial interpretation given to it by some patristic writers. Again, *Genesis* 14.20 records that after Melchizedek blessed Abram "he paid him a tithe of everything." Ever since the time of Jerome (*Epistles* 73.6; Corpus scriptorum ecclesiasticorum Latinorum 55.20), the ambiguity of the statement about tithes has been noted: Who paid whom? No subject of the verb is expressed in either the Masoretic Text or the Septuagint, and the subject of the preceding verb is Melchizedek. The Genesis Apocryphon (1QapGen) xxii.17, however, solves the problem: "And he gave him a tenth of all the flocks of the king of Elam and his confederates." Thus Abram paid tithes to Melchizedek, and so the ambiguous text gets the same interpretation as *Hebrews* 7.2, where *Abraam* has been inserted.

When Melchizedek exercises his priestly office in blessing Abram, he invokes not "the most high God, the creator of heaven and earth" (*Gn.* 14.19) but "the most high God, lord of heaven and earth" (1QapGen xxii.16). The latter title is undoubtedly venerable in Jewish tradition but not often found (see *Tb.* 7.17; Septuagint mss. B,A [unfortunately not preserved in Tobit[a–e] 4Q196–200]). It has its Greek counterpart in *Matthew* 11.25 and *Luke* 10.21. Lastly, when Abram swears that he will take none of the booty of the king of Sodom, he raises his hand "to the most high God, the lord of heaven and earth" (1QapGen xxii.21), and the Tetragrammaton of *Genesis* 14.22 (*el YHVH el ʿelyon*) is lacking. It thus confirms the suspicion of modern scholars who have regarded YHVH as a gloss in the Masoretic Text, since its counterpart is absent in the Septuagint and Peshitta.

BIBLIOGRAPHY

Avigad, Nahman, and Yigael Yadin. *A Genesis Apocryphon: A Scroll from the Wilderness of Judaea: Description and Contents of the Scroll, Facsimiles, Transcription and Translation of Columns II, XIX–XXII.* Jerusalem, 1956. The main publication of the Genesis Apocryphon. Currently out of print.

Fitzmyer, Joseph A. *The Genesis Apocryphon of Qumran Cave I: A Commentary.* Biblica et Orientalia, 18A. 2d ed. Rome, 1971. Introduction, text, translation, and detailed commentary, with a grammatical analysis of the text and glossary. Being revised.

Greenfield, Jonas C., and Elisha Qimron. "The Genesis Apocryphon Col. xii." In *Studies in Qumran Aramaic,* edited by T. Muraoka, pp. 70–77. *Abr-Nahrain* Supplement 3. Louvain, 1992. Publication of 1QapGen xii.1–21, 27. The same authors are to publish other badly preserved intermediary columns, recently studied with new photographic techniques (e.g., cols. xvi–xvii).

Kutscher, E. Y. "Dating the Language of the Genesis Apocryphon." *Journal of Biblical Literature* 76 (1957), 288–292. The basic discussion of the kind of Aramaic in which the Genesis Apocryphon was written.

Kutscher, E. Y. "The Language of the 'Genesis Apocryphon': A Preliminary Study." In *Aspects of the Dead Sea Scrolls,* edited by Chaim Rabin and Yigael Yadin, pp. 1–35. Scripta hierosolymitana, 4. Jerusalem, 1958. Continues the preceding article in greater detail.

Milik, Józef T. "Apocalypse de Lamech." In *Qumran Cave I,* edited by D. Barthélemy and J. T. Milik, pp. 86–87. Discoveries in the Judaean Desert, 1. Oxford, 1955. Publication of fragment 1Q20, known to be related to the Genesis Apocryphon. It was called "Apocalypse de Lamech" because, before the unrolling of the scroll and its official publication by Avigad and Yadin, the name "Lamech" appeared on a fragment that had come loose from the rolled-up scroll.

Muraoka, T. "Notes on the Aramaic of the Genesis Apocryphon." *Revue de Qumrân* 8 (1972–1976), 7–51. Further grammatical analysis of the Genesis Apocryphon going beyond that of Fitzmyer.

Qimron, Elisha. "Towards a New Edition of the Genesis Apocryphon." *Journal for the Study of the Pseudepigrapha* 10 (1992), 11–18.

JOSEPH A. FITZMYER, S.J.

GENTILES. The view of the non-Jewish nations, known as gentiles, in Jewish literature of the Second Temple period embodies both the deprecation of paganism and the universalism inherent in prophetic teaching. This duality may already be illustrated in the later components of the *Book of Isaiah*, where the nations are esteemed as nothing before the Lord (*Is.* 40.17), yet the foreigner is beckoned not to remain separate but to join his covenant with Israel (*Is.* 56.3–8). Hellenistic Jewish literature comprises not only cosmopolitan works, such as the *Letter of Aristeas*, in which the Torah is portrayed as compatible with the finest gentile ethics and wisdom, but also works such as *3 Maccabees*, which has a point of view characterized as narrowly Jewish and antigentile. Among Judean writings the latter view is most prominent in the *Psalms of Solomon*, where the depiction of gentiles reflects the oppression by the Roman conquerors. *Jubilees* (23.23) likewise describes the "sinners of the nations" who have no mercy for old or young. Qumran writings have many affinities with these works and share their pejorative estimate of pagan culture. Among heathen "abominations," Temple Scroll[a] singles out their burial of the dead in homes (11Q19 xlviii.12), the cult of Molech (lx.17), and necromancy (lx.19). The savagery of the *Kittim*, who are generally identified as the Romans, is vividly portrayed in Pesher Habakkuk (1QpHab).

As one might expect, the deprecation of pagans is most pronounced in the War Scroll (1QM), where expressions such as "nations of wickedness" and "nations of futility" are frequently found. In accordance with the deterministic bent of Qumran theology, the contrasting character between Israel and the nations was attributed to divine destiny. The expulsion liturgy found at the end of the Damascus Document blesses God, "who established peoples in accordance with their families and tongues for their nations, but made them go astray in a trackless void; but our ancestors you did choose and to their descendants you gave your truthful statutes" (4Q266 11.9–11). The depiction of the contrasting destiny of Israel and the gentiles may have been influenced by *Deuteronomy* 4.19 and has some similarities with the rabbinic *ʿAleinu* prayer. However, the latter was customarily followed by the expressed hope for the end of paganism through the recognition of God's kingdom by all mankind, a redemptive hope not compatible with the fatalistic view of evil at Qumran.

In the Qumran legal sphere, there are a number of rules that pertain to relations with non-Jews. It has been suggested that these support the hypothesis of a diaspora origin for the Qumran community (Murphy-O'Connor, 1974). Actually, the rules seem more to reflect the treatment of gentiles living in areas under Jewish control. According to the law code of the Damascus Document, violence against non-Jews or their property is prohibited, unless sanctioned by Ḥibbur Yiśra'el, a Jewish governing authority (CD xii.6–8). The reason given, "so that they will not blaspheme," implies a sensitivity to blasphemy on the part of gentiles. One may not send a gentile to do his business on the Sabbath (4Q266 11.2). It is improper to spend the Sabbath day in a place near pagans (4Q266 11.14). One should not sell clean animals to gentiles in order that they not sacrifice them (4Q266 12.8–9). Conversely, metals from which heathen images were fashioned were defiled for reuse (e.g., 4Q269 8.ii and parallel Damascus Document fragments from Cave 4 at Qumran). A priest who was in captivity among gentiles or who migrated into areas under their jurisdiction is disqualified for Temple service (4Q266 5.ii.5–9). Slaves and maidservants of a Jewish household who entered the "covenant of Abraham" may not be sold to pagans (4Q266 12.10–11).

The foregoing laws are largely compatible with the picture of Jewish–pagan coexistence in Second Temple Palestine as depicted by David Flusser. Even though they lived side by side, Jews and gentiles went their separate ways. As early as the Persian period most Jews do not appear to have been greatly attracted to paganism. In Jewish regions they were very careful to keep out pagan symbols, and Roman governors for the most part respected their sensibilities. Jews accepted the reality of paganism, though they longed for its final disappearance from the Holy Land.

The Damascus Document states that "Any man who destroys a man among men by the statutes of the gentiles is to be put to death," a law formulated somewhat ambiguously (CD ix.1). It was construed by Chaim Rabin to mean that "those condemned to death by the sect are to be handed over to the gentiles for execution." This interpretation was based on the notion "that the sect would hardly have added to the biblical death penalties" (Rabin, 1954). In Temple Scroll[a], however, we clearly have additional capital penalties, including death by hanging, prescribed for one who betrays his people to a foreign nation or curses his people after fleeing to the gentiles (11Q19, lxiv.6–11). The crime of revealing a secret of the people to the gentiles is also listed in the catalog of transgressions appended to the laws in the Damascus Document[e] (4Q270 2.ii.13). It is, therefore, highly probable that the Damascus Document (CD ix.1) intended that the death penalty be imposed on anyone who brought about the death of a Jew by gentile authorities.

Despite the aforementioned legal barriers and the self-enclosed nature of the Qumran community, one should by no means assume that the latter was impervious to foreign influences. Among the possible borrowings from the Greek world, scholars have compared the disciplinary and procedural rules of the Qumran community with those of Hellenistic associations. The hypothesis of Pythagorean influence upon the Essenes, already recorded by Josephus (*Jewish Antiquities* 15.371), has been reevaluated since the finding of the Dead Sea Scrolls. Possible Pythagorean influences have been noted in the honoring of the founder, procedural rules at assemblies, common meals, initiation rules, and ethical standards. (Cf. Hengel, vol. 1, pp. 243–247.) [*See* Pythagoreans.] The unprecedented theological credo in the Rule of the Community (iii–iv) with which the *maskil* (instructor) was to indoctrinate all the Sons of Light is part of what Martin Hengel terms the "intellectualization of piety" (1974). Iranian influence may be seen in the sharp dualism between light and darkness that is used in the War Scroll (1QM) to describe the apocalyptic battle of Israel with the gentile nations. It has also been suggested by David Flusser that this very dualism, in which the wicked of Israel are consigned to the realm of darkness together with pagans, served ultimately to redraw the moral boundaries between good and evil along ethical rather than ethnic lines.

BIBLIOGRAPHY

Baumgarten, Joseph M. "The 'Halakha' in Miqṣat Ma'aśe ha-Torah (MMT)." *Journal of the American Oriental Society* 116 (1996), 512–516.

Fitzmyer, Joseph A. *Responses to 101 Questions on the Dead Sea Scrolls*. New York, 1992. See pages 93–94, which deal with the gentiles.

Flusser, David. "Paganism in Palestine." In *The Jewish People in the*

First Century, edited by S. Safrai and M. Stern, pp. 1065–1100. Compendia Rerum Iudaicarum ad Novum Testamentum, vol. 1, fasc. 2. Assen/Maastricht/Philadelphia, 1987.

Flusser, David. *Judaism and the Origins of Christianity*. Jerusalem, 1988.

Hengel, Martin. *Judaism and Hellenism*. Philadelphia, 1974.

Murphy-O'Connor, Jerome. "The Essenes and Their History." *Revue biblique* 81 (1974), 215–244.

Qimron, Elisha, and John Strugnell. *Qumran Cave 4, V: Miqṣat Ma'aśe ha-Torah*. Discoveries in the Judaean Desert, 10. Oxford, 1994.

Rabin, Chaim. *The Zadokite Documents*. Oxford, 1954.

Schürer, Emil. *The History of the Jewish People in the Age of Jesus Christ, 175 B.C.–A.D. 135*. 3 vols., revised and edited by Geza Vermes, Fergus Millar, et al. Edinburgh, 1973–1987.

Schwartz, Daniel R. *Studies in the Jewish Background of Christianity*. Wissenschaftliche Untersuchungen zum Neuen Testament, 60. Tübingen, 1992.

JOSEPH M. BAUMGARTEN

GEOGRAPHY IN THE DOCUMENTS. The geography of the Qumran literature requires special discussion in two respects. First, a very small number of the texts are documentary rather than literary in character—that is, they preserve records of the current activities of the people to whom they belonged—and they contain references to the contemporary geography of the region. Second, the literary texts that are sectarian in character, reflecting the distinctive religious ideas of the Qumran community, often envision geography in idealized ways, so that the place names they contain may be symbolic or cryptic. Otherwise, the geography of the Qumran library is the geography of the Bible and of Judea in the Hasmonean and Herodian periods.

Apart from coins, the only Qumran texts of undisputed documentary character are two inscribed potsherds found at the base of the eastern perimeter wall of Khirbet Qumran in 1996. Only one of the two broken ostraca is sufficiently well preserved for decipherment, and it contains a single geographical reference, evidently naming Jericho as the place where the transaction recorded on the ostracon occurred. An increasing number of scholars believe that the Copper Scroll is a documentary text, despite the conclusion of its first official editor that its catalog of hidden property is traditional and legendary rather than real. If this is true, the list of documentary references to geographical locations becomes much longer, and in any case the Copper Scroll provides the most complete picture of the geography of the Judean wilderness that survives from the time of the Qumran community. [*See* Copper Scroll.]

Since it is an inventory of hiding places, the Copper Scroll is replete with place names and references to topographic features. Many of these correspond to places known from other ancient sources, but only a few can be identified with modern sites. For example, Koḥelit (*kḥlt*), one of the key sites in the inventory, is mentioned in the Babylonian Talmud (B.T., *Qid.* 66a) as a wilderness region containing sixty fortresses conquered by John Hyrcanus, but the scroll mentions a specific place, a mound or tell, and the opinions of scholars about its location differ widely. In general, however, it is clear that the majority of the Copper Scroll caches are in the northern part of the Judean desert, east of Bethlehem and Jerusalem, and as far north as the wilderness region above Jericho.

The list begins at a place called Ḥarubah (*ḥrbh*, "ruin"?) in the Valley of Achor, the location of a number of caches at the beginning of the list and elsewhere. According to *Joshua* 15.7 this valley lay on the northern border of Judah near Jericho. Thus it was the biblical name of the Judean Buqeia, the level basin that lies above the cliffs overlooking the terrace where Khirbet Qumran is located, but there is some evidence that by the Roman period the name Achor had shifted north to a valley system above Jericho. A significant number of places in the vicinity of Jericho are mentioned, and some are identifiable, such as Doq, the ancient name of the Jebel Qarantal, which was surmounted by the Hasmonean fortress mentioned in *1 Maccabees* 16.15 as the site of the murder of Simon (the Hasmonean). The spring of Kozeba is probably the place where the 'Ein Qilt empties into the Wadi Qilt, near which are Herodian aqueducts and the fifth-century monastery of Saint George of Kozeba. A location in the Jericho region is probably also to be sought for the Copper Scroll's reference to Mount Gerizim. Sources from late antiquity consistently place Ebal and Gerizim near Jericho, despite the traditional biblical location of the two mountains at Shechem (Nablus). Anti-Samaritan polemic is the likely explanation for this change of position, which is also presupposed in the arrangement of the story of the Israelites' entry into the Promised Land in Josephus (*Jewish Antiquities* 5.19–20) and in a Qumran biblical manuscript (4QJosh[a]).

A large number of Copper Scroll caches are located in the Judean wilderness south of Jericho in the wadi systems running from Jerusalem to the Jordan Valley and the Dead Sea. These include, from north to south, the Wadi Kippa (*kp'*), possibly the Wadi Kuteif where the modern Jerusalem-Jericho road passes, the Wadi el-'Aṣla (*'tsl'*), part of the large system of deep wadis extending from the Mukellik to the Daber, the Valley of Secacah (*skk'*), which drains the central Buqeia, and the Qidron (*qdrwn*), which forms the southern boundary of the Buqeia. The last two names in this list are biblical. The Qidron, figuring in the Bible primarily in its upper reaches where it divides the central hills of Jerusalem from the Mount of Olives (see, for example, *2 Sm.* 15.23), gouges a deep channel through the Judean wilderness on its way to the sea, and it is here, in the gorge (*tsuq*) of the Qidron that one of the Copper Scroll caches was concealed. Secacah is included in a biblical list of six "villages" (actually small forts) in the wilderness district of Judah (*Jos.* 15.61–62). It appears prominently in the scroll, once as the name of a dammed valley (*ge'*) and elsewhere as that of a village or fortress where several caches were hidden. An argument can be made for identifying Secacah with Khirbet Qumran itself, since it was occupied in the biblical period and since the nearby Wadi Qumran is a suitable candidate for the Valley of Secacah. A more widely accepted identification of Secacah, however, is with Khirbet Samra, the central ruin of the Buqeia, and Khirbet Qumran is believed to have been the biblical City of Salt, another of the forts in the wilderness district. If this is correct, we are forced to the surprising conclusion that the community center is not mentioned by name in the Copper Scroll or any other document from the eleven caves.

The Copper Scroll also provides the contemporary names of a number of places on the outskirts of Jerusalem, east and southeast of the city, where several caches of property were hidden. The Natof (*ntp*), the location of at least one and perhaps as many as four caches, is probably the 'Ein Natuf, which empties into the deep Wadi Khareitun (Naḥal Teqoa') southeast of Bethlehem; the spring preserves the name of the biblical village of Netophah (see, for example, *Ezr.* 2.22), probably Khirbet Bedd Faluh. Beth-haccherem (*beit ha-kerem*), where there was a reservoir in which two caches were concealed, is a biblical toponym—it was the residence of a district governor in the time of Nehemiah (*Neh.* 3.14)—and it is also mentioned in the Genesis Apocryphon and the rabbinical writings. The modern site is believed to be Ramat Raḥel, midway between Bethlehem and Jerusalem. Two caches are said to have been hidden in the Shaveh. This was the valley where, according to *Genesis* 14.17–18, Abraham was greeted by Melchizedek, king of Jerusalem, and the king of Sodom after his victory over the coalition of Chedorlaomer. The name there is glossed as "the King's Valley," which is also mentioned in *2 Samuel* 18.18 in a context that suggests a location very close to Jerusalem; it is usually thought to be the upper Qidron or part of it.

The eastern bank of the upper Qidron, today a vast necropolis, was already a traditional burial ground in antiquity, and a number of Copper Scroll caches are distributed here and there in the cemetery and other locations southeast and east of the Temple platform. The grave marker called "Absalom's Monument" (*yad Avshalom*) is also mentioned by Josephus. It is less likely to have been the actual pillar referred to in *2 Samuel* 18.18 than a later monument to which the name became attached, possibly the same prominent first-century BCE tomb that bears the name today. The reservoir of Bethesda (*byt 'shdtyn*) may correspond to the twin pools of Iron Age and Seleucid date near Saint Anne's Church, northeast of the Temple mount.

Just as the Copper Scroll provides an inventory of the real geography of the region in which the Qumran community lived, the sectarian literature reveals an idealized picture of the same geography. Like other apocalyptic groups, the Qumran covenanters viewed the world in which they lived as a temporary facade that would be altered or swept away with the dawn of the new age. Apparent realities were untrustworthy. The truth was hidden and revealed itself only in cryptic or symbolic language. Even geography was described in idealized terms. From this point of view, the failure noted above of the contemporary name of Qumran itself to appear in the community's literature is less surprising. It is probable, in fact, that the residence of the community is mentioned in the sectarian literature, but by its ideal or apocalyptic designation, "the land of Damascus." According to the Damascus Document (CD vi.5), this was the place to which the community migrated when it went into exile from the land of Judea. Some scholars have taken this to mean that there was an early migration to the actual city of Damascus in Syria, following which the community returned to Judea and settled in the wilderness, or that "the land of Damascus" was the name of the larger administrative district to which Qumran belonged. In all probability, however, "the land of Damascus" was a code name for Qumran itself.

Such code names—and the ideal geography in general—were derived from the distinctively apocalyptic interpretation of scripture as reflected in the sectarian literature. The understanding of the place of exile as Damascus, for example, was derived from the exegesis of *Amos* 5.26–27, which refers to Israelites carrying a "star" into exile beyond Damascus. Though the star in Amos is an image of a foreign god, for whose worship the Israelites are condemned to exile, the Qumran sectarians understood it to refer to their own divinely inspired Interpreter of the Law, who went into exile in "Damascus," that is, Qumran (CD vii.18–19).

At the center of this ideal, scripture-based geography was Jerusalem, which was understood, according to the same kind of apocalyptic exegesis, not only as the chosen place of *Deuteronomy* 12 (4Q395 32–33, 60–61) but also as the camp in the wilderness as described in *Numbers* 1–10 (4Q395 29–30, 58–62). The language of the wilderness camp is also used, especially in the Rule of the Community (1QS) but also in other sectarian literature, to describe the residence of the sectarian community, which was organized on the pattern of the tribes encamped in the wilderness in Mosaic times. In the logic of apocalyptic ways of thinking, these two ways of understanding the wilderness camp are not contradictory, for the camp represented the sacred center of Israel, which was supposed to be Jerusalem and would eventually return to Jerusalem, but which during the present world age was exiled in the wilderness. In Jerusalem the Temple was the sanctuary, corresponding to the tabernacle in the wilderness camp, but in the sectarian community center the Community Council served in lieu of the sanctuary (1QS viii.4–9, ix.3–6). This equation of the Community Council with the Temple permitted the interpretation of Habakkuk's reference to "the violence done to Lebanon" (*Hb.* 2.7) as an allusion to the Wicked Priest's mistreatment of the Community Council (1QpHab xii.3–4), since "Lebanon," even apart from Qumran apocalypticism, was a traditional way of referring to the Temple (see, for example, B.T., *Yoma* 39b).

As the last example shows, it is in the *pesher* material that the use of ideal geographical terms becomes most arcane. Biblical toponyms are often interpreted apocalyptically, while their interpretations are expressed in code names, so that the uninitiated reader is twice removed from real geography. Elsewhere in Pesher Habakkuk (ii.10–12), for example, a statement about the Chaldeans in *Habakkuk* 1.6 is interpreted as a reference to the *Kittim*, a biblical term for Cypriotes or, more generally, the coastal peoples of the Mediterranean basin, which in Qumran sectarian literature is the standard code word for the Romans. Using these principles it was possible in Pesher Nahum (4Q169) to find allusions to the Qumran community's rivals, the Pharisees and the Sadducees, in the text of *Nahum* 3.7–8. These verses are part of Nahum's taunt against the Assyrian city Nineveh on the eve of its destruction (612 BCE). In the *pesher* (iii.5–7), Nineveh is interpreted as "the Seekers of Smooth Things," the Qumran sobriquet for the Pharisees, who earlier in the *pesher* (ii.2) are referred to by another code name, "Ephraim." The biblical text continues with a comparison of the destruction of Nineveh to that of the Egyptian city Amon (Thebes), "situated by the Nile," and in the *pesher* (iii.9) Amon is identified as "Manasseh," the code name for the Sadducees, and the Nile (a grammatical plural in Hebrew) is identified as "the great men of Manasseh," that is, the Sadducee leaders.

P. KYLE MCCARTER, JR.

GHWEIR, WADI. Naḥal Qaneh (in Hebrew) is the name of a short precipitous ravine descending from the steep escarpment fault to the Dead Sea approximately 15 kilometers (9 miles) to the south of Qumran. At its outlet, a two-kilometer (1 mile) long oasis of thick and swampy vegetation, the Wadi extends from ʿEin-el-Ghweir (called *ʿEin Ghazal* by the bedouin; *ʿEinot Qaneh* in Hebrew) in the north to ʿEin et-Trâbeh or ʿEin at-Turaba (*ʿEnot Samar* in Hebrew) in the south. The spring water of ʿEin-el-Ghweir is of a better quality than that of ʿEin-Feshkha, which has a very high salt content. Archaeological remains of the Iron Age II and the Late Hellenistic/Early Roman periods are scattered along the moderate, narrow strip of land between the foothills and this oasis. The remains scattered along more than 1 kilometer of the northern part of the oasis, referred to by P. Bar Adon as ʿEin-el-Ghuweir, were divided by him into six areas, designated A to F, from north to south. Bar Adon identified the site with biblical Nibshan of *Joshua* 15.62. Qasr at-Turaba located near ʿEin at-Turaba, at the southern end of the oasis, was considered to be a separate settlement, which he suggested was biblical *ʿIr Ha-Melaḥ* (Town of Salt).

The archaeological remains were first explored in the years 1964–1966 on behalf of the British School of Archaeology at Jerusalem by I. Blake, and then between 1967 and 1976 on behalf of the Israel Department of Antiquities by P. Bar Adon.

Iron Age II Remains (eighth–seventh centuries BCE). A 600 meter (1,968 feet) long fenced wall (designated as area D) with eighteen rooms dispersed on either side along its course, some of them with rounded corners, is the most peculiar feature of the site. A similar fenced wall, dated to the same period, was traced by de Vaux in the area between ʿEin-Feshkha and Qumran. The rooms were built against the wall, most of them on the eastern side; some on the western. A layer of ashes was found in most of the rooms. A few finds of the Roman period were located on the upper layer. Another structure with similar finds was excavated in area E farther to the south.

A building—presumably a workshop for the manufacture of perfumes—was excavated by Bar Adon, near ʿEin-el-Ghweir. Rectangular in shape, it is 8 by 11 meters (26 by 36 feet), with five rooms and a courtyard of 9.5 by 10.5 meters (31 by 34 feet) to its east. The walls were 0.7–1 meter (2–3 feet) thick, and there were plastered floors. The entrance room was the largest—3.20 by 6.50 meters (10 by 21 feet) in dimension. A raised plastered platform, a drain, and traces of fires point to an industrial installation.

Qasr at-Turaba, approximately 2 kilometers (1 mile) from ʿEin-el-Ghweir to the south, was a fortified tower adjacent to the southern springs of ʿEin at-Turaba, located near the southern end of Area D. It was first excavated by Blake, and then in 1971 by Bar Adon. The tower, 15 by 13 meters (49 by 43 feet), was appended on the north by a 19.5 by 18.5 meter (64 by 61 foot) courtyard. The building, constructed of clay/bulrush blocks, was destroyed by an intense fire. In the adjacent cliffs to the west, two caves yielding Chalcolithic–Early Bronze, Iron

Age II, and Hellenistic pot sherds were explored by Bar Adon. In a cave explored by Blake, jars and a Greek ostracon were found, presumably of a Byzantine hermit.

All buildings were abandoned at the destruction of the First Temple. A cave above ʿEin-el-Ghweir yielded Iron Age II pot sherds.

Second Temple Period Remains. Besides a reoccupation of the earlier structures, a settlement (designated by Bar Adon as area C) contemporary with Qumran Ib and II was established near ʿEin-el-Ghweir, with a Qumran-type cemetery adjacent to it. [*See* Cemeteries.] The central building occupied an area of 43 by 19.5 meters (141 by 64 feet), consisting of a wall 0.7 meters (2 feet) thick enclosing a courtyard. A 27.5 meter (90 feet) elongated structure on the southern side was entered through a 1 meter (3 foot) wide opening. This elongated structure consisted of an open space (I) 9.2 meters (30 feet) wide (too wide to substantiate Bar Adon's interpretation of it as a hall), flanked on the north by a shaded area (II) 15.5 meters (51 feet) long by 3.2 meters (10 feet) wide. This part had a light roof (presumably of local bulrush), supported by four wooden posts resting on bases of stones. Stone partitions extending from the western wall and running between the two western posts converted this section to a more closed area. Two ovens and two granaries found east of them suggest that this part served as a kitchen. Two other rooms (III and IV), 7.9 meters (26 feet) and 5.1 meters (17 feet) wide respectively, were located farther to the east, but their southern part was almost entirely washed away. It seems that they were storerooms. A 10–30 centimeter (4–12 inch) thick layer of ash covered the floor of these rooms. A sounding in the northern end of the shaded space II uncovered two level pavements, each covered by a 10–20 centimeter (4–8 inch) thick layer of ash. These two layers of ash were uncovered in other places as well. It was not possible to distinguish between the two phases by the pottery. Seven identifiable coins were found: five in area I, adjacent to the western wall, retrieved in an intervening stratum and two from room III. Five coins are of Herod, one of Archelaus, and one of Agrippa I. The pottery finds include sherds of jars, cooking pots, kraters, bowls, jugs, flasks, and two "Herodian" lamps. Also were found a bronze nail and buckle, and a fragment of a stone measuring vessel. No *miqveh* was found so far at the site, but Bar Adon mentions structures north of the large building, which were not excavated. The site was abandoned in the First Jewish Revolt (66–70 BCE).

On a hill approximately 800 meters (one half mile) north of the principal building was the cemetery of the settlement. Eighteen graves were excavated; most are oriented north-south, four slightly deviate to the northwest, and one (tomb 15) is oriented east-west. The pit graves, resembling those of Qumran, are cut in the ground to a depth of about 2 meters (7 feet). A large stone juts out on the southern end of the tomb, where the skeleton head is to be found. The skeleton was placed in a niche at the bottom of the grave, but along the east wall. The niche was covered by slanting stone slabs set perpendicular to the niche. Sherds of bowls or jars were placed over the covering stones. An almost completely restorable jar found in tomb 18 bears a Hebrew inscription of which only the name *Yehoḥanan*, written in black ink on the shoulder near its handle, was decipherable. The remains of twelve men and three women were found in the graves. A second cemetery located on a second hill to the south seems to be a small bedouin cemetery, since the graves here are oriented east-west. Two tombs were opened on this hill, yielding the remains of a man and a seven-year-old child.

Two unpublished fragments are labeled in the archives of the Rockefeller Museum (PAM) as coming, presumably, from Wadi Ghweir: Ghweir? 1 is a papyrus fragment written in cursive Greek and Ghweir? 2 is a fragment bearing Semitic script. The exact spot where they were found is unknown (Reed, 1994, pp. xlii, 281).

BIBLIOGRAPHY

Bar Adon, P. "Another Settlement of the Judean Desert Sect at ʿEn el-Ghuweir on the Shores of the Dead Sea." *Bulletin of the American Schools of Oriental Research* 227 (1977), 1–25.

Bar Adon, P. "Ein el-Ghuweir." In *Excavations in the Judean Desert. ʿAtiqot* (Hebrew Series) 9 (1989), 33–40.

Blake, I. "Rivage occidental de la Mer Morte." *Revue biblique* 73 (1966), 565–566, Pl. XXXIV, XXXV.

Blake, I. "Dead Sea Sites of 'the Utter Wilderness.'" *Illustrated London News*, 4 March 1967, 27–29.

Reed, S. A. *The Dead Sea Scrolls Catalogue: Documents, Photographs and Museum Inventory Numbers*. SBL Resources for Biblical Study, 32. Atlanta, 1994.

JOSEPH PATRICH

GIANTS, BOOK OF. The name given to a literary work represented by a group of Aramaic fragments recovered from several Qumran caves is the *Book of Giants*. The contents of these fragments suggest the existence of an extended narrative whose exegetical anchor was the terse biblical story about the birth of "giants" found in *Genesis* 6.1–4. Such an expansion is extant in the first part of the Enochic "Book of Watchers" (*1 En.* 6–16), but the surviving portions of the Aramaic Book of Giants (as well as later testimonies) indicate that the latter work was considerably more elaborate than its *1 Enoch* analogue, featuring frequent dialogue between the main characters, descriptions of martial encounters, symbolic dreams, journeys to distant regions, and emotion-laden soliloquies. Moreover, there are indications that the *Book of*

Giants may have once contained a variant version of the Flood narrative.

Credit for the identification of the Qumran Book of Giants as a narrative entity belongs to Józef T. Milik, who in two 1971 articles and subsequently in his 1976 edition of the Qumran Aramaic Enoch manuscripts published much of the relevant textual corpus. Therein Milik identified fragments from at least six separate copies of the *Book of Giants* (1QEnoch Giants[a] [1Q23], 4QEnoch Giants[a] [4Q203], 4QBook of Giants[b–c] [4Q530–531], so-called 4QEnGi[e] [= 4Q533?], and 6Q8). He also called attention to additional manuscripts that might possibly stem from the *Book of Giants* (Enoch Giants[b] [1Q24], 2QEnoch Giants [2Q26], 4QEnoch[e] [4Q206], 4QBook of Giants[d] [4Q532], and so-called 4QEnGi[f] [=?]). Milik's recognition of these disparate fragments as portions of an integral work was grounded in his brilliant discovery that the Qumran fragments bore a close resemblance to the surviving Middle Iranian fragments of the Manichaean *Book of Giants*, a writing allegedly authored by Mani, the third-century CE founder of a Mesopotamian gnostic religious community that rapidly achieved an almost worldwide dispersal. [*See* Manichaeans.] The Manichaean *Book of Giants* enjoyed canonical status within that religion, and to judge from the prominent appearance of its title in Greek, Coptic, Middle Iranian, Arabic, and Chinese testimonia, must have been extensively distributed by Manichaean missionaries. Portions of the Manichaean *Book of Giants* were recovered earlier this century from Turfan in Central Asia and published by W. B. Henning (1943–1946) and W. Sundermann (1973). Despite the damaged condition of both manuscript collections, the surviving references to the characters and the narrative events confirm Milik's suspicion that the Qumran Book of Giants is the literary ancestor of the Manichaean text.

Intriguing references and allusions to certain characters and events presented therein suggest that copies or later versions of the *Book of Giants* circulated among certain Jewish, Christian, and Muslim circles well into the medieval era.

Contents of the Work. The *Book of Giants* is an extrabiblical narrative embellishment and expansion of the cryptic *Genesis* 6.1–4, the infamous passage about the illicit intercourse between the sons of God and mortal women, which resulted in the appearance of *giborim*, "giants." A reconstruction of the narrative would appear to have the following form.

In the generation of Jared, the father of Enoch, two hundred angels ("Watchers") descend from heaven to earth under the leadership of Shemiḥazah. Beholding the beauty of mortal women, they are seized by sexual desire and unite with them, thereby engendering a hybrid race of lawless Giants. The Giants quickly overrun hapless humankind by engaging in widespread slaughter, destruction, and moral corruption.

Apparently sometime prior to the manifestation of these disasters, Enoch had been removed from human society (*Gn.* 5.24). The distressful situation upon earth is now revealed to Enoch, and Enoch in turn beseeches God to exact judgment upon the Watchers and Giants for their wickedness. God resolves to bring the Flood, but apparently in keeping with his attribute of mercy, decides to give the Giants an opportunity for repentance. He dispatches symbolic dreams to the two Giant sons of Shemiḥazah, identified by name as Ohyah and Hahyah. These dreams presage an impending universal destruction, which only four individuals will survive. Despite the transparency of the dream imagery to the modern exegete, Ohyah and Hahyah are perplexed by the dreams, but are sufficiently alarmed to relate their dreams before an assembly of gathered Giants. The assembled Giants are also baffled by the dreams. To secure an authoritative interpretation of the dreams, they resolve to send one of their number to visit Enoch for a consultation.

They accordingly commission a Giant named Mahaway, the son of the Watcher Baraq'el, to go to Enoch's abode "beyond the wastelands" in order to procure an interpretation. Mahaway makes this journey and receives two tablets from Enoch inscribed with the true meaning of the dreams and God's impending judgment. He returns to the Giants with the tablets, and they are read aloud before their assembly. The terrible message elicits two distinct responses. Some of the Giants are chastened by the message and counsel repentance, but others, apparently the majority, react with open defiance and arrogantly challenge God to act against them. At this point in the story the Qumran fragments break off, leaving us with a hint that the Flood was eventually described in that text. The Manichaean fragments testify that fierce battles break out between the archangelic hosts of God and the arrogant Giants, who were with difficulty finally subdued.

One particularly exciting feature of the contents of the *Book of Giants* in both its Qumran and Manichaean versions involves the appearance within it of characters from the Mesopotamian Epic of Gilgamesh. In the Qumran *Book of Giants*, the names Gilgamesh and Hobabish (i.e., Humbaba) occur, but lack an intelligible narrative context. However, the Manichaean *Book of Giants* preserves the name Hobabish in a context that identifies him as one of the Giants engendered by the fallen Watchers. Apparently the Jewish author(s) of the *Book of Giants* considered these renowned epic characters to be simply two of the wicked Giants. Newly published fragments from the

Manichaean *Book of Giants* include mention of the Giant Atambish, whose name seems to be a later reflex of the name Utnapishtim, the Mesopotamian Flood-hero featured in Tablet XI of the Epic of Gilgamesh. The appearance of this name within the Manichaean *Book of Giants*, like that of Hobabish, was presumably dependent upon the occurrence of the name Utnapishtim within the Qumran Book of Giants. The appearance of these names within a Jewish composition of the Second Temple era attests to the vitality of Mesopotamian literary traditions among literate circles of the ancient Near East, probably transmitted via Aramaic versions.

Milik proposed that the *Book of Giants* was originally a part of *1 Enoch*, occupying the space later taken by the so-called Similitudes (*1 En.* 37–71), but few scholars have accepted his arguments. Obviously, the *Book of Giants* is closely related to the Enochic corpus of writings, particularly *1 Enoch* 6–16. The figure of Enoch plays an important narrative role in the *Book of Giants*, but is not credited (in the extant fragments) with the work's authorship. It seems more likely that the *Book of Giants* circulated as an independent composition among intellectual circles interested in the exegesis of *Genesis* 6.1–4.

Dating the production of the *Book of Giants* is extremely problematic: Milik's suggested time frame of 125–100 BCE rests upon several arguable points. Subsequently, Florentino García Martínez (1992) and K. Beyer (1984) have proposed alternative dates for the composition of the work, the latter suggesting the late third century BCE as a possible time of origin. Insofar as the *Book of Giants* appears to be allied with those circles responsible for the production of the Enochic "Book of Watchers," a date in the late third or early second centuries BCE would not be unreasonable.

BIBLIOGRAPHY

Beyer, K. *Die aramäischen Texte vom Toten Meer*. Göttingen, 1984. See pages 258–268.

García Martínez, Florentino. *Qumran and Apocalyptic: Studies on the Aramaic Texts from Qumran*. Leiden, 1992. See pages 97–115.

Henning, W. B. "The Book of the Giants." *Bulletin of the School of Oriental and African Studies* 11 (1943–1946), 52–74. Manichaean fragments of the *Book of Giants*.

Milik, J. T. "Problèmes de la littérature hénochique à la lumière des fragments araméens de Qumran." *Harvard Theological Review* 64 (1971), 366–372.

Milik, J. T. "Turfan et Qumran: Livre des Géants juif et manichéen." In *Tradition und Glaube: Das frühe Christentum in seiner Umwelt*, edited by G. Jeremias, et al., pp. 117–127. Göttingen, 1971.

Milik, J. T. *The Books of Enoch: Aramaic Fragments of Qumran Cave 4*, pp. 298–339. Oxford, 1976. Identification, publication, and translation of many of the Aramaic fragments belonging to the *Book of Giants*, recapitulating and revising the material presented in his 1971 articles.

Reeves, John C. *Jewish Lore in Manichaean Cosmogony: Studies in the Book of Giants Traditions*. Monographs of the Hebrew Union College, 14. Cincinnati, 1992. A synthesis of the Qumran and Manichaean evidence, along with its religio-historical implications.

Reeves, John C. "Utnapishtim in the Book of Giants?" *Journal of Biblical Literature* 112 (1993), 110–115. Exploration of the likelihood that the Mesopotamian Flood-hero was named in the Aramaic *Book of Giants*.

Stuckenbruck, L. T. *The Book of Giants from Qumran*. Texte und Studien zum Antiken Judentum, 63. Tübingen, 1997. This new study arrived too late to be of service in the article; a new edition, translation, and commentary.

Sundermann, Werner. *Mittelpersische und parthische kosmogonische und Parabeltexte der Manichäer*. Berliner Turfantexte, 4. Berlin, 1973. See pages 76–78. Additional Manichaean fragments of the *Book of Giants*.

Sundermann, Werner. "Ein weiteres Fragment aus Manis Gigantenbuch." In *Orientalia J. Duchesne-Guillemin emerito oblata*, pp. 491–505. Acta Iranica, 23. Leiden, 1984. Yet more fragments.

JOHN C. REEVES

GLASSWARE. Many of the Judean Desert sites have yielded a wealth of material culture, and glass forms a significant portion of these finds. Found in association with datable texts, the glassware from the sites where the Judean Desert texts were found provide a unique opportunity for the dating of such wares. It was during the first and/or the second centuries CE that several sites such as Masada, ʿEin-Gedi, and Qumran flourished and that the caves of the region were used as hiding places during periods of strife. The occupants, even when seeking temporary refuge, left behind remains of their daily lives, and glass had become an everyday household item by this period. Highly prized luxury items were also taken to the caves for safekeeping.

Glass recovered from these sites generally survives in a remarkably good state, with little corrosion or deterioration. Glass tends to deteriorate in more humid environments, often forming heavy skins of corrosion and leaving little of the original material intact. Glass from the desert, however, can survive in a clean, fresh state, often revealing the original appearance of the vessels.

Although most of the glass excavated in the region is well preserved, it is unfortunate that relatively little has been fully studied. It is principally one scholar, Dr. Dan Barag of the Hebrew University, who has examined and written the existing reports about this glass, many in the form of preliminary notes.

The Cave Sites. The Israeli Judean Desert Expedition of 1961–1962 conducted the first systematic archaeological expedition to explore the caves in the valleys between ʿEin-Gedi and Masada. Finds from these explorations revealed that numerous caves had been occupied during the Roman period and many could be dated to the period of the Bar Kokhba Revolt. At the outset of this project, four areas were defined. Expedition A, supervised by Nahman Avigad, covered one of these areas and first examined Naḥal Ṣe'elim and later Naḥal David at ʿEin-Gedi. Among the caves of Naḥal David, the team excavated the Cave of the Pool, revealing fourteen fragments of glass vessels (Barag, 1962, pp. 167–183). Like other finds in the cave, the glass was dated to the first or first third of the second century CE.

The glass from this cave, as at other sites in the Judean Desert, was well preserved due to climatic stability. The color, which could be viewed without distortion by the iridescence of weathering, was generally a bright bluish green, with the exceptions of one fragment that was clear and one other that was bright green. All were blown vessels of normal household types.

The remains are quite fragmentary and support the excavators' conclusion that the cave served as a refuge for families from ʿEin-Gedi during the last days of the Bar Kokhba Revolt and that, owing to the pool constructed as a water source, these people did not perish in this cave. Further supported by the lack of any human remains, this theory concludes that the fortunate refugees survived to depart from the cave, taking with them any possessions of value and leaving behind only broken and discarded material. It was, therefore, only the most fragmentary glass remains that were discovered in this cave.

Among the examples were four fragments of tall-necked bottles. These included a neck fragment of a type well known throughout Syria and Palestine on pear-shaped and "candlestick" bottles (Barag, 1962). Two fragments from a lesser-known type of bottle were also discovered. These pieces come from a ribbed bottle, also dated after the late first century CE and are comparable to another from the Cave of Horror. Rims and bases from bowls were also recovered, consistent with types dating to the second century. One rim has a double fold in the wall just below the lip. Another preserves remains of a crimped handle, a type known into the third century, but best dated from this and other Judean Desert finds such as the one described by Barag (Yadin, 1963, pp. 104–105, no. 7).

The caves of Naḥal Ḥever were explored by the Israel Department of Antiquities and Museums in 1953, followed in 1955 by the exploration of the Cave of Horror, so called because of the skeletal remains found within it. Yohanan Aharoni directed these expeditions as well as the later excavations (1960–1961) as part of Expedition B of the Judean Desert Expedition. The glass was published by Barag (1962, pp. 208–214, figs. 1–18). Unlike the scanty finds in the Cave of the Pool, this expedition recovered two complete bowls and approximately two hundred other glass fragments, making it the most extensive group of glass found in the Judean caves. Dates for these finds were consistently in the second century CE. While most were identified as Syro-Palestinian types, there were also imports. The vessels were predominantly everyday wares, although several were fine wares.

Vessel types included deep bowls, some with folded walls like the example from the Cave of the Pool (Barag, 1962). Barag notes (p. 210) that deep bowls of this type were common from the last third of the first century CE onward, but that these rim types are rather uncommon. The same sort of rim also appeared on a few shallow bowls, one with a crimped handle. Several other bowls are recognized as imports. These consist of very clear glass with just a slight yellow-green color, and were mold-made and polished. Barag cites parallels from Karanis and Britain, dated no later than the mid-second century CE. Fragments of candlestick bottles were also found and represent Syro-Palestinian production. Also of interest are several fragments from a number of mold-blown vessels, which form a class of fine ware produced in Syria-Palestine. Included is an example of a ribbed bowl like the one discovered in the Cave of the Pool.

Located on the opposite side of Naḥal Ḥever is the Cave of the Letters, excavated by Yadin in 1960–1961 as Expedition D of the Judean Desert Expedition. Barag summarized the glass finds in Yadin (1963, pp. 101–110). Although the number of glass finds was far smaller than that discovered in the Cave of Horror, the nature of these finds is remarkable. Because they were uncovered from many loci, some carefully concealed among the rocks and some strewn over the floor, Barag concluded that the glass finds had been broken and scattered or hidden in antiquity. Most of the vessels were presumably of Syro-Palestinian production, blown and generally a pale bluish green, some ranging to green or yellow green in color. There were three complete vessels and approximately fifty fragments. In contrast to these remains, there were three mold-made vessels of a color and style pointing to a foreign manufacture (Yadin, 1963, pp. 106–108).

The blown vessels were types well known in Syria-Palestine, including candlestick bottles, a cylindrical jug, a deep bowl with crimped handles, and a globular flask. Most are types that appeared from the second half of the first century CE onward.

The mold-made vessels are far more extraordinary. Since blown glass had almost completely supplanted the mold-made forms by the second century, these are noteworthy in their contexts. Furthermore, perfect preservation and the quality of these three vessels contribute to the richness of this discovery. Almost colorless, the two plates and the bowl are in pristine condition. They were found still carefully wrapped in palm fibers and hidden in the cave. It was assumed that such luxury possessions were there for safekeeping, but not used while in the cave. The two plates are very similar to one another and like the bowl have a base ring, convex sides, and a broad overhanging rim. They are each incised with a small circle at the interior center. The bowl is more ornate, decorated with bands of cut circles and lines. Parallels come from Karanis from second- to third-century CE contexts, and while most scholars agree that these seem to have come from the same production center, one outside Syria-Palestine, that center is not yet known. Donald B. Harden believed the center of production to have been in Egypt, perhaps Alexandria (Harden, 1936).

The Permanent Occupation Sites. Although glass from stratified excavation of occupational sites in the Judean Desert is certainly abundant, almost none has been studied. While the very rich finds from the Cave of the Letters reveal something of the nature and diversity of glass owned by refugees from ʿEin-Gedi, glass finds from the oasis site itself remain virtually unpublished. A brief passage by Barag (1979, pp. 78–79) refers to Avigad's examination of a number of Hasmonean tombs at this site and his discovery of both a mold-made and a blown vessel in a tomb dated no later than 31 BCE. Little else can be gleaned from the literature about the glass from this site.

Masada's glass is barely any better known in publication. Barag, however, has given his preliminary impressions concerning this important corpus (Barag, 1991, pp. 137–140). Archaeological investigation has indicated that most of the glass finds date to no later than 73/74 CE. While most of the finds are Julio-Claudian, there are also remains from the period of the later Roman garrison, present until 115 CE. There is also some Byzantine glass, probably in association with the small late fifth- to early-sixth-century CE chapel.

Glass finds from Masada, mostly fragments, number into the thousands and are the largest corpus of their period known in the eastern provinces. There is some diversity, but by far the majority of the remains are pale bluish green, the color generally associated with the Syro-Palestinian wares. Some examples of imported wares include dark-colored luxury materials. Hellenistic forms, probably of the Herodian period, are well attested; several core-form vessels are perhaps the earliest examples. A few pieces of Early Roman mosaic glass are also present, as are numerous fragments of pillar-molded bowls of this period. Of later date in the first century CE are many fragments from bowls, drinking vessels, small bottles, and a large number of long-necked, pear-shaped bottles, some intact. Conspicuously absent are the candlestick bottles, with only two examples of early variants of this type, supporting a Flavian date (69–96 CE) for their development. A number of mold-blown types are also well represented. Cylindrical beakers, some with inscriptions, also offer well-dated comparative material. Some western types are attested at Masada while generally unknown in most other sites of the eastern provinces. These include ribbed bowls with marvered white-thread decoration and dark blue bowls with enameled polychrome paintings. Barag concludes that their discovery in this area points to a more eastern origin than the often proposed northern Italy, perhaps Alexandria, instead. The study and publication of the glass from Masada are crucial.

Another corpus of glass, still inaccessible, which will certainly provide valuable data, is the material from Qumran. In this case the nature of the small finds can certainly shed light on the ongoing debate regarding the function of the site. Again, this important class of artifacts remains to be published.

BIBLIOGRAPHY

Barag, Dan. "Glass Vessels from the Cave of Horror." *Israel Exploration Journal* 12 (1962), 208–214.

Barag, Dan. "Towards a Chronology of Syro-Palestinian Glass." In *Annales du Congrés de l'association internationale pour l'Histoire d'Verre*, pp. 78–79. London-Liverpool, 1979.

Barag, Dan. "The Contribution of Masada to the History of Early Roman Glass." In *Roman Glass: Two Centuries of Art and Invention*, edited by Martine Newby and Kenneth Painter, pp. 137–140. London, 1991.

Donceel, Robert, and Pauline Donceel-Voûte. "The Archaeology of Khirbet Qumran." In *Methods of Investigation of the Dead Sea Scrolls and the Qumran Site*, edited by Michael O. Wise et al. in the Annals of the New York Academy of Sciences, 722, 1–38. 1994. The Donceels make the case for the site as a villa and in part base that finding on their unpublished small finds. Jodi Magness refutes their theory in her article "Qumran: Not a Country Villa." *Biblical Archaeology Review* 22 (1996), 38–76.

Harden, Donald B. *Roman Glass from Karanis Found by the University of Michigan Archaeological Expedition in Egypt, 1924–1929.* Ann Arbor, 1936.

Yadin, Yigael. *The Finds from the Bar Kokhba Period in the Cave of Letters*. Jerusalem, 1963. Chapter 5, "The Glassware," was prepared by Dan Barag.

LISA KAHN

GNOSTICISM. A term first used in the seventeenth century to refer to the doctrines of various heretics mentioned by the early church fathers, here Gnosticism refers to a religion of salvation based on revealed knowledge (*gnosis*) that arose around the turn of the common era. Gnosticism influenced, and was influenced by, both Judaism and Christianity.

Gnostic Religion. In the Gnostic religion, *gnosis* ("knowledge") is requisite to salvation. This knowledge, communicated in a revealed myth, changes the status of the knowers (gnostics) by revealing to them the transcendent God, their own original consubstantiality with God, and their heavenly origins and destiny. The transcendent

God is above and beyond the creator of the world and his archons. The world-creating and world-ruling powers try to keep the elect shackled and somnolent in their material bodies, which are the product of these lower powers. The basic Gnostic myth seems to have been developed by Gnostic teachers familiar with Platonist metaphysics as popularized in the Mediterranean world from the first century BCE, but the chief components of the myth itself reflect the use and reinterpretation of biblical texts and Jewish exegetical traditions.

Until comparatively recently, the chief sources for the study of Gnosticism consisted of reports prepared by their opponents, mainly the fathers of the church and other ancient writers, including Plotinus (*Enneads* 2.9). The church fathers, starting with Justin Martyr, traced the Gnostic heresies back to the Samaritan wonder worker Simon Magus, first mentioned in the *Acts of the Apostles* (8.9–24).

The discovery of a whole library of Gnostic texts in Upper Egypt, near the modern town of Nag Hammadi, has put the scholarly study of the Gnostic religion on an entirely new footing, resulting in a better understanding of Gnosticism: its essential features, its origins, and the history of its early development.

The Gnostic religion, in the form of Manichaeism, became a world religion that survived in China until the seventeenth century. Another branch of ancient Gnosticism survives to this day in the form of Mandeanism (Mandaic, a form of Eastern Aramaic, *manda*ʿ means *gnosis*). The home of the Mandaeans ("Gnostics") is the marshlands of modern Iraq and Iran, though they trace their ancient origins to the Jordan Valley.

Nag Hammadi Codices. In December 1945, some months before the discovery of the first of the Dead Sea Scrolls, two brothers, Muhammad and Khalifa Ali, peasants from the village of Hamra Dom, were digging for *sebakh* (a nitrate soil used for fertilizer) at the base of the Jabal et-Tarif when they uncovered a jar. Muhammad Ali broke the jar and out came thirteen leather-bound books, papyrus codices inscribed in Coptic. The story of this discovery and the subsequent history of the codices is now well known as a result of the careful research of James M. Robinson of Claremont University in Claremont, California, who also was the driving force in the publication of the manuscripts. The Nag Hammadi Codices have been published in a facsimile edition (1972–1977) and in various critical editions in several languages. A one-volume English translation of all forty-six tractates in the Nag Hammadi collection, plus two from a related Coptic codex (Papyrus Berolinensis 8502), appeared first in 1977.

The Nag Hammadi Codices were inscribed and bound toward the end of the fourth century CE, probably in a monastic setting, and buried shortly afterward. All the tractates are Coptic translations of texts originally produced earlier in Greek. Not all the tractates are Gnostic, and those that are represent various sects and groups with differing beliefs and practices. By far the most important of the Nag Hammadi tractates for the study of Gnosticism is the *Apocryphon of John*, preserved in four different copies, plus an excerpt corresponding to part of this text found in Irenaeus's treatise *Adversus omnes Haereses* 1.29, composed in approximately 185 CE. The myth found in this tractate can be said to represent that of classic (or Sethian) Gnosticism, circulating among people referred to by Irenaeus as Gnostics and the Gnostic sect (*Adversus omnes Haereses* 1.29.1 and 1.11.1, respectively). This variety of Gnosticism was the basis for the Christian sect founded in the early second century by the influential heresiarch Valentinus, according to Irenaeus (*Adversus omnes Haereses* 1.11.1). Some of the tractates in the Nag Hammadi library come from the Valentinian sect.

Gnosticism and the Dead Sea Scrolls. Gnosticism and the religion of the Dead Sea Scrolls have in common certain features that offer interesting points of comparison and contrast. The contrasts are such as to make it clear that the religion of the Essene sect, the sect of the Dead Sea Scrolls, cannot be subsumed under the category of Gnosticism.

Knowledge. A key concept in the writings of the Qumran community, the idea of knowledge (*gnosis, da*ʿ*at*) is especially prominent in Hodayot^a from Cave 1 at Qumran (1QH^a) and in the hymnic material at the end of the Rule of the Community from Cave 1 at Qumran (hereafter 1QRule of the Community; 1QS). Several Hebrew words are used for the verb *to know* and the noun *knowledge*, but the most frequent words are *yada*ʿ and *da*ʿ*at*, respectively. In the Qumran sectarian literature, *da*ʿ*at* has an important role to play in salvation. The object of this knowledge is God (see 1QH^a xii.11, for example) and the "mysteries" or "secrets" (*razekhah*, "your secrets") that he reveals to his elect (1QH^a xii.20; cf. 1QS xi.5). One of the fragmentary Qumran texts is Mysteries (1Q27; Mysteries^{a-c} 4Q299–301), detailing various kinds of mysteries, including the "mystery that was coming into being" (*raz nihyeh*, 1Q27 [twice], as translated by Lawrence Schiffman in his edition of Mysteries^{a-c}, pp. 35–36), which ordinary people "did not know." The knowledge of God's mysteries or secrets is clearly an esoteric knowledge, reserved for the elect. Those in possession of this knowledge can even be referred to as *yode*ʿ*im* ("knowers," 1QH^a xi.14; cf. *gnostikoi*). Thus the concept of revealed *da*ʿ*at* at Qumran invites comparison with the revealed *gnosis* of the Gnostic literature. But the contrasts are crucial: in Gnosticism the God who is revealed is a transcendent being above the lower creator of the world. The self-knowledge of the

Gnostic relates to the divine spark currently trapped in a material body and not to the weakness of his flesh or his sinful condition as in the Qumran literature. Finally, in Gnosticism it is *gnosis* that is the very basis of salvation, whereas in the Qumran literature *da'at* relates to a salvation based on repentance, forgiveness, and observance of covenant law.

Dualism. An important feature of the religion of the Dead Sea Scrolls, dualism is important to the Jewish apocalyptic worldview in general. [*See* Dualism.] Dualism characterizes all of the sectarian literature, though with variations in detail from one text to another. A classic text representative of Qumran dualism is the section of 1QRule of the Community that deals with the two opposing spirits (1QS iii.13–iv.26). This text teaches that God, in the beginning, created two spirits or angels, one good and the other evil. The good spirit is associated with light, truth, and righteousness; the evil spirit is associated with darkness, falsehood, and sin. The dualism is qualified in that God is the ultimate creator of both, and the evil spirit, elsewhere called Belial, has a fixed time for his activity in the world ("the dominion of Belial," e.g., 1QS i.18), after which he will be destroyed. Gnostic dualism is comparable with that of Qumran in some respects: it is not absolute, for in the Gnostic myth good and evil are posterior to the transcendent God and subject to dissolution at the end. But in Gnostic dualism the transcendent God is not the creator of the world. The world is the product of a lower being (e.g., Yaldabaoth-Saklas-Samael in the *Apocryphon of John*) or beings (e.g., the seven creator-angels of Saturninus's system, according to Irenaeus, *Adversus omnes Haereses* 1.24). In classic Gnostic texts the creator of the world is at once the God of the Bible and a world ruler comparable to Belial, the evil spirit of the Qumran literature. Moreover, the Gnostic dualism of spirit versus matter is clearly grounded in Platonist metaphysics, though modified with features drawn from Jewish apocalyptic traditions.

The divine vs. the earthly. The Qumran literature sets up a strong contrast between human beings and God. Humans are formed from dust, and to dust they will return (e.g., 1QH[a] x.3–4), a teaching derived from the Bible (*Gn.* 3.19). The basic biblical view of the human as a creature of weakness, mortality, and sin is heightened in the Qumran literature with its doctrine of the "flesh" (*basar*) as the locus of sin, and "righteousness" as something wholly given by God (e.g., 1QS xi.5–12). The Gnostic view of the human constitution is very different. Though the Gnostics despise the flesh, they look upon the essential human being as a "spark" of the divine: Gnostic humanity comes from God as a part of God, and to God it will return. *Gnosis* thus provides its own answer to the basic human questions: "what we were, what we became; where we were, whither we have been thrown, whither we hasten, whence we are delivered; what birth is, what rebirth" (Clement of Alexandria, *Excerpta ex Theodoto* 78). Gnostic anthropology is essentially dualistic and grounded in Platonist traditions relating to the soul.

Dualism does impinge in a way on the Qumran anthropology, too. This is especially clear in its classification of human beings into two groups: the sons of light governed by the spirit of light and the sons of darkness governed by the spirit of darkness (1QS iii.14–iv.16). This predestinarian doctrine has a counterpart in Gnosticism. The *Apocryphon of John* contains a Gnostic catechism very much like that of the aforementioned passage from 1QRule of the Community. In this passage (Nag Hammadi Codices 2.25, 16–27, 30, and parallels) the fate of human souls, salvation or reprobation, is tied to the operation of two spirits, the spirit of life and the imitation spirit. An apocalyptic Jewish source may, in fact, be posited for this passage, though with a Gnostic twist in that three groups of people are in view: the "perfect," who are saved, "ignorant" souls who are given another chance in another incarnation, and "those who did know but have turned away" who are "punished with eternal punishment."

Baptism. Ritual washing—baptism—was an important feature of the communal life of the Qumran sectaries, though the Dead Sea Scrolls provide surprisingly little information about it. Josephus reports that the Essenes practiced a purificatory immersion twice daily before meals (*The Jewish War* 2.129, 132), and this is likely to have been the case among the Qumran sectaries. The emphasis, of course, is on ritual purity. Some fragments of the Baptismal Liturgy (4Q414) recently have been published, and these fragments reflect a repeatable community rite of ritual purification. Concern for ritual purity naturally also would enter into the process of initiation into the community. The references to "purifying water" and cleansing by the "spirit of holiness" in 1QRule of the Community (1QS iii.4–12) very likely reflect a ceremony of initiation into the covenant, as the context would imply (cf. Josephus, *The Jewish War* 2.138).

Baptism was an important feature of Gnostic ritual as well, though in Gnosticism the initiatory feature predominates over the concern for ritual purity. The Nag Hammadi texts, especially those reflecting a Sethian provenance, are replete with allusions to baptismal initiations. Some Gnostic groups, however, rejected water baptism altogether (e.g., the Manichaeans; cf. Nag Hammadi Codices *Paraphrase of Shem* [8.1] and *Testimony of Truth* [9, 3]). On the other hand, repeatable ritual washings, comparable to those of the Qumran sectarians, are a feature of the one Gnostic group surviving from antiquity, the Mandeans. Indeed, there even may have been a close relationship between the original Mandeans and Jewish baptismal sects of the Jordan Valley, such as the Essenes of Qumran. In any case, it seems clear that Gnostic baptism, as attested in our sources, is rooted in the ritual practices of sectarian Judaism.

Shared Traditions. Some ancient Gnostic writers used, in addition to the Bible, Jewish traditions and writings also represented among the Dead Sea Scrolls.

Melchizedek lore. One of the Nag Hammadi tractates, *Melchizedek* (9.2; unfortunately very fragmentary), is formally an "apocalypse of Melchizedek" in which the "priest of God most high" (12, 10–22; cf. *Gn.* 14.18b) receives and transmits revelations mediated by heavenly emissaries. The core of the revealed material has to do with the future career of Jesus Christ and the ultimate identification of Jesus with the recipient of the revelation, Melchizedek himself. This text in its present form obviously is a Christian text, and its view of Melchizedek is based in large part on *Hebrews* 7. However, there are also aspects of the interpretation of Melchizedek that are traceable to Jewish apocalyptic speculation, unmediated by Christianity. Melchizedek is depicted as a heavenly holy warrior who, as a heavenly high priest, emerges victorious in an eschatological battle with demonic forces. The only known Jewish apocalyptic text that contains precisely this combination of roles and attributes is Melchizedek from Cave 11 at Qumran (11Q13). That text (also unfortunately fragmentary) features Melchizedek as a heavenly warrior-priest virtually identical to the archangel Michael. He appears in the tenth and final jubilee of world history (11Q13 ii.7) to rescue the "men of the lot of Melchizedek" (11Q13 ii.8) from Belial and his fellow spirits (11Q13 ii.13). Melchizedek's triumph is described as a high-priestly act of "expiation" (11Q13 ii.8). While it cannot be demonstrated that the author of the Nag Hammadi tractate *Melchizedek* knew and used the Dead Sea Scroll Melchizedek, it nevertheless is clear that he was familiar with Jewish apocalyptic traditions about Melchizedek very much like those found in the Melchizedek manuscript from Cave 11.

Enochic "Book of Watchers." A number of Gnostic texts refer to the biblical patriarch Enoch and cite revelations attributed to him. In some cases it is possible to see in the Gnostic material influence from specific Enochic writings. Probably the clearest case of this is the use in the *Apocryphon of John* of the "Book of Watchers," the first and perhaps oldest of the parts that make up what we now know as *1 Enoch*. *Apocryphon of John* 2.29, 16–30, 11 is a Gnostic reinterpretation of the myth of the fallen angels found in *1 Enoch* 6–11 and 15. In the Gnostic version the chief archon, that is, the biblical Creator, plays the role of the wicked Shemiḥazah, chief of the watchers (the "sons of God" of *Gn.* 6.2). The Qumran sectarians had several copies of the various parts of *1 Enoch* in their library (except the "Book of Parables" [chapters 37–71]), as attested in Aramaic fragments found in Qumran. The myth of the fallen watchers not only was part of the Enoch literature kept at Qumran but also was incorporated into the sect's own teachings (see Damascus Document CD ii.17–19). [*See* Enoch, Books of.]

Enochic "Book of Giants." Among the books used by the Manicheans was one called the *Book of Giants*. From the eighteenth century it was thought that this book was somehow related to the Enoch literature, especially the "Book of Watchers." (The giants are the progeny of the watchers, according to the Enochic myth.) Fragments of this Manichean book exist in several Oriental languages, and now its association with the Enoch literature has been proven by the discovery among the Dead Sea Scrolls of Aramaic fragments of a Jewish Book of Giants ascribed to Enoch. Its place in Manichaean literature can be accounted for by positing that the prophet Mani knew of the Jewish *Book of Giants* circulating in Aramaic in the Jewish Christian Elkesaite community in which he was reared. Mani liked the book and adapted it for use in the communities that he founded.

From Jewish Apocalyptic Thought to Gnosis. All of the available evidence indicates that Gnosticism arose among circles in which Jewish apocalyptic traditions were current. The Dead Sea Scrolls are important for the study of Gnosticism because the literature produced by the Qumran sect and other Jewish literature circulating in it attest to the kinds of apocalyptic traditions that play such a prominent role in the origins and early development of the Gnostic religion.

BIBLIOGRAPHY

Hauschild, Wolf-Dieter. "Judentum—Gnosis—Christentum: Die Pneumatologie im Apokryphon des Johannes." In *Gottes Geist und der Mensch: Studien zur frühchristlichen Pneumatologie*, by Wolf-Dieter Hauschild, pp. 224–272. Munich, 1972. An important study of the catechism on the classes of human souls in the *Apocryphon of John*.

Layton, Bentley. *The Gnostic Scriptures*. Garden City, N.Y., 1987. Contains translations of what Layton calls "classic gnostic" scripture, plus related material, with valuable introductions and annotations.

Mansoor, Menahem. "The Nature of Gnosticism in Qumran." In *Le origini dello gnosticismo: Colloquio di Messina 13–18 Aprile 1966*, edited by Ugo Bianchi, pp. 389–400. Studies in the History of Religions, 12. Leiden, 1970. A comparative study of the Dead Sea Scrolls and Gnosticism.

Milik, Józef T. *The Books of Enoch: Aramaic Fragments of Qumrân Cave 4*. Oxford, 1976. Publication, with full commentary, of the Aramaic fragments of the Enochic literature found at Qumran.

Osten-Sacken, Peter von den. *Gott und Belial: Traditionsgeschichtliche Untersuchungen zum Dualismus in den Texten aus Qumran*. Studien zur Umwelt des Neuen Testaments, 6. Göttingen, 1969. An important study of dualism in the Qumran literature.

Pearson, Birger A. "The Figure of Melchizedek in Gnostic Literature."

In *Gnosticism, Judaism, and Egyptian Christianity*, by Birger A. Pearson, pp. 108–123. Minneapolis, 1990. Includes a discussion of Nag Hammadi Codex *Melchizedek* (ix,1) and its relation to Melchizedek from Cave 11 at Qumran (11Q13).

Pearson, Birger A. "*1 Enoch* in the *Apocryphon of John*." In *Texts and Contexts: Biblical Texts in Their Textual and Situational Contexts*, edited by Tord Fornberg and David Hellholm, pp. 355–367. Oslo, 1995. A study of the appropriation by the *Apocryphon of John* of the myth of the fallen angels in *1 Enoch*.

Ringgren, Helmer. "Qumran and Gnosticism." In *Le origini dello gnosticismo: Colloquio di Messina 13–18 Aprile 1966*, edited by Ugo Bianchi, pp. 379–384. A comparative study of the concept of knowledge in Qumran and in Gnosticism.

Robinson, James M., and Richard Smith, eds. *The Nag Hammadi Library in English*, 3d ed. Leiden and San Francisco, 1988. English translation of all of the tractates of the Nag Hammadi Codices plus two from the Berlin Codex.

Rudolph, Kurt. *Gnosis: The Nature and History of Gnosticism.* Translated by R. McL. Wilson. Edinburgh and San Francisco, 1983. A standard comprehensive work on Gnosticism by a prominent historian of religions.

Rudolph, Kurt. "Antike Baptisten: Zu den Überlieferungen über frühjüdische und -christliche Taufsekten." In *Gnosis und spätantike Religionsgeschichte: Gesammelte Aufsätze*, by Kurt Rudolph, pp. 569–606. Nag Hammadi and Manichaean Studies, 42. Leiden, 1996. Discusses the ancient evidence for Jewish baptismal sects and related groups.

Schiffman, Lawrence H. "Mysteries." In *Qumran Cave 4, XV: The Sapiential Texts*, edited by T. Elgvin et al., pp. 31–123. Discoveries in the Judaean Desert, 20. Oxford, 1997.

Segelberg, Eric. *Maṣbutā: Studies in the Ritual of the Mandaean Baptism.* Uppsala, 1958. A detailed historical and comparative study of Mandaean baptism.

Sevren, Jean-Marie. *Le dossier baptismal séthien: Études sur la sacramentaire gnostique.* Bibliothèque Copte de Nag Hammadi, Études 2. Quebec, 1986. An important study of the baptismal passages in the Sethian texts from Nag Hammadi, with a phenomenological and historical reconstruction of Sethian baptism.

BIRGER A. PEARSON

GOD. The community reflected in the texts that have been found at Qumran, as far as we can see from the scrolls, oriented its entire life to God and his commandments. The Qumran community used a calendar with 364 days, which corresponded to God's plan of salvation as it seemed to be expressed in the Sabbath scheme of Creation and the history of Israel. Although the literature of this community deals in detail with instructions for a life in accordance with the will of God, indications are sparse as to how they imagined God and what kind of theology they may have had. Therefore, it has to be reconstructed first by examining the variety of terminology and attributes, and then by analyzing the development of concepts of God in their historical context.

Attributes of God. God is regarded by the covenanters of Qumran as the one majestic almighty ruler, all his creatures being infinitely below him. This is shown by the hymns and prayers at Qumran, which take up the tradition of *Genesis* 2, that man is made of the dust of the ground in order to emphasize the immense distance between the creator (cf. liturgy, 4Q409) and human beings (cf. Hodayot[a] from Cave 1 at Qumran [1QHodayot[a]] 1QH[a] xx.27, vii.34 [xii.24, xv.21]). But God can also be named as the loving one (e.g., Rule of the Community from Cave 1 at Qumran [hereafter 1QRule of the Community], 1QS iii.26). [*See* Rule of the Community.] He has done just deeds and given his merciful favors to Israel (1QS i.21–22). His justice can cleanse and atone for the sins of the community (1QS ii.14); all his acts are true and just, from the times of the fathers he bestowed his grace and mercy on those who live according to the covenant (1QS i.26; cf. the reconstruction of S. E. Scheepstra).

God acting directly. There are some texts that quite definitely show God speaking or acting directly. In Temple Scroll[a] from Cave 11 (11Q19), the Tetragrammaton YHVH is used and God speaks to the community of Moses in the first person. [*See* Temple Scroll.] There are even some instances where the biblical text has been changed from the third to the first person (cf. *Nm.* 30.3–4 in 11Q19 liii.14–15). Presenting God in this way, as speaking directly, emphasizes the authority of this document, which presents itself as a Torah and binding commandment.

The Aramaic Genesis Apocryphon from Cave 1 at Qumran (1QapGen) has to be seen differently. According to column xx, God intervenes directly after a prayer of Abraham by sending a chastising spirit. [*See* Genesis Apocryphon.] In columns xxi and xxii he appears and speaks directly to Abraham. In this text the portrayal of God's immediate effectiveness promotes the concreteness of the narrative and arouses confidence in God's intervention. Even if we do not know whether these two texts (Temple Scroll[a] and the Genesis Apocryphon) were written at Qumran, they were copied and used there. The experience of God acting directly is also witnessed in Pesher Habakkuk (1QpHab vii.4–5), according to which "God has disclosed to the Teacher of Righteousness all the mysteries of the words of his servants, the prophets." [*See* Pesher Habakkuk.] In a similar way, the elect of God knows the mysteries of all living things (Elect of God, 4Q534). It is not certain whether this title refers to a messianic figure or not. [*See* Messiahs.]

God and the gods. The majority of texts from Qumran no longer speak of God as acting directly. His effectiveness can only be imagined as mediated by other celestial beings. This phenomenon can also be detected in other documents from the late postexilic period, above all the *Book of Daniel*. It is the consequence of a more transcendent, strictly monotheistic conception of God. The celestial beings can be named as Gods, for example, in Songs of the Sabbath Sacrifice[a] (4Q400 1–2; *elim* or *elohim*). [*See* Songs of the Sabbath Sacrifice.] God himself therefore is regarded as "God of gods" (cf. Songs of the Sage[a] 1.2 [4Q510]). Further names are "gods of the light" (Songs of the Sabbath Sacrifice[d] 4Q403 1.ii.35) or "gods of knowledge" (cf. 4Q400 2.8); the latter designation is surely to be connected with the name *El ha-deʿot*, "God of knowledge" for the one God (e.g., 1QS iii.15). In other instances they are called "cherubim of knowledge" (4Q400 1.6), "eternal holy ones" (1.15) or "most holy ones" (Songs of the Sabbath Sacrifice[b], 4Q401 14.i.7). Also individual figures like Melchizedek can be designated as "angel" and therefore as "God" (cf. Melchizedek 11Q13 ii.9–11 as an interpretation of Ps. 82.1). [*See* Melchizedek.]

An apocalyptic work (4Q246) that is only fragmentarily preserved even speaks of a "son of God," a "son of the Most High," who also belongs to the angelic sphere (García Martínez, 1992). He can be compared with figures like Melchizedek or the "splendid counselor" from 1QHodayot[a] (1QH[a] iii.10). The Florilegium (4Q174 i.10) explains the son of God from *2 Samuel* 7.12 as the messianic branch of David, who will rise up in Zion in the last days. In other texts the members of the community seem to be designated as sons of God (cf. 11Q13 ii.8–14 and Words of the Luminaries, 4Q504[a] iii). [*See* Words of the Luminaries.] The angel-Gods are called *benei shamayim*, "sons of heaven," according to 1QRule of the Community (1QS xi.8).

Further designations for celestial beings are *mal'akhim*, "angels" (so in the Songs of the Sabbath Sacrifice) and *ruḥot*, "spirits" (cf. 1QS iii.14). [*See* Angels.] Both of these terms can be applied to good and bad powers because of the dualistic ideas of the covenanters. [*See* Dualism.] Songs of the Sabbath Sacrifice (11Q17) offers a collection of designations for those spirits, showing the whole range of what was possible. The marking of single angels by giving them proper names, which is well known from other texts, is found at Qumran, too. One can find, for example, Gabriel, Michael, Sariel, and Raphael (War Scroll, 1QM ix.15–16) or Uriel (Astronomical Enoch[b], 4Q209 25.3). According to the Songs of the Sabbath Sacrifice it is the primary function of the angels to praise and worship God, the king of glory, in their heavenly service. When the community fulfills the cultic regulations of the Torah, its worship is in harmony with that of the angels.

This merging of earthly cult and divine sphere can also be traced in the Songs of the Sage[a–b] (4Q510–511). In reciting these collected prayers and praises, thus exalting the name of God (4Q511 35.6), the *maskil* ("instructor") is expelling the bastard spirits. In effect, he is protecting the sons of light from their seductions. The *maskil* thus participates in a magical way in the divine power. The distinctions between earthly and heavenly spheres become fluid.

Epithets for God. To show the goodness and majesty of God, many attributes and epithets were used, especially in hymnic contexts. In fact there are some instances where one can read about God's anger, his angry face, or the God of vengeance (cf. 1QS ii.9; iv.12). But as a rule, positive designations were used to describe God. He is characterized by truth and justice (1QS i.26); he is a God of salvation (1QS i.19). He, the God of Israel, the God of the fathers, is a God of mercy (Catena[a] 4Q177 10.9); he can be addressed as "foundation of my well-being, source of knowing, spring of holiness, peak of glory, and all-powerful one of eternal majesty" (1QS x.12). God is the most high (*ʿelyon*; cf. 1QS x.12), the Lord of the universe (*Adon ha-kol*; cf. 4Q409 1.6), Lord of eternity (Words of Michael 4Q529 11) or Lord of the heaven (1QapGen ix.17). The same epithets can be used with "king" (*melekh*) instead of "lord" without a recognizable difference in meaning (cf. 1QM xii.8). In using those epithets, the covenanters showed their deeply felt reverence for God and his helpful acts for those observing his Torah.

God in Historical Context. The Dead Sea Scrolls show how biblical traditions (including *1 Enoch* and *Jubilees*) are used as the primary sources to develop a more or less coherent concept of what is meant by the terms used for God. They reflect the ambivalence of particularistic and universalistic, empirical and eschatological modes of speaking about God, which are already present in the Bible.

God the creator. The basic confession of faith in God as creator of heaven and earth is put at the beginning of the Torah by the first creation account in *Genesis* 1. In some Dead Sea Scrolls the meaning of God's acts of creation is specified further and combined with his words attested in the prophetic literature. This specific view is interested in the long perspective of the connection between the heavenly and earthly realms: From God's side the spirits become agents of the continuation of the process of creation, while from the side of humanity right knowledge and religious practices open the gates of heaven to reach affirmation about the eschatological purpose/goal of the divine intention. The intersection of both areas of reality is dominated by the works fulfilled by good and evil spirits, which correspond to good and evil knowledge/work within humanity and its surroundings (cf. 1QS iii.13–iv.26). Both aspects of spirits are authored by God; they build the bridge between anthropology, cosmology, and eschatology (cf. liturgical work, 4Q392). This concept in the Dead Sea Scrolls is influenced by earlier texts like *1 Enoch* 15, which speaks about the fact that the fall of the watchers produced in humanity a mixture of spirit and flesh, and *Jubilees* 2, which reports the creation of natural phenomena together with corresponding spirits.

The implied dynamic of God's salvation history, which is produced by the ambivalence of creation, by light and darkness, is an elaboration emerging from God's self-declarations primarily given in *Isaiah*, the prophetic book that was most frequently copied among the Dead Sea Scrolls. [*See* Light and Darkness.] One can compare *Isaiah* 45.7, where emphasis is given to the creation of darkness as well as to the making of light. In *Isaiah* the shift to the eschatological situation is also promised: God "will arise upon thee, and his glory shall be seen upon thee" (*Is*. 60.2). The theophany of God himself "will be the eternal light" (*Is*. 60.19; cf. Osten-Sacken, 1969, p. 82).

God as a man of war. God's activity becomes more indirect in the War Scroll. He acts through the ones whom he has enlightened, that is, the heavenly and earthly "sons of light": "the sons of justice shall shine" and fight "the war of extermination against the sons of darkness" (1QM i.8–10). [*See* War of the Sons of Light against the Sons of Darkness.]

God's history with its cosmological and anthropological background is displayed for the end time as a war. This is a development of biblical tradition where God is called "a man of war" (*Ex*. 15.3). God and his "exalted greatness will shine for all the [eternal] times" (1QM xi.8), only after the last victory of those who demonstrate his power up to the ends of the earth.

Demonstrating God's power by warlike acts has ancient precedents in the Hebrew scriptures. It has to be stated that this is only a mode of language, not an actual pattern of behavior. The addition of liturgical material in the War Scroll as well as in several other Dead Sea Scrolls shows that not only cultic assemblies in the desert tradition of camps but also liturgical practices are the framework for understanding this language.

With the Song of the Sea, the biblical tradition offers a starting point for an integration of military and liturgical metaphors that are used up to modern times in synagogal services: God, "the man of war" (*Ex*. 15.3) "shall reign for ever and ever" (*Ex*. 15.18). The second element, with the confession of divine kingship, occurs in many psalms as well. But this kingship required development to a higher level, when even earthly kings claimed to be "king of kings," as is the case at least from Persian times on (cf. *Dn*. 2.37). The concept of a heavenly kingdom that incorporates even foreign kings and rulers, combined with the monotheistic idea of God, requires a universal confession: "God is the God of gods, and the Lord of kings. . . ." (*Dn*. 2.47). Within the Dead Sea Scrolls, one further step in the correspondence of the earthly and heavenly realms can be seen in the use of the double designation that is "God of gods of all the chiefs of the heights, and king of kings of all the eternal councils" (4Q403 1.34; cf. *1 En*. 9.4). Within the thirteen Songs of the Sabbath Sacrifice this central statement is made as the climax reached on the seventh Sabbath and again at the center of the seven praises of this day (Schwemer, 1991, p. 95).

God's dwellings. This concept of the heavenly kingdom and worship oriented to the celestial temple breaks down the barriers between the earthly and heavenly realms and brings together all the tongues of praise in one common service. The certainty that angels are accompanying the communities is one of the characteristics of many of the Dead Sea Scrolls, requiring purity and holiness on the part of the members. Because of their cultic assemblies, both realms are merged with each other; it is even possible to state that God's temple is represented by the community that forms a "temple of men" (4Q174 i.6 as an interpretation of *Ex*. 15.17–18; Brooke, 1997, p. 70).

This temple seems to be a proleptic representation of God's theophany, which will result in a new creation and a new temple when, according to the prophets, God will "dwell in the midst of them forever" (*Ezek*. 43.9; cf. *Lv*. 26.11; 11Q19 xxix.8–10). In *Jubilees* 1.16–18 this hope is combined with the imagery of the "righteous plant" that God himself takes care of at all times. This metaphor of the eternal plant gives an important key for the self-understanding and theology of the groups behind the Dead Sea Scrolls (e.g., 1QS viii.5; xi.8; CD i.7; 1QH[a] vi.15, viii.6, viii.9, viii.10). [*See* Eternal Planting.]

They see certain texts as a coherent chain of motifs.

- the announcement by Moses that God himself enables the planting of his people in the promised inheritance (*Ex*. 15.17)
- the throne vision seen by Isaiah in which God decrees that a remnant of the stable root will remain (*Is*. 6.13)
- the words of Isaiah about future salvation, where the growing of the plants is announced together with enlightenment and anointing by God's spirit (*Is*. 60.19–61.3)

These eschatological plant metaphors of the Hebrew scriptures were already fundamental in the Apocrypha and pseudepigrapha predating most of the Dead Sea Scrolls (e.g., *1 En*. 10.16–19, 84.6, 93.2, 93.5, 93.10; *Jub*. 7.34–37, 16.26, 21.24, 36.6).

God's revelation. A further important development in speech about God and his modes of action is visible in *1 Enoch* 2–5, where in a mode of wisdom teaching, the addressees are requested to observe natural phenomena. Their signs are used to demonstrate the connection between heaven and earth as well as to make inferences from God's creation regarding the hope of fulfillment of his blessings and curses in the end time. [*See* Blessings and Curses.] The experiences of seasons, times of heat and rain that determine the appearance of trees, permit indirect speech about God. This chain of affirmative metaphoric language is taken up in the parables of growing in New Testament and rabbinic literature.

But even this empirical approach needs the right spirit of understanding. To interpret the meaning of things as authored by God makes it necessary to know how good and evil spirits are connected with creation and how they provide the real background of the visible phenomena, which fulfill God's hidden plans. The realization of this "mystery" of all things (already in existence and to come) marks in many Dead Sea Scrolls the revelatory process (e.g., 1QS xi.3, 5, 9). A counterpart to this is the confession of sin and self-humiliation of those who want their eyes, ears, and heart to be prepared for the perception of God's mysteries and to be members of his covenant (cf. *Is.* 6.10 against *Dt.* 29.3). As in *Isaiah* 55.7–9, people are able to return to God and are confronted with God's thoughts, which seem to reveal no simple mode of predestination.

God's blessings and his appointed times. The affirmation of the right knowledge about God and the possession of the right spirit given by God himself are enacted in the lifestyle and rituals of the communities: They study documents that reveal his will and they practice a cultic-liturgical life that guarantees that it is his light that shines upon and through the covenanters. The priestly blessing from *Nm.* 6.24–26 marks the fate of each individual as an effect of God's activity: may God "bless you, . . . make his face to shine upon you, . . . and give you peace." But according to the prophetic tradition of Isaiah, this is not applicable to the wicked, who will have "no peace" (*Is.* 48.22, 57.21). This sentence is taken over as a central message of *Enoch* to the fallen watchers and their followers (*1 En.* 12.5–6, 13.1, 16.4). It corresponds to the message of judgment. In *1 Enoch* 1.8 only the righteous ones receive the blessing of *Numbers* 6, with the eschatological announcement of mercy, peace, and God's saving light upon them. The wicked, in contrast, have to expect God's firelike theophany as judgment that brings the curses upon them: they will have "no peace" (*1 En.* 1.9, 5.4–7). Among the appointed times the main festivity in the communities of the Dead Sea Scrolls is depicted as a covenantal festival of the Torah (*Dt.* 27–28; 29–30). They assemble according to the precept of Moses and perform "your passing over into the covenant of YHVH" (*Dt.* 29:11) in connection with the ritual of blessings and curses that are invoked upon each of the participants (1QS i.16–ii.18; cf. Berakhot[a], 4Q286 7.i–ii). A similar yearly ceremony is dated in the final column of Damascus Document[b] (4Q266 11–17) to the third month, the month of the giving of the Torah on Mount Sinai and the corresponding festival of weeks or oaths (Shavuʿot; cf. *2 Chr.* 15.12–15). [*See* Damascus Document.] Here on the one hand are curses for the wicked who do not walk in God's Torah. But on the other hand the confession of faith in God as creator and in "the people of your ransom" is the basis for hope. It corresponds to the willingness to stand in his service "during the ages of anger and in their steps to all those who [dwell in their camps and in their cities]" (4Q267 18.v.9–12, 18.v.18–20). In reenacting this biblical situation the community reaffirms the final intention of God's Torah and his covenant.

[*See also* Creation; Eschatology.]

BIBLIOGRAPHY

Baumgarten, Joseph M. "A New Qumran Substitute for the Divine Name and Mishnah Sukkah 4.5." *Jewish Quarterly Review* 83 (1992), 1–5.

Brooke, George J. "The Qumran Scrolls and Old Testament Theology." *Problems in Biblical Theology: Essays in Honor of Rolf Knierim*, edited by Henry T. C. Sun, and Keith L. Eades, pp. 59–75. Grand Rapids, Mich., 1997.

Davila, James R. "The Name of God at Moriah: An Unpublished Fragment from 4QGenExod[a]." *Journal of Biblical Literature* 110 (1991), 577–582.

Dombrowski, B. W. "The Idea of God in IQ Serek." *Revue de Qumrân* 7 (1971), 515–531.

Fitzmyer, Joseph A. "The Aramaic 'Elect of God' Text from Qumran Cave IV." *Catholic Biblical Quarterly* 27 (1965), 348–372.

Fitzmyer, Joseph A. "4Q246: The 'Son of God' Document from Qumran." *Biblica* 74 (1993), 153–174.

García Martínez, F. "The Eschatological Figure of 4Q246." *Qumran and Apocalyptic: Studies on the Aramaic Texts from Qumran*, pp. 162–179. Leiden, 1992.

Hengel, Martin, and Anna Marie Schwemer, eds. *Königsherrschaft Gottes und himmlischer Kult im Judentum, Urchristentum und in der hellenistischen Welt*. Wissenschaftliche Untersuchungen zum Neuen Testament, 55. Tübingen, 1991.

Osten-Sacken, Peter von der. *Gott und Belial. Traditionsgeschichtliche Untersuchungen zum Dualismus in den Texten aus Qumran*. Studien zur Umwelt des Neuen Testaments, 6. Göttingen, 1969.

Puech, Émile. "Fragment d'une Apocalypse en araméen (4Q246= pseudo-Dan[d]) et le 'Royaume de Dieu.'" *Revue biblique* 99 (1992), 98–131.

Qimron, Elisha. "Times for Praising God: A Fragment of a Scroll from Qumran (4Q409)." *Jewish Quarterly Review* 80 (1989/1990), 341–347.

Ringgren, Helmer. *The Faith of Qumran. Theology of the Dead Sea Scrolls*, edited with a new introduction by James H. Charlesworth. New York, 1995.

Scheepstra, S. E. "True and Righteous are All the Works of God: A Proposal for Reconstruction of 1QS i.26." *Revue de Qumrân* 16 (1995), 641–646.

Schuller, Eileen M. "Some Observations on Blessings of God in Texts from Qumran." *Of Scribes and Scrolls: Studies on the Hebrew Bible, Intertestamental Judaism, and Christian Origins Presented to John Strugnell on the Occasion of His Sixtieth Birthday*, edited by Harold W. Attridge, John J. Collins, and Thomas H. Tobin, pp. 133–143. Lanham, Md., 1990.

Schwemer, Anna Marie, and M. Hengel, eds. "Gott als König und seine Königsherrschaft in den Sabbatliedern aus Qumran." In *Königsherrschaft Gottes und himmlischer Kult im Judentum, Urchris-*

tentum und in der hellenistischen Welt, pp. 45–118. Wissenschaftliche Untersuchungen zum Neuen Testament, 55. Tübingen, 1991.

Weinfeld, Moshe. "God versus Moses in the Temple Scroll—'I do not speak on my own authority but on God's authority' (Sifre: Deut. sec. 5; John 12, 48f)." *Revue de Qumrân* 15 (1991), 175–180.

MARTIN RÖSEL
UWE GLEßMER

GREAT REVOLT, THE. *See* First Jewish Revolt.

GRECO-ROMAN GUILDS. Trade guilds and voluntary associations abounded in the Greco-Roman world from the fourth century BCE to the late Roman period. One theory to explain the popularity of the guilds is that they provided a sense of community and belonging at a time when real participation in the life of the *polis* had been diminished under the changed conditions of first the Hellenistic kingdoms and then the Roman Empire. They appeared under various names such as *eranos*, *thiasos*, and *koinon* in Greek and *collegium*, *secta*, and *factio* in Latin.

Classification and Organization. Although these and other terms are used in the sources without any clear distinction, making it difficult to come up with any neat system of classification based on terminology alone, most scholars recognize three basic types of associations: trade guilds, religious associations, and burial clubs. A certain amount of overlap exists between these categories, however. For instance, many of the trade guilds were devoted to the worship of a patron deity, and religious associations often contributed toward the funeral expenses of deceased members, as did the burial clubs. Hence, the distinction between the types should not be seen as one of function but rather of emphasis and organizing principle. Indeed, most guilds functioned to meet a variety of needs ranging from social to religious to economic.

The economic activity of the guilds, however, was mostly directed to helping poorer members with personal expenses. In contrast with modern labor unions, the main goal of ancient trade guilds was not to improve the working conditions of members, and only in a few instances does one find guilds acting to protect a perceived threat to their livelihood (cf. *Acts* 19.24–25). Also infrequent is any mention of political activity. An exception is found at Pompeii, where "election posters" inscribed on the facades of buildings show that *collegia* supported candidates for office in the first century CE. In the earlier period such activity was likely more common, since Rome passed laws strictly controlling the formation of new guilds from 64 BCE onward.

The organization of the guilds in many ways mirrored that of the *polis*. Thus, they were rather democratic institutions with a set of rules ratified by the members and serving as a constitution of sorts. The rules usually had to do with the meetings of the association and stipulated such things as when meetings were to be held, who was to contribute what, and how members were to act toward each other. Breaking of the rules was punishable by fine or, for more serious offenses, exclusion. Periodically, the rules were read and assented to by the membership. They also had elected officials to carry out the routine business of the group.

The guilds usually were organized and functioned only on the local level, though a few did apparently extend over a province. The local nature of the guilds meant that their membership was limited. The average size was about thirty to thirty-five people, though a few had as many as two hundred to three hundred (cf. Marcus Tod [1974] and John Kloppenborg and Stephen Wilson [1996]). The composition of the membership also varied from group to group. Some associations had an all-male membership, some all-female, while others were mixed and some even included children. There were also associations made up of poorer people for whom the group provided the certainty of a decent burial at death. In the most inclusive guilds, however, men and women, slaves and freeborn, and rich and poor would all come together.

Qumran as a Guild. H. Bardtke (1961) was the first scholar to raise the question of whether the Qumran group was organized along the lines of a guild or voluntary association. His work was furthered by C. Schneider (1963), B. Dombrowski (1966), and W. Tyloch (1967), and set in a wider context by M. Hengel (1974). The fullest study to date, however, is the monograph of Moshe Weinfeld titled *The Organizational Pattern and the Penal Code of the Qumran Sect* (1986).

All these investigations have shown that there are a number of parallels between Qumran and the guilds. Thus, for example, the term that the Qumran group uses to refer to itself is *yaḥad* ("community"), which is quite similar to the Greek words *koinon* and *koinōnia*, used to refer to Greek guilds. Indeed, if one accepts that the Qumran group was in some way related to the Essenes, then it is significant that both Philo and Josephus use the same two Greek terms, *koinon* and *koinōnia*, when describing the Essenes.

Also like the guilds, the Qumranites had works such as the Rule of the Community (1QS) and the Damascus Document (CD) outlining the organization and rules of their group. Although differing slightly in their details, both these documents describe a community that is structured remarkably like a voluntary association with a governing council, various officers having clearly defined duties, and a specific process of initiation. Importantly, it is just such matters as initiation, for which there is clearly no biblical precedent, that strengthen the likelihood of direct imitation of the guilds.

The same is true with regard to the various rules that govern conduct within the group. The requirement of unwavering fidelity, the regulations stipulating what is acceptable behavior at meetings, the prescribing of a fixed seating order at meetings and meals, the establishment of a fund for mutual aid of members, and the process for resolving disputes and misconduct all have analogies with practices in the guilds. Once again, it is just in those areas where there is no specific biblical prescription that the parallels with the guilds are revealed.

Still, in spite of the similarities just noted, there are also some differences. Both the Rule of the Community and the Damascus Document are longer and more detailed than the statutes of the societies. The range of issues dealt with in the Qumran works is more extensive, covering marriage laws, diseases, bodily emissions, and tithes. All these topics reflect issues that derive from the Torah and were of specific concern to Jews. At the same time, certain issues that were commonly mentioned in association statutes, such as provision for sacrifices at meetings and proper burial for deceased members, are absent from the Qumran compositions (though the absence of the former is undoubtedly because of the unique requirement in Judaism that sacrifice be offered only in Jerusalem).

Different also is the inclusion of poetry (cf. 1QS i.25–ii.17; x.1–xi.22) and religious instruction (cf. 1QS iii.13–iv.26, the so-called Treatise on the Two Spirits) that is missing from the pagan statutes but common in the Torah. Finally, one notices a polemical tone to both the Qumran works that is not found in the pagan statutes. This controversial element has to do specifically with the proper observance of the Torah. It is not merely a reflection of Israel's conviction of the exclusive claims of monotheism vis-à-vis paganism, however, for while the Qumran literature evidences no great esteem for gentiles, it is equally harsh on Jews not belonging to the group who are viewed as transgressing God's law.

The question thus becomes how to account for both the similarities and the differences between Qumran and the guilds. Weinfeld's view is that while the organization and structure of the Qumran community clearly reflect those of the guilds, the overall purpose and many of the specific practices of the community took their inspiration from uniquely Jewish religious ideals. His conclusion, however, has been challenged from two very different perspectives by Matthias Klinghardt (1994) and Sandra Walker-Ramisch (1996).

Klinghardt criticizes Weinfeld for recognizing most of the parallels but failing to draw the only proper conclusion, namely that Qumran was an association pure and simple. Furthermore, since he accepts that Jewish synagogues in the Diaspora were organized as associations, the type of association described in 1QRule of the Community is best understood as a Palestinian synagogue. Contrary to Klinghardt, Walker-Ramisch maintains that Weinfeld has failed to realize that parallels between groups such as the Greco-Roman guilds and the community of the Damascus Document can only be validated in light of their overall systems of belief and practice. She finds that it is the sectarian mentality of the latter group, based on religious ideology, antagonistic to the rest of society, and informing every aspect of its organization and conduct, that ultimately distinguishes it from the associations.

Of the three views, that of Klinghardt is the most problematic. Leaving aside the rather dubious assumption that since synagogues were associations, any Jewish association must be a synagogue, Klinghardt's theory fails to account satisfactorily for the differences between Qumran and the guilds, such as the all-encompassing nature of Qumran law, the translocal nature of the community (especially the references to "camps" in the Damascus Document, but cf. also 1QRule of the Community vi), and the sectarian outlook of the *yaḥad*. It is primarily what Walker-Ramisch sees as the pervasive influence of the last of these that leads her to conclude that the group behind the Damascus Document was not an association. The problem with her study is that after having drawn this fundamental conclusion, she is totally silent concerning the origin of the striking parallels that led to the whole discussion in the first place.

Strangely lacking in all three studies is the question of what the Qumranites themselves intended. Did they consciously set out to establish an association in imitation of their pagan neighbors and did they intentionally pattern their behavior after the guilds? Given the general attitude toward gentiles in the scrolls, the answer is likely no (see also Hengel [1974]). Of course, the lack of intentional borrowing does not mean that there has not been any influence at all. But such influence was likely indirect at most. This is corroborated by the fact that some of the most prominent shared traits between the guilds and Qumran also show up in other Jewish groups. Thus, with regard to initiation, S. Lieberman (1952) has shown that rabbinic literature describes a similar process for joining the *ḥavurah* in the time of the Mishnah, though it is perhaps of even earlier Pharisaic origin. Similarly, the closest parallel to the brotherly reproof described in 1QRule of the Community (v.24–vi.1) and the Damascus Document (CD ix.17–23) is not that of the guilds but that of the early church as outlined in *Matthew* 18.15–17.

In sum, then, the most important differences distinguishing Qumran from the guilds are the all-encompassing legislation of the Qumran rules, the polemical tone (which entails a different motive for membership than merely choice—it is a matter of being faithful to God), and the translocal nature of the community (as envisioned in CD and perhaps in 1QS vi). Where the parallels to the guilds do exist, they may in part be coincidental, but more likely represent some kind of indirect Hellenistic influence exerted upon Judaism as a whole during the Greco-Roman period.

BIBLIOGRAPHY

Bardtke, Hans. "Die Rechstellung der Qumran Gemeinde." *Theologische Literaturzeitung* 86 (1961), 93–104.

Dombrowski, B. "HYḤD in 1QS and τὸ κοινόν." *Harvard Theological Review* 59 (1966), 293–307.

Hengel, M. *Judaism and Hellenism: Studies in Their Encounter in Palestine in the Early Hellenistic Period*. 2 vols. Philadelphia, 1974. See pages 243–247.

Klinghardt, Matthias. "The Manual of Discipline in the Light of Statutes of Hellenistic Associations." In *Methods of Investigation of the Dead Sea Scrolls and the Khirbet Qumran Site: Present Realities and Future Prospects*, edited by Michael Wise et al., pp. 251–270. New York, 1994.

Kloppenborg, John S., and Stephen G. Wilson, eds. *Voluntary Associations in the Graeco-Roman World*. London, 1996. An exemplary collection of essays that explores the usefulness of the concept "association" in understanding groups such as synagogues, churches, mystery religions, and philosophical schools.

Lieberman, S. "The Discipline in the So-Called Dead Sea Manual of Discipline." *Journal of Biblical Literature* 71 (1952), 199–206. Shows the similarities between initiation at Qumran and the rabbinic/Pharisaic *ḥavurah*.

Schneider, C. "Zur Problematik des Hellenistischen in den Qumrantexten." In *Qumran-Probleme*, edited by H. Bardtke, pp. 299–314. Berlin, 1963.

Tod, Marcus N. "Clubs and Societies in the Greek World." In *Ancient Inscriptions: Sidelights on Greek History*, pages 71–96. Chicago, 1974, reprint of 1932. A brief but useful survey.

Tyloch, W. "Les thiases et la communauté de Qumran." In *Fourth World Congress of Jewish Studies: Papers I*, pages 225–228. Jerusalem, 1967.

Walker-Ramisch, Sandra. "Graeco-Roman Voluntary Associations and the Damascus Document: A Sociological Analysis." In *Voluntary Associations in the Graeco-Roman World*, edited by John S. Kloppenborg and Stephen G. Wilson, pp. 128–148. London, 1996.

Weinfeld, Moshe. *The Organizational Pattern and the Penal Code of the Qumran Sect*. Novum Testamentum et Orbis Antiquus, 2. Fribourg, 1986. The most important study of the issue.

ERIK W. LARSON

GREECE. The long history of Greece can be only partly reviewed here. At the beginning of the fifth century BCE, the Greeks found themselves locked in a struggle with the Achaemenid dynasty of Persia, which some forty years earlier had allowed the Jews to return to their homeland. This struggle was brought on by the rebellion of the Greek-speaking cities of Ionia in southwest Asia Minor in 499 BCE and resulted in two Persian invasions of the Greek mainland in the years 490 and 480–479 BCE, respectively. The Greeks, led by the two powerful city-states of Athens and Sparta, decisively defeated the Persians. The city of Athens, destroyed during the war, was rebuilt, and it was often there in the succeeding century and a half that brilliant new elements were added to the Greek heritage, forming what is often called classical Greek civilization. Among its characteristics were the ideal of democratic rule, a distinctive style of architecture and city planning, sophisticated art and sculpture, the development of tragedy and comedy, the rise of the discipline of history writing, and the flowering of philosophy.

Unfortunately, the political situation in Greece was not as propitious. From 431 to 404 BCE Athens and Sparta fought the Peloponnesian War, which resulted in a rather pyrrhic victory for Sparta. After the war, continued struggles between various city-states exhausted Greek military strength. Meanwhile, to the north of Greece a new power was rising in the person of Philip II, king of Macedonia. In 338 BCE Philip defeated the combined forces of Athens and Thebes at the battle of Chaeronea and became the undisputed master of the entire Greek world. Two years later he died by poisoning and was succeeded by his young son Alexander, later called the Great.

Shortly after his accession, Alexander was ready to avenge the Persian invasions of a century and a half earlier. In 334 BCE he crossed the Hellespont and in a series of battles crushed the numerically superior Persian forces. East and West were now united in one vast empire, and Greek language and culture were spread throughout the Near East, a process known as Hellenization, by the founding of Greek-style cities such as Alexandria in Egypt. In 323 BCE Alexander died, as did his empire, which was immediately divided up between certain of his generals. In Egypt, Ptolemy founded a dynasty that lasted from 323–30 BCE, while in Syria, Seleucus established a kingdom that lasted from 312 to 64 BCE. It was during the rule of the Seleucid Antiochus IV Epiphanes (175–164 BCE) that the Maccabean Rebellion broke out in Judea, partly as a reaction against the spread of Greek culture.

The Hebrew word for Greece is *Yavan*. This term is clearly derived from the Greek word *Ionia*, which as noted above refers to the area of southwest Asia Minor inhabited by Greek-speaking peoples since at least 1000 BCE. It is with this meaning that *Yavan* is used in biblical passages such as *Isaiah* 66.19; *Ezekiel* 27.13, 19(?); *Joel* 4.6; and *Zechariah* 9.13. In the genealogies of *Genesis* and *1 Chronicles*, *Yavan* is the eponymous ancestor of these peoples.

By the time of the *Book of Daniel*, the use of the word

was extended to include the Greek-speaking territories on the western side of the Aegean too, and particularly the area ruled by Alexander the Great (cf. *Dn.* 8.21, 10.20, 11.3). In a similar way, the word *Kittim*, connected to *Yavan* in the biblical genealogies and originally signifying Cyprus, also underwent an extension in meaning so that it too could denote Greeks in general. The semantic overlap between *Yavan* and *Kittim* in Second Temple literature is well illustrated by the fact that in *Daniel* 8.21 Alexander is associated with *Yavan*, but in *1 Maccabees* 1.1 with *Kittim*. However, in Pesher Nahum (4Q169) 3–4.i.3 a clear distinction is made between *Yavan* and *Kittim*, so that the former refers to Greeks and the latter to Romans.

In the nonbiblical texts from Qumran, the word *Yavan* occurs twice in Pesher Nahum 3–4.i.2–3, twice in the Damascus Document (viii.11, xix.24), and once in Genesis Apocryphon 12.xii. Another possible instance occurs in Tanḥumim (4Q176) 34.2 where *ywnym* (in plural, cf. *Jl.* 4.6) is found, but not enough context is provided to determine whether one should translate it as "Greeks" or "doves."

Pesher Nahum 3–4.i.2–3 is one of the most noteworthy passages in the *pesharim* since it actually provides names and events that can be correlated to other historical sources. Line 2 mentions Demetrius III Eukerus (95–88 BCE) and calls him "king of *Yavan*," *Yavan* here clearly meaning the Seleucid realm. Line 3 further mentions a series of kings of *Yavan*, "from Antiochus until the appearance of the rulers of the *Kittim*." Again, this is a clear reference to the Seleucid dynasty, with Antiochus being either Antiochus III (223–187 BCE) or more likely Antiochus IV (175–164 BCE), and the coming of the *Kittim* referring to the end of the dynasty at the hands of the Roman general Pompey in 64 BCE.

The two instances of *Yavan* in the Damascus Document actually represent the same sentence as found in the two slightly different versions of the Cairo Genizah manuscripts. The lines immediately preceding contain a condemnation of a certain group called "the princes of Judah," who acted wickedly and followed the ways of the gentiles. Fittingly, these apostates will be punished by one called "the chief of the kings of Greece (Yavan)" who will come to execute vengeance on them. The fact that the author of the Damascus Document envisions the activity of this king as taking place in the future makes it impossible to know precisely whom, if anyone in particular, he had in mind. Nevertheless, it is likely that one of the Seleucids is intended, as is certainly the case in Pesher Nahum.

BIBLIOGRAPHY

Bickerman, Elias J. *The Jews in the Greek Age*. Cambridge, Mass., 1988.

Hengel, Martin. *Judaism and Hellenism*. Philadelphia, 1974.

Horgan, Maurya P. *Pesharim: Qumran Interpretations of Biblical Books*. Catholic Biblical Quarterly Monograph Series, 8. Washington, D.C., 1979. Includes a fine study of Pesher Nahum (4Q169).

Knibb, Michael A. *The Qumran Community*. Cambridge Commentaries on Writing of the Jewish and Christian World 200 BCE to AD 200. Cambridge, 1987. Contains an excellent discussion on the passages in the Damascus Document.

ERIK W. LARSON

GREEK. The Greek of the texts from the Judean Desert, both literary and nonliterary, is the *koine*, a common language which replaced the variety of dialects of classical Greek, and can be seen as a transitional stage between classical and modern Greek. This is the language of Hellenistic prose, both pagan and Jewish, the Septuagint and other translations of the Hebrew scriptures, the New Testament, and the inscriptions; in its nonliterary form it is the language of the papyri and the ostraca. Following Alexander's conquests, Greek supplanted Official Aramaic as the language of government in the Near East. It retained this status even after Rome had ousted the Hellenistic kingdoms. Nevertheless, the majority of the texts from the Judean Desert are written in dialects of Aramaic—Jewish Aramaic and Nabataean—and Hebrew. Furthermore, Qumran texts evince a deliberate and conscious avoidance of Greek loanwords. This runs counter to the prevailing trend in spoken and written Aramaic and Hebrew at the time. On the other hand, the Greek of the documentary texts, which mostly involve Jews, reflects the influence of the local spoken Aramaic language of the writers. The pervasive Semitisms in the papyri from the Judean Desert stand in sharp contrast to the resistance of the Greek language to native influences in the Greek papyri from Egypt. Certain lexicographic features of our texts, shared with Greek papyri from other parts of the Near East, are either not attested at all in the Greek papyri from Egypt, or occur in them only at a much later period. This feature may well be a product of the influence of the Aramaic world in which they were written. The influence of Latin, the language of the Roman administration and army, is limited: it expresses itself mainly in the use of the Roman calendar, the literal translation of legal formulas and transcriptions of Latin words.

Literary Texts. With one exception, no Greek literary texts were found in the Judean Desert. The exception is Mur 108, not a "philosophical text," as its first editor suggested, but iambic trimeters, and thus a fragment of a comedy (see C. Austin, *Comicorum Graecorum Fragmenta in papyris reperta*, 1973, no. 360). Mas739, a fragment of a line dated to the first century CE, and Mur 109–112, fragments of literary texts of the first half of the second century CE, scarcely alter the picture.

Nor did the caves yield a rich crop of biblical texts in Greek. The most important text is undoubtedly the Greek translation of the Minor Prophets, 8ḤevXIIgr, which comes from Cave 8, the "Cave of Horror," in Naḥal Ḥever. The fragments belong to a single manuscript, of which more than half has survived, written on leather in two different book-hands which can be dated to the later first century BCE. The translation is a revision of the Septuagint translation, based on the same Hebrew text. Its literal and pedantic tendencies are especially noticeable in the attempt to render every Hebrew word by its Greek equivalent.

Fragments of Greek translations of the Hebrew scriptures come from Qumran Cave 7 and Cave 4. 7Q1, which contains two small fragments of *Exodus* 28.4–6 and 28.7, is dated to c.100 BCE; 4Q119 and 120, Septuagint Leviticus[a,b], are dated to the first century BCE—they thus antedate other Greek witnesses to Leviticus by approximately four centuries; 4Q121, Septuagint Numbers, could be somewhat later than the previous two; 4Q122, Septuagint Deuteronomy, may belong to the earlier or mid–second century BCE. In addition, there are texts which may not have a Hebrew *Vorlage*: The Cave 7 Epistle of Jeremiah is dated to c.100 BCE and the Cave 4 Greek Paraphrase of Exodus to the first century BCE or early first century CE.

Kh. Mird P.A.M. 2 + 1 of the eighth or ninth century CE, a private copy of a liturgical hymn (*tropologion*), and Kh. Mird P.A.M. 22 of the eighth century, a series of metrical units called *doxastika*, were both written in book-hands of the early Byzantine period. Almost the entire corpus of Greek texts from Khirbet Mird (approximately two hundred texts) has so far remained unpublished. It may well contain more literary texts from these centuries. Mur 156, a fragment of Christian liturgy, is dated paleographically to the eleventh century CE.

Documentary Texts. The Greek texts from Masada are the earliest dated Greek documentary texts from the Judean Desert. With the exception of one Byzantine papyrus (Mas742), all the Greek documentary texts from Masada come from a Jewish milieu, and thus date from no later than 73 (or 74) CE, when the fortress fell to the Romans. These texts include papyri (Mas739–741, 743–747), ostraca (Mas772–794), and jar inscriptions (Mas854–914). Some of the ostraca (Mas772–777) show signs of having been used for daily transactions and are therefore likely to have been written by the Sicarii who occupied the fortress from 66 to 73 (74).

The Greek texts from Wadi Murabbaʿat, Naḥal Ḥever (Cave 5/6, the Cave of Letters, and Cave 8, the Cave of Horror), Naḥal Ṣe'elim, Naḥal Mishmar, and Ketef Yeriḥo are likely to have been written no later than the last part of 135 CE (the conclusion of the Bar Kokhba Revolt). Those which bear dates fall between 99 or 109 (XḤev/Se Gr. 66) and 132 (P.Yadin 35). From Wadi Murabbaʿat come documents on leather (Mur 89–107) and on papyrus (Mur 113–125 and the tiny fragments 126–155). From Naḥal Ḥever come the Babatha archive (of which P.Yadin 5, 11–35 are in Greek), the archive of Salome Komaïse daughter of Levi (XḤev/Se Gr. 60–65), two letters from the Bar Kokhba circles (P.Yadin 52 and 59; there may be more among the unpublished material in the Rockefeller Museum), and probably also XḤev/Se Gr. 67–73 and the unidentified fragments XḤev/Se Gr. 74–169. The material from Naḥal Ṣe'elim, Naḥal Mishmar, and Ketef Yeriḥo will be published in the series Discoveries in the Judaean Desert (Oxford, 1955–).

The second-century documentary hands from the Judean Desert have been studied by Crisci and others, and the conclusions are summarized by Thomas:

> The hands from the Judaean Desert have affinities with contemporary Egyptian documentary hands, but at the same time show features similar to those found in some of the hands from Dura . . . The general impression we get from them is of less cursive scripts with fewer ligatures than would be normal in papyri from Egypt of a similar type. None of the scripts makes a serious attempt at bilinearity, and indeed the variable size of the letters . . . is a notable feature of most of the texts.

Mas742 and Kh. Mird P.A.M. 22 and 8(b) are Byzantine.

BIBLIOGRAPHY

Cotton, H. M. "The Languages of the Legal and Administrative Documents from the Judaean Desert." *Zeitschrift für Papyrologie und Epigraphik* 125 (1999), 219–231.

Cotton, H. M. "Introduction to the Greek Documentary Texts." In *Aramaic, Hebrew and Greek Texts from Naḥal Ḥever and Other Sites with an Appendix Containing Alleged Qumran Texts* (*The Seiyâl Collection*, vol. 2), edited by H. M. Cotton and A. Yardeni, pp. 133–136, 141–157. Discoveries in the Judaean Desert, 27. Oxford, 1997.

Cotton, H. M., W. Cockle, and F. Millar, "The Papyrology of the Roman Near East: A Survey." *Journal of Roman Studies* 85 (1995), 214–235.

Crisci, E. *Scrivere Greco fuori d'Egitto*, Papyrologia Florentina, 27, 1996. Survey of the paleography of Greek texts, literary and documentary, outside Egypt, with plates and drawings.

Lewis, N. "General Introduction." In N. Lewis, *The Documents from the Bar-Kokhba Period in the Cave of Letters. Greek Papyri*. Judean Desert Studies, 2. Jerusalem, 1989, pp. 3–28.

Lifshitz, B. "The Greek Documents from Naḥal Ṣe'elim and Naḥal Mishmar." *Israel Exploration Journal* 11 (1961), 53–61. First publication, with several errors, of the Greek papyri from Naḥal Ṣe'elim and Naḥal Mishmar, to be read with J. Schwartz, "Remarques sur des fragments grecs du Désert de Juda." *Revue biblique* 69 (1962), 61–63.

Lifshitz, B. "The 'Greek Documents' from the Cave of Horror." *Israel Exploration Journal* 12 (1962), 206–207.

Mussies, G. "Greek in Palestine and the Diaspora." In *The Jewish People in the First Century*, edited by S. Safrai and M. Stern, vol. 2, pp. 1040–1065. Philadelphia, 1976.

Parsons, P. J. "The Scripts and Their Date." In *The Greek Minor Prophets Scroll from Naḥal Ḥever (8ḤevXIIgr)* (*The Seiyâl Collection*, vol. 1), edited by E. Tov, pp. 19–26. Discoveries in the Judaean Desert, 8. Oxford, 1990.

Parsons, P. J. "The Palaeography and Date of the Greek Manuscripts." In *Qumran Cave 4, IV: Palaeo-Hebrew and Greek Biblical Manuscripts*, pp. 7–13. Discoveries in the Judaean Desert, 9. Oxford, 1992.

Rosén, H. "Die Sprachsituation im römischen Palästina." In *Die Sprachen im römischen Reich der Kaiserzeit*, pp. 215–239. Beihefte der Bonner Jahrbücher, 40, 1980.

Sevenster, J. N. *Do You Know Greek? How Much Greek Could the First Jewish Christians Have Known?* Supplements to Novum Testamentum, 19. Leiden, 1968.

Thomas, J. D. "Paleographical Notes." In *Aramaic, Hebrew and Greek Texts from Naḥal Ḥever and Other Sites with an Appendix Containing Alleged Qumran Texts* (*The Seiyâl Collection*, vol. 2), edited by H. M. Cotton and A. Yardeni, pp. 137–140. Discoveries in the Judaean Desert, 27. Oxford, 1997.

Van Haelst, J. "Cinq textes provenant de Khirbet Mird." *Ancient Society* 22 (1991), 297–317.

HANNAH M. COTTON

H

HABAKKUK, BOOK OF. *See* Minor Prophets; Pesher Habakkuk.

HAGGAI, BOOK OF. *See* Minor Prophets.

HAGU, BOOK OF. The expression, appearing either as *spr hhgw* or *spr hhgy*, and usually translated as the "Book of Meditation," occurs four times (one occurrence is restored) in the Dead Sea Scrolls. It is not attested in either the Hebrew scriptures or other ancient Jewish writings. Therefore, its correct vocalization (*sefer he-hago/he-hagu/he-hagi/ha-hagi/he-hegi/ha-hegeh*) and meaning have been a matter of debate. Three out of the four passages in which the expression appears are in the Damascus Document (CD x.6; xiii.2; xiv.8 [restored]; Rule of the Congregation 1Q28a i.7). In the last passage the reading is clearly *hhgy*, whereas in the first two it could be *hhgw* or *hhgy*, the letters *vav* and *yod* not being clearly differentiated by the scribe. The latter is favored by Elisha Qimron in his transcription of the Damascus Document (CD) in *The Damascus Document Reconsidered* (Jerusalem, 1992) and appears to be confirmed by fragments of the Damascus Document found in Cave 4 at Qumran (4Q266 8.iii.3.5; 4Q267 9.v.12; 4Q270 6.iv.17; see Baumgarten, 1996, p. 67).

In each occurrence, the expression is the object of study or learning. In the Damascus Document (CD), it is used to denote the expert learning of a leading priest, or judges, characterized as "learned (*mevonen*) in the Book of Meditation." In the Rule of the Congregation it refers to youth who are to be "instructed in the Book of Meditation." In two of the four passages (CD x.6; 1Q28a i.7), expertise or instruction in the Book of Hagu is to include communal laws, (*yesodei ha-berit*; *ḥuqqei ha-berit*); whereas in another passage (CD xiv.9 [restored]) it is linked to "all the judgments of the Torah (*mishpeṭei ha-torah*)."

Scholars have been divided about whether the phrase refers to what is elsewhere called "the Torah of Moses" (e.g., 1QS v.8; viii.22; CD xv.9 xv.12; xvi.2; xvi.5; 4Q266 11.8) or "the Book of Torah" (e.g., CD v.2; 4Q266 5.ii.2–3; 4Q177 3.14; 4Q396 10), or to some more esoteric, sectarian collection of rules, whether extant (e.g., the Temple Scroll [11Q19] or the Rule of the Community from Cave 1 [1QS]) or not.

While there is no consensus, most scholars appear to prefer the first alternative. In an apparent parallel to a sentence in the Damascus Document (CD xiii.2–3), "And in a place of ten, there shall not be lacking (*'al-yamush*) a priest learned in the Book of Meditation," we find, "And in the place where there are ten, there shall not be lacking (*'al-yamush*) a man who studies the Torah day and night continually" (1QS vi.6–8). Both passages are commonly understood to be reworkings of *Joshua* 1.8 (with an echo of Psalm 1.2), in which God charges Joshua: "Let this Book of Torah not cease (*lo' yamush*) from your lips, but recite (*hagita*) it day and night, so that you may observe faithfully all that is written in it." Thus it is argued that the Book of Torah, which is to be recited or meditated upon continually, is sometimes called "the Book of Meditation" in the Dead Sea Scrolls and set alongside the study of the community's own esoteric laws and teachings.

[*See also* Cairo Genizah; Damascus Document; *and* Rule of the Community.]

BIBLIOGRAPHY

Baumgarten, Joseph M., ed. *Qumran Cave 4, XIII: The Damascus Document (4Q266–273)*. Discoveries in the Judaean Desert, 18. Oxford, 1996.

Ginzberg, Louis. *An Unknown Jewish Sect*, pp. 49–51, 123–190, 197, 286. New York, 1976. Updated translation of German original, *Eine unbekannte jüdische Sekte*. New York, 1922. Based on three occurrences of the expression in the Damascus (Zadokite) Document, known prior to discovery of the Dead Sea Scrolls from Qumran. Takes the term to refer to an authoritative sectarian book of laws or legal scriptural interpretations.

Goshen-Gottstein, Moshe. "Sefer Hagu: The End of a Puzzle." *Vetus Testamentum* 8 (1958), 286–288. Understands the term to refer to a book containing the basic commandments and customs of the sect.

Rabinowitz, Isaac. "The Qumran Authors' *SPR HHGW/Y*." *Journal of Near Eastern Studies* 20 (1961), 109–114. Understands this expression to refer to the Hebrew scriptures, which the sect studied.

Wieder, Naphtali. *The Judean Scrolls and Karaism*, pp. 215–251. London, 1962. Understands the terms to refer to the Hebrew Bible as a whole.

Yadin, Yigael. *The Temple Scroll*. 3 vols., vol. 1, pp. 393–394. Jerusalem, 1983. Must refer to a sectarian book of laws or legal exegesis, perhaps to the Temple Scroll.

STEVEN D. FRAADE

HALAKHIC LETTER. *See* Miqtsat Ma'asei ha-Torah.

HALAKHIC WORKS. *See* Legal Works.

HASIDEANS. The Greek term *Asidaioi*, which is a transliteration of the Hebrew *ḥasidim* ("pious ones") and perhaps the Aramaic *ḥasidayya'*, is used to designate a specific group of Jews who participated in events at the time of the Maccabean Revolt. The three references to this body in the books of the *Maccabees* constitute the primary evidence for its existence: *1 Maccabees* 2.42, 7.13 and *2 Maccabees* 14.6. The textual evidence for their appearance in *1 Maccabees* 2.42 is not above dispute. While the name appears to be rooted in the use of the term *ḥasid* in the Hebrew scriptures, there is no evidence to postulate that Psalm 149.1 or other references in the *Psalms* should be taken as evidence for the existence of this group.

The term *ḥasidim* is found rather infrequently in the Qumran corpus. While the allusions in the Messianic Apocalypse (4Q521 2+4.ii.5, 7) and the Apocryphal Psalms[a] (11Q11 xviii.10, xix.7, xxii.3, 6) have sometimes been cited as evidence of this group, the fact that the term is used as a synonym for "the righteous," "the humble," and other such designations suggests a general reference to piety rather than to the group mentioned in *1* and *2 Maccabees*. Other references, such as those in the Florilegium (4Q174 6–7.3) and the Testimonia (4Q175 14), are merely biblical quotations. Possible allusions to the term in the Apocryphon of Moses (4Q377 2.i.8, 2.ii.12) and the Apocryphon of Joshua[a] (4Q378 26.6) are so fragmentary as to contribute little to the discussion. They do appear to contain the phrase *ish ḥasadim*, used to describe David in 4QMMT (398) 14–17.ii.1. The name *Ḥisday*, found on an ostracon from Qumran, is attested elsewhere as a common personal name from that era.

This group has often been viewed in modern scholarship as the forerunners of the Pharisees and the Essenes of the Second Temple period. Many scholars argue that the term *Essenoi* is derived from the plural form of the Aramaic term *ḥasya'*, the supposed equivalent of the Hebrew *ḥasid*. Due to their role in the events of the Maccabean era, scholars have also considered them to be part of the apocalyptic tradition. The frequent references to the *hosioi* (the Greek translation of *ḥasidim*) in the *Psalms of Solomon*, and especially to the "synagogue of the pious" in 17.16, have also been considered evidence of these connections. None of these identifications is beyond dispute.

The first reference in *1 Maccabees* 2.42 includes the *Ḥasidim* within the account of the growth and development of the Hasmonean movement. *1 Maccabees* 2.39–48 describes the origins of the Maccabean Revolt as stemming from the actions of Mattathias and his friends. The *Ḥasidim* are included among those forces which allied themselves with Mattathias after the king's troops attacked on the Sabbath those Jews who had fled to the wilderness for refuge, as described in *1 Maccabees* 2.29–38. The *Ḥasidim* are described in *1 Maccabees* 2.42 as *ischyroi dynamei*, usually translated "mighty warriors" but which could equally well refer to "mighty men," a group of leading citizens of Judea. The members of this elite group "offered themselves willingly for the Law," pledging to violate the prohibition instituted by Antiochus IV against its observance (*1 Mc.* 1.41–50). Included among the prohibitions were sacrifices and offerings in the Temple as well as the observance of Sabbaths, festivals, and the rite of circumcision.

The leading role of this group is attested in the story of *1 Maccabees* 7.12–18. In verse 12 they are identified as a "company of scribes" and in verse 13 they are said to be "first among the Israelites." The political significance, however, of this leading group is discounted by the pro-Hasmonean author of this dynastic history. The *Ḥasidim* are said to have trusted the "peaceable words" of Alcimus and Bacchides in verse 15, a confidence badly misplaced, since it resulted in the murder of sixty members of their company in one day (*1 Mc.* 7.16). Judas and his brothers had already rejected the "peaceable but treacherous words" of Alcimus and Bacchides in *1 Maccabees* 7.10–11. It appears that the trust of the *Ḥasidim* was based upon the presence of Alcimus, "a priest of the line of Aaron." The Hasmonean historian who authored *1 Maccabees* thought that the *Ḥasidim* naively trusted a Greek general due to the presence of a Jewish priest with the army. So the *Ḥasidim* are portrayed in this account as an important but misguided group of leaders at this crucial stage in Israelite history during which the foundation was laid for the establishment of the Hasmonean dynasty. The use in *1 Maccabees* 7.17 of Psalm 79.2–3 as a proof text explaining the fate of the *Ḥasidim* suggests that the author did regard them as legitimate martyrs on behalf of Israel.

The reference to the *Ḥasidim* in *2 Maccabees* 14.6 is placed in the context of a direct quotation attributed to Alcimus. Identifying Judah the Maccabee as their leader, Alcimus accuses the *Ḥasidim* of "fighting and causing insurrection, not permitting the kingdom to find stability." From the viewpoint of the epitomist of this history, this is a positive statement about Judah. The role of these leading citizens of Israel in the insurrection is used as evidence of the military leadership and accomplishments, as well as the piety and purity, of Judah the Maccabee, the hero of this account.

The appearance of the name in Greek transliteration rather than translation also attests its significance. At the very least, the translator of *1 Maccabees* in the second century BCE, the editor of *2 Maccabees*, and, almost certainly, Jason of Cyrene (whose five-volume history is summarized in *2 Maccabees*) understood the name to be a proper noun. Any argument that claims these references merely allude to pious Jews in general must be rejected on this account.

The foregoing description demonstrates that any simplistic presentation of the *Ḥasidim* as either pacifists who deviated from their basic ideology in support of Mattathias or as the religious wing of the revolution that broke ranks with the Hasmoneans when their religious objectives were accomplished does not find support in these sources. Clearly, the history of this important Jewish group is much more complicated than either of those perspectives would suggest. The details are, however, irretrievable from our limited sources. The literary evidence does not support a link between the *Ḥasidim* and the refugees in the desert "who were seeking righteousness and justice," described in *1 Maccabees* 2:29–38. This link has been regarded as a crucial piece of evidence for connecting the *Ḥasidim* with the Essenes.

References to the term *ḥasid* in both the singular and plural are to be found in early rabbinic literature. Individuals such as Ḥoni the Circle Drawer and Hillel the Elder bear this designation. While some scholars have considered Ḥanina ben Dosa, a miracle worker in the rabbinic tradition, to be a *ḥasid*, he is not referred to with this epithet in early rabbinic texts. Actions attributed to him resemble incidents and activities ascribed to the "early *Ḥasidim*" in related rabbinic accounts. The major references to the "first" or "early *Ḥasidim*," Mishnah, *Berakhot* 5.1, Tosefta, *Baba Qamma* 2.6, Babylonian Talmud *Niddah* 38a–b, Babylonian Talmud *Nedarim* 10a, and Babylonian Talmud *Menaḥot* 40b–41a, show that this group was used in the Talmudic tradition to demonstrate exemplary behavior rather than as authorities in Talmudic disputes or as evidence of a divergent halakhic tradition.

BIBLIOGRAPHY

Berman, Dennis. "Hasidim in Rabbinic Traditions." *Society of Biblical Literature Seminar Papers* 2 (1979), 2:15–33. Best recent analysis of rabbinic citations.

Black, Matthew. *The Scrolls and Christian Origins: Studies in the Jewish Background of the New Testament*. Brown Judaic Studies, 48. Chico, Calif. 1983. Reflects the earlier consensus concerning the relationship of the Essenes and the Hasidim.

Cross, Frank Moore. *The Ancient Library of Qumran*, 3d ed. Minneapolis, 1995. Revision of classic work which makes Essenes a development out of the Hasidic movement.

Davies, Philip R. "Ḥasidim in the Maccabean Period." *Journal of Jewish Studies* 28 (1977), 127–140. Good critical analysis of the references in Maccabees.

Hengel, Martin. *Judaism and Hellenism: Studies in their Encounter in Palestine during the Early Hellenistic Period*. Trans. by J. Bowden. 2 vols. Philadelphia, 1974. Classic study arguing the Hasidim are central for the development of Essenes and Pharisees and are authors of apocalyptic literature.

Jacobs, Louis. "The Concept of *Hasid* in the Biblical and Rabbinic Literatures." *Journal of Jewish Studies* 8 (1957), 143–154.

Kampen, John. *The Hasideans and the Origin of Pharisaism: A Study in 1 and 2 Maccabees*. Septuagint and Cognate Studies, 24. Atlanta, 1988. Monograph surveying all the literature on this subject and providing the basis for the viewpoint in this article.

Schwartz, Daniel R. "Hasidim in I Maccabees 2:42?" *Scripta Classica Israelitica* 13 (1994), 7–18. Argues that the best reading of the Greek text at *1 Maccabees* 2:42 does not include the *Ḥasidim*.

Sievers, Joseph. *The Hasmoneans and Their Supporters: From Mattathias to the Death of John Hyrcanus I*. South Florida Studies in the History of Judaism, no. 6. Atlanta, 1990. Contains an excursus on the *Ḥasidim* from pp. 38–40.

Stegemann, Hartmut. "The Qumran Essenes—Local Members of the Main Jewish Union in Late Second Temple Times." In *The Madrid Qumran Congress: Proceedings of the International Congress on the Dead Sea Scrolls Madrid 18–21 March 1991*, edited by Julio Trebolle Barrera and Luis Vegas Montaner, vol. 1, pp. 83–166. Leiden, 1992. Argues that the *Ḥasidim* were the major Jewish group in the desert and east of the Jordan during the Maccabean era.

JOHN I. KAMPEN

HASMONEANS are the family of priests who played the leading role in the Jewish rebellion against the Seleucid Empire (beginning in 167 BCE), an uprising that ultimately led to the establishment of an independent Jewish state. The origins of the title Hasmonean are unclear; while it was known to Josephus and frequently mentioned in rabbinic literature, the *Books of the Maccabees* and other sources of the Second Temple period make no reference to it. Josephus states that "Asamonaios" was the great-grandfather of Mattathias (*Jewish Antiquities* 12.265), and also claims that his own mother was a descendant of Asamonaois, whose offspring "for a very considerable period were kings, as well as high-priests, of our nation" (*Life* 2). Rabbinic literature refers at times to "[the Kingdom of] the House of Hashmonay" or "the Sons of Hashmonay," which merely suggests the name as that of an eponymous family ancestor. The text of the rabbinic prayer (*'Al ha-Nissim*) commemorating the victory of the Hasmoneans, however, refers to Mattathias as "son of Yohanan, great priest, Hashmonay and his sons," and this has led certain scholars to claim that the name was an additional one for Mattathias himself (Goldstein, 1976, p. 18, n. 34). Most scholars tend to view the title as alluding to a geographical origin, probably the village of Heshmon (*Jos.* 15.27).

The Hasmonean chapter in Jewish history can be divided into two sections: (a) the years of the revolt, beginning with the initial opposition of Mattathias to any submission to the religious decrees issued by Antiochus IV Epiphanes (168–167 BCE) and culminating with the removal of all vestiges of Seleucid political control in Judea

(142 BCE); and (b) the emergence of an independent Jewish state ruled by the descendants of Mattathias, initially in their capacity as high priests but at a later stage assuming royal title as well. The independent Hasmonean state was conquered by Pompey in 63 BCE, and the Hasmonean monarchy was also abolished at that time. However, a vassal Jewish state, ruled by Hyrcanus II as high priest and ethnarch, extended Hasmonean control of the Jewish portions of Judea until 40 BCE. The Parthian invasion and short-lived conquest of much of the Near East in 40 BCE restored Hasmonean glory to Judea, and for one final time a member of the family, Mattathias Antigonus, briefly ruled as king in Jerusalem. His defeat and the reconquest of the land by Rome (37 BCE), with the assistance of Herod, brought Hasmonean rule to a close, and Herod was appointed by Rome to succeed the Hasmoneans as king of Judea. The new king considered the Hasmoneans his natural enemies, and while his marriage to the Hasmonean Mariamme extended the family's prominence by a few generations, most notably through the reign of Agrippa I (41–44 CE), Herod would also be remembered in subsequent Jewish literature as the monarch who systematically persecuted the Hasmoneans (*Ass. Mos.* 6.2; B.T., *B. B.* 3b).

Unless stated otherwise, the following historical outline until the end of Simon's rule depends largely on the narrative of *1 Maccabees*, and thereafter on the accounts of Josephus. The first member of the Hasmonean family for whom we have any historical information is Mattathias, a priest of the prominent family of Joarib (*1 Chr.* 24.7), who settled at some unknown stage in the village of Modi'in (*1 Mc.* 2.1), on the border between Judea and Samaria. It was to this village that Greek officers were dispatched at the early stages of forced implementation of the religious decrees issued by Antiochus IV Epiphanes, and Mattathias is described as refusing the Greek request to set an example by submitting to the king's demands. Mattathias proceeded to kill both a potential Jewish collaborator as well as the Greek official on the scene, and this event was projected as the raising of the banner of rebellion against Seleucid attempts forcibly to change the religious character of the Jewish nation (*1 Mc.* 2.19–22).

Mattathias, his sons, and supporters abandoned Modi'in for the hills north of Jerusalem, and thus began a classic guerrilla war. The Jewish fighters appear initially devoid of any military tradition, and even refuse to defend themselves when attacked on the Sabbath, causing the deaths of one thousand Jewish men, women, and children. Mattathias is credited with proclaiming it permissible to fight when attacked on the Sabbath (*1 Mc.* 2.41), and the transition from episodic clashes and isolated opposition to an organized and popular uprising is formulated ideologically in Mattathias's deathbed exhortation to his five sons (166 BCE; *1 Mc.* 2.49–68). Of these, Judah Maccabee was appointed military leader, and his leadership raised the level of organized Jewish opposition.

Support for the Hasmonean uprising in the hills surrounding Jerusalem created a situation whereby the Greek garrison in the city, as well as the pro-Seleucid Jewish party in it, slowly found themselves under siege. For three years Seleucid armies attempted to link up with Jerusalem, but were repeatedly surprised and defeated by the growing forces under Judah's command. By December 164 BCE Judah was sufficiently in control of the area surrounding Jerusalem, and after retaking the city had the Temple cleansed of the various impurities introduced into it while under Hellenistic rule. The ensuing rededication of the Temple established the basis for the annual festival of Ḥanukkah, and in one sense marks the culmination of the initial stage of the Hasmonean uprising.

Under Judah, who continued to clash with Seleucid forces for the next four years (164–160 BCE), a gradual transition from religious uprising to a quest for national autonomy occurred. To this end, Judah entered into an alliance with Rome (161 BCE; *1 Mc.* 8), which shared, for its own reasons, the objective of weakening Seleucid control over the Near East. This alliance between Rome and the Hasmoneans was destined to become a mainstay of Hasmonean policy, both before and after the achievement of complete independence.

Judah's death in battle in 160 BCE served only to slow down Hasmonean progress toward independence. He was succeeded by Mattathias's remaining sons, Jonathan (160–142 BCE) and Simon (142–135 BCE), under whom the final steps were taken toward a complete removal of Seleucid rule in Judea. More than military genius, it was brilliant political instinct that now advanced Hasmonean goals. In particular, the growing weakness within the Seleucid monarchy provided the Hasmonean leaders with the opportunity to offer their support to one or another of a series of contenders to the Syrian throne, all of whom eagerly vied for such support by granting the Hasmonean brothers greater authority within Judea. In 152 BCE Jonathan was recognized as high priest by one of these Syrian pretenders, Alexander Balas (*1 Mc.* 10.18–20), and this office would remain in Hasmonean hands for more than a century, ending only in 35 BCE with the drowning in Jericho, under Herod's orders, of Aristobulus III, the last of the Hasmonean high priests.

Jonathan and Simon consolidated their position by annexing the districts of Lydda, Ramathaim, Ephraim, and Ekron, on the northern and western borders of Judea, to the territory already under their control. With the conquest of the port city of Jaffa, the Hasmoneans secured an outlet to the Mediterranean. Hasmonean designs on statehood also were evident through an active diplomatic initiative undertaken by Jonathan. Not only did he renew the pact with Rome (*1 Mc.* 12.1), but he also embarked on a correspondence with Sparta, in which it was even suggested that the two nations enjoyed a common kinship (*1 Mc.* 12.2–23). Indeed, it was this enhanced Hasmonean political fervor that momentarily proved their undoing. In 142 BCE, Jonathan was taken captive by the Syrian general Tryphon, a supporter of yet another Seleucid pretender, and ultimately executed. This setback, however, was shortlived, and immediately upon the succession of the last son of Mattathias, Simon, the final trappings of independence were achieved. In 142–141 BCE, Simon succeeded in gaining control of the Greek citadel in Jerusalem (*1 Mc.* 13.49–52), the last vestige of Seleucid rule in the land.

The establishment of Jewish independence under the Hasmoneans was formally recognized through a declaration issued by "a great synagogue of priests and people and leaders of the nation and elders of the community" that convened on the eighteenth day of Elul in "the third year of the reign of Simon the high priest" (140 BCE). The declaration in essence serves as the constitutional basis and formal recognition of the Hasmonean dynasty, both as political leaders as well as high priests "until a true prophet should arise" (*1 Mc.* 14.27–49). This last clause, which seems to downplay the overwhelming power now in Hasmonean hands, may in fact be an attempt at pacifying the first stirrings of opposition to the family, either for usurping the high priesthood or for joining that office with supreme political control over the nation. It is not surprising, therefore, that a majority of scholars have identified "the Wicked Priest who was called by the name of truth at the beginning, but when he ruled over Israel his heart became haughty" (Pesher Habakkuk [1QpHab] viii.8–13) as the Dead Sea sect's description of either Jonathan or Simon. The fact that the Wicked Priest also "took the wealth of the nations" might easily correspond to the conquests carried out by the last two sons of Mattathias, and inasmuch as this same priest is also accused of pursuing "the Teacher of Righteousness" (Pesher Habakkuk xi.5–8; Pesher Psalms[a] [4Q171] 1–10.iv.8–9), it is highly probable that the establishment of the Hasmonean state also served as one of the crucial junctures in the formation of the Dead Sea sect. These events may provide the backdrop for the composition of 4QMMT.

Pesher Habakkuk (1QpHab ix.8–12) claims that the Wicked Priest ultimately met with a violent end at the hands of his enemies, and indeed Simon, like his brother Jonathan, was also murdered, together with most of his sons, by his own son-in-law while at a feast at the Fortress of Duk overlooking Jericho (*1 Mc.* 16.16–21; some have connected Simon's murder with certain violent events at Jericho related in Apocryphon of Joshua[b] [4Q379] 22.ii.7–14 = Testimonia [4Q175] 21–40). One of Simon's sons, John Hyrcanus I (134–104 BCE) survived the massacre, and under his lengthy rule the Hasmonean state expanded significantly. In fact, it was under Hyrcanus I that major portions of Judea not inhabited by Jews now came under Hasmonean rule. These areas included Idumea, Samaria, and Scythopolis (Beth Shean) as well as portions of the Transjordan, and no less noteworthy is Hyrcanus's forcible conversion of the Idumeans to Judaism.

A major expression of Jewish independence under Hyrcanus I is the appearance for the first time of Hasmonean coins. The inscriptions on these early Hasmonean coins project the major components of Jewish sovereignty, for they mention "Johanan high priest and the congregation [or nation] of the Jews (*ḥever ha-yehudim*)." Some coins describe Hyrcanus as "head of the congregation of the Jews" (*ro'sh ḥever ha-yehudim*), and the monarchical implications in such titles may be one of the causes leading to the dissonance between the Hasmonean ruler and the Pharisees (*Jewish Antiquities* 13.288–296; compare B.T., *Qid.* 66a and B.T., *Ber.* 29a). Nevertheless, John Hyrcanus I is the first of the Hasmoneans (other than Mattathias) to be mentioned in rabbinic sources by name, with a number of references made to ordinances established by him in matters of Temple procedure (which may lie behind some matters discussed in the Temple Scroll[a] [11Q19] xxxiv) as well as regarding the tithing of agricultural produce (*Ma'as. Sh.* 5.15; T. *Sot.* 3.10). One legendary rabbinic source claims that John Hyrcanus I heard a voice from the sanctuary proclaim the victory of his sons in battle "at Antioch" (T., *Sot.* 13.5; cf. *Jewish Antiquities* 13.282–283), probably an allusion to their victory over Antiochus IX Cyzicenus at Samaria.

Hyrcanus's heir, Aristobulus I, ruled for only one year (104–103 BCE), during which the Hasmonean conquest of Galilee was completed. Like his father John Hyrcanus I, he too imposed conversion on a local Semitic tribe, in this case the Itureans, who had moved from the Lebanon into Northern Galilee (*Jewish Antiquities* 13.318). Josephus states that Aristobulus I was the first to place a royal crown on his head (*Jewish Antiquities* 13.301, *The Jewish War* 1.70) while the Greek geographer Strabo of Amaseia claims that it was his brother and successor Alexander Jannaeus who "was first to declare himself king instead of priest" (*Geography* 16.2.40). Scholars have attempted to reconcile these diverse claims by suggesting that the Hasmonean move to monarchy was carried out in stages: Aristobulus I assumed the title of king primarily for foreign consumption, while remaining high priest in Jewish eyes (hence the sole title of "high priest" on his coins), whereas Jannaeus completely transformed the government of Judea into a monarchy (Stern, 1974, p.

307). Jannaeus, in any case, proclaimed his royal status on his coins in Hebrew, Aramaic, and Greek, and so is the best candidate with whom "Jonathan the King" (probable reading) should be identified (Apocryphal Psalm and Prayer [4Q448] B2).

Under Alexander Jannaeus (103–76 BCE) the Hasmoneans reached the zenith of their power and territorial expansion. The entire coast of Palestine (save for Ashkelon) came under Jewish rule, as did many of the Greek cities of the Transjordan. However, Jannaeus's reign was marked by a period of internal dissension (90–83 BCE), possibly a result of opposition to his extended military campaigns, not all of which were successful, but also a reflection of growing displeasure with the direction that the Hasmonean dynasty had taken. Josephus describes the slaughter of thousands of Jews at the hands of Jannaeus (*Jewish Antiquities* 13.376), and even relates that Jews joined the forces of the Seleucid King Demetrius III Eukerus (95–88 BCE) in his campaign against the Hasmonean king. These rebels were ultimately defeated by Jannaeus, who reportedly had eight hundred of them crucified (*Jewish Antiquities* 13.380). The events are almost certainly alluded to in Pesher Nahum, which describes "[Deme]trius, king of Greece, who sought to enter Jerusalem with the counsel of the interpreters of false laws" and who also made war "against the Lion of Wrath" (Pesher Nahum, 4Q169 3–4.i.2–6). The "Lion of Wrath," almost universally assumed to be Jannaeus, took revenge "in that he hanged men alive" (Pesher Nahum, 4Q169 3–4.i.7–8), descriptions all closely mirroring those of Josephus. The Hasmonean state, in its final stages, indeed takes on a decidedly negative appearance in the writing of Josephus, but this fact must be tempered by the realization that Josephus's primary source for this era was not a Jewish one, but rather Nicolaus of Damascus, the court historian and ally of Herod, and certainly not one expected to portray the Hasmoneans in a positive light (Stern, 1974, p. 230). Jannaeus's attitude and exploits or those of his father may have provoked some of the restrictions on the king aspired to in the "Law of the King" (Temple Scroll^a, 11Q19 lvi.12–lix).

Jannaeus was succeeded by his widow Shelamzion Alexandra (76–67 BCE), who is mentioned in Calendrical Document C^a (4Q322) ii.4 and Calendrical Document C^c (4Q324b) 1.ii.7. Save for isolated forays (an attempt to capture Damascus) the queen's rule was for the most part peaceful. Some internal unrest resulted from her decision to join ranks with the Pharisees. They may now have tried to settle old scores with their opponents, who had earlier enjoyed considerable influence under previous Hasmonean rulers. Later rabbinic sources, not surprisingly, portrayed Shelamzion's rule in idyllic colors (B.T., *Ta'an.* 23a). In fact, however, harbingers of the demise of the state began to appear during her rule. Her sons Hyrcanus II and Aristobulus II were already jockeying for position, and upon her death Aristobulus assumed power forcibly. His elder brother, Hyrcanus, was convinced by Antipater, the governor of Idumea, not to concede his rightful claim to the high priesthood, and the years 67–63 BCE were marked by civil war. The dispute was resolved with the appearance of Roman legions in Judea under the command of Pompey, who was probably accompanied by Aemilius Scaurus (cf. Calendrical Document C^d, 4Q324a 2.iv.8). Hyrcanus II was granted the high priesthood, Aristobulus and his sons were taken prisoner, and most of the non-Jewish territories conquered by Hyrcanus's predecessors were now torn from the truncated Hasmonean vassal state established by Pompey. Opponents to the Roman conquest would nevertheless continue to rally around the Aristobulan branch of the Hasmonean family, and the legacy of the Hasmonean era assumed a significance far exceeding the years of independent statehood. The success of the Hasmonean rebellion and the state that followed in its wake preserved Jewish self-identity for more than a century, and the failure of Roman attempts to divide the nation into separate administrative districts (under Gabinius, 57–55 BCE) attests to the Hasmonean success in forging a common Jewish identity throughout their territories. This legacy assured an enduring Jewish presence in Judea.

BIBLIOGRAPHY

Bar-Kochva, Bezalel. *Judas Maccabaeus: The Jewish Struggle against the Seleucids.* Cambridge, 1989. A biography of the heroic leader of the Hasmonean uprising in its earliest stages, the work represents a critical appraisal of the historicity of the accounts in *1 Maccabees.* A major stress is placed on an analysis of the military history of the uprising.

Bickerman, Elias. *The God of the Maccabees: Studies on the Meaning and Origin of the Maccabean Revolt.* Leiden, 1979. An attempt to determine the sequence of events leading to the Hasmonean uprising, with special attention to the nature of the Jewish parties that aimed at a reform of the ancestral faith in the spirit of Hellenism.

Efron, Joshua. *Studies on the Hasmonean Period.* Leiden, 1987. Collected studies on various stages of the Hasmonean period as shaped through ancient and modern historiography.

Goldstein, Jonathan A. *I Maccabees.* Garden City, N.Y., 1976. An introduction, translation, and exhaustive commentary on the primary source for the first stage of the Hasmonean period.

Mendels, Doron. *The Land of Israel as a Political Concept in Hasmonean Literature.* Tübingen, 1987. A study of the role of biblical attitudes toward the Land of Israel in the literature describing the Hasmonean uprising, and in books written at various stages of the Hasmonean era.

Meshorer, Ya'akov. *Ancient Jewish Coinage*, vol. 1, *Persian Period through Hasmoneans*, pp. 35–98. Dix Hills, N.Y., 1982. A comprehensive description of all the numismatic material from the Hasmonean state, with discussions of the inscriptions, titles, symbols, characteristics, and groupings of Hasmonean coins.

Rajak, Tessa. "The Hasmoneans and the Uses of Hellenism." In *A Tribute to Geza Vermes: Essays on Jewish and Christian Literature and History*, edited by Philip R. Davies and Richard T. White, pp. 261–280. Sheffield, 1990. An analysis of the validity of the common distinction between Hellenism and Judaism, with a focus on the "Hellenization" of the Hasmoneans.

Schürer, Emil. *The History of the Jewish People in the Age of Jesus Christ (175 B.C.–A.D. 135)*. New English edition by G. Vermes et al., vol. 1, pp. 125–286. Edinburgh, 1973. An updated version of one of the most thorough histories of the period, with bibliographies and discussions on all aspects of the Hasmonean period.

Shatzman, Israel. *The Armies of the Hasmoneans and Herod*, pp. 1–125. Tübingen, 1991. An analysis of the military achievements of the Hasmoneans, from the earliest stages of the revolt under Judah until the major conquests of Jannaeus.

Sievers, J. *The Hasmoneans and Their Supporters, from Mattathias to the Death of John Hyrcanus I*. Atlanta, 1990.

Stern, Menahem. "The Hasmonean Revolt and Its Place in the History of Jewish Society and Religion." In *Jewish Society through the Ages*, edited by H. H. Ben-Sasson and S. Ettinger, pp. 92–106. London, 1971. An appraisal of the significance of the Hasmonean episode for the survival of the Jewish religion, and the role it played in the reshaping of Jewish society.

Stern, Menahem. *Greek and Latin Authors on Jews and Judaism*, vol. 1. Jerusalem, 1974.

Tcherikover, Victor. *Hellenistic Civilization and the Jews*, pp. 1–265. Philadelphia, 1959. A survey of the history of Palestine from the Hellenistic conquest under Alexander the Great until the end of the Hasmonean state. Tcherikover presents a novel approach to understanding the events leading up to religious persecution under Antiochus IV, with major implications for appraising the nature of the pro-Hellenistic Jewish party in Jerusalem.

ISAIAH M. GAFNI

ḤAVERIM. The term *ḥaver* was used in Jewish society during the last decades of the Second Temple period and apparently occurs only in sources compiled after 70 CE. It refers in particular to a male individual who belonged to a *ḥavurah* (fellowship), which was very strict about the setting aside of *terumot* (priestly portions) and *maʿaserot* (tithes), as well as about the observance of the laws of ritual purity. Organization into *ḥavurot* was an accepted phenomenon at the time for meeting certain mutual needs or achieving certain common ideals. Some of these *ḥavurot* had rules and ways of living that required segregation and even total withdrawal from normative society, as with the Judean Desert sect, while other *ḥavurot* continued to live in settled areas and within the community. These latter included *ḥaverim*, who formed a kind of elite stratum among the Pharisees.

There is relatively little evidence on the customs, lifestyle, and day-to-day life of these *ḥavurot* because no book or document written by a *ḥaver* has survived with evidence of this kind. Evidence about the *ḥavurah* is all drawn from Talmudic literature, which for the most part reflects the period after the destruction of the Second Temple. Moreover, the obligations undertaken by the members of the *ḥavurah* did not usually become religious laws that were binding on most Jews, and were never a central concern in the discussion of the sages. In a number of places in Talmudic literature, however, collections of religious laws have been preserved, which include the obligations of a *ḥaver* and the conditions for his acceptance into a *ḥavurah* (M. *Dem.* 2.2–3; T., *Dem.* 2.2–3, 15, [Lieberman edition, pp. 68–77]; J.T., *Dem.* 2.22d–23a; B.T., *Bekh.* 30b–31a). The majority of these religious laws and sayings present *ḥaverim* in contrast with the *ʿammei ha-ʾarets*, Jews who were defined in the Second Temple period as people who neglected precisely those areas of religious law that the *ḥaverim* observed with the greatest stringency. Thus, the *ḥaver* stands at the top of the social scale in the eyes of Pharisaic religious law, while the *ʿammei ha-ʾarets* are considered to be at the bottom.

A candidate for membership in a *ḥavurah* had to undergo a probationary period. During this time, he gradually took on the obligations of a *ḥaver*, and correspondingly gradually joined in and was accepted as a member of the *ḥavurah*. These conditions of membership were obligatory for all candidates, even sages. The sources do not give an exact description of the entry stages and how long they lasted. Nevertheless, it is clear that the criterion for the graduated entry into the *ḥavurah* was the extent of the stringency with which the laws of purity were observed. There is a considerable degree of similarity between the entry stages described in the collections of religious laws noted above, and the levels of impurity in Pharisaic law, so that a person outside the *ḥavurah* who was not scrupulous about the laws of purity was considered to be a generator of impurity (*av ha-ṭumʾah*), like a man with a genital discharge, and was defined as an *ʿam ha-ʾarets*. A candidate for membership in a *ḥavurah* at the beginning of his probationary period was considered to be subject to the first degree of impurity, by which he conveyed impurity to ordinary things. He was therefore forbidden to come near the pure *ḥavurah* at this stage. In the second stage of his probationary period, he was considered to be subject to the second degree of impurity, whereby he no longer conveyed impurity to food and utensils, so he was now allowed to approach the pure *ḥavurah*. However, he was still liable to contaminate drink, for the laws of purity are more stringent about liquids than about solid food. Consequently, he was still not allowed to touch liquids belonging to the *ḥavurah*. After he had undergone all the stages of acceptance, the candidate became a *ḥaver*: he was considered completely free of all impurity, and was accepted into the *ḥavurah* with all the obligations and rights of a full member.

Some scholars think that the halakhic commitment undertaken by the members of a *ḥavurah* was no stricter than normative halakhic practice and that the main goal of forming these fellowships was to make it easier for the members to observe the laws of the Torah as the Pharisees interpreted them. But the stringent long-drawn-out acceptance procedures, and the situation reflected in the various religious laws, which mention the obligations of a *ḥaver* and the lifestyle of a *ḥavurah*, produce what is almost a picture of life in a total institution. The conclusion to be drawn is that the *ḥavurah* took on themselves exceptional stringencies in various areas, and especially in the laws of purity and impurity, where the peak of their achievement was eating ordinary nonconsecrated food in a state of total purity. Their extreme scrupulousness about ritual purity in their daily lives was normally only demanded of priests in connection with the Temple rites and with the eating of consecrated food.

It is very probable that the *ḥavurah* held communal meals, as has been implied already in the stages of acceptance to the *ḥavurah*. The term *ḥavurah* is often mentioned in Talmudic literature with reference to communal meals. Thus the Mishnah mentions meals held by a *ḥavurah* in connection with the sanctification of the month (*San.* 8.2) was well as the *ḥavurot* who ate the Passover meal together (e.g., *Pes.* 7.13; 8.4) and so on. Communal meals are known among the Essenes and the Judean Desert sect; the early Christians also held communal meals, as did some pagan societies, such as the Nabateans. At Petra, the Nabatean capital, special rooms have been found cut out of the rock for this purpose. Judaism gave a value of its own to these communal meals, in that their ceremonial aspects were compared to the rites of sacrifice in the Temple, so that the table was seen as equivalent to the altar and the grace before and after the meal was parallel to the prayers before and after the offering. The formal invitation to the grace after meals was largely intentionally produced for the communal meals of the *ḥavurah*.

As a member of a *ḥavurah*, a *ḥaver* had to be scrupulous in carrying out his obligations and also had to relate with the strictest discipline toward his *ḥavurah* and its institutions. A *ḥaver* was obliged to give a full account of his actions: as the Jerusalem Talmud puts it, he was to "answer to the *ḥavurah*" (J.T., *Dem.* 2, 23a). If he departed from the principles laid down by the *ḥavurah*, he was liable to sanctions and punishment. In extreme cases he was excluded from the social framework of the *ḥavurah*: "They send him away from his *ḥavurah*" (J.T., *Dem.* 2, 23a), and in some instances he was not allowed to atone for his actions and be reinstated. The members of a *ḥavurah* kept their own property and had the right to own land and slaves. They continued to have reciprocal relations with neighbors who did not belong to a *ḥavurah*, but they were careful not to contract impurity from them or to receive untithed produce. *Ḥaverim* also preserved the framework of the family. The wife of a *ḥaver*, his nuclear family, and his slaves had to take on themselves all the principles that were obligatory for the *ḥavurah*. However, they were not obliged to go through a period of candidacy or trial, but had to promise the *ḥaver*, who was master of their household, that they would carry out these obligations. They were accountable to him, not to the institutions of the *ḥavurah*. Thus, they formed a sort of periphery to the *ḥavurah* and belonged to it passively; all relations with it were via the *ḥaver* who was head of the family. Thus it is clear that the *ḥavurot* preferred to preserve the framework of the family rather than adopt the stricter policy of celibacy.

There is a great deal of similarity between the description of the *ḥavurot* in Talmudic literature and between the membership conditions, obligations, and customs of the Judean Desert sect. In particular, scholars agree that *ḥaverim* are similar to the members of the community of the *yaḥad*, whose rules are to be found in the Rule of the Community (*Serekh ha-Yaḥad*). A comparison of the conditions for membership makes it clear that, both in the case of the *ḥaverim* and in the case of the Judean Desert community, there was a public undertaking of the obligations of the *ḥavurah*; a period of learning the rules; a trial period and graduated acceptance based on the measure of reliability in the area of purity; and a final stage of acceptance, which allowed the new member access to liquids (see the Rule of the Community vi.14–23; compare also the entry conditions of the Essenes [*The Jewish War* 2.137–142]). The central importance of communal meals is noteworthy both with the *ḥaverim* and with the Judean Desert sect.

In spite of these similarities, the contention that the *ḥavurot* and their members are identical to the Judean Desert sect cannot be upheld. First, it should be noted that such comparisons must by their nature be forced because the surviving evidence is so fragmentary and lacking in particulars, and because everything related to *ḥaverim* is contained in works edited at the earliest well over a hundred years after the time of the *ḥavurot*. Second, even the evidence that has been preserved points to essential differences between the *ḥaverim* and the sect. The most essential of these differences is the way in which the sect broke away from normative Jewish society as well as its ascetic way of life (it is probable that there were no women in the dominant group of the sect, for they are not mentioned in some sources), and its communal ownership of the use of property (according to the majority of scholars). *Ḥaverim*, in contrast, remained part of their hometowns and villages, maintained their families and their private property, and participated in local life.

A particular phenomenon among the *ḥavurot* who continued to be part of normative society were those *ḥavurot* whose rules and lifestyles included social and religious obligations to the community within which they lived.

The outstanding examples of this are the "*ḥavurot* which were in Jerusalem," which worked for the good of the general Jewish community and its poor. There is evidence about these *ḥavurot* from Rabbi Eleazar the son of Rabbi Zadok, who was active around the time of the destruction of the Temple and in the Yavneh period (after 70 CE), and who provides many descriptions of the customs of different groups in Jerusalem at the end of the Second Temple period.

"Rabbi Eleazar the son of Rabbi Zadok said: 'The *ḥavurot* which were in Jerusalem used to operate like this: some [helped] with meals to celebrate engagements, some with wedding meals, some with circumcision feasts and some with collecting bones, some [helped] with celebrations and others with mourning'" (T., *Meg.* 3.15; Lieberman edition p. 357). These *ḥavurot* were typified by the help they gave to the individual in the community in times of joy and sorrow (cf. the work of the *beit ha-ḥever* of Damascus Document[a] [4Q266] 10.i.10). They contributed to the ritually prescribed feasts celebrated by the individual, as well as providing for the needs of the sick and the bereaved. Indeed, there are parallels between the communal meals that were a central part of the lifestyle of *ḥaverim* and the ritually prescribed meals in which the "*ḥavurot* which were in Jerusalem" took part. In the Damascus Document[a] (4Q266 10.i.10) the rules for groups related to the *yaḥad* in some way include one mention of the communal house (*beit ha-ḥever*), which is the focus for the care of the disadvantaged members of the group; this is the only instance of a phrase terminologically comparable with the *ḥavurah* of later rabbinic sources. It is necessary to understand "the counsel of the joint communal body of Israel" (*ʿatsat ḥever yisrael*: Damascus Document[b] [4Q267] 9.iii.3 = CD xii.8 [*ḥavur*]) in some other way, perhaps as comparable with the designation *ḥever ha-yehudim* on Hasmonean coins.

Another term that is connected both to *ḥaverim* and to the "*ḥavurot* which were in Jerusalem" is *ḥever ʿir*, which appears to be defined as *ḥavurah*, rather than an individual, in relation to a town or village. From the sources it is clear that the *ḥever ʿir* carried out certain functions in the local leadership of the settlements. The *ḥever ʿir* is mentioned in religious laws dealing with mourning, so that it is clear that this institution was engaged in charitable activities. It was also active in carrying out the religious laws that depend on settlement in the Land of Israel and have social repercussions, like the poor man's tithe and the sabbatical year. Religious law stresses the special place of the *ḥever ʿir* in the synagogue and in relation to the prayers. Here, too, there is a connection between the *ḥever ʿir* and the "*ḥavurot* which were in Jerusalem," for Rabbi Eleazar the son of Rabbi Zadok notes that the people in Jerusalem who engaged in social help were connected with the synagogue (T., *Suk.* 2.10, Lieberman edition p. 265), and it would appear that he is referring to the "*ḥavurot* which were in Jerusalem." There are also similarities between *ḥaverim* and the "*ḥavurot* which were in Jerusalem," and between the early *ḥasidim*. All of these groups stress the importance of help for the individual in social and communal life. [*See* Hasideans.]

Another socially active group that appears to be connected to *ḥaverim* and to the "*ḥavurot* which were in Jerusalem" is that of the "pure-minded of Jerusalem," whose actions are highly praised. Communal meals are noted among their customs (for example: B.T., *San.* 23a), and they too were to be found in Jerusalem. Jerusalem at the end of the Second Temple period was a spiritual center for different groups of *ḥavurot*, another facet of the city's special status as a socially unifying force.

It is especially interesting to compare the two extremes of the social spectrum, the *ḥaverim* and the *ʿammei ha-ʾarets*, and the way they related to each other before and after the destruction of the Temple. The *ḥaverim* of Temple times kept their distance from the *ʿammei ha-ʾarets*, but this was simply because they did not want to be contaminated with impurity or to receive untithed produce. Religious law recognized the possibility of forming family ties between *ḥaverim* and *ʿammei ha-ʾarets*, and there are records of *ḥaverim* and *ʿammei ha-ʾarets* who lived as very close neighbors. After the destruction of the Temple, when the study of the Torah took pride of place in Jewish life instead of the Temple and the laws connected with it (such as offerings, ritual purity, and tithes), the terms used to describe different classes of the community changed accordingly. The term *ḥaver*, used in connection with tithes and purity, disappeared. Its place in society was taken over by the learned sage, who then took over the title *ḥaver* as well: "There are no *ḥaverim* apart from the sages," states the Babylonian Talmud (B.T., *B.B.* 70a). In contrast, the term *ʿam ha-ʾarets* became a description of an ignoramus, far removed from the world of Torah study. The tolerance shown by the *ḥaverim* in their relations with the *ʿammei ha-ʾarets* at the end of the Second Temple period gave way to mutual hatred between the sages and the illiterate *ʿammei ha-ʾarets* after the destruction.

It is not possible to pinpoint the exact time when the *ḥaverim* and *ḥavurot* began to appear during the Second Temple period, but the spread of the phenomenon probably took place in the period's last decades. This was a time of institutional decline and decay, which also gave rise to sectarianism, preparing the ground for the appearance of different sorts of groups. Indeed, some of the disagreements between the schools of Hillel and Shammai include religious laws that deal with *ḥaverim*. The destruction of the Temple brought about the decline of the *ḥavurot*: the *ḥavurah* ceased to be the definitive form of organization, and its place was taken by the community. But the ideals of the *ḥaverim* and the "*ḥavurot* which were in Jerusalem" continued to exist, and they are found to a certain extent in the world of the sages, to a greater extent among the circles of *ḥasidim* who operated on the fringes of that world, and to an even greater extent in various sporadic phenomena like the *ḥavurah* that was called the "Holy Community of Jerusalem." This *ḥavurah* was active in Jerusalem in the days of Rabbi Judah ha-Nasi [the Patriarch] more than a hundred years after the destruction of the Temple.

BIBLIOGRAPHY

Alon, Gedaliahu. "The Bounds of the Laws of Levitical Cleanness." In *Jews and Judaism and the Classical World*, pp. 190–234. Jerusalem, 1977.

Heinemann, Joseph. "Birkath ha-Zimmun and Ḥavurah Meals." *Journal of Jewish Studies* 13 (1962), 23–29.

Oppenheimer, Aharon. *The ʿAm ha-Aretz: A Study in the Social History of the Jewish People in the Hellenistic-Roman Period*, pp. 118–179. Leiden, 1977.

Oppenheimer, Aharon. "Benevolent Societies in Jerusalem at the End of the Second Temple Period." In *Intertestamental Essays in Honour of Józef T. Milik*, edited by Z. J. Kapera, pp. 149–165. Kraków, 1992.

Neusner, Jacob. "The Fellowship in the Second Jewish Commonwealth." *HTR* 53 (1960), 125–142.

Neusner, Jacob. "ḤBR and N'MN." *Revue de Qumrân* 5 (1964), 119–127.

Neusner, Jacob. "Fellowship through Law: The Ancient Ḥavurah." In *Contemporary Judaic Fellowship in Theory and in Practice*, edited by J. Neusner, pp. 13–30. New York, 1972.

Spiro, Solomon J. "Who Was the Ḥaver? A New Approach to an Ancient Institution." *Journal for the Study of Judaism* 11 (1980), 186–216.

Urbach, Ephraim E. *The Sages: Their Concepts and Beliefs*, pp. 582–642. Jerusalem, 1987.

AHARON OPPENHEIMER

HEALING. Historical demographers agree that the average life expectancy of prehistoric and early historic peoples was less than thirty years, perhaps substantially less. Where mortality rates are high, the health of the living is likewise poor. The majority of inhabitants of the Mediterranean region in the Greco-Roman period, especially those who lived in cities, suffered from one chronic health problem or another; sickness was everywhere.

Eye diseases, skin rashes, and missing limbs are mentioned again and again in ancient sources describing urban life. Contracts of the period described the parties involved in terms of disfigurements, mostly scars, for purposes of identification One papyrus in particular (*P.Abinn.* 67.v) comprises a fairly long list of debtors, all of whom were scarred. Further, ancient letter writers constantly mention matters of health, both their own and that of their recipients. Formulas such as the Latin *salve* were not polite banalities—they were often expressions of real concern. Women were particularly afflicted by ill health because of infections that accompanied childbirth and abortion. Given this dismal reality, it is only to be expected that healing would be a central aspect of both paganism and Judaism. Numerous Dead Sea Scrolls touch on the matter from a variety of perspectives.

In Judaism, poor health was often equated with sin. Numerous precedents could be drawn from the Hebrew scriptures to support this outlook: the plague that followed David's census, for example (*2 Sm.* 24). New Testament authors certainly believed in this equation: "Therefore, confess your sins to one another, and pray for one another, that you may be healed" (*Jas.* 5.16). The assumption behind this exhortation is that if one can somehow expunge sin, health will return. The equation of forgiveness with healing—often to be accomplished through prayer—appears at more than one juncture in the Dead Sea Scrolls. The clearest passage lies in the Genesis Apocryphon (1QapGen xx.21–29 [xxi.21–29, if 1Q20 fragments are included as the original column]).

The story is told of Pharaoh's taking Sarai from Abram. [*See* Abraham; Sarah.] Pharaoh and his court are then stricken with disease—gonorrhea, perhaps—and no Egyptian medicine successfully cures the condition. A courtier of the pharaoh, Hyrcanos, discovers that the seizure of Sarai lies behind the problem and comes to Abram:

> Then Hyrcanos came to me, asking me to come pray for the king, and to lay hands upon him and cure him—for [he had seen me] in a dream. . . . Hyrcanos told the king, "All these smitings and plagues by which my lord the king has been smitten and afflicted are because of Sarai, the wife of Abram! Let him return Sarai to Abram, her husband, and this plague will depart from you, that is, the spirit causing the discharges of pus." So he called me to himself and asked me, "What have you done to me because of your wife [Sar]ai? . . . Here she is; take her, go. . . . But first, pray for me and my house that this evil spirit may be exorcised from us." So I prayed for him, that blasphemer, and laid my hands upon his [he]ad. Thereupon the plague was removed from him, the evil [spirit] exorcised [from him,] and he was healed.

A further aspect of healing in the scrolls, and in Judaism more generally, is prominent here: an evil spirit as the agent of disease. To be cured, one must be forgiven of the sin that was the root cause, but one had also to deal with the evil spirit(s). That might involve exorcism, as in the Genesis Apocryphon above or the Prayer of Nabonidus below.

Nabonidus, the last of the Neo-Babylonian kings, is portrayed as describing what happened to him while he was in Teima:

> [I, Nabonidus,] was smitten [with severe inflammation] lasting seven years. Beca[use] I was thus changed, [becoming like a beast, I prayed to the most high,] and he forgave my sins.

> An exorcist—a Jew, in fact, a mem[ber of the community of exiles—came to me and said,] "Declare and write down this story, and so ascribe glory and gre[at]ness to the name of [God most high"]. (4Q242 i–iii.2–5)

The connection between sin and disease is very clear in the Prayer of Nabonidus, but less clear is the role of the exorcist. Some scholars reconstruct and read the text differently, with the result that the exorcist, not God, is the one forgiving the king's sin. Given the fragmentary textual remains, the debate cannot be settled decisively, but it does seem unlikely that any Jewish text of the period would suggest that someone other than God could forgive sin. In reply, of course, advocates of the forgiving exorcist point to the Gospels and Jesus's claiming the power to do just that.

Proverbs(?) (4Q560) concerns itself with the prevention of demon possession rather with than its treatment. The work is actually not a collection of proverbs, as it was once supposed, but an apotropaic formula(s) for protection against demons. The surviving rubric mentions childbirth and attendant health concerns, consumption or tuberculosis, fevers, chills, and chest pain—all addressed as their eponymous demons. The author adjures them in "[the Name of YHVH, 'He who re]moves iniquity and transgression'" (*Ex.* 34.7). Songs of the Sage[a–b] (4Q510–511) and Apocryphal Psalms[a] (11Q11) are similarly involved with the binding of demons to prevent sin and disease.

In Songs of the Sage[a] the *maskil* ("instructor," an officer of the sect or sects that composed some of the scrolls) declares "I, the *maskil*, proclaim His [God's] glorious splendor, so as to frighten and te[rrify] all the spirits of the destroying angels, and of the bastards, demons, Lilith, howlers and [desert dwellers . . .] and those who fall upon men without warning, to lead them astray from a spirit of understanding . . ." (4Q510 i.4–6). Having sinned, of course, people would be subject to punishment in the form of disease; better to prevent the entire cycle before it begins. So, too, Apocryphal Psalms[a], which preserves an incantation attributed to David and intended to be uttered against Resheph, an ancient Semitic deity whom the Jews now cast as a demon. Here the chief weapon is mockery: "Who are you? [Withdraw from] humanity and from the ho[ly] race. For your appearance is [nothing], and your horns are horns of sand" (11Q11 iv.6–7). It has been suggested that the apotropaic psalms of Apocryphal Psalms[a] are those mentioned at the conclusion of Psalms[a] (11Q5). Here, included in a list of writings attributed to David, one reads of "four songs for charming the demon-possessed with music" (11Q5 xxvii.10). In light of the extremely fragmentary condition of Apocryphal Psalms[a], however, this possibility must remain only that.

An intriguing and almost universally misunderstood passage on the legal aspects of demonic possession and healing appears in one of the central sectarian works, the Damascus Document. It reads:

> Any man whom the spirits of Belial rule so that he preaches apostasy shall be judged in accordance with the law of the necromancer and the medium. But anyone he leads astray so as to profane the Sabbath or the festivals should not be executed; rather, his confinement becomes a human responsibility. If then he should be healed of it (the evil spirit), then they must observe him for seven years (to assure proper behavior). Afterwards, he may re-enter the congregation. (CD xii.2–6)

The "law of the necromancer and the medium" is an allusion to *Leviticus* 20.27, which requires that such people be stoned to death. The phrase "preaches apostasy" is a reference to *Deuteronomy* 13.6, a passage describing prophets or diviners who "preach apostasy" and must therefore be purged from Israel. False prophets were thought to operate under the influence of evil spirits, as did mediums, diviners, and necromancers; they must all be executed in the same manner. The content of the apostasy is defined: breach of laws that would result in profanation of the Sabbath or festivals. Included in such preaching of apostasy would be advocacy of the false (Pharisaic) calendar. [*See* Calendars and Mishmarot.] Members of the group who fell under the inimical influence of false prophets were not to suffer the same penalty as the prophets themselves. Being deceived in such a way was only possible, it was believed, because a person was possessed by demons—"led astray" (compare the wording of the Damascus Document text with that of 4Q510 above). The hope was that such victims might be healed, presumably by exorcism, though the passage does not specify the means.

Finally, there is a significant passage in the scrolls that refers to the healing of mortal wounds, even resurrection from the dead, in the messianic era. In reference to the coming of "God's messiah," the scroll Messianic Apocalypse describes a wondrous era when God will "honor the pious upon the th[ro]ne of his eternal kingdom" (4Q521 ii.7). At that time, God or his messianic agent (certainty about which is precluded because of damage to the text, though of course God is involved either way) will "heal the mortally wounded, revive the dead, [and] bring glad tidings to the poor" (ii.12). This description of the messianic era, it has been noted, is precisely that of the Gospels at a certain juncture (*Mt.* 11.4–6, *Lk.* 7.22–23 [Q source]). In that day, impossible healings would become possible, for God himself would act.

In view of the frequent connection made between the scrolls and the Essenes, this discussion would not be complete without noting the suggestion of Geza Vermes, that the term *Essene* derives etymologically from an Aramaic term for healing, *ʾasa*. No linguistic obstacle disallows this possibility. On the other hand, the Aramaic word in question occurs only a few times in the scrolls (in the Genesis Apocryphon) and is never used in the sectarian texts at all, much less as a self-designation for the group.

BIBLIOGRAPHY

Fitzmyer, Joseph A. *The Genesis Apocryphon of Qumran Cave I: A Commentary.* 2d rev. edition. Biblica et Orientalia, 18A. Rome, 1971. Detailed commentary on the entire text, including the passage on exorcism and healing discussed above. Includes full bibliography on the passage as well.

Hogan, Larry P. *Healing in the Second Temple Period.* Novum Testamentum et orbis antiquus, 21. Göttingen, 1992. Very useful collection of relevant references.

MacMullen, Ramsay. *Paganism in the Roman Empire.* New Haven, 1981. At more than a dozen points, MacMullen touches on healing in the context of various Greco-Roman cults.

Nitzan, Bilhah. "Hymns from Qumran: 4Q510–511." *The Dead Sea Scrolls: Forty Years of Research,* edited by Devorah Dimant and Uriel Rappaport, pp. 53–63. Leiden and Jerusalem, 1992. Brief discussion of the texts and their import for healing, with guidance to fuller and more technical discussions.

Penney, Douglas L., and Michael O. Wise. "By the Power of Beelzebub: An Aramaic Incantation Formula from Qumran (4Q560)." *Journal of Biblical Literature* 113 (1994), 627–650. Full analysis of 4Q560 in the context of ancient Near Eastern and Greco-Roman incantations against demons. Makes the argument that the text is indeed an incantation, not a collection of proverbs.

Stark, Rodney. *The Rise of Christianity: A Sociologist Reconsiders History.* Princeton, 1996. Chapters four and seven discuss aspects of health and healing in the Greco-Roman world, with particular application to earliest Christianity and the Judaism out of which it arose. Excellent for its detailed description of the poor state of health of individuals.

Wise, Michael. "The Messiah at Qumran." *Biblical Archaeology Review* 18.6 (1992), 60–65. An accessible discussion of 4Q521 and the passage about healing and resurrection, exploring the connections with the Gospels.

MICHAEL O. WISE

HEAVEN. In contrast to the speculations about the contents and spatial configuration of the heavens that one finds in many apocalypses (e.g., *1 Enoch, 2 Enoch, 2 Baruch, Apocalypse of Abraham, Testament of Abraham*), sectarian literature from the Dead Sea Scrolls shows comparatively little interest in such matters. Presumably, the descriptive tradition of apocalypticism was known to the Qumran community, since copies of *1 Enoch* were preserved there. In their own literature, however, and in the texts that seem most closely related to it, references to heaven tend to be brief and nondescriptive. The one partial exception to this generalization is Songs of the Sabbath Sacrifice (4Q400–407, 11Q17, Mas1k). Similarly, in the nonapocalyptic, nonsectarian literature found at Qumran, references to heaven are brief and incidental. [*See* Songs of the Sabbath Sacrifice.]

In *1 Enoch* 14, Enoch describes a visionary journey to heaven, specifically, to the palace that contains the throne of God. [*See* Throne.] This heavenly structure consists of two rooms, the second more splendid than the first. The outer room is described numinously through the use of contradictory images. It is "hot as fire and cold as snow," constructed of what appears to be hailstones and snow but also of burning fire. Cosmological and meteorological images are invoked to describe the roof of the structure, which is like the path of the stars with lightning flashing in it. Images of cherubim, also described in terms of fire and water, suggest a connection between this heavenly structure and the Temple (cf. *1 Kgs.* 6.29–32). The description of the inner throne rooms is similar although more glorious. The throne itself appears like ice, with rivers of fire flowing from it, and the figure whom Enoch sees sitting upon it is described in terms of the radiance of the sun (cf. *Dn.* 7.9–10, *Ezek.* 1.26–28). In attendance upon the enthroned God are cherubim, myriads of angels, and the high ranking angels called the "holy ones." [*See* Angels.]

Nothing comparable to this detailed description is to be found in the hymns and liturgical compositions from Qumran. As in the Hebrew scriptures, "the heavens," the paired terms *heaven and earth*, and *angels in heaven* often occur in hymns of praise, as part of a descriptive catalog of God's creative acts (as in Hodayot[a] from Qumran Cave 1, hereafter 1QHodayot[a], 1QH ix.10–14 [i.8–12]; Noncanonical Psalms B, 4Q381 1.3; Psalms[a] from Qumran Cave 11, hereafter, 11QPs[a], 11Q5 xxvi.14–15), as those called upon to praise God (as in the War Scroll, 1QM xii.1; Psalms[f], 4Q88 10.5–6; Words of the Luminaries[a], 4Q504 7.4–12), or occasionally in connection with times for praise (Daily Prayers, 4Q503 3.1; cf. 1QH[a] xx.4–9 [xii.1–6]). Little can be gathered from these texts concerning the nature of heaven, although one fragmentary liturgical work (4Q392) refers to heaven not only as the dwelling of God but also as a place of perpetual light, in contrast to the earth, where light and darkness are separated. [*See* Light and Darkness.]

A little more information about the heavens is disclosed in those texts that share aspects of the religious ideology of apocalypses. Incantations and songs against demons speak of a divine judgment, which occurs in heaven against divine beings and on earth against humans (Songs of the Sage[b], 4Q511 10.11–12; Apocryphal Psalms[a], 11Q11 2.6–8), a motif that also occurs in wisdom texts and *pesharim* that display eschatological interest (Sapiential Work A[b], 4Q416 1.10–16; Melchizedek, 11Q13 2.8–11). The heavens are also said to contain tablets upon which are inscribed the predetermined acts for every age, apparently including the deeds and judgments of both the "sons of heaven" and humans (Ages of Creation, 4Q180–181; Apocryphon of Jacob, 4Q537).

Heaven is, above all, the place of God's presence and

rule, as well as the place of the holy angels who serve God and have knowledge of truth and mysteries. One of the distinctive features of Qumran sectarian literature is that it speaks of membership in the community as an entry into a communion with "the congregation of the sons of heaven" (1QH[a] xi.19–22 [iii.18–21], xix.11–14 [xi.8–11]; Rule of the Community from Qumran Cave 1, hereafter, 1QRule of the Community, 1QS xi.7–8; Ages of Creation from Qumran Cave 4, 4Q181 1.3–5). Although emphasis in these references is on the communion with the angels, heaven is described in terms of its opposition to the *pit*, *Sheol*, and *Abaddon* (terms for the underworld), as an "everlasting height," and as a "limitless plain" (1QH[a] xi.19–20 [iii.18–19]). The eschatological blessing of the high priest speaks of his serving in the "holy dwelling," that is, the heavenly temple, like an Angel of the Presence (Rule of the Blessings, 1Q28b iv.24–28); and a covenant liturgy (Berakhot[a–b], 4Q286–287) includes in its blessings brief descriptions of the glories of heaven, the multiple chariot thrones that attend God, and the heavenly spirits.

The most extensive description of the heavenly realm in Qumran literature, however, is found in the Songs of the Sabbath Sacrifice. Since this text is a liturgical composition that invokes angelic praise in the heavenly temple, its descriptive passages occur within the context of acts of praise, not, as in apocalypses, in a narrative context. Also, whereas apocalyptic descriptions often mention the heavenly temple as one part of what is found in the heavens (e.g., *Testament of Levi* 3), in Songs of the Sabbath Sacrifice the heavenly temple is not related to other heavenly structures but is the sole focus of attention.

In continuity with biblical and other Qumran literature, heaven in the Songs of the Sabbath Sacrifice is often referred to as "the highest height" and as the "dwelling" of God and the angels. Most of the description, however, refers to the structure of the heavenly temple itself. The terminology is partly drawn from the various biblical accounts of the Tabernacle (*Ex.* 25–27) and the Solomonic Temple (*1 Kgs.* 7–8) but is particularly indebted to Ezekiel's description of the ideal temple (*Ezek.* 40–48). Various general expressions are used to identify the heavenly temple (e.g., "temple," "sanctuary," "holy place," "tabernacle," "building"), along with numerous references to the particular architectural features of the temple (e.g., gates, portals, vestibules, pillars, corners, beams). Relatively little reference to the furnishings of the heavenly temple occurs, although figures engraved on the walls of the temple chambers and embroidered on the *parokhet* veil are mentioned, as well as the divine throne and footstool. Considerable attention is given to describing the heavenly *devir* ("holy of holies") and the *merkavah* ("chariot throne"), with its attendant cherubim and *ʾofanim* ("wheels"). In addition to the chariot throne upon which God is enthroned, there are also multiple chariot thrones that praise God in the heavenly temple, a feature that is known from later Jewish mystical literature (*Maʿaseh Merkavah* 6; cf. also 4Q286). The heavenly temple is not an inanimate structure but rather a construction of spirits, so that the various features of the temple are capable of praising God. The numinous quality of the temple is also suggested by recurrent references to fiery phenomena, light, and colors. Serving in the heavenly temple are various priestly councils, headed by the seven chief and deputy princes, who praise and bless. The splendid garments of the high priestly angels are described in technical terms that evoke the garments of Israel's high priest (e.g., *ḥoshen* ["breast-piece"], *ephod*) and the techniques for making them (brocade, woven work), yet their ineffable quality is so suggested. Although praise is one of the primary features of the heavenly temple, the Songs of the Sabbath Sacrifice also refer to offerings that are made there (e.g., sacrifices, grain offerings, drink offerings).

Several passages in Songs of the Sabbath Sacrifice refer to seven territories or sanctuaries, and in one passage antiphonal praise from multiple chariot thrones is said to pass from "*devir* to *devir*." In other passages, however, only one heavenly temple and *devir* seem to be envisioned. Parallels exist in later Jewish mystical literature for the notion of seven heavens, each with its own chariot throne (*Reʾuyot Yeḥezqel*), but these heavens are not envisaged as sanctuaries. Certain Jewish mystical texts, however, speak of seven *heikhalot* ("palaces," "temples") where praise is offered to God by thousands of chariot thrones (*Maʿaseh Merkavah* 6). Other texts depict the seven *heikhalot* as concentrically arranged, with an inner shrine at the center (*3 En.* 1.1–2, *Heikhalot Rabbati* 15–16). How closely the Songs of the Sabbath Sacrifice scrolls compare to these later traditions is difficult to say, since the Qumran texts never specify a spatial or hierarchical relationship among the seven sanctuaries. Perhaps the Heikhalot literature represents a later rationalization of the elusive and numinous evocation of the heavenly temple as both one and seven in Songs of the Sabbath Sacrifice.

[*See also* Apocalyptic Texts; Religious Beliefs, Qumran Sect.]

BIBLIOGRAPHY

Bietenhard, Hans. *Die himmlische Welt im Urchristentum und Spätjudentum*. Wissenschaftliche Untersuchungen zum Neuen Testament, 2. Tübingen, 1951.

Gruenwald, Ithamar. *Apocalyptic and Merkavah Mysticism*. Arbeiten zur Geschichte des Antiken Judentums und des Urchristentums, 14. Leiden, 1980.

Halperin, David J. *The Faces of the Chariot: Early Jewish Responses to Ezekiel's Vision*. Texte und Studien zum Antiken Judentum, 16. Tübingen, 1988.

Kuhn, Heinz-Wolfgang. *Enderwartung und gegenwärtiges Heil.* Studien zur Umwelt des Neuen Testaments, 4. Göttingen, 1966.

Newsom, Carol A. *Songs of the Sabbath Sacrifice: A Critical Edition.* Harvard Semitic Studies, 27. Atlanta, 1985.

Rowland, Christopher. *The Open Heaven: A Study of Apocalyptic in Judaism and Early Christianity.* New York, 1982.

CAROL A. NEWSOM

HEBREW. Hebrew accounts for the largest portion of the Judean Desert documents among the languages in which they are written. The remaining languages are Aramaic, Greek, Nabatean, Syriac, Christian Palestinian Aramaic, Arabic, and Latin. Besides a large amount of mostly fragmentary manuscripts of biblical books, the corpus includes a sizable collection of nonbiblical, original compositions in Hebrew as well as ephemeral documents such as letters and deeds. According to one recent estimate, the total length of these Hebrew texts amounts roughly to 11 percent of the Hebrew Bible. This sheer quantity of new documents and the fact that their general provenance and date—at least that of the manuscripts—can be determined with reasonable certainty add to their considerable importance as valuable primary sources for advancing and extending our knowledge of the Hebrew language of the period concerned, approximately the early second century BCE to the middle of the second century CE.

Although the great majority of the Hebrew Dead Sea Scrolls were actually unearthed, or are at least assumed to have been unearthed, in one of the eleven caves in Khirbet Qumran, other adjacent sites in the wilderness of Judea such as Masada, Wadi Murabbaʿat, Naḥal Ḥever, Naḥal Ṣeʾelim, and Naḥal Mishmar have also produced a quantity of documents, some of great importance for their contents as well as their language.

While the provenance of a given manuscript does not necessarily mean that it was composed at the site or in the general area, some documents such as deeds, contracts, and Bar Kokhba letters leave no doubt in this regard. Even when no internal evidence enables us to identify a document's provenance or place of composition, paleographical considerations and the very fact that it was read by or addressed to individuals or members of the various sites in and around Qumran and stored there justify our use of these documents as witnesses to Hebrew as it was used and understood in Palestine of the above-mentioned time span, roughly 200 BCE–150 CE. In this sense, the use of the generic designation Qumran Hebrew is admissible.

Varieties within Qumran Hebrew. Over a period of 350 years a natural language could undergo considerable changes. Partly due to our still insufficient knowledge of Qumran Hebrew, no clear, historical changes within it have been identified.

On the other hand, certain linguistic features occur exclusively or predominantly in certain documents, as has been noted in one of the pioneering studies by Goshen-Gottstein (1958) on Qumran Hebrew. The striking syntagm <*t* noun> for the standard <*ʾt* + noun> is to be found only in Bar Kokhba letters: *mʿyd ʾny ʿly t shmym*, "I invoke Heaven" (Mur 43.3). The periphrastic syntagm <*hyh* + participle> to indicate a durative, repetitive, or habitual action is extremely frequent in certain parts of the Temple Scroll. However, a single document may attest to two features each of which is considered to be characteristic of a different phase of Hebrew or a different tradition of it. Thus, Miqtsat Maʿasei ha-Torah from Qumran Cave 4 shows a definite preference for the relative pronoun *sh-*, which is typical of late Biblical Hebrew and Mishnaic Hebrew, though we once encounter the standard Biblical Hebrew equivalent *ʾshr* (B 32).

The quality of the language can also vary, as can be gauged, for instance, from the varying number of corrected scribal errors. The bewildering variety of spellings in Miqtsat Maʿasei ha-Torah (for example, *ṭmʾ* versus *ṭmh* "impure"; *hyh* versus *hyʾ* "was"; *hbrkh [wh]qlʾ* "the blessing and curse") has led Shelomo Morag (1996) to conclude that the Teacher of Righteousness or his circle, to whom the document has been attributed by some, would be embarrassed by such an ascription. On the other hand, a phonetic spelling such as *t shmym* in a Bar Kokhba letter mentioned above may be excused on the ground of the document's ephemeral nature.

Though we still know too little about the nature of Qumran Hebrew to speak of chronological developments or local dialects, it is clear that the language is far from uniform, and this is not to speak of varieties of style and vocabulary, which are largely a function of the content of the documents in question.

Orthography and Phonology. Since Qumran Hebrew is written totally unvocalized and there is no tradition whatsoever of pronunciation represented by the documents written in it, one's knowledge of the phonology of Qumran Hebrew is largely dependent on spelling variations within the documents and their deviations from the traditions of Hebrew about whose orthography and phonology one possesses more information. Some orthographical features also provide clues as to the morphology of words.

Scriptio plena. One of the orthographic features that characterize many Qumran Hebrew (and Aramaic) documents is a rather liberal use of certain letters of the alphabet to indicate vowels within a word, in particular, the letter *vav* and, though to a much lesser extent, the letter *yod*. These originally indicated, and still do, a presumably bilabial semivowel /w/ and a palatal semivowel /y/, respectively. The former is now often found marking a variety of either *o* or *u* vowels, and the latter a variety of *i* or *e* vowels. The emergence of these so-called *matres lectionis*, "vowel letters," had been a gradual process, and no absolute consistency in their use and nonuse (the latter known as *scriptio defectiva* as against *scriptio plena*) can be assumed for any ancient Hebrew or Aramaic document of any meaningful length. Thus, words or forms that are never spelled *plene* in the Masoretic Text are so spelled almost as a rule: for example, *mwšh* /moshe/ "Moses" (1QIsaiah[a] at *Is.* 63.12), *shlwmwh* /shlomo/ "Solomon" (4QMMT C 1—for the standard spelling *shlmh*), and *kwhn* /kohen/ "priest." The use of *yod* as a *mater lectionis* is exemplified by spellings like *ʿyṣh* (with a supralinear *yod*) /ʿeṣah/ "her wood" (Pesher Habakkuk, 1QpHab x.1) and *ryʿykh* /reʿekha/ "your fellow-man" (Temple Scroll[a], 11Q19 liv.20). The spellings *rʾwsh* and *rwʾsh* instead of the standard spelling *rʾsh* /rosh/ "head," also attest to the same orthographic tendency. Eduard Kutscher's (1974, pp. 20–23) suggestion that this tendency was due to the scribe's desire to avoid possible confusion between Hebrew and Aramaic applies only to a small number of instances.

In view of this prevailing *plene* orthography, one is puzzled by spellings in Bar Kokhba letters such as *ntn*, *dʾgn*, and *ʾkln*, all *Qal* principles for which one would expect a *vav* after the first letter.

In Hebrew and Aramaic texts evincing the more "orthodox" orthography, the two vowel letters were, as a rule, used, though never consistently, in word-medial positions when the vowels in question were historically long. In Qumran Hebrew, however, such a constraint does not necessarily apply: *mwkh* /mukke/ (1QIsa[a] at *Is.* 53.4); *ṭwhrh* "purity" (Rule of the Community from Qumran Cave 1, hereafter, 1QRule of the Community, 1QS vi.22), and *ḥwdshyhm* "their months" (War Scroll, ii.4), which correspond to /ṭohora/ and /ḥodshehem/, respectively, in the Tiberian Masoretic tradition.

The abundance of *matres lectionis* or the origin of their use does not necessarily have to do with the poor command of the language on the part of scribes or the declining knowledge of the language on the part of the reader. The feature is attested almost from the earliest Hebrew (and Aramaic) documents, though admittedly on a more modest scale.

As Józef Milik (1962, p. 224) appositely remarks, the bilingualism led to some orthographic rules that were equally applicable to Hebrew and Aramaic: the use of *alef* to indicate word-final *a* (*hgdwlʾ*, *bʾ* "in her," *hḥwmʾ* "the wall") or *e* (*zʾ* "this" [masculine], *ṣwpʾ* "looking toward"), and the use of *alef* in word-final digraphs (see below).

Digraphs. The phenomenon of the digraph, namely, the use of two consecutive letters to mark a single vowel, especially at the end of a word with *alef* as the second, otiose letter, is another notable feature of Qumran Hebrew (and Aramaic). It is attested by the ubiquitous *kyʾ*, which is the conjunction /ki/ spelled *ky* in the standard orthography. Likewise, *yʾmynwʾ* "they will believe" (1QpHab ii.6), *lwʾ* /lo/ "to him" (1QS vi.27). The negator *lwʾ* does not belong here, since the final *alef* was originally consonantal.

This feature is not unique to Qumran Hebrew (and Aramaic): there are two instances of it in an Aramaic text from the fifth century BCE (Sheikh Fadl cave inscription)—*prʿh nkwʾ* "Pharaoh Necho," and in Biblical Aramaic—*shyṣyʾ* "he completed" (*Ezra* 6.15).

Weakening of gutturals. The frequent deletion of guttural letters, by which are meant *alef*, *he*, *ḥet*, and *ʿayin*, and their indiscriminate interchange, as eloquently illustrated by four conflicting spellings of the demonstrative pronoun—phonetically, /zot/—*zʾt*, *zʾwt*, *zwʾt*, and *zwt*, attest to the general weakening of these consonants in Qumran Hebrew. Examples of missing guttural letters are *nspym* (1QIsa[a] at *Is.* 13.4) for the Masoretic Text's *nʾspym* /neʾesafim/, *ybwr* (1QIsa[a] at *Is.* 28.15) for the Masoretic Text's *yʿbr* /yaʿavor/, *lhtlk* (1QS v.10) for the standard *lhthlk* /lehithallekh/. Examples of arbitrary substitution are *bʾwpyʿ* (1QS x.2) for the standard *bhwpyʿ* /behofiaʿ/ "in appearing," *nrhb* (1QIsa[a] at *Is.* 30.23) for the Masoretic Text's *nrḥb* /nirḥav/, *ʿmsym* (1QIsa[a] at *Is.* 64.1) for the Masoretic Text's *hmsym* /hamasim/, *hṣlkm* for *ʾṣlkm* "with you" (Mur 43.4), *hthzq* "take courage" (Mur 44.7), followed by *ḥzq* "fortify." All this, however, does not have to mean that the gutturals had become weakened throughout Palestine already at this period, an invalid conclusion as has been cogently argued by Kutscher in his *Studies in Galilean Aramaic* (Ramat-Gan, 1976), pages 67–96.

Penultimate stress. Tiberian Hebrew shows a marked drift toward the ultima stress. There are indications, however, that in some categories of verb morphology, Qumran Hebrew still retained the earlier stress on the penultimate syllable. While in Tiberian Hebrew the penultimate stress is well-nigh confined to finite verb forms with vocalic morphemes—thus, typically, /yishmoru/ and /shamaru/—which also appear in pausal position, the penultimate stress appears to be almost the rule in the imperfect and imperative *Qal* where *plene* spellings occur, and that irrespective of pause: for example, *yshqwlw yskwrw* . . . *ysgwdw* (1QIsa[a] at *Is.* 46.6) for the Tiberian /yishqolu yiskeru . . . yisgedu/, *ʿbwrw* . . . *sqwlw* (1QIsa[a] at *Is.* 62.10–11) for the Tiberian /ʿivru . . . saqqelu/, and *zkwrw* (1QM xvii.2) for *zkrw* /zikhru/. Ben-Ḥayyim (1958, pp. 202–203) rightly pointed out the affinity of Qumran Hebrew with Samaritan Hebrew, though general penultimate stress as in Samaritan Hebrew is not likely since nouns of the *quṭl* pattern are very often spelled *qṭwl* in the *status con-*

structus, whereas in the *status absolutus* they are spelled *qwṭl* with a mere handful of exceptions of the *qṭwl* type, as shown by Elisha Qimron (1986, p. 38). One would also hesitate in postulating penultimate stress for *Qal* imperfects and imperatives of the types mentioned above when they are "defectively" spelled.

Sibilants. One set of spellings with the twenty-first letter of the Hebrew alphabet where the sound represented corresponds to Proto-Semitic /s/, and hence the letter *samekh* is expected, remains puzzling: for example, *m'sˇw* "they despised" (1QpHab i.11), *mnsˇh* "testing" (11Q19 liv.12), *pšḥ* "Passover" (4QPhylactery i.8). If /s/ had changed to /š/, the change could not have come about via Greek, which lacks the latter consonant.

Morphology. There are two features that typify the morphology of the personal pronouns in Qumran Hebrew. The first is unique to Qumran Hebrew, not shared by any tradition of Hebrew either prior to or after it: the third-person singular masculine *hw'h* and feminine *hy'h*, which occur very frequently, the latter being as common as the standard *hy'* (nineteen times as against twenty-one times according to Qimron 1986, p. 57). They confirm that the final *alef* of the traditional forms was not originally a vowel letter. That the forms ended with a second vowel, *a*, is known from Arabic and Ugaritic. In Arabic, it is, however, short, and the spelling with *he* may go back to *-at*—the corresponding forms in Assyrian, Old Phoenician, and Classical Ethiopic end with *t*. Finally, the glottal stop, /ʾ/, as a constituent of these pronouns, occurs in Old Phoenician and Classical Ethiopic. Thus, the Qumran forms have every appearance of great antiquity: Carl Brockelmann (*Grundriss der vergleichenden Grammatik der semitischen Sprachen*, I, 1908, p. 303) holds *hūʾa* to be the earliest Proto-Semitic form for "he." They are hardly artificial creations, though one does not know how such archaic forms managed to survive in this isolated speech community and in this relatively late phase of Hebrew.

That these archaic forms coexisted in Qumran Hebrew along with their younger and shorter forms is evident from such phonetic spellings as *hw* (Copper Scroll 3Q15 x.20) and *hy* (Mur 42.4). Therefore, not every *hw'* or *hy'* can be a defective spelling of the long, archaic form.

The second noteworthy feature is the presence of doublets, short and long forms: second masculine plural *'tmh* versus *'tm*, third masculine plural *hmh* versus *hm*, third feminine plural *hnh* versus *hn*. As a matter of fact, already in Biblical Hebrew the long form is much more common for the third-person masculine, and the feminine form is generally assumed to have been originally long, the long masculine form being an analogical extension of it. Qumran Hebrew may then be said to have extended this analogy a step further.

These long morphemes are also found in suffixal pronouns and personal endings of the verb in the perfect tense: third-person feminine singular *-hh* or *-h'* alongside *-h*, second-person masculine plural *-kmh* alongside *-km* as in *lkmh* "to you" (1QMysteries, 1Q27 1.i.8), third-person masculine plural *-mh* alongside *-m* as in *npsˇmh* "their soul" (1Q27 1.i.4), third-person common plural *-hmh* versus *-hm* as in *lhmh* "to them" (Apocryphal Prophecy, 1Q25 i.5), *'kltmh* "you ate" (Apocryphal Prophecy from Qumran Cave 2, 2Q23 3). In Biblical Hebrew, according to the Tiberian tradition, these long, suffixal morphemes are virtually unknown.

These long forms, whether suffixal or not, constitute another important isogloss shared by Qumran Hebrew and Samaritan Hebrew, as emphasized by Ben-Ḥayyim (1958, p. 202). On the other hand, the long second- and third-person morphemes are one of several significant features that indicate that Qumran Hebrew and Mishnaic Hebrew are distinct, for the latter attests to the short form only, though they may have developed as a result of the apocopation of word-final, unstressed vowels. But how does one explain *'t* "you (masculine singular)" in Mishnaic Hebrew?

Another feature that contrasts Qumran and Mishnaic Hebrew is the separate pronoun for the first-person plural, for which Biblical Hebrew uses *'nḥnw*, while Mishnaic Hebrew knows only *'nw*, which occurs only once in *Jeremiah* 42.6 as *Qere*. In contrast to other Qumran documents, Miqtsat Maʿasei ha-Torah uses only the long form, as many as ten times.

Another interesting matter is the spelling of the third-person masculine singular suffix attached to a masculine plural noun. Besides the standard spellings *-w* with a singular noun and *-yw* with a plural noun, one often comes across cases of the reverse situation as in *ydyw* in *ydyw nṭwyh* "his hand extended" (1QIsa[a] at *Is.* 5.25), *wryqh npshyw'* "and his soul is empty" (1QIsa[a] at *Is.* 29.8), on the one hand, and *ytdwtw* "its stakes" (1QIsa[a] at *Is.* 33.20) and *m'ḥrw* "from after him" (1QS i.17), on the other, though there is no consistency. The latter category can be explained as cases of defective spellings, as is attested not infrequently in the Masoretic Text. Such an explanation, however, cannot account for the former category. Many scholars see here another isogloss shared by Qumran Hebrew and Samaritan Hebrew, where the diphthong /aw/ of the plural suffix has contracted to /o/ or /u/.

Finally, the abundance in Qumran Hebrew of *plene* spellings of the possessive suffix *-kh* next to *-k* and the perfect tense suffix *-th* next to *-t* for the second-person masculine singular has laid to rest P. Kahle's theory that the long morphemes are articifial forms created by the Tiberian scholars under the influence of Arabic.

Biblical Hebrew already attests to a small number of Aramaizing masculine plural (and dual) endings /-in/.

Given the multilingual milieu in Palestine in our period as delineated by Joseph Fitzmyer (1979), it is not surprising to see this trend reinforced in Qumran Hebrew, particularly the Copper Scroll and Bar Kokhba documents: for example, *ʿsryn* "twenty" (next to *shty[m]* "two"—Mur 24 B 1), *ḥmsht kwryn ḥ[ty]n* "five *kors* of wheat" (Mur 44.2–3), *m'tyn* "two hundred" (3Q15 iv.10), *hmym hqrwbyn* "the approaching water" (3Q15 ix.11–12). It should be remembered that Bar Kokhba's circle has also left us documents written in Aramaic, tinged in their turn with some Hebraisms. The feature in question was, to a certain extent, reinforced by the general neutralization of the phonological distinction between the two nasals in word-final position, a phenomenon evident from the Second Temple period onward, as shown by Kutscher in his *Studies in Galilean Aramaic*, pages 58–67.

Judging from the way certain nouns are spelled in Qumran Hebrew, one may conclude that they represent a formation pattern different than the Tiberian one: for example, *lwhb* (1QM vi.2) or *lhwb* (Hodayot[a] from Qumran Cave 1, hereafter, 1QHodayot[a], 1QH[a] iii.30) "flame" for the Tiberian /lahav/, *ʿrwl* for /ʿorel/ "uncircumcised" for /ʿerel/ or /ʿ^{a}ral/; *ṭm'h*, possibly to be read as /ṭim'a/ as in the Babylonian pronunciation of Hebrew as against the Tiberian /ṭum'a/; *sdwm* or *swdm* "Sodom" for the Tiberian /sedom/ (compare Sodoma in the Septuagint). In some of these cases our decision depends on the paleographic choice between *waw* and *yod*, two letters that are notoriously difficult to tell apart in many Dead Sea documents. Thus, if we read *k'yb* at 1QIsaiah[a] at *Is.* 17.11, it would be a *plene* spelling of the Tiberian form /ke'ev/ "pain."

The *Qal* imperfect, the imperative, and the infinitive construct with an object suffix, notably that of the third-person singular, synthetically attached display some striking forms: *ydrwsˇhw* "they will examine him" (1QS vi.17), *ydwrsˇhw* (1QS vi.14), same meaning. These are explained by Qimron (1986, p. 52) as analogical developments based on the infinitive construct with an object suffix of the types *qṭwlny* and *qwṭlny* in the Tiberian tradition of Biblical Hebrew. The difficulty with this view is that the first pattern is not attested when a vowel intervenes between the last root letter and the suffix, which is the case with the first- and third-person pronouns. One is reminded, however, that even the Tiberian phonology is not averse to a vowel in an unstressed, open, and pretonic syllable in the case of the *yiqṭal* imperfect (and the related imperative) as can be seen in forms such as /yiqra'úhu/ and /shmaʿénna/.

The infinitive absolute had become almost obsolete: rare examples are *y'yrw . . . hlwk w'wr* "they will continue to shine . . ." (1QM i.8), *bkw tbkh* "she shall surely weep" (Apocryphal Lamentations A, 4Q179 ii.9), *hkh tkh* "you shall surely smite" (11Q19 lv.6). The use of the infinitive absolute continuing a finite verb, a syntagm typical of late Biblical Hebrew, is attested once in Miqtsat Maʿasei ha-Torah: *hy' nṣl . . . wnslwḥ lw* /haya niṣṣal . . . venisloaḥ lo/ "he was being rescued . . . and pardoned" (C 26). Otherwise, the infinitive absolute has disappeared from Mishnaic Hebrew.

Qumran Hebrew appears to be continuing the trend already visible in late Biblical Hebrew in which a verb used intransitively in *Qal* may also be used in *Hifil* (and possibly *Piel*) without any functional opposition. For example, *Qal rshʿ* "to act wickedly" occurs in *2 Samuel* (once; also in the parallel psalm), *Kings* (once; also in the parallel passage in *Chronicles*), *Daniel* (once), *Ecclesiastes* (once), while its *Hifil* occurs in *Chronicles* (twice), *Nehemiah* (once), *Daniel* (twice), as well as in *Job* (once) and *Psalms* (once). The *Hifil* of this verb occurs as an intransitive verb in *hrshʿnw* "we acted wickedly" (1QS i.25) in a confessional formula, though the same formula in the Damascus Document (CD xx.29) uses the *Qal* form: *rshʿnw*. One cannot speak here of a general drift. Each lexeme needs to be examined separately. Thus, still in the same formula (and in quite a few additional Qumran texts), we find a synonymous verb root *ʿwh* used in *Nifal*, while early Biblical Hebrew prefers *Hifil* and late Biblical Hebrew the *Qal*.

In the *Hifil* perfect, the first and second persons of hollow roots show a separating vowel as in *h'yrwth* "you have illumined" (1QH[a] iii.3), while Mishnaic Hebrew and Samaritan Hebrew do without such a vowel: the form just quoted would be *h'rth*.

Morphosyntax and Syntax. The process of deterioration of the inverted tenses characteristic of the classical Hebrew narrative style had started in late Biblical Hebrew, culminating in Mishnaic Hebrew, from which such forms virtually disappeared. Kutscher (1974, pp. 350–358) noted not a few examples in which the scribe of 1QIsaiah[a] had changed conversive imperfects of the Masoretic Text to perfects, and, conversely, conversive perfects to imperfects. However, as shown by Mark Smith (1991), Qumran Hebrew, taken as a whole, presents a rather complex picture in this respect. The system of inverted tenses is far from dead. On the contrary, there is every indication that authors of "classical" Qumran Hebrew documents were quite at home with this system of tenses. While it is not surprising to find plenty of inverted imperfects attached to the conjunction *vav* in parabiblical narrative texts, one comes across a few examples even in 4QMMT, the language of which is thought by some to be a specimen of Hebrew spoken in the Qumran community: *shyglḥ wkbs* "that he should shave and wash" (4QMMT B 66), *shytqn 't ʿtstk whrḥyq mmk . . . wnḥshbh lk ltsdqh* "that he strengthen your will and remove from you . . . and it will be counted for you as credit" (4QMMT C 28–31).

The proclitic particle *sh-*, though undoubtedly of ancient origin as shown by its occurrences in the oldest layer of the biblical literature (see the Song of Deborah in *Judges* 5), had become an unmistakable hallmark of late Biblical Hebrew and would subsequently take the place of *asher* in Mishnaic Hebrew. However, that the shorter particle was felt to be alien to a certain register of Qumran Hebrew is shown by its pattern of distribution. The scribe of 1QIsaiah[a], despite his various efforts to make the language of the ancient prophet easier to comprehend for his contemporary readership, did not find it right to modernize and popularize even a single *asher* in his original text by converting it to *sh-*. Elsewhere the shorter particle is confined to documents such as the Bar Kokhba letters, Copper Scroll, and 4QMMT, which is couched in the form of a halakhic dialogue. Absolute consistency, however, is not to be expected, for even in 4QMMT we find *asher* at B 32. That the language of 4QMMT is not entirely Mishnaic in this respect is rightly emphasized by Qimron (1994, pp. 74–75), for it retains *ky* as a particle of cause, a function that in Mishnaic Hebrew is also covered by *sh-*.

While Qumran Hebrew still maintains the classic mode of synthetically connecting two substantives by means of the construct chain, certain documents attest to an alternative, analytical syntagm mediated by the particle *shel*, most likely reinforced by its formal equivalent in contemporary Aramaic idioms with *zil* or *dil*, although a related Hebrew syntagm is already attested thrice in the *Song of Songs*: *karmi shelli* "my own vineyard" (*Song* 1.6, 8.12), and *miṭṭato shellishlomo* "Solomon's couch" (*Song* 3.7). Examples are *hprnsyn shl byt mshkw* "the managers of Beth-Mashko" (Mur 42.1), *mʿrt hʿmwd shl shny [h]ptḥyn* "the cave of the column of the two entrances" (3Q15 vi.1). The second constituent may be a personal pronoun as in *lymwmyt shlw* "to its small water basin" (3Q15 xi.13). The particle *shel* is also found without the preceding noun head in *shhy shlw* "which was his" (Mur 42.4) and *shhyw shl hgwʾyn* "who were of the gentiles" (5/6Ḥev 5). Further, we also find examples of the anticipatory pronoun (prolepsis) exactly as in the above-quoted *Song of Songs* 3.7: *ʾshtw shl dwsts zh* "the wife of this Dostheus" (Mur 30.25). Note, however, that unlike Mishnaic Hebrew and the *Song of Songs* 3.7, Qumran Hebrew spells *shl* as a separate word when followed by a substantive. Another difference from Mishnaic Hebrew is that the second noun in this analytic syntagm often has the definitive article: for example, *bmʿrʾ shl hknʾ shl hrgm* "in the cavity of the base of the rock (3Q15 vi.7).

Vocabulary. Qimron's provisional list of words, forms, meanings, or usages of words in Qumran Hebrew not previously known from Biblical or Mishnaic Hebrew goes up to nearly three hundred (Qimron, 1986, pp. 105–115). Examples of new words are *bdn* "form," and *zrq* "dart." New forms of known roots: *Hifil* (instead of *Qal*) *gyl* "to rejoice," *byn* "understanding" (for /bina/). New meanings: *Qal gʿr* "to exorcize," *bʿwl* /baʿul/ "well-versed, accustomed," *yḥd* "community." New collocations: *byt rʾsh* "helmet," *hʾyr lb* "to enlighten the mind."

Qumran Hebrew in the History of the Hebrew Language. Even this necessarily limited overview of Qumran Hebrew makes it plain that, as Qimron (1992 and 1994) emphasized, it is too simplistic to characterize Qumran Hebrew in terms of a linear chronological development, early or classical Biblical Hebrew → late Biblical Hebrew → Qumran Hebrew → Mishnaic Hebrew. We have shown, on one hand, that Qumran Hebrew itself is not entirely uniform, and, on the other hand, that there are features that cannot have developed from late Biblical Hebrew as well as features that cannot have later developed into Mishnaic Hebrew features. The long forms of the third-person singular pronouns are unique to Qumran Hebrew.

Against the current, well-nigh universal consensus that, during the period represented by the Dead Sea documents, Hebrew was only one of the languages of Palestine, or more precisely, of Judea, Qumran Hebrew reveals features that are so organically integrated into the texture of the language and other features that can be adequately accounted for only in terms of phonological processes and development such that it must have had its basis in a community that used Hebrew as a means of oral communication. It is hardly an artificial and merely biblicizing means of literary creativity, but a natural, vibrant idiom. Since the notion of writing as one talks is a fairly modern development, none of the documents is likely to reveal the writer's spoken Hebrew in full, which equally holds for Mishnaic Hebrew. As is the case with every natural language, the written register constantly feeds on its spoken form. Joshua Blau (1997), however, has rightly cautioned us against invoking the notion of *diglossia* in evaluating Qumran Hebrew.

Lines of isoglosses extend in various directions: late Biblical Hebrew, Aramaic, Samaritan Hebrew, the Babylonian tradition of Hebrew, and others, but not in one direction only. Nevertheless, Qumran Hebrew, despite some signs of internal diversity observable even within the bulk of the documents originating from a single location, namely Qumran itself, appears to constitute a distinct idiom of its own.

BIBLIOGRAPHY

Ben-Ḥayyim, Ze'ev. "Traditions in the Hebrew Language, with Special Reference to the Dead Sea Scrolls." *Scripta Hierosolymitana* 4

(1958), 200–214. The first significant study to point to close affinities between Qumran Hebrew and Samaritan Hebrew.

Blau, Joshua. "The Structure of Biblical and Dead Sea Scrolls Hebrew in Light of Arabic Diglossia and Middle Arabic." *Leshonenu* 60 (1997), 21–32. Pleads for the earlier view on Qumran Hebrew as a mixture of Biblical and Mishnaic Hebrew, drawing on Middle Arabic for comparison.

Fitzmyer, Joseph Augustine. "The Languages of Palestine in the First Century A.D." In Fitzmyer, *A Wandering Aramean: Collected Aramaic Essays*. Society of Biblical Literature Monograph Series, 25 (Missoula, Mont., 1979), pp. 29–56. Originally published in *Catholic Biblical Quarterly* 32 (1970), 501–531. Good sketch of the situation with abundant data.

Goshen-Gottstein, Moshe Henry. "Linguistic Structure and Tradition in the Qumran Documents." *Scripta Hierosolymitana* 4 (1958), 101–137. A pioneering and still useful discussion of significant linguistic features of the then-known major Qumran documents and the distribution of the features among them.

Kaddari, Menaḥem Zevi. *Semantic Fields in the Language of the Dead Sea Scrolls* (in Hebrew). Jerusalem, 1968. An interesting semantic study on terms denoting obligation. English summary.

Kutscher, Eduard Yechezkel. "Hebrew Language: Dead Sea Scrolls." In *Encyclopedia Judaica* cols. 1,583–1,590. Jerusalem, 1971.

Kutscher, Eduard Yechezkel. *The Language and Linguistic Background of the Isaiah Scroll (1QIsa[a])*. Studies on the Texts of the Desert of Judah, 6. Leiden, 1974. An English translation of the Hebrew original published in 1959. A pioneering and thorough study of Qumran Hebrew focused on the Isaiah scroll, 1QIsa[a].

Kutscher, Eduard Yechezkel. "Hebrew and Aramaic Letters of Bar Koseba and His Contemporaries. Part II: The Hebrew Letters" (in Hebrew). In *Hebrew and Aramaic Studies*, edited by Z. Ben-Ḥayyim, A. Dothan, and G. Sarfatti. Jerusalem, 1977. Originally published in *Leshonenu* 26 (1961), 7–23. Valuable philological studies on Bar Kokhba's Hebrew letters.

Milik, Józef T. Succinct Characterization of the Language of the Copper Scroll (3Q15). In *Les 'Petites Grottes' de Qumran*, edited by M. Baillet, J. T. Milik, and R. de Vaux, pp. 221–235. Discoveries in the Judaean Desert, 3. Oxford, 1962.

Morag, Shelomo. "Qumran Hebrew: Some Typological Observations." *Vetus Testamentum* 38 (1988), 148–164. Instructive evaluation of select features for characterizing general Qumran Hebrew.

Morag, Shelomo. "Language and Style in *Miqṣat Maʿaśe ha-Torah*—Did *Moreh ha-Ṣedeq* Write This Document?" *Tarbiz* 65 (1996), 209–223. In Hebrew with an English summary. Answers the question in the negative on the basis of the nature and quality of the Hebrew of the document, and introduces the notion of mixing levels.

Muraoka, Takamitsu, and John Francis Elwolde, eds. *The Hebrew of the Dead Sea Scrolls and Ben Sira: Proceedings of a Symposium Held at Leiden University, 11–14 December 1995*. Studies on the Texts of the Desert of Judah, 26. Leiden, 1997.

Qimron, Elisha. *The Hebrew of the Dead Sea Scrolls*. Harvard Semitic Studies, 29. Atlanta, 1986. An abridged and updated English version of the author's 1976 Hebrew University Ph.D. dissertation (in Hebrew). Currently the best and most up-to-date description of Qumran Hebrew focused on nonbiblical texts. Includes a treatment of the vocabulary. For fuller data, reference to the author's dissertation (Jerusalem, 1976) is essential.

Qimron, Elisha. "Observations on the History of Early Hebrew (1000 BCE–200 CE) in the Light of the Dead Sea Documents." In *The Dead Sea Scrolls: Forty Years of Research*, edited by D. Dimant and U. Rappaport, pp. 349–361. Leiden, 1992. Insightful attempt to characterize Qumran Hebrew against other varieties of early Hebrew.

Qimron, Elisha. "A Careful and Detailed Description of the Salient Isoglosses of the Hebrew of 4QMMT in Comparison with Other Qumran Hebrew Documents, Biblical Hebrew and Mishnaic Hebrew." In *Qumran Cave 4, V: Miqṣat Maʿaśe ha-Torah*, edited by E. Qimron and J. Strugnell, pp. 65–108. Discoveries in the Judaean Desert, 10. Oxford, 1994.

Qimron, Elisha. "The Biblical Lexicon in Light of the Dead Sea Scrolls." *Dead Sea Discoveries* 2 (1995), 295–329. Study of how difficult words in the Hebrew Bible were understood by Qumran authors.

Rabin, Chaim. "Historical Background of Qumran Hebrew." *Scripta Hierosolymitana* 4 (1958), 144–161. A useful discussion of Qumran Hebrew against its historical and social background.

Segert, Stanislav. "Zur Habakuk-Rolle aus dem Funde am Toten Meer, I." *Archiv Orientální* 21 (1953), 218–239. Five more subsequent studies with same title in the same journal: 22 (1954), 99–113, 444–459; 23 (1955), 178–183, 364–373, 575–619.

Smith, Mark S. *The Origins and Development of the* Waw-*consecutive Northwest Semitic Evidence from Ugarit to Qumran*. Harvard Semitic Studies, 39. Atlanta, 1991. Good analysis of an important feature of Hebrew syntax, focused on data in the major Qumran documents. See pages 35–63.

Yalon, Henoch. *Studies in the Dead Sea Scrolls. Philological Essays (1949–1952)*. Jerusalem, 1967. A collection of still valuable and original studies. In Hebrew with English summaries.

TAKAMITSU MURAOKA

HEBREWS, LETTER TO THE. An elaborate, anonymous homily urging an early Christian community to renew its commitment to Christ, who is portrayed as the cause of their salvation (2.10, 5.9, 9.14) and the model for their behavior (12.1–2), the *Letter to the Hebrews* drives its message home through forceful exhortations and various elaborate interpretations of passages from the Hebrew scriptures. The parallels with the Dead Sea Scrolls arise primarily in these exegetical arguments.

Publication of the first scrolls prompted suggestions by, among others, Yigael Yadin and Celas Spicq, that *Hebrews* was directly influenced by the piety of the scrolls. Yadin, for example, maintained that *Hebrews* was written to oppose Christians who knew of the Qumran community, anticipated resumption of the Temple cult, and took the Israelite organization in the desert period as their model. Critical reviews of the suggested parallels followed by F. F. Bruce and Herbert Braun, among others. Most scholars today find the scrolls useful for illustrating first-century exegetical techniques and some strains of eschatological thinking relevant to *Hebrews*. Specialized studies of individual works, such as Paul Kobelski's treatment of Melchizedek (11Q13) and related texts, have been fruitful for illuminating the background to *Hebrews*.

The opening chapter of *Hebrews* (*Heb.* 1.5–14), consisting of a series of citations primarily from the *Psalms*, argues that Christ is superior to the angels. The series is formally similar to a group of citations interpreted messianically (Testimonia, 4Q175; Florilegium, 4Q174). The

Florilegium cites two passages also joined in *Hebrews* 1.5, *2 Samuel* 7.14, and Psalm 2.7. The overall argument of the first chapter of *Hebrews* may reflect a kind of piety in which angels, particularly angels involved in heavenly worship, played a role. Such piety is amply attested in the scrolls, particularly in Songs of the Sabbath Sacrifice (4Q400–407). Hebrews, however, does not directly criticize such mystical traditions.

A central feature of *Hebrews* is its portrait of Christ as a heavenly high priest. The text bases that portrait on its application of Psalm 110.4 to Christ. Early Christians frequently used the first verse of that royal psalm as a description of Christ's heavenly exaltation. The fourth verse, designating the royal figure a "priest after the order of Melchizedek," understood as an address to Christ, enables the author to consider him a priest. Through an interpretation of the "order of Melchizedek" as a heavenly and eternal reality (*Heb.* 7), the verse permits the construing of Christ as a special kind of high priest. This conceit is necessary for the central argument of *Hebrews* 8–10, that Christ at his death performed a definitive atoning sacrifice. The Melchizedek text (11Q13) indicates the presence of speculation on the mysterious figure of Melchizedek, who appears only in *Genesis* 14 and Psalm 110. The fragmentary eschatological *midrash* ("interpretation") apparently identifies Melchizedek as one of the Elohim ("divine beings") of Psalm 82.1 and attributes to him an eschatological role as judge; it also refers to Yom Kippur and speaks of Melchizedek's atoning work. The Qumran text thus illustrates one strand of speculation on Melchizedek as a heavenly entity, perhaps associated with or identical to the angel Michael. Although *Hebrews* is careful not to commit itself to any definite statement about the status of Melchizedek, such speculative traditions in the Judean Desert documents may lie behind its argument about the "order of Melchizedek."

There may be some remote analogy between the priestly messianism of *Hebrews* and the expectation of the scrolls that there would be in the end time a messianic priest who accompanies the Messiah of Israel. He is called the Messiah of Aaron (1QS ix.11; see also CD xii.23–xiii.1, xiv.18–19, xix.10–11, xix.33–xx.1), the Interpreter of the Law (4Q174 1.10–13; CD vii.18–19; 4Q177 10–11.5), or simply chief priest or priest (often in the War Scroll, 1QM; cf. 4Q161 8–10.17–29; 4Q285 3–5). In one passage he and the Messiah of Israel carry out an atoning function at the end of this era (CD xiv.18–19). *Hebrews*, however, argues that Jesus cannot be a messiah in the line of Levi (7.13).

Having established that Christ is a heavenly high priest, *Hebrews* considers the character of his priestly work. To do so, the homilist argues that Christ's death was a sacrifice, like the sacrifices of Yom Kippur, but more definitively effective. *Hebrews* also considers this sacrifice to parallel the covenant-inaugurating ritual of *Exodus* 24.8, when Moses sprinkled blood on the Israelites. Thus, for *Hebrews*, Christ's death fulfilled the promise of a "new covenant" found in *Jeremiah* 31.31–34, cited in *Hebrews* 8.8–12. The notion of a new covenant, and the fidelity that it requires, is essential to the hortatory program of *Hebrews*. The community of the Damascus Document also understood itself to be involved in a new covenant (CD vi.19, xx.12) and explicitly invoked the prophecy of Jeremiah (CD viii.21). The notion that the followers of Jesus constituted a community of a new covenant is found in other early Christian sources (*Mt.* 26.28 and parallels; *1 Cor.* 11.25; *2 Cor.* 3.6).

Hebrews exhorts renewed fidelity to Christ in the light of his imminent coming in judgment (10.25, 10.37–38, 12.25–29). To support that exhortation, it cites *Habakkuk* 2.3–4, a text that receives extended treatment in Pesher Habakkuk (1QpHab vii.10–viii.3). Both *Hebrews* and the Qumran *pesher* call for continued fidelity but construe its objects differently. Pesher Habakkuk insists, in view of the approaching eschatological judgment, upon fidelity to Torah and to the Teacher of Righteousness. *Hebrews*, using a Greek translation, construes the prophecy to apply to Christ's second coming and urges imitation of Christ's fidelity to God in the face of persecution (*Heb.* 12.1–2).

The eschatological tableau sketched in *Hebrews* 12.22–25 has points of contact with imagery in the scrolls, including images of the heavenly court (1QS x.8; 1Q28a ii.8; 1QM vii.6) or the new Jerusalem (1Q32, 2Q24, 4Q554–555, 5Q15, 11Q18). Similarly, *Hebrews* 13.15 and Rule of the Community (1QS ix.4–5) share the widespread use of cultic language as a metaphor for prayer. Strands of Jewish piety thus attested in the scrolls survive in an altered form in *Hebrews*.

[*See also* Melchizedek; Messiahs; *and* New Testament.]

BIBLIOGRAPHY

Attridge, Harold W. *The Epistle to the Hebrews*. Hermeneia. Philadelphia, 1989.

Braun, Herbert. *Qumran und das Neue Testament*, 2 vols. Tübingen, 1966. See vol. 1, pages 241–278 and vol. 2, pages 181–194.

Bruce, F. F. "'To the Hebrews' or 'To the Essenes'?" *New Testament Studies* 9 (1962–63), 217–232.

Kobelski, P. *Melchizedek and Melchireša'*. Catholic Biblical Quarterly, Monograph Series, 10. Washington, D.C., 1981.

Koester, Craig R. *The Dwelling of God: The Tabernacle in the Old Testament, Intertestamental Jewish Literature, and the New Testament*. Catholic Biblical Quarterly, Monograph Series, 22. Washington, D.C., 1989.

Kosmala, Hans. *Hebräer-Essener-Christen*. Leiden, 1959.

Spicq, Celas. "L'Épître aux Hébreux: Apollos, Jean-Baptiste, les Hellénistes et Qumran." *Revue de Qumrân* 1 (1958–1959), 36–55.

Yadin, Yigael. "The Dead Sea Scrolls and the Epistle to the Hebrews." *Scripta Hierosolymitana* 4 (1958), 36–55.

HAROLD W. ATTRIDGE

HEBREW UNIVERSITY OF JERUSALEM. As one of the oldest institutions of higher learning in Israel, the Hebrew University of Jerusalem has played an important role in the study and preservation of the Judean Desert manuscripts from the time of their discovery. During the early 1950s, the university was actively involved in the acquisition, study, and publication of documents from Cave 1 at Qumran. In the early 1960s, the institution served as co-sponsor of the excavations conducted by Professor Yigael Yadin in the Judean Desert caves and at Masada, which resulted in the recovery of important manuscripts. Although the bulk of the primary publications of Qumran material came from the International Team at the Palestine Archaeological Museum in the Jordanian sector of Jerusalem during the later 1950s and 1960s, the Hebrew University Institute of Archaeology was a cosponsor of Yadin's research on the Bar Kokhba and Masada documents, and, after 1967, of Yadin's publication of the Temple Scroll[a] (11Q19). Following the administrative reorganization of the International Scrolls publication project in 1991, the Hebrew University once again became a central institution and clearinghouse for Dead Sea Scrolls scholars all over the world. [*See* Masada; Palestine Archaeological Museum; *and the biography of Yadin*.]

Despite later developments, the initial contacts of officials of the Hebrew University with Qumran texts were singularly unproductive. In August 1947, soon after his acquisition of four scrolls from Cave 1, the Metropolitan Athanasius Yeshue Samuel sought the advice of two (still unidentified) staff members of the Jewish National Library, affiliated with the university, about the value of the texts. They mistakenly regarded them as relatively modern copies of biblical manuscripts. In October 1947, Archbishop Samuel consulted Hebrew University linguist Tuvia Wechsler, who offered an even more discouraging assessment. According to Samuel, Wechsler expressed skepticism that manuscripts from the Second Temple period could have survived. He reportedly asserted to Samuel that "If that table were a box and you filled it full of pound notes, you couldn't even then measure the value of these scrolls if they are two thousand years old as you say!" (Trever, 1964, p. 110) [*See also the biography of Samuel*.]

Yet in November 1947, when Hebrew University archaeology professor Eleazar L. Sukenik was approached by Jerusalem antiquities dealer Nasri Ohan with an offer to purchase another group of scrolls from Cave 1 that had come into the hands of Bethlehem dealer Feidi al-Alami, the result was dramatically different. Sukenik immediately recognized that the scrolls' script closely resembled that of inscribed ossuaries from the Second Temple period. Thus recognizing the scrolls' probable date and potential value, Sukenik immediately sought to purchase these manuscripts for the Hebrew University. By December 1947, with the support and financial intervention of university president Judah L. Magnes, Sukenik was able to acquire the War Scroll (1QM), 1QHodayot[a] (1QH), and Isaiah[b] (1Q8). Although Sukenik was not initially successful in acquiring the texts still in the possession of Archbishop Samuel, he was able to examine them in March 1947 and compiled a report on the style and contents of all seven of the complete texts from Cave 1. This report was published in August 1948, with a second installment in 1950. [*See also the biography of Sukenik*.]

Throughout the early 1950s, Sukenik worked steadily on the transcription and publication of the three Cave 1 scrolls he had obtained for the Hebrew University, closely assisted by Nahman Avigad and Jacob Licht. [*See also the biography of Licht*.] Other scholars at the Hebrew University who took an early interest in the study of the Judean Desert documents and contributed to the ongoing scholarly discussions included David Flusser, whose main interest lay in the relationship of this literature to known apocalyptic texts and to the origins of Christianity, and Shemaryahu Talmon, who contributed important insights on the implications of the Qumran calendar. Sukenik's death in 1953 temporarily brought the work of publication of the Hebrew University scrolls to a halt. However, it was resumed at an intensified pace with the eventual purchase of Samuel's scrolls by Sukenik's son, Yigael Yadin, in the summer of 1954. Sukenik's longtime assistant, Nahman Avigad, completed the final publication of Sukenik's scrolls in 1955. Yadin published his transcription and commentary on the War Scroll in the same year, and Yadin and Avigad collaborated on an initial publication of the Genesis Apocryphon (1QapGen) that was produced by the Magnes Press of the Hebrew University in 1956. The Hebrew University also played a role in the first public exhibition of the scrolls in Israel in 1955, when they were displayed in the university's main administration building at the Givat Ram campus.

The combined Hebrew University-Israel Department of Antiquities-Israel Exploration Society expedition to the Judean Desert caves in 1960/1961 brought to light a wealth of new documents, particularly from Yadin's excavations in the Cave of the Letters in Naḥal Ḥever. [*See* Israel Antiquities Authority; Israel Exploration Fund; *and* Ḥever, Naḥal.] Additional important manuscript finds came from Yadin's large-scale excavations at Masada (1963–1965), also cosponsored by the Hebrew University. Yadin's acquisition of the Temple Scroll (11Q19) during the 1967 Arab-Israeli War and its publication in 1977 by the Israel Exploration Society and the Hebrew University added an important new text to the corpus. The Temple Scroll transformed the direction of the study of the Dead Sea Scrolls, challenging the accepted interpretations of the nonlegal character of the finds and offering some intriguing new links to the origins and crystallization of *halakhah*. [*See* Temple Scroll.]

With the reconstitution of the International Dead Sea Scrolls Publication Team in the autumn of 1991, several faculty members of the Hebrew University took important leadership roles. Emanuel Tov was designated editor in chief, and Shemaryahu Talmon and Jonas C. Greenfield, along with Tov, were appointed to the Israel Antiquities Authority scroll advisory board, entrusted with the task of overseeing the pace and character of future publications. The Hebrew University also became the headquarters of the Orion Center for the Study of the Dead Sea Scrolls, established October 1995 under the direction of Michael Stone. The center began to serve as a clearing house for the work of Dead Sea Scrolls scholars from all over the world, organizing and promoting public lectures and scholarly conferences and maintaining a World Wide Web site for the study of the Dead Sea Scrolls and related literature.

[*See also* Museums and Collections; Publication; *and* Scrolls Research.]

BIBLIOGRAPHY

Samuel, Archbishop Athanasius Yeshue. *Treasure of Qumran: My Story of the Dead Sea Scrolls*. Philadelphia, 1966. Samuel's autobiography.

Silberman, Neil Asher. *The Hidden Scrolls: Christianity, Judaism, and the War for the Dead Sea Scrolls*. New York, 1994. A popular account of the discovery, study, and clash for control of the scrolls.

Sukenik, E. L. "Twenty-five Years of Archaeology." In *Hebrew University Garland: A Silver Jubilee Symposium*, edited by Norman Bentwich, pp. 43–57. London, 1952. Sukenik's record of Hebrew University participation in the study of the scrolls.

Tov, Emanuel. "Expanded Team of Editors Hard at Work on Variety of Texts." *Biblical Archaeology Review* 18.4 (July/August 1992), 69, 72–75. A report on the reconstituted Publication Project.

Trever, John C. *The Untold Story of Qumran*. Westwood, N.J., 1964. A first-person story of the discovery of the scrolls, from an American perspective.

Yadin, Yigael. *The Message of the Scrolls*. New York, 1957. A personal account of the acquisition of the Cave 1 scrolls by Sukenik and Yadin with a brief introduction to the main documents.

Yadin, Yigael. *The Temple Scroll*, 3 vols. Jerusalem, 1983. The definitive publication of this important document with an introduction on its discovery and publication.

NEIL ASHER SILBERMAN

HEGESIPPUS was a second-century CE Christian church historian. Most of our knowledge of Hegesippus's life and works comes from Eusebius (c.260–339 CE), who writes that Hegesippus was a converted Jew who "belonged to the first generation after the Apostles" (*Historia ecclesiastica* 2.23.3; 4.22.8). Hegesippus wrote five short books entitled *The Memoirs*, fragments of which are preserved in Eusebius. These works contain a history of the early church and a refutation of the heresies that had sprung up since the time of the Apostles.

After quoting Hegesippus's account of the Christian heresies that had emerged since the Apostles, Eusebius notes that Hegesippus also names the Jewish sects. He quotes as follows from Hegesippus: "There were various groups in the circumcision, among the children of Israel, all hostile to the tribe of Judah and the Christ. They were these—Essenes, Galileans, Hemerobaptists, Masbotheans, Samaritans, Sadducees, and Pharisees" (*Historia ecclesiastica* 4.22.7).

For Hegesippus, then, the Essenes were part of a group of seven Jewish sects. Unlike the later (fourth century) testimony of Epiphanius, who lists the Essenes as a sect under the Samaritans, Hegesippus recognizes both the Essenes and the Samaritans as Jewish sects. This is consistent with the earlier sources such as Josephus and Philo.

Hegesippus's statement that the Essenes were "hostile to the tribe of Judah and the Christ" is intriguing. Does this mean that the Essenes also comprised the beginnings of a Christian sect? His mention of exactly seven Jewish sects (immediately after describing seven Christian heretical sects) may indicate that Hegesippus is trying to link the origin of the Christian sects back to these Jewish sects. Since we have only fragments of Hegesippus rather than a complete text, it is impossible to be certain on this point. Nonetheless, there is no indication either from the other ancient sources concerning the Essenes or from Qumran literature that the Essenes had any particular hostility toward Jesus or the early Christian Church.

Another excerpt of Hegesippus states that "the sects mentioned above did not believe either in a resurrection or in one who is coming to give every man what his deeds deserve," though some from these sects did come to believe in Jesus (*Historia ecclesiastica* 2.23.8–9). Since scribes and Pharisees are mentioned later in this same excerpt, it is probable that Hegesippus is referring to the seven Jewish sects. If so, Hegesippus is saying that none of the Jewish sects, including the Essenes, Pharisees, and Sadducees, believed there would be a resurrection. With respect to the Essenes, Hippolytus states that they did believe in a resurrection (*Refutation of All Heresies* 9.27.1), while Josephus says that they believed the soul was immortal (similar to the Greeks; *The Jewish War* 2.154–157). Certainly the Sadducees did not believe in resurrection, but the Pharisees did. Thus, the testimony of Hegesippus appears to be of limited value in determining the Essene attitude toward resurrection.

BIBLIOGRAPHY

Adam, Alfred. *Antike Berichte über die Essener*. 2d ed. Berlin, 1972. Greek text and brief commentary on all the ancient accounts of the Essenes.

Black, Matthew. *The Scrolls and Christian Origins: Studies in the Jewish Background of the New Testament*. Brown Judaic Studies, 48. Chico, Calif., 1983. A brief discussion of Hegesippus's account of the Essenes.

Eusebius. *The History of the Church from Christ to Constantine*. Translated by G. A. Williamson. New York, 1965. One of the many good English translations of Eusebius's *Ecclesiastical History*.

Grant, Robert M. *Eusebius as Church Historian*. Oxford, 1980. Provides an evaluation of Eusebius's citations of Hegesippus. See pages 67–70.

Puech, Émile. *La croyance des Esséniens en la vie future: Immortalité, résurrection, vie éternelle? Histoire d'une croyance dans le Judaisime ancien*. Études bibliques, 21. Paris, 1993. A detailed treatment of the scrolls and other sources, including Hegesippus, in relation to resurrection.

Quasten, Johannes. "Hegesippus." In *Patrology*, by Johannes Quasten, vol. 1, pp. 284–287. Westminster, Md., 1983. Brief biography of Hegesippus and discussion of his writings.

Schwartz, Edvard. *Eusebius*. Die griechischen christlichen Schriftsteller der ersten drei Jahrhunderte. Leipzig, 1903, 1908, 1909. The standard Greek edition of Eusebius's *Ecclesiastical History*.

TODD S. BEALL

HEIKHALOT LITERATURE. The first major expression of mysticism in postbiblical Judaism can be found in the writings that make up the Heikhalot literature. [*See* Mysticism.] This corpus comprises a number of discrete textual units that were composed and redacted over a period of several centuries. Two central themes run through the Heikhalot texts: the mystical ascent through the heavenly realms, culminating with an ecstatic vision of the luminous form on the throne located in the seventh palace of the seventh heaven; and the adjuration of angels through mentioning the divine names and displaying the magical seals, which facilitates the acquisition of knowledge of the secrets of Torah. [*See* Angels; Throne.] It is virtually impossible to separate mysticism and magic, either conceptually or textually, in these compositions: the mystical component embraces in a fundamental way magical techniques, and the magical component is frequently linked to an experience of a mystical nature. [*See* Magic and Magical Texts.] From a redactional standpoint, therefore, there is little justification to employ the terms *mysticism* and *magic* to refer to distinct phenomena reflected in these texts, nor is there sufficient reason to ascribe priority to the one over the other. Certainly the medieval authors, who received and in some instances helped to shape these sources, made no discernible attempt to isolate the mystical and magical elements.

The six most important texts that provide descriptions of the mystical ascent to the throne of glory are *Heikhalot Zutarti; Heikhalot Rabbati; Sefer Heikhalot,* also known as *3 Enoch;* the treatise published by Gershom Scholem with the title *Ma'aseh Merkavah; Ḥotam ha-Merkavah,* a fragment from the Cairo Genizah referred to by scholars as the Ozhayah text; and *Massekhet Heikhalot*. The protagonists of these ascent texts are Yishma'el, 'Aqiva, and Neḥunya ben ha-Qanah. The use of these rabbinic figures, however, must be seen as merely a literary device to transmit the mystical teachings in the name of established authorities. The precise historical and social context of the authors who produced these works is not at all clear, but it is likely that this mystical praxis was cultivated in Babylonia sometime in the amoraic period (fourth through fifth centuries). It may be assumed that the texts in the form in which they have been preserved were redacted sometime between the seventh and twelfth centuries. Not only do the first explicit references to Heikhalot compositions occur in geonic material, but the first account of mystical techniques employed for ascent is provided by Hai Gaon (939–1038). Additionally, there is substantial textual evidence from this period to show that interest in the mystical and magical traditions (especially connected with divine names) continued to have a decisive impact.

There has been a tendency in some current scholarship to reclaim the view expressed by several nineteenth-century scholars concerning the influence of Islamic mysticism on Jewish mystics in general and on the Heikhalot mystics in particular. In addition to the possible impact of specific Sufi techniques, the combination of ancient gnostic and philosophic ideas characteristic of various forms of Islamic esotericism (especially Isma'ili sources) may prove important in future research on the evolution of Jewish mysticism from late antiquity to the Middle Ages. It must be pointed out, however, that another important milieu for understanding the cultivation and transmission of Heikhalot texts and traditions was southern Italy. The presence of this material in the Islamic and Byzantine-Christian context underscores the centrality of speculation on the throne in the religious history of the Jews, and it is likely that a common source for both currents lies in Palestine.

The details of the vision of the divine chariot were first recorded in the *Book of Ezekiel*. While many of the themes in the biblical prophecy served as the exegetical basis for the visionary experiences elaborated in Heikhalot literature, the essential difference between the prophetic theophany and mystical vision is evident. Closer to the spirit of the experience described in the Heikhalot texts are remnants of heavenly ascents recorded in Jewish and Christian apocalyptic literature from the second century BCE to roughly the third century CE. Some scholars have argued that the mystical praxis preserved in the Heikhalot literature is an outgrowth of Jewish apocalypticism. An important link in this chain is the angelic liturgy of the Qumran sectarians, the Songs of the Sabbath

Sacrifice (4Q400–407) as well as other liturgical fragments found in the Qumran collection. [*See* Songs of the Sabbath Sacrifice.] While there is some uncertainty regarding the appropriateness of the term *mystical* to refer to the poetic descriptions of the angelic realm and the throne contained in these documents, there can be little doubt that the motifs discussed in these sources bear a striking resemblance to the main concerns of the Heikhalot literature. Chariot speculation was an essential aspect of the religious worldview of the Qumran sect. This interest should be seen as part of a much larger phenomenon that involves the profound impact that the *Book of Ezekiel* had on the sectarians. The particular interest in the chariot vision of Ezekiel is attested as well in *Second Ezekiel*, which is rich in exegetical elaborations of the biblical text. The major methodological question is, however, was this interest in the chariot merely speculative in nature; or was it related to specific liturgical practices that the sectarians believed enabled them to bridge the gap between the human and angelic realms? The textual evidence allows us to conclude that this gap was closed in the minds of the sectarians by the angels descending to join their camp, but was it also closed by the humans ascending to join the angels in the heavenly heights? [*See* Heaven.]

Recent attempts to assign the Heikhalot to a later date in Jewish history may be valid from a textual point of view, but it is nevertheless evident that incorporated in these sources are older materials. In particular, the hymns in Qumran fragments provide an important perspective for the evaluation and the possible dating of the liturgical components embedded in the Heikhalot corpus to the Second Temple period. The philological similarities of the Qumran hymns and the liturgical poems contextualized in the larger redactional settings of the Heikhalot texts may also provide important clues for determining the identity and social standing of the composers of the latter. [*See* Poetry; Psalms, Hymns, and Prayers.] Furthermore, the connection between the priestly ritual and the angelic liturgy found in the relevant Dead Sea Scrolls may help the scholar determine the provenance of the Heikhalot writings. It seems likely that the visionary ascent to the heavenly throne and the participation in the angelic worship would have been a preoccupation of a priestly group who, in the absence of an earthly temple, turned their attention to its celestial counterpart. The similar turn from the earthly to the heavenly temple that one finds in the priests who decided to leave Jerusalem to establish a sectarian community in the desert provides the scholar with one of the best tools to appreciate the religious motivation underlying the intense experiences related in the Heikhalot corpus.

BIBLIOGRAPHY

Baumgarten, Joseph M. "The Qumran Sabbath Shirot and the Rabbinic Merkabah Traditions." *Revue de Qumrân* 13 (1988), 199–213.

Elior, Rachel. "From Earthly Temple to Heavenly Shrines: Prayer and Sacred Song in the Hekhalot Literature and Its Relation to Temple Traditions." *Jewish Studies Quarterly* 4 (1997), 217–267.

Gruenwald, Ithamar. *Apocalyptic and Merkavah Mysticism*. Leiden, 1980.

Halperin, David J. *The Faces of the Chariot: Early Jewish Responses to Ezekiel's Vision*. Tübingen, 1988.

Newsom, Carol. *Songs of the Sabbath Sacrifice: A Critical Edition*. Harvard Semitic Studies, 27. Atlanta, 1985.

Nitzan, Bilhah. *Qumran Prayer and Religious Poetry*. Translated by Jonathan Chipman. Studies on the Texts of the Desert of Judah, 12. Leiden, 1994.

Nitzan, Bilhah. "Harmonic and Mystical Characteristics in Poetic and Liturgical Writings from Qumran." *Jewish Quarterly Review* 85 (1994–1995), 163–183.

Schäfer, Peter. *The Hidden and Manifest God: Some Major Themes in Early Jewish Mysticism*. Translated by Aubrey Pomerance. SUNY Series in Judaica. Albany, 1992.

Schiffman, Lawrence H. "Merkavah Speculation at Qumran: The 4Q Serekh Shirot ʿOlat ha-Shabbat." In *Mystics, Philosophers, and Politicians: Essays in Jewish Intellectual History in Honor of Alexander Altmann*, edited by Jehuda Reinharz and Daniel Swetschinski, with the collaboration of Kalman P. Bland, pp. 15–47. Durham, 1982.

Schiffman, Lawrence H. "Heikhalot Mysticism and the Qumran Literature" (in Hebrew). *Jerusalem Studies in Jewish Thought* 6. 1–2 (1987), 121–138.

Scholem, Gershom. *Major Trends in Jewish Mysticism*. New York, 1956.

Scholem, Gershom. *Jewish Gnosticism, Merkabah Mysticism, and Talmudic Tradition*. 2d ed. New York, 1965.

Wolfson, Elliot R. "*Yeridah la-Merkavah:* Typology of Ecstasy and Enthronement in Ancient Jewish Mysticism." In *Mystics of the Book: Themes, Topics and Typologies*, edited by Robert A. Herrera, pp. 13–44. New York, 1993.

Wolfson, Elliot R. *Through a Speculum That Shines: Vision and Imagination in Medieval Jewish Mysticism*. Princeton, 1994. See pages 74–124.

Wolfson, Elliot R. "Mysticism and the Poetic-Liturgical Compositions from Qumran: A Response to Bilhah Nitzan." *Jewish Quarterly Review* 85 (1994–1995), 185–202.

ELLIOT R. WOLFSON

HELLENISM. Modern scholars identify the process by which the eastern Mediterranean basin and western Asia adopted Greek culture after the conquests of Alexander the Great (d. 323 BCE) as *Hellenism*. The main channels of transmission were the Greek cities founded by Alexander and his successors in the newly conquered territories and the waves of Macedonian and Greek immigrants. The language spoken in this much-expanded Greek world was a common (Grk., *koine*) dialect that replaced the hitherto prevailing local Greek dialects, but many of the native languages, including Egyptian, Aramaic, Hebrew, and several languages of Asia Minor, remained in use throughout the Greco-Roman period. Moreover, the spread of Hellenistic culture was far from homogeneous: in the Phoenician cities, for example, close commercial ties brought about substantial Greek influence long before Alexander's conquest; in Judea, a land further removed from the sea and lacking any economic appeal for Greek merchants or settlers, Hellenization was a much slower process. Here too, however, the process began even before Alexander's campaign, as can be seen, for example, from the Greek elements in the Wadi ed-Daliyeh seals. The Greeks' sophisticated culture, their conviction of its superiority over all "barbarian" cultures (*barbarians* are people who say *bar bar* and cannot speak intelligibly, i.e., in Greek), and their firm control of most political and economic activities throughout much of the then-known world, created an enormous incentive for the higher echelons of the native populations to become like Greeks. Moreover, for the Greek elite it was education, even more than ancestry, that made one truly Greek: all non-Greeks could learn the Greek language, immerse themselves in Greek culture, and share in the nurturing of a vibrant cosmopolitan civilization. Thus, one important aspect of Hellenistic culture was the extensive participation of non-Greeks—including, occasionally, such Jews as Caecilius of Caleacte (a rhetor of the late first century BCE)—and the subsequent enrichment of that culture.

A second significant aspect of Hellenistic culture was that the Greek language was used by non-Greeks who sought to preserve their ethnic and cultural uniqueness. Romans, Egyptians, Babylonians, Jews, and others could express their distinct cultures, and trace their national histories in the only language they could expect their non-compatriots to read (with growing Roman assertiveness, Latin, too, became a possible medium for literary creativity, at least in the western Mediterranean). In some instances, religious literature was also translated into Greek; for example, Egyptian texts, occasionally rendered in Greek, or the far more extensive translation of Jewish religious texts into Greek (like the Septuagint).

Hellenistic civilization exerted a great influence even on those individuals who never learned the Greek language: numerous Greek words entered the vocabularies of all other languages. Moreover, decidedly Greek literary motifs appeared in Egyptian and Jewish literature. Roman culture borrowed extensively from the Greek world, and numerous cross-cultural influences can be detected in the fields of art, architecture, law, medicine, religion, and magic. In effect, the global spread of Hellenistic culture enabled such extensive contacts and transformations even across the linguistic barriers separating Greek-speakers from "barbarians."

The Hellenization of Judea was a relatively slow process. Although the spread of new cultural modes was welcomed by many Jews, some aspects of Hellenistic culture—its cosmopolitan tendencies, its inherently polytheistic outlook, its occasional insensitivity to ethnic and religious taboos, and its emphases on the human body and on physical images—were seen by many as irreconcilable with the Jewish way of life. Thus, much of the history of Jewish civilization in the Greco-Roman world can be seen as a struggle to define how exactly Jews should relate to this foreign culture. Within this context, the Dead Sea Scrolls clearly stand out as representing an extremely conservative Jewish milieu. The few Greek texts found at Qumran, including Septuagint manuscripts and fragments of unidentified works of Judeo-Greek literature, bear clear testimony to the Qumranites' contacts with Greek-speaking Jews and their culture. The references in the *pesharim* and related literature to the Seleucid and Roman military presence in Judea demonstrate the Qumranites' awareness of the non-Jewish world around them. And yet, their extensive writings in Hebrew and Aramaic display no interest in Greek culture, not even in the Judeo-Greek world. The Dead Sea Scrolls often evince their authors' deliberate attempt to avoid using Greek words in their writings, in spite of the use of numerous Greek words in contemporary Hebrew and Aramaic (as can be seen from the *Book of Daniel*, from the Copper Scroll [3Q15]). Such aversion to foreign words was in no way unique. In Egyptian (Demotic) documents, a similar phenomenon is apparent, and Latin speakers too sometimes objected to the incursion of Greek words into their language; however, the Qumran authors certainly stand out in their tenacity on this score.

The general lack of Greek loan-words in the Qumran scrolls, and of references to specifically Hellenistic ideas or practices, makes the assessment of the impact of Hellenism on the Qumran community an extremely complex issue. Numerous parallels can be drawn between the Qumranites' social organization, for example, and those of contemporary non-Jewish social and religious associations. Yet such parallels need not be interpreted as reflecting direct cross-cultural influences from one direction or the other, for similar phenomena can often develop independently in unrelated social contexts. Even the obvious parallels between such texts as Zodiology and Brontology (4Q318) and the Greek brontological literature, too specific to be attributed to mere chance, need not reflect a direct Greek influence on the Qumran texts, as both the Aramaic and the Greek astrological traditions owe much to the older Babylonian texts. Overall, it seems clear that at a time when the Hasmonean dynasty was adopting many of the characteristics of the other Hellenistic kingdoms, and when the subsequent Roman and

Herodian regimes opened Judea even further to the non-Jewish world, the Qumranites stood out in their refusal to accept the new realities. This refusal might help explain their marginal position within the Jewish society of the time, and their limited influence on future Jewish history.

If the Qumran scrolls testify to their owners' relative success in insulating themselves against Hellenic culture, that success must be interpreted in part as a sign of the relatively slow Hellenization of Judea and in part as resulting from the sect's close-knit character and the small number of its members. This also explains why the texts found elsewhere in the Judean Desert, and dating from the late first and the second centuries CE, amply testify to the pervasiveness of Greek culture in Roman Judea and to the exposure to that culture of many strata of Jewish society. This is seen not only in the Greek translation of the Minor Prophets found at Naḥal Ḥever, but also from the many Greek documents included in the Babatha archive and from the Greek letters found in the Cave of the Letters and belonging to Bar Kokhba and his comrades. Both sets of documents attest to daily contacts between Jews and non-Jews and testify to the numerous transactions that were carried out, even among the Jews themselves, in the Greek language and within the legal conventions of the Hellenized Near East. In an age characterized by a growing foreign presence in Judea, by a much-weakened Jewish community, and by the end of isolationist sectarianism, Jews were more exposed to the influence of Hellenic culture than ever before. As the rabbis were soon to demonstrate, such exposure need not imply a compromise of one's Jewish identity.

BIBLIOGRAPHY

Avi-Yonah, Michael. *Hellenism and the East: Contacts and Interrelations from Alexander to the Roman Conquest*. Ann Arbor, Mich., 1978.

Bickerman, E. J. *The Jews in the Greek Age*. Cambridge, Mass., 1988.

Goodman, Martin (ed.). *Jews in a Graeco-Roman World*, Oxford, 1998.

Hadas, Moses. *Hellenistic Culture: Fusion and Diffusion*. New York, 1959.

Hengel, Martin. *Judaism and Hellenism*, 2 vols. Translated by John Bowden. Philadelphia, 1974.

Klinghardt, M. "The Manual of Discipline in the Light of Statutes of Hellenistic Associations." In *Methods of Investigation of the Dead Sea Scrolls and the Khirbet Qumran Site*, edited by M. O. Wise et al., pp. 251–270. Annals of the New York Academy of Sciences, 722, New York, 1994.

Millar, Fergus. *The Roman Near East 31 BC–AD 337*. Cambridge, Mass., 1993.

Levine, Lee I. *Judaism & Hellenism in Antiquity: Conflict or Confluence?* Seattle, 1998.

Momigliano, A. *Alien Wisdom: The Limits of Hellenization*. Cambridge, 1975.

Tarn, W. W. *Hellenistic Civilisation*, 3d ed., rev. by G. T. Griffith. London, 1952.

Tcherikover, Victor. *Hellenistic Civilization and the Jews*. Translated by S. Applebaum. Philadelphia, 1959.

Walbank, F. W. *The Hellenistic World*, rev. ed. Cambridge, Mass., 1993.

Weinfeld, M. *The Organizational Pattern and the Penal Code of the Qumran Sect: A Comparison with Guilds and Religious Associations of the Hellenistic-Roman Period*. Novum Testamentum et Orbis Antiquus, 2, Göttingen, 1986.

GIDEON BOHAK

HEMEROBAPTISTS. The Greek *Hēmerobaptistai* (= *kath' hēmeran baptizomenoi*) can be translated as the Hebrew term *ṭovelei yom*, "those who bathe (immerse) daily." The preserved information about the Jewish sect of hemerobaptists is extremely scant. It is mentioned by the Christian authors Justin Martyr (c.100–165 CE) in *Dialogue with Trypho* 80.4 (here, it is called the sect of "Baptists"), Eusebius of Caesarea (ca. 263–339 CE) in *Ecclesiastical History* IV.22.7 (quotation from the unpreserved *Hypomnemata* [*Memoirs*] by the Christian historian of the second century CE Hegesippus), Epiphanius of Salamis (ca. 315–403 CE) in the *Panarion*, Heresy XVII, and in the *Apostolic Constitutions* (ca. 380 CE) VI.6.5 mentioned along with the sects of Pharisees, Sadducees, Essenes, and some others. Pseudo-Clementine *Homilies* (third–fourth centuries CE) 2.23.1 use the term with respect to John the Baptist. According to Epiphanius, the sect "has the same ideas as the scribes and Pharisees," but "unlike the Sadducees, however, in their [the Sadducees'] denial of resurrection." The members of the sect "were always baptized every day . . . and thus came to be called Hemerobaptists. For they made the claim that there is no life for a man unless he is baptized daily with water, and washed and purified from every fault" (*Panarion* 17.1.1–2). According to the *Apostolic Constitutions*, the Hemerobaptists "unless they wash every day, do not eat, and unless they cleanse their beds and tables, or platters and cups and seats, do not make use of any of them." It is possible that the Hemerobaptists are identical with the *ṭovelei* (*ṭovelanei*) *shaḥarit*, "morning bathers," mentioned in Rabbinic literature (e.g. T., *Yad.*, II, 20; B.T., *Ber.*, 22a; J.T., *Ber.*, 3.6c). Some scholars (e.g., H. Graetz, J. D. Amusin) identified the latter with the Essenes. The Hemerobaptists were probably close to (if not identical with) the Jewish sect of Masbotheans (the Greek *Masbōtheoi/Masbōthaioi* is apparently derived from the Syro-Palestinian *mtsbwʿth*, "baptism") mentioned, in particular, in the *Ecclesiastical History* 4.22.7 and *Apostolic Constitutions*, 6.6.4. According to the latter composition, the Masbotheans "deny Providence, and say that the world is made by spontaneous motion, and take away the immortality of the soul."

According to Epiphanius's *Panarion* 30.15.3, the apostle Peter and the sect of Ebionites were "baptized daily for purification." [*See* Ebionites.]

The resemblance of the Hemerobaptists to the Essenes is evident. According to *The Jewish War*, 2.129, 138, 168 by the Jewish historian Flavius Josephus (37/38–after 100 CE), the Essenes practiced daily ritual purifying ablutions (baths) probably not long before noon (2.129).

Purification and sanctification by water are mentioned in the Qumran Rule of the Community (1QS) iii.4–9, iv.21, v.13–14 (see also the fragments of the Rule from Cave 4: 4Q255, frg. 2, 1–4; 4Q257, frg. 1, 2.6–13; 4Q262, 1–4). Judging from these passages, the Qumranites seem to have stipulated purifying ablutions (the frequency and order of which are unknown) by the obligatory repentance and spiritual cleansing preceding them (cf. *Ezek*. 36.25–26). If the term *Hemerobaptist* reflects *ṭevul yom* in some form, then texts found in Qumran that reflect a debate about this issue may indicate a trajectory found both in the late Second Temple period (cf. Miqtsat Ma'asei ha-Torah[b] [4Q395 13–16, 64–72]) and in an early Jewish Christian group. According to Josephus's *Jewish Antiquities*, 18.117, *Matthew* 3.11, *Mark* 1.4, and *Luke* 3.8 (cf. also *Panarion*, 30.13.6; 14.3 [a fragment of the so-called *Gospel of Ebionites*; for further reference, *see* Ebionites]), John the Baptist (who, according to some scholars, had close connections with the Qumran community) preached the "baptism of (preliminary) repentance." [*See* John the Baptist.]

In connection with the description of the Hemerobaptists attested in the *Apostolic Constitutions* it is appropriate to mention that the ritual meal of the Qumranites is designated in the Dead Sea Scrolls as *ṭohorah*, "purity" (e.g., the Rule of the Community 4Q255–4Q264 [1QS, 4QS[a–j]], passim; the *Damascus Document* [CD] ix.21, 23). In Rabbinic literature the term *ṭohorah* is used to designate ritually pure articles—tableware, utensils, cloths, and especially food.

BIBLIOGRAPHY

Friedländer, M. *Die religiösen Bewegungen innerhalb des Judentums im Zeitalter Jesu*. Berlin, 1905.

Lieberman, Saul. "The Discipline in the So-Called Dead Sea Manual of Discipline." *Journal of Biblical Literature* 71 (1952), 199–206 (= Lieberman, Saul. *Texts and Studies*. New York, 1974, pp. 200–207).

Simon, Marcel. *Les Sectes Juives au temps de Jésus*. Paris, 1960. (*Jewish Sects at the Time of Jesus*. Translated from French by J. H. Farley. Philadelphia, 1967).

Thomas, J. *Le mouvement baptiste en Palestine et en Syrie*. Gembloux, 1935.

IGOR R. TANTLEVSKIJ

HEROD AGRIPPA. *See* Herodian Rulers.

HEROD ANTIPAS. *See* Herodian Rulers.

HERODIAN RULERS. The Herodian dynasty followed the Hasmonean one, which had ruled Judea under various forms from the middle of the second century BCE until 37 BCE.

The rise of the Herodians to power had already begun under the Hasmoneans (*Jewish Antiquities* 14.10) and was precipitated by the internal rivalry within the Hasmonean family. The roots of the Herodians were in Idumea, where they were counted among the leading noble families. They became Jewish when John Hyrcanus I conquered Idumea. Antipas, Herod the Great's grandfather, became governor of Idumea under Alexander Jannaeus. His son Antipater, Herod's father, inherited this post and was also a close friend and counsellor of Hyrcanus II (*Jewish Antiquities* 14.8).

This family belonged to the Judean nobility of the later Hasmonean period, even though its members were considered as *homines novi*, in the eyes of the more veteran or priestly Jewish nobility. The Dead Sea Scrolls are vehemently critical of this nobility. They are blamed for belligerency and social inequity, and doomed to destruction. In the early stages of Roman rule in the land of Israel, Antipater and his sons, Phasael and Herod, forged strong links with Roman governors and generals. These connections, the upheaval of the Parthian invasion of Syria in 40 BCE, and the instability of later Hasmonean rule, paved the way for Herod to the throne of Judea (for the history of this period and Herod's rule see *Jewish Antiquities*, books 14 to the middle of 17).

Herod's rule lasted for thirty-four years (37–4 BCE). It consolidated the political situation in Judea after a long period of instability, which had already begun under the later Hasmoneans. Yet it did not solve social problems, ideological unrest, and national aspirations, although it suppressed them all with an iron fist.

How did this affect the Jewish sects? The answer is not easy, as we should not suppose a common attitude on Herod's part toward all the sects, and because our sources are very limited. Be that as it may, it seems that both the Sadducees and the Pharisees were forced to abstain from political activity and were restricted to religious matters, the Sadducees mainly to the priestly activity around the Temple, although even there they were obliged to accept Pharisaic intervention, and the Pharisees mainly to juristic and communal activity. As both sects were active within Jewish society, they were forced, haphazardly, to keep aloof of any interference with Herod's state and family affairs.

The Essenes were the most tolerated among these three "classical" Jewish sects (*Jewish Antiquities* 15.373–378).

From a political point of view, Herod's tolerance toward the Essenes is explicable, since the Essenes, though ideologically extremists, were a closed sect, waiting for metaphysical deliverance from the corrupt existence in this world, and inactive as far as public and political life were concerned.

Assuming that the Essenes are to be identified with the Qumran community, and that all, or many, of the manuscripts found there were part of a sectarian collection of books, and that some of them express a sectarian ideology, we may conclude that under Herod the Dead Sea sect lived undisturbed on the outskirts of society. According to Flusser, they survived the famine in the land in 25–24 BCE, which is referred to in some of the Dead Sea Scrolls (Flusser, 1987).

It seems that the creative period of the sect preceded Herod's days. Yet, as many manuscripts from Qumran are dated paleographically to the Herodian period, it is clear that the sect's ideological activity did not stop. The fact that some of the sectarian writings, composed at an earlier period, were copied in Herod's time means that interest in their content still existed.

Yet, interestingly enough, no major composition seems to have been written down later than the early Roman period, and even meaningful editing in the Herodian period cannot be detected in the Dead Sea Scrolls. Archaeology also does not show any major events at the Qumran settlement between the earthquake of 31 BCE, which, according to Roland de Vaux brought severe destruction at Qumran, and the destruction of Qumran in 68 CE, in the course of the First Jewish Revolt of 66–70.

Additionally, Herod is only rarely mentioned in the Jewish literature of the Second Temple period, the Apocrypha and pseudepigrapha. The *Assumption of Moses* is the one work that refers to Herod, although not by name, as is the rule in apocalyptic literature.

Our main source for Herod's time and activity is Josephus (see *The Jewish War* 1.204–666; *Jewish Antiquities* as cited above), who was dependent on Herod's friend, Nicolaus of Damascus as a source. The main turning points in Herod's career were:

- His appointment by his father Antipater as governor of Galilee (in 47 BCE) and the friendly relations he forged with influential Romans.
- The Parthian invasion (40 BCE) of Syria, the death of his elder brother Phasael, his flight to Rome, and his crowning as king of Judea in the same year.
- The conquest of the land of Israel from the last Hasmonean ruler—Mattathias Antigonus—and the beginning of his *de facto* rule in Judea (37 BCE).
- The struggles within his family involving Hyrcanus II, Hyrcanus II's daughter Shelamzion Alexandra, and Miriamme, Shelamzion Alexandra's daughter and Herod's wife, who was executed by him (29 BCE).
- The confirmation of Herod in his position by Octavian (31 BCE), which was a major step in consolidating his rule over Judea.
- His building activity, crowned by such projects as the Temple Mount, Caesarea, Masada, and Herodion, of which traces are still to be seen in the land of Israel.

Herod was hated by many of his Jewish subjects and was regarded by them as a Roman puppet. Although the economic situation was improved under his rule, he represented foreign domination and was king of a binational state. His "Greek" subjects and his Jewish subjects hated each other, and both hated him.

Nevertheless in some areas, Herod continued trends that were already visible under the Hasmoneans. One of them was developing and strengthening relations with the Jewish Diaspora. It seems that there Herod achieved a certain degree of popularity, which he could not achieve in the Land of Israel.

Some of Herod's progeny continued to serve as rulers in the Land of Israel under Roman patronage, including three of his sons: Archelaus as ethnarch of Judea, Samaria, and Idumea (4 BCE–6 CE); Herod Antipas as tetrarch in the Galilee and the Perea (4 BCE–39 CE); and Philip as tetrarch in the Golan and its surroundings (4 BCE–33/34 CE). Archelaus's failure as a ruler brought his part of Herod's kingdom under the direct control of Roman governors. His two brothers ruled much longer, and their princedoms were gradually inherited by Herod's most distinguished successor, Agrippa I, his grandson through the Hasmonean Miriamme.

Agrippa I's reign constituted a kind of a short blooming period of Herodian rule, at least from a Jewish point of view. In 37 CE Agrippa was appointed king of the former princedom of his uncle Philip and two years later of Antipas's tetrarchy. Agrippa's meteoric career was due to his friendship with Caligula, the Roman emperor (37–41 CE). Caligula's murder opened the way for a new emperor, Claudius, also a friend of Agrippa, who made him king over all the land of Israel by adding Judea, Samaria, and Idumea, the three of which were a Roman province (6–41 CE), to his kingdom.

Agrippa's kingdom was as large as that of his grandfather Herod the Great, but, unlike him, he was popular among his Jewish subjects. Yet this flourishing of an autonomous Judea under him was shortlived. In 44 CE Agrippa suddenly died; some think he was poisoned. He was replaced by Roman governors, who ruled over most of the land of Israel.

There is little that links Herod's successors with the Dead Sea sect. One may find indirect relation in Herod Antipas's treatment of John the Baptist (*Antiquities* 18.117–119; New Testament: *Mt.* 14.3f; *Mk.* 6.17–18; *Lk.* 3.19–20), if we assume some connection of John with the Essenes/Qumranites.

It is thought that Agrippa I inclined toward the Pharisees, an inclination that cannot be proven, and in any case contributes nothing to our knowledge of the Dead Sea Scrolls. Both rulers are mentioned in the Gospels and *Acts*, and like Herod, they too are presented in a negative light.

The last Herodians who play a role in Jewish history are Agrippa I's children, Agrippa II and Berenice. After some interval, Agrippa II was appointed king of Philip's tetrarchy, to which the eastern Galilee, along with Tiberias, were later added. Berenice was active at the side of her unmarried brother to such a degree that they were suspected of incest. They both played a role in Jewish society until the end of the First Jewish Revolt of 66–70 CE, but with the destruction of the Temple they seem to disappear politically from the Judean scene.

Some other Herodians of lesser position also played a part in Jewish life and usually sided with the pro-Roman party in Judea, like most of the Judean nobility. Others served the Romans as rulers of regions outside Judea. Most distinguished among them were Herod of Chalcis, Agrippa I's brother, and his son Aristobulus, who ruled Chalcis in the Lebanon.

Although the Herodian dynasty and its offshoots played a major role in Jewish society for about 110 years (40 BCE–70 CE at least), its activity is not reflected in the Dead Sea Scrolls, and is only very slightly reflected in the Apocrypha and pseudepigrapha, which may be partially related to the Dead Sea Scrolls. In the Talmudic literature there are some references to Herodians, but their historical value is very doubtful.

If we consider the later existence of the Qumran settlement as contemporary with the Herodian dynasty, and draw conclusions from the silence of the literary sources, then we may propose that from Herod the Great until the destruction of Jerusalem, the Essenes/Qumranites lived undisturbed in their place. They, for their part, were more active in copying older works than in developing new attitudes toward the rulers of Judea, both Herodian and Roman.

BIBLIOGRAPHY

Flusser, David. "Qumran and the Famine during the Reign of Herod." *Israel Museum Journal* 6 (1987), 7–16.

Hoehner, Harold W. *Herod Antipas*. Cambridge, 1972.

Kokkinos, Nikos. *The Herodian Dynasty: Origins, Role in Society and Eclipse*. Journal for the Study of Pseudepigrapha Supplement Series, 30. Sheffield, 1998.

Schalit, Abraham. *König Herodes, der Mann und sein Werk*. Berlin, 1969.

Schwartz, Daniel R. *Agrippa I: The Last King of Judea*. Tübingen, 1990.

URIEL RAPPAPORT

HERODIANS were referred to in the New Testament and in Josephus, but not in the scrolls, on which various theories have been held (H. Rowley identifies twelve: more could be added). The Gospels suggest that Herodians had a social-religious program, though Josephus implies that they were a political, not well-defined group. The relatively late evidence has encouraged proposals that behind the Herodians are Agrippa I or II.

Mark 3.6 and 12.13 (c.70 CE) claim that at the time of Jesus, Herodians (using the latinized Greek form *hêrôdianoi*) were associated with Pharisees, but only one parallel (*Mt.* 22.16; c.85 CE) follows *Mark*. *Mark* 8.15 has a variant, "Herodians," for "leaven of Herod," but neither Matthew nor Luke refers to either Herodians or Herod, suggesting that neither knows the group; Mark, or his source, knows them only slightly.

Josephus's earlier work, *The Jewish War* (c.75 CE), describes conditions in the period 40–37 BCE when Herod's supporters appear as a loose coalition (*The Jewish War* 1.319, 326, 356; using the Greek forms *hêrôdeioi, tous ta hêrôdou phronesantas, tous ta autou phronêsantas eunousterous*). In only one case does *Jewish Antiquities* (c.95 CE) use this vocabulary (*Antiquities* 14.450; contrast 14.436?, 15.1–2). Josephus, like the Synoptic Gospels and at about the same time, minimizes the group's significance as he moves farther from his source (Nicolaus of Damascus). The Gospels and Josephus do not support the view that the term *Herodians* refers primarily to supporters of Agrippa I or II.

Proposals that the scrolls allude to Herodians have been made. Yigael Yadin argued that the Temple Scroll's allusion to seven baskets of bread in an Essene ordination ritual (11QT[a] xv.3–5) is reflected in the reference in *Mark* to seven baskets of crumbs (*Mk.* 8.14–21), and that Jesus' warning against the leaven of Herodians in 8.15 (v. 1) supports Constantin Daniel's argument that Herodians are simply Essenes, a view dismissed by Willi Braun. Eisenman and Wise suggest that marriage with nieces and relationship with gentiles in the Damascus Document should be linked with marriage questions in Miqtsat Maʿasei ha-Torah (4QMMT B39–49, 81–82; CD v.7–9; iv.14–19; cf. 11QT[a] lxvi.15–17) and understood as prohibitions against Herodians in the period 40–66 CE. The dating of the texts, however, makes it unlikely that either intends to refer to Herodians.

Some hold that the group originated under Antipas (4

BCE–38 CE; see Bikerman). More logically, it derives from Herod the Great's reign, as a sociopolitical movement upon which Herod depended for legitimacy. While it probably began with members of the elite who agreed with Herod's entente with Rome and supported his hold on power, it may have developed later as a group with quasi-religious features, possibly including views of Essenes and others such as Boethos (Hoehner), who owed his position to Herod. There is no evidence that Herodians viewed Herod as the Messiah (contra Epiphanius). [*See* Herodian Rulers.]

BIBLIOGRAPHY

Bennett, W. J. Jr. "The Herodians of Mark's Gospel." *Novum Testamentum* 17 (1975), 9–14. Herodians are a creation of Mark.

Bikerman, E. "Les Hérodiens." *Revue biblique* 47 (1938), 184–197. Patristic and linguistic evidence suggests that Herodians first appear about 30 CE.

Braun, Willi. "Were the New Testament Herodians Essenes? A Critique of an Hypothesis." *Revue de Qumrân* 14 (1989), 75–88. The Daniel/Yadin hypothesis—that the Herodians are Essenes—fails to persuade.

Daniel, Constantin. "Les 'Hérodiens' du Nouveau Testament sont-ils des Esséniens?" *Revue de Qumrân* 6 (1967), 31–53.

Hoehner, Harold. "The Herodians." In *Herod Antipas*, pp. 331–342. Grand Rapids, Mich., 1980 [1972], Appendix X. Herodians are Boethusians.

Rowley, H. H. "The Herodians in the Gospels." *Journal of Theological Studies* 41 (1940), 14–27. A useful survey of various patristic and modern views.

PETER RICHARDSON

HERODIUM. Lying 5 kilometers (3.1 miles) southeast of Bethlehem and 12 kilometers (7.5 miles) south of Jerusalem, the truncated, conical mountain Herodium (Gk., *Herodion*) is described by Josephus as having the shape of a woman's breast (*Jewish Antiquities* 15.324). The Arabic name of the site, Jebel Fureidis, seems to preserve the name *Herodis* ("Herod's mountain"), the site's designation during the period of the Bar Kokhba Revolt against Rome (see below). Herodium was constructed by Herod some time between the years 24/22 and 15 BCE. According to Josephus, it was intended to serve as a fortress, as the capital of a toparchy (administrative district), and ultimately as a memorial to Herod (*The Jewish War* 1.419, 3.55; *Antiquities* 15.324). Josephus also describes the procession accompanying Herod's funeral and burial at Herodium (*The Jewish War* 1.670–673; *Antiquities* 17.196–199). During the First Jewish Revolt against the Romans (66–70 CE), Herodium was occupied by Jewish rebels and was one of the last three strongholds to fall to the Romans after the destruction of Jerusalem (*The Jewish War* 4.518–520, 4.555, 7.163). According to documents from Wadi Murabba'at dating to the time of the Bar Kokhba Revolt (c.132–135 CE), Shim'on Bar Kokhba had a command post at Herodium.

Exploration of the Site. During the eighteenth and nineteenth centuries, Herodium was visited and described by a number of explorers, including Richard Pococke (1738), Edward Robinson (1838), Félicien du Saulcy (1863), Conrad Schick (1879), and Claude Reignier Condor and Horatio Herbert Kitchener (1881). Excavations on top of the mountain were conducted by Virgilio C. Corbo from 1962 to 1967 on behalf of the Studium Biblicum Franciscanum. In 1967 and 1970, conservation and restoration works were carried out by Gideon Foerster on behalf of the Israel National Parks Authority. Between 1970 and 1987, excavations were conducted in Lower Herodium by Ehud Netzer of the Hebrew University of Jerusalem. Although no documents have been found at any of the excavations at Herodium, there are graffiti scratched on the plaster of walls, ostraca, and inscriptions on jars in Hebrew, Aramaic, and Greek from all phases of occupation. [*See* Names and Naming.]

Upper Herodium. The site of Herodium consists of a palace/fortress on top of the mountain and a Lower City. The palace/fortress is located inside the top of an artificial mountain that was created by pouring an earth and stone fill around the outside of a double circular wall, the diameter of which is 62 meters (203 feet). A round tower, 18 meters (59 feet) in diameter, was set into the double circular wall on the east. A semicircular tower projected from the wall at each of the other three cardinal points. The double wall and towers were constructed on a series of vaults and rose several stories in height, with their tops originally protruding above the earth and stone fill. Herod's palace/fortress was built inside the double circular wall, as if set into the mouth of a volcano. A stepped, vaulted passage was cut through the fill from the base of the mountain to an entrance on the northeast side of the top.

The circular area on top of the mountain was divided into two symmetrical halves. The eastern half was occupied by a peristyle garden flanked by exedrae (semicircular recesses). The palatial rooms, including dwellings, service rooms, a triclinium (dining room), and a bathhouse, occupied the western half. During the period of the First Jewish Revolt the triclinium was converted into a synagogue. A small monastic community occupied the top of the mountain during the Byzantine period (fifth–early seventh centuries CE).

Lower Herodium. The buildings in the Lower City have the same axial orientation as those on top of the mountain and were apparently constructed as part of the same overall plan. A large (46 by 70 by 3 meters [151 by

227 by 9.8 feet] deep) pool with a circular pavilion in the center dominated the Lower City. The pool was surrounded by a garden with porticoes along the sides. To the southeast of the pool complex was a long, narrow racecourse or track (350 meters [1148 feet] long by 30 meters [98 feet] wide), with a large palace just above it to the north. The racecourse is too narrow to have served as a hippodrome. An elaborate structure described by Netzer as a "monumental building" faces directly onto the western edge of the racecourse. It consisted of a single rectangular hall of ashlar masonry, whose bottom part was cut into bedrock. The interior of the hall is surrounded by niches with half-columns set on pedestals between them. The thickness of the side walls indicates that there was a vaulted ceiling and perhaps a monumental roof above. Netzer has considered but rejected the possibility that the "monumental building" was Herod's tomb, but he believes that the tomb may have been located in the vicinity and that the "racecourse" may have been used for Herod's funeral procession. Noting the similarity between the interior of the "monumental building" and the triclinium of the Roman Soldier Tomb at Petra, he has suggested that the building served as a grave marker for Herod's tomb. This suggestion has been refuted by Foerster, who identifies the building as a triclinium.

Like Masada and Machaerus, Herodium remained in the hands of Jewish rebels or Zealots after the fall of Jerusalem in 70 CE but was the first of the three to be captured by the Romans. Post-Herodian remains at Lower Herodium include a network of tunnels that served mostly as hiding places during the Bar Kokhba Revolt (mostly at the northeastern edge of the mountain) and three churches of the Byzantine period. [*See* Bar Kokhba Revolt.]

Prototype for Herodium. Herodium's distinctive truncated, conical shape, combined with the fact that Herod's architecture in general was inspired by contemporary Hellenistic and Italic models, has led scholars to search for a prototype. The most plausible candidate until now has been the Mausoleum of Augustus in Rome, the similarities of which to Herodium in function and design were noted by Arthur Segal. This is not supported by the known chronology, however, since Herod made no recorded visits to Rome before the construction of Herodium was well under way or even completed. Instead, the similarities between the two monuments reflect the inspiration of a common prototype: the lost Mausoleum of Alexander the Great in Alexandria. This is supported by ancient descriptions of the mausoleum and by the fact that Herod accompanied Augustus to Alexandria in 30 BCE, at which time Augustus visited the mausoleum and paid homage to Alexander's remains. Herod probably followed Augustus's example and modeled his own mausoleum after that of Alexander the Great.

BIBLIOGRAPHY

Corbo, Virgilio C. *Herodion 1: Gli Edifici della Reggia Fortezza.* Jerusalem, 1989. The publication of the Italian expedition's excavations on top of the mountain.

Foerster, Gideon. "Herodium." In *The New Encyclopedia of Archaeological Excavations in the Holy Land,* edited by Ephraim Stern, vol. 2, pp. 618–622. New York, 1993. An excellent, up-to-date description of the archaeological excavations and remains on top of the mountain.

Netzer, Ehud. *Herodium, An Archaeological Guide.* Jerusalem, 1978. This is a slender paperback guidebook to the site.

Netzer, Ehud. *Greater Herodium.* Qedem, 13. Jerusalem, 1981. The publication of the author's excavations at Lower Herodium from 1972 to 1978.

Netzer, Ehud. "Lower Herodium." In *The New Encyclopedia of Archaeological Excavations in the Holy Land,* vol. 2, edited by Ephraim Stern, pp. 621–626. New York, 1993. An excellent, up-to-date description of the archaeological excavations and remains of Lower Herodium.

Segal, Arthur. "Herodium." *Israel Exploration Journal* 23 (1973), 27–29. Segal establishes the construction date of Herodium and suggests that the Mausoleum of Augustus in Rome served as the prototype.

Tsafrir, Yoram. "The Desert Fortresses of Judaea in the Second Temple Period." In *The Jerusalem Cathedra 2,* edited by Lee I. Levine, pp. 120–145. Jerusalem, 1982. A good overview of the Hasmonean and Herodian fortresses of the Judean Desert.

JODI MAGNESS

HEROD THE GREAT. *See* Herodian Rulers.

ḤEVER, NAḤAL. [*This entry is divided into two articles:* Archaeology *and* Written Material.]

Archaeology

In the autumn of 1953, Yoḥanan Aharoni conducted a survey of Naḥal Ḥever, where he found ten caves (which he designated Caves 1 through 10). Aharoni likewise discovered two Roman siege camps, the first on a plateau north of Naḥal Ḥever and a second camp on the southern bank. In both camps, as well as in the cave below the northern camp, he discovered evidence that the bedouin had preceded him and undertaken excavations for the purpose of plundering. In the course of his examination, it was ascertained that the cave under the northern bank was a large cave with two openings (designated as openings number 5 and 6; therefore, the northern cave is identified as 5/6Ḥev). During the spring of 1955 Aharoni returned to the caves of Naḥal Ḥever, this time to examine Cave 8 on the southern bank of the river below the southern Roman camp. It was determined that excavations had been conducted by the bedouin in this cave as well. Here, Aharoni discovered more than forty skeletons and named the southern cave the Cave of Horror. Within the framework of the Judean Desert Expeditions in 1960, Yigael Yadin excavated the northern cave. He found in it many artifacts from the era of the Bar Kokhba Revolt. [*See* Bar Kokhba Revolt.] The most significant find was a leather flask containing fifteen letters that Shimʿon bar Kosiba' (Bar Kokhba's real name) had sent. [*See* Bar Kokhba, Shimʿon.] Following this discovery, the northern cave was named the Cave of the Letters.

In 1961, within the framework of the second part of the Judean Desert Expeditions, Yadin returned to the northern bank of Naḥal Ḥever. This time he excavated the Roman camp, Caves 3 and 4 (where he found pottery from the era of the Bar Kokhba Revolt), and he returned to the Cave of the Letters. During the course of this project, Yadin discovered the Babatha archive. [*See* Babatha.] In the course of part two of the Judean Desert Expeditions, Aharoni excavated the Cave of Horror, where he found a number of scroll fragments, among them fragments of the Greek Minor Prophets scroll, proving that the main section of this scroll was discovered by the bedouin in this cave.

In 1991 an additional cave was discovered in the western portion of Naḥal Ḥever, where refugees had fled at the end of the Bar Kokhba Revolt. This cave was excavated by David Amit and Hanan Eshel. Signs of pillaging excavations conducted by the bedouin also were found in this cave. Despite this, a silver coin from the time of the Bar Kokhba Revolt was discovered. One can assume that the two documents included in the Naḥal Ṣe'elim collection originated in this cave.

Cave of the Letters. This cave is the largest on the northern bank of Naḥal Ḥever. The cave's two openings are 7 meters (23 feet) apart. The length of the cave is approximately 150 meters (457 feet), and it contains three chambers. The two openings lead to chamber A, the northeastern side of which is rounded. Chamber A is full of huge masses of boulders. A tunnel approximately half a meter (1.6 feet) high leads from chamber A to chamber B. It is necessary to crawl through it in order to enter chamber B. From chamber B a tunnel extends to the east, while chamber C opens from the north into chamber B west of the tunnel.

In 1960 a burial chamber containing the skeletons of nineteen people and an abundance of fabric was found in the cave. At the foot of the cave a Bar Kokhba coin, a hoard of bronze articles used for ritual worship, and a fragment of a scroll of the *Book of Psalms* were found. The most significant findings in the cave, fifteen of Bar Kokhba's letters, also were discovered in 1960. In 1961, hoards of pottery, metal, and glass vessels were discovered in the inner portion of the cave. [*See* Glassware; Metal Utensils; *and* Pottery.] Among them was an archive containing the documents of Babatha. Arrowheads, a whole arrow, fragments of a scroll from the *Book of Numbers*, as well as a fragment of papyrus including a Nabatean document published by Starcky (5/6Ḥev 36 = XḤev/Se Nab. 1) were found at the entrance to the cave in 1961. Hence, we can deduce that some of the documents included in the Naḥal Ṣe'elim collection originated in the Cave of the Letters. A hoard of nineteen bronze vessels and a fragment of a scroll of the *Book of Psalms* were found in the first chamber. In the second chamber there were few finds: primarily, pottery, mats, and a Greek papyrus, which is the inner section of a marriage contract (5/6Ḥev 37). The majority of the finds were discovered in the third chamber: metal finds, a collection of rings, a cooking pot, a set of glassware, a Bar Kokhba coin, and baskets. The most significant find was a basket containing, among other items, the Babatha archive—thirty-five documents written between 93 and 132 CE in various languages—Greek, Nabatean, and Aramaic. Adjacent to the Babatha archive were six documents from the era of the Bar Kokhba Revolt belonging to Eleazar ben Samuel, a farmer from ʿEin-Gedi who had leased land from Bar Kokhba.

Cave of Horror. This cave is situated on the southern bank of Naḥal Ḥever. It resembles a corridor 65 meters (213 feet) long, winding a little toward the north and culminating in a chamber that is reached by a short tunnel. The bedouin conducted pillaging excavations in the cave, and it was excavated entirely by Aharoni in 1961. During the course of this excavation, many clay vessels from the era of the Bar Kokhba Revolt were found in the cave, among them a significant group of ceramic oil lamps, glass vessels, and four bronze coins that were minted by Bar Kokhba. Also discovered were three *ostraca*, bearing names of the deceased placed on top of the skeletons, as well as fragments of two documents written on a papyrus, one in Aramaic and another in Greek, and fragments of a scroll written in Hebrew containing what most likely is a prayer (8Ḥev 2). Especially important are nine fragments of the Greek Minor Prophets (8Ḥev 1) discovered by Aharoni, the remainder of which were found by the bedouin, who designated their origin as Naḥal Ṣe'elim. Consequently, one can assume that a portion of the documents included in the Naḥal Ṣe'elim collection originated in the Cave of Horror.

Cave of the Tetradrachm. This is a large cave on the upper west side of Naḥal Ḥever approximately 12 kilometers (7.5 miles) west of the Cave of the Letters and the Cave of Horror. This cave has three openings and three chambers; however, it is larger than the Cave of the Letters, and it is 200 meters (656 feet) long. This cave was discovered and excavated in 1991 by David Amit and Hanan Eshel. In it were found many clay vessels from the era of the Bar Kokhba Revolt, two short inscriptions written in ink upon sherds itemizing the contents of jars, and a silver tetradrachm from which the cave gets its name. An assumption can be made that two of the documents (XḤev/Se 9 [deed]; XḤev/Se Gr. 2 [double contract; marriage contract]) included in the Naḥal Ṣe'elim collection were discovered by the bedouin in this cave, since these documents originated in Yakim, which is only about 5 kilometers (3.1 miles) from the Cave of the Letters, whereas the rest of the documents of the Naḥal Ṣe'elim collection originated in the eastern region of Transjordan. The documents under discussion mention the village Aristoboulias and the capital of the toparchy Zif—both in the southern region of Mount Hebron. The Aramaic document is dated by paleographic analysis to the Herodian period, and it documents the transaction of Yehudah ben Shimon selling an orchard in Yakim to a man by the name of Yehudah. [*See* Deeds of Sale.] The Greek document is a canceled marriage document from the year 130 CE, of a bride from Aristoboulias and a man from Yakim.

[*See also* Archaeological Surveys; Archaeology; Qumran, *article on* Archaeology; *and biography of Yadin.*]

BIBLIOGRAPHY

Aharoni, Y. "The Cave of Naḥal Ḥever." *ʿAtiqot*, English Series 3 (1961), 148–162.

Aharoni, Y. "Expedition B—The Cave of Horror." *Israel Exploration Journal 12* (1962), 186–199.

Amit, David, and Hanan Eshel. "A Tetradrachm of Bar Kokhba from a Cave in Naḥal Ḥever." *Israel Numismatic Journal* 11 (1990–1991), 33–35.

Amit, David, and Hanan Eshel. "Selaʿ Cave." *Excavations and Surveys in Israel* 13 (1993), 107–108.

Barag, D. "Glass Vessels from the Cave of Horror." *Israel Exploration Journal* 12 (1962), 208–214.

Tov, Emanuel, ed. *The Greek Minor Prophets Scroll from Naḥal Ḥever (8ḤevXIIgr): The Seiyal Collection*. Discoveries in the Judaean Desert, 8. Oxford, 1990.

Yadin, Yigael. "Expedition D." *Israel Exploration Journal* 11 (1961), 36–52.

Yadin, Yigael. "Expedition D—The Cave of the Letters." *Israel Exploration Journal* 12 (1962), 227–257.

Yadin, Yigael. *The Finds from the Bar Kokhba Period in the Cave of Letters*. Judean Desert Studies. Jerusalem, 1963.

Yadin, Yigael. *Bar-Kokhba: The Rediscovery of the Legendary Hero of the Second Jewish Revolt against Rome*. London, 1971.

HANAN ESHEL

Written Material

The written material from Naḥal Ḥever falls into three groups: Group I contains documents found in Cave 5/6 (the Cave of the Letters) and Cave 8 (the Cave of Horror) in the course of controlled excavations; Group II contains documents which, although they can be traced definitely to two caves in Naḥal Ḥever, were not found there in the course of controlled excavations; Group III contains material about which there are reasons to believe that it comes from Naḥal Ḥever, although this cannot be said with absolute certainty. Fragments from this group sometimes match those found in the first two groups, for example, the Greek Minor Prophets Scroll (8Ḥev 1).

Group I. This group was discovered in Naḥal Ḥever by Israeli archaeological missions as part of a large-scale Judean Desert survey in 1960–1961. [*See* Archaeology.]

Documents from the Cave of the Letters. Cave 5/6, the Cave of the Letters, was excavated by Expedition B, led by Yigael Yadin, during two seasons of excavations, in 1960 and 1961. [*See also biography on Yadin.*] With the exception of two literary texts, Numbers ([5/6Ḥev 1a] and Psalms [5/6Ḥev 1b]), all of the material excavated by Yadin's mission is composed of documentary texts from the last decade of the first century CE to the end of the Bar Kokhba Revolt in 135 CE. [*See* Bar Kokhba Revolt.] This documentary corpus, designated P.Yadin (olim 5/6Ḥev), falls into three groups.

First are the letters of Bar Kokhba and his supporters (5/6Ḥev 49–63). The majority of these letters were written by Bar Kokhba himself. [*See* Bar Kokhba, Shimʿon.] They are written in Hebrew, Aramaic, and Greek. None of the letters is dated. Most are addressed to Jonathan son of Baianos and Masabalah (5/6Ḥev 49–56, 58–60), Bar Kokhba's administrators in ʿEin-Gedi, and are, therefore, likely to come from their archives. [*See* ʿEin-Gedi.] These letters should be studied together with two letters of Bar Kokhba to Yeshuʿa son of Galgula found in Wadi Murabbaʿat (Mur 43–44; Benoit, 1961), both of which, like the letter from Beit-Mashiko to Yeshuʿa ben Galgula (Mur 42), must have come from the latter's archive. The fragmentary letters Mur 45–52 may belong to the Bar Kokhba circle as well. The only letter addressing Bar Kokhba himself is part of the Naḥal Ṣe'elim collection (XḤev/Se 30; Cotton and Yardeni, 1997). [*See* Ṣe'elim, Naḥal.]

The second set consists of leases and subleases of the Bar Kokhba administration in ʿEin-Gedi in Hebrew and Aramaic (5/6Ḥev 42–46) and one private deed from the time of the revolt (5/6Ḥev 47a–b). The leases should be considered in conjunction with a deed of sale and farming contracts from Murabbaʿat (Mur 24), also recording leases of land. These leases and subleases suggest that Bar Kokhba took possession of public land, that is, parts of the imperial domain in Judea.

A deed of sale of half of a garden (5/6Ḥev 47a–b) in ʿEin-Gedi is dated by the era of the Bar Kokhba Revolt. It should be considered together with nine private legal deeds written during the revolt and using the same dating system. Four are deeds of sale from Wadi Murabbaʿat (Mur 22, 23, and 25; Benoit, 1961); from Naḥal Ṣeʾelim come three other deeds of sale (XḤev/Se 7–8a), a confirmation of divorce (XḤev/Se 13), and a deed of land sale (XḤev/Se 49) (Cotton and Yardeni, 1997). [*See* Deeds of Sale; Murabbaʿat, Wadi.]

It should be noted that the private-law procedures visible in the documents from the Bar Kokhba period are continuous with those from the immediately preceding "provincial" period both in Judea and Arabia. What changes dramatically after the outbreak of the revolt is language use: Hebrew now appears alongside Aramaic (Nabatean) and Greek.

The third set of documents is the Babatha archive (5/6Ḥev 1–35), which contains legal documents in Nabatean (5/6Ḥev 1–4, 6, and 9), Aramaic (5/6Ḥev 7–8 and 10), and Greek (5/6Ḥev 5, 11–35) of a Jewish woman who lived in the village of Maḥoz ʿEglatain on the southern shore of the Dead Sea, in what used to be the Nabatean kingdom which in 106 CE became the Roman province of Arabia. [*See* Babatha.] The Babatha archive begins on 11 August 94 CE and concludes on 19 August 132 CE—not long after the outbreak of the Bar Kokhba Revolt in Judea. The close ties with ʿEin-Gedi, evident throughout the archive, may explain the presence of the Babatha archive in the same cave where documents belonging to Jonathan son of Baianos and Masabalah were found. The Babatha archive should be studied closely together with the archive of Salome Komaïse daughter of Levi (XḤev/Se 12, XḤev/Se gr 60–65), which also revolves around the affairs of a Jewish family from the village of Maḥoz ʿEglatain, and whose documents are dated between 30 January 125 and 7 August 131 CE. The two archives contain deeds of sale, deeds of gift, petitions, land registrations, receipts, mortgages, promissory notes, and marriage contracts. The two women must have known each other since their families' properties were abutted by the same neighbors and the same witnesses signed their documents. Like Babatha and her family, Salome Komaïse left her home in Arabia with her precious documents and probably perished in the Bar Kokhba Revolt. Neither Babatha nor Salome Komaïse retrieved her documents.

Of all the material found in the Cave of the Letters at Naḥal Ḥever by Yadin, only the Greek part of the Babatha archive has received its final publication (Lewis, 1989). The rest will be published by Y. Yadin, J. C. Greenfield, A. Yardeni, and B. Levine, *The Documents from the Bar Kokhba Period in the Cave of Letters*, vol. 2: *Hebrew, Aramaic and Nabatean Documents* (Judean Desert Studies, 3). [*See* Family Life; Marriage and Divorce; *and* Names and Naming.]

Documents from the Cave of Horror. Cave 8, the Cave of Horror, was excavated by expedition B, led by Y. Aharoni, in 1960. Fragments of the Greek Minor Prophets scroll (8Ḥev 1), fragments of parchment containing a prayer (8Ḥev 2), and a fragment of a letter (?) written in Greek on papyrus (8Ḥev 4) were found there.

Group II. The second group contains most of the so-called Seiyal collection. The original Seiyal collection was composed of documents that were not discovered in the course of controlled excavations but rather were found by bedouin and brought in August 1952 and July 1953 to the Rockefeller Museum (then the Palestine Archaeological Museum), where they are kept to this day. [*See* Palestine Archaeological Museum.] The plates were labeled *Se*, that is, Seiyal (Naḥal Ṣeʾelim). Although the labeling suggested that the papyri came from Naḥal Ṣeʾelim, those directly in charge of the documents at the time of their discovery never made this claim anywhere in print. Most of the original Seiyal collection has been published (Tov, 1990; Cotton and Yardeni, 1997).

Seiyal Collection, Volume 1. The first volume (Tov, 1990) contains the Greek translation of the Minor Prophets (8Ḥev 1). The fragments of this translation, discovered by Aharoni in 1960 in the Cave of Horror in Naḥal Ḥever, established that the larger fragments of the text designated on the plates in the Rockefeller Museum as coming from Seiyal also came from Cave 8 of Naḥal Ḥever. Thus the entire first volume of the Seiyal collection originated in Naḥal Ḥever. The fragments belong to a single manuscript written in two different hands that can be dated to the late first century BCE. The translation follows the sequence of books of the Masoretic Text and not that of the Septuagint. It contains portions from the books of *Joel*, *Micah*, *Nahum*, *Habakkuk*, *Zephaniah* and *Zechariah*. If the scroll had contained all the Minor Prophets, it would have reached approximately 10 meters, longer than any published Qumran scroll.

Seiyal Collection, Volume 2. The second volume (Cotton and Yardeni, 1997) contains exclusively documentary texts, in Hebrew, Aramaic, and Greek. Depending on the language in which they are written, the documents are designated XḤev/Se and XḤev/Se ar, respectively, for the Hebrew and Aramaic documents and XḤev/Se gr for the Greek documents. Many of these texts can be safely traced to the Cave of the Letters—above all, those documents that belong to the archive of Salome Komaïse, daughter of Levi. The striking similarities between the archive of Salome Komaïse and Babatha, and the identity of some of the people who figure in both archives, would constitute reasons strong enough to postulate that the Cave of the Letters is the source of Salome's archive as well, were it not for the more tangible proof that one document from the archive (XḤev/Se gr 65) was found by Yadin in the Cave of the Letters. The unity of the archive seems to be the best proof that the other documents in this archive, XḤev/Se ar 12, XḤev/Se gr 60, 61, 62, 63, and 64 (possibly also XḤev/Se ar 32), originally part of the Seiyal collection, come from the Cave of the Letters as well. In addition, XḤev/Se gr 67, 68, 70, and 71, located on a plate in the Rockefeller Museum (XḤev/Se gr. 5), which contains several documents from the archive of Salome Komaïse daughter of Levi, must come from the Cave of the Letters as well. And finally the Aramaic deed XḤev/Se 7 and the Aramaic renunciation of claims following a divorce XḤev/Se 13 safely can be traced to the Cave of the Letters for reasons of identity of hands and names.

Volume 2 of the Seiyal collection also includes an Appendix Containing Alleged Qumran Texts, two of which, 4Q347 (a fragment of XḤev/Se ar 32) and 4Q359, can be traced to the Cave of the Letters; both were not part of the original Seiyal collection. On the other hand, there are items that are part of the original Seiyal collection, but that are not included in volume 2, that can be traced to the Cave of the Letters: Numbers? (XḤev/Se 1) and Psalms (XḤev/Se 4), which are from the same manuscripts as the smaller fragments from the same books found by Yadin in the Cave of the Letters (5/6Ḥev 1a and 1b); and contracts XḤev/Se Nab. 1–5 (6). Fragments of contract XḤev/Se Nab. 1 (Starcky, 1954) were discovered by Yadin in the Cave of the Letters in 1961. Since all the Nabatean documents according to Starcky were found in the same place, contracts XḤev/Se Nab. 2–5 (6) were surely found in the Cave of the Letters too. Furthermore, it is possible that contract XḤev/Se Nab. 1 belongs to the Babatha archive, whereas contract XḤev/Se Nab. 2 belongs to the archive of Salome Komaïse daughter of Levi.

Group III. The third group is composed of documents that are likely to have come from Naḥal Ḥever. Thus there are good reasons for believing that the contracts XḤev/Se 8 and XḤev/Se 8a (two deeds written in Kefar Baru), the deeds XḤev/Se 26 (written in the same hand as the former two documents), and the deed of land sale XḤev/Se 49—all four of which are included in volume 2 of the Seiyal collection—come from Naḥal Ḥever. A deed of sale XḤev/Se 9 (written in Yakim) and a canceled marriage contract XḤev/Se gr 69 (written in Aristoboulias)—both included in volume 2 of the Seiyal collection—are likely to have come from a cave in the upper part of Naḥal Ḥever (some 12 kilometers west of the Cave of Horror and the Cave of the Letters), excavated in December 1991. Both locations, Yakim (present-day Khirbet Yuqin or Khirbet Bani Dār) and Aristoboulias (present-day Khirbet Istabûl), are close to the cave (Khirbet Istabûl lies only 3 kilometers west of the cave).

As regards Group III generally it can be assumed that whatever belongs to the original Seiyal collection may have come from Naḥal Ḥever, as do the single documents from the collection that belong to Group II. This consideration lies behind the decision to designate all of them XḤev/Se. The *X* indicates that the cave number is unknown, the *Ḥev* expresses their likely provenance (Ḥever), whereas the *Se* (Seiyal) is there to remind us of the alleged provenance of the documents as well as to preserve the connection with the collection as a whole.

[*See* Aramaic; Greek; *and* Hebrew.]

BIBLIOGRAPHY

Aharoni, Y. "Expedition B—The Cave of Horror." *Israel Exploration Journal* 12 (1962), 186–199. Description of the discoveries in the Cave of Horror in Naḥal Ḥever.

Benoit, P., J. T. Malik, and R. de Vaux. *Les Grottes de Murabbaʿat*. Discoveries in the Judaean Desert, 2. Oxford, 1961.

Cotton, H. M., and A. Yardeni. *Aramaic, Hebrew, and Greek Texts from Naḥal Ḥever and Other Sites, with an Appendix Containing Alleged Qumran Texts. The Seiyâl Collection*, vol. 2. Discoveries in the Judaean Desert, 27. Oxford, 1997.

Greenfield, Jonas C. "The Texts from Nahal Ṣe'elim (Wadi Seiyâl)." In *The Madrid Qumran Congress: Proceedings of the International Congress on the Dead Sea Scrolls, Madrid, 18–21 March 1991*, vol. 2, edited by J. Trebolle Barrera and L. Vegas Montaner, pp. 661–665. Studies on the Texts of the Desert of Judah, 11. Leiden, 1992. A survey of the Seiyal collection.

Lewis, N. *The Documents from the Bar Kokhba Period in the Cave of the Letters*, vol. 1, *Greek Papyri*. Judean Desert Studies, 2, edited by Yigael Yadin and Jonas C. Greenfield. Jerusalem, 1989. The Greek documents of the Babatha archive and Aramaic and Nabatean Signatures and Subscriptions.

Starcky, J. "Un contrat Nabatéen sur papyrus." *Revue biblique* 61 (1954), 161–181. Preliminary publication of XḤev/Se Nab. 1.

Tov, Emanuel. *The Greek Minor Prophets Scroll from Naḥal Ḥever (8ḤevXIIgr). The Seiyâl Collection*, vol. 1. Discoveries in the Judaean Desert, 8. Oxford, 1990.

Tov, Emanuel, with collaboration of Stephen J. Pfann. In *Companion Volume to the Dead Sea Scrolls on Microfiche Edition*, rev. ed. Leiden, 1995.

Yadin, Yigael. "Expedition D." *Israel Exploration Journal* 11 (1961), 36–52.

Yadin, Yigael. "Expedition D—The Cave of the Letters." *Israel Exploration Journal* 12 (1962), 227–257.

Yadin, Yigael. "The Nabtaean Kingdom, Provincia Arabia, Petra and En-Gedi in the Documents from Naḥal Ḥever." *Phoenix. Ex Oriente Lux* 17 (1963), 227–241. The three articles by Yadin contain preliminary and partial transcriptions of the texts found in Naḥal Ḥever in 1961 and 1962.

HANNAH M. COTTON

HIGH PRIESTS. With the end of the Davidic dynasty in the Persian period, the office of high priest increased in importance and absorbed many royal prerogatives, becoming effectively the political representative of the Jewish people. The terminology reflects this development. The most common biblical designation for the head priest was simply *ha-kohen*. Occasionally he was called *(ha-)kohen ha-ro'sh (2 Kgs*. 25.18; *Jer*. 52.24; *Ezr*. 7.5; *2 Chr*. 19.11, 24.11, 26.20, 31.10) or *ha-kohen ha-gadol*

(*Lv*. 21.10; *Num*. 35.25, 35.28; *Jos*. 20.6; *2 Kgs*. 22.4, 22.8, 23.4; *Hg*. 1.1, 1.12, 1.14, 2.2, 2.4; *Zec*. 3.1, 3.8, 6.11; *Neh*. 3.1, 3.20, 13.28; *2 Chr*. 34.9; *Sir*. 50.1), but mostly in postexilic texts. Apparently, the titular use of *ha-kohen ha-gadol* became established by the adoption of the pagan title *archiereus* (Gr.)—used for the head of the state religion—as the title for the Jewish high priest, beginning with the Hasmonean Jonathan (*1 Mc*. 10.20). Thus *ha-kohen ha-gadol* (occasionally *kohen gadol* or *ha-kohen*) is the usual title for the high priest on Hasmonean coins and in the Mishnah, and *archiereus* is the common designation for the high priest in the books of the Maccabees, Josephus, and the New Testament.

Among the Dead Sea Scrolls, *ha-kohen ha-gadol* occurs only in the Copper Scroll (3Q15 vi.14–vii.1, high priest's burial chamber) and in Temple Scroll[a] (cultic activities on festivals and Yom Kippur: 11Q19 xv.15, xxiii.9, xxv.16, xxvi.3; consultation before engaging in war; lviii.18). [*See* Copper Scroll; Temple Scroll.] The War Scroll (1QM; 4Q491–496) refers to the high priest who will take leadership in the final battle against the Sons of Darkness as *kohen ha-ro'sh*. [*See* War of the Sons of Light against the Sons of Darkness.] Assisted by his deputy (*mishneh*; cf. 11Q19 xxxi.4), he stands at the head of the chiefs of the priests (*ra'shei ha-kohanim*), Levites, and lay leaders (1QM ii.1; 4Q494 4), and fulfills various liturgical functions in the time of battle (1QM xv.4, xvi.13; 4Q491 11.ii.11, 18.5, 19.11; cf. 13.1).

Given that the Copper Scroll is unlikely to be of Qumran origin, and that Temple Scroll[a] and the War Scroll express ideals rather than history (and may derive from pre-Qumran sources), the sectarian scrolls noticeably avoid applying the titles of high priest or chief priest to any contemporary figure. Rather, the high priest is otherwise simply *ha-kohen*, sometimes with a descriptor. On the one hand, the biblical commentaries (*pesharim*) polemicize against one or more ruling high priests as "the priest who rebelled" (Pesher Habakkuk, 1QpHab viii.16), "the priest whose shame exceeded his glory" (1QpHab xi.12), and "the last priest" (Pesher Hosea[b], 4Q167 ii.3), but more commonly as "the Wicked Priest" (*ha-kohen ha-rasha'*: 1QpHab viii.8, ix.9, xi.4, xii.2, xii.8; Pesher Isaiah[c], 4Q163 30.3; Pesher Psalms[a], 4Q171 4.8), which may be a derogatory pun on *ha-kohen ha-ro'sh*. [*See* Pesher Habakkuk; Pesher Hosea *and* Wicked Priest.] On the other hand, several positive uses of *ha-kohen* may intend to designate a past, rightful ideal, or future high priest: the "anointed priest" *ha-kohen ha-mashiaḥ*, Apocryphon of Moses B[a], 4Q375 1.i.9 and Apocryphon of Moses B[b], 4Q376 1.i.1), the Teacher of Righteousness (*ha-kohen moreh ha-[tsedeq]*, Pesher Psalms[a], 4Q171 1, 3–4.iii.15; cf. ii.19; 1QpHab ii.2, ii.8), "[the pri]est at the end" (Pesher Psalms[b] 4Q173 1.5), and the priest who presides over the messianic banquet (Rule of the Congregation, 1Q28a ii.12. [*See* Pesher Psalms; Rule of the Congregation; *and* Teacher of Righteousness.] Although the relevant heading is lost, it is probable that Rule of the Blessings includes a benediction blessing the high priest in the last days (1Q28b iv.22–28), and that the New Jerusalem text pictures an ideal high priest who outranks elders and other priests (New Jerusalem, 2Q24 iv.13). [*See* New Jerusalem.]

According to Joachim Jeremias (1969), the plural, *archiereis*, in the New Testament and Josephus probably designates the upper hierarchy of priests who held permanent offices at the Temple, including the high priest. In support of this, chief priests in the War Rule (*ra'shei ha-kohanim*, 1QM ii.1) are the leading priests who continually serve before God and oversee other priestly, Levitical, and lay leaders (cf. *kohanei ra'shei-deviro*, etc., in the Songs of the Sabbath Sacrifice (4Q400–4Q407, 11Q17; Mas1k). [*See* Songs of the Sabbath Sacrifice.]

Josephus (*Jewish Antiquities* 11–20; summary in 20.224–251) is the main source about high priests from Alexander the Great until the destruction of the Temple. [*See* Josephus Flavius.] From the time of Herod the Great on (Books 15–20), his information can be regarded as substantially accurate, probably derived ultimately from Temple archives. Other sources include the books of *Maccabees* (Onias III to John Hyrcanus), the Gospels and *Acts of the Apostles* (Ananus, Caiaphas, Ananias), and the Mishnah and Tosefta. *Ben Sira* 50 (Simon the son of Onias-Simon the Just), *Daniel* 9.25–6 and 11.22 (Onias III), and the Qumran *pesharim* (Hasmoneans) also allude to high priests. [*See* Pesharim.]

Under the Seleucids, Zadokite high priests functioned as princes of a self-governing ethnos and representatives of the king at the head of a priestly aristocracy. By virtue of the mythology of an unbroken dynasty extending back to Aaron, they wielded tremendous spiritual (e.g., *Sir*. 50) and political influence.

After the last two legitimate successions, Simon II (the Just, c.200 BCE) and Onias III (through 175 BCE), the Zadokite dynasty fell victim to personal ambition and party politics when Jason (175–172 BCE) bribed the Seleucid king, Antiochus IV Epiphanes, to depose his brother Onias III and appoint him. [*See* Antiochus IV Epiphanes.] Three years later he, in turn, was outbid by Menelaus (172–162 BCE), a non-Zadokite priest who arranged the murder of Onias III. The Zadokite Onias IV fled to Egypt and initiated a rival temple there. Menelaus's successor, Alcimus (162–159 BCE), being at least an Aaronide, won the support of the Hasideans until he betrayed their trust and executed a group. All three of these high priests actively promoted the Hellenization of Jews, bringing the high priesthood into disrepute in the eyes of pious Jews.

Josephus knew of no high priest during the seven years following Alcimus (*Antiquities* 20.237), but some (e.g., Hartmut Stegemann, Jerome Murphy-O'Connor) have speculated that the Teacher of Righteousness may have been serving as a Zadokite high priest during part of this time (on the question, see Wise, 1990, pp. 587–613). Following his military successes, Jonathan (Hasmonean, 152–143/42 BCE) accepted appointment as high priest from Alexander Balas, pretender to the Seleucid throne. [*See* Jonathan (Hasmonean).] It is most commonly held that the epithet Wicked Priest in the Qumran *pesharim* refers to Jonathan, and that it was for accepting the title of high priest without being of Zadokite lineage that he lost favor with the *yaḥad* ("called by the name of truth when he first appeared," 1QpHab viii.8b–9a). [*See* Wicked Priest.] Numerous other interpretations have been offered for Wicked Priest, almost always regarded as an acting high priest (or succession of high priests). The pre-Christian dating of the *pesharim* discounts identifications in the Christian era, such as Robert Eisenman's theory (1996) that the Teacher of Righteousness was James the Just, promoted as high priest by his supporters and executed by Ananus (high priest in 62 CE), the "Wicked Priest" (collected studies in *The Dead Sea Scrolls and the First Christians*. Essays and Translations, Shaftesbury, Dorset, 1996). Of more value is his questioning the importance of genealogical lineage in determining Zadokite succession. There is no hint that the lineage of the Wicked Priest was a point of contention with the *yaḥad*.

Following Jonathan's death, his brother Simon (142/41–134 BCE) was confirmed as high priest by the Seleucid king Demetrius II, and the Jewish people additionally bestowed on him the title ethnarch. Under the Hasmonean dynasty the office of high priest attained its zenith of power. Simon's son John Hyrcanus (134–104 BCE) added the title king and was followed by his son Aristobulus I (104–103 BCE). [*See* John Hyrcanus; Hasmoneans.] With Alexander Jannaeus (103–76 BCE), the prestige of the high priesthood declined, as he was blamed for military failures and clashed violently with his Jewish opponents. [*See* Alexander Jannaeus.] Pesher Nahum (4Q169) alludes to the horror of his crucifixion of many Pharisees. [*See* Crucifixion; Pesher Nahum.] Warfare between Alexander's sons—Hyrcanus II (76–67, 63–40 BCE) and Aristobulus II (67–63 BCE)—further degraded the high priestly office, which once again involved the intervention of foreign rulers. Regularly, the Dead Sea Scrolls accuse the Hasmonean high priests (e.g., "the last priests of Jerusalem," 1QpHab ix.4–5) of arrogance, defilement, and unjust accumulation of wealth.

Herod terminated the Hasmonean dynasty by executing Antigonus II (40–37 BCE) as well as Aristobulus III, whom he himself had appointed high priest (35 BCE) for political reasons. [*See* Herodian Rulers.] Instead, Herod created a new oligarchy, loyal to himself, by appointing high priests from a few select nonlocal families (especially Boethus, Phiabi, Ananus, and Camithus), mostly drawn from the Diaspora. From this time on, the power of the high priestly office was seriously curtailed as the Herodian rulers and the Romans deposed and appointed at will. Herodian appointments included: Ananel (37–36, 34 BCE); Jesus (c.22 BCE), Simon (c.22–5 BCE), Matthias (5–4 BCE), Joseph (5 BCE), Joazar (4, 6 BCE), Eleazar (4–? BCE), and Jesus (6 CE). Roman appointments included Ananus (6–15 CE), Ishmael I (15–16 CE), Eleazar (16–17 CE), Simon (17–18 CE), Joseph Caiaphas (c.18–37 CE), Jonathan ben Ananus (37 CE), and Theophilus (37 CE–?). Later Herodian appointments included Simon Cantheras (41 CE–?), Matthias (?), Elionaeus (c.44 CE), Joseph (?), Ananias (47–55? CE), Ishmael II (?–61 CE), Joseph Cabi (61–62? CE), Ananus (62 CE), Jesus (c.62–65 CE), Joshua (c.63–65 CE), and Matthias (65–67 CE).

During the revolt, the Zealots appointed by lot an uneducated stonemason named Phineas (67–70 CE) to the high priesthood.

BIBLIOGRAPHY

Alon, Gedalyahu. *Jews and the Classical World: Studies in Jewish History in the Times of the Second Temple and Talmud*, translated by Israel Abrahams. Jerusalem, 1977. See pages 48–88.

de Vaux, Roland. *Ancient Israel: Its Life and Institutions*, translated by John McHugh. London, 1961. See pages 378 and 397–403 for a discussion of the biblical use of the terms *high priest* and *chief priest*.

Eisenman, Robert. *The Dead Sea Scrolls and the First Christians. Essays and Translations*. Dorset, 1996.

Hölscher, Gustav. *Die Hohenpriesterliste bei Josephus und die evangelische Chronologie*. Sitzungsberichte der Heidelberger Akademie der Wissenschaften. Philosophisch-historische Klasse. Heidelberg, 1940. Important evaluation of Josephus's list of high priests and his sources.

Jeremias, Joachim. "The Clergy." In *Jerusalem in the Time of Jesus: An Investigation into Economic and Social Conditions during the New Testament Period*, translated by F. H. Cave and C. H. Cave, pp. 147–221. Philadelphia, 1969. A classic discussion of high priests that introduced an influential theory about the plural term; an appendix (pp. 377–378) lists all high priests from 200 BCE–70 CE.

Sanders, E. P. *Judaism: Practice and Belief, 63 BCE–66 CE*. London, 1992. See pages 317–340. General overview.

Schrenk, Gottlob. "Archiereus (in Greek)." *Theological Dictionary of the New Testament*, vol. 3, edited and translated by G. W. Bromiley, pp. 265–283. Grand Rapids, Mich., 1965. Technical discussion of terminology for high priests in Judaism and the New Testament.

Schürer, Emil. *The History of the Jewish People in the Age of Jesus Christ (175 B.C.–A.D. 135): A New English Edition*, revised and edited by Geza Vermes, Fergus Millar, and Matthew Black, literary editor Pamela Vermes. 3 vols. in 4 parts. Edinburgh 1973, 1979, 1986, 1987. See volume 1, pages 125–242 and 281–286, for a detailed treatment of the Hasmonean high priests. See volume 2, pages 227–236, for an annotated list and discussion of high priests from the time of Herod the Great until the destruction of the Temple.

Smallwood, E. Mary. "High Priests and Politics in Roman Palestine." *Journal of Theological Studies* 13 (1962), 14–34. A classic examination of the role of politics in the Herodian and Roman appointments and depositions of high priests.

Stern, Menahem. "Aspects of Jewish Society: The Priesthood and Other Classes." In *The Jewish People in the First Century. Section 1. Historical Geography, Political History, Social, Cultural and Religious Life and Institutions*, vol. 2, edited by S. Safrai and M. Stern in cooperation with D. Flusser and W. C. van Unnik, pp. 561–630. Compendia Rerum Iudaicarum ad Novum Testamentum. Assen, 1976. See pages 600–612.

Wise, Michael O. "The Teacher of Righteousness and the High Priest of the Intersacerdotium: Two Approaches." *Revue de Qumrân* 14 (1990), 587–613. Argues that *ha-kohen* was never a title for the high priest on the basis of biblical, numismatic, and inscriptional evidence.

DANIEL K. FALK

HIPPOLYTUS (c.170–235 CE), Roman presbyter and rival bishop to Callistus (217–22 CE), Urban (222–30 CE), and Pontianus (230–35 CE). Under the persecution of the Roman emperor Maximinus, he was exiled to Sardinia in 235 CE along with Pontianus, with whom he became reconciled before their martyrdom.

Hippolytus was one of the most prolific writers of the early Western Church, and the last Christian author from Rome to write in Greek. Whether because of his deviant Christology (his view of the Logos as generated at the Incarnation), his tendency toward schism with other church leaders, or the decline of a knowledge of Greek, few works of Hippolytus have survived in Greek. Among his writings are biblical commentaries, homilies, chronological treatments, religious poetry, and antiheretical treatises. His most famous work is the *Refutation of All Heresies* (written c.225 CE), also called the *Philosophumena*. This ten-book treatise was originally considered Origen's, but is now almost universally regarded as the work of Hippolytus. Books 1–4 deal with the different pagan systems (books 2 and 3 are lost), while books 5–10 link each of thirty-three heresies to these pagan systems.

In book 9 of *Refutation of All Heresies*, Hippolytus discusses the Essenes as one of three heretical Jewish sects. He gives much more space to the Essenes than to the Pharisees or Sadducees. His account is so similar to Josephus's description of the Essenes in *The Jewish War* (2.119–161) that some scholars believe that Hippolytus used Josephus as a source. However, in light of the large number of differences between the two accounts, it is more likely that Hippolytus was using a paraphrase of Josephus's work written by a second-century Christian author or that Hippolytus and Josephus both used a common source. If the latter scenario is correct, then Hippolytus's account should not automatically be considered inferior to that of Josephus.

Some of the more significant differences from Josephus's account follow. In discussing the Essene piety toward God, Josephus states that the Essenes direct certain ancestral prayers toward the sun, "as if entreating it to rise" (*The Jewish War* 2.viii.5 sec. 128). Hippolytus, however, omits the intriguing reference to the sun, saying only that they "pray from early dawn" (*Refutation of All Heresies* 9.21). Further, while Josephus says that the Essene took an oath to "hate forever the unjust" (*The Jewish War* 2.viii.7 sec. 139), Hippolytus states that the Essene swore "that he will not hate a person who injures him, or is hostile to him, but pray for them" (*Refutation of All Heresies* 9.23). These sentiments may have been borrowed from Jesus' Sermon on the Mount rather than reflecting genuine Essene beliefs (see *Mt.* 5.44).

Hippolytus also has an extensive paragraph which discusses three divisions of Essenes. One group is characterized by excessive avoidance of idols; another by the practice of killing those who refuse to be circumcised (these are called Zealots or Sicarii); and a third by refusing to call anyone "lord" but God. None of this information is attributed by Josephus to the Essenes, though he does ascribe similar tendencies to other groups. In this paragraph, Hippolytus appears to have incorrectly attributed to the Essenes views held by the Zealots and others.

But the most important difference between Hippolytus and Josephus is in their discussion of the afterlife and the final judgment. For the Essenes, Josephus says, "bodies are corruptible and their matter is not lasting, but their souls are immortal and continue forever": in fact, the souls are imprisoned in the bodies and are "set free" upon death. Good souls go to a refreshing place "beyond the ocean," while evil souls are assigned to "a gloomy and tempestuous recess, filled with incessant punishments" (*The Jewish War* 2.viii.11 sec. 154–155). By contrast, Hippolytus states clearly that the Essenes believe in the resurrection of the body as well as the soul: "The doctrine of the resurrection is firmly established among them. They declare, in fact, that flesh will rise again and be immortal, just as the soul is already immortal." Furthermore, Hippolytus says that the Essenes "affirm that there will be both a judgment and a conflagration of the universe, and that the wicked will be eternally punished" (*Refutation of All Heresies* 9.27).

Once again, it is not clear whether Josephus is simply attempting to express (and even alter) Essene beliefs in terms of Greek thought in order to appeal to his gentile readership, or whether Hippolytus is giving a "Christianized" version of Essene teachings. While it is evident why Josephus would wish to adapt Essene thought to a Greek model, it is not so apparent why Hippolytus, in describing a heretical Jewish sect, would wish to make it more appealing to his Christian audience. It should be noted that one text from Qumran, the Messianic Apocalypse, may speak of bodily resurrection (4Q521 2.11.12: "For he shall heal the slain, and he shall cause the dead to live"), while another appears to describe a universal conflagration at the end of the world in terms similar to those of Hippolytus (1QH[a] xi.29–36 [iii.3.29–36]). If these Qumran documents are of Essene origin, they would provide evidence, as Émile Puech has argued, that in these instances the account of Hippolytus more accurately reflects Essene thought.

BIBLIOGRAPHY

Adam, A. *Antike Berichte über die Essener*. 2d ed. Berlin, 1972. Greek text of and brief commentary on all the ancient accounts of the Essenes.

Black, Matthew. *The Scrolls and Christian Origins: Studies in the Jewish Background of the New Testament*. Chico, Calif., 1983. In Appendix B, Black gives a brief yet helpful comparison of the Essene accounts in Josephus and Hippolytus.

Puech, Émile. *La Croyance des Esséniens en la vie Future: immortalité, résurrection, vie éternelle? Histoire d'une croyance dans le Judaïsme ancien*. Études bibliques, 21–22. Paris, 1993. Chapter 13 is the most extensive recent discussion of Hippolytus on resurrection.

Quasten, Johannes. "Hippolytus of Rome." In *Patrology*, vol. 2, pp. 163–207. Westminster, Md., 1983. Brief biography of Hippolytus and discussion of his writings and theology.

Smith, Morton. "The Description of the Essenes in Josephus and the Philosophumena." *Hebrew Union College Annual* 29 (1958), 273–313. An extensive comparison of the Essene texts of Josephus and Hippolytus.

Vermes, Geza, and Martin Goodman. *The Essenes according to the Classical Sources*. Sheffield, 1989. Provides Greek/Latin text, English translation, and brief introduction for the major classical sources describing the Essenes.

Wendland, Paul. *Hippolytus*. Dritter Band. GCS, 26. Leipzig, 1916. The standard Greek edition of *Refutation of All Heresies* (*Refutatio Omnium Haeresium*).

TODD S. BEALL

HODAYOT. Among the literary genres recognized in the Essene literature from the Qumran library, the genre of hymns holds an important place.

The Scrolls. Among the seven large scrolls discovered by the bedouin in the spring of 1947 in the first cave with manuscripts, one manuscript was identified that contained a collection of hymns (Hodayot[a] [1QH[a]] hereafter called 1QHodayot[a]), which expressed the ideas and feelings of a member or members of the Qumran Community. These poetic compositions of variable length imitate the biblical Psalms in giving thanks to God the Creator and the one who exercises Divine Providence for his deeds of kindness toward their author(s). Since most of the hymns begin with the formula *ʾodekha ʾadonay*, "I give you thanks, Lord," and since no title has been preserved for the composition, the editor gave the manuscript the Hebrew title *hodayot*, rendered in English as *Thanksgiving Psalms/Hymns/Scroll*.

The *editio princeps* of the scroll, published in 1954–1955, presented 1QHodayot[a] in eighteen columns and sixty-six fragments as belonging to several manuscripts. Eleazar Sukenik, the editor, judged that the fragments discovered by the archeologists during the excavation of the cave in 1949 belonged to one of them (1QHodayot[b] [1Q35]). The editor of 1QHodayot[b] concurred in this opinion (Milik, 1955). In 1958, Jean Carmignac proposed differentiating two scrolls in Cave 1: 1QHodayot[a] and Hodayot[b]. The first would include columns xiii to xvi of the edition plus fragments 15, 18, 22 and 1QHodayot[b], while the second would include all the rest (Carmignac, *Biblica* 1958, *Revue de Qumrân* 2 [1958] and 4 [1960]). However, a closer study led to the conclusion that two scrolls were divided as follows: 1QHodayot[a] includes all the columns and all the fragments of the *editio princeps* plus some thirty other as yet untitled fragments; 1QHodayot[b] constitutes a second scroll (1QH[b]), which overlaps with 1QHodayot[a] (column vii and viii of the *editio princeps*) (see Puech, 1987, 1988, and 1995). In an unpublished work/study, Stegemann arrived at a similar result, although he integrated somewhat fewer fragments (see Kuhn, 1964, 16f.).

The reconstruction of the scroll by positioning all of the columns and most of the preserved fragments (about one hundred in number) makes it possible to recover its original appearance. The scroll originally included at least seven leather sheets of four columns each, all of essentially equal size. The impeccable material crafting of the scroll, which to our knowledge is unique among the manuscripts that have been found, would in itself show the great esteem and importance the scribe-copyist accorded to this text, on a level with the great biblical manuscripts. There are forty-one lines for columns i and xviii, according to the new numbering, and forty-two lines starting from column xix (= xii of the edition), which is where there is a change in handwriting; the second copyist took over from that point to the end of the scroll. Reconstructing the scroll was greatly facilitated by the change in handwriting at column xix (= xii), by the direct joining points of numerous fragments and the sheets to be juxtaposed, and by the shapes of the breaks that were repeated at regular spaces in the rolled scroll, all proving that the fragments came from one and the same scroll. Thus column xviii of the edition should be considered an erroneous column, and its fragments—which certainly do not fit together—should be separated from it. The same holds true for "fragment 15" with its misleading points of juncture (Puech, *Revue de Qumrân* 13 [1988]). At the present state of research, some twenty small published fragments, as well as the unclassified manuscripts, still remain to be repositioned. As for 1QHodayot[b], it has a minimum of twenty-eight lines per column, but more likely thirty-three or thirty-four, or even more, thus approaching the dimensions of 1QHodayot[a] (Puech, 1995). Some fragments of other copies have been found in Cave 4, and these have been grouped into six different manuscripts, Hodayot[a–f] (= 4Q427–432, hereafter 4QHodayot[a–f]); five of them are on leather and one is on papyrus (Hodayot[f] = 4Q432).

Dating. While 1QHodayot[a–b], with its beautiful calligraphy, largely dates from the beginning of our era or shortly before, the manuscripts from Cave 4 are certainly older: 4QHodayot[d–f], the most recent, would date from the third quarter of the first century BCE (early Herodian), 4QHodayot[a] and 4QHodayot[c] from the middle of the first century BCE (late Hasmonean–early Herodian), and 4QHodayot[b], the most ancient, from the first quarter of the first century BCE, shortly after 100 BCE (middle Hasmonean).

Although in Aramaic script, all these scrolls are in the Hebrew language, as is the case for the majority of the Essene writings. However, the copyists of Hodayot[a] and Hodayot[b] sometimes write the divine name *el* and *eli* in Hebrew script, incorrectly called "paleo-Hebrew," thus imitating a custom of copyists from the Herodian era, at least for the divine names. But the question as to the composition of the Hymns remains open. 1QHodayot[b] follows the order of 1QHodayot[a], as does 4QHodayot[b] with its seventy-five fragments (= Hodayot[a] x.35–xxvi.42), 4QHodayot[f] with its twenty-nine fragments (= Hodayot[a] ix.15–xvi.10), and 4QHodayot[c] with its ten fragments (= 1QHodayot[a] xiii–xiv). In contrast, 4QHodayot[c] with its sixteen fragments deviates from that order on at least one point. This manuscript corresponds to some Hymns at the end of 1QHodayot[a] xix–xxvi+, but fragment 3.i–ii attests to a different sequence affecting at least three Hymns. (It must be acknowledged, and it is the only case, that the placement of fragment 10 of 1QHodayot[a] in column vii is uncertain.) Must we then conclude from this that 4QHodayot[a] did not contain the "Hymns of the Teacher," those attributed by scholars to the Teacher of Righteousness? The question will have to be studied more closely after the publication of these fragments. Manuscripts 4QHodayot[d] and 4QHodayot[e], which are represented only by a single fragment containing a few lines, do not bring any information to bear on this question.

From these first indications, one important conclusion ought to be drawn. Indeed, the most ancient manuscript, 4QHodayot[b], the copy of which dates back to about the beginning of the first century BCE, may well attest to the same Hymns and in the same order as does 1QHodayot[a], and this on the basis of significant remainders of seventeen columns = 1QHodayot[a] x.35–xxvi.42. A single manuscript, from the middle of the century, 4QHodayot[a], attests to a somewhat different sequence in a single passage on two columns (fragment 3.i–ii) and involving three Hymns. But it is far from being proven that 4QHodayot[c] contained only the "Hymns of the Teacher" on twelve line columns; the same also holds true for 4QHodayot[f]. Since it is rather likely that 4QHodayot[b] is merely a copy of a scroll of the Hymns, one must logically conclude that the sequence of the Hymns in 1QHodayot[a] was known at least by about 100 BCE. The presence of this type of Hymn at the end of the Rule of the Community (1QS ix.26–xi.22), itself a nonautograph scroll and dated to about 100 BCE or the beginning of the first century BCE, confirms this conclusion and calls for dating the composition of this type of Hymn to the second half of the second century BCE. Thus, from a chronological standpoint, it appears plausible to attribute at least a part of the Hymns to the Teacher of Righteousness or to his disciples and contemporaries. This becomes even highly likely if not certain, if one wishes to account for the quality of inspiration and the exalted conceptions expressed by their author concerning the relationship of humans with their creator, features rarely encountered in other compositions.

Author. The authorial unity of the Hymns, at first held to be likely, is now questioned and the trend of current research is to distinguish two types of Hymns: the "Hymns of the Teacher," or Thanksgiving Hymns on occasion of a revelation or of a personal release, and the "Hymns of the Community," soteriological confession Hymns (*soteriologisches Bekenntnis*) by different authors where the "I" has no autobiographical coloring but refers to the members of the Community (Morawe, Jeremias, Kuhn, and so forth). However, a systematic attribution of authorship probably does not do justice to the reality, since the Teacher of Righteousness was no doubt capable of expressing himself according to various literary approaches and could vary his vocabulary wherever necessary. His strong personality was certainly not limited to a single type of hymn composition, and could vary between expressing himself in his own name and using his own spiritual experience as a pattern, or composing in a more impersonal manner for his group and for community praise of God. This would better explain an unmistakable unity of style and vocabulary that is rather striking in these Hymns, and better accounts for the repeated expressions such as *mizmor la-maskil* or *la-maskil hodot u-tefillah, la-maskil mizmor*, and *la-maskil mizmor*, showing that those hymns were intended for the prayer and meditation of the disciples and those committed to the Covenant. The presence of these expressions similar to "rubrics" found in columns v.12–15, vii.21, xx.7–14, and xxv.34 lead us to suppose there was another such expression at the beginning of the scroll (compare 1QRule of the Community ix.26 ff. to 1QHodayot[a] v.12 ff. and xx.7 ff. in particular). These five "rubrics" suggest grouping the Hymns of 1QHodayot[a] into five sets, which cannot help but be reminiscent of the ordering of the scroll of the 150 biblical Psalms into five small books. It is thus possible, and even likely, that the Hodayot Scroll, or at least most of the Hymns, rather early on (about 100 BCE at the latest) had a liturgical purpose, just like the "hebdomadary" (i.e., seven fold structure) of the Words of the Luminaries[a–c] (4Q504–4Q506) with a prayer for each day of the week or the Songs of the Sabbath Sacrifice with its thirteen compositions. The liturgical life of the Community, having been cut off from the Temple, must have become organized already in the second half of the second century BCE, at the time when the original core group grew very quickly, thanks to the arrival of newcomers (see the transition from stratum Ia to stratum Ib in the archaeological levels according to Roland de Vaux, based on his excavations). Thus nothing proves that totally independent sources, which would have been gathered and combined in different ways in manuscript families like 1QHodayot[a] and 4QHodayot[a], are involved. Since the composition of these Hymns must have taken a certain amount of time, it would be normal for some groups or sections to be enriched or revised. Thus 4QHodayot[a], with a somewhat different arrangement, might be a copy of an older manuscript.

In the present state of the documentation, it can be reasonably surmised that the Hymns of 1QHodayot[a] were composed during the lifetime of the Teacher of Righteousness. This is all that can be said for certain, until the publication of the manuscripts from Cave 4, which will give us a clearer picture, since the preliminary publications of passages from 4QHodayot are not without contradictions in the scholarly distinctions between "Hymns of the Teacher" and "Hymns of the Community." Whatever the case may be, whether they be compositions by the Teacher or compositions by his contemporary disciples, these Hymns certainly date back to the second half of the second century BCE. In this connection, we may recall the observations by Philo about the Therapeutae of Egypt, that they had preserved some hymns composed by the first leaders of their sect, which they sang in their cultic assemblies, with everyone joining in together on the refrains (*On the Contemplative Life* secs. 29, 80, 83–84).

Related Texts. According to the preliminary indications of the editors, these manuscripts should be seen in comparison to manuscripts like the Hodayot-like texts 4Q433 and 4Q440, although at present it appears there is no overlap. Other fragments that should also be included within this literary genre are the fragments of the hymnic compositions such as 1Q36–40, 3Q6, 6Q18, 8Q5, 11Q15–16, the end of 1QRule of the Community ix.26–xi, the Hymns that are scattered throughout the War Scroll (1QM xii–xix) and the parallels in War Scroll[b] (4Q492), War Scroll[e] (4Q495) and particularly War Scroll[a] (4Q491 11), which attests to some overlaps with 4QHodayot[a], the Prayer of Michael, and 1QHodayot[a] xxvi. More broadly, they ought to be related to the Songs of the Sage[a–b] (4Q510–4Q511), the Songs of the Sabbath Sacrifice[a–h] (4Q400–407, as well as 11Q17), the Words of the Luminaries[a–c] (4Q504–506), the Blessings (*Berakhot*), and the Noncanonical Psalms (4Q380–381, 11Q5[a], 4Q88[f], 4Q448, 4QPsAp[a] among the most notable Qumran compositions), as well as to the *Psalms of Solomon*, the *Psalms*, and Song of the Hebrew Scriptures, as well as the *Benedictus* and *Magnificat* (*Lk.* 1) or some passages from the *Gospel of John* (the Prologue of *Jn.* 1) in the New Testament.

Contents. The style of the author (authors?) of these Hymns, which are steeped in the Bible, abounds with biblical formulas. According to the first decipherment, some 673 (Carmignac, 1960) or 679 (Holm-Nielsen, 1960) quotations or allusions, often mixed with anthological tirades and more personal theological considerations, have been located and identified. The underlying unity of the Hymns is that they are a kind of meditation in which the theological subject is generally dealt with according to three major areas of focus: God, the salvation of the just, and the final doom of the godless—beginning with their leader Belial—in an eschatological war. God's greatness and perfection is described, along with his justice and kindness, and his forgiveness. God's creation of the universe is contrasted with the wretchedness and smallness of a human being, a creature of clay who is dependent on divine help. The Hymns speak of the persecution and suffering to which the faithful person falls victim and of his hope for the victory of God the Father, and for the punishment of the wicked. The author and, in turn, the one who prays, express their feelings of adoration, praise, gratitude, trust, and faithfulness, while at the same time acknowledging their weakness, fear, guilt, repentance, and sometimes their desire for vengeance for the wickedness of their adversaries and the sinners. This meditation sometimes takes the form of thanksgiving, or praise, or lament, or supplication, but always in a composed spirit of devotion and prayer, both day and night. It also serves as a kind of instruction, since God has revealed the secrets of the mysteries and the understanding of his marvelous works to the Teacher of Righteousness, who is charged with conveying this knowledge and enlightenment. In the "Hymns of the Teacher," it is God himself who has placed in his mouth these Hymns of praise for the instruction of the lowly and the poor and who has placed him at the wellspring of a lush planted field or of a luxuriant and blossoming tree; in short, it is God who has established him as the Teacher of the Community. By his life and his teaching, he shows the way of the "healing" that is to come. Unquestionably he remains a sinner, but God has purified him of the great sin and will purify him by his holy spirit, and will not allow him to be carried away. Together with his faithful ones, he is sheltered in a fortified city over which God keeps watch.

To enter the Community is to enter into God's Covenant with the resolve to fortify oneself and to persevere (compare the Rule of the Community and the Damascus Document). Thus a member belongs to the group of the just or to the small remnant for whom God is already manifesting his power and mercy, while he will fully manifest his power and justice at the Visitation-Judgment, when all the wicked are destroyed, both Jews and pagans alike (compare the War Scroll). For the just, it will be a time of rejoicing, rewards, delights of Paradise, eternal glory, and peace in the world that has been renewed and purified in the universal conflagration, while Belial will be cast into the burning place of eternal Doom. The conception of eschatology is the same, whether it be in the "Hymns of the Teacher" or in the "Hymns of the Community." The allusions to the total eschatological war, the final and decisive judgment in the heights on earth and in the underworld Abyss, as well as reference to punishment in the infernal Sheol, and to reward with the sons of heaven are found in both categories. The elect knows what end awaits the wicked, those who refuse to observe the commandments of God and the instructions of the Teacher. For the just man, the return to dust is not the end; rather glorification is to follow because he will be restored to the glory of Adam with an abundance of days in a life of intimacy with God as a servant in the company of the angels. Indeed, although depicted in language full of imagery, the belief in the resurrection of the just is not totally absent from these texts (1QHodayot[a] xiv, xiii, xix). In the present, a life of communion with the angels signifies for the Community a kind of return to the earlier purity of the people of God, a certain communing with the divine world while awaiting the complete restoration with God and freedom from sin at the end of days, a kind of return to the original paradise from which sin and death will have disappeared forever.

The same theological and anthropological conception underlies these Hymns as underlies the great Essene texts, such as the Rule of the Community and the War Scroll, in particular. In both places, there is a certain degree of dualism and determinism, without predestination however, since the faithful must respond actively by a life in conformity with the will of God. Angelology plays a similar role in these texts: Belial and his demons are the inspirers of evil and in the end they will be the victims of punishment. The angels, as servants of God, will take part in the eschatological war but, since they dwell before God, they are already watching over the faithful and preparing the successful outcome of the battle.

The theology of these texts takes no account of the oracles of the biblical prophets that foretell the conversion of the pagans. Rather, they remain centered on the community that is closed in upon itself, thus lacking any universalism. In contrast, the liturgical worship at the Temple, which is very much present in the Hebrew Scriptures, has no place in this literature. This fact shows to what extent the Community had broken away from the Temple, which had been defiled by wicked hands. All collective prayer in these Hymns is outside the Temple and without reference to it.

The points that these Hymns have in common with the Rule of the Community and the War Scroll in particular, and perhaps also the Damascus Document, argue for their having been composed in the same community at about the same time, that is the second half of the second century BCE, the generation of the Teacher of Righteousness. It is not surprising that these foundation documents of the life of the community were carefully copied onto large-format scrolls, just as normative texts such as the Torah, the Prophets, and so forth were. The Scroll of Hymns must have had "authoritative" value for the followers of the Community before they had time to go through a long series of editions. At the present state of research there are hardly any variants except those owing to copying errors, for the most part. The Hymns most certainly occupied a primary place among the Essene compositions by the first generation of the founding of the Community.

BIBLIOGRAPHY

EDITIONS

Milik, Józef T. *Qumrân Cave 1*. In Discoveries in the Judaean Desert, 1, edited by D. Barthélemy and J. T. Milik. Oxford, 1955. Editions of 1Q35 = 1QH[b].

Sukenik, Eleazar L. *Oṣar hammegillôt haggenuzôt šebîdê ha-universitah ha-ʿvivrît*. Jerusalem, 1954. *The Dead Sea Scrolls of the Hebrew University*, Jerusalem, 1955. Edition of 1QH[a] in Hebrew and in English.

STUDIES

Carmignac, Jean. "Remarques sur le texte des Hymnes de Qumrân." *Biblica* 39 (1958), 139–155. Attempt to reconstruct scroll 1QH.

Carmignac, Jean. "Localisation des fragments 15, 18 et 22 des Hymnes." *Revue de Qumrân* 1.3 (1958), 425–430. Attempt to reconstruct scroll 1QH[a].

Carmignac, Jean. "Compléments au texte des Hymnes de Qumrân." *Revue de Qumrân* 2.2 and 4 (1960), 267–276 and 549–558. Attempt to reconstruct scroll 1QH.

Carmignac, Jean. "Les citations de l'Ancien Testament, et spécialement des Poèmes du Serviteur, dans les Hymnes de Qumrân." *Revue de Qumrân* 2.3 (1960), 357–394. Citations from the Old Testament in the 1QH Hymns.

Carmignac, Jean. *Les Hymnes*. In *Les Textes de Qumrân traduits et annotés, I—Règle de la Communauté—la Règle de la Guerre—les Hymnes*, edited by J. Carmignac and P. Guilbert. Paris, 1961. Introduction, translation, and detailed commentary.

García Martínez, Florentino. *The Dead Sea Scrolls Translated: The*

Qumran Texts in English, translated by W. G. E. Watson. Leiden, New York, Cologne, 1994.

Holm-Nielsen, Svend. *Hodayot—Psalms from Qumran*. Acta Theologica Danica, 2. Aarhus, 1960. Translation and detailed commentary.

Holm-Nielsen, Svend. "'Ich' in den Hodajoth und Qumran Gemeinde." *Qumran Probleme (Vorträge des leipziger Symposions über Qumran-Probleme vom 9. bis 14. Oktober 1961)*, edited by H. Bardtke. German Academy of Sciences at Berlin (Schriften der Sektion für Altertumswissenschaft, pp. 217–229). Publications of the Section for Ancient Studies, 42. Berlin, 1963. Study of the use of "I" in the Hymns.

Jeremias, Gert. *Der Lehrer der Gerechtigkeit*. Studien zur Umwelt des Neuen Testaments, 2. Göttingen, 1963. Study of the personality of the Teacher of Righteousness according to the Hymns.

Kittel, Bonnie P. *The Hymns of Qumran, Translation and Commentary*. SBL Dissertation Series, 50. Chico, Calif., 1981. Study of a few composition techniques.

Kuhn, Hans W. *Enderwartung und gegenwärtiges Heil. Untersuchungen zu den Gemeindeliedern von Qumran, mit einem Anhang über Eschatologie und Gegenwart in der Verkündigung Jesu*. Studien zur Umwelt des Neuen Testaments, 4. Göttingen, 1964. Studies on the Hymns, classification, and eschatology.

Morawe, Günther. *Aufbau und Abgrenzung der Loblieder von Qumrân. Studien zur gattungsgeschichtlichen Einordnung der Hodajôth*. Theologische Arbeiten, 16. Berlin, 1961. Study of the literary genre of the Hymns.

Puech, Émile. "Quelques aspects de la restauration du Rouleau des Hymnes (1QH)." *Journal of Jewish Studies* 39 (1988), 38–55. Attempt to reconstruct scroll 1QH[a].

Puech, Émile. "Un hymne essénien en partie retrouvé et les Béatitudes. 1QH V 12–VI 18 (= col XIII–XIV 7) and 4QBéat." Mémorial Jean Carmignac. Études qumraniennes, edited by F. García Martínez and É. Puech. *Revue de Qumrân* 13 (1988), 59–88. Reconstruction of an important passage from 1QH[a].

Puech, Émile. *La croyance des Esséniens en la vie future: Immortalité, résurrection, vie éternelle? Histoire d'une croyance dans le Judaïsme ancien. I—La Résurrection des morts et le contexte scripturaire, II—Les Données qumraniennes et classiques*. Études Bibliques N.S. 21–22, 335–419. Paris, 1993. Reconstruction, translation, and commentary on the Hymns in relation to Essene eschatology.

Puech, Émile. "Restauration d'un texte hymnique à partir de trois manuscrits fragmentaires: 1QH[a] XV 37–XVI 4 (VII 34–VIII 3), 1Q35 (H[b]) 1, 9–14, 4Q428 (H[b]) 7." *Revue de Qumrân* 16 (1995), 543–558. Example of the restoration of a very fragmentary Hymn from three manuscripts.

Schuller, E. "The Cave 4 Hodayot Manuscripts: A Preliminary Description." *Jewish Quarterly Review* 85 (1994), 137–150. Description of the fragments of the manuscripts from Cave 4.

Schuller, E., and L. Di Tomaso. "A Bibliography of the Hodayot 1968–1996." *Dead Sea Discoveries* 4.1 (1997), 55–101.

Vermès, Geza. *The Dead Sea Scrolls in English*. Baltimore, 1962.

ÉMILE PUECH

Translated from French by Robert E. Shillenn

HOLY CONGREGATION OF JERUSALEM. The *qahala qaddisha* or *ʿedah qedoshah* in Jerusalem of Talmudic and later sources was an ascetic conventicle that cannot be confidently dated earlier than the second half of the second century CE. J.T., *Maʿaser Sheni* 2.10, 53d links the group with Yose ben [ha-]Meshullam and Simeon ben Menasyah (c.180 CE). *Qoheleth Rabba* 9.9 explains its name by their practice of dividing the day into three parts, devoting a third to study of the Torah, a third to prayer, and a third to work. Other authorities suggested that they pursued agricultural work in the summer but study in the winter. The collective daily division of time, which restricts work to less than laborers' typical hours, and the description *ʿedah*, suggest a closely integrated social group with a substantially independent economy, geared to the maintenance of study. The adjective *qedoshah* refers principally to abstinence and ritual purity. The group's interpretation of a principal scriptural injunction regarding marriage suggests a membership of males who were unmarried or had separated themselves from family life for the purpose of study. Some nineteenth-century scholars saw the group as a survival of the Essene sect. The Rule of the Community from Qumran has since indicated a community structure that is to some extent analogous. In particular, 1QRule of the Community (1QS) vi.6–7 attests a similar, but not identical, division of time. Wherever an Essene community numbered at least ten celibate males, a rota ensured that at least one member was studying day and night; the community kept watch for a third of each night of the year, possibly according to a sequential rota. While 1QRule of the Community suggests full sharing of property, however, the practice of the Holy Congregation implies that members held their own land. The extreme sanctity of Jerusalem probably accounts for the group's rigorous purity, as mentioned in four texts of the Babylonian Talmud whereby bedding of forbidden mixed composition is prohibited even if ten coverlets are interposed. In B.T., *Betsah* 14b and *Yoma* 69a, the Holy Congregation is located prior to Rabbi Yehudah the Prince (died 217 CE) in chains of tradition; *Tamid* 27b omits his name. *Betsah* 27a has Simeon ben Menasyah attribute the *halakhah* to Rabbi Meir, but records the slightly opaque objection that "these [the Holy Congregation] are much older than he [apparently Rabbi Meir, but conceivably Simeon himself]." This may imply that the group began with disciples of Rabbi Meir (mid-second century CE), in the Yavneh period, or even earlier. The Holy Congregation itself suggests, along with other evidence, that the prohibition of Jews entering Jerusalem following the Bar Kokhba Revolt was relaxed under the Severan emperors. That a scholarly community observing rigorous standards of purity later clung tenaciously to the holy city suggests that it must have had precursors in an earlier time, including the probable opportunistic removal of the Qumran community to Jerusalem during its absence from the Dead Sea site in the reign of the Essene-friendly Herod the Great, before and after which related, Qumran-influenced conventicles may have existed in the city.

BIBLIOGRAPHY

Jeremias, Joachim. *Jerusalem in the Time of Jesus*. London, 1969. Argues for pre–70 CE origins of the Holy Congregation. See pages 247–249.

Rabin, Chaim. *Qumran Studies*. Oxford, 1957. Relates origins of the Holy Congregation in the Yavneh period. See pages 37–52.

Safrai, Shmuel. "The Holy Congregation in Jerusalem." *Scripta Hierosolymitana* 23 (Jerusalem, 1972), 62–78. Seeks to relate the practice of the Holy Congregation to the teachings of Rabbi Meir.

BRIAN J. CAPPER

HOROSCOPES. Horoscopy (or genethlialogy) is understood as the prediction of an individual's future based on the positions of the planets, the sun, and the moon in the zodiac at the instant of his or her conception or birth. The Greek term, *horoskopos*, refers to a star or the point of the zodiacal circle rising just above the eastern horizon at the moment of birth or ruling over the current hour.

Among the Dead Sea Scrolls, only one text could belong to the astrological genre of horoscopic literature: 4Q186. Although even this text lacks some typical features of horoscopes (see below), for convenience's sake it is called here *horoscope*. The astrological character of two other texts, Elect of God (4Q534) and Physiognomy/Horoscope (4Q561), is still under discussion. [*See* Elect of God.] Another document, Zodiology and Brontology (4Q318), undoubtedly astrological, is by definition not a horoscope but describes the course of the moon through the twelve signs of the zodiac during the twelve months of the year and predicts future mundane events based on the phenomena of thunder in a particular zodiacal sign.

Unlike astrology, brontology-based oracles concern events of national interest (wars, weather, crops, etc.) rather than the fate of individuals. While Zodiology and Brontology need not be discussed here, the text clearly attests an interest in astrology as well as knowledge of the zodiac at Qumran. One common feature of horoscope (4Q186), Elect of God, and Physiognomy/Horoscope is the detailed description of physiognomic characteristics of particular persons. But only horoscope (4Q186) exhibits a clear astrological background because of the relation between physiognomic traits and the zodiacal sign at the moment of the birth (*ha-molad*) of various individuals.

Horoscope (4Q186). In 1964 Allegro first drew attention to the existence of a cryptographic astrological document from Qumran, which he published in 1968. In 1965 Carmignac presented a preliminary analysis of horoscope (4Q186). Since that time this text has been the object of numerous studies. According to Milik and Starcky, the text was copied in the second half of the first century BCE. It consists of the remains of six columns with portions of four different horoscopes. The surviving text, however, is so fragmentary that many questions remain unanswered. In addition it is cryptographic in a double sense: the script is a mixture of Proto-Hebrew, Greek, and cryptic characters, and characters and word order proceed from left to right (the single exception being 1.ii.2). In terms of content, the following elements are discernible in horoscope (4Q186): the physiognomic description of an individual; the reference to a certain *ʿamud* ("position") combined with a number ("e.g., he is in the second position"); the reference to a ratio of portions in the "house of light" and the "house/pit of darkness" concerning the *ruaḥ* ("spirit/room"?); the sign of the zodiac for the moment of birth; and a prediction of the individual's fate (e.g., "he will be poor").

Unlike other ancient horoscopes, this text gives no information about the position of the sun, moon, or planets in relation to the zodiac or to the horizon. A person is said to have been born "in the foot of the bull" (*be-regel ha-shor*), a key phrase commonly interpreted as a reference to the position of the sun within the zodiacal sign of Taurus. In this case horoscope (4Q186) would not be a horoscope needing sophisticated astronomical calculations but would belong to the astrological genre of zodiologies, which required knowledge only of the position of the sun, something easily gleaned from a solar calendar. Physiognomic characterization is a typical feature of this sort of astrological text. The phrase "in the second position" also may refer to the zodiacal sign of Taurus, because this sign is second behind Aries, which in antiquity was regarded as the first sign of the zodiac. The formulation "in the foot of Taurus," however, points to a more specific meaning of the phrase. Does it stand for a particular part of the constellation, in which the position of a certain celestial body is to be observed? Since the position of the sun within a zodiacal sign cannot be observed by day, it has been suggested that the phrase refers to the position of the moon in Taurus. The first part of Zodiology and Brontology (4Q318) would seem to support this assumption because it attests interest in the observation and schematic computation of lunar movements through the zodiac. The observation of the moon in the "feet of Taurus" also is attested in astrological texts from antiquity, for example in the work of Firmicus Maternus (*Mathesis* VI 31, 88). But what is the meaning of the ratio of portions (always a total of nine) in the "house of light" and the "house/pit of darkness"? Is there an astrological explanation for this enigmatic phrase? In the Hellenistic astrological compendium, *Book of Hermes Trismegistos*, we find the ideas that each zodiacal sign is divided into light and dark parts and that the position of sun, moon, and planets in the dark and light parts at birth determines the fate of an individual born at that moment. Even if horoscope (4Q186) is interpreted against this background, however, some problems remain: The scroll does not mention celestial bodies, and there is no explanation for the light–darkness ratio of six to three in connection with the "foot of Taurus."

Most of the problems are solved if we interpret horoscope (4Q186) in light of a Greek zodiacal text attributed to the Hellenistic astrologer Teukros (about 100 BCE) and delivered by the Byzantine collector of astrological literature Rhetorios (Catalogus Codicum Astrologorum Graecorum 7 p. 197 24ff.) nine parts (1.1°–3°, head; 2.4°–7°, horns; 3.8°–10°, neck; 4.11°–13°, breast; 5.14°–18°, hip; 6.19°–21°, loins; 7.22°–24° feet (!); 8.25°–27°, tail; 9.28°–30°, claws). The nine parts of the body of Taurus rise over the eastern horizon one after the other in the order of one to nine. Thus, the "foot of Taurus" in horoscope (4Q186) could designate the ascendant, the rising point of the ecliptic at the moment of birth, which was of importance in casting a horoscope. The ascendant interpretation does not need the additional hypothesis of solar, lunar, or planetary positions in horoscope (4Q186). The ninefold partition of the zodiacal sign of Taurus also explains the light–darkness ratio of 6:3 in 7–8 4Q186 1.ii.7–8 because the "feet" of Taurus appear in position seven: Six parts of Taurus have already risen (above the horizon = "in the house of light") and three parts are still beneath the horizon ("in the house/pit of darkness"). The horizon is the boundary between light and darkness (cf. Job 26.10). The famous Greek astronomer Hipparchus (190–125 BCE), for example, discusses in his commentary on the *phainomena* of Aratus and Eudoxus the statements there about the risings and settings of the constellations. In one place (Lib. II Cap. II. secs. 15–17) he explains that the space above the earth is called the diurnal one whereas that below the horizon is called the nocturnal one and that a constellation sets at the western horizon after becoming satiated with light.

This interpretation can be combined with a proposal by Gordis to translate the word *ruaḥ* in horoscope (4Q186) 1.ii.1 and 1.iii.5; 2.i.6 as "space" instead of the usual "spirit," using the vocalization of *Genesis* 32.17 (*revaḥ*). Thus the translation: "He has space in the house of light of six (parts) three (parts) in the house/pit of darkness." That way the ascendant divides the rising zodiacal sign at the moment of birth into parts of light and darkness that determine the physiognomic features and the fate of the person concerned. Presumably there was the assumption of an analogy between the nine parts of the body of the rising zodiacal sign and the human body (nine parts?) born at this moment. However, to speculate further about the way the relationship was seen would be guesswork.

Elect of God and Physiognomy/Horoscope. The astrological character of these two texts is highly questionable. The Elect of God text (4Q534) which was first published by Jean Starcky in 1964 presents some fragmentary statements about the outward appearance and the future development of a newborn child which is designated as the Elect of God. Starcky called this text *astrologique*, and most researchers followed him in this respect. However, there is no reference to zodiacal signs, planetary positions, etc., which might suggest its horoscopic nature, as Fitzmyer correctly noticed. Of course an astrological background of the Elect of God is imaginable, but it cannot be demonstrated with any degree of certainty.

The Aramaic text Physiognomy/Horoscope (4Q561) contains physiognomic descriptions comparable to those in horoscope (4Q186), but we find in this highly fragmentary text no astrological or horoscopic elements, either. Some scholars regard it as a copy in Aramaic of horoscope (4Q186) (e.g., Florentino García Martínez, *The Dead Sea Scrolls Translated*, Leiden, 1994, p. 508), but this assumption is hypothetical.

Significance of Horoscopes in Qumran. Most scholars explain the significance of horoscope (4Q186) against the background of the teaching of the two spirits in the Rule of the Community from Cave 1 ([hereafter, 1QRule of the Community] 1QS iii.13–iv.26). The connecting link is the statement "His spirit has six [parts] in the house of light and three in the pit of darkness" (*ruaḥ lo be-veit ha-ʾor shesh ve-shalosh be-veit / be-vor ha-ḥoshekh*) (4Q186 1.ii.7–8). It is common opinion that in horoscope (4Q186) and 1QS iv.15ff. people are seen as composed of different portions of the spirit of light and the spirit of darkness, nine altogether. On the other hand, the different ratio of the two spirits in an individual effects different physiognomic features. All this is then related to the zodiacal sign or, more exactly, to the part of the zodiacal sign in which a person was born. The physical appearance of individuals, the composition of their spirit of light and darkness, and their fate are finally determined by the zodiacal constellation at the moment of birth. Thus, astrological wisdom enables the diviner to identify the people who were made up more of darkness than of light and to know the secrets of divine predestination. Astrological knowledge, this interpretation suggests, was an integral part of the religious ideas of the Jewish group (Essenes, Proto-Essenes?) who composed writings like those which contain the teaching of the two spirits. The cryptographic script in horoscope (4Q186) would have served as a means to emphasize the importance of astrology at Qumran by the esoteric form of writing.

However, if one assumes a relationship between the teaching of the two spirits and horoscope (4Q186), the question arises why topics like justice and sin, and living in truth and knowledge, emphasized in 1QRule of the Community (1QS iv.2ff.), do not play any role in horoscope (4Q186) where only external traits like physiognomic characteristics are mentioned. According to 1QRule of the Community (1QS iv.15ff.) the spiritual quality of human beings is recognized by their deeds (*ma'seihem*), not by their physiognomy. Moreover, the objection has been raised that influential works such as *Jubilees* and *1 Enoch* condemn astrology as the sinful wisdom of the Chaldeans, which was taught to humankind by the fallen Heavenly Watchers (*1 En.* 8.3; *Jub.* 8.3; cf. *Jub.* 11.8, 12.6–21; 1Q23, lines 9,14,15; *Is.* 47.13; *Jer.* 8.2). It is therefore advisable to look for an alternative interpretation.

The ascendant theory suggested above renders unnecessary the need to construct a connection to 1QRule of the Community (1QS iii–iv). If this theory is correct, horoscope (4Q186) might be regarded as a common astrological text, comparable to Hellenistic parallels and without deeper theological significance. The use of a cryptic script could be interpreted as a means of literary style for marking the esoteric character of the contents, but it could also be understood as a quasi-prohibition sign for unauthorized readers within the community. Indeed, it is quite easy to decode the text, but the cryptic and reversed manner of writing could have been an unmistakable signal for unauthorized readers that they had in their hands a forbidden text of pagan provenance (wisdom of the Chaldeans).

It should be emphasized that the ascendant theory does not automatically exclude a connection with the teaching about the two spirits (1QS iii–iv). For example, the partition of the rising zodiacal sign by the ascendant in dark and light parts may be interpreted as determining the ratio of light and darkness within the spirit of the individual who is born according to 1QRule of the Community (1QS iv.15–26). The sparse information conveyed by horoscope (4Q186) does not permit a final decision about the relative merits of the various interpretations. What is certain is that, in whatever way, horoscopy was an object of interest in the Qumran community.

[*See also* Cryptic Scripts; Determinism; *and* Rule of the Community.]

BIBLIOGRAPHY

Albani, Matthias. "Horoscopes in the Qumran Scrolls." In Peter W. Flint and James C. VanderKam (eds.), *The Dead Sea Scrolls after Fifty Years. A Comprehensive Assessment*, vol. 2, pp. 279–330. Leiden and Boston, 1999. Including among others a detailed discussion of the ascendant-theory of horoscope 4Q186.

Allegro, J. M. "An Astrological Cryptic Document from Qumran." *Journal of Semitic Studies* 9 (1964), 291–294. First study concerning the Qumran horoscope 4Q186.

Allegro, J. M. "4Q186." In *Qumran Cave 4, I. (4Q158–4Q186)*, pp. 88–91. Discoveries in the Judaean Desert, 5. Oxford, 1968. Including the authorized facsimile edition of the Qumran horoscope 4Q186.

Bergmeier, R. *Glaube als Gabe nach Johannes*. Religions- und theologiegeschichtliche Studien zum prädestinationischen Dualismus im vierten Evangelium. Stuttgart 1980. On pages 78–81 there is a very interesting excursus ("Astrologie, Prädestination und Dualismus") discussing the theological significance of the horoscopes in the Dead Sea Scrolls. The author pleads for a pure astrological interpretation of 4Q186 and argues against a connection between the teaching of the two spirits (1QS iii/iv) and the Qumran horoscopes in 4Q186.

Carmignac, J. "Les horoscopes de Qumrân." *Revue de Qumrân* 5 (1965), 199–217. The author discusses the reconstruction of the text of the Qumran horoscopes.

Catalogus Codicum Astrologorum Graecorum VII—Codices Germanicos, descripsit Franciscus Boll, Brussels 1908. Important collection of Greek astrological texts with critical apparatus, including the zodiacal text of Teukros, which is the basis of the ascendant interpretation of horoscope (4Q186).

Charlesworth, J. H. "Jewish Interest in Astrology during the Hellenistic and Roman Period." In *Aufstieg und Niedergang der römischen Welt II*, Band 20.2. pp. 926–950. Berlin and New York, 1987. Including a brief chapter on the Qumran horoscopes ("IV. Astrology and the Dead Sea Scrolls," pages 938–940) and their significance in the Qumran Community.

Delcor, M. "Recherches sur un horoscopes en langue hébraïque provenant de Qumrân." *Revue de Qumrân* 5 (1965–1966), 521–542. A very extensive study of the Qumran horoscopes including interesting analogies and parallels from ancient writings.

Fitzmyer, J. A. "The Aramaic 'Elect of God' Text from Qumrân Cave IV." *Catholic Biblical Quarterly* 27 (1965), 348–372. Fitzmyer's view of the Elect of God (4Q534) is that the designation of the text as horoscope is not justified and that it is better to see it against the background of Greco-Roman physiognomic literature.

García Martínez, F. *Qumran and Apocalyptic: Studies on the Aramaic Texts from Qumran*. Leiden, 1992. Including a detailed analysis of the scroll originally known as a horoscope of the Messiah (4Q534), which the author considers as part of the oldest known (but lost) apocalypse, the *Book of Noah*. The author sees an interrelationship between the Qumran horoscopes in 4Q186 and Talmudic passages and expresses a hypothesis on the use of astrology in the Qumran community.

Lichtenberger, H. *Studien zum Menschenbild in den Texten der Qumrangemeinde*. Tübingen, 1980. The author includes not only a very important discussion of the anthropological aspects of the Qumran horoscopes on pages 142–148, but also offers some interesting ideas for the astrological and astronomical understanding of the text 4Q186.

Schmidt, F. "Ancient Jewish Astrology—An Attempt to Interpret 4QCryptic (4Q186)." In M. E. Stone and E. G. Chazon (eds.), *Biblical Perspectives: Early Use and Interpretation of the Bible in the Light of the Dead Sea Scrolls. Proceedings of the First International Symposium of the Orion Center for the Study of the Dead Sea Scrolls and Associated Literature, 12–14 May, 1996*, pp. 189–205. Leiden and Boston, 1998. Most recent study on horoscope 4Q186. Schmidt offers some very interesting new ideas for understanding the puzzling details of horoscope 4Q186: He explains the changing parts in the house of light or darkness, attributed to every individual, on the one hand by the subdivision of the zodiacal signs into 36 *decans*—three for each zodiacal sign—and on the other hand by the moment of conception and not that of birth; for Schmidt's intriguing theory, see the detailed discussion in an addendum of my article "Horoscopes in the Dead Sea Scrolls" in *The Dead Sea Scrolls after Fifty Years*.

Starcky, J. "Un texte messianique araméen de la grotte 4 de Qumrân." In *École des langues orientales anciennes de l'Institut Catholique de Paris. Mémorial du cinquantenaire 1914–1964*, pp. 51–66. Paris, 1964. First edition of the text 4Q534 (= 4QElect of God ar/ 4QMessᶜ aram = 4QNoah), which the editor thought had preserved a horoscope of the Messiah.

Strugnell, J. "Notes en marge du Volume V des 'Discoveries in the Judaean Desert of Jordan.'" *Revue de Qumrân* 7 (1969/1971), 163–276. Including corrections of the text reconstruction of the Qumran horoscope 4Q186 in the DJD (Discoveries in the Judaean Desert) edition by Allegro on pages 274–276.

Stuckrad, Kocku von. *Frömmigkeit und Wissenschaft. Astrologie in Tanach, Qumran und frührabbinischer Literatur*. Frankfurt and New York, 1996. The author offers a useful overview of the use and significance of astrology in ancient Judaism against the background of Babylonian, Egyptian, and Hellenistic astrology, including an interesting discussion of the Qumran horoscopes on pages 117–132.

MATTHIAS ALBANI

HOSEA, BOOK OF. *See* Minor Prophets; Pesher Hosea.

HOUSE OF PROSTRATION. *See* Synagogues.

HYMNS AND PSALMS. *See* Psalms, Hymns, and Prayers.

HYMN SCROLL. *See* Hodayot.

HYMN TO THE CREATOR. *See* Psalms Scroll.

HYRCANIUM. *See* Mird, Khirbet.

HYRCANUS II. *See* Alexander Jannaeus; Hasmoneans; *and* Shelamzion Alexandra.

I

INKWELLS. At Qumran at least four inkwells were discovered: three by Roland de Vaux and one by Solomon Steckoll. De Vaux unearthed two in locus 30, the room below the scriptorium, and the third in locus 31, which is adjacent to and east of locus 30. The fourth was found by Steckoll in an unspecified location. One of de Vaux's inkwells is made of bronze, whereas the other two as well as Steckoll's are ceramic.

After the Qumran pottery inkwells were found, other examples of the same type—now called Qumran pottery inkwells—were also discovered in other sites in early Roman Palestine. Produced on a wheel, the type has the form of a cylindrical "pillbox" with a flat base and top attached at a sharp angle—both top and base are uncharacteristic of ceramics but natural to bronze inkwells, which the Qumran-type vessels try to imitate. The ware is usually reddish or pinkish, but certain inkwells are gray, another feature derived from the metal utensils.

The concave top and a "sleeve" below the opening are designed to prevent spilling and are common features in inkwells from antiquity to our own times. A feature peculiar to the Qumran type is the ring handle, which is preserved only on rare occasions. The Steckoll inkwell is 5.5 centimeters (2.2 inches) tall and 3.9 centimeters (1.5 inches) in diameter, and the dimensions of those found by de Vaux are similar. This type has been found so far only in Palestinian Jewish sites of the first century CE.

The Qumran bronze vessel is made from a rectangular sheet turned into a cylinder with the two ends soldered together. The existence of a lid, now missing, is attested by a hinge still riveted near the filling hole. Similar to the pottery receptacles, it stands 5.2 centimeters (2 inches) high with a diameter of 3 centimeters (1.2 inches) and is of a type quite common to Roman inkwells from the first and second centuries CE.

Various collections (in Florida, Oslo, Munich, and elsewhere) include inkwells, both ceramic and metal, bought from a Jerusalem dealer and allegedly found at Qumran. There is good reason to doubt the claims for a Qumranic origin of these inkpots—an alleged Qumranic pedigree must have made them more attractive on the antiquities market. Even so, the four inkwells found at Qumran are of great significance and attest to at least serious, if not intensive, scribal activity.

[*See also* Scribal Practices; Scribes.]

BIBLIOGRAPHY

de Vaux, Roland. "Fouilles au Khirbet Qumrân. Rapport préliminaire sur la deuxième campagne." *Revue biblique* 61 (1954), 212. See plate X:b.

de Vaux, Roland. *Archaeology and the Dead Sea Scrolls: The Schweich Lectures 1959*. London, 1973. See pages 29–33 and 104.

Goranson, Stephen. "Qumran—The Evidence of the Inkwells." *British Archaeological Reports* 19.6 (1993), 67.

Goranson, Stephen. "Qumran—A Hub of Scribal Activity." *British Archaeological Reports* 20.5 (1994), 36–39.

Khairy, Nabil I. "Ink-Wells of the Roman Period from Jordan." *Levant* 12 (1980), 155–162.

Olenik, Y. "Early Roman Period Pottery Inkwells from Eretz Israel." In *Israel—People and Land.* Haaretz Museum Yearbook, 1. Tel Aviv, 1983–1984. See pages 55–66; English abstract appears on pages 10–11. This is the most comprehensive study of the subject.

MAGEN BROSHI

INSCRIPTIONS. Ancient Hebrew and Aramaic inscriptions of Palestine from the ninth–eighth century BCE onward are limited to nonliterary documents, mainly ostraca of the following types: alphabets, school exercises, letters, and economic documents, which tell of the political, juridical, economic, and social conditions of their time.

Regarding the discoveries in the Judean desert, nonliterary documents consist mainly of papyri, some leather fragments, and a few inscriptions on jars and potsherds. Of the latter, ostraca were discovered in Wadi Murabba'at (Mur 72–87), Wadi Khabra (Naḥal Ḥever) (8Ḥev 5–8), Masada (Mas 1–701, 750–794), the area of southern Judea (fourteen ostraca with lists of goods, dating to the first century CE), and in the ruins of Khirbet Qumran and the caves nearby.

These inscriptions are written in black ink or charcoal or in incised letters on jars and potsherds. In instances where they show more than few letters (writing exercises, alphabets), they contain lists of personal names together with numeral signs and abbreviations, accounts, invoices, letters (Mas 554–552), reports (Mur 72), and a tomb inscription (8Ḥev 5). [*See* Deeds of Sale; Names and Naming.]

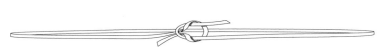

The script of the Hebrew and Aramaic ostraca is mainly cursive (derived from the Jewish square script) or a more or less fine bookhand. [*See* Paleography.] The languages of these inscriptions are Hebrew (Khirbet Qumran; the Qumran caves; 8Ḥev; Mas [Beyer, 1994, pp. 209–212]), Aramaic Mas; (Beyer, 1994, pp. 209–213), Greek (Khirbet Qumran; Mas 772–794), and Latin (Mas 750–771).

In the ruins of Khirbet Qumran, inscriptions on jars with personal names (Hebrew, Latin, and Greek) were discovered as well as more than twenty ostraca with personal names and alphabets.

The caves near Khirbet Qumran preserved the following inscriptions: Cave 3, one jar inscription with the impression "Ṭ"; Cave 4, one jar inscription with the wish/greeting "Peace/Greeting. May he enlighten your face"; Cave 6, two inscriptions on jars about a quantity; Cave 7, one inscription on a jar with the personal name "RM"; Cave 10, one ostracon with traces of a personal name.

These few inscriptions on jars and potsherds from Khirbet Qumran and from the caves nearby give very little information about the everyday life of the Qumran Hasidean-Essene community; however, this statement now may need revision. One of the volunteers of a small expedition to Khirbet Qumran led by J. F. Strange in the winter of 1996 found two inscribed sherds at the base of the eastern face of the outer wall. Both ostraca contain Hebrew inscriptions. The script is very similar to that of the Copper scroll (3Q15) and seems to belong to the middle or end of the first century CE. The reading of the second ostracon yields only some personal names (. . . . P BN NTN . . . and perhaps [B]NYW Mʿ YN [GDY ?]). Ostracon number one is broken in two parts and contains fifteen more or less preserved lines. It represents a deed of gift from 67/68 CE ("in year two of [the freedom of . . ."], written at Jericho, the place of execution of the contract). The donor's name is Ḥoni b. . . . , the name of the recipient is Eleazar b. Naḥamani. The donation consists of the slave Ḥisday from Ḥolon and other property; through it the donor fulfills his obligation to the Qumran community (*yḥd*). If this interpretation is correct, this ostracon is one of the most convincing links between the community at Khirbet Qumran during the First Jewish Revolt and the Rule of the Community, providing for the first time the name of a *mevaqqer* of the community (see CD xi.13). It should be noted, however, that some scholars question the reading of the word *yaḥad* and see this inscription as irrelevant to the Qumran community.

BIBLIOGRAPHY

Beyer, K. *Die Aramäischen Texte vom Toten Meer*. Göttingen, 1984.

Cotton, Hannah, and Joseph Geiger. *Masada II. The Latin and Greek Documents*, Jerusalem, 1989.

Cross, F. M., and E. Eshel. "Ostraca from Khirbet Qumran." *Israel Exploration Journal* 47 (1997), 17–28.

Humbert, J.-B. *Fouilles de Khirbet Qumrân et de Aïn Feshka IV: Numismatique, Inscriptions et Graffiti*. Göttingen-Fribourg (forthcoming).

Nebe, G. W. "Qumran IV." *Zeitschrift für Althebräistik* 12 (1999), forthcoming.

Tov, Emanuel, ed. *The Dead Sea Scrolls on Microfiche*. Leiden, 1993.

Yadin, Yigael, and Joseph Naveh. *The Yigael Yadin Excavation, 1961–65. Final Reports: Masada I.* The Aramaic and Hebrew Ostraca and Jar Inscriptions. Jerusalem, 1989.

Yardeni, Ada. "New Jewish Aramaic Ostraca." *Israel Exploration Journal* 40 (1990), 130–152.

G. Wilhelm Nebe

INTERPRETATION OF SCRIPTURES. The picture of biblical interpretation at Qumran is but a piece of the larger mosaic of Jewish biblical interpretation in antiquity. Although it may not have comprised a major component of that body of exegesis during the Second Temple period, Qumran biblical interpretation now constitutes a principal element in our delineation of the overall system of early biblical interpretation. The significance of the Dead Sea Scrolls in this area is based not merely upon the number of manuscripts discovered, but also on the diversity in its corpus and the way in which the collection seems to mirror Second Temple Jewish literature as a whole. It can thus serve as a virtual representative of a much broader body of material.

Nearly all of the writings of the Qumran community, whether formally linked with scripture or not, are pervaded with scriptural interpretation. Fragments of all books of the Hebrew scriptures, with the exception of *Esther*, have been found at Qumran. Clearly then, the raw material for scriptural interpretation was available. Regardless of whether there was a biblical "canon" at Qumran and what its contents might have been, it is generally conceded that, however it was defined by the Qumranites, and whatever books it contained, the books of what is now known as the Hebrew scriptures frequently functioned as both the source and the framework for what the Qumran writers wanted to say and the way in which they said it. The genres employed for interpretation are so diverse, and the various parts of scripture are employed in such diverse fashions, that they force us to focus on the important fact that any picture that is drawn of Qumran scriptural interpretation must be a highly variegated one. Diversity of texts commented upon, methods of interpretation, genres of commentary, functions of commentary, and modes of presentation make variety itself a characteristic feature.

It should also be stressed that the very notion "Qumran interpretation of scripture" is a virtual misnomer, for there is no reason to assume that the Qumran documents, deposited in the caves over a lengthy period of time, whether brought to the caves or written in the Qumran community, derive from a group or groups that had a unified sense of the way in which scripture was to be read or a single conception of the message that it was to convey. Our classification of the texts, their characteristics, and their methods of interpretation should not be taken as intended to produce an integrated portrait of what is actually at best a mosaic. We can view the biblical interpretation of the Qumran scrolls as presenting a representative variety of the kinds of biblical interpretation that were presumably being carried out in Second Temple Judaism as a whole, with an admixture of uniquely Qumranic material such as, perhaps, the *pesharim*. [*See* Pesharim.]

The history of scholarship on Qumran biblical interpretation is instructive, since in many ways it serves as a microcosm of Qumran studies as a whole. The order in which the Qumran documents were discovered was responsible to a large degree for the guidelines and categories by which the genres of Qumran literature were described, and biblical interpretation was no exception. Thus the *pesharim*, especially the nearly complete Pesher Habakkuk (1QpHab), were the focal point of much early study, while the other biblical commentary from Cave 1, the Genesis Apocryphon (1QapGen), lagged behind in attracting academic interest because of its poor state of preservation. It has only been with the publication of a broader range of Qumran texts that focus on the Bible, such as the many *pesharim* (4Q161–173), Florilegium (4Q174), and the Temple Scroll (11Q19), that properly nuanced discussion of scriptural interpretation at Qumran could be carried on.

Unsurprisingly, the books of the Pentateuch dominate at Qumran as objects of interpretation. In addition to texts such as the Genesis Commentaries, the Genesis Apocryphon, the Reworked Pentateuch, and the Temple Scroll, we find substantial literature pertaining to Enoch, Noah, and Levi, "Moses-pseudepigrapha," other legal texts related to the Torah, as well as *Jubilees* and works related to *Jubilees* within the Qumran corpus. A very substantial proportion of Qumran pentateuchal interpretation pertains to *Genesis*, and even as far as that biblical book, there seems to be particularly heavy interest in the narrative of *Genesis* from Creation through the Aqedah (the binding of Isaac, *Gn*. 22.1–19). The other divisions of the Hebrew scriptures in their later form, the Prophets and Writings (cf. Miqtsat Maʿasei ha-Torah [4QMMT C 10]), attracted less written attention. Among the latter prophets, *Isaiah, Hosea, Micah, Habakkuk, Zephaniah*, and *Nahum* were the object of *pesharim*, while *Jeremiah* and *Ezekiel* engendered works that have been classified by scholars as "Apocryphon of Jeremiah" and "Pseudo-Ezekiel." It is somewhat striking that there is no generic overlap in the treatment of the two groups of prophetic texts.

The Aramaic Targum of Job (11Q10, hereafter 11QTargum of Job) represents the most extended interpretation on any book of the Writings. Beyond translation, focused and sustained interpretation of the Writings is to be found primarily in *pesharim* on Psalms from Caves 1 and 4, with only one of the manuscripts, Pesher Psalms[a] (4Q171), being at all substantial. Three so-called "thematic" *pesharim*, Florilegium (4Q174), Catena[a] (4Q177), and Melchizedek (11Q13), also contain interpretive material on Psalms, with the latter commenting on *Daniel* as well. Based on the extant fragments, it is difficult to classify the pseudo-Danielic material (4Q243–245) as scriptural interpretation.

The study of biblical interpretation at Qumran (once again, like that of early Jewish interpretation generally) can be approached from a variety of valid perspectives. This survey is organized around the following categories: types of biblical interpretation; forms or genres of biblical interpretation; and methods of biblical interpretation. The first of these categories characterizes briefly the typological varieties of interpretation that are found in those works; the second, in somewhat greater detail and from a formal perspective, the kinds of works wherein we find biblical interpretation at Qumran; and the third, the techniques and methods through which those interpretations are derived from the biblical text.

Types of Interpretation. Classifying the types of biblical interpretation that are found at Qumran is more difficult then surveying its genres or describing its methodologies. One utilitarian perspective arranges types of interpretation along a range, which stretches from a straightforward literal exegesis demanded by a text (along the lines of that which is described as *peshaṭ* in later Jewish literature) to the most extreme eisegesis, wherein the biblical text becomes the pretext for an ideologically or theologically colored "reading" that is superimposed upon it. In between these we find simple sense readings, which conform to, but are not demanded by, the text, and readings that might be the sense of the text, but that are selected by the interpreter largely for ideological reasons. At Qumran we can find types that range across this whole spectrum, and the boundaries between the "types" are usually not clearly delineated.

The Qumran (or other Second Temple) interpreter faced a variety of difficulties: some real; some imagined. Linguistic problems had to be solved; perceived gaps in a narrative had to be filled in; repetitive or contradictory stories and laws had to be integrated or harmonized; stories that contained matter at variance with the moral tastes of later generations needed to be adjusted. At the same time, the interpreter could also delve into the text in order to attain the fullest meaning of God's word for his generation, as he searched scripture for answers to questions, which, from the perspective of the modern reader, scripture does not seem even to ask. The interpreters in the Dead Sea Scrolls were offering only one (or more) of a range of interpretive options that existed in

Second Temple Judaism, and their readings must often be read as in dialogue with, or as polemic against, those of other Jewish groups. G. Vermes has distinguished between these two types as "pure" and "applied" exegesis, respectively, but it is not at all clear whether the ancient interpreter would have made such a distinction. Indeed, although the distinction is at times quite valuable, it is often difficult, even with our hindsight, to draw the line between "pure" and "applied."

The question is further complicated if we allow for the possibility that not everything we consider as "interpretation" is textually generated, even by the standards of very close reading and gap-filling, which seem to have characterized ancient exegetes. The expansions of biblical narratives (and occasionally biblical legal material) with completely extrabiblical material, which need not be exegetically linked to the Hebrew text, certainly belong to the category of interpretation, but are hard to classify according to type.

If we try to classify some of the interpretive texts from Qumran against this background, we will find that most interpretive texts contain different sorts of exegesis side-by-side. The Genesis Apocryphon works out and smooths out details of the narratives in the Bible about Noah and Abraham in a manner that responds to the "bumps" in the biblical text, but also seems to find place for introduction into its narrative of legal practices that were of particular interest to the Qumran sect. Portions of Commentary on Genesis A (4Q252) seem to be directed at resolving "simple sense" exegetical difficulties (4Q252 ii.5–7, 8–10), but others seem to be focused on sectarian interests such as the chronology of the Pentateuch (i.1–ii.5) or on locating certain sectarian beliefs within the biblical text (v.1–5).

The *pesharim*, of course, stand at one extreme of the spectrum; almost all of the interpretation in them aims at locating sectarian history and theology within the interpretation of the biblical text of the Prophets or Psalms through the identification and association of names and events from the Bible with the personalities and history of the authors' own day. Any attempt to *interpret* the biblical text in the modern sense appears to be very secondary to the prophet's hidden message, which the authors are striving to reveal.

In the case of virtually all legal texts from Qumran that have scriptural interpretation, a spectrum of interpretive types may be observed. Generically diverse works such as the Temple Scroll[a] (11Q19), Damascus Document[a–h] (4Q266–273; CD), and 4QMMT (4Q394–399) all contain exegesis of the legal portions of the Torah. The reading of the biblical text is often of the sort that can comfortably be described as "simple sense," but the textual support is often for laws that are the subject of debate between the Qumran group and its opponents. "Simple sense" interpretation thus serves tendentiously as the support of a legal system.

Genres of Biblical Interpretation at Qumran. When we turn to the forms of interpretive works, we observe the range of literary genres wherein biblical interpretation is to be found either as a primary or secondary function. It is especially necessary to distinguish between these two groups because, on the one hand, formal commentary differs generically from the other types, and, on the other, because to omit the nonformal commentaries would be to overlook the very pervasive nature of biblical interpretation in the Qumran scrolls as a whole. It also should be stressed that Qumran biblical interpretation, like other forms of biblical interpretation in antiquity, often did not resemble modern, "objective," reading of the text. The Bible was not merely the object of study for the Qumranites, it pervaded their lives, prescribing both practice and belief. The study of, or meditation on, scripture was part of their daily (and nightly) religious and intellectual activity (see Rule of the Community [1QS vi.6–7]), and the unidentifiable Teacher of Righteousness was an inspired interpreter of prophetic texts (Pesher Habakkuk [1QpHab vii.3–5]).

Interpretation in interpretive genres. Biblical interpretation can be seen immediately as the goal of a variety of works from Qumran, particularly those labeled by modern scholars as *pesher* or "commentary." These at times resemble the commentary form, which persists to the present day. The structure of such works, with the presentation of a lemma from the biblical text followed by interpretive remarks, makes it obvious that the Bible is the object of what we describe as interpretation. When the *pesharim* were discovered and read, beginning with Pesher Habakkuk in the early 1950s and followed by about fifteen other subsequently published exemplars, they provided scholars with a completely new type of ancient biblical commentary. Its form was indisputably commentary, although the kind of commentary it contained was not the straightforward explication of the text to which modern readers were accustomed, but one that located the message of the biblical text in the interpreter's day, with the fulfillment of the biblical prophecy being seen in contemporary events. The commentary's solution to the enigmatic prophecies often remains enigmatic to the modern student, and perhaps to some ancient readers as well, because the identities of groups and characters alluded to in the Bible are hidden behind "code" terms, which must have been clear to the author and the initiates of his group.

In the 1980s and 1990s, it became clear that the *pesharim* were not the only commentary form to be found at Qumran, and that the books of the prophets were not the only objects of commentary. In particular, four texts (4Q252–254a) containing remarks on different parts of *Genesis* were labeled "Commentaries on Genesis A-D." Although their remains, with the exception of Commentary on Genesis A (4Q252), are meager, that one manuscript exhibits a number of significant features for the classification of Qumran interpretation. Not all of Commentary on Genesis A is lemma + comment-type, and parts of it seem to derive from something resembling "Rewritten Bible," but what is clear is that it is not a systematic retelling of the biblical text, and therefore must be distinguished generically from "Rewritten Bible." It is also not even a commentary on all parts of *Genesis*, and that distinguishes it from many of the *pesher*-type commentaries, the discovery of which preceded it, because those commentaries usually present a verse by verse exegesis on the biblical text. What appears to characterize these commentaries, if we may use the best-preserved Commentary on Genesis A as a paradigm, is their selectivity and their willingness to comment, in whatever fashion, on specific texts and not on the biblical book as a whole.

The other major interpretive genre at Qumran is the so-called "Rewritten Bible." Under this term we include texts that retell, summarize, or present in altered fashion the narratives or laws of the Hebrew scriptures. All rewriting is commentary, and the methodology of selection, rearrangement, supplementation, and omission in the process of rewriting is a form of commentary, even if the interpretive aspect is not always overt at first glance to the reader who is not closely attentive to the original text being rewritten. It is possible that "Rewritten Bible" represents the earliest generic attempt to comment on the Bible before the more economical "commentary" form was developed. Before the Qumran discoveries this ancient genre was extant only in such works as *Jubilees*, Josephus's *Jewish Antiquities*, and pseudo-Philo's *Biblical Antiquities*. [*See* Rewritten Bible.]

The Qumran caves enriched considerably the range of extant examples of this literary type, while simultaneously presenting some problems to the modern interpreter. At one end of the spectrum, on the border between biblical texts and biblical interpretation, stand the "Rewritten Bible" texts, which have been named by their editors "Reworked Pentateuch" (4Q158 and 4Q364–367). Inclusion of these works under the rubric of "interpretation" can be taken to imply that they are not biblical texts, but it is possible that, from the standpoint of their authors, as opposed to that of the modern scholar, they are biblical, with the process of interpretation taking place within rather than upon a text (cf. the relationship of the Samaritan Pentateuch and the Masoretic Text). [*See* Reworked Pentateuch.]

The lengthy rewriting of the Pentateuch in this modified form, which, it must be stressed, differs considerably among the several manuscripts given this title, rearranges segments for the sake of clarity, introduces interpretive comments, and occasionally adds new material. For long stretches some of these texts resemble some form of the biblical text itself. Thus the breadth of the rewriting, together with the fact that there are few major additions, makes the interpretive aspect of these manuscripts rather small in proportion to their lengths (4Q158 may be an exception to this description). In a like fashion, some of the "deviations" from the Masoretic Text in a biblical manuscript like 1QIsaiah[a] may not all be due to variant textual traditions, but rather to interpretive rewriting. Distinguishing between variant text and exegetical rephrasing is a delicate matter regarding which scholars are virtually bound to disagree, and in the case of some of the Reworked Pentateuch material from Cave 4 a final decision has yet to be rendered as to their "biblical" or "nonbiblical" nature.

When we turn to works that are clearly distinguishable as nonscriptural, Cave 1, once again, provides an early example, the Genesis Apocryphon, which, in its extant portions, retells in Aramaic parts of the Noah and Abraham narratives of *Genesis*. Occasionally close enough to the Hebrew text to be a virtual *targum*, it also offers paraphrase and "midrashic" expansion of the biblical story. The Temple Scroll, discovered later, is rewritten Bible of a legal sort. The first part of the scroll describes the festivals and their sacrifices and the construction of the Temple in a fashion both structurally and stylistically modeled on the Pentateuch. The latter section of the scroll (li.11–lxvi.17, called by some the "Deuteronomic paraphrase") gathers biblical laws under common rubrics, rearranging the pentateuchal legal material, and occasionally adding laws that have no overt scriptural basis. Because its language remains so closely modeled on the biblical, we can often follow the Temple Scroll's manipulation of the pentateuchal text with great ease, and detect the places in which it has altered the original or handled it in such a fashion as to indicate a particular reading of the original. [*See* Genesis Apocryphon.]

A genre that is interpretive in a somewhat different fashion is the so-called thematic *pesher* mentioned earlier, which collects and interprets verses from diverse parts of the Bible around a particular issue. Both the anthologizing itself and the comments on the texts constitute scriptural interpretation. In particular, the employment of material from one book of the Bible as part of the exegesis of another demonstrates the sense of the interrelationship of various parts of the Bible held by the authors of the texts. Florilegium (4Q174) and Catena[a] (4Q177) focus on *Psalms*, but cite texts from the Pentateuch and the Prophets in the course of their interpretation, while Melchizedek (11Q13) does not appear to be as firmly located in a single biblical book and follows its theme through the Pentateuch, *Isaiah*, *Psalms*, and *Daniel*. One of the Isaiah *pesharim* (Pesher Isaiah[c] [4Q163]) also introduces references to other prophetic books (*Hosea*, *Jeremiah*, *Zechariah*) into its commentary on Isaiah.

Interpretation in noninterpretive genres. Not all Qumran biblical interpretation, however, is to be found in texts that focus on the Bible. In texts that are heavily legal in content, such as the Damascus Document (CD), the Rule of the Community (1QS), and 4QMMT (4Q394–399), we find exegesis in both legal and nonlegal sections. The orientation of the Qumran group to the Bible appears to have demanded biblical support for theology as well as law. Thus, the Damascus Document or Zadokite Fragments (CD) interprets and employs biblical passages in both of the sections into which it has been divided, the Admonition and the Laws (a distinction that has grown progressively difficult to assert after the full publication of the 4QDamascus Document texts). The Bible is in no way the framework for either so-called division of the work, but its influence is pervasive on both of them.

Miqtsat Maʿasei ha-Torah (4Q394–399), the so-called halakhic letter, is clearly not as scripturally based as the Temple Scroll, but it is difficult to deny its connection with scripture. It does not derive laws from scripture, but in listing the *halakhot* which it addresses, Miqtsat Maʿasei ha-Torah actually employs scripture as the model for its language. The legal section B of Miqtsat Maʿasei ha-Torah is heavily influenced by *Leviticus* and *Numbers*.

There are other literary forms at Qumran, such as prayers and others of less easily identifiable genres, that have been given such names as "paraphrase," "exposition," "admonition," and the like by modern editors, which also include or reflect scriptural interpretation. If a biblical narrative is employed in a hortatory fashion or made part of a historical survey contained in a prayer, scriptural interpretation is inevitably present. Thus in the final section of Miqtsat Maʿasei ha-Torah, the so-called "Exhortation," the phraseology is heavily influenced by the diction and theological themes of *Deuteronomy*. Finally, although perhaps furthest removed generically from "interpretation," the Hodayot are composed in language that is saturated with that of the Bible, and the employment of biblical phraseology in the poetry often sheds light on the way in which the poet of the Hodayot would have interpreted Scripture.

Methods and Techniques of Interpretation: A Selection. The methods, or techniques, of interpretation at Qumran, with the exception of *pesharim*, are not unique to this corpus of literature, but are shared with other Second Temple documents and rabbinic texts as well, and some may even find their origins within the Hebrew Bible itself. They are not linked exclusively to the ideology of the Qumran group although they are sometimes employed in support of that ideology.

Thematic association. Thematic association is one of the most prominent methods of interpretation found in the Qumran texts, and it includes a variety of specific interpretive methods. Thus, the juxtaposition of biblical passages that share a common theme, whether legal or nonlegal; the harmonization of passages on the same or similar theme; and the linking of passages through common vocabulary are all forms of thematic association employed in Qumran biblical interpretation.

Harmonization and rearrangement are aspects of this procedure employed by the Qumran biblical interpreters in both legal and narrative material. At times their goal is the convenient assembly of material, found originally in diverse parts of the biblical text, into a single location. This systematization and collocation of related material is one fundamental form of interpretation. These methods are also employed in order to resolve difficulties in the text, whether of contradiction between two biblical passages or the apparent lack of sequentiality within a biblical narrative.

The Reworked Pentateuch texts omit the laws of *Numbers* 5–6 so that the narrative proceeds from the appointment of the Levites in *Numbers* 4.47 to the construction of the Tabernacle in *Numbers* 7.1 (4Q365 28). The laws of the festival of Sukkot, which appear in *Numbers* 29 and *Deuteronomy* 16, are juxtaposed in 4Q366 4 and may have been followed, according to the editors of the Reworked Pentateuch texts, by the laws of Sukkot in *Leviticus* 23. In their narrative portions, as well, we find the dialogue between the Israelites and the Edomite king harmonizing the accounts of *Numbers* 20 and *Deuteronomy* 2 (4Q364 23a–b i) in a manner similar to, but not identical with, that of the Samaritan Pentateuch. In Reworked Pentateuch[c] (4Q365 36), the two incidents pertaining to the daughters of Zelophehad (*Nm.* 27 and 36) are placed together (cf. Numbers[b] [4Q27 31–32]).

Temple Scroll[a] shows an even greater tendency toward the gathering of legal material with similar subjects from different places in the Torah into common locations. The intent was apparently to produce a "better organized" Torah than the Mosaic one. An extended example can be found in 11Q19 lii–lv where the biblical text *Deuteronomy* 17.1, which prohibits the sacrificing of blemished animals, engenders a series of laws about slaughtering, some biblical and some extrabiblical, including the laws against sacrificing a mother and her child on the same day (*Lv.* 22.28). Other laws about animal slaughter deriving from *Deuteronomy* 12 and 15 and *Leviticus* 17 are introduced in a harmonizing fashion. Moving from the laws on slaughter in *Deuteronomy* 12 to a law on vows in *Deu-*

teronomy 12.26, the Temple Scroll then moves to *Deuteronomy* 23.24 on vows, followed by the major pentateuchal passage on vows deriving from *Numbers* 30. This is then followed by *Deuteronomy* 13, several laws pertaining to idolatry, and then by the equivalent of *Deuteronomy* 17.2 introducing another passage on idolatry and continuing from the point at which the rearrangement within this section began.

The Genesis Apocryphon has minor rearrangements of material at several points in the extant fragments, the goal of which appears to be the creation of smoother narrative by furnishing information to the reader at an earlier point than its appearance in the biblical text. Thus Hagar is introduced into the Apocryphon's narrative at the point of Abram's leaving Egypt in order to account for her presence in *Genesis* 16.1. The words from *Genesis* 20.13, which Abram is said to have spoken to Sarai at the beginning of their wanderings, are actually inserted into the narrative's equivalent of *Genesis* 12.12–13, thus making the biblical narrative smoother and consistent.

Specification and atomization. Since the biblical text is often terse and nonspecific, the interpreter often must employ what might be termed *specification*, assigning specific identification or meaning to nonspecific references. This technique, employed by Qumran interpreters of both legal and nonlegal biblical texts, might be said to underlie much *pesher* exegesis in which the interpreter assigns specific meaning to the nonspecific words of the prophet, thereby revealing to his reader the hidden intention of the prophet. Thus the "wicked one" of *Habakkuk* 1.13 is "the man of the lie" in Pesher Habakkuk (1QpHab v.11); the "righteous one" who will live by his faith (2.4) is associated with the "keepers of the law in the house of Judah" (v.1); and the "arrogant man" of *Habakkuk* 2.5 is associated with the Wicked Priest (1QpHab viii.8). The "wicked" of Psalm 37 are taken in Pesher Psalms[a] (4Q171) to refer to the opponents of the Qumran group, while the "righteous" are claimed by the author to be himself and his colleagues. In a non*pesher* context, the unidentified escapee (*Gn*. 14.13) who tells Abraham about the capture of Lot at Sodom is identified as "one of the herdsmen of the flock which Abram gave to Lot" in the Genesis Apocryphon (1QapGen xxii.1–2).

Such *pesher*-type readings (whether or not they appear in formal *pesharim*) are often "atomized," ignoring the contextual meaning of the phrase or clause under consideration, or the punctuation between verses in order to decode its contemporary referent. Thus when the author of Damascus Document iv.12–19 interprets the "terror, pit and snare" of *Isaiah* 24.17 as referring to three sorts of sins of which his opponents are guilty, he has stripped the verse of its probable contextual sense according to which the three terms represent the catastrophic disasters of an apocalyptic day of judgment. In a legal context, the key word in the phrase "*Observe* the sabbath day to keep it holy" (*Dt*. 5.12) is not taken as a general prescription, but as regulating one's behavior by avoiding forbidden activity late Friday afternoon (CD x.14–17).

Legal methods. In legal contexts, it is clear that the Qumran interpreters at times read the biblical text strictly rather than loosely. Thus in 4QMMT, the gifts of the first planting of fruit trees and the animal tithe (Miqtsat Ma'asei ha-Torah B 62–64) are assigned to the priests (unlike their treatment in rabbinic *halakhah*), based on the strict reading of *Leviticus* 19.23–24 and 27.32, "holy to the Lord." The priest who burns the ashes of the red heifer must be totally purified (once again in opposition to the rabbinic position) because Qumran law insisted on reading the biblical "pure" (*Nm*. 19.9) in the most limiting fashion.

At the same time, legal exegesis may expand the meaning of the pentateuchal text. The prohibition against defrauding (*Lv*. 25.14) is interpreted to mean in Damascus Document[f] (4Q271 3.4–6) that the seller must disclose defects in his wares to the buyer, and the failure to disclose the faults in a prospective bride to the potential groom (7–10) is characterized as "leading the blind astray from the road" (*Dt*. 27.18). Opposition to divorce (CD iv.21–v.2) is grounded in two narrative passages, "male and female he created them" (*Gn*. 1.27), and "they went into the ark two by two" (*Gn*. 7.9), coupled with the interpretation of *Deuteronomy* 17.17, "he shall not multiply wives for himself," as meaning that *even* the king may not take many wives.

Linguistic analogy (similar to the rabbinic *gezerah shavah*) is implicitly employed in Temple Scroll[a] (11Q19 l.17–18). The texts regarding the false prophet (*Dt*. 18.22) and a dishonest judge (*Dt*. 1.17) are the only pentateuchal occurrences of the phrase *lo' tagur(u)* ("you shall not be afraid"). Since a false prophet is to be put to death, reasons the scroll, so is a judge who takes bribes. A logical form of analogy seems to be employed in the argument that the laws of consanguinity operate for both males and females, so that uncle-niece marriage is to be prohibited on the same grounds as aunt-nephew marriage (*Lv*. 18.13; CD v.7–10).

Introduction of completely new material. Finally, scriptural interpretation at Qumran must also be taken to include the introduction of material that is virtually wholly new into readings of the biblical text without any stimulus for it within the text. On a legal level, the lengthy section of Temple Scroll[a] that is generally referred to as the "Law of the King" departs at great length from the straightforward interpretation of the passage in *Deuteronomy* about the appointment and regulation of a king, and incorporates the treatment of topics that are completely unfounded on the scriptural material. Yet it is located within the running paraphrase of deuteronomic legislation set out by the author. The same is true of nonscriptural details in Pseudo-Jubilees[a] (4Q225) or in lengthy passages of the Genesis Apocryphon where, in the course of retelling the biblical narrative, the narrator includes details not exegetically derived from the Bible. The extrabiblical speech of Rebecca in Reworked Pentateuch[b] (4Q364 3.ii.1–6) is typical of this type.

Comparison with Other Biblical Interpretation in Late Antiquity. Although it is clear that the Qumran scrolls are geographically isolated as a collection, it must be stressed that they nevertheless constitute a perhaps nonisolated selection of Jewish literature in late antiquity, and, as has been noted, this is as true in the area of biblical interpretation as in any other. The methods and terminology employed in citing biblical texts at Qumran are strikingly similar to those employed both in the New Testament and in rabbinic literature. The Aramaic *targum* (translation) of *Job* from Qumran can clearly be seen to stand on the same continuum as the later Aramaic versions, while the Genesis Apocryphon straddles the boundary that is drawn later between midrash and targum.

The kinds of legal interpretation that are found in the Qumran scrolls are similar to the types of readings that are found in later rabbinic and targumic literatures. Even when the rabbis derive a different law from the text than the Qumran exegete, the way in which Scripture is read to extrapolate the law is often the same. In that fashion, later rabbinic legal and nonlegal exegesis is part of the same continuum with the forms of interpretation that we find at Qumran, even if it is not literally a continuation of that interpretation. Like the Qumran interpreters, the rabbis specify what is nonspecific in the Bible, atomize texts by decontextualizing them, introduce new material (*aggadot*) into narratives, and associate and harmonize related texts with each other. Many of the problems that challenged Qumran interpreters confronted the rabbis as well, and after allowances have been made for the differing theological stances of the two groups, we can see how similar difficulties were often faced in similar ways.

Not all aspects of Qumran interpretation, however, found their continuation in rabbinic literature; *pesher*-type exegesis especially seems to be lacking. That type of prophecy-fulfillment interpretation, however, seems to survive in early Christianity, the other heir of Second Temple Judaism. In this model, texts from the Hebrew prophets are taken to be applicable to the days of the commentator. For the Qumran commentator, the eschatological prophecies were to be fulfilled in the era of the Teacher of Righteousness, while for the authors of the New Testament it was during the time of Jesus. Furthermore, such documents as Melchizedek may be seen as belonging to the exegetical milieu that generates the interpretation of the Hebrew Bible in the *Epistle to the Hebrews*.

BIBLIOGRAPHY

Bernstein, Moshe J. "Contours of Genesis Interpretation at Qumran: Contents, Context and Nomenclature." In *Ancient Biblical Interpretation*, edited by James L. Kugel. Cambridge, in press.

Bernstein, Moshe J. "Pentateuchal Interpretation at Qumran." In *The Dead Sea Scrolls after Fifty Years: A Comprehensive Assessment*, edited by Peter W. Flint and James C. VanderKam, vol. 1, pp. 128–159. Leiden, 1998.

Bernstein, Moshe J. "4Q252: From Re-Written Bible to Biblical Commentary." *Journal of Jewish Studies* 45 (1994), 1–27.

Bernstein, Moshe J. "The Employment and Interpretation of Scripture in 4QMMT: Preliminary Observations." In *Reading 4QMMT: New Perspectives on Qumran Law and History*, edited by John Kampen and Moshe J. Bernstein, pp. 29–51. Society of Biblical Literature Symposium Series, 2. Atlanta, 1996.

Bernstein, Moshe J. "Re-arrangement, Anticipation and Harmonization as Exegetical Features in the Genesis Apocryphon." *Dead Sea Discoveries* 3 (1996), 37–57.

Brin, Gershon. "Concerning Some Uses of the Bible in the Temple Scroll." *Revue de Qumrân* 12 (1987), 519–528.

Brooke, George J. "4Q252 as Early Jewish Commentary." *Revue de Qumrân* 17 (1996), 385–401.

Brooke, George J. "The Explicit Presentation of Scripture in 4QMMT." In *Legal Texts and Legal Issues: Second Meeting of the IOQS, Cambridge 1995. Published in Honour of Joseph M. Baumgarten*, edited by Moshe J. Bernstein, Florentino García Martínez, and John Kampen, pp. 67–88. Studies on the Texts of the Desert of Judah, 23. Leiden, 1997.

Brooke, George J. *Exegesis at Qumran: 4QFlorilegium in Its Jewish Context*. Sheffield, 1985.

Brooke, George J. "Parabiblical Prophetic Narratives." In *The Dead Sea Scrolls after Fifty Years: A Comprehensive Assessment*, edited by Peter W. Flint and James C. VanderKam, vol. 1, pp. 271–301. Leiden, 1998.

Brownlee, William H. "Biblical Interpretation among the Sectaries of the Dead Sea Scrolls." *Biblical Archaeologist* 14 (1951), 54–76.

Brownlee, William H. *The Meaning of the Qumran Scrolls for the Bible*. New York, 1964.

Bruce, Frederick F. *Biblical Exegesis in the Qumran Texts*. The Hague, 1959.

Campbell, Jonathan G. *The Use of Scripture in the Damascus Document 1–8, 19–20*. Beihefte zur Zeitschrift für die alttestamentliche Wissenschaft, 228. Berlin, 1995.

Dimant, Devorah, "Qumran Sectarian Literature." In *Jewish Writings of the Second Temple Period*, edited by Michael E. Stone, pp. 503–514. Compendia Rerum Iudaicarum ad Novum Testamentum, section 2, vol. 2. Philadelphia, 1984.

Eshel, Esther. "Hermeneutical Approaches to Genesis in the Dead Sea Scrolls." In *The Book of Genesis in Jewish and Oriental Christian Interpretation: A Collection of Essays*, edited by Judith Frishman and Lucas Van Rompay, pp. 1–12. Traditio Exegetica Graeca, 5. Leuven, 1997.

Fishbane, Michael. "Use, Authority, and Interpretation of Mikra at Qumran." In *Mikra: Text, Translation, Reading, and Interpretation of the Hebrew Bible in Ancient Judaism and Early Christianity*, edited by Martin J. Mulder, pp. 339–377. Compendia Rerum Iudaicaram ad Novum Testamentum, 2.1. Assen, 1988.

Gabrion, Henri. "L'interprétation de l'Ecriture dans la littérature de Qumrân." *Aufstieg und Niedergang der Römischen Welt* 19.1, (1979), 779–848.

Horgan, Maurya P. *Pesharim: Qumran Interpretations of Biblical Books*. Washington, D.C., 1979.
Kister, Menahem. "Biblical Phrases and Hidden Biblical Interpretations and Pesharim." In *The Dead Sea Scrolls: Forty Years of Research*, edited by Devorah Dimant and Uriel Rappaport, pp. 27–39. Leiden, 1992.
Maier, Johann. "Early Biblical Interpretation in the Qumran Literature." In *Hebrew Bible/Old Testament: The History of Its Interpretation*, I.1 *From the Beginnings to the Middle Ages (Until 1300): Antiquity*, edited by M. Sæbø, pp. 108–129. Göttingen, 1996.
Milgrom, Jacob. "The Qumran Cult: Its Exegetical Principles." In *Temple Scroll Studies*, edited by George J. Brooke, pp. 165–180. Sheffield, 1989.
Patte, Daniel. *Early Jewish Hermeneutic in Palestine*. Missoula, Mont., 1975.
Segal, Michael. "Biblical Exegesis in 4Q158: Techniques and Genre." *Textus* 19 (1998), 45–62.
Slomovic, Eliezer. "Toward an Understanding of the Exegesis in the Dead Sea Scrolls." *Revue de Qumrân* 7 (1969–1971), 3–15.
Swanson, Dwight D. *The Temple Scroll and the Bible: The Methodology of 11QT*. Leiden, 1995.
Tov, Emanuel. "Biblical Texts as Reworked in Some Qumran Manuscripts with Special Attention to 4QRP and 4QParaGen-Exod." In *The Community of the Renewed Covenant: The Notre Dame Symposium on the Dead Sea Scrolls*, edited by Eugene Ulrich and James VanderKam, pp. 111–134. Notre Dame, 1994.
Vermes, Geza. "Bible Interpretation at Qumran." *Eretz-Israel* 20 (1989), 184–191.
Vermes, Geza. *Scripture and Tradition in Judaism*. Leiden, 1973.
Vermes, Geza. *Post-Biblical Jewish Studies*. Leiden, 1975.
Wernberg-Møller, Preben. "Some Reflexions on the Biblical Material in the Manual of Discipline." *Studia Theologica* 9 (1955), 40–66.

MOSHE J. BERNSTEIN

INTERPRETER OF THE LAW is a title (Heb. *doresh ha-torah*) that occurs four times in the Dead Sea Scrolls but it is used in different ways. The Damascus Document describes in CD v.20–vi.11 the origins of the group that lies behind the Qumran scrolls. [*See* Damascus Document.] The core of the passage consists of an interpretation of *Numbers* 21.18 ("the well that the princes dug, that the nobles of the people laid open with the scepter"; CD vi.3–4), in which the well is taken as a symbol for the law. This passage refers first to the raising up by God of a group responsible for the law (CD vi.2–3), and then to the designation by God of an individual called the Interpreter of the Law (CD vi.7), who is identified with the "scepter" of *Numbers* 21.18 and whose rulings are held to have binding authority until the appearance of "the one who shall teach righteousness at the End of Days" (CD vi.11). It is quite clear that in CD vi.7 the Interpreter of the Law is a figure of the past, and in view of the parallel between CD v.20–vi.11 and CD i.3–12—the key passage concerned with the origins of the group behind the scrolls—it further seems clear that the Interpreter of CD vi.7 is to be identified with the Teacher of Righteousness of CD i.11. The use of the title Interpreter of the Law for the Teacher derives naturally from the context of CD v.20–vi.11, in which the emphasis is on the role of the Teacher as the one whose legal decisions alone are authoritative.

However, in the work from Cave 4 known as the Florilegium (4Q174), which is perhaps better described as the Midrash on Eschatology, the title Interpreter of the Law is unambiguously used to refer to a figure of the future, a messianic figure. [*See* Florilegium.] The Florilegium is a thematic *pesher*, which brings together a number of Old Testament texts that are interpreteted by the author to refer to the "End of Days." [*See* Pesharim.] In the Florilegium (4Q174 iii.10–12) the quotation of *2 Samuel* 7.11c–14a is followed by the explanation: "This is the Branch of David who will appear with the Interpreter of the Law, [whom he will raise up] in Zi[on at the] End of Days."

The passage is concerned primarily with the expectation of a royal messiah, who will be a descendant of David and is referred to here by the title *Branch of David* (cf. *Jer.* 23.5; Commentary on Genesis A [4Q252 v.3–4]. The Interpreter of the Law will accompany the Branch of David, and it is clear that in this context the Interpreter is a messianic figure. Although nothing is said here about the status and the duties of the Interpreter, it seems certain that he was regarded as a priestly figure and that his role, just like that of the historical Interpreter of CD vi.7, was to give authoritative legal decisions—in this case, decisions binding on the royal Messiah.

The Florilegium thus contains the expectation of two messianic figures acting side by side, the figures described elsewhere in the scrolls as the Messiahs of Aaron and Israel. The role of the priestly Messiah/Interpreter of the Law in giving legal instruction is indicated in the Testimonia (4Q175), which consists of a collection of messianic proof texts. *Deuteronomy* 33.8–11, the text quoted in reference to the priestly Messiah, includes specific mention of the role of Levi in giving instruction in the law, and it is perhaps not without significance that this text is also quoted in one of the fragments of the Florilegium, the Midrash on Eschatology. The role of the priestly Messiah in giving instruction is also indicated in Pesher Isaiah[a] (4Q161 iii.24) where it is said of the Davidic Messiah: "According to what they (i.e., the priests) teach him, he will judge."

The Interpreter of the Law is further mentioned in Catena[a] (4Q177 ii.5). It has recently been argued that Catena[a] is another copy of the Midrash on Eschatology; in any case the work has a strong eschatological emphasis. Unfortunately, however, too little of the text has survived at the crucial point for it to be possible to determine whether the Interpreter in Catena[a] belongs to the past or to the future.

The final reference to the Interpreter of the Law occurs in CD vii.18–19 in the context of a complex passage (CD vii.9–viii.2) referring to the origins of the group that lies behind the scrolls. The passage includes an abbreviated quotation from Amos (*Am.* 5.26–27), which is a prophecy of judgment on Israel but is interpreted in the Damascus Document as a prophecy of salvation relating to this group. The abbreviated quotation omits mention of the "star-god" in its version of *Amos* 5.26, but the author nonetheless added an explanation of "the star" in his comment on the passage; this in turn triggered a quotation of, and comment on, *Numbers* 24.17: "The star is the Interpreter of the Law who will come (or who came) to Damascus, as it is written: 'A star shall come out of Jacob, and a scepter shall rise out of Israel.' The scepter is the prince of the whole congregation, and when he appears he shall beat down all the sons of Seth" (CD vii.18–21). The Interpreter of the Law is here mentioned alongside the prince of the whole congregation who manifestly is a messianic figure. This fact, combined with the fact that *Numbers* 24.17 was frequently interpreted in Jewish and Christian texts in a messianic sense, suggests very strongly that the Interpreter of the Law of CD vii.18–19 is a messianic figure. Further, although it has sometimes been argued that the Interpreter in this passage is a prophetic figure, it seems much more likely—for the reasons indicated above in relation to the Florilegium—that he is a priestly figure. However, the Hebrew expression translated "who will come" is ambiguous, and it could also be translated as "who came." This has suggested to some scholars that the Interpreter here is a figure of the past. Certainty is impossible, but the balance of probability favors the messianic interpretation.

[*See also* Messiahs; Priests; Prince of the Congregation; *and* Teacher of Righteousness.]

BIBLIOGRAPHY

Brooke, George J. "The Messiah of Aaron in the Damascus Document." *Revue de Qumrân* 15 (1991), 215–230. Recent study of CD vii.13–viii.1.

Caquot, André. "Le Messianisme qumrânien." In *Qumrân: Sa piété, sa théologie et son milieu,* edited by M. Delcor, pp. 231–247. Bibliotheca ephemeridium theologicarum lovaniensium, 46. Paris, 1978. Representative of the view that the Interpreter of the Law of CD vii.18–19 is a figure of the past.

Collins, John J. *The Scepter and the Star: The Messiahs of the Dead Sea Scrolls and Other Ancient Literature.* The Anchor Bible Reference Library. New York, 1995.

García Martínez, Florentino. "Messianic Hopes in the Qumran Writings." In *The People of the Dead Sea Scrolls: Their Writings, Beliefs, and Practices,* edited by Florentino García Martínez and Julio Trebolle Barrera, pp. 159–189. Leiden, 1995. Representative of the view that the Interpreter of the Law of CD vii.18–19 is a prophetic figure.

Knibb, Michael A. "The Interpretation of Damascus Document VI, 9b–VII, 2a and XIX, 5b–14." *Revue de Qumrân* 15 (1991), 243–251.

Steudel, Annette. *Der Midrasch zur Eschatologie aus der Qumrangemeinde (4QMidrEschat[a–b])*. Studies on the Texts of the Desert of Judah, 13. Leiden, 1994. Recent study of 4Q174 and 4Q177.

MICHAEL A. KNIBB

ISAIAH, BOOK OF.

ISAIAH, BOOK OF. One of the most important, revered, and influential works for the community gathered at Qumran was the *Book of Isaiah*. It held a similarly special place for the early Christians, who used *Isaiah* heavily in order to understand and depict Jesus.

One complete copy of the book (1QIsaiah[a]) was found at Qumran, the only biblical manuscript that survived intact over the intervening two millennia. It was found inside a pottery jar in Cave 1, presumably placed there, quite effectively, for safe preservation. Though there are a few small damaged places, its text is virtually completely preserved. Generous fragments from a second copy of the book (1QIsaiah[b]) were also found in that cave, while the fragmentary remains of eighteen more manuscripts were recovered from Cave 4 and a couple of fragments from an additional copy in nearby Cave 5. Another was found at Murabbaʿat a few miles south. The total of twenty-one manuscripts at Qumran places Isaiah as one of the three most popular books there, along with Psalms (thirty-six manuscripts in the Qumran caves) and Deuteronomy (twenty-nine) manuscripts. This popularity was presumably shared among a wider group within general Judaism as well, since the biblical scrolls found at Qumran appear to be representative of the scriptures of general Judaism of the period, and since quotations from those three books rank statistically as the highest in the New Testament. Authors from the Qumran community, believing that Isaiah foretold God's plan for the period in which the community lived, explicitly quoted the book as authoritative scripture, wrote commentaries on it, and even quoted it to give expression to their self-identity.

Isaiah Manuscripts Found in the Judean Desert. The following list gives the designations of the manuscripts of the *Book of Isaiah* found in the Judean Desert:

1QIsaiah[a] (1QIsa[a])	4QIsaiah[j] (4Q63)
1QIsaiah[b] (1Q8)	4QIsaiah[k] (4Q64)
4QIsaiah[a] (4Q55)	4QIsaiah[l] (4Q65)
4QIsaiah[b] (4Q56)	4QIsaiah[m] (4Q66)
4QIsaiah[c] (4Q57)	4QIsaiah[n] (4Q67)
4QIsaiah[d] (4Q58)	4QIsaiah[o] (4Q68)
4QIsaiah[e] (4Q59)	4QIsaiah[p] (4Q69)
4QIsaiah[f] (4Q60)	4QIsaiah[q] (4Q69a)
4QIsaiah[g] (4Q61)	4QIsaiah[r] (4Q69b)
4QIsaiah[h] (4Q62)	5QIsaiah (5Q3)
4QIsaiah[i] (4Q62a)	Murabbaʿat Isaiah (Mur 3)

1QIsaiah[a] is the oldest manuscript of the book preserved, dating from the early Hasmonean period, around 125 BCE, or perhaps even a bit earlier. It presents an image much more realistic than that provided by the Masoretic Text of the kind of scroll from which the translator of the Septuagint must have worked, probably in the latter third century BCE, and of the difficulties involved in understanding the text to be translated. In contrast to some earlier views before the scrolls were known and their significance digested, it is quite likely that the translator of the Old Greek faithfully translated the Hebrew text he had before him, as best he could understand it. The orthographic practice is not systematic in any of the scrolls or in the Masoretic Text, but the spelling is generally fuller in 1QIsaiah^{a} than in the Masoretic Text or any of the other Isaiah scrolls except 4QIsaiah^{c}. Some of its more interesting textual features will be discussed below.

1QIsaiah^{b} was published by Eleazar Sukenik of the Hebrew University, but further fragments were found in the systematic excavation of the cave and published in Discoveries in the Judaean Desert (1955) by Dominique Barthélemy working at the Palestine Archaeological Museum in east Jerusalem. Its Herodian script places it near the turn of the era. Its text is closely allied with the tradition transmitted in the Masoretic Text, but not quite as closely as is commonly described. Many unclear or mostly lost letters were restored according to the reading in the Masoretic Text, but some of these restorations need correction.

With regard to date, the Cave 4 scrolls can be grouped into four categories. From the Hasmonean period generally (approximately the first half of the first century BCE) come 4QIsaiah^{f,h,i,l,m,n,o,p,r}. From the late Hasmonean period (the middle or third quarter of the first century BCE) come 4QIsaiah^{a,j,k}, or (moving perhaps into the early Herodian period) 4QIsaiah^{b,g}. From the early Herodian period (the late first century BCE), come 4QIsaiah^{e,q}. And from the late Herodian period (toward the middle of the first century CE), come 4QIsaiah^{c,d}.

For the most part, both the orthography and the text of the Cave 4 scrolls display only minor differences from other witnesses, of interest primarily to the specialist. The scribe of 4QIsaiah^{a} used forms somewhat more full than those of the Masoretic Text but less full than those of 1QIsaiah^{a}; he seemed intent upon expanding Qal participial forms, sometimes adding a superlinear *vav* after the first radical. He also divides some verses differently than the Masoretic Text, in one instance illuminating that the Greek translator had made the same judgment:

Isaiah 23.1–2

1QIsaiah^{a} *nglh lmw dmw* (ambiguous)

4QIsaiah^{a} *nglh* ^{2}*lmwdmw* (no division; *w* and *y* look alike)

Septuagint *nglh* ^{2}*lmy dmw* ("she is taken captive. ^{2}To whom are they like?")

Masoretic Text *nglh lmw* ^{2}*dmw* ("it is revealed to them. ^{2}Be silent!")

4QIsaiah^{a} contains about forty variants in its fifteen fragments. For this and all the Cave 4 Isaiah scrolls, the variants are mostly quite minor and show no particular pattern of textual affiliation for any of the texts, Hebrew or Greek.

4QIsaiah^{b} has numerous small fragments, fortunately containing both the first verse and the last verse (66.24) of the book. Its scribe also divides verses differently than 1QIsaiah^{a}, the Masoretic Text, and the Septuagint at 19.15–16. This extensive scroll displays numerous corrections, but all by the original scribe, and has more than 130 variants.

4QIsaiah^{c}, one of the latest of the scrolls, uses the ancient Paleo-Hebrew script for writing the divine name. As in 1QIsaiah^{a}, the orthography is full, and the longer morphological forms for suffixes are used. It has only eight corrections, all by the original scribe, and has about a hundred variants.

4QIsaiah^{d} preserves fragments from nine out of twelve successive columns, covering chapters 45–58. Its orthography is shorter than that of the Masoretic Text and considerably shorter than that of 1QIsaiah^{a}. It is carefully written with only three or four corrections, all by the original scribe. It has about seventy variants.

Whereas numerous fragments of 4QIsaiah^{b} and 4QIsaiah^{c} survive, 4QIsaiah^{a,d,e,f} have only a modest number, 4QIsaiah^{g} has eight from a single column, and 4QIsaiah^{h-r} have only one to five fragments each. 4QIsaiah^{p} was written on papyrus, whereas all the others were written on leather. For the scrolls with only a few fragments, it seems likely but is not always certain that they represent a manuscript of the full *Book of Isaiah*. The possibility remains that they could represent a *pesher* ("commentary"), an excerpted text, or another work that had simply quoted Isaiah, but, since only biblical text is preserved, they are classified as scrolls of Isaiah.

In addition to the twenty-two scrolls of the *Book of Isaiah*, six *pesharim* on the book were found, underscoring the community's recognition of *Isaiah* as authoritative scripture: 3QPesher Isaiah (3Q4) and 4QPesher Isaiah^{a,b,c,d,e} (4Q161–165). 4QPesher Isaiah^{c} (4Q163) was written on papyrus, the others on leather. Most of the *pesharim* are dated near the turn of the era, and though it is thought by some that they were composed then, there are indications that those manuscripts may have been copied from somewhat earlier originals. The *pesharim* generally are unconcerned with the original historical context of the words of Isaiah but eagerly apply the ancient words to events happening in their own time period, which they saw as the end time.

Characteristics and Significance of the Isaiah Manuscripts. Literary criticism has long since demonstrated that most of the books of the Hebrew scriptures are the product of a lengthy and complex compositional process, and the earliest extant textual evidence at times preserves documentation of the latter stages of these processes. This general picture holds also for the *Book of Isaiah* in particular. It is a highly composite work, with a rich history of growth and development. Starting with a collection of oracles from the eighth-century BCE prophet Isaiah of Jerusalem, the work served as a magnet for a rich and variegated heritage of prophetic materials. These range from the large collections of high theology expressed in lyric poetry by an unknown exilic author called Deutero-Isaiah in Babylon and the late-sixth-century follow-up in Trito-Isaiah in Jerusalem, to hundreds of minor insertions expressing divergent theological points over the passing centuries. But in contrast to a number of other books, such as *Exodus*, *Numbers*, *Jeremiah*, and *Psalms*, for which textual evidence is preserved of variant literary editions of the book, only a single literary edition is preserved for *Isaiah*, though the individual variants number over a thousand. All the evidence that is extant is limited to minor developments, pointing to a single organic text that grew incrementally.

The variants highlighted by a comparison of the various Qumran manuscripts, the Masoretic Text, and the Greek translation display the complete range of categories of textual variants known from general textual criticism of the Hebrew scriptures. These include simple errors, large and small losses and insertions, transpositions, misdivisions, obscurities, awareness of mistakes already in the manuscript from which the copy is being made, and some successful and some unsuccessful attempts to correct or smooth the text. These are evident in the Masoretic Text, the Septuagint, and the Qumran texts.

The extant textual evidence, however, from the scrolls, the Masoretic Text, and the Old Greek, all points to a single main edition of the work circulating in Judaism in the late Second Temple period. Although there are numerous variants displayed by all witnesses, as well as numerous types of variants, they all appear to be what can be classified as individual textual variants; that is, each of the variants seems to be an isolated instance, in contrast to there being a general tendency or pattern displayed by a significant group of variants indicating that someone had intentionally set about making a systematic or large-scale revision of the book.

It will prove illuminating to consider some examples of the larger, apparently intentional, insertions characteristic of the latter stages of the development of the book. Already in chapter two there are two large insertions, both looking like isolated thoughts only loosely connected with the surrounding text, which display different patterns of textual witness. The first was not in 1QIsaiah[a] but it occurs (with variants) in the Masoretic Text, 4Q-Isaiah[a], 4QIsaiah[b], and the Septuagint: "Do not forgive them! Enter into a rock, and hide in the dust from before the terror of the Lord and from the splendor of his majesty!" (*Is*. 2.9b–10). The second was not in the Greek or presumably the Hebrew text from which the Greek was translated, but it is in 1QIsaiah[a] and the Masoretic Text: "Have no more to do with mortals, who have but a breath in their nostrils, for what they are worth?" (*Is*. 2.22).

The possibility should be considered, of course, that these passages were just lost from a single witness, and sometimes this does happen. Whereas 4QIsaiah[a], the Masoretic Text, and the Septuagint all preserve Isaiah 4.5–6 intact, the scribe of 1QIsaiah[a] or his predecessor clearly skipped from "by day" in verse 5 to "by day" in verse 6, losing a line of text. But occasionally two or more manuscripts attest the integrity of the short text that makes sense on its own. In the well-known call narrative of Deutero-Isaiah, the original scribe of 1QIsaiah[a] and the Septuagint wrote:

> All flesh is grass and all its beauty like the flowers of the field.
> The grass withers, the flowers fade,
> but the word of our God stands forever. (*Is*. 40.6–8)

A later scribe has inserted into 1QIsaiah[a], prior to the final affirmation, this addition also present in the Masoretic Text:

> All flesh is grass and all its beauty like the flowers of the field.
> The grass withers, the flowers fade,
> when the breath of the Lord blows on it.
> (Surely the people is the grass.)
> The grass withers, the flowers fade,
> but the word of our God stands forever. (*Is*. 40.6–8)

Similar long insertions can be highlighted in both 1QIsaiah[a] and the Septuagint by noting the shorter text that stands on its own, in contrast to a sentence or two which gives the appearance of a secondary insertion. For 1QIsaiah[a], see, for example, 34.17–35.2; 37.5–7; and 40.14b–16, in contrast to the Masoretic Text, usually accompanied by the Septuagint. For the Septuagint, see, for example, 36.7b,c, where the secondary character of the insertion (between dashes) as a theological commonplace within the Assyrian Rabshakeh's threat to Judah seems clear:

> But if you say to me, We trust in the Lord our God—
> is he not the one whose high place and altars Hezekiah removed,
> after which he said to Judah and Jerusalem,
> You will worship before this altar in Jerusalem?—
> come now, make a wager with my lord the king of Assyria.
> (*Is*. 36.7–8).

It is noteworthy that the Masoretic Text has the longer, later form in all the above examples. 1QIsaiah[a] and the other scrolls give evidence that texts were occasionally corrected when errors were noticed, and were expanded when additional supplements were known and able to be added. In 1QIsaiah[a] at least four scribes made revisions in the scroll, in addition to the original scribe's corrections. Since the insertions were sporadically entered secondarily into various texts, it is quite likely that the textual tradition transmitted in the Masoretic Text attempted to incorporate as much material associated with the developing Isaiah heritage as possible. Further, it is quite unlikely that all the passages now universally attested in the Septuagint were present in the original translation of the book into Greek but were picked up in the transmission process as the Greek text was copied generation after generation. After all the thousand-plus variants in the Isaiah manuscript corpus are reviewed, no evidence appears that would ground a pattern of intentional change according to consistent principles which would constitute evidence for variant literary editions of the book. That type of large-scale editorial work had ended for Isaiah before the period from which manuscript evidence is preserved. What we can see from the second century BCE onward is a much loved and heavily used book that was studied closely and occasionally supplemented with individual reflections.

The Prophet Isaiah and the Qumran Community. Unlike such figures as Enoch, Moses, and Daniel, the person of Isaiah does not emerge as a clear actor in the writings found at Qumran, whether in those composed there or in those brought in from Palestine generally. In fact, very little curiosity about the person of Isaiah is evident in either Judaism or Christianity. The *Martyrdom and Ascension of Isaiah* stands somewhat alone in this regard, even though it demonstrates both Jewish and Christian interest. The oldest section, the core of the *Martyrdom*, was a Jewish composition from approximately the second century BCE, and rabbinic interest in the death of Isaiah continued in the Talmuds. The *Martyrdom* itself was complemented by Christian additions in the "Testament of Hezekiah" and "Vision" sections.

Rather than the person of the prophet, it was God's message revealed through the prophet and recorded in the book that seems to have been the basis of its great influence at Qumran and in the early Church. Within the general belief that life should be guided by the scriptures, the Qumran community believed that God spoke through Isaiah specifically as one of the vehicles of revelation. The introduction to the Rule of the Community instructs that the *maskil* should teach the members of the Qumran community to live according to its rules, "that they may seek God [with a whole heart and soul and] do what is good and right before him as he commanded through Moses and all his servants the prophets" (1QS i.1–3). The same Rule cites Isaiah with the traditional formula for introducing scriptural quotations ("as it is written"): "No member of the community shall follow them . . . , as it is written saying, Have no more to do with mortals, who have but a breath in their nostrils, for what are they worth?" (1QS v.17; *Is*. 2.22).

Some further quotations of Isaiah introduced by that formula occur in the following:

11QMelchizedek (11Q13) ii.23	quoting *Isaiah* 52.7
Damascus Document vii.10–12	quoting *Isaiah* 7.17
4QFlorilegium (4Q174) 1–2.i.15–16	quoting *Isaiah* 8.11
4QMiscellaneous Rules (4Q265) 2.3–5	quoting *Isaiah* 54.1–2

The War Scroll (1QM, 1Q33) goes further and equates the text of Isaiah with God's word, but without mentioning Isaiah by name: "Long ago you [God] foretold . . . , saying, "Assyria will fall by a sword not mortal, a sword not human will devour him" (1QM xi.11–12; *Is*. 31.8). But the Damascus Document (CD, with a highly fragmentary parallel in 4Q266) makes it explicit: " . . . as God spoke through Isaiah the prophet son of Amoz, "Terror, the pit, and the trap will come upon you, O inhabitant of earth" (CD iv.13–14 = 4Q266 3.i.7; *Is*. 24.17).

Over and above recognizing and using the *Book of Isaiah* as authoritative scripture, the community at Qumran even looked to that book to express its self-identity:

> When they have become a community in Israel according to these rules, they must separate . . . and go into the wilderness to prepare there the way of him as it is written, "In the wilderness prepare the way of . . . , in the desert make a smooth highway for our God." (1QS viii.12–14; *Is*. 40.3)

In both their heavy use of *Isaiah* as scripture and their application of *Isaiah* 40.3 specifically to their contemporary religious situation, the community at Qumran parallels the early Christian movement in that *Isaiah* is one of the three most quoted books in the New Testament and in that all four Gospels cite *Isaiah* 40.3 in reference to John the Baptist's ministry in the desert preparing the way for Christ (*Mt*. 3.3; *Mk*. 1.3; *Lk*. 3.4; *Jn*. 1.23). Moreover, there was a particular way of understanding *Isaiah* and revelation that was shared by Jewish groups including the Qumran community and early Christians. Revelation was seen as verbal, and the words of Isaiah, the rest of the prophets, and even the totality of the Hebrew scriptures were seen as the ancient word of God spoken long ago but with primary relevance to the contemporary or imminent situation of later Israel (whether in its Jewish or Christian continuation). This particular approach was common in the apocalyptic period (200 BCE–200 CE), including the latest works of the Hebrew scriptures (see *Dn.* 9.2, 24–27), the Qumran writings (especially the *pesharim*), and the New Testament (envisioning Jesus as the fulfillment of prophecy).

BIBLIOGRAPHY

Baillet, Maurice, Józef T. Milik, and Roland de Vaux. *Les 'Petites Grottes' de Qumrân*. Discoveries in the Judaean Desert, 3. Oxford, 1962. Critical edition of 5QIsaiah.

Barthélemy, Dominique, and Józef T. Milik. *Qumrân Cave 1*. Discoveries in the Judaean Desert, 1. Oxford, 1955. Critical edition of the remaining fragments of 1QIsaiah[b] recovered in the excavations of Cave 1; complements Sukenik's edition.

Benoit, Pierre, Józef T. Milik, and Roland de Vaux. *Les Grottes de Murabbaʿât*. Discoveries in the Judaean Desert, 2. Oxford, 1961.

Brooke, George J. "Isaiah 40.3 and the Wilderness Community." In *New Qumran Texts and Studies: Proceedings of the First Meeting of the International Organization for Qumran Studies. Paris 1992*, edited by George J. Brooke with Florentino García Martínez, pp. 117–132. Studies on the Texts of the Desert of Judah, 15. Leiden, 1994.

Burrows, Millar, ed., with John C. Trever and William H. Brownlee. *The Dead Sea Scrolls of St. Mark's Monastery*, vol. 1, *The Isaiah Manuscript and the Habakkuk Commentary*. New Haven, 1950. Good photographs with a transcription on facing pages. This early transcription inevitably contained inaccuracies, some of which were revised in a second printing.

Cross, Frank Moore, David Noel Freedman, and James A. Sanders, eds. *Scrolls from Qumran Cave 1: The Great Isaiah Scroll, the Order of the Community, the Pesher to Habakkuk, from Photographs by J. C. Trever*. Jerusalem, 1972. Color and black-and-white photographs of the scrolls on facing pages; good for comparison.

Horgan, Maurya P. *Pesharim: Qumran Interpretations of Biblical Books*. Catholic Biblical Quarterly Monograph Series, 8. Washington, D.C., 1979.

Kutscher, E. Y. *The Language and Linguistic Background of the Isaiah Scroll (1QIsa[a])*. Studies on the Texts of the Desert of Judah, 6. Leiden, 1974. An extensive analysis of the language exhibited in 1QIsaiah[a].

Parry, Donald W., and Elisha Qimron, eds. *The Great Isaiah Scroll (1QIsa[a]): A New Edition*. Studies on the Texts of the Desert of Judah, 32. Leiden, 1999. Good photographs of the scroll, with a fresh transcription (based on examination of the original scroll plus digitally enhanced images) on facing pages.

Qimron, Elisha. *The Language and Linguistic Background of the Isaiah Scroll by E. Y. Kutscher: Indices and Corrections*. Studies on the Texts of the Desert of Judah, 6A. Leiden, 1979.

Sukenik, Eleazar L. *The Dead Sea Scrolls of the Hebrew University*. Edited by N. Avigad and Y. Yadin. Jerusalem, 1955. Photographs and transcription of 1QIsaiah[b].

Tov, Emanuel. "The Text of Isaiah at Qumran." In *Writing and Reading the Scroll of Isaiah: Studies of an Interpretive Tradition*, edited by Craig C. Broyles and Craig A. Evans, pp. 491–511. Formation and Interpretation of Old Testament Literature, 1.2. Leiden, 1997. A rich analysis of the Qumran texts and the history of scholarship on them.

Ulrich, Eugene et al. *Qumran Cave 4, X: The Prophets*. Discoveries in the Judaean Desert, 15. Oxford, 1997. Critical editions of the eighteen Cave 4 Isaiah scrolls.

EUGENE ULRICH

ISRAEL. The term *Israel*, Hebrew *Yisraʾel*, was used in the Hebrew scriptures in a number of ways. It served as the collective name for the twelve tribes who traced their ancestry to Jacob, whose name was changed to Israel after he wrestled with an angel (*Gn.* 32.28, 35.10). The Israelites were also known as *children of Israel*, often translated "people of Israel." While this term often designated the nation as a whole, during the period of the Divided Monarchy (924–721 BCE) it referred only to the northern kingdom, as distinct from Judah, the southern kingdom. After the destruction of the North, the term *Israel* was again used for the entire people. In accord with this usage, the land occupied by the people of Israel was termed the Land of Israel in the Prophets and the Writings. In Jewish sources of the Second Temple period, Israel was synonymous with the Jewish people (or with the non-priestly and non-Levitical members of the Jewish people), and the term *Land of Israel* was used to denote its ancestral homeland.

These terms are used in the same sense in the Qumran scrolls and either simply continue the biblical tradition, or provide examples of uniquely sectarian understandings of the people and land of Israel. There are no significant data available in the other Judean Desert documents.

The People of Israel. Israel had been a term for the entire nation in biblical times. From the Second Temple period on, in the absence of the old tribal system, Jews saw themselves as divided into four groupings: priests, Levites, Israelites, and proselytes. In several Qumran passages that describe the mustering ceremony and the lists of members of the sect that were kept by the examiner (*mevaqqer*), this division is maintained (CD xiv.3–6; Damascus Document[b], 4Q267 9.v.7–10; Damascus Document[c], 4Q268 2; cf. also Rule of the Community, 1QS ii.19–22 and War Scroll, 1QM ii.1–3 where the proselytes are not mentioned). This same division into four groups appears in Four Lots (4Q279 formerly, Purification Rules D), where each group is called a "lot" (*goral*). This division presumed that the tribe of Levi continued to be divided into the Aaronide priestly group and the rest of the Levites who served in the Temple as singers or assisted in various aspects of the maintenance of the sanctuary. All other born Jews, who were not immediately descended from converts to Judaism, constituted the main part of *Israel*—the Jewish people.

The final group, maintained as a separate group in the sectarian approach, was the converts. From their listing as a separate group, it is clear that the sectarian scrolls would have agreed with the Temple Scroll[a] (11Q19), which did not accord proselytes the same status as full Israelites. Thus, they were not permitted to enter the

Temple until the fourth generation (11Q19 xl.5–7). This approach to the status of proselytes has some parallels in minority opinions in tannaitic literature (B.T., *Qid.* 5.1; *Sifrei Dt.* 247) but was rejected by the rabbinic tradition, which saw proselytes as full Jews with exactly the same status as born Jews.

The author of Florilegium excluded proselytes altogether from the messianic Temple (4Q174 1–2.i.4). This opinion accords well with the notion that the messianic deliverance, rather than a universal experience, was to be enjoyed by the most chosen of God's holy people, the sect alone. Despite the large wealth of Qumran literature, there is no discussion of the manner in which the sectarians determined the status of a born Jew. It is most likely that the sectarians shared the notion later codified in rabbinic literature that Jewish status was determined by birth to a Jewish mother. This approach seems to have been the norm among Jews in the Land of Israel in Second Temple times and it is in this context that we must understand the opposition to intermarriage in *Jubilees* (30.7–17) and the Temple Scroll.

For the sectarians, one final additional aspect must be emphasized. They understood the history of Israel in biblical times as essentially a period of religious and moral decline leading to the destruction of the First Temple. This process, described in theological terms in the Admonition at the beginning of the Damascus Document (CD i–viii), meant that God's covenant with Israel was transferred to the righteous remnant—the members of the Qumran sect and those who would join them in the End of Days. In effect, then, the sectarians saw themselves as the true Israel, the people of God. This special holiness was also manifested, according to their beliefs, in the presence of holy angels among them.

Jews and Non-Jews. The Qumran sectarians defined themselves as separate from non-Jews in two ways. On the one hand, they condemned the practices of the nations surrounding them, specifically idolatry, and distanced themselves from these pagans. On the other hand, they identified themselves as the chosen people whose merit it was to inherit the land in the End of Days.

The most objectionable feature of pagan religion to Jews was the worship of idols or a multiplicity of gods. The Damascus Document prohibits even indirect support of idolatrous practices by outlawing the selling of kosher animals and fowl to non-Jews for pagan sacrificial purposes (CD xii.8–10), and the Temple Scroll recapitulates the law of *Exodus* 34.10–17 stating that idolatrous cult places must be destroyed (11Q19 ii.6–12). Similarly, any object or material once used for idolatry may not be used in Jewish worship, such as meat of idolatrous offerings. In a passage based on *Deuteronomy* 16.21–22 (cf. *Lv.* 26.1) the author of the Temple Scroll warns against the erection of Asherot, pillars, and figured stones to which to bow down (11Q19 lx.19–lii.3).

Indeed, idolaters may be put to death (*Dt.* 12.2–7; 11Q19 lv.15–lvi.4) if they can legally be convicted in court. The law of an idolatrous city (11Q19 lv.2–14) intends to interpret the biblical commandment (*Dt.* 13.13–19) that requires destruction by the sword of a Jewish city that has turned to idol worship.

The Temple Scroll[a] (11Q19 ii.1–15) requires that pagan cultic objects be destroyed, and this passage also invokes the biblical prohibition (*Ex.* 34.10–16) on making covenants with the Canaanite nations lest there be intermarriage between them and the Jewish people. Other passages in the Temple Scroll indicate that all marriage between Jews and non-Jews was prohibited (11Q19 lvii.15–17).

Idolatry carries with it an impurity that can be contracted. Therefore, the Dead Sea Scrolls recommend that the sectarians distance themselves from non-Jews. On the Sabbath, the Damascus Document recommends that Jews not spend the Sabbath "in a place close to the gentiles" (xi.14–15). Non-Jews were forbidden from entering the Temple (11Q19 xxxix.5–7) and, according to Florilegium (1Q174 1–2.i.4), will also be excluded from the Temple in the End of Days.

Miqtsat Maʿasei ha-Torah (B3–5) prohibits the acceptance of grain offerings (*terumah*) from non-Jews for the Temple. Similarly, Miqtsat Maʿasei ha-Torah (B8) condemns the acceptance of sacrifices that non-Jews bring to the Temple, a practice current in the time of the Hasmoneans. Both these laws accord with the view of the sectarians that in the End of Days the non-Jewish nations will disappear. Pharisaic-rabbinic tradition taught the opposite: that in the End of Days the nations will come to worship God and will voluntarily appear to sacrifice at the Jerusalem Temple.

A poetic section of the War Scroll (1QM xii.12–14), which most probably predated its final authorship, calls upon the city of Jerusalem in the End of Days to accept the wealth of the nations who will now be subservient to Jerusalem. This poem would imply that the nations survive the final cataclysm and, based on *Isaiah* 60.10–14, become vassals of Israel. The same notion is found in Pesher Isaiah[a] (4Q161 7.25). However, the overwhelming notion of the War Scroll is the destruction of the nations of the world by the sectarians at the End of Days.

Chosen People. The notion that Israel is God's chosen people is prominent in the sectarian documents. The War Scroll (1QM x.9–10; 4Q495 frag. 1) proclaims: "Who is like unto your people Israel which you have chosen for yourself from all the nations of the lands, a people of those holy through the covenant!" The text continues by stating that Israel has expressed its chosenness by accepting the revelation and God's commandments (lines 10–11).

Liturgical passages repeat this motif often. In a Passover prayer, God "cho[se] us from among [the] nations" (Daily Prayers [4Q503] 24–25.vii.4; cf. Noncanonical Psalms 76–77 15). Similarly, "you have loved Israel more than the [other] peoples. . . . All the nations saw your glory in that you were sanctified among your people Israel" (Words of the Luminaries[a] [4Q504] 1–2.iv.4–9). The festival prayer states that God chose the Jewish people and set them apart as holy, renewing his covenant with them (1Q34bis ii.5–7 = 4Q509 97–98.i.7–10).

The Land of Israel in the Qumran Scrolls. The biblical usage of the expression *Land of Israel* (*Erets Yisra'el*) became increasingly prominent in the Second Temple period and is used in the scrolls. This expression occurs only rarely in the preserved Qumran scrolls (cf. Paraphrase of Kings [4Q382] 1.4 [restored]). Often, the area of Judea is termed *Land of Judah* in the scrolls, apparently a reference to the present political realities of the Greco-Roman period. Two passages are significant: In Miqtsat Ma'asei ha-Torah B 63, *Land of Israel* serves as a legal term for the area that is subject according to Jewish law to the laws of tithing of produce and the offering of fourth-year produce. While this legal usage certainly indicates a geographical entity, it need not assume a governmental or administrative significance. In the Temple Scroll (11Q19 lviii.6) it is used as a geographical and governmental term for the area under the sovereignty of the ideal king of Israel whose constitution is set forth in the Law of the King (11Q19 lvi–lix).

Despite the fact that the only mention of this term in the Temple Scroll is in a governmental context, this scroll presents an ideal vision of how the people of Israel should live in the Land of Israel. Throughout, the author is informed by a notion of concentric spheres of holiness, as well as by distinct concern for the sanctity of the entire Land of Israel as sacred space.

The preserved portion of the Temple Scroll begins with the assertion of God's covenant with Israel regarding the Land of Israel (col. ii). This section, adapted from *Exodus* 34.10–16 and *Deuteronomy* 7.5, 25, relates that God will expel the Canaanite nations from the Land of Israel. The Israelites, in turn, are commanded to destroy pagan cult objects and to avoid any covenants with the Canaanite nations since such alliances would lead to idolatry and intermarriage. The laws of war in the scroll (lx.9–16) concern the destruction of the pagan inhabitants of the land as well.

The notion that Israel is given the land conditionally also appears in the scroll. Bribery and corruption in judgment must be avoided, "in order that you live, and come and take (or retain) possession of the land which I am giving you as a possession for ever" (li.15–16). In other words, judicial corruption will result in the destruction of the land and exile (lxx.2–9). Only after repentance (line 11) will Israel return to its land.

For the Temple Scroll, the central point of the Land of Israel was the Temple and the surrounding complex. Here the scroll provides for a Temple plan of very different proportions from that which existed in First or Second Temple times. This new Temple plan would be characterized by the enclosure of the Temple building itself by three concentric courtyards. This entire plan has behind it the assumption that the Temple is the center of sanctity for the entire land. The scroll makes clear repeatedly that it is the indwelling of the divine presence in the Temple that imparts to the land this level of sanctity.

Beyond the Temple city which, for the scroll, symbolized the desert camp, was located the hinterland of Israel. *Ezekiel* 48.1–10 had adopted an ideal view of the land, seeing the tribal allotments as a series of east-west strips of land. The Temple Scroll also took an ideal view, but for its author it is most likely that the tribes were to dwell outside the respective gates through which they were to enter the Temple precincts. Indeed, it was through these gates that the tribal territory was to be tied to the sanctity of the central shrine and the divine presence, which dwelled there.

Throughout the Temple Scroll there is a persistent notion that the people of Israel will dwell in cities. The scroll envisaged the people, including priests and Levites, as living in the cities of Israel, which were to be scattered about the central sanctuary, each tribe opposite its respective gate. Burial in the cities was forbidden (11Q19 xlviii.11). Burial places were to be set aside, one for each four cities (xlviii.11–13). The limitation of burial to specified places was designed to avoid rendering the land impure (xlviii.10).

All in all, the authors of the various sectarian texts found at Qumran saw both the people and the Land of Israel in ideal terms. They expected that as the true Israel, separated from both errant Jews and from the non-Jewish world, they could live a life of perfect holiness and sanctity in their ancestral land. Yet in the eyes of the author/redactor of the Temple Scroll, this land, even before the End of Days, had to be reconfigured and idealized in order to represent the level of holiness to which the sectarians aspired.

BIBLIOGRAPHY

Alexander, Philip S., and Geza Vermes. *Qumran Cave 4, XIX: Serekh ha-Yaḥad and Two Related Texts,* pp. 217–223. Discoveries in the Judaean Desert, 26. Oxford, 1998. Text and commentary on 4QFour Lots indicating division of Jewish people into priests, Levites, Israelites, and proselytes.

Qimron, Elisha, and John Strugnell. *Qumran Cave 4, V: Miqṣat Ma'aśe ha-Torah*, p. 88. Discoveries in the Judaean Desert, 10. Oxford, 1994. Discussion of the term Land of Israel in the Dead Sea Scrolls.

Schiffman, Lawrence H. "Sacred Space: The Land of Israel in the Temple Scroll." In *Biblical Archaeology Today, 1990: Proceedings of the Second International Congress on Biblical Archaeology, Jerusalem, June–July 1990*, pp. 398–410. Jerusalem, 1993. A study of the idealized picture of the Temple, the city of Jerusalem, and the surrounding land as understood by the Temple Scroll.

Schiffman, Lawrence H. *Who Was a Jew? Rabbinic and Halakhic Perspectives on the Jewish Christian Schism*. Hoboken, N.J., 1985. A study of Second Temple and early rabbinic ideas on Jewish status.

LAWRENCE H. SCHIFFMAN

ISRAEL ANTIQUITIES AUTHORITY. Founded on April 1, 1990, the Israel Antiquities Authority (IAA) assumed the role and functions of the Israel Department of Antiquities and Museums (IDAM), which had operated since the founding of the State of Israel (1948) as an integral part of the Israel Ministry of Education and Culture. This legal and administrative change was made in order to facilitate the actions taken by this institution in its main capacity, which is to safeguard the antiquity sites and antiquities in Israel and to enforce the Israel Law of Antiquities. In this respect it continued the function of the Department of Antiquities of the British Mandate over Palestine (1920–1948). The IAA headquarters are located at the Rockefeller Museum in Jerusalem.

The protection of antiquity sites in Israel is carried out in different ways. Legal protection is given by the Israel Law of Antiquities (1978), which defines the nature of an antiquity site (any place where a construction or artifact produced by humans prior to the year 1700 CE has been found) and specifies certain limitations regarding the use of the land that encompasses an antiquity site. The IAA maintains a large number of inspectors of antiquities, organized into five divisions (North, Center, Jerusalem, South, and Judea and Samaria). Their function is mainly to participate in the planning and building commissions and to ensure that development projects do not endanger antiquities sites. In many cases ad hoc archaeological surveys are carried out as a preparatory action before major building projects are initiated, or when a rescue excavation is required.

A special unit for the prevention of clandestine excavations tries to minimize destruction of antiquities caused by unlicensed excavations. The Department of Excavation and Surveys performs all rescue excavations required to salvage archaeological data in cases of chance discoveries of ancient remains during the development of a site. It also carries out archaeological surveys of predesignated areas. On the average, more than two hundred excavations and surveys are undertaken each year. In recent years the IAA has begun several major preplanned excavations on sites chosen for tourist development, such as Beth-Shean, Caesarea Maritima, Banyas, Beth Guvrin, Maresha, 'Ein Hazeva and Robinson's Arch at the Temple mount in Jerusalem. The Department of Conservation of Monuments carries out conservation and selected reconstructions of ancient monuments, adopting the guidelines of the ICOMOS Venice Charter (1964).

The IAA is the custodian of all antiquities objects and maintains the State Collections. This department lends all antiquities required for local museums as well as for exhibitions in foreign countries. The IAA organizes a selected number of exhibitions (see below). The IAA maintains and develops most of the laboratories and technical services for archaeological work, as well as laboratories for conservation of antiquities. The IAA also has its own department of publications. Major periodicals are *Ḥadashot Arkheologiyot (Archaeological News)*, published twice a year (since 1961) with an English edition, *Excavations and Surveys in Israel* (since 1982); *'Atiqot*, the main journal for scientific studies and archaeological reports, with articles in English and Hebrew (with English summaries); the systematic publication of the *Archaeological Survey of Israel*, each issue covering an area 10 by 10 kilometers in size (with about twenty issues published per year). Special monographs include L. Y. Rahmani, *Corpus of Jewish Ossuaries at the State Collections*. The popular publications include a series of guides to antiquities sites (e.g., Tiberias, Khirbet Susiya, Ḥammat Gader, the Monastery at Ma'ale Adummim) and an album of aerial photographs of antiquities sites.

The IAA established the Education and Public Relations Department, which disseminates archaeological information. It sponsors several archaeological educational centers in Jerusalem, Nahariya, Karmiel, and Arad where groups of school classes are instructed. Since archaeology is taught in Israel in selected high schools, the IAA supports the education of high school teachers in this field. The IAA maintains an excellent library and archive (at the Rockefeller Museum) and for several years has been developing an elaborate computer database of archaeological information, which will soon be opened to the public. The IAA's Archaeological Advisory Board, of which representatives of all major Israel archaeological institutions are members, gives the Director of Antiquities professional advice on important archaeological issues and serves as the committee for licensing excavations.

IDAM, IAA, and the Dead Sea Scrolls. Following rumors of the discoveries made by a group of bedouin in the desert on both sides of the Israel-Jordan border, and following discoveries made by Yohanan Aharoni in Naḥal Ṣe'elim (in 1953, 1955, 1956, and 1960), the archaeological institutions of Israel at that time (including IDAM, the Hebrew University of Jerusalem, and the Israel Exploration Society) decided on an active approach to recovering scrolls. The Judean Desert Expedition was sent on a mission to survey and excavate the southern part of the desert that at the time was already included within the boundaries of the state of Israel. Four subexpeditions, headed by Aharoni (Naḥal Ṣe'elim, northern bank), Nahman Avigad (Naḥal Ṣe'elim, southern bank, followed by Naḥal David), Pessah Bar-Adon (Naḥal Mishmar and vicinity), and Yigael Yadin (Naḥal Ḥever, northern bank and Naḥal 'Arugot) were active during the spring of 1960 and 1961. Scrolls of the type discovered at Qumran were not found here. Other significant finds, however, were made, such as the discovery of the Bar Kokhba letters.

On 7 June 1967, while the fighting in Jerusalem was still raging (the Six Day War), Israeli archaeologists Professor A. Biran, director of IDAM, Professor Avigad of the Hebrew University, and J. Aviram, director of the Israel Exploration Society, entered the Rockefeller Museum, with the assistance of the Israeli Defense Forces, in order to survey and secure the building and its collections, among which were the Dead Sea Scrolls. The fighting in Jerusalem (including on the perimeter of the museum's premises) caused minor damage to some of the collections, but none to the Dead Sea Scrolls. When shortly afterward the headquarters of IDAM were transferred to the Rockefeller Museum, the direct custody of IDAM over the Dead Sea Scrolls was established. It should be noted that the Dead Sea Scrolls at the Rockefeller Museum came under a new legal status due to two actions: (1) the nationalization of the museum, its collections, and all its other assets by the Jordanian Government (November 1966), which relieved the international board of trustees that had run the museum since the end of the British Mandate over Palestine in May 1948 of its authority; and (2) the Israeli capture of east Jerusalem, including the Rockefeller Museum, by action of war (June 1967).

Shortly after the war, an inventory of the Dead Sea Scroll fragments at the Rockefeller Museum was prepared. Soon informal talks (of which no minutes were recorded) were held between Professor A. Biran, director of IDAM, Professor Yigael Yadin, chairman of the Shrine of the Book of the Israel Museum, and Roland de Vaux, editor in chief of the Dead Sea Scrolls. The Israeli authorities expressed their policy that they would retain the role of custodian of the Dead Sea Scrolls, while de Vaux retained the full rights and obligations as editor, including the responsibility for the policy of assigning manuscripts to scholars for study and publication—matters in which the IDAM did not interfere. This policy obtained as well under subsequent editors, Pierre Benoit (1971–1982) and John Strugnell (1982–1990). In the first twenty years of the Dead Sea Scrolls under Israeli responsibility (with Biran followed by A. Eitan as Director of Antiquities), IDAM's interference in all editorial matters of the Dead Sea Scrolls was minimal. IDAM initiated two actions intended to improve the long-term preparation of the Dead Sea Scrolls. First, it initiated the movement of the fragments from the sunlit Room of Records at the Rockefeller Museum to a dark vault in the basement and provided the necessary climate-control equipment. Second, after E. Bechtel's suggestion and support, for reasons of security, duplicates of the Dead Sea Scroll negatives were created in Jerusalem to be kept in separate locations (the Center for Ancient Biblical Manuscripts, Claremont, California, and the Huntington Library, San Marino, California).

Major changes in the publication of the Dead Sea Scrolls, as well as the conservation of the fragments, began when A. Drori was appointed Director of IDAM (1988), and especially after IDAM was transformed into IAA. As a result of these changes, the legal status of the Dead Sea Scrolls and the direct responsibility of the IAA concerning all matters related to the scrolls was reassessed. An advisory and oversight committee to the director on Dead Sea Scroll matters was created, which included Professor S. Talmon, Professor J. Greenfield, and Magen Broshi. For the first time a timetable for the full publication of the still unpublished Dead Sea Scroll fragments (especially the Qumran Cave 4 fragments) was demanded of and received from the editor in chief. In 1990, Emanuel Tov was appointed deputy editor, and he later replaced Strugnell as editor in chief. A major step in the acceleration of publication was the reassigning of Dead Sea Scroll fragments to a larger group of scholars and the amendment of the publication timetable.

The IAA organized a major project for enhancing the state of conservation of the Dead Sea Scrolls. This meant removing the Scotch tape, which the scholars in the 1950s had used to glue scroll fragments together, and the careful cleaning of the fragments. The fragments were removed from the double glass plates in which they had originally been placed and were inserted into new containers made from inert paper and other tissues. In addition, the negatives were restored. [*See* Conservation.]

The IAA initiated and organized an exhibition of the Dead Sea Scrolls (curated by Ayala Sussman and Ruth Peled), which included twelve fragments, most of which had never been exhibited (e.g., a fragment of the Cairo Damascus Document, Miqtsat Ma'asei ha-Torah [4QMMT], prayer for King Jonathan [4Q448], and Songs of the Sabbath Sacrifice). These fragments, augmented with a collection of artifacts from Qumran (pottery, coins, etc.)

were displayed in 1993–1994 at the Library of Congress, Washington D.C.; the New York Public Library; the de Young Memorial Museum in San Francisco; the Vatican Library in Rome; and the Shrine of the Book at the Israel Museum in Jerusalem. In collaboration with E. J. Brill located in Leiden (the Netherlands) the photographs of all scroll fragments were published by the IAA in microfiche form, edited by Tov in 1993. The IAA also collaborated with A. Witkin and Pixel Multimedia to publish a popular work on the story of the Dead Sea Scrolls aimed at the general public. It appeared in CD-ROM form (written and edited by R. Reich). Another CD-ROM project of the IAA aimed at the academic readership was designed to make available all the photographs of Dead Sea Scroll fragments.

In November 1993, the IAA conducted for several weeks an archaeological survey in the caves of the Judean Desert (in the regions of Jericho, Qumran, and further south) aimed at locating additional ancient manuscripts. At this time, the IAA also carried out excavations in selected caves and performed several probes at Khirbet Qumran itself (named Operation Scroll). As a result of these operations, several inscribed papyri were discovered in a cave above Jericho, and at Qumran an installation to produce date "honey" was excavated. The various Judean Desert caves also produced a wealth of organic items (e.g., textiles) and important Early Bronze finds.

BIBLIOGRAPHY

Reich, Ronny. "The Israel Antiquities Authority." In *Biblical Archaeology Today, 1990. Proceedings of the Second International Congress on Biblical Archaeology, Jerusalem, June–July 1990*, edited by A. Biran and J. Aviram, pp. 27–30. Jerusalem, 1993.

Silberman, Neil Asher. *The Hidden Scrolls: Christianity, Judaism and the War for the Dead Sea Scrolls*. London, 1995.

Sussman, A., and R. Reich. "The History of the Rockefeller Museum" (in Hebrew). In *Zev Vilnay Jubilee Volume*, edited by E. Schiller, vol. 2, pp. 83–91. Jerusalem, 1987.

Sussman, Ayala, and Ruth Peled. *Scrolls from the Dead Sea, An Exhibition of Scrolls and Archaeological Artifacts from the Collections of the Israel Antiquities Authority*. Washington, D.C., 1993.

RONNY REICH

ISRAEL DEPARTMENT OF ANTIQUITIES AND MUSEUMS. *See* Israel Antiquities Authority.

ISRAEL EXPLORATION SOCIETY. Founded in Jerusalem in 1914 with the name Jewish Palestine Exploration Society, the Israel Exploration Society (IES; as it was known in 1948 with the creation of the state of Israel) was modeled after the foreign societies engaged in the study and exploration of the history and antiquities of the Holy Land. The IES has played a major role over the years in four main areas: sponsorship, organization, and financing of archaeological excavations in Israel; publication of the results of current archaeological, historical, and geographical research; sponsorship of forums for the exchange of scholarly information and reporting of current research; and the promotion of public interest in archaeology by providing nonspecialists with opportunities to increase their knowledge through membership in the society, publication of the popular Hebrew journal *Qadmoniot*, and participation in lectures and field trips to archaeological sites in Israel and neighboring lands. The IES is governed by an executive committee and council representing all the major institutions involved in archaeology in Israel, including universities, research institutes, museums, and the Israel Antiquities Authority.

The following archaeological excavations were carried out under IES sponsorship: Ḥammath Tiberias Synagogue, 1921; Absalom's Tomb (Jerusalem), 1924; Third Wall (Jerusalem), 1925–1927, 1940; Ramat Raḥel, 1931; Beth-She'arim, 1936–1940, 1953–1956, 1958–1959; Tell Qasile, 1948–1950, 1982–1989; Hazor, 1955–1958, 1968, 1990–1998; Judean Desert Caves, 1960–1961; Masada, 1963–1965; 'Ein-Gedi, 1970–1972; Arad, 1962–1966, 1971–1978, 1980–1984; Temple Mount (Jerusalem), 1968–1977; Jewish Quarter (Jerusalem), 1969–1985; City of David (Jerusalem), 1976–1985; Herodium, 1970–1988; Jericho, 1973–1983, 1986–1987; Aphek, 1972–1985; Lachish, 1973–1987; Dor, 1982–1998; and Sepphoris, 1985–1997.

Current serial publications of the IES include *Eretz-Israel: Archaeological, Historical and Geographical Studies* (1951–); *Qadmoniot: A Journal for the Antiquities of Eretz-Israel and Bible Lands* (in Hebrew; 1968–); *Studies in the Geography of Israel* (1960–); and *Israel Exploration Journal* (1951–). In addition, the IES publishes books in English and Hebrew concerning the archaeology, history, and geography of Israel and Bible lands.

Over the years, the IES has played a significant role in Judean Desert text research. Of particular importance were its sponsorship and coordination of the archaeological excavations at Masada directed by Yigael Yadin. Exploration and excavation of caves in Naḥal Ḥever and Naḥal Ṣe'elim, which yielded a significant portion of existing Judean Desert texts, were carried out as part of the 1960–1961 Judean Desert Expedition, a joint project sponsored by the IES, Hebrew University of Jerusalem, and the Israel Antiquities Authority to explore the area between 'Ein-Gedi and Masada. Documents found during the 1963–1965 Masada excavations include ostraca (fragments of incribed pottery; tags, inscriptions, and letters); apocryphal, biblical, and sectarian scrolls; and papyri (letters, documents, and fragments). At Naḥal Ṣe'elim, Cave 34 (the Cave of the Scrolls) yielded phylacteries, a scroll fragment, and fragments of Aramaic and Greek papyri. The Cave of the Letters at Naḥal Ḥever yielded a group of fifteen letters, all from Shim'on Bar Kokhba to leaders of the revolt in the 'Ein-Gedi region, as well as biblical scroll fragments, the archive of Babatha, a group of Nabatean documents, and the archive of the people of 'Ein-Gedi. Several papyrus fragments were found at Naḥal Mishmar. It was at IES annual meetings that the discovery of these texts was first publicly announced. Likewise, the acquisition in 1967 of Temple Scroll[a], probably from Cave 11 at Qumran, was first publicized at the IES annual meeting.

Following these discoveries, the IES has exercised a significant role in their publication. In addition to popular articles relating to Judean Desert texts that appeared in the Hebrew-language journal *Qadmoniot* and scholarly articles in the *Israel Exploration Journal*, IES publications dealing with Judean Desert texts include *The Judean Desert Caves I. Survey and Excavations, 1960* (Avigad, Aharoni, Bar-Adon, and Yadin, 1961); *The Judean Desert Caves II. Survey and Excavations, 1961* (Avigad, Aharoni, Bar-Adon, and Yadin, 1962); *The Finds from the Bar Kokhba Period in the Cave of Letters* (Yadin, 1963); *The Ben Sira Scroll from Masada* (Yadin, ed., 1965); *The Documents from the Bar Kokhba Period in the Cave of Letters,* which presents Greek papyri (Lewis, ed., 1989) and Aramaic and Nabatean signatures and subscriptions (Yadin and Greenfield, eds., 1989); *The Temple Scroll* (three volumes and a supplement; Yadin, ed., 1977 and 1983; Hebrew- and English-language editions); *The Damascus Document Reconsidered* (Broshi, ed., 1992); *Naḥal Ṣe'elim Documents* (Yardeni, 1995); *The Temple Scroll: A Critical Edition with Extensive Reconstructions* (Qimron, 1996); *The Documents from the Bar Kokhba Period in the Cave of Letters II,* which presents Hebrew, Aramaic, and Nabatean documents (Greenfield, Levine, and Yardeni, eds., forthcoming); and *The Masada Final Reports* (vols. 1–6; the final volume includes "Hebrew Biblical and Non-Biblical Fragments from Masada" [Talmon, ed.].

In addition to this active publications program, two international congresses devoted to biblical archaeology were held in Jerusalem, in 1984 and 1990, under IES sponsorship. Each included an entire session devoted to Dead Sea text research at which many of the world's foremost scholars in the field presented original papers. These were published in the volumes *Biblical Archaeology Today* (1985) and *Biblical Archaeology Today 1990* (1993). In cooperation with the Israel Museum, Shrine of the Book, and Israel Antiquities Authority, an international congress was held in Jerusalem in 1997 to celebrate the fiftieth anniversary of the discovery of the Dead Sea Scrolls and fifty years of Dead Sea text research. The proceedings of this congress will be published by the IES in conjunction with other organizations involved in research on the Dead Sea documents.

[*See also* Ḥever, Naḥal; Israel Antiquities Authority; Masada; Ṣe'elim, Naḥal; *and the biography of Yadin.*]

JOSEPH AVIRAM

J

JACOB, the younger twin son of Isaac and Rebecca. His life is presented as a struggle with both human beings and God (*Gn.* 32.28), beginning from the womb with Esau from whom he took the birthright and blessing. As a result, he was forced to flee to his uncle Laban. On the way he had a dream at Bethel and saw a ladder joining earth to heaven (*Gn.* 28.12, 17–19). After struggling under Laban's employment he left with two wives, becoming the father of one daughter and of twelve sons from whom descended the tribes of Israel. In his final testament (*Gn.* 49), Jacob blesses his sons and alludes to the future of the tribes.

The most significant Judean Desert writings that mention Jacob are fragments related to Second Temple works such as *Jubilees* and the *Testaments of the Twelve Patriarchs*, which retell and expand biblical stories. [*See* Jubilees, Book of; Twelve Patriarchs, Testaments of the.] In *Jubilees*, Jacob is a central figure, much more frequently praised and blessed than in the Hebrew scriptures. In the *Testaments of the Twelve Patriarchs*, which follow the pattern of Jacob's final testament (*Gn.* 41–50), his sons recount an episode in their life to illustrate a vice or virtue that becomes the subject of exhortation to their sons. In the *Testaments of the Twelve Patriarchs*, Jacob prays for his sons (*Testament of Reuben* 1.7; *Testament of Judah* 19.2), and in *Jubilees* he exhorts against evil (*Jub.* 39.6). In both *Jubilees* and the *Testaments of the Twelve Patriarchs*, Jacob's struggles culminate in victory over the Amorites and his killing of Esau (*Jub.* 34, 38; *Testament of Judah* 3, 9, cf. *Gn.* 48.22).

The Judean Desert texts contain a number of references to Jacob. Many are references to the sons of Jacob (e.g., 4Q372 1.13), or the nation as a whole is called Jacob (e.g., 4Q175 1.12, 17). At least eight passages relate to Jacob's life. There are a number of Aramaic fragments dating from about 100 BCE of a work that has been called the Apocryphon of Jacob (4Q537). This work may be a reworking from the third person to the first person of *Jubilees* 32.21 (Jacob's return to Bethel where he confers the priesthood on Levi, cf. *Gn.* 35.7). The first fragment mentions a dream in which an angel brings Jacob tablets on which were written what would happen to him during his life and perhaps (the text is broken) forbids the building of a temple at Bethel. The second fragment gives instructions concerning the temple, the priesthood, and sacrifices (lacking in *Jubilees*). The Temple Scroll (11Q19 xxix.10) also associates the temple with God's covenant with Jacob at Bethel, as does the Apocryphon of Joseph (4Q372 3.9). Two Hebrew fragments of *Jubilees* at Qumran contain the section that mentions Jacob's first journey to Bethel (1Q17, cf. *Jub.* 27.19–21) and Rebecca's request to Isaac to make Esau swear not to harm Jacob (1Q18, cf. 35.8–10). Jubilees[f] (4Q221) fragment 4 preserves parts of the story about Reuben's sin with his father's concubine (*Jub.* 33.12–15); fragments 5 and 6 have parts of the narrative about his war with Esau (37.11–15; 38.6–8), and Jubilees[g] (4Q222) fragment 1 contains Jacob's discussion with Rebecca about a wife for him (25.9–12; cf. 27.6–7). In Jubilees[h] (4Q223–224) several sections from the Jacob stories are extant 32.18–21; 34.4–5, 35.7–12, 12–22; 36.7–10, 10–23; 37.13, 17–38. Reworked Pentateuch[a] (4Q158 7–9) expands *Genesis* 32.29 by giving the content of God's blessing at Penuel—that Jacob would be fertile, blessed with knowledge and intelligence, and freed from all violence. Commentary on Genesis A (4Q252 iv.5–7) contains a *pesher* ("commentary") on Jacob's blessing of Reuben in *Genesis* 49.3–4. The commentary mentions that Jacob reproved Reuben because he lay with Bilhah and comments on his status as the firstborn. Column v follows with a *pesher* of Jacob's blessing of Judah in *Genesis* 49.10. [*See* Judah.]

The New Testament refers to Jacob in connection with the other patriarchs or with his sons, for example, in the genealogies (*Mt.* 1.2; *Lk.* 3.34) or with blessing Joseph's sons (*Hb.* 11.21). Jacob is an example of God's selection (*Rom.* 9.13), and Christ as the Son of Man is seen as the focus of his dream at Bethel (*Jn.* 1.51). Rabbinic writings elevate Jacob as the greatest of the patriarchs (*Gn. Rab.* 76.1). They justify his gaining the birthright and blessing, and desiring Rachel; they disapprove of his marriage to two sisters (B.T., *Pes.* 119b), his treatment of Leah (Ag. *Ber.* 48(49).2), favoritism toward Joseph (B.T., *Shab.* 10b; B.T., *Meg.* 16b; *Gn. Rab.* 84.8), and prolonged absence from home (B.T., *Meg.* 16b ff.).

BIBLIOGRAPHY

Milik, Józef T. "Écrits préesséniens de Qumrân: d'Hénoch à Amram." In *Qumrân: Sa piété, sa théologie et son milieu*, edited by M. Delcor, pp. 91–106. Paris, 1978. Contains a transliteration, notes, and comments on the Apocryphon of Jacob.

Peuch, Émile. "Fragments d'un apocryphe de Lévi." In *The Madrid Qumran Congress*, vol. 2, edited by Julio Trebolle Barrera and Luis

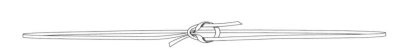

Vegas Montaner, pp. 449–501. Studies on the Texts of the Desert of Judah, 11. Leiden, 1992. Contains the text, transliteration, notes, and comments on the Apocryphon of Jacob.

ROGER GOOD

JAMES, LETTER OF. One of the New Testament's seven so-called Catholic Epistles (Eusebius *H.E.* 2.23.25), the *Letter of James* is named after its author rather than its addressees. The letter is attributed to James, the brother of Jesus (*Gal.* 1.19; *Mt.* 13.55; *Mk.* 6.3) and leader of the early church in Jerusalem (*Acts* 12.17, 15.13; *Gal.* 2.9, 2.12), who by the third century CE was known in some writings as James the Just (Eusebius, *H.E.* 2.23.4). Though much in the letter may stem from this James, the work was probably compiled in its final form by an unknown Christian teacher in the last quarter of the first century CE. It is very difficult to determine more precisely the date of the epistle and its geographical setting.

The work is not really a letter at all but a collection of wisdom instructions that can be grouped loosely as follows: the benefits of trials (1.2–18); true religion (1.19–27); impartiality (2.1–13); faith and works (2.14–26); true wisdom (3.1–18); godliness and worldliness (4.1–5:6); and matters of encouragement (5.7–20).

The Jewishness of much of the letter's content is often pointed out. Apart from the two references to Jesus Christ (*Jas.* 1.1, 2.1), the letter lacks anything distinctively Christian. This has led some to argue that most of the content was strictly Jewish, not Christian-Jewish, in origin. Shortly after the discoveries of the Dead Sea Scrolls, several aspects of the letter were linked with the Qumran sectarians. For example, the "righteous one" of *James* 5.6 was seen as a designation applied to Jesus under the influence of the Qumran writings (Leaney, 1958, p. 93). In light of the *Letter of James,* it was even suggested that the community of Jewish Christians gathered around James in Jerusalem had at one time been "the urban brethren of the hardier souls that betook themselves to Qumran" (Gaster, 1976, p. 16). Such direct association was also dismissed as "fanciful" (Driver, 1965, pp. 543–44). Aspects of these proposals have been revived and exhaustively elaborated by Robert H. Eisenman (1996; 1997), who identifies the sectarian teacher of the scrolls as James the Just. The majority of scholars dismiss Eisenman's proposal on the basis of the dating of the evidence, its oversimplified view of the history of early Judaism, and the nonspecific character of the word-plays on which much of his theory relies.

Similarities between the letter and the clearly sectarian scrolls are relatively limited and seem almost incidental. Some of these similarities are matters of terminology. "Father of lights" (*Jas.* 1.17), a title which relates God to the stars and which has no sure precedent in Judaism (cf. *T. Abr.* B 7.5), can be compared to the angelic "Prince of lights" in the Rule of the Community (1QS iii.20; CD v.18). The technical idiom "cycle of becoming" (*Jas.* 3.6) may be such a cycle as is described, though not labeled as such, in 1QH[a] xx.5–8.

Some similarities are based in a common representation of exegetical traditions. For example, the letter is addressed to the twelve tribes (*Jas.* 1.1), a scriptural image also probably applied to sectarian community organization in Rule of the Community (1QS viii.1). In *James* 4.14 transitoriness is likened to smoke as in *Hosea* 13.3 (cf. the War Scroll [1QM xv.10]). In *James* 1.25 the law is described as a "law of freedom," a play on the consonants of *ḥrwt* in *Exodus* 32.16, which may also have been known to the author of Rule of the Community (1QS x.6–8), where most scholars take the play in the sense of "engraved." In *James* 2.23, Abraham is described as a friend of God (cf. *Is.* 41.8; *2 Chr.* 20.7; *Sg. of 3* 12; *Jub.* 19.9; CD iii.2; Commentary on Genesis A [4Q252 ii.8]; *Ap. Ab.* 9.6; 10.5; *T. Ab. A* 1.6 and often).

Some similarities are found in ethical instruction. The most explicit seem to lie with the Treatise on the Two Spirits of the Rule of the Community (1QS iii–iv), which may in any case be nonsectarian in origin. For example, *James* 1.6–8 speaks of the double-minded person and *James* 4.1 of the battle within a person (cf. 1QS iii.17–18, iv.23; also *Didache* 4.4; *Epistle of Barnabus* 19.5). However, in contrast with Qumran, there is no suggestion of a cosmic or angelic dualism lying behind the letter's anthropology. The term "way" (*Jas.* 5.19–20) is used of ethical and halakhic teaching from *Proverbs* 4.14 through to the *Didache* (cf. 1QS iii.13–iv.26, viii.15). The characteristics of wisdom (*Jas.* 3.14) are echoed in several Jewish texts (*Prv.* 8; *Wis.* 7; cf. 1QS iv.3–8).

The description of the teacher (*Jas.* 3.1) is an echo of the standard Jewish role of both priest and sage; at Qumran this role is variously taken up by both *mevaqqer* ("guardian"; CD xiii.7–8) and *maskil* ("wise teacher"; 1QS ix.12–20). *James* 2.10 insists on the keeping the whole of law (cf. 1QS viii.15–17; 4 *Mc.* 5.19; *Mt.* 5.19; *Test. Asher* 2:5–10; *Gal.* 5.3; B.T., *Shab.* 70b). *James* 5.19–20 urges that the community members be dealt with suitably (cf. 1QS v.25–6.1). With regard to the instruction against oaths (*Jas.* 5.12), both Philo and Josephus describe the Essenes as forbidding oaths (*Every Good Man Is Free* 84; *The Jewish War* 2.135; *Antiquities* 15.371), though they made oaths on entry (*The Jewish War* 2.139, 142). This is echoed in the Damascus Document where there are oaths on entry (CD xv.5ff.) but restrictions thereafter (CD xv.1).

There are plenty of significant differences between the *Letter of James* and the form of Judaism represented in the sectarian scrolls. In general, the letter shares little or none of the explicit form of scriptural exegesis found in the scrolls, which identifies prophecies as fulfilled in the experiences of the community. There is no narrow nationalism, no evidence of a hierarchical community, no restricted legal discipline, and no exclusion of outsiders from its meetings (2.2). In 5.14–15 there is a discussion of healing, but no mention of the laying on of hands that is common in other Christian and Jewish texts (cf. Genesis Apocryphon [1QapGen xx.25–30]).

The publication of the predominantly nonsectarian wisdom compositions found in the Qumran caves has provided a clearer perspective on the Jewishness of the *Letter of James*. It is now most likely that the sectarian scrolls and the *Letter of James* reflect varying receptions of a wide range of Jewish wisdom writings. Similarities between the letter and the nonsectarian wisdom traditions found in many of the scrolls are plentiful, but not precise. Standard idioms and common subjects for instruction can be found here: advice on how to carry on business dealings (Sapiential Work A[b] [4Q416 2.ii.4–15]; *Jas.* 4.13–17), teaching on how to treat the wealthy and the poor (4Q416 2.iii.8–19; *Jas.* 2.1–13; 5.1–6), and advice on how to treat weaker members of society (untitled sapiential work [4Q424 3.9–19]; *Jas.* 1.27). Some of the ideas, such as business dealings (CD xii.7–11) and wealth (CD iv.17), are also discussed in the sectarian scrolls. As elsewhere, in both the scrolls (Prayer of Nabonidus [4Q242 1–3, 3–4]) and *James* (5.15), healing and forgiveness of sins are linked.

BIBLIOGRAPHY

Driver, G. R. *The Judaean Scrolls*. Oxford, 1965. Draws attention to several parallels between the *Letter of James* and the scrolls, but is cautious about how they should be explained.

Eisenman, Robert H. *The Dead Sea Scrolls and the First Christians*. Shaftesbury, 1996. Reprints conveniently a collection of Eisenman's studies; chapter 6 on rain imagery is a good example of his attempt at discussing a word play that is supposedly present in both the scrolls and the *Letter of James*.

Eisenman, Robert H. *James the Brother of Jesus: Recovering the True History of Early Christianity*. London, 1997. Eisenman develops his theory beyond the New Testament period. The *Letter of James* is a key to understanding the kind of Christianity that was largely suppressed.

Gaster, Theodor H. *The Dead Sea Scriptures: With Introduction and Notes*. Garden City, N.Y., 1976. An enthusiast for seeing the *Letter of James* as representing the kind of Judaism that is also to be found in the sectarian scrolls.

Laws, Sophie. *A Commentary on the Epistle of James*. London, 1980. A detailed and well-balanced commentary on the *Letter of James* with several cross-references to the scrolls.

Leaney, A . Robert C. *A Guide to the Scrolls*. London, 1958. An early attempt for the nonspecialist at describing some of the parallels between the *Letter of James* and the scrolls.

Marcus, Joel. "The Evil Inclination in the Epistle of James." *Catholic Biblical Quarterly* 44 (1982), 606–621. A detailed study of the anthropology behind the ethics of the *Letter of James* with reference to the scrolls.

Nauck, W. "Lex insculpta (*ḥwq ḥrwt* [in Hebrew]) in der Sektenschrift." *Zeitschrift für die Neutestamentliche Wissenschaft* 46 (1955), 138–140. Argues against reading 1QS x.6, 8, 11 as being about a "Law of Freedom."

Nötscher, F. "'Gesetz der Freiheit' im NT und in der Mönchsgemeinde am Toten Meer." *Biblica* 34 (1953), 193–194. Juxtaposes *James* 1.25 with the scrolls.

GEORGE J. BROOKE

JANNES AND JAMBRES. *See* Yohanah and His Brother.

JEREMIAH, BOOK OF. [*This entry comprises two articles:* Biblical Text *and* Pseudo-Jeremiah.]

Biblical Text

Six fragmentary manuscripts from the *Book of Jeremiah* were discovered in the caves of Qumran. At other sites in the Judean Desert where biblical manuscripts were discovered, no remnants of this book were found.

In Cave 2 one manuscript—Jeremiah (2Q13)—was discovered. In Cave 4 two manuscripts of the *Book of Jeremiah*—Jeremiah[a] and Jeremiah[b] (4Q70 and 4Q71)—were identified in the 1950s; however, during the course of preparing these manuscripts for publication, Emanuel Tov and Esther Eshel realized that the fragments listed as Jeremiah[b] belonged to several separate manuscripts, so the total from Cave 4 is five manuscripts:

1. Jeremiah[a] (4Q70)
2. Jeremiah[b] (4Q71)
3. Jeremiah[c] (4Q72)
4. Jeremiah[d] (4Q71a) and
5. Jeremiah[e] (4Q71b).

These fragments represent a large part of the book, from the middle of chapter 4 until the beginning of chapter 40.

Comparing the texts of these manuscripts to the known versions of the *Book of Jeremiah* shows that it is possible to connect them to two major textual groups: One group includes texts similar to the Masoretic Text, more commonly referred to as the "Proto-Masoretic Text," in which Jeremiah (2Q13) and the two large manuscripts from Cave 4—Jeremiah[a] and Jeremiah[c]—as well as an additional manuscript from which only one fragment remains—Jeremiah[e]—are included. In the second group there are two manuscripts, from each of which just one fragment remains: Jeremiah[b] and Jeremiah[d]. These manuscripts are similar to the text of the Septuagint, and despite their small size it should be assumed that they belong to the group of manuscripts called "Proto-Septuagint Text." These texts probably reflect the *Vorlage*, used by the translators of the Septuagint.

The Manuscripts of *Jeremiah* from Qumran. As noted above, six manuscripts of the *Book of Jeremiah* have survived at Qumran.

Jeremiah (2Q13). The scroll of *Jeremiah* that was discovered in Cave 2 includes twenty-seven fragments with text from *Jeremiah* 42–49 (only one complete column has been reconstructed from four fragments). The manuscript dates from the Herodian period, and it was written in the unique script familiar to us from the scrolls of Qumran (with forms such as: *ky'*, *zw't*, etc.). Although a number of minor textual discrepancies exist between Jeremiah (2Q13) and the Masoretic Text, it is possible to characterize this manuscript as reflecting the Masoretic type of text, and to connect it to the group of manuscripts called "Proto-Masoretic Text."

In this scroll there is a case of difference in content: in fragments 9–12.ii.13 (*Jer.* 48[31].35) the word "[in] them" is added above the words "is sacrificing and] burning incense." This results in the reading "sacrifices in] them [and] burning incense," which is similar to the Masoretic Text.

Jeremiah[a]. In this scroll fifteen columns were reconstructed. The manuscript was dated by paleography to the period between the end of the third century BCE and the beginning of the second century BCE. This is one of the most ancient manuscripts discovered in Qumran. The text of the scroll is also similar to the Masoretic Text, and the spelling in the scroll is similar to the spelling documented in the Masoretic Text (however, see the debate regarding the reconstruction of col. iii). The manuscript is characterized by a large number of corrections. Thus, for example, in lines 7–9 in column xi it is possible to count eight corrections, including erasures and/or additions above the line. These are corrections mainly of scribal errors (such as haplography). It appears that a second scribe proofread the spelling according to a manuscript identical in its text to the Masoretic Text; however, it is possible that from the start the manuscript was similar to the Masoretic Text, and the mistakes stem from the copyist of this manuscript. Particularly interesting is an addition in column iii. In the original copying of the manuscript one entire paragraph, which exists in the rest of the textual witnesses (*Jer.* 7.30–8.3), was not included. The addition of this paragraph was made in small script, in the following way: The copyist added three rows, which begin above the line, continue in the space between the columns, and end beneath the third line of the column, where they are written upside-down. This style of correction is unique among the more than eight hundred manuscripts from Qumran. The motive for the correction is not clear, but it is possible to offer a number of possible explanations:

1. The original text before the correction may document an ancient and shorter version of chapter 7, which is a different edition of the book earlier than the Masoretic and Septuagint versions.
2. The omission of the paragraph from the original version may have been intentional.
3. The omission may have resulted from a scribal error.

It is difficult to explain an intentional omission. Regarding the possibility of an earlier version, it should be noted that it is perhaps possible to define the missing words as an independent unit, possessing Deuteronomistic characteristics. From a more precise examination of the section at hand, it seems that the verses appearing before and after the missing passage were written in a poetic fashion.

> 7.29
> Cut off and discard your hair
> and bear upon the hills a lament
> for God has rejected
> and abandoned the generation of his fury
>
> [7.30–8.3 absent]
> 8.4
> They shall fall and not arise
> if they will repent or not repent. . . .

The missing paragraph 7.30–8.3, however, was written in prose: "For the people of Judea did wrong in my eyes said the Lord. They put their abominations in the house which is called by my name to contaminate it and they built altars to Topeth . . . which remain in all the places." This paragraph belongs to the prose sections written in the Deuteronomistic style and which scholars have identified as an addition of a later editor.

As for the theory that one is dealing with an ancient source and not a scribal error, it should be noted that it is difficult to assume that the translator specifically omitted the prose passage. The difficulty in this explanation is that we do not have another textual witness to support this theory; that is, the stage of early editing preceding that which is documented in the Septuagint is not known to us from other sources, and we do not have additional examples of this early stage in other fragments of Jeremiah[a].

An additional explanation for the omission of the passage is parablepsis—that is, the skipping of the copyist's eye from one section to another. Similar instances of the omission of a passage between open portions are not known to us, although other types of omissions due to similarities are known to us and are widespread at Qumran.

The text of Jeremiah[a] is most similar to the Masoretic Text. Of particular interest is the exceptional correspondence in col. xii, line 8 of the scroll: *tiheyenah* ("will be," with a single *yod*) is shared by the Masoretic Text of *Jeremiah* 18.21, although the common form in the Masoretic Text is the spelling *tiheyyenah* (with a double *yod*).

Also, in the large addition in column iii between the lines and in the margins, there are eight minor corrections that make the text of the addition and the Masoretic Text more similar to each other. One example is in col. xi, line 5, where after "my glory" the word "you" was added, as in the Masoretic Text (*Jer.* 17.14). In line 6 the word "not" was added: "And I did not hasten" (*Jer.* 17.16). And in line 8 the word *tishberem* ("you will brea(k) them") was corrected to *shavrem* ("break them!") by the erasure of the letter *tav*, as in the Masoretic Text of *Jeremiah* 17.18. To this it is possible to add minor corrections involving guttural letters, which were added or switched in order to reconcile them with a text identical to the Masoretic Text. For example, *shefa'im* ("hills," with an *alef*), was corrected to *shefaim* (without an *alef*) (*Jer.* 14.6). There are also changes in forms. For example, the word *temru* ("you will say") in the scroll was changed with the aid of a final letter *nun* to the form *temrun*, which agrees with the Masoretic Text of *Jeremiah* 10.11. There are also cases of textual changes in the direction of the Masoretic Text, as in the example from *Jeremiah* 17.19 of the changing from the singular *melekh* ("king"), to the plural *melakhim* ("kings of Judah," with a final *kaf* in the middle of the word, which is closer to the medial *kaf* used in the Masoretic Text).

In contrast, there are corrections that distance the text from the Masoretic Text, as in the example of *ya'azvenu* ("will leave us"), found in the Masoretic Text (17.11), which was corrected in the scroll by the erasure of *nun* and the addition of *he* to the form *ya'azvehu* ("he will leave him").

From the many corrections in this scroll it is possible to conclude that the first scribe was careless, and that the scribe who proofread the text corrected it according to another text, which was very close to the Masoretic Text.

***Jeremiah*[b].** After separating this manuscript from the rest of the manuscripts that had been grouped with it, only one fragment remained, which includes *Jeremiah* 9.22–10.21. It was dated by paleography to the first half of the second century BCE. The text of this fragment is very similar to the Hebrew text before the translator of the Septuagint, and therefore it is possible to define it as "Proto-Septuagintal Text." According to this version, verses 6–8 and 10 in chapter 10 were not included, and the order of the verses reconstructed according to Jeremiah[b] is identical to the text of the Septuagint—4, 5a, 9, 5b.

***Jeremiah*[c].** From this manuscript parts of twenty-five columns have survived and between sixty-three and seventy other columns were reconstructed. The scroll includes remnants of *Jeremiah* 4.5–33.20 (altogether between eighty-eight and ninety-five columns were reconstructed).

The text of this scroll, like Jeremiah[a], is similar to the Masoretic Text and is different from the abridged text of the Septuagint in the parallel chapters, with the exception of a small number of insignificant differences, and therefore it is possible to define it as "Proto-Masoretic Text." The spelling is similar to the spelling in the Masoretic Text, although in a number of instances it is fuller than the Masoretic Text (e.g., *ya'aqov* ["Jacob"] appears with *plene* spelling).

***Jeremiah*[d].** A small fragment represents this manuscript and it contains *Jeremiah* 43.2–10 (those verses were also preserved in Jeremiah [2Q13]). The spelling is similar to the spelling in the Masoretic Text. The manuscript is similar to the version of the Septuagint, and documented in it are instances of the use of shorter versions of names: "Yoḥanan" in the scroll and in the Septuagint, as opposed to "Yoḥanan son of Koraḥ" in the Masoretic Text.

***Jeremiah*[e].** From this manuscript a small fragment of *Jeremiah* 4.5–6 has been preserved. This is apparently the first column in a sheet of parchment. At the beginning there is a correction of the words "and at those time" to "and at that time." The source of the error is probably in the phrase, "in those days," which appears earlier in the verse.

The Contribution of the Scrolls to the Textual Criticism of the *Book of Jeremiah*. With the beginning of the study of the *Book of Jeremiah* it became clear that the version of it in the Septuagint is approximately one-eighth shorter than in the Masoretic Text. There are words, phrases, sentences, and even whole paragraphs found exclusively in the Masoretic Text. In addition, the order of the paragraphs and verses is not identical in the Septuagint and the Masoretic Text, while the most noticeable differences between these textual witnesses are the prophecies against the nations. According to the Masoretic Text, their place is at the end of the book (chapters 46–51), while in the Septuagint they are inserted after chapter 25.13. In addition, there are many differences in readings between the sources. The elaborations of the Masoretic Text are customarily classified into a number of categories: there are additions defined as "expansive language," meaning additions of names (e.g., "Baruch *son of Neriah* [8.36]), repetitions of expressions such as "before . . . *before*" (37.49), or additions of formulas (e.g., "as the Lord said" or "utterance of the Lord") in many prophecies in the book; there are also additions taken from other verses in the *Book of Jeremiah*, some of them resulting from immediate contexts, and others from similar contexts, as well as additions of editorial matters, among them the addition of introductory words and conclusions, which were written by the later editor. Additionally, repetitions of sections mentioned in other places in the *Book of Jeremiah* (e.g., the addition in *Jer.* 30.10–46.28) exist in the Masoretic Text. Likewise, textual material from Jeremiah was added to the Masoretic Text, as well as elaborations characterized as Deuteronomistic additions.

The question of whether the short version of the Septuagint is original stood at the center of the study of the *Book of Jeremiah* even before the discovery of the Qumran scrolls, and different explanations were given for the question of the relation between the different versions. There were those who claimed that the Masoretic Text constitutes an elaboration of the *Book of Jeremiah* that was close to the *Vorlage* of the Septuagint. Others suggested that it is a matter of two different editions of the *Book of Jeremiah*, which reflect a different tradition of editing (between which there is a historical connection).

With the discovery of the scrolls, ancient biblical texts written in Hebrew were found, and among them were found versions documented in the Septuagint as well. Two large manuscripts were discovered at Qumran, Jeremiah^a and Jeremiah^c, the texts of which are closest to the Masoretic Text, as well as two fragments that remained from scrolls that were also closest to the Masoretic Text. In contrast, a group of texts similar to the Septuagint were also discovered. Particularly close to this text is Jeremiah^b. In this manuscript, as in the Septuagint, there is a short version of the *Book of Jeremiah*, and in it the order of the verses is different from the one in the Masoretic Text. An important new item for the study of the text comes from Jeremiah^a in which a correction of the text of the scroll to the Masoretic Text, although not entirely consistent, is documented. And so we possess different witnesses of the text, side by side, which testify to the literary development of the *Book of Jeremiah*.

It should be noted that in these manuscripts there is no evidence of the scrolls' source, and hence there is no proof that they were copied at Qumran. Whether these texts were copied at Qumran or were brought to Qumran, it is possible to ascertain that in the Land of Israel during the Second Temple era, at least two different versions of the *Book of Jeremiah* were in use, one similar to the Septuagint, and one similar to the Masoretic Text. For Jeremiah^a it is possible to determine that this scroll was brought to Qumran, since it was dated paleographically to the years between 200 and 175 BCE, prior to the establishment of the communal center at Qumran.

BIBLIOGRAPHY

Baillet, M. "Textes des grottes 2Q, 3Q, 6Q, 7Q, a 10Q." In *Les 'Petites Grottes' de Qumrân* by M. Baillet, J. T. Milik, and R. de Vaux, pp. 62–69. Discoveries in the Judaean Desert, 3. Oxford, 1962.

Janzen, Gerald. *Studies in the Text of Jeremiah*. Harvard Semitic Monographs, 6. Cambridge, Mass., 1973.

Tov, E. "The Literary History of the Book of Jeremiah in the Light of Its Textual History." In *Empirical Models for Biblical Criticism*, edited by J. H. Tigay, pp. 211–237. Philadelphia, 1985.

Tov, E. "4QJer^c (4Q72)." In *Tradition of the Text: Studies Offered to Dominique Barthélemy in Celebration of his 70th Birthday*, edited by Gerard J. Norton and Stephen Pisano, pp. 249–276. Freiburg and Göttingen, 1991.

Tov, E. "Three Fragments of Jeremiah from Qumran Cave 4." *Revue de Qumrân* 15 (1992), 531–541.

Tov, E. "4QJer^a—A Preliminary Edition." *Textus* 17 (1994), 1–41.

Tov, E. "4QJer^a, 4QJer^b, 4QJer^c, 4QJer^d, 4QJer^e." In *Qumran Cave 4.X the Prophets*, by E. Ulrich, et al. Discoveries in the Judaean Desert, 15. Oxford, 1997.

ESTHER ESHEL
Translated from Hebrew by Daphna Krupp

Pseudo-Jeremiah

A group of works related to the career of the biblical prophet Jeremiah or based on the biblical *Book of Jeremiah* is indicated by the title *Pseudo-Jeremiah*. Although these works purport to be written by the prophet Jeremiah (or his scribe Baruch; see *Jer.* 36.4), they are all clearly pseudonymous. These pseudo-Jeremianic works include the *Epistle of Jeremiah*, the *Paraleipomena Ieremiou* ("The Rest of the Words of Jeremiah" or *4 Baruch*), and the previously unknown *Apocryphon of Jeremiah*. Related texts, including those attributed to Baruch, are the first, second, and third books of *Baruch* and the *Lives of Prophets*. All these works date to the Hellenistic and Roman periods (late fourth century BCE–first century CE). With one exception (see below), they were all known prior to the discoveries at Qumran, and none displays any specific sectarian characteristics.

Two of this group of texts have been found among the Qumran scrolls. The first, the *Apocryphon of Jeremiah*, was not known prior to the discovery of the scrolls. It exists in five manuscripts from Cave 4: 4Q383, 4Q384, 4Q385b, 4Q387b, and 4Q389a. All of these manuscripts are extremely fragmentary, and the largest, 4Q385b, dates paleographically to c.50–25 BCE. The Apocryphon of Jeremiah B (4Q384) is a papyrus manuscript that dates to the Herodian period (c.50–1 BCE). All the manuscripts are in Hebrew; however, since there are no overlaps among the five manuscripts it is impossible to tell if they are all from the same composition. The manuscripts also do not contain any overlaps with the biblical *Book of Jeremiah*. In fact, three of the manuscripts—4Q385b, 4Q387b, and 4Q389a—were identified by their original editor, J. Strugnell, as part of a work entitled "Pseudo-Ezekiel." However, their present editor, D. Dimant, has identified these manuscripts, along with 4Q383 and 4Q384, as an *Apocryphon of Jeremiah* on the basis of content.

The largest of the manuscripts, 4Q385b, contains two columns of material. The first fragment, column 1, concerns Jeremiah and the destruction of Jerusalem. Its context draws on *Jeremiah* 40–44 and 52.12–13. Jeremiah is identified as a prophet; the content includes the exile to Babylon and the Temple vessels, as well as the mention of Nabuzaradan, the Babylonian "captain of the guard" (*Jer.* 39.11, 52.12). All of the material agrees with the biblical narrative, except the text seems to imply that Jeremiah went to Babylon with the exiles (line 6), as opposed to the biblical text, which states that he remained in Judah (*Jer.* 39.14, 40.6). The tradition that Jeremiah accompanied the exiles to Babylon agrees with other pseudo-Jeremianic works, for example, *Paraleipomena Ieremiou* 4.5 and the *Apocalypse of Baruch* 10 and 33, as well as certain rabbinic traditions, for example, *Seder Olam* 26 and J. T., *Sanhedrin* 1, 19a, both of which place Jeremiah in Babylon.

Fragment 1, column ii, of 4Q385b concerns Jeremiah in Egypt. Lines 1 and 6 mention Taphnes (or Tahpanes), a location of Jewish settlement in Egypt given in *Jeremiah* 2.16, 43.7–9, 44.1, 46.14 and *Ezekiel* 30.18. Lines 6–10 seem to contain an oracle of Jeremiah delivered in Egypt to the exiles, an oracle that line 2 may imply they do not understand ("do not interpret for them"). This notion of the people's obtuseness coincides with the biblical text, which declares that Jeremiah's prophecies in Egypt continued to meet with disbelief and rejection (*Jer.* 43.1–3, 44.15–19). In fact, the later work *Lives of the Prophets* and the *Midrash Aggadah* on *Numbers* 30.15 both declare that Jeremiah was stoned to death by the Jews in Egypt.

Apocryphon of Jeremiah D (4Q387b), fragment 1, also concerns Jeremiah in Egypt (line 4). Jeremiah is identified as the son of Hilkiah (*Jer.* 1.1). Line 5 mentions "x]–six" years of exile from Israel. This may agree with a tradition found in the *Paraleipomena Ieremiou*, which states that Jeremiah returned to Jerusalem from Babylon after sixty-six years of exile. In line 6 the name of the river Sor or Sud is given. This name, otherwise unidentified, is probably identical to the river Sud mentioned in *Baruch* 1.4 (in the Apocrypha) as the place of exile of King Jeconiah and his fellow captives in Babylon.

All of the correlations given above between the *Apocryphon of Jeremiah* and the other pseudo-Jeremianic works, as well as the biblical *Book of Jeremiah* and the rabbinic traditions, indicate that the *Apocryphon* was not a unique composition but part of a wider corpus of compositions based on the life and oracles of the prophet Jeremiah. Therefore, it is unlikely that the *Apocryphon of Jeremiah* was a sectarian composition; rather, it was a work of the general literature of the Second Temple period that was read at Qumran. In this it is like other nonsectarian compositions based on biblical books found at Qumran, such as the Genesis Apocryphon.

The second pseudo-Jeremianic composition found at Qumran is the *Epistle of Jeremiah*. The *Epistle of Jeremiah* is supposed to be a copy of the letter which Jeremiah sent to the exiles in Babylon (*Jer.* 29). It is actually a satirical polemic against idolatry composed in the late fourth century BCE. Now extant only in Greek, the original language of the epistle may have been Hebrew. The epistle is part of the Greek Septuagint, where it is placed after *Lamentations* (also attributed to Jeremiah) and before *Ezekiel*. However, in the Latin Vulgate it is appended as a sixth chapter to the *Book of Baruch* (in the Apocrypha), since it was rejected by Jerome as pseudepigraphical.

The Qumran copy was discovered in Cave 7 (7Q2), a cave containing only Greek manuscripts. The manuscript is papyrus, written in uncials without separation between the words. Its editor, M. Baillet, dates it on the basis of paleography to c.100 BCE. The text of 7Q2 contains verses 43b–44 of the *Epistle of Jeremiah*, with only one significant variant.

Finally, a reference to a pseudo-Jeremianic work may occur in the Damascus Document viii.20, which reads, "This is the word which Jeremiah spoke to Baruch, son of Neriah, and Elisha to Gehazi his servant." This line is neither preceded nor followed by a biblical quotation, so it is uncertain as to what it refers. The context refers to the punishment of those who forsake the covenant, so the implication may be that Baruch has been unfaithful. There is no reference in either the *Book of Jeremiah* or any of the known pseudo-Jeremianic works, however, to an episode in which Baruch is unfaithful; in fact, Baruch is the epitome of faithfulness. It is possible that this line in the Damascus Document refers to some unknown pseudo-Jeremianic work. However, it is significant that this line comes from Cairo Damascus Document-A, at a point where it deviates sharply from manuscript B, and is not found in any of the Qumran Damascus Document manuscripts. Therefore, this line probably reflects a variant (and possibly post-Qumran) tradition within the composition history of the Damascus Document.

BIBLIOGRAPHY

Baillet, M. "Lettre de Jérémie." In *Les 'petites grottes' de Qumran*, p. 143, edited by M. Baillet, J. T. Milik, and R. de Vaux. Discoveries in the Judaean Desert, 3. Oxford, 1962.

Davies, Philip R. *The Damascus Covenant*. Journal for the Study of the Old Testament Supplement Series, 25. Sheffield, 1983.

Dimant, Devorah. "An Apocryphon of Jeremiah from Cave 4 (4Q385b = 4Q385 16)." In *New Qumran Texts and Studies: Proceedings of the First Meeting of the International Organization for Qumran Studies, Paris 1992*, edited by George J. Brooke, pp. 11–30. Leiden, 1994.

Smith, Mark. "Apocryphon of Jeremiah." In *Qumran Cave 4, XIV: Parabiblical Texts, Part 2,* edited by M. Broshi et al., pp. 137–152. Discoveries in the Judaean Desert, 19. Oxford, 1995.

SIDNIE WHITE CRAWFORD

JERUSALEM. The form *Urushalim* is first attested in the Amarna letters of the fourteenth century BCE. It is a combination of two elements *yrw* and *shlm,* which means "the foundation of *Shalem.*" In the Ugaritic pantheon, *Shalem* was the god of Twilight. The name appears in *Genesis* 14.18; *Psalms* 76.2 as Salem. The city is sited on the crest of the central mountain range of Palestine at an altitude of 750 meters (2,500 feet). It is separated from the Mount of Olives on the east by the Kidron Valley, and limited on the west by the Hinnom Valley. The Tyropoeon Valley divides the higher western hill from the eastern hill, which is the oldest part of the city.

History. Sometime around 1,000 BCE David took the little Jebusite city on the Ophel ridge (*2 Sm* 5.6–10). In order to house the Ark of the Covenant, he bought a threshing floor to the north of the city from Araunah (*2 Sm* 24:18–25), which is a personal name in Ugaritic and a title in Hittite. It was here that Solomon built the first Temple (*1 Kgs*. 6–7). In 722 BCE, refugees from the defeated northern kingdom settled outside the crowded city. When Sennacherib menaced Jerusalem in 701 BCE, these had to be protected. King Hezekiah enclosed (*Is*. 22.10) the two new quarters on the western hill, the *mishneh* (*2 Kgs*. 22.14) and the *makhtesh* (*Zep*. 1.11), and guaranteed the water supply by cutting a tunnel from the Gihon spring to the Siloam pool (*2 Chr*. 32).

In 587/586 BCE the Babylonians devastated Jerusalem and deported its inhabitants to Babylonia. Only a fraction returned 60 years later, and the city contracted to the original eastern hill, where the Temple was restored by Zerubbabel (*Ezr*. 5–6). Jerusalem expanded to the west again only in the mid-second century BCE when the Maccabees built the First Wall to enclose the western hill (Josephus, *The Jewish War* 5.142–145). Subsequently the north and south walls moved backward and forward but always between the fixed east and west walls. Sometime in the early first century BCE the need for more space forced the construction of the Second (Northern) Wall (*The Jewish War* 5.146).

When Judas Maccabeus, after his first victories, returned to the city, he "found the sanctuary deserted, the altar desecrated, the gates burnt down, and vegetation growing in the courts as it might in a wood or on some mountain, while the store rooms were in ruins" (*1 Mc*. 4.38). This demanded extensive rebuilding (*1 Mc*. 4.48, 60; 12:37). The square platform was extended on the south to bury the Syrian Akra (*1 Mc*. 1.29–35). Herod the Great's construction of the Antonia fortress (*The Jewish War* 5.238–245) north of the Temple, and of his new palace on the western hill (*The Jewish War* 5.161–182), highlighted the shabbiness of the much restored Temple. It took him nine and a half years to rebuild it completely (*The Jewish War* 5.184–247).

After the return from exile in Babylon (587–538 BCE), political and religious authority in Jerusalem was invested in the high priest. This office was hereditary in the Zadokite line (*1 Chr*. 6:3–15; *Neh*. 12:10–11; Josephus, *Jewish Antiquities* 11.347–12.239) until the legitimate succession was broken by Antiochus IV Epiphanes (175–164 BCE), who replaced Onias III by his brother Jason (*2 Mc*. 4.7–20). In 172 BCE Antiochus went a step further by appointing a non-Zadokite, Menelaus, as high priest (*2 Mc*. 4.23–24). His successor, Alcimus (162–159 BCE), again named by the Syrians, was of Zadokite stock (*1 Mc*. 7.14), though not of the high priestly line (*Jewish Antiquities* 12.387). The rupture with sacrosanct tradition became definitive when, in autumn 152 BCE, Jonathan Maccabeus invested himself as high priest by putting on the sacred vestments (*1 Mc*. 10.21). Thereafter, the high priesthood became hereditary in the Hasmonean dynasty until Herod the Great had Aristobulus III murdered in 35 BCE (*The Jewish War* 1.437).

Thereafter, Herod nominated "insignificant persons who were merely of priestly descent" (*Jewish Antiquities* 20.247). The consequence was the promotion of four families—Boethus, Hannas, Phiabi, and Kamith—from which twenty-two of the twenty-five illegitimate high priests of the period 37 BCE–70 CE were drawn. Inevitably, nepotism was rife throughout the sacerdotal system. Understandably, traditionalists foresaw a horrible fate for "the last priests of Jerusalem, who will accumulate riches and loot from plundering the peoples. However, in the last days their riches and their loot will fall into the hands of the *Kittim*" (Pesher Habakkuk, 1QpHab xii.7–9).

References in the Scrolls. The scrolls contain a number of simple factual references to Jerusalem. Geographically, it is "the high mountain of Israel" (Pesher Psalms[a], 4Q171 iii.11). This essential physical characteristic of the city is highlighted in the citation of *Isaiah* 10.32, which puts "the mount of the daughter of Zion" in parallelism with "the hill of Jerusalem" (Pesher Isaiah[a], 4Q161 2–6.21). The allusion of the War Scroll (1QM) to "the desert of Jerusalem" (ii.2–3) may have been inspired by the immediately preceding reference to "the desert of the peoples," i.e., the Syrian desert, which is drawn from *Ezekiel* 20.35, but for the Bible the desert began on the eastern slopes of the Mount of Olives (Funk, 1959).

On the historical level, Salem is identified as Jerusalem (Genesis Apocryphon, 1QapGen xxii.12). "The capture of

Jerusalem and of Zedekiah, king of Judah" (MMT[e], 4Q398 1.1–2) is used to specify the *terminus ad quem* of curses which came upon the southern kingdom from the time of Jeroboam son of Nebat (cf. *1 Kgs*. 11.26–25.7). Pesher Nahum (4Q169) 3–4.i.2–3 interprets *Nahum* 2.12 as a reference to the abortive effort of Demetrius III Eukerus to take Jerusalem at the invitation of the opponents of Alexander Jannaeus (*The Jewish War* 1.92–98). There is a similar neutral usage in the War Scroll, "No young boy or any women at all shall enter the camps when they leave Jerusalem to go to war" (vii.3–4).

A number of texts already quoted suggest that, as in the Bible, Zion, or the daughter of Zion, is a fully interchangeable synonym for Jerusalem. Confirmation is furnished by the juxtaposition "Mount Zion, Jerusalem" in Ages of Creation (4Q180) 5–6.4. "Jerusalem [the city which you c]hose from the whole earth" is "Zion, your holy city" (Words of Luminaries, 1–2.iv 3.12; cf. Noncanonical Psalms A, 4Q380 1.i.2–7). "The ramparts of the daughter of Zion" is equivalent to "the precincts of Jerusalem" (Testimonia, 4Q175 29–30). The "Rock of Zion" is the site of the "house of the God of Israel" (Work with Place Names, "Rock of Zion," 4Q522 8.ii.3–4).

Such value-free references to Jerusalem are relatively rare in the scrolls. The majority of the texts reflect either an idealistic vision of the holiness of the city or a harshly condemnatory assessment of its real situation. The latter, of course, was conditioned by the former.

Both the Temple Scroll and Miqtsat Ma'asei ha-Torah devote particular attention to Jerusalem. The context is a debate concerning the contemporary interpretation of the Pentateuchal laws of purity. How were laws enacted to govern behavior in the tent of meeting and in the camp of the Israelites on their long journey from Egypt to the Promised Land to be applied in very different physical circumstances? Should they be given a limited or wide extension?

That there were different opinions is clear from the formulation of Miqtsat Ma'asei ha-Torah (B29–33):

> We are of the opinion that the sanctuary [is the "tent of meeting"] and that Jerusalem is the "camp", and that "outside the camp" [is outside Jerusalem], that is, the encampment of their settlements. It is "outside the c]amp" where one should . . . the purification-offering and] take out the ashes of [the] altar and bu[rn the purification-offering. For Jerusalem] is the place which [He has chosen] from among all the tribes [of Israel. . . .]

Later in the same document we read, "One must not let dogs enter the holy camp, since they may eat some of the bones of the sanctuary while the flesh is (still) on them. For Jerusalem is the camp of holiness, and is the place which He has chosen from among all the tribes of Israel. For Jerusalem is the capital of the camps of Israel" (B58–61).

The authors evidently reject an alternative view which identified "the tent of meeting" and "the camp" with different parts of the Temple. For its supporters, Jerusalem was "outside the camp" and thus subject to much less stringent standards of ritual purity. The authors of Miqtsat Ma'asei ha-Torah, on the contrary, insist not only that Jerusalem is "the camp" but that it is also "the place which He has chosen," a phrase that could easily be restricted to the Temple (Qimron and Strugnell, 1994, 144).

The same approach to the level of purity required of those who enter Jerusalem appears in the Temple Scroll (11Q19). "And if a man lies with his wife and has an emission of semen, for three days he shall not come into any part of the city of the Temple, where I will settle my name. No blind man shall enter it all their days, so that they will not defile the city in which I dwell" (xlv.11–13). The enlargement of *Leviticus* 15.18 is paralleled by what is said of the blind; the original restriction applied only to priests (*Lv*. 21.17–21). The Damascus Document (CD) formally articulates the logical consequence of this legislation. Sexual intercourse should not take place in "the city of the temple" (xii.1–2). Yadin (vol. 1, 289) considers this the basis of Essene celibacy. Prior to the publication of Miqtsat Ma'asei ha-Torah there were those who believed that "the city of the Temple" did not mean Jerusalem but the Temple complex (Levine, 1978; Schiffman, 1989).

Those whose state of purity permitted them to enter "the holy city" (Damascus Document, CD xx.22) were not necessarily in a state to enter the Temple. Hence, "you shall make a ditch around the Temple, 100 cubits in width, which will separate the holy temple from the city, so that they may not come suddenly into my temple and desecrate it" (Temple Scroll, 11Q19 xlvi.9–11). The distinction is between the holy and the most holy and, while there is little difference in exclusions, positive qualifications assume great importance (Milgrom, 1980, 96). Those resident in Jerusalem could eat meat only from animals that had been sacrificed in the Temple, and all the skins they used for wine and oil must come from such animals (Temple Scroll, 11Q19 xlvii.8–18). The standard of other cities was not adequate for Jerusalem.

The sanctity of Jerusalem was due to the presence in it of the Temple. The Temple Scroll speaks of "the city which I will hallow by settling my name and [my] temp[le within (it)]" (xlvii.3–4). The theme recurs in the form of a command, "You shall not defile the city in which I settle my name and my temple" (xlvii.10–11); "you shall not defile my temple and my city in which I dwell" (xlvii.17–18). The only biblical parallel to "my city" is *Isaiah* 45.13, where Jerusalem is certainly in view.

The other scrolls to focus particularly on Jerusalem are

the *pesharim*. Their attitude, however, is significantly different, because they speak about the reality of the authors' relationships with the city. Note the criticism of the priests of Jerusalem (see Pesher Micah [1Q14] 11, 1).

One priest is singled out for particular notice. Commenting on "owing to the blood of the city" (*Hab.* 2.17) the Pesher Habakkuk (1QpHab) writes, "Its interpretation: the 'city' is Jerusalem since in it the Wicked Priest performed repulsive acts and defiled the Temple of God" (xii.7–9). The second charge was inevitable, given the standards of impurity demanded by the scrolls, and the illegitimacy of all high priests since Onias III. The first probably refers to the persecution of the Teacher of Righteousness and his followers (Pesher Habakkuk, 1QpHab ix.9–10; xi.4–7; xii.2–6).

Pesher Isaiah[b] (4Q162) interprets *Isaiah* 5.14 and 25 as referring to "the congregation of arrogant men who are in Jerusalem" (1.ii.6–7, 10). If the underlying allusion is to *Isaiah* 28.14 the *pesher* has the authorities in view. These are certainly to be distinguished from "the congregation of Jerusalem" (War Scroll, 1QM iii.11), but their relationship to "the congregation of those [looking] for easy interpretations who are in Jerusalem" (Pesher Isaiah[c], 4Q163 23.10–11) is an open question. The latter group also appear in Pesher Nahum (4Q169) in association with Jerusalem (3–4.i.2) and with "the city of Ephraim" (3–4.ii.2). The name identifes them as lax by the strict standards of the authors of these *pesharim*.

The tension between the ideal Jerusalem and what actually went on in the holy city provoked different reactions. There were those who dreamt of a new Jerusalem unmarked by any sins of the past. Even though the name appears nowhere in any copy of an extremely fragmentary text, in which the seer is shown around an immense immaculate city by an angel with a measuring rod, the title accepted by all is "Description of the New Jerusalem" (García Martínez, 1986).

Others believed in a transformation of the existing city, "And of the book of Isaiah: Words of consolation [Be consoled, consoled, my people! (*Is.* 40.1–5)] says your God; speak to the heart of Jerusalem and sho[ut to her that her service is done,] that her fault has been forgiven, that from the hand of [the Lord] she has received double for all her sins" (Tanḥumin [4Q176] 1–2.i.4–6). The same hope inspired the great poetry of the Hymns to Zion (4QPs11[f] vii–viii; 11Q5 xxii.8–15).

Finally some, on the grounds that their standard of observance alone befitted the holiness of Jerusalem, tended to identify their community with the holy city, as they did with the Temple (Rule of the Community, 1QS vii.5–6). Thus, the sapphire foundations of the New Jerusalem in *Isaiah* 54.11 mean "the council of the community, the priests and the people" (Isaiah Pesher[d], 4Q164 1.2). Similarly *2 Samuel* 7.12–14 was understood to refer to "the branch of David," who will arise with the "Interpreter of the Law who [will rise up] in Zi[on in] the last days" (Florilegium, 4Q174 1–3.10–12; cf. Rule of the Congregation 1Q28a ii.11–17).

BIBLIOGRAPHY

Funk, R. "The Wilderness." *Journal of Biblical Literature* 78 (1959), 205–214.

García Martínez, F. "La 'Nueva Jerusalen' y el Templo Futuro de los MSS. de Qumran." In *Salvación en la Palabra. Targum—Derash—Berith. En memoria del profesor Alejandro Diez Macho*, edited by Domingo Muños Leon, pp. 563–590. Madrid, 1986.

Levine, B. "The Temple Scroll—Aspects of Its Historical Provenance and Literary Character." *Bulletin of the American Schools of Oriental Research* 232 (1978), 13–17.

Mazar, B., Y. Shiloh, N. Avigad, and H. Geva. "Jerusalem." *The New Encyclopedia of Archaeological Excavations in the Holy Land*, edited by E. Stern, A. Lweinson-Gilboa, and A. Aviram, pp. 698–757. Jerusalem, 1993.

Milgrom, J. "Further Studies in the Temple Scroll." *Jewish Quarterly Review* 71 (1980), 1–17, 89–106.

Qimron, E., and J. Strugnell. *Qumran Cave 4, V: Miqṣat Maʿaśe Ha-Torah*. Discoveries in the Judaean Desert, 10. Oxford, 1994.

Schiffman, L. H. "Architecture and Law: The Temple and Its Courtyards in the Temple Scroll." In *From Ancient Israel to Modern Judaism. Intellect in Quest of Understanding*, pp. 267–284. Brown Judaic Studies, 159. Atlanta 1989.

Yadin, Y. *The Temple Scroll*. 3 vols. Jerusalem, 1983.

JEROME MURPHY-O'CONNOR

JESUS. The following article deals with Jesus only inasmuch as he can be understood through historical research. A comparison with Jesus will be made using only the texts discovered in the eleven caves at or near Qumran. Within the Qumran texts, as far as possible, a distinction will be drawn between texts that go back directly to the Qumran community or the wider movement of which it was a part (the Essenes) and those which were merely part of their library. Throughout (in keeping with the Rule of the Community), the "Qumran community" is taken to mean wherever members lived (1QS vi.2). In general, the Rule of the Community is cited only according to 1QS, without any reference to the parallel manuscripts.

The State of Research on Jesus. Sources for the historical Jesus include the four canonical Gospels (the oldest, the *Gospel of Mark*, dates from about 70 CE) and also the Gospel of Thomas from among the documents found at Nag Hammadi. Jesus grew up as a Jew in Nazareth in Galilee. That he was baptized by John the Baptist is historically certain, but whether the Baptist originally belonged to the Qumran community cannot be ascertained. A critical reading of the Gospels indicates that the locations of Jesus' activity were in Galilee and Gaulanitis, around Capernaum, Bethsaida, and Chorazin—largely at the northern end of the Sea of Galilee. Jesus came on the scene as a kind of itinerant preacher and wonder worker, neither of which has virtually any equivalent in the Qumran texts (However, with regard to the laying on of the hands for healing, which was performed by Jesus, according to *Mark* 8.23, 8.25 and *Luke* 13.13 see the parallels in 1QGenesis Apocryphon xx.22, xx.29). Jesus and Qumran share the basic presupposition that the end of time was imminent, in other words, that a new and definitive divinely ordained world was expected in the near future. The principal theme in the preaching of Jesus was the "Kingdom of God" (*basileia tou theou*) understood eschatologically, while the genre that was characteristic of Jesus' preaching was the parable. There is hardly any instance of either in the Qumran texts. That Jesus understood himself to be the Messiah has been almost unanimously ruled out by critical research. Around 30 CE the Roman prefect Pontius Pilate (26–36 CE) had Jesus crucified.

Jesus and the Qumran Texts. In this article only the main points of comparison can be covered. The theories that Jesus was an Essene, and even that he should be identified with a particular figure in the Qumran texts, have been judged too far-fetched by critical researchers and therefore are not dealt with here. Neither are theories that are overly speculative, such as the conjecture that Jesus may have celebrated his Last Supper according to the Essene calendar, since it is difficult to determine historically that Jesus even had a last supper on the basis of the New Testament accounts of it. (Accordingly, there will be no attempt at a comparison between the Last Supper accounts and the Qumran meal texts in 1QRule of the Congregation [1Q28a] ii.11–22 and 1QRule of the Community vi.2–6.) Unconnected parallels, such as those between the Beatitudes from the Sermon on the Mount (*Mt.* 5.3–12) and the Qumran texts (see particularly the 4Q Wisdom Text with Beatitudes [4Q525]), must likewise be left undiscussed. In the Qumran texts there is no reference of any kind to Jesus or to early Christians (nor have any New Testament texts been found in Cave 7), and this also holds true vice versa—New Testament texts do not make direct reference to the Qumran sectarians or their compositions.

Discipleship or community. The basic difference between the Qumran community and the Jesus movement lies in group sociology: The Qumran covenanters organized themselves into a closed community (*yaḥad*), while Jesus called only certain individual disciples to follow him (since the number of "the twelve" as representing the whole of Israel should probably not be read back into Jesus' lifetime, the representation of the twelve tribes by twelve men in 1QRule of the Community viii.1–4 is not discussed here). To all who encountered him, particularly his fellow Jews, Jesus preached the Kingdom of God, but he did not gather his followers into communities. This was done by Christians only after the crucifixion, when they began to understand themselves as a "church" (*ekklêsia*). Thus, from a sociological standpoint, these later Christian communities (*ekklêsiai*) are more similar to the Qumran community or communities than the earliest Jesus movement.

Christians' identification of themselves as "children of light" (*huioi tou photos/benei ʾor*), a phrase reminiscent of the Qumran community and found in the parable of the unjust steward (*Lk.* 16.1ff.) should not be attributed to Jesus, because verse 8 is almost certainly a later addition to the parable.

The Torah. Jesus' attitude toward the Torah is difficult to characterize, and it is even less clear to what extent his activity in Galilee and Gaulanitis was influenced by the local attitude to the Torah, which certainly differed somewhat from that which prevailed in Jerusalem. Nevertheless, the contrast between the strict understanding of the Torah as it is found in the Qumran texts, and Jesus' behavior, particularly with regard to the Sabbath and questions of ritual purity, is unmistakable.

Perhaps the most controversial passage in the canonical Gospels regarding Jesus' stance on the Torah is *Mark* 7.15; it is a statement that probably goes back to Jesus. On the one hand, Jesus makes the Torah more stringent by contrasting the external eating of food with ethical behavior; on the other hand, he barely stops short of abrogating the Torah (see *Leviticus* 11 and *Deuteronomy* 14).

One constant characteristic of Jesus' preaching and practice was his table fellowship with tax collectors and sinners (see *Mk.* 2.15–17 and *Lk.* 5.29–30, *Lk.* 7.34 parallels *Mt.* 11.19, *Lk.* 15.2, 19.7). In the Qumran community, by way of contrast, not even the novices who had already spent a whole year in the community were allowed "to touch the purity of the Many (i.e. the full members)" (1QS vi.16–17) and even after an additional year, they were not yet allowed to partake of "the drink of the Many" (1QS vi.20). Furthermore, in 1QRule of the Congregation ii.3–11, following *Leviticus* 21.16–24, the Qumran community provides for the exclusion of all those with physical impairments (the lame, the crippled, and the blind, among others) from the actual community (perhaps only in the eschaton). It almost seems as if Jesus were presenting an opposing agenda when (in a saying in *Luke* 14.12–14) he clearly proclaims that "the crippled, the lame and the blind" are to be invited as partakers at the table, in addition to the "poor" (a positive self-designation that the Qumran community used of itself). This is repeated in *Luke* 14.21 in the parable of the banquet in the Kingdom of God.

Jesus' attitude toward the Sabbath is likewise inconsistent with that of the Qumran community. In addition to the doubtlessly authentic saying of Jesus in *Mark* 2.27, which argues from the account of Creation, *Mark* 3.1–5 seems characteristic of Jesus, because he equates doing good on the Sabbath with saving a life, which was permissible in any case, and thus reduces his opponents to an absurd position. The Qumran texts, by contrast, advocate the strictest observance of the Sabbath, as the Damascus Document x.14–xi.18, for example, shows (partly preserved in 4Q266, 267, 270, 271). The prohibition in Damascus Document xi.13–14 (also in part in the parallel manuscript copies from Cave 4) and 4QSerekh Damascus (4Q265 7.i.6–7) against helping to save an animal that has fallen into a cistern or a pit would have struck Jesus as absurd, since the saying in *Luke* 14.5 (parallels *Matthew* 12.11–12) shows that he starts from the opposite assumption.

In *Mark* 10.2–9 (parallels *Matthew* 19.1ff.) Jesus argues from Creation (*apo archês ktiseôs*) against the possibility of divorce, which "Moses" allowed. Precisely this approach, arguing from Creation, is also found once in the Damascus Document iv.20–21 (partly preserved in the parallel manuscript copies 4Q269 and 6Q15), where the same passage, *Genesis* 1.27 is cited. While in *Mark* 10.9 (parallels *Matthew* 19.6) Jesus forbids divorce, the Qumran community seems to go even further by requiring men to be married to only one woman during their lifetime. Of course, the Qumran texts make no reference to any exception quoted by Moses.

In the so-called antitheses in the Sermon on the Mount (*Mt*. 5.21–48), of which particularly the first and the second are probably authentic, Jesus juxtaposes "but I say to you" to another tradition. This has a certain parallel in 4QMMT (4Q394–99), a document which comes from the earliest period of the Qumran community. There, the opposing opinion is frequently rejected with the words "(but) we say" (B 55, 65, 73 along with the common "but we think"; see also "but you know" in B 68, 80; C8).

The command to love. In the Damascus Document vi.20–21 the commandment of *Leviticus* 19.18 "You shall love your neighbor as yourself" is reflected in the version "one should love his brother (see *Lv*. 19.17) as himself." This also includes strangers: "one should look after the stranger" (Damascus Document vi.20–21 is also partly preserved in 4Q269 and 6Q15). In the smaller catalogs of virtues in 1Q Rule of the Community "love" is "faithful love" (*ahavat ḥesed*—see ii.24, v.4, v.25, viii.2, x.26), and in the large catalog of virtues (1QS iv.3aβ–6a) "unending goodness" (*ṭov ʿolamim*) occurs (1QS iv.3). There can be little doubt that in all these cases it is the community members who are understood as the objects of these virtuous attitudes.

Repeatedly, Jesus' command to love one's enemies (*Mt*. 5.44 [parallels *Lk*. 6.27, 6.35]) stands in contrast with the Qumran texts. The Rule of the Community explicitly says that one should "love all the children of light," and "hate all the children of darkness" (1QS i.9–10; see also ix.21–22, also partially preserved in 4Q256, 258, 259). Whether Jesus is here inveighing against the Qumran community cannot be determined. Jesus seems to have used "hate" in a general sense, but in the Qumran texts "hate" is used in particular dualistic religious contexts and presupposes a picture of God that is alien to Jesus. (It is a different matter in *midrash Sifra Leviticus* 19.18, where hate as "vengeance" and "rage" against gentiles is allowed.) Explicit love for enemies, in the stark wording that we find with Jesus, has no parallels in the Jewish literature of antiquity. Clearly, it must go back to Jesus himself, who again argues from Creation (the more original version is probably in *Matthew* 5.45 as opposed to *Luke* 6.35).

Eschatology. The Qumran texts turn out to be particularly helpful for reaching a better understanding of Jesus' eschatology, which is characterized by its combination of future and present aspects. For Jesus, salvation is not only hoped for but also already experienced. Until the discovery of the Qumran texts, the common opinion was either that Jesus had a completely new understanding of eschatology over and against his own Jewish milieu (W. G. Kümmel), or that Jesus' eschatology was falsely attributed to him, because it was not attested in the Judaism of the time (R. Bultmann). Recently, the so-called Jesus Seminar in North America has even supposed that Jesus' teaching completely lacked any eschatology or apocalypticism, but his view is exegetically untenable (one has only to cite the petition in the Lord's Prayer "Thy kingdom come" in *Luke* 11.2 [parallels *Matthew* 6.10] and some of the parables of Jesus). Among the most important authentic sayings of Jesus which speak of the presence of future salvation are *Luke* 11.20 (parallels *Matthew* 12.28) (as Jesus was casting out demons, the Kingdom of God has already begun to break through), and also *Luke* 10.23–24 (parallels *Matthew* 13.16–17); *Luke* 7.22–23 (parallels *Matthew* 11.5–6); and *Mark* 2.19a (parallels *Matthew* 9.15a and *Luke* 5.34).

There is no significant anticipation of future salvation as such in the Qumran texts. However, in the frequently encountered references to the community's communion with the angels (e.g., 1QHodayot[a] xi [formerly iii] 21–23, xix [formerly xi] 14–15; 4QAges of Creation [4Q181] 1.ii.4–5; the Songs of the Sabbath Sacrifice [4Q400–407; 11Q17; Mas1k], which perhaps did not originate in the Qumran community) and from the fact that the community understood itself to be the Temple of God (see particularly 1QS viii.5, viii.8–9), it is clear that the present for them is no longer devoid of salvation, as is the case in the apocalyptic literature. This is the background for the transposition of future eschatological concepts into the present that was made by the Qumran community (H.-W. Kuhn) in, for example, the community songs in 1Q Hodayot[a] (especially xi.19–23, xix.10–14), in the closing song of 1QRule of the Community (xi.7–9), and most likely also in other texts (4QWar Scroll[a] [4Q491] 11.i, particularly line 1; 4QAges of Creation 1.ii.4 and in particular also 4QHodayot[a] 7.ii [now part of 1QHodayot[a] xxvi] and 4QHodayot[e] [4Q431 1]). The Qumran community's members, upon their entrance into the community, saw themselves as having already been transported into heaven (1QHodayot[a] xi.20, and perhaps also 4QWar Scroll[a] 11.i.11). Indeed, the Qumran devotee had already experienced a new creation (1QHodayot[a] xi.21, xix.13; compare vii [formerly xv] 16–17).

With respect to the much-debated 1QHodayot[a] xi.21, on the basis of its context and the parallels with 1QHodayot[a] xi.20–23 in 1QHodayot[a] xix.10–14, it is clear that the words *yatsarta me-ʿafar* ("you have created from the dust") in xi.21 do not refer to the first creation of humanity from dust, but rather to its new creation out of what is transitory, out of an existence marked by sin. 4QHodayot[a] 7.ii.8 is now additional confirmation that what is meant by creation "from the dust" (*me-ʿafar*) in 1QHodayot[a] xi is the new creation of humanity as expressed by the phrase *wa-yarem me-ʿafar evyon le-[rum ʿolam]* ("and thus he has raised the poor man out of the dust to the [everlasting heights]"). The corresponding sayings of Jesus, however, should not be understood against a cultic backdrop. They should rather be interpreted as Jesus expressing that the coming Kingdom of God is already present in his activity.

One of the sayings of Jesus about the immediacy of the end time, *Matthew* 11.5–6 (parallels *Luke* 7.22–23), now has a parallel in 4Q521; however, this Qumran text speaks in a traditional manner only about the future. In the text from the Sayings Source (Q) that can be extrapolated from *Matthew* and *Luke*, Jesus uses words from the *Book of Isaiah* (35.5–6, 29.18–19, 26.19, 61.1) to paint a picture of the future eschatological salvation, which he understands as being already present. The high point of the recounting of the eschatological salvific events is Jesus' tidings to the poor. The Qumran manuscript (4Q521) contains the remains of a document which has been misnamed the "Messianic Apocalypse" (where *mshyḥy* [which should be read as *meshiḥay* and not as *meshiḥo*] in 2.ii.1 undoubtedly means the biblical prophets corresponding to 8.9). This text did not necessarily originate in the Qumran community. Fragment 2.ii contains two lists, which, like Q 7.22–23, use biblical sayings to describe eschatological salvation, but whose subject is God. In the first list (line 8), the correspondences with Q primarily concern healing from blindness; in the second list (lines 12ff.) 4Q521 and Q have the same sequence of the raising of the dead (*Is.* 26.19) and the preaching to the poor (*Is.* 61.1). After citing the preaching to the poor, the Qumran text continues with further matters, so that the climax of the text is different. Behind Jesus' saying and behind 4Q521 there may well stand a common Jewish tradition that describes the time of salvation.

Jesus and the Teacher of Righteousness. The external circumstances of the lives of these two individuals were very different. The Teacher of Righteousness was a priest (Pesher Psalms[a] [4Q171] iii.15; compare Pesher Habakkuk ii.8) and perhaps even the high priest (H. Stegemann), while Jesus came from a humble family. Despite this, there are some amazing correspondences between Jesus' consciousness of being sent and that of the Teacher of Righteousness. According to the so-called Songs of the Teacher in the Hodayot, God has not only made known all the mysteries of the prophets to the Teacher of Righteousness (Pesher Habakkuk vii.4–5), but God has even made him "a banner for the righteous elect" (1QHodayot[a] x [formerly ii] 13) and "a father to the children of grace" (xv [formerly vii] 20). The Teacher of Righteousness becomes a "trap for the rebellious, but healing for all those who turn from sin" (x.8–9).

This corresponds with Jesus' basically authentic saying that salvation is decided in accordance with the position that one takes with respect to him, because this will be the criterion used by the future Son of Man at the Judgment (see the older version in Q [*Lk.* 12.8–9] and in *Mark* 8.38). The cities that Jesus condemns, through his words, come under the judgment of God (*Lk.* 10.13–15, parallels *Mt.* 11.21–22). His activity is already the irruption of the Kingdom of God. This clearly goes beyond the claims of the Teacher of Righteousness.

The Teacher of Righteousness became the founder of one of the most important pious associations of the time. Jesus gathered about himself a few people from the outermost edges of Israel/Palestine. Although the Teacher of Righteousness had the "Wicked Priest" after his blood (Pesher Psalms[a] iv.8; see also Pesher Habakkuk xi.4–8), it seems that he died a natural death (at about the end of the second century BCE). Jesus, however, was evidently handed over by the authorities of his own people (according to all four canonical Gospels, through the connivance of the high priest Caiaphas), and was falsely put to death as a revolutionary by the Roman prefect of Judea, Pontius Pilate, through the ignominious punishment of crucifixion.

The Teacher of Righteousness had a major impact on his own extraordinarily well-organized Qumran community that endured for at least a century and a half (the Damascus Document vi.10–11 does not support any belief that he would return). But, while the Jews on the whole managed to overcome the catastrophes of the two revolts in the first and second centuries CE, the Teacher of Righteousness and his followers no longer played any role after the destruction of the Qumran settlement by the Romans in 68 CE, after which the whole community eventually died out. The followers of Jesus, on the other hand, after his death, began to appeal to eyewitnesses, saying that God had raised him from the dead (see particularly *1 Corinthians* 15.3–5). On the basis of Jewish categories, among other things, Christians understood Jesus as the Messiah. Using more Hellenistic categories, they saw him as the preexisting Son of God (e.g., *Philippians* 2.6–11), and the Jesus movement that had begun as a Jewish splinter group soon covered almost the whole world as it was known at that time.

BIBLIOGRAPHY

Becker, Michael. "4Q521 und die Gesalbten." *Revue de Qumrân*, forthcoming. The author shows that the messianic understanding of the text is not correct.

Berger, Klaus. *The Truth under Lock and Key? Jesus and the Dead Sea Scrolls*. Translated by James S. Currie. Louisville, Kent., 1995. The chapters on Qumran and the New Testament have to be read very critically.

Bergmeier, Roland. "Beobachtungen zu 4Q 521 f 2, II, 1–13." In *Zeitschrift der Deutschen Morgenländischen Gesellschaft* 145 (1995), 38–48.

Betz, Otto, and Rainer Riesner. *Jesus, Qumran and the Vatican: Clarifications*. New York, 1994. Giessen and Basel, 1993.

Charlesworth, James H., ed. *Jesus and the Dead Sea Scrolls*. New York, 1993, 1995. In this book covering a broad variety of aspects the papers of Charlesworth (general overview on Qumran and the historical Jesus, pp. 1–74), James G. D. Dunn (on table fellowship, pp. 254–272) and Howard C. Kee (written from a sociological point of view, pp. 104–122) are of special interest for the preceding article. Well indexed; "Selected Bibliography," pp. 333–338.

Evans, Craig A. "Appendix: The Recently Published Dead Sea Scrolls and the Historical Jesus." In *Studying the Historical Jesus*, edited by Bruce Chilton and Craig A. Evans, pp. 547–565. Leiden and New York, 1994.

Evans, Craig A. "Jesus and the Messianic Texts from Qumran: A Preliminary Assessment of the Recently Published Materials." In *Jesus and His Contemporaries: Comparative Studies* by Craig A. Evans, pp. 83–154. Leiden and New York, 1995.

Flusser, David. *Judaism and the Origins of Christianity*. Jerusalem, 1988. Several articles on Qumran and the Jesus tradition.

Jeremias, Gert. *Der Lehrer der Gerechtigkeit*. Studien zur Umwelt des Neuen Testaments, 2. Göttingen, 1963. Basic study for all further research.

Kuhn, Heinz-Wolfgang. *Enderwartung und gegenwärtiges Heil: Untersuchungen zu den Gemeindeliedern von Qumran mit einem Anhang über Eschatologie und Gegenwart in der Verkündigung Jesu*. Studien zur Umwelt des Neuen Testaments, 4. Göttingen, 1966.

Murphy-O'Connor, Jerome. "Qumran and the New Testament." In *The New Testament and Its Modern Interpreters*, edited by Eldon Jay Epp and George W. MacRae, pp. 55–71. Atlanta, Ga., 1989. On Jesus, see pages 57–60.

Söding, Thomas. "Feindeshass und Bruderliebe: Beobachtungen zur essenischen Ethik." *Revue de Qumrân* 16.64 (1995), 601–619.

Stegemann, Hartmut. "Jesus and the Teacher of Righteousness. Similarities and Differences." In *Bible Review* 10.1 (1994), 42–47.63.

Stegemann, Hartmut. *The Library of Qumran: On the Essenes, Qumran, John the Baptist and Jesus*. Grand Rapids, Mich., 1996. The author is one of the leading experts in Qumran research.

Wilcox, Max. "Jesus in the Light of his Jewish Environment." III.3: "The Essene Movement." In *Principat*, edited by Wolfgang Haase, pp. 164–169. Aufstieg und Niedergang der Römischen Welt, 2. vol. 25.1. Berlin and New York, 1982.

HEINZ-WOLFGANG KUHN

Translated from German by ROBERT E. SHILLEN

JEWELRY is among the earliest artifacts and includes practically all items used for personal adornment. Gold jewelry was considered an expression of wealth, social standing, and economic security and at the same time valued most highly as an amulet *(apotropaion)* for the living and the dead, transmitting magical power and protecting the bearer against evil. Thus, many pieces were found among grave goods. Jewish women were permitted to wear jewelry and did so especially on special occasions (e.g., as a bride) and on festivals; jewels were not worn at times of mourning.

In Hellenistic and Roman times the art of jewelry making flourished, and Alexandria in Egypt was one of the major centers. Goldsmiths created elaborate and aesthetic jewelry, combining gold with precious and semiprecious stones and colored glass. In comparison, the standard of local Judean craftmanship was moderate in forms, motifs, and techniques. Gold and silver were not readily available, so simpler versions in bronze, stone, glass, frit, and faience were used. It is nearly impossible to classify jewelry according to ethnic and religious contexts, not to mention the separate pagan, Jewish, and Christian contexts. Because of the economic situation in the late Second Temple period and afterward, the amount of jewelry unearthed is not large, particularly in Jewish areas, thus the paucity of finds in the Judean Desert.

The most common types of jewelry are necklaces, pendants, diadems, finger rings, earrings, and nose rings. The *qaṭla* (*Kel.* 11.8) is a necklace formed by pendants and strung beads of different materials. Representative is a necklace from the late second-century CE tomb in Jerusalem and one in the collection of the Ha'aretz Museum in Tel Aviv. Images for pendants include the amphora, basket, lamp, key, hand, phallus, Hercules' club, bull's head, Egyptian gods like Bes, cluster of grapes, and pomegranate. Particularly common is the crescent-shaped gold pendant (*lunula*), a motif that can be traced back to Neolithic times and has always been very popular in the Near East. In Roman imperial times it was worn by women and children and was meant to protect the bearer against evil spirits and to guarantee life and prosperity. The hoard from Beth-Guvrin–Eleutheropolis, buried during the Bar Kokhba Revolt, contained two chain necklaces with crescent pendants. In addition, a spherical, bell-shaped silver pendant from the Cave of the Letters was found together with beads.

A miniature soft-stone pendant from a Jerusalem tomb proves to be unusual; the material from which it was made was not susceptible to ritual impurity. The diadem from a third-century CE burial at Kefar Giladi (northern Israel) is made of a band of thin-ribbed gold foil with nine applied gems of stone, glass, and mother-of-pearl. It is a good example of Roman polychrome style. Finger rings of gold, silver, bronze, and iron are very common, depending on the wealth of the owner. Several bronze and iron rings from Cave 4 at Murabba'at are either plain or engraved. Precious gold rings carry gems with figures and scenes in miniature carving known as intaglio (i.e., engraved into the surface and thus giving the impression of a stamp). The known rings from the first century BCE to the third century CE bear classical motifs with magical and religious significance; they were personal seals or amulets. In Jewish sources the finger ring *('etsba' shel taba'at)* was separated into two classifications: rings with seals *(ṭaba'ot ḥotam)* were worn by men and used for sealing documents; the rings without seals were considered women's jewels (B.T., *Shab.* 59.2).

Earrings display quite a variety of shapes. Hoop- and boat-shaped earrings were made by beating gold foil over a core made of paste and were sometimes decorated with stones and rows or clusters of granulation (the application of minute grains of gold directly to the sheet metal). This type is represented in the Beth-Guvrin–Eleutheropolis hoard. A ceramic mold for mass-producing earrings consisting of a hoop with two concentric rows of globules came to light in the City of David excavations in Jerusalem predating the city's destruction in 70 CE. In Jerusalem several pairs occur in male burials of the early third century. Since at that time only women wore earrings in the Near East, the deceased must have been Roman legionaries whose wives placed the jewels as grave offerings. A pair of earrings from another third-century CE tomb in Jerusalem belongs to the so-called shield-cross-bar-and-pendant type, which continues a widespread Hellenistic group. The shield is an openwork circular frame of lotus blossoms, holding a female head in chalcedony. Three movable pendants of pearls and glass beads hang from a horizontal bar. Simpler and popular Eastern Mediterranean versions are crescent-shaped earrings with movable pendants and those consisting of a convex shield with one or two pendants. These types occur in the Beth-Guvrin hoard and in Ketef Hinnom to the west of Jerusalem. A pair of basket-shaped earrings from a tomb at Hamat-Tiberias of the second–third century CE is decorated with minute rosettes in filigree, a technique in which wires in the shape of the decorative elements are soldered to pieces of sheet gold.

The custom of wearing nose rings is known: on Shabbat Jewish women were not permitted to go out "with a necklace or nose ring or with a ring that bears no seal or with a needle that has no eye" (B.T., *Shab.* 6.1). Gold nose rings were identified at Mampsis and Oboda in the Negev and at Petra in Nabatean contexts. Needles were considered jewelry when used as hairpins (B.T., *Shab.* 60.a): some of these found in the Judean Desert caves could have been used in this way. In a wider sense, personal items such as mirrors, combs, and cosmetic articles related to eye makeup can be counted among female jewelry and are treated as such in Jewish writings. A rectangular box with a vaulted top and a sliding lid at the bottom, found in the Cave of the Letters, could have been used as a jewelry box.

Most of the items described here are of local workmanship, although individual workshops have not yet been identified; however, the number of ceramic and stone molds for casting jewelry found in nonstratified contexts is relatively large and needs further study.

BIBLIOGRAPHY

Barkay, Gabriel. *Ketef Hinnom: A Treasure Facing Jerusalem's Walls*. Exhibition Catalog, Israel Museum. Jerusalem, 1986. Earrings from Roman-period burials.

Benoit, P., J. T. Milik, and R. de Vaux. *Les grottes de Murabba'at*. Discoveries in the Judaean Desert, 2. Oxford, 1961.

Rahmani, L. Y. "Jewish Rock-Cut Tombs in Jerusalem." *'Atiqot* 3 (1961), 93–120. For the soft-stone pendant, see page 104 and plate XIII:7, right.

Rahmani, L. Y. "A Roman Tomb at Manahat, Jerusalem." *Israel Exploration Journal* 27 (1977), 209–214. Jewelry and ethnic identification.

Rosenthal, Renate. *Jewellery in Ancient Times*. London, 1973. A popular presentation of several important finds, including Nabatean jewelry.

Rosenthal-Heginbottom, Renate. "Two Jewelry Moulds." In *Excavations at the City of David 1978–1985 Directed by Yigal Shiloh III* (Qedem 33), edited by A. De Groot and D. T. Ariel, pp. 275–278. Jerusalem, 1992.

Yadin, Yigael. *The Finds from the Bar Kokhba Period in the Cave of the Letters*. Jerusalem, 1963. For the pendant, see page 92, for the beads, page 115, and for the box, pages 123–124.

Zevulun, Uza, and Yael Olenik. *Function and Design in the Talmudic Period*. Exhibition Catalog, Haaretz Museum. Tel Aviv, 1978. Some jewelry finds and literary references.

RENATE ROSENTHAL-HEGINBOTTOM

JEWISH CHRISTIANS. Discussions of Jewish Christians (not a term used in the ancient sources, except once in Jerome [*Zach.* 3.14.9]) and Jewish Christianity have been plagued by problems of definition. An adequate definition must recognize that the distinctiveness of so-called Jewish Christians lies in the fact they were both Jews and Christians and must take account of their evolving relationships both to other Jews and to other Christians over the four centuries (first through fourth centuries CE) in which something of their history can be traced. Definition by means of a particular set of beliefs is impossible, since, while all Jewish Christian groups differed from non-Christian Jews in the status they attributed to Jesus (though not all Jewish Christian groups had the same kind of Christology), doctrinal beliefs cannot distinguish Jewish Christians from other Christians. Some Jewish Christians (those whom Epiphanius calls "Nazoreans") did not differ in beliefs from the "catholic" Christians of their time. [*See* Epiphanius.] What distinguished them, as well as other Jewish Christian groups, from other Christians were their Jewish observances.

So Jewish Christians should be defined as Jews who held Jesus to be the Messiah (or some equivalent term) and also continued to live as Jews, observing Torah. By their observance of circumcision, Sabbath, dietary laws, and purity regulations, they maintained their Jewish identity, unlike Christians of Jewish ethnic origin who gave up observing Torah. Thus Christology distinguished them from other Jews; Torah observance distinguished them from other Christians. Their identity as both Christians and Jews, which increasingly led to their being disowned as Christians by other Christians and as Jews by other Jews, means that the term Christian Jews should be regarded as just as appropriate as the more usual Jewish Christians. Considering them more Christian than Jewish or more Jewish than Christian depends on perspectives that define Christianity in non-Jewish terms or define Judaism in non-Christian terms. This was what other Jews and other Christians did in the process of marginalizing and disowning Jewish Christians (cf. Jerome, *Epistle* 112.3: "since they want to be both Jews and Christians, they are neither Jews nor Christians"), but in their own self-understanding their identity as both Jews and Christians was unproblematic.

History and Character. In the earliest period, up to the fall of Jerusalem in 70 CE, most Christians of Jewish origin were, according to our definition, Jewish Christians. They retained their Jewish identity by observing Torah. There are few indications of debate about observance of Torah by Jews within the Christian movement in this period. (This was a quite different issue from, and should not be confused with, the question of whether gentile Christians should observe Torah, which was debated.) The Jerusalem church in particular, along with other Jewish Christians visiting Jerusalem, maintained its clearly Jewish identity by continuing to participate in the worship at the Temple, so that the destruction of the Temple was a factor in the growing marginalization of Jewish Christians with respect to the rest of Judaism in the post–70 period. This marginalization and, subsequently, separation accompanied the growing dominance of rabbinic Judaism and the marginalization of all other forms of Judaism. In this process Jewish Christians were disowned not only because of their Christology and their association with gentile Christianity, but also because they did not follow rabbinic *halakhah* in their observance of Torah. Their alienation from other Jews can probably also be associated with their geographical location: From the second century onward there seem to have been rather few Jewish Christians in Palestine west of the Jordan, while their main concentrations were in areas to the east of the Jordan, the northeastern parts of Palestine and Syria.

That Jewish and Christian identity were incompatible became not only the general Jewish view but also, from the second century onward, the general Christian view. Justin Martyr (c.100–163/165) advocated full fellowship with Jewish Christians who continued to observe the Torah, unless they tried to persuade gentile Christians to do the same, but admitted that this tolerance was not shared by all gentile Christians in his time (*Dialogue with Trypho* 47.1–2). After his time it was rare. The view that came to prevail was that observing the Torah was incompatible with belief in Jesus Christ. Probably most Christians of Jewish ethnic origin lost their Jewish identity, and those who continued to observe the Torah were confined to sectarian groups regarded as schismatic or even heretical by the gentile church. Epiphanius, who knows of no heretical beliefs he can ascribe to the Nazoreans, as he can to other Jewish Christian groups, nevertheless calls them "nothing but Jews" (*Panarion* 29.9.1), cursed by God for their vain attempt to observe the Law (29.8.1–7).

The nature and origins of the various different Jewish Christian groups are debatable. The Nazoreans or Nazarenes should probably be seen as the most direct heirs of the earliest Jerusalem church. [*See* Nazoreans.] Their beliefs, including the virginal conception and divinity of Jesus, were orthodox by the standards of catholic Christianity, and they even took a positive view of the Pauline mission. Though the church fathers sometimes seem to have called all Jewish Christians Ebionites, the term should more properly be applied to a form of Jewish Christianity which, diverging from the Nazarenes, adopted positions that were less orthodox from both mainstream Christian and Jewish perspectives. [*See* Ebionites.] Their Christology had no place for the virginal conception and divinity of Jesus, while their acceptance of the Torah was strongly qualified by a rejection of the sacrificial cultus. Their bitter polemic against Paul no doubt reflects catholic Christianity's interpretation of Paul as disallowing Torah observance by Christians. The divergence between Nazorean and Ebionite forms of Jewish Christianity may derive from the schism in Palestinian Jewish Christianity, which, according to Hegesippus, occurred at the time of the election of Simeon as second bishop of Jerusalem (quoted in Eusebius, *Ecclesiastical History* 4.22.4–5). The distinctively Ebionite critique of sacrifice is probably a response to the destruction of the Temple. Ebionism thus would have developed east of the Jordan in the period after 70 CE, but it may have taken several forms. The fragments of the *Gospel of the Ebionites* portray Jesus as condemning and abolishing sacrifices and reflect the Ebionite prohibition against eating meat. The Jewish Christian source in the Pseudo-Clementine *Recognitions* 1.27–71 seems Ebionite in regarding sacrifices as a Mosaic concession to Israel which Jesus came to abolish, but it does not engage in the more radical criticism of the Hebrew scriptures or in the speculative elaboration of the idea of the True Prophet that is characteristic of the more certainly Ebionite material in Pseudo-Clementine literature. The Elkesaites, [*See* Pseudo-Clementine Literature.] who also rejected sacrifice, can plausibly be seen as originating from the Ebionite movement at an early stage of its history. [*See* Elkesaites.]

The Dead Sea Scrolls and Jewish Christians. A number of scholars, beginning with J. L. Teicher, soon after the first publication of scrolls, have identified the Qumran sect with a Jewish Christian group. The mere fact that none of the scrolls refers to Jesus, whereas all Jewish Christian literature of which we know does, is sufficient to discredit such a view. More plausible are theories that explain the parallels and resemblances between the scrolls and what is known of Jewish Christianity by postulating the Essene origin of the scrolls and a greater or lesser degree of Essene influence on Jewish Christianity. Such theories can be divided into two types: those that postulate Essene influence on the early Jerusalem church (and therefore depend largely on the New Testament's evidence about early Jewish Christianity) and those that postulate Essene influence on Jewish Christian groups at a later stage in order to explain certain features of such groups according to the patristic evidence. Sometimes it has been argued that significant numbers of Essenes became Christians in the period after the destruction of the Qumran settlement, with the result that either Ebionism (Cullmann, 1954, pp. 35–51; Daniélou, 1964, pp. 55–64) or Elkesaitism (Reeves, 1996, pp. 47–48) can be seen as essentially a sort of Essene Christianity. [*See* Elkesaites.]

Qumran and the Early Jerusalem Church. There are a number of important parallels between the Qumran community and the early Jerusalem church.

Both groups saw themselves as the true Israel of the last days. But whereas the Essenes understood this in an exclusive, sectarian sense, the first Jewish Christians more probably understood themselves as the beginning of the messianic renewal of Israel, which potentially included all Israel.

Both groups applied the image of the temple of God to their own community and are the only two Jewish groups known to have done so. This theme, which is widespread in early Christian literature, can be traced back to the early Jerusalem church by means of *Galatians* 2.9, which reports that James, Peter, and John were known as "pillars." This identification of leaders of the community with specific architectural features of the new temple can be paralleled in Pesher Isaiah[d] (4Q164) and by the reference in Pesher Psalms[a] (4Q171) to the Teacher of Righteousness as the pillar of the building that is the community.

Two differences should be noted. The early church probably saw itself as the messianic temple of the eschatological age, whereas the Qumran sect saw itself functioning as a temple only until the building of the eschatological temple in Jerusalem. Secondly, whereas the Qumran community boycotted the Jerusalem Temple, the Jerusalem church continued to worship in it (*Acts* 2.46). This again shows the Jewish Christians to be less sectarian in relation to the rest of Judaism than the Qumran community was.

Each group referred to itself or its way of life as "the Way" (Rule of the Community from Cave 1 at Qumran 1QS viii.13–14; ix.17–18, x.20–21; *Acts* 9.2), probably both in dependence on *Isaiah* 40.3. However, the Qumran interpretation of this as the study and practice of Torah (1QS viii.15–16) differs from the Christian usage.

Both groups practiced a community of goods (*Acts* 2.44–45, 4.32–5.11; 1QS vi.19–20, vi.22, vi.24–25) and are the only two Palestinian Jewish groups known to have done so. How close the resemblance is is debatable, but similarities of organization have been argued (Capper, 1995, pp. 323–356). Both groups also practiced common meals (*Acts* 2.42, 2.46; 1QS vi.4–5). In addition, both groups engaged in the *pesher* exegesis characteristic of the Qumran commentaries (Ellis, 1978; R. Bauckham, 1990, chap. 4). The role of the Twelve in the Jerusalem church can be compared with that of the ruling group of twelve in the Qumran community (1QS viii.1).

Qumran and the Ebionites. Three resemblances have been observed between the Qumran community and the Ebionites. First, the name of the Ebionites (meaning "the poor") is paralleled by the occasional use of "the poor" as a self-description by the community in the Dead Sea Scrolls (4Q171 2.9–10, 3.10; War Scroll 1QM xi.9, xi.13, xiii.12–14). Second, there are some resemblances between the dualism of the Qumran texts and that attributed to the Ebionites by Epiphanius (*Panarion* 30.16) and found in the Ebionite sources of the Pseudo-Clementines, but there are also significant differences. Finally, both groups practiced frequent ritual ablutions, but the widespread popularity of ritual purification in late Second Temple Judaism makes this resemblance less remarkable. [*See* Epiphanius.]

Against these resemblances must be set major differences. Unparalleled at Qumran are the Ebionites' abstention from wine and meat, their radical rejection of the sacrificial cultus as not commanded by God, their rejection of the "false pericopes" in the Pentateuch, and their rejection of the Prophets. These make any significant Essene influence on Ebionism implausible. If a particular Jewish sectarian influence accounts for the special character of Ebionism, the Nazarenes (a non-Christian Jewish group described by Epiphanius [*Panarion* 18]) should be considered a more likely candidate, since they rejected sacrifice, abstained from meat, were critical of the Pentateuch, and lived in Transjordan.

[*See also* Essenes; Nazoreans.]

BIBLIOGRAPHY

Alexander, Philip S. "'The Parting of the Ways' from the Perspective of Rabbinic Judaism." In *Jews and Christians: The Parting of the Ways A.D. 70 to 135*, edited by J. D. G. Dunn, pp. 1–25. Wissenschaftliche Untersuchungen zum Neuen Testament, 66. Tübingen, 1992. On Jewish Christians from the rabbinic perspective.

Bauckham, Richard. *Jude and the Relatives of Jesus in the Early Church.* Edinburgh, 1990. See chapter four.

Betz, Otto, and Rainer Riesner. *Jesus, Qumran and the Vatican: Clarifications*. Translated by John Bowden. London, 1994. Accessible and critical discussion of arguments for connections between Qumran and early Jewish Christianity.

Capper, B. "The Palestine Cultural Context of Earliest Christian Community of Goods." In *The Book of Acts in Its Palestinian Setting*, edited by Richard Bauckham, pp. 323–356. The Book of Acts in the First Century Setting, 4. Grand Rapids, 1995.

Cullmann, O. "Die neuentdeckten Qumrantexte und das Judenchristentum der Pseudoklementinen." In *Neutestamentliche Studien für Rudolf Bultmann.* Beihefte zur Zeitschrift für die neutestamentliche Wissenschaft, 21, pp. 35–51. Berlin, 1954.

Daniélou, J. *The Theology of Jewish Christianity*. Translated by J. A. Baker. London, 1964. See pp. 55–64.

Ellis, E. E. *Prophecy and Hermeneutic in Early Christianity*. Wissenschaftliche Untersuchungen zum Neuen Testament, 18. Tübingen, 1978.

Fitzmyer, Joseph A. "Jewish Christianity in Acts in the Light of the Qumran Scrolls." In *Essays on the Semitic Background of the New Testament*, pp. 271–303. London, 1971. Careful examination of the case for influence.

Fitzmyer, Joseph A. "The Qumran Scrolls, the Ebionites, and their Literature." In *Essays on the Semitic Background of the New Testament*, pp. 435–480. London, 1971.

Grego, Igino. *I Giudeo-Cristiani nel IV Secolo: reazione-influssi*. Jerusalem, 1982. A study of all the later patristic evidence.

Klijn, A. F. J., and G. J. Reinink. *Patristic Evidence for Jewish-Christian Sects.* Supplements to Novum Testamentum, 36. Leiden, 1973. Collection of the patristic texts.

Mimouni, Simon C. "Pour une définition nouvelle du Judéo-christianisme ancien." *New Testament Studies* 38 (1992), 161–186. Important for definition.

Pritz, Ray A. *Nazarene Jewish Christianity.* Leiden and Jerusalem, 1988. The only detailed study that correctly distinguishes Nazarenes from Ebionites.

Reeves, J. C. *Heralds of That Good Realm: Syro-Mesopotamian Gnosis and Jewish Traditions.* Nag Hammadi and Manichean Studies, 41. Leiden, 1996. See pages 47–48.

Riesner, R. "Das Jerusalemer Essenerviertel und das Urgemeinde." In *Aufstieg und Niedergang der römischen Welt*, vol. 2. 26/2. Berlin, 1995.

RICHARD BAUCKHAM

JOB, BOOK OF. Four fragmentary manuscripts from Qumran Caves 2 and 4 preserve portions of the book of *Job*. The Cave 2 Job (2Q15), a manuscript written in Herodian script, is represented by only a single fragment, containing portions of five words. Despite the small size, the fragment can be securely identified as containing material from Job 33:28–30, part of Elihu's speech. 4QJob[a] (4Q99) and Job[b] (4Q100), are written in Hasmonean scripts and consist of twenty-two and six fragments, respectively. 4QJob[a] preserves parts of Job 31.14–19, 32.3–4, 33.10–11, 24–26, 28–30, 35.16, 36.7–11, 13–27, 32–33, 37.1–5, 14–15. The fragments of 4QJob[b] preserve parts of *Job* 8.15–17, 9.27, 13.4, 14.4–6, 31.20–21. The text of 4QJob[a] is written stichometrically, each line usually containing two cola. In several instances Job[a] differs from the Masoretic Text, including divergences in orthography, grammatical forms, and readings. Although these manuscripts contain relatively little of the text of the book of *Job*, they provide evidence that the Elihu speeches (*Job* 32–37), which many scholars consider to be a secondary part of the composition, were part of the book by the turn of the era.

The most interesting manuscript is Paleo-Job[c] (4Q101), written in Paleo-Hebrew script. Three fragments of this manuscript survive, containing portions of *Job* 13.18–20, 23–27, 14.13–18. Although Paleo-Hebrew texts are difficult to date, Paleo-Job[c] has been estimated to come from some time in the period 225–150 BCE, probably toward the earlier part of the period (McLean, 1982, p. 52). The text was written stichometrically, each line beginning with a new stich. Typical of Paleo-Hebrew manuscripts, dots or strokes serve as word dividers within each line. Since the great majority of manuscripts written in Paleo-Hebrew are books of the Torah, it is somewhat surprising to find the book of *Job* written in Paleo-Hebrew. Perhaps, as the editor of Paleo-Job[c] suggests, the use of Paleo-Hebrew script reflects the tradition that Moses wrote the book of Job (see B.T., *B.B.*, 14b, 15a). The orthography of Paleo-Job[c] is more conservative than that of the Masoretic Text, using no internal *matres lectionis* (consonantal letters which indicate the presence of a vowel). In other respects it appears to preserve the same text as the Masoretic Text, with only one or two minor variations.

In addition to the four Hebrew manuscripts of *Job* the Qumran caves have also yielded two copies of an Aramaic *targum* ("translation") of *Job*, a text known as Targum of Job (4Q157), which preserves in Aramaic translation only *Job* 3.5–9, 4.16–5.4, and the much more extensive Targum of Job from Cave 11 (11Q10), which preserves portions of the text from *Job* 17–42. The script of the Cave 11 Targum of Job dates from the early first century CE, although the date of the translation may be earlier. This Targum of Job appears to have been translated from a text closely similar to the Masoretic Text, with most divergences appearing to be the result of the translator's attempt to produce a clear and understandable translation. The end of the *targum*, however, differs significantly from the Masoretic Text both in detail and in extent, the *targum* ending with lines which correspond to *Job* 42.9–11, whereas the Masoretic Text continues on to 42.17. [*See* Job, Targum of.]

BIBLIOGRAPHY

Baillet, M., J. T. Milik, and R. de Vaux, *Les 'Petites Grottes' de Qumrân*, Discoveries in the Judaean Desert, 3. Oxford, 1962.

McLean, M. D. "The Use and Development of Palaeo-Hebrew in the Hellenistic and Roman Period." Ph.D. diss, Harvard University, 1982.

Skehan, P. W., E. Ulrich, and J. E. Sanderson. *Qumran Cave 4, IV: Palaeo-Hebrew and Greek Biblical Manuscripts*. Discoveries in the Judaean Desert, 9. Oxford, 1992.

CAROL A. NEWSOM

JOB, TARGUM OF. Among the Dead Sea Scrolls, remains of two manuscripts of a Targum of Job were discovered, one in Cave 4 at Qumran (4Q157), the other in Cave 11 (11Q10). Only two fragments from Cave 4 (hereafter, 4QTargum of Job), dating to the middle of the first century CE, have survived. Frg. 2 is so small that its contents cannot be identified, although it is known that it comes from the same manuscript. Frg. 1 shows the remains of two columns and contains text portions that virtually correspond to passages from *Job* 3.5–6 and 4.17–5.4.

About 15 percent of the original text of the Targum of Job from Cave 11 (hereafter, 11QTargum of Job), has survived. Discovered by the bedouin in 1956, the rights to study and publish the document were procured from the Palestine Archaeological Museum in 1961 by the Royal Dutch Academy of Sciences and Arts, which entrusted its editing to J. P. M. van der Ploeg and A. S. van der Woude. The Aramaic text of the document, written in an elegant Herodian script from the first decades of the first century CE, is a fairly faithful rendering of its biblical base text, allowing the conclusion that the complete scroll measured about 7 meters (23 feet) by 12–13 centimeters (5 inches) and contained about sixty-eight columns of sixteen or seventeen lines. In its present state, the end of the manuscript, containing portions of ten columns (11Q10 xxix–xxxviii) corresponding to passages from *Job* 37.10–42.11, is still in the form of a fragmentary scroll 109 by 4 to 6 centimeters (43 by 2 inches) in size (the lost bottom of column xxxviii and the top of column xxxix may have contained a paraphrase of *Job* 42.12–17).

Twenty-three tiny fragments (A 1–5, B–C, D 1–2, E–R), which contain only a few letters each, also derive from this "small scroll." From the preceding section of the document only twenty-eight fragments deriving from twenty-nine columns (including the fragment published by B. Zuckerman and S. A. Reed, 1993) remain, the text of which corresponds to passages from *Job* 17.14–26.33. Because the beginning of the manuscript is lost we do not know whether 11QTargum of Job belonged to the same work as 4QTargum of Job.

It is extremely difficult to state precisely when the original text of the Targum of Job was composed. The exegetical traditions used by the translator lack specific elements for dating their provenance, and, despite some assertions to the contrary, there are no clear indications of a sectarian origin for the work. Linguistic criteria may point to a date between the final redaction of the *Book of Daniel* (about 165 BCE) and the Genesis Apocryphon (1QapGen), which probably was composed in the first half of the first century BCE. The origin of the text of 11QTargum of Job must therefore in all likelihood be dated to the last decades of the second century BCE or a bit later. For linguistic reasons, T. Muraoka has, however, argued for an earlier origin (between 250 and 150 BCE) by asserting that the Targum is of Babylonian, not Palestinian, provenance (there is also use of some Persian loanwords).

The base text used by the interpreter for his Aramaic rendition was almost the same as the Hebrew tradition of the *Book of Job* known to us from the Masoretic Text. The conspicuous omissions and transpositions that are characteristic of the Septuagint version of the *Book of Job* are not found in the Targum, although in a number of cases its translation concurs with the Greek text. Over and against the singular of the Hebrew base text, 11QTargum of Job sometimes has a plural (especially in the case of collective nouns) or the other way around. Now and then a vocalization of the Hebrew consonantal text, which differs from later tradition, seems to be presupposed. In other cases the Aramaic rendition tries to clarify biblical passages by adding certain elements, for example, pronouns. The hermeneutical principles that guided the interpreter manifest themselves in a number of cases. He shows a certain inclination toward rationalization (cf. 11Q10 xxx.4 [= *Job* 38.7]), where the morning stars are said "to have shone" instead of "to have sung." In the translation the base text is often changed in order to accentuate God's sovereignty and omnipotence (e.g.,

11Q10 x.2 [= *Job* 26.11a], 11Q10 xxiv.7 [= *Job* 34.13], and in particular 11Q10 xxvi.8 [= *Job* 35.13a], where the interpreter, in contrast to the Hebrew text, states that the omnipresent God hears vanity). Special stress is laid on God's creative power (e.g., the elaboration of the Hebrew base text in 11Q10 xxix.2–3 [= *Job* 37.12]). Sometimes passages that might infringe on God's majesty are changed (cf. 11Q10 xxxiv.4, *Job* 40.8). In other cases words are omitted because the translator considered their contents shocking (cf. 11Q10 xviii.3, where the second part of *Job* 31.10 is left untranslated). Sometimes the rendition seems to forestall false interpretations and to prevent erroneous exegetical conclusions.

Most conspicuous from a hermeneutical point of view is the way in which Job is presented as a knowing and righteous man. Over and against the biblical text of *Job* 42.6, where Job is depicted as repenting because, in spite of the righteousness of his cause, he failed to recognize God's overpowering sovereignty, in the interpreter's rendition (11Q10 xxxvii.8–9), Job remains the innocent sufferer ("I am poured out and fall to pieces, and I become dust and ashes").

Except for the small fragments of the Targum of Leviticus (4Q156; about 100 BCE), 11QTargum of Job is the oldest *targum* we possess. It proves that Aramaic paraphrases of biblical texts were in existence well before the Common Era. In this respect, the reference in the Jerusalem (J.T., *Shab.* 15c) and Babylonian Talmuds (B.T., *Shab.* 115a) to an Aramaic *Book of Job*, which at the command of Rabban Gamli'el the Elder (who flourished between 25 and 50 CE) was hidden by a mason under a layer of stones in the Temple area, is noteworthy, although we cannot be sure that the contents of this text were identical with the text of 11QTargum of Job. It is certain however, that 11QTargum of Job has nothing to do with the later rabbinic Targum of Job.

The Targum of Job from Cave 11 is important because it sheds light on the history of the *targums*, presents us with linguistic data about written Aramaic at the beginning of the Common Era, and offers us some aid in the field of textual criticism of the book in question. But its main significance is to be sought in the hermeneutical principles that guided the interpretation of a biblical text in early Jewish circles.

[*See also* Aramaic; Targumim.]

BIBLIOGRAPHY

Aufrecht, W. E. "A Bibliography of Job Targumim." *Newsletter for Targumic and Cognate Studies*, Supplement 3 (1987), 1–13.

Brownlee, William H. "The Cosmic Role of Angels in 11QTargum of Job." *Journal for the Study of Judaism* 8 (1977), 83–84. On column 29.

García Martínez, Florentino, Eibert J. C. Tigchelaar, and Adam S. van der Woude. *Qumran Cave 11. II. 11Q2–18 11Q20–31*. Discoveries in the Judaean Desert, 23. Oxford, 1998. See pages 79–180.

Muraoka, Takamitsu. "The Aramaic of the Old Targum of Job from Qumran Cave XI." *Journal of Jewish Studies* 25 (1974), 425–443. Early dating of the *targum*, which in the author's opinion originates from Babylonia.

Muraoka, Takamitsu. "Notes on the Old Targum of Job from Qumran Cave XI." *Revue de Qumrân* 9 (1977–1978), 117–125.

Ploeg, J. P. M. van der, A. S. van der Woude, in collaboration with Bastiaan Jongeling. *Le targum de Job de la grotte XI de Qumran*. Leiden, 1971. *Editio princeps*.

Puech, Émile, and Florentino García Martínez. "Remarques sur la colonne XXXVIII de 11QtgJob." *Revue de Qumrân* 9 (1977–1978), 401–407.

Sokoloff, Michael. *The Targum to Job from Qumran Cave XI*. Bar-Ilan Studies in Near Eastern Languages and Culture. Ramat-Gan, 1974. A thorough introduction to the language of the *targum* and a new annotated text edition.

Zuckerman, Bruce, and S. A. Reed. "A Fragment of an Unstudied Column of 11QgJob. A Preliminary Report." *The Comprehensive Aramaic Lexicon Newsletter* 10 (1993), 1–7.

ADAM S. VAN DER WOUDE

JOEL, BOOK OF. *See* Minor Prophets.

JOHN, GOSPEL AND LETTERS OF. The Dead Sea Scrolls cast general light on Judaism in the last two centuries BCE and the first century CE and thus on the writings of the Christian community that emerged from Judaism. However, to investigate the specific relationship of the scrolls to one group of those writings, we must lay aside as too imprecise, incidental, or implausible some of the similarities that are cited in the literature comparing the scrolls to *John*. For instance, the scrolls illustrate Jewish messianic expectations and the use of "son of god," but none of that applies exclusively to Johannine usage. For the community hero, an honorific title rather than a personal name is used both by the scrolls (the Teacher of Righteousness) and John (the disciple whom Jesus loved), but that could be pure coincidence. The Copper Scroll (3Q15 xi.12–13) speaks of Bet 'Eshdatayin, seemingly the pool of Bethesda (*Jn.* 5.2); and Temple Scroll[a] (11Q19 l.10–16) warns that a house is rendered ritually impure once an unclean person has entered, supplying background for the fear that entering Pilate's praetorium might bring contamination (*Jn.* 18.28). Yet, such incidental background does not establish a Johannine relationship to the scrolls.

Moving on to factors that could plausibly establish a specific relationship, the discussion is affected by presuppositions about both sets of writings. As for the Dead Sea Scrolls, the following positions are not seriously objectionable and will be assumed. Although the community at Qumran probably consisted of Essenes, a neutral designation is the neologism "Qumranians." The main Qumran compositions with which we shall be concerned date from the second and first centuries BCE, particularly the

Rule of the Community of Qumran Cave 1 (hereafter, 1QRule of the Community, 1QS) and the Damascus Document (CD). (In the instance of 1QRule of the Community, it should be noted that in the many Cave 4 copies that may be earlier than the Cave 1 scroll, the key dualistic two-spirits passage of column iii is not found. If that absence is not by chance, it may tell us that strong dualism developed only later.) In these basic scrolls there is no evidence of a knowledge of Christianity or of quotations from the New Testament. Therefore, the possible influence would have been from Qumran to *John*, not vice versa.

As for the Johannine writings, it is not easy to list positions that might be unobjectionable and assumed, for there is a great deal of dispute. Despite attempts at early dating, most scholars would date the *Gospel of John* to the 90s CE (with a possible final editing between 100 and 110 CE) and the three Johannine Epistles to approximately 100 CE following the Gospel (but perhaps preceding the final editing). Traditionally, the author has been identified as John, son of Zebedee and one of the Twelve Apostles, who was thought to have been "the disciple whom Jesus loved," an unnamed figure who appears in the second half of the Gospel (*Jn*. 13–21). Now, however, the majority view would probably distinguish that disciple (who may have been the source of Johannine tradition about Jesus) and the evangelist (even if he was a follower of the disciple), and leave both unidentified. Often, different authorship is posited for the Epistles, so that a Johannine school of writers is envisioned. The traditional place of composition, Ephesus, continues to have many supporters, but frequently with the qualification that the tradition-bearers and parts of the Johannine community had moved there from Palestine or adjacent Syria where the early stages of the tradition behind the Gospel had taken shape.

Although *John* shares some outline and content similarities with the synoptic Gospels, it is unique among the four in content, style, and thought patterns. As for the similarities, did the evangelist know the other Gospels or, simply, was a general approach to Jesus also known to them, and Mark in particular? Do the differences have a root in genuine tradition about Jesus or are they the product of external Hellenistic influences on the evangelist and/or his tradition, for example, Gnosticism? A significant body of scholars contends that amid the diversity of pre-70 CE Judaism in Palestine, Jews of Jerusalem provenance, different from the Galileans who made up the Twelve, came into the following of Jesus during his lifetime and subsequently shaped a tradition about him. It was partially similar to the tradition found in the Synoptics but basically independent. How might Qumran Judaism have been an element in this picture?

The Johannine writings contain no clear quotation from a Qumran document and no reference to the Qumran community history. Therefore, the discussion has to concentrate on possible contacts in ideas and vocabulary. Many suggested parallels are attractive but quite speculative. For instance, the presence at Qumran of the Temple Scroll and various calendars of feasts has been related to the emphatic and early position of the cleansing of the Temple in *John* (2.13–22), the stress that Jesus' risen body is the replacement for the earthly Temple, and the framework of feasts that holds together chapters 5–12. 1QRule of the Community (1QS ix.11) speaks of "the coming of a prophet and the Messiahs of Aaron and Israel [i.e., priestly and Davidic messiahs]"; and the Messianic Apocalypse (4Q521 2.1, 2.5, 5.6), which speaks of the Messiah without further qualification, has the Lord calling the just by name and making the dead of his people rise. The Johannine Jesus is thought to be the prophet (6.14, 7.40), the Messiah (1.41, 4.25–26), and perhaps a high priest (17.19, 19.23–24); he calls his sheep by name (10.30), and when those in the tombs hear his voice they will come forth (5.28–29). Wisdom Text with Beatitudes, in a context of beatitudes, presents a personified Wisdom who is juxtaposed to the Law; John's Jesus, who is a greater gift than the Mosaic Law (4Q525 1.17), is God's word and wisdom made flesh. Nevertheless, one could explain most parallels of this type overall by invoking themes in the protocanonical and deuterocanonical Old Testament; the parallels show Jewish influence on *John* but are not precise enough to establish scroll influence on the book.

In fact, there is only one major area of relatively precise similarity, and so most of the comparison will center on dualism and its corollaries. The more speculative question of the channel of any direct or indirect influence will be raised at the end.

Modified Dualism. Theological dualism pictures the universe under the dominion of two opposing principles—one good, the other evil; modified dualism adds that such principles are dependent on a God who is over all. In the Old Testament there is no dominant, systematic dualism, even though there are evil agents (such as the tempter of *Genesis* 3) and evil people who are opposed to good people. In the Qumran literature (and related noncanonical works written in the last centuries BCE), we find a new outlook. All human beings are aligned in two opposing camps, one of light and truth and the other of darkness and falsehood, with each faction ruled by a spirit or prince. This is not a physical dualism wherein the nonmaterial is good and the material is evil; rather, it is ethical and cosmic. Although the synoptic Gospels portray Jesus in conflict with the devil or demons who possess people, *John* more clearly articulates a cosmic struggle between Jesus and the Prince of this world. The language in which Qumran documents and *John* express dualism is remarkably the same: light and darkness, truth and falsehood; Spirit of Truth and falsehood (see below); children of light and darkness (1QS i.9–10, iii.13, xiii.24, xiii.25; *Jn.* 12.36); those who walk in light and darkness (1QS iii.20, iv.11, xi.10; *Jn.* 8.12, 12.35; *1 Jn.* 1.6–7, 2.11); or walk in truth or falsehood (1QS iv.6, 15; *2 Jn.* 4; *3 Jn.* 3–4); do truth/falsehood (1QS i.5, v.3, viii.2; *Jn.* 3.21; *1 Jn.* 1.6; [3.18]); witness to truth (1QS viii.6; *Jn.* 5.33, 18.37; *3 Jn.* 3); purge or sanctify truth (1QS iv.20; *Jn.* 17.17). Some of these expressions occur elsewhere in the New Testament, but not with Johannine frequency.

Both Qumran and John take for granted the biblical doctrine of creation. 1QRule of the Community reads, "From the God of knowledge exists all that is and will be" (1QS iii.15) and "By his knowledge everything has been brought into being" (1QS xi.11). (Compare this passage to *John* 1.3: "Through him [the Word] all things came into being, and apart from him not a thing came to be.") In particular, 1QRule of the Community (1QS iii.17–25) teaches that God created the spirits of light and darkness and that human beings will walk by these spirits of truth and deceit until the moment of God's visitation. Visions of Amram[b] (4Q544 1.12) makes it clear that people choose between the rulers of light and darkness; the sons of light go to everlasting happiness, and the sons of darkness to annihilation (4Q548 1.12–14). In the hand of the Prince of Light is dominion over all the children of righteousness, but because of the Angel of Darkness, all the children of righteousness go astray. The dominion mentioned here is not purely external, for 1QRule of the Community (iv.23–24) reports that until now, the spirits of truth and perversion feud in the hearts of people so that they walk in wisdom and foolishness. Those whose inheritance is truth and righteousness hate evil; those whose inheritance is perversity and wickedness abominate truth. The ultimate outcome is not in doubt, for God and God's Angel of Truth help all the children of light. God's wisdom determines a period for the existence of wrongdoing; but God's visitation will destroy it forever, and the truth will appear (1QS iv.18–19). The Qumran text on Mysteries (1Q27 1.i.5) promises that when those born of sin are locked up, evil will disappear before justice as darkness before light. The Qumranians lived in the period immediately before the divine visitation, to be introduced by the great battle described in the Qumran War Scroll (1QM).

In the Johannine writings, the exalted image of Jesus makes a difference; he is not on the same level as the Prince of this world. The Word that has become flesh existed before creation and brought it into being (*Jn.* 1.1–3), while the devil was a murderer and liar from the beginning (*Jn.* 8.44; that is, from the post-Creation period narrated in *Genesis* 2–3). The darkness did not overcome the light (*Jn.* 1.5), and Jesus is the light come into the world (*Jn.* 1.9, 9.5). This coming of light produces judgment: Those who practice wickedness hate the light, while those who do truth come to the light so that it may be shown that their deeds are done in God (*Jn.* 3.17–21). Jesus urges, "Walk while you have the light, or the darkness will come over you" (*Jn.* 12.35–36). Those who have faith in Jesus become children of the light; those who do not love Jesus belong to the devil (*Jn.* 8.41–44). Within the community of believers, people who hate their "brothers" or "sisters" are still in darkness, but those who love their "brothers" or "sisters" abide in the light (*1 Jn.* 2.9–10). Those claiming communion with God while continuing to walk in darkness do not do truth (*Jn.* 1.6). As for the struggle, Jesus gives the assurance: "The Prince of this world has been condemned" (*Jn.* 16.11) and "Take courage, I have overcome the world" (*Jn.* 16.33). The *First Letter of John* (2.8) confirms: "The darkness has passed away, and the true light is already shining." Believers in Jesus are begotten by God (*Jn.* 1.12–13), and all begotten by God conquer the world through their faith (*1 Jn.* 5.1, 5.4–5).

Corollaries of the Dualism. Other parallels of thought between the scrolls and the Johannine writings have been proposed, for instance, a special emphasis on knowing, and a sense of predestination as if God had chosen beforehand those who would be sons of light. In addition, there are various parallels of vocabulary. For example, "the light of life" (1QS iii.7; *Jn.* 8.12); "living water" (1QH[a] viii[16].7; CD xix.34; *Jn.* 4.10–11, 7.38); God as light/enlightener (1QH[a] iv[12].23; *1 Jn.* 1.5). Yet, among all such suggestions, two parallels, both corollaries of dualism, are the most persuasive.

Spirit of Truth. Among the various Qumranian terms for the good principle are Prince of Light and Spirit of Truth. The Johannine writings have two good principles, one following the other, both necessary to accomplish God's plan. Jesus is the light and the truth, but after his departure comes the Paraclete who is the Holy Spirit and the Spirit of Truth. Several unique characteristics mark the Johannine concept and bring it very close to Qumranian thought. First, only the Johannine writings (*Jn.* 14.17, 15.26, 16.13; *1 Jn.* 4.6) use the term *Spirit of Truth*, an expression absent from the Old Testament but found at Qumran (1QS iii.18–19; iv.21, 23) and in the *Testaments of the Twelve Patriarchs* (*Testament of Judah* 20.1–5), a dualistic work that has many parallels with Qumran literature. Second, the Qumranian Spirit of Truth functions at times as an angel (Michael) and thus as a personal being. John is uniquely clear about the personal characteristics of the Spirit of Truth. Besides the Greek neuter noun *pneuma* ("spirit"), *John* alone uses the masculine *paraklētos* ("Paraclete, advocate, counselor"). The Paraclete-Spirit is almost another Jesus (himself called a Paraclete implicitly in *John* 14.16 and explicitly in *1 John* 2.1), coming after Jesus leaves (*Jn.* 16.7), taking his place as teacher (*Jn.* 14.26), and proving that the Prince of this world has been condemned (*Jn.* 16.8, 11). Third, the Johannine Holy Spirit, even more than Jesus, has the internal aspect of the dominion of the Spirit of Truth at Qumran; for the spirit is invisible and dwells within the disciples (*Jn.* 14.17). Therefore, one must test a person's spirit to know whether it is the spirit of God or the spirit of the Antichrist (*1 Jn.* 4.1–6), a passage that resembles the rule for those entering the Qumran community: "They shall test their spirits" (1QS v.20–21, 24).

Love for community members. The Qumranians formed a tightly knit community, committed to the Teacher of Righteousness's interpretation of the law and shaped by a rigorous formation. The biblical encouragement to love what is good in God's sight and to hate what is evil (1QS i.3–4) is extended to the divided humanity ruled by the two spirits—love the children of light and hate the children of darkness (1QS i.9–10). Although 1QRule of the Community curses the children of Belial (1QS ii.4–8), it also gives a warning not to speak to one's "brother" in anger (1QS v.25–26). God will obliterate those who backslide from the community (*Jn.* 2.11–17); and when the glory of God is revealed, such unfaithful covenanters will be condemned and delivered to Belial (CD xx.25–26; 4Q269 3.iv.11–12).

The Johannine writings make Jesus' teaching on love his commandment par excellence and include followers of John the Baptist, whom the Fourth Gospel describes as the first disciples of Jesus. Did such Baptist disciples who had been Qumranians filter what they heard from Jesus through the prism of their own dualistic outlook? In any case, Qumranian parallels fortify the thesis that the Johannine tradition arose in Palestine.

BIBLIOGRAPHY

Brown, Raymond E. "The Qumran Scrolls and the Johannine Gospel and Epistles." *Catholic Biblical Quarterly* 17 (1955), 403–419, 559–574. Reprinted, corrected, and abbreviated in his *New Testament Essays*, 3d ed.; pp. 102–131. New York, 1982. Covers the basic comparable points.

Charlesworth, James H., ed. *John and Qumran*. London, 1972. Reprinted as *John and the Dead Sea Scrolls*. New York, 1990. Collection of important essays from the first two decades of scroll research, covering most aspects of the relationship.

Charlesworth, James H. "Reinterpreting John: How the Dead Sea Scrolls Have Revolutionized Our Understanding of John." *Bible Review* 9.1 (1993), 18–25, 53. Somewhat exaggerates the importance of the scrolls for Johannine research (in terms of "revolution").

Leaney, A. R. C. "John and Qumran." *Studia Evangelica* 6 (1973), 296–310. Significant points of comparison.

Painter, John. "John and Qumran." In *The Quest for the Messiah*, pp. 29–39. Edinburgh, 1991. Well-balanced summary.

Shafaat, A. "*Geber* of the Qumran Scrolls and the Spirit-Paraclete in the Gospel of John." *New Testament Studies* 27 (1980–1981), 263–269. Speculative: a debatable interpretation of two difficult passages.

RAYMOND E. BROWN, S.S.

JOHN HYRCANUS, ethnarch (leader) of Judea and high priest from 135 to 104 BCE. He rose to power following the murder of his father and two brothers by his brother-in-law Ptolemy. John Hyrcanus attempted to punish his father's murderer; however, his mother was taken hostage by Ptolemy, and Ptolemy escaped without punishment. In 135 BCE a serious threat to the safety of Judea occurred when Antiochus VII Sidetes (138–129 BCE) sought to restore to the Seleucid kingdom provinces that had gained their independence. John Hyrcanus was compelled to surrender Jerusalem to the Selucid king, agreeing to pay him a tariff in exchange for Jaffa and other cities conquered by Simon outside Judea. Although John Hyrcanus maintained his position as high priest and governor of Judea, it was still a subject state to the Seleucids for six years, until Antiochus VII Sidetes was killed in a military campaign against the Parthians. John Hyrcanus expressed the independence of Judea by minting coins that bore the slogan "John high priest and friend of the Jews."

Like his predecessors, he maintained good relations with Rome; during his reign the Roman senate passed resolutions in favor of Judea. Diplomatic ties with Pergamum and Ptolemiac Egypt were even established.

From 114 to 108 BCE, John Hyrcanus set out on a long series of conquests. He conquered Idumea, which was south of Judea, Samaria, portions of Transjordan, and apparently the Galilee as well. He destroyed the Samaritan city built on Mount Gerizim and the Samaritan Temple at its center. The conquering of Samaria and Scythopolis/Beth-Shean led to the unsuccessful Seleucid intervention in an effort to save the inhabitants of the Hellenistic cities. John Hyrcanus subsequently compelled the Idumeans to convert or be forced into exile. During the rule of John Hyrcanus, the territorial boundaries of the Hasmonean state were established. John Hyrcanus's followers claimed that he was merited to wear three crowns: the crown of priesthood, the crown of government, and the crown of prophecy.

Josephus's writings describe how John Hyrcanus observed the priestly laws as documented in the scrolls. In the description of John Hyrcanus's attempt to punish his father Simon's murderer, it is noted that Ptolemy was saved due to the sabbatical year in which Jews do not fight (*The Jewish War* 1.60; *Jewish Antiquities* 13.234). The War Scroll testifies that it is forbidden to fight during the sabbatical year (1QM ii.6). Likewise, Josephus noted that in its campaign in Babylonia, the Seleucid army with its Jewish allies was compelled to camp for two days due to Shavu'ot (*Jewish Antiquities* 13.251–252).

One of the scrolls found in Qumran Cave 4, Testimonia (4Q175), is a single page containing four paragraphs. The first three paragraphs are quotations from the Pentateuch describing positive leaders, a true prophet, a ruler chosen by the Lord who would govern Moab, and a priest. The last paragraph explains *Joshua* 6.26 and describes a negative character nicknamed "the man Belial" who had built Jericho and appointed his sons as rulers. It is upon them that the curse of Joshua falls. It is accepted that Testimonia is a collection of quotations taken from *Exodus, Numbers*, and *Deuteronomy*, and that the last paragraph is quoted from the Apocryphon of Joshua (4Q378–379).

The last paragraph in Testimonia is similar in nature to a *pesher* in that it contains exegesis to a biblical verse and its author assumes that the curse of Joshua was in effect in his days. Beginning in 1973, an archaeological expedition headed by E. Netzer excavated a cluster of palaces built by John Hyrcanus, fortified and surrounded by a ditch dug by his heirs. Thus, archaeological evidence together with the description of Josephus support Jean Starcky's suggestion that the author of the last paragraph of Testimonia claimed that the curse of Joshua was applicable to John Hyrcanus I and his sons, on account of the deaths of Aristobulus and Antigonus, who both died from unnatural causes in 104/103 BCE. Josephus in *The Jewish War* 1.69 and in *Jewish Antiquities* 13.299–300, in his summary of the period of John Hyrcanus's activity, noted that he merited the high priesthood, prophecy, and power.

In Qumran Cave 4, an additional composition connected to John Hyrcanus was found. This is the Prayer of Joseph (4Q371–372) describing what is probably the conquest of Mount Gerizim and the destruction of the Samaritan Temple by John Hyrcanus in 111 BCE. In this prayer it is said that Joseph is thrown into unknown lands, and scoundrels built altars for themselves on Joseph's desolate mountains. *Scoundrels* is a nickname for the Samaritans in the *Book of Ben Sira* and in the *Testament of Levi*. It is proposed that this prayer was composed following the conquest of Mount Gerizim by John Hyrcanus and was customarily said on the day that was designated as a holiday in honor of the destruction of the Samaritan Temple. It is possible that on a small fragment of papyrus found at Masada mentioning Mount Gerizim was also a hymn thanking the Lord for the destruction of the Temple on Mount Gerizim.

A third scroll, which is possibly connected to John Hyrcanus, is Calendrical Document C[a] (4Q322). In one of its paragraphs, the high priest is most likely mentioned. One line below that, the name John is mentioned. Since this is a very fragmented scroll, and Shelamzion Alexandra and Aemilius (one of Pompey's generals) were mentioned in the other paragraphs, it seems that the events mentioned are not from the second century BCE but from the first century BCE, so that the reference is not to John Hyrcanus but to Hyrcanus II, son of Alexander Jannaeus and Shelamzion Alexandra. [*See* Hasmoneans.]

BIBLIOGRAPHY

Barag, D. "New Evidence on the Foreign Policy of John Hyrcanus I." *Israel Numismatic Journal* 12 (1992–1993), 1–12.

Eshel, H. "The Prayer of Joseph, a Papyrus from Masada and the Samaritan Temple on APTAPIZIN (in Hebrew)." *Zion* 56 (1991), 125–136.

Eshel, H. "The Historical Background of the Pesher Interpreting Joshua's Curse on the Rebuilder of Jericho." *Revue de Qumrân* 15 (1992), 411–420.

Nezer, E. "The Winter Palaces of the Judean Kings at Jericho at the End of the Second Temple Period." *Bulletin of the American Schools of Oriental Research* 228 (1977), 1–14.

Schuller, E. "4Q372:1 A Text about Joseph." *Revue de Qumrân* 14 (1990), 349–376.

Starcky, J. "Les Maitres de Justice et la chronologie de Qumrân." In *Qumrân: sa piété, sa théologie et son milieu*, edited by M. Delcor, p. 253. Louvain, 1978.

Vermes, G. "Qumran Forum Miscellanea I." *Journal of Jewish Studies* 43 (1992), 304–305.

Wise, M. O. "An Annalistic Calendar from Qumran." In *Methods of Investigation of the Dead Sea Scrolls and the Khirbet Qumran Site: Present Realities and Future Prospects*, edited by M. O. Wise et al., pp. 389–408. New York, 1994.

HANAN ESHEL
Translated from Hebrew by Daphna Krupp

JOHN THE BAPTIST, a first-century CE Jewish figure, engaged in a prophetic ministry in the region of the Judean Wilderness (sometime around 25–28 CE). Integral to this prophetic ministry was baptism, a religious rite involving an act of immersing in water, thus providing John with his nickname, "the baptizer" or "the Baptist." The primary sources of information about John include a variety of texts in the New Testament Gospels (e.g., *Mt.* 3.1–17 = *Mk.* 1.2–11 = *Lk.* 3.1–22) and Josephus's *Jewish Antiquities* (18.116–119).

The similarities between John's ministry and the ideas and practices expressed in the Dead Sea Scrolls, and the close proximity of the locale of John's ministry to Khirbet

Qumran have led scholars to consider the relationship between John the Baptist and the Qumran Community. To understand the issues we first describe John the Baptist briefly and then examine the evidence of a link between him and this community.

Description of John the Baptist. It is possible that John was of priestly descent (*Lk.* 1.5), but otherwise his origins are shrouded in obscurity. He appeared on the stage of Palestinian history as an adult and became known for his practice of baptism and his prophetic announcements (*Mt.* 3.1–17 = *Mk.* 1.2–11 = *Lk.* 3.1–22).

The use of water for ritual ablutions was a widespread and varied practice in Second Temple Judaism, and included handwashing, footwashing, sprinkling, and bathing. It is this latter practice of immersion that John adopted as a significant rite, but at the same time he adapted its practice and significance. John's baptism was associated with the Jordan River (e.g., *Mt.* 3.6 = *Mk.* 1.5; though not exclusively, *Jn.* 3.23), and the New Testament describes John as explaining that his baptism was "a baptism of repentance for the forgiveness of sins" (e.g., *Mk.* 1.4 = *Lk.* 3.3; cf. Josephus's interaction with this explanation in *Jewish Antiquities* 18.117). As an immersion in flowing water (e.g., *Mt.* 3.6 = *Mk.* 1.5), John's baptism would have been understood in Second Temple Judaism as an act that cleansed from more severe forms of uncleanness (e.g., *Lv.* 15.13; *Miq.* 1.6–8; cf. *Jewish Antiquities* 18.117). For John, this severe uncleanness was caused by sin, and in Second Temple Judaism flowing water or rivers were associated with repentance and forgiveness (e.g., *Sib. Or.* 4.165–167; *Apoc. Mos.* 29.11–13). Immersion rites in John's day were self-administered, but John appears to have played some role in the act of baptizing (*Mk.* 1.5, 8; *Mt.* 3.11 = *Lk.* 3.16), thus contributing to his nickname "the baptizer."

John's baptism functioned in several interrelated ways for those who participated in it (John's opponents would, of course, deny these functions; cf. *Mt.* 3.7–10). The first three of these are related to the issue of sin. First, John's baptism was an expression of conversionary repentance, in which those baptized were returning to a relationship with God (e.g., *Mk.* 1.4 = *Lk.* 3.3; *Mt.* 3.8 = *Lk.* 3.8; *Mt.* 3.2; cf. *Jewish Antiquities* 18.117). Second, it mediated divine forgiveness; that is, it was "for the forgiveness of sins" (*Mk.* 1.4 = *Lk.* 3.3). John's participation in the act of baptism may have implied some mediatorial role (cf. the possibility that John was of priestly descent). Third, John's baptism probably also cleansed from uncleanness caused by sin. The function of immersions in Second Temple Judaism was usually concerned with such cleansing and, as noted above, John's use of flowing water is probably related to this function. Fourth, John's baptism foreshadowed the future activity of an expected figure whom John proclaimed as one who would imminently bring judgment and restoration to Israel. John contrasted his own baptism with the activity of this figure, but continued to use the metaphorical language of baptism to describe this activity: "I baptize you with water . . . ; he will baptize you with holy spirit and fire" (*Mt.* 3.11 = *Lk.* 3.16; cf. *Mk.* 1.8; *Jn.* 1.26–27). Fifth, John's baptism was probably an initiatory rite into what we might call the "true Israel." His proclamation of repentance was addressed to Israel, and his baptism effectively distinguished between those who would experience the expected figure's restoration and those who would be judged. The net effect of his baptism, then, was to prepare a remnant for the eschaton. Finally, it is possible that John's baptism may have been an implicit protest against the Temple establishment, especially as it functioned as an alternate means of forgiveness (cf. a similar link in *Sib. Or.* 4.8, 27–30 with 4.162–170).

As a prophet, John not only called on the people to express repentance through his baptism, he also announced the imminent coming of a figure who would bring judgment and restoration (*Mk.* 1.7–8; *Mt.* 3.11–12 = *Lk.* 3.16–17). The nature of John's proclamation places his expectation within a Jewish eschatological framework, but the descriptions of this expected figure are sufficiently vague as to make it difficult to identify him with any particular expected figure within Second Temple Jewish thought (e.g., Messiah, Elijah-*redivivus,* Son of Man). The early Christian movement was later to interpret Jesus the Messiah as a fulfillment of John's announcement, but this does not necessitate attributing a particular messianic view to John himself.

A number of different types of prophetic figures arose in the late Second Temple period, including "clerical prophet," "sapiential prophet," and "popular prophet" ("popular" in the sense of relating to the common people). Some scholars understand John as a "solitary popular prophet." But John the Baptist is better understood to be a "leadership popular prophet" (like Theudas, *Jewish Antiquities* 20.97–98; or the Egyptian, *Jewish Antiquities* 20.169–72) because in his prophetic role he was a leader of a movement, preparing the true Israel for the eschaton (cf. *Jewish Antiquities* 18.118).

John the Baptist was arrested by Herod Antipas and later executed at Machaerus, one of Herod's palace fortresses (*Jewish Antiquities* 18.119; *Mk.* 6.17–29). The New Testament explains that Herod's actions were caused by John's condemnation of Herod's second marriage as immoral (*Mk.* 6.17–19), while Josephus explains that Herod feared that John was creating turmoil among the people (*Jewish Antiquities* 18.118). These two explanations are probably complementary: the latter is the political fallout created by the moral condemnation.

Parallels between John the Baptist and the Qumran Community. Shortly after the discovery of the Dead Sea Scrolls, a number of scholars proposed that John the Baptist was related in some way to the Qumran community (e.g., Brownlee, 1958; Robinson, 1962; and most recently Sefa-Dapaah, 1995). The grounds for such a proposal are based on a number of parallels that may be observed between John and the Qumran community. Some of these parallels are quite intriguing but, as we shall see, they are also problematic, leading other scholars to reject an explicit link between them (e.g., Rowley, 1959; Sutcliffe, 1960; Webb, 1991; and most recently Taylor, 1997).

First (and probably most significant), both John and the Qumran Community practiced a ritual immersion. A number of Dead Sea Scrolls allude to or regulate such immersions (e.g., Damascus Document, CD x.10–13, x.23–xi.2, xi.21–22; Temple Scroll, 11Q19 xlv.7–10), but it is in Rule of the Community [1QS] where we may perceive something of the function and ideology of immersions. It has been argued (e.g., Webb) that the Rule of the Community, 1QS ii.25–iii.9 (esp. iii.6–9) and v.7–15 (especially v.13–14) points to a special initiatory immersion, which changed a person's status from a candidate to a member of the community. Whether or not one accepts this particular interpretation of one aspect of the Qumran immersion practices, the verbal parallels between John's baptism and the description contained in these texts are noteworthy: both John's and Qumran's immersions are linked to repentance (1QS v.1, 8, 14), atonement of sins (1QS iii.6–9), a spirit of holiness (1QS iii.7, iv.21), and the expectation of an eschatological cleansing (1QS iv.19–22). Yet, while there are similarities of ritual and language, it must be noted that there are also conceptual differences. For example, in the passages of the Rule of the Community it is repentance that makes efficacious both the atonement (resulting in forgiveness) and the immersion (resulting in cleansing), whereas with respect to John it is baptism linked with repentance that accomplishes both.

Second, the New Testament uses *Isaiah* 40.3 to interpret John as "the voice of one crying in the wilderness . . . ", and the Qumran community used the same text in the Rule of the Community (1QS) viii.12–16 and ix.19–20 to express the community's reason for its existence in the Judean Wilderness. Yet, a number of factors weigh against this similarity being evidence for a link between John and the Qumran Community. First, the prophecy of *Isaiah* was part of the scriptures for all first-century Jews, not just John and the Qumran Community. Second, the text each quotes is different. In the Rule of the Community (following Isaiah[a] [1QIsa[a]] and the later Masoretic Text) the text states: "A voice cries out, 'In the wilderness prepare the way of YHVH'"; whereas the New Testament, following the Septuagint, describes John as "the voice of one crying in the wilderness, [to] 'prepare the way of the Lord'" (*Mt.* 3.3 = *Mk.* 1.3 = *Lk.* 3.4; *Jn.* 1.23). Third, the New Testament use of *Isaiah* 40.3 is expressed as a Christian interpretation of John and is not attributed to John himself (except in *Jn.* 1.23 where it is placed on the lips of John—a typical device used by the fourth evangelist). It is unlikely that John would have used a reading from the Greek Septuagint to express his self-understanding. While it is quite possible that John did use *Isaiah* 40.3 to understand his prophetic call, the specific way it is used in the New Testament is more likely derived from early Christian reflection on John's significance than from John himself.

Third, John's teaching incorporates eschatological themes such as the expectation of eschatological judgment and of an eschatological figure who is God's agent of judgment and restoration (*Mt.* 3.11–12 = *Mk.* 1.7–8 = *Lk.* 3.15–17; *Mt.* 3.7–10 = *Lk.* 3.7–9). Such an eschatological orientation is also found in the Dead Sea Scrolls (e.g., IQS iv.18–25; Rule of the Blessings [1Q28b] v.20–29; Florilegium [4Q174] i.11–13; Pesher Isaiah[d] [4Q164]; Melchizedek, 11Q13 ii.4–20). However, such similarities may also be noted among other groups in first-century Judaism. The points at which similarities may be noted are not unique to the Qumran community and John. Since all groups drew upon the common tradition of the Hebrew Bible and did so in a context where such ideas were in the air, these similarities do not constitute evidence that John was specifically related to the Qumran community.

Fourth, John is described as being associated with the wilderness (*Mt.* 3.1 = *Mk.* 1.4 = *Lk.* 3.2–3) and baptizing in the Jordan River (*Mt.* 3.5 = *Mk.* 1.5; *Jn.* 1.28; according to Josephus, *The Jewish War* 3.515, the Jordan River flowed through a wilderness area, which would have included the Judean Wilderness). The Qumran community, located near the northwest bank of the Dead Sea in the Judean Wilderness, was only a few kilometers away from where the Jordan River flowed into the Dead Sea. Clearly John and Qumran were in close geographical proximity. In addition, some scholars observe that *Luke* 1.80 states: "And the child grew and became strong in spirit, and he was in the wilderness until the day of his public appearance to Israel." They suggest that John lived in the wilderness as a child and that he was raised by the Essenes—a practice described by Josephus (*The Jewish War* 2.120). However, *Luke* 1.80 is better read as a transitional verse, with verse 80a summarizing his spiritual growth as a child and verse 80b preparing the reader for his appearing in the wilderness as an adult (*Lk.* 3.1–2). Finally, it must be noted that geographical proximity is just that, proximity; it does not provide evidence of a relationship.

Other possible links include John being an ascetic like the members of the Qumran community, and both John and the Qumran community being critical of the Temple establishment. But, while asceticism may be attributable to John (*Mt.* 11.18 = *Lk.* 7.33; *Mt.* 3.4b = *Mk.* 1.6b; cf. *Lk.* 1.15), the Qumran community only stressed purity according to the Torah, and this would not have been considered asceticism at all. And a critical stance with respect to the Jerusalem Temple establishment was hardly unique to John and the Qumran community.

While there are significant similarities between John and the Qumran community, there are also significant differences. Generally, those who propose that there was a link between John and the community admit that John must have broken with them in order to engage in his prophetic ministry as we know it. Such an admission is made in light of the evidential weight of these differences. Recognizing the differences and realizing that all the evidence is, at best, circumstantial and implicit suggest the more judicious conclusion that there was no direct link between John and the Qumran community. It is quite possible that they knew of each other (and that is all it is—a possibility), but the similarities are better explained as deriving from a common milieu. Some of this common milieu was widespread in first-century Judaism (e.g., concern for purity), while other elements of the common milieu may be traced to an eschatological orientation associated with motifs of a "wilderness mentality." Only in this sense are John and the Qumran Community linked—an indirect link through their common heritage, milieu, and orientation derived from elements in first-century Judaism.

BIBLIOGRAPHY

Betz, O. "Was John the Baptist an Essene?" *Bible Review* 6 (December 1990), 18–25. Reprinted in *Understanding the Dead Sea Scrolls*, edited by Hershel Shanks, pp. 205–214. New York, 1992. A popular-level argument for John's being a member of the Qumran community.

Brownlee, W. H. "A Comparison of the Covenanters of the Dead Sea Scrolls with Pre-Christian Jewish Sects." *BA* 13 (1950), 50–72. One of the first to argue for a relationship between John and the Qumran community.

Brownlee, W. H. "John the Baptist in the New Light of Ancient Scrolls." In *The Scrolls and the New Testament*, edited by K. Stendahl, pp. 33–53, 252–256. London, 1958.

Chilton, Bruce. "John the Purifier." In *Judaic Approaches to the Gospels*, pp. 1–37. Atlanta, 1994. An intriguing article examining John's baptism. He rejects a link between John and the Qumran Community.

Davies, S. L. "John the Baptist and Essene Kashruth." *New Testament Studies* 29 (1983), 569–571. Links John's unusual diet with Essene kosher practices.

Geyser, A. S. "The Youth of John the Baptist: A Deduction from the Break in the Parallel Account of the Lucan Infancy Story."' *Novum Testamentum* 1 (1956), 70–75. Proposes that John was raised by the Essenes.

Gnilka, J. "Die Essenischen Tauchbäder und die Johannestaufe." *Revue de Qumrân* 3.2 (1961), 185–207. A careful comparison of Essene immersions and John's baptism.

Pryke, J. "John the Baptist and the Qumran Community." *Revue de Qumrân* 4 (1964), 483–496. Argues that John was not linked to the Qumran community because the differences are greater than the similarities.

Robinson, J. A. T. "The Baptism of John and the Qumran Community." In *Twelve New Testament Studies*, pp. 11–27. London, 1962. Argues that John was linked to the Qumran community.

Rowley, H. H. "The Baptism of John and the Qumran Sect." In *New Testament Essays: Studies in Memory of T. W. Manson*, edited by A. J. B. Higgins, pp. 218–229. Manchester, 1959. One of the early articles to reject the relationship between John and the Qumran community.

Scobie, C. H. H. *John the Baptist*. London, 1964. One of the first monograph-length works on John the Baptist after the discovery of the Dead Sea Scrolls.

Scobie, C. H. H. "John the Baptist." In *The Scrolls and Christianity*, edited by M. Black, pp. 58–69. Theological Collections 11. London, 1969. A summary of Scobie's point of view with respect to John and Qumran.

Sefa-Dapaah, Daniel. "An Investigation into the Relationship between John the Baptist and Jesus of Nazareth: A Socio-Historical Study." Ph.D. diss., University of Oxford, 1995. Argues that John was brought up by the Essenes and then left them to begin his prophetic, baptizing ministry.

Sutcliffe, E. F. "Baptism and Baptismal Rites at Qumran?" *Heythrop Journal* 1 (1960), 179–188. Argues against any link between John and the Qumran Community.

Taylor, Joan E. *The Immerser: John the Baptist within Second Temple Judaism*. Studies in the Historical Jesus. Grand Rapids, Mich., 1997. Contains a careful analysis of the arguments for a link between John and the Qumran community and concludes that they are inadequate to support a relationship between them.

Webb, Robert L. *John the Baptizer and Prophet: A Socio-Historical Study*. Journal for the Study of the New Testament Supplement Series, 62. Sheffield, 1991. An analysis of John's public roles of baptizer and prophet in light of Second Temple Judaism. It contains an examination of the immersions at Qumran in relationship to John's baptism and concludes that John was not directly linked with the Qumran community.

Webb, Robert L. "John the Baptist and His Relationship to Jesus." In *Studying the Historical Jesus: Evaluations of the State of Current Research*, edited by Bruce D. Chilton and Craig A. Evans, pp. 179–229. New Testament Tools and Studies, 19. Leiden, 1994. A summary of Webb's earlier monograph, extending the discussion to John's relationship to Jesus.

Wink, Walter. "John the Baptist and the Gospel." Ph.D. diss., Union Theological Seminary, 1963. Contains an extensive critique of the claim that John was related to the Qumran community. Unfortunately this section was not included in the published revision of Wink's work.

ROBERT L. WEBB

JOHN THE ESSENE. *See* Essenes.

JONAH, BOOK OF. *See* Minor Prophets.

JONATHAN (HASMONEAN), son of Mattathias was high priest from 152 to 143 BCE. Jonathan was the younger brother of Judah the Maccabee and together with him fought in battles from the beginning of the Hasmonean rebellion. After Judah fell in battle in 161 BCE, his friends elected Jonathan as their leader. Shortly thereafter, Jacimus was appointed high priest by Bacchides, military commander of Demetrius I of Syria, causing Jonathan and his followers to flee to the desert of Tekoa. When Jonathan's brother Yoḥanan was killed by a hostile Arab tribe, Jonathan took revenge against them. Bacchides attempted to punish Jonathan for the injury to the Arabs, but then formed an alliance with him. When a pretender to the crown, Alexander Balas, rose against Demetrius I in 152–145 BCE, both parties made offers to Jonathan to appoint him as high priest in 152 BCE in exchange for aid. Henceforth, Jonathan did not need to fight the Seleucids in order to strengthen his position; rather, he acted in the diplomatic realm in order to further his objectives. In 147 BCE, Demetrius II arose as a competitor to Alexander Balas. Jonathan defeated him in a battle that took place near Jaffa and Ashdod. As a reward, Jonathan received the Akra and its surroundings from Alexander Balas. After Demetrius II returned to Antioch, he faced a revolt of soldiers and residents. Demetrius II was compelled to ask for Jonathan's help, and as compensation he promised Jonathan to evacuate the Seleucid soldiers from the Akra. A force of three thousand Jewish soldiers departed for Antioch and protected Demetrius II, who then evaded his promises to Jonathan.

Toward the end of 145 BCE, the power of Tryphon (who was a pretender to the Seleucid throne) and Antiochus VI became stronger, and Jonathan formed an alliance with them. They authorized Jonathan's rule over the northern regions and added a fourth region to Judea (most likely Transjordan). Tryphon even appointed Simon, the brother of Jonathan, as governor of the coastal district. In 143 BCE, Jonathan formed political alliances with Rome and Sparta. Tryphon reached the conclusion that Jonathan was overly independent. Tryphon captured Jonathan at Acre and subsequently attempted to invade Judea, which was defended by Simon. Tryphon attempted to reach Jerusalem via the Judean Desert; however, as a result of a snowstorm, he was forced to return to the Jordan Valley. Following the failure of his campaign, Tryphon executed Jonathan in 143 BCE.

Among scholars of the Qumran scrolls, there has been a lengthy controversy regarding the identity of the Wicked Priest who is mentioned five times in Pesher Habakkuk (1QpHab) and an additional two times in two *pesharim* from Qumran Cave 4 (4Q171 and 4Q163). [*See* Wicked Priest.] The majority of scholars have accepted the suggestions of Geza Vermes and Józef Milik in identifying the high priest as Jonathan son of Mattathias.

The following details about the Wicked Priest are elucidated in the *pesharim*: Pesher Habakkuk says that the evil priest was originally considered legitimate at the beginning of his service, and only when he ruled over Israel did he abandon the Lord and begin to betray the statutes for wealth (1QpHab viii.3–13). Likewise, it is noted that the Wicked Priest committed abominations in Jerusalem, defiled the Temple, and robbed the riches of orphans (1QpHab xii.7–10). The attempt of the Wicked Priest to kill the Teacher of Righteousness is mentioned twice. In Pesher Habakkuk it is said that the Wicked Priest attacked the Teacher of Righteousness on Yom Kippur, while the Teacher of Righteousness fasted in his place of exile (1QpHab xi.2–8). [*See* Teacher of Righteousness.] From this description it seems that one of the arguments between the Teacher of Righteousness and the Wicked Priest was the question of the calendar, since the Wicked Priest, who was probably the high priest, could not leave the Temple on the Day of Atonement. Therefore, it seems that the Wicked Priest attacked the Teacher of Righteousness on his Yom Kippur, which was not Yom Kippur for the Wicked Priest. [*See* Calendars and Mishmarot.]

In Pesher Psalms[a] it was noted that the Wicked Priest tried to kill the Teacher of Righteousness on account of the statute and the law which the Teacher of Righteousness sent to the Wicked Priest (4Q171 4.7–9). In Pesher Habakkuk it is said that the Lord took vengeance upon the Wicked Priest because he attempted to hurt the people of the sect (1QpHab xii.2–6). Likewise, there are two descriptions in this *pesher* which note that the Wicked Priest's enemies caught him, tortured him, and took revenge upon his corpse (1QpHab vii.13–ix.2; ix.99–12). The mention of the Wicked Priest in Pesher Isaiah[c] is fragmented and nothing can be learned from it (4Q163 30.3).

The widespread opinion that the treatise Miqtsat Maʿasei ha-Torah was sent by the Teacher of Righteousness to the Wicked Priest also explains why the author of Pesher Habakkuk took the trouble to differentiate between the beginning of the Wicked Priest's life in which he was a positive leader and the end of his life in which he betrayed the statutes for wealth. The last paragraph in Miqtsat Maʿasei ha-Torah is formulated in a very positive tone, and the writer notes that the addressee excels in the study of the law and understanding of the statutes. [*See* Miqtsat Maʿasei ha-Torah.]

Some scholars have suggested that Jonathan son of Mattathias was mentioned in one of the scrolls, Apocryphal Psalm and Prayer (4Q448). This scroll contains a prayer for the welfare of King Jonathan and his kingdom.

Yet Jonathan was not a king but a high priest, and there is no evidence that his followers called him *king*. Thus, the king mentioned in Apocryphal Psalm and Prayer must be Alexander Jannaeus, the only king whose Hebrew name was Jonathan.

[*See also* Alexander Jannaeus; Hasmoneans.]

BIBLIOGRAPHY

Cross, Frank Moore. *The Ancient Library of Qumran and Modern Biblical Studies*. Garden City, N.Y., 1961. See pages 141–156.

Eshel, H. "4QMMT and the History of the Hasmonean Period." In *Reading 4QMMT: New Perspectives on Qumran Law and History*, edited by J. Kampen and M. S. Bernstein, pp. 53–65. Atlanta, 1996.

Jeremias, G. *Der Lehrer der Gerechtigkeit*. Göttingen, 1963.

Milik, Józef T. *Ten Years of Discovery in the Wilderness of Judaea*, translated by John Strugnell. Studies in Biblical Theology, 26. Naperville, Ill., 1959. See pages 74–87.

Murphy-O'Connor, J. "The Essenes and Their History." *Revue biblique* 81 (1974), 215–244.

Murphy-O'Connor, J. "Demetrius I and the Teacher of Righteousness." *Revue biblique* 83 (1976), 400–420.

Qimron, E., and J. Strugnell. "An Unpublished Halakhic Letter from Qumran." In *Biblical Archaeology Today*, edited by J. Amitai, pp. 400–407. Jerusalem, 1985.

Stegemann, Hartmut. *Die Entstehung der Qumrangemeinde*. Bonn, 1971.

Talmon, S. "Yom Hakkippurim in the Habakkuk Scroll." *Biblica* 32 (1951), 549–563.

Vermes, Geza. *Discoveries in the Judean Desert*. New York, 1956. See pages 89–97.

Vermes, Geza. "The So-Called King Jonathan Fragment (4Q448)." *Journal of Jewish Studies* 44 (1993), 294–300.

Yadin, Yigael. *The Temple Scroll*, vol. 1. Jerusalem, 1983. See page 396.

HANAN ESHEL

JORDAN VALLEY. The Jordan Valley is part of the great Syrian-African Rift, in which significant volcanic and tectonic activity took place. Flowing through it and dividing it longitudinally into two parts, east and west, is the Jordan River, the longest flowing river in the Land of Israel. The Wadi ed-Daliyeh is located to the west of the Jordan Valley north of Jericho, while Qumran lies to the southwest of the point where the river enters the Dead Sea. The valley, whose waters originate in Mount Hermon in the north at an altitude of 2,840 meters above sea level, and drop into the Dead Sea at 395 meters below sea level, is differentiated into two parts (Har-El and Nir, 1995):

The Upper Jordan Valley, from the sources of the Jordan to the Sea of Galilee, is about 80 kilometers long, with the Hula marshes spreading in the upper part and rugged basalt rocks in the lower; this section has a pleasant Mediterranean climate.

The Lower Jordan Valley, from the Sea of Galilee to the Dead Sea, includes the saline, marly Lisan hills, a distance of 105 kilometers; its northern section has a steppe-like climate, whereas the southern section has an arid, desert climate. The valley is between 4 kilometers and 20 kilometers wide.

The Jordan Valley is referred to by different names in the Bible, each relating to a different section: the Jordan Steppe (ʿArava; Willow), the Jordan Plain, and Pride of the Jordan. Each name has geographic significance and a different economic function, and each is bounded by a different district in the valley:

The Jordan Steppe (ʿArava; Willow) extends from the Sea of Galilee to the Dead Sea (*Jos*. 12.3) and is so called because of the large willow trees on the banks of the Jordan River. It has deep, fertile alluvial soils washed down from the mountains, and/or barren Lisan marl earth, which was deposited on the bottom of the ancient Lisan lake, the precursor of the Dead Sea.

The Jordan Plain (Har-El, 1984) is a low, richly watered plain, surrounded by mountains and extensive streams throughout the Jordan and Dead Sea valleys. Three fertile valleys are noted in the Bible:

1. "cities of the plain" and "land of the plain" to the south of the Dead Sea (*Gn*. 13.12; 19.28–29) fed by the Zered and Nimrin wadis in Moab,
2. "the plain," in the Jericho valley (*Dt*. 34.3; *Neh*. 3.22; 12.28) fed by the Qilt and Nueima wadis west of Jericho, and
3. "the Jordan Plain" in the Sukkot valley fed by the Jabbok River in Gilead, which spills into the Jordan (*1 Kgs*. 7.46; *2 Chr*. 2.4, 17).

Pride of the Jordan (Har-El, 1978) is the lowest section in the Jordan Valley (*Jer*. 12.5; 49.19; 50.44; *Zec*. 11.3). Here occurred or were found earthquakes, high and low tides, thick forests, grassland and pasture for livestock, and a habitat for wild animals and predators.

Although the distance between the Sea of Galilee and the Dead Sea as the crow flies is 105 kilometers, it is 217 kilometers when following the meandering of the Jordan River. The average width of the river in summer is 30 meters, but in winter, with the swell of floodwaters, it reaches a width between 60 and 1,500 meters. During the ebb tide, with low energy flow, it is between 1 and 3 meters deep. Before the establishment of the National Water Carrier in Israel in 1956, 1 billion cubic meters of water flowed into the Dead Sea from the Jordan River annually. Crossing the river, connecting the two sides of the valley were fifty-five fords (*Jos*. 2.7; *Jgs*. 3.28; 12.5–6), fifty of which were north of the Jabbok River in Gilead and only five south of it.

Roadways. The Jordan Valley provided longitudinal and transverse arteries of transportation between the two sides of the river. The valley's lengthwise structure and water sources enabled comfortable passage from the north to the south and back. The convenient connection between the settlers in the Galilee, Samaria, and Judea in the west and those in the Golan, Gilead, and Ammon in the east was through fords across the Jordan River and the valleys of its tributaries. There were five roads branching from the Via Maris that ascended from the Galilee to the Golan. The transverse valleys of Shechem (Nablus), Farah in Samaria and the Yarmouk, and Jabesh Gilead and the Jabbok in the Golan and Gilead enabled convenient passage between the two sides of the Jordan.

Settlements, Security, and the Economy. There were three centers of settlement in the Jordan Valley. In the Hula Valley there was a concentration of frontier settlements connecting inhabitants of the valley in southern Lebanon to the settlements of northern Israel and the Golan. Among them were Dan (*Jgs*. 18.29), which was established at the headwaters of the Dan River, at 204 meters above sea level; Abel Beth-maacah (*2 Sm*. 20.14) on Naḥal Ijon (ʿAyoun) at an altitude of 414 meters above sea level; Ijon (*2 Chr*. 16.4) at 700 meters above sea level, at the headwaters of Naḥal Ijon; and Panias or Caesarea Phillipi (*Mt*. 16.13; *Mk*. 8.27; Josephus, *Antiquities* 18.2.1) at 350 meters above sea level on the Panias (Senir) River. The inhabitants of these cities engaged in dry and irrigated farming and serviced the international commercial caravans. In the southwest Hula Valley, Hazor was founded, at 200 meters above sea level; its king was head of the Canaanite kings (*Jos*. 11.10). The Canaanite inhabitants of Hazor had an army of iron chariots (*Jgs*. 4.2–3) by which they ruled the other kings in the area and controlled the Via Maris and the international trade in the north of the country. Built southwest of the Sea of Galilee were Hammath and Rakkath (*Jos*. 19.35), and Tiberias of Second Temple and Roman times, which controlled the Via Maris and its branches leading to the Golan and Damascus. Its inhabitants engaged in dry farming and fishing in the Sea of Galilee, and they made a living from the hot springs at Hammath, from trade with the international caravans, and from the sites holy to Christian tourists. The Sea of Galilee is considered holy by Christians, since Jesus performed the miracle of multiplying loaves and fish at Tabgha (*Mk*. 6.34–44), preached in the synagogue at Capernaum, performed wonders, and healed the sick (*Mk*. 1.21; *Mt*. 8).

In the Lower Jordan Valley the following important cities were built:

Beth-Shean (Scythopolis) and its towns (*Jos*. 17.11) were located 120 meters below sea level. The city had the largest amount of irrigated crops in the country because it annually received 130 million cubic meters of water, which flowed at the foot of Mount Gilboa, at the eastern opening of the fertile Jezreel Valley. The city was established midway along the Via Maris, at the important junction of all four directions in the country, and was the capital of the Decapolis alliance of ten Roman cities on the eastern side of the Jordan (Josephus, *The Jewish War* 3.9.7) and the capital of the district of Second Palestine in Byzantine times. In the days of Byzantine Christian rule, in the fourth to sixth centuries CE, Christian monks from Jerusalem and the Judean Desert came to the Jordan Valley and the Beth-Shean and Galilee valleys (Chitty, 1966).

Succoth and its towns (*Jgs*. 8.14–15; *Ps*. 60.8) were founded on the fertile Jordan Plain, at the mouth of the Jabbok River, which yielded 80 million cubic meters of water a year. North of Naḥal Reggev (*Men*. 8.3) (Rajib) the Philistines and Israelites produced their iron implements, and King Solomon cast his copper vessels for the temple there (*1 Kgs*. 7.46).

Jericho (*Jos*. 4.13) was founded in the fertile steppes as a desert oasis at the mouth of Wadi Nueima and Wadi Qilt, 215 meters below Mediterranean sea level. It was the city of palm trees and flax at the time of the First Temple (*Dt*. 34.3; *Jgs*. 3.3) and of balsam from the time of the Second Temple onward (Josephus, *The Jewish War* 1.6.6; 4.8.3; and Har-El, 1981).

The Jericho district and the mouth of the Jordan, where it spills into the Dead Sea, are sites in the country that have been sanctified in the Christian tradition. At Bet Hogla, on the Jordan's shore (*Jos*. 15.6), Jesus came to his teacher, John, who baptized him in the Jordan's water, and the "spirit of God rested upon him" (*Mt*. 3.13–17). The devil brought Jesus to Jebel Qarantal, the Mount of Temptation, which is above Jericho, to be tested; there he fasted for forty days and forty nights (*Mt*. 4.1). Thus the district of Wadi Qilt, Jericho, and the Jordan River became a center of Christian monastaries in Byzantine times and onward.

When Jesus and his twelve disciples went up to Judea and Jerusalem from the Galilee by way of the Jordan Valley and Jericho, rather than through Samaria, they increased the importance of these areas for their followers in later times. Hence, along this same route through the Jordan Valley, monks migrated and established monastaries in the Beth-Shean Valley and in the Hula Valley in Galilee.

BIBLIOGRAPHY

Chitty, D. J. *The Desert: A City*. Oxford, 1966. The author, who is also an archaeologist, describes in detail the history of the monks and asceticism in the Land of Israel and of their spread throughout the country.

Har-El, Menashe. "The Valley of Craftsmen (Ge' ha-Ḥarashim)." *Palestine Exploration Quarterly* 109 (1977), 75–86. The only iron mines in the country were discovered in the Sukkot Valley. They were first exploited by the Philistines and the Israelites in the twelfth century BCE and formed the basis for the wood, stone, and metal industries in the Land of Israel.

Har-El, Menashe. "The Pride of the Jordan—The Jungle of the Jordan." *Biblical Archaeologist* 41.2 (1978), 64–75. The Jungle of the Jordan is a lush tropical strip of land bordering the Jordan River, which contrasts sharply with the barren hills on either side of the valley.

Har-El, Menashe. *The Judean Desert and the Dead Sea* (in Hebrew). Tel Aviv, 1981. A handbook for teachers and hikers, which gives a description of the important sites in the Judean Wilderness and details of its seven deserts and their inhabitants. The approach is geographic, historical, and archaeological, with information on the domiciles of the Judean Desert sects, the Christian monks and their monastaries, the fortresses of the desert, the agricultural inhabitants of the desert oases, and the history and fluctuations of the Dead Sea level.

Har-El, Menashe. *Landscape, Nature and Man in the Bible* (in Hebrew). Tel Aviv, 1984. The author gives a geographic interpretation of the landscape, nature, and human events in biblical times. He describes life in the settlements of the different regions; their economy, crafts, and industry; road paving in the mountains and deserts; and the water installations and their sources. He discusses the wars against tribes and countries, and the relations between the Israelite nation and its close and distant neighbors.

Har-El, Menashe and Dov Nir. *Geography of the Land of Israel* (in Hebrew). Tel Aviv, 1995 (new edition). A textbook for high-school and teachers'-college students. The authors deal with the country-wide and regional geography. They discuss physical properties, settlements, economic topics in the geographic regions, and also special problems of each and every region, emphasizing the anthropogenic activities that changed the landscape.

MENASHE HAR-EL

JOSEPH, the eleventh and favorite son of Jacob, and the principal character in *Genesis* 37–50. The narrative tells of Joseph's dreams, his being sold by his brothers into Egypt, his success in enduring temptation from Potiphar's wife, his rise to become Pharaoh's chief officer in charge of the distribution of Egyptian food resources, and his reunion with his family in Egypt.

The most significant Judean Desert documents that refer to Joseph are fragments of a work called Apocryphon of Joseph[a-c] (4Q371–373) in Hebrew and an Aramaic Apocryphon of Joseph (4Q539). [*See* Joseph, Apocryphon of.] Only the Aramaic Apocryphon of Joseph has some resemblance to the Testament of Joseph, which focuses on and embellishes two aspects of the Joseph narrative—Joseph's resisting the seduction of the wife of Pentephris (Potiphar) and his selfless dealing with his brothers.

The Apocryphon of Joseph[a], a copy of the same text as the Apocryphon of Joseph[b] (lines 5–13), is written in a middle Hasmonean script and dated earlier than the Apocryphon of Joseph[b]. The Apocryphon of Joseph[b] consists of three major fragments and twenty-four much smaller fragments and is dated paleographically to the late Hasmonean or early Herodian period. One fragment of about thirty lines contains a psalm of Joseph uttered in a foreign land. It is either an exegetical reflection on *Genesis* or a composition that takes Joseph as a designation for the northern tribes suffering in exile. A second fragment of about fourteen lines also contains a psalm of praise. The Apocryphon of Joseph[c], which mentions a battle against Og, has been assigned to the Apocryphon of Joseph but may be better assigned to the Apocryphon of David? (2Q22).

The Apocryphon of Joseph contains Aramaic fragments dating from the late Hasmonean period. One fragment consists of a couple of words that may be related to the *Testament of Joseph* 14.4–5, which describes the schemes of the Egyptian (Memphian) woman to seduce Joseph. Two other fragments have a certain resemblance to *Testament of Joseph* 15.1–17.2, which mentions Joseph's being sold to the sons of his uncle Ishmael, his father Jacob's mourning, and his not wanting to bring scorn upon his brothers. Jubilees[b] from Cave 2 at Qumran (2Q20) consists of three Hebrew fragments, only one of which is identified. This fragment corresponds to *Jubilees* 46.1–3, which describes the prosperity of Israel in Egypt until the time of Joseph's death. Joseph is also mentioned in two Aramaic fragments of the Apocryphon of Judah (4Q538), which recount the second journey to Egypt when the brothers finally recognize Joseph (cf. *Jub.* 42.25–43.18, *Gn.* 44.1–45.10). [*See also* Judah.] There is an additional Hebrew fragment, a Text Concerning Rachel and Joseph (4Q474), in which Joseph is referred to as a "beloved son." Joseph also is referred to a number of times in Temple Scroll[a] (11Q19) in connection with the other tribes (e.g., 11Q19 xxiii.1).

In the New Testament, Joseph figures prominently in Stephen's speech. Stephen retells the *Genesis* narrative including Joseph's being sold into Egypt, God being with him to rescue him, and God granting him favor and wisdom before Pharaoh so that he was appointed governor over Egypt (*Acts* 7.9–18). Joseph's provisions for his burial are mentioned in *Hebrews* 11.22. While the images of Jacob and Judah are elevated above the corresponding biblical accounts in the Second Temple and rabbinic writings, Joseph's steadfastness in facing temptation, his loyalty to and love for his family, and his conduct in high office, they also point out his various faults and shortcomings. His troubles are due to his pride in his physical appearance (he "painted his eyes, curled his hair, and walked with a mincing step," [*Gn. Rab.* 84.7]) and his wrongly charging his brothers with serious offenses (*Gn. Rab.* 87.3).

BIBLIOGRAPHY

Milik, Józef T. "Écrits préesséniens de Qumrân: D'Hénoch à Amram." In *Qumrân: Sa piété, sa théologie et son milieu*, edited by M. Delcor, pp. 91–106. Paris and Gembloux, 1978. Contains transliterations, notes, and comments on the Apocryphon of Joseph.

Schuller, Eileen. "4Q372 1: A Text about Joseph." *Revue de Qumrân* 14 (1990), 349–376. Contains notes, transcriptions, photographs, translation, commentary, and general comments on the Apocryphon of Joseph[b] (4Q372 1), which, so it is argued, reflects Samaritan and Jewish polemics and was written before John Hyrcanus's attack on Shechem in 126 BCE.

Schuller, Eileen. "A Preliminary Study of 4Q373 and Some Related Fragments." In *The Madrid Qumran Congress*, (?) edited by Julio Trebolle Barrera and Luis Vegas Montaner, pp. 515–530. Studies on the Texts of the Desert of Judah, 11. Leiden, 1992. Links the Apocryphon of Joseph[c] to the Apocryphon of David.

ROGER GOOD

JOSEPH, APOCRYPHON OF. The work known as the Apocryphon of Joseph, which is contained in scrolls Apocryphon of Joseph[a] (4Q371) and Apocryphon of Joseph[b] (4Q372), was given this title because the largest fragment is concerned with Joseph, but parallels with two related manuscripts, the Apocryphon of Joseph[c] (4Q373) and the Apocryphon of David? (2Q22), indicate that the work was concerned with other biblical figures as well. The interpretation of the work as a whole remains uncertain, but it is clear that the extant fragments consist largely of narrative and psalmic material, and it appears that the narrative sections provided a historical setting for autobiographical psalms in which heroes from the past acknowledged God's actions on their behalf or appealed for God's help. The work belongs to the category of parabiblical literature.

The greatest amount of text is preserved in the Apocryphon of Joseph[b], which consists of twenty-four small fragments and three somewhat larger pieces. Of the latter, the text concerned with Joseph (4Q372 1) is far longer than that of any of the fragments of the other manuscripts of this work. The Joseph text is also represented in seven of the twelve small fragments of the Apocryphon of Joseph[a], which overlap with fragment 1 of the Apocryphon of Joseph[b]. The text consists of a narrative and a psalm of lament, and, although the psalmist is not named, it is clear that Joseph is the speaker. The narrative makes use of the "sin-exile-return" pattern and alludes to the fate of the northern and southern kingdoms, the return from exile, and the postexilic period, which is presented as a time of continuing oppression. But the real concern of the text is with the fate of Joseph, seen here primarily as representative of the northern tribes: Joseph, in exile, prays for deliverance and for the destruction of the hostile people—probably the Samaritans—who had erected a "high place" in the land. However, although the concern is with Joseph as representative of the northern tribes, it is possible that the fate of the patriarch Joseph, who was himself sent into exile, has been transferred to a much later time and situation, that of an anti-Samaritan polemic in the Maccabean period, and used to shed light on the fate of the exiled northern tribes.

Such a transference of an incident from Israel's past to a contemporary situation may provide the key to understanding the references to David and Goliath and to figures from the *Book of Numbers* that are also contained in the fragments of the four interrelated manuscripts, but the fragments are too small for this to be clear. The Apocryphon of David?, with which the Apocryphon of Joseph[b] (4Q372 19) and the fragments of the Apocryphon of Joseph[c] overlap, appears to contain a narrative in which David described his battle with Goliath and a psalm of thanksgiving. The Apocryphon of Joseph[b] (4Q372 3) is a psalm that refers to Zimri son of Salu (*Nm.* 25.14) and to the five kings of Midian (*Nm.* 31.8).

The fragments contain no hint that the work is sectarian in character. The manuscripts date from the first half of the first century BCE to the first half of the first century CE, but the work itself probably dates from the second century BCE.

To be distinguished from the above work composed in Hebrew is the Aramaic Apocryphon of Joseph (4Q539), of which five small fragments dating from the middle of the first century BCE survive. The two largest fragments (2a–b) appear to lie behind the Greek Testament of Joseph (15.1–17.2) from the *Testament of the Twelve Patriarchs*, but although the Aramaic work has been called a testament, it is not certain that it had this literary form.

Equally distinct from both the Hebrew and the Aramaic Apocryphons of Joseph is the Text Concerning Rachel and Joseph (4Q474), which mentions Rachel and appears to refer to Joseph as a "beloved son." This Hebrew text is represented by one small fragment and apparently contains a prayer to God for the birth of another son (cf. *Gn.* 30.24); it may also contain a prophecy on the future of Israel, but this part of the text is too fragmentary for the meaning to be completely clear. The manuscript dates from the end of the first century BCE, but the text itself could have originated in the second century BCE.

[*See also* Samaritans; Twelve Patriarchs, Testaments of the.]

BIBLIOGRAPHY

Beyer, Klaus. "Die Abschiedsrede Josephs." In *Die aramäischen Texte vom Toten Meer*, p. 188; *Ergänzungsband*, p. 71. Göttingen, 1994. Edition of the fragments of the Aramaic Apocryphon of Joseph.

Elgvin, Torleif. "4Q474: A Joseph Apocryphon?" *Revue de Qumrân* 18 (1997), 97–108.

Elgvin, Torleif. "A Joseph Apocryphon from Qumran." In *At slutte medens legen er god: Festschrift for E. E. Knudsen*, pp. 70–81. Oslo, 1997.

García Martínez, Florentino. "Nuevos textos no bíblicos procedentes de Qumran." *Estudios Biblicos* 49 (1991), 97–134. Discussion of the interpretation of the Apocryphon of Joseph.

Schuller, Eileen. "4Q372 1: A Text about Joseph." *Revue de Qumrân* 14 (1990), 349–376.

Schuller, Eileen. "A Preliminary Study of 4Q373 and Some Related (?) Fragments." In *The Madrid Qumran Congress: Proceedings of the International Congress on the Dead Sea Scrolls, Madrid, 18–21 March 1991*, vol. 2, edited by Julio Trebolle Barrera and Luis Vegas Montaner, pp. 515–530. Studies on the Texts of the Desert of Judah, 11. Leiden and New York, 1992.

MICHAEL A. KNIBB

JOSEPHUS FLAVIUS. From the very time when the scrolls were first discovered, the most important ancient author for determining the historical context of the scrolls has been Josephus, especially since it is precisely for the period to which the scrolls are dated (c.225 BCE–68 CE) that Josephus, himself a contemporary, writes at greatest length. Any attempt at identifying allusions in the scrolls to Judean history would naturally have to be verified in Josephus. Moreover, inasmuch as most of the earliest scholars who dealt with the scrolls identified them as Essene documents, one would turn to Josephus, who has left us by far our most comprehensive description of them. Where the Dead Sea fragments disagree with the Masoretic or Septuagint texts of the Bible, one turns to Josephus to see whether there are parallels in his paraphrase of the Bible. Finally, where the Dead Sea fragments disagree in their versions of Jewish law as later codified in the Mishnah (c.200 CE), one turns to their contemporary, Josephus, for parallels.

Josephus Flavius was born in 37 CE and was given the Hebrew name of Yosef ben Mattityahu. His mother was a descendant of the Hasmonean family (*The Life* 2) that had ruled Judea a century earlier. By birth, he was a priest, and, indeed, he belonged to the first of the twenty-four courses of priests—a fact to be borne in mind in view of the sharp antagonism of the Qumran community to the established priesthood of the Temple in Jerusalem. According to his own statement, he tried out membership in different sects. So prominent was he that at the young age of twenty-seven (in 64 CE) he was selected to go to Rome to seek the freedom of some priests, a mission in which he was successful through the intervention of Poppaea Sabina, the Emperor Nero's consort (*The Life* 16) and a "sympathizer" with Judaism, that is, one who observed some of the practices of Judaism without actually converting (*Jewish Antiquities* 20.195). Two years later, despite a lack of previous military experience, he was chosen either to induce the Jewish revolutionaries in Galilee to lay down their arms (*The Life* 29) or, in what appears to be a contradictory passage, to serve as general of the Jewish forces in Galilee in the revolt against Rome (*The Jewish War* 2.568). After showing considerable ingenuity in the latter task, he surrendered to the Romans at Jotapata (*The Jewish War* 3.391), predicted General Vespasian's succession as emperor (*The Jewish War* 3.401), and received various gifts from the Romans, including lodging in the house of Vespasian in Rome, citizenship, and a pension (*The Life* 423). In Rome, so far as we can tell, he devoted himself primarily to writing: first, *The Jewish War*, dealing with the revolution against the Romans, in seven books in Aramaic, which he later (c.79–81 CE) translated into Greek (*The Jewish War* 1.3), then (in 93 CE), the *Jewish Antiquities* in twenty books, starting with creation and ending with the outbreak of the Jewish War. Finally, some time before his death (c.100 CE) he wrote an autobiography (primarily intended to defend his conduct during the Jewish War) and the essay, in two books, *Against Apion*, an apologetic defense of Judaism against maligners.

One must recognize that Josephus should be approached with caution. In the first place, though he writes in Greek, this is not his first language, which was Aramaic, or even his second language, which was Hebrew. He himself (*Jewish Antiquities* 20.263) admits that though he labored strenuously to master Greek prose and poetry, his habitual use of his native tongue prevented him from attaining precision in the pronunciation. He also admits (*Against Apion* 1.50) that he needed the help of assistants in rendering into Greek his first work, *The Jewish War*, which is precisely the one that contains by far his longest account of the Essenes (*The Jewish War* 2.119–161) and the passage most important for students of the Dead Sea Scrolls. Hence, it is not surprising that the understanding of his Greek presents considerable difficulty. Moreover, Josephus is hardly impartial, being an apologist for his patrons the Romans, as well as for the Jewish religion, and, of course, for himself in his dubious role during the war against the Romans. We are seldom in a position to check up on him in his account of the Essenes, inasmuch as only Philo (*Every Good Man Is Free* 75–91 and *Hypothetica* 11.1–18) and a brief passage in Pliny the Elder (*Natural History* 5.15.73) have anything of importance to say about them, and the Talmud is completely silent about them. Moreover, we may well be skeptical of Josephus' attempt to equate Jewish movements and ideas with those of the Greeks, for example, the Essenes with the Pythagoreans (*Jewish Antiquities* 15.371) and the Essenes' view of the afterlife with that of the Greeks (*The Jewish War* 2.155–158). Finally, the manuscript tradition of Josephus is relatively late, the earliest manuscript (Codex Ambrosianus) dating from the tenth or eleventh century; and we have only one brief (third century) papyrus fragment of his works (*The Jewish War* 2.576–579, 2.582–594).

The Scrolls as a Source of Historical Information Confirmed by Josephus. In a very few instances the scrolls seem to corroborate information found in Josephus. One such case is in connection with Alexander Jannaeus' conflict with his political opponents. Some have identified the Wicked Priest in the Pesher Habakkuk (1QpHab i.12–15, xi.4–8) as a Hasmonean ruler, whether Jonathan (161–142 BCE), Simon (142–134 BCE), or Alexander Jannaeus (103–76 BCE), as described by Josephus. Pesher Nahum (4Q169) mentions "Demetrius King of Greece who sought, on the counsel of those who seek smooth things, to enter Jerusalem" (4Q169 3–4.i.2), the reference probably being to Demetrius III Eukerus (95–88 BCE), who, upon being summoned by the Jewish opponents of King Alexander Jannaeus of Judea (*Jewish Antiquities* 13.376–378), defeated him in battle. Pesher Nahum (4Q169 3–4.i.7) also refers to the "Lion of Wrath" "who would hang men up alive, [a thing never done] formerly in Israel"; this has been identified by most scholars as a reference to Alexander Jannaeus, who, after his defeat by Demetrius, according to Josephus (*The Jewish War* 1.97, *Jewish Antiquities* 13.380), ordered eight hundred of his Jewish opponents to be crucified and slaughtered their wives and children before their very eyes while he feasted with his concubines. Though these opponents are not specifically referred to here as the Pharisees, elsewhere (*Jewish Antiquities* 13.398–406) it is clear that Alexander Jannaeus' chief Jewish opponents were the Pharisees, and it is thus that we may identify them as the Seekers after Smooth Things who summoned Demetrius III.

The publication of Miqtsat Maʿasei ha-Torah, with its statement that "you [plural] know that we have separated ourselves from *rov ha-ʿam* [multitude of the people]" (4QMMT C 7), would seem to support Josephus' claim that the Pharisees, who are apparently the opponents of the authors of this document and whose *halakhah* (i.e., law) is, to a considerable degree, the object of their attacks, were extremely influential among the masses (*Jewish Antiquities* 18.15). This would apply to the early Hasmonean period when MMT was apparently composed, but, admittedly, the question of whether this also applies to the period of Josephus himself, two centuries later, is open to debate.

There are a number of historical references in the scrolls, particularly in the *pesharim* and in the War Scroll, to a greatly feared and merciless military power, the *Kittim*, who, it is thought, are to be identified with the Romans. The *Kittim* are said (1QPesher Habakkuk vi.3–5) to sacrifice to their standards, as indeed Josephus tells us (*The Jewish War* 6.316) was true of the Romans. Josephus declares (*The Jewish War* 2.152–153) that the war with the Romans tested the souls of the Essenes, who are usually identified with the Qumran community, and the fact that the latest Jewish coins found at Qumran date from 68 CE while the earliest Roman coins date from that year would seem to indicate that the settlement was destroyed in that year by the Romans.

Josephus as an Aid in Identifying the Qumran Community. For a group such as the Qumran community with its huge library, it would seem surprising if Josephus had not even heard of them. In his autobiography—the earliest that has come down to us from antiquity—which consists of 430 paragraphs in Niese's standard Greek text, only twenty-one do not deal with the war against the Romans in which he served as a general in Galilee. Yet a major highlight of these twenty-one paragraphs is Josephus' account (*The Life* 10–12) of how, at the age of sixteen, after receiving a thorough education and achieving an excellent reputation for his learning, he had determined to gain personal "experience of the sects [*haireseis*, "systems of philosophical principles, sects, schools, factions, parties"] among us," the clear implication being that he intended to try all the sects (though such a search is a commonplace, similar to the motif found in the lives of Nicolaus of Damascus, Apollonius of Tyana, Justin, and Galen). Josephus proceeds to state that "these are three [in number]," after which he names them as the Pharisees, the Sadducees, and the Essenes. In the three other places (*The Jewish War* 2.119, *Jewish Antiquities* 13.171, 18.11) where he mentions the sects, he likewise specifies that they are three in number. Josephus (*The Life* 10) says that he determined to choose the best of these sects after "becoming thoroughly acquainted [*katamathoimi*, "searching out, observing well, examining carefully"] with all" of them. He then spent three years (*The Life* 11) with a hermit named Bannus, but it is clear that he did not regard Bannus as being connected with a sect. To be sure, in the Jerusalem Talmud (J.T., *San.* 10.6) the third-century Rabbi Yoḥanan is quoted as saying that "Israel was not exiled until twenty-four sects [*kitot*, "parties, classes"] of heretics [*minim*, "sectarians"] had come into being," but this may reflect rabbinic preoccupation, especially in the third century and thereafter, with speculating on the causes of the destruction of the Temple in Jerusalem in the year 70 CE.

Like Josephus, Pesher Nahum (4Q169 3–4.ii.2–iv.1–7) mentions three separate Jewish groups, referring to them as Ephraim (the "Seekers after Smooth Things," probably to be identified with the Pharisees, though the term "Pharisees" does not appear thus far in any of the scrolls), Manasseh (probably to be identified with the Sadducees, though this term likewise does not appear thus far in any of the scrolls), and Judea (probably to be identified with the Qumran community itself), though it must now be admitted that 4QMMT (Miqtsat Maʿasei ha-Torah), with its indication that the sect followed Sadducean *halakhah*, would lead us to question these identifications.

As a result of these passages in Josephus referring to

the sects, most scholars, when the first Dead Sea Scrolls were discovered, assumed that they belonged to one of these sects, especially since the Qumran community was clearly not a small, ephemeral group restricted to Qumran and since it persisted for at least two centuries. Based largely on Josephus, most scholars identified the sect as the Essenes, even though the name Essenes is probably not found in any of the scrolls. In the first place, the Essenes are first mentioned by Josephus (*Jewish Antiquities* 13.171–173) in his account of Jonathan the Hasmonean, who ruled in the middle of the second century BCE, which is the approximate date of some of the earlier finds of the Qumran community. This identity seems to be confirmed by the statement of Pliny the Elder (*Natural History*, 5.15.73), who specifically locates the Essenes on the western shore of the Dead Sea.

A number of parallels have been noted between the Qumran community, especially as seen in the Rule of the Community (1QS), and Josephus' description of the Essenes:

1. Both separate themselves from other Jews, whereas members are extremely close to one another (Josephus, *The Jewish War* 2.119, 124; 1QS ii.23–25).
2. Both exercise extreme asceticism, shunning all pleasures (*The Jewish War* 2.120; 1QS iv.9–11).
3. Both educate young children according to their customs (*The Jewish War* 2.120; 1Q28a i.4–5).
4. Both look upon women as wanton (*The Jewish War* 2.121; 4Q184 i.13–14).
5. Both despise riches (*The Jewish War* 2.122; 1QS ix.21–24, CD iv.17, 1QpHab viii.10–13).
6. They pool their property (*The Jewish War* 2.122, *Jewish Antiquities* 18.20; 1QS i.11–12).
7. Both regard oil as a defilement (*The Jewish War* 2.123; CD xii.15–17).
8. They dress in white (*The Jewish War* 2.123; 1QM vii.9–10).
9. Both have treasurers in charge of their funds and various activities (*The Jewish War* 2.123; 1QS vi.20, CD xiii.16).
10. They replace their clothing only when totally worn out (*The Jewish War* 2.126; 1QS vii.13–14).
11. Both pray at dawn (*The Jewish War* 2.128; 1QS x.1–3).
12. Both practice purificatory washings (*The Jewish War* 2.129; 1QS iii.4–5).
13. Both have common meals (*The Jewish War* 2.129; 1QS vi.2–3).
14. The meal is restricted to initiated members (*The Jewish War* 2.129; 1QS v.13).
15. The priest blesses the food before the meal (*The Jewish War* 2.131; 1QS vi.4–5).
16. They speak in turn, each making way for the other (*The Jewish War* 2.132; 1QS vi.10–13).
17. Both strictly follow the orders of their overseers (*The Jewish War* 2.134, 2.146; 1QS v.2–3).
18. Both are masters of their temper (*The Jewish War* 2.135; 1QS iv.10).
19. Both are champions of fidelity (*The Jewish War* 2.135; 1QS viii.1–3).
20. Both are peace loving (*The Jewish War* 2.135; CD vi.21–vii.3).
21. Both are zealous students of the ancient writings (*The Jewish War* 2.136; 1QS vi.6–8, CD xiii.2).
22. Both are greatly interested in the healing of diseases (*The Jewish War* 2.136; *Jub.* 10.10–14).
23. Both describe an initiation period for entrance into the sect, there being a two-year period of initiation within the community itself (*The Jewish War* 2.137–142; 1QS vi.13–16).
24. Both declare that those entering the community must take an oath (*The Jewish War* 2.139; 1QS v.8–9, CD xv.7–11), though the Essenes do so at the end of the initiation period, whereas the sect does so at the beginning.
25. Both hide nothing from fellow members of the sect nor disclose anything about themselves to others (*The Jewish War* 2.141; 1QS iv.5–6, viii.11–12).
26. Both transmit their teachings precisely as they have received them (*The Jewish War* 2.142; 1QS ix.16–19).
27. Both refrain from brigandage (*The Jewish War* 2.142; 1QS x.19).
28. Both preserve the names of the angels (*The Jewish War* 2.142; 1QM ix.14–16).
29. Both obey the elders and the majority (*The Jewish War* 2.146; 1QS v.2–3, v.9).
30. Both avoid spitting (*The Jewish War* 2.147; 1QS vii.13).
31. They are particularly strict in observance of the Sabbath (*The Jewish War* 2.147; CD x.14–xi.18).
32. Both follow a strict rule of discipline, demanding absolute obedience by junior members toward senior members (*The Jewish War* 2.150; 1QS v.23, vi.2).
33. They are fearless in the face of danger (*The Jewish War* 2.151; 1QS i.16–17).
34. Some of the sect are able to foretell the future (*The Jewish War* 2.159; 1QpHab vii.4–5).
35. Both believe in determinism (*Jewish Antiquities* 18.18; 1QS iii.15–16).
36. Both disagree with the ritual practiced in the Temple in Jerusalem (*Jewish Antiquities* 18.19; CD vi.11–13).

However, there are a number of differences: (1) the members of the main Essene community (in contrast to one offshoot, cf. *The Jewish War* 2.160–161) do not marry, seeking to protect themselves, as they stated, against women's wantonness (*The Jewish War* 2.120–121), whereas marriage was practiced in the Qumran community, as we see, for example, in the Damascus Document iv.19–v.2, xvi.10–12; (2) the Essenes (*The Jewish War* 2.122) shared their property, whereas the members of the community retained ownership of their possessions (1QS vii.6–8, CD xiv.12–13); (3) Josephus (*The Jewish War* 2.135) says that the Essenes avoid swearing except when finally being admitted to the sect (*The Jewish War* 2.139), whereas the Temple Scroll (11Q19 liii.9–liv.5) has a long passage on oaths and permits the husband to annul a wife's oath; (4) Josephus (*The Jewish War* 2.145) says that the Essenes never pass sentence in a court of less than a hundred members, whereas the Damascus Document x.4–7 speaks of a court of ten, and another fragment (4Q334 2–4.i.3–4) speaks of a court of ten men and two priests; (5) Josephus (*The Jewish War* 2.145) says that the penalty for blasphemy against the lawgiver, presumably Moses, is death, but there is no such mention in any of the scrolls; (6) the community does have slaves (CD xi.12, xii.10–11), whereas the Essenes do not (*Jewish Antiquities* 18.21); (7) there is no mention in Josephus of the community's use of a solar calendar (cf. 11Q5 xxvii.6); (8) there is no mention in Josephus of the Teacher of Righteousness; (9) there is no mention in Josephus of the community's eschatological views. The number of parallels is much greater than the number of discrepancies. Moreover, some of the discrepancies are between the Damascus Document and the Rule of the Community and may indicate the composition of the texts during different time periods.

Josephus and the Biblical Texts of the Scrolls. Since so many of the fragments of the Dead Sea Scrolls are either biblical texts or paraphrases or commentaries thereon, Josephus is of particular value, inasmuch as in the first eleven books of the *Jewish Antiquities* he presents a comprehensive and often close paraphrase of most of the Bible, the earliest systematic "rewritten" Bible that has come down to us. What is important for students of the scrolls is that he is contemporary with those writings. Hence, he is a most important source for our knowledge of the biblical text and the interpretation thereof. Indeed, such a document as 4Q252, a Commentary on Genesis, is not unlike Josephus' *Jewish Antiquities* or Pseudo-Philo's *Biblical Antiquities* in focusing on selected incidents, while abbreviating or expanding as the author deems appropriate. Josephus' value is particularly great because our earliest extant complete Hebrew texts of the Bible date from the tenth century CE; and our other sources, notably the Septuagint, the Samaritan text, and biblical quotations in the Talmud and Midrash are fraught with incredibly complex problems of their own.

Josephus himself (*The Life* 418) states that he received from Titus, the Roman commander at the capture of Jerusalem, a gift of sacred books, presumably the Bible in Hebrew. It is this text that we may speculate was a major basis of his version in the *Jewish Antiquities*; there is, moreover, reason to think that this version was the basis of the text known to the Qumran community. Thus, for the *Book of Joshua* we may note that in Josephus the account of the crossing of the Jordan River (*Jewish Antiquities* 5.16–19) by Joshua's army is followed by the account of Joshua's erection of an altar and his sacrificing upon it (*Antiquities* 5.20), precisely as in a Dead Sea fragment (4Q47), and, by implication, in the Mishnah (*Sot.* 7.5) and the Tosefta (T., *Sot.* 8.7), whereas in the Bible the altar is built later at Mount Ebal (*Jos.* 8.30–35), a passage omitted by Josephus. For the *Book of Samuel* there are at least four readings (*1 Sm.* 1.22, *Jewish Antiquities* 5.347; *1 Sm.* 11.1, *Jewish Antiquities* 6.68–69; *1 Sm.* 28.1, *Jewish Antiquities* 6.325; *2 Sm.* 11.3, *Jewish Antiquities* 7.131) in which the biblical scroll used by Josephus agrees with a Qumran scroll of Samuel (4Q51) against the Masoretic Text, whereas there are no readings where Josephus agrees with the Masoretic Text against the Qumran scroll.

Moreover, in his interpretation of the Bible Josephus is sometimes in accord with the scrolls against the simple understanding of the Bible itself. An example may be seen in the case of King Zedekiah of Judah. The Bible asserts that Zedekiah did what was evil in the sight of the Lord (*2 Kgs.* 24.19). Josephus (*Jewish Antiquities* 10.120) goes out of his way to mention Zedekiah's goodness and sense of justice in apparent contradiction to his own earlier statement (*Jewish Antiquities* 10.103) that Zedekiah was contemptuous of justice and duty. This same positive portrayal of Zedekiah appears to be reflected in several fragments (4Q470) discovered at Qumran.

Furthermore, in the realm of *halakhah*, Josephus' *Jewish Antiquities* and the scrolls share, to some degree, the interpretation of the Torah's laws. There are even parallels in points of detail: for example, both the Temple Scroll (lxiii.5—like the Septuagint) and Josephus (*Jewish Antiquities* 4.222) assert that the public officers of the nearest town are to wash their hands in holy water over the head of a heifer in expiation for an undetected murderer, whereas the Bible (*Dt.* 21.6) states that they are to wash their hands over the heifer, without specifying the head. Likewise, whereas according to both the Hebrew Scriptures (*1 Kgs.* 21.13) and the Septuagint (*1 Kgs.* 20.13) there were two false witnesses against Naboth while Josephus (*Jewish Antiquities* 8.358) speaks of three, Josephus may be following an earlier *halakhah*, which required three witnesses (that is, one accuser and two witnesses) in cases of capital punishment. In this connection, we may note that the Damascus Document (CD ix.17, ix.22) similarly requires three witness in capital cases. Indeed, the very fact that the Temple Scroll records laws, including much oral law, in a systematic way should lead us to think that perhaps such a written compendium might have been available for Josephus.

[*See also* Demetrius III Eukerus; Pesher Nahum.]

BIBLIOGRAPHY

Beall, Todd S. *Josephus' Description of the Essenes Illustrated by the Dead Sea Scrolls*. Cambridge, 1988. Extensive and judicious commentary on all the passages in Josephus dealing with the Essenes, noting parallels with the Dead Sea Scrolls.

Bilde, Per. *Flavius Josephus between Jerusalem and Rome: His Life, His Works, and Their Importance*. Sheffield, 1998. A critical evaluation of scholarship on Josephus, with special attention to the most recent scholarship.

Feldman, Louis H. "Josephus." In *Anchor Bible Dictionary*, edited by David Noel Freedman, vol. 3, pp. 981–998. Garden City, 1992. Summary of Josephus' works, his views on Jewish law, his language and style, his influence, the text of his works, paraphrases and translations, and scholarship on Josephus.

Feldman, Louis H. *Josephus and Modern Scholarship (1937–1980)*. Berlin, 1984. A critical bibliography, arranged topically, of books and articles dealing with Josephus, including an extensive section on the Dead Sea Scrolls.

Feldman, Louis H. *Josephus: A Supplementary Bibliography*. New York, 1986. Corrects and supplements Schreckenberg's bibliographies, particularly adding summaries for items where these had been omitted.

Feldman, Louis H., and Hata, Gohei, eds. *Josephus, the Bible, and History*. Detroit, 1989. A collection of essays by various contributors.

Niese, Benedictus. *Flavii Iosephi Opera*. 7 vols. Berlin, 1885–1895. The definitive edition of the Greek text of Josephus. Very conservative in avoiding emendations wherever possible.

Rabin, Chaim. "Alexander Jannaeus and the Pharisees." *Journal of Jewish Studies* 7 (1956), 3–11. Drawing on references in the Dead Sea Scrolls, argues that Josephus does not identify the Jewish opponents of Jannaeus as Pharisees.

Rajak, Tessa. *Josephus: The Historian and His Society*. London, 1983. Interprets Josephus' social, educational, and linguistic background in light of what can be known about his contemporaries and their attitudes. Focuses on the Jewish revolt against the Romans.

Rajak, Tessa. "Ciò che Flavio Giuseppe vide: Josephus and the Essenes." In *Josephus and the History of the Greco-Roman Period: Essays in Memory of Morton Smith*, edited by Fausto Parente and Joseph Sievers, pp. 141–160. Stresses the Greek models behind Josephus' account of the Essenes in *The Jewish War* and suggests that this explains to a considerable degree what Josephus overlooks in describing the Dead Sea sect to his readers.

Rengstorf, Karl H., ed. *A Complete Concordance to Flavius Josephus*. 4 vols. Leiden, 1973–1983. Extraordinarily accurate and complete, except for the small portion of *Against Apion* (2.51–133), which is extant only in the Latin version.

Schreckenberg, Heinz. *Bibliographie zu Flavius Josephus*. Leiden, 1968. Supplementary volume, 1979. Lists books and articles, with brief summaries for most entries in German.

Strugnell, John. "Flavius Josephus and the Essenes: *Antiquities* XVIII, 18–22." *Journal of Biblical Literature* 77 (1958), 106–115. Argues convincingly, identifying the Essenes and the Dead Sea sect, that the Essenes did send sacrifices to the Temple in Jerusalem but used a different method of purification.

Thackeray, Henry St. J., Ralph Marcus, Allen Wikgren, and Louis H. Feldman. *Josephus*. Loeb Classical Library. 10 vols. London, 1926–65. Critical edition of the Greek text, translation into English, with brief commentary. Generally regarded as the standard translation but not very literal.

Thackeray, Henry St. J. *Josephus: The Man and the Historian*. New York, 1929; reissued 1967. Semipopular, highly readable work. Surveys the life and works of Josephus.

Ulrich, Eugene. "Josephus' Biblical Text for the Books of Samuel." In *Josephus, the Bible, and History*, edited by Louis H. Feldman and Gohei Hata, pp. 81–96. Concludes convincingly that Josephus' biblical text was in Greek, not Hebrew or Aramaic, and was intimately related to the Dead Sea Scroll of Samuel (4Q51).

Ulrich, Eugene C. *The Qumran Text of Samuel and Josephus*. Harvard Semitic Monographs, 19. Missoula, 1978. Extremely thorough, systematic comparison of Josephus' paraphrase of the Books of Samuel as compared with the fragmentary Dead Sea Scroll of Samuel.

Ulrich, Eugene. "4QJoshua[a] and Joshua's First Altar in the Promised Land." In *New Qumran Texts and Studies: Proceedings of the First Meeting of the International Organization for Qumran Studies, Paris 1992*, edited by George J. Brooke with Florentino García Martínez, pp. 89–104. Leiden, 1994.

LOUIS H. FELDMAN

JOSHUA, BOOK OF. If the number of the copies of manuscripts found at Qumran is an indication of their popularity with the Qumran community, Joshua was not a popular book, represented by merely two copies in Cave 4 (4Q47, 4Q48), published by Ulrich and Tov (1995). At the same time, Joshua is a central figure in five different copies of a Joshua apocryphon.

Before the discoveries at Qumran the main representatives of the text of Joshua were the Masoretic Text and Septuagint, which differ rather much from each other. Several scholars presented these two texts as reflecting two different text editions (recensions) of Joshua, representing different stages in the development of the biblical book. The Septuagint often presents a shorter text than the Masoretic Text, but it also contains substantial pluses, and it reflects other significant differences as well. The relation between the two texts should probably be portrayed in general lines as parallel editions of the book of Joshua, each of which are on occasion longer. The often earlier elements of the Septuagint of Joshua were analyzed especially by Auld (1978), Rofé (1994), Tov (1986), and Mazor (1994). A third textual witness of Joshua is the Samaritan version of the book of Joshua which, among other things, contains several readings agreeing with the Septuagint as against the Masoretic Text (see Gaster, 1906). Readings agreeing with the Septuagint are also reflected in Joshua[a], and less significantly also in 4QapocrJosh[a,b] and Joshua[b].

The medieval Masoretic Text is now joined by the few fragments of Joshua[b] (late Hasmonean, six fragments of chapters 2, 3, 4, 17), although that text also contains some readings which are found in the Septuagint (note a supralinear correction in *Joshua* 3.15 agreeing with the Septuagint), as well as some independent readings.

The suggestion that the Masoretic Text and Septuagint reflect two different recensions can be expanded by reference to Joshua[a], which reflects yet a third recension, although at times it is also significantly close to either the Masoretic Text or the Septuagint.

Joshua[a] (dated to the Hasmonean period) contains twenty-two fragments covering chapters 5–10. As a rule, that text goes with the Masoretic Text against the Septuagint, but in two important pericopes it behaves differently.

Fragments 1–2, named "col. 1" by the editor, Eugene Ulrich, reflect the following sequence: 8.34–35 (the covenant at Ebal connected with the erecting of the altar described in the previous verses), two lines containing previously unknown verses (the preserved words refer to the crossing of the Jordan and the reading of the Torah), 5.2–7 (the circumcision ceremony), immediately followed by fragment 3 containing chapter 6 of *Joshua*. The sequence of events in Joshua[a] presents Joshua as building an altar immediately upon crossing the Jordan (chapter 4), rather than as in the other textual witnesses, in which the altar is built after several military operations at the end of chapter 8. It is not likely that fragments 1–2 contain a doublet of 8.30–35, which would also have occurred in the section which contains chapter 8 in Joshua[a] (not preserved in Qumran), because in that case Joshua would have built two altars and probably would have performed two similar ceremonies.

Based on the assumption that Joshua[a] presents a different chronological sequence of events, it should be understood as reflecting a different edition of the book of *Joshua*, at least in this regard. This rival version was possibly known to Josephus, since, according to *Jewish Antiquities* (5.20), Joshua built an altar upon crossing the Jordan, even though, later in the story, he built another altar in connection with the reading of the Torah (5.59).

When comparing the different attestations of the pericope of the building of the altar and the reading of the Torah, one clearly recognizes their secondary nature. This section was meant to stress Joshua's faithfulness to the commands of the Torah: As soon as the Israelites crossed the Jordan, they implemented the command of *Deuteronomy* 27, which ordered the Israelites to build an altar on Mount Ebal (or Mount Gerizim, according to the Old Latin and the Samaritan Pentateuch). This pericope was inserted secondarily in some manuscripts of Joshua in the course of the development of that book, and, as often happens, it was inserted in three different places in the different textual witnesses.

But, while in the traditions behind the Masoretic Text and Septuagint, this pericope is secondary, its position in Joshua[a] seems to be original. The version of Joshua[a] is therefore hailed by Ulrich and Rofé as presenting an earlier and more logical version of *Joshua* than the Masoretic Text and Septuagint, since it presents the Israelites as building an altar as soon as they had safely traversed the Jordan. The secondary nature of 8.30–35 in its present context in the Masoretic Text is evident, as this section is very loosely connected with the context. This pertains also to the Septuagint in which it occurs at a slightly different place (after 9.2).

Kempinski (1993) stresses different aspects of Joshua[a] by explaining the juxtaposition in that scroll of the covenant near Shechem and the circumcision ceremony. According to him, the conquest was sealed with a covenant and a circumcision (for which cf. *Gn.* 15 and 17). Kempinski finds parallels between this celebration far away from the temple in Jerusalem and the views of the Qumran covenanters whose cultic center was also outside Jerusalem. However, the Qumranic origin of Joshua[a] is not a likely assumption.

In fragments 15–16 of the scroll (col. vi in Ulrich's reconstruction, *Jos.* 8.10–18) the (reconstructed) text is significantly shorter than the Masoretic Text, thus more closely resembling the shorter text of the Septuagint. According to the reconstruction, verses 11b–13 are lacking in the scroll as in the Septuagint, and this pertains also to 14b–17, which are present in the Septuagint. On the whole, Joshua[a] presents a more smoothly flowing text. The shortness of the Septuagint is one of its recensional traits, as opposed to the longer Masoretic Text. In this fragment the text of Joshua[a] is even shorter than that of the Septuagint.

Five different groups of fragments of compositions from Qumran and two fragments of a similar composition from Masada rewrite the book of *Joshua* and most, if not all, of them may derive from the same composition (an apocryphon of *Joshua*). This composition, unknown before the Qumran finds, contains traditions about Joshua, several of which are not known from the Bible and may therefore be described as an example of the genre Rewritten Bible. [*See* Rewritten Bible.] These manuscripts cover different episodes and themes from the book of *Joshua*. Two copies of a composition rewriting the book of *Joshua*, Apocryphon of Joshua[a,b] (4Q378–9), are poorly preserved in a great number of fragments published preliminarily and later in a final form (Discoveries in the Judaean Desert, 22, Oxford, 1996) by Newsom. Many of the fragments of these two manuscripts reflect speeches, blessings, and prayers by Joshua not contained in the biblical text, built on the model of the speeches of Joshua in chapters 1 and 23–24, and on those of Moses in *Deuteronomy* chapters 1–3 and 28–31. Apocryphon of Joshua[a] (4Q378), previously named 4QPsalms Joshua[a], dating to the Herodian period, covers the earlier part of Joshua's career. It probably started off with the Israelites' mourning for Moses (frg. 14), and it contained an account of the transfer of the leadership from Moses to Joshua (frg. 3). Several other fragments contain speeches of Joshua to the people (cf. the speeches of Joshua scattered in the biblical book, and especially in chapters 18–21). The incident of Achan (Joshua 7) is probably described in fragment 6.i, the ruse of the Gibeonites (Joshua 9) in fragment 22, Joshua's restraining the sun (chapter 10) in fragment 26 (cf. especially line 5), and a summary of the conquests in accordance with God's plan (*Joshua* 21.43–45) in fragment 11.

Apocryphon of Joshua[b] (4Q379), dating to the Hasmonean period, contains more identifiable parts of the book of *Joshua*. It contains a description of the crossing of the Jordan (frg. 12 and probably additional fragments) and of the curse pronounced on the rebuilder of Jericho (*Jos.* 6:26), together with a prophetic vision on the identity of that rebuilder (frg. 22.ii). The blessings mentioned in fragments 15–16 of that manuscript may reflect the ceremony on or opposite Mount Gerizim (*Jos.* 8.30–35). A summary of Joshua's victories over the inhabitants of Canaan is reflected in fragment 3 (parallel to *Joshua* 13). Fragment 17 probably reflects Joshua's final speech.

The fragments of Work with Place Names (4Q522) probably reflect 4QapocrJosh[c] (Qimron and Tov speak about "Joshua Cycles"), and not a text dealing with "David and his son as well as the temple and tabernacle" (Puech). Only a minority of the identifiable elements in fragment 8.ii pertain exclusively to the period of Joshua. In the explanation by Puech, they feature as the central elements of this document, while for Qimron and Tov they are a mere digression in a document containing the memoirs of Joshua.

Fragment 8.i and additional fragments list names of places conquered by the Israelite tribes, in the north of the country and in the territories of Judah and Joseph, and they further contain fragments of narratives about the places which had not been conquered. The second column of that fragment contains a speech by Joshua (to Eleazar and the people?) explaining why he was unable to conquer Jerusalem, that the tent of the meeting would have to be transferred to an unnamed locality (Shiloh?), but that in the future the city would be conquered by David and that the tent of the meeting would be moved there, and eventually the temple would be established.

4QpaleoParaJosh, probably dating to the last half of the second century BCE, contains several phrases which were identified by Ulrich as deriving from *Joshua* 21. Since no coherent biblical text is identifiable in this very fragmentary text, Ulrich regards it as a paraphrase, but he does not rule out the possibility that this is a variant edition of the biblical book of *Joshua*. However, the writing of this scroll in the Paleo-Hebrew script is unusual for a paraphrase, since almost all texts which have been preserved in this script are biblical.

A list of geographical names similar to the list in Work with Place Names (8.i) is contained in 5Q9 (5Qapocr-Josh? published in Discoveries in the Judaean Desert as 5QWork with Place Names). This list mentions the figure of Joshua and a list of geographical names from the same areas as those in Work with Place Names from Cave 4, namely from the north of the country and from the tribes of Judah and Joseph. If the link between 4Q522 8.i and 5Q9 is understood correctly, this manuscript contains an additional copy of the apocryphon of Joshua contained in Apocryphon of Joshua[a] (4Q378), Apocryphon of Joshua[b] (4Q379), and Work with Place Names (4Q522) (Tov).

Paraphrase of Joshua from Masada was described by Talmon as an apocryphon based on *Joshua* 23–24 (described as an apocryphon on Samuel by Yadin at an earlier stage of research). The text is very fragmentary, but there are a few similarities in motifs and literary texture between this text and Apocryphon of Joshua, which may suffice to assign them to the same literary composition.

Because of the uncertainties concerning the relation between the six different manuscripts, the issue of their possible Qumran authorship has to be dealt with separately, and may be answered positively for some manuscripts, although the evidence is not clear. The curse against the rebuilder of Jericho in Apocryphon of Joshua[b] fragment 22.ii is the only datable element for the composition (in addition to the date of the individual manuscripts). Several scholars have suggested that the object of that curse is Simon or John Hyrcanus, and in that case the composition should be considered anti-Hasmonean. If this assumption is correct, the composition would have been written either in the late second or early first century BCE. The theological discussion in Work with Place Names (4Q522) as to why Jerusalem was not made a religious center in the days of Joshua is probably written from the point of view of the Jerusalem priesthood (Tov), but this element is not datable.

Beyond the aforementioned compositions devoted to Joshua, the figure of Joshua is mentioned only rarely in the Qumran texts: Words of Moses, 12 (1Q22); Damascus Document, CD v.4.

BIBLIOGRAPHY

Auld, Graeme G. "Textual and Literary Studies in the Book of Joshua." *Zeitschrift für die alttestamentliche Wissenschaft* 90 (1978), 412–417.

Bieberstein, Klaus. *Lukian und Theodotion im Josuabuch, Mit einem Beitrag zu den Josuarollen von Hirbet Qumran*. Biblische Notizen, Beiheft 7. Munich, 1994.

Eshel, Hanan. "The Historical Background of 4QTest in the Light of Archaeological Discoveries" (in Hebrew). *Zion* 55 (1990), 141–150.

Gaster, Moses. "Das Buch Josua in hebräisch-samaritanischer Rezension." *Zeitschrift der deutschen Morgenländischen Gesellschaft* 62 (1906), 209–279, 494–549.

Greenspoon, Leonard. "The Qumran Fragments of Joshua: Which Puzzle Are They Part of and Where Do They Fit?" In *Septuagint, Scrolls and Cognate Writings: Papers Presented to the International Symposium on the Septuagint and Its Relations to the Dead Sea Scrolls and Other Writings (Manchester, 1990)*, edited by G. J. Brooke and B. Lindars, pp. 159–194. Septuagint and Cognate Studies, 33. Atlanta, 1992.

Kempinski, Aharon. "'When History Sleeps, Theology Arises': A Note on *Joshua* 8:30–35 and the Archaeology of the 'Settlement Period'" (in Hebrew). *Eretz Israel* 24 (1993), 175–183.

Mazor, Lea. "The Septuagint Translation of the Book of Joshua—Its Contribution to the Understanding of the Textual Transmission of the Book and Its Literary and Ideological Development" (in Hebrew). Ph.D. Diss., Hebrew University. Jerusalem, 1994.

Puech, Émile. "La pierre de Sion et l'autel des holocaustes d'après un manuscrit hébreu de la grotte 4 (4Q522)." *Revue biblique* 99 (1992), 676–696.

Qimron, Elisha. "Concerning 'Joshua Cycles' from Qumran" (in Hebrew). *Tarbiz* 63 (1994), 503–508. English summary.

Rofé, Alexander. "The Editing of the Book of Joshua in the Light of 4QJosh[a]." In *New Qumran Texts and Studies: Proceedings of the First Meeting of the International Organization for Qumran Studies, Paris 1992*, edited by G. J. Brooke with F. García Martínez, pp. 73–80. Studies on the Texts of the Desert of Judah, 15. Leiden, 1994.

Talmon, Shemaryahu. "A Joshua Apocryphon from Masada." In *Studies on Hebrew and Other Semitic Languages Presented to Professor Chaim Rabin on the Occasion of His Seventy-Fifth Birthday*, edited by M. Goshen-Gottstein, S. Morag, and S. Kogut, pp. 147–157. Jerusalem, 1990.

Tov, Emanuel. "The Growth of the Book of Joshua in the Light of the Evidence of the Septuagint Translation." *Scripta Hierosolymitana* 31 (1986), 321–339.

Tov, Emanuel. "The Rewritten Book of Joshua as Found at Qumran and Masada." In press.

Ulrich, Eugene. "4QJoshua[a] and Joshua's First Altar in the Promised Land." In *New Qumran Texts and Studies: Proceedings of the First Meeting of the International Organization for Qumran Studies, Paris 1992*, edited by G. J. Brooke with F. García Martínez, pp. 89–104. Studies on the Texts of the Desert of Judah, 15. Leiden, 1994.

EMANUEL TOV

JUBILEES, BOOK OF, a retelling of the stories in *Genesis* and the first parts of *Exodus* set within the literary context of a divine revelation to Moses while he was on Mount Sinai. In the first chapter, God himself converses with Moses about Israel's future apostasy and restoration, but in the remaining chapters (2–50) an Angel of the Presence reveals the contents of heavenly tablets to Moses. The scriptural material that is revealed by the angel begins with the creation story in *Genesis* 1 and continues until the Israelites have departed from Egypt, crossed the sea, and entered the wilderness, that is, from *Genesis* 1 to *Exodus* 19. The biblical stories are placed within a chronological framework provided by the author's system of dividing time into units of forty-nine years, called jubilees, each of which is subdivided into seven units of seven weeks of years. Numerous events from *Genesis* and *Exodus* are thus introduced with a formula such as the one found in *Jubilees* 4.29: "At the end of the nineteenth jubilee, during the seventh week—in its sixth year—Adam died" (the date in question is the year 930 from creation; see *Gn*. 5.5). References to the book by its Hebrew title *Jubilees*, derived from the frequently recurring chronological unit of forty-nine years, are found in Hebrew, Greek, and Syriac sources, while another title—*The Book of the Division of the Times* (taken from the prologue and *Jub*. 1.4)—which was probably its original name, is attested in Hebrew and Ethiopic sources.

It is highly likely that the book was written in the mid-second century BCE or even a little earlier. While scholars such as R. H. Charles defended a late-second-century date, new evidence now makes the midsecond-century date more likely. Externally, the earliest copy of any part of the book is Jubilees[a] (4Q216), whose script indicates that it was copied during the Hasmonean period, probably between 125 and 100 BCE. *Jubilees* is mentioned by name and cited as an authority in the Damascus Document (CD xvi.2–4). The earliest copy of the Damascus Document from Cave 4 can be dated paleographically to between 100 and 50 BCE. Thus, the dates of the earliest copy of *Jubilees* itself and of the earliest reference to it indicate that it was written no later than approximately 100 BCE. Internally, the book contains some clues that it was written after most of the booklets included in *1 Enoch* had been composed. The section about Enoch (*Jub*. 4.15–26) betrays knowledge of the "Astronomical Book" (*1 Enoch* 72–82), the "Book of Watchers" (*1 Enoch* 1–36), the "Epistle of Enoch" (*1 Enoch* 91–107), and the "Book of Dreams" (*1 Enoch* 83–90). The "Book of Dreams" appears to be the latest among them, and, judging by historical allusions in the "Animal Apocalypse" (chaps. 85–90), it was written no earlier than c.164 BCE. Hence, *Jubilees*, which refers to this section, was written after 164 BCE. While many of the concerns in *Jubilees* resemble those found in the sectarian texts at Qumran (see below), there is no evidence in the book that the author advocated withdrawal from Jewish society. Consequently, it may have been written before the exodus to Qumran, which may have occurred c.150–140 BCE. A date of composition somewhere between 160 and 150 BCE seems highly likely for the complete book. Several scholars (Goldstein

[1983], Knibb [1989]) have argued that a slightly earlier date is more likely, perhaps about 170 BCE. Their reasoning is that the book demonstrates the author's knowledge of events that occurred early in the reign of Antiochus IV (175–164 BCE) but not of his infamous decrees banning the practice of Judaism in 167—an event the writer would certainly have noted had he been aware of it. It is not obvious, however, that, within the framework of the book, the author would have had occasion to comment on or allude to these decrees; moreover, a date of composition in approximately 170 BCE would not explain the writer's knowledge of the later "Book of Dreams." There is no textual or manuscript evidence for any subsequent redactions of *Jubilees* or parts of it.

Jubilees was composed in Hebrew and was subsequently translated into Greek and possibly into Syriac. The Greek translation served as the basis for renderings into Latin and Ethiopic. Some textual evidence from each of these versions has survived, but the complete book is extant only in the Ethiopic (Geʿez) language. The Hebrew text of the book seems to have passed out of use in antiquity; nothing was thought to have survived of it, apart from a citation of its title in the Damascus Document (CD xvi.3–4), until the Qumran discoveries. In the Qumran caves, fragmentary copies of fourteen (possibly fifteen) manuscripts were found (see VanderKam [1992], p. 642). They are listed here with their paleographically determined dates (Hasmonean = 150–30 BCE; Herodian = 30 BCE–70 CE) and chapters and verses that are attested (usually only partially) in them:

1Q17	Herodian	27.19–20
1Q18	Hasmonean	35.8–10
2Q19	Herodian	23.7–8
2Q20	Herodian	46.1–3
3Q5 frgs. 3, 1	Herodian	23.6–7, 12–13
4Q176a frgs. 19–21	Herodian	23.21–23, 30–31
4Q216	Hasmonean	Prologue + 1.1–2, 4–7, 7–15, 26–28; 2.1–4, 7–12, 13–24
2Q217 (?)	Hasmonean	1.29–2.1; 2.29–30 (?)
4Q218	Herodian	2.26–27
4Q219	Herodian	21.1–2, 7–10, 12–16, 18–22.1
4Q220	Herodian	21.5–10
4Q221	Herodian	21.22–24; 22.22, (30?); 23.10–13; 33.12–15; 37.11–15; 38.6–8; 39.4–9
4Q222	Hasmonean	25.9–12; 27.6–7; 48.5 (?)
4Q223–224	Hasmonean	32.18–21; 34.4–5; 35.7–22; 36.7–23; 37.17–38.13; 39.9–40.7; 41.7–10
11Q12	Herodian	4.7–11, 13–14, 16–17, 29–30; 5.1–2; 12.15–17, 28–29

As all fifteen (or fourteen if 4Q217 is omitted) of these copies are written in Hebrew, there can be no doubt that Hebrew was the original language of the book. It has been claimed that a copy of *Jubilees* was found at Masada (1276–1786), but the fragmentary text is related to parts of the book in theme only and is not from a copy of *Jubilees* itself. Unlike the Qumran copies of *1 Enoch*, the *Jubilees* manuscripts show that the Ethiopic version has preserved the text of the book in an accurate fashion. The Greek version has disappeared; all that survives is a series of allusions to and quotations from it in the writings of various Christian authors such as Epiphanius, Syncellus, and Cedrenus (see the list in VanderKam, [1989], 1, xii). The same situation obtains for the Syriac version, if there ever was a complete translation of *Jubilees* in this language: only a series of nineteen excerpts in the *Chronicon ad annum Christi 1234* has survived. A Latin version is attested by one fifth–sixth century palimpsest manuscript on which approximately one-third of the text from twenty-five different sections (beginning at *Jub.* 13.10) is preserved. The full text of *Jubilees* is extant in the Ethiopic language, and twenty-seven copies of it have been identified (cf. VanderKam, 1989).

Although the name of the author remains unknown, the concerns that led him to write the book are evident throughout. He chose to present his work as a divine revelation, with God himself speaking in the first chapter and the Angel of the Presence, reading from the heavenly tablets, in chapters 2–50. In large part he reproduced the scriptural base, but through additions and other modifications he was able to insert his own views into the older text and thus to clothe them with the same revealed authority. One of his principal emphases was to present the patriarchs as faithfully obedient to divine laws that, according to the Pentateuch, were revealed only in postpatriarchal times. Hence, Noah celebrated Shavuʿot (*Jub.* 6.17–18), and Abraham observed it (*Jub.* 15.1–10) and Sukkot (*Jub.* 16.15–31) as well. The writer may have been combating a current opinion that there had once been a time when the laws that came to separate Jewish people from others were not in existence. His point is that there was never such a time; the chosen race had always been distinguished from other nations by special laws that they observed from the earliest days.

Another overarching theme is chronological. The period from the first day of creation to the future entry into Canaan extends exactly fifty jubilee periods of forty-nine years each, that is, 2,450 years. Such language reminds the reader of the biblical jubilee legislation requiring that at the end of a jubilee (in the fiftieth year according to *Lv.* 25.8–17) slaves were to be freed and land was to be returned to its original owners. In *Jubilees* the same happens in the fiftieth jubilee period but on a national scale: early in the jubilee period (the year 2410) the Hebrew slaves are freed from Egyptian bondage, and at the end of it (the year 2450) they enter the promised land, which had rightfully been theirs since the division of the earth following the Flood. The importance of chronology is also evident from the numerous dates that the author assigns to biblical events and from his teachings about the correct calendar. He attributes the beginning of calendrical knowledge to Enoch (*Jub.* 4.17–18, 21) but discloses the details about it in connection with the story of the Flood (*Jub.* 6.20–38). The revealed calendar is a solar one of 364 days (exactly fifty-two weeks), with each quarter having ninety-one days (thirteen weeks). Within this arrangement each festival has an exact time when it is to be celebrated, and the weekly rhythm of time is marked by the all-important Sabbath, which is to be observed scrupulously. The writer insists that lunar movements play no calendrical role; they mislead one into following the calendar of the nations. Several passages in the book imply that Shavuʿot was celebrated on the fifteenth day of the third month. The Qumran calendars specify the same date for the holiday and thus show that these exegetes understood the phrase "the day after the Sabbath" in *Leviticus* 23.15—the date that serves as the starting point of the fifty-day count leading to Shavuʿot—to mean the twenty-sixth day of the first month. This date is the occasion for making or remembering covenants in *Jubilees* (with Noah, *Jub.* 6.17–22; Abraham, *Jub.* 14.20; and Moses, *Jub.* 1.1) and is now known to be the time when the Qumran community annually renewed its covenantal vows (Damascus Document[a] [4Q266 ii.16–18] = Damascus Document[e] [4Q270 ii.11–12]).

Early in the history of scrolls scholarship, Annie Jaubert proposed that *Jubilees'* solar calendar provided the information needed to solve the problem of the conflicting days for the Last Supper in the Gospels. The synoptic Gospels identify the supper as a Passover meal, whereas John places it on the evening before Passover. Jaubert proposed that the synoptic writers followed the *Jubilees* calendar, but John used the lunar-solar arrangement practiced at the time in the larger Jewish community. Her proposal has not received much support because there is no evidence in the New Testament for the 364-day solar calendar; moreover, the differences in the gospel chronologies seem to be theologically motivated.

A third entity emphasized in *Jubilees* is the priesthood. In the book the priestly line extends back to Adam, who offered sacrifices as he left the garden of Eden (*Jub.* 3.27), and continues through to Levi who is the biblical ancestor of the priests. The sacred writings are entrusted to the members of this line. Levi, the third son of Leah and Jacob, is presented far more favorably in *Jubilees* 30–32 than in the corresponding parts of *Genesis*. The writer makes it abundantly clear that priestly authority, represented especially by Levi, who was divinely chosen for the position, is superior to temporal power, embodied particularly in Judah.

Fourth, unlike the biblical texts that undergird the book, *Jubilees* shows an interest in the last times. In the future, God, after punishing his recalcitrant people, will purify and restore them and will dwell with them in a new creation when human life will again be as long as it was for the antediluvian patriarchs (see chaps. 1 and 23).

A final intriguing point that the writer highlights is the importance of women in the chosen line. Unlike the biblical writers, he names the wives of all the patriarchs and supplies genealogical information about them. In this way he assures the purity of the line by documenting the proper family connections of both mother and father (Halpern-Amaru, 1994). Mention should also be made here of the significant role that Rebekah plays in the book (Endres, 1987).

Jubilees enjoys the closest ideological kinship with the Enochic literature, the Levi texts—especially Aramaic Levi—and the sectarian literature from Qumran. The writer's knowledge of the early Enoch booklets—the "Astronomical Book," the "Book of Watchers," the "Epistle," and the "Book of Dreams"—is clear in *Jubilees* 4.16–25, the paragraph about Enoch. One specific theme common to *Jubilees* and the Enochic works is the angelic interpretation of *Genesis* 6.1–4: the sons of God (= angels) married the daughters of men who gave birth to giants. Their violent and evil exploits served as an explanation for the monstrous increase of evil in the world before the Flood, and their punishment prefigured the final judgment. A second theme that they share is the 364-day solar calendar. *Jubilees* disagrees with the "Astronomical Book," however, in according no valid place to a lunar element in calendrical matters. *Jubilees* also borrows, whether directly or indirectly, from Aramaic Levi for its extremely positive portrait of the ancestral priest and his divine election to the priesthood (similar themes continue particularly in the *Testament of Levi* and *Testament of Judah* in the *Testaments of the Twelve Patriarchs*).

The Qumran caves have also revealed, besides the fourteen or fifteen copies of *Jubilees* found in them, a series of texts that have affinities with *Jubilees*. Several calendrical texts offer or presuppose the same 364-day solar calendar; among them are Calendrical Document A (4Q320, which, however, correlates solar and lunar calendars), Calendrical Document E[b] (4Q327, which correlates Sabbaths and festivals with dates in the 364-day system), Miqtsat Maʿasei ha-Torah (4QMMT), the Temple Scroll (11Q19 and 11Q20), Songs of the Sabbath Sacrifice (4Q400–407 and Mas1k), and the Compositions of David in Psalms[a] xxvii.5–7 from Qumran Cave 11 (11Q5). Other texts from Qumran that show similarities with *Jubilees* are the Pseudo-Jubilees texts (4Q225–227); 4Q228, which may cite *Jubilees* as an authority; Commentary on Genesis A (4Q252), whose chronology for the Flood account seems to offer a slight correction of the one in *Jubilees*; and the Genesis Apocryphon, whose story about the division of the earth among Noah's offspring, for example, closely resembles *Jubilees* 8–9.

There is strong reason for believing that *Jubilees* was considered authoritative at Qumran. The number of copies of the book is unusually high for any work, including the ones that became recognized as biblical. Only *Psalms* (thirty-six), *Deuteronomy* (twenty-nine), *Isaiah* (twenty-one), and *Exodus* (seventeen) among the scriptural writings are represented in more copies than *Jubilees*. Interestingly, there are as many copies of *Genesis* (fifteen) as of *Jubilees* (if 4Q217 is counted). No other text found in the caves is attested as frequently. In addition to the relatively large number of manuscripts, *Jubilees* is recognized as an authority in the Damascus Document. The Damascus Document (CD xvi.2–4) refers to it and employs its Hebrew title ("The Book of the Divisions"): "And the exact interpretation of their ages about the blindness of Israel in all these matters, behold, it is defined in the book of the divisions of the periods according to their jubilees and their weeks" (translation of García Martínez, p. 39; compare also CD x.7–10 with *Jubilees* 23.11 for a possible second reference). The text 4Q228 (work with citation of *Jubilees?*) may mention the book in 1.i.2 ("[in the divi]s[ion]s of the times") and 1.i.9 ("For thus is it written in the divisions"; cf. lines 4 and 7). The citation formula that introduces the reference in line 9 is familiar from scriptural quotations at Qumran and elsewhere.

The status of *Jubilees* at Qumran is complicated by several other considerations. It may seem to have served as an authority in calendrical matters in that its 364-day solar calendar is attested in a series of Qumran texts, but the Qumran calendars are more closely related to the Enochic "Astronomical Book" because they also reckon with a lunar calendar, which is anathema to the author of *Jubilees*. Moreover, Commentary on Genesis A (hereafter, 4Q252) offers an interpretation of the dates in the Flood story that seems to correct the one presented in *Jubilees:* where *Jubilees* 5.27, following *Genesis* 7.24, states that "[t]he waters remained standing on the surface of the earth for five months—150 days," the author of 4Q252 recognized that in the 364-day calendar the five months in question would total 152 days. Hence he added two days to the 150 to achieve five complete months. That is, the verdict of *Jubilees* was not taken as authoritative.

While there are no indications that *Jubilees* ever became more widely authoritative in Jewish circles, it was used by later writers. An example is the eleventh-century rabbi Moses the Preacher of Narbonne, who derived the *Jubilees* material that he incorporated in his writings from Byzantine excerpts from Jewish pseudepigrapha (Himmelfarb, 1994). The book was transmitted in Christian circles, although, apart from Ethiopia, little textual evidence remains. In the Abyssinian Church, *Jubilees* achieved canonical status and is often listed together with the works of the Pentateuch.

BIBLIOGRAPHY

Berger, K. *Das Buch der Jubiläen*. Jüdische Schriften aus hellenistisch-römischer Zeit, 2.3. Gütersloh, 1981. The latest German translation that includes a full introduction, and detailed textual notes.

Charles, R. H. *The Book of Jubilees or the Little Genesis*. London, 1902. Charles's translation, introduction, and brief commentary have been the standard treatments in English until recently.

Charles, R. H. "The Book of Jubilees." In *Apocrypha and Pseudepigrapha of the Old Testament*, edited by R. H. Charles, 2.1–82. Oxford, 1913. Charles's contribution to his standard collection contains much the same material as the 1902 volume but is more easily accessible.

Cowley, R. W. "The Biblical Canon of the Ethiopian Orthodox Church Today." *Ostkirchliche Studien* 223 (1974), 318–323. Cowley explains the place of *Jubilees* in the Ethiopian Orthodox Church's canon of scripture.

Cowley, R. W. "Old Testament Introduction in the Andemta Commentary Tradition." *Journal of Ethiopian Studies* 12 (1974), 133–175. Cowley includes a translation of the introductory comments on *Jubilees* in the Andemta tradition.

Davenport, G. L. *The Eschatology of the Book of Jubilees*. Studia Post-Biblica, 20. Leiden, 1971. Davenport finds that *Jubilees* has gone through two revisions, both of which have altered the eschatological message of the book.

Endres, J. C. *Biblical Interpretation in the Book of Jubilees.* Catholic Biblical Quarterly Monograph Series, 18. Washington, D.C., 1987. Endres focuses on the extended *Jacob* material and explores the ways in which the author has worked with the biblical text.

Goldstein, J. "The Date of the Book of Jubilees." *Proceedings of the American Academy for Jewish Research* 50 (1983), 63–86. Goldstein argues for a pre-167 BCE date for *Jubilees*.

Halpern-Amaru, B. "The First Woman, Wives, and Mothers in Jubilees." *Journal of Biblical Literature* 113 (1994), 609–626. Halpern-Amaru demonstrates that concern for the purity of the chosen line has led the author to name the matriarchs and to give their family connections.

Himmelfarb, M. "Some Echoes of *Jubilees* in Medieval Hebrew Literature." In *Tracing the Threads: Studies in the Vitality of Jewish Pseudepigrapha*, edited by John C. Reeves, pp. 115–141. Early Judaism and Its Literature, 6. Atlanta, 1994. Himmelfarb explores the evidence for use of *Jubilees* in later sources and the ways in which the authors obtained the information from the book.

Jaubert, A. *The Date of the Last Supper*. Staten Island, 1965 (translation of *La date de la cène*. Paris, 1957). Jaubert argues that the calendar of *Jubilees* underlies the priestly parts of the Old Testament and was used by the authors of Matthew, Mark, and Luke.

Knibb, M. "Jubilees and the Origins of the Qumran Community." Inaugural lecture, Department of Biblical Studies, King's College, London, 17 January 1989. Knibb also formulates a case for a pre-167 date for *Jubilees*.

Rabin, C. "Jubilees." In *The Apocryphal Old Testament*. Edited by H. F. D. Sparks, pp. 1–139. Oxford, 1984. Rabin has revised Charles's translation for this easily accessible collection.

Talmon, S. "Hebrew Written Fragments from Masada." *Dead Sea Discoveries* 3 (1996), 168–176. Talmon reassesses Masada 1276–1786 and recognizes that it is related to the text of *Jubilees* but is not from a copy of the book.

VanderKam, J. C. *Textual and Historical Studies in the Book of Jubilees*. Harvard Semitic Monographs, 14. Missoula, Mont., 1977. VanderKam defends the accuracy of the Ethiopic version, examines the textual affiliations of the book's citations from the Bible, and defends a date of composition between c.160 and 150 BCE.

VanderKam, J. C. *The Book of Jubilees*. 2 vols. Corpus Scriptorum Christianorum Orientalium, 510–511, Scriptores Aethiopici, 87–88. Louvain, 1989. The first volume contains a critical Ethiopic text and all the then-available versions, and the second volume gives a translation of the Ethiopic text and of the versions and adds a textual commentary.

VanderKam, J. C. "The Jubilees Fragments from Qumran Cave 4." In *The Madrid Qumran Congress*, edited by Julio Trebolle Barrera and Luis Vegas Montaner, pp. 635–648. Leiden, 1992. A survey of all the Qumran textual evidence for *Jubilees*.

VanderKam, J. C., and J. T. Milik. "Jubilees." In *Qumran Cave 4: VIII Parabiblical Texts Part I*, pp. 1–185. Discoveries in the Judaean Desert, 13. Oxford, 1994. The official publication of the Qumran Cave 4 copies of *Jubilees* and pseudo-Jubilees texts.

Wintermute, O. "Jubilees." In *The Old Testament Pseudepigrapha*, edited by J. H. Charlesworth, pp. 2.35–142. Garden City, N.Y., 1983, 1985. Wintermute introduces, translates, and comments briefly on *Jubilees* in this widely distributed collection of pseudepigrapha.

JAMES C. VANDERKAM

JUDAH, the fourth son of Jacob and Leah, who persuaded his brothers to sell Joseph to the Midianites rather than to kill him (*Gn.* 37.26–28). He took a Canaanite wife who bore him three sons and had twins through Tamar, the wife of his firstborn son (*Gn.* 38). He was blessed with the scepter (of kingship) that would not depart from him (*Gn.* 49.10), and from him kings and eventually the Messiah would descend.

The most significant Judean Desert documents that refer to Judah are fragments that resemble, but have no direct correspondence to, *Jubilees* and the *Testament of Judah*. The *Testament of Judah* (1.5) attributes the assignment of kingship to Judah's obedience and honoring his parents, and also mentions his military exploits (chaps. 3–7). *The Testament of Judah* puts much of the blame for Judah's actions in *Genesis* 38 on his Canaanite wife, who opposed her sons having children by the Amorite Tamar (10.1–6), and on drunkenness, the love of money, and gazing at the beauty of women, which caused him to take a Canaanite woman as his wife and enter into relations with Tamar (14.1–6). Because of this, his tribe would be doomed to wickedness (17.1–2). The termination of his rule by an alien race is foretold (22.2) and the coming of his descendant, the star of Jacob, as a savior (24.1, 24.6). *Jubilees*, which retells *Genesis*, also elevates Judah, including his repentance for having had relations with Tamar, his forgiveness, as well as his command for strict punishment for those who do likewise in the future (*Jub.* 41.34–28; cf. *Gn.* 38).

Judean Desert documents contain numerous references to the tribe of Judah in connection with the other tribes (e.g., the War Scroll; 1QM i.2) or the land of Judah (e.g., Testimonia; 4Q175 27). The works that mention Judah's life are the Testament of Judah? from Cave 3 at Qumran (hereafter, 3QTestament of Judah?; 3Q7), Testament of Judah? from Cave 4 at Qumran (hereafter, 4QTestament of Judah?; 4Q484), Apocryphon of Judah (4Q538), and Commentary on Genesis A (4Q252). The first three are very fragmented, and it is difficult to say very much about the precise nature of these works. 3QTestament of Judah? consists of a number of Hebrew fragments that seem to be a list of tribes among whom Judah (the name Judah must be restored) is included, who are blessed by the Angel of the Presence. 3QTestament of Judah? is similar to *Testament of Judah* 25.1–2, which also mentions the Angel of the Presence. 4QTestament of Judah consists of twenty tiny fragments (the largest contains only five letters) dated to the first century CE, three of which may be related to the *Testament of Judah* 24 and 25. There are two Aramaic fragments of late Hasmonean date entitled the Apocryphon of Judah that recount the second journey of Jacob's sons to Egypt, in which Judah offers himself instead of Benjamin before the brothers recognize Joseph (cf. *Jub.* 42.25–43.18; *Gn.* 44.1–45.10). Commentary on Genesis A (4Q252 v.1–6) dates to around the second half of the first century BCE and contains a commentary or *pesher* on *Genesis* 49.10, predicting the coming of Judah's descendant, the Messiah of Righteousness, the Branch of David.

Judah's main significance in the New Testament is as the forefather of Jesus Christ, the priestly Messiah descended from Judah (*Heb.* 7.14) and lion of the tribe of Judah (*Rv.* 5.5). Matthew's genealogy of Christ also mentions Tamar, recalling Judah's relationship with her (*Mt.* 1.3). Rabbinic writings tend to elevate Judah, attributing his kingship to admirable character traits. He was distinguished by saving Joseph's life, openly confessing his relationship with Tamar, and his profound wisdom and physical strength. The death of his wife and sons is explained as divine retribution for the suffering he caused

Jacob by selling Joseph (Tanḥ B, *Gn.* 209). His sinning with Tamar was due to an "angel of desire" who enticed him because kings and redeemers were to issue from this union (*Gn. Rab.* 95.2).

BIBLIOGRAPHY

Allegro, John M. "Further Messianic References in Qumran Literature." *Journal of Biblical Literature* 74.2 (1956), 174–176. Discusses one fragment of Commentary on Genesis A, which gives the text of *Genesis* 49.10 (the Blessing of Judah) and a commentary on it; the commentary identifies the Messiah of Righteousness as the Qumran sect's Teacher of Righteousness.

Milik, Józef T. "Écrits préesséniens de Qumrân: D'Hénoch à Amram." In *Qumrân: Sa piété, sa théologie et son milieu*, edited by M. Delcor, pp. 91–106. Paris and Gembloux, 1978. Contains transliterations, notes, and comments on the Testament of Judah? from Caves 3 and 4.

ROGER GOOD

JUDAH, HOUSE OF. There are four certain occurrences of the term *house of Judah* in the Dead Sea Scrolls: the Damascus Document (CD iv.11); Pesher Habakkuk (1QpHab viii.1); Pesher Psalms[a] (4Q171 1–10. ii.14); and the Florilegium (4Q174 4.4; 1–3. ii.1 is usually restored with this sobriquet also). Several questions arise in the understanding of this appellation. First, is it specific, not to be conflated with other uses of the term *Judah*, or could it overlap in meaning with Judah? Second, is the intended referent of the term the same in every document?

In the Cairo Damascus Document, the sobriquet appears in a brief passage following a *midrash* on *1 Samuel* 2.35–36 and *Ezekiel* 44. Both are accounts of the selection of a new priesthood, and both are interpreted as referring to the founding of the Qumran community. Thus the reference to "joining the house" appears to play on the "house" promised in *1 Samuel* 2.35–36 to which the old priesthood of Eli's line will beg in vain to be joined. The *midrash* on *Ezekiel* also plays on "joining," and probably alludes to *Isaiah* 14.1 as well. The passage in the Damascus Document concludes with the warning that the time for "joining with the house of Judah" is or will soon be over. If this is so, the *house of Judah* refers to the Qumran community; the passage suggests that the community saw itself as the beginning of the true eschatological Judah, which they hoped others would join before it was too late.

In Pesher Habakkuk the sobriquet is found in a passage that is an interpretation of *Habakkuk* 2.4b. The faithfulness that leads to life in Habakkuk is interpreted as faithfulness to the Teacher of Righteousness. The ones who are faithful are "those who observe the Law in the house of Judah." It is uncertain whether "in the house of Judah" refers to the place in which the observance happens, in which case the house of Judah is to be identified with the Qumran community, or whether "in the house of Judah" suggests all Israel. Quite possibly, elements of both senses of the sobriquet were intended. The community (or the author) recognized the existence of an Israel apart from the gentile nations. Within this community of Israel the author recognized some who were faithful to the covenant although they had not yet joined the author's community. At the same time, the community considered itself the true Israel.

The discussion of how the sobriquet in Pesher Psalms[a] is to be understood usually hinges on the understanding of the phrase "ruthless ones of the covenant." This could refer to those who are violent against the covenant; in this case, either the "covenant" is in the house of Judah or the violent ones are in the house of Judah. A more likely understanding of the passage begins with the subject "ruthless ones of the covenant," about whom two things are said: first, "they are in the house of Judah," and second, they "plotted to destroy those who do the Law." According to this understanding, being "in the covenant" is the same as being "in the house of Judah." The sobriquet would then refer to all Israel, some of whom are hostile to the community.

The example in the Florilegium ("[. . .] to the house of Judah, severe things, to cherish animosity against them [. . .]") occurs in a small fragment that provides little context for an understanding of the sobriquet.

[*See also* Covenant; Qumran Community.]

BIBLIOGRAPHY

Davies, Philip R. *The Damascus Covenant: An Interpretation of the "Damascus Document."* Journal for the Study of the Old Testament, Supplement Series, 25. Sheffield, 1983. See, in particular, pages 103–104, in which he argues that the sobriquet refers to the community.

Horgan, Maurya P. *Pesharim: Qumran Interpretations of Biblical Books.* Catholic Biblical Quarterly, Monograph Series, 8. Washington, D.C., 1979. Brief commentary on the sobriquet in the Pesharim. Leans toward the view that the term refers to the Qumran community.

Murphy-O'Connor, Jerome. "The Essenes and Their History." *Revue biblique* 81 (1974), 215–244. Discusses a number of previous attempts to understand the sobriquet in the context of reconstructions of the history of the community. Suggests that the term can refer to the community or to Judaism at large, depending on the document.

Rabin, Chaim. *The Zadokite Documents.* 2d. rev. ed. Oxford, 1958. Rabin suggests that the term refers to a group distinct from both Judaism at large and from the sect.

Schwartz, D. "'To Join Oneself to the House of Judah' (Damascus Document IV, 11)." *Revue de Qumrân* 10 (1981), 435–446. A discussion of the entire passage in the Damascus Document (CD iii3.18b–iv.12a).

RICHARD RATZLAFF

JUDAH THE MACCABEE. *See* Hasmoneans; Jonathan (Hasmonean).

JUDAS THE ESSENE. *See* Essenes.

JUDE, LETTER OF. This New Testament work has often been treated as a product of early Catholic Christianity and dated late, but recent study has shown that it probably derives from early Palestinian Jewish Christianity. There is no good reason to deny its attribution to Jude, that is, Judas the brother of Jesus, who was a leader of the early Christian movement in Jewish Palestine. [*See* Jewish Christians.] The work's striking affinities with the Dead Sea Scrolls are one element in the case for its origin in a Palestinian Jewish context. They are not such as to prove any particular historical connection with the Qumran community, but probably reflect the common milieu that the Qumran community and earliest Christianity shared. Of special interest are the shared exegetical methods and traditions, which are evidence of the degree to which exegesis at Qumran was in many ways typical of first-century Judaism.

Jude 4–19 is the most elaborate and carefully structured piece of formal exegesis in the style of the Qumran *pesharim* to be found in the New Testament; this was first observed by Ellis (1978, pp. 220–226), and is studied particularly by Bauckham (1983; 1990, chap. 4). The structure resembles the thematic *pesharim* of Qumran, which provide commentary on a collection of scriptural texts on a theme (e.g., Florilegium [4Q174], Tanḥumim [4Q176], Melchizedek [11Q13]). The passage shares with the Qumran *pesharim* in general exegetical formulas, exegetical techniques, and hermeneutical principles. Although it has no equivalent to the most common exegetical formulas in the Qumran *pesharim* (those that use the word *pesher*), its use of formulas including "these" (*Jude* 8, 10, 12, 16, 19) to identify contemporaries to whom scripture prophetically refers is best paralleled in the Qumran *pesharim* (e.g., Pesher Isaiah[b] 4Q162 2.6–7, 4Q174 1.16). Exegetical techniques that can be paralleled in the Qumran *pesharim* include the use of catchwords to link texts and to link texts and their interpretation. *Jude* shares with the Qumran *pesharim* the hermeneutical presupposition that scripture speaks of the last days in which he and his contemporaries live and of the events in which his community takes part. Jude's use of eschatological typology, which understands biblical persons and events as prefiguring those of the last days, is not typical of Qumran *pesharim* but is found elsewhere in Qumran literature. [*See* Pesharim.]

Other points of contact between *Jude* and the Dead Sea Scrolls are as follows. In addition to an explicit citation from *1 Enoch* (*Jude* 14–15 = *1 En.* 1.9 = Enoch[c] 4Q204 1.i.15–17), *Jude* contains several clear allusions to the Enochic literature, indicating an evaluation of the work similar to that attested by the several copies of *Enoch* found at Qumran. [*See* Enoch; Enoch, Books of.] *Jude* 5–7 makes use of a traditional schema of examples of divine judgment that is also attested in the Damascus Document (CD ii.17–iii.12) as well as elsewhere (*Sir.* 16.7–10, *3 Mc.* 2.4–7, *Testament of Naphtali* 3.4–5, *San.* 10.3). The story of the dispute over the body of Moses to which *Jude* 9 refers belongs to a tradition of stories of dispute between good and bad angels, to which Visions of Amram[a–f?] (4Q543–548) also belong and which accounts for some striking verbal parallels (cf. 4Q544 1.10–12). J. T. Milik (1972) thought Jude's source, the *Assumption of Moses*, depended on the Visions of Amram (but against this and for studies of the whole tradition, see Berger [1973] and Bauckham [1983, pp. 65–76; and especially 1990, chap. 5]). C. Daniel [1968] identified the dreamers of *Jude* 8 as Essenes, but this ignores the clear evidence that Jude's opponents are antinomians. The allusion to *Isaiah* 57.20 as a prophetic reference to Jude's opponents in *Jude* 13 is paralleled by allusions to the same text in Hodayot[a] from Cave 1 at Qumran (1QH[a] x.14–15; xvi.15–16; cf. x.29–30; xiv.26 [ii.12–13; viii.14–15; cf. ii.27–28; vi.23])

BIBLIOGRAPHY

Bauckham, Richard. *Jude, 2 Peter*. World Biblical Commentary, 50. Waco, Tex., 1983. The most detailed recent commentary, with fullest references to the Dead Sea Scrolls.

Bauckman, Richard. *Jude and the Relatives of Jesus in the Early Church*. Edinburgh, 1990. Chapters 3 through 5 discuss parallels with the Dead Sea Scrolls.

Berger, K. "Der Streit des guten und des bösen Engels um die Seele: Beobachtungen zu 4QAmr[b] und Judas 9." *Journal of Semitic Studies* 61 (1973), 1–18.

Daniel, C. "La Mention des Esséniens dans le texte grec de l'épître de S. Jude." *Muséon* 81 (1968), 503–521.

Ellis, E. E. "Prophecy and Hermeneutic in Jude." In *Prophecy and Hermeneutic in Early Christianity*. Wissenschaftliche Untersuchungen zum Neuen Testament, 18, pp. 220–226. Tübingen, 1978.

Milik, J. T. "4Q Visions de 'Amram et une citation d'Origène." *Revue biblique* 79 (1972), 77–97.

RICHARD BAUCKHAM

JUDEA. [*This entry is divided into five articles:* Economy, Fauna, Flora, Geography, *and* History.]

Economy

Judea possessed a mixed economy in the Second Temple period, characterized by growth and change. [*See* Economic Life.] Until the Hasmonean uprising, Judea had been a small province divided into a number of districts.

A mixed but characteristically closed agricultural economy with a combination of crops and flocks was dominant in most of these districts. [*See* Agriculture.] The Greek cities were patently more open to commerce, and their economy was based on trade and the import of foodstuffs from within various parts of the country and from other provinces. The collapse of the Seleucid empire and the growth of the Hasmonean kingdom not only effected a change in the political situation, but also altered the economic conditions in the new kingdom.

The Hasmonean Revolt (166–164 BCE) caused much damage to the Hellenistic urban sector. According to Josephus, the Hasmoneans destroyed all the Hellenistic cities, but that description is exaggerated. At least some of these cities continued to be active, though to a lesser degree. On the other hand, there was a distinct economic and demographic increase throughout all regions of the land, especially in the Judean hill country, which was the heartland of the new kingdom. The Hasmonean kingdom was freed from the yoke of the taxes that had formerly been given to the Seleucid rulers, and these monies were now transferred to Jerusalem and the members of the Hasmonean elite. The tax burden imposed upon the farmer did not change, but the economy of the entire state benefited, since taxes ceased to constitute the export of capital.

The Roman conquest of 63 BCE liberated the majority of the Hellenistic cities; in other words, they were reestablished as autonomous cities that were detached from the vassal state of Judea and placed under direct Roman rule. There is no archaeological evidence for any surge of growth in these cities, but logic dictates that the lifting of the restrictions imposed by the hostile Hasmonean rule benefited the Hellenistic cities. No fundamental changes took place in the agrarian sector. The placement of Judea under the sheltering wings of the Pax Romana and the uniform system of Roman commerce and civilization contributed to the growth of the land. New technology, norms of consumption, and commercial arrangements all entered the land, and each exerted a positive influence upon the Judean economy.

Productive Economic Branch. The major productive economic branch was agriculture. Three agricultural products dominated the economy of Judea: grains (primarily wheat with some barley, mainly in the desert fringe); olives, which were used mainly as a source of oil; and wine, which was the primary source of sugars and which was drunk diluted with water in a ratio of 1:2 or 1:3. There were also a number of other crops that played an important role such as figs, dates grown in the Jordan Valley region, and pome fruits from Galilee. The raising of flocks and some cattle was another major sector of Judean agricultural production. The raising of flocks constituted a maximal utilization of the desert fringe areas in the southern Hebron hill country and in the Judean Desert. In the hill country regions, in contrast, such activity was wasteful. A sheep or goat requires an average of four to five dunams for grazing, and the area required for two or three of these animals would suffice to raise food for an entire nuclear family. Nonetheless, Josephus's enthusiastic description portrays Galilee, Judea, and Samaria as grazing lands (*The Jewish War* 3.35–50), thus indicating that the economy was mixed and that some potential agricultural lands were being used extensively as pasture. Such mixed agriculture is characteristic of less well-developed economies, for in more advanced phases this branch is shunted to areas with lower economic potential.

A Closed or Open Economy? The rural farm was basically a closed economic unit. The farmers supplied by themselves almost all their own needs. Nonetheless, the few manufactured goods that the common person required had to be imported. Thus, for example, there were no iron and copper deposits in the Land of Israel, and all metals would have to have been imported, as was the case regarding additional vessels. Few imported pottery vessels were found in rural areas, and Rhodian seals, for example, are extremely rare. Josephus explains the lack of attention by Roman authors to the people of Israel because "ours is not a maritime country; neither commerce nor the intercourse which it promotes with the outside world has any attraction for us . . . and we devote ourselves to the cultivation of the productive country with which we are blessed" (*Against Apion* 12.60). This description is somewhat tendentious and apologetic, and was meant to explain the disregard by Hellenistic culture of the ancient and venerable people of Israel. Another description by Josephus alludes to the existence of many ports and the possibilities of trade (*The Jewish War* 3.35–58). Nonetheless, the emphasis upon the agricultural nature of the land is essentially correct and recurs in the writings of many authors who stress the fertility and maximal utilization of the land.

Notwithstanding the above, there were pockets of open economies in certain regions of the land where specialized economies developed. In other words, special crops were raised in these areas that would then be exported, balanced by the need to import regular consumer goods. This required a market that would absorb the special crop and enable the marketing and purchase of standard consumer items. Galilee characteristically produced olive oil, while Judea specialized in the raising of grapes, but this did not suffice to change the structure of the economy. A different situation prevailed in Jericho, which produced dates and the ingredients of spices (myrrh and balsam). The plots devoted to spices were limited in area, but such crops were extremely profitable, and when expropriated by the authorities, became a monopoly of the house of Herod and later of the Roman authorities. Clearly, the inhabitants of the region did not supply by themselves all their needs, but rather relied, in some measure, upon an open market.

Jerusalem and its Temple constituted another focal point of an open economy. The members of the elite streamed to the city from throughout the land, as did myriads of pilgrims a number of times during the year. Taxes, *terumot* ("heave offerings"), tithes, and many freewill offerings were brought to Jerusalem. The Mishnah attests that all the produce within a day's distance from Jerusalem was produced in a state of ritual purity and was regarded as potentially for Temple use. Jerusalem was a true metropolis, and the influence of its wealth and prosperity was felt throughout the entire province of Judea. Thousands of columbarium caves, used for the raising of doves most likely intended for sacrificial use in the Temple, were discovered in the Shephelah of Judea. Regardless of the intended economic function of the birds, it is clear that the commercial opportunities offered by Jerusalem's expanding urban market served as a major catalyst for this area's development as a dove-raising center.

The Hellenistic cities were also commercial centers. Some cities were agriculturally oriented to a great degree, while others were less so. Caesarea, for example, was a commercial city in all respects. It was here that Herod built the largest port between Alexandria and Antioch, and it also took part in the grain trade between Egypt and Rome. The agricultural potential of the area was low because of its sand dunes (which were used agriculturally only in the Early Arab period), and the city naturally relied heavily upon its commercial markets. The royal court and the homes of the rich located in Caesarea constituted another focal point of the city's open economy.

Evidence of magnificent buildings and international economic ties was uncovered in the excavations of cities in Judea. Rhodian seals and imported pottery vessels were found in almost every excavation. Thus, for example, the palace at Masada contained evidence of the import of foodstuffs for members of the Herodian dynasty from Italy and other Roman provinces. All the above-described factors, then, combined to produce a complex situation in which two economic systems—one open and the other closed—existed concurrently.

The Agrarian Situation and Socioeconomic Stratification. Before the Hasmonean rebellion Judean society consisted primarily of three socioeconomic entities: small, independent farmers; a few wealthy individuals; and officials involved with the government and operating out of governmental estates. A large governmental estate was located in the eastern Jezreel Valley, and the Zenon papyri speak of additional estates. The scope of the governmental estates has not been determined, but there is no reason to assume that they occupied a large portion of the lands of Judea since the Jewish *halakhah* offered only a few ways in which the Temple might control extensive lands (in contrast with the land ownership policies of pagan temples in antiquity). Nonetheless, the Temple most likely possessed lands on a small scale.

The Hasmonean rebellion and the subsequent development of the Hasmonean kingdom provided the ideal background for agrarian changes that greatly affected the socioeconomic structure of Judean society. The new rulers inherited the lands of the Seleucid kings, and their conquests engendered a plethora of opportunities for land appropriations. The demographic increase in Judea led to the creation of landless masses. Jerusalem underwent a process of development and massive growth, and the small town became a tumultuous metropolis. A portion of the demographic increase was absorbed by Jerusalem, where landless masses earned their livelihood by providing services to the wealthy inhabitants of the city, in the construction work in the city, and, mainly, in the building of the Temple. The late Second Temple period was characterized by frequent changes of government. Each such change was followed by the exchange of elites, and probably by the expropriation of lands belonging to the members of the former ruling class. A number of estate buildings to the north of Jerusalem were abandoned at different times in the late Second Temple period and may attest to this ongoing process of the exchange of elites.

Some scholars are of the opinion that the agrarian tension and the constant upheavals caused by it to the socioeconomic stratification of Judean society were the primary reasons for both the First Jewish Revolt (66–73 CE) and various other social phenomena (e.g., messianic sects). Although there is no explicit proof of any direct link, many agrarian changes undoubtedly occurred in this period.

Many excavations have uncovered residential structures, the majority of which are simple houses without the characteristic components of Hellenistic architectural structures. The use of marble or ornamented capitals was not common among the masses. Economic prosperity, on the other hand, is evident, and the dwellings, though built simply, do not reflect poverty. There is insufficient evidence regarding the dwellings of the masses in Jerusalem itself. Only some of the patrician houses that were excavated throughout the land and in Jerusalem exhibit the influences of the Roman building style, and, with the exception of the palaces of Herod, no magnificent Roman villas on the highest imperial level were found in Judea.

Based on the archaeological finds to date, we are unable to identify any established stratum of the extremely wealthy.

In summary, despite the relative stability of every identifiable factor in the different production branches of the Judean economy, the overall economic situation of Judea was characterized by organizational and economic mobility and underwent recurring processes of structural change.

ZE'EV SAFRAI

Fauna

The Levantine region comprises a biogeographical crossroads between Africa and Eurasia where several biogeographical zones overlap and coexist and thus constitute one of the most complicated ecosystems in the world. Up until the Miocene (24 million years ago) the Levant was an integral part of Africa, but during the later part of the early Miocene (19 million years ago), due to a long-term gradual northward shift, the Afro-Arabian continental plate eventually coupled with the southwest corner of Asia. This created a land-bridge between the two continents through which an extensive biotic exchange between the Paleoarctic domain and the African continent took place.

Thus the southern Levant became a melting pot for Ethiopian, Oriental, Paleoarctic, and even Nearctic elements. During the latter part of the Miocene and the Pliocene (12–2 million years ago) the Saharo-Arabian desert belt was steadily developing, eventually creating a barrier between tropical Africa and the Levant and causing the original African organisms to become partially or totally isolated within the Levantine region.

The fluctuating environmental changes that took place in southwest Asia during the Pleistocene Age (1.7–0.1 million years ago) were significant enough to induce oscillating alterations of the faunal composition of the southern Levantine desert in accordance with the glacial-interglacial climatic changes. The abrupt increase in the postglacial world temperature (last 10,000 years), followed by an intense process of desiccation, compelled many Paleoarctic and Paleotropic elements to become completely isolated from their main center of distribution, surviving in ecological enclaves, mainly in desert oases around the Dead Sea, and forced less tolerant species to the brink of extinction. At present, the region is paved with islands of coexisting Afro-tropical and Eurasian relicts.

The Judean region has been occupied for thousands of years. Population density began to grow rapidly in the late Epipaleolithic and Neolithic periods. The following Holocene period is characterized by an overall deteriorating climate and reduction in forest lands. Starting with the Canaanites and the ancient Israelite tribes, wildlife resources have been intensively exploited.

During the last few centuries, the pressure on the ecosystem by hunting and intensive herding has led to severe land attrition. The introduction of firearms has proved to be almost disastrous to the local biodiversity. Thus the extant fauna cannot faithfully represent the original animal community of Judea during the biblical period. Animals like the hartebeest (*Alcelaphus buselaphus*), the Arabian oryx (*Oryx leucoryx*), the Persian wild ass (*Equus hemionus*), the lion (*Panthera leo*), the ostrich (*Struthio camelus*), and most species of vultures have disappeared.

The extremely diversified composition of the Levantine biota comes to its full expressiveness in and around the Dead Sea area, which supports an impressive number of Paleotropic elements; at present it is completely isolated within an extreme eremian region. A few examples among birds are the fan-tailed raven (*Corvus rhipidurus*), the sooty falcon (*Falco concolor*), the Tristram's grackle (*Onychognathus tristrami*), and the blackstart (*Cercomela melanura*), all of which delineate an essential "Syro-African Rift Valley" pattern of distribution, with a significant disjunction between the Levantine and the African realms. To them we may add the rock hyrax, or the coney (*Procavia capensis*), and the Nubian ibex (*Capra ibex nubiana*).

During the last decade, leopards (*Panthera pardus*) almost disappeared from the Judean Desert. Among other cats, the caracal lynx (*Lynx caracal*) is especially common along the Dead Sea Rift, the sand cat (*Felis margarita*) is rare, and the wild cat (*Felis silvestris*) is probably extinct. Among the three species of foxes found in Judea—the Rüppel's sand fox (*Vulpes rüpelli*), the tiny Blanford's fox (*Vulpes cana*), and the red fox (*Vulpes vulpes*)—the latter is by no means the most common predator. Other carnivores are the Egyptian mongoose (*Vormela peregusna*) and the badger (*Meles meles*). Hyenas (*Hyaena hyaena*) and wolves (*Canis lupus*) are extremely rare in this region. Among the artiodactyls the dorcas gazelle (*Gazella dorcas*), a graceful open plain antelope, is still found in the region. The mountain gazelle (*Gazella gazella*) is mainly restricted to semidesert habitats. A pygmy race of the wild boar (*Sus scrofa*) occupies the marshes of the southern Dead Sea region.

No less than four species of venomous snakes are found in the Judean Desert: the Palestinian horned viper (*Pseudocerastes persicus fieldi*), the carpet viper (*Echis coloratus*), the burrowing black mole viper (*Atractaspis endaddensis*), and the desert cobra (*Walterinnesia aegyptia*).

The springs along the Dead Sea may be occupied by freshwater animals originating from extremely distant regions, like the two tooth carps (*Cyprinodontidae*) species, *Apahanius dispar*, of a Paleo-Mediterranean origin, and *Aphanius mento*, which much like the endemic freshwater mollusk *Pseudamnicola solitaria* is an old species from the ancient Tethys region. Both species of fish live alongside the African copepod crustacean *Darwinula*.

BIBLIOGRAPHY

Tchernov, E., and L. K. Horwitz. "Herd Management in the Past and Its Impact on the Landscape of the Southern Levant." In *Man's Role in the Shaping of the Eastern Mediterranean Landscape*, edited by S. Bottema, G. Entjes-Nieborg, and W. van Zeist, pp. 207–218. Rotterdam, 1990.

Tchernov, E. *An Early Neolithic Village in the Jordan Valley. Part II: The Fauna of Netiv Hagdud*. American School of Prehistoric Research Bulletin, 44. Cambridge, Mass., 1994.

Yom-Tov, Y., and E. Tchernov. *The Zoogeography of Israel*. Dordrecht, 1988.

EITAN TCHERNOV

Flora

The Dead Sea Scrolls add little to our knowledge of Judean plants and their use. The plants cited are the same as those in the Bible. The most commonly named are vine (*Vitis vinifera*), olive (*Olea europeae*), wheat (*Triticum durum*), cedar (*Cedrus libani*), cypress (*Cupressus sempervirens*), and hyssop (*Origanum syriacum*); we also find more generic terms such as vineyard and grain. An interesting list of types of wood that produce a pleasing sacrificial odor is given in the pre-Qumran Aramaic Levi Document (4Q213–214); it names the cedar (*Cedrus libani*), juniper (*Juniperus phoenicea*), mastic pine (*Pistacia lentiscus*), fir pine (*Abies cilicica*), tamarisk (*Tamarix manifera*), cypress (*Cupressus sempervirens*), fig (*Ficus carica*), oleaster (*Elaeagnus angustifolia*), laurel (*Laurus nobilis*), myrtle (*Myrtus communis*), and aspalathus (*Alhogi camelorum*). This list is similar to the twelve trees listed in *Jubilees* (21.12) and mentioned, but not listed, in the *Testament of Levi* (9.12). The sequence is different: twelve rather than ten trees are provided; also oleaster and ash are missing while savin (*Juniperus sabina*), almond (*Amygdalus communis*), myrrh (*Commiphora myrrha*), and olive (*Olea europeae*) have been added. The identification of most of the plants is tentative. Both lists differ from the requirements cited in the Mishnah (*Tam*. 2.3, 4), which named the olive (*Olea europeae*) and vine (*Vitis vinifera*) as not used on the sacrificial altar and the fig (*Ficus carica*) and walnut (*Juglans regia*) as generally utilized. Plants were used in poetic imagery in, for example, Psalms[f] (4Q88) or Hodayot[b] (4Q428), but much less frequently than in the Bible. Many plants figure in biblical citations, for example, Words of Moses (1Q22) and Commentary on Genesis A (4Q252).

With regard to the plant material found in Judea, we should assume that the agriculture was conservative and only the 128 species mentioned in the Hebrew Bible were known. Insofar as the borders of Judea were fluid throughout this period, all plants of the Land of Israel would be included except perhaps those found in the Jordan River Rift Valley, such as papyrus (*Cyperus papyrus*), cattail (*Typha sp.*), or reed (*Phragmites australis*). These subtropical species were unlikely to be found elsewhere in the land. Some mountain species such as the cedar of Lebanon (*Cedrus libanus*), as well as various kinds of evergreen (*Cuperus sempervirens*, *Abies cilicia*, or *Juniperus excelsa*), would not be found even though their wood may have been used.

Approximately a dozen species from the New Testament, the Apocrypha, and pseudepigrapha must be added. Josephus mentioned a few more plants. The Mishnah, edited at the end of the second century, added several hundred plants to those known from the Bible. Other plants are mentioned in the *baraitot* of the Talmud, a literary form usually considered as old as the Mishnah. No study of plants specifically mentioned in the Tosefta or the partially contemporary tannaitic literature (*Mekhilta*, *Sifrei*, *Sifra*) has been undertaken.

A plant assessment for this area and the entire Near East is difficult because of plant introductions presumably made through the newly established Greek cities in and around Judea. The Greek botanist and plant explorer, Theophrastus, who accompanied Alexander on his route of conquest into India, introduced a variety of new plants, many of which were later mentioned in the Mishnah. Some, like the citrus (*Citrus medica*), spread through Persia to the lands of the Middle East. We do not know what other plants spread or how quickly this occurred. We may assume that the spread of any new plants among the agricultural population was very slow. A more adequate knowledge of the plants of this period awaits the results of pollen and other studies, which have recently begun.

BIBLIOGRAPHY

Feliks, Y. *Plants and Animals of the Mishna* (in Hebrew). Jerusalem, 1983.

Jacob, Irene, and Walter Jacob. "Flora." In *Anchor Bible Dictionary*. New York, 1992.

Kottek, S. S. *Medicine and Hygiene in the Works of Flavius Josephus*. Leiden, 1994.

Löw, I. *Die Flora der Juden*. Vienna, 1928.

Moldenke, H., and A. Moldenke. *Plants of the Bible*. New York, 1952.

Zohary, M. *Plants of the Bible*. New York, 1982.

WALTER JACOB
IRENE JACOB

Geography

Judea comprises four north-south geographic strips: the coastal plain, the foothills (Shephelah), the Judean

Mountains, and the Judean Desert. The Judean Mountains are a high, wide consolidated block to the west of the Dead Sea and the Judean Desert, extending about 100 kilometers in length from Mount Baal Hazor in the north to the Beersheba Valley in the south; they are about 50 kilometers wide. Unlike the other mountains on the western side of the Jordan, the backbone of the Judean Mountains forms a continuous water divide. The Shephelah to the west and the Judean Desert to the east, made mostly of soft chalk, form two lanes alongside the mountains, through which entrance and exit was gained to pathways in the mountains themselves. Thus, fortresses were built in the mountains for the defense and security of their inhabitants.

The Judean Mountains are unique in both their landscape and climatic conditions, differing from all the other mountains west of the Jordan River. Their ridges are made of hard, rugged limestone. As a result of erosion, they have little soil and very few springs; both are swallowed up in the rocky terrain. The mountains were forested by sturdy oak trees, which were hard to uproot. Because of the rocks and the steep slopes, it was difficult to pave roads in the mountains, and extending east of them is the desolate Judean Desert. There was, therefore, never any intensive settlement in the area before that of the Israelites.

The Judean Mountains are divided into three transverse blocks:

1. In the south are the Hebron Mountains, reaching a maximum of 1,027 meters above sea level and extending lengthwise about 50 kilometers, most of which comprise the Judean Desert. On the west, toward the Shephelah, the Hebron Mountains have steep slopes, and on the east, toward the desert and the Dead Sea, the slopes are even steeper.
2. In the center are the Jerusalem Mountains, reaching altitudes just under 900 meters above sea level and extending 20 kilometers in length; they include three ranges that face west and serve as an agricultural hinterland for the capital, Jerusalem.
3. In the north are the Bethel Mountains, rising 1,016 meters above sea level and extending 20 kilometers in length; they are more of a plateau that constitutes a fertile agricultural base. Throughout the Judean Mountains there are observation points, which were utilized for signal fires and communication, as well as many caves for hiding.

Five streams flow out of the Judean Mountains into the Mediterranean Sea; these served as arteries of transport and communication between the mountain settlements and the port cities on the coast in the days before the Israelite settlement.

Routes and Trade. The uniformity and continuity of the high Judean Mountains enable passage along their length over the "mountain route," which follows the water divide, without any ups and downs. Founded on the "mountain route," on the narrow part of the water divide and east of it, Jerusalem's position was special. From the days of the Israelite settlement in the mountains and onward through the Second Temple, Roman, and Byzantine times, forty roads and ascents were paved in the Judean Mountains: twenty from the Dead Sea and the Judean Desert, thirteen from the coast, three from the north, and four from the Beersheba Valley. This unique phenomenon occurs only in the Judean Mountains because of Jerusalem, which was the capital, and because of the temple there. Jerusalem, on the "parting of the way" (*Ezek*. 21.26) and "where the paths meet" (*Prv*. 8.2), was positioned at the important crossroad of the longitudinal "mountain route," where it intersects the transverse Jaffa-Jericho-Rabbat Ammon connection of the Via Maris in the west with the King's Highway in Transjordan in the east.

Because of Jerusalem's low position, in a saddle straddling the Judean Mountains, the only stream penetrating the heart of the mountains and flowing to the west was Naḥal Soreq-Rephaim, which served for convenient passage from Jaffa to Jerusalem. The only stream in the Judean Desert with water flowing its entire length is Naḥal Perat (Wadi Qilt), which flows from north of Jerusalem eastward, spilling into the Jordan River east of Jericho. This intersection established Jerusalem as a principal commercial center not only for the Judean Mountains, but also for the coastal plain and the Shephelah foothills to the west, and for the kingdoms of Ammon and Moab in the east (*Letter of Aristeas*, 114).

Defense and Security. Jerusalem was built on two elongated hills surrounded by deep valleys, whereas most of the towns in the Judean Mountains were built at the top of the mountains with no valleys protecting them. The city was spread on the lower hill in the east; it was the first capital of the Land of Israel and within it was the only temple holy to the Israelites. Its maximum height was 743 meters above sea level, whereas the upper hill to the west was 777 meters high. Jerusalem was called Zion, from the Hebrew *tsiyyah*, which means "wilderness," a dry, desolate, parched, and weary land (Ps. 63.2; *Is*. 35.1; *Jer*. 2.6; and others), because it is the lowest, easternmost city on the water divide, close to the Judean Wilderness and the Dead Sea.

The Judean Mountains could be easily breached by enemies from the coast and the Shephelah in the west. On the other hand, the mountains had both natural and human fortifications, and thus in times of war the inhabitants of Judea sought protection in the mountain strongholds and desert fortifications, as urged by Jeremiah (*Jer.* 4.5; 8.14). Jerusalem was protected by four concentric rings of tens of fortifications distributed throughout all the mountain districts, as well as by tens of thousands of agricultural terraces that were obstacles to approaching enemies (*Ezek.* 13.5; *Ps.* 80.13, 89.41–42; Har-El, 1981).

The Judean Desert. The Judean Desert is long and narrow: about 100 kilometers long and about 22 kilometers wide in the north near Jerusalem and narrower, about 13 kilometers wide in the south, east of the Arad Valley. It includes the area to the east of the mountains with steep slopes, inhabited by shepherds, and the desert oases at the edge of the Dead Sea. The Judean Desert comprises both the biblical pastureland desert, which receives 100 to 200 millimeters of rain annually, sufficient for raising flocks of sheep and goats, and the wilderness, which receives less than 100 millimeters annually and is sufficient only for raising camels.

The Judean Desert differs from other deserts in Israel. It is the smallest of all the deserts, has no lack of water since it is part of the Judean Mountains and gets the mountain runoff, and contains many springs emerging in the Dead Sea Rift. The breadth of the desert, the Dead Sea, and the mountains of Moab can all be observed from the summits of the frontier settlements: Anatot, Tekoa, Ziph, Maon, and Arad. Therefore, in most of the periods in which the country was under Jewish rule, the desert was part of the Judean Mountain settlements, bustling with life and filling important functions:

Communication connected the tribes that were historically on both sides of the Jordan, through Jericho and the northern Dead Sea and also from the middle of the desert; at that time the Dead Sea terminated at the tongue (el-Lisan), east of Masada (Neev and Emery, 1995).

Those raising livestock drove their choice cattle and flocks from northern Edom and southern Moab to the market centers in Hebron and Jerusalem by way of the southern Dead Sea.

Shepherds tending their flocks in the Judean Desert in summer (*Is.* 32.14; *Ezek.* 34.14; and others) migrated with them in winter to the Dead Sea coast and returned to the mountains in summer for the birthing and shearing seasons.

The desert oases on both sides of the Dead Sea attracted those raising cattle and also merchants.

The curative spring waters on both sides of the Dead Sea attracted persons recuperating from illness and injury (Josephus, *The Jewish War* 1.33.5).

Export both of dates from Jericho, ʿEin-Gedi, and Zoar (*Dt.* 34.3; *Jgs.* 1.16; *2 Chr.* 20.2; and others) and of balsam from ʿEin-Gedi, Ramatha, and Jericho (*Shab.* 26, p. 1) enriched the country, according to the *Onomasticon* of Eusebius.

Vital salt from Mount Sedom and the Dead Sea (*Lv.* 2.13) and asphalt from the Dead Sea and its shore (*Gn.* 14.10; Josephus, *The Jewish War* 4.8.4) served to seal cracks in Phoenician ships and to mummify the dead in Egypt.

Refugees, zealots, and rebels found refuge in the hilltop strongholds, caves, and canyons in the desert.

Jewish and Christian monastic sects settled at the mouths of streams and in caves in the canyons of Naḥal Hemar, Zohar, Ṣeʾelim, Mishmar, Ḥever, ʾArugot, Hazezon, and Wadi Murabbaʿat, en-Nar, Mukallik, Qumran, and Qilt, and pilgrims were baptized in the Jordan (*Jn.* 3.22–23), all adding life to the desert.

Settlement and the Stronghold. Settlement in the Judean Desert dates back to biblical times, beginning with the settlement of the tribes of Israel in the Land of Israel. Six cities were established then: Beth-Arabah, Secacah, Middin, Nibshan, City of Salt (ʿIr Ha-Melaḥ), and ʿEin-Gedi (*Jos.* 15.61–62); these cities on the western shore of the Dead Sea were excavated by Bar-Adon (Bar-Adon, 1989).

King David and his men joined together at the "stronghold" (*1 Sm.* 24.23; *1 Chr.* 12.9), which apparently was Masada, and there the foundations were laid for the establishment of the Judean army, headed by David and his chief of the army, Joab, a native of the Judean Desert (*1 Kgs.* 2.34). The Rechabites, keepers of the Lord's covenant and his laws, established settlements in the Judean Desert (*2 Kgs.* 10.15, 23; *Jer.* 35.2–10), thereby renewing the days of their forefathers, who dwelt in the Sinai and Negev deserts. In the days of the Judean Kingdom, the Hasmoneans, and the Second Temple, huge fortresses were established at the frontiers of the Judean Mountains, the Judean Desert, and the Dead Sea as a protective ring around the cities of Judea and Jerusalem.

The Pastureland Desert of the Shepherds. Its seven deserts are evidence of the Judean Desert's value to sheep breeders.

1. Beth-Aven, or Bethel (*Jos.* 18.12),
2. Gibeon (*2 Sm.* 2.24),
3. Jeruel (Jerusalem) (*2 Chr.* 20.16),
4. Tekoa (*2 Chr.* 20.20; *1 Mc.* 9.33),
5. ʿEin-Gedi (*1 Sm.* 24.1),
6. Ziph (*1 Sm.* 23.14–15; 26.2), and
7. Maon (*1 Sm.* 23.24–25).

Though just 10 km apart from each other, each encompasses several streams and their sources. Thus, with water and pasturelands available at each place for their flocks and herds, and comfortable climatic conditions for every season, the shepherds wandered from one to the other, coming full circle in the course of the year. The livestock served as raw material for a variety of industries: milk products, wool cloth, leather goods, saddles and reins, containers for liquid, and parchment for holy writings.

The Desert as a Refuge and Passage for War Convoys. In times of war in Jerusalem, the proximity of the Judean Desert made it an accessible refuge, either as a permanent or temporary haven, for zealots and rebels and persecuted religious sects, who could preserve their liberty and/or religious freedom there. Sometimes they returned to the capital to free it from their enemies. Nature endowed the desert with places and conditions for hiding, namely, thirty canyons full of caves and streams that spill into the Dead Sea. This configuration helped those dwelling in the caves and strongholds to defend themselves against their pursuers. In addition to the desert oases that served the persecuted as a source of livelihood, centers of learning (Torah) were established by the Rechabites and the sects of priests, based on principles of justice, righteousness, and truth. These bequeathed to the world the concepts of cooperation in work, brotherhood, peace, and frugality.

Thus the desert inspired prophets and kings, priests and monks, commanders of armies and rebels, husbandmen and shepherds. Here in the desert the settlements symbolized by the plow—Jericho, ʿEin-Gedi, Zoar, and Ramatha—merged with those symbolizing Torah learning—Qumran, ʿEin-Feshkha, Turaba, Ghuweir, and ʿEin-Gedi—and with the strongholds symbolizing independence and freedom—Masada, Herodium, Hyrcanium (Khirbet Mird), Machaerus, and others.

BIBLIOGRAPHY

Bar-Adon, Pesash. *Excavations in the Judean Desert*. *ʿAtiqot* (Hebrew series) 9 (1989). Report of the author's excavations; English summaries.

Har-El, Menashe. "Jerusalem and Judea: Roads and Fortifications." *Biblical Archaeologist* 4.1 (1981), 8–19. The author explains the reasons for the unusually large number of roads built in the Judean hills, which were among the most desolate mountains of Judea during the Canaanite period.

Har-El, Menashe. *The Judean Desert and the Dead Sea* (in Hebrew). Tel Aviv, 1981. A handbook for teachers and hikers.

Har-El, Menashe. *This Is Jerusalem*. Los Angeles, 1983. A handbook for teachers and hikers.

Har-El, Menashe, and Dov Nir. *Geography of the Land of Israel* (in Hebrew). Tel Aviv, 1995. A textbook for high school and teachers' college students.

Neev, David, and K. O. Emery. *The Destruction of Sodom, Gomorrah, and Jericho: Geological, Climatological and Archaeological Background*. New York, 1995. Historical fluctuations of the Dead Sea level and relevant settlement of the Dead Sea region are discussed.

MENASHE HAR-EL

History

In the summer of 586 BCE, the Babylonians ruled by Nebuchadnezzar captured the rebellious city of Jerusalem for the second time. As on the former occasion (16 March 597 BCE), the reigning king, now Zedekiah, and members of the royal family were carried away into exile along with military and religious leaders, wealthy landowners, artisans, and potential troublemakers. The number taken into exile remains uncertain: *2 Kings* 25.11 contains only general statements without figures while *Jeremiah* 52.29 says 832 persons (only males?) from Jerusalem, but places the deportation in the eighteenth year of Nebuchadnezzar, a year earlier than *2 Kings* 25. In spite of the lack of precision, a sizable number of Judeans must have been deported, although by no means the majority of the surviving population.

The city and the Solomonic Temple were looted and burned and the walls of the town were demolished (*2 Kgs*. 25.8–17). Vessels from the Temple were taken to Babylon as booty (*2 Kgs*. 25.14–15). Most of the Judean cities, especially to the south and west of Jerusalem, lay in ruins. The rule of the royal house of David, which had supplied monarchs for the country for more than four hundred years, was brought to an end.

The Babylonians took limited actions to stabilize and control the newly conquered region. Unlike the earlier Assyrians, the Babylonians neither restored destroyed capitals nor settled foreigners, deported from other conquests, in the area. Nebuchadnezzar appointed Gedaliah, who was from a prominent pro-Babylonian family with governmental experience (*2 Kgs*. 25.22; *Jer*. 40.5), over the people left in the land (*Jer*. 40.7, 11; 41.2, 18) but to what office (king? governor?) remains uncertain. The Babylonians redistributed land among the population left in the country, turning the poor into vinedressers and plowmen (*2 Kgs*. 25.12; *Jer* 39.10). This newly enfranchised class probably worked the land of the deported wealthy Judean aristocracy, sharing the benefits with the Babylonian authorities.

The Benjaminite city of Mizpah, about seven miles north of Jerusalem, served as the capital for Gedaliah's short-lived rule. He was eventually assassinated by a certain Ishmael, a member of the Davidic family who, along with numerous associates, had sought refuge with the Ammonite king Baalis and thus escaped the Babylonians (*2 Kgs*. 25.22–25; *Jer*. 41.1–10). A contingent of Babylonian forces was slaughtered along with Gedaliah's troops and supporters, and a third deportation of Jews into exile may have resulted from this episode (see *Jer*. 52.30, which says that another 745 persons were exiled in Nebuchadnezzar's twenty-third year, which along with 3,023 exiles in 597 BCE and the 832 in 586 BCE, made a grand total of 4,600). Numerous Judeans took refuge in Egypt following Gedaliah's assassination (*2 Kgs*. 25.26; *Jer*. 41.17–18), including the recalcitrant prophet Jeremiah (*Jer*. 42.1–43.7).

The Persian Period (539–333 BCE). Nothing of consequence is directly reported about Judean history in biblical and nonbiblical texts from the assassination of Gedaliah until the collapse of the Babylonian empire and its replacement by the Persians. The city of Babylon fell into Persian hands without a battle in October 539 BCE. The Persian ruler Cyrus (539–530 BCE) thus added the Babylonian empire to the territory previously taken from the Medes to the east and north of Mesopotamia and from various kingdoms in Asia Minor. The Babylonian province of Judea thus acquired a new overlord although exactly when Persian authority was initially asserted in the region remains uncertain. Certainly by the time Cyrus's successor Cambyses (530–522 BCE) invaded and conquered Egypt in 525 BCE, the west was firmly under Persian authority.

Evidence, both textual and archaeological, is more plentiful for the Persian than for the preceding Babylonian period. In spite of this increase of evidence, however, numerous problems remain unsolved. Was Judea a separate province in the Persian satrapy of "Beyond the River" or was it a part of the province of Samaria until the time of Nehemiah? Although some scholars defend the latter position, the preponderance of evidence seems to indicate that Judea was inherited by the Persians from the Babylonians as a separate province and retained that status. Since Jerusalem, the main city in Judah, had not been refortified and repopulated, Samaria may have been the most important regional center and thus have wielded more significant influence in the area than Jerusalem.

Persia apparently administered the province through an appointed native governor and his staff. From the Hebrew Bible, the Elephantine papyri, and coins and seals, the names of eight governors of the Persian province of Yehud (Judea) are known, but there is uncertainty about the order of some of these: Sheshbazzar, Zerubbabel, Elnathan, Nehemiah, Bagohi, Yehʿezer, Ahzai, and Hezekiah. (This list is based on the assumption that the terms *peḥah* and *tirshata*ʾ, translated "governor," are always used in this technical sense.)

The borders of the Persian province of Yehud are not completely certain, especially in the northwest. The southern boundary seems to have run between Beth-Zur and Hebron, the western between Azekah and Gath, the northern between Bethel and Samaria, and the eastern along the Jordan Valley and the Dead Sea. (The boundaries are reconstructed on the basis of *Ezra* and *Nehemiah* 3 and 7.) The region was about 25 miles by 30 miles or between 750 and 800 square miles. The province was divided into five or six districts with district capitals and sub-capitals (see *Nehemiah* 3, which lists the workers participating in the reconstruction of the walls of Jerusalem by districts).

Cyrus, the founder of the Persian empire, carried through on elements widespread in Near Eastern royal ideology, namely, playing the role of "the gatherer of the dispersed" and "the restorer of the gods and their sanctuaries." Thus, he allowed the return of religious relics and encouraged local religious communities and the restoration of sanctuaries. His "decree" regarding the exiled Judeans and their Temple occurs three times in the Hebrew Bible: twice in the Hebrew language in *Ezra* 1.1–5 and *2 Chronicles* 36.22–23, the latter probably merely restating the former, and once in Aramaic in *Ezra* 6.3–5 (see also *Is*. 44.28). The Aramaic form, described as the official record of Cyrus's edict, stipulates the size of the restored Temple, the method of construction, royal financing, and the return of the exiled Temple vessels, but makes no reference to the return of Judeans to their homeland. The Hebrew form is more general in content, noting the privilege of exiles to return to Jerusalem to rebuild the Temple and the right of nonreturning exiles to contribute financially to the undertaking, but lacks the other stipulations of the Aramaic text.

How many Judean exiles returned to Jerusalem and when remain uncertain. *Ezra* 1.5–6 speak of a return, but provide little detail. The exiled Temple vessels were said to be turned over to Sheshbazzar (*Ezr*. 1.7–11; 5.14–15; see *Is*. 52.11–12), "the prince of Judah," perhaps the Babylonian-appointed head of the province of Yehud who was confirmed or appointed as governor by Cyrus (*Ezr*. 5.15). The two, almost identical, lists of returnees in *Ezra* 2 and *Nehemiah* 7 appear to come from a later time because the leaders are Zerubbabel, Jeshua, and others, not Sheshbazzar.

The reconstruction of the Temple in Jerusalem did not occur during Cyrus's reign nor under his patronage. The rebuilt Temple was dedicated during the reign of Darius I (522–486 BCE); according to *Ezra* 6.15 it was dedicated in the Persian king's sixth year (516 BCE), which would have been seventy years after its destruction (see *Jer*. 25.11; 27.7; 29.10). The biblical evidence concerning the stages by which religious life was restored in Jerusalem, culminating in the rededication of the Temple, is complex and somewhat contradictory. In *Ezra* 1 and 5.6–17, Sheshbazzar is said to have begun reconstruction during the reign of Cyrus. In *Ezra* 3 and 6.19–22, Zeruabbabel and Jeshua act as the restorers, whereas in *Ezra* 5.1–5 and 6.1–18, as in the prophetical books of *Haggai* and *Zechariah*, Zerubbabel and Jeshua carry out the work in conjunction with these two prophets. (In *2 Mc*. 1.18–2.15, Nehemiah is said to have been the restorer of the Temple and the altar.)

Two figures dominate the biblical portrayal of restored Jewish life in Jerusalem during the fifth century—Ezra and Nehemiah. Although the final form of the biblical text has their activity overlapping (see *Neh.* 8.9; 12.26, 36), the two probably worked separately. In *Ezra* 7.7–8 and *Nehemiah* 2.1 both return to Judah under Persian sanction during the reign of an Artaxerxes. Three Persian kings bore this name: I Longimanus (465–424 BCE), II Memnon (405–359 BCE), and III Ochus (359–338 BCE). Artaxerxes III Ochus is easily excluded as a candidate. That Nehemiah returned in the twentieth year of Artaxerxes I (445 BCE) has been almost universally accepted. Throughout the twentieth century, however, scholars have been divided over whether Ezra returned to Jerusalem under the first (in 458 BCE) or second Artaxerxes (in 398 BCE). No conclusive verdict on this issue is possible.

The materials on Ezra are found in *Ezra* 7–10 and *Nehemiah* 7.73b–10.39. *Ezra* 7.11–9.15 are in autobiographical or memoir form. Apparently Ezra returned with special prerogatives and powers granted by the royal court (*Ezr.* 7.11–26). In addition, he possessed the "law of God" in his hand. The identity of this law, whether the Pentateuch, one of its sources, or some collection now unknown, remains uncertain. The Persians, as is known from nonbiblical sources, encouraged local communities to draw up collections of their laws and customs, and this factor may have influenced the codification of Jewish law. *Nehemiah* 8.1–38 report the reading, interpretation, and observance of Ezra's law as well as the covenanting of the people to obey its stipulations. Ezra also opposed the intermarriage of Jewish males with non-Jewish females and forced a covenant agreement to implement putting away these wives and their children (*Ezr.* 10; see 10.3). The consequences of a societal survey by a commission, which determined those so intermarried, including priests and Levites, are not given, and the *Book of Ezra* breaks off abruptly.

The Nehemiah materials in *Nehemiah* 1.1–7.73a and chapters 11–13 are autobiographical and were probably written to be placed as a memoir in the sanctuary. As cupbearer to the Persian king, Nehemiah would have had immediate access to the monarch. The biblical narrative indicates that he initiated the course of action that led to his return to Jerusalem (*Neh.* 1.1–2.8) accompanied by a military escort, "officers of the army and horsemen" (*Neh.* 2.9). The following activities are attributed to Nehemiah: The city of Jerusalem was refortified in spite of the threat of local rulers (*Neh.* 2.11–4.23; 5.15; 12.17–43); economic measures were taken to alleviate the indebtedness of the local population because of interest charging (*Neh.* 5.1–13; see *Dt.* 23.19–20) and to grant remission from some taxes (*Neh.* 5.14–19); and people from the region were moved into Jerusalem to repopulate the city (*Neh.* 11.1–2). It may have been at this time that Jerusalem replaced Mizpah as the capital of the province of Yehud.

Nehemiah apparently served two stints as governor of the province (see *Neh.* 5.14 and 13.6), the first lasting twelve years and the second of unknown duration. His second period of service was recalled as a time when he expelled Tobiah the Ammonite from the Temple precincts (*Neh.* 13.4–9), took measures to ensure that the Levites received their designated income (*Neh.* 13.10–14), sought to enforce observance of the Sabbath (*Neh.* 13.15–27), and confronted the problem of mixed marriages, expelling a son of the high priest because of his intermarriage (*Neh.* 13.23–29).

The work of Ezra and Nehemiah was sanctioned by the Persians, who no doubt wanted to encourage loyal and stable communities in Syria-Palestine. Throughout the fifth and fourth centuries, Persia was not only warring with the Greeks but also had to confront rebellions by the Egyptians and revolts by Persian governors in the west.

The following internal developments during the period are noteworthy.

1. Various conflicts existed between the Jewish community and its neighbors. These conflicts tended to stimulate xenophobic reaction in the community.
2. The literature of the period suggests that a sharp distinction was drawn between those who had returned from exile (the *benei ha-golah*) and those Judeans who remained in Judea.
3. The swearing of agreements over the issues of marriage to foreigners and observance of the law (*Ezr.* 10.3; *Neh.* 9.38; 10.28–39) tended to create groups of "covenanters," perhaps the forerunners of later sectarian movements.

The Hellenistic Period (333–63 BCE). In 334 BCE, Alexander the Great crossed the Bosporus into Asia to carry out plans formulated by his father, Philip II. Although Alexander's immediate goal was the Persian capital at Persepolis, he moved first down the eastern Mediterranean seaboard toward Egypt in order to secure his flank when he later moved eastward. The Jewish community in Judea was part of his acquisitions from the Persians. Legends about Alexander's meeting and obeisance to the Jerusalem high priest have been preserved in Josephus (*Jewish Antiquities* 11.331–339) and the Babylonian Talmud (B.T., *Yoma* 69a), but what contact the community had with the Macedonian remains unknown. Presumably, transition from Persian to Greek rule went smoothly in Jerusalem, unlike the trouble that developed in Samaria.

With the death of Alexander in Babylon in June 323

BCE, his generals inaugurated a struggle over the division of his kingdom, which reached something of a state of equilibrium only in 301 BCE. At that time, Ptolemy I was ruling in Egypt and Seleucus I in Babylon. Syria-Palestine had been assigned to Seleucus but was occupied by Ptolemy. Throughout the next century, five major wars were fought between the two royal houses. Both wished to control southern Syria and Palestine as an economically and commercially valuable buffer zone in addition to its military importance.

Ptolemaic rule resulted in several significant consequences for the Jewish community.

1. The continued struggle with the Seleucids over control produced pro-Ptolemaic and pro-Seleucid factions within the community, thereby polarizing elements in the society.
2. Ptolemaic control brought with it administrative and economic control that involved heavy taxation, royal monopolies, royal ownership of large estates, and royal land-lease policies.
3. The old office of Judean governor disappeared. Some of its functions were taken over by the overlay of Ptolemaic administrators, and others were absorbed by the high priest of the Jerusalem Temple, who became the primary leader of the community.
4. The operation of the government was based on use of the Greek language. Local persons wishing to rise in Ptolemaic administration and to participate in commercial activity had to adjust to the demands of Hellenized culture.

In the Fifth Syrian War (202–200 BCE), Antiochus III the Great (223–187 BCE) wrested control of southern Syria-Palestine from the Ptolemies. The pro-Seleucid elements among the Jews not only welcomed the change but also fought against Ptolemaic forces. Antiochus rewarded the Jews and the city of Jerusalem with various privileges (*Jewish Antiquities* 12.138–144, 145–146): funds for sacrifices, support and goods for construction work on the city and Temple, reduction in taxes, and so forth, as well as the right of Jews to return from elsewhere to their homeland. These edicts are generally dated to about 198 to 196 BCE.

The year 196 BCE also witnessed the Isthmian Proclamation made by the Roman general Flamininus at the Isthmian games. Supported by the Roman Senate, the proclamation and subsequent Isthmian Doctrine declared Rome to be the protector of all Hellenes in both Europe and Asia (Polybius, 18.46; Livy, 33.32–33). The application of this perspective involved the Romans in eastern Mediterranean affairs from the first decade of the second century BCE.

Good relations between the Seleucids and the Jewish community began to deteriorate during the reign of Seleucus IV (187–175 BCE), when factional strife broke out in Jerusalem. Eventually, four major families vied for control of the local Jewish community: the Oniads, from whose ranks high priests had traditionally been chosen; the Tobiads, one of whose earlier ancestors had purchased tax collection rights in the region from the Ptolemies (see *Jewish Antiquities* 12.154–241); the Simonites, whose head was captain of the Temple and who apparently sought control over the Jerusalem market (*2 Mc.* 3.1–4); and the Maccabeans (or Hasmoneans), who were members of the priestly course of Jehoiarib (*1 Chr.* 9.10–13; 24.1–7) and owned an estate in the hill country northwest of Jerusalem.

Jason, an Oniad, secured the office of high priest from the new Seleucid king, Antiochus IV Epiphanes (175–164 BCE), while his brother, Onias III, was at the Seleucid court attempting to remove a cloud of suspicion about his loyalty (*2 Mc.* 4.7–17). For a price, Jason also secured the right to establish a Hellenistic city in Jerusalem called Antioch-in-Jerusalem. This involved determining who would hold citizenship and attendant privileges in the new city, the construction of a gymnasium, and the creation of an *ephebeion* or youth corps to be educated in and to utilize the gymnasium. The establishment of Antioch-in-Jerusalem was no doubt intended to bring the city into fuller participation in the commercial and political activities of the time. Contact with Rome may have been made to "establish friendship and alliance" (*2 Mc.* 4.11).

Menelaus, a Simonite with Tobiad support, outbid Jason and secured the high priestly office (in ca. 172 BCE) and forced the latter to withdraw across the Jordan River (*2 Mc.* 2.23–26). Actions by Menelaus, including some looting of Temple objects, led to a popular uprising (*2 Mc.* 4.27–50).

Open civil war erupted in Jerusalem when an attempt to take Egypt by Antiochus was cut short by Rome and rumor spread that Antiochus had died. Jason then led an army against Menelaus (*Dn.* 11.25–29; *2 Mc.* 5.1–10). The Seleucid king, who was returning home from Egypt, attacked Jerusalem and took actions to repress the fighting and establish order. The Temple was looted. Either in conjunction with this activity or sometime thereafter, Seleucid troops were stationed in a new citadel (the Akra) in Jerusalem, land was taken over, and the Temple was used for non-Yahwistic worship (*Dn.* 11.30–31; *1 Mc.* 1.16–40; *2 Mc.* 5.11–26).

At this stage, the Maccabean family became an important player both in the civil struggles among the Jews and in opposition to Seleucid control (*2 Mc.* 5.27). The stories about Mattathias, the father of the Maccabean brothers, in *1 Mc.* 2, go unmentioned in *2 Mc.* and are probably legendary. Judah Maccabee raised an army, took action against fellow Jews sympathetic to the Seleucids, and won several strategic battles against Antiochus's forces. Seleucid persecution of the Jews to suppress their religious practices probably occurred during this period (see *1 Mc.* 1.41–64; *2 Mc.* 6–7), although it is doubtful if there was an official edict circulated throughout the kingdom (see *1 Mc.* 1.41–42).

The Seleucids had been placed under heavy indemnity after their military loss to the Romans at Magnesia (190 BCE) and the Treaty of Apamaea (188 BCE) and were battling the Parthians to the east. Thus they were unable to commit full military power against the Maccabean forces.

Maccabean success in the field and Seleucid preoccupation elsewhere led to negotiations to settle the conflict. Four documents in *2 Maccabees* 11.16–38 reflect these negotiations, although they are neither in their proper literary context nor in chronological order. One document addressed to the Jewish senate in 11.27–34 suggests that Antiochus IV offered amnesty and relaxation of oppression after the intercession of the high priest Menelaus. Another document, from the general Lysias in 11.16–21, probably addressed to the Maccabean faction, suggests that some matters between the parties were settled. Roman envoys gave their support to efforts and suggested further negotiations, according to the document in 11.34–38. The final document in 11.22–26, which dates to after the death of Antiochus IV (in late November or early December 164 BCE), has the new young king (Antiochus V) ordering the complete surrender to the Judeans of the Temple in Jerusalem and the cessation of religious repression.

No doubt, Antiochus V and the general Lysias intended that the Jerusalem Temple revert to the control of the high priest Menelaus, who was recognized by the Seleucids. Judah and his followers, however, captured the Temple precincts before the death of Antiochus IV, according to *1 Maccabees* 4.36–61, but after his death according to *2 Maccabees* 10.1–8. The Temple was cleansed, rededicated, and the sacrificial cult reinstituted on the twenty-fifth of Kislev (in December 164 BCE).

Several actions were subsequently carried out under Judah.

1. The Temple Mount was fortified as well as the city of Beth-Zur (*1 Mc.* 4.60–61).
2. Raids were carried out against local powers, and Jews were brought to Judea from Galilee and Gilead (*1 Mc.* 5; *2 Mc.* 10.10–38).
3. Negotiations were conducted in Rome, and a treaty of friendship and alliance was concluded between the Jews and the Romans (*1 Mc.* 8) in which the Maccabeans became a client state to Rome.
4. According to Josephus (*Jewish Antiquities* 12.414, 410, 434), Judah assumed the office of high priest, probably after the Seleucids had put Menelaus to death (*2 Mc.* 13.3–8) and appointed Alcimus his successor (*1 Mc.* 7.9). If Judah was recognized as high priest (see *Antiquities* 12.414) by any external government, it would have to have been the Romans.
5. The Maccabean forces unsuccessfully besieged the Akra, which was garrisoned with Seleucid forces and sympathetic Judeans (*2 Mc.* 5.18–20).

Political rivalry in the Seleucid kingdom had aided Judah's exploits. But a new king, Demetrius I (162–150 BCE), sent a major force against the Maccabeans. In the consequent battle, in 160 BCE, Judah, who was supported by a force of only eight hundred warriors, was killed (*1 Mc.* 9.1–18).

The Maccabean movement was taken over by Judah's brother Jonathan and for several years exercised little or no authority in Judea, functioning primarily as a guerrilla force, harassing and avoiding the Seleucids and their supporters (*1 Mc.* 9.23–69). By 152 BCE, conditions changed for Jonathan when renewed rivalry racked the Seleucid kingdom. To gain his support, the rivals bestowed upon Jonathan various positions and privileges, recognizing him as client ruler of Judea. In a matter of months, Jonathan rose to become military, civil, and religious leader of Judea, not always to the delight of the local population (*1 Mc.* 10.7–8). Jonathan assumed the office of high priest in 152 BCE, having been appointed by Alexander Balas, the Seleucid pretender to the throne (*1 Mc.* 10.18–21); his appointment brought to an end the interregnum in the post that had existed since the death of Alcimus in 159 BCE (*1 Mc.* 9.54–57). The Maccabeans, however, were not members of the families from which the high priests had traditionally been chosen. King Demetrius I subsequently bestowed upon the Judeans various concessions as well as additional territory (*1 Mc.* 10.22–45).

With the Seleucid kingdom in turmoil, Jonathan became a major power in the region, headed up a large military force, campaigned as far afield as Damascus, and renewed the treaty with Rome. But he was unable to eradicate completely Seleucid power in Judea (*1 Mc.* 10.67–12.38) and eventually fell victim in the Seleucid power struggles (*1 Mc.* 12.39–53). He was seized, through deception, by Tryphon, a pretender to the Seleucid throne, and was executed in 143/42 BCE by Tryphon when the latter's march on Jerusalem was thwarted by Maccabean forces under Jonathan's brother Simon and by an unusually heavy snowfall (*1 Mc.* 13.1–24).

Simon, earlier appointed by the Seleucids as governor of the Mediterranean coastal plain (*1 Mc.* 11.59), was the last of the original family to lead the Maccabean movement. Simon was confirmed in the high priestly office by

Demetrius II (146–140 BCE), who also granted various privileges after receiving initiatives and gifts from Simon (*1 Mc.* 13.31–40). During Simon's rule (142–135 BCE), the following noteworthy developments occurred.

1. Simon assumed full civil, military, and religious authority, and the practice of dating documents by his rule affirmed an expression of independence granted by the Seleucids (*1 Mc.* 13.41–43).
2. Tribute was no longer paid to the Seleucids (*1 Mc.*10.29–30).
3. Judean territorial control was extended toward the Mediterranean Sea in the west (see *1 Mc.* 13.29; 14.34) where Gazara (Gezer) was captured and resettled with loyal Judeans, analogous to Antiochus IV's earlier settlement of Syrians in Jerusalem (*1 Mc.* 13.43–48).
4. The anti-Maccabeans and Seleucids in the Akra were starved into submission, and the fortress fell into Maccabean hands amid joyous celebration (*1 Mc.* 13.49–52a).
5. The Temple Mount was fortified (*1 Mc.* 13.52b) as well as other places in Judea (*1 Mc.* 14.33–35).
6. The client-state relationship with Rome was reaffirmed (*1 Mc.* 14.16–19, 24; 15.15–24), and friendship greetings were received from Sparta (*1 Mc.* 14.20–23).
7. "The Jews and their priests" granted Simon and his family hereditary leadership with full civil, military, and religious prerogatives (*1 Mc.* 14.41–43). (*1 Mc.* 14.4–15 eulogizes Simon as if he were a messianic redeemer.)
8. The Seleucid king, Antiochus VII (138–129 BCE), recognized the "independence" of Judea under Simon, and granted him the right to mint coinage (*1 Mc.* 14.1–9). These grants seem to have been rescinded once the new king secured the throne (*1 Mc.* 15.10–36), and an expedition was sent to reconquer Judea (*1 Mc.* 15.37–16.10).
9. Simon and two of his sons were killed by his son-in-law, Ptolemy, and his supporters at a feast at Dok near Jericho (*1 Mc.* 15.11–17). The assassination was part of a major plan to seize power throughout the country, but was unsuccessful because Simon's son John Hyrcanus (135–105 BCE) was able to succeed his father (*1 Mc.* 16.18–22).

Evidence in the two books of *Maccabees* and in Josephus's works indicates that the Maccabean movement was never supported by an overwhelming majority of the Judeans and often faced considerable internal opposition. This conclusion is supported by the following factors.

1. *1 Maccabees* 2.29–38 mentions those who refused to participate in military actions against the Seleucids, relying instead on the hope of divine intervention (see *Dn.* 11.34).
2. When Alcimus was appointed high priest, elements that had fought with Judah abandoned him (*1 Mc.* 7.12–17).
3. Letters from Rome noted the need to return to Judea for punishment "any pestilent men who had fled" to other countries (*1 Mc.* 15.15–24).
4. Privileges granted to Simon in *1 Maccabees* 14.31–44 are matched by restrictions imposed upon various elements in the society, limiting their freedom (*1 Mc.* 14.44–45).
5. Josephus first mentions the existence of the groups Pharisees, Sadducees, and Essenes during this period (*Jewish Antiquities* 13.171–173). To the existence of these groups, one could surely add the Qumran community.

After a period of Seleucid military success over John Hyrcanus (*Jewish Antiquities* 13.236–248), the latter eventually was able, because of Seleucid strife over rulership, to assert some independence (*Jewish Antiquities* 13.273). Hyrcanus then conquered regions in Transjordan to the east, in Idumea to the south and west, and in Samaria to the north, eventually destroying the city of Shechem, the Samaritan temple on Mount Gerizim, and the city of Samaria (*Jewish Antiquities* 13.254–281). The Idumeans and others were forced to submit to circumcision (to convert) or abandon their homes (*Jewish Antiquities* 13.257–258). Hyrcanus also employed foreign mercenaries and was faced with various internal factions and oppositions, to which he responded with repressive actions (*Jewish Antiquities* 13.249, 299; *The Jewish War* 1.67). According to Josephus, Hyrcanus broke with the Pharisees, who had widespread support (*Jewish Antiquities* 13.288–298).

Aristobulus I (104–103 BCE) seized power upon his father's death. He assumed the titles "king" and "Philhellene" (friend of the Greeks) and extended Judean holdings in the north (*Jewish Antiquities* 13.301–314). He died quickly, however, and through the intervention of the queen, Shelamzion Alexandra, Alexander Jannaeus (103–76 BCE) succeeded to the offices of high priest and king (*Jewish Antiquities* 13.320).

The rule of Jannaeus was characterized by territorial expansion of the Hasmonean (Maccabean) kingdom and by rising internal opposition, which was suppressed harshly. Jerusalemite control was extended to include major portions of the Mediterranean coast south of Mount Carmel. The districts of Judea, Samaria, Galilee, and Transjordan were under the rule of Jannaeus. Newly captured areas were required to convert or be destroyed (see *Jewish Antiquities* 13.397). Expressions of internal opposition to Jannaeus ranged from crowds pelting him with festival fruit, to open civil war, to an appeal to the rival Seleucid king Demetrius III (in 88 BCE) to invade the land aided by some Jewish military support (*Jewish Antiquities* 13.372–383). Numerous Jewish opponents were put to death by Jannaeus, some by crucifixion.

Shelamzion Alexandra (76–67 BCE), succeeded her husband Jannaeus, and her son Hyrcanus II was made high priest. Josephus states that she ruled with the support of the Pharisees and their adherents, who used their power to take revenge on their enemies (*Jewish Antiquities* 13.405–409).

Before the queen's death, her son Aristobulus II began moves to seize power from his less assertive older brother. Upon the queen's death, civil war erupted between the two brothers, with Hyrcanus II being advised by Antipater, governor of the Jewish district of Idumea (*Jewish Antiquities* 13.417–432; 14.4–21).

The Roman Period (63 BCE–135 CE). With civil war raging in Judea and Aristobulus II, who had temporarily assumed the title of king, besieged in the Temple by Hyrcanus II and the Edomites, Rome moved to bring order to its client state. The Roman general Pompey, in the east to secure Rome's borders and to subdue piracy, eventually captured Jerusalem and the Temple (*Jewish Antiquities* 14.29–73). Pompey reorganized the political structure of Judea, greatly reducing its territory (*Jewish Antiquities* 14.74–76). Hyrcanus II was recognized as high priest (*Jewish Antiquities* 14.73), and Aristobulus II and his family were carried off to Rome (*Jewish Antiquities* 14.79). Judea was placed under the oversight of the Roman legate ruling Syria, which had been annexed by Rome from the Seleucids.

As far as possible, Rome exercised its rule through the use of local power groups. This was to Rome's financial advantage and involved fewer of its troops. Over the years, various forms of administration were utilized to govern Judea.

In the period from 63 to 37 BCE, two factors characterized local Judean politics. First, Aristobulus II and his family, building upon local support, sought to reassert Hasmonean dominance in the area. At various times, Aristobulus II and his sons, Alexander and Antigonus, led uprisings with some initial success (*Jewish Antiquities* 14.82–97, 101–102). However, Aristobulus II was eventually poisoned and Alexander beheaded. When the Parthians overran Palestine in 40 BCE, Antigonus was made king. He mutilated Hyrcanus II, rendering him unfit to serve as high priest. After his defeat, Antigonus was beheaded by Antony (*Jewish Antiquities* 14.330–336, 363–366; 15.5–10). Second, the family of Antipater rose to prominence. After the Roman takeover, Antipater was gradually granted more and more power (*Jewish Antiquities* 14.103, 127, 139) through being able to support the winning side in Roman politics (*Jewish Antiquities* 14.143–157). His eldest son, Phasael, was made governor of Jerusalem and his second son, Herod, was made governor of Galilee (*Jewish Antiquities* 14.158–162). Although Antipater was poisoned (*Jewish Antiquities* 14.280–284) and Phasael was killed or committed suicide while Antigonus held Jerusalem (*Jewish Antiquities* 14.367–369), Herod proved to be a skilled survivor.

Herod fled from the Parthians and made his way to Rome, where he was designated king over Judea in 40 BCE (*Jewish Antiquities* 14.381–389). However, only in 37 BCE was Herod able to overcome his opponents and capture the city of Jerusalem (*Jewish Antiquities* 14.465–491).

For convenience, Herod's reign may be divided into three phases. The first, 37 to 30 BCE, coincided with the final phase of struggle for the control of Rome, which saw the triumph of Octavian (Augustus Caesar). During this period, Herod faced continued opposition from elements in the local population, as well as threats against his territory by the ambitions of Cleopatra.

The second phase, 30–10 BCE, witnessed Herod in the good graces of Rome after his pledge of allegiance to Octavian. His territory was expanded to the Mediterranean Sea, into northern Transjordan, and eventually was almost as large as that controlled by the Hasmoneans at the height of their rule (*Jewish Antiquities* 15.217, 343–348; *The Jewish War* 1.400). He rebuilt cities throughout his kingdom and developed major fortresses, some with palaces, as retreats and defense posts. Jerusalem and its Temple were rebuilt to become what Pliny the Elder called "the most outstanding city in the East" (*Natural History* 5.70). Herod made contributions to many cities outside his kingdom as well. During this time, Herod put to death several members of his extended family, including his Hasmonean wife Mariamme.

In the final phase of his rule, 10–4 BCE, Herod became more and more paranoid and, with some justification, took out his frustration on his immediate family, executing his two sons by Mariamme (*Jewish Antiquities* 15.361–394) and Antipater, the son of his wife Doris (*Jewish Antiquities* 17.182–186). As an old man, he attempted to elicit a pledge of loyalty from some of the religious leaders. On their refusal, he reacted violently (*Jewish Antiquities* 17.41–67). Herod died, probably early in 4 BCE, just before Passover (*Jewish Antiquities* 17.188–192, 213).

Herod had executed a succession of wills. His last was generally followed by Octavian, but not completely and not immediately (*Jewish Antiquities* 17.317–324; *The Jewish War* 2. 93–100). Before Rome made a final settlement, several civil disturbances erupted: pretenders to the throne vied for support, anti-Roman sentiment abounded, and messianic hopefuls arose. In addition, Roman leadership in the area proved less than competent and more than greedy. Such features of the situation were an indication of things to come.

Herod's kingdom was somewhat reduced by the Romans and the remainder divided between three sons: Archelaus (4 BCE–6 CE), made ethnarch, a position lower than king, received Judea, Idumea, and Samaria; Herod Antipas (4 BCE–39 CE) was made tetrarch over Galilee and Perea in Transjordan; and Philip (4 BCE–33/34 CE) received territory in the northeast, which included Gaulanitis, Trachonitis, Batanea, Panias, and Auranitis (*Jewish Antiquities* 17.317–320).

Archelaus's incompetent rule was terminated by the Romans, who banished him to Gaul (*Jewish Antiquities* 17.339–355; *The Jewish War* 2.111–116). This time, Rome decided to govern the region directly and added it to the province of Syria. A census, carried out at the time (6/7 CE) by Quirinius, met with widespread opposition because the new political status involved increased taxation and direct Roman rule (*Jewish Antiquities* 18.4–10; *The Jewish War* 2.118). Judea was governed locally by Romans of the lower administrative echelon of the equestrian rank. Called "prefects," later "procurators," these officials resided in Caesarea.

The most famous Judean prefect was Pontius Pilate (ca. 26–36 CE), under whom several civil outbreaks occurred and Jesus was tried and condemned (*Jewish Antiquities* 18.55–64, 85–89; *The Jewish War* 2.169–177). Pilate was eventually removed from office and banished by the Romans for excessive cruelty.

Relations between Judeans and Romans were almost in a constant downward spiral. Roman ineptitude, greed and looting by the prefects, local gangs and thievery, group rivalry, freedom movements, political use of the office of high priest, and messianic enthusiasm all contributed their part. For example, when the emperor Gaius Caligula (37–41 CE) ordered that a statue of himself be set up in the Jerusalem Temple, widespread opposition erupted and general rebellion was averted only through administrative delays and Gaius's assassination (*Jewish Antiquities* 18.261–309; *The Jewish War* 2.184–203).

The grandson of Herod the Great, Agrippa I, was appointed king over the whole of Judea, Idumea, and Samaria by the emperor Claudius (41–54 CE) in 41 CE. This arrangement, restoring native Jewish rule, ended, however, with Agrippa's death in 44 CE (*Jewish Antiquities* 19.274–277, 350–352; *The Jewish War* 2.214–220).

Rome then decided to place Judea again under direct rule. Most of the procurators from 44 to 66 CE were confronted with periodic turmoil in the country and ruled with less than competency so that "matters were constantly going from bad to worse" (*Jewish Antiquities* 20.160).

During the procuratorship of Gessius Florus (64–66 CE), matters became so tense and anarchy so widespread that open rebellion broke out. Jewish rebels seized several fortresses, including first of all Masada, which overlooked the Dead Sea, and sacrifices for the emperor were canceled in the Jerusalem Temple (*The Jewish War* 2.408–410). Battles between Jewish factions broke out in Jerusalem, and rebellious elements seized most of the city and the Temple, and in the process burned state records and archives (*The Jewish War* 2.411–456). The Roman governor of Syria, Cestius Gallus, took the field in early fall of 66 CE with the twelfth legion, but his army was devastated when it retreated from Jerusalem (*The Jewish War* 2.499–555). After the defeat of the Roman force, Jewish leadership set up a government, appointed generals to conduct the war, and began the minting of coins (*The Jewish War* 2.562–568). Vespasian was appointed to head the Roman forces, but Emperor Nero died and struggles in Rome erupted before Vespasian could subdue the region. Roman military activity was focused on isolating Jerusalem until Vespasian returned to Rome as emperor (69 CE), leaving his son Titus to take the Jewish capital.

In Jerusalem's final days, the anti-Roman forces in the city were divided into three factions, which fought one another until the Roman siege was well underway (Tacitus, *Histories* 5.12.3). The city was besieged in early spring of 70 CE and captured in stages. The Temple was burned in August and the upper city captured in September (*The Jewish War* 6.252–317, 358–408). Masada was not taken until 73/74 CE.

Radical changes in Judean life followed the revolt. Judea was made into an independent province ruled by legates of senatorial rank, and the Roman army was enlarged to legionary status. The Jewish sacrificial cult ended with the destruction of the Temple, and Jewish religious practices took on new features and orientations. Much of the agricultural land was taken over by Romans.

Little is known of Jewish life in Palestine from the end of the First Jewish Revolt until the Bar Kokhba Revolt (ca. 132–135 CE). Under the emperor Trajan (98–117 CE), widespread Jewish rebellion broke out in Egypt, Cyrene, Cyprus, and Mesopotamia, but the extent of Judea's involvement remains unknown. The causes of the second major war with Rome, the Bar Kokhba Revolt, are not clear. According to Dio Cassius (*Roman History* 69. 12. 1–14. 3), conflict occurred when Emperor Hadrian (117–138 CE) rebuilt the city of Jerusalem and constructed a pagan sanctuary on the Temple Mount. In the *Historia Augusta*, Roman prohibition of circumcision is noted as the reason (Hadrian 14.2). During the revolt, Judean forces led by Shim'on Bar Kokhba were able to control Jerusalem for a time, set up a government, and mint coins. Recent discoveries in Judean caves reveal some of the realia of the war.

BIBLIOGRAPHY

Bickermann, E. J. *From Ezra to the Last of the Maccabees: Foundations of Postbiblical Judaism*. New York, 1962.

Bickermann, E. J. *The Jews in the Greek Age*. Cambridge, Mass., 1988.

Cohen, S. J. D. *From the Maccabees to the Mishnah*. Philadelphia, 1987.

Feldman, L. H., and M. Reinhold. *Jewish Life and Thought among Greeks and Romans: Primary Readings*. Minneapolis, 1996.

Gera, D. *Judaea and Mediterranean Politics 219 to 161* BCE. Leiden, 1997.

Grabbe, L. L. *Judaism from Cyrus to Hadrian*. 2 vols. Minneapolis, 1992.

Hayes, J. H., and S. R. Mandell. *The Jewish People in Classical Antiquity: From Alexander to Bar Kochba*. Louisville, Ky., 1998.

Schiffman, L. H. *From Text to Tradition: A History of Second Temple and Rabbinic Judaism*. Hoboken, N.J., 1991.

Schürer, E. *The History of the Jewish People in the Age of Jesus Christ*. 3 vols. in 4. Rev. ed. Edinburgh, 1973–1987.

Smallwood, E. M. *The Jews under Roman Rule: From Pompey to Diocletian*. Leiden, 1976.

JOHN H. HAYES

JUDGES, BOOK OF. At Qumran the *Book of Judges* is represented by three manuscripts: Judges, Judges[a], and Judges[b].

Judges (1Q6) from the first century CE is preserved in nine identified fragments containing portions of the text of *Judges* 6.20–22; 8.1 (?); 9.1–4, 4–6, 28–31 (frgs. 5 and 6), 40–42, 40–43, 48–49. Thirty-one small pieces are unidentified fragments. Judges presents two unique readings and agrees three times with the Septuagint against the Masoretic Text, in two of them with support of the Vulgate (Barthélemy and Milik, 1955).

Judges[a] (4Q49) is extant in two contiguous pieces of a single fragment and contains portions of *Judges* 6.2–13. The script is a late Hasmonean or early Herodian bookhand from approximately 50 to 25 BCE. This manuscript offers new data for a better understanding of the textual history and the literary development of *Judges*. It represents a form of the text independent from any other known text type. In six instances of a total of ten variant readings, the manuscript goes its own way, disagreeing with the Masoretic Text and the Greek tradition. [*See* Septuagint.]

It is the only extant witness that does not include *Judges* 6.7–10, although two Hebrew medieval manuscripts and the Septuagint[B] text also omit verse 7a. Verses 8 through 10 generally have been recognized by modern critics as a literary insertion, attributed in the past to an Elohist source (G. F. Moore, *ICC*, 1895) and now generally considered (for example, by Wellhausen, Gray, Boling, and Soggin) a piece of late Deuteronomic redaction.

A lacuna in line 4 (verse 5) allows room for no more than ten letters, those corresponding to a shorter reading, *ve-lahem '[ein mispar va-ya]vo'u*, attested only by the Old Latin *quorum non erat numerus . . .* , as against the Masoretic Text *ve-lahem ve-ligmalleihem 'ein mispar . . .* , "and neither they nor their camels could be numbered." In line 3 the counting of letters per line gives the reading *ve'-ohaleihem u-gemalleihem yav[i]'u*, which Judges[a] shares with the proto-Lucianic text and the Old Latin, which here witness to the Old Greek.

The use in *Judges* 6.13 of *š* instead of the Masoretic Text *'šr* is characteristic of Qumran texts, which stand between late Biblical and Mishnaic Hebrew.

Judges[b] (4Q50) is extant in only three fragments, containing portions of *Judges* 19.5–7 and 21.12–25. Fragments 2 and 3, although not contiguous, preserve parts of three lines in common. The reconstruction of the text shows an irregularity in the number of characters per line that may be explained by the fact that fragments 2 through 3 belong to the last column of the book. The preserved readings of Judges[b] are very close to the Masoretic Text (Trebolle Barrera, 1995).

The identification of the proto-Theodotionic (also called *kaige*) recension with the help of the Greek Minor Prophets (8Ḥev 1) also has a bearing on the textual history of the Septuagint of *Judges*. [*See* Minor Prophets.]

The B group of manuscripts (B efj[m]qsz) with the subgroup irua[2] are related to that recension (Bodine, 1980). The A group (A G abd[k]x Syr) is very close to the Old Greek, except for its hexaplaric characteristics. The Lucianic group (K Z glnw) is prehexaplaric and forms the best witness to the Old Greek in *Judges*.

BIBLIOGRAPHY

Barthélemy, D., and J. T. Milik. *Qumran Cave 1*. Discoveries in the Judaean Desert, 1. Oxford, 1955.

Bodine, Walter Ray. *The Greek Text of Judges: Recensional Developments*. Harvard Semitic Monographs, 23. Chico, Calif., 1980.

Boling, Robert G. "Judges: Introduction, Translation and Commentary." *The Anchor Bible*, vol. 6A. Garden City, N.Y., 1975.

Trebolle Barrera, Julio. "4QJudg[b]." In *Qumran Cave 4, IX: Deuteronomy, Joshua, Judges, Kings*, edited by Eugene Ulrich and Frank Moore Cross, pp. 165–170. Discoveries in the Judaean Desert, 14. Oxford, 1995.

JULIO TREBOLLE BARRERA

JUDICIAL PROCEDURES. For what is generally considered to have been a small, self-enclosed community, the multiple references in the Qumran texts to juridical bodies are noteworthy. The Damascus Document includes a *serekh* ("rule") "for the judges of the congregation," which describes the standard court consisting of ten men chosen from the congregation, "four from the tribe of Levi and Aaron and from Israel six" (CD x.4–6). The judges must be between twenty-five and sixty years old and well versed in the "Book of Hagu," probably a compendium of communal rulings. The passage does not define the nature of the cases that fall under the jurisdiction of the court of ten. It has been suggested that the quorum may be derived from the ten elders in *Ruth* 4.2, although the latter were apparently convened on an *ad hoc* basis. According to the Rule of the Community (1QS vi.3–4) ten was also the minimum quorum for a functioning unit of the sect, including deliberations "for their counsel on any matter." For capital offenses, this quorum was augmented by the presence of two priests (Ordinances[a] [4Q159 2–4]). [*See* Hagu, Book of.]

A "council of the community" consisting of twelve lay and three priestly members is referred to in the Rule of the Community (1QS viii.1), but the broad description of its functions makes it likely that this was a leadership council rather than a judicial body. In fact, the term "council of the community" is also used for the community as a whole (1QS iii.2; v.7 etc.). Among matters brought before the whole "session of the many" were the acceptance of candidates (1QS vi.16 and parallels), the indictment of sinners (1QS vi.1), and questions about legal matters (Rule of the Community[d] [4Q258 1.i.2]). These functions and the fact that participation in legal proceedings (*torah* and *mishpaṭ*) was a privilege of all members in good standing within the community add to the difficulty of discerning the sect's specifically juridical bodies.

In addition to the courts that apparently functioned within the community, the Temple Scroll[a] (11Q19) describes a royal council that was to guide the king in matters of judgment: "He will have twelve princes of his people with him and twelve priests and twelve Levites who shall sit next to him [to counsel him] concerning matters of law and Torah. Let him not act presumptuously toward them nor do anything requiring counsel without them" (11Q19 lvii.11–15).

The duodecimal pattern employed here to make up a quorum of thirty-six is the same as that employed in the War Scroll (1QM ii.1–3) for the representation of the people at the Temple cult. As the highest court of the community, this council appears to have functions similar to those that rabbinic tradition ascribed to the Great Sanhedrin. The quorum of the latter, which varies in different sources between seventy, seventy-one, and seventy-two members, was apparently viewed by some as also having a duodecimal basis. The principle that courts should always be odd-numbered to prevent a deadlock is reflected in Talmudic theory and in the quorums of Greek courts. It was apparently ignored by Qumran legists.

The duodecimal system also is reflected in the Qumran interpretation of a prophetic vision. Pesher Isaiah[d] (4Q164), a *pesher* on *Isaiah* 54.11–12, alludes to "the twelve [chief priests who] give light by the judgment of the Urim and Thummim" and "the heads of the tribes of Israel." Together these twenty-four constitute the council of the community, which is likened to the sapphire stone and the radiance of the sun (4Q1641).

Witnesses. According to Deuteronomic law "two or three witnesses" are required to establish guilt for any offense (*Dt.* 17.6, 19.15). Qumran legists had an elaborate way of resolving this ambiguity:

> Any trespass committed by a man against the Torah, which is witnessed by his fellow—he being but one—if it is a capital offense, he shall report it in [the wrongdoer's] presence with reproof to the Overseer. And the Overseer shall write it down with his hand until [the man] does it again before one, who again reports it to the Overseer. If [the man] is again caught in the presence of one, his judgment is complete. And if they are two, testifying about different things, the man shall only be separated from the purity. . . . And concerning property they shall receive two reliable witnesses, while one suffices [only] to separate [him from] the pure (food and vessels).
>
> (CD ix.16–23)

A distinction is drawn in this passage between capital cases, which require three witnesses or occurrences, and monetary cases, which require only two. The testimony may combine discrete violations, each one observed by only one witness, a procedure excluded in rabbinic *halakhah*. Scholars differ with regard to a single capital offense seen by two witnesses. *Deuteronomy* 17.6 and Temple Scroll[a] (11Q19 lxiv.8) favor the view that two simultaneous witnesses would suffice to impose a death sentence; it is only for sequential testimony ("different things") that three are required.

The cumulative procedure requires that after each violation the offender is to be reproved before the Overseer who records the offense. Failure to do so was seen as a violation of *Leviticus* 19.17: "You shall surely rebuke your fellow and not bear sin on his account" (Rule of the Community [1QS v.26–vi.1]). *Matthew* 18.15–17 has a similar procedure for disciplining sinners, except that the initial chastisement is private. It has also been noted that rabbinic *halakhah* requires a warning (*hatraʾah*) by witnesses before corporal punishment can be imposed, but this warning precedes rather than follows the offense. Its purpose was to verify that the offender was aware of the crime and its penalty.

An interesting communal record of chastisement is extant in Rebukes by the Overseer (4Q477), which refers to the rebuke of several named individuals for being short-tempered, possessed of a haughty spirit, and gluttonous. Here the reproof apparently concerns moral shortcomings of character, rather than specific offenses, but it no doubt derives from the same source, *Leviticus* 19.1, which was the basis of the juridical rebukes recorded by the Overseer.

The qualifications for witnesses are indicated in the Damascus Document: "No witness shall be received by the judges to put someone to death on the basis of his testimony unless he has reached the age to pass among those who are mustered (and) is God-fearing. No man shall be believed against his neighbor as a witness who transgresses a commandment deliberately until he is cleansed by repentance" (CD ix.23–x.3).

The biblical age for mustering was twenty, which is also indicated in the Rule of the Congregation as the age when one "shall be received so as to witness the precepts of the Torah" (1Q28a 1.11). This passage, which has some syntactical ambiguities, is part of the description of the stages in the maturation of a youth within the congregation. Twenty is also the minimum age for a man's marriage, and this has led some translators to read the verb "receive" (*tequbat*) as a feminine passive referring to the wife being received to testify against her husband and to take part in judicial hearings. Others, including this writer, proposed emending the text in accordance with the above-cited law in the Damascus Document, to refer to the husband's eligibility to give testimony after he reaches the age of maturity. However, in view of now available rules barring nonreproductive and unnatural intercourse in the Damascus Document[e] (4Q270) it seems more cogent to retain the form *teqabel* and to translate it in the sense of a promise by the wife to admonish her husband about the laws pertaining to licit and illicit conjugal relations. Marital responsibilities to differentiate "between good and evil" would thus devolve upon both partners.

Oaths. The pronouncement of oaths, other than those sworn upon entering the covenant (CD xv.5–9), was lawful only in a judicial setting. This is stated as the first rule under the rubric Concerning Oaths found in the Damascus Document: "As to that which he said, 'Let not your hand help you,' a man who causes an oath to be sworn in the open field that is not in the presence of the judges or by their bidding has let his hand help him" (CD ix.8–10). The injunction not to resort to violence ("letting one's hand help him") derives from *1 Samuel* 25.25–33; it is here extended to oaths, which not only involve the raising of one's hand (*Gn.* 14.22) but the use of the sacrosanct name of God.

Among oaths that may be sanctioned by the court, mention is made of one imposed upon someone suspected of misappropriating the property of others (CD xv.3) and an oath curse to elicit information about a theft (CD ix.10–12).

Penalties. Despite occasional assertions by scholars to the contrary, it is clear that Qumran legal teachings did not eliminate the biblical death penalties. The Damascus Document (CD xii.2–5) explicates the distinction between erroneous and flagrant offenses (see table 1): "Any man who is ruled by the spirits of Belial and speaks apostasy, in accordance with the judgment of the [one who communicates with] a ghost, or a familiar spirit shall he be judged. But each man who errs and profanes the Sabbath or the holy days shall not be put to death."

The court of twelve referred to in the Ordinances texts from Cave 4 at Qumran had the authority to execute deliberate transgressors of capital laws. The same text refers to the death penalty for a bride who has proved not to have been a virgin. This accords with the literal reading of *Deuteronomy* 22.13–21 (cf. Temple Scroll[a] [11Q19 lxv.7–15]). Rabbinic *halakhah* limited the death penalty to cases of proven promiscuity after betrothal (B.T., *Ket.* 44b).

In its paraphrastic version of Deuteronomic laws, Temple Scroll[a] not only preserves their capital penalties, but also adds some new ones including a law dealing with treason: "If a man informs against his people, and delivers his people up to a foreign nation, and does harm to his people, you shall hang him on the tree, and he shall die" (11Q19 lxiv.7–8). This law, and the related one concerning one who leaves his people and goes over to the gentiles, derives its phraseology from *Deuteronomy* 21.22, "And if a man commits a sin worthy of death, and he is put to death, and you hang him on a tree, his body shall not remain all night upon the tree, but you shall surely bury him that day." However, as Yigael Yadin pointed out, the author of Temple Scroll[a] has deliberately reversed the sequence of execution and hanging. This led Yadin to the inference, followed by a number of other scholars, that "hanging" meant death by crucifixion. Baumgarten maintains that hanging was more likely a form of strangulation (*ḥeneq* in tannaitic literature) and has questioned Yadin's inference on several grounds (Yadin, 1971, pp. 1–12; Baumgarten, 1982, pp. 7–16). One objection is that the protracted death by crucifixion would make the insistence in Temple Scroll[a] (11Q19 lxiv.11) on burial before sundown impossible to fulfill. Another is that Pesher Nahum (4Q169) emphatically denounced Alexander Jannaeus's crucifixion ("hanging alive") of his Pharisaic enemies, who were guilty of precisely the kind of high treason to which Temple Scroll[a] refers, as an unprecedented atrocity, for which the "Lion of Wrath" was to face divine retribution (Pesher Nahum, 4Q169 3–4.i.6–8; see also Baumgarten, 1977, pp. 172–182). The premise that crucifixion was a legally sanc-

JUDICIAL PROCEDURES. TABLE 1. *Penalties for Infractions of the Communal Rule.*

OFFENSE	1QS	4Q266	4Q270	4Q265
Walking out of assembly 3 times	Penance: 10 days	Penance: 10 days		
Walking out while assembly stands	Penance: 30 days	Penance: [30] days		
Going naked before others	Penance: 6 months	Exclusion: 6 months	[Exclusion: 6 months Penance ?]	
Spitting at assembly	Penance: 30 days			
Indecent exposure	Penance: 30 days	Exclusion: 30 days Penance: 10 days	[Penance: 30 days]	
Guffawing foolishly	Penance: 30 days	Exclusion: 30 days Penance: 15 days	[Exclusion: 30 days Penance 15 days]	Exclusion: [30 days] Penance: [15 days]
Gesticulating with left hand	Penance: 10 days	Exclusion ? Penance: [10 days]	Penance [10 days]	
Slandering another	Exclusion and Penance: 1 year	[Exclusion: 1 year Penance ?]	Exclusion: 1 year Penance: ?	
Slandering community	Expulsion		Expulsion	
Murmuring against community	Expulsion			
Murmuring against Fathers			Expulsion	
Murmuring against Mothers			Penance: 10 days	
Murmuring against another	Penance: 6 months			
Deviating from fundamentals	Penance: 2 years		Exclusion: [2 years] Penance: 60 days	
Despising communal law			Expulsion	
Apostasy after ten years	Expulsion			
Fornication with wife			Expulsion	
Lying about property	Exclusion: 1 year Penance: ¾ food	Exclusion: [1 year] Penance: ?		
Disobeying a senior	Penance: 1 year			Exclusion: ? Penance: ½ food
Improper use of divine name	Expulsion			
Speaking against priests				
a. deliberately	Exclusion and penance: 1 year			
b. unwittingly	Penance: 6 months			
Lying (against intimate)	Penance: 6 months			Exclusion: 6 months Penance: ½ food
Insulting (?) another	Exclusion and penance: 1 year	Exclusion: 1 year Penance: ?		? Penance: 30 days
Deceiving intimate	Penance: 6 months			Exclusion: [6] months Penance: ½ food

JUDICIAL PROCEDURES. TABLE 1. *Penalties for Infractions of the Communal Rule (continued).*

Offense	1QS	4Q266	4Q270	4Q265
Deceiving another	Penance: 3 months			
Losing communal property	Compensation or penance: 60 days			
Malice or revenge against another	Penance: 6 months (var. 1 year)	Exclusion: [200?] days Penance: 100 days		
Malice in capital case		Expulsion		
Unseemly speech	Penance: 3 months	Exclusion: 3 months Penance: 20 (?) days		
Interrupting another	Penance: 10 days	Penance: [10] days		
Dozing at assembly	Penance: 30 days	Exclusion: 30 days Penance: 10 days		Penance: 30 days
Dozing 3 times while Book is read				Penance: ?

tioned form of execution in Qumran law thus remains open to question [*See* Crucifixion.]

Another nonbiblical death penalty is prescribed for "the man who takes a bribe and perverts righteous judgment" (Temple Scroll[a] li.16–18). The phraseology derives from *Deuteronomy* 15.19 but not the capital penalty. Yadin (1983, p. 229) suggested that the injunction, "and you shall not fear him [the corrupt judge]" echoes a similar one concerning the false prophet in *Deuteronomy* 18.22, which led to the inference that both were to be executed. This seems rather circuitous. It is noteworthy that Josephus also states flatly that "a judge who accepts bribes suffers capital punishment" (*Against Apion* 2, 27). *Jubilees* 21.20, however, apparently alludes to a heavenly reward to he who does not accept bribes to avoid executing a murderer; this judge will be saved from all death.

Next to death the most severe penalty in the Qumran penal code was expulsion. In his description of the Essenes, Josephus observes that expulsion was often tantamount to death, since the ejected member was still bound by his oath not to partake of the food of outsiders (*The Jewish War* 2.143). In the version of the code preserved in the Rule of the Community, expulsion was specified for blasphemy (1QS vii.1), slander or grumbling against the community (vii.16–17), apostasy by a senior of ten or more years standing (vii.22), and flagrant transgression of a Pentateuchal law (1QS viii.22). A Cave 4 version of the penal code adds grumbling against the fathers and "one who approaches to fornicate with his wife contrary to the law" (Damascus Document[e] 4Q270, 7.i.12–13). The latter apparently refers to a violation of some sexual ban, perhaps of unnatural intercourse.

For lesser offenses the Qumran penal codes list suspensions of varying durations from access to purity rituals to reductions in one's food ration. The nature of most of these offenses is substantially similar in the Rule of the Community and the Cave 4 versions of the penal code (Serekh Damascus, 4Q265; Damascus Document[a,e], 4Q266, 4Q270). They involve infractions of communal order and discipline, rather than transgressions of biblical laws. Lawrence Schiffman suggests that these selections from the penal code served a central role in the initiation rites for new members. This is a plausible suggestion, to which, however, should be added the observation that in the Cave 4 manuscripts of the Damascus Document the penal code is placed just before the expulsion rite for recalcitrant offenders.

The formulation of the penalties in the different versions of the code is not uniform (see table). While the Rule of the Community generally prescribes only one penalty for each infraction, the Cave 4 Damascus Document texts have compound penalties consisting of a specified period of suspension (*havdalah*) and a period of penance (*ne'enash*). In one case, deception involving property, the Rule of the Community (1QS vi.25) spells out a compound penalty: "he shall be excluded from the purity of the many for one year, and be fined one-fourth his bread." A fragmentary passage in the Damascus Document (CD xiv.20–21) refers to the same crime but has suspension and a penalty of only "six days," which may be a corrupt reading. In the case of lying to one's fellow, Serekh Damascus (4Q265) refers to a rather severe fine of one-half his bread and also indicates that the offender was excluded from participating in communal deliberations. For unjustified malice against a fellow the Rule of the Community (1QS, vii.8) has a suspension of six months, but a correction above the line of the text reads "one year." Such corrections, erasures, and variations among parallel sources have led scholars to postulate different stages in the evolution of the community, but no firm evidence for the direction of the evolution of the penal system has yet been put forth.

A number of scholars have drawn attention to the similarity in its emphasis on rules of order between the Qumran code and the constitutions of various Hellenistic associations. The parallels concerning fixed seating, speaking in order, avoidance of disturbances, and other procedural rules are of great interest. However, they do not suffice to establish direct dependence. What they do suggest is that even the self-enclosed Qumran community, which some have characterized as the least Hellenized of ancient Jewish societies, was not impervious to the cross-currents of contemporary influence. [*See* Greco-Roman Guilds.]

[*See also* Cairo Genizah; Damascus Document; *and* Rule of the Community.]

BIBLIOGRAPHY

Baumgarten, Joseph M. *Studies in Qumran Law*. Leiden, 1977.

Baumgarten, Joseph M. "Hanging and Treason in Qumran and Roman Law." *Eretz-Israel* 16 (1982), 7–16.

Baumgarten, Joseph M. "The Cave 4 Versions of the Qumran Penal Code." *Journal of Jewish Studies* 43 (1992), 268–276.

Baumgarten, Joseph M., ed. *Qumran Cave 4, XIII: The Damascus Document (4Q266–273)*. Discoveries in the Judaean Desert, 18. Oxford, 1996.

Schiffman, Lawrence H. *Sectarian Law in the Dead Sea Scrolls: Courts, Testimony, and the Penal Code*. Brown Judaic Studies, 33. Chico, Calif., 1983.

Weinfeld, Moshe. *The Organizational Pattern and the Penal Code of the Qumran Sect*. Novum Testamentum et Orbis Antiquus, 2. Fribourg, 1986.

Yadin, Yigael. "Pesher Naḥum Reconsidered." *Israel Exploration Journal* 21 (1971), 1–12.

Yadin, Yigael. *The Temple Scroll*, vol. 2. Jerusalem, 1983.

JOSEPH M. BAUMGARTEN

K

KABBALAH. From the Middle Ages, *Kabbalah* is the generic term used to refer to a multiplicity of esoteric currents in Judaism that impart knowledge about God, the self, and the universe. Kabbalistic literature is not a monolithic phenomenon that can be delimited in a simplistic or straightforward manner. On the contrary, the works of Kabbalah comprise a multifaceted and complex set of phenomena that have evolved over an extensive period of time and in many geographical regions. It is commonplace to think of Kabbalah as interchangeable with Jewish mysticism, but in fact the mystical element (whether related to intense revelatory or unitive experiences of the divine) is only one component of the Kabbalistic lore. A more suitable term to characterize Kabbalah in its diversity is esotericism, which conveys the notion that there are inner, secretive traditions that cannot be conveyed except to select individuals. These traditions encompass both speculative and practical matters, theological beliefs and cultic rituals.

A recurring claim in Kabbalistic literature is that the mysteries have been transmitted orally through the generations from master to disciple in an uninterrupted chain. Nothing is more important for understanding the mentality of the Kabbalist than the correlation of esotericism and orality. According to one of the more popular chains of tradition found in a number of sources, the first link in the chain is Elijah, who revealed himself to a particular individual. The choice of Elijah as the one who revealed esoteric truths helped to guarantee the traditional and authoritative status of the content of the revelation, even while tacitly alluding to the fact that something novel had occurred in history. Whether the Kabbalistic traditions were legitimated by prophetic revelation or oral transmission, the presumption of Kabbalists is that these traditions are encoded in the Torah. The master of Kabbalah possesses the exegetical means to draw the mysteries out of the scriptural text. Indeed, a belief widely affirmed by Kabbalists (often expressed in the language used by Maimonides) is that the Torah has two complementary parts: the revealed or exoteric (*nigleh*) and the hidden or esoteric (*nistar*). What the Kabbalist discloses through his interpretive powers is the inner meaning of Torah that sheds light on the external meaning as well.

The possession of secret gnosis empowers the Kabbalist, for he alone has the keys to unlock the hidden treasures of the tradition. One must suppose that Kabbalistic circles functioned as autonomous fraternities, laying claim to a secretive knowledge that explained the essence of Judaism but that was not readily available to all Jews in an equal manner. The implicit elitism of Kabbalistic literature is reinforced by the claim repeated by many Kabbalistic authors regarding the inability of human reason to ascertain the esoteric truths. Even after Kabbalistic literature became a greater force in shaping popular religious culture, especially in the sixteenth and seventeenth centuries, it is still fair to say that the more recondite doctrines and more intense spiritual practices remained the exclusive property of small circles of initiates. This is the case as well in the Hasidic communities that evolved in the Ukraine, Poland, and Russia in the eighteenth and nineteenth centuries.

There are no discernible historical links connecting the members of the sectarian Qumran community and the medieval Kabbalistic fraternities. Yet, there are interesting conceptual and sociological parallels that make a comparison of the two worthwhile. Both the sectarian community and the Kabbalistic fraternities were organized socially as an elitist, secret society. One major difference is, of course, that, unlike the Qumran community, the Kabbalistic fraternities were never geographically removed from the larger Jewish society. One must presume that in practical matters Kabbalists availed themselves of the religious institutions that served the rest of their extended communities. Nevertheless, the theological calling of both the Qumran community and the Kabbalistic circles is related to a shared sense of being the spiritual elite led by an enlightened leader (*maskil,* a term used in the Dead Sea Scrolls and in Kabbalistic literature due to the mutual influence of the *Book of Daniel*). It is also of interest to consider the role of the Kabbalist as the inspired interpreter of scripture and that of the Teacher of Righteousness. [*See* Teacher of Righteousness.] Just as the sectarian belief was that the Teacher of Righteousness revealed the secrets of scripture to the members of the community, the Kabbalistic literature imparts a similar task to the master of esoteric lore (although in a technical sense there is no genre of the *pesharim* in works of Kabbalah). More importantly, both the Teacher of Righteousness and the Kabbalist engage in pneumatic exegesis, and thus their interpretations have the status of prophecy. For both the Qumran sectarians and the medieval Kabbalists, authority of interpretation derives from its being divinely inspired. Closely connected to this belief is the hermeneutical assumption regarding the dual nature of scripture as yielding both exoteric and esoteric meaning, which is shared in one form or another by the sectarian community and the Kabbalists.

Another fruitful area of comparison is the strong interest in magic and the occult in both the Qumran community and the Kabbalists. In particular, the Qumran fragments and the Kabbalistic compositions indicate that the magical arts of physiognomy and chiromancy, as well as astrology, were cultivated and considered to be part of the esoteric tradition. [*See* Horoscopes; Magic and Magical Texts.] Moreover, it is clear that the Qumran sect had an extensive angelology and demonology that is developed in later Jewish magical texts. [*See* Angels; Demons.] The technical use of hymns and spells to adjure angels or to ward off demons found in the Dead Sea Scrolls bears a striking similarity to techniques elaborated in the practical Kabbalah. [*See* Psalms, Hymns, and Prayers.]

A final point worthy of comparison is the attitude toward evil and suffering. The Kabbalists did not embrace the idea of predestination and the doctrine of ethical dualism so central in the Qumran texts, but there is a very strong emphasis in Kabbalistic literature on the cosmic struggle between the forces of light and darkness. [*See* Dualism.] The Kabbalistic notion of the holy *sefirot* (luminous emanations) competing with the impure *sefirot* is in some measure reminiscent of the sectarian view regarding the Sons of Light and the Sons of Darkness. [*See* War of the Sons of Light against the Sons of Darkness.] The discussions on evil in Kabbalistic texts are far more complex than the sectarian approach. Nevertheless, there is a similar psychological tendency found in both contexts, which serves as the basis for the assumption regarding the ontological tension between good and evil and the eschatological hope in the eventual overcoming of evil by good.

BIBLIOGRAPHY

Fine, Lawrence, ed. *Essential Papers on Kabbalah.* New York, 1995.

Hallamish, Moshe. *Introduction to the Kabbalah* (in Hebrew). Jerusalem, 1992.

Idel, Moshe. *Kabbalah: New Perspectives.* New Haven, 1988.

Liebes, Yehuda. *Studies in Jewish Myth and Jewish Messianism.* Translated by Batya Stein. Albany, 1993.

Liebes, Yehuda. *Studies in the Zohar.* Translated by Arnold Schwartz, Stephanie Nakache, and Penina Peli. Albany, 1993.

Scholem, Gershom. *Major Trends in Jewish Mysticism.* New York, 1956.

Scholem, Gershom. *On the Kabbalah and Its Symbolism.* Translated by Ralph Manheim. New York, 1965.

Scholem, Gershom. *Kabbalah.* Jerusalem, 1974.

Scholem, Gershom. *Origins of the Kabbalah.* Edited by R. J. Zwi Werblowsky and translated by Allan Arkush. Princeton, 1987.

Scholem, Gershom. *On the Mystical Shape of the Godhead: Basic Concepts in the Kabbalah.* Translated by Joachim Neugroschel and edited by Jonathan Chipman. New York, 1991.

Tishby, Isaiah. *Studies in the Kabbalah and Its Branches* (in Hebrew). 3 vols. Jerusalem, 1982–1993.

Tishby, Isaiah. *The Wisdom of the Zohar: An Anthology of Texts.* Translated by David Goldstein. Oxford, 1989.

Wolfson, Elliot R. *Through a Speculum That Shines: Vision and Imagination in Medieval Jewish Mysticism.* Princeton, 1994.

Wolfson, Elliot R. *Along the Path: Studies in Kabbalistic Myth, Symbolism, and Hermeneutics.* Albany, N.Y., 1995.

Wolfson, Elliot R. *Circle in the Square: Studies in the Use of Gender in Kabbalistic Symbolism.* Albany, N.Y., 1995.

ELLIOT R. WOLFSON

KANDO. *See* Shahin, Khalil Iskandar (Kando).

KARAITES were a Jewish sect whose teachings rejected the authority of rabbinic Jewish (Rabbanite) tradition and leadership, and did not acknowledge the concept of oral law and its literature, the Mishnah and Talmud. Karaites recognized only the Hebrew scriptures as a divinely revealed authoritative source of law. Karaism posed a serious challenge for rabbinic leadership from the late ninth through the eleventh centuries, and still exists today, mainly in Israel.

The name Karaite (*Qara'im* or *Benei Miqra'*) is derived from the Hebrew root *qara'*, meaning "to read," indicating the scripturalist aspect of Karaite ideology. Alternately, it can mean "to call" or "summon," denoting the missionizing aspect of medieval Karaism, which sought to summon Jews to their movement. The earliest attestation of the name comes from the Karaite Benjamin al-Nahāwendī in the mid-ninth century, although it may have been coined by Rabbanite Jews.

Parallels in ideology, exegetical method, and vocabulary can be identified in the Dead Sea Scrolls and Karaism. In its medieval phase, Karaism, like the ideology of the scrolls, was eschatological and messianic, resulting in constructions of the community and its laws that were predicated upon working toward the imminent end of time. These ideologies were sectarian in that they were formulated in opposition to dominant forms of Judaism by adopting a posture of resistance based upon a critique of the ruling elements of Jewish society. The Karaites believed that the rabbis were responsible for the exile because they perpetuated the evils that brought about the destruction of the Temple and that they benefited from their hegemonic position as leaders of the community.

History. The origins of Karaism are rooted in the great variety of nonrabbinic Jewish religious activity in the Near East of the early Muslim era. The consolidation of the political and social order of Islam was mirrored by similar developments within Rabbanite Jewry. A rejection of rabbinic hegemony among some Jews resulted from a complex set of social and religious conditions, including class distinctions, forms of Jewish localism that had always had a nonrabbinic character, and messianism. The primary witness to Near Eastern Jewish heterodoxy of the eighth and ninth centuries is the Karaite Yaʿqūb al-Qirqisānī, who in 937 CE described groups that differed widely in regard to law, messianism, revolution, and syncretism. Several of these groups would later contribute to the more fully articulated Karaite movement of the tenth and eleventh centuries.

One of these movements began with Anan ben David in the middle of the eighth century, according to a narrative that may have originated among Rabbanites but was recorded by the twelfth-century Byzantine Karaite Elijah ben Abraham. Anan, of the Jewish princely family in Iraq, was passed over in the succession to the office of the exilarchate on account of his heterodox ideas. By presenting himself to the Muslim authorities as leader of a religion different from that of the rabbis, and not merely a sectarian group, he was able to secure governmental protection for himself and his followers. The narrative describes these so-called Ananites, who were acknowledged by later Karaites as the first of their movement, as "remnants of the Sadducees and Boethusians."

By the late ninth century, several heterodox trends came together to constitute Karaism, including antirabbinism, scripturalism, the Ananites, and perhaps remnants of defunct messianic followings. Under the leadership of Daniel al-Qūmisī, an ideology emerged that actively called for Jews to return to the land of Israel, in expectation of messianic times. Known as the "Mourners for Zion" (*Avelei Tsiyyon*), this group combined a millenarian perspective with ascetic tendencies. By choosing immigration to Palestine, they sought to negate the exile in preparation for the coming of the Messiah.

In the tenth and eleventh centuries, Jerusalem became a center for Karaite life and scholarly activity. This period is identified by some modern scholars as its "classical period" or "golden age" on account of the literary production in Hebrew and Arabic by a series of eminent scholars, including al-Qūmisī and al-Qirqisānī. These authors wrote works on biblical commentary, Karaite *halakhah*, philosophy, antirabbinic polemic, and Hebrew language and masoretic studies. This range of works has attracted attention on the part of modern scholars interested in correlations between the Karaites and the Dead Sea Scrolls.

Karaite *halakhah* for the most part is based upon scripturalism, a concentration on authority in scripture to the exclusion of received tradition. In order to develop a comprehensive legal system without making claims to tradition, Karaites used the entire Hebrew scriptures for legal purposes and had recourse to the hermeneutical methods of analogy (*heqqesh*) and consensus of the community (*qibbuts* or *ʿedah*). Nonetheless, scripturalism generated a great deal of individualism in jurisprudence, resulting in wide halakhic variation. It is noted by al-Qirqisānī that one could hardly find two Karaites who agreed. Many Karaites addressed diversity in their *halakhah* by turning to rationalism in the form of Kalām philosophy, which lent itself to efforts at systematization and provided an intellectually acknowledged methodology that could rival rabbinic traditionalism.

After dissolution of the Jerusalem center in the latter half of the eleventh century, Karaites continued to live in the Islamic Near East, with an important community in Cairo. However, a new intellectual center was established at Constantinople, where Karaism lost some of its millenarian emphasis as the immediacy of messianic belief was tempered by accommodation to the notion of exile. A great literary project translated the Arabic works of previous generations into Hebrew for use in the non-Islamic environment. Balkan and Constantinopolitan Karaites experienced a second period of florescence under the Ottomans (fourteenth through sixteenth centuries), producing important works of biblical commentary, law, and philosophy.

In the early modern period, Karaites were found in the Crimea and Poland-Lithuania, where a few Karaite scholars of distinction were influenced by contacts with Protestant academics in the sixteenth through eighteenth centuries. In the nineteenth century, eastern European Karaites distanced their group from Judaism, and, as a result of the Holocaust and Soviet policies, have virtually disappeared. In the twentieth century, the majority of Near Eastern Karaites immigrated with other Jews from Arab lands to Israel. Contemporary Israeli Karaites have focused some attention on the Dead Sea Scrolls in an effort to claim Second Temple origins for their community.

Karaism and the Scrolls. Scholars have suggested connections between the Dead Sea Scrolls and Karaism, but their many theories are weakened by an inherent twofold problem. If, on the one hand, the Karaites are intellectual and/or communal descendants of the Qumran community, then one needs to demonstrate some kind of historical continuity across a little-known period in Jewish history spanning the seven or eight centuries that intervened between the destruction of Qumran (68 CE) and the era to which we traditionally assign Karaite origins. If, on the other hand, the Karaite phenomenon is a medieval movement independent of Second Temple period antecedents, then one must be able to explain striking similarities shared by these two groups.

What is perhaps the most plausible of theories is that medieval Karaites had access to Dead Sea Scroll literature or materials cognate to the scrolls and used them to formulate their own ideology. The Damascus Document was known to medieval Jews, having been found among the documents of the Cairo Genizah, and medieval Karaites claimed to be in possession of Zadokite texts. This theory is supported by a ninth-century letter from the Nestorian Catholicos of Seleucia-Baghdad, Timotheus, who reports that a desert chamber was discovered near Jericho filled with Hebrew manuscripts, which subsequently were declared heretical by local rabbinic authorities. It has been suggested that this was a medieval discovery of Cave 1 or some other known or unknown cave, and that these heretical documents became the bases for later medieval Jewish heterodoxy. Such a view finds further support in reports of other ancient and medieval manuscript finds (by Eusebius, by the Magharians, and in the Khazar correspondence).

A wide range of speculation has generated other theories. Naphtali Wieder suggests in *The Judean Scrolls and Karaism* that the Dead Sea Scroll community survived into the Islamic period as the Karaites, or as a group that joined and greatly influenced the larger nexus of groups forming the Karaites. In "The Damascus Document Revisited" (*Revue biblique* 92, 1985), Jerome Murphy-O'Connor states that Karaism is a medieval continuation of the teachings and community of the Essenes, originally an ancient Babylonian movement. It was subsequently imported to Qumran in Palestine in the Second Temple period, but its medieval Babylonian (Iraqi) continuators are understood to be Anan and the earliest Karaites. Another theory associates scripturalist ideologies found in Karaism with the scrolls and with forms of eastern Christianity, especially the writings of the Syrian Father Aphrahat, who died c.345 CE (Jean Ouellete, "Aphraate, Qumrân, et les Qaraïtes," an appendix in Jacob Neusner, *A History of the Mishnaic Law of Purities*, Leiden, 1976). An important link in this theory is Dāwūd ibn Marwān al-Muqammiṣ, a ninth-century convert to Christianity who later returned to Judaism and became an important source for al-Qirqisānī. One must also mention the now-discredited theories reviewed by H. Rowley that claim the Dead Sea Scrolls are of medieval origin, either Karaite forgeries fabricated in order to establish an ancient origin for Karaism (Solomon Zeitlin), or documents of the ʿIsawite sect, followers of Abū ʿĪsa al-Isfahānī, the messianic leader of a rebellion against the Muslim Caliphate in eighth-century Iran (P. R. Weiss).

Comparisons of Karaism and the Dead Sea Scrolls often begin with *halakhah*. Karaite *halakhah* differs from rabbinic *halakhah* on many particular points, with the findings of the former often in agreement with the *halakhah* of the scrolls. The following three examples illustrate this: a marked tendency toward asceticism (compare asceticism in the scrolls to the ninth-century Daniel al-Qūmisī of Leon Nemoy, *Karaite Anthology*, p. 34ff., or the tenth-century Sahl ben Maṣliah, *Karaite Anthology*, p. 113f.); the presence of a calendar designed so that some or all holidays fall on a particular day of the week (compare the calendar behind the Temple Scroll [11QT] or Calendrical Document A (4Q320) to Samuel al-Maghribī in Nemoy, *Karaite Anthology*, p. 222, or the discussion in Zvi Ankori, *Karaites in Byzantium*, p. 275ff.); and strict notions of consanguinity, including rejection of niece-marriage (compare Damascus Document, CD v.7–11, and 11QT[a] lxvi.15–17 to Daniel al-Qūmisī in Nemoy, *Karaite Anthology*, p. 40, or the discussion in Bernard Revel, "The Karaite Halakah," pp. 66–78).

On the other hand, there are many instances where Karaite and rabbinic rulings correspond but are opposed to those found in the Dead Sea Scrolls. Furthermore, Karaite *halakhah* can find both agreement and disagreement with Sadducean legal positions known from rabbinic literature. The wide difference in the results of these comparisons is compounded by the lack of consistency in Karaite *halakhah*. As a result, it is problematic to postulate a systematic halakhic correspondence between the scrolls and the Karaites.

Karaite literature and the Dead Sea Scrolls exhibit similarities in outlook and vocabulary, a correspondence most markedly noted in the writing of Daniel al-Qūmisī, but continued thereafter as part of Karaite literary tradition. Both Karaites and the Qumran community utilized the idea of the perfection of the Torah (*Torah temimah*) as an ideological foundation and as a critique of their opponents, who were characterized as false interpreters and liars. The Karaites also used this notion of the Torah as the basis for scripturalism, postulating the self-sufficiency of the Torah for human understanding, and thereby denying a need for rabbinic tradition. For both sects, the method by which the knowable or "revealed" Torah became comprehensible was *midrash*, understood to mean "inquiry," "study," or "seeking," perhaps to be contrasted to the narrower rabbinic definition of "homiletic exposition" (compare CD vi.7; Rule of the Community, 1QS vi.6; viii.11–12, 15–16; Florilegium, 4Q174 i.11 to the discussion in Wieder, *The Judean Scrolls*, pp. 77–79).

This type of inquiry into scripture was the domain of the *maskil*, translated as "man of understanding"; or "teacher, enlightener," whose scriptural exegesis often utilized the *pesher* method known from the Dead Sea Scrolls (CD xii.21; xiii.22; 1QS iii.13; ix.12; ix.21; War Scroll, 1QM x.10; Hodayot[a], 1QH[a] xx.11). Karaite exegetes often employed the term *pashar* (or its cognate, *patar*), and even utilized verses and their *pesharim* as found in the scrolls. For example, a *pesher* is used in the Damascus Document (CD iv.15–18; v.6), Pesher Psalms[a] (4QpPs[a], ii.9–12), Pesher Habakkuk (1QpHab, xii.8–9, and several Karaite sources (including al-Qūmisī) to identify sins of the writers' opponents, known as the "nets of Belial."

Karaites used many other terms also found in the Dead Sea Scrolls to denounce their opponents, particularly in the Damascus Document. These include "changers of boundaries" (CD v.20–vi.2), "builders of the wall" (CD iv.19; viii.12; xix.24–25), "lying and deceiving interpreters" (1QH[a] x.31; xii.7, 9–10), "shepherds" (". . . of the exile," for Karaites) (CD xix.5–13), and "deflectors from the way" (CD i.13; ii.6; 1QS x.21).

Similarly, other Dead Sea Scroll terminology was used by Karaites to portray themselves, including "perfect in the way" (there are many instances of *temimei derekh* in the Damascus Document and the Rule of the Community, e.g., 1QS iv.22, as well as 1QM xiv.7, 1QH[a] x.36, and the Rule of the Blessings 1Q28b v.22), as well as "those who turn from transgression" (CD ii.5; xx.17; 1QS x.20; 1QH[a] vi.24; x.9; xiv.6), and the idea of "the remnant."

Both Karaism and the scrolls speak of "returning to the Torah of Moses" to indicate conversion to their brand of Judaism (CD xv.9, 12; xvi.1–2, 4–5; 1QS v.8). Eschatological expectation in both sects included a doctrine of two messiahs (CD xii.23; xiv.19; 1QS ix.11; Wieder, "Doctrine of Two Messiahs"), one of whom would be the Teacher of Righteousness (*Moreh Tsedeq*) (CD i.11; xx.32; 1QpHab i.13; ii.2; v.10; vii.4; viii.3; ix.9–10; xi.5; 4QpPs[a] iii.15).

In spite of many shared elements, it must be noted that the Dead Sea Scroll community withdrew from Second Temple society at large to create a separate quasi-monastic society, whereas the Karaites created their subculture in Jerusalem and among the widely dispersed Jewish communities of the medieval Near East. Unlike the Qumran community, the Karaites never established a hierarchy of initiation, and Karaite theology included neither the dualism of light and darkness nor spirits of truth and evil.

BIBLIOGRAPHY

Ankori, Zvi. *Karaites in Byzantium: The Formative Years, 970–1100*. New York and Jerusalem, 1959. Authoritative study of medieval Karaite history describing the translation of Karaism from the Islamic world to the Byzantine Empire.

Birnbaum, Philip. *Karaite Studies*. New York, 1971. Collection of important journal articles by various authors.

Chiesa, Bruno, and Wilfrid Lockwood, eds. *Ya'qūb al-Qirqisānī on Jewish Sects and Christianity*. Judentum und Umwelt, 10. Frankfurt am Main, 1984. Translation and two studies of this significant source on medieval Jewish sects.

Erder, Yoram. "When Did the Karaites First Encounter Apocryphic Literature Akin to the Dead Sea Scrolls?" *Cathedra* 42 (1987), 54–68. With comments by Haggai Ben-Shammai; other articles by this author should be consulted.

Gil, Moshe. *A History of Palestine, 634–1099*. Cambridge and New York, 1992. Excellent up-to-date history of medieval Palestinian Karaism; see pages 777–820.

Mann, Jacob. *Texts and Studies in Jewish History and Literature*, vol. 2: *Karaitica*. New York, 1972. Authoritative studies on Karaite texts from the Middle Ages through the nineteenth century.

Nemoy, Leon. *Karaite Anthology: Excerpts from the Early Literature*. New Haven and London, 1952. Standard reference and collection of translated texts from the eighth to fifteenth centuries. Journal articles by this author are also important.

Paul André. *Écrits de Qumran et sectes juives aux premiers siècles de l'Islam, Recherches sur l'origine du Qaraïsme*. Paris, 1969. Theoretical and synthetic treatment that views Karaism as a Judaic reform movement that was influenced in the tenth century by the discovery of Dead Sea Scroll materials.

Revel, Bernard. "The Karaite Halakah and Its Relation to Sadducean, Samaritan and Philonian Halakah." In *Karaite Studies*, edited by Philip Birnbaum, pp. 1–88 [reprint of *Jewish Quarterly Review*, n.s. 2 (1911–1912) and 3 (1912–1913)]. Analysis of Karaite *halakhah* showing agreements and disagreements with Damascus Document as known from the Cairo Genizah. Written before the discovery of the Dead Sea Scrolls.

Rowley, H. H. *The Zadokite Fragments and the Dead Sea Scrolls*. Oxford, 1952. Includes a good review of possible connections between the Damascus Document and Karaites (pp. 21–30), even though it was written before the Damascus Document was known from Qumran Caves 4 and 6.

Wieder, Naphtali. "The Doctrine of the Two Messiahs among the Karaites." *Journal of Jewish Studies* 6 (1955), 14–25. Compares Karaite and Dead Sea Scroll notions of dual messiahs.

Wieder, Naphtali. "The Qumran Sectaries and the Karaites." *Jewish Quarterly Review*, n.s. 47 (1956–1957), 97–113, 269–292. Analysis of certain terminology found in the Dead Sea Scrolls and Karaite literature.

Wieder, Naphtali. *The Judean Scrolls and Karaism*. London, 1962. Standard work on the subject; suggests that remnants of the Dead Sea Scroll community survived to influence the Karaites.

FRED ASTREN

KETEF JERICHO. *See* Mafjar, Wadi el-.

KHABRA, WADI. *See* Ḥever, Naḥal.

KILNS. In his excavations at Qumran, Roland de Vaux discovered the remains of potters' kilns belonging to periods Ia, Ib, and II (last third of the second century BCE to 68 CE). They were in potters' workshops located on the southeastern edge of the site, with those of periods Ib and II lying a little farther to the east due to the expansion of the later settlement. The remains of two poorly preserved kilns of period Ia were found side by side beneath Locus

66. Both were circular and measured approximately two to three meters internally and four meters externally in diameter. The opening of the eastern kiln faced south, while the western kiln opened to the north. The western kiln also had a round central pillar supporting the floor, a feature that was either lacking or not preserved in the eastern kiln.

In Period Ib, a new potters' workshop was established in the triangular enclosure just to the east of the period Ia kilns. It continued in use to the end of period II. Again there were two kilns, adjacent to each other. The southern kiln, which was circular and opened toward the north, either had no central support for the floor or it was not preserved. The pots were put into the kiln through an opening in its upper part and placed on a bench that encircled the floor. Steps led down to another opening below, where the fire chamber was located. The kiln measured approximately two meters internally and four meters externally in diameter. The northern kiln opened toward the south. It appears to have been roughly circular in the interior and square or rectangular on the exterior. A round central pillar that supported the floor was found, and part of the floor was still pierced by five flues. It was smaller than the southern kiln, measuring a little over one meter in diameter internally and about two meters externally. De Vaux suggested that the openings of these two kilns were oriented to take advantage of the prevailing winds along the Dead Sea and that the southern kiln was used to fire larger vessels.

These two kilns lay in a sunken area on the eastern edge of the triangular enclosure, which was approached on the southwest by five steps. An iron hook, perhaps for stirring the fire, was found lying on the steps. Other parts of the potters' workshop were discovered outside the sunken area. About four meters to the southwest of the steps, de Vaux uncovered a circular cavity made of stones, measuring about one meter in diameter internally, which he identified as the site of a potter's wheel. Just to the south lay two plastered basins, which de Vaux associated with the workshop. The southern basin is shallow and roughly rectangular in shape, and was bordered by a line of standing stone slabs. According to de Vaux, it was filled with fairly clean clay. This basin received water from a small channel that branched off from the main supply channel of the adjacent cistern. The water flowed into a small decantation basin before entering the southern basin. De Vaux proposed that the potters washed their clay in the southern basin. Just to its north lay an L-shaped basin. The southern part of the basin is shallower and was filled with yellow clay. De Vaux suggested that this represents the stock of cleaned clay, which was mixed in the deeper northern part of the basin.

Samples of clay from Qumran were analyzed by Fredrick E. Zeuner (1960). The results indicated that neither the marl deposits of the Qumran terrace nor the deposits that formed in the cisterns and decantation basins in the settlement could have provided suitable raw material for pottery manufacture. Thus, though the presence of the workshops at Qumran indicates that at least some of the pottery was locally produced, the source of the clay is still unknown. On the other hand, neutron activation analysis has demonstrated that the pottery vessels from Wadi Ghweir and Qumran were made from different clays.

In de Vaux's field notes, the western kiln (the one with the central pillar) of period Ia is described as being made of baked clay. The materials from which the other Qumran kilns are constructed are not described, though in the published photographs they appear to consist of fieldstone and mud. Their heights also are not recorded, and in no case was the upper part of the kiln preserved. Presumably, it would have been destroyed and rebuilt between firings to allow for the insertion and removal of the vessels. Despite their variation in size, materials, and the presence or absence of a central pillar, all of the Qumran kilns are of the usual Roman updraft type. The pots were stacked on a floor that was pierced by flues and that separated the oven compartment from the fire chamber below. The round plan of the Qumran kilns also conforms to the standard Roman type. At least two of the Qumran kilns had a central pillar to support the floor. Perhaps the other two kilns originally had a similar arrangement that was not preserved, since kilns without any internal support seldom measure more than one meter in diameter internally. On the other hand, in none of the Qumran kilns is the flue spanned by a complex of arches, which is usually found in kilns measuring more than three to four meters in diameter.

The Qumran kilns are unparalleled in the Judean Desert, and published examples from other parts of Hellenistic and Roman Palestine are rare. A contemporary round kiln was found in the Nabatean potters' workshop at Avdat (Oboda) in the Negev Desert. The workshop at Avdat, like that at Qumran, was located on the eastern outskirts of the settlement. According to the excavator, Avraham Negev (1974), this is because the prevailing winds blow from north-northwest to south-southeast. Other examples of kilns and potters' workshops in Roman Palestine are found at Kefar Ḥananya and Kfar Naḥf in the Galilee, and at Givat Ram in Jerusalem. The discovery of potters' workshops at Qumran constitutes important evidence for local ceramic production. It also accounts for some of the peculiar characteristics of the ceramic repertoire at Qumran, including the unusual types and the rarity of decoration. Rachel Bar-Nathan (1988) has noted a similar phenomenon at Jericho, where she believes much of the pottery found in the excavations was produced. In light of the similarities between the Jericho and Qumran assemblages, she has suggested that local potters' workshops supplied settlements along the Jordan Valley and Dead Sea.

[*See also* Qumran, *article on* Archaeology.]

BIBLIOGRAPHY

Adan-Bayewitz, David. *Common Pottery in Roman Galilee: A Study of Local Trade*. Ramat-Gan, Israel, 1993. Discusses pottery manufacture at Kefar Ḥananya and other Roman period sites in Galilee.

Arubas, Benny, and Haim Goldfus. "The Kilnworks of the Tenth Legion Fretensis." In *The Roman and Byzantine Near East: Some Recent Archaeological Research*. Journal of Roman Archaeology Supplementary Series, 14, edited by John H. Humphrey, pp. 95–107. Ann Arbor, Mich., 1995. Preliminary report of the excavations of this kiln site in Jerusalem.

Bar-Nathan, Rachel. "The Pottery of Jericho in the Hasmonean Period and the Time of Herod, and the Problem of the Transition from Hasmonean Pottery Types to Pottery Types of the Time of Herod." M. A. thesis, Hebrew University of Jerusalem, 1988. A typology of the Hasmonean and Herodian pottery from Ehud Netzer's excavations.

Broshi, Magen. "The Archaeology of Qumran—A Reconsideration." In *The Dead Sea Scrolls: Forty Years of Research*, edited by Devorah Dimant and Uriel Rappaport, pp. 103–115. Jerusalem, 1992. Describes the results of neutron activation analysis of pottery samples from Qumran and Wadi Ghweir.

de Vaux, Roland. *Archaeology and the Dead Sea Scrolls*. Oxford, 1973. Contains a synthetic description and discussion of the potters' workshops at Qumran.

Humbert, Jean-Baptiste, and Alain Chambon. *Fouilles de Khirbet Qumrân et de Aïn Feshkha I*. Göttingen, 1994. The publication of Roland de Vaux's field notes and photographs from the time of the excavations.

Negev, Avraham. *The Nabataean Potter's Workshop at Oboda*. Bonn, 1974. Publication of the potters' workshop at Avdat in the Negev Desert.

Peacock, David P. S. *Pottery in the Roman World, an Ethnoarchaeological Approach*. New York, 1982. Excellent overview of pottery production in the Roman world.

Vitto, Fanny. "Potter's Kilns at Kfar Naḥf." *Israel Exploration Journal* 30 (1980), 205–206. Preliminary report of the late Roman to early Byzantine potters' workshop at this Galilean site.

Zeuner, Fredrick E. "Notes on Qumran." *Palestine Exploration Quarterly* 92 (1960), 27–36.

JODI MAGNESS

KINGS, FIRST AND SECOND BOOKS OF. Three Qumran manuscripts of *Kings* are extant. Kings from Cave 4 at Qumran (hereafter, 4QKings, 4Q54) dates from the middle of the first century BCE. The seven identified fragments contain portions of *1 Kings* 7.20–21, 25–27, 29–42, 50(?), 51; 8.1–9; 16–18; fragment 8 is unidentified. 4QKings stands in the proto-masoretic textual tradition, agreeing with the Masoretic Text of *Kings* (and *Chronicles*) against the Septuagint in all the minuses and transpositions that give the Old Greek its peculiar textual character here. Fragment 7 preserves a reading in *1 Kings* 8.16, lost by homoioteleuton in the Masoretic Text but present in the parallel *2 Chronicles* 6.5b and 6.6a and also partly preserved in the Old Greek of *Kings* (Trebolle Barrera, 1995). [*See* Septuagint.]

Kings from Cave 5 at Qumran (5Q2) dates to the late second century BCE. Three fragments from the first column contain parts of *1 Kings* 1, verses 16–17 and 27–37, its text agreeing, except for spelling, with the Masoretic Text and the Greek (Milik, 1962).

Kings from Cave 6 at Qumran (hereafter, 6QKings, 6Q4), on papyrus, is from the late second century BCE. The orthography is full at times. Fragments 1–17 contain portions of *1 Kings* 3.12b–14, 12.28b–31, and 22.28–31 and *2 Kings* 5.26; 6.32; 7.8–10, 20; 8.1–5; 9.1–2; 10.19–21 fragments 18–94 are unidentified. The text of *2 Kings* 7.20–8.5 in 6QKings is sometimes shorter than the Masoretic Text (Baillet, 1962).

Furthermore, three fragments of the Book of the Kings (4Q235) in the Nabatean script have been preserved. [*See* Nabatean.]

The Isaiah scrolls also have a bearing on the text of *Kings* in the passages they have in common (*Is*. 36.1–39.8, *2 Kgs*. 18.13–20.19). Isaiah[a] from Cave 1 at Qumran (1QIsa[a]) preserves the entire parallel text, Isaiah[b] from Cave 1 at Qumran (1Q8) has 37.8–12 and 38.12–39.8, and Isaiah[b] from Cave 4 at Qumran (4Q56) contains 36.1–2, 37.29–32, 39.1–8.

In Paraphrase of Kings et al. (4Q382), fragments 1–5, 9, 11, 30 (40?) appear to be a paraphrase or part of a work rewriting the Elijah-Elisha stories (*2 Kgs*. 2.3–4; 17.1; 18.4; 19.16, 19). [*See* Elijah *and* Elisha.] The text is more closely related to the Hebrew underlying the Old Greek than to the Masoretic Text. Fragment 2 of the fragment mentioning Elisha (4Q481a) quotes and paraphrases *2 Kings* 2.14–14.16. The seventy-two fragments of Apocryphon on Samuel-Kings (6Q9) contain only scanty material related to these books and *Chronicles* (Baillet, 1962). [*See* Chronicles, First and Second Books of.]

Other Judean Desert biblical manuscripts shed light on the textual history of *Kings*. The Greek Minor Prophets (8Ḥev 1) contains the text of the proto-Theodotionic recension that is also found in two sections of the Septuagint *Kings*: *1 Kings* 1.1–2.11 and *1 Kings* 22.1–*2 Kings* 25.30 (Barthélemy, 1972). [*See* Minor Prophets.] In these sections the *Codex Vaticanus* (B), followed in Rahlf's Septuagint edition, reproduces the text of the proto-Theodotionic recension, while the Lucianic manuscripts (boc_2e_2) preserve a text that is very close or substantially identical to that of the Old Greek. The identification of a proto-Lucianic recension was prompted by the observation that Lucianic readings of *Samuel* agree with the Hebrew of

Samuel[a] (4Q52) against the Masoretic Text and the Old Greek, which in such cases does not show traces of recensional activity (Cross, 1975, p. 315; Ulrich, 1978, pp. 95–96). [*See* Samuel, First and Second Books of.]

Qumran confirms the antiquity of the Masoretic Text of *Kings* (for the defective orthography, for example), but also the text-critical value of the Old Greek. The considerable variations (pluses and minuses, transpositions, different chronological systems, etc.) that the Old Greek offers with respect to the Masoretic Text are not due so much to the work of the Greek translator but rather reflect a different text from that transmitted by the masoretic tradition. In not a few cases the Hebrew original of the Greek version represents a literary edition of *Kings* that is older and shorter than that known in the Masoretic Text. However, the question of whether the Septuagint differs in recension from the Masoretic Text or reflects later Midrashic developments has not yet been answered.

BIBLIOGRAPHY

Baillet, M., J. T. Milik, and R. de Vaux. *Les 'Petites Grottes' de Qumran*. Discoveries in the Judaean Desert, 3. Oxford, 1962.

Barthélemy, Dominique. "Les problèmes textuels de 2 Sam 11,2–1 Rois 2,11 reconsidérés à la lumière de certaines critiques des *Devanciers d'Aquila*." *1972 Proceedings (IOSCS* (1972), 16–89.

Cross, Frank Moore. "The Evolution of a Theory of Local Texts." In *Qumran and the History of the Biblical Text*, edited by Frank Moore Cross and Shemaryahu Talmon, pp. 306–320. Cambridge and London, 1975.

Trebolle Barrera, Julio. "4QKgs." In *Qumran Cave 4, IX: Deuteronomy, Joshua, Judges, Kings*, edited by Eugene Ulrich and Frank Moore Cross, pp. 171–183. Discoveries in the Judaean Desert, 14. Oxford, 1995.

Ulrich, Eugene Charles. *The Qumran Text of Samuel and Josephus*. Harvard Semitic Monographs, 19. Missoula, Mont., 1978.

JULIO TREBOLLE BARRERA

KINGSHIP. Although foreign kings ruled Judea during most of the Second Temple period, Hasmonean rulers claimed the royal title, beginning with Aristobulus I (r.104–103 BCE), continuing through the reigns of Alexander Jannaeus (103–76 BCE), Shelamzion Alexander (76–67 BCE), Aristobulus II (67–63 BCE), and ending with Antigonus II (40–37 BCE). Herod the Great (37–4 BCE) also received the title, while it was denied to his son Herod Archelaus (4 BCE–6 CE; but see *Mt*. 2.2, *Jewish Antiquities* 18.93). Herod Agrippa I also ruled as king (41–44 CE). [*See* Hasmoneans; Herodian Rulers.]

According to Judean Desert documents, the ideal Jewish society also included the institution of kingship, yet the status and duties of the king were to be carefully circumscribed. The primary sources for determining the view of kingship expressed in the scrolls are the Law of the King section of Temple Scroll[a] (11Q19 lvi.12–lix.21) and several fragmentary texts that refer to kings or kingship.

The Law of the King interprets and augments *Deuteronomy* 17.14–20. Following this biblical text, it refers to the monarch as *melekh* ("king") and requires that the king be an Israelite, be chosen by God, and refrain from accumulating horses and wealth. Other items in the biblical text are modified, however. The prohibition against acquiring many wives is elaborated so that it explicitly requires the king to be monogamous, selecting a lifelong partner from his father's house, and whereas *Deuteronomy* 17.18–19 instructs the king to write out for himself a copy of the law that he might rule in accord with it—presumably referring to the deuteronomic law, Temple Scroll[a] apparently directs the priests in charge of the law to write out for the king the Law of the King. If the king obeys the law, God promises to deliver him from his enemies, make him prosperous, and grant him and his descendants long rule. Disobedience, however, would result in exile for his people and the end of his dynasty. In short, dynastic continuance is strictly conditioned on obedience to the law of God.

The king's duties consist of military and judicial affairs. He must appoint from the tribes of Israel the army and its leaders, as well as a royal guard of twelve thousand soldiers of character and valor, whose primary task is to protect the king from capture by a foreign nation. Detailed rules for war restrict the number of soldiers a monarch may muster in a defensive war, limit his share of the plunder to one-tenth, and place the decision of whether to engage in a nondefensive war in the hands of the high priest. The king's judicial activities are to be distinguished by righteous judgments; he may not take bribes or covet the possessions of his subjects. Furthermore, he must exercise judgment in consultation with a judicial council composed of twelve leaders of the people, twelve priests, and twelve Levites: "his heart may not be lifted up above them" and "he may not do anything by any counsel apart from them" (11Q19 lvii.14–15).

The Law of the King sets forth a decidedly limited version of Jewish kingship, one that stands in contrast to the authority and prerogatives exercised by ancient Israelite kings. Conspicuously absent from the Law of the King are ideas associated with the Judean royal ideology, such as Davidic lineage, divine sonship of the king, and unconditional rule sealed by covenant; nor is there any role reserved for the king in cultic matters. Instead, the Law of the King reflects reservations about kingship and its abuses found in the Hebrew scriptures (cf. *1 Sm*. 8). The emphasis on priestly oversight of royal activities reflects similar misgivings about the power of kings. Accordingly, while monarchy is still viewed as a divinely approved institution for Israel, its character appears to be shaped by biblical texts favoring restricted kingship and conditional rule (cf. *Ezek*. 40–48; Psalm 132).

Several provisions in the Law of the King probably represent a reaction to problems associated with the Hasmonean rulers. For example, the need for a loyal guard to protect the king from capture may constitute a response to the seizure and execution of Jonathan (the Hasmonean) in 143 or 142 BCE by the Seleucid Trypho. Furthermore, it is likely that prohibitions against the accumulation of wealth and restrictions against offensive wars reflect a critique of Hasmonean leaders such as John Hyrcanus (135–104 BCE), who amassed great riches and embarked on wars of conquest. Most importantly, in the Law of the King the office of king is distinct from the office of high priest, yielding a model of diarchic governance at odds with Hasmonean rulers who were both high priests and chief lay leaders or kings.

Despite claims to the contrary by some scholars, the Law of the King does not envision eschatological kingship; nor is the ideal king a messianic figure. [*See* Messiahs.] The need to fight defensive wars, the possibility of exile, and the potential for the king's dynasty coming to an end support this conclusion. Hence, while the ideal king of Temple Scroll[a] shares with the Qumran royal Messiah a military and judicial role and subordination to priests, these figures are to be distinguished. [*See* Hasmoneans.]

Like the Law of the King, other Judean Desert documents speak of devotion to the law as fundamental to Jewish kingship. For instance, in Miqtsat Ma'asei ha-Torah[a–f] (4Q394–399) the recipient of this halakhic document is exhorted to remember the example of the kings of Israel, including David, who were delivered from their troubles and forgiven their sins because of their piety and faithfulness to the law. Also, in a fragmentary text mentioning Zedekiah (4Q470), this biblical king is portrayed as recommitting himself to the law of God.

Scholars have generally found in Judean Desert documents a negative attitude toward Hasmonean rule, in part because of the implicit critique of Hasmonean leadership in Temple Scroll[a] and the absence of documents with a pro-Hasmonean slant among the scrolls. However, with the decipherment and publication of the Apocryphal Psalm and Prayer (4Q448), this conclusion has been challenged. Some scholars argue that this text contains a prayer for the welfare of King Jonathan, identified as the Hasmonean king Alexander Jannaeus. Yet the reading of the name *Jonathan*, the text's interpretation, and its provenance are all matters of dispute. On the other hand, Herodian kings are never specifically mentioned in Judean Desert documents, but their loyalty to the Romans and penchant for impiety suggest that the sectarians at Qumran viewed them as illegitimate.

The concept of kingship in Judean Desert documents can be compared to other ideas about this institution expressed during the Second Temple period. Thus, Josephus reports that during the struggle between Hyrcanus II and Aristobulus II for the Hasmonean throne (63 BCE), the nation declared its desire to be ruled by priests instead of a king (*Antiquities* 14.41). On the other hand, *Psalms of Solomon* 17 (c.60 BCE) envisions a Davidic king of power, wisdom, and holiness, whose reign leaves little role for priests. However, leadership through a king and a high priest is paralleled in some portions of the *Testaments of the Twelve Patriarchs* and on coins minted by the Jewish revolutionary Shim'on Bar Kokhba (c.132 BCE).

[*See also* Temple Scroll.]

BIBLIOGRAPHY

Eshel, Esther, Hanan Eshel, and Ada Yardeni. "A Qumran Composition Containing Part of Ps. 154 and a Prayer for the Welfare of King Jonathan and his Kingdom." *Israel Exploration Journal* 42 (1992), 199–229. Initial publication and interpretation of Apocryphal Psalm and Prayer (4Q448).

Schiffman, Lawrence H. "The King, His Guard, and the Royal Council in the *Temple Scroll*." *Proceedings of the American Academy for Jewish Research* 54 (1987), 237–259. Particularly helpful in placing the Law of the King within the context of Second Temple Jewish history and thought.

Vermes, Geza. "The So-Called King Jonathan Fragment (4Q448)." *Journal of Jewish Studies* 44 (1993), 294–300. Offers a different interpretation of the Apocryphal Psalm and Prayer text (4Q448) than Eshel, Eshel, and Yardeni.

Yadin, Yigael. *The Temple Scroll*. 3 vols. with a supplement. Jerusalem, 1983. Definitive publication and expert discussion of all facets of Temple Scroll[a], including the Law of the King.

KENNETH E. POMYKALA

KITTIM. A group referred to as the *Kittim* figure prominently in the Qumran scrolls. The name occurs several times in the *pesharim* (Pesher Habakkuk, 1QpHab; Pesher Nahum, 4Q169; Pesher Isaiah[a], 4Q161; Pesher Psalms, 1Q16), the War Scroll (1Q33, 4Q471, and 4Q491–497), and the War Rule (4Q285). There is consensus that the reference is to the Romans.

Biblical Use of Kittim. The spelling of the name *Kittim* in the Hebrew scriptures varies between *ktyym* and *ktym*. Deriving from the Phoenician *kt* and *kty*, which originally referred to Citium, a town on the southeastern coast of Cyprus near modern Larnaca, and its residents (Harris, 1936, p. 113), the Hebrew term (always in the plural) came to have several meanings: the son of Javan, son of Japheth (*Gn*. 10.4; *1 Chr*. 1.7); Cyprus, or the coastlands generally (*Jer*. 2.10; *Ezek*. 27.6). In Jewish and Christian traditions, the word *kittim* likewise had a range of geographical and ethnic referents. The author of *1 Maccabees* understood it as Macedonia when he states that Alexander the Great defeated Darius after marching from the "the land of the *Kittim*" (*1 Mc.* 1.1; Perseus is called "king of the *Kittim*" in *1 Maccabees* 8.5). Both Targum Onkelos and the Vulgate rendered *Numbers* 24.24 ("but ships shall come from the coast of *Kittim*") as a reference to the Romans (cf. *Dn.* 11.30 [*rōmaioi* in the Septuagint, but *kitioi* in Theodotion]). Josephus explains that the name is given "to all islands and to most maritime countries" (*Jewish Antiquities* 1.128).

In the Qumran scrolls, *Kittim* is spelled, as in some of the biblical texts, as *ktyym* (4QpNah 1–2.ii.[3]; 3–4.i.3; 1QM i.2, 4, 6, 9; xi.11; xv.9; xvi.3; xvi.6, 9; xvii.12, 14; xviii.2, 4; xix.10, 13; 4QM[b] 1.9; 4Q285 5.6) or with the digraph as *kty'ym* (1QpHab ii.12, 14; iii.4, 9; iv.5, 10; vi.1, 10; ix.7; 1QpPs 9.4; 4QpIsa[a] 7–10.iii.7, 9, 11, 12; 4QM[a] 10.ii.8, 10, 12; 11.ii.8, 19; 13.5).

Kittim as Romans. The identification of the *Kittim* as Romans in the Qumran scrolls is based primarily upon the historical allusions in the *pesharim*. In the fragmentary interpretation of *Nahum* 2.12b, the author reveals that "[Deme]trius, king of Greece, sought to enter Jerusalem on the advice of the Seekers after Smooth Things" and that the biblical phrase also foretold the actions of "the kings of Greece, from Antiochus until the rise of the rulers of the *Kittim*, and afterwards she [Jerusalem] will be downtrodden" (4Q169 3–4.i.2–3).

These statements are understood to refer to the broad historical context as well as to specific events. From the time of Antiochus IV Epiphanes (c.170 BCE) no Greek king had entered Jerusalem. Demetrius (most probably Eukerus, c.88 BCE), the Seleucid king who ruled in Syria, on the advice of the Pharisees known by their sobriquet *Seekers after Smooth Things*, sought to enter Jerusalem but withdrew when out of pity for the defeated Alexander Jannaeus six thousand Jews gathered in support of him (Josephus, *Antiquities* 13.372–383; *The Jewish War* 1.90–98). The phrase "until the rise of the rulers of the *Kittim*" then appears to be a reference to Pompey's intervention in 63 BCE in the Jewish civil war in 63 BCE when Jerusalem was finally captured by the Romans. [*See* Seekers after Smooth Things.]

One particularly telling passage (1QpHab vi.4) states that the *Kittim* "sacrifice to their standards," a practice characteristic of the Roman veneration of their military standards (*signa*). Josephus, in recounting the dramatic climax of the First Jewish Revolt, reports that when the rebels had fled and while the sanctuary of Jerusalem was in flames, the Romans carried their standards into the Temple court, sacrificed to them at the eastern gate, and with a loud acclamation hailed Titus as *imperator* (*The Jewish War* 6.316).

There may also be a reference to the Roman senate, which continued to send governors and military commanders to Judea, when the author of Pesher Habakkuk interprets *Habakkuk* 1.11 as referring to "the commanders of the *Kittim* who, by the council of their guilty house (Roman senate?), cause each man to pass before his neighbor; [their] rulers one after another will come to destroy the la[nd]" (1QpHab iv.10–13).

Qumran Attitudes toward the Kittim. It has been suggested (Vermes, 1994) that the Qumran community came to regard the *Kittim*/Romans as its chief enemy, even though earlier it depicted them simply as instruments of divine punishment of the "last priests of Jerusalem" (1QpHab ix.4). This developmental view involves seeing the *pesharim* to Habakkuk and Nahum as representing the earlier, more neutral stage, and the War Scroll, the War Rule, and Pesher Isaiah[a] the later, hostile repositioning.

The key to this approach is to be found in the different terms used to describe the leaders of the *Kittim*. In Pesher Habakkuk and Pesher Nahum, the *Kittim* are led by "commanders" (*moshelim*; 1QpHab iv.5, 10, 12; 4Q169 3–4.i.2–3). By contrast, in the War Scroll there is only one leader who stands with the army of Belial against the sons of light, and he is described as the "the king (*melekh*) of the *Kittim*" (1QM xv.2). The singular use of "king" is significant because it indicates that the *Kittim*/Romans are now ruled by an emperor (27 BCE onward). Notable, too, for comparison is the use of the royal terminology to describe Antiochus and Demetrius in Pesher Nahum (4Q169 3–4.i.2–3). Republican Rome is assumed in the former, while the latter presupposes that the *imperium* now lay in the hands of a single man.

In this view, then, the king of the *Kittim*, the emperor of the Romans, stands at the front of a satanic army that must be subjugated by the sons of light in the apocalyptic and eschatological battle envisioned in the War Scroll. The *Kittim*, who are the biblical Lebanon of *Isaiah* 10.34 in Pesher Isaiah[a] (4Q161 7–10.iii.7), will fall, and their king will be put to death by the Prince of the Congregation (War Rule, 4Q285 5).

Other References to Kittim. Since Jewish tradition often used *Kittim* to refer in a general way to the last foreign enemy, it is possible that other groups represented the *Kittim*. In Pesher Habakkuk, the *Kittim* are equated with the Chaldeans of biblical prophecy. Like the Chaldeans, the *Kittim* are "swift and mighty in war" (IQpHab ii.12–13), "and merciless" (vi.10–12); "fear and dread of them are upon all the nations; (iii.4–5). They "scoff at the fortresses of the nations and lay siege to them" (iv.5–8), and they "amass their booty" (vi.1–2) and "annually apportion their yoke and tribute upon all the peoples" (vi.6–8). The War Scroll may have had another group in mind when it used the phrases "the *Kittim* of Ashur" and "the *Kittim* in Egypt" (1QM i.4; xv.2–3; xix.10). It has been suggested that these may be references to the Seleucids and Ptolemies. Alternatively, the phrase "*Kittim* of Ashur" may be a straightforward terminological reflex due to the fact that *Kittim* and Ashur occur together at least three times in the Bible.

[*See also* Hasmoneans; Pesharim; Pesher Habakkuk; Pesher Isaiah; Pesher Nahum; Rome; *and* War of the Sons of Light against the Sons of Darkness.]

BIBLIOGRAPHY

Abegg, Martin G., Jr. "Messianic Hope and 4Q285: A Reassessment." *Journal of Biblical Literature* 113 (1994), 81–91.

Atkinson, K. M. T. "The Historical Setting of the War of the Sons of Light and the Sons of Darkness." *Journal of Semitic Studies* 4 (1954), 246–255.

Baker, David W. "Kittim." In *Anchor Bible Dictionary*, edited by David Noel Freedman, vol. 4, p. 93. New York, 1992.

Carmignac, Jean. *Le règle de la guerre des fils de lumière contre les fils de ténebres: Texte restaurè, traduit et commenté.* Paris, 1958.

Collins, John J. *Daniel.* Hermeneia. Minneapolis, 1993.

Davies, P. R. *1QM, the War Scroll from Qumran: Its Structure and History.* Rome, 1977. Important literary analysis of 1QM.

Duhaime, Jean. "War Scroll (1QM; 1Q33; 4Q491–496 = 4QM1–6; 4Q497)." In *Damascus Document, War Scroll and Related Documents,* edited by James H. Charlesworth et al., pp. 80–203. Tübingen, 1995. Includes transcription and translation of material from Cave 4.

Harris, Zellig S. *A Grammar of the Phoenician Language.* New Haven, 1936.

Horgan, Maurya P. *Pesharim: Qumran Interpretations of Biblical Books.* Catholic Biblical Quarterly, Monograph Series, 8. Washington, D.C., 1979. Texts, translations, and notes.

Schürer Emil. *The History of the Jewish People in the Age of Jesus Christ (175 B.C.–A.D. 135)*, revised by G. Vermes, Fergus Millar, M. Goodman et al., vol. 1 (1973), pp. 241–242; vol. 3.1 (1986), pp. 403–404, 425–426, 431, 434–436.

Vermes, Geza. *The Dead Sea Scrolls. Qumran in Perspective.* Rev. ed. London, 1994. Includes a synthesis of recently published texts.

Vermes, Geza, Timothy H. Lim, and Robert P. Gordon. "The Oxford Forum for Qumran Research Seminar on the Rule of War from Cave 4 (4Q285)." *Journal of Jewish Studies* 43 (1992), 85–94. Reading the alleged "slain messiah" fragment in context.

Yadin, Yigael. *The Scroll of the War of the Sons of Light against the Sons of Darkness.* Oxford, 1962. Basic work for the study of the War Scroll.

TIMOTHY H. LIM

KOHATH. *See* Qahat.

L

LAMECH. *See* Genesis Apocryphon.

LAMENTATIONS, BOOK OF. *See* Five Scrolls.

LANGUAGES. Among the languages used in the eastern Mediterranean world from roughly 150 BCE to 135 CE, four mainly have to be considered: Greek, Hebrew, Aramaic, and Latin. The language most commonly used at that time was Greek, the Indo-European language proper to Greece (Attica, Achaia, Macedonia, Peloponnesus). Its classical form flourished earlier and reached its apogee in the Attic dialect of the fifth and fourth centuries BCE. A developed form of Attic Greek spread throughout the eastern Mediterranean area, after Alexander the Great (356–323 BCE) conquered the Persian empire and Asia (334–324 BCE). It became the Hellenistic form of the language called *Koine*, which gradually replaced Aramaic as the *lingua franca*, or international language, of the area controlled by the successors of Alexander, the Lagides or Ptolemies in Egypt and the Seleucids in Syria, who actively worked for the spread of Hellenistic culture. Even later, under the Romans who dominated the Mediterranean world in the first century BCE, Greek continued to be the commonly used language, but its use never led to the demise of other languages.

After the fall of Jerusalem to the Babylonians in 587 BCE and the return of Jews from the Babylonian Captivity, their land, Judah, was dominated by the Persians. Jews of that land had earlier spoken their own Semitic language, Hebrew, sometimes called *yehudit*, "language of Judah" (*2 Kgs*. 18.26, 28; *Is*. 36.11, 13), and even *sefat Kena'an*, "language of Canaan" (*Is*. 19.18), because it was related to the Canaanite family of Northwest Semitic (along with Ugaritic, Phoenician, Ammonite, and Moabite). Hebrew is often thought to have been a more important Semitic language than Aramaic, because the bulk of the Hebrew scriptures is written in it. It was, however, spoken only by Jews in ancient Israel and Judah, whereas Aramaic was used by many peoples throughout Asia, Asia Minor, and Egypt. Jews deported to Babylonia adopted this commonly used cognate Semitic language. On their return to Judah under Cyrus in 538 BCE, they continued to use Aramaic, but Hebrew never completely died out among them, remaining as a spoken language in certain areas and in certain strata of society. The Scriptures were still read in Jewish religious services in Hebrew; the composition of *Daniel* 1 and 8–12 and of *Ben Sira* provides evidence of its continued use (see *Sir*. 50.27). It is usually thought that an effort was made to revive the use of Hebrew in the second century BCE after the Maccabean revolt. This was true at least of the Qumran sectarians, whose sectarian literature (rulebooks, hymnbooks, liturgical prayers, War Scroll, and *pesharim*) was composed by them in a form of postbiblical Hebrew, which was transitional between the late postexilic form and Mishnaic Hebrew. The majority of the Qumran scrolls were in Hebrew.

The most commonly used language in the eastern Mediterranean world prior to the conquest of Alexander was Aramaic, a sister language of Hebrew in the Northwest Semitic family. It had already become the *lingua franca* during the time of the Neo-Assyrian empire, used by diverse peoples from the Indus Valley (modern Pakistan) across the Fertile Crescent to the southernmost parts of Egypt. Most of the evidence of this language and of its widespread literary, inscriptional, epistolary, legal, and commercial use has come to light only in the last eighty years. Many Aramaic literary texts, dating from the first centuries BCE and CE, were recovered from the Qumran caves between 1947 and 1956. Some of the Babatha archive material found in the Cave of the Letters of Naḥal Ḥever (second century CE) is formulated in Greek with an Aramaic summary of its contents. The amount of Greek vocabulary, however, that infiltrated the Middle Aramaic of Judea in this period is rather small in contrast to the abundant influx of Greek into the targumic and rabbinic forms of Late Aramaic. About 120 Qumran texts were written in Aramaic.

Even prior to the golden age of fifth-century Greece, its pottery, coinage, and culture had begun to spread to the eastern Mediterranean, and Judah was affected. Only when Alexander the Great annexed Judah (332 BCE) was the Greek language gradually introduced, eventually becoming widely spoken along with Aramaic. Evidence for the use of Greek in Judah prior to the third century BCE is very sparse. The oldest extant Greek text from Judah is an Edomite-Greek bilingual ostracon from Khirbet el-Kom dated to the sixth year of Ptolemy II Philadelphus

(277 BCE); and the next Greek inscription recalls the victory of Antiochus III (the Great) at Raphia in 217 BCE.

Aramaized Greek names for musical instruments are recorded in *Daniel* 3.5; *qaytros* = Greek *kitharis*, "lyre"; *pesanterin* = *psalterion*, "harp"; *symponyah* = *symphonia*, "bagpipe." Even the full form of the *Book of Daniel* attests Hellenistic influence: to the protocanonical parts in Aramaic and Hebrew are added the Greek deuterocanonical chapters (as also in *Esther*). Many Judeans wrote in Greek, (e.g., Josephus). A letter written by *Soumaios*, usually taken to be Shimʿon Bar Kokhba, even says, "(This) has been written in Greek because a [des]ire has not be[en] found to w[ri]te in Hebrew" (5/6 Ḥev 52.11–15). In *Acts of the Apostles* 6.1, *Hellenistai*, Jews who spoke only Greek, disputed with *Hebraioi*, Greek-speaking Jews who also spoke a Semitic language (probably Aramaic) in the early Christian community of Jerusalem. Many of the texts recovered from Murabbaʿat and Naḥal Ḥever were composed in Greek.

Under the Roman domination of the Mediterranean world, Latin, the language of central and northern Italy, was introduced into the eastern Mediterranean world. There it was mainly used by Roman officials and the Roman army, sometimes for official announcements or signs (e.g., dedicatory inscriptions on buildings and aqueducts, milestones for the direction of Roman legions, funerary inscriptions of legionnaires, warnings against entry). A fragmentary inscription of the Tiberieum, a building in Caesarea Maritima, tells of "[Po]ntivs Pilatvs / [Praef]ectvs Ivda[ea]e]." It shows that Pilate's title was not *procurator*, but *praefectus*, as Roman historians had often maintained. Evidence of the use of Latin in Judea is, however, sparse, because Roman administrators normally used Greek in dealing with the indigenous populace. Fragments of seven Latin texts were recovered from Murabbaʿat (Mur 158–163, 168).

BIBLIOGRAPHY

Fitzmyer, Joseph A. "The Languages of Palestine in the First Century A.D." In *A Wandering Aramean: Collected Aramaic Essays*, pp. 29–56. Society of Biblical Literature Monograph, 25. Missoula, Mont., 1979.

Fitzmyer, Joseph A. "Did Jesus Speak Greek?" *Biblical Archaeology Review* 18.5 (1992), 58–63, 76–77. Discussion of the evidence that Jesus of Nazareth spoke Greek at times, even though he probably did not teach in it.

Fitzmyer, Joseph A., and Daniel J. Harrington. *A Manual of Palestinian Aramaic Texts (Second Century BC–Second Century AD)*. Biblica et Orientalia, 34. Rome, 1978. A collection of 150 Middle Aramaic texts from Judea with translation, brief comments, and bibliography. The appendix contains further synagogal and funerary texts of Late Aramaic to facilitate comparison.

Frova, A. "L'iscrizione di Ponzio Pilato a Cesarea." *Rendiconti dell'Istituto Lombardo, Accademia di scienze e lettere* 95 (1961), 419–434. Main publication of the Pilate inscription mentioned in the text above.

Geraty, L. T. "The Khirbet el-Kom Bilingual Ostracon." *Bulletin of the American Schools of Oriental Research* 220 (1975), 55–61. Publication of the Edomite-Greek inscription of 277 BCE mentioned above.

Greenfield, Jonas C. "The Languages of Palestine, 200 BCE–200 CE." In *Jewish Languages: Theme and Variation*, edited by H. H. Paper, pp. 143–154. Cambridge, Mass., 1978. Discusses the use of Hebrew, Aramaic, and Greek by Judeans in the period indicated.

Kitchen, K. A. "The Aramaic of Daniel." In *Notes on Some Problems in the Book of Daniel*, pp. 31–79. London, 1965. Discussion of the Aramaic of Daniel along with the evidence for the spread of Greek throughout the eastern Mediterranean.

Lifshitz, B. "Beiträge zur palästinischen Epigraphik." *Zeitschrift des deutschen Palästina-Vereins* 78 (1962), 64–88. Discusses the Raphia inscription of 217 BCE.

Safrai, S. "Spoken Languages in the Time of Jesus." *Jerusalem Perspective* 4.1 (1991), 3–8, 13.

Sevenster, J. N. *Do You Know Greek? How Much Greek Could the First Jewish Christians Have Known?* Novum Testamentum Supplement, 19. Leiden, 1968. A good discussion of all the evidence needed to answer the question asked in the subtitle.

Sherk, Robert K. *Roman Documents from the Greek East*: Senatus Consulta *and* Epistulae *to the Age of Augustus*. Baltimore, 1969. An important collection of official and administrative texts issued in Greek pertaining to the eastern Mediterranean world.

Vardaman, J. "A New Inscription Which Mentions Pilate as 'Prefect.'" *Journal of Biblical Literature* 81 (1962), 70–71.

JOSEPH A. FITZMYER, S.J.

LATIN. Only two sites from the Judean Desert have yielded Latin documents: Masada and Wadi Murabbaʿat.

The Masada material includes inscriptions on jars (*tituli picti*), papyri, and ostraca. The *tituli picti* are inscribed on imported storage jars (Mas793–852). Some of these advertise the luxury products contained in the jars: "apples from Cumae" (*mala Cumana*, Mas822), fish sauce (*garum*, Mas826), Philonian wine (*Philonianum*, Mas804–816), Masic wine (*Masicum*, Mas819), and so forth; they could have inspired Josephus' lavish praise of Herod's stores on Masada (*Jewish Antiquities*, 7.295ff.). Herodian dates are found on seventeen jars: The bilingual (Latin and Greek) Mas795–796 carry the consular dates 27 and 26 BCE, respectively, a series of wine jars, Mas804–817, carry the name of a (single) consul of 19 BCE, and Mas818 is datable to 14 BCE. Although most of the corpus of *tituli picti* is likely to date to the Herodian period at Masada, there are some exceptions (Rea 1999). They are written in capital letters resembling the so-called *capitalis rustica* used in literary texts and in headings for military documents (see below).

The papyri and ostraca come from a Roman military context. The papyri constitute a haphazard and mostly fragmentary collection of discarded texts, found in the rubbish pile assembled in locus 1039 on Masada, probably from the fall of the fortress in spring 73 (or 74) CE. The most important items are an elegantly written line from Virgil (*Aeneid* 4.9, Mas721a), a pay record of a legionary cavalryman from 72 CE—the only dated papyrus from Masada (Mas722)—a list of hospital supplies (Mas723), a letter to Iulius Lupus, perhaps to be identified with the homonymous governor of Egypt after February 73 (Mas724), and two items mentioning the *xylobalsamum*, a by-product of the famous balsam growing in Jericho and ʿEin-Gedi (Mas725 and 749b). The nomenclature points unambiguously to soldiers of the Tenth Legion as the source of the Latin papyri and ostraca. It was this legion, the standing provincial garrison of the province of Judea, that laid siege to the fortress, leaving one of its units behind after its fall (Josephus *Antiquities* 7.407, probably in Camp F^2).

All the Latin documents found on Masada thus have a precise historical context and date, the early seventies of the first century CE. This enhances their paleographical value. With the exception of the heading of Mas722 and the *tituli picti*, written in *capitalis rustica* (see above), the writing used in the corpus can be given the general description of Old Roman Cursive, also known as Capital Cursive (in contrast to the minuscule cursive or New Roman Cursive in use from 300 CE onward). Despite the word "cursive," ligature is almost absent throughout the Masada papyri. Mallon's definition of the script as "l'écriture commune classique" emphasizes the fact that a common Latin script was in use throughout the Roman Empire at that period—a fact confirmed by the similarity between the Masada papyri and contemporary materials from military contexts in Egypt and Vindolanda in Britain.

The twenty-two ostraca each carry a single Roman name, some well known and well worn and some rare or even unattested names, a feature which proves that they belong to Roman citizen soldiers, that is to say, legionaries. The purpose of these ostraca is unknown.

The only Jewish items in Latin are Mas936, a bread stamp carrying the name "Josepu" and a bilingual (Latin and Greek) papyrus with Jewish names, Mas748.

The scanty Latin fragments from Wadi Murabbaʿat (Mur 158–163) are paleographically and tentatively dated to the first and second century CE.

BIBLIOGRAPHY

Benoit, P. "Papyrus Latins." In P. Benoit, J. T. Milik, and R. de Vaux, *Les Grottes de Murabbaʿat*, pp. 270–274. Discoveries in the Judaean Desert, 2. Oxford, 1961.

Cotton, H. M. and J. Geiger. *Masada II: The Latin and Greek Documents*. Final Reports. Jerusalem, 1989. Doc.Mas. refers to the papyri published in this volume.

Cotton, H. M., O. Lernau, and Y. Goren, "Fish Sauces from Herodian Masada." *Journal of Roman Archaeology* 9 (1996), 223–238. Argues that the inscribed jars which contained luxury products from Italy and Spain are of Herodian date.

Cotton, H. M. "The Date of the Fall of Masada: The Evidence of the Masada Papyri." *Zeitschrift für Papyrologie und Epigraphik* 78 (1989), 157–162. Weighs the evidence for maintaining the traditional date for the fall of Masada, Spring 73, against the new date of Spring 74 proposed by W. Eck in "Die Eroberung von Masada und eine neue Inschrift des L. Flavius Silva Nonius Bassus." *Zeitschrift für die neutestamentliche Wissenschaft* 60 (1969), 282–289, and more fully argued in *id. Senatoren von Vespasian bis Hadrian*. Vestigia, vol. 13. Munich, 1970, pp. 93–102.

Rea, J. "Masada and Pompeii: Another Link." *Scripta Classica Israelica* 18 (1999), 121–124.

Roth, J. "The Length of the Siege of Masada." *Scripta Classica Israelica* 14 (1995), 87–110. Argues convincingly that the siege did not last more than eight weeks.

Thomas, J. D. "The Palaeography of the Latin Papyri." In H. M. Cotton and J. Geiger, *Masada II: The Latin and Greek Documents*. Final Reports, Jerusalem, 1989, pp. 27–31.

HANNAH M. COTTON

LATTER DAYS. *See* Eschatology.

LAW AND LAWGIVING. The Torah of Moses posed real problems for the interpreters of the Bible in the Second Temple period. Two problems proved quite challenging to these early Jewish readers. First, the Law code of Moses was not known by the patriarchs in *Genesis*. This baffled Jewish readers for a number of reasons, but most problematic was the question of God's providential plan: if the Law code of Moses was so central to the religion of Israel, why did it take so long to be revealed? The second problem is to be found within the Law code itself. As any careful reader of the Torah knows, there are many legal statements that stand in outright contradiction to one another. If one is obligated to keep the whole Torah, then what does one do when the commands themselves stand in contradiction? Every Jewish exegete of the Second Temple period found himself forced to grapple with both these questions.

The book of *Jubilees* represents one solution to this problem. In this book, itself a grand expansion of *Genesis*, the Angel of the Presence makes clear to Moses at nearly every turn just how the actions of the patriarchs are to be understood in light of the legislation given at Sinai. Sometimes *Jubilees* rewrites the biblical story in such a way that the patriarchs actually know and observe Sinaitic legislation. For example, one frequently reads of certain patriarchs celebrating Israelite religious festivals (e.g., *Jub.* 7.3–6). At other times, the voice of the angelic interlocutor interrupts the *Genesis* narrative to make clear how a certain event is to be understood after the revelation of that law. Thus the recounting of the sin of Reuben's violation of his father's concubine is linked to the corresponding Mosaic injunctions against such behavior (*Jub.* 33.13–14): "And you Moses, command the children of Israel and let them keep this word because it is a judgment worthy of death. . . . Let them not say that Reuben had life and forgiveness . . . for the [Torah] had not yet been revealed then." In this case, the narrator correlates Sinaitic law with a figure in *Genesis*, Reuben, but expressly to show that he was ignorant of that legislation and hence not fully accountable.

At Qumran, we have clear parallels to such exegetical examinations and expansions. But the members of the sect were faced with an additional problem. Because they did not believe that the era of the exile had come to an end with the founding of the Second Temple by Zerubbabel (cf. *Hg.* 2.1–8), they still awaited the era of restoration. For them, the most urgent problem was that of returning to a full obedience to the Torah of Moses. They often referred to themselves as the "penitents of Israel" (cf. CD iv.2), for they were the ones who had initiated the path to renewal.

When the sect took root, its leaders began to expound on what this renewed covenant would look like. In their view, the restored community of Israel was under a twofold legal obligation that looked both forward and backward. On the one hand, when they joined the group, they reobligated themselves to the "revealed" (*niglot*) laws of Moses given at Mount Sinai. On the other hand, they also obligated themselves, for the first time, to an ever-growing corpus of "hidden" (*nistarot*) laws, which were just now being discovered by the sect through inspired exegesis. The best textual illustration of this fundamental point is to be found in the Rule of the Community from Cave 1 at Qumran (1QS v.7–12):

> Everyone who enters the council of the community shall enter the covenant of God in the presence of all those who have freely entered [in the past]. And they shall take upon themselves a binding oath [*Nm.* 30.3] to return to the Torah of Moses according to all which he commanded with all [their] heart and soul [*Dt.* 30.2] and to all which has been revealed from it by the sons of Zadok, the priests, the guarders of the covenant, and interpreters of his will . . . .[They shall separate themselves] from all evil men who walk in a wicked path. For they are not reckoned among [those of] his covenant because they do not search out nor interpret his statutes so as to discern "the hidden laws" (*nistarot*). For [in these hidden matters] they have strayed so as to incur guilt. But toward "the revealed laws" (*niglot*) they have acted in a high-handed fashion so as to raise up wrath for judgment and the executing of revenge according to the curses of the covenant [*Dt.* 29.18, 19, 20].

This text indicates that the rite of entry into the sect depended on a return to fidelity to the Torah of Moses and an obligation to place oneself in a posture of obedience to the hidden commandments, which were only now being revealed. These commandments provided a new avenue of sanctification for the sectarians but also allowed them another means of condemning greater Israel. As to Israel as a whole, or, perhaps better, Israel outside the sect, it was guilty of violating both the Mosaic and the sectarian Torah.

A well-known example of how the sect extended the force of biblical Law is found in the Damascus Document (CD iv.20–21). In considering the sins that comprise the "three nets of Belial" that have ensnared the people of Israel, the writer underscores the sin of unchastity (*zenut*). What is surprising is how it is defined. In contrast to the Hebrew scriptures, the author of the Damascus Document declares that any man possessing more than one wife is in violation of divine law. This point, which is absent from the Sinaitic legislation itself, is argued on the basis of the creation account. God created humanity as male and female (*Gn.* 1.27), implying that the marriage bond was to be between two people alone. In this example, we can see the boundaries of biblical law subject to dramatic extension with an end toward both shaping sectarian conduct and condemning the ways of wayward Israel: "[with these three nets Belial] entrapped Israel and made them appear as forms of righteousness." What may appear as righteous practice from a simple reading of biblical law is subject to dramatic reformulation in the hands of the sectarians.

In their own self-understanding, the Covenanters were in a legal position similar to that of the patriarchs in *Genesis*. For just as the patriarchs themselves faced a set of legal obligations that existed before them (e.g., the commandments given to Noah [cf. *Gn.* 9. 1–17]) while they awaited the fuller revelation to come at Mount Sinai, so the Covenanters stood under the prior obligations of the Mosaic Torah while they, in turn, awaited the full revelation of the Messianic Torah at the End of Days. This correlation of the patriarchal period with their own is not dissimilar, in formal terms, to the correlation drawn in the New Testament by Paul (cf. *Rom.* 4). For Paul, the issue of legal obedience in the patriarchal period also paralleled the position of the believer in the messianic age. Yet, one must emphasize that patriarchal nonobservance of the Torah was, for Paul, matched in the *eschaton* by a similar nonobservance on the part of Christians.

A different set of problems regarding the Torah and its status is to be found in a document like Temple Scroll[a] (11Q19). This text purports to be a direct revelation to Moses, which he, in turn, narrates in the first person to the Israelites. The narrative has all the appearances of being an "inspired text" in its own right, perhaps of higher status than the other "interpretive" texts found at Qumran, which presume an authoritative biblical text as the point of departure for exposition. The language of the scroll (which is quite distinct from the rest of the scrolls) and its unique pseudepigraphic style have led some to question whether it was composed by the sectarians themselves or whether it was simply brought to Qumran from the outside. The current tendency is to see the document as a nonsectarian composition. As to the text's "inspired" character and its relationship to the "canonical" Torah, one must be cautious. Careful examination of the document shows that the writer was quite conscious of those laws in the Torah that contradicted one another, and he took special care to harmonize them in Temple Scroll[a]. Perhaps the text was simply another example of a very common literary form of this period known as Rewritten Bible. [*See* Rewritten Bible.]

The fact that the Torah contained conflicting laws, especially in such crucial matters as ritual purity and sacrificial practice, meant that a great deal of exegetical energy was spent trying to solve these incongruities. The cult was slowly being transformed by their learned exegetical reflection. In fact, the exegetical solutions to the problems of sacrifice began to absorb as much creative spiritual energy as the actual habit of Temple worship itself. [*See* Sacrifice.] We can see the beginnings of this process in Temple Scroll[a], a process that would gather steam and assume much more significance in the post-70 CE era, when the Temple was no longer standing. [*See* Temple Scroll.]

Regardless of whether Temple Scroll[a] was sectarian, it and other legal works in the Qumran caves show that the people of Qumran possessed written law codes and thus did not adhere to the principle that extrabiblical legal traditions were to remain oral and not be put in writing.

It is also interesting that the caves contained not only earlier texts such as Aramaic Levi and *Jubilees*, which highlight legal points, but also booklets from the Enochic tradition in which the Law of Moses plays virtually no part. Even when relating the events at Mount Sinai, the "Animal Apocalypse" says nothing about the giving of the law (see *1 En.* 89.28–36). The Enoch literature, true to the pseudepigraphic identification of its hero as an antediluvian sage, emphasizes the pre-Flood revelations given to Enoch, not the later disclosures to him.

[*See also* Covenant; Scriptures, *article on* Texts; *and* Worship, Qumran Sect.]

BIBLIOGRAPHY

Anderson, Gary A. "The Status of the Torah before Sinai: The Retelling of the Bible in the Damascus Covenant and the Book of Jubilees." *Dead Sea Discoveries* 1 (1994), 1–29. Discussion of the problems of revealed and hidden law in the legal rulings of the sect, the exegesis of the narratives about the patriarchs, and the teaching of Saint Paul.

Baumgarten, Joseph M. "A 'Scriptural' Citation in 4Q Fragments of the Damascus Document." *Journal of Jewish Studies* 43 (1992), 95–98. This article shows how the sect came to understand "the ban" as a replacement for sacrificial expiation.

Brooke, George J. *Temple Scroll Studies: Papers Presented at the International Symposium on the Temple Scroll, Manchester, December 1987.* Journal for the Study of the Pseudepigrapha Supplement Series, 7. Sheffield, 1989. A fine collection of recent work on this scroll.

Schiffman, Lawrence H. *The Halakhah at Qumran.* Studies in Judaism in Late Antiquity, 16. Leiden, 1975. Classic discussion of the problem of revealed and hidden law.

Stegemann, Hartmut. "The Origins of the Temple Scroll." In *Congress Volume, Jerusalem 1986,* edited by J. A. Emerton, pp. 235–256. Supplement to Vetus Testamentum, 40. Leiden, 1988. He argues that the Temple Scroll was composed outside of Qumran and consists of archaic laws, some dating from as early as the fourth century BCE.

GARY A. ANDERSON

LEATHER GOODS. Due to the extremely dry conditions in the Judean Desert, numerous leather objects of daily used have been preserved. The best published collection of leather artifacts, dating to the period of the Bar Kokhba Revolt (132–135 CE), is from the Cave of the Letters (Naḥal Ḥever). [*See* Ḥever, Naḥal.] Additional examples have been recovered from contemporary caves in Naḥal Ḥever, Wadi Murabbaʿat, Naḥal Mishmar, and Naḥal David, and at the Second Temple period sites of Masada and the Jewish cemeteries in Naḥal David (ʿEin-Gedi) and Jericho. [*See* ʿEin-Gedi; Masada; Mishmar, Naḥal; Murabbaʿat, Wadi.]

In general, the leather objects from the Judean Desert indicate a high level of craftsmanship. Contemporary written sources describe in detail the manufacture of leather. It entails three main stage of production. First, the animal pelt must be cured in preparation for tanning. It is salted or dried in the sun or shade, followed by soaking, the removal of the hair and epidermis, and scudding the grain surface in order to remove the last traces of hair and debris. The next stage is tanning, which causes chemical changes in the pelt and renders it imputrescible and water-resistant. Lastly, the finishing of the leather can include rolling, lubrication, dyeing, and other treatments that improve the texture of the skin or hide. Parchment is also prepared from a pelt but is dried and worked, usually without tanning, while under tension on a stretching frame.

An installation, possibly used for preparation of leather or parchment, was uncovered at ʿEin-Feshkha, located south of Qumran. [*See* ʿEin-Feshkha.] It comprised a large rectangular building with a central courtyard surrounded by rooms with several plastered basins to the north and a system of canals and reservoirs. The excavator, Roland de Vaux, identified this complex as a tannery because of its numerous plastered vats, water channels and abundant supply of water. However, the plan of the ʿEin-Feshkha complex does not correspond to that of known Roman tanneries, where depilation and tanning pits are small and numerous. In addition, no traces of tannin were discernible during chemical analyses of the sediments inside the basins. In light of the absence of tannin in the sediments, de Vaux subsequently suggested that this building complex was set up for the preparation of parchment. Alternative theories propose that the basins were used in the retting of flax for linen or as ponds for breeding fish.

Leather goods found in the Judean Desert include sandals, shoes, pouches or purses, waterskins, garments, leather phylactery cases (Wadi Murabbaʿat), fragments of colored leather covers for wooden boxes (Cave of Horror) and a sheath (Cave of the Letters). Most of them were of sheepskin, and occasionally, usually the accessory parts, were of goat- and calfskin. Analyses of the leather objects from the Judean Desert, and especially the Cave of the Letters, reveal that they were vegetable tanned, often with galls and pomegranates.

Sandals and shoes, especially their soles, are by far the most numerous type of leather object. Many examples have been found at Masada, ʿEin-Gedi, the Jericho cemetery, Naḥal Ḥever, Naḥal Mishmar, Wadi Murabbaʿat (Cave 1), and Wadi el-Habibi. The best preserved sandals were discovered at Masada, found with three skeletons on the lower terrace of the Northern Palace, and in the Cave of the Letters. All the sandal-soles, whether men's, women's, or children's, were formed of several layers of leather, stitched together by leather thongs. The sandals were fashioned only of leather, in contrast to the *caligae*—the nail-studded sandals of the Roman soldiers—and seem to be the type of sandal mentioned in later rabbinic texts (on the prohibition of wearing nail-studded sandals on the Sabbath, see, e.g., *Shab*. 6.2 and B.T., *Shab*. 60a). In the ʿEin-Gedi cemetery, a pair of leather shoes was found on the feet of the deceased interred in a wooden coffin. In the contemporary first century BCE Jericho cemetery, several similar sandal-soles were found inside wooden coffins, but placed under the skull of the deceased. In addition to adult sandals and shoes, a well-preserved child's shoe (Cave 5/6 [Cave of the Letters], Naḥal Ḥever) and a child's sandal (Cave 1, Wadi Murabbaʿat) were recovered.

Three purses, or pouches, were discovered during Yigael Yadin's excavation in the Cave of the Letters. One purse, inside a waterskin, contained thirty-five documents dating from 93 to 132 CE, including the Archive of Babatha. A second purse, square in shape, was made of a long piece of red-dyed leather, folded over in the middle. A single black rosette applique and red and black fringes, also made out of leather, decorate both sides of the purse. It was closed by pulling on the draw string at the top. Fragments of leather strips from Wadi Murabbaʿat (Cave 1) may have originally belonged to a similar purse or to military equipment.

Several waterskins, most in a poorly preserved condition, were recovered from the Cave of the Letters. The waterskins were formed by closing off the animal skin at the neck with a round piece of leather. The ends of the forelegs were tied together, functioning as a handle. The hind-end of the skin was left open until filled, and then it was closed by winding and tying it with a rope. In the Cave of the Letters they also served as containers for the Bar-Kokhba letters, bronze vessels, and other personal belongings such as cosmetic items and balls of wool or linen threads.

Leather garment fragments from the Naḥal Ḥever (Cave of the Letters and the Cave of Horror) and Naḥal Mishmar (Scouts' Cave) have been identified as tunics or jackets. It is not clear if they were of a military nature. Similar leather remains were found in Wadi Murabbaʿat where they were described as tunics belonging to Roman soldiers.

The leather goods from the Judean Desert reflect accessories and clothing typical of the Second Temple period and later. Several leather objects found in close proximity to the Judean Desert documents, especially in the Cave of the Letters, served as containers for the documents themselves. From the nature of the artifacts, it is clear that women and children were also among the refugees hiding in the Judean Desert during the First and Second Jewish Revolts. It has also been suggested that some of these leather goods may have belonged to Roman soldiers involved in quelling these revolts.

BIBLIOGRAPHY

Aharoni, Yohanan. "The Caves of Nahal Hever." *ʿAtiqot*, English Series, vol. 3 (1961), 148–162. Includes a description of the initial 1953 excavations in Naḥal Ḥever.

Aharoni, Yohanan, Nahman Avigad, Pessah Bar-Adon, and Yigael Yadin. "The Expedition to the Judean Desert, 1960." *Israel Exploration Journal* 11 (1961), 3–52. Includes a description of the artifacts found during the 1960 expedition to the Judean Desert.

Aharoni, Yohanan, Nahman Avigad, Pessah Bar-Adon, and Yigael Yadin. "The Expedition to the Judean Desert, 1961." *Israel Exploration Journal* 12 (1962), 168–183; 186–199; 215–257. Includes a description of the artifacts found during the 1961 expedition to the Judean Desert.

de Vaux, Roland. *Archaeology and the Dead Sea Scrolls*. The Schweich Lectures of the British Academy. Oxford, 1959. For a presentation of the evidence in favor of a "tannery" at ʿEin-Feshkha, see pages 75–83.

de Vaux, Roland. "Archéologie." In *Qumran Cave I*, edited by Dominique Barthélemy and Józef T. Milik, pp. 35–44. Discoveries in the Judaean Desert, 1. Oxford, 1955. A description of Roman period artifacts excavated in Cave 1.

Forbes, R. J. "Leather in Antiquity." In *Studies in Ancient Technology*, pp. 1–77. Leiden, 1957. General discussion of leather and its preparation in antiquity.

Poole, J. B., and R. Reed. "The 'Tannery' of ʿAin Feshkha." *Palestine Exploration Quarterly* 93 (1961), 114–123. Disputes the identification of ʿEin-Feshkha installation as "tannery."

Reed, R. *Ancient Skins, Parchments and Leathers*. Studies in Archaeological Science. New York, 1972. A thorough discussion of leather and parchment and their preparation in a historical context.

Yadin, Yigael. "Leather Objects." *The Finds from the Bar Kokhba Period in the Cave of Letters*, pp. 157–168. Jerusalem, 1963. Detailed description of leather objects found during the second series of excavations of Naḥal Ḥever.

ANN E. KILLEBREW

LEGAL WORKS. Several minor Hebrew works dealing with issues of Jewish law are found at Qumran; they are termed *minor* only because of their present state of preservation. In antiquity, these texts may have been much more extensive. This article does not discuss the major legal works, such as the Rule of the Community, the Rule of the Congregation, Damascus Document, Temple Scroll, or Miqtsat Maʿasei ha-Torah. Also not discussed here, since they are the subject of specific articles, are the Serekh Damascus document (4Q265) and Ordinances (4Q159, 513–514). No legal tracts have been found among the Masada or Bar Kokhba period collections. The numerous legal documents from the Judean Desert are covered elsewhere.

Halakhah A from Cave 4. This document (4Q251) contains a series of laws on a variety of subjects and probably represents only a small part of what was originally a larger text. Some of its many prescriptions (of which only a few will be mentioned here) overlap with laws known from the Damascus Document, Temple Scroll, and Miqtsat Maʿasei ha-Torah from Cave 4 (4QMMT), and include some prescriptions that are typical of the Sadduccean-type legal system we encounter in the sectarian materials. In general, the literary form of this text is much closer to that of Rewritten Bible than to abstractly formulated laws.

Some Sabbath laws (frgs. 1–2) overlap with prescriptions found in the Sabbath code of the Damascus Document, as well as in the Serekh Damascus. Important here is the reference in a broken context to what seems to be public scriptural reading on the Sabbath. Most of the preserved text is a rewriting of various laws in *Exodus* 21–22. Also described here are laws of first fruits and new grain, following a scheme similar to that in the Festival Calendar of the Temple Scroll (11QT xviii–xxiii). Other laws address the selling of ancestral lands (based on *Lv*. 25.14–17), the giving of fourth-year produce, or "first fruit," to priests (as opposed to eating it in Jerusalem as the Pharisees ruled), a practice also mandated in the Temple Scroll ($11QT^a$ lx.3–4) and Miqtsat Maʿasei ha-Torah (4QMMT; B 62–63). The text also prohibits eating an animal that did not live for seven days (*Lv*. 22.27) and the slaughter of pregnant animals, again shared with the Temple Scroll (11QT lii.5) and Miqtsat Maʿasei ha-Torah (4QMMT; B 36), but permitted by Pharisaic rabbinic *halakhah*. The text also includes a list of forbidden consanguineous marriages similar to that in the Temple Scroll (11QT lxvi.11–17). Among the laws here are a prohibition of intermarriage with non-Jews and of a priest marrying his daughter to a nonpriest.

Purification Rules (Tohorot) A. This fragmentary text (4Q274) deals with the laws of impurity resulting from the disease *tsaraʿat*, usually mistranslated as "leprosy." As in the Temple Scroll ($11QT^a$ xlviii.14–15), this text provides for special places for the quarantine of those with this disease, and they must remain at least 12 cubits from the pure food to the northeast of each dwelling, probably from each town or village. Such people are forbidden to come in contact even with those already impure, as they would still require ritual cleansing from such contact. This indicates that impurity can be contracted in successively stronger layers, so that those with lesser impurity may not come in contact with those with this skin disease. The requirement of separation, even for the impure, indicates a consciousness also of the contagious nature of such diseases—in the same way a woman with a nonmenstrual discharge of blood may not touch a gonorrheic or anything upon which he may have sat or with which he may have come in contact. If she does, she must undergo purification, even if she remains in her own original state of impurity. The text provides several examples to make this general point.

Another issue addressed in Tohorot A, also found in the Temple Scroll (e.g., $11QT^a$ xlv.7–10), is the requirement that one who is to undergo a seven-day purification period, with sprinkling on the third and seventh days, must undergo ablutions as well on the first day to peel off the initial level of impurity and to allow him or her to begin the normal purification required by the Torah. Until this first-day ablution, he or she may not eat anything. Further, all sprinkling for purification is forbidden on the Sabbath. Also discussed in this text is the impurity of semen and of reptiles.

Purification Rules (Tohorot) B^b (4Q276) and B^c (4Q277). These two texts deal with the ritual of the Red Cow as the means of purification from impurity of the dead as prescribed in *Numbers* 19. Purification Rules B^b (4Q276) seems to refer at the beginning to the high priest who ministers at this ritual. The text describes the slaughter of the animal and the sprinkling of its blood, as well as other aspects of the ritual as outlined in the Torah.

Purification Rules B^c (4Q277) also mentions the fact that the one who performs this ritual is rendered impure as a result, a paradox mentioned already in the Bible. As in Miqtsat Maʿasei ha-Torah (4QMMT; B 13–17), all participants in the ritual are explicitly mentioned, indicating that they are all rendered impure by their participation. Also hinted at is the requirement, specified in Miqtsat Maʿasei ha-Torah as well, that the priest who officiates must be totally pure himself. In case he has just completed a purification ritual, the sun must have set on his last day of purification. The Pharisaic-rabbinic tradition would have allowed one still awaiting sunset on his last day of purification to perform the ritual. The Sadducees and those who followed their halakhic tradition disagreed. Further, the text lists a number of ways in which the impurity of the dead can be passed from one person to another, expanded to include categories that the Bible specifies for the gonorrheic (*Lv*. 15.4–15).

Tohorot B[a] (4Q275), as presently preserved, has no specific legal content, but does refer to the inspector (*mevaqqer*) and to the cursing of someone, perhaps one who is being expelled from the community. Expulsion as a punishment is mentioned in the Rule of the Community (1QS vii.1–2, 18–19, 22–25, viii.21–ix.2) and Damascus Document (CD xx.1–8), and a ritual for expulsion is found in the Qumran fragments of the Damascus Document (4Q266 7.i–ii. 5–15). Tohorot C? (4Q278) is extremely fragmentary and relates to impurity that can be transferred by contact, referring to the bed that can be rendered impure if one who contracted impurity has sat on it.

Harvesting (Leqet). This text (4Q284a) is extremely fragmentary and deals with the requirements for gleaning. According to *Leviticus* 19.9–10 and 23.22, grain left in the field may not be collected after the harvest is completed, but must be left for the poor. The Bible supplies no specific requirements for the gleaners, but this text requires that they be ritually pure. Little more can be derived from this text, but it no doubt included specifics of this requirement and may have included other agricultural laws.

Rebukes by the Overseer. This document (4Q477) clearly stems from the Qumran sectarian community and records actual dockets reflecting sectarian legal proceedings against those who violated the sect's prescriptions. According to sectarian law, it was required to perform reproof of one who violated the law in front of the overseer (*mevaqqer*) and in front of witnesses. Only if this procedure had taken place could a sectarian be punished for a later infraction of the same law. This fragmentary text lists by name specific individuals who had been rebuked, as well as their transgressions.

BIBLIOGRAPHY

Baumgarten, Joseph M. "4QHalakhah[a], the Law of Ḥadash, and the Pentacontad Calendar." *Journal of Jewish Studies* 27 (1976), 36–46. A study of the law of new grain and its relationship to the Qumran calendar.

Baumgarten, Joseph M. "Liquids and Susceptibility to Defilement in New 4Q Texts." *Jewish Quarterly Review* 85 (1994), 91–101.

Baumgarten, Joseph M. "The Laws about Fluxes in 4QTohora[a] (4Q274)." In *Time to Prepare the Way in the Wilderness*, edited by Devorah Dimant and Lawrence H. Schiffman, pp. 1–8. Studies on the Texts of the Desert of Judah, 16. Leiden, 1995. A study of purity laws.

Baumgarten, Joseph M. "The Red Cow Purification Rites in Qumran Texts." *Journal of Jewish Studies* 46 (1995), 112–119.

Baumgarten, Joseph M. et al. *Qumran Cave 4, XXV: Halakhic Texts*. Discoveries in the Judaean Desert, 25. Oxford, forthcoming.

Eshel, E. "4Q477: The Rebukes of the Overseer." *Journal of Jewish Studies* 45 (1994), 111–122.

Milgrom, Jacob. "Studies in the Temple Scroll." *Journal of Biblical Literature* 97 (1978), 501–523.

Milgrom, Jacob. "4QTohora[a]: An Unpublished Qumran Text on Purities." In *Time to Prepare the Way in the Wilderness*, edited by Devorah Dimant and Lawrence H. Schiffman, pp. 59–68. Studies on the Texts of the Desert of Judah, 16. Leiden, 1995.

Milik, Józef T. "Milkî-ṣedeq et Milkî-rešaʿ dans les anciens écrits juifs et chrétiens." *Journal of Jewish Studies* 23 (1972), 95–144.

LAWRENCE H. SCHIFFMAN

LETTERS. The Judean Desert Scrolls include an extremely diverse corpus of letters. Discovered at five or six different sites, the manuscripts were written over a timespan far broader than any other nonbiblical genre of material found in the Judean Desert—from the period of the Judean monarchy to the Umayyad period following the Muslim conquest—some fifteen centuries. (A few fragments are even later.) Linguistically, they are equally diverse, being composed in Hebrew and Aramaic (two distinct forms of each), Latin, Greek, and Arabic. The subject matter encompasses a wide variety of administrative, military, economic, and purely personal matters (see table 1).

Leaving Miqtsat Maʿasei ha-Torah (4Q394–4Q399) aside, all but a handful of these are written on papyrus. The only exceptions are two letters on leather (4Q342 and 343), the three Aramaic letters from Masada (ostraca), and one Bar Kokhba letter (5/6Ḥev 54) written on a wooden board.

Site-by-Site Summary. A letter fragment from post-exilic Judah (Mur 17), though it comes from Wadi Murabbaʿat, where a number of the Bar Kokhba letters were found, is in a class by itself. There is not much of it, but with a probable date of composition from the early seventh century BCE, it is perhaps the oldest Hebrew letter known. A palimpsest, it is extremely difficult to read, and only part of the opening has survived.

From the Qumran caves themselves, there are virtually no traces of true letters. The concluding section of the Ethiopic Book of Enoch (*1 En*. 91–108) has been known since ancient times as the "Epistle of Enoch." Two Ara-

LETTERS. TABLE 1. *Sample Letters in Idiomatic Translation.*

Letter	Text
A. Mur 17: (7th century BCE):	[. . .]yahu says to you: I send very warmest greetings to your household! . . . Now pay no attention to [anything . . .] may say to you. . . .
B. 5/6 Ḥev 54 (132–135 CE):	Shimʿon bar Kosiba, ruler over Israel, to Yehonatan and Masabbala. Greetings! You are to seek out and confiscate any wheat which Taḥnun bar Ishmaʿel may have, and send [X] *seahs* of wheat to [PN] under guard. . . . you shall do so. If you have sentenced any of your men to punishment, send the man to me under guard. If there are any of the Ṭekoans whose houses were promised to you, but who are still living in them, summon them, and I will carry out their punishment, and the punishment of Yeshuaʿ bar Tadmorayya. Arrest them and send them to me under guard. Do not shrink from taking up the sword against him! And send Shemuʿel bar ʿAmi.
C. 5/6 Ḥev 57 (132–135 CE):	Shimʿon to Yehudah bar Menashe of Kiryat ʿArabayya. I have sent you two donkeys, with which you are to send two men to Yehonatan bar Baʿayan and Masabbala. They should load them up with palm branches and citrons and send them to you at the camp. You are to send others from where you are to bring you myrtle branches and willow boughs. Prepare them and send them to the camp, because the number of the soldiers (?) is large. Greetings!
D. papMird A (7th–10th century CE):	From the one blessed by the Lord, Gabriel the sinner, to the Superior of the community of our "lords and fathers." I entreat you to pray for me because of the "clan" (?) on account of whom my heart trembles (?). Peace to you from the Father and the Son and the Holy Spirit.
E. APHM 49 (8th century CE):	In the name of the Father and the Son and the Holy Spirit in one substance. To Ḥabban ibn Yusuf from Majnille the preacher. The elder inquires after you. . . .
F. APHM 18 (7th century CE):	In the name of God, the compassionate, the merciful. To Dirʿ ibn ʿAbdallah from ʿUmar ibn ʿUbaidallah. Greetings to you! I praise God to you, beside whom there is no other god. Further, may God grant you the fullness of his well-being in this world and the world to come. Now you have written me concerning Umm Iyas, daughter of Muʿarik, about the matter she raised with you concerning her [hus]band's taking away her property and her maintenance. I have confronted them, and asked him about the matter you mentioned. He acknowledged her property, so I gave it back to her. But he disowned her maintenance. So the wife requested that I bring him with her to you. I did this; I ordered them both to go to you. Now you have written me ordering me to do what. . . .

maic manuscripts of Enoch from Cave 4 contain fragments of this "Epistle" (Enoch^{g} [4Q212] and Enoch^{e} [4Q206]). [*See* Enoch, Books of.] Józef T. Milik (1976) reconstructs Enoch^{g} as containing references to Enoch's writing a letter for Methuselah and his grandsons, but the extant text has no epistolary features and it is not included here.

The Hebrew halakhic text Miqtsat Maʿasei ha-Torah has been generally described as a "letter." Generically mixed, it contains calendric, halakhic, and hortatory material, and many details of its interpretation are still controversial. It is quite unlike the personal letters described below, with no close parallels to their structure and formulation.

It has been observed by Elisha Qimron and John Strugnell (1994) that the legal section of the text introduces each new topic with the phrase, "Now concerning so-and so . . . ," a pattern paralleled in some of Paul's ethical instructions in the New Testament (*1 Cor.* 7.1, 25; 8.1, 4; 12.1; cf. *1 Thes.* 5.1). In both cases the ensuing discussions frequently contain such phrases as "We (I) think. . . ," "We (I) say. . . ," etc.

Early attempts to identify the writer of Miqtsat Maʿasei ha-Torah as the Teacher of Righteousness have generally been abandoned. The official editors identify its genre provisionally as that of the corporate or public letter, or a treatise. Lawrence H. Schiffman (1995, p. 87) dates the work to the earliest period of the Qumran community's existence, and proposes that it was addressed by its unnamed leaders to the high priest in Jerusalem. Whatever the historical origin of Miqtsat Maʿasei ha-Torah, it is clear from the number of copies of it found (six, dating variously between ca.75 BCE to 50 BCE) that it was treated as a literary text rather than an occasional communication. It is not included in the discussion of letter-forms below. [*See* Miqtsat Maʿasei ha-Torah.]

Other epistolary remains from Qumran are meager. Letter 4Q342 consists of a few fragments of a letter in Jewish Aramaic, and letter 4Q343 contains three small scraps of a Nabatean letter (Cotton and Yardeni, 1997). In fact, the editors of these texts believe that their provenance must be placed elsewhere in the Judean Desert area.

Epistolary material from Masada is both scanty and fragmentary. A partially legible Aramaic ostracon of six lines (Mas554) pleads for payment of money owed for a purchase of bread (?). Another Aramaic ostracon (Mas556) found in the southern storeroom complex gives instructions for deliveries of myrrh in clay jars. A broken portion of a papyrus letter in Greek (Mas741) from a certain Abakantos to one Judah mentions a shipment of lettuce.

There are two fragments of Latin letters, apparently from the time of the Roman siege of the site. One (Mas724) bears little more than the names of the sender (Titulenus Vindex) and the recipient (Julius Lupus), followed by a stylized greeting (*salutem*). The addressee is an officer known from the history of the period. Tiberius Julius Lupus served in the Roman army during the siege of Masada, and while on duty there was promoted to the position of prefect of Egypt. In the letter, the recipient's name is followed by the phrase, [*do*]*mesticum m*[*eum*], "my familiar," meaning "well-known to me," identifying it as personal letter of reference. In the other Latin letter (Mas726), the words ". . . will be in danger . . . I will send a centurion to inspect whether . . ." can be made out. There are additional small fragments of letters from Masada.

Wadi Murabbaʿat and Naḥal Ḥever have yielded a significant collection of letters from the time of the Bar Kokhba Revolt against Rome (132–135 CE). These have become known as the Bar Kokhba letters (Aramaic "Son of the Star," an allusion to *Nm.* 24.17). As is now known from the letters, most of which were written or dictated by him, his name was Shimʿon ben Kosiba (S. bar Kosiba in Aramaic).

The Murabbaʿat letters are all in Hebrew to subordinates in the vicinity, particularly one Yeshuaʿ ben Galgulaʾ. Those from Naḥal Ḥever are mainly to one or both of the co-commanders of the ʿEin-Gedi region, Yehonatan and Masabbala.

One of the most interesting features of the letters from Naḥal Ḥever is that they are in three languages, Hebrew, Aramaic, and Greek. It is difficult to give the exact number of letters from each site, because some of the papyri are so fragmentary, and also because much of the material from Naḥal Ḥever is not fully published. From Murabbaʿat, there are five Hebrew letters, plus a number of fragments. From Naḥal Ḥever, there are definitely eight letters in Aramaic, three in Hebrew (including one letter to Bar Kokhba [XḤev/Se 30], whose provenance is uncertain), two in Greek, and at least two more whose language is uncertain, but which are thought to be Hebrew.

The Bar Kokhba letters do not deal with matters of major military importance, but give vivid glimpses into the day-to-day problems faced by the Jewish commander: casualties (Mur 45), the difficulty of provisioning soldiers and maintaining supply lines (Mur 44, 5/6Ḥev 58, 59), the expropriation of food and living space (5/6Ḥev 54), and above all, the difficulty of maintaining morale (Mur 44). There is evidence of regional dissension (Mur 43), insubordination (Mur 43), apathy (Mur 49), food shortages (Mur 45), and various threats of punishment (Mur 43, 5/6Ḥev 54, 55). One fragmentary letter cites a subordinate for selfless actions—burying the dead and (caring for?) the poor—(Mur 46), another sarcastically accuses the recipients, "You sit, eat, and drink from the goods of the House of Israel, and care nothing for your brothers!" (5/6Ḥev 49). One letter (Mur 45) mentions a fortress Meṣad-Ḥasidim, which some have suggested may be Qumran.

The seriousness with which Bar Kokhba maintained Jewish religious observance in the midst of difficult wartime conditions has often been noted. This is clearest in 5/6Ḥev 57, in which he orders the transport of "palm branches, citrons, myrtle branches and willow boughs" for the soldiers, the so-called four species required for the celebration of the festival of Sukkot (*Lv.* 23.39–43). [*See* Sukkot.] Letter 5/6Ḥev 52, which refers to "citrons" and a "festival," probably has a similar intent, though the Greek text is less clear. Sabbath was carefully observed (Mur 44, 50), and one letter, in an unclear context, mentions a Rabbi (5/6Ḥev 56).

The manuscripts discovered at Khirbet Mird near the ruins of a Christian monastery of the Byzantine period include a number of letters from a much later era. The desert region between Jerusalem and the northeast shore of the Dead Sea became a favorite place of withdrawal for Christian hermits from at least as early as the fourth century CE. Sometimes there grew up around such an anchorite a loosely organized association of other solitaries, known as a *laura* (Greek). The monks acknowledged the authority of one of themselves as superior, but lived in isolation. [*See* Mird, Khirbet.]

One papyrus letter from Khirbet Mird (papMird A), dating from the seventh century or later, was composed in Christian Palestinian Aramaic by a member of such a community. In it, a monk named Gabriel asks the head of his community for prayers, concluding with a benediction in the name of the Trinity. Józef T. Milik (1953, pp. 536–537) interprets the short body of the letter as expressing fear of attack from desert bedouin. However, the word translated "the clan" (*ahla'*, a loan-word from Arabic not otherwise found in Aramaic) normally expresses intimacy rather than hostility and may refer to the monastic community itself ("the brotherhood") and Gabriel's concern for them. In addition to providing a personal glimpse into the piety and concerns of the writer, the letter is also of interest in demonstrating the use of Christian Palestinian Aramaic for everyday purposes of communication. Virtually all known texts in this dialect are liturgical and biblical, most of them translated somewhat stiffly from Greek.

Of the Arabic letters from Khirbet Mird, only a few are explicitly Christian. Private letter APHM 45 is an eighth-century note from a Christian writer, Anba Majnille (= Greek Magnilios), who styles himself "the preacher," and appears to have been abbot of a monastic community at or near Khirbet Mird. He opens the letter with an invocation of the Trinity, adding the phrase "in one substance."

This brief phrase is worthy of comment in the light of the Christological controversies of the early church. The Nicene Creed (325 CE) affirmed that Christ was "of one substance (Greek *homoousion*) with the Father"; however, the interpretation of this phrase occasioned immense debate. The Council of Chalcedon (451 CE) attempted to resolve the question with a more precise definition.

In the aftermath of Chalcedon, the Palestinian monasteries were deeply divided. A few accepted the "orthodox" Chalcedonian position. But the majority of Aramaic- and Arabic-speaking Christians in Palestine followed the less philosophically nuanced Monophysite position, that one need affirm only that Christ is human and divine "in one nature (*physis*)," and the phrase "one nature" became a code-word identifying an anti-Chalcedonian position. By the sixth century, the Palestinian church had become solidly Monophysite. The phrase in private letter APHM 45 ". . . in one *jawhar*^{un}," uses an Arabic word commonly used to translate Nicene *homoousion*; hence it is translated here as "one substance." But the meaning of the Arabic word is sufficiently broad that it also may be understood in the Monophysite sense as "one nature," perhaps indicating the relative indifference of the Arabic-speaking church to the philosophical nuances so beloved by the Greek theologians (see table 1: sample letter E).

A shorter version of the Trinitarian formula appears at the head of the reply (private letter APHM 46), on the verso of the same papyrus. Private letter APHM 49 also refers, in a badly broken context, to a Christian abbot, Anba Yusuf.

Most of the Arabic letters appear to be communications between Muslim correspondents, though one cannot in every case be sure. In later times at least, some theological formulations common in Islam were also utilized by Christians, for example, the *Basmala* ("In the name of God, the compassionate, the merciful"). The letters date mainly from the Umayyad Period (661–750 CE) of Muslim administration in Palestine, a few being as late as the ninth century (Abbassid Period). The great majority of the letters in Khirbet Mird are damaged or fragmentary. Beyond common formulas, only a few can be understood in any detail.

Official letters APHM 10–32 deal with administrative matters of local and regional concern: a wife's legal claim against her husband (18; see table 1: sample letter F), an allegation of theft (19), a suspected case of fraud (24), and fragments referring to a grain tax (26–28). The personal letters (APHM 42–70, also some fragments in 79–99) are even more difficult to interpret, since they often allude obliquely to matters known to both correspondents. One refers to "the food of Ramadan" (42), another to a land tax (50), and many contain personal greetings to family or friends. These letters add a few details to our knowledge of lower-level government administration and everyday life in a rather poorly documented period.

The Forms and Formulas. The seventh-century Hebrew letter from Wadi Murabba'at is so poorly legible it is difficult to draw many conclusions (see table 1: sample letter A). If correctly understood, it has an *initial address* beginning with the form of the verb "to say," though the syntax of the following clause is not clear. Dennis Pardee (1982, p. 121) suggests that a second form of the same verb (imperative?) may have been lost in the lacuna. In any case, the "say" formula is not otherwise known in ancient Hebrew letters, and has its closest parallels in letters from Edom, Ammon, and Phoenicia. The precise form of the *greeting* that follows is also unknown, but the transition to the *body* with *wʿt* ("and now") is a common construction in both Hebrew and Aramaic letters of the early period.

Compared to older Hebrew and Aramaic letters, the Bar Kokhba letters are quite simple in their form. Most (in all three languages) begin with an *initial address* in the form "from A to B," or simply "A to B" (so also in Mas741). The more ancient usage known from preexilic Judah (Hebrew) and Achaemenid Egypt (Aramaic), according to which the preferred order is "to B from A," occurs only in XḤev/Se 30. Either or both names may be accompanied by a patronymic ("son of so-and-so"). Rarely, the sender is also identified by a title or epithet, "the administrators of Beth-Mashiko" (Mur 42); and most interestingly, in two letters the name of Shimʿon bar/ben Kosiba is followed by the title "ruler over Israel" (5/6 Ḥev 54, Aramaic; similarly in XḤev/Se 30, Hebrew), a title by which he is also known in the Talmud. In the much later letter from the monk Gabriel to an abbot (papMird A), the writer styles himself "the one blessed by the Lord" and "the sinner."

In some cases, the initial address is followed by an *initial greeting*, a single word meaning "peace, greetings" in Hebrew (Mur 42, 43, 44, 46; 5/6Ḥev 49), Greek (5/6Ḥev 52, 59; so also Mas741), and less commonly in Aramaic (5/6Ḥev 54 and 58). Letter 5/6Ḥev 53 is unique, opening with "A letter of Shimʿon bar Kosiba, greetings!" with the name of the recipient following.

Sometimes the *body* of the letter begins immediately thereafter, with no transition (Mur 43, 46; 5/6Ḥev 49). Frequently, the body is introduced with a relative pronoun (Hebrew *she-*, Aramaic *di*), literally "that. . . ." Since in virtually every case the next sentence is a direct command (one or more jussive-imperfect verbs), it appears that the relative pronoun is not a simple transitional particle, but part of a newly developed command-form (*she-* in Mur 42, 44; *di* in 5/6Ḥev 50, 54, 57, 58; so also Mas554.)

Following the body, there is often a brief *closing greeting*, any of several similar phrases meaning "best wishes" or "may it be well with you" (Mur 46; 5/6Ḥev 52, 53, 57, 59). A *signature* is not a regular feature, though the ends of many of the letters are lost or unreadable. Letter 5/6Ḥev 50 concludes with the words "dictated by Shimʿon bar Yehuda" (literally, "S. bar Y. wrote it," but the usage of the phrase in other contemporary documents makes it clear this is not an indication of a personally written signature). The ending of the letter from Beth-Mashiko to Yeshuʿa ben Galgula (Mur 42), a mixed-genre letter intended to be used as a legal document, uses the same phrase with the name of each of the two senders, followed by the signatures of the principal party, two witnesses, and a notary.

The letters from Khirbet Mird, both Muslim and Christian, belong to much later and different traditions. The Christian Palestinian Aramaic letter (papMird A) concludes with a Trinitarian blessing (see Table 1: sample letter D), and the two Christian Arabic letters (APHM 49 [see table 1: sample letter E] and 50) begin with one. The Muslim letters regularly begin with the *Basmala*, then the initial address in the form "to B from A," followed by "greetings to you" and other, often lengthy, religious formulas. Private letter APHM 49 (see Table 1: sample letter F) is typical.

A more comprehensive formal analysis of the letters is beyond the scope of this article, but several recent studies have exhaustively analyzed the form of the letters from the Bar Kokhba period in the light of earlier Hebrew and Aramaic correspondence. [*See also* Ḥever, Naḥal; Murabbaʿat, Wadi.]

BIBLIOGRAPHY

Beyer, Klaus. *Die aramäischen Texte vom Toten Meer*. Göttingen, 1984. A German work roughly comparable in scope and content to the work of Fitzmyer and Harrington (below). Only six of the Bar Kokhba Aramaic letters, partially deciphered in some cases, are included. Beyer makes a number of advances in reading the texts. Glossary, bibliographies, and an extensive grammatical introduction are included. Line numbers do not always correspond to those of the originals.

Cotton, Hannah M., Joseph Geiger, and J. David Thomas. *Masada II: The Latin and Greek Documents*. The Yigael Yadin Excavations 1963–1965, Final Reports. Jerusalem, 1989. Official publication (texts, translations, photographs) of the Greek and Latin letters. An especially thorough and helpful commentary on Mas724.

Cotton, Hannah, M., and Ada Yardeni. *Aramaic, Hebrew, and Greek Documentary Texts from Naḥal Ḥever and Other Sites, with an Appendix Containing Alleged Qumran Texts. (The Seiyâl Collection II)*. Discoveries in the Judaean Desert, 27. Oxford, 1997.

Fitzmyer, Joseph A. "Aramaic Epistolography." *Semeia* 22 (1981), 25–56. Inventory, bibliography, and brief form-critical study of Aramaic letters, including Bar Kokhba letters from Naḥal Ḥever and papMird A.

Fitzmyer, Joseph A., and Daniel J. Harrington. *A Manual of Palestinian Aramaic Texts*. Biblica et Orientalia, 34. Rome, 1978. Texts, translations (reliable, but preliminary), with extensive bibliographies, of eight of the more legible Bar Kokhba Aramaic letters from Naḥal Ḥever. Many of the texts are only partially deciphered, based on earlier publications. Line numbers in some cases do not correspond with those of the originals. Includes a complete glossary, making it particularly useful to the student.

Grohmann, Adolf. *Arabic Papyri from Ḥirbet el-Mird*. Bibliothèque du Muséon, 52. Louvain, 1963. Text, translations, brief commentary, and selected photographs of the Arabic texts from Khirbet Mird.

Kutscher, Eduard Yechezkel. "The Hebrew and Aramaic Letters of Bar Koseba and His Contemporaries." In *Hebrew and Aramaic Studies*, pp. 36–53; 54–70 (Hebrew section). Jerusalem, 1977. The first major publication of the Bar Kokhba letters, with partial transcription and valuable commentary.

Lifshitz, Baruch. "Papyrus grecs du désert de Juda." *Aegyptus* 42 (1962), 240–256. Edition with French translation, notes, and photographs of the Greek letters from Naḥal Ḥever: 5/6Ḥev 52 and 59.

Lifshitz, Baruch. "The Greek Documents from the Cave of Horror." *Israel Exploration Journal* 12 (1962), 201–207. Text, translation, and photograph of the Greek fragment 8Ḥev 4.

Lindenberger, James M. *Ancient Aramaic and Hebrew Letters*. Atlanta, 1994. Anthology of Aramaic and Hebrew letters down to 400 BCE. Includes a brief formal analysis of the older corpus, and recently published letters in Edomite and Ammonite.

Milik, Józef T. "Une inscription et une lettre en araméen christo-palestinien." *Revue biblique* 60 (1953), 526–539. First publication (text, translation, excellent notes, and photograph) of the Christian Palestinian Aramaic letter from Khirbet Mird.

Milik, Józef T. "Textes hébreux et araméens." In *Les grottes de Murabbaʿat* by Pierre Benoit, Józef T. Milik, and Roland de Vaux, pp. 67–205. Discoveries in the Judaean Desert, 2. Oxford, 1961. Official publication of the Hebrew letters: Mur 17 (his hand copy and notes, pp. 93–96, are particularly valuable); Mur 42–52, the Murabbaʿat Hebrew letters and fragments (pp. 155–169). Texts, translation, commentary, and photographs.

Milik, Józef T. *The Books of Enoch*, pp. 260–265. Oxford, 1976.

Pardee, Dennis. *Handbook of Ancient Hebrew Letters*. SBL Sources for Biblical Study, 15. Chico, Calif., 1982. The definitive work on Hebrew letters through the Bar Kokhba period, with an appendix on tannaitic letters in rabbinic literature. Texts (in transliteration) and translations, commentary, and detailed form-critical analysis. Extensive bibliography of earlier publications, including a number of his own on Hebrew epistolography. In many passages Pardee improves on the readings of Milik in Discoveries in the Judaean Desert, 2.

Pardee, Dennis, Paul E. Dion, and Stanley K. Stowers. "Letters." In *The Anchor Bible Dictionary*, edited by David Noel Freedman, vol. 4, pp. 282–293. New York, 1992. A concise, well-documented study of the types, formulas, and structure of letters in ancient Hebrew (Pardee), Aramaic (Dion), and Greek and Latin (Stowers).

Qimron, Elisha, and John Strugnell. *Qumran Cave 4, V: Miqṣat Maʿaśe ha-Torah*, pp. 113–114. Discoveries in the Judaean Desert, 10. Oxford, 1994.

Schiffman, Lawrence H. *Reclaiming the Dead Sea Scrolls*. New York, 1995.

White, John L. *Light from Ancient Letters*. Philadelphia, 1986. Anthology of Greek letters from Hellenistic and Roman Egypt, with formal analysis.

Yadin, Yigael, Joseph Naveh, and Yaacov, Meshorer. *Masada I: The Aramaic and Hebrew Ostraca and Jar Inscriptions, the Coins of Masada*. The Yigael Yadin Excavations 1963–1965, Final Reports. Jerusalem, 1989. Official publication of the Aramaic texts (including the three Aramaic letters) from Masada. Texts, translations, brief commentary, and photographs; includes a hand copy by Ada Yardeni of Mas554.

Yadin, Yigael. "Expedition D." *Israel Exploration Journal* 11 (1962), 36–52. First major English publication on the Bar Kokhba letters from Naḥal Ḥever. Excerpts from fifteen Hebrew, Aramaic, and Greek letters with preliminary translations and brief commentary. His readings have been the basis of most subsequent studies of the texts, and his serial numbering system is still widely used.

JAMES M. LINDENBERGER

LEVI, the third son of Jacob and Leah (*Gn.* 29.34) and the eponymous ancestor of the tribe of the Levites. With Simeon he took fearful vengeance on the men of Shechem for violating his sister Dinah (*Gn.* 34). Jacob's blessing of Levi in *Genesis* 49.5–7 also refers to this incident (without mentioning a priesthood). The ideas about Levi in the blessing of Moses differ (*Dt.* 33.8–11). There, both cultic and teaching functions are attributed to him. These verses are cited in the Testimonia (4Q175 14–20) as characteristic of Levi. His three sons were Gerson, Qahat, and Merari; the high priests are descended from Qahat. The Levites served as one of the orders of servitors in the Temple, and there are numerous references to the Levites in the Hebrew scriptures.

The Levites, and consequently Levi, were important during the Second Temple period, playing a special role in the Dead Sea sect. In Jewish writings of the Second Temple period the relationship of Levi with Jacob, the incident in Shechem, and Levi's cultic and teaching functions are particularly central. Behind these themes is the idea of a covenant between God and Levi (*Dt.* 33.9, *Mal.* 2.4–9).

A saying of Levi, son of Jacob, is cited in the Damascus Document (CD iv.15). *Jubilees* 45.16 refers to the transmission of teaching through Levi, and this idea is reinforced by the Testament of Qahat (4Q542) and the Visions of Amram (4Q543–548). The transmission of teaching though the Levitical line was central to these documents. The Apocryphon of Joshua[b] (4Q379 1.2) refers to "Levi, the beloved."

The most important single source relating to Levi is *Aramaic Levi Document*. This document focuses on a number of themes: the Shechem incident; Levi's installation as a priest and the recognition of his status by Jacob; Levi's prayer and vision; Levi's instruction by Abraham in cultic practices from the "Book of Noah"; and Levi's teaching of reading, writing, and wisdom to his children. Other characteristics of Levi may have been mentioned in this document, which survives only in fragments. These major biblical themes relating to Levi, as in *Genesis* 49 and *Deuteronomy* 33 were later developed in particular ways. Since Aramaic Levi is probably of the third century BCE, that a number of these ideas about Levi were taken up in *Jubilees* and in the later Qahat and Amram documents is not surprising.

Levi appears in other works as well. In the *Testaments of the Twelve Patriarchs* (the date of which is much debated), particularly in the *Testament of Levi*, Levi and Judah play central roles, with Levi holding pride of place. This relationship is already expressed in *Jubilees* 31.13–20, and earlier the exclusive eschatological dominance of Levi is mentioned in Aramaic Levi Document 66. In *Joseph and Asenath* 23.14, the Shechem incident figures in connection with Simeon and Levi's prowess. This incident is also described graphically by Theodotus (frag. 8; Eusebius, *Preparation for the Gospel* 9.22.10–12) and in *Jubilees* 30.3–4. *The Testament of Simeon* 5.4–6 refers to a future war between the descendants of Simeon and Levi, in which the Levites prevail.

[*See also* High Priests; Jubilees, Book of; Levi, Aramaic; Priests; Testaments; *and* Twelve Patriarchs, Testaments of the.]

BIBLIOGRAPHY

Brooke, George J. "Levi and the Levites in the Dead Sea Scrolls and the New Testament." In *Mogilany 1989: Papers on the Dead Sea Scrolls Offered in Memory of Jean Carmignac*, edited by Z. J. Kapera, pp. 105–129. Kraków, 1993. A survey of the relevant material.

de Jonge, M. "The Testament of Levi and 'Aramaic Levi.'" *Revue de Qumrân* 13 (1988), 367–385. An analysis of the relationship between these documents.

Fuller, Russell. "The Blessing of Levi in Dtn 33, Mal 2 and Qumran." In *Konsequente Traditionsgeschichte: Festschrift für Klaus Baltzer zum 65. Geburtstag*, edited by Rüdiger Bartelmus, Thomas Krüger, and Helmut Utzschneider, pp. 31–44. Göttingen, 1993. Discussion of the development of this text and its use in light of changing views of Levi.

Greenfield, Jonas C. "The Words of Levi Son of Jacob in *Damascus Document* IV, 15–19 (CD)." *Revue de Qumrân* 13 (1988), 319–322. An assessment of this citation.

Kugel, James. "Levi's Elevation to the Priesthood in Second Temple Writings." *Harvard Theological Review* 86 (1993), 1–64.

Kugler, Robert A. *From Patriarch to Priest: The Levi-Priestly Tradition from Aramaic Levi to* Testament of Levi. Society of Biblical Literature, Early Judaism and Its Literature, 9. Atlanta, 1996. A substantial study of the growth of these traditions.

Stallman, Robert C. "Levi and the Levites in the Dead Sea Scrolls." *Journal for the Study of the Pseudepigrapha* 10 (1992), 163–189. Collection and analysis of the main sources.

MICHAEL E. STONE

LEVI, ARAMAIC. An important document of early, postbiblical Judaism, Aramaic Levi reflects attitudes toward the priesthood that differ strongly from those of another more or less contemporary work, the *Book of Ben Sira*. Aramaic Levi stresses the transmission of the cultic commandments from Noah to Abraham to Levi in a striking fashion. The authority of the Levitical priesthood is anchored in the actions of Noah, who founded postdiluvian humanity, and relates to the very first sacrifice he offered upon exiting the ark. The actual cultic instructions are unparalleled in detail and are one of the very earliest examples of postbiblical Jewish law. They are legitimated by an appeal to ancient tradition, perhaps because the Mosaic revelation had not taken place at the time assumed by the pseudepigraphal framework of the book. Yet the stress laid upon literacy and teaching raises the question of whether more is at stake here than providing legitimacy for priestly teaching before the revelation at Mount Sinai.

Sometimes called Aramaic Testament of Levi, Aramaic Levi was discovered in the early part of the century in two fragments from the Cairo Genizah; one being Cambridge Geniza, published in 1900 by H. L. Pass and J. Arendzen and the other, Bodleian Geniza, published in 1907 by R. H. Charles and A. Cowley. The relationship between Aramaic Levi and the Greek *Testament of Levi* included in the *Testaments of the Twelve Patriarchs* immediately was apparent. In addition, an insertion in one of the Greek manuscripts of the *Testaments of the Twelve Patriarchs* (Athos Koutloumous 39) was recognized as extracts from a Greek translation of Aramaic Levi. Among the Dead Sea Scrolls seven copies of Aramaic Levi have been identified, one from Cave 1 (Aramaic Levi, 1Q21) and six from Cave 4 (Aramaic Levi^{a-f}, 4Q213, 4Q213a, 4Q213b, 4Q214, 4Q214a, 4Q214b).

The fragments from Cave 4, among which J. T. Milik recognized three manuscripts, have been found to stem from six manuscripts (Greenfield and Stone, 1979). It is quite striking that all the Qumran copies date from the same period. The manuscripts are in scripts that resemble those typical of late Hasmonean, or in one or two instances early Herodian, writing. Significantly, two of the manuscripts (Aramaic Levi^{d} and Aramaic Levi^{e}) present variant shorter texts of the Cairo Genizah Aramaic Levi document.

Aramaic Levi seems to have been written originally in Aramaic, though some scholars, such as Grelot (1956), have maintained that the original was written in Hebrew and that it was translated into Aramaic in antiquity. This view has not met with general acceptance.

There is good reason to date Aramaic Levi to the third century or to the very early second century BCE. Aramaic Levi (or something very much like it) seems to have served as a source for *Jubilees*, which is usually dated to the first half of the second century BCE, as well as for the *Testaments of the Twelve Patriarchs*, and it is cited by the Damascus Document (CD), which is somewhat later than *Jubilees*. This date makes Aramaic Levi one of the most ancient of the pseudepigrapha.

Aramaic Levi relates nothing directly about its provenance, nor would such statements be expected in a pseudepigraphon. It employs a solar calendar resembling the one promoted by *1 Enoch*, *Jubilees*, and the Qumran sectarian writings. In contrast to *1 Enoch* and *Jubilees*, the surviving fragments contain no polemics regarding the use of the solar calendar. In addition to its adoption of the solar calendar, Aramaic Levi expresses distinctive ideas about two spirits, apotropaic prayer, and demonology, as well as oppositional views about the priesthood, including the unusual idea of an exclusively Levitical messianism. Aramaic Levi does not bear the distinctive marks of Qumran sectarian language, however, and should be attributed to a third-century wing of Judaism from which the Qumran sectarians are but one group of descendants.

It is possible to reconstruct the original order of the Oxford (Bodleian) and Cambridge fragments of Aramaic Levi from the Cairo Genizah. They are apparently parts of the two middle leaves of a quire (a collection of four sheets, folded in half). The Cambridge sheet preserves part of the recto of a right-hand column of a right-hand folio and part of the verso of the same folio, which is from the following left-hand column. The single Bodleian leaf was the right-hand leaf of the innermost sheet of the quire. The left-hand leaf is lost, but its contents are preserved in the Greek fragment (Athos Koutloumous 39, see above). Then the recto and verso of another left-hand leaf (Cambridge) follow. Thus the structure of these fragments is: *lr-*lv (Cambridge); *2r-*2v (Oxford); [*3r-*3v Greek]; *4r-*4v (Cambridge).

The sequence of the fragments is important because it fixes the order of events in part of the original document. It is, however, incomplete in two respects. We do not know what material came between the fragmentary quarter columns of the first recto and verso in the Cambridge fragment and between them and the first column of the Bodleian fragment. Moreover, the Cairo Genizah fragments preserve neither the beginning nor the end of the work.

There is some further evidence that Aramaic Levi was longer, perhaps substantially longer, than the Cairo Genizah and Athos material. First, the Prayer of Levi that was preserved as an insertion in the Greek *Testament of Levi* (3.2) also occurs in a fragment of Aramaic Levi^{b}. This confirms the position of the Prayer of Levi as part of Aramaic Levi. Second, some of the other Qumran fragments overlap with the material known from the Cairo Genizah, but numerous fragments of the Qumran Aramaic text have no parallels at all in the Cairo Genizah-Athos material. These must have come from parts of Aramaic Levi that did not survive in the Cairo or Athos finds. Third, a citation attributed to Levi is given by Ammonas, a successor of Saint Anthony. If this is from Aramaic Levi, it is from some other part of the manuscript than those preserved in the surviving Greek and Aramaic fragments. Finally, Puech (1992) has claimed that the two copies of Aaronic Text A (4Q540–541), which show certain parallels to the Greek *Testament of Levi* 18, also derive from Aramaic Levi. This is not certain, but if it were true it would hint at the inclusion of this eschatological material in the book. We regard only those manuscripts with some textual overlap with the Cairo Genizah-Athos material as being a definite part of Aramaic Levi. Puech also refers to Milik's suggestion that the narrative 4Q458 contains the closing passage of Aramaic Levi.

R. Kugler (1996) has proposed an overall history and structure of Aramaic Levi that is of considerable interest, though debatable at some points. The surviving substantial fragments of Aramaic Levi deal with the following topics.

Levi's prayer and vision (Prayer of Levi) is a separate piece that may have originally preceded the Cairo Genizah-Athos material, though not directly (Aramaic Levi^{b} 1–2). It has been suggested that 1QAramaic Levi fragment 1 might have occurred in the material preceding section 4 of the Genizah text. Levi's investiture and the recognition of his priesthood by Abraham, Isaac, and Jacob is found in Cairo Genizah, 1QAramaic Levi (3, 4), and Aramaic Levi^{c}:

4–10 = Genizah
4–6 = Aramaic Levi frg. 3
7–9 = Aramaic Levi^{c}
9 = Aramaic Levi frg. 4

Isaac's exhortation and cultic instructions to Levi (4Q214 1; 4Q214b 2–6; 4Q214a; 4Q214 2; 1Q21 45):

14–61 = Genizah
20–23 = Aramaic Levi^{d} frg. 1
22–27 = Aramaic Levi^{f} frgs. 2–6
24–25 = Aramaic Levi^{e} frg. 1
25–30 = Aramaic Levi^{d} frg. 2
26–27 = Aramaic Levi frg. 45

The birth of Levi's children and the major events of his life (4Q214a 2–3.i):

62–81 = Genizah
69–72 resembles Aramaic Levi^{e} frgs. 2–3 col. i

Levi's address to his children before his death, which is a wisdom poem (4Q213 1 and 2; 4Q214a 2–; 4Q214b 8):

82–95 = Genizah
Aramaic Levi^{a} frgs. 1 and 2 overlap with this and have further text
Aramaic Levi^{e} frgs. 2–3 = 95 and text from 4QLevi^{a}
4QLevi^{f} frg. 8 overlaps with the preceding.

This was not the end of the work, as is clear from parts of Aramaic Levi^{a} (1.ii and 2), which overlap with the end of the poem and which are followed by an eschatological exhortation.

Other substantial fragments that cannot be placed by reference to the continuous text of Aramaic Levi mentioned above include a piece of hortatory text (4Q213 4) and a reference to the Dinah incident, which also contains some eschatological words (4Q213a 3–4). Numerous other fragments of the Qumran Aramaic Levi manuscripts do not parallel any of the Qumran material noted above, and there seems to be no sure way of fixing their sequence in Aramaic Levi. It seems likely that Aramaic Levi formed the inspiration for two other works found at Qumran, the Testament of Qahat (4Q542) and Visions of Amram^{a-f} (4Q543–548). Thus a series of three compositions were attributed to the fathers of the priestly line.

[*See also* Amram; Ben Sira, Book of; Levi; Qahat; Testaments; *and* Twelve Patriarchs, Testaments of the.]

BIBLIOGRAPHY

de Jonge, M. "Notes on Testament of Levi II–VII." In *Travels in the World of the Old Testament*, edited by M. S. H. G. Heerma van Voss, Ph. H. J. Houwink ten Cate, and N. A. van Uchelen, pp. 132–145. Assen, 1974. Also available in *Studies on the Testaments of the Twelve Patriarchs*, edited by M. de Jonge. Leiden, 1975.

de Jonge, M. "The Testament of Levi and 'Aramaic Levi'." *Revue de Qumrân* 13 (1988), 376–385. Examines the relationship of the Greek and Aramaic documents.

Greenfield, Jonas C. "The Words of Levi Son of Jacob in Damascus Document 4.15–19." *Revue de Qumrân* 13 (1988), 319–322. Shows that Aramaic Levi is cited in the Damascus Document.

Greenfield, Jonas C., and Michael E. Stone. "Remarks on the Aramaic Testament of Levi from the Geniza." *Revue biblique* 85 (1979), 214–230. A study of the Genizah Aramaic text.

Grelot, Pierre. "Notes sur le Testament araméen de Lévi." *Revue biblique* 63 (1956), 391–406. A study of the Genizah Aramaic text.

Kugler, Robert A. *From Patriarch to Priest: The Levi-Priestly Tradition from Aramaic Levi to* Testament of Levi. Society of Biblical Literature, Early Judaism and Its Literature, 9. Atlanta, 1996. Important study also containing full edition and translation of the texts.

Puech, É. "Fragments d'un apocryphe de Lévi et le personnage eschatologique, 4QTestLévi[c–d] (?) et 4 QAJa." In *The Madrid Qumran Congress: Proceedings of the International Congress on the Dead Sea Scrolls, Madrid, 18–21 March 1991*, edited by J. Trebolle Barrera and L. Vegas Montaner, pp. 449–501. Studies on the Texts of the Desert of Judah, 11. Madrid, 1992. Proposes that 540 and 541 come from Aramaic Levi.

Milik, Józef T. "Le testament de Lévi in araméen: Fragment de la grotte 4 de Qumrân." *Revue biblique* 62 (1955), 398–406.

Milik, Józef T. *The Books of Enoch: Aramaic Fragments of Qumrân Cave 4*. Oxford, 1976. Publishes a fragment of Aramaic Levi.

Stone, Michael E. "Enoch, Aramaic Levi and Sectarian Origins." *Journal for the Study of Judaism* 19 (1988), 159–170. Role of Aramaic Levi in early postbiblical Judaism.

Stone, Michael E., and Jonas C. Greenfield. "4 Q Levi ar." In *Qumran Cave 4: Parabiblical Texts, Part 3*, edited by George Brooke et al., pp. 1–72. Discoveries in the Judaean Desert, 22. Oxford, 1997.

Stone, Michael E., and Jonas C. Greenfield. "The Aramaic Levi Document." In *The Testaments of the Twelve Patriarchs: A Commentary*, edited by H. W. Hollander and M. de Jonge, pp. 457–469. Leiden, 1985. English translation.

Stone, Michael E., and Jonas C. Greenfield. "The First Manuscript of Aramaic Levi Document from Qumran (4 Q Levi[a] aram)." *Le Muséon* 107 (1994), 257–281.

Stone, Michael E., and Jonas C. Greenfield. "The Second Manuscript of Aramaic Levi from Cave 4 at Qumran (4QArLevi[b])." *Le Muséon* 109 (1996), 1–15.

MICHAEL E. STONE

LEVI, TESTAMENT OF. *See* Levi, Aramaic; Testaments.

LEVITICUS, BOOK OF. Thirteen manuscripts of the *Book of Leviticus* were discovered in the Judean Desert. Eleven of them were found at Qumran and two at Masada. Besides paleo-Leviticus 1Q3 (hereafter 1Qpaleo-Leviticus) and paleo-Leviticus 2Q5 (hereafter 2Qpaleo-Leviticus) (approximately one third of the manuscripts discovered in Qumran were written in paleo-Hebrew), four manuscripts were discovered in Cave 4. During the course of the preparation of these four manuscripts for publication, E. Tov separated the fourth copy into three manuscripts, so that now we possess six manuscripts from Cave 4, while on the first copy the *Books of Leviticus* and *Numbers* are found:

1. Leviticus-Numbers[a] (4Q23)
2. Leviticus[b] (4Q24; hereafter 4QLeviticus[b])
3. Leviticus[c] (4Q25)
4. Leviticus[d] (4Q26)
5. Leviticus[e] (4Q26a)
6. Leviticus[g] (4Q26b).

In addition, there is one manuscript from Cave 11, Leviticus[b] (11Q2). Two manuscripts of *Leviticus* were discovered at Masada and given the sigla Masla and Maslb.

Two manuscripts of a Greek translation of the *Book of Leviticus* were discovered in Cave 4 (Septuagint Leviticus[a] [4Q119] and Septuagint Leviticus[b] [4Q120]); there is also one manuscript from Cave 4 in which there are fragments of an Aramaic translation of the book (Targum of Leviticus [4Q156]).

The Hebrew Manuscripts of *Leviticus* from Qumran. From 1Qpaleo-Leviticus we have twenty-four fragments containing parts of chapters 11–23 of *Leviticus*, as well as a number of fragments belonging to the *Book of Numbers*. The editor claims that the *Books of Leviticus* and *Numbers* were copied in order on the same scroll. The text of the scroll is identical to that of the Masoretic Text, except for a number of spelling variations. The spelling in the scroll is primarily "defective."

From 2Qpaleo-Leviticus there is only a single fragment, which contains parts of chapter 11, verses 22–29. The text in this small fragment is different from that of the Masoretic Text, and in two cases it is similar to the Samaritan Pentateuch and to the Septuagint. In verse 25 there is space for inserting the words "and bathe in water":

verse 25.
Masoretic Text: "whoever bears (*nose*ʾ, in defective spelling) from their carcasses shall wash his clothes and be impure until the evening"
scroll, Samaritan Pentateuch: "[and whoever bears (*nose*ʾ, in "plene" spelling) from their carcasses] shall wash his clothes [and bathe in water and be impure until the evening]"
verse 26.
Masoretic Text: "to every beast that spreads its hooves and does not chew the cud"
scroll, Septuagint: "[to every beast that spr]eads its hooves and chews its cud"

It appears that the texts of the scroll and the Septuagint preserve a harmonistic change that was made in the verse on the basis of the introduction to chapter 11, verse 3:

"Everyone that spreads its hooves and chews its cud." The spelling in the scroll is usually "plene" (*we-ha-nogea*ʿ, he who touched, as opposed to *we-ha-nogea*ʿ). In the scroll and in the Samaritan Pentateuch the spelling *mafrisat* ("spread") is attested as opposed to *mafreset* in the Masoretic Text. This spelling is consistent in the Samaritan Pentateuch in all of the occurrences of this word.

Leviticus-Numbers[a] includes 104 fragments, among them 30 particularly small ones, which were not identified by the editor. According to the reconstruction, the scroll included 21.5 columns from the *Book of Leviticus* (the first eight were lost). After several blank lines comes the *Book of Numbers*, which included according to reconstruction 29.5 additional columns.

The script is an Early Hasmonean formal hand, dating from approximately the middle or later half of the second century BCE. The spelling is similar to that in the Masoretic Text and the Samaritan Pentateuch, but there are a number of discrepancies between them. It is not possible to see consistency in the method of the spelling in the different texts. In two cases the copyist omitted an entire verse: In *Leviticus* 14.24 and 14.45 the verse was added above the line, most likely by a second scribe. In an additional instance (14.43) a fragment remained that was too small to determine whether the copyist used a shorter original version (which is not attested in other witnesses), or perhaps made an omission by parablepsis. Also, missing vowel letters were added above the line and a number of letters were corrected between the lines.

4QLeviticus[b] includes thirty fragments and is dated paleographically to the Late Hasmonean period, from approximately the mid-first century BCE. The spelling is similar to that in the Masoretic Text and in the Samaritan Pentateuch, but a number of discrepancies exist between them and it is not possible to discern a consistent pattern in the different texts. The text of the scroll is similar to the Masoretic Text and the Samaritan Pentateuch, but it seems that it did not contain *Leviticus* 3.1–11. Since verses 1–5 and 6–11 are similar, the omission can be explained in two ways: either the scribe skipped from verse 2 to verse 8, "and the sons of Aaron (the priests) threw the blood/its blood," because of the similarity of the expressions; or the copyist's *Vorlage* was a shorter version and did not contain these verses and in it the two units were combined. Similarly, in *Leviticus* 22.22 there is a small addition that is not attested in the remaining witnesses, the Masoretic Text, Samaritan Pentateuch, and Septuagint: ". . . either a wart or eczema or moist skin eruption." Leviticus[b]: ". . . either a wart o[r eczema or moist sk]in eruption or bruised [testic]les."

Of Leviticus[c] only six fragments have survived along with three small fragments that were not identified (they may belong to Leviticus[e] [4Q26a]). The manuscript contains sections from chapters 1, 3–5, and 8. The spelling is generally similar to the spelling of the Masoretic Text and Samaritan Pentateuch, with slight differences. Also, the differences in the text are few and lack textual significance. In fragment 4, a correction of 4.23, which was partially erased, corrects the text and brings it closer to the other textual testimonies.

Leviticus[d] contains four identified fragments, in which there are sections from chapters 14, 15, and 17, with seven small fragments that have not been identified.

Leviticus[d] is written in an early Herodian script and is to be dated between 30 BCE and 20 CE. The spelling in the scroll is fuller than in the parallel passages of the Masoretic Text and the Samaritan Pentateuch. The condition of the scroll's preservation is extremely bad, and in fragment 6 it is possible to read primarily the impression made by the letters, but the text preserved in it is important. In fragment 4, which contains some of *Leviticus* 17, there are a number of textual differences:

Leviticus 17.3
Masoretic Text, Samaritan Pentateuch: "Each man from the house of Israel."
Leviticus[d]: "[Each man from the house of Israel and the sojourner who] sojourns in Israel."
Septuagint: "Each man from the children of Israel and the sojourner who sojourns among you."

This difference concerns the inclusion of resident aliens in the prohibition in verse 3 (they are mentioned in other prohibitions in the chapter [vv. 8, 10, 12, 15]). *Sifra* 8.6 includes resident aliens in the prohibition of slaughtering inside the camp: "(It is written) 'The Israelites'. I know only that it includes the Israelites; how do I know it includes the strangers and the slaves? Because it is stated 'say to them'" (Weiss, p. 83b). Some scholars offer explanations for the omission of the resident aliens in the Masoretic Text formulation of the Law. It is possible that the scroll has the original version, and the words "and the sojourner who sojourns in Israel" have been omitted in the other versions due to parablepsis.

Leviticus 17:
Samaritan Pentateuch, Masoretic Text: "from outside (*mi-ḥuts*) the camp"
Leviticus[d]: "from outside (*mi-ḥutsah*) the camp"

Here we find a use of the locative ending on a word preceded by a preposition.

This difference relates to whether the text refers to *ḥullin* (the slaughter of "nonsacred" animals), or *qodashim* (the slaughter of sacred animals). Lines 3–5 of fragment 4 read as follows:

Leviticus[d]: "and [t]o the entran[ce of the Tent of Meeting he did not bring it in order to make it a burnt-offering] or peace offering to the Lord as [a pleasing aroma and he is to slaughter it outside and to the entrance of the Tent of Meeting] he is not to bring it to offer it as a sac[rifice to the Lord]."

Masoretic Text: "and to the entrance of the Tent of Meeting he did not bring it to offer as a sacrifice to the Lord."

Samaritan Pentateuch: "And to the entrance of the Tent of Meeting he did not bring it in order to make it a burnt-offering or a peace offering to the Lord acceptable on your behalf as a pleasing aroma and he is to slaughter it outside and to the entrance of the Tent of Meeting he did not bring it to offer it as a sacrifice to the Lord."

R. Ishmael and R. Akiba as well as contemporary commentators have disagreed about the contents of this passage. In *Leviticus Rabbah* one reads: R. Ishmael and R. Akiba (are in dispute). R. Ishmael says that this is a case of a

> permissive law arising out of a prohibition, for owing to the fact that in the wilderness Israel were forbidden to eat the meat for enjoyment, the scriptures come and permit it to them, only stipulating that it is to be ritually slaughtered. R. Akiba says: It is a case of a prohibition arising out of that which was permitted, for since in the wilderness Israel used to kill the animals by stabbing and eat the meat, the scriptures come and forbid them to do so, laying down that they must perform ritual slaughter. (*Lev. Rab.* 22:7, Slotki ed., p. 285)

The law of slaughtering *ḥullin* in the Temple City, according to the Temple Scroll, states:

> You shall not eat the flesh of an ox [or a sheep] or a goat within my city—which I consecrate to put my name there within it—which is not to enter my temple; and they shall slaughter (it) there, and throw its blood on the base of the altar of burnt offering; and its fat they shall burn. (lii.19–21)

The author of the Temple Scroll held the view that *ḥullin* was forbidden when the Israelites were in the wilderness, and for the same reason it is not permitted to eat *ḥullin* in Jerusalem. The same view was shared by the author of *Miqtsat Maʿasei ha-Torah* (4Q 394–399), who writes:

> [for the sons] of the priest should [take care] concerning all [these] practices, [so as not to] cause the people to bear punishment. [And concerning] that it is written: [if a person slaughters inside the camp, or slaughters] outside the camp cattle or sheep or goat. (B.25–28)

Leviticus[d] as well as the Samaritan Pentateuch and the Septuagint reflect the same view as that held later by R. Ishmael—that the law of *Leviticus* 17 deals with the slaughtering of *ḥullin* and meat eaten for enjoyment. This view is opposed to that of R. Akiba, who explained that *Leviticus* 17 deals with *qodashim*. We may assume that a version similar to Leviticus[d] was used as a source by the authors of the Temple Scroll and *Miqtsat Maʿasei ha-Torah*. Those authors thought that *Leviticus* 17 forbids slaughtering *ḥullin* near the altar. Thus during the time of the wilderness as well as in Jerusalem, *ḥullin* should be brought as offerings to the Temple. On the other hand, those authors thought that *Deuteronomy* 12 speaks about people who are living at a distance from the Temple, and therefore they are not obligated to bring their *ḥullin* to the Temple.

From reconstructing this fragment it seems that the phrase "This shall be to them a law for all time, throughout the ages" (v. 7) is probably missing from Leviticus[d]. In this way there is no contradiction between *Leviticus* 17 and *Deuteronomy* 12.

Leviticus[e] contains nine fragments from chapter 3, 19–22. The spelling is almost identical to that of the Masoretic Text and the Samaritan Pentateuch, and in the manuscript there is an omission that most likely is a result of homoeoteleuton.

Leviticus 19.36

Masoretic Text, Samaritan Pentateuch, and the Septuagint: "From the ears of the righteous stones of righteousness"

scroll: "Stones of righteousness"

The other differences are small and lack textual significance.

Leviticus[g] contains only one fragment from *Leviticus* 7.19–26. The spelling in it is more plene than in the Masoretic and Samaritan texts, and the name of God is written in paleo-Hebrew script.

From 6Qpaleo-Leviticus only one fragment remains, and in it are remnants from *Leviticus* 13:12–13, written in paleo-Hebrew script. The spelling in the scroll is plene (for example, *roʾsh* ["head," with the vowel spelled out] and *kutn(o)t* ["tunics," with the second vowel spelled out]). Since ample spacing exists which enables reconstruction of two additional letters to the word *avneṭ* ("belt") found in the Masoretic Text, the editor reconstructs the word *avneṭim* ("belts"), as in the Samaritan Pentateuch.

11Qpaleo-Leviticus[a] is written in paleo-Hebrew as well, and includes between six and nine lines from the last fourteen columns of the scroll of *Leviticus*. This is the longest scroll discovered in Qumran that is written in paleo-Hebrew. Of it there have survived fragments from chapters 4, 10–11, 13–22, as well as the entire text of chapters 22–27.

Following the publication of the edition by K. A. Mathews and D. N. Freedman, E. Puech identified a number of fragments that had not been identified by the editors and claimed that the original scroll contained twenty-three columns. In the text there is evidence of the use of a symbol for a passage that is out of place:

Leviticus 18.27
Samaritan Pentateuch, Masoretic Text: "The people of the land committed"
11Qpaleo-Leviticus[a]: "You, the people of the land, committed [and he was disgusted with them and said to you y]ou shall inherit their la[n]d."

This addition, taken from 20.23–24, does not fit the context, and has a harmonistic character, since the two passages deal with the abominations of the nations that were committed in the land. The copyist perceived the secondary character of the addition, and put a mark similar to a parenthesis, the antisigma, which is found in classical texts (similar to the upside-down *nuns* in the Masoretic Text before and after *Numbers* 10.35–36), at the end of the passage (after the word "their land").

In the scroll there are a large number of independent readings, some of them significant:

Leviticus 22.22
Masoretic Text, Samaritan Pentateuch: "Either a wart or eczema or a moist skin eruption"
11Qpaleo-Leviticus[a]: "Either a moist skin eruption or eczema or a wart"
Leviticus 26.24
Masoretic Text: "and I also went with you"
Samaritan Pentateuch: "and I too went with you"
11Qpaleo-Leviticus[a]: "and I went with you."

There are also a number of scribal errors in the scroll, which in part are a result of homoeoteleuton, such as the example of the omission of the words "and to his sons" in 17.2.

Masoretic Text, Samaritan Pentateuch: "To Aaron and to his sons and to . . ."
11Qpaleo-Leviticus[a]: "To Aaron and to . . ."

Although there are readings shared by the scroll and the other textual witnesses, the text of the scroll is not especially close to any one of those witnesses. There are a number of independent readings in it that are not attested in other witnesses to the text, but it is difficult to define them as having a unique character or particular *Tendenz*. It appears that the uniqueness of the scroll is in its being different from the other textual witnesses. It is possible that in this there is evidence of the existence of more than the three groups of textual witnesses that were known to us. According to E. Tov, the variance of the scroll is not surprising, since every ancient source is likely to contain elements found in the Masoretic Text, and/or the Samaritan Pentateuch and/or the Septuagint without having to come to typological conclusions regarding the nature of this source.

11QLeviticus[b] includes fragments from chapters 7–10, 14–15, and 25, and is written in a late Herodian hand (ca. 50 CE). It is written with plene spellings and has readings that agree with the Septuagint against the Masoretic Text in three cases, with the Masoretic Text against the Septuagint in three instances, and it has five unique readings.

The Hebrew Manuscript of *Leviticus* from Masada. During excavations conducted by Y. Yadin at Masada two copies of the *Book of Leviticus*, which were written on parchment, were found.

Leviticus[a] (Mas1a) was written in a formal Herodian script from the second half of the first century BCE, by a skilled scribe. The text of this fragment is identical to the Masoretic Text of *Leviticus* 4:3–9, except for the word "will pour" (written plene) as opposed to "will pour" (defective spelling) in the Masoretic Text (4.7).

From Leviticus[b] (Mas1b) forty-five fragments of different sizes have survived, some of them very small. The manuscript is dated to the later Herodian period—from the middle of the first century CE. The text of the scroll is identical to the Masoretic Text, including its spelling, and sections of *Leviticus* 8.31–11.40 are preserved in it. A number of corrections, which were most likely made by the scribe himself, are found in the scroll. The only difference is in the word "they" (*hemmah*, with the final form of *mem* in middle of the word). It appears that this evidences unobserved use of writing the letters *mem, nun, tsadi, pe(fe)*, and *kaf* in their initial and final forms. The similarity between the text of the scroll and the Masoretic Text extends to its division into sections.

In addition to the Hebrew copies of *Leviticus*, there are two manuscripts from Cave 4 of Qumran that contain a Greek translation of the book.

Greek Translations of Leviticus. From Septuagint Leviticus[a] an entire column has survived, which contains the Old Greek translation of *Leviticus* 26.2–16, and an additional tiny fragment (on which one can identify only the word *kai*). The manuscript dates from about the late second or first century BCE.

The spelling is more or less similar to the spelling of the Septuagint. This manuscript is approximately four hundred years earlier than the earliest manuscripts of the Old Greek translation of the book. There are fifteen textual differences between the scroll and the Septuagint (Göttingen edition), among them seven are unique, and three are attested in other manuscripts. These differences stem primarily from a free translation of a text similar or identical to the Masoretic Text. On account of the antiquity of its script and the evidence of its text, one can conclude that this is an authentic textual witness to the Old Greek translation.

Septuagint Leviticus[b] was copied on papyrus. Thirty-one identified fragments and sixty-six small unidentified fragments have survived from this manuscript. This is a text of the Septuagint of *Leviticus*, which should probably be dated to the first century BCE. The spelling is similar to the spelling of the Septuagint, and it contains a few scribal errors and scribal marks signaling the beginning of a paragraph. This manuscript too, like Septuagint Leviticus[a], is about four hundred years earlier than the oldest manuscripts of the Old Greek translation of the book.

Aramaic Translation of *Leviticus*. From Targum of Leviticus, two small Aramaic fragments were identified by J. T. Milik as an Aramaic translation of the *Book of Leviticus*. The manuscript is dated to the second century BCE. Vermes suggested the possibility that these small fragments were part of a larger composition, which contained in addition to a translation of sections of *Leviticus* liturgical sections or other texts. But there is no additional evidence that supports this suggestion. The fragments contain a translation of verses from *Leviticus* 16, in which there is a description of the Day of Atonement. A comparison of the fragments to the Masoretic Text and the other Aramaic translations of the *Book of Leviticus* shows that this is a literal translation, similar to Targum Onkelos and Targum Neofiti I. Of interest is the use of the word *kasi'*, from the root *ksy* (meaning to hide, cover) as a translation of the word *kaporet* as opposed to *kaporta'* in the rest of the Aramaic translations.

The Contribution of the Scrolls to the Textual Criticism of the *Book of Leviticus*. In the manuscripts of the *Book of Leviticus* discovered at Qumran the diverse nature of the different texts is especially prominent. Among the fragments that remain are manuscripts that are close in their text to the Masoretic Text, and in others readings that are found in the Septuagint and the Samaritan Pentateuch are attested. However, the evidence of many manuscripts, principally 11Qpaleo-Leviticus[a] (11Q1), in which are found a large number of independent readings that were unknown to us from other textual witnesses, is of special importance. Yet it is difficult to characterize these readings as having a common denominator or a certain tendency. Moreover, it is possible to explain a large portion of these readings as arising from different scribal errors, mainly as a result of parablepsis, etc. This variation raises the possibility that there may have been more than three groups of textual witnesses in the Second Temple period that were assumed prior to the discovery of the scrolls.

The picture from the other fragmented and limited discoveries is entirely different. The manuscripts from Masada are absolutely identical to the Masoretic Text. Combined with this are the textual discoveries from the caves of the Judean Desert, in which biblical scrolls from the period of the Bar Kokhba Revolt were found (fragments from the *Book of Leviticus* have not survived). These biblical fragments are also identical in their text to the Masoretic Text. It appears that we will not be mistaken if we conclude from this that during the first century CE a decision was made to choose the Masoretic Text as the normative one. During this stage, it appears the other versions were rejected, and this is the reason that only texts identical to that of the Masoretic Text were discovered in Masada and later on in the caves of the Judean Desert.

Additional evidence of great significance is the discovery of the two Greek manuscripts of the *Book of Leviticus* from Cave 4 and one manuscript containing an Aramaic translation of the book. The Greek manuscripts form the most ancient evidence of the original text of the Old Greek, and they precede by approximately four hundred years the oldest manuscripts of the Old Greek that we had possessed. The Aramaic translation, although it is limited in its scope, is the only evidence that we presently have of a literal Aramaic translation, similar in its character to Targum Onkelos and Targum Neofiti I.

BIBLIOGRAPHY

Baillet, M. "Textes des grottes 2Q, 3Q, 6Q, 7Q a 10Q." In *Les 'Petites Grottes' de Qumran* by M. Baillet, J. T. Milik, and R. de Vaux, pp. 56–57, 106. Discoveries in the Judaean Desert, 3. Oxford, 1962.

Barthélemy D., and J. T. Milik. "Lévitique et autres fragments en écriture 'Phénicienne'." In *Qumran Cave I*, edited by D. Barthélemy and J. T. Milik, pp. 51–54. Discoveries in the Judaean Desert, 1. Oxford, 1955.

Eshel, E. "4QLev[d]: A Possible Source for the Temple Scroll and Miqṣat Maʿase ha-Torah." *Dead Sea Discoveries* 2 (1995), 1–13.

Fitzmyer, J. A. "The Targum of Leviticus from Cave 4." *Maarav* 1 (1978–1979), pp. 5–23.

Freedman, D. N., and K. A. Mathews. *The Paleo-Hebrew Leviticus Scroll (11QpaleoLev)*. Winona Lake, Ind., 1985.

García Martínez, F., A. S. Van der Woude, and E. J. C. Tigchelaar. *Qumran Cave 11.II 11Q2–18, 11Q20–31*. Discoveries in the Judaean Desert, 23. Oxford, 1998.

Mathews, K. A. "The Leviticus Scroll (11QPaleLev) and the Text of the Hebrew Bible." *CBQ* 48 (1986), 171–207.

Milik, J. T. "Targum du Lévitique (4Q156)." In *Qumran Grotte 4, II 4Q128–4Q157*, edited by R. de Vaux and J. T. Milik, pp. 86–89. Discoveries in the Judaean Desert, 6. Oxford, 1977.

Puech, É. "Notes en marge de 11QPaléoLévitique: Le fragment L, des fragments inédits et une jarre de la grotte 11." *Revue biblique* 96 (1989), 161–183.

Qimron, E., and J. Strugnell. *Qumran Cave 4, V: Miqṣat Maʿasé ha-Torah*. Discoveries in the Judaean Desert, 10. Oxford, 1994.

Schiffman, L. H. "Sacral and Non-Sacral Slaughter according to the *Temple Scroll*." In *Time to Prepare the Way in the Wilderness: Papers on the Qumran Scrolls by Fellows of the Institute for Advanced Studies of the Hebrew University, Jerusalem, 1989–1990*, edited by D. Dimant and L. H. Schiffman, pp. 69–84. Leiden, 1995.

Skehan, P. W. "The Qumran Manuscripts and Textual Criticism." *Volume du Congrès, Strasburg 1956*. VTSup 4, Leiden, 1957.

Talmon, S. "Fragments of Two Scrolls of the Book of Leviticus from Masada" (in Hebrew). *Eretz Israel* 24 (1993), 99–110.

Talmon, S. "Hebrew Fragments from Masada." In *Masada VI: Yigael*

Yadin Excavations 1963–1965, Final Reports, pp. 36–50. Jerusalem, 1999.

Tov, E. "Textual Character of the Leviticus Scroll from Qumran Cave 11" (in Hebrew). *Shnaton: An Annual for Biblical and Ancient Near Eastern Studies* 3 (1978–1979), 238–244.

Tov, E. "4QLev[d] (4Q26)." In *The Scriptures and the Scrolls: Studies in Honor of A. S. van der Woude*, edited by F. García Martínez, A. Hilhorst, and C. J. Labuschagne, pp. 1–5. Leiden and New York, 1992.

Tov, E. "4QLev[c]," "4QLev[d]," "4QLev[e]," "4QLev[g]." In *Qumran Cave 4, VII: Genesis to Numbers*, edited by E. Ulrich and F. M. Cross, pp. 189–204. Discoveries in the Judaean Desert, 12. Oxford, 1994.

Tov, E. "4QLev[c,e,g] (4Q25, 26a, 26b)." In *Pomegranates and Golden Bells: Studies in Biblical, Jewish, and Near Eastern Ritual, Law, and Literature in Honor of Jacob Milgrom*, edited by D. P. Wright, D. N. Freedman, and A. Hurvitz, pp. 257–266. Winona Lake, Ind., 1995.

Ulrich, E. "The Greek Manuscripts of the Pentateuch from Qumran, including Newly-Identified Fragments of Deuteronomy (4QLXX-Deut)." In *De Septuaginta: Studies in Honor of John William Wevers on His Sixty-fifth Birthday*, edited by A. Pietersma and C. Cox, pp. 71–82. Mississauga, Ont., 1984.

Ulrich, E. "4QLXXLeviticus[a]," "pap4QLXXLeviticus[b]." In *Qumran Cave 4, IV: Paleo-Hebrew and Greek Biblical Manuscripts*, by P. W. Skehan, E. Ulrich, and J. E. Sanderson, pp. 161–186. Discoveries in the Judaean Desert, 9. Oxford, 1992.

Ulrich, E. "The Septuagint Manuscripts from Qumran: A Reappraisal of Their Value." In *Septuagint, Scrolls and Cognate Writings*, pp. 49–80. *Septuagint and Cognate Studies*, edited by G. J. Brooke and B. Lindars. Atlanta, 1992.

Ulrich, E. "4QLev-Num[a]," "4QLev[b]." In *Qumran Cave 4, VII: Genesis to Numbers*, edited by E. Ulrich and F. M. Cross, pp. 153–187. Discoveries in the Judaean Desert, 12. Oxford, 1994.

van der Ploeg, J. P. M. "Lev. IX, 23-X 2 dans un texte de Qumran." In *Bibel und Qumran: Festschrift H. Bardtke*, pp. 153–155. Berlin, 1968.

ESTHER ESHEL

Translated from Hebrew by Daphna Krupp

LIAR. The figure referred to variously by scholars as "the Liar" or "the man of the lie" (*ish ha-kazav*; 1QpHab ii.2; v.11; xi.[1]; CD xx.15); "the spouter (or preacher) of the lie" (*maṭṭif ha-kazav*; 1QpHab, 10.9; 1Q14 10.[2]; CD viii.13; xix.26), or "the scoffer" (*ish ha-lashon*; CD i.14) is widely held to be a rival expositor of the law to the Teacher of Righteousness. The legal dispute between the two is thought to have led to schisms, but the nature of these divisions is disputed. Some believe that the Liar was a competitor from within the Essene movement, given that it is prohibited to argue with the "men of the pit" (Rule of the Community 1QS ix.16–18), while others argue that he must have been outside the community.

Liar and Wicked Priest. While many scholars are convinced that the Liar is a different person from the Wicked Priest, the view that they are one and the same is not without its supporters. Geza Vermes sees the significance of these sobriquets in Jonathan Maccabee, whom the Qumran community originally considered to have been "called by the name of truth" before his heart became haughty (1QpHab viii.8–9). The implication is that he has become "wicked" because he has been teaching what the Qumran community considers to be lies. The author of Pesher Habakkuk, however, does not make this point.

The Liar may be distinguished from the Wicked Priest as scholars like Gert Jeremias and Hartmut Stegemann have done, but such a thesis is not without its problems. In Pesher Habakkuk (v.8–12) "the man of the lie" is identified as "the wicked one" of the biblical citation—a corollary to the equation of "the righteous one" with the Teacher of Righteousness. A similar identification of the wicked and righteous occurs in Pesher Psalms[a] (4Q171 1–10. iv.7–10), but here it is between the Teacher of Righteousness and the Wicked Priest. Both the Wicked Priest and Liar, if they are different figures, are "wicked" in the eyes of the Qumran community. Moreover, both are associated with some form of building program (1QpHab ix.16–x.13).

Proper caution must be exercised in distinguishing between different figures in the text on the basis of slight changes in terminology, since the scrolls themselves do not always maintain these perceived distinctions. The Liar is known as "the man of the lie" or "preacher of the lie," but the same figure seems to be referred to as "the scoffer" or "the man of scorn who dripped waters of lie over Israel" in the Damascus Document (CD i.14–17) Moreover, the term *scoffing* is also found in Pesher Isaiah[b], in connection with a certain group who are called "scoffers who are in Jerusalem" (4Q162 2.6).

The figurative description of a false prophet or teacher as one who "drips lies" is biblical (*Mi.* 2.6, 2.11; *Am.* 7.16, 9.13), and this term is also used to describe the curious figure of *tsav*, the enigmatic personification of judgment in *Hosea* 5.11, as "he who is the one who drips." In Hodayot[a] there are furthermore "scoffers of lie" (2.31 and 4.10) and "prophets of lie" (4.16).

Role of the Liar. As the Liar is understood by several scholars, he is the rival of the Teacher of Righteousness on the matter of legal interpretation. Central to this understanding of the Liar is the passage in Pesher Habakkuk (1QpHab v.8–12) where the Teacher of Righteousness and his rival confront each other in the midst of their congregation. The precise translation and interpretation of the events recorded in this passage are disputed: Who are "the house of Absalom" and the men of their council, and what part, if any, did they play in the dispute between the two leaders?

One translation of the problematic lines 9 and 10 is "its interpretation concerns the house of Absalom and the men of their council who remained silent at the rebuke of the Teacher of Righteousness and did not help him against the man of the lie." This renders "the house of Absalom" (cf. *1 Mc.* 11.70, 13.11; *2 Mc.* 11.17) and its men as remaining guiltily neutral for not taking the side of the Teacher of Righteousness. The biblical lemma that precedes it similarly asks why there is silence when the righteous is being swallowed up by the wicked. If this is correct, then it would appear that the Liar reprimanded the Teacher of Righteousness, and this reprimand is a rejection of the law.

There are, however, good linguistic reasons for translating the verb *ndmw* in the passive, as "they were silenced," and the "rebuke" in the active sense (see Williamson). This would mean that the men of the house of Absalom were silenced at the Teacher's reprimand and thus did not help him against the Liar who rejected the law in the midst of their congregation. If this translation is to be preferred, then the Teacher of Righteousness is seen both to be correcting the men of the house of Absalom as well as resisting the teachings of the Liar.

The Liar was a halakhic teacher, and his teachings are polemically described in Pesher Habakkuk as having "rejected the Torah" (1QpHab v.11–12). In the Damascus Document (CD i.14–17) the liar is described as a scoffer who preached lies to Israel. With his teachings, he led many astray and they sought smooth things and twisted righteousness and justice beyond recognition. In Pesher Habakkuk the Liar likewise is said to have led many astray in the building of a city of vanity and in instructing them with "[pre]cepts of falsehood" (x.9–13). His followers are called "traitors" in Pesher Habakkuk (1QpHab ii.2–10) because they did not believe that the eschatological interpretation of the Teacher of Righteousness was divinely ordained.

[*See also* Absalom, House of; Pesher Habakkuk; Pesher Psalms; Teacher of Righteousness; *and* Wicked Priest.]

BIBLIOGRAPHY

Baumgarten, Joseph, and Daniel Schwartz. "Damascus Document (CD)." In *Damascus Document: War Scroll and Related Documents*, edited by J. H. Charlesworth, pp. 4–58. Tübingen, 1995.

Collins, John J. "The Origin of the Qumran Community: A Review of the Evidence." In *To Touch the Text: Biblical and Related Studies in Honor of Joseph A. Fitzmyer, S.J.*, edited by Maurya P. Horgan and Paul J. Kobelski, pp. 159–178. New York, 1989.

García Martínez, Florentino. "Qumran Origins and Early History: A Groningen Hypothesis." *Folia Orientalia* 25 (1988), 113–136. An analysis of the dispute between the Liar and the Teacher of Righteousness as key to the creation of a daughter Qumran community.

Horgan, Maurya P. *Pesharim: Qumran Interpretations of Biblical Books*. Catholic Biblical Quarterly Series, 8. Washington, D.C., 1979.

Jeremias, Gert. *Der Lehrer der Gerechtigkeit*, pp. 79–89. Göttingen, 1963. Seminal study that distinguishes the Liar from the Wicked Priest.

Knibb, M. A. *The Qumran Community*. Cambridge, 1987. Recommended commentary on some key Qumran texts.

Lim, Timothy H. "The Wicked Priests of the Groningen Hypothesis." *Journal of Biblical Literature* 112 (1993), 415–425.

Murphy-O'Connor, Jerome. "The Essenes and Their History." *Revue biblique* 81 (1974), 215–244.

Stegemann, Hartmut. "Die Entstehung der Qumrangemeinde." Ph.D. diss., Rheinischen Friedrich-Wilhelms-Universität, Bonn, 1971.

Vermes, Geza. *The Dead Sea Scrolls: Qumran in Perspective*. Rev. ed. London, 1994.

Williamson, H. G. M. "The Translation of *1QpHab* V, 10." *Revue de Qumrân* 9 (1977), 263–265. Suggests that the House of Absalom was reduced to silence by the reprimand of the Teacher of Righteousness.

TIMOTHY H. LIM

LICHT, JACOB, (1922–1992), one of the earliest scholars of the Dead Sea Scrolls and one of the principal editors of the *Encyclopaedia Biblica*, was born in Vienna and raised in Brno, Czechoslovakia. He was educated in both the German and Czech cultures and in the renascent Hebrew-Zionist culture. In 1940, thanks to a student certificate, he immigrated to Erets Yisra'el and thus was saved from the horrors of the Holocaust. Licht served as professor of Bible at Tel Aviv University and was a member of the Israel Academy of Sciences and Humanities.

Upon the discovery of the Dead Sea Scrolls, Licht was invited to assist Professor Eleazar L. Sukenik in preparing the publication of the texts of the scrolls from Cave 1 at Qumran, which had been acquired by the Hebrew University of Jerusalem. [*See biography of Sukenik*.] Together with Sukenik and Nahman Avigad, Licht participated in all aspects of this task—reconstruction of the fragmented material, preparation of the Hebrew transcription, assistance in the English translation, et cetera (Licht, 1993). However, his major task involved the preparation of a philological and comparative commentary, and it was this that marked his role in the research and exegesis of the scrolls. In 1957 Licht published his critical edition of Hodayot[a] (1QH), which was his doctoral dissertation at the Hebrew University of Jerusalem, and in 1965 he published a critical edition of the Rule of the Community (1QS; hereafter, 1QRule of the Community). For this latter work he received the Warburg Prize. [*See* Hodayot; Rule of the Community.]

Licht focused upon the work of philological exegesis, concentrating most of his efforts on understanding the written text as such, and deliberately refrained from engaging in philosophical approaches based upon speculative theories. Licht's close adherence to the written text assisted him not only in the interpretation of words and ideas in context but also in tracing the styles of the authors of the scrolls and their literary approaches (Licht, 1957, pp. 10–17; 1965, pp. 25–38). The distinctions among the different stylistic features were useful in isolating the groups of laws gathered in 1QRule of the Community at different stages of its editing, which Licht saw as the result of an ongoing, developing process of legislation that required adjustment to changing conditions (Licht, 1965, p. 22). In his close reading of the text, Licht occasionally noted inner contradictions among the different testimonies of the sect of the *yaḥad*. However, he refrained from explaining the existence of these contradictions, preferring to recognize in them different approaches that were necessarily created during the course of everyday life, on the one hand, and the development of ideas, on the other.

Licht recognized the possible affinity between the sect of the *yaḥad* and that of the Essenes but refrained from making a definite identification between the two. On the other hand, he wrote extensively about the common ideological ground of the Qumran authors and a number of the noncanonical books in the postbiblical apocalyptic stream (Licht, 1965, pp. 83–85). Licht placed the apocalyptic vision of the future alongside the sect's doctrine of eras, thereby showing that both fit within one united system of postbiblical thought (1965).

Licht's adherence to the written word—of the Bible, of the extrabiblical writings, and of the Qumran scrolls—made it possible for him to distinguish among the different layers of the development of Jewish religious thought and the religious atmosphere that gradually changed over the course of generations (Licht, 1973). By doing so, he laid the groundwork for understanding the phenomenon of the *yaḥad* sect upon the stage of history and its religious and literary activities.

BIBLIOGRAPHY

WORKS BY LICHT

"The Attitude to Past Events in the Bible and in Apocalyptic Literature" (in Hebrew). *Tarbiz* 60 (1990), 1–18.

"From Brünn to Jerusalem" (in Hebrew). *Epistle of the Israel Academy of Sciences and Humanities* 12. Jerusalem, 1993.

"The Plant Eternal and the People of Divine Deliverance." In *Essays on the Dead Sea Scrolls: In Memory of E. L. Sukenik*, edited by C. Rabin, Yigael Yadin, and J. Licht, pp. 49–75. Jerusalem, 1961.

The Rule Scroll: A Scroll from the Wilderness of Judea. 1QS, 1QSa, 1QSb (in Hebrew). Jerusalem, 1965.

Testing in the Hebrew Scripture and in Postbiblical Judaism (in Hebrew). Jerusalem, 1973.

The Thanksgiving Scroll: A Scroll from the Wilderness of Judea (in Hebrew). Jerusalem, 1957.

"Time and Eschatology in Apocalyptic Literature and in Qumran." *Journal of Jewish Studies* 16 (1965), 177–182.

BILHA NITZAN

LIGHT AND DARKNESS play an important role in the Hebrew Bible. The creation begins with the separation between light and darkness, and the statement that light is "good." The sun, moon, and stars are set into the firmament to rule over day and night and to indicate the season, the years, and the festivals (*Gn.* 1.4,14–19). Light and darkness are also associated, respectively, with wisdom and folly, righteousness and wickedness, salvation and destruction (*Eccl.* 2.13–14; *Prov.* 2.13; *Is.* 2.3–5 *Am.* 5.18–20; etc.). Light is elsewhere a visible expression of God's glory (*Ezek.* 1.26–28; 10.4; Ps. 104.2). The Qumran literature builds on these foundations and makes use of the image of light and darkness mainly to convey its unerstanding of the cosmic order and its dualistic teachings. [*See* Determinism; Dualism.]

The Songs of the Sabbath Sacrifice (4Q403; 4Q405; 11Q17) locate the most perfect light in the heavenly sanctuary, where God, the glorious king, is served by radiant angels and spirits, the most prominent among them being "gods of light." In a liturgical work the light of God's dwelling is not separated from darkness, contrary to what happens in the cosmos (4Q392 1.4–7). At Qumran great attention is paid to this cosmic division of light and darkness, and especially to the monthly phases of the moon and to the yearly course of the sun, which are detailed in works such as Jubilees[a,c–g] (4Q216, 4Q218–222), Astronomical Enoch[a–d] (4Q208–211), and Phases of the Moon (4Q317). An archeological witness to this is an astronomical instrument that measures the solstices and equinoxes, the horizontal position of the sun at each season, the fraction of the days according to seasonal hours, etc. The complex balance between light and darkness and their respective luminaries is understood as a manifestation of the knowledge, strength, and wisdom of the "God of lights" who had set their permanent laws (1QHodayot[a] 1QH[a] ix.10–12; xxiii 1–3; Liturgical Prayers, 1Q34 3.ii.1–4; War Scroll, 1QM x.11, Daily Prayers[a], 4Q503 13–16; 29–32; 11QPsalms[a], 11Q5 xxvi.9–15). Therefore, the turning points of days and nights are the most appropriate times for prayers and blessings (Rule of the Community, 1QS x.1–10; 1QHodayot[a] 1QH[a] xx.4–11; Daily Prayers 4Q503, 1–6; 10–11; 33–36; 39; 48–50; compare Josephus *The Jewish War* 2. 128; Philo *On the Contemplative Life* 27; 89); feasts and festivals, as well as priestly rosters, are also linked to the calendar (cf. Calendrical Document A–H, 4Q320–330).

Humanity, in God's mysterious design, is divided between "sons of light" and "sons of darkness" (Rule of the Community, 1QS 1.9–11; iii.13; and so forth). The two ethical spheres of light and darkness are the respective domains of a spirit or Prince of lights and of an Angel of darkness, heading heavenly hosts and having dominion over human beings, the first "over all sons of justice" who "walk in the paths of light," the second over "sons of deceit" who "walk in paths of darkness" (Rule of the Community, 1QS iii.17–25; cf. War Scroll, 1QM xiii.1–6, 9–12; Berakhot[a], 4Q286 7 ii.1–5; Apocryphal Psalms[a], 11Q11 i.5–6; iii.8–12; iv.4–13; and so forth). Depending on the time of his conception or birth, each individual inherits various parts of light and darkness; hence everyone partly belongs to "evil humankind," to "the assembly those who walk in darkness" (Rule of the Community, 1QS xi.9–10; cf. 1Q Hodayot[a], 1QH[a] xx.24–25). But God discloses his light to those whom he favors, and he makes them know "the great plans of his intellect"; he illuminates their hearts "with the discernment of life," through a spirit of truth, and through their gathering in a community of salvation around inspired teachers and priests who are also instrumental in their enlightenment. A model for them is the great figure of David, praised for having been "wise, a luminary like the light of the sun, learned, knowledgeable, and perfect in all his paths before God and men" (Rule of the Community, IQS ii.3–4; iii.7; iv.2; xi.3; Damascus Document, CD xiii.11–12; 1QHodayot[a], 1QH[a] xii.5–6.23–27; xxiii.2 11–12; Rule of the Blessings, 1Q28b iv.27–28; Barkhi Nafshi[a], 4Q434 1.1–8; Testament of Qahat, 4Q452 i.1–3; Daily Prayers, 4Q503 7–9; 51–55; Psalms,[a] 11Q5, xxvii.2–4). On the contrary, the sons of darkness who follow Belial's leadership have their heart hardened and behave with evil cunning (Rule of the Community, 1QS iv.11; War Rule, 1QM xv.9–10; Wiles of the Wicked Woman, 4Q184 4–7; etc.).

The members of the community are watchful of false converts who, while joining, still continue to regard "darkness as paths to light" (1QS ii.16; iii.8). In addition, the sons of light are threatened by Belial, who dominates during periods of wickedness and, together with the spirits of his lot, attempts to trap them and cause them to fall (1QS iii.24; Damascus Document, CD v.18; Catena[a], 4Q177 ii.7; iii.8; Florilegium, 4Q174 1–3 7–9; Aramaic Levi[a], 4Q213 5 iii.8–10; Narrative, 4Q462 9–10). The torments experienced by the faithful are expressed with various metaphors, including that of light and darkness: "The light of my face has become gloomy with deep darkness, my radiance has changed into gloom" (1QH[a] xiii.32). A way to resist the assaults of evil spirits is to proclaim against them the grandeur of the radiance of God (Songs of the Sage[a] [4Q510] 1.4–7). When finally delivered from his enemies, the righteous states that God, his everlasting luminary, has caused his light to shine from darkness or that he made him "radiant with sevenfold light" (1QH[a] xi.3; xv.24–25; xvii.24).

In spite of opposition, the sons of light will shine until the completion of the periods of darkness; then, on the day appointed by God, there will take place an eschatological battle between both camps, along with their respective angelic counterparts, the result of which will be the complete destruction of wickedness, with "no escape for the sons of darkness" (1QM; iii.6–9; xiii.14–16; xiv.16–18; xv–xix). On the contrary, God's lot is promised peace and blessing, while the covenant of Israel will "shine with joy" (1QM xvii. 6–7). This double expectation is found in other documents as well, with minor variations: "Evil will disappear in front of justice as darkness disappears in front of light . . . and justice will be revealed like a sun which regulates the world" (Mysteries [1Q27] i 5–6); "The angel of his truth will ransom all the sons of light from the power of Belial. . . . Belial and all the men of his lot will be finished for ever, and all the sons of light will be reunited" (4Q177 iv.12–16); "The sons of light] will go to the light, to [everlasting] happiness, [to rejoicing;] and all the sons of dark[ness will go to the shades, to death] and to annihilation" (Visions of Amram[f]? [4Q548] 12–14; cf. also Hodayot[b] from Cave 4 at Qumran, hereafter 4QHodayot[b] [4Q428] 7.ii.4–5). The fate of Belial's lot is also described as "being sentenced to the gloom of everlasting fire," "humiliation of destruction by the fire of the dark regions," etc. (1QS ii.7; iv.13–14; 1QH[a] xiv.17–18; Sapiential Work A[a] [4Q418] 69.7). The followers of the spirit of truth are promised "a crown of glory with majestic raiment in eternal light," joy "in eternal light," or a place "in the everlasting residence, in the light of dawn for ever" (1QS iv.6–8; 1QH[a] xxi.13–15; Aramaic Levi[d], 4Q541 24.ii.5–6). The deliverance of God's people is depicted elsewhere as a mission of atonement and enlightenment by an eschatological priest: "His eternal sun will shine and his fire will burn in all the ends of the earth; above the darkness his sun will shine. Then, darkness will vanish from the earth, and gloom from the globe . . . " (Aramaic Levi[d], 4Q541 9.2–5).

Because it is experienced at various levels in the daily life of every human being, the separation of light and darkness provided the Qumranites with a powerful and multifaceted means to conceive and express some of their basic doctrines, as was also the case for other groups in Judaism, Gnosticism, and Christianity (e.g., the *Gospel of John*) during the same period and later on up to modern times.

BIBLIOGRAPHY

Aalen, Sverre. "ʾwr." In *Theological Dictionary of the Old Testament*, edited by G. Johannes Botterwick and Helmer Ringgren, translated by John T. Willis, vol. 1, pp. 147–167. Grand Rapids, Mich., 1977.

Mitchel, L. A., et al. "*ḥšk*." In *Theological Dictionary of the Old Testament*, edited by G. Johannes Botterwick and Helmer Ringgren, translated by John T. Willis, vol. 5, pp. 245–259. Grand Rapids, Mich., 1977.

Nötscher, Friedrich. "Licht und Finsternis." In *Zur theologischen Terminologie des Qumran-Texte*, pp. 92–148. Bonner Biblische Beiträge, 10. Bonn, 1956. A comprehensive study of the symbolic use of the notions of light and darkness in major texts from Qumran Cave 1 and in the Damascus Document.

JEAN DUHAIME

LITURGICAL TEXTS. *See* Psalms, Hymns, and Prayers.

LUKE, GOSPEL OF, the first volume of a two-volume work, Luke-Acts, which narrates the career of Jesus of Nazareth as the founder of Christianity.

The Gospel. The third gospel opens with a literary preface that identifies the programmatic concerns of the text (*Lk.* 1.1–4). The preface compares unnamed earlier works (verses 1–2) with the present work (verses 3–4). We can identify two of the predecessors: Q, the sayings gospel, and *Mark*. It is quite likely that the author knew others. In contrast to these, the author claims to present a fuller and more reliable version of the apostolic tradition about Jesus. The *testimonia* of the early church tell us that the author was Luke, a second-generation Christian and the sometime traveling companion of Paul (e.g., the Muratorian Canon 2–8, 34–39; Irenaeus, *Against Heresies* 3.1.1, 3.14.1; and the Old Independent Prologue or Anti-Marcionite Prologue). However, the preface suggests that the author was a third-generation Christian. Most place the author in the last twenty years of the first century CE. The geographical locale of the author and readers is impossible to pinpoint since the text was probably addressed to more than one community. The literary nature of the prologue is important for understanding the work and its relationship to the finds in the Judean Desert: it is the only text in the New Testament that self-consciously situates itself in the Greco-Roman world by means of a literary preface.

At the same time, the narrative is unabashedly Jewish. It begins with an infancy narrative (*Lk.* 1.5–2.52) that has an unmistakable Semitic ambience. A sketch of the career of John the Baptist and Jesus' appointment as the kingdom-proclaimer (*Lk.* 3.1–4.13) serves as an introduction to Jesus' Galilean ministry (*Lk.* 4.14–9.50). The most distinctive structural feature of the gospel is the long travelogue in which the author places Jesus' teaching in thematic groupings (*Lk.* 9.51–19.27). The Jerusalem ministry (*Lk.* 19.28–21.38) sets up the passion narrative that emphasizes the political charges against Jesus (*Lk.* 22.1–23.58). Unlike Mark, who championed the death of Jesus, this gospel accentuates Jesus' entrance into glory by narrating a series of resurrection appearances and an ascension (*Lk.* 23.50–24.52).

Luke and the Dead Sea Scrolls. The third gospel thus has a paradoxical relationship to the world of Qumran: it wants to claim continuity with Judaism and, at the same time, it opens up Christianity to the larger world by engaging it on its own terms. The paradox is complicated by the creation of the apostolic tradition. Christianity was not simply a variation of Greek-speaking Judaism, but a movement in the process of acquiring its own identity.

The similarities with the Dead Sea Scrolls belong to the effort to anchor Christianity within Judaism. Yet the author clearly knew Judaism in several different forms, including the Septuagint, Greek-speaking Judaism, and Jewish Christianity. The echoes of the Dead Sea Scrolls must therefore be heard as one tradition among several. For the sake of convenience, I will cluster these reverberations into three groups.

The first is the general atmosphere of the earliest sections. As previously noted, the infancy narrative creates a Jewish milieu. While this world depends heavily on the Septuagint, the canticles of Mary and Zechariah (1.46b–55, 68–79) remind the reader of the hymns among the scrolls (1QH^a and the hymns in 1QM; e.g., *Lk.* 1.52 and 1QM xiv.10–11; *Lk.* 1.71 and 1QM xviii.11–12). The heavy Semitic cast of the hymns suggests that they were taken over from earlier Jewish Christians who composed them in much the same spirit as the Covenanters at Qumran did their hymns. The scrolls have even helped to clarify a line in another canticle. Scholars were divided over whether "goodwill" in "people of goodwill" (*Lk.* 2.14) referred to humans or to the deity. The discovery of the same phrase at Qumran where it means "people whom God favors" (1QH^a iv.32–33 [xvii.20–21], xi.9 [iii.8]) has settled the debate. Another section of the narrative that is redolent of Qumran is the presentation of John the Baptist (e.g., 3.1–20; cf. *Lk.* 3.4 and 1QS viii.12–16; *Lk.* 3.16 and 1QS iv.20–21). However, we must not overdraw this portrait since *Luke*, like the *Jewish Antiquities* of Josephus (18.116–19), presents John more as a Hellenistic moral reformer (cf. 3.10–14) than as an apocalyptic prophet.

A second area is the interpretation of scripture. Like the author of *Luke* (24.44), the Essenes know a threefold division of sacred texts (4QMMT 95). Both understand the scriptures eschatologically although the specific vantage point is different: The Christian author can look back to Jesus as the interpreter, whereas the Essenes understood the Teacher of Righteousness to be the interpreter and still anticipated the Messiah(s) (1QpHab vii.4–5). Their hermeneutics are quite similar as the introductory formulas for citations demonstrate (e.g., *Lk.* 3.4 and 4QFlor 1.15; *Lk.* 4.10 and CD xi.20; *Lk.* 7.27 and 4QFlor 1.16). At times they even cite the same texts (*Is.* 40.3 in *Lk.* 3.4 and 1QS viii.14; *Is.* 61.1–2 in *Lk.* 4.18; 7.22 and 1QH^a xviii.14 [x.12]; 11QMelch ii.18–19; cf. 4Q521 2).

The third area comprises the speculations about eschatological figures. The most impressive is *Luke* 1.32 and 35 and the Aramaic Apocalypse (4Q246) ii.1–8, which share four phrases, three virtually identical. Each claims the figure "will be great," "will be called son of most high," "will be called son of God," and will have an everlasting reign. While *Luke* clearly refers to the Messiah, the Aramaic Apocalypse could refer to a number of different figures: a historical figure such as Alexander Balas, the Messiah, the anti-Christ, an angelic figure such as Melchizedek, or Israel, collectively. At a minimum, the two texts demonstrate that early Christians applied known eschatological formulas to Christ. Another example is the common use of *Isaiah* 61.1–2 in the eschatological speculations of both groups: *Luke* 4.18 and 7.22 use it to refer to Jesus; one of the Hodayot (1QH[a] xviii.14 [x.12]) alludes to it as the revelation of God's truth to the speaker (the Teacher of Righteousness?); Melchizedek (11QMelch) applies it to the "messenger" of *Isaiah* 52.7, who appears to be Melchizedek; the Messianic Apocalypse (4Q521) ii.12 associates *Isaiah* 61.1 with God's activities in the messianic era. While there are variations, they all point to the association of *Isaiah* 61.1–2 with the announcement of eschatological salvation.

These similarities should not lead us to think that the Covenanters who produced the Judean Desert documents represent the primary source for Judaism in *Luke*. We have one text that may record a polemic against the Essenes. Luke insists that Christians include "the poor, the crippled, the lame, and the blind" (*Lk*. 14.13, 21) and warns against preferential seating arrangements (*Lk*. 14.7–11, 22.24–26). The Essenes, as described in the Qumran texts, explicitly exclude three of the former (1QSa ii.5–9; 1QM vii.4–6) and have rigid rules for seating arrangements (1QSa ii.11–22). Whether or not these statements were addressed against the Essenes at an earlier stage of the tradition, they represent the values of Jesus and his tradition, which stand at the heart of *Luke*.

Perhaps it is appropriate that a fragment of *Luke* has been found at Khirbet Mird (*Lk*. 13.1, 3–4) in the Judean wilderness. It represents a full circle for *Luke*, which used the traditions from Judea to create a portrait of a branch of Judaism that became Christianity in the larger world and then returned to the homeland.

BIBLIOGRAPHY

Braun, Herbert. *Qumran und das Neue Testament*. 2 vols. Tübingen, 1966. Volume 1 works through the parallels systematically in the order of the text of *Luke*; volume 2 deals with the material thematically.

Brown, Raymond E. *The Birth of the Messiah: A Commentary on the Infancy Narratives in the Gospels of Matthew and Luke*. Anchor Bible Reference Library. New York, 1993. Indispensable discussion of *Luke* 1–2, especially the canticles.

Collins, John J. *The Scepter and the Star: The Messiah of the Dead Sea Scrolls and Other Ancient Literature*. New York, 1995. Important treatment of messianic texts.

Fitzmyer, Joseph A. *The Gospel according to Luke*. 2 vols. The Anchor Bible 28–28A. Garden City, N. Y., 1981–1985. The best critical commentary on *Luke* by an expert on the New Testament and Dead Sea Scrolls.

Gregory E. Sterling

M

MACHAERUS. The fortress of Machaerus is located on an isolated spur of the Jordanian plateau in the southern region of Madaba, between the Wadi Zarqa Maʿin and the Wadi Moujib-Arnon. It is geographically connected to the hot springs of Baaru to the north (today Hammamat Maʿin) and the hot springs of Callirhoe to the west on the shore of the Dead Sea (present-day Zara).

The name of the fortress, known by the Arabs as Qalʿat al-Mishnaqa, was preserved in the ruins of the Roman-Byzantine village of Mechaberos-Mekawer, situated on the high plateau in front of the fortress (Georgii Cyprii *Descriptio*, n. 1082; Cyrilli *Vita Sabae*, 82). U. Seetzen registered the name of the village in 1807 and correctly identified the site, which was later visited by explorers. August Strobel drew a topographical map of the ruins in 1973, focusing on the Roman siege works with the *vallum* (siege wall), the camps, and the towers still clearly visible. Archaeological excavations were directed by V. Corbo on behalf of the Studium Biblicum Franciscanum between 1978 and 1981. Restoration work, followed by the resumption of archaeological research, was conducted in 1992 and 1993 by the Jordanian Ministry of Tourism and Antiquities.

According to Josephus, Alexander Jannaeus chose this naturally defended site, building the fortress on the southern boundary of the eastern province of Jewish Perea as a protection against the Nabateans of Petra (*The Jewish War* 7.6.2). It was demolished by Gabinius (57 BCE). Aristobulus and his son Alexander sought refuge among the ruins (*The Jewish War* 1.8.6). King Herod rebuilt the fortress (*The Jewish War* 7.6.2–3), which was inherited by his son Herod Antipas. In the fortress John the Baptist was thrown into prison and put to death (*Jewish Antiquities* 18.5.1–2). On the death of King Herod Agrippa I (44 CE), the fortress came under the direct control of the Roman army. It was held by the Zealots from the outbreak of the First Jewish Revolt (66 CE) until 72 CE (*The Jewish War* 2.18.6). In that year Lucilius Bassus besieged the fortress, took it, and destroyed it (*The Jewish War* 7.6).

Excavations have clarified the distinction made in Josephus's description between the upper city on the top of the mountain and the lower city built on the steep northern slope.

The structure constituting the first phase of the upper city has been identified as the Hasmonean fortress, but it has not yet been excavated. A later phase, possibly Herodian, was built above it and was differently aligned. The Herodian fortress is defended by four towers, three of which have been identified, and is divided into two main wings by a paved corridor stretching north to south. In the eastern wing, a central court possibly is related to the main entrance, and has thermae (baths) on the southern side and rectangular rooms on the northern side. The main feature of the central court of the western wing is a colonnaded peristilium with a possible double triclinium (reception or banquet hall) on the southern side. Both central courtyards covered a single water cistern. Columns and capitals of Doric and Ionic styles decorated with painted stuccoes found in the central cistern suggest a possible double order for the colonnade.

During the final phase of the occupation, possibly during the First Jewish Revolt, a polygonal defensive wall was built on the outer perimeter of the upper city. Two ovens on the mosaic floor of the *apoditerium* (disrobing room), a *miqveh* (Jewish ritual bath) and a poorly executed wall inside the north tower—the tower being the most exposed to the attack of the Roman legions—should be identified as traces of the Jewish revolt.

In the lower city, built on terraces inside a defensive retaining wall, only a few houses have been excavated. The city wall was defended on both sides by a tower. The northwest tower protected the opening of a large cistern hewn in the mountain.

The lower and upper city were connected to the high plateau on the east through an aqueduct 15 meters (49 feet) high, which diverted rainwater to the cisterns hewn in the northern slope of the mountain. A lower aqueduct served the same purpose for the cisterns at a lower height.

The fortress was razed to the foundation. The siege works built by the Roman legionaries are still well preserved: the *vallum*, with its camps and towers, which encircles the fortress; and the ramp, which was left unfinished because, Josephus relates (*The Jewish War* 7.6), the besieged surrendered. There is no evidence of a later occupation except for two coins of the Roman Provincia Arabia struck at the time of the Emperor Trajan.

[*See also* Alexander Jannaeus; John the Baptist.]

BIBLIOGRAPHY

Corbo, V. "La Fortezza di Macheronte. Rapporto preliminare della prima campagna di scavo: 8.09–28.10. 1978." *Liber Annus Studii Biblici Franciscani* 28. Jerusalem, 1978: 217–238.

Corbo, V. "Macheronte: La Reggia-Fortezza Erodiana. Rapporto preliminare alla seconda campagnia di scavo: 3.09–20.10. 1979." *Liber Annus Studii Biblici Franciscani* 29 (1979), 315–326.

Corbo, V. "La Fortezza di Macheronte (Al Mishnaqa). Rapporto preliminare alla terza campagna di scavo: 8.9.–11.10. 1980." *Liber Annus Studii Biblici Franciscani* 30 (1980), 365–376.

Corbo, V., and S. Loffreda. "Nuove Scoperte alla Fortezza di Macheronte. Rapporto preliminare alla quarta campagna di scavo: 7.9.–10.10. 1981." *Liber Annus Studii Biblici Franciscani* 31 (1981), 257–286.

Loffreda, S. *La ceramica di Macheronte e dell' Herodiun* (90 e.c–135 d.c). Studium Biblicum Franciscanum Collectio Maior. Jerusalem, 1996.

Piccirillo, Michelle. "Le monte della Fortezza di Macheronte (El-Mishnaqa)." *Liber Annus Studii Biblici Franciscani* 30 (1980), 403–414.

Piccirillo, Michelle. "Le antichita' oristiane del villaggio di Mekawer." *Liber Annus Studii Biblici Franciscani* 45 (1995), 293–318, tauv. 25–42.

Strobel, August. "Das römische Belagerungswerk um Macharus. Topographische Untersuchungen." *Zeitschrift des deutschen Palästina-Vereins* 90 (1974), 128–184.

MICHELLE PICCIRILLO

MAFJAR, WADI EL-. In a series of waterfalls west of Jericho, Wadi el-Mafjar spills into the Jericho plain. During the Hasmonean era, the Fortress of Duk or the Fortress of Dagon was built north of the stream where Simon (Hasmonean) was murdered in 135 BCE [*See* Simon (Hasmonean).] Near the openings of several caves on the northern bank of Wadi el-Mafjar, a monastery named Duka was built during the fourth century CE. This was the second monastery built in the Judean Desert by Saint Chariton. Since the Middle Ages, the monastery has been associated with the tradition in the New Testament that Satan had tempted Jesus for the duration of forty days; therefore, the monastery is named Karantel, for the forty days Jesus stayed there (see *Lk.* 4.1–13, Mt. 4.1–11, and 1.12–13). In comparison to the caves on the northern bank that are part of the Karantel monastery, the caves south of the stream remained more or less in their natural state. In 1979 the Israel Cave Research Center explored the southern bank of Wadi el-Mafjar. The discovery in 1984 of a wooden comb characteristic of the Bar Kokhba era prompted my excavations in 1986 [*See* Bar Kokhba Revolt.] During this excavation, fragments of four different documents from the Bar Kokhba era and an almost complete document, dated to the fourth century BCE according to paleographic considerations, were discovered. Because the name Avi'or is mentioned in this document, the cave is called the Cave of Avi'or. At the end of 1993, excavation of Wadi el-Mafjar continued under the leadership of Hanan Eshel and B. Zissu. Fragments of twenty fiscal documents from the Bar Kokhba era were found below the Cave of Avi'or. Excavations were conducted in the adjacent Cave of the Sandal, situated approximately 300 meters (984 feet) south of the Cave of Avi'or, where additional finds from the Bar Kokhba era, among them two small fragments of economic documents written in Greek, were discovered.

Cave of Avi'or. The small cave known as the Cave of Avi'or is 25 meters (85 feet) deep. It has three openings, a low one, approximately 5 meters (16.4 feet) high above the natural terrace south of Wadi el-Mafjar, as well as two higher ones. From the high northern entrance a tunnel connects to the main hollow of the cave, which is located at its center. From this point, the tunnel continues into an inner chamber. It is impossible to stand erect in the Cave of Avi'or, except for the areas of the lower entrance and the high southern entrance. Finds date from the Chalcolithic period, the Middle Bronze Age, the Roman era (second century CE), the Mamluk dynasty (fourteenth century CE), 1948, and 1967.

The majority of the finds in the cave are from the Roman era. Thirty-eight disarticulated skeletons were found in the inner chamber. The skeletons were of men, women, and children who most likely choked to death when the Roman army discovered the cave and ignited a bonfire under it. The oldest person to escape to the Cave of Avi'or was sixty-five years old, and the youngest was a girl of three. Special significance is given to remnants of a studded sandal, meaning a Roman boot, found in the cave, since it illustrates nicely a tradition appearing in rabbinic literature that the Jews who fled to the caves at the end of the Bar Kokhba Revolt used this type of sandal. The ceramic and organic findings discovered in the cave verify that the refugees fleeing to the cave did not prepare sufficient provisions and were therefore compelled to gather wild fruit, which ripens in the months of September and October, outside the cave. Consequently, it can be assumed that the people of Jericho escaped to the caves west of their city in October of the year 135 CE like the people of Herodian who fled to Wadi Murabba'at at the same time, since the latest document. Fragments of four economic documents from the Bar Kokhba era were found in the Cave of Avi'or: two in Aramaic and two in Greek. One of the Aramaic documents is a loan contract in which Neḥunia ben ha-Levi borrowed an amount of money he was obligated to repay in four installments. An additional Aramaic document describes the sale of agriculture goods. A Greek certificate document mentions a man named Yehudah, while the fourth document is a receipt for the sale of seeds. [*See* Deeds of Sale.] The documents were discovered in a crevice in the cave's floor and in the terrace built above the lower entrance.

A document from the fourth century BCE was discovered above the Roman documents on this terrace. This document was written on both sides of the papyrus and contains two lists of Jewish names. Written beside each name is a sum of money in shekels, quarters, and *meʿah*s (ancient coins). Several of the names are rare while others are typical of the Second Temple era. [*See* Names and Naming.] At the end of each side is a summary. On side A, the sum is twenty-one shekels, while the sum on side B most likely reads: "all shekels twelve . . . the remaining shekels eight, coins of small change two." Because some of the names are mentioned on both sides of the papyrus and the sum on side B is always lower than the sum on side A, one can assume that sums of money given as loans were written on side A, while the repayments of these were written on side B. Since the documents and other finds were discovered on the terrace in inverted stratigraphy, meaning that the finds from the Roman era were discovered under finds from the fourth century BCE, one can assume that the terrace was built during the Mamluk era.

Because all the documents were discovered in the cave, in the terrace, or in a crevice in the floor, it was thought that it was possible that in the Mamluk era the cave was clean of soil (excluding the soil in the crevice and on the terrace), and therefore in 1993 excavations were carried out beneath the lower entrance. During this excavation a group of approximately twenty fragments of economic documents written on papyri from the Bar Kokhba era were discovered. [*See* Economic Life.] Four are in Greek, and the remainder are in Aramaic. The most complete among them is an Aramaic text documenting the sale of a date crop by a lawyer for an orphan.

Cave of the Sandal. This is a small cave, similar to the Cave of Aviʾor. Approximately 300 meters (98 feet) south of the Cave of Aviʾor, the Cave of the Sandal has a single entrance, the height of which is approximately 8 meters (26 feet) above its terrace. Its length is roughly 15 meters (49 feet). The Chalcolithic period and Early Bronze Age are represented as is the Roman era: the cave served as a burial place in earlier periods and as a place of refuge during the Roman era. Twelve skeletons, seven of them dated to earlier periods, while the five others are most likely from the Roman era, were discovered in the cave. It can be assumed that those who hid in this cave met a similar death to those in the Cave of Aviʾor, suffocating from the smoke of a fire set by the Roman army after they found the cave. The finds from the Bar Kokhba era include pottery, as well as two complete oil lamps and remnants of glass vessels. [*See* Glassware; Pottery.] Likewise, parts of leather sandals, processed leather, ropes strings, and parts of baskets and mats were discovered. [*See* Basketry; Leather Goods.] The metal finds include coins and jewelry, consisting of a pair of gold rings, a gold earring, and a silver makeup spoon. [*See* Jewelry; Numismatics.] Twenty-six silver and bronze coins were discovered in the cave, the earliest among them is a silver dinar from the days of Vitellius from the year 69 CE, and the latest are dinars from the days of Hadrian. Especially interesting is a collection of six bronze coins with counter marks of the Tenth Legion. Two torn fragments of papyri with Greek letters were found at the entrance to the cave.

[*See also* Archaeology.]

BIBLIOGRAPHY

Eshel, Esther, and Hanan Eshel. "Fragments of Two Aramaic Documents that Were Brought to the Abiʾor Cave during the Bar Kokhba Revolt" (in Hebrew). *Eretz-Israel* 23 (1992), 276–285.

Eshel, Hanan, and Hagai Misgav. "A Fourth Century BCE Document from Ketef Yeriho." *Israel Exploration Journal* 38 (1988), 158–176.

Eshel, Hanan. "How I Found a Fourth-Century B.C. Papyrus Scroll on My First Time Out." *Biblical Archaeology Review* 15/5 (1989), 44–53.

Eshel, Hanan, and Boaz Zissu. "Ketef Jericho, 1993." *Israel Exploration Journal* 45 (1995), 292–298.

Kislev, M. E. "Vegetable Food of Bar Kokhba Rebels at Abiʾor Cave near Jericho." *Review of Palaeobotany and Palynology* 73 (1992), 153–160.

HANAN ESHEL

Translated from Hebrew by Daphna Krupp

MAGHARIANS. Named after the Arabic term meaning "people of the caves" (*maghār* means "cave"), the Magharians are described as a pre-Christian Jewish sect by the tenth-century Karaite Jew Yaqub Qirqisani. Some modern scholars prefer to date the Magharians to the medieval period. Although Qirqisani understands the name to mean that "their books were found in a cave," it is not clear whether in the distant past the Magharians themselves found books in a cave or their books were recovered from a cave in later times. Qirqisani also mentions that among these were the book of the "Alexandrian," who has been identified by some scholars as Philo, and a *Sefer Yaduʿa* (or *Yadoʿa*), the identification of which is problematic.

One of two primary distinguishing features of the Magharians is a calendar the months of which begin with the appearance of the full moon. The Muslim scholar al-Bīrūnī (973–1048) suggests that the Magharians observed both Roʾsh ha-Shanah and Passover only on a Wednesday, since that was the day of the week on which the sun and moon were created. The other distinguishing feature is the idea of the existence of a mediating angel used to explain anthropomorphisms in the Bible, thereby preserving the ultimate transcendence of God. This angel was described by the Muslim heresiographer al-Shahrastānī (d. 1153) as the creator of the world who acted as God's "viceroy" and "elect" on earth and may reflect possible Gnostic connections. Both Qirqisani and al-Shahrastānī connect this point of Magharian theology with that of the ninth-century Karaite Binyamin ben Mosheh Nahawendi, who held a similar view. Both authors also attribute ascetic tendencies to the Magharians.

Even before the discovery of the Dead Sea Scrolls the Magharians were identified by some scholars with the Essenes, but afterward they were explicitly identified as the Essene-Qumran community based upon the following: the association with caves; the approximate dating of the sect by Qirqisani and al-Shahrastānī to the first century BCE; the identification of the Alexandrian as Philo, whose description of the Therapeutae in *The Contemplative Life* has been thought to describe the Essene-Qumran community; the purported similarities of the Magharian calendar to the calendar of *Jubilees* and other calendars seemingly used by the Qumran community; and the association of the Magharian creator-angel with dualism in the angelology of the scrolls.

Scholars also have identified the Magharians as a link between the Dead Sea Scrolls and medieval sectarian phenomena, postulating that as a medieval sect their ideology was based upon manuscripts found in a cave in the vicinity of Qumran, as reported by Timotheus, the ninth-century Nestorian Catholicos of Seleucia-Baghdad. It is further suggested that the Magharians influenced the development of Karaism, especially by those who identify the Magharians and Karaites as medieval continuators of the Essenes. Magharian dualism and the doctrine of a mediating angel support a Gnostic identification, either as a pre-Christian sect or as a Jewish Gnostic sect in the medieval Islamic world.

BIBLIOGRAPHY

Bammel, Ernst. "Höhlenmenschen." *Zeitschrift für die neutestamentliche Wissenschaft* 49 (1958), 77–88.

Erder, Yorham. "The Observance of the Commandments in the Diaspora on the Eve of the Redemption in the Doctrine of the Karaite Mourners of Zion." *Henoch* 19 (1997), 175–202. Identifies the Magharians specifically as the Dead Sea Scroll community and cites other scholars who made this identification; scroll literature is primary source for medieval Karaism.

Fossum, Jarl. "The Magharians: A Pre-Christian Jewish Sect and Its Significance for the Study of Gnosticism and Christianity." *Henoch* 9 (1987), 303–344. Careful analysis of sources; identifies the Magharians as a Second Temple Jewish Gnostic sect.

Golb, Norman. "Who Were the Maġārīya?" *Journal of the American Oriental Society* 80 (1960), 347–359. Standard overview of the sources and critical problems; understands the Magharians as an ancient Jewish sect.

Wasserstrom, Steven M. "Shahrastānī on the Maghāriyya." *Israel Oriental Series* 17 (1998), 127–155. Understands the Magharians as a medieval Jewish Gnostic sect.

Wolfson, Harry Austryn. "The Pre-Existent Angel of the Magharians and al-Nahāwandī." *Jewish Quarterly Review* 51 (1960–1961), 89–106. The Magharians began as a Judaized pagan syncretism, became a Christian Gnostic sect, and ended up as a medieval Arabized Jewish Gnostic sect influencing the ninth-century Karaite Binyamin ben Moshe Nahawendi.

FRED ASTREN

MAGIC AND MAGICAL TEXTS. Though the Qumran community knew of the biblical prohibition against magic (11Q19 lx.16–21; cf. *Dt.* 18.9–14), both sectarian and nonsectarian texts from the Judean Desert prove that, like most of their contemporaries, they believed in and practiced certain types of magic. These magic and magical texts concern two areas: exorcism, healing, and protection against demons (4Q510, 4Q511, 4Q560, 11Q11), and divination, augury, and prediction of the future, specifically through physiognomy (4Q186, 4Q561), zodiology and brontology (4Q318), and astrology (4Q186, 4Q318).

Proverbs(?). This very fragmentary text (4Q560) is an adjuration against demons, which attack pregnant women, cause various illnesses, and disturb sleep. Though the categories of demons listed are sometimes hard to identify, a complex demonology is clearly implied. Beelzebub, the prince of the demons, may be mentioned by name (4Q560 i.1). The text probably comes from a book of spells that contained a collection of such adjurations. A healer or exorcist would have copied an appropriate spell from the book onto leather, papyrus, or a thin sheet of metal and personalized it for a client by inserting his name. This text, encased in a small container, would then have been worn as an amulet or buried in a suitable spot in a house (e.g., at the threshold). Proverbs(?) is almost certainly not itself the amulet, since the leather shows no signs of rolling or folding; the spell is a general charm to prevent demonic attack. Such amulets may be compared with *tefillin* and *mezuzot*, examples of which have been found at Qumran. It is unclear, however, whether the Qumran community considered *tefillin* and *mezuzot* as protection against demons or simply as the literal fulfillment of the injunctions in *Deuteronomy* 6.8–9.

Songs of the Sage$^{a–b}$. These texts (4Q510–511) contain fragments from an extensive collection of Hebrew songs of a strongly incantatory character. The songs were recited by the *maskil* ("sage"), who declares the power and majesty of God in order

> to frighten and ter[rify] all the spirits of the destroying angels and the spirits of the bastards, the demons, Lilith, the howlers and [the yelpers], those who strike suddenly to lead astray the spirit of understanding and to appall their [the members of the Qumran community's] heart and their so[uls] in the age of the dominion of wickedness. (4Q510 i.4–6)

The text is probably sectarian in origin and reflects the belief of the Qumran community that it is engaged through its liturgy in spiritual warfare against the forces of evil. The sage above all was charged with the spiritual defense of the community. These songs, which have a general apotropaic function, illustrate how fine is the line dividing prayer and hymn, on the one hand, from magical incantation, on the other. They recall such texts as the Rule of the Community from Qumran Cave 1 (hereafter, 1QRule of the Community; 1QS ii.4–9), the War Scroll (1QM xiii.4–5), Berakhot[f] (4Q280), Berakhot[a] (4Q286), and, possibly, Curses (5Q14), in which Belial and his minions (both demonic and human) are ritually damned. In the latter texts the curses are uttered by the priests and Levites, or even by the community as a whole, whereas Songs of the Sage[a–b] contain liturgies apparently falling specifically within the province of the sage and reflecting his particular role in the community. [*See* Songs of the Sage.]

Apocryphal Psalms[a]. Of these four incantations attributed to David, the first three are apocryphal, and the fourth is a version of Psalm 91, the use of which for protection against demons is well attested in rabbinic sources (J.T., *ʿEruv.* 10.11 [26c]; B.T., *Shev.* 15b). These four texts have been plausibly linked to the four "songs for singing over the afflicted" mentioned in the list of David's writings in Psalms[a] from Qumran Cave 11 (11Q5 xxvii.9–10). Though they share many motifs with Songs of the Sage[a–b], the situation they envisage is specific and not general. The outer defensive ring represented by Songs of the Sage[a–b] and Proverbs(?) has been breached. An evil spirit has successfully attacked a member of the community causing illness and has to be expelled. Apocryphal Psalms[a] contains the texts recited over the victim, perhaps by the sage, to effect the exorcism. The victim responds after each incantation with the formula "Amen, amen. Selah" (cf. 11Q11 v.14). The first three texts are hortatory in tone. The victim is exhorted to exert himself, to confront the evil spirt, and to remind it of the creative power of God, of the mighty guardian angels whom the righteous man can summon to his aid, and of the incarceration in the abyss that they can inflict. Consequently, an element of self-healing seems to be involved. The text also may contain a remarkable allusion to the physiognomy of Belial if "face" and "horns" are to be taken literally (11Q11 iv.6–7). An early mention of Solomon appears in the context of spells against demons (11Q11 i.3).

Apocryphal Psalms[a] may be compared with descriptions of healings in a number of literary narratives in the Dead Sea Scrolls. The most complex example is in the *Book of Tobit*, a novelistic work of nonsectarian origin but apparently popular at Qumran, in which Tobias expels the demon Asmodeus from his bridal chamber through a combination of prayer and magical praxis (the burning of parts of the heart and liver of a fish on ashes of incense). The warrior angel Raphael is also involved in the action, both in advising Tobias and in pursuing and binding Asmodeus (*Tb.* 6.16–17, 8.1–8; cf. 4Q196, 4Q197). [*See* Tobit, Book of.] A second example is the Genesis Apocryphon (1QapGen xx.16–29), in which Abraham prays and lays his hands on Pharaoh's head to expel an evil spirit that has afflicted him because he took Sarah into his house (cf. *Gn.* 12.10–20, 20.1–18). The third example is in the Prayer of Nabonidus (4Q242): Nabonidus is cured of an "evil ulcer" through praying to God and through the attentions of a Jewish "exorcist" who "forgave" his sin. The account of the healing is very compressed and unclear, and it has been suggested that, in fact, the word is "resident alien" rather than "exorcist."

Horoscope and Physiognomy/Horoscope. Both of these texts (4Q186 and 4Q561, respectively) are physiognomic texts that attempt to determine the character of a person's "spirit" from the color of his eyes, the sound of his voice, the shape of various parts of his body, and other observable physical features. Though the two texts are very similar, it is unlikely that one is a straightforward copy of the other. Horoscope is in Hebrew; Physiognomy/Horoscope is in Aramaic. Horoscope is in code; Physiognomy/Horoscope is not. Above all, Horoscope links physiognomy with astrology (the sign under which one is born determines the nature of one's spirit, and this in turn registers on one's physiognomy), whereas Physiognomy/Horoscope, at least in the preserved portions, does not. The divinatory science of physiognomy is well attested in antiquity, with an extensive literature in Akkadian, Greek, and Latin, but before the discovery of Horoscope and Physiognomy/Horoscope, the earliest Jewish texts on these subjects dated to the Middle Ages. The expressions "house of light" and "pit of darkness" in Horoscope link it with the "Treatise on the Two Spirits" in 1QRule of the Community (1QS iii.13–iv.26) and suggest that the Qumran community, like the Pythagoreans, applied physiognomic criteria to determine who was fit to join their group. [*See* Pythagoreans.] The astrological element in Horoscope fits in well with the community's broader knowledge of calendrical and astronomical lore. [*See* Horoscopes.]

Two narrative texts from Qumran also show an interest in physiognomy. The first, Elect of God (4Q534), describes the birth of a wonder child (probably Noah), whose special qualities and destiny are marked by certain physiognomic features. The reference to "lentils" (freckles) and "moles" is paralleled in medieval Jewish physiognomies. The second is the description of Sarah's beauty in the Genesis Apocryphon (1QapGen xx.2–8), where long, supple fingers are seen as a positive physical characteristic, in contrast to the negative characterization of short, fat fingers in Horoscope. [*See* Elect of God; Genesis Apocryphon.]

Zodiology and Brontology. This scroll (4Q318), a type of divinatory text, found also in Akkadian, Greek, and medieval Hebrew, interprets thunder as an omen portending important events. Zodiology and Brontology is complex. It opens with a table that assigns the moon to one of the twelve signs of the zodiac for each day of each month of the year. This table was then used in the second half of the work to explain the significance of thunder. If it thundered on a day when the moon was in a given sign, certain things, it was believed, would follow. For example, "If thunder occurs [when the moon is] in Gemini, [it portends] fear and distress caused by foreigners." Brontology did not necessarily involve astrology. The astrological element in Zodiology and Brontology is, therefore, significant, as is its use of the moon to link thunder to the zodiac. Josephus (*The Jewish War* 6.291) states that portents were eagerly studied in first-century CE Palestine and that the interpretation of omens required great skill. It may have been seen specifically as a priestly prerogative. An interest in portents at Qumran would also fit well with the community's eschatological perspective. It is a commonplace of apocalyptic literature that signs and wonders in the heavens would foretell the end of history.

Though the basic ideas and praxis of Qumran magic were common in antiquity, the high level of theological reflection behind the magic at Qumran is unusual. Magic is fully integrated into the Qumran worldview. The Qumran group knew and accepted the remarkable account of the origin of the demons from the bodies of the antediluvian giants (*1 En.* 7.2–6, 10.4–15, 15.8–16.2, cf. 4Q201, 4Q202, and 4Q204). *1 Enoch* lies behind the expression "the spirits of the bastards" in Songs of the Sage[a], and Apocryphal Psalms[a] alludes to the judgment of the angelic watchers from whose illicit union with women the giants were born. The Qumran community also may have known the parallel passage in *Jubilees* 10.1–14 and noted its claim that the angels taught Noah all the "medicines" to counteract the harmful activities of the demons. Behind magic at Qumran lies the dualism of the Two Spirits (1QS iii.13–iv.26). Good and evil are at present locked in a cosmic conflict. Ranged on one side are Satan/Belial/Melchiresha' and his servants—the demons and the wicked human opponents of the sect. Ranged on the other side are Michael/Melchizedek, the good angels and the members of the sect. The sect's spells, incantations, and prayers are weapons in its fight against the forces of darkness. The "Treatise on the Two Spirits," with its determinism, lies behind even the Qumran physiognomies. The magic is restrained: the praxis on the whole is not theurgic or mechanistic but relies heavily on petitioning divine agencies to intervene on the community's behalf. The Qumran community's reluctance to pronounce the names of God (1QS vi.27–vii.2, CD xv.1–2; and the letter *yod* as the abbreviation for YHVH in 4Q511) may have inhibited the development of the *nomina barbara* ("strange names") so characteristic of later Jewish magic and mysticism. This is not the magic of the marketplace, but a high-level, learned magic, comparable in sophistication to that found later in the Great Magical Papyrus of Paris, written in Greek, or in the Hebrew *Sefer ha-Razim* (Book of Secrets). Qumran magic probably formed part of the doctrine and tradition that the *maskil*, as the guardian of the community's spiritual and physical wellbeing, was expected to master and transmit.

BIBLIOGRAPHY

Alexander, P. S. "Incantations and Books of Magic." In *The History of the Jewish People in the Age of Jesus Christ*, vol. 3, revised and edited by G. Vermes, Fergus Millar, and Martin Goodman, pp. 342–379. A general survey of early Jewish magic, including that of the Qumran community.

Alexander, P. S. "Physiognomy, Initiation, and Rank in the Qumran Community." In *Festschrift for Martin Hengel zum 70. Geburtstag, Judentum*, vol. 1, pp. 385–394. Discusses the role that physiognomy may have played in the life of the Qumran community.

Nitzan, Bilhah. *Qumran Prayer and Religious Poetry*, pp. 227–272. Studies on the Texts of the Desert of Judah, 12. Leiden, 1994. Detailed literary analysis of 4Q510–511 and 11Q11.

Penney, Douglas L., and Michael O. Wise. "By the Power of Beelzebub: An Aramaic Incantation Formula from Qumran (4Q560)." *Journal of Biblical Literature* 113 (1994), 627–650. The best reading to date of the difficult text 4Q560 (proverbs?).

Wise, Michael O. *Thunder in Gemini and Other Essays on the History, Language and Literature of Second Temple Palestine*, pp. 13–50. Sheffield, 1994. Sets Zodiology and Brontology (4Q318) in the context of early brontological literature.

PHILIP S. ALEXANDER

MALACHI, APOCRYPHON OF. *See* Minor Prophets.

MALACHI, BOOK OF. *See* Minor Prophets.

MANASSEH. *See* Ephraim and Manasseh.

MANASSEH, KING. Noncanonical Psalms B includes a fragmentary composition entitled "A Prayer of Manasseh, King of Judah, when the King of Assyria Imprisoned Him" (4Q381 33.8). This superscription refers to the Judean king who ruled from approximately 687 to 642 BCE. The Qumran psalm recalls the unusual summary of Manasseh's reign in *2 Chronicles:* "Manasseh's deeds, his prayer to his God, and the words of the seers who spoke to him in the name of the Lord God of Israel are in the annals of the kings of Israel. His prayer, and how God received his entreaty, all his sin and faithlessness, the places where he built high places and set up the sacred poles and images, before he humbled himself, these are written in the records of the seers" (*2 Chr.* 33.18–19). In spite of Manasseh's alleged prayer and repentance, his legacy is quite mixed. According to *Kings*, Manasseh was the most wicked of the Judean kings, and exilic writers point to his sins to explain the Judean exile (e.g., *2 Kgs.* 21.10–15, 24.3–4; *Jer.* 15.4). Further elaborations of Manasseh's sins are described in *2 Baruch* (64– 65), *Martyrdom and the Ascension of Isaiah* (2.1–6), and rabbinic tradtions. Yet according to *Chronicles*, Manasseh was exiled to Babylon for his sins but repented and prayed to God and was returned to Jerusalem (*2 Chr.* 33.10–17).

The Qumran Prayer of Manasseh follows the predominantly positive view of Manasseh in later Jewish sources where the wayward king becomes a paradigm of the repentant sinner (for example, in Josephus, *Jewish Antiquities*, 10.40–46). Manasseh's prayer speaks of his "sins" and "multiplied guilt" (4Q381 33.9). Manasseh acknowledges that he "did not serve" or even "remember" God (line 11), and yet he looks to God's "salvation" and "saving presence" (lines 8–9). The Prayer of Manasseh also highlights the competing explanations for the Babylonian exile. In the tradition represented by *Kings*, the exile is blamed on one individual—Manasseh. In the other tradition, this individual becomes the paradigm for a whole nation that was exiled in sin and restored in repentance.

The language and style of the Qumran Prayer of Manasseh indicate a close relationship with biblical psalmody. Although the biblical story obviously was known, the Qumran text surprisingly betrays no direct dependence on *Chronicles*. It speaks only in the most general terms of Manasseh's "great sins" and "shame" and his "seeking salvation" from God. This seems especially unusual when compared with the Greek Prayer of Manasseh, which depends directly on *Chronicles*. The Greek Prayer is typical of apocryphal and pseudepigraphal literature, which draw heavily on biblical language, themes, and motifs. It also raises the question of whether the *Chronicles* tradition may actually be derived from the Qumran Prayer of Manasseh. Alternatively, the Qumran prayer and *Chronicles* draw on an earlier tradition.

[*See also* Sadducees.]

BIBLIOGRAPHY

Charlesworth, James H. "Prayer of Manasseh." In *Old Testament Pseudepigraph*, vol. 2, edited by James H. Charlesworth, pp. 625–637. Garden City, 1985. Introduction to and translation of the Greek Prayer of Manasseh.

Schniedewind, William M. "The Source Citations of Manasseh: King Manasseh in History and Homily." *Vetus Testamentum* 41 (1991), 450–461. Argument that the reference to Manasseh's prayer derives from an early source.

Schniedewind, William M. "A Qumran Fragment of the Ancient 'Prayer of Manasseh'?" *Zeitschrift für die Alttestamentliche Wissenschaft* 108.1 (1996), 105–107.

Schuller, Eileen M. *Non-Canonical Psalms from Qumran: A Pseudepigraphic Collection.* Harvard Semitic Studies, 28. Atlanta, 1986. Publication of noncanonical psalms.

WILLIAM M. SCHNIEDEWIND

MANICHAEANS were a religious community whose name stems from that of its founder, Mani, a third-century CE Mesopotamian gnostic sage. Due to its aggressive promulgation within both the Roman and Sassanian Empires, Manichaeism rapidly became a major rival of their indigenous religions, particularly Christianity. Vigorous state-supported suppression insured the demise of Manichaeism in the West by the sixth century. Similar persecutions by Zoroastrian and eventually Muslim zealots were less successful in the East, and Manichaeism survived as a viable religious identity within the Islamic realm well into the ʿAbbasid period. There also exists evidence that attests to its persistent survival even as late as the seventeenth century in China.

Sources for Manichaeism. Our knowledge of Manichaeism derives largely from two broad categories of data. First in importance are the extant remnants of authentic Manichaean writings recovered by archaeological investigations of sites in Egypt and in central Asia. Manichaean literature from Egypt survives in Syriac, Greek, and Coptic, with the latest evidence indicating that the Greek and Coptic works are local translations of earlier Syriac versions. The central Asian finds are rendered in a variety of Middle Iranian languages, as well as Old Turkic, and lexical clues once again point to a prior eastern Aramaic stratum. Given Mani's Mesopotamian roots, as well as the explicit statement of later tradent, that Mani composed the bulk of his writings "in Syriac," this is, on its surface, an unremarkable state of affairs, yet scholars have been surprisingly unappreciative of the implications of the Semitic linguistic background for Mani's conceptual development. Unfortunately, most of these recovered works are in an extremely fragmentary condition, and a substantial quantity of the material remains unpublished.

Also of signal value in the reconstruction of Manichaean ideology are a small number of testimonia supplied by later Christian and Muslim heresiologists. Their general veracity, once suspect, has been confirmed by portions of the aforementioned primary sources. The most important of these testimonia are contributed by Ephrem Syrus (fourth century), Theodore bar Konai (eighth century), Ibn al-Nadim (tenth century), al-Biruni (eleventh century), and al-Shahrastani (twelfth century).

In addition to providing valuable historical information about the founder and the subsequent fortunes of his community, these sources also utilize (and sometimes quote) Manichaean literature when illustrating particular facets of that religion's doctrine. Since Ephrem and Theodore present their material in Syriac, their reports are of especial significance in the task of the recovery of original Manichaean terminology and locutions.

Ideology and Ethos. The cosmogonical teachings of Mani, derived in large part from a creative exegesis of the Bible and works like *1 Enoch*, form the structural basis for the typical attitudes and behavior associated with Manichaeism. According to both authentic Manichaean writings and summaries supplied by hostile witnesses, the following myth is the fundamental expression of Manichaean religiosity. [*See* Enoch, Book of.]

In the beginning there existed two Realms in a primal, unsullied state: the Realm of Light or of Goodness, and the Realm of Darkness or Wickedness, each Realm populated with entities sharing those respective qualities, the "Sons of Light" and the "Sons of Darkness." The Sons of Darkness, depicted as filled with lust for violence and sensual gratification, gradually became aware of the paradisiacal qualities of the neighboring Realm of Light, and launched an assault against it with the aim of acquiring it for themselves. The ruler of the Realm of Light, termed the *Father of Greatness*, responded to this attack by invoking a champion, the so-called Primal Man, who went into battle armed with various component entities from the Realm of Light. Primal Man proceeded to the Realm of Darkness, but was promptly defeated, taken captive, and stripped of his lustrous armor, which was then consumed like food by the Sons of Darkness. This catastrophic defeat marks the initial "mixture" or "mingling" of the two previously separate Realms, a state of affairs which the eventual creation of the physical cosmos and the course of human history will be dedicated to alleviating.

Primal Man was soon delivered from his predicament by other forces from the Realm of Light, but the rescue of the now hopelessly dispersed and entrapped elements of Light consumed by the Sons of Darkness required a more imaginative stratagem. This plan involved the creation of the present universe as the arena wherein the captured elements of Light could be recovered. Sun, moon, and stars were created in order to attract the earthbound particles of Light upward toward their original home in the Realm of Light. Furthermore, a certain number of the Sons of Darkness, termed *archons* or *demons*, were taken into custody by the forces of Light. [*See* War of the Sons of Light against the Sons of Darkness.] Some of these archons were killed and dismembered so as to construct from their carcasses the physical surface of the earth. The remainder of the archons were imprisoned upon the firmament (literally, "affixed" or "nailed") and kept under guard in preparation for the next step of recovery, a stage labeled by modern scholars the *seduction of the archons*.

The seduction of the archons was effected by an emissary of the Realm of Light who was androgynous in form. This emissary paraded nude before the captive archons, displaying a female form to the male archons and a male form to the female archons. Excited by their lust for this unattainable form, the male archons ejaculated semen wherein the previously engulfed particles of Light were now concentrated. This seed fell to earth and became the origin of plant life. Similarly, the female archons, who were depicted as being pregnant, miscarried, and their fetuses fell to earth where they became animal life, as well as other monstrous beings, termed *abortions*. The abortions fed upon the plants and each other, engaged in generally riotous, violent behavior, and further dispersed and mixed the entrapped elements of Light. They, however, wistfully recalled the beautiful forms of the emissary which their archon parents had seen in the heavens, and decided to create facsimiles of those male and female forms upon earth. By a gruesome process of cannibalism and sexual activity, the first human couple, Adam and Eve, was created.

Alarmed by these new developments upon earth, the Father of Greatness dispatched a heavenly messenger, the "Apostle of Light," to Adam in order to instruct him regarding the ways in which he and his offspring could assist in the process of recovering the trapped elements of Light from the material universe. These instructions form the core of the Manichaean ethos: complete abstinence from sexual activity, strict dietary regulations, and elaborate rules for prayer and purification. If followed, these prescriptions would eventually produce the liberation of the captured particles of Light and restore the primal uncontaminated status of the Realm of Light, as well as the destruction of the physical universe. During the course of human history, the Apostle of Light has periodically journeyed to earth and assumed human guise in order to repeat these instructions to subsequent generations of humanity. The advent of Mani was viewed as the final stage of the Apostle's didactic mission.

Relationship to the Scrolls. One of the more intriguing aspects of modern research into the history of Near Eastern religions during late antiquity involves the growing recognition that there is a conceptual and literary nexus between Second Temple Jewish scribal circles and certain subsequent Syro-Mesopotamian religious movements, including, most prominently, Manichaeism. The mechanisms underlying this gradual eastward transmission of traditions and texts remain, however, tantalizingly obscure.

Thanks to the recent discovery and publication of the Cologne Mani Codex, a fourth- or fifth-century Greek hagiographic life of the heresiarch, we know that Mani spent his formative years among a southern Mesopotamian branch of the Elkesaite sect, a Jewish-Christian group allegedly founded by a prophet named Elkesai. This sect originated in the Transjordan and Dead Sea region during the final decades of the first century CE. Interestingly, some suggestive similarities have been observed between the communal structure and ritual behavior of the Elkesaites and the earlier Second Temple Jewish sect of the Essenes, a group that has been prominently linked by many scholars to the composition and/or preservation of the Qumran library. A possible connection between these two sectarian communities receives important support from the testimony of Epiphanius, a prominent fourth-century Christian bishop and heresiologist who was intimately familiar with the late antique Palestinian religious landscape. [*See* Ephiphanius.] According to this source, there was present in the region around the Dead Sea a Jewish sect of "Ossaeans," a designation which is strikingly reminiscent of "Essenes." However, "during the reign of the Emperor Trajan . . . these were then joined by one called Elksai, who was a false prophet" (*Panarion* 19.1.4). Epiphanius reports that this sect is "now called Sampsaeans," but adds at another place that "the Sampsaeans are now called Elkesaites" (*Panarion* 53.1.1). If Epiphanius's information can be trusted on this point, we have discovered one plausible way by which Second Temple Jewish extrabiblical literature came into the possession of the Elkesaite sect and ultimately to the attention of Mani.

The posited linkage between the Essenes and the Elkesaites need not be the sole means of this ideological and textual migration. Some scholars have speculated about the possible survival of subterranean sectarian currents within classical Judaism until the geonic period, at which time one or more reemerge in the Karaite schism. There are sporadic references in Christian, Muslim, and even medieval Jewish literature to the continued existence of the "Zadokite" (usually rendered "Sadducee") sect, a group which moreover displays some interesting affinities with its alleged forebears at Qumran. [*See* Sadducees.] Finally, the presence of "apocryphal" works like the Damascus Document, Aramaic Levi, and *Ben Sira* among the Cairo Genizah hoard demonstrates the persistent vitality of sectarian literary traditions among certain segments of Islamic Jewry. It is possible that Mani (and others) were exposed to traditions of this sort via occasional interactions with representatives of such groups.

Careful study of Manichaean literature and traditions has systematically uncovered Mani's reliance upon and esteem for older pseudepigraphic works, particularly those allegedly authored by biblical primal forefathers, such as Adam, Seth, or Enoch. His indebtedness to Enochic literature is especially profound, inasmuch as certain structural features of his cosmogony, cosmology, and eschatology betray the influence of the revelatory wisdom transmitted in what are today termed *1 Enoch* and *2 Enoch*. Most importantly, conclusive evidence for Mani's acquaintance with specifically Qumranic literature comes from his expropriation and adaptation of the so-called *Book of Giants*, an aggadic expansion of *Genesis* 6.1–4 and *1 Enoch* 6–11 that is presently attested only in two literary collections; namely, the Qumran library and Manichaean scriptures. This work, originally a Jewish composition, eventually achieved canonical status within Manichaeism.

[*See also* Elkesaites; Ephraim and Manasseh; *and* Light and Darkness.]

BIBLIOGRAPHY

Reeves, John C. *Heralds of That Good Realm: Syro-Mesopotamian Gnosis and Jewish Traditions*. Nag Hammadi and Manichaean Studies, 41. Leiden, 1996.

Reeves, John C. *Jewish Lore in Manichaean Cosmogony: Studies in the Book of Giants Traditions*. Monographs of the Hebrew Union College, 14. Cincinnati, 1992.

Reeves, John C. "Jewish Pseudepigrapha in Manichaean Literature: The Influence of the Enochic Library." In *Tracing the Threads: Studies in the Vitality of Jewish Pseudepigrapha*, edited by J. C. Reeves, pp. 173–203. Atlanta, 1994.

JOHN C. REEVES

MANUAL OF DISCIPLINE. *See* Rule of the Community.

MARK, GOSPEL OF. While much has been written concerning the dubious identification of certain of the papyrus fragments discovered in Cave 7 at Qumran (7Q1–18) as fragments of the *Gospel of Mark* (Fitzmyer, 1990), there has been relatively little discussion of the specific relation of Mark's gospel to the scrolls except within the general context of their relation to Christian origins (Black, 1961, 1969), the New Testament (Braun, 1966, Stendahl, 1958), the Gospels (Betz, 1987), John the Baptist, and Jesus (Berger, 1995; Charlesworth, 1993; Stegemann, 1994).

Introduced by a proof text (*Is.* 40.3) that the Qumran community also used to account for its presence in the wilderness (see Rule of the Community [1QS viii.12–16] where "preparing the way of the Lord" meant the study of the Law), John the Baptist is the first character to appear on the Markan stage (*Mk.* 1.4). A connection between John and the Qumran community has frequently been posited, reference being made to the proximity of Qumran to his sphere of activity (*Mk.* 1.4, 5), and to the similarity of their respective teaching (eschatological judgment and messianic expectation) and practice (baptism and asceticism), as the Markan evangelist presents these (cf. *Mk.* 1.4–8; 2.18–19). Appeal has been made in particular to the remarkable (but disputed) conjunction, common to both, between baptism and entry into the eschatological community, between baptism, repentance, and the confession of sin (cf. *Mk.* 1.4, 5 and 1QS i.24–ii.1; v.13–14), and between such cleansing and the Holy Spirit (cf. *Mk.* 1.8 and 1QS iii.6–9; iv.20–22). On the other hand, the Markan Baptist is not concerned with founding a community, but calls on the nation as a whole for what is an unrepeatable act of moral obedience rather than for the regular ritual washings that otherwise characterize the Qumran community. Significant in *Mark* solely for his witness to Jesus, he proclaims furthermore only a single messiah (1.7), in contrast to the two or more messianic figures of Qumran expectation.

Although described as a "true" teacher (*Mk.* 12.14), the principal character of Mark's gospel is hardly to be identified with the "Teacher of Righteousness" of the scrolls, as some have suggested, far less with the Wicked Priest (see Thiering, 1981). There is little indeed to establish a connection between the Markan Jesus and the Qumran community other than his links with John. His attitude to wealth or to marriage is comparable to theirs, but these have an Old Testament foundation and may not be significant. A healer and exorcist like the Essenes, he too invests eschatological significance in cures and exorcisms (cf. *Mk.* 3.22–30 and 1QS iv.19–22; War Scroll, 1QM xiv.9–10), which he accomplishes with the laying on of hands (cf. *Mk.* 7.32 ff. and Genesis Apocryphon, 1QapGen xx.21–22, 28–29, hereafter called 1QGenesis Apocryphon). As teacher and prophet, he proclaims "the good news" (cf. *Mk.* 1.14–15), a messianic act according to Melchizedek (11Q13) ii.15–20. In priestly fashion, he can expiate sins (cf. *Mk.* 2.5, 10), a role predicated of the expected Messiah of Aaron and Israel (cf. Cairo Damascus Document[a], CD-A xiv.18–19 = 4Q Damascus Document[b], 4Q267 18 iii.12–13), and as "shepherd" of his flock (cf. *Mk.* 6.34; 14.27) he fulfils the words of *Zechariah* 13.7, a passage quoted in Cairo Damascus Document[b] (CD-B) xix.7–11 in connection with the same figure(s).

Principal Parallels. Although the linguistic medium of the respective texts is different—Mark is written in Hellenistic Greek (*Koine*); almost all of the Qumran documents, in Biblical Hebrew or Aramaic—the aforementioned parallels exist because the author of *Mark* has taken over a Palestinian Jesus (and John) tradition already forged in the common crucible of apocalyptic Judaism and the ideas associated with it. These ideas are a dualism, both cosmic (two powers, God and Satan, in continuous warfare; cf. *Mk.* 3.22–30 and 1QS iii.17–iv.1) and temporal (two ages, the present wicked, the future blessed); the battle of God's elect with temptation (*peirasmos*), sin, and the flesh (cf. *Mk.* 1.12–13; 4.17; 8.33; 13.21–22; 14.38; 1QS iii.13–iv.26); an emphasis on eschatology (the present age, in fulfilment of prophecy, as the final age of blessing for the righteous and judgment [by fire] for the wicked; cf. *Mk.* 1.14–15; 9.43ff.; 13.1ff. and Pesher Habakkuk, 1QpHab vii.1–14; 1QS ii.7–8; iv.11–14; 1QHodayot[a], 1QH[a] xiv.17–19; CD-A ii.5–7); the coming of the reign or kingdom of God (cf. *Mk.* 1.14–15; 9.1; 14.25; 15.43; Assumption of Moses 7–10 and, among the scrolls, where it is not, however, a dominant theme, 1QM vi.6; xiv.16); the advent of messianic agents prosecuting God's will.

While the scrolls appear to testify to a plurality of messianic figures (CD-A vii.18–21 = 4Q267 3.iv.7–10 = Damascus Document[f], 4Q271 5.2–4; xii.22–xiii.2; xiv.18–19 = 4Q267 18.iii.12–13 = 4Q271 13.2–3; CD-B xix.10–11, 35–xx.1; 1QS ix.9–11; Rule of the Congregation, 1Q28a ii.11–14, 17–22; Florilegium, 4Q174 i.10–13; 11Q13 ii.15–19), a Davidic messiah or messiah of Israel (cf. also Commentary on Genesis A, 4Q252 v.1–7; War Rule, 4Q285 5.1–6; Messianic Apocalypse, 4Q521 2.ii: a priestly messiah or messiah of Aaron [cf. also Aaronic Text A = Aramaic Levi[d]?, 4Q541 9.i]), an anointed prophet and/or "Interpreter of the Law" (cf. *Mk.* 9.4) and, more controversially a heavenly figure or "Son of God," cf. Aramaic Apocalypse, 4Q246 i.1–ii.8), such expectations are attached in *Mark* either, in a subordinate way, to John the Baptist (cf., e.g., *Mk.* 1.2; 9.12–13, "prophet") or, in a major way, to the figure of Jesus (cf., e.g., "prophet" *Mk.* 6.14–16; 8.27–28; "Son of David" 10.47–48; 11.9–10; "Son of God" 1.1, 11; 3.11; 5.7; 9.7; 12.6; 13.32; 15.39), whose messianic role, unlike that of the scrolls, involves his redemptive death and resurrection as "Son of Man" (the titular use of which, incidentally, is unknown in the scrolls). [*See* Messiahs.]

Turning from parallels in ideas to those in institutions, we can observe certain similarities and differences between the Markan community and that (or those, if more than one community is represented by these diverse texts) of the scrolls. While both shared a conception of being an "elect" or "covenant" community (cf. *Mk.* 4.11–12; 13.22; 14.24; 1QS viii.5–10), with, in addition to "the many" (cf. 1QS vi.1, 7–25; CD-A xiii.7 = 4QDamascus Document[d], 4Q269 11.i.4; xiv.6–8 = 4Q269 11.ii.10–12), a special body or inner circle of members (the twelve laymen of Qumran, 1QS viii.1, who probably represented the twelve lay tribes of Israel, offering, some claim, a certain parallel with the twelve disciples in Mark), Qumran's highly developed hierarchical structure (cf. 1Q28a i.28–ii.1) and stringent rules for membership (cf. Josephus, *The Jewish War*, 2.8.7 and 1QS vi.14–23) were in sharp contrast to the inclusiveness and disregard of rank urged on Mark's community (cf. e.g. *Mk.* 9.33–41; 10.13–16, 35–45).

Jesus' rigid attitude to the marriage law, on the other hand, is paralleled only in the scrolls, both advocating lifelong monogamy (cf. *Mk.* 10.2–9 and Temple Scroll[a], 11Q19 lvii.17–18) and making a similar, though not identical, appeal to *Genesis* 1.27 (cf. CD-A iv.20–21 = Damascus Document[f], 4Q271 3 1–2). [*See* Marriage and Divorce.]

As reflected in *Mark* 1.9–11 (cf. also *Mk.* 10.38–39), baptism was clearly the significant non-repeatable initiation rite for the Markan community, whereas regular purificatory lustrations, which most Jewish sects practiced but to which, in another context, the Markan Jesus was averse (cf. *Mk.* 7.1–8), were the primary emphasis of Qumran practice (cf. CD-A x.10–13; 1QS iii.4–6; v.13–14; 1QM xiv.2–3). Adopted only after membership, however, and therefore signifying admission into the covenant community, Qumran baptismal practice offers then a partial parallel to the Christian rite. [*See* Baths and Baptism.]

Poverty and the sharing of goods also appear to have been a religious ideal for both communities (cf. *Mk.* 10.21ff.; 12.41–44; 1QS vi.18–23), members admitted to the Qumran sect being required to surrender private property and possessions, thereby placing them at the disposal of the group. Itinerant sectarians, therefore, could expect to carry little with them, and to be given extraordinary hospitality when travelling (cf. *Mk.* 6.7–13; Josephus, *The Jewish War,* 2.8.4).

Common meals, in which the writer of Mark's gospel seems to have taken an inordinate interest (cf. e.g., *Mk.* 2.15ff; 6.21ff.; 6.30–44; 7.1ff.; 8.1–21; 14.3, 12–25), were a daily feature of Qumran life, together with special ceremonial meals of a more sacramental or priestly character (1QS vi.3–6; 1Q28a ii.2–10). These may have been connected with the weekly eating of the shewbread, or "bread of the presence" (cf. *Mk.* 2.26), and looked forward to the meal (of bread and wine) that would be eaten in the new age in the presence of the anointed priest and Messiah of Israel (cf. 1Q28a ii.11–22 and *Mk.* 14.25). Features of the Markan account of the Last Supper (*Mk.* 14.12–25), which are inexplicable in relation to a Passover meal (e.g., the secrecy surrounding the event, the lack of mention of the lamb, the presence of men only, the absence of the *pater familias*), but which cohere with the Essene cult meal (e.g., the participation of an inner circle only, the presidency of the appointed leader of the community, the blessing of both the bread and the wine at the beginning of the meal), have been taken by some to argue for Qumran influence on the primitive eucharist. On the other hand, the absence in the Markan account of certain distinctive Qumran features (e.g., the strict observance of precedence), the presence of certain distinctive Christian features (e.g., the central significance accorded the leader and his death), and similarities to other Jewish religious or ritual meals (e.g., the "brotherhood" meals of the Pharisees) have made the majority of scholars more cautious in positing a specific Essene connection. [*See* Meals.]

One problem to which Qumran practice has been deemed to offer a solution is the discrepancy between the dating of the Last Supper and Jesus' crucifixion as they are given in the separate Markan and Johannine accounts. In Mark, Jesus eats (on the evening of 14 Nisan) what is described as a Passover meal with his disciples (cf. *Mk.* 14.12ff.) and is crucified the following day (cf. *Mk.* 15.1ff.), while in John the meal takes place at least twenty-four hours before the Passover, and Jesus is crucified on the day of preparation (cf. *Jn.* 13.1; 18.28; 19.14, 31). Arguing for the operation of two calendrical systems, one the official luni-solar calendar used in the Temple (which calculated the day of the Passover, 14 Nisan, as commencing on Friday evening), the other the solar calendar used by the Qumran sectarians (which calculated the Passover, 14 Nisan, as commencing on Tuesday evening), A. Jaubert (1957) argued that Jesus, following Essene practice, had celebrated the Passover according to the latter. *Mark* was therefore correct in making Jesus' Last Supper with his disciples a Passover meal, but celebrated, according to the solar calendar, three days earlier, and *John* is correct in giving Jesus' crucifixion as the day of preparation for the official Passover. Such harmonization is not without its problems, however, since there is no evidence elsewhere that Jesus followed the solar calendar, nor any indication why he would wish to follow the Qumran community in this matter. [*See* Passover.]

One point of similarity between the Markan evangelist and the Qumran sectarians is their use of scripture, and in particular their common conviction that the biblical text held a contemporary relevance for their community's beliefs and experience (both present and future). Both had a particular preference for the prophetic writings (especially *Isaiah*) and for the Psalms (cf. the "*pesher*" use of *Is.* 40.3 previously referred to, or the use of Ps. 118.22–23 in *Mk.* 12.10–11). Where the *Gospel of Mark* makes Jesus the subject of Old Testament prophecies, as well as the revealer of divine secrets (cf. *Mk.* 4.11–12; 13.1ff.), the Teacher of Righteousness is the final interpreter of the words of God's servants, the prophets (cf. 1QpHab vii.4–5). [*See* Teacher of Righteousness.]

The attitude of both communities to the Law, however, cannot have stood in sharper contrast, the Qumran sectarians evidencing a strictness that exceeded that of the Pharisees, the Markan community demonstrating a laxness for which there is no parallel in the scrolls. This can be seen, for example, in their respective attitude to Sabbath observance (cf. *Mk.* 2.23ff.; 3.1–6 and CD-A x.14–xi.18 = Damascus Document[e], 4Q270 10 v.1–21), or the purity laws (cf. *Mk.* 7.1ff., 14ff. and CD-A x.10–13; xii.11–15). Where the Markan Jesus is content to heal a non-life-threatening condition on the Sabbath (3.1–6), and the Pharisees only if danger to life were involved (cf. B.T., *Yoma* 86a), the Essenes were given instruction that if anyone fell into a "place of water . . . no one should take him out with a ladder, or a rope, or a utensil" (CD-A xi.16–17 = Damascus Document[c], 4Q268 3.10–11). Where ritual purity was of little concern to the Markan community, the laws of cleanness and uncleanness were a major occupation of the Qumran sectarians: the avoidance of sources of contamination (corpses, non-members, gentiles, etc.), the observance of dietary regulations, the practice of the daily ritual bath, etc. While penitence was essential, and spirituality atoned for transgression (cf. 1QS iii.6–12), sin tended to be equated with impurity, and forgiveness with ritual cleansing. The Markan approach to defilement, by contrast, is moral ("the things which come out of a man are what defile him," *Mk.* 7.15) and the solution a Christocentric one ("the Son of Man has authority on earth to forgive sins," *Mk.* 2.10). [*See* Purity.]

These conflicting attitudes to purity, on the other hand, converge when we consider their respective posture toward that ultimate monument to official ritual purity, the Jerusalem Temple. While retaining some kind of connection with it—by making offerings, for example (CD-A xi.17–21 = 4Q268 3 i.11–15; cf. also *Mk.* 1.44)—each regarded this institution as corrupt (cf. *Mk.* 11.15–18 and CD-A vi.11ff.; 1QpHab ix.3–8, 9–15; xii.1–10). Regarding righteousness as more important than sacrifices (1QS ix.3–6; *Mk.* 12.32–33), they each held a spiritualized view of sacrificial worship and the Temple. The Qumran sect indeed saw the community itself as a substitute for the Temple (1QS viii.1–ix.11 and esp. viii.5–10), hence their stringent efforts to maintain its purity. A similar idea is found in *Mark*, which implies that the community is the new Temple brought about by Jesus' death (*Mk.* 14.58; 15.38). Some have argued for a common tradition here (cf. Gärtner, 1965), although Qumran's hierarchical distinctions within the new Temple (between laity and priesthood, or "holy dwelling" and "holy of holies") are not in evidence in the Markan community. The sectarians, moreover, intended to restore the Temple to its proper worship (cf. 1QM ii.1–6) whereas the Markan community appears to have been reconciled to its demise (cf. *Mk.* 11.15ff. read in conjunction with 11.12–14, 20ff.; 13.1–2; 14.58; 15.38).

Traditio-Historical Links. The principal parallels between the Qumran scrolls and the *Gospel of Mark,* and their respective communities, then, where traditio-historical links are concerned, lie primarily with the figure of John the Baptist, and only secondarily with Jesus. As for ideas, the major resemblances reside in their eschatological worldview, and (to a qualified extent) in their messianic expectations. With regard to institutions, there are similarities to be observed in their common conception of the elect or covenant community; their stringent views on marriage, the place given to baptism, the attitude taken to wealth, poverty, the community of goods, and hospitality; the significance attached to communal and sacred meals; their use of scripture; and last but not least their common posture toward the Temple. These similarities are outweighed, however, by radical differences regarding admission to and membership of the community, as well as to rank and hierarchy within it, and by extreme contrasts in their attitudes to the law, the Sabbath, and matters of ritual purity. Where the ideological parallels are concerned, a common debt to the Hebrew scriptures and to apocalyptic Judaism may supply a satisfactory explanation. While Qumran may have exerted some influence on primitive Christianity in matters of practice, the sharp divergences here point to the very different nature of the communities represented by the scrolls and the *Gospel of Mark.* The first reflects a sectarian movement with an esoteric impulse, the second a universal thrust, the former emphasizing retreat from the world, the latter outreach to it, the one stressing exclusiveness, the other inclusiveness. The study of each therefore highlights the various polarities that existed in first century Judaism as Jews and Christians sought to give expression to their different understandings of being God's people in and for the world.

Qumran Cave 7 and Khirbet Mird. No discussion of *Mark* and the Dead Sea Scrolls would be complete without some reference to the debate, mentioned at the start, over the question of the identification of certain of the papyrus fragments discovered in Cave 7 at Qumran (7Q1–18) as fragments of Mark's gospel, particularly that known as biblical text? 7Q5. One of eighteen such fragments in Greek, discovered in 1955 and published in 1962, biblical text? 7Q5 has been identified (O'Callaghan, 1972, and Thiede, 1992) as part of *Mark* 6.52–53. Three more of the nine alleged New Testament fragments in this group have also been attributed to *Mark* (7Q6 1 = *Mk.* 4.28; 7Q7 = *Mk.* 12.17; and 7Q15 = *Mk.* 6.48), although the case for these has not been as compelling. Apart from the intrinsic unlikelihood of the Qumran sectarians preserving a copy (indeed four copies, since the fragments do not all come from the same manuscript!) of a Gospel with such divergent teachings and practice, the uncertainty of its date (the fragment could be dated earlier than the Christian era), and the possibility, were it genuine, that the cave had been re-used and someone other than a sectarian had placed it there, scholars have pointed out a number of technical difficulties with the biblical text? 7Q5 identification: The minute size of the fragment (twenty letters), its illegibility and the consequent problems in transcription (only nine letters, on four lines, are certain), the presumption of textual variants (to make the fragment fit, two emendations to the traditional text of *Mark* have to be accepted), and the possibility of other identifications (*Ex.* 36.10–11, *2 Sm.* 4.12–5.1; 5.13–14, *2 Kgs.* 5.13–14, *Zec.* 7.4–5) have all been suggested. For these reasons, this controversial hypothesis has not received widespread acceptance.

Uncontroversial, on the other hand, have been the Greek manuscript fragments of the *Gospel of Mark* (*Mk.* 2.3–5, 8–9; 6.30–31, 33–34, 36–37, 39–41) found among the wider body of Judean Desert Scrolls. Part of an uncial biblical codex (p^{84}) dating to the sixth century, these texts were found near Qumran at Khirbet Mird, the site of the former monastery of Castellion, and are now in the Louvain University Library.

BIBLIOGRAPHY

Berger, K. *The Truth under Lock and Key? Jesus and the Dead Sea Scrolls.* Louisville, 1995. English version of *Qumran und Jesus: Wahrheit unter Verschluss?* (1993). Discusses the relation between the Qumran Scrolls and the New Testament.

Betz, O. "Die Bedeutung der Qumranschriften für die Evangelien des Neuen Testaments." In *Jesus. Der Messias Israels. Aufsätze zur biblischen Theologie,* edited by O. Betz, pp. 318–332. Tübingen, 1987. Affirms the value of the Qumran Scrolls for understanding the Gospels and Jesus. Considers the close connection of John the Baptist to the Qumran community.

Black, M. *The Scrolls and Christian Origins: Studies in the Jewish Background of the New Testament.* London, 1961. Early classic work by a celebrated scholar in the field.

Black, M., ed. *The Scrolls and Christianity.* Theological Collections, 11. London, 1969. A classic collection of essays by a number of scholars on various topics, including C. H. H. Scobie on "John the Baptist," pp. 58–69.

Braun, H. *Qumran und das Neue Testament.* Tübingen, 1966. Useful treatment (esp. pp. 60–77).

Charlesworth, J. H., ed. *Jesus and the Dead Sea Scrolls.* Garden City, N.Y., 1993. A collection of essays by a number of scholars on various aspects of the subject.

Fitzmyer, J. A., ed. *The Dead Sea Scrolls: Major Publications and Tools for Study.* Society of Biblical Literature Resources for Biblical Study. Atlanta, 1990. A standard tool. On *Mark* and the Dead Sea Scrolls, see especially pages 168–172.

García Martínez, F. *The Dead Sea Scrolls Translated: The Qumran Texts in English,* translated by W. G. E. Watson. Leiden, 1994. Offers a brief introduction to the Dead Sea Scrolls and translations of the 270 most important manuscripts from Qumran.

García Martínez, F., and J. Trebolle Barrera. *The People of the Dead Sea Scrolls: Their Writings, Beliefs and Practices.* Leiden and New York, 1993. Especially useful for its sections on "Messianic Hopes in the Qumran Writings" (pp. 159ff.) and "Qumran and the Origins of Christianity" (pp. 191ff.).

Gärtner, B. E. *The Temple and the Community in Qumran and the New Testament: A Comparative Study in the Temple Symbolism of the Qumran Texts and the New Testament.* Society of New Testament Studies Monograph Series, 1. Cambridge, 1965.

Jaubert, A. *La date de la Cène. Calendrier biblique et liturgie chrétienne.* Études bibliques. Paris, 1957.

O'Callaghan, J. "New Testament Papyri in Qumran Cave 7?" *Supplement to Journal of Biblical Literature* 91.2 (1972), 1–14.

Stanton, G. N. *Gospel Truth? New Light on Jesus and the Gospels.* London, 1995. Contains a recent critical examination of the O'Callaghan and Thiede hypothesis.

Stegemann, H. *Die Essener, Qumran, Johannes der Täufer und Jesus. Ein Sachbuch.* 4th ed. Freiburg, 1994. Offers reflections on what the Qumran scrolls can tell us about John the Baptist, Jesus, and Christian origins.

Stendahl, K., ed. *The Scrolls and the New Testament.* London, 1958. A classic collection of essays by a number of scholars on various topics, including K. G. Kuhn on "New Light on Temptation, Sin, and Flesh in the New Testament."

Thiede, C. P. *The Earliest Gospel Manuscript? The Qumran Papyrus 7Q5 and Its Significance for New Testament Studies.* Exeter, 1992.

Thiering, B. E. *The Gospels and Qumran: A New Hypothesis.* Sydney, 1981.

W. R. TELFORD

MARRIAGE AND DIVORCE. Among the documents from the Judean Desert are texts that shed light on the matrimonial practices of Judean Jews. Some of these texts give information about Essene ideas on marriage and divorce, and others preserve marriage contracts and writs of divorce used by Judean Jews of a later period. Some scholars maintain that the Qumran Jews were not Essenes; others that they were Christians. This article shares the conviction of the majority of scholars that the Jews of Qumran were Essenes.

Essene Marriage. Josephus tells us that many Essenes were celibate (*The Jewish War* 2.8.2, sec. 120; *Jewish Antiquities* 18.1.5, sec. 21; cf. Philo, *Hypothetica* 11.14: "No Essene takes a wife") but that there was a second "order" of Essenes that married (*The Jewish War* 2.8.13, sec. 160). Some Qumran texts support both statements. There is no mention of marriage or of women in the Rule of the Community from Qumran Cave 1 (hereafter, 1QRule of the Community, 1QS); not even *perut zera*ʿ ("fruitfulness of seed"; 1QS iv.7) is necessarily understood to mean human progeny. [*See* Celibacy.]

The appendix to 1QRule of the Community, the Rule of the Congregation, however, mentions "toddlers and women" (1Q28a 1.4) and "every head of a family" (1Q28a i.16); it also forbids a youthful member to enter into marriage before he is twenty years old (1Q28a i.9–10). These phrases, then, seem to refer to married members of the community. Moreover, the Damascus Document explicitly mentions "marrying and begetting children" and recognizes the "ordinances 'between a man and his wife'" (CD vii.6b–8, quoting *Nm.* 30.17).

1QRule of the Community was mostly likely the rule book for celibate Essenes living at Qumran, for whom life in the community symbolized life in "the camp of holiness," that is, Jerusalem, which called for no marital intercourse, whereas the Rule of the Congregation and the Damascus Document regulated the life of Essenes living in towns and villages throughout Judea, the other "camps," where Essenes did marry and beget children. The difference between 1QRule of the Community and the Rule of the Congregation may be explained rather as the difference between an earlier celibate form of the community and a community that only later admitted married members and women among its ranks. This too may be the reason why in the large main part of the Qumran cemetery, which was carefully planned, all the skeletons are male (de Vaux, 1973, p. 47), whereas skeletons of women and children were found in the extensions of the cemetery. [*See* Cemeteries.]

Essenes had an exalted view of married life. Full maturity was required of the youth who would enter into marriage: twenty years of age, "when he knows good and evil" (1Q28a i.10–11). This age differs from the later rabbinic requirement that viewed twenty as the *terminus ante quem*, the age by which a youth should have entered into marriage (B.T., *Qid.* 29b). Nothing in the Qumran texts supports what Josephus reports about the marrying Essenes who gave their wives a three-year probation and married them only after they gave proof of fecundity by three periods of purification, or who had no intercourse with their wives during pregnancy, engaging in it only for the procreation of children (*The Jewish War* 2.8.13, sec. 161; contrast Philo, *On the Special Laws* 3.6, sec. 35).

Qumran Marriage. Among Qumran texts there is no example of a marriage contract, but a fragmentary document, the Rule of Marriage (4Q502), was called by the original editor a wedding ritual; others have considered it a ritual celebrating the golden age of elderly married couples (*zeqenim u-zeqenot*; 4Q502 19.2, 24.4) in the community. This text mentions the "procreation of offspring" (4Q502 1–3.4), but its broken context does not permit one to gather whether that was understood as the sole reason for intercourse. Intercourse with one's wife, however, was regarded as a source of ritual defilement and prohibited an Essene from entering any part of the city of Jerusalem for three days thereafter (11Q19 xlv.11–12), for there God had established his name: "the camp of holiness is Jerusalem" (4Q394 8.iv.10). "No one should sleep with his wife in the city of the Temple, defiling the city of the Temple with their impurity" (CD xii.1–2). This was apparently the Essene way of interpreting *Exodus* 19.15b and of extending the sense of *Leviticus* 15.18. [*See* Purity.]

The Qumran community forbade marriage within close degrees of kinship (between uncle and niece or aunt and nephew), interpreting *Leviticus* 18 strictly. They regarded such marriages as being caught in *zenut*, one of "the three nets of Belial" (CD iv.15): "They take [as wives], each one [of them], the daughter of his brother and the daughter of his sister, whereas Moses said, You shall not approach [sexually] your mother's sister; she is your mother's kin" [*Lv.* 18.13]. The regulation for incest is written for males, but it applies equally to women: "so if a brother's daughter uncovers the nakedness of her father's brother, whereas she is his kin . . . " (CD v.7–11).

Polygamy was also denounced by the Qumran Jews, who considered it a second way of being caught in *zenut*, "by taking two wives in their lifetime, whereas the principle of creation [is] 'Male and female he created them' [*Gn.* 1.27]; and those who entered [Noah's] ark, 'two [by] two went into the ark' [*Gn.* 7.9]. And concerning the prince [it is] written, 'He shall not multiply wives for himself' [*Dt.* 17.17]" (CD iv.20–v.2a). This denunciation of polygamy stands in contrast to Mosaic regulations permitting it (*Dt.* 21.15–17; cf. *Gn.* 16.3, 29.18, 29.25–30; *1 Kgs.* 11.1–3).

Essene Divorce. The Essene attitude toward divorce and remarriage after divorce was complicated. Although Temple Scroll[a] (11Q19 liv.4) asserts that the vow made by "a widow or a divorcee," by which "she binds herself formally, will hold good," it is not clear that Qumran Essenes considered divorce legal or tolerated marriage after it. Some interpreters have understood the Damascus Document (CD iv.20–v.2a), cited above, to forbid not only polygamy but also divorce, especially in light of Temple Scroll[a] (11Q19 lvii.17–19, which elaborates the prohibition of polygamy for a king stated in *Dt.* 17.17): "He shall not take in addition to her another wife, for she alone shall be with him all the days of her life; and if she dies, he shall take for himself another [wife] from his father's house, from his clan." Although this prohibition is found among the statutes for the king in Temple Scroll[a], it is usually judged that what was legislated for the king was to be observed by the commoner as well. So marriage was regarded as an alliance between one man and one woman "in their lifetime." Hence, it would be a prohibition not only of polygamy but also of divorce. If so, then this attitude differs from the Mosaic legislation tolerating divorce (*Dt.* 24.1–4; cf. *Jer.* 3.8). But so the Essenes honored God's words recorded in *Malachi* 2.14b–16a.

Qumran Divorce and the New Testament. The prohibition of divorce in Qumran texts provides an important Palestinian Jewish background for the New Testament prohibition of it. Its most primitive formulation is found in the isolated dominical saying in *Luke* 16.18: "Everyone who divorces his wife and marries another commits adultery." Jesus' absolute prohibition of divorce and remarriage is formulated from the viewpoint of Palestinian Judaism: the man must not divorce his wife. Moreover, such divorce is equated with adultery, itself proscribed in *Exodus* 20.14 and *Deuteronomy* 5.18. An absolute prohibition of divorce is also found in *1 Corinthians* 7.10–11 and in *Mark* 10.11–12, where it is preceded by another pronouncement of Jesus: "What God has joined together let no human put asunder" (*Mk.* 10.9). Both Pauline and Marcan texts were formulated to address divorce practices in the Hellenistic world outside Judea, where a woman could divorce her husband. Such prohibition of divorce stands in contrast to the allowance of it according to "the laws of the Jews" (Josephus, *Jewish Antiquities* 15.7.10, sec. 259; cf. H. L. Strack and P. Billerbeck, *Kommentar zum Neuen Testament aus Talmud und Midrasch*, 6 vols. [Munich, 1922–1961], vol. 1, pp. 319–320). Because some Palestinian Jews (Qumran Essenes) apparently did forbid divorce, the *Sitz im Leben* for Jesus' debate with the Pharisees, "Is it lawful for a man to divorce his wife?" (*Mk.* 10.2), must be considered. The question, as formulated in *Mark*, is not as inconceivable in a Palestinian milieu as some commentators have maintained. Pharisees, knowing the Essene prohibition of divorce, would have asked Jesus the question to find out where he stood: "Do you side with Essenes or Pharisees in the matter of divorce?"

In *Matthew* 5.31–32 (corresponding to the formulation in *Luke* 16.18) and 19.9 (corresponding to *Mark* 10.11), an exceptive phrase is added, "except for *porneia*." [*See* Q Source.] The meaning of the Greek term *porneia* has been long debated. Etymologically, it corresponds to the Hebrew *zenut* ("fornication"). With the recent light shed on one of the two forms of *zenut* (CD iv.17) by Temple Scroll[a] (11Q19 lvii.17–19), one realizes that the best meaning of *porneia* is now "illicit marital union" (that is, a marriage within degrees of kinship forbidden by *Leviticus* 18). This makes it intelligible why the evangelist, writing for a mixed, but predominantly Jewish-Christian, community, would have added the exceptive phrase, allowing divorce for gentile converts who would already have been married within degrees of kinship unacceptable to Jewish-Christians. Moreover, the question posed by Pharisees in *Matthew* 19.3, "Is it lawful to divorce one's wife 'for any cause?'" would represent the evangelist's reformulation of it in terms of an inner-Pharisee dispute, between the schools of Hillel and Shamm'ai.

Non-Qumran Documents. Eleven documents found at Judean Desert sites other than Qumran—Naḥal Ḥever, Naḥal Ṣe'elim, and Wadi Murabba'at, preserve examples of a dowry settlement, marriage contracts, and writs of divorce. One of these is written in Nabatean, five are written in Greek (one with an Aramaic subscription and signature), and the rest are written in Aramaic. The *ketubbah* ("marriage contract") and the *geṭ* ("writ of divorce") reveal ancient formulas that have persisted in such documents for centuries.

5/6Ḥev 1 Nab.	Babatha Archive dowry settlement? (94 CE; as yet unpublished)
5/6Ḥev 10 Aram.	contract of Babatha's second marriage (P.Yadin 10, 122–125 CE)
5/6Ḥev 18 Gr.	contract of marriage of Shelamzion and Kimber (with Aramaic subscription and signature; P.Yadin 18, 128 CE)
5/6Ḥev 37 Gr.	marriage contract (P.Yadin 37, 131 CE)
XḤev/Se 13 Aram.	confirmation of divorce (135 CE)
XḤev/Se Gr. 2 Gr.	marriage contract (canceled after 130 CE)
Mur 19 Aram.	writ of divorce (111 CE)
Mur 20 Aram.	marriage contract (117 CE)
Mur 21 Aram.	marriage contract (? CE)
Mur 115 Gr.	remarriage contract (124 CE)
Mur 116 Gr.	marriage contract (? CE)

Marriage Contract 5/6Ḥev 18 is a so-called double document, with the text of the *ketubbah* written twice: the upper part is the *scriptura interior* (folded over and sealed by thread), and the lower part is the *scriptura exterior* for normal consultation. (If someone contested the *scriptura exterior*'s text, the upper part could be opened in order to check the text of the lower part.) According to it, Judah son of Eleazar/Chthousion gives his virgin daughter Shelamzion to Judah, son of Hananiah, surnamed Kimber, to be his wedded wife according to the laws (*kata tous nomous* [Greek]). Shelamzion was apparently a minor (under twelve years of age) and could not legally be a party to the contract; so she is given away by her father. Her dowry (*prosphora* [Greek]) consists of feminine adornment in silver, gold, and clothing appraised by mutual agreement at two hundred silver denarii, given by her father; another three hundred silver denarii are promised by the groom for her support and that of the children to come "according to Greek custom." Judah Kimber agrees that the total dowry is repayable on demand in exchange for the return of the contract (that is, if the marriage is dissolved). The contract was signed by the father, the groom, and five witnesses: one in Greek and the rest in Aramaic. The bride's father, Judah son of Eleazar/Chthousion was the second husband of Babatha daughter of Simon whose *ketubbah* was written in Aramaic (5/6Ḥev 10), whereas that of Shelamzion (a younger generation) is in Greek. Judah son of Eleazar/Chthousion was also married to Miriam daughter of Beianos and on his death his two wives disputed over his possessions (5/6Ḥev 26 7–8, 13–14). [*See* Babatha *and* Family Life.]

Text 5/6Ḥev 37 is part of the *scriptura interior* of another Greek double document, a contract of the marriage of Jesus son of Menaham, domiciled in Soffathe, with Salome surnamed Komaïs, a resident of Maoza. Her dowry is stated to be worth ninety-six silver denarii (feminine adornment in silver, gold, clothing, and other articles).

Papyrus fragment Mur 20 preserves the beginning of seventeen lines of the Aramaic marriage contract of Judah son of Yeho[ ] son of Menashsheh of the Benê Eliashib, with [ ] (the bride's name is lost). The fragment preserves the essential formula [*ʾat*]*y tihviʾ li le-anttah kedin M*[*osheh*] ("[yo]u shall be my wife according to the law of M[oses]"). Part of the dowry is given as *kesef zuzin* ("silver denarii"). If the wife dies before the husband, the dowry will be inherited by the sons to be born; the daughters will continue to live and be cared for in the husband's house until their marriage.

Marriage contract Mur 21 is another fragmentary papyrus *ketubbah* preserving the beginning of five lines of the *scriptura interior* and most of the twenty lines of the *scriptura exterior*. The groom's name is Menahem son of [ ], and the bride's name is Leʿuthon daughter of [ ]. A bit of the essential formula is preserved (as above), but most of the extant text deals with provisions for the care of children to be born and for inheritance of the dowry by sons in case the wife dies before the husband. If he dies first, she will be provided for from his possessions.

Writ of divorce Mur 19, another double document, records the divorce of Joseph son of Naqsan, resident of Masada, and Miriam daughter of Jonathan, from Hanablaṭa. It states that she has been his wife up to that time but that she is now free to go and become the wife of any Jewish man she chooses. It mentions the return of her dowry and reimbursement for ruined or damaged goods and promises the replacement of the writ, if necessary. It is signed in Aramaic on the reverse by Joseph and three witnesses.

Text XḤev/Se 13 is a receipt of confirmation of divorce, which, written in the name of the divorced wife, has been interpreted as revealing that a woman could initiate divorce; but lines 6–7 are far from clear in this regard (See Benoit et al., 1961, p. 108).

Document Mur 115 is a contract of remarriage. Eleaios son of Simon and Salome daughter of John Galgoula had been married; subsequently, Eleaios separated and divorced (*apallagenai kai apolyein*) Salome. Later Eleaios was reconciled and took again (*katallaxai kai proslabesthai*) the same Salome for his wedded wife. Her dowry was two hundred denarii, of which fifty were Tyrian shekels. The rest of the document mentions the usual details found in contemporary Greek marriage contracts.

Only the *scriptura exterior* of a marriage contract remains of double document XḤev/Se Gr. 2. Its text has been canceled by diagonal pen strokes across the lines and signatures on the back, indicating that the marriage had been terminated (by divorce?).

[*See also* Contracts; Murabbaʿat, Wadi, *article on* Written Material; Ḥever, Naḥal; Ṣe'elim, Naḥal; *and* Rule of the Congregation.]

BIBLIOGRAPHY

Archer, L. J. *Her Price Is Beyond Rubies: The Jewish Woman in Graeco-Roman Palestine.* Journal for the Study of the Old Testament Supplement Series, 60. Sheffield, 1990. A modern discussion of the status and marriage of women in ancient Judea.

Baumgarten, Joseph M. "4Q502, Marriage or Golden Age Ritual?" *Journal of Jewish Studies* 34 (1983), 125–135.

Baumgarten, Joseph M. "The Qumran-Essene Restraints on Marriage." In *Archaeology and History in the Dead Sea Scrolls: The New York University Conference in Memory of Yigael Yadin*, edited by Lawrence H. Schiffman, pp. 13–24. Journal for the Study of Pseudepigrapha Supplement Series, 8. Sheffield, 1990.

Beall, Todd S. *Josephus' Description of the Essenes Illustrated by the Dead Sea Scrolls*, pp. 38–42. Society for New Testament Studies Monograph Series, 58. Cambridge, 1988.

Benoit, Pierre, Józef T. Milik, and Roland de Vaux, eds. *Les Grottes de Murabbaʿat*. Discoveries in the Judaean Desert, 2. Oxford, 1961. *Editio princeps* of the Murabbaʿat documents.

Cotton, Hannah. "A Cancelled Marriage Contract from the Judaean Desert (*XHev/Se Gr.* 2)." *Journal of Roman Studies* 84 (1994), 64–86.

de Vaux, R. *Archaeology and the Dead Sea Scrolls: The Schweich Lectures of the British Academy 1959*. London, 1973. Discusses the archaeological evidence for women and children at Qumran.

Epstein, Louis M. *The Jewish Marriage Contract: A Study in the Status of Women in Jewish Law*. New York, 1973.

Fitzmyer, Joseph A. "Divorce among First-Century Palestinian Jews." In *H. L. Ginsberg Volume*, edited by M. Haran, pp. 103–110. Eretz-Israel, 14. Jerusalem, 1978.

Fitzmyer, Joseph A. "The Matthean Divorce Texts and Some New Palestinean Evidence." *Theological Studies* 37 (1976), 197–226. Reprinted with slight revision in *To Advance the Gospel: New Testament Studies*, pp. 79–111. New York, 1981. More extended discussion of many of the topics and texts used in this article.

Fitzmyer, Joseph A. "The So-called Aramaic Divorce Text from Wadi Seiyal." In *Frank Moore Cross Volume*, pp. 16–22. Eretz-Israel, 26. Jerusalem, 1966. Discussion of XḤev/Se 13.

Friedman, M. A. *Jewish Marriage in Palestine: A Cairo Geniza Study*. 2 vols. Tel Aviv and New York, 1980–1981. Important contribution to the topic, but utilizing mostly later documentation.

Greenfield, J. C. "736. Nahal Se'elim 13." Discoveries in the Judaean Desert, 29. Oxford, forthcoming. *Editio princeps* of XḤev/Se 13.

Isaksson, Abel. *Marriage and Ministry in the New Temple: A Study with Special Reference to Mr. 19.13–12* [*sic*] *and 1. Cor 11.3–16*. Acta seminarii neotestamentici upsaliensis, 24. Lund, 1965. Good discussion of marriage and divorce in Hebrew scriptures, the Qumran texts, and the New Testament.

Lewis, Naphtali. *The Documents from the Bar Kokhba Period in the Cave of Letters: Greek Papyri*. Judean Desert Studies, 2. Jerusalem, 1989. Publication of the Greek texts of 5/6Ḥev. 18, 26, and 37.

Qimron, Elisha. "Celibacy in the Dead Sea Scrolls and the Two Kinds of Sectarians." In *The Madrid Qumran Congress: Proceedings of the International Congress on the Dead Sea Scrolls, Madrid, 18–21 March 1991*, edited by Julio Trebolle Barrera and Luis Vegas Montaner, vol. 1, pp. 287–294. Studies on the Texts of the Desert of Judah, 11. Leiden, 1992. Discusses celibate and marrying Essenes.

Yadin, Yigael, Jonas C. Greenfield, and Ada Yardeni. "Babatha's *Ketubba.*" *Israel Exploration Journal* 44 (1994), 75–101. *Editio princeps* of 5/6Ḥev 10.

Yardeni, Ada, and Jonas C. Greenfield. "*Shwbr shl ktwbh nḥl ṣ'lym* 13." In *Mḥqryn lzkrn shl M̆nḥm Šhṭrn*, edited by I. M. Gafni et al., pp. 197–208. Jerusalem, 1996. *Editio princips* of XḤev/Se 13.

JOSEPH A. FITZMYER, S.J.

MASADA. [*This entry consists of three parts:* Archaeology, History, *and* Written Material.]

Archaeology

The mountain of Masada, located on the southwestern shore of the Dead Sea, is one of the most famous archaeological sites in Israel. The mountain stands in isolation, surrounded on all sides by sheer cliffs, and rises to a height of over 1,300 feet above the shores of the Dead Sea. In the first century BCE, the Roman client king of Judea, Herod the Great, fortified the mountain and built a series of structures on the top, including two large palaces, storehouses, and water cisterns. Seventy years after his death, the Jews of Judea and Galilee revolted against Roman rule, and a band of about 960 Jewish rebels, known as Sicarii, took over the site. They continued to occupy Masada even after the fall of Jerusalem in 70 CE, until the arrival of the Tenth Roman Legion at the site two years later. The Romans set up a siege and managed to breach the walls around the top of the fortress by moving a battering ram up a ramp of earth and stones they had constructed on the western side of the mountain. When the Sicarii realized they had no more hopes of holding out against the Romans, they committed suicide in order to rob the Romans of their hard-won victory and to ensure their death as free people (in 73 or 74 CE). The story of Masada is told in detail by the Jewish historian Josephus Flavius, who lived at the time of the First Jewish Revolt.

Exploration of the Site. The American scholar Edward Robinson and his traveling companion Eli Smith, who visited the area in 1838, first proposed the identification of the site as Masada. The scholars who followed in their footsteps added their own observations and surveyed parts of the site. Among them were the French scholar Felicién de Saulcy (1851), the British explorer Captain Charles Warren (1867), and the German scholar Adolph Schulten (1932). In 1953 Shemaryahu Gutman started a systematic survey of the site. In 1955–1956 an excavation was carried out under the direction of Nahman Avigad, Michael Avi-Yonah, Yohanan Aharoni, and Immanuel Dunayevsky on behalf of the Hebrew University of Jerusalem and the Israel Exploration Society. Two extensive seasons of excavation were conducted between 1963 and 1965 under the direction of Yigael Yadin on behalf of the Hebrew University of Jerusalem, the Israel Exploration Society, and the Israel Department of Antiquities. Yadin also reconstructed the site. During the 1970s Gutman reconstructed one of the Roman siege camps. At the time of Yadin's death in 1984, only preliminary reports and a popular book had appeared in print. Since then, a number of scholars have undertaken the publication of the final excavation report, six volumes, in a series produced by the Israel Exploration Society and the Hebrew University of Jerusalem.

Small-scale excavations in selected areas were conducted on top of the mountain from 1994 to 1996 under the direction of Ehud Netzer of the Hebrew University. Another expedition in 1995, under the direction of Gideon Foerster, Benny Arubas (Hebrew University), Haim Goldfus (Ben-Gurion University) and me (Magness) (Tufts University), conducted excavations in the Roman siege camp F and cut a section through the Roman siege camp.

Phases of Occupation. On the basis of Josephus's testimony and the archaeological evidence, a number of occupational phases can be distinguished at Masada. The earliest phases, which are represented mainly by scattered potsherds rather than architectural remains, belong to the Chalcolithic period (fourth millennium BCE) and the Iron Age (tenth to seventh centuries BCE). According to Josephus, the site was first fortified by "Jonathan the High Priest." This probably refers to the Hasmonean king Alexander Jannaeus (103–76 BCE) or perhaps to Jonathan the brother of Judah the Maccabee (152–143 BCE). However, architectural remains from the Hasmonean period have proven difficult to identify. Instead, most of the buildings at Masada were erected by Herod the Great (40–4 BCE). Netzer, who published the final report on the architecture, has distinguished a number of building phases during the reign of Herod. Following Herod's death the site was occupied and maintained by a Roman garrison that seems to have made few if any architectural changes. During the period of the First Jewish Revolt (66–70 CE), the Sicarii occupied and modified the Herodian buildings and erected some structures of their own. Many of the Herodian buildings were destroyed during the siege and the subsequent fall of Masada to the Romans in 73 or 74 CE. The Romans left a small garrison to guard the site until 115 or 116 CE at the latest. An earthquake destroyed many of the remaining buildings on the mountain some time between the second and fourth centuries CE. The last phase of occupation at Masada consisted of a small Byzantine monastic settlement (fifth to early seventh centuries CE). A well-preserved church on the summit of the mountain is associated with this community.

Archaeological Remains. Herod fortified the top of Masada with a casemate wall (a double wall divided into rooms that could serve as barracks or as an arsenal for storing weapons; many of the casemate rooms were used as dwellings by the Sicarii). The wall, which runs along the edge of the mountain, has towers located at intervals and gates leading into the site. One gate is located at the top of the snake path, which ascends the steep eastern side of the mountain in a winding, serpentine manner. Another gate is located on the other side of the mountain, by Herod's western palace. It was approached by a path that was covered by the Roman siege ramp, and in the Byzantine period another gate (which is still visible) was erected on this spot. A third gate is located on the northwestern side of the mountain. It provided access to a path that led to two rows of cisterns hewn into the rocky slope below. These cisterns were filled by flash-flood waters channeled through an aqueduct from riverbeds (wadis) in the vicinity of Masada. The Herodian buildings are concentrated at the northern end of the mountain. They include a three-tiered palace-villa (with a small bathhouse), a large bathhouse, storehouses, and an administrative building. Another complex constituting the western palace is located about midway along the western side of the site. A number of small palace buildings that apparently date to the earliest Herodian phase are scattered around the top of the mountain. Except for these and a large open pool, the southern and eastern parts of the site are almost empty of structures. The following description proceeds from north to south.

At the heart of the northern palace complex is the palace itself, which is spectacularly constructed on a series of three buttressed terraces overhanging the northern edge of the mountain. The palace is separated from the rest of the site by a large, white plaster wall. Originally the only access was around the eastern end of the wall, where a guardhouse was located. From here one entered the upper terrace of the northern palace, which consisted of a rectangular wing in the south and a semicircular structure in the north. The rectangular wing contained two pairs of rooms paved with simple black and white mosaics. These rooms apparently served as the king's bedrooms; in the Byzantine period this area was reoccupied by monks. The bedrooms opened on to the semicircular structure, which formed a balcony with a view to the north. The middle terrace was a circular structure. (*tholos*) that seems to have been a colonnaded, covered hall. Vertical niches in the cliff face on the southern side of the terrace originally may have contained rows of wooden shelves for a library. The lower terrace carried a rectangular colonnaded hall, which was probably roofed. Well-preserved wall paintings (frescoes) that imitate multicolored stone and marble panels can still be seen on some of the walls of the lower terrace. The columns and some of the architectural details are covered with molded plaster (stucco), again in imitation of marble. The structure on this terrace apparently functioned as a dining room (triclinium). Thus, while the upper terrace contained a suite of private bedrooms, the buildings on the middle and lower terraces were intended primarily for recreation and the entertainment of guests. The three terraces originally were connected by a staircase whose remains still can be traced. A small bathhouse associated with the lower terrace contained a group of important finds from the time of the First Jewish Revolt.

Upon the steps leading to the cold-water pool of the bathhouse and on the ground nearby were the remains of three human skeletons: a man about twenty years of age, a young woman, and a child (these and twenty-five other skeletons found in a cave on the southeastern side of the mountain were the only human remains discovered in the excavations). The woman's hair was still preserved, and the associated finds included scale armor, arrows, leather sandals, fragments of a prayer shawl (*tallit*), and an ostracon (inscribed potsherd) with Hebrew letters. Yadin suggested that these were the remains of some of the Sicarii defenders of Masada, perhaps the last to commit suicide. According to Josephus the last zealot, after verifying that all the others were dead, set fire to the palace and killed himself near the bodies of his family. The finds in the bathhouse were buried in the debris of the collapse of the palace rooms above. The human skeletal remains from Masada were the subject of a recent article by Joseph Zias, a physical anthropologist. According to Zias, there were only seven or eight human skeletons in the cave on the southeastern side of the mountain. In addition, the presence of pig bones in the cave indicates that these are probably the remains of Romans, not Jews. Zias has also suggested that the fragmentary nature of the three skeletons from the northern palace indicates that they did not belong to a single family, but were deposited at this point by hyenas (Zias, 1998).

The northern palace was serviced by a complex adjacent to the upper terrace, which includes a large bathhouse, storerooms, and an administrative building. The bathhouse was entered through a colonnaded courtyard with a mosaic-paved floor and painted (frescoed) walls. It is typical of Roman bathhouses of the first century BCE, having been equipped with a "dressing room" (*apodyterium*), "cold-water pool" (*frigidarium*), "tepid room" (*tepidarium*), and "steam room" (*caldarium*). The heat in the steam room was provided by a hypocaust system, in which dozens of small pillars supported the floor. Hot air from an adjacent furnace circulated among the pillars and through terra-cotta pipes along the walls. Water thrown onto the floor and walls from bathtubs in the niches at either end of the room created steam. The walls of the bathhouse were painted with paneled frescoes, and the floors were paved with black and while tiles (*opus sectile*).

The storehouses consist of rows of long, narrow rooms oriented more or less north-south. Broken storage jars found in these rooms originally contained oil, wine, and grain. Latin inscriptions identify some as wine jars imported by Herod from Italy. Other jars and potsherds found at Masada bear inscriptions in Aramaic, Greek, and Hebrew, often consisting of Jewish names or titles. These include a group of eleven or twelve ostraca discovered near the entrance to the storehouses. Each is inscribed in the same handwriting with a single name or nickname in Hebrew or Aramaic. One that bears the name Ben Ya'ir probably refers to Eleazar ben Ya'ir, the leader of the Sicarii at Masada. Yadin identified these ostraca as the "lots" drawn by the Sicarii at the time of the suicide, since Josephus states that after the men had killed their wives and children, they chose ten men by lot to slay the other men. These ten men drew lots again, and the last one killed the remaining nine men and then himself. However, as Joseph Naveh has pointed out, there are more than ten "lots" in this group, and they do not differ in character from many of the other ostraca found at Masada. Thus, their identification as lots remains uncertain. Another potsherd found by Netzer in his recent excavations on the northwest side of the mountain bears the Latin inscription "Herod the Great, King of the Jews (or Judea)." It is the first inscription found at Masada containing Herod's full title.

On the northwestern side of the mountain is a large hall set into the line of the casemate wall. During the Herodian period, it contained a porch or anteroom that led into a colonnaded hall. During the time of the First Jewish Revolt, the Sicarii removed the wall separating the anteroom from the hall and added rows of benches along the walls and a room at the back. The addition of the benches and the discovery of scroll fragments under the floor of the back room (which suggest that the room served as a repository, or *genizah*) indicate that this structure was used as a synagogue by the Sicarii. Yadin believed that this structure functioned as a synagogue already in the time of Herod, but this has not been accepted by all scholars. In the final report, Netzer has raised the possibility that the hall originally may have functioned as a stable (a purpose it apparently served between the death of Herod and the outbreak of the revolt). Fragments of other scrolls were found at Masada, especially in another casemate room on the northwestern side of the mountain. They include biblical texts and a fragment of an apparently Essene document (Songs of the Sabbath Sacrifice); copies of the same work have been found among the Dead Sea Scrolls from the caves of Qumran. The presence of the latter led Yadin to suggest that after the fall of Qumran to the Romans (probably in 68 CE), some of the inhabitants joined the Sicarii forces at Masada.

The western palace complex is located about midway along the western side of the mountain. It is made up of a wing containing the official rooms (the "core"), another wing with a group of storehouses, and a service wing that includes servants' quarters, workshops, and administrative rooms. At the heart of the official wing is a room that contained four rectangular postholes that are thought to have held the base of a canopied throne. One of the rooms that provided access to the throne room was paved with a polychrome mosaic floor decorated with intricate geometric and floral designs. The official wing also contained a bathhouse, which is paved with more polychrome mosaics. Netzer disagrees with Yadin's conclusion that the western palace served as Herod's ceremonial palace, believing instead that the northern palace fulfilled this function.

As mentioned above, the Sicarii occupied many of the casemate rooms and converted the hall set into the casemate wall on the northwestern side of the mountain into a synagogue. They also constructed two ritual baths (*miqva'ot*), one in the administrative wing of the northern palace complex, and the other in a casemate room at the southeastern edge of the site. Netzer has suggested that some of the other pools at Masada, such as the frigidarium in the large bathhouse in the northern palace complex, also may have functioned as *miqva'ot*. Two of the rooms in the northern palace (Loci 442 and 456), one of which was paved with the polychrome mosaic described above, were apparently used by the Sicarii as workshops or smithies for the forging of iron arrowheads.

Roman Siege. The signs of the Roman siege are still clearly visible at Masada. When they arrived at the foot of the mountain, the Roman forces (which included the Tenth Legion and numbered up to ten thousand soldiers) constructed a circumvallation wall with guard towers around the bottom of the site. The soldiers were housed in eight walled camps (designated by the letters A through H) surrounding the base of the mountain. Flavius Silva, the Roman commander, communicated with his forces by means of messages sent with runners along a path connecting the camps. [*See* Roman Camps.] The Romans managed to take Masada by constructing a ramp of earth and stones that can still be seen on the western side of the mountain. Silva's headquarters are believed to have been located in the two largest Camps, B on the eastern side of the mountain, and F on the western side near the foot of the ramp. Among the remains uncovered in the excavations in Camp F is a huge three-sided rectilinear structure that opened toward the east, perhaps the officers' triclinium or dining room. A tent unit nearby probably served as officers' quarters, judging from its size, central location, and unusually rich finds. Next to this unit stood a raised, square stone podium, apparently the tribunal from which the commander addressed his troops and reviewed parades. The headquarters itself might be represented by another unit just to the west that had beautifully plastered walls. Also uncovered in the excavations were rows of mess units (*contubernia*), individual tent units housing groups of eight enlisted men. Each consists of a small rectangular room encircled on three sides by earth and stone benches, on which the men ate and slept, with a small vestibule or anteroom in front. The remains of hearths, where the soldiers who shared the tent cooked their food, occupy the corners of the vestibules. All of the units in Camp F were constructed of dry-laid fieldstone walls, which originally stood three to four feet high. Leather tents pitched above these walls would have been held in place by iron pegs. The section cut through the Roman siege ramp revealed that it was constructed of fieldstones, each of which could be lifted by a single man. The stones were held in place by a framework made of horizontally and vertically laid pieces of tamarisk and date palm wood. Once the ramp was constructed, the Romans were able to drag their siege machinery to the top of the mountain and break through the Herodian casemate wall. At this point, according to Josephus, Eleazar ben Ya'ir gathered the Sicarii together and convinced them to commit suicide.

Suicide Controversy. Josephus describes the site of Masada and the events that transpired there in great detail. Just a few years earlier, he had participated in the First Jewish Revolt as the commander of the Jewish forces of the Galilee. Much of his testimony has been borne out by the archaeological finds at Masada. Yadin understood Josephus's account literally, and clearly it influenced his interpretation of the archaeological remains (such as the "lots"). However, the accuracy of Josephus's account, and especially the veracity of the suicide story, have been called into question by a number of scholars. One of them is Shaye J. D. Cohen, who has pointed out that, among other things, there are a number of mass suicide stories in Greco-Roman works of literature. He therefore has suggested that Josephus used the suicide as a literary device to enhance the drama of his story about Masada (Cohen, 1982).

The archaeological evidence has been interpreted as both supporting and contradicting Josephus's account. For example, Netzer has pointed out that only about 10 percent of the buildings at Masada showed signs of burning. He argues that the others were not burned because their wooden roof beams had been dismantled by the Sicarii for use in the wood and earth wall they constructed at the top of the Roman siege ramp, as described by Josephus. On the other hand, Hillel Geva recently has proposed that the debris piled against the outside of the large white plaster wall separating the northern palace from the rest of the mountain represents a siege ramp constructed by the Romans (Geva, 1996). If this is the case, it suggests that there was a battle on top of the mountain during which at least some of the Sicarii took refuge in the northern palace, thereby contradicting Josephus's account.

BIBLIOGRAPHY

Aviram, Joseph, Gideon Foerster, and Ehud Netzer, eds. *Masada IV: The Yigael Yadin Excavations 1963–1965 Final Reports.* Jerusalem, 1994. Contains the final publication of the oil lamps; textiles, basketry, cordage, and related artifacts; wood remains; ballista balls; and an addendum on the human skeletal remains.

Cohen, Shaye J. D. "Masada: Literary Tradition, Archaeological Remains, and the Credibility of Josephus." *Journal of Jewish Studies* 33 (1982), 385–405. A critical analysis of Josephus's reliability as a historian, focusing on the suicide story at Masada.

Cotton, Hannah M., and Joseph Geiger. *The Latin and Greek Documents. Masada II: The Yigael Yadin Excavations 1963–1965 Final Reports.* Jerusalem, 1989. The final publication of the Latin and Greek documents from Yadin's excavations.

Foerster, Gideon. *Art and Architecture. Masada V: The Yigael Yadin Excavations 1963–1965 Final Reports.* Jerusalem, 1995. The final publication of the art and architecture of Herod's buildings at Masada, including the wall paintings (frescoes) and molded plaster (stucco). This complements Ehud Netzer's volume on the architecture (see below).

Geva, Hillel. "The Siege Ramp Laid by the Romans to Conquer the Northern Palace at Masada" (in Hebrew with English summary). *Eretz-Israel* 26 (1996), 297–306. Geva interprets the debris piled against the large white plaster wall separating the northern palace from the rest of the mountain as a siege ramp constructed by the Romans.

Magness, Jodi. "Masada 1995: Discoveries at Camp F." *Biblical Archaeologist* 59 (1996), 181. A brief report on the 1995 excavations in Roman siege camp F.

Meshorer, Yaacov. *The Coins of Masada. Masada I: The Yigael Yadin Excavations 1963–1965 Final Reports.* Jerusalem, 1989. The final publication of the coins from Yadin's excavations.

Netzer, Ehud. *The Buildings, Stratigraphy and Architecture. Masada III: The Yigael Yadin Excavations 1963–1965 Final Reports.* Jerusalem, 1991. The final publication of the architectural remains uncovered in Yadin's excavations. See pages 69–132, plates 61–81.

Tsafrir, Yoram. "The Desert Fortresses of Judaea in the Second Temple Period." In *The Jerusalem Cathedra 2,* edited by Lee I. Levine, pp. 120–145. Jerusalem, 1982. A good overview of the Hasmonean and Herodian fortresses of the Judean Desert.

Yadin, Yigael. "The Excavation of Masada—1963/64, Preliminary Report." *Israel Exploration Journal* 15 (1965), 1–120. The preliminary report on the first season of Yadin's excavations at Masada containing twenty-four plates and a pullout plan of the site.

Yadin, Yigael. *Masada: Herod's Fortress and the Zealots' Last Stand.* London, 1966. Yadin's popular account of his excavations at Masada.

Yadin, Yigael, and Joseph Naveh. *The Aramaic and Hebrew Ostraca and Jar Inscriptions. Masada I: The Yigael Yadin Excavations 1963–1965 Final Reports.* Jerusalem, 1989. The final publication of the

Aramaic and Hebrew inscriptions from Yadin's excavations. See pages 1–68 and plates 1–60.

Zias, Joseph. "Whose Bones? Were They Really Jewish Defenders? Did Yadin Deliberately Obfuscate?" *Biblical Archaeology Review* 24 (1998), 40–45, 64–66. A reevaluation of the number and identity of the human skeletal remains found by Yadin at Masada.

JODI MAGNESS

History

According to Josephus (*The Jewish War* 7.285), Jonathan the High Priest built Masada. Opinions concerning the identity of this Jonathan are divided. Some say that the reference is to Alexander Jannaeus, king of Judea from 103 to 76 BCE. Others theorize that the source before Josephus utilized the Hebrew name of Alexander Jannaeus—Jonathan—which was unknown to Josephus. Josephus therefore may have assumed that Jonathan the Hasmonean built Masada. Another possibility is that because the coins of Alexander Jannaeus are inscribed in Greek with Aleksandros Basileus and in Hebrew with Jonathan the High Priest, whoever used the Hebrew name designated Alexander Jannaeus as High Priest. Josephus explicitly writes that Aleksandros, king of the Jews, is the one who built Machaerus (*The Jewish War* 7.171) at approximately the same time as the construction of Masada. The discovery of twelve Ptolemaic coins and five Seleucid coins near Masada makes it possible that Jonathan the Hasmonean built Masada during the years that he spent in the desert after the death of his brother Judah (between 161 and 152 BCE). Alternatively, it is entirely possible that Masada was only built later, at the beginning of the first century BCE by Alexander Jannaeus.

The similarity between the western palace on Masada and the twin palaces of Shelamzion Alexandra, which were discovered in Jericho by A. Netzer, enables us to date the western palace at Masada to the days of Jannaeus. Likewise, there is proof that some of the wells were built during the Hasmonean era. Masada is mentioned in ostraca (fragments of ancient pottery engraved with writing) discovered at Wadi Murabbaʿat and paleographically dated between the years 125–120 BCE.

In the year 42 BCE Jewish rebels who were opposed to the house of Antipater gained control of Masada. They held the fort until they were forced to surrender to Herod (*The Jewish War* 1.236–238, *Jewish Antiquities* 14.296). In 40 BCE, when Herod fled from the Parthians and Antigonus in Judea, he left eight hundred of his family and close friends at Masada (*The Jewish War* 1.246–267, *Jewish Antiquities* 14.361–362). Antigonus besieged the fortress during one of the winters between 40 and 37 BCE, in an attempt to capture Herod's family. It is possible that there is archaeological evidence of the seige works Antigonus had erected beneath one of the Roman camps surrounding Masada. Josephus notes that the occupants of Masada debated whether to escape to the Nabateans because of the lack of water; however, sudden rainfall at Masada replenished the wells in the fortress, and Herod's family succeeded in surviving until Herod's return to Judea in 37 BCE (*The Jewish War* 1.286–287, 293–294; *Jewish Antiquities* 14.390–391, 400). An assumption can be made that Masada was not besieged during the entire rule of Antigonus, since three coins minted in Jerusalem during his reign were found in his fortress.

King Herod (37–4 BCE) is credited with building the majority of the existing structures at Masada, including the three-tiered palace, the bathhouse, and the storehouses. Herod also ordered the construction of dams and water conduits leading to the western pools. In 31 BCE, when Herod went to meet Augustus after the battle of Actium, he again left his family at Masada (*Antiquities* 15.184).

It is difficult to determine when the colossal building projects that Herod initiated at Masada were completed. Intriguingly, during Marcus Agrippa's visit to Judea in 15 BCE, Herod took him to Alexandrion, Herodium, and Hyrcania (Khirbet Mird), but not to Masada (*Jewish Antiquities* 16.14). Therefore, it is quite possible that the building projects at Masada had not yet been completed. While thirteen pitchers bearing Latin inscriptions mentioning Herod king of Judea were found in the northern storehouses and dated to the year 19 BCE, they cannot prove when building activity in the area ceased.

After the death of Herod, Masada passed into the hands of Archelaus (4 BCE–6 CE), 176 of whose coins were discovered in the fortress. After the exile of Archelaus, a force of Roman guards remained at Masada. Coins of all the Roman commanders were discovered at Masada (517 coins in all). It is not known whether the soldiers staying at Masada in the days of Agrippa I (41–43 CE) were Jewish or Roman (114 coins of Agrippa I were found in Masada). There is no doubt that Masada was manned with guards and equipped with large amounts of provisions and weapons before the First Jewish Revolt.

In 66 CE the Sicarii, headed by Menahem ben Yehudah the Galilean, gained control of Masada (*The Jewish War* 2.433–434). When Menahem was killed during a power struggle in Jerusalem, some of his followers, headed by his relative Eleazar ben Yaʾir, fled back to Masada (*The Jewish War* 2.446–447). Josephus mentions that "the robbers dwelling in Masada destroyed all the villages around the fortress and razed the entire land." Apparently, Josephus had a personal interest in representing the followers of Eleazar ben Yaʾir in a negative light.

Masada was not cut off from Jerusalem during the course of the First Jewish Revolt, as evidenced by thousands of bronze and silver coins from Jerusalem, which reached the fortress. Refugees escaping to Masada during the revolt settled in the various buildings and implemented architectural changes. The Sicarii and refugees lived within the enclosing wall of the western palace and in the buildings adjacent to it. They strictly adhered to the laws governing ritual purity and impurity as the writings discovered upon the pitchers found in the fortress substantiate. Various people fled to the fortress, among them priests of respectable lineage, as the writing upon a pitcher bearing the name of "ʿAqaviah ben Ḥananiah the High Priest" proves. (Ḥananiah was most likely Ḥananyah ben Nadivi, who served as High Priest between 59 and 47 BCE.) The refugees were probably divided into different groups, and they distributed coupons, most likely as a method of rationing provisions. Two coins minted during the reign of Agrippa II in Banyas and discovered in Masada prove that refugees from the Galilee reached Masada as well.

Y. Yadin claims, based on a Qumran manuscript (Songs of the Sabbath Sacrifice) found near the synagogue at Masada, that members of the sect of Qumran fled to Masada to escape from the Roman army. Talmon, meanwhile, hypothesized that a small fragment of a papyrus mentioning Mount Gerizim, which was also found near the synagogue, confirms that Samaritans fled from the Roman army to Masada. Both these theories can be questioned. The discovery of the Songs of the Sabbath Sacrifice at Masada does not prove that anyone from Qumran fled to Masada; perhaps its presence at Masada merely indicates that it was extremely popular during the Second Temple era among people who adhered to the solar calender. Likewise, the papyrus containing the name Mount Gerizim does not prove that Samaritans escaped to Masada. Indeed, it is possible that it is an anti-Samaritan prayer praising the Lord for the destruction of the temple on Mount Gerizim. Similar prayers were discovered at Qumran in Apocryphon of Joseph[a] (4Q371).

After the destruction of Jerusalem, three fortresses remained in the hands of the rebels: Herodium, Machaerus, and Masada (*The Jewish War* 4.55). It is difficult to determine the number of people who escaped to Masada following the destruction of Jerusalem in 70 CE. Meshorer theorized that until 73 CE people were still arriving at Masada, since coins that were minted in Ashkelon during the year 72/73 CE were found in the fortress (Meshorer, 1989). Meshorer is of the opinion that these coins were brought to Masada by Jewish rebels and not by Roman soldiers.

It was most likely during the winter of the year 73 CE (some suggest that the event occurred during the winter of 74 CE) that Flavius Silva, the commander of the tenth legion and governor of Judea, besieged Masada. One may suppose that the siege lasted about three months. Masada fell, therefore, during the spring of 73 CE. The Roman army surrounded Masada with a wall 3.5 kilometers long and patrolled by guards to prevent escape. In addition to the wall, the Roman army erected eight camps surrounding Masada and a rampart west of the fortress on which the army raised siege machines. At this stage the defenders of Masada disassembled the wooden ceilings of some structures in Masada in order to build an inner wall. This wall did not last and in the end it went up in flames ignited by the Roman army (*The Jewish War* 7.275–319).

Josephus attests that 960 people fell at Masada and seven were spared. During excavations conducted at Masada, 25 skeletons, some of women and children, were discovered in one of the caves on the southern cliff. Three additional skeletons of a man, woman, and child were likewise discovered on the lowest step of the northern palace. It can be assumed that during the fall of Masada the majority of the skeletons were thrown by Roman soldiers into the abyss surrounding the cliff.

Josephus states that a number of the defenders of Masada committed suicide on the night before the conquering of the fortress following the burning of the inner wall (*The Jewish War* 7.389–406). The words that Josephus put into the mouths of Agrippa II (*The Jewish War* 2.345–401) and Eleazar ben Yaʾir (*The Jewish War* 7.323–388) are a historical convention of the time, calculated to give the reader background material and express the historian's point of view. Therefore, we cannot accept Josephus's description as a historically accurate description. Although it must be assumed that a few of the people of Masada indeed committed suicide as Josephus says, suicides occurred in other places conquered by the Roman army. Of the rest of the Jews at Masada, some of them fought and met their deaths in combat; a portion of them were executed after the conclusion of the war; and some of them were sold into slavery. It should be noted that in the northern region of Masada, Roman soldiers were compelled to draw an additional rampart in order to conquer the northern palace, demonstrating that at least a few of the warriors of Masada continued to fight even after the Romans burst into the fortress.

Yadin claimed that the ostraca he found in the fortress served as the lots which the rebels cast when they decided to commit suicide. This description does not coincide with the description of Josephus, although it is interesting that "ben Yair," the name of Masada's commander, is written on one of the ostraca.

After the fall of Masada the Roman army returned to guard the fortress. On the summit of Masada were found documents of Roman soldiers who had participated in the siege, among them two soldiers' pay stubs, letters, and a list of medical equipment for the wounded. Also discovered at Masada were five coins of conquered Judea (*Judea Capta*), which Titus had minted in Caesarea between the years 71 and 81 CE. The latest Roman coin found at the site is a silver coin from the days of Trajan; it was minted in Provincia Arabia in 112 CE (coin no. 3840). It should be noted that a treasure of thirteen tetradrachmas from the days of Nero, Vespasian, and Trajan, which a Roman soldier probably hid, was also discovered.

At the beginning of the sixth century a group of Christian monks settled at Masada. This monastery most likely functioned until the Persian conquest in 614 CE. It seems that these monks wrote Syriac, as an ostracon found near Masada testifies. Approximately twenty monks resided on the western side of Masada, in an area that lay near the Roman bulwark. The presence of a very small number of monks is evidenced by only five coins.

BIBLIOGRAPHY

Cohen, S. J. D. "Masada: Literary Tradition, Archaeological Remains, and the Credibility of Josephus." *Journal of Jewish Studies* 33 (1982), 385–405.

Cotton, H. M. "The Date of the Fall of Masada: The Evidence of the Masada Papyri." *Zeitschrift für Papyrologie und Epigraphik* 78 (1989), 157–162.

Gichon, M. "A Further Camp at Masada." *Bulletin du Centre Interdisciplinaire de Recherches Aeriennes* 18 (1995), 25–27.

Meshorer, Ya'acov. *Masada I: The Coins of Masada*. Jerusalem, 1989.

Richmond, I. A. "The Roman Siege-Works of Masada, Israel." *Journal of Roman Studies* 52 (1962), 145–155.

Roth, J. "The Length of the Siege of Masada." *Scripta Classica Israelica* 14 (1995), 87–110.

Schulten, A. "Masada: Die Burg des Herodes und die Römischen Lager." *Zeitschrift des Deutschen Palästina-Vereins* 66 (1933), 1–184.

Yadin, Yigael. "The Excavation of Masada—1963/64: Preliminary Report." *Israel Exploration Journal* 15 (1965).

Yadin, Yigael. *Masada: Herod's Fortress and the Zealot's Last Stand*. London, 1966.

Yadin, Yigael, and Joseph Naveh. *Masada I: The Aramaic and Hebrew Ostraca and Jar Inscriptions*. Jerusalem, 1989.

HANAN ESHEL

Written Material

The excavations at Masada (1963–1965) led by Yigael Yadin yielded not only a considerable amount of materials inscribed in Greek and Latin, but also the remains of fourteen parchment documents written in Hebrew (one possibly in Aramaic) and in Hebrew square characters, and one Hebrew papyrus fragment penned in Paleo-Hebrew. These fragments were discovered in various locations at the desert fortress. They are identified by the first set of figures in the *siglum* of each piece, whereas the second set of figures indicates the number of the find in a given locus (excavated archaeological feature), e.g. 1039–270. While some items were found *in situ*, others were discovered in places where presumably they had been discarded by Roman soldiers. Casemate 1039 (a storage room in the rampart), in which seven items were found, together with Hebrew and Aramaic ostraca (inscribed pottery fragments) and Latin and Greek papyri, stands out in this respect, giving "the impression that articles from various rooms were thrown in disorder into this one and heaped up there." The Hebrew fragments stem from works of a variety of literary genres.

Scrolls of Biblical Books. Fragments of seven manuscripts of books of the Hebrew scriptures, two scrolls each of *Leviticus* and *Psalms*, and one each of *Genesis*, *Deuteronomy*, and *Ezekiel*, were discovered. Not one is preserved in one piece, even the smallest, Psalms[b] (Mas1f), consists of two bits of parchment. The straight margins of some fragments seemingly evince willful tearing, presumably by Roman soldiers who, as Josephus alleges, vented their rage on the sacred writings of the Jewish defenders after the conquest of Masada. The condition of these fragments is probably not caused by deterioration or damage caused by insects, the effects of which can be observed most prominently in other Qumran scrolls.

Jubilees from Masada (Mas1i; 1039–317) contains one fairly sizable piece and five scraps of parchment, almost all of which can be fitted together on the basis of edge contours and extant letters. In the reconstituted fragment, measuring 5.6 by 4.5 centimeters, a part of the text of *Genesis* 46.7–11 is preserved, in which are listed the names of Jacob's sons who went down with him to Egypt.

Leviticus[a] (Mas1a; 1039–270) consists of two pieces of parchment, which can be joined to form one fragment measuring 9.7 by 11.5 centimeters. It contains most of the text of *Leviticus* 4.3–9, which deals with expiation offerings.

Leviticus[b] (Mas1b; 92–480) consists of over forty pieces, ranging in size from mere snippets of parchment to fragments as large as the palm of a hand. The preserved bits of text are practically identical with the Masoretic Text of *Leviticus* 8.31–11.40. Therefore, every piece can be integrated mosaic-fashion in five partly restorable columns. The mock-up sheet reconstituted in this way measures approximately 54.0 by 21.5 centimeters. The portion of text preserved in the five reconstructed columns comprises somewhat less than one-tenth of the text of *Leviticus*, both by a verse and a page count in modern editions. We may therefore conclude that forty-eight to fifty columns would have been required to accommodate the entire text of the book. The fully rolled-out scroll would have measured approximately 5.4 to 5.6 meters, without taking into account a handle sheet (see below), if such a sheet was attached to it.

The four fragments of *Deuteronomy* from Masada (Mas1c; 1034/1–4) evidently are remains of the final two columns of the last sheet of a *Deuteronomy* scroll and contain parts of *Deuteronomy* 33.17–34.6, including the Song of Moses. In fragment 1 the beginnings of seven lines, which constitute the main portion of the preserved text, are extant. Together with the 3.4-centimeter-wide top margin, fragment 1 measures 8.0 by 8.0 centimeters. The largest fragment, fragment 2, measures 13.8 by 10.0 centimeters. It holds seven line endings, of which five are the continuation of the parallel lines on fragment 1; next to them is a strip of the left-hand margin. A blank stretch of parchment measuring 9.7 by 11.0 centimeters is sewn to the margin. Needle holes are still discernible with a snip of thread running through them. This blank piece is evidently the remainder of the handle sheet, which enfolded the written columns of the rolled-up scroll, serving as their protective wrapper. Fragment 3 measures 4.0 by 3.3 centimeters and contains parts of four lines. On the strength of edge contours and textual sequence it can be joined with fragment 4, measuring 2.0 by 4.5 centimeters, in which fractions of text from the middle parts of six lines are extant.

Ezekiel from Masada (Mas1d; 1043–2220) consists of over fifty pieces of varying size forming the four columns that originally held the text of *Ezekiel* 35.11–38.8, including the "Vision of the Dry Bones." All four columns can be reconstructed in large measure because of the virtual identity of the recoverable text portions with the Masoretic Text. The resulting mock-up sheet measures 41.0 by 29.5 centimeters and contains 85 of the 1,273 verses that the Masoretes counted in the book of *Ezekiel*, approximately one-fifteenth of the book. Therefore, the entire text of the book would have taken up approximately sixty columns of forty-two lines each. The fully unrolled scroll originally may have attained a length of approximately 5.75 to 6.15 meters, and approximately 6.0 to 6.4 meters with a handle sheet.

The two pieces of Psalms[a] from Masada (Mas1e; 1039–160) can be comfortably joined on the strength of their edge contours and the extant or restorable text portions of three columns. The upper column (i) measures 18.0 by 14.7 centimeters, and the lower column (ii) 20.2 by 13.5 centimeters. A spur at the top of column ii projects almost perfectly into a concave indentation at the bottom of column i. The combination of both columns makes up a fragment that is 25.5 centimeters high. The apparent loss of some 2.7 centimeters results from the ingress of the spur of column ii into the concavity of column i. Four partial lines of text at the joint were lost in a fairly large lacuna that extends from the middle of the second column to its left edge. The ruggedness of the edges, which is especially noticeable on the right side of fragment 1, seems to evince deterioration of the parchment rather than willful tearing, as Yadin assumed (1965, p. 103). The column is 20 centimeters high and holds twenty-seven written lines and divider blanks between psalms that equal the width of approximately two more lines. The fully extant bottom margin measures 3.4 centimeters; the top margin 2.1 centimeters. Thus, the scroll originally attained a height of about 25.5 centimeters.

Psalms[a] from Masada encompasses the text of Psalms 81.2b–85.6a in one complete and two partial columns of hemistichs (half lines). The middle column (ii) is the best preserved. It contains the text of Psalms 81.16b–83.17a in twenty-seven lines. A 2.1-centimeter-wide blank in the column separates Psalm 81 from Psalm 82, except for the latter's superscription, *mizmor le-ʾAsaf* ("a song of Asaph") which is kept apart from the last word of Psalm 81, *asbiʿeka*, by a somewhat broader than regular space between the line. Variants on the Masoretic Text, which are more numerous in Psalms[a] than in other biblical fragments, are concentrated in the lower half of this column (Ps. 83.8–15).

The right-hand part of column i is lost. The extant left-hand side holds parts of the line endings of Psalms 81.2–18. Equally, the left-hand length of column iii is missing. But in the right-hand length, which is fully extant, all the first hemistichs of Psalms 83.17b–85.6 are preserved. A blank of 1.2 centimeters separates Psalm 83 from Psalm 84, and a slightly larger one keeps Psalm 84 apart from Psalm 85.

In contrast to the color of the other fragments, which ranges from light brown to almost black, the two small pieces of Psalms[b] (Mas1f; 1103–1742) are practically paper white. They can be combined easily in one fragment measuring 7.5 by 4.4 centimeters, which contains Psalm 150 written in especially small letters as poetry in sense units separated by blank spaces.

Comparison with Masoretic Text. Some textual variants between the biblical fragments from Masada and the Masoretic Text should be noted. Psalms[a] (Mas1e ii.19) reads *ʾlhy ʾdwm* ("the gods of Edom"); Masoretic Text for Psalm 83.7 reads *ohelei Edom* ("the tents of Edom"). MasGen 1.2 reads *mitsrayi]m et yaʿaqov ha-baʾim mitsraymah yaʿaqov uvanav* ("to Egypt with Jacob"); the Masoretic Text for *Genesis* 46.8 reads *ha-baʾim mitsraymah yaʿaqov uvanav*. MasGen reflects here possibly the reading *et yaʿaqov avihem* ("with Jacob their father"), which is preserved in the expanded Ethiopic version of the passage in *Jubilees* 44.11–13.

There are further variants with respect to *plene* and defective spellings. In several instances, Masada fragments exhibit a *plene* spelling vis-à-vis a defective spelling in the Masoretic Text, or vice versa. But, in general, the Masada texts appear to exhibit the same fluctuation in the use of *plene* and defective spellings as the Masoretic Text. In this respect, the Masada scrolls differ decidedly from many Qumran biblical and nonbiblical scrolls, which are marked by a tendency to use *superplene* spellings.

For all intents and purposes, the text preserved in the Masada fragments is identical to the Masoretic Text. The textual congruence is highlighted by instances in which a Masada fragment agrees with the Masoretic Text against a variant preserved in a practically contemporaneous Qumran source. The same holds true for variants in other ancient versions of the scriptures, particularly in the Septuagint, especially where additions or deletions are involved. Special mention should be made of the two-word divine epithet (*Adonay Elohim*) of the Masoretic Text of the *Book of Ezekiel*. The Septuagint often renders the epithet by one word only, *Kurios*. In all recoverable instances, the Ezekiel scroll discovered at Masada exhibits the Masoretic reading.

Most important for gauging the relation between Ezekiel found at Masada and the Masoretic Text are variants in the Septuagint that show either the translator's misunderstanding of the Hebrew text or his deliberate deviation from it, or else a derivation from a divergent Hebrew text. For example, the Masoretic Text of *Ezekiel* 35.12 reads: "I have heard all [*kol*] your blasphemies. . . . The mountains of Israel have been given to us to devour [*le-ʾokhlah*]." The Septuagint reads: "I heard the voice [*qol*] of your blasphemies. . . . You have said the mountains of Israel are desolate and have been given to us as an inheritance [*le-naḥalah*]."

Parashot: the section system. In the Masada texts of Leviticus[b] and Ezekiel, in which large enough portions of text are preserved, one notes an overall although not complete agreement of internal divisions with the masoretic section system, as exhibited by other major medieval Masoretic Text manuscripts, the Aleppo Codex (A), Codex Leningradensis B19a (L), the Cairo Codex of the Prophets (C), and Codex Sassoon (S), which indeed differ among themselves in this respect. But a section indicated in a Masada text by a blank in the line or one that can be restored with confidence on the strength of space calculations always coincides with a section in one or more of the above codices.

In summary, similar to fragments of biblical scrolls discovered at Wadi Murabbaʿat, Naḥal Ḥever, and Naḥal Ṣeʾelim, the Masada scrolls exhibit a text tradition that is virtually identical to the Masoretic Text and thus give witness to the great antiquity of the Masoretic Text. Furthermore, unlike practically all Qumran scrolls of the Hebrew scriptures, which contain a plethora of diverse textual deviations from the Masoretic Text, only very few true variants vis-à-vis the Masoretic Text can be identified with certainty in the Masada biblical fragments. This circumstance prompts the conclusion that in the late Second Temple period, mainstream Judaism affirmed as authoritative a proto-masoretic text tradition, the forerunner of the text that ultimately gained exclusive acceptance.

Extrabiblical Compositions. This category includes fragments of previously known apocryphal writings discovered at Masada.

Twenty-six fragments of a Hebrew scroll of Ben Sira (Mas1h) were discovered in a casemate in the fortress wall, not far from the gate of the "Snake Path." These biblical fragments, written in a middle or late Hasmonean hand and therefore older than the fragments from the Herodian period discussed above, contain *Ben Sira* 37.27–43.30. They represent the earliest copy of this important apocryphal book, whether in Hebrew or in translation. Until the end of the last century, *Ben Sira* had been known only in Greek and Syriac renditions. The presence at Masada of a fragmentary copy of the Hebrew original, written within a century after the production of the Greek translation, strongly suggests that in the Second Temple period, *Ben Sira* also had currency in mainstream Judaism. [*See* Ben Sira, Book of.]

Fragments of previously unknown compositions of the apocryphal genre were also discovered at Masada. This category includes two items whose literary character suggests a Qumran origin. Phrases that echo expressions from the biblical story of Joseph indicate that the tiny fragments 1045–1350/1–4 and 1375 (Mas1m) survived from a work woven around the Joseph tale or from an apocryphal composition based on the entire *Book of Genesis*. A Joshua Apocryphon (Mas1c; 1039–211) consists of one main fragment measuring 9.5 by 5.8 centimeters and a scrap measuring 3.3 by 2.5 centimeters. The restored composite fragment holds parts of ten inscribed lines. The ink is very well preserved, and the script is legible with the exception of a few letters. The preserved text, in which God is praised for having come to the aid of his people, evidently echoes matters related in the last chapters (23–24) of the *Book of Joshua*. It should be noted that fragments of the Apocryphon of Joshua[a–b] from Qumran (4Q378–4Q379) manifestly reflect events related in the first part of the biblical book. [*See* Apocrypha and Pseudepigrapha; Joshua, Book of.]

Songs of the Sabbath Sacrifice (Mas1k; 1039–200) consists of two pieces of parchment in which the partial text of two columns is preserved. This work, known from remains of several copies found at Qumran (4Q400–407, 11Q17), most probably contained individual compositions for each Sabbath of the year. Songs for the first thirteen Sabbaths, namely for the first quarter of the solar year of 52 weeks (364 days), are partially extant in the Qumran finds. Substantial overlaps between the Masada and the Qumran fragments "allow for important mutual supplementation and the reconstruction of a significant amount of continuous text" (Newsom and Yadin, 1984, pp. 78–80). The Masada fragments appear to derive from a copy of the work brought to the fortress by members of the Qumran community who fled there when the Romans overran their communal center. [*See* Songs of the Sabbath Sacrifice.]

Additional finds at Masada include small pieces of parchment with only a few broken lines or letters that make it impossible to identify the works from which they originate. The legible bits of text suggest that all are remnants of nonbiblical compositions, which exhibit linguistic peculiarities known from discoveries in the Qumran caves.

A work similar to Jubilees (Mas1j; 1276–1786) contains seven partial lines of two columns. At the end of line 5 of the right-hand column, the collocation *sar ha-masṭemah* ("prince of evil") can be read. The noun *masṭemah* is used recurrently in the covenanters' ideoreligious vocabulary. But the specific term *sar ha-masṭemah* turns up at Qumran only in fragments of *Jubilees*, in which it designates the head angel of the forces of evil and darkness. It may, therefore, be surmised that this Masada fragment, too, stems from a copy of Jubilees or Pseudo-Jubilees imported from Qumran. [*See* Jubilees, Book of.]

In line 3 of the small fragment (Mas1n; 1063–147), seemingly written by an untrained hand, the third-person, masculine pronoun is given in the typical Qumran *plene* spelling *hu'ah*. Equally, the *plene* spelling *qudsho* (line 2) and the indication of the third-person, masculine, possessive pronoun by *heh* in *le-nevu'ateh* (line 4) give reason for positing that this small piece remained of a document that a covenanter had brought to Masada.

Masada 1039–274 consists of a piece of dark brown parchment measuring 3.0 by 2.8 centimeters, on which the beginnings of four lines are preserved with the partly preserved right-hand margin. At the edge, traces of stitching can be discerned. The few extant legible words do not allow for an identification of the contents of this text.

A small papyrus fragment of Samaritan origin, about the size of the palm of a hand (Mas1o; 1039–320), inscribed on both sides in Paleo-Hebrew, holds five partial lines written by different hands. Dividers in the form of large dots separate one word from the next. On one side, *li-r nanah* ("to praise") can be read at the beginning of lines 2 and 3, possibly followed there by *tselo*[*ta'*], an Aramaic word for "prayer." In line 4, the word *har-geri-*[*zz*]*i*[*m*] ("Mount Gerizim") can be restored, written as one word as is customary in the Samaritan tradition. We may therefore conclude that this papyrus originated from a Samaritan liturgical composition.

Scribal Conventions. The scribes of all the above documents, foremost of the biblical scrolls, follow rabbinic instructions for writing holy books. Most letters measure 0.3 by 0.3 centimeters and hang from horizontal dry rulings, as is the custom in ancient Hebrew manuscripts. In some cases, a perpendicular line of dots guides the scribe in the marking of the dry rulings, and where these are missing, the letter tops form a straight line. Larger letters like *lamed*, *qof*, and the final forms of *kaf*, *nun*, *pe*, and *tsadi* are 0.6 centimeters high, protruding above the heads or descending below the foot bars of the other letters. However, the occasional use of a final letter in mid-position and of a medial form at the end of a word, as in Qumran documents, suggests that the differentiation between medial and final forms had not yet stabilized at that time.

Letters are clearly separated by a fraction of a millimeter, and words by a space of approximately 0.1 centimeters. But now and then, two or more letters will flow together. Words will sometimes coalesce when a larger-than-usual length of text forced the scribe to crowd the writing, usually at the end of a hemistich or a line. In some instances, the last word or words of a line or a hemistich will spill over into the interhemistich space or the left margin. This also occurs when vertical dry rulings are provided for the guidance of the scribe.

The several columns of a manuscript usually hold the same number of lines, plus or minus one. But the numbers vary from one manuscript to another, from the twenty-five to twenty-six lines of Leviticus[a] to the forty-two lines of Ezekiel.

Top and bottom margins come to "two finger-breadths," namely 3.0 to 3.5 centimeters, and intercolumn margins to "a thumb's breadth," approximately 2.0 centimeters, as prescribed by rabbinic tradition (B.T., *Men.* 30a).

Dating the Fragments. The site of Masada provides a definite and indisputable *terminus ante quem* for the written material, 73 or 74 CE, the year in which the fortress fell to the Romans. There are no tangible indications that any of the scrolls and documents were penned on the site. Rather, all the items were brought there by the defenders and fugitives. There are reasons for assuming that the documents were originally produced quite some time before the fall of Masada to the Romans.

The fragments of *Deuteronomy* and *Ezekiel* were found at Masada on the very last day of the excavation in two shallow pits, covered with sand and dirt, under the only partly uncovered floor of the "synagogue." Yadin believed that these pits served as a *genizah*. In later times, this technical term came to designate a special room set aside in a synagogue for the storage of tattered or faulty copies of holy books, which had become unfit for use in public worship. They were taken out of circulation but were saved from desecration. The most famous example of a rich repository of this kind is the Cairo Genizah. [*See* Cairo Genizah.] If Yadin's conjecture is correct, this would imply that the holy scrolls of *Deuteronomy* and *Ezekiel* at Masada had become tattered through handling over an appreciably long period. Since they were unfit for cultic use, they were deposited in the pits to prevent their profanation. It is not unreasonable to assume that by this criterion alone these scrolls may be dated to the beginning of the first century CE or to the second half of the last century BCE.

Paleography permits further precision in dating the Masada texts. With the exception of one small piece of papyrus inscribed in Paleo-Hebrew characters, thirteen of the remaining fragments are penned in varying forms of the Hebrew square script of the Herodian period and the Ben Sira scroll is written in a late Hasmonean hand. They help us to trace diverse stages in the development of Hebrew script at the height of the Second Temple period (Cross, 1961). On the strength of linguistic criteria and/or content, several Masada documents are shown to be akin to certain Qumran works. They were probably carried to Masada by refugee covenanters. Therefore, the above findings reflect indirectly on the dating of at least some Qumran scrolls.

The discovery at Masada of remnants of compositions of Qumran vintage, on the one hand, and a piece of Samaritan origin, on the other, next to remains of the literary heritage of mainstream Judaism, points to the heterogeneity of the groups of people who had fled to the desert fortress before it fell to the Romans. In this context, attention should be drawn to the excavators' explanation of alterations made within the complex of the large Western Palace, which fact "clearly testifies to occupation either by a group of military commanders (perhaps without their families), an important family, or a coherent community such as the group of Essenes who might have joined the Zealots in their life on Masada" (Netzer, 1991, p. 634).

Yadin and Carol Newsom stress the significance of the presence at Masada of a fragment of the Songs of the Sabbath Sacrifice scroll extant at Qumran "because it implies the participation of members of the Qumran community, almost certainly to be identified with the Essenes, in the revolt against Rome" (Newsom and Yadin, 1984, p. 77). Vermes (1977, p. 124) weighs this possibility but also offers another interpretation of the circumstances:

> the discovery of a Qumran writing at Masada . . . does not *ipso facto* equate the inhabitants of the Dead Sea establishment with the garrison of Masada. It is more likely to mean either that some of the Qumran sectaries made common cause with the revolution during the last stage of the Community's history and brought their manuscripts to Masada with them, or that the Masada rebels considered the Qumran Community politically unreliable and seized its settlement as the Romans advanced towards the Dead Sea.

But the presence of a Samaritan piece among the Masada finds, in addition to documents of apparent Qumran vintage, suggests a more inclusive explanation: in times of distress and mortal danger, the desert fortress offered refuge not only to members of the mainstream community but also to various groups of dissenters—Zealots, Samaritans, and adherents of the "Community of the Renewed Covenant."

[*See also* Documentary Texts; Inscriptions; Interpretation of Scriptures; Letters; *and* Scriptures, *article on* Texts.]

BIBLIOGRAPHY

Cross, Frank Moore. "The Development of the Jewish Script." In *The Bible and the Ancient Near East*, edited by George Ernest Wright. Garden City, N.Y., 1961.

Netzer, Ehud. *Masada III. The Yigael Yadin Excavations, 1963–1965: Final Reports—The Buildings, Stratigraphy, and Architecture*. Jerusalem, 1991.

Newsom, Carol, and Yigael Yadin. "The Masada Fragment of the Qumran Songs of the Sabbath Sacrifice." *Israel Exploration Journal* 34 (1984), 77–84.

Talmon, Shemaryahu. "Fragments of a Psalms Scroll from Masada, MPs[b] (Masada 1103–1742)." In *Minḥah le Naḥum: Biblical and Other Studies Presented to Nahum M. Sarna in Honour of His Seventieth Birthday*, edited by Marc Brettler and Michael Fishbane, pp. 318–327. Journal for the Study of the Old Testament Supplement Series, 154. Sheffield, 1993.

Talmon, Shemaryahu. "Fragments of an Apocryphal Book of Joshua from Masada." *Journal of Jewish Studies* 47 (1996), 129–139.

Talmon, Shemaryahu. "Fragments of an Ezekiel Scroll from Masada (*Ezek*. 35.11–38.14) 1043–2220, Mas1d," *Orientalia Lovaniensia Periodica* 27 (1996), 29–49.

Talmon, Shemaryahu. "Hebrew Written Fragments from Masada." *Dead Sea Discoveries* 3 (1996), 168–177.

Vermes, Geza. *The Dead Sea Scrolls: Qumran in Perspective*. 2d ed. London, 1977.

Yadin, Yigael. *The Ben Sira Scroll from Masada*. Jerusalem, 1965. Hebrew text with English translation. Introduction and commentary in Hebrew and English.

Yadin, Yigael. "The Excavation of Masada, 1963–1964: Preliminary Report." *Israel Exploration Journal* 15 (1965), 1–120.

Yadin, Yigael. "Masada." In *Encyclopedia of Archaeological Excavations*, edited by Michael Avi-Yonah, pp. 791–816. Jerusalem, 1975. Concise overview of the excavation.

SHEMARYAHU TALMON

MASTEMAH. *See* Demons.

MATTHEW, GOSPEL OF. The connection between various portions of the *Gospel of Matthew* and the texts found around the Dead Sea has been the subject of a good deal of speculation and discussion since the initial discovery of the Dead Sea Scrolls in 1947. The results of this research have been significant for our understanding of various portions of the text of *Matthew* as well as for the exploration of the social context in which it was written.

Sermon on the Mount. *Matthew* 5–7, the Sermon on the Mount, rightly has attracted the most attention from researchers. Important similarities with *Matthew* 5.3–11 are found in the Wisdom Text with Beatitudes (4Q525 2.ii.1–6). Both texts develop themes from Psalm 37 and share the use of the phrase *lev ṭahor* ("pure heart"), which appears in Greek in the Septuagint as *katharoi tei kardiai* ("pure in heart"). Other references also are apparent. The similarity of *Matthew* 5.3–5 to Hodayot[a] from Cave 1 at Qumran (hereafter 1QHodayot[a] xxiii [xviii].14–15) has been argued, noting the presence of phrases such as "poor in spirit," "the meek," and "those who mourn" in both texts, each of which utilizes *Isaiah* 66.2 and 61.21–22 in a similar manner. The Messianic Apocalypse (4Q521) and Melchizedek (11Q13) also use this same language from Isaiah. The presence of these terms already was noted in the first scrolls from Cave 1. Other terms such as the "merciful" in *Matthew* 5.7 and "righteousness" in *Matthew* 5.6 and 10 also are attested in the Qumran texts.

Sectarian centers such as Qumran around the "Salt Sea" could be the image behind *Matthew* 5.13, just as the dualistic context of the sons of light and the sons of darkness would be evoked by the references to light in *Matthew* 5.14–16. It also is possible that salt refers to wisdom and light to the law. In either case these few verses could reflect a Matthean response to the kind of sectarianism represented in a large portion of the nonbiblical scrolls from the Qumran finds. If so they constitute a bridge between the eschatological outlook of the Beatitudes and the following pronouncements concerning the role of the law.

The antitheses (*Mt.* 5.21–48) are introduced by a statement on the role of the law (*Mt.* 5.17–20). This paragraph begins with a declaration concerning its continuing validity, "Do not think that I have come to abolish the law or the prophets," and concludes with an appeal for a greater righteousness. The extent to which a sectarian identity associated with the Qumran texts was rooted in a very particular interpretation of the legal prescriptions of the Torah is well documented in Miqtsat Maʿasei ha-Torah[a–e] (4Q394–399), as well as a host of other works such as Temple Scroll[a] (11Q19), the Rule of the Community from Cave 1 (1QS; hereafter 1QRule of the Community), the Damascus Document (CD), and the Cave 4 texts of these compositions, to name only a few. The antitheses conclude in *Matthew* 5.48 with the injunction "be perfect," a term also utilized in *Matthew* 19.21 and found nowhere else in the New Testament Gospels but familiar in the legal literature of the Dead Sea corpus. The antitheses are bracketed by statements using central concepts undergirding the communal legislation of the Qumran scrolls.

A number of studies of the antitheses (*Mt.* 5. 21–48) have pointed to the similarities between their structure in *Matthew* and the literary form of Miqtsat Maʿasei ha-Torah. The difference between the first person plural of Miqtsat Maʿasei ha-Torah and the first person singular of *Matthew* can be ascribed to the latter's Christological interests. It appears that the rather direct polemical approach of Miqtsat Maʿasei ha-Torah may be closer to the Matthean formulation than previous hypotheses based on either Greek or other Hebrew literature.

The stringent rules concerning divorce shared by the New Testament and the Qumran scrolls in contrast to most of the remainder of Second Temple Judaism have resulted in the close examination of those features of the Matthean legislation (*Mt.* 5.31–32 and 19.1–12) that make it unique within the New Testament. The prohibition against both polygamy and divorce is spelled out and justified in the Qumran legislation (Temple Scroll[a] [11Q19 lvi.18, lvii.17–18, lxvi.8–11]; CD iv.12–v.11, etc.). These texts are the earliest record of a tradition of the prohibition against divorce that is then picked up by the followers of Jesus. The Matthean texts are distinguished by the clause "except on the grounds of *porneia*," frequently translated as "fornication." This Greek term in the Septuagint is a translation of the Hebrew *zenut*, a term used in the Damascus Document to designate a variety of sexual activities regarded as illegal by the sect, including divorce, polygamy, and a broadened definition of incest (CD ii.16, iv.17, iv.10, vii.1, viii.5, ix.17). One of the Cave 4 manuscripts of the Damascus Document possibly refers to a violation of the laws of menstruation (Damascus Document[e] [4Q270 11.i.12–13], Damascus Document[b] [4Q267 12.4–5]). In Miqtsat Maʿasei ha-Torah the term is used to designate the intermarriage of priests and common Israelites (4Q396 1–2.iv.4–11, 4Q397 12–15). A broad sectarian definition for *porneia* may lie behind *Matthew* 5.32 and 19.9.

Interesting parallels to the injunction against swearing oaths in *Matthew* 5.33–37 (cf. *Mt.* 23.16–22) are found in the descriptions of the Essenes in Josephus (*The Jewish War* 2.135) and in Philo (*Every Good Man Is Free* 84), as well as in 1QRule of the Community (1QS vi.27–vii.1) and the Damascus Document (CD xv.1–15, xvi.1–2). In these same materials we also find descriptions of the oaths required upon admission into the group (*The Jewish War* 2.139–142; 1QRule of the Community v.7–11; CD xv.1–13). Other stipulations concerning oaths and vows can be found in the Damascus Document (CD vii.8) and Temple

Scroll[a] (liii.9–liv.7). Texts such as Damascus Document (CD xv) suggest that further oaths were unnecessary following the loyalty oaths required upon admission.

The second clause of *Matthew* 5.48, "You shall love your neighbor and hate your enemy," is not found in *Leviticus* 19.18, its presumed biblical antecedent. While 1QRule of the Community and other texts itemize legislation concerning the meaning of the mandate to love your neighbor, that is, other members of the sect (e.g., 1QRule of the Community v.24–vi.1, vi.25–27, vii.4–17; CD ix.2–8, etc.), they also contain sections closer to the Matthean appropriation of this legislation. Among the perspectives to be taught new initiates to the sect was "that they may love all that he has chosen and hate all that he has rejected" (1QRule of the Community i.4; cf. CD viii.15–19, xix.29–32). Upon admission to the "covenant of grace," they pledged that they would "hate all the sons of darkness, each according to his guilt in God's vengeance" (1QRule of the Community i.9–11; cf. 9.15–23).

Righteousness. Within the New Testament *Matthew* employs the term *righteousness* in a unique manner. Out of a total of seven references in the work the term appears only in *Matthew* 3.15 and 21.32 outside of the Sermon on the Mount. *Matthew* 5.20 and 6.33 (cf. *Mt.* 6.1) both use this term to point to the very particular understanding of Judaism and the attendant lifestyle the author of the first gospel expected of the followers of Jesus. Within the Beatitudes we learn that "those who are persecuted for the sake of righteousness" in *Matthew* 5.10 (cf. 5.6) are really suffering for the sake of Jesus in *Matthew* 5.11. This same term also is used to designate the sectarian lifestyle within the legal literature from the Dead Sea. The author of the Damascus Document is upset because the opposition has described "the three nets of Belial . . . in which Israel is ensnared" as "three kinds of righteousness" (CD iv.17). These "nets of Belial" are listed as fornication, wealth, and defilement of the Temple, issues at the heart of the sectarian identity spelled out in this composition. Within the viewpoint developed in the Damascus Document, however, it is the adherents of the new covenant in the land of Damascus who have the correct understanding of righteousness. The first line of the Damascus Document reads "And now listen all who know righteousness." Both this composition and the first gospel use the same term to designate their own particular viewpoint within Judaism.

Wisdom. While the beatitudes of the Wisdom Text with Beatitudes emphasize wisdom and law in a manner not immediately apparent in the Matthean version, certain parallels in structure are striking, and both works share an eschatological interest, certainly more highly developed in the latter. Elsewhere in *Matthew*, particularly *Matthew* 11.25–30, Jesus is regarded as the representative of wisdom. In light of this identification, also mentioned in *Matthew* 11.19, 12.42, and 13.54, the equation of wisdom with law in the Sermon on the Mount becomes evident, emphasized in *Matthew* 5.17–20. This link is common throughout the Qumran corpus (e.g., Wiles of the Wicked Woman [4Q184 14–15]; 1QRule of the Community i.12, iii.1, viii.9, ix.17–18), where law is fundamental for a number of the basic compositions undergirding the life of the sect. Eschatological interests are another important feature of Qumran wisdom (Mysteries [1Q27 i.1–7]; Sapiential Work A[a] [4Q418 69.5–15, 81.1–11]). The wisdom associated with Jesus is the occasion for persecution and suffering on the part of those who adopt it (*Mt.* 5.10–12, 7.6, 23.34–36); those who embrace the sectarian wisdom share the same lot in Wisdom Text with Beatitudes 1.ii.3–6. Thus we see that the connection of eschatological themes with wisdom statements in *Matthew*, evident in both the Sermon on the Mount and in chapter 11, also is evident in wisdom compositions from Qumran. The utilization of the wisdom theme as one argument for the authority of Jesus as lawgiver also is evident in *Matthew* 11.27.

Communal Discipline. The discussion of communal discipline in *Matthew* 18.15–18 reflects a particular interpretive tradition of the laws of reproof in *Leviticus* 19.17–18. These same verses are the source of the serious obligation in the Damascus Document (CD vii.2–3, ix.2–8), Damascus Document[a] (4Q266 18.ii), and 1QRule of the Community (1QS v.25–vi.1, vii.8–9) to reprove a fellow member of the sect when necessary and the attendant steps to be taken. Berakhot[a] and Berakhot[c] (4Q286, 4Q288) also contain evidence of similar traditions. As in *Matthew* the emphasis is on internal discussion and rebuke, even though these Qumran texts outline specific punishments in many instances. The fragmentary remains of Rebukes by the Overseer (4Q477) suggest a written record of rebuke. When this process does not yield results, the unrepentant must be excommunicated. The Damascus Document (CD ix.16–22) deals with the procedure in capital cases.

Use of Scripture. One of the distinctive features of the Matthean usage of the Hebrew scriptures is the employment of the formula quotation "to fulfill the word . . . ," followed by a citation from the Hebrew scriptures. Some studies have found an explanation for the origin of these texts within the evidence from the Qumran scrolls. While the formula employed in the two literatures is different, there is a good deal of similarity between their interpretive interests and techniques. These quotations do resemble the *pesher* literature in their shared interest in questions of the relationship between eschatology and the events narrated in the text. The *pesharim*, however, employ the biblical verse as the beginning point of the argument followed by an exegetical explanation, while the author of *Matthew* employs the verse as an explanation (or justification) for the preceding narrative or statement.

A related argument that precedes the Qumran discoveries is that the author of this gospel possessed a collection of "testimonies" that were integrated into the composition. Further evidence for this kind of collection was found among the Qumran scrolls in Testimonia (4Q175). Since the citations introduced by the formula quotations appear to reflect very closely the theology of the gospel's author, it is questionable whether these citations were based on an independent collection. Even if they were, the creative work of the author is apparent in their usage. The evidence from the Dead Sea Scrolls does make it clear that Jewish readers of the *Gospel of Matthew* could have been familiar with hermeneutical approaches to the Hebrew scriptures that were centered in concepts of eschatological fulfillment.

Matthew is the gospel with the greatest number of explicit quotations from the Hebrew scriptures, containing approximately sixty citations. Some studies prior to the discovery of the Dead Sea Scrolls found a significant variation between those texts cited in connection with formula quotations and the remainder that were seen to reflect Septuagint readings. Subsequent research has suggested a more complicated picture. The pluriform character of the textual traditions attested in the Qumran manuscripts provides new evidence for evaluating the Matthean citations of the Hebrew scriptures.

Prophet Like Moses. It is relatively clear that the figure of Moses is an important character for *Matthew*'s depiction of Jesus. Whether the author deliberately intended to portray Jesus as the new Moses or as one greater than Moses or whether the author used a variety of less systematic allusions is the subject of continuing debate. The centrality of allusions to the figure of Moses in both *Matthew* and in significant compositions among the Dead Sea Scrolls cannot be contested. Mosaic allusions pervade the birth and infancy narratives. The story in *Matthew* 2 of Joseph and Mary's flight to Egypt and subsequent return is built on imagery of Moses and the Exodus, including the use of *Hosea* 11.1 in *Matthew* 2.15, Herod's murder of the children, and the reference to "those who were seeking the child's life" in verse 20 and elsewhere. There also is evidence for proposing that by the first century CE Jewish traditions about Moses included some of the more miraculous elements present in *Matthew* such as the birth narrative and Jesus' ability to perform miracles. Many of these traditions are rooted in the statement of *Deuteronomy* 18.15–18 concerning the "prophet like Moses." The Transfiguration story in *Matthew* 17.1–13 is another example. Evidence of Moses as the prophet-king is found within this tradition. Good evidence for understanding this use of the Mosaic imagery in an eschatological and possibly messianic sense can be found in 1QRule of the Community ix.11, "until there shall come the prophet and the anointed ones of Aaron and Israel," and in the inclusion of *Deuteronomy* 18.18–20 in Testimonia. Some scholars have suggested that Elijah redivivus was identified with the Mosaic eschatological prophet in Apocryphon of Moses B[a] (4Q375) and some other Qumran texts.

All of these allusions to Moses pale in significance when compared to his overarching significance as lawgiver, recognized most obviously in *Matthew* 23.2. Moses' paramount role as lawgiver is presupposed in texts such as 1QRule of the Community v.8 and Damascus Document (CD) xv.2 and xv.12, where his name is used to designate the Pentateuch. The same obvious point is evident in the phrase "Moses says" in Damascus Document (CD) v.8, viii.14, and xix.26–27. The entire Temple Scroll[a], an authoritative statement of the will of God based upon the Pentateuch and written in the first person, is attributed to Moses. While not written in its entirety in the first person, *Jubilees*, amply attested in the Qumran fragments, makes a similar claim. There is adequate evidence to suggest that the sectarian legislation found among these compositions represented a unique attempt in Second Temple Judaism to interpret and live by the law of Moses. While the argument that the five major discourse sections of *Matthew* suggest a structure deliberately based upon the Pentateuch is less than convincing, it is clear that the interpretation of the Mosaic law is an issue throughout the work, most notably in *Matthew* 5.17–18 and throughout the Sermon on the Mount. In the case of this gospel the assertions concerning the authority of Jesus have to do with his priority as the fundamental lawgiver-interpreter (e.g., *Mt.* 5.17–20, 11.25–30, 23.9, 28.18).

Jewish Sectarianism. The greatest contribution of the Dead Sea Scrolls to the study of *Matthew* is their contribution to our understanding of Jewish sectarianism in the late Second Temple period. A Jewish sectarianism informed by these perspectives provides a logical context for understanding the *Gospel of Matthew*. The Jewish religious and intellectual environment in which the *Gospel of Matthew* could be composed and understood becomes much clearer on the basis of the evidence from the scrolls. It is from this perspective that we evaluate the shared thematic and literary features identified above. Both literatures provide evidence of Jewish sects with a particular interest in issues of both law and eschatology. The interrelationship of these themes and other relevant materials in *Matthew* also aids in the interpretation of fragmentary remains of the scrolls where limited material on isolated topics makes comprehension and interpretation rather difficult. The complicated nature of Jewish communities in the latter half of the Second Temple era becomes more evident as we attempt to understand these literatures within their social and historical context, and in relationship to one another.

Khirbet Mird. A few fragments of Greek papyri containing the text of *Matthew* were found at Khirbet Mird. Mird 16 and 29 have been labeled p83 in the Aland listing of New Testament manuscripts. Mird 16 contains portions of *Matthew* 20.23–25 and 16B may include *Matthew* 20.30–31.

BIBLIOGRAPHY

Allison, Dale C., Jr. *The New Moses: A Matthean Typology*. Minneapolis, 1993. Allison covers many allusions to Qumran materials in the course of his argument.

Brooke, George J. "The Wisdom of Matthew's Beatitudes (4Q Béat and Mt. 5.3–12)." *Scripture Bulletin* 19.2 (Summer 1989), 35–41. Good brief summary of the significance of the Qumran beatitudes for *Matthew*.

Davies, W. D. *The Setting of the Sermon on the Mount*. London, 1964. The most important study of *Matthew* in its Jewish setting, including a chapter on Qumran.

Davies, W. D., and Dale C. Allison, Jr. *A Critical and Exegetical Commentary on the Gospel According to St. Matthew*. The International Critical Commentary. 3 vols. Edinburgh, 1988 (vol. 1), 1991 (vol. 2). Includes extensive references to Second Temple Jewish material including Qumran and a bibliography for each section.

Eshel, Esther. "4Q477: The Rebukes by the Overseer." *Journal of Jewish Studies* 45 (1994), 111–122. Preliminary publication and discussion of this fragment related to *Matthew* 18.15–18.

Fitzmyer, Joseph A. "The Matthean Divorce Texts and Some New Palestinian Evidence." In *To Advance the Gospel*, pp. 79–111. New York, 1981. Good summary and analysis of Qumran evidence.

Flusser, David. *Judaism and the Origins of Christianity*. Jerusalem, 1988. See pages 102–125 for essays on the Beatitudes.

Kampen, John. "The Matthean Divorce Texts Reexamined." In *New Qumran Texts and Studies: Proceedings of the First Meeting of the International Organization for Qumran Studies, Paris, 1992*, edited by George J. Brooke, pp. 149–167. Studies on the Texts of the Desert of Judah, 15. Leiden, 1994. An analysis of the Matthean divorce texts in the context of Qumran literature.

Kampen, John. "The Sectarian Form of the Antitheses within the Social World of the Matthean Community." *Dead Sea Discoveries* 1 (1994), 338–363. An examination of recent studies of *Matthew* from a sociological perspective, comparing the antitheses with Miqtsat Maʿasei ha-Torah.

Nitzan, Bilhah. "The Laws of Reproof in *4QBerakhot* (4Q286–290) in Light of Their Parallels in the Damascus Covenant and Other Texts from Qumran." In *Legal Texts and Legal Issues: Proceedings of the Second Meeting of the International Organization for Qumran Studies, Cambridge, 1995. Published in Honour of J. Baumgarten*, edited by Moshe Bernstein, Florentino García Martínez, and John Kampen, pp. 149–165. Studies on the Texts of the Desert of Judah, 23. Leiden, 1997. A preliminary publication of this Qumran text related to *Matthew* 18.15–18.

Overman, J. Andrew. *Matthew's Gospel and Formative Judaism: The Social World of the Matthean Community*. Minneapolis, 1990. A social analysis that attempts to take seriously the sectarian context of *Matthew* derived partially from examination of the Qumran evidence.

Przybylski, Benno. *Righteousness in Matthew and His World of Thought*. Cambridge, 1980. Notes the uniqueness of the Matthean usage of this term within the context of Second Temple Judaism.

Schubert, Kurt. "The Sermon on the Mount and the Qumran Texts." In *The Scrolls and the New Testament*, edited by Krister Stendahl, pp. 118–128. New York, 1957. Early study noting parallels between the bodies of literature.

Stanton, Graham N. *A Gospel for a New People: Studies in Matthew*. Edinburgh, 1992. Includes studies on a comparison with the Damascus Document and on the use of the Hebrew Scriptures.

Stendahl, Krister. *The School of St. Matthew and Its Use of the Old Testament*. Philadelphia, 1968. Study of the formula quotations and Matthean use of biblical textual traditions.

Viviano, Benedict T. "Beatitudes Found among Dead Sea Scrolls." *Biblical Archaeology Review* 18 (November–December 1992), 53–55, 66. Includes translation of text of the Qumran beatitudes and a brief analysis.

John I. Kampen

MAZIN, KHIRBET. Also known as Qasr el-Yahud or Khirbet el Yahoud (de Saulcy, 1853), Khirbet Mazin is a prominent Hasmonean ruin located in the delta of Wadi Mazin, approximately 500 meters to the north of the confluence of Naḥal Kidron (Wadi en-Nar) to the Dead Sea. The structure had been erected at the foot of an ascent from the Dead Sea to the Buqeia. The perennial springs of ʿEin-Feshkha are 3.5 kilometers to the north. The ruin was explored in 1953 by the Belgian expedition working at Khirbet Mird; it was excavated in December 1960 and January 1961 by Howard Stutchbury and G. R. Nicholl (1962), and again in 1971, 1974, and 1976 by P. Bar Adon (1989). The site was identified by Bar Adon as the biblical Middin (*Jos.* 15.61–62). He attributes its first construction to Uzziah, king of Judah, as related in *2 Chronicles* 26.10.

The ruin consists of a large courtyard or hall, 31 meters long and 11 meters wide inside, with a rectangular watchtower 9 by 18 meters in dimension, two to three stories high, attached to its northeastern corner. The tower was divided by lateral walls into five rooms and two interconnected, plastered water cisterns, 4 meters deep. The rooms served for dwelling and storage. The entrance to the courtyard was from a single opening, 5.2 meters wide, on the east, facing the Dead Sea. The jambs were built of carefully cut ashlars. Several worked sandstones were attributed to a frieze and cornice; others had marginal drafting and masons' marks, dry painted plaster (*secco*) in red and black, and molded stucco. A slanting ramp, approximately 6 meters wide, supported by walls on either side, descended from the opening eastward. A curvilinear wall approximately 4 meters wide to the east of the tower might have served as a breakwater to prevent the sea water from flooding in. The level of both courtyard and ramp was sunk below the external, surrounding ground level.

The courtyard walls, approximately 2 meters thick at

the bottom and tapering upward, were built of large local boulders on both sides, with a core of smaller stones packed between them. The large boulders were laid roughly in courses, with lacings of smaller stones embedded in mud mortar. The western and northern walls of the courtyard had an outer retaining wall with an external face built of undressed smaller stones. The 2.5-meter space between this and the inner wall was filled with rubble. The stone walls were covered by an external layer of plaster. The tower walls are preserved to an elevation of 6 meters. Sounding near the gate, especially on the southern side, yielded iron and bronze nails from the timber doors, fired pieces of which were also found. In the 1960–1961 excavations distinctive molded ware, coins, a ring, and a large lamp of lead were found. The pottery finds in the Bar Adon excavations are mainly from the second century BCE to the first century CE. The coins are from the time of Alexander Jannaeus to the time of the First Jewish Revolt. Iron Age II (eighth century BCE to seventh century BCE) pottery shards found by Bar Adon indicate that the Hasmonean fortress was preceded by an earlier one. Occupation by "squatters" during the Byzantine period is indicated by several fireplaces and small amounts of pottery shards, and by crude blocking of the entrance.

A cave, 6 meters wide and 12 meters deep, was excavated by Bar Adon in the cliffs to the west of Khirbet Mazin. The pottery finds are from the second and first centuries BCE. Another cave, referred to as the Coin Cave and yielding similar finds and a coin from the First Jewish Revolt, was excavated by Bar Adon 2 kilometers south of the site.

According to Bar Adon, Khirbet Mazin was a military and maritime trading post. Ehud Netzer (1989) had suggested that the site, which once stood very near the water's edge, was a fortified Hasmonean dry anchorage for royal boats, which could have been dragged from the sea along the ramp. The boats would have been protected inside the walled area. The courtyard could have been covered by a cloth curtain if not by a wooden roof. In this case the boats actually were protected inside a roofed hall. A small unit of soldiers occupied the tower. Four boats, 14 meters long and 4 to 4.5 meters wide, could have been housed in this dry anchorage. The boats were at the service of the Hasmonean kings and their retinues in sailing from Jerusalem or Jericho to ʿEin-Gedi, Masada, Mikhwar, or Zoara, since land traffic from Jericho and Qumran southward along the seashore was impossible.

BIBLIOGRAPHY

Bar Adon, Pessah. "Qasr el-Yahud" (in Hebrew). *ʿAtiqot* 9 (1989), 18–29.

De Saulcy, Felicién. *Voyage autour de la Mer Morte et dans les Terres Bibliques: Atlas.* Paris, 1853.

Netzer, Ehud. "The Hasmonean Building Projects" (in Hebrew). In *Greece and Rome in Eretz Israel: Collected Essays,* edited by A. Kasher, G. Fuks, and U. Rappaport, pp. 225–227. Jerusalem, 1989.

Stutchbury, Howard E., and G. R. Nicholl. "Khirbet Mazin." In *Annual of the Department of Antiquities of Jordan* 6–7 (1962), pp. 96–103, pls. XVIII–XXII, figs. 1–10.

JOSEPH PATRICH

MEALS. The Dead Sea Scrolls testify to the regular practice of communal meals in the Qumran community. Facilities for dining have also been identified among the Qumran remains. The importance of the communal meal at Qumran is indicated in this summary statement from the Rule of the Community from Cave 1 regarding community life. "They shall eat in common and bless in common and deliberate in common" (hereafter, 1QRule of the Community, 1QS vi.2–3). Descriptions of Essene meal practices in Philo and Josephus coordinate with what we find in the Dead Sea Scrolls and lend weight to the theory that the inhabitants of Qumran were Essenes.

Although the scrolls do not indicate how often the communal meals were held, Josephus notes that the Essene meals took place twice a day, once in the late morning, when they took a break from their morning labors, and once in the late afternoon, when they finished their labors for the day (*The Jewish War* 2.129–132). Before each meal, Josephus writes, they would purify themselves with a bath and put on special garments. The scrolls also connect purificatory ablutions with entrance to the "pure meal" of the community (1QS v.13–14).

Documentation. The Rule of the Community from Cave 1 describes the common meal as follows:

> Wherever there are ten men of the council of the community there shall not lack a priest among them. And they shall all sit before him according to their rank and shall be asked their counsel in all things in that order. And when the table has been prepared for eating, and the new wine for drinking, the priest shall be the first to stretch out his hand to bless the first fruits of the bread and new wine. (1QS vi.3–6)

Like other gatherings of the community, the common meal required at least ten men and the presence of a priest. No mention is made of women participating in the meal, a point also made by Josephus (*The Jewish War* 2.120–121). When they arrived in the dining room, the men were to sit "according to rank," which corresponds to Josephus's note that they were served "in order" (*The Jewish War* 2.130). The meal began with a benediction by the priest, also emphasized by Josephus, who adds: "none may partake until after the prayer" (*The Jewish War* 2.131). Josephus also mentions a prayer by the priest at the end of the meal, a practice not referred to in the scrolls.

The Rule of the Community specifies prayers over both the bread and the "new wine." This does not mean that only bread was eaten; rather, the prayer over the bread would be intended to cover all the food. According to Josephus the menu included bread and an unspecified common dish that was served to each participant (*The Jewish War* 2.130). The reference in the Rule of the Community to "new wine" is unusual since it is not the normal term for wine but rather refers either to lightly fermented new wine or simply to grape juice. Though later rabbinic usage connects the term with grape juice, the Temple Scroll[a] (11Q19) connects it with the feast of new wine. In either case, the limited alcoholic content of their wine correlates with the sobriety of the community.

One component of their cuisine appears to have been meat. At various locations at the Qumran site, burials of animal bones encased in pottery vessels have been found. The bones appear clearly to be the remains of meals since they derive from edible animals (goats, sheep, oxen) and have been separated and cleaned of flesh. Why the remains of meals were buried so carefully continues to be a mystery. It has been suggested that they were remains of sacrificial meals, but no signs of sacrifice have been found at the site, and burial of sacrificial remains in this manner is unprecedented, so this interpretation is problematic.

Archaeological Remains. Two separate rooms among the archaeological remains at Qumran have been proposed as dining halls. Roland de Vaux identified a large rectangular room, 22 meters by 4.5 meters wide (72 feet by 15 feet), as the community dining hall because an adjacent room contained a cache of some one thousand serving vessels. He also noted that the room was designed so that it could be washed with water and drained, consistent with its proposed use for dining. There is no indication as to what the furnishings of the room might have been.

A reexamination of the excavation data by Pauline Donceel-Voûte has resulted in a new theory that the collapsed second floor of locus 30, previously identified as the scriptorium, was instead used as a dining room. The plastered furnishings found in the debris from the room, originally identified by de Vaux as a bench and writing table (1973, pp. 29–33, pl. XXIa), would in this reconstruction be identified as a low platform placed along the wall on which the couches (formerly identified as "writing tables") would rest. Donceel-Voûte argues that this reconstruction better fits the form of the remains and, furthermore, corresponds more accurately to a known architectural pattern in the ancient world, since there are many examples of dining rooms being designed in this way, whereas the proposed bench and writing table are unprecedented architecturally (as acknowledged by de Vaux). Donceel-Voûte's reconstruction of the arrangement of the furnishings suggests that the room could have held at least nine and possibly more reclining diners. While it was common for diners to recline at ancient banquets, it must be noted that the scrolls describe diners at the community meal as sitting (1QS vi.3–5).

Symbolism. The community meal was known as a "pure meal," indicating its function as a centerpiece for the elaborate purity rules specific to this community. Just as the community saw itself as set apart from the rest of humanity, and even the rest of Judaism, by its purity, so the meal was one in which only the pure could participate.

In many ways participation at the common table symbolized membership in the community. There was a two-year trial period for each initiate before being accepted into full membership, during which time "he shall not touch the pure meal of the congregation until one full year is completed . . . he shall not touch the drink of the congregation until he has completed a second year among the men of the community" (1QS vi.16–17). Josephus states: "Before he may touch the common food, he is made to swear tremendous oaths" (*The Jewish War* 2.139). Similarly, exclusion from the meal for a specified time, usually a year, was the primary way in which members were disciplined (1QS vi.24–25, vii.15–16, vii.18–20).

This function of the meal as a boundary marker, setting the community apart from the outside world, is a feature it shared with meals in the culture at large. Meals functioned as a central activity for groups of various kinds in the Greco-Roman world, such as clubs, funerary societies, and philosophical societies, as well as sectarian groups within Judaism, such as the Therapeutae (described in Philo's *On the Contemplative Life*) and the early Christians. Other features of the Qumran meals were also consistent with Greco-Roman banquets, including prayer before the meal (which for the Greeks was usually in the form of a libation), the ranking of guests at the table, and reclining, if indeed reclining was practiced at Qumran (as Donceel-Voûte argues, but the evidence is inconclusive).

Another interpretation of the meal is found in the Rule of the Congregation (1Q28a). Here the community meal is said to include not only the community, but also "the priest," "the whole congregation of Israel," "the sons of Aaron the Priests," "the chiefs of the clans of Israel," and "the Messiah of Israel." The entire company proceeds in and sits "each in the order of his dignity." After the priest says the benediction over the bread, "the Messiah of Israel shall extend his hand over the bread, and all the congregation of the community shall utter a blessing, each man in the order of his dignity" (1Q28a ii.11–22). This text superimposes over the formula of the regular community meal a description of a banquet with the Messiah. The motif is that of the messianic or eschatological banquet, the banquet of the end time, a theme that is widely reflected in biblical and extrabiblical tradition (e.g., *Is.* 25.6–8, *2 Bar.* 29.1–8). Based on this text, Frank Moore Cross, among others, has suggested that the Qumran community celebrated their common meals as a "liturgical anticipation of the messianic banquet."

Comparison with Christianity and Other Sects. Comparisons are often drawn between the Qumran meal and the Christian Lord's Supper. However, the centrality of the meal to the life of the community and the prominence of bread and wine are common features of all ancient meals. More distinctive is the eschatological focus and the idealization of the meal as a messianic banquet, which the Lord's Supper emphasizes as well in such texts as *Mark* 14.25 and *Luke* 22.15–18. But these texts contrast the Lord's Supper with the Passover meal and make no reference to the Qumran (or Essene) tradition, so it is unlikely that Christian practices were drawn directly from Qumran practices.

The Qumran meal has also been identified as a "sacred meal" in its resemblance to the Christian sacramental interpretation of the Lord's Supper. These arguments often derive from an inadequate definition of "sacred meal" and an inadequate appreciation for the widespread practice of communal meals in the ancient world. The closest one gets to such a concept is Josephus's reference to the Essenes entering the dining hall "as into some holy shrine" and practicing silence at the table so as to appear "to those outside . . . like some awful mystery" (*The Jewish War* 2.129, 2.133). Notice, however, that Josephus is not referring to the meaning of the meal per se, but rather to the effect it might have had on outside observers. It is a style of argument meant to persuade the reader that these meals were not run-of-the-mill pagan affairs but rather had a form consistent with the strict rules of purity with which they were circumscribed.

Qumran meal practices have also been compared to these of the *ḥavurah* ("fellowship," "brotherhood"), a term mentioned in *Dema'i* 2.2–3. The *ḥaver* was one who maintained a table of ritual purity and refrained from eating with *ʿam ha-ʾarets*. Whether the *ḥaverim* were actually a sectarian group, like the Qumran community, or whether this terminology simply referred to gatherings with one's social intimates are matters of scholarly debate. But at the least the category of the *ḥavurah* illustrates the phenomenon of separation on the basis of laws of purity elsewhere in Judaism.

[*See also* Eschatology; Essenes; Messiahs; Priests; Purity; Qumran, *article on* Archaeology; *and* Rule of the Community.]

BIBLIOGRAPHY

Beall, Todd S. *Josephus' Description of the Essenes Illustrated by the Dead Sea Scrolls,* pp. 52–64. Society for New Testament Studies, Monograph Series, 58. Cambridge, 1988. Provides a judicious, up-to-date, and comprehensive discussion of the Qumran meal.

Cross, Frank Moore. *The Ancient Library of Qumran,* 3d. ed., pp. 74–78. Minneapolis, 1995. Classic interpretation of the Qumran meal as a messianic banquet.

de Vaux, Roland. *Archaeology and the Dead Sea Scrolls.* London, 1973. English translation with revisions of 1959 Schweich Lectures: originally published in French in 1961. An abbreviated excavation report by the original excavator. De Vaux died before a final report could be prepared.

Donceel-Voûte, Pauline H. E. "Coenaculum la salle à l'étage du *locus* 30 à Khirbet Qumrân sur la Mer Morte." In *Banquets d'Orient,* pp. 61–84. Res Orientales, 4. Leuven, 1992. Presents a new interpretation of the archaeological data regarding the scriptorium and proposes that it is a dining room instead.

Donceel, Robert, and Pauline Donceel-Voûte. "The Archaeology of Khirbet Qumran." In *Methods of Investigation of the Dead Sea Scrolls and the Khirbet Qumran Site: Present Realities and Future Prospects,* edited by Michael O. Wise, Norman Golb, John J. Collins, and Dennis G. Pardee, pp. 1–31. Annals of the New York Academy of Sciences, 722. New York, 1994. Provides an English-language summary of the arguments in the article above.

Kuhn, Karl Georg. "The Lord's Supper and the Communal Meal at Qumran." In *The Scrolls and the New Testament,* edited by Krister Stendahl, pp. 65–93. New York, 1957. The classic case for the relation of the Qumran meal to the Christian Lord's Supper.

Lieberman, Saul. "Discipline in the So-Called Dead Sea Manual of Discipline." *Journal of Biblical Literature* 71 (1951), 199–206.

Schiffman, Lawrence H. *Reclaiming the Dead Sea Scrolls: The History of Judaism, the Background of Christianity, the Lost Library at Qumran.* See pages 333–338 for an argument that the Qumran meal was not a sacred meal.

Smith, Dennis E. "The Messianic Banquet Reconsidered." In *The Future of Early Christianity: Essays in Honor of Helmut Koester,* edited by Birger A. Pearson, pp. 64–73. Minneapolis, 1991. A comprehensive presentation of the messianic banquet motif in Jewish and Christian traditions.

VanderKam, James C. *The Dead Sea Scrolls Today,* Grand Rapids, Mich., 1994. See pp. 84–86, 173–175 provides a useful summary of interpretations of the meal at Qumran.

DENNIS E. SMITH

MEDIA. Over the years, coverage of the Dead Sea Scrolls in mass-circulation newspapers and magazines, popular books, and broadcast media has played an important role in arousing worldwide public interest in and even fascination with the Judean Desert manuscripts. Yet on more than a few occasions, media coverage of the scrolls has transcended strictly scientific reporting to become deeply intertwined with wider modern political and religious controversies. In some cases, extensive media coverage of the scrolls' supposed hidden religious significance or their interpretation and publication by scholars has sparked public protests and political controversies so serious that they have profoundly influenced governmental policies regarding the scrolls in both Jordan and Israel.

Discovery and Conflicting Scholarly Claims. The first announcement of the discovery of the scrolls from Cave 1 at Qumran, made by Professor Millar Burrows on behalf of the American Schools of Oriental Research in a carefully worded statement datelined New Haven, 25 April 1948, ignited a storm of controversy over the legal status of the scrolls. Though initial details were sketchy (in one of the published versions, ten scrolls were reportedly found near ʿEin-Gedi), this press release, carried in the *New York Times* and on wire services all over the world, brought an immediate, angry response from Professor Eleazar L. Sukenik of the Hebrew University of Jerusalem who believed that his scholarly rights had been violated by the American scholars. [*See biography of Sukenik.*] Calling his own press conference on the following day (April 26) at the Jewish Agency building in Jerusalem, Sukenik reported on the Cave 1 scrolls that had come into his possession during the previous autumn and asserted that his negotiations to acquire the remaining Cave 1 manuscripts, though interrupted by the outbreak of the 1948 war, had established his prior scholarly claim. Public recriminations intensified in August 1949 with the publication in the London *Times* of a letter by Professor Godfrey Driver of Oxford, who criticized Burrows and his American colleagues for encouraging Archbishop Athanasius Yeshue Samuel to leave Palestine with his scrolls (in direct violation of British Mandatory antiquities laws) and for being "non-cooperative" in sharing details about the scrolls with other scholars. [*See biography of Samuel.*]

Questions of Authenticity. Through 1949, disputes over scholarly priority gradually gave way to enthusiastic reports about the antiquity and historical value of the scrolls. For the most part, these reports faithfully conveyed the general scholarly consensus, yet in the wake of the publicity and popular interest that accompanied public exhibitions of scrolls in London and at the Library of Congress in Washington, Professor Solomon Zeitlin of Dropsie College began to raise serious questions in the press about the scrolls' antiquity and even authenticity. Zeitlin's outspoken condemnations of what he believed to be scholarly credulity were soon countered in the press by prominent biblical scholars, including W. F. Albright, who rallied to the defense of the scrolls' value and early date. By 1950, criticism of the scrolls' authenticity and pre-Christian date had been effectively rebutted, but a pattern had been established in which future scholarly debates about the scrolls would be extensively covered by the news media and have a profound effect in shaping public opinion.

The Dead Sea Scrolls and Christianity. Although the discovery of the cache from Cave 4 at Qumran in September 1952 attracted immediate attention in the mass media, the issues that captured the imagination of the general public in the mid-1950s were mainly theological. In 1950, wide coverage was given to Professor André Dupont-Sommer's theory, based on his interpretation of Pesher Habakkuk (1QpHab), that the community's veneration and expectation of the return of their martyred Teacher of Righteousness was a hitherto unknown precursor of the Christian tradition. [*See* Pesher Habakkuk *and biography of Dupont-Sommer.*] This theory was elaborated further by the American critic and novelist Edmund Wilson whose extensive 1955 feature article in *The New Yorker* later became a bestselling book entitled *The Scrolls from the Dead Sea.* The underlying theological implication—hinted at by Dupont-Sommer and deftly sidestepped by Wilson—was that the scrolls showed Christianity not to be the result of a sudden, unique revelation but a development of preexisting Jewish messianic ideas. That assertion was stated bluntly by John M. Allegro, a member of the international team of scroll scholars, who was featured in a series of British Broadcasting Corporation (BBC) radio interviews in the spring of 1956. [*See biography of Allegro.*] Allegro's description of his own work on the scrolls (notably Pesher Nahum 4Q169, with its references to crucifixion) was, by his own later admission, meant to undermine orthodox faith in the uniqueness of Christianity. [*See* Crucifixion; Pesher Nahum.] Moreover, his insinuation that other members of the international team were intentionally concealing the true theological implications of the scrolls' sectarian texts led to a public confrontation. A letter of protest, condemning Allegro and repudiating his conclusions, signed by other members of the international team, was published in the London *Times* on 16 March 1956. These accusations and countercharges between scroll scholars forever planted the suspicion in the public consciousness that the scrolls contained explosive religious secrets about the origins of Christianity that were being hidden or suppressed.

Warfare and Politics. Considering the time and place of their discovery around the outbreak of the Arab-Israeli conflict, the Dead Sea Scrolls were almost certainly destined to become contested objects of nationalistic pride. From the beginning, Sukenik had always stressed the emotional significance that the ancient Hebrew and Aramaic documents held for the people of the newly established State of Israel and for Jews all over the world. Indeed, the secret purchase by Sukenik's son Yigael Yadin of the remaining Cave 1 scrolls from Archbishop Samuel in the summer of 1954 was seen as a national triumph when it was officially announced in a press conference held by Prime Minister Moshe Sharett of Israel in February 1955. [*See biography of Yadin.*] In Jordan, the scrolls also became objects of national attention; in the rising tide of Arab nationalism in the months leading up to the Suez Crisis of 1956, articles and editorials began to appear in the Jordanian press opposing the export of any of the scrolls to foreign institutions that had subsidized their purchase from the Ta'amireh bedouin and demanding that the scrolls—as well as the Palestine Archaeological Museum—be nationalized. In 1960, John Allegro gained official Jordanian government support for his widely publicized (and ultimately unsuccessful) search for the treasures of the Copper Scroll. In Israel, the political significance of scroll discoveries was further underlined in the press and in the public consciousness by Yadin's decision in March 1960 to announce the discovery of the Bar Kokhba Letters from Naḥal Ḥever in the residence of the president of Israel. [*See* Ḥever, Naḥal, *article on* Written Material.] Likewise, the Masada expedition, funded and covered exclusively by the London *Observer,* was portrayed throughout the world as a national undertaking by the people of modern Israel in an attempt to uncover their ancient heritage. [*See* Masada.]

Publication Rights and the International Team. The Israeli conquest of East Jerusalem and the West Bank in the 1967 Arab-Israeli War brought both the scrolls and the Qumran site under Israeli administration, yet the previous arrangements regarding scholarly rights were retained. Yadin's 1967 announcement that he had obtained Temple Scroll[a] (11Q19) from the Bethlehem antiquities dealer Khalil Iskander (Kando) Shahin was widely publicized in the press and viewed with excitement by many scholars, but a full decade would pass before the scrolls once again became an international *cause célèbre.* [*See* Temple Scroll *and biography of Shahin.*] In the late 1970s, Professors Geza Vermes and Morton Smith began to criticize the slow pace of publication of texts by the members of the original publication team. By 1984 their protests were joined by a powerful new voice on the archaeological scene: Hershel Shanks, the founder and editor of the widely circulated *Biblical Archaeology Review.* In the pages of his journal and in lectures and interviews, Shanks energetically campaigned for strict timetables for scholarly publication and, eventually, for open access by all qualified scholars to the entire corpus of the Qumran scrolls. Before long, Shanks's crusade was taken up by the general media as an issue of academic freedom, and the pressure exerted in public forums on the members of the international team and on the Israel Antiquities Authority eventually forced the establishment of a new and more open regime for the study and publication of the scrolls. During the height of the public uproar, the editor in chief of the scrolls publication project, Professor John Strugnell, granted a personal interview to a correspondent for the Israeli daily *Ha-'Arets.* Strugnell's outspoken reflections on religion and politics in the modern Middle East greatly intensified the controversy. [*See biography of Strugnell.*] In addition, the broadcast in the United States of a documentary on the scrolls controversy by the Public Broadcasting Service (PBS) series *Nova* proved instrumental in turning public opinion against the international team. Even though the public controversy died down with the reconstitution of the publication project in the autumn of 1991, journalistic interest in the newly released scrolls and their historical significance remained high.

New Theories, New Celebrities. Part of the intensity of the media campaign to gain access to the unpublished scrolls was fueled by the lobbying of scholars who opposed the general consensus on dating and identification of the authors of the scrolls. Reviving Allegro's claims that the international team members harbored private political or religious reasons for suppressing certain documents, a new wave of popular books and articles condemning scholarly abuses appeared side by side with new theories about the relation of Qumran to early Christianity. Most prominent in this respect were the works of Professors Barbara Thiering and Robert Eisenman, who identified members of the Qumran community with personalities mentioned in the New Testament. Another outspoken voice against the old order was Professor Norman Golb who had formulated a "Jerusalem Theory" of scroll origins, which linked the Qumran manuscripts not to a sectarian group in the wilderness, but to the efforts of individuals from Jerusalem to preserve the manuscripts of the city's libraries from destruction by the Romans during the First Jewish Revolt.

By the mid-1990s, however, emotions had cooled, and new leaders of mainstream Qumran research such as Professors Lawrence H. Schiffman, James C. VanderKam, Emanuel Tov, and Eugene Ulrich had emerged as effective spokespersons in press interviews and documentary films. At the same time, the new technologies of CD-ROM and the Internet served to diffuse unfounded, sensationalist press coverage by disseminating the latest developments of scroll research to an ever wider general audience.

BIBLIOGRAPHY

Baigent, Michael, and Richard Leigh. *The Dead Sea Scrolls Deception.* New York, 1991. A history of scrolls discovery and interpretation, highlighting the authors' view of the role played by the Vatican.

Betz, Otto, and Rainer Riesner. *Jesus, Qumran, and the Vatican: Clarifications.* New York, 1994. A history of scrolls discovery and interpretation, refuting various conspiracy theories.

Golb, Norman. *Who Wrote the Dead Sea Scrolls: The Search for the Secret of Qumran.* New York, 1995. An alternative explanation of scroll origins and a detailed account of the campaign to open access to the Qumran texts by one of the participants.

Kapera, Zdzislaw. "The Unfortunate Story of Qumran Cave Four." In *Qumran Cave Four: Special Report,* edited by Zdzislaw J. Kapera, pp. 5–67. Kraków, 1991. An excellent summary of the public controversies with an extensive bibliography of press references. *The Qumran Chronicle I, no. 2.3 (1990–1991).*

Shanks, Hershel. *Understanding the Dead Sea Scrolls. A Reader from the Biblical Archaeology Review.* New York, 1992. A collection of essays on the history and interpretation of the scrolls, including several essays on the public controversies and involvement and role of public media.

Silberman, Neil Asher. *The Hidden Scrolls: Christianity, Judaism, and the War for the Dead Sea Scrolls.* New York, 1994. A history of scrolls discovery and interpretation, with bibliographical notes on media sources.

Trever, John C. *The Untold Story of Qumran.* Westwood, N.J., 1965. The most comprehensive account of the discovery of the scrolls from Cave 1 at Qumran and the initial American contacts with the press.

Wilson, Edmund. *The Scrolls from the Dead Sea.* New York, 1955.

Yadin, Yigael. *The Message of the Scrolls.* London, 1957.

NEIL ASHER SILBERMAN

MEDITATION ON CREATION. *See* Wisdom Texts.

MELCHIZEDEK. The name *Melchizedek* first appears in the Hebrew scriptures and became popular in some lines of Jewish and Christian traditions. It is to be understood as "king of righteousness" or "righteous king," and not "my king is righteous[ness]." This understanding of the name is attested by Josephus (*Jewish Antiquities* 1, 180). Nevertheless, a primitive meaning, "my king is Zedek" (Zedek was god of the city of Jerusalem), is possible. Its English pronounciation derives from the Septuagint.

The origin of the figure Melchizedek is not clear. Was he a purely mythical figure, even a Canaanite God (Bodinger, 1994), or was he a historical person from patriarchal times (e.g., Horton, 1976), to whom mythical features later were attributed?

Hebrew Scriptures. The name *Melchizedek* occurs twice in the Hebrew scriptures, in *Genesis* 14.18 and in Psalm 110.4. The age of these texts is disputed, though they surely are not extremely old; Psalm 110 recently has been dated to Hasmonean times (Donner, 1994), but, among other arguments, the use of the Tetragrammaton, which died out in the second century BCE, speaks against a late date. Neither *Genesis* 14.18 nor Psalm 110 is represented among the biblical manuscripts at Qumran, a fact that is best explained by the fragmentary state of preservation of the *Genesis* and *Psalms* manuscripts there. The *terminus ad quem* for the origin of *Genesis* 14.18–20 is the Greek translation about the middle of the third century BCE; the first reference to Psalm 110 might be found in 4Q183.

The short Melchizedek passage in *Genesis* 14.18–20 obviously is an insertion into the story of Abram meeting the king of Sodom after he came back from his victory over Chedorlaomer in *Genesis* 14.17–24. Melchizedek is presented as king of Salem, which the later tradition explicitly identifies with Jerusalem (e.g., Genesis Apocryphon 1QapGen xx.13; cf. Ps. 76.2), and as priest of *ʾEl ʿElyon* (kings who act as priests are well attested in the ancient Near East). Melchizedek brings out bread and wine to Abram, blesses him, and praises *ʾEl ʿElyon*, the creator of heaven and earth, who is responsible for the victory of Abram. The positive description of Melchizedek contrasts with the characterization of the king of Sodom in this story. This led J. T. Milik to the assumption that the confrontation of Melchizedek and the king of Sodom here might be an image of the battle between the two chief spirits, Melchizedek and Melchireshaʿ. The meaning of verse 20 is uncertain. It simply is reported that "he" gave one tenth to "him"; later it generally was assumed that Abram was the subject of the action (e.g., 1QapGen xx.17; Josephus, *Antiquities* 1, 180; *Heb.* 7.2), but the problem is still discussed in rabbinic literature.

Psalm 110 is a psalm with many textual difficulties. It deals with a king, obviously the royal Messiah, to whom God has sworn the oath "You are a priest forever according to the order of Melchizedek" (v 4). Assuming that verses 5b through 6 refer to the Messiah and not to God ("When he grows angry he shatters kings, he gives the nations their deserts, smashing their skulls, he heaps the wide world with corpses."), it is this king who will also execute the final judgment of the nations.

Apocrypha and Pseudepigrapha. There hardly are any traces of Melchizedek in apocryphal and pseudepigraphal texts. *Jubilees* (chap. 13) originally may have referred to Melchizedek, but the existing copies of the book do not mention him in its retelling of *Genesis* 14. Instead the tithe is given to an anonymous collective, to "the priests." This might be an intentional avoidance by the author of *Jubilees*, who favors Levitical priestly interests.

Qumran. Melchizedek appears in the Genesis Apocryphon and in Melchizedek from Cave 11 at Qumran (11Q13). In Songs of the Sabbath Sacrifice[b] (4Q401) Melchizedek could be the seventh and highest of the heavenly chief princes; the restoration of his name in this text is uncertain (4Q401 11.3, 22.3; cf. Songs of the Sabbath Sacrifice[d] 4Q403 1.ii.24) but possible. In the fragmentary, pre-Qumran Aramaic text Visions of Amram[b] (4Q544), the name Melchizedek probably occurred in a lacuna (2.1–b, 3.1–3) as one of the three names of the angel of light, the opponent of Melchireshaʿ (see Puech, 1993 p. 536).

In the Genesis Apocryphon (1QapGen) xxii.14–17 the Melchizedek story basically is the same as in *Genesis* 14, but some difficult points of interpretation regarding Salem and the tithe are clarified. The identification of *ʾEl ʿElyon* with YHVH (*Gn.* 14.22) is missing in verse 21, and the general avoidance of the Tetragrammaton in the Genesis Apocryphon might suggest an origin only in the second century BCE; other aspects of the language point to the first century BCE (Kutscher, 1965).

The most interesting text is Melchizedek from Cave 11 at Qumran, a manuscript that consists of fourteen fragments from three successive columns (*Editio princeps* by van der Woude, 1965; new edition and reconstruction by Puech, 1987). Paleographically this copy dates from the middle of the first century BCE or slightly later. From column i only parts of a supralinear writing that continues in the margin are preserved; column ii probably had twenty-seven lines and can be restored extensively; column iii is represented by small remains. Unfortunately, the character and the length of the composition as a whole are unknown, as well as the original position of the three columns. The work probably dates from the end of the second half of the second century BCE; formal criteria, such as the use of certain quotation and interpretation formulas, suggest this date. Melchizedek is the oldest purely exegetical text from Qumran, older than the *pesharim*, 4Q174 and 4Q177. At the center of the manuscript from Cave 11 is the figure of Melchizedek, heavenly high priest, eschatological savior of the righteous ones; as the instrument of God, he will be judge on the "day of atonement" at the time of God's final judgment, when Belial and the spirits of his lot will be defeated. Melchizedek is not an earthly messianic figure. Rather he seems to be almost identical (only with nuances in function like cult, war, etc.) with the prince of light (cf. Rule of the Community, 1QS iii.20), the archangel Michael (cf. War Scroll 1QM xvii.6–8), the angel of truth (1QS iii.24), and the great hand of God (cf. 4Q177 xi.14); he further exhibits parallels to the Son of Man. The eschatological scenario of history in Melchizedek from Cave 11, which is understood as being divided into jubilees, is described with the help of citations from different biblical books (*Leviticus* 25 and *Isaiah* 61 seem to play a kind of guiding role). Melchizedek ii.18 contains the oldest known explicit citation from the *Book of Daniel*. It is an unsolved problem whether the one who announces the release in the first week of the tenth jubilee (11Q13 ii.7) is identical with Melchizedek, who will bring about the release at the end of the tenth jubilee (11Q13 ii.7), or whether they are two distinct figures. Some scholars (e.g., Milik 1972, Puech 1987) have proposed identifying the one who announces the release with the Teacher of Righteousness, who, as "messenger of good news" (11Q13 ii.16), proclaims salvation for the just and consoles them by giving them insight into the sequence of the periods of history (11Q13 ii.18–20), including its end (according to Melchizedek and the Damascus Document CD ii, the end was expected probably around the year 70 BCE; see Steudel 1993).

Philo and Josephus. Both Philo and Josephus highly valued the virtuous figure of Melchizedek. Philo mentions him in *De Abr*. 235, *De Congr*. 99, and *Legum allegoriarum* III 79–82, always in the context of the Abram story. In *De Abr*. Melchizedek is designated as high priest, in *De Congr*. he is said to be self-taught, and in *Legum allegoriarum* the "king of Salem" is interpreted as "king of peace" (cf. *Heb*. 7.2). Josephus discusses Melchizedek in *Jewish Antiquities* I 180–181. There he explains that Melchizedek means "righteous king," and that for his righteousness, Melchizedek was made priest of God. In *The Jewish War* VI, 438 Josephus states that the original founder of Jerusalem was a Canaanite chief, who was the first to officiate as priest of God and the first to build the temple.

Christianity. In the New Testament Melchizedek figures only in the *Letter to the Hebrews* (chaps. 4–10). The influence of the ideas of the Qumran community on the particular Christology of the *Letter to the Hebrews*—via converted Essenes—often has been assumed, and indeed there are some characteristic parallels in the concept and the use of the figure of Melchizedek, but differences also exist. God makes Jesus, his son, high priest according to the order of Melchizedek. Jesus has entered the heavenly sanctuary once and for all, having won eternal redemption by his own blood for the pious. Melchizedek and his priesthood are depicted as eternal; the Melchizedekian priesthood is superior to the Levitical priesthood.

The Slavonic *Apocalypse of Enoch* refers to three Melchizedeks. Chapters 71 through 73 of *2 Enoch* exibit clear Christian interpolation; an early redactor seems to have been interested in a Melchizedek-Christ typology when he revised the Jewish Melchizedek legend of these chapters. These chapters tell about the supernatural birth of the priest of priests Melchizedek, son of Nir and nephew of Noah, who was brought to paradise for eternity by Michael in order to be protected from the Flood; another Melchizedek is priest and king in Salem; the third and final one is obviously Christ.

Melchizedek appears in the Gnostic texts *Pistis Sophia*, the *Books of Jeu*, and the fragmentary *Melchizedek* tractate of the Nag Hammadi Codices (Codex IX, 1). Epiphanius (Haer. 55) reports on the sect of the Melchizedekians. The Gnostic ideas about Melchizedek, which characterize him, for example, as heavenly, as carrier of the light, as high priest, identical with Michael, identical with Christ, are influenced by the traditions found in Melchizedek from Cave 11 at Qumran and the *Letter to the Hebrews*.

The church fathers stress especially the identity of Melchizedek's offering of bread and wine with the Eucharist (e.g. Cyprian, Epistle 63, 4).

Targumim and Rabbinic Literature. The Targumim as well as the rabbis identified Melchizedek with Shem, son of Noah (e.g., Targum Pseudo-Jonathan on *Gn*. 14.18;

B.T., *Ned.* 32b). Apart from Targum *Neophyti* 1, the Targumim avoid speaking of Melchizedek's priesthood. Instead of calling him "priest," as *Genesis* 14.18 does, they use a verbal form of the word meaning "to minister" (Targum Onkelos, Targum Pseudo-Jonathan). The same tendency is seen in rabbinic texts. It was Melchizedek's mistake to bless Abraham before blessing God (*Gn.* 14.19–20). For this reason God took the priesthood from Melchizedek and gave it to Abraham (the difficult expression in Ps. 110.4 is understood as "because of the words of Melchizedek," i.e., because of his erroneous blessing, B.T., *Ned.* 32b; *Lv. Rab.* 25). These texts might reflect a reaction to Christian ideas of the superiority of Jesus' priesthood compared with that of Melchizedek, though already in *Jubilees* there seems to be an antipathy on the part of Levitical priestly circles to the idea of a Melchizedekian priesthood. Nevertheless, in Pesiq. 51a Melchizedek is seen positively, as an eschatological figure, one of the four craftsmen of *Zechariah* 2.3 (cf. Rashi, B.T., *Suk.* 52b).

BIBLIOGRAPHY

Beauchamp, Paul. "Quelle typologie dans l'Epître aux Hébreux?" In *Cahiers Ratisbonne* 2. Jerusalem, 1997. See pp. 10–32.

Bodinger, Martin. "L'énigme de Melkisédeq." *Revue de l'Histoire des Religions* 211 (1994), 297–333.

Carmignac, Jean. "Le document de Qumrân sur Melki sédeq." *Revue de Qumrân* 7 (1970), 343–378.

Donner, Herbert. "Der verläßliche Prophet. Betrachtungen zu I Makk 14, 41 ff und zu Ps 110." In *Aufsätze zum Alten Testament: Aus vier Jahrzehnten*, edited by H. Donner. Berlin, 1994. See pp. 213–223.

Flusser, D. *Judaism and the Origins of Christianity*. Jerusalem, 1988. See pp. 186–192.

Horton, Fred L. *The Melchizedek Tradition: A Critical Examination of the Sources to the Fifth Century* A.D. *and in the Epistle to the Hebrews*. Society for New Testament Studies Monograph Series, 30. Cambridge, 1976.

Kobelski, Paul J. *Melchizedek and Melchireša'*. Catholic Biblical Quarterly Monograph Series, 10. Washington, D.C., 1981.

Kutscher, Eduard Y. "The Language of the 'Genesis Apocryphon.'" *Scripta Hierosolymitana* 4 (1965), 1–35.

Milik, Józef T. "Milkî-ṣedeq et Milkî-reša' dans les anciens écrits juifs et chrétiens." *Journal of Jewish Studies* 23 (1972), 95–144.

Puech, Émile. "Notes sur le manuscrit de 11Qmelkîsédeq." *Revue de Qumrân* 12 (1987), 483–513.

Puech, Émile. *La croyance des Esséniens en la vie future: immortalité, résurrection, vie éternelle?*, vol. 2. In Études Bibliques, Nouvelle série. No. 22. Paris, 1993.

Schenke, Hans-Martin. "Die jüdische Melchisedek-Gestalt als Thema der Gnosis." In *Altes Testament—Frühjudentum—Gnosis: Neue Studien zu Gnosis und Bibel*, edited by K.-W. Tröger, pp. 111–136. Berlin, 1980.

Steudel, Annette. "*'aḥarit ha-yamim* in the Texts from Qumran." *Revue de Qumrân* 16 (1993), 225–246.

Van der Toorn, K., et al, eds. *Dictionary of Deities and Demons in the Bible*. Leiden, New York, Cologne, 1995.

Van der Woude, Adam S. "Melchisedek als himmlische Erlösergestalt in den neugefundenen eschatologischen Midraschim aus Qumran Höhle XI." *Oudtestamentische Studien* 14 (1965), 354–373.

ANNETTE STEUDEL

MENAHEM THE ESSENE. *See* Essenes.

MESSIAH OF AARON. *See* Messiahs.

MESSIAH OF ISRAEL. *See* Messiahs.

MESSIAHS. Some thirty texts in the Dead Sea Scrolls speak of anointed personages—the literal definition of messiah—and although only about half refer to what is probably the traditional, royal Messiah, most of the other texts refer to the prophets. A few refer to the priest, and one is in reference to Moses. The language is drawn from the Hebrew scriptures and is found in numerous writings and bodies of literature produced by Jews and Christians in late antiquity.

Derivation of the Term Messiah. The word *messiah* comes from the Greek *messias* (cf. *John* 1.41; 4.25), which itself is a transliteration of the Hebrew *mashiaḥ* (*2 Sm.* 22.51; 23.1), meaning one who is "anointed" (with oil). *Mashiaḥ* occurs some thirty-eight times in the Hebrew scriptures. The Greek equivalent is *christos* (cf. Septuagint, *2 Sm.* 22.51; 23.1), which occurs some 529 times in the New Testament (about half in Paul; more than half if one includes the Pastorals). The nominal form is derived from the verbs *mashaḥ* (Hebrew) and *chriein* (Greek), which mean "to anoint" or "to smear (with oil)." When the nominal form is definite (Heb., *ham-mashiaḥ*; Aram., *mashiḥa'*), it is usually translated "the Messiah." The Greek definite form, *ho christos*, is usually translated "the Christ."

Israel's tradition of anointing the priest is ancient (cf. *Ex.* 28.41; 30.30; 40.13–15; *Lv.* 16.32, *Nm.* 3.3). Of special interest is the anointing of the high priest (*Ex.* 40.13; *Lv.* 7.35), who in *Numbers* 35.25 is said to be "anointed with the holy oil." Ben Sira eulogizes Aaron, stating that "Moses ordained him, and anointed him with holy oil" (*Sir.* 45.15). Early rabbinic literature is keenly interested in the "anointed high priest" (cf. *Hor.* 2.1–3, 2.6–7; 3.1–2; 3.4; 3.6; *Zev.* 4.3; *Men.* 5.3; 5.5, 6.2; 6.4; *Me'il.* 2.9), much more than it is in the royal Messiah (cf. *Sot.* 9.15).

The kings of Judah and Israel were anointed, usually by prophets as well as by priests. Especially important is Samuel's anointing of Saul (*1 Sm.* 9.9; 9.16; 10.1; 15.1; 15.17) and David (*1 Sm.* 16.1–3; 16.12–13; *2 Sm.* 12.7; cf. *Sir.* 46.13). Nathan the prophet and Zadok the priest anointed Solomon (*1 Kgs.* 1.34; cf. *1 Kgs.* 1.39; 1.45). Elijah was commanded to anoint Hazael to be king over Aram and Jehu to be king over Israel (*1 Kgs.* 19.15–16), though Elisha actually carries out the task (*2 Kgs.* 9.1–3, 9.6; 9.12; cf. *Sir.* 48.8). Even in the period of the judges we find the tradition of someone being anointed king

(*Jgs*. 9.8, 9.15). Frequently the anointed king is called "the Lord's anointed" (*1 Sm*. 16.6; 24.6; 24.10; 26.9; 26.11; 26.16; 26.23; *2 Sm*. 1.14, 1.16; 19.21; cf. Ps. 2.2; 18.50; 20.6; 28.8). The psalmist, on behalf of the anointed, sometimes appeals to God for help (Ps. 84.9; 89.38; 89.51; 132.10; 132.17).

Elijah anointed Elisha, his prophetic successor (*1 Kgs*. 19.15–16; cf. *2 Kgs*. 9.1–3, 9.6; 9.12, where Elisha in turn anoints Jehu king). The anointing of Elisha is the only instance of an anointed prophet. However, one should recall that the prophetic speaker in *Isaiah* 61 claims to have the spirit of the Lord and to have been "anointed" to preach (cf. *Tg. Is*. 61.1: "The prophet said: 'A spirit of prophecy before the Lord God is upon me'"). The association in a sermon attributed to Jesus (*Lk*. 4.18–27) of this passage from *Isaiah* with the ministries of Elijah and Elisha is probably not accidental but reflects the tradition of the anointed prophet.

Perhaps reflecting on Psalm 105.15 and *1 Chronicles* 16.22 ("Touch not my anointed ones, and do my prophets no harm!"), the Dead Sea Scrolls often refer to the prophets as "anointed ones" (cf. CD ii.12; v.21–vi.1 = 4Q267 2.6 = 6Q15 3.4; 1QM xi.7–8; 1Q30 1.2[?]; 4Q270 9.ii.13–14; 4Q287 10.13; 4Q521 8.9 [or anointed priests]). They are "anointed by the Holy Spirit, the seers of truth" (CD ii.12). These anointed prophets have spoken the words that the Qumran community in its own time has been able to interpret (cf. Pesher Habakkuk, 1QpHab vii.1–5). They spoke to an unbelieving and idolatrous Israel in times past (Damascus Document, CD v.21–vi.1), but they also spoke of the last days: "By the hand of your anointed ones, seers of things appointed, you have told us about the ti[mes] of the wars of your hands" (War Scroll, 1QM xi.7–8).

Messianic Interpretation and the Rise of Messianism. The Hebrew scriptures speak of anointed priests, kings, and prophets. But none of these anointed persons is to be understood as an eschatological figure of deliverance. Sometime in the third or second century BCE, *messiah* takes on this eschatological nuance. In reaction to the oppression of Greek and Roman rule, and in response to what was perceived as usurpation of the high priesthood on the part of the Hasmoneans and their successors, hopes for the appearance of a righteous king and/or priest began to be expressed. The later usurpation of Israel's throne by Herod and his successors only fueled these hopes. The literature of this time speaks of the appearance of worthy anointed persons through whom the restoration of Israel might take place. These hopes and predictions drew upon passages of scripture that spoke of anointed persons and upon passages that spoke in more indirect ways of individuals or symbols that lent themselves to eschatological or salvific interpretations.

Three passages played an important, generative role in the rise of messianism: *Genesis* 49.10, *Numbers* 24.17, and *Isaiah* 11.1–6. All these passages are interpreted in a messianic sense in the Dead Sea Scrolls and other early Jewish and Christian writings.

In the Commentary on Genesis A (4Q252 1.v.1–7). *Genesis* 49.10–11 is cited and is understood to refer to the "Branch of David." The passage also may be alluded to in Pesher Isaiah[a] (4Q161 7–10.iii.25), again in a messianic sense. The messianic potential appears to have been enhanced in the Septuagint. All four Targums to the Pentateuch (Targum Onkelos, Targum Pseudo-Jonathan, Targum Neophyti, and the Fragmentary Targum) render the *Genesis* passage in an explicitly messianic sense ("King Messiah" is mentioned in verses 10, 11, and 12). Jacob's blessing (*Gn*. 49.8–12) is referred to in the *Testament of Judah* 1.6 ("my father declared to me, 'You shall be king'") and in the *Testament of Judah* 22.3 seems to be understood in a messianic sense. The description of the warrior Messiah in *Revelation* 19.11–16 may have this passage, as well as *Isaiah* 11, as a source (compare *Rv*. 19.13 with *Gn*. 49.11); and it may be alluded to in *Hebrews* 7.14. Christian messianic interpretation of the passage becomes commonplace in the second century (cf. Justin Martyr, *1 Apologies* 32 and 54, *Dialogue with Trypho* 52 and 120; Clement of Alexandria, *Pedagogue* 1.5 and 1.6; Irenaeus, *Against Heresies* 4.10.2).

The interpretation of *Numbers* 24.17 is similar to that of *Genesis* 49.10. All four *targums* to the Pentateuch paraphrase the passage in explicitly messianic terms. The Hebrew text's "a star shall come forth out of Jacob, and a scepter shall rise out of Israel" becomes in the Aramaic "a king shall arise out of Jacob and be anointed the Messiah out of Israel." Messianic interpretation of *Numbers* 24.17 is widely attested in traditions dating to the first century CE and earlier (*Testament of Judah* 24.1–6; CD vii.20; 1Q28b v.27–28; 1QM xi.4–9; 4Q175 1.9–13; possibly Philo, *De Vita Mosis* 1.52 secs. 290; *De praemiis et poenis*, 16 sec. 95; Orphica 31 [Aristobulus fragment 4.5]). It is probably to this passage that Josephus refers when he says that his countrymen were misled by an "ambiguous oracle" that promised that "one from their country would become ruler of the world" (*The Jewish War*, 6.312–313; cf 3.400–402). The "star" that "stood over the city" of Jerusalem would have only fueled such speculation (*The Jewish War*, 6.289). At issue was not the messianic orientation of the oracle; rather, the question was to whom the oracle applied. Of course, Josephus here is being disingenuous. It is very probable that he too understood the passage in the way his contemporaries did. Instead, Josephus deliberately distanced himself from popular Jewish interpretation and applied the oracle to Vespasian his patron, "who was proclaimed emperor on

Jewish soil." Early Christians were also aware of the passage's messianic potential, as seen in the "star" of *Matthew* 2.2 and the Magi's assumption that it pointed to the birthplace of the "king of the Jews." The nickname of Shim'on bar Kosiba', "Bar Kokhba'" ("son of the star"), apparently was inspired by this passage. According to rabbinic tradition, this man claimed to be the Messiah, or at least was proclaimed as such by some of his followers (cf. J.T., *Ta'an*. 4.5/8; B.T., *San*. 93b; Justin Martyr, *1 Apologies* 31 and *Dialogue with Trypho* 106; Irenaeus, *Against Heresies* 3.9.2).

In the Hebrew text, the oracle of *Isaiah* 11.1–6 anticipates the coming forth of "a shoot from the stock of Jesse, even a branch shall grow out of his roots" (v. 1). The *Isaiah* Targum, which represents later interpretive tradition, renders the verse, "And a king shall come forth from the sons of Jesse, and the Messiah shall be exalted from the sons of his sons." Much earlier the Septuagint had enhanced the messianic potential of *Isaiah* 11.10: "And there shall be in that day the root of Jesse, even he who arises to rule over nations. . . ."). Paul quotes this passage and applies it to Jesus (*Rom*. 15.12; cf. *Rv*. 5.5, 22.16; Clement of Alexandria, *Stromateis* 5.6). *Isaiah* 11 is taken in a messianic sense in Pesher Isaiah[a] (4Q161 7–10.iii.22–29 and is echoed in a passage in the Rule of the Blessings (1Q28b v.21–26), which describes the blessing that is to be pronounced upon the Prince of the Congregation. In *4 Ezra* 13.2–10, *Isaiah* 11.4 is alluded to and applied to the man who "flew with the clouds of heaven" (cf. *Daniel* 7.13). Messianic interpretation of *Isaiah* 11 probably underlies the War Rule (4Q285 5.1–6) and *Testament of Levi* 18.7 as well. Early Christian writers were especially fond of *Isaiah* 11 (for v. 1, cf. *Mt*. 2.23; *Acts* 13.23; *Heb*. 7.14; *Rv*. 5.5, 22.16; Justin Martyr, *1 Apologies* 32, and *Dialogue with Trypho* 87; Clement of Alexandria, *Pedagogue* 1.7; Irenaeus, *Against Heresies* 3.9.3; *Sib. Or*. 6.8, 6.16, 7.38, 8.254; for v. 2, cf. *Eph*. 1.17; *1 Pet*., 4.14; Irenaeus, *Against Heresies* 3.17.1; for v. 3, cf. *Jn*. 7.24; Clement of Alexandria, *Pedagogue* 1.7; for v. 4, cf. *Jn*. 7.24; *Eph*. 6.17; *2 Thes*. 2.8; *Rv*. 19.11; Clement of Alexandria, *Pedagogue* 1.7; Irenaeus, *Against Heresies* 4.33.1; for v. 5, cf. *Eph*. 6.14).

The data therefore suggest that the messianism of the Dead Sea Scrolls coheres with what can be ascertained from other Jewish sources from this period. The scrolls contain some distinctive ideas in certain details (such as the nature of the final war at the End of Days and the Messiah's role in it, or the Messiah's submission to the priests), but it would appear that in most of the major points Qumran messianism is not much different from that of other pious, hopeful Jews.

The "Anointed of Aaron and of Israel." One of the interesting features of Qumran messianism is the epithet "anointed (ones) of Aaron and of Israel" (CD xii.23; xiv.19; xix.10–11; xx.1; 1QS ix.11). The coupling of the "anointed of Aaron and of Israel" reflects the frequent association of Aaron and Israel in the Pentateuch (cf. *Ex*. 16.9, 18.12, 34.30; *Lv*. 17.2, 21.24, 22.18; *Nm*. 13.26) as well as in liturgical expressions, such as "(God) will bless the house of Israel; he will bless the house of Aaron" (Ps. 115.12, cf. vv. 9–10; 135.19). The story of the simultaneous anointing of Solomon, the son of David, and of Zadok the high priest (*1 Chr*. 29.22), combined with Zechariah's vision of the two "sons of oil" (*Zec*. 4.14; cf. 4Q254 4.2), that is, the priest and the political ruler (cf. *Zec*. 3–4), probably informed the Damascus Document's expectation of the eventual appearance of the "anointed of Aaron and of Israel" (see also *1 Sm*. 2.35).

The epithet "anointed of Aaron" reflects passages that refer to the anointing of Aaron (*Ex*. 40.13; *Lv*. 7.35). To the passages from the better known scrolls one may now add the Apocryphon of Moses B[a] (4Q375 1.i.9; "the anointed priest upon whose head the oil of anointing has been poured") and the Apocryphon of Moses B[b] (4Q376 1.i.1; "the anointed priest"). Although these texts are fragmentary, they broaden the field of reference.

Many scholars of the Dead Sea Scrolls are convinced that at Qumran the "anointed of Aaron," along with his priestly colleagues, would be equal to, if not superior to, the royal Messiah (but see Abegg [1995] for important caveats). Again, the history of Solomon, the son of David, may have been viewed as exemplary: "Let Zadok the priest and Nathan the prophet there anoint him (Solomon) king over Israel" (*1 Kgs*. 1.34; cf. vv. 39, 45). In the commentary on *Isaiah* 11, it is anticipated that the "Branch of David" will submit to the instruction of the priests (4Q161 7–10.iii.22–29). One is reminded also of the prominence of the high priest and his priestly colleagues in the War Scroll (1QM) in the direction of the holy war against the sons of darkness. This royal priestly cooperation is probably at work in the related War Rule (cf. 4Q285 5.1–6), where the "Branch of David" battles the Romans (the Kittim), and the priests take charge of the disposal of the slain to avoid the defilement of the land. [*See* Kittim.]

Qumran's epithet "anointed of Israel" derives from passages in the Hebrew scriptures that speak of figures being "anointed king over Israel" (as in *1 Kgs*. 1.34; *2 Sm*. 12.7). The description of David prefaced to his final words may be relevant: "Now these are the last words of David: The oracle of David, the son of Jesse, the oracle of the man who was raised on high, the anointed of the God of Jacob, the sweet psalmist of Israel" (*2 Sm*. 23.1; cf. *Mk*. 15.32: "The anointed one, the king of Israel").

According to the Dead Sea Scrolls the "anointed of Israel" will engage in battle with the forces of darkness. Israel's enemies "will be delivered up to the sword at the coming of the anointed of Aaron and of Israel" (CD xix.10–11). Indeed, the Davidic Branch "will kill him" (War Rule, 4Q285 5.4), by which we probably should understand that the Messiah was expected to kill the leader of the Romans (the *Kittim*), perhaps meaning the Roman emperor himself. The Messiah will also serve faithfully alongside the priests (1Q28a ii.20–21). The Messiah of the Messianic Apocalypse (4Q521), though perhaps a messianic figure of prophetic stripe, adds to our picture. According to this scroll (1.ii.1) "heaven and earth will obey his anointed" (cf. *Dt.* 32.1; *Is.* 1.2; Ps. 146.6). When this Messiah comes, God "will honor the pious upon the th[ro]ne of the eternal kingdom, setting prisoners free, opening the eyes of the blind, raising up those who are bo[wed down]" (1.ii.7–8). At this time the Lord "will do glorious things that have not been done, just as he said. For he will heal the wounded, he will revive the dead, he will proclaim good news to the afflicted" (1.ii.11–12). The echoes of *Isaiah* 61.1–2 and 35.5–6 are interesting; especially noteworthy is the parallel between the scroll and a saying attributed to Jesus that echoes these passages in *Isaiah* and that also speaks of raising the dead (*Mt.* 11.4–5 = *Lk.* 7.22), an element not found in the passages from *Isaiah*. This is an important point of coherence between Jesus and the Messianic Apocalypse that must be explored.

The much debated "anointed of Aaron and of Israel" raises an important question: Do some of the Scrolls envision messianism as a diarchy? Many scholars think that they do. The idea of a priest and an anointed royal personage is found in *1 Samuel* 2.35: "And I will raise up for myself a faithful priest, who shall do according to what is in my heart and in my mind; and I will build him a sure house, and he shall go in and out before my anointed forever." The *targum* translates "sure house" as "lasting kingdom" and "anointed" as "Messiah." Part of the Hebrew expansion of *Sir.* 51.12 praises God who "makes the horn to sprout for the house of Israel" and who "elects the sons of Zadok to be priests" (cf. Ps. 132.16–17). As has already been mentioned, Qumran's "anointed of Aaron and of Israel" may reflect the diarchy of Zechariah. The alternating emphasis on descendants from the lines of Levi and Judah in the *Testaments of the Twelve Patriarchs* may be open to the same explanation (on the ruler from Levi, see *Testament of Reuben* 6.11–12 and *Testament of Levi* 18.1–14; for the ruler from Judah, see *Testament of Judah* 24.5–6 and *Testament of Naphtali* 4.5).

There is nothing novel about Qumran's messianic diarchy; it has its roots in the Hebrew scriptures (especially in the Masoretic Text and the Targum of *Zechariah* 3.6–10, 6.9–15; cf. juxtaposition of Aaron/Israel, for example in Ps. 115.9–10, 115.12, 118.3, 135.19) and is probably the presupposition of the *Testaments of the Twelve Patriarchs* (cf. *Testament of Dan* 5.10: "And there shall arise for you the tribe of Judah and of Levi the Lord's salvation"; *Testament of Joseph* 19.11: "honor Levi and Judah, because from them shall arise the salvation of Israel"). It is not necessary to conclude, as did R. H. Charles long ago, that the *Testaments of the Twelve Patriarchs* exhibit two competing messiahships—one priestly (of Levi), the other Davidic (of Judah). Rather, the *Testaments of the Twelve Patriarchs* may reflect the understanding of the diarchy as it arose in the Second Temple period. Side by side a royal descendant of David and a Zadokite high priest would rule over restored Israel. It is possible that the emphasis on the two Messiahs, one of Aaron and one of Israel, may have originated as a corrective of the merger of the high priestly and royal offices during the Hasmonean period.

The reading and interpretation of the Rule of the Congregation (1Q28a ii.11–12) have been controversial. D. Barthélemy (1955, p. 110) originally read the text "[This is the sit]ting of the men of renown [called] to assembly for the council of the community when [God] will have be[got]ten [*yolid*] the Messiah among them." But he thought the text should be emended to read "when God will have brought [*yolikh*] the Messiah" (1955, p. 117). Other emendations have been proposed. Although it remains disputed, the original reading enjoys a measure of support from Psalms 2.2 and 2.7: "The kings of the earth set themselves, and the rulers take counsel together, against the Lord and his Messiah. . . . He said to me: 'You are My son, today I have begotten you [*yelidtikha*].'" Given the language of Psalms 2.2 and 2.7, there is nothing unusual or unexpected in restoring the Rule of the Congregation (1Q28a ii.11–12) to read: "when God will have begotten the Messiah." This reading, however, does not necessarily imply that the author of the Rule of the Congregation expected the Messiah to experience an unusual or miraculous birth. (See, however, the objection to this reading by Puech [1994], who defends the reading "when God will reveal the Messiah.")

Related Messianic Epithets in the Dead Sea Scrolls. There are several other names and epithets given to the royal Messiah, the "anointed of Israel." He is explicitly identified as the "Branch of David" (*tsemaḥ David*). The epithet "Branch of David" occurs five times in the Dead Sea Scrolls (sometimes reconstructed) and derives from prophetic language (4Q161 7–10.iii.22; 4Q174 1–3.i.11; 4Q252 1.v.3–4; 4Q285 5.3, 4). Jeremiah's promise, "I will raise up for David a branch of righteousness [*le-David tsemaḥ tsaddiq*]" (Jer. 23.5; cf. 33.15), appears to be the principal text. But Zechariah's semititular usage ("Behold, the man whose name is 'Branch' [*tsemaḥ shemo*]") has probably made a contribution as well (*Zec.* 6.12; cf. 3.8; *Is.* 11.1). In Commentary on Genesis A (4Q252 1.v.3–4) the Branch is called the "Messiah of righteousness." In narrative (4Q458 2.ii.6) he is described as "one anointed with the oil of the kingdom" (cf. *1 Sm.* 10.1, 16.13; esp. Ps. 89.21 [English v.20]). According to Melchizedek from Qumran Cave 11 (11Q13) "the herald is the [one] anointed of the Spir[it], of whom Dan[iel spoke]" (ii.18). This passage alludes to *Daniel* 9, which originally may have spoken of an anointed priest. But in Melchizedek it refers to the herald of *Isaiah* 52.7, who may have been understood as an anointed prophet or as an anointed royal Messiah. The "herald" of Melchizedek may have something to do with the Messiah of the Messianic Apocalypse, who also proclaims good news (4Q521 1.ii.12).

The Messiah is also called the "prince." The "prince" [*nasi*ʾ] of the (whole) congregation" occurs some ten times in the Dead Sea Scrolls (CD vii.19–20; 1Q28b v.20; 1QM v.1; 4Q161 2–6.ii.19; 4Q266 3.iv.9; 4Q285 4.2, 6; 5.4; 6.2; 4Q376 1.iii.1). All these occurrences are messianic. Four other references to *nasi*ʾ probably refer to this personage: the isolated reading "to the prince" in the Apocryphon of Moses B[b] (4Q376 1.iii.3; which probably refers to the *nasi*ʾ mentioned in 1.iii.1); the "prince of the myriad" in the War Scroll (1QM iii.16), who is distinct from the tribal chieftains; and the fragmentary and partially superscripted twin references in the War Scroll[f] (4Q496 10.3–4; cf. 1QM v.1). The messianic epithet "prince" is apparently derived from *Ezekiel*, which speaks of a coming prince (*nasi*ʾ) who will shepherd Israel faithfully: "My servant David, a prince among them" (*Ezek.* 34.24); "My servant David shall be their prince forever" (*Ezek.* 37.25).

The "prince" is further identified as the "rod [that] is risen from Israel (*Nm.* 24.17). The rod is the prince of the whole congregation" (CD vii.19–20 [Damascus Document[a], 4Q266 3.iv.9; cf. Pesher Isaiah[a], 4Q161 2–6.ii.19). In War Rule (4Q285 5.4) the "prince of the congregation" is equated with the "Bran[ch of David]." Thus, we have at Qumran the messianic matrix Messiah = Prince = Branch of David.

The tradition of Israel's monarch as a divine son (Ps. 2.7; *2 Sm.* 7.14) gave rise to a variety of "son" epithets. Within the Dead Sea Scrolls this language appears seven times, although it is unclear how many of them actually refer to a messianic figure. The epithets include "son" (*ben*; cf. 4Q174 1–3.i.11), "son of God" (*bereh di el*; cf. 4Q246 ii.1), "son of the Most High" (*bar ʿelyon*; cf. 4Q246 ii.1), "firstborn son" (*ben bekhor*; cf. 4Q369 1.ii.6), and "two sons of oil" (*shenei benei ha-yitshar*; cf. 4Q254 4.2). The common rabbinic epithet, "son of David," has not been found at Qumran. Only the reference in the Florilegium (4Q174) is indisputably messianic. In this passage, not only is the "son" of *2 Samuel* 7.14 identified as the "Branch of David," but this figure is also understood to be the fulfillment of the prophecy of *Amos* 9.11 (cf. 4Q174 1–3.i.12), while the quotation and interpretation of Psalm 2.1–2, with which column i of the Aramaic Apocalypse concludes (lines 18–19), probably apply to him as well.

The references in (4Q246 i.9; ii.1) are much disputed. It has been proposed that the son of God figure is an angel or an evil person, perhaps even an antichrist figure, who blasphemously applies these epithets to himself. Others argue that this figure is the son of a Jewish king, but that the son of God language is not messianic. And, of course, it has been contended that this figure is indeed a messianic figure, as the parallels with *Luke* 1.32–35, *2 Samuel* 7, and the Florilegium would seem to suggest.

The "firstborn son" in the Prayer of Enosh? (4Q369 1.ii.6) may be messianic, but the text is so fragmentary that it is difficult to gain a clear picture of the document's perspective. It may be looking to the past, or it may be looking to the future (in which case the figure is probably messianic). The reference to the "two sons of oil" in the Commentary on Genesis (4Q254 4.2) is drawn from *Zechariah* 4.14 and may be messianic, especially if fragment 4 has been placed in its proper sequence and if it does indeed preserve a portion of the commentary on *Genesis* 49.8–12 (Jacob's blessing of Judah).

There are other texts that from time to time have been regarded as having messianic significance, either by association with a messianic figure, such as "star," or by identification with certain personages thought to be messianic, such as the Teacher of Righteousness. For "seeker of the law" (*doresh ha-torah*) passages see the Damascus Document (CD and 4Q266–267), Florilegium (4Q174) and Catena[a] (4Q177). For "teacher" (*moreh [ha-]tsedeq*) passages, see the Damascus Document (CD); Pesher Habakkuk (1QpHab); Pesher Psalms[a] (4Q171); unidentified *pesher* (4Q172); Pesher Psalms[b] (4Q173); the Damascus Document[b] (4Q267); the Damascus Document (CD, *yoreh ha-tsedeq*); Pesher Habakkuk (*moreh ha-tsedaqah*); Pesher Micah (1Q14); Pesher Isaiah (4Q163); Noncanonical Psalms (4Q381). For "star (*kokhav*) passages (all involving *Num.* 24.17) see the Damascus Document (CD, where "star" is read as the "seeker of the law"); War Scroll (1QM); Testimonia (4Q175). For "staff"/"leader"/"decree" (*meḥoqeq*) passages, see the Damascus Document (CD, 4Q266–267, where "staff" is read as the "teacher of the Law"); Commentary on Genesis A (4Q252, where the "staff" is read as the "covenant of the kingdom"); Paraphrase of Kings et al. (4Q382); and Sapiential Work A[c] (where reference is to the "degree" of God).

[*See also* Aaron; Aramaic Apocalypse; Elect of God; Interpreter of the Law; Levi; Prince of the Congregation; War of the Sons of Light against the Sons of Darkness; *and* Women.]

BIBLIOGRAPHY

Abegg, Martin G., Jr. "Messianic Hope and 4Q285: A Reassessment." *Journal of Biblical Literature* 133 (1994), 81–91. Provides decisive arguments against the controversial claim that 4Q285 speaks of the killing of the Messiah.

Abegg, Martin G., Jr. "The Messiah at Qumran: Are We Still Seeing Double?" *Dead Sea Discoveries* 2 (1995), 125–144. Raises concerns about the widely held view that the scrolls speak of two Messiahs.

Allegro, John Marco. "Further Messianic References in Qumran Literature." *Journal of Biblical Literature* 75 (1956), 174–187. Provides text and discussion of several messianic texts from Cave 4.

Allegro, John Marco. *Qumran Cave 4 I. (4Q158–4Q186)*. Discoveries in the Judaean Desert, 5. Oxford, 1968. Provides Hebrew text, (English) translation, and discussion of many texts from Cave 4, including the *pesharim* (commentaries), the Florilegium, and Testimonia texts, several of which speak of messianic figures.

Barthélemy, D., and J. T. Milik, eds. *Qumran Cave I*. Discoveries in the Judaean Desert, 1. Oxford, 1955. Provides Hebrew text, (French) translation, and discussion of 1QSa and 1QSb (texts which refer to the Messiah), as well as many other scrolls from the first cave discovered.

Brown, Raymond E. "J. Starcky's Theory of Qumran Messianic Development." *Catholic Biblical Quarterly* 28 (1966), 51–57. Calls into question Jean Starcky's proposal that Qumran's messianic beliefs evolved through four distinct stages.

Charlesworth, James H., ed. *The Messiah: Developments in Earliest Judaism and Christianity*. Minneapolis, 1992. Very helpful collection of studies by major scholars treating several facets of messianism at Qumran and in early Judaism and Christianity in general.

Collins, John J. *The Scepter and the Star: The Messiahs of the Dead Sea Scrolls and Other Ancient Literature*. Anchor Bible Reference Library. New York, 1995. Excellent, up-to-date discussion of Qumran messianism and its relationship to messianic ideas expressed in early Jewish and Christian texts.

Davies, Philip R. "The Teacher of Righteousness and the 'End of Days.'" *Revue de Qumrân* 13 (1988), 313–317. Argues that the "Teacher of Righteousness" was a messianic figure.

Evans, Craig A. "Jesus and the Messianic Texts from Qumran: A Preliminary Assessment of the Recently Published materials." In *Jesus and His Contemporaries: Comparative Studies*, pp. 83–154. Arbeiten zur Geschichte des antiken Judentums und des Urchristentums, 25. Leiden, 1995. Examines recently published material from Cave 4 and compares it with the previously published scrolls; concludes that new material lends further support to the proposal that the scrolls anticipate two Messiahs, one priestly and the other royal, and that Jesus' own messianic ideas may have been similar.

Fitzmyer, Joseph A. "The Aramaic 'Elect of God' Text from Qumran Cave." *Catholic Biblical Quarterly* 27 (1965), 348–372. Reprinted in *Essays on the Semitic Background of the New Testament*, pp. 127–160. London, 1971. Reprinted as Society of Biblical Literature Sources for Biblical Study, 5 Missoula, Mont., 1974. Critical discussion of 4Q534; doubts that the text is messianic.

Fitzmyer, Joseph A. "4Q246: The 'Son of God' Document from Qumran." *Biblica* 74 (1993), 153–174. Critical discussion of 4Q246 ("Son of God text"); asserts that text speaks of an awaited Jewish king, but is not messianic.

García Martínez, Florentino. "The Eschatological Figure of 4Q246." In *Qumran and Apocalyptic: Studies on the Aramaic Texts from Qumran*, pp. 162–179. Studies on the Texts of the Desert of Judah, 9. Leiden, 1992. Critical discussion of 4Q246; thinks it may be speaking of an angel, perhaps Michael (as in 1QM xvii.5–8).

García Martínez, Florentino. "Messianic Hopes in the Qumran Writings." In *The People of the Dead Sea Scrolls*, by Florentino García Martínez and Julio Trebolle Barrera, pp. 159–189. Leiden, 1995. Very helpful overview of the messianic hopes expressed in the Dead Sea Scrolls.

Horsley, Richard A., and John S. Hanson. *Bandits, Prophets, and Messiahs: Popular Movements in the Time of Jesus*. Minneapolis, 1985. Reprinted San Francisco, 1988. Studies the restoration movements in the time of Jesus described by Josephus; concludes that several movements were messianic in nature.

Jonge, Marinus de. "Messiah." In *Anchor Bible Dictionary*, edited by David Noel Freedman, vol. 4, pp. 777–788. New York, 1991. Helpful overview of major issues.

Knibb, Michael A. "The Teacher of Righteousness—a Messianic Title?" In *A Tribute to Geza Vermes: Essays on Jewish and Christian Literature and History*, edited by Philip R. Davies and Richard T. White, pp. 51–65. Journal for the Study of the Old Testament, Supplement, 100. Sheffield, 1990. Author does not think that the members of the Qumran community regarded the Teacher of Righteousness as the awaited Messiah.

Kuhn, Karl Georg. "The Two Messiahs of Aaron and Israel." *New Testament Studies* 1 (1954–1955), 168–180. Reprinted in *The Scrolls and the New Testament*, edited by Krister Stendhal, pp. 54–64, 256–259. New York, 1957. Reprinted New York, 1992. Classic proposal that members of the Qumran community awaited two Messiahs: an anointed priest and an anointed king.

Levey, Samson H. *The Messiah: An Aramaic Interpretation: The Messianic Exegesis of the Targum*. Monographs of the Hebrew Union College, 2. Cincinnati, 1974. Very convenient collection and interpretation of the messianic passages in the Targums (the Aramaic paraphrases of the Old Testament).

Neusner, Jacob. *Messiah in Context*. Philadelphia, 1984. A critical study of messianic passages in the rabbinic literature; concludes that the familiar rabbinic image of the Messiah is a late development.

Neusner, Jacob, William Scott Green, and Ernest S. Frerichs. *Judaisms and Their Messiahs at the Turn of the Christian Era*. Cambridge, 1987. An important collection of studies, in which the diversity and pluralism of eschatology and messianism of early Judaism and Christianity are emphasized.

Puech, Émile. "Préséance sacerdotale et Messie-Roi dans la Règle de la Congregation (1QSa ii 11-22)." *Revue de Qumrân* 63 (1994), 351–365.

Starcky, Jean. "Les quatres étapes du messianisme à Qumrân." *Revue biblique* 70 (1963), 481–505. Synthetic study, in which it is concluded that messianism at Qumran evolved through four distinct steps.

van der Woude, Adam S. *Die messianischen Vorstellungen der Gemeinde von Qumrân*. Studia semitica neerlandica, 3. Assen, 1957. Classic study on the messianic ideas of Qumran; though dated, still valuable.

VanderKam, James C. "Messianism in the Scrolls." In *The Community of the Renewed Covenant: The Notre Dame Symposium on the Dead Sea Scrolls*, edited by Eugene Ulrich and James C. VanderKam, pp. 211–234. Notre Dame, 1994. Provides helpful discussion of the messianism at Qumran; concludes that there is a "dual messianism, with one messiah being priestly and the other davidic" (page 234).

CRAIG A. EVANS

MESSIANIC APOCALYPSE. A few of the fragments of the Hebrew Messianic Apocalypse (4Q521) manuscript have a great importance for the history of religions. The copy of the manuscript is dated paleographically to the first quarter of the first century BCE; the various corrections made to it entail that it be considered a copy and not the original. The discovery of this single copy bearing the scribal characteristics of the Qumran copyists makes it most likely that it is a product of the local scriptorium.

The use of the word *Adonay*, along with the absence of the Tetragrammaton and its systematic elimination in the direct quotations of Psalm 146.7–8, make it possible to conclude that the author of the composition followed the same procedure as the author of the Damascus Document (CD vii.11) or of Hodayot[a] from Cave 1 at Qumran (1QH; hereafter 1QHodayot[a]), in observing the warning against an abusive or misplaced use of the Tetragrammaton as expressed in the Rule of the Community from Cave 1 at Qumran (1QS vi.27f; hereafter 1QRule of the Community). [*See* Damascus Document, Hodayot, *and* Rule of the Community.] Other similarities in the vocabulary relate the Messianic Apocalypse to certain passages of 1QHodayot[a] xxiii.13–16 (= xviii 12–15) referring to *Isaiah* 61.1–2. The mention of the *ḥasidim, tsadiqim, qedoshim,* and *ʾamunim* on the one hand, and the insistence on seeking the Lord in worship on the other (4Q521 2.ii.3), a worship set apart (4Q521 5.i.4) by faithful people who keep the covenant (4Q521 10.2), who adhere to its commandments (4Q521 2.ii.1–2), in the midst of whom unrighteousness should no longer be found (4Q521 10.3), for whom the priesthood holds an important place (4Q521 8–9, 11–12) and who await the coming of the Messiah-king (4Q521 2.iii.2ff), of the New Elijah (4Q521 2.iii.1f), and of the coming of the priest-prophet (4Q521 2.ii.1), seem to fit the Essenes-*ḥasidim* best. It is more than likely that this is an Essene composition dating from the second half of the second century BC, which might be attributed to the Teacher of Righteousness himself. [*See* Teacher of Righteousness.]

The set of fragments, including Messianic Apocalypse 2–7, arranged on four successive columns, although very incomplete, makes it possible to draw some important conclusions. Because of the gap preceding Messianic Apocalypse 2.ii.1, the interpretation of *mshyḥw* is not very clear: "its messiah" (*meshiḥo*) or "its messiahs" (*meshiḥav*)? Still it does seem that the plural is possible because the word may mean the king and the priest, which in turn may also be the prophet and the eschatological interpreter. [*See* Messiahs.] If it is read in the singular, then it has to be understood as the priest-prophet of messianic times and not the prophet who is never consecrated (in *1 Kgs*. 19.16 due to the parallelism). The second paragraph (4Q521 2.ii.4ff. + 4) describes in poetic style and in the form of an exhortation the eschatological blessings that God will accomplish in the messianic era (compare *Mt*. 11.5 and *Lk*. 7.22). After a change in structure, the remaining fragments of Messianic Apocalypse 2.ii.1, which most certainly refer to *Malachi* 3.24 and *Ben Sira* 48.10, allude to the new Elijah and the revelation of the king-Messiah in the time of the blessing of the Lord in his divine goodness, which is at the origin of the general exultation and the later mention of the scepter. This passage is followed by a few hints about the prosperity of the messianic kingdom (4Q521 5.i + 6). It seems that the new Elijah, referred to in the first person, is the teacher of the last times, the high priest who is the contemporary of the Messiah-king, the combined teacher-prophet (4Q521 2.ii.1), as understood by some Karaite authors (Daniel al-Qumisi, Yefet ben ʿEli, and Avraham al-Fasi) who became aware of other Qumran scrolls discovered at the end of the eighth century. [*See* Karaites.]

Then comes the description of the End (4Q521 7, 5.ii). Just as God created the heavens and the earth and all that they contain, he also is able to raise up the just of his people, the blessed ones, while the damned shall be for death. He will deliver(?) from death mortal men, open the tombs of those who have died, and proceed to the judgment. The beginnings of lines 11 to 15, "and the valley of death . .[.], the bridge of the Aby[ss . . .], the damned are petrified [. . .], the heavens welcome [. . . and all] the angels [. . ." can only be referring to the Last Judgment, the eternal rewards of the just and the eternal punishments of the damned, of the just and the wicked (cf. *Mt*. 25.31–46). When they cross the "Bridge of the Abyss," the damned fall stiff and lifeless into hell, while the just are welcomed by the angels into heaven. This new and unique presentation recalls the "Bridge of the Sorter" of Zoroastrianism and the life of the just transformed into glory in the company of the angels in Paradise, which was borrowed from Persian religion but adapted to a Semitic background and anthropology. This suggests that the resurrection is not conceived as a return to life, a simple reanimation, but as a transformation into glory of the just, whether living or dead (4Q521 7), on a new Earth.

These various partially preserved motifs belong more to the genre of exhortation based on the eschatological blessings and punishments that God will carry out in the messianic days. In language that is half prophetic and half apocalyptic, the author invites the "devout just" to persevere in the observance of the Law and the orthodox practice of worship. He recalls God's judgment in favor of the just and the wages of the wicked. The *eschaton* will see the fulfillment of the prophecies (*Is*. 40–6, *Mal*. 3). The various allusions to the day of Yahveh of *Malachi* 3.18–24, to the glorious deeds that have not yet taken place, belong to a kind of *midrash* of Psalm 146, a hymn to a God who stands ready to help, presenting its central themes: God as creator and savior, the distinction between the just and the wicked. The main parallels in the Old and New Testament, and the apocryphal texts justify this kind of interpretation. Thus the dominant messianic and eschatological theme suggests classifying this text in the apocalyptic genre of Jewish circles of the second century BC, as in the proposed designation Messianic Apocalypse.

[*See also* Apocalyptic Texts.]

BIBLIOGRAPHY

Collins, John J. "The Works of the Messiah." *Dead Sea Discoveries* 1 (1994), 98–112.

Puech, Émile. "Une Apocalypse messianique (4Q521)." *Revue de Qumrân* 15 (1992), 475–522.

Puech, Émile. *La croyance des Esséniens en la vie future; immortalité, résurrection, vie éternelle? Histoire d'une croyance dans le Judaïsme ancien*. Études Bibliques, 21–22. Paris, 1993. See pages 627–692.

ÉMILE PUECH
Translated from French by Robert E. Shillenn

METAL UTENSILS. Though not found in great numbers, the metal utensils from the Judean Desert display typological diversity. Made of bronze, iron, and lead, they will be discussed in the following categories: vessels, tools, and weights.

Vessels. The bronze tableware found in the Cave of the Letters includes four shovels, two bowls, a *patera* (saucer), and fourteen jugs. Another jug and three ladles were found at the ʿEin-Gedi tombs and three ladles exist from the Cave of the Pool in Wadi Sdeir. The shovels comprise a rectangular pan, two small cups set on its rim in the corners, four feet on its bottom and a tubular handle. Traces of burning in the center of the pans suggest identifying it as an incense shovel. The coals were placed in the pan, while the incense was kept in the cups and sprinkled from time to time over the coals. This ritual was performed by pagans, Jews, and Christians. Common all over the Roman Empire, more than a dozen bronze and iron shovels are from Palestine, the earliest among the cult vessels from the Hellenistic temple at Beersheba, others from tombs in Jerusalem near Tell Ab-Shusha, and at Ḥeshbon. In the Talmud, the *maḥtah* (incense burner) is mentioned when finishing a meal with the smelling of incense (J.T., *Shab*. 3.7). In the Byzantine period, the shovel is represented with ritual objects such as a *shofar*, *lulav*, and *etrog* flanking the menorah on synagogue mosaic pavements. Besides being used for burning incense, the shovels are also thought to have been used for bone collection in secondary burials, as a snuff box or a lamp-cleaning utensil in the synagogue, or as cult objects associated with the festivals.

Two hemispherical bowls or basins are provided with feet and a pair of omega-shaped swing handles ending in bird and animal heads.

The *patera*, a bowl with a central decorated medallion, depicts Thetis riding a centaur to bring weapons to her son Achilles, and has a tubular handle formed like a fluted column, terminating in a ram's head. The faces of Thetis and the centaur were partially obliterated after the vessel had come into Jewish hands; such deliberate erasure of images was sufficient to allow the vessel's use (J.T., *ʿA.Z.* 4.5) and shows that the leaders of the Bar Kokhba Revolt observed the rabbinic rulings. Another *patera* from Lajjun, ancient Caparcotna south of Megiddo, is a second type with a high boss [umbo] in the center of the bowl and a handle terminating in the bearded face of Pan (the shepherd god) turned up level with the vessel interior. Both *paterae* show no traces of soot and were never used over a fire, but were used for ceremonial purposes when wine was poured for libation. Occasionally found with jugs, thus forming a set, their cultic use is not undisputed, for it was a Roman custom to have water brought by slaves during and at the end of meals for cleaning hands and fingers. The slaves poured water from the jugs over the hands, which was collected in the *patera*. The same ritual, using the *kiton* (water canteen) and *leves* (basin), was obligatory for Jews with the blessing over wine before, during, and after the meal (M., *Ber*. 8.2–4; T., *Ber*. 4.8–9).

The jugs have a slender, squat, or biconical body. Some have a pinched spout or a trefoilmouth for convenient pouring of liquids. The elegantly shaped handles are decorated. Some decorations include: geometrical and floral patterns, human masks, the bust of a robed figure (a winged Victory?), a youth (possibly young Bacchus), a festooned bucranium [a bull's head], lion heads, griffons, and birds. A single jug is adorned with a frieze of a hound chasing an animal. The human faces have been partially rubbed out to permit the vessel's use by Jews. Similar jugs are known from all over the Roman Empire. In Jewish sources they are termed *lagin*, serving primarily as wine decanters filled from the *ḥavit* (M., *Ṭev. Y.* 4.4).

The ladle (*simpulum*, *tarvad*) for scooping liquids served also as a liquid measure (T., *Cholot* 2.2) and ceremonial vessel in offerings. There are two shapes, both found in the ʿEin-Gedi tombs: a handleless form and another with a long handle rising vertically from a bowl (T., *B.B.* 7.8), the handle sometimes ending with an animal head finial. The most common kitchen vessel, the bucket (*situla*), is represented by a bronze bucket with an iron handle from the Qumran Caves and a handle from the Cave of the Letters. In the so-called scriptorium at Qumran (Locus 30) a cylindrical, handleless, bronze inkwell was found, its lid missing (the *qalmarin*, J. T., *Miq*. 10.1). Dated to the first century CE, it is one of five inkwells, the others are made of ceramic. A rod flattened at both ends and twisted in the middle from the Cave of the Letters appears to be a stylus, a writing pen. The only iron vessel from the same findspot, a flat frying pan with two horseshoe-shaped handles, shows heavy traces of soot (the *teigan*, T., *ʿA.Z.* 8[9].2).

The iron pan is of local manufacture. The bronze tableware from the Cave of the Letters, considered booty taken by the revolutionaries from the Roman army, originated from the area of Capua in southern Italy and likely dates from the mid-first century to the early second century CE. The vessels from the ʿEin-Gedi tombs represent the personal effects of the deceased. Altogether, a date range from the second century BCE to the third century CE can be demonstrated.

Tools. Iron blades were fastened into wooden or bone handles with rivets and collars. A chopper with a long broad blade, the *hopis* of J.T., *Sotah* 9.5., served for slaughtering animals and cutting bones as well as chopping wood (Cave of the Letters). A hatchet from Cave 11 at Qumran has double blades flanking the circular hole for the insertion of the wooden shank: a wide flat one and a pointed one offset to the hole. A common type in the Roman period, the *dolabra* or pickax was used for land cultivation, excavating, and mining. The tool is identified by de Vaux as the Essene hatchet and the *axinidion* or *skalis* mentioned by Josephus (c.75–79 CE) as being used by the Essenes for covering up their excrement in a hole in the ground, dug with the pointed blade (*The Jewish War* 2.8.9). An ax blade with a wide cutting edge was found in the Cave of Horror. Sickle blades with an inner sharp slightly saw-toothed edge and knife blades were noted in several caves. Of special interest is a clasp knife from the Cave of the Letters, which folds into its handle on a pivot. Such a tool was helpful during weaving for cutting the weft or thread from a ball. Two blades—one of a knife, the other of an adz—were found at Masada. Metallurgical study showed that the knife was not specially hardened during fabrication and was thus made for activities not requiring great hardness, such as food preparation, while the adz was deliberately hardened. A hoe in the shape of a modern turieh is reported from Wadi Murabbaʿat. An S-shaped hook found in the Cave of the Letters was used for hanging meat or for moving a door bolt and must have been very convenient for hauling baskets and jars up to the cave. A hook from Masada was heavily cold worked, only then could it bear a heavy load.

Fine bronze and iron tools include needles, crochet hooks, and awls from several caves, as well as some surgical instruments, including a lancet, spatulae, and spoons from Murabbaʿat Cave 4.

An iron peg from Masada, forged from wrought iron with no attempt made to strengthen it, could have been a construction element or simply a digging tool. Iron nails with a broad head and a shank square in cross section are common. The analysis of a nail from Masada showed that it could have served to reinforce two slabs of limestone connected with a layer of mortar. In the caves of the Judean Desert only sandals without nails were found, supporting the prohibition of wearing nail-studded sandals on Shabbat (M., *Shab*. 6.2) and in general. Yigael Yadin argues that this was done for security reasons, pointing out that the clatter of Roman soldiers wearing hob-nailed sandals could be heard. His suggestion is contradicted by the find from the Ketef Jericho Cave: a heel, piece of sole, and eighteen bronze nails.

Iron keys, twelve from the Cave of the Letters, and one from Murabbaʿat, are of two types: ring and elbow keys. The ring key has two parts, the ring for carrying and the bit for opening or closing the lock. Used to secure locks on chests and boxes, this key is probably referred to in Tosephta, *Shabbat* 4.11. In an elbow or knee key the shank is not straight but bent in a right angle, forming the upper arm and the forearm to which the bit is attached. Made for locks on heavy and light doors, elbow keys are discussed in M., *Kelim* 13.6 and 14.8.

Weights. Several lead weights of the Bar Kokhba administration are known, one from an underground hiding complex in the Beit Guvrin area, decorated on both sides with a rosette. The Hebrew inscription confirms the name and titles of the revolt's leader, already known from the papyri.

Taking into account the mobile mint at Ḥorvat Eqed halfway between Jaffa and Jerusalem, operating under Bar Kokhba, the iron tools and lead objects illustrate the standards of metallurgical industrial manufacture in the first and second centuries CE.

BIBLIOGRAPHY

Aharoni, Yohanan. "The Caves of Nahal Hever." *ʿAtiqot* 3 (1961), 148–162. A crochet hook from Cave No. 5–6.

Aharoni, Yohanan. "Expedition B—The Cave of Horror, The Expedition to the Judean Desert, 1961." *Israel Exploration Journal* 12 (1962), 186–199. Illustration of needles, nails, awls, a knife, and an ax blade.

Avigad, Nahman. "Expedition A, The Expedition to the Judean Desert, 1960." *Israel Exploration Journal* 11 (1961), 6–10. A needle from the Cave of the Pool.

Baillet, M., J. T. Milik, and R. de Vaux. *Les 'Petites Grottes' de Qumrân*. Discoveries in the Judaean Desert, vol. 3. Oxford, 1962.

Benoit, P., J. T. Milik, and R. de Vaux. *Les grottes de Murabbaʿat*. Discoveries in the Judaean Desert, vol. 2. Oxford, 1961.

de Vaux, Roland. "Une hachette essénienne?" *Vetus Testamentum* 9 (1959), 399–407.

Eshel, Hanan. "How I Found a Fourth-Century B.C. Papyrus Scroll on My First Time Out!" *Biblical Archaeology Review* 15.5 (1989), 44–53. Discovery of the first nail-studded sandal.

Function and Design in the Talmudic Period. Exhibition Catalogue, Haaretz Museum, Tel Aviv, 1978. Parallels to the finds from the Cave of the Letters with literary references.

Goranson, Stephen. "An Inkwell from Qumran." *Michmanim* 6 (1992), 37–40. A thorough presentation of the inkwells from Qumran.

Hadas, Gideon. *Nine Tombs of the Second Temple Period at 'En Gedi* (Hebrew). 'Atiqot 14, Jerusalem, 1994. Close parallels for the finds from the Judean Desert. English abstract.

Khairy, Nabil I. "Ink-wells of the Roman Period from Jordan." *Levant* 12 (1980), 155–162. The bronze inkwell from Qumran with several parallels.

Kloner, Amos. "Lead Weights of Bar Kokhba's Administration." *Israel Exploration Journal* 40 (1990), 58–67.

Knox, Reed, Robert Maddin, James D. Muhly, and Tamara Stech. "Iron Objects from Masada: Metallurgical Studies." *Israel Exploration Journal* 33 (1983), 97–107. Many details on manufacturing procedures and techniques.

Magness, Jodi. "Two Notes on the Archaeology of Qumran, A Toilet at Qumran." *Bulletin of the American Schools of Oriental Research* 312 (1998), 37–40.

Rahmani, L. Y. "A Roman Patera from Lajjun." *Israel Exploration Journal* 31 (1981), 190–196. A thorough survey with numerous comparisons.

Yadin, Yigael. *The Finds from the Bar-Kokhba Period in the Cave of the Letters*, Judean Desert Studies. Jerusalem, 1963. A detailed, well-illustrated presentation of the finds.

RENATE ROSENTHAL-HEGINBOTTOM

MEZUZOT. *See* Phylacteries and Mezuzot.

MICAH, BOOK OF. *See* Minor Prophets.

MICHAEL. The name *Michael* means "who is like God" and is used in the scrolls to refer to the prominent archangel known from a wide variety of Second Temple texts. The name *Michael* occurs ten times in the scrolls in their current state of preservation: four times in the War Scroll (1QM), once each in the Enochic manuscripts Enoch[a,b] (4Q201–202) once in War Rule (4Q285), twice in fragment mentioning Zedekiah (4Q470), and once in Words of Michael (4Q529). However, there are also a number of texts that mention an angelic figure not explicitly called *Michael* but perhaps referring to him nevertheless. This article will briefly review both the certain and the possible references to Michael.

The War Scroll and War Rule. The War Scroll (1QM ix.15–16) refers to Michael twice in an injunction to inscribe his name on certain shields used in battle formations called *towers*. Other shields will have the names Gabriel, Sariel, or Raphael. Yigael Yadin noted that this same group of four archangels occurs in many other Jewish texts, particularly the *Book of Enoch*. The reason for inscribing their names on shields is probably connected to the belief that the angels will fight with the sons of light against the sons of darkness.

In the War Scroll (1QM xvii.6–7) Michael is mentioned twice in a speech given by the high priest who says that God will exalt Michael's authority above that of all the gods and cause the covenant of Israel to shine with joy. As often elsewhere, a clear connection is made here between the authority of Michael and the fortunes of Israel. According to Jean Duhaime, War Scroll xvi.11–xvii.9 is a later addition to the text, indicating a developing doctrine of dualism within the Qumran sect. On this theory, Michael's role in the struggle against Belial is emphasized to protect God's sovereignty. A possible reference to Michael occurs in War Scroll xiii:10–11 which mentions a "prince of light" who is contrasted with Belial.

The text known as War Rule (4Q285) is related to the War Scroll though clearly not a copy of it. Fragment 10.3 preserves the names of both Michael and Gabriel followed by a lacuna. Unfortunately, the small size of the fragment does not allow any certainty as to what function Michael may have had in this composition, though it is not unreasonable to hypothesize that it was similar to that in the War Scroll.

Enoch. The name *Michael* is preserved at *1 Enoch* 9.1 in Enoch[a,b]. However, since both texts in their original condition probably contained all of the "Book of Watchers," one must also consider *1 Enoch* 10.11; 20.5; and 24.6 where Michael is mentioned in the extant Greek and Ethiopic manuscripts. In these four passages Michael appears in roles related to either judgment or revelation.

At *1 Enoch* 9.1 Michael is again mentioned along with Sariel, Raphael, and Gabriel, just as in the War Scroll. These angels behold the blood being shed on earth by the giants of the antediluvian age and intercede on behalf of perishing humanity. In *1 Enoch* 10.11, God sends Michael to pronounce judgment against both the angels and their progeny. Later, at *1 Enoch* 20.5, Michael appears as part of a group of seven angels who are said to keep watch and are assigned specific tasks. Michael is appointed to be "over the good things of the people [of Israel]." *1 Enoch* 24.6 portrays Michael as the interpreting angel (*angelus interpres*) who explains to Enoch the things that he sees on his heavenly tour.

In addition to these four explicit references, two other verses may refer to Michael indirectly. *1 Enoch* 87.2 mentions a group of seven archangels that would likely have included Michael and *1 Enoch* 90.14 refers to an angelic being who fights for the people of Israel. Both verses come from the "Book of Dream Visions" (*1 En.* 83–90) of which four copies were found at Qumran.

Fragment Mentioning Zedekiah. In this fragment, Michael acts as God's representative in establishing a covenant with a certain Zedekiah, apparently to be identified as the last ruler of the kingdom of Judah. The Hebrew scriptures make no mention of any covenant mediated by Michael, but somewhat proximate parallels may be found in the New Testament, which contains statements to the effect that the Sinaitic covenant was mediated by angels (*Acts* 7.53; *Gal.* 3.19; *Heb.* 2.2). Note also that War Scroll xvii.6–17 links God's exaltation of Michael with his causing the covenant of Israel to shine. But the latter is still not the same as having Michael act as God's agent in establishing the covenant.

Words of Michael. This Aramaic work consists of an account, written in the first person singular, of the words that Michael spoke to certain of the angels. After some kind of geographical description ending with the statement, "I saw Gabriel there," Michael relates a vision, perhaps given to him by Gabriel, describing various future events, including the building of a city. Although Michael appears in the familiar role of revealer of divine mysteries in this text, what is unusual is that he delivers his message not to humans but to angels.

Daniel. The only canonical book to mention Michael is *Daniel*. This happens three times at *Daniel* 10.13, 21; 12.1. Although none of the *Daniel* manuscripts from Qumran actually preserves the name *Michael*, the close agreement of all of them with the Masoretic Text indicates that they originally contained all three references. In these verses, Michael acts as protector of the people of Israel and struggles against those angels who represent other peoples, namely Persia and Greece. Furthermore, *Daniel* 7.13 mentions "one like a son of man." Many recent commentators believe that this enigmatic figure is none other than Michael (so Collins, 1993).

Other Possible References. The text known as Melchizedek (11Q13) mentions an angelic being who is set in charge of the Sons of Light and contends with Satan and the spirits of his lot. Some scholars believe that the similarity in roles played by Melchizedek here and Michael elsewhere warrants considering them to be one and the same figure. The fact that the text itself does not explicitly make this equation, however, suggests that some caution be exercised. Similar to Melchizedek is Visions of Amram[b] (4Q544) which describes two watchers struggling for control of Amram. The evil watcher is Melchiresha'. The good watcher is said to have three names but none of these is preserved due to a lacuna in the text. Again, on analogy with those texts that describe a struggle between Michael and Belial, many scholars believe that one of the names of the good watcher must have been Michael.

War Scroll[a] (4Q491) and Prayer of Michael (4Q471b) contain textual overlap and both describe a glorious and exalted figure who will be "reckoned among the gods" (4Q491 11.i.14) and who asks rhetorically, "Who is like me among the gods?" (4Q471b 6.4). Maurice Baillet, the original editor of War Scroll[a], believed that the text spoke of Michael since War Scroll xvii.7 says that Michael is given authority above all the gods. However, Baillet's views have recently been challenged by Collins (1995) and Eshel (1996) who argue convincingly that both works speak of the exaltation of a human, perhaps priestly, figure.

The Rule of the Community (1QS iii.20, 24) mentions respectively a "Prince of Lights" and an "Angel of his Truth." Both are said to aid the Sons of Light against the Sons of Darkness and their leader, the Angel of Darkness. Comparison with the War Scroll again suggests that Michael may be in mind. Damascus Document v.17–19 likewise mentions the Prince of Lights who helped Moses and Aaron when Belial raised up Jannes and Jambres. Aramaic Apocalypse (4Q246) refers to a figure called the *Son of God* who is involved in an eschatological struggle with evil and whom Florentino García Martínez (1992) has identified as Michael, though other scholars take the *Son of God* as a messianic title or a title for a Greek ruler. Finally, *Tobit* 12.15 mentions a group of seven angels that likely included Michael. Five copies of the book have been recovered at Qumran (4Q196–200), two of which contain chapter 12.

Implications. Michael plays a variety of roles in the texts surveyed: protector of God's people, bearer of divine judgment, revealer of heavenly mysteries, and mediator of a covenant. All these roles are consistent with what is known about the development and expansion in the Second Temple period of ideas concerning angelic activity in general and of Michael in particular. Furthermore, Michael often appears in connection with other archangels, such as Gabriel. Usually the number of such angels is given as four, though sometimes seven.

It is important to note that Michael is often associated with the idea of dualism that is so prominent at Qumran. [*See* Dualism.] In such a context he fights on the side of good against Belial and the forces of evil. Some scholars suggest that Michael is introduced to downplay the idea, expressed in some scrolls nevertheless (e.g., 1QM i.5), that God himself struggles against Belial.

Other scholars have gone even farther and suggested that in certain Qumran texts, such as Melchizedek, Michael functions as God's hypostasis or his visible form when he appears to men. This is surely an overstatement of the case. While Michael is often closely associated with God, the distinction between them is clear: God commands and Michael obeys, God will exalt the authority of Michael, etc. It is best, therefore, simply to see Michael as the servant of God, a role which he fills nevertheless with unique distinction.

The prominence of Michael in the Qumran texts may have one further implication. Larry Hurtado has recently suggested that the unique status of Michael as agent of the divine provided an analogy to the early Christians in their thinking about the person and role of Jesus and had a powerful impact upon Christological developments in the nascent church. Though a full evaluation of this hypothesis is outside the scope of this article, it once again raises interesting questions regarding the Jewish background of the New Testament and early Christian belief.

BIBLIOGRAPHY

Collins, John J. *Daniel*. Hermeneia. Minneapolis, 1993. The best commentary on this book.

Collins, John J. *The Scepter and Star: The Messiahs of the Dead Sea Scrolls and Other Ancient Literature*. New York, 1995. Good evaluations of 4Q246, 4Q471b, and 4Q491.

Duhaime, Jean. "Dualistic Reworking in the Scrolls from Qumran." *Catholic Biblical Quarterly* 49 (1987), 32–56. Important study on the connection between Michael and the theology of Qumran.

Eshel, Esther. "4Q471[b]: A Self Glorification Hymn." *Revue de Qumrân* 17 (1996), 175–203. Denies that 4Q471[b] should be interpreted as referring to Michael.

García Martínez, Florentino. *Qumran and Apocalyptic. Studies on the Aramaic Texts from Qumran*. Studies on the Texts of the Desert of Judah, 9. Leiden, 1992.

Hurtado, Larry. *One God, One Lord. Early Christian Devotion and Ancient Jewish Monotheism*. Philadelphia, 1988. A stimulating discussion of the significance of Jewish beliefs about angels on the development of Christology in the early church.

Kobelski, Paul J. *Melchizedek and Melchireša'*. Catholic Biblical Quarterly Monograph Series, 10. Washington, D.C., 1981. Thorough study of Melchizedek and visions of Amram.

Larson, E. "4Q470 and the Angelic Rehabilitation of King Zedekiah." *Dead Sea Discoveries* 1 (1994), 210–228. Examination of the role of Michael in 4Q470.

Yadin, Yigael. *The Scroll of the War of the Sons of Light against the Sons of Darkness*. Oxford, 1962. Still an important commentary on the War Scroll.

ERIK W. LARSON

MICHMASH, NAḤAL. The northern tributary of Wadi Qilt, Naḥal Michmash (Wadi Suweinit) originates from Bethel Hills near Ramallah, and joins Wadi Qilt west of ʿEin-Fawar. Its canyon-like section starts east of the villages of Jabaʾ and Mukhmas, whose names preserve the biblical names of Gaba and Michmash (*1 Sm.* 13.16). This canyon is perhaps "the ravine of Beth Tamar" mentioned in the Copper Scroll (3Q15 xi.14–15, ed. Milik), unless the reference is to the cliffs of ʿEin-Fara. [*See* ʿEin-Fara.] Between 1983 and 1985, in the framework of the Archaeological Survey of the Judean Desert Caves, carried out on behalf of the Institute of Archaeology of the Hebrew University of Jerusalem, directed by J. Patrich, the caves along this canyon were explored, as well as those in Wadi al-Habibi, the northern tributary of Naḥal Michmash. Along an approximately 5 kilometer section of Naḥal Michmash fifteen artificial caves were found, some isolated, and some in groups of a few caves each; eight caves were found in Wadi al-Habibi. The caves were cut by Jews in the Second Temple period, probably as part of a deliberate emergency project aimed at providing shelter and hideout for families of the nearby villages of Michmash and Gaba. Some of these caves were reused during the Bar Kokhba Revolt.

A large space in the rock was hollowed beyond the natural face of a crevice or a natural rock ledge, through which access was maintained. The caves were classified into six different types according to the size and shape of the cave or group of caves. Most had built-in cisterns for water. A particularly interesting type is the single chamber cave (10–30 square meters in area) with a vertical chimney or shaft (approximately 1 meter square in cross section and several meters deep) cut into its floor. Projections or depressions cut in the vertical walls of the shaft aided climbing; the entrance at the bottom was sealed by a door, probably of stone, which revolved on hinges. In one place a circular stone (approximately 1 meter in diameter) was found in situ. The stone could roll in a groove carved especially in the rock to keep the entrance open. In some caves a concealed upper cell was cut near the ceiling. A leather sandal similar to those found at Masada and in other caves in the Judean Desert was found in Wadi al-Habibi Cave 4.

Some of the caves had been reused during the Byzantine period by the monks of the Byzantine laura of Saint Firminus. [*See* Monasteries.] This laura was established in this ravine in the sixth century CE (Cyril of Scythopolis, *Vita Sabae* 16.89). Its ruined remains, explored by R. Rubin, are scattered along the wadi, mainly on its northern bank, but some hermitages were also built on the southern bank. They included two chapels. A Syriac inscription in a mosaic floor was found in a hermitage on this bank, near ʿEin-Suweinit (Haloun and Rubin, 1981). A secondary, eastern center of the laura, comprising some ruined buildings and cisterns, a burial chapel, and a large water reservoir, was found near the confluence of Wadi al-Habibi with Naḥal Michmash.

The most complex groups of caves, known in Arabic as el-Aliliyat ("the upper chambers"), are located in the cliffs of the northern bank. There are two adjacent groups, one to the east and one to the west. The caves of the eastern group are located along a rock ledge 56 meters long, 30 meters above the foot of the cliff. The complex consists of two rock-cut dwelling rooms, a ritual bath (*miqveh*), and a cistern. On the plaster covering the walls of the cistern are charcoal sketches of seven branched menorahs, a pentagram, and inscriptions. The inscriptions include two lines of an abecedary, which, along with the drawings, probably should be interpreted as magic formulas to protect the writers. Another Aramaic inscription reads: "Yoʿezer has been uprooted, the guards have entered." This may have been the writer's last message, telling of the wounding or death of one Yoʿezer—a common name in priestly circles—and indicating that the besieging guards had penetrated this almost inaccessible place.

The script is typical of late Second Temple period. Below the pentagram another inscription reads: "Peace, peace, amen." During the Byzantine period monks lived in the caves and inscribed crosses and Syriac and Greek inscriptions in red paint on the rock walls and on the sides of the cistern and the *miqveh*. These were noticed already in 1928 by M. Marcoff and D. Chitty. This complex was reexamined in 1978 by a team of scholars on behalf of the École Biblique et Archéologique Français in Jerusalem, who had published a plan and the Syriac inscriptions on the plastered wall of the *miqveh*—a verse from *Psalm* 29.3 repeating three times: "The voice of the Lord is upon the waters." The three Greek inscriptions accompanied by crosses read: IC XC; IC XC NI KA; and IC XC *Basileue*.

The western group of caves consisted of four systems, one above the other toward the top of the cliff, interconnected by a tunnel and rock-hewn steps. The water collection system served all four systems of caves. Its plastered rock-cut channel collected runoff from the cliff, which was then directed to the cisterns as it descended from level to level. Typical shards from the time of of the Bar Kokhba Revolt were found in this group of caves. Other finds from this period, including five bronze coins, were found in el-Ji Cave, the largest cave on the southern bank of the wadi (Eshel, 1997).

BIBLIOGRAPHY

Eshel, H. "Jerusalem No More." *Biblical Archaeology Review* 23.6 (1997), 48, 73.

Finkelstein, I., ed. *Archaeological Survey of the Hill Country of Benjamin* (sites no. 232, 543, 544). Jerusalem, 1993.

Halloun, M., and R. Rubin. "Palestinian Syriac Inscription from 'En Sueinit'." *Liber Annuus* 31 (1981), 291–298, pls. 59–62.

Hirschfeld, Y. "List of Byzantine Monasteries in the Judean Desert." In *Christian Archaeology in the Holy Land: New Discoveries* [*Archaeological Essays in Honour of Virgilio C. Corbo ofm*], edited by G. C. Bottini, L. DiSegni, and E. Alliata, pp. 44–45. Jerusalem, 1990.

Patrich, J. "Hiding Caves and Jewish Inscriptions on the Cliffs of Naḥal Michmas" (in Hebrew). *Eretz Israel* (Avigad Volume) 18 (1985), 153–166, pls. 24–27.

Patrich, J. "Inscriptions araméennes juives dans les grottes d'el Aleiliyat, Wadi Suweinit." *Revue biblique* 92 (1985), 265–273.

Patrich, J. "Chronique Archéologique: Refuges juifs dans les gorges du Wadi Mukhamas." *Revue biblique* 96 (1989), pp. 235–239, pl. XV.

Patrich, J. "Hideouts in the Judean Wilderness." *Biblical Archaeology Review* 15.5 (1989), 32–42.

Patrich, J., and R. Rubin. "Les grottes de el-Aleiliyat et la laure de Saint Firmin." *Revue biblique* 91 (1984), 379–387.

JOSEPH PATRICH

MIDRASHIM. The term *midrash* in the context of early rabbinic literature has three levels of meaning: the activity of interpretive study of Hebrew scriptures, the discrete exegetical results of such study, and the literary collections (*midrashim*) of such exegeses. Within the last level, it is common first to distinguish chronologically between the collections. The earliest ones, containing Midrashic traditions attributed to the tannaitic sages (c.70–220 CE), are referred to as tannaitic *midrashim* or *midreshei halakhah* ("legal *midrashim*"). Both terms are somewhat imprecise, since these collections in their present form are most likely the products of amoraic redactors of the mid- to late-third century CE and their contents are both halakhic (legal) and aggadic (narrative/hortatory), depending on the mix of law and narrative in the biblical books upon which they comment. The biblical books covered, but not necessarily completely, by these collections are *Exodus* (by the *midrash Mekhilta*), *Leviticus* (*Sifra*), and *Numbers* and *Deuteronomy* (*Sifrei*), with evidence of there having been two recensions of each collection, only one of which in most cases is fully preserved, the other requiring reconstruction.

In the later Midrashic commentaries of the amoraic period (third through fifth centuries CE), a further distinction is drawn between those that take the form of running expository commentaries following the order of the biblical books (the Pentateuch and the Five Scrolls, but not the Prophets), and those that are more thematically and homiletically structured around the opening verses of weekly or festival scriptural lections. Among the latter, particular scholarly attention has been paid to the rhetorical artistry of the *mashal* ("parable") and the *petiḥta'* ("proem"). But this distinction between expository and homiletical collections should not be drawn too sharply, as nascent homiletical structures can be found in the earlier (tannaitic) collections as well.

As to language, both early and late Midrashic collections of the rabbinic period are written in rabbinic Hebrew, but the later (amoraic) collections contain a higher admixture of Palestinian Aramaic and aramaized Hebrew, in all cases with a liberal peppering of Greek and Latin loanwords. While these *midrashim* are all collective, edited anthologies rather than authored or pseudepigraphic compositions, their constituent traditions are frequently (more so in the amoraic collections) attributed to named rabbinic sages, the veracity of such attributions being difficult to determine with certainty.

Although the extant collections of rabbinic *midrash* all date in their present form to the third century CE and later, it is generally assumed that they transmit earlier traditions, deriving not only from earlier rabbinic generations, but from prerabbinic antecedents of Second Temple times. Until the discovery of the Dead Sea Scrolls, the evidence for such prerabbinic Jewish scriptural interpretation was limited largely to writings preserved in Greek and other non-Semitic languages, and transmitted, with varying degrees of tampering, by later Christian denominations. The extent to which such writings could be identified with specific Jewish social groups was extremely limited. Even the Hebrew word *midrash*, in its rabbinic sense of biblical interpretation, was unknown in prerabbinic Jewish sources. Thus, it was difficult to judge whether, or to what extent, rabbinic *midrash*'s own claims for great antiquity (extending ultimately to Moses at Mount Sinai) had any basis in fact. In the area of Jewish law, did the rabbinically preserved legal exegeses that derived rabbinic legal theory and practice from scriptural verses represent scriptural justifications of received legal traditions, originally transmitted nonexegetically, or the very methods by which Jewish law developed in the Second Temple period? In other words, was Jewish law of Second Temple times taught and transmitted through or independently of Midrashic interpretation? While the discovery and publication of the Dead Sea Scrolls and related literature have not fully answered these questions, they have revolutionized the way in which they are approached.

To begin with, the Hebrew word *midrash* appears some eight times in the Dead Sea Scrolls (Rule of the Community from Qumran Cave 1, hereafter, 1QRule of the Community, 1QS vi.24, viii.15, viii.26; Florilegium, 4Q174 1.14; 4Q269 (verso); Damascus Document, CD xx.6; Damascus Document^{a}, 4Q266 5.i.17 (restored), 11.20; Damascus Document^{e}, 4Q270 7.ii.15), in five cases of which it is followed by the word *torah*. However, in such usages often it is not clear whether the word *midrash* has the specific connotation of scriptural exegesis or the more general sense of study. The same ambiguity pertains in the Dead Sea Scrolls to the use of the verb *lidrosh* in conjunction with a text or body of laws.

With the discovery of the Dead Sea Scrolls, many exegetical traditions, formerly known only from early rabbinic *midrash*, are now known to have circulated in late Second Temple times, minimally within the Qumran community and related groups, but probably more broadly. This sharing of exegetical traditions is as true for legal as for nonlegal understandings of scripture. Less certain is whether or to what extent these shared traditions are the products of direct or indirect contact between the Qumran sectaries and the Pharisees or the later rabbis, independent exegesis by the two groups, or a broader, more commonly shared body of tradition upon which both drew.

When we examine the variety of literary forms in which the two communities collected and transmitted their exegetical traditions, there are striking differences as well as similarities to be noted. For example, we find in the Dead Sea Scrolls some of our earliest known running scriptural commentaries, in the form of the *pesharim* to biblical books of the Prophets and *Psalms*. [*See* Pesharim.] These tend to decode in sequence the terms of the biblical verses in specific reference to events, personalities, or groups in the life and history of the Qumran community, much like the interpretation of a dream, thereby affirming that the prophetic predictions have been or will shortly be actualized in the community. The term *pesher* and its form bear striking resemblance to the later rabbinic exegetical form and cognate term *petirah*. However, there are significant differences between the two. Rabbinic *midrash* often decodes an indeterminate scriptural verse or phrase, but not just from the Prophets, so as to refer intertextually to a specific biblical figure or event. Furthermore, it commonly provides a series of such decodings, each referring to a different referent or set of referents. Thus, rabbinic *midrash* commonly adduces a multiple of intrascriptural decoding possibilities, whereas the Qumran *pesher* commonly gives a single extrascriptural one. Finally, the rabbinic *petirah*, like rabbinic *midrash* in general, achieves its results through the exegetical juxtaposition of verses from different parts of the Hebrew scriptures, while the continuous *pesharim* refer only to the base verse being commented upon. However, intertextual interpretation is displayed in the several noncontinuous, or thematic, *pesher* or *pesher*-like interpretations in the Damascus Document (e.g., CD vi.2–11, vii.9–viii.2) and the Florilegium. Similarly, the thematic stringing together of scriptural verses from diverse locations (rabbinic *ḥarizah*) is evidenced in Catena^{a-b} (4Q177, 182). All these Qumran forms, however, lack the dialogical rhetoric of rabbinic *midrash* (for example, question and answer, the rhetorical raising of alternative exegetical possibilities to be disproved) and the attribution of particular interpretations to named authorities.

Although Qumran texts evidence, besides the *pesher* terminology, stock terms for scriptural citation (e.g., *asher katuv/amar*; "as it is written/said") similar to those in rabbinic *midrash*, the frequency of actual scriptural citation is far less in Dead Sea Scroll interpretation than in rabbinic *midrash*. In some cases, especially in Miqtsat Maʿasei ha-Torah (MMT^{a-e}, 4Q394–399), what follows such seeming citation terminology cannot be identified with any known biblical verse but rather represents a biblical paraphrase or common biblical idea. [*See* Miqtsat Maʿasei ha-Torah.] Much more commonly, and especially in legal texts such as Temple Scroll^{a} (11Q19) and the Damascus Document, the Dead Sea Scrolls present the results of the community's (or its leadership's) exegetical activity in nonexegetical, paraphrastic form (referred to by some as "rewritten Bible"). [*See* Rewritten Bible.] Thus, as in early rabbinic literature where laws are taught both exegetically (*midrash*) and nonexegetically (Mishnah), both forms can be found in the Dead Sea Scrolls, but with a larger preponderance of the latter. So, while the Dead Sea Scrolls contain many antecedents to rabbinic exegetical traditions, the fact that the exegetical underpinnings of those antecedents are expressed more implicitly than explicitly makes the search for antecedents to specific rabbinic hermeneutical methods rather difficult and the results minimal. Unlike early rabbinic literature, there is no evidence among the Dead Sea Scrolls for the explicit articulation of the hermeneutical rules that govern exegesis.

Being aware of these differences and limitations, it is important to acknowledge significant similarities between the two communities' employment of scriptural exegesis in relation to their respective social and ideological self-understandings. For both communities, the ritualized activity of interpretive study of scriptures was a central religious activity that defined the community and socialized its members to its ethos and place within the larger sacred history of Israel. In both cases, the scrutiny of scripture required close attention to the particulars of scriptural language in its smallest details, wherein lay deeper levels of meaning to be uncovered. For both communities, such highly engaged activity of *midrash* was not simply a utility for deriving or justifying their laws and teachings. Rather, it was a form of intensive religious expression and experience in itself, veritably a form of worship, a locus for experiencing the divine presence in their midst. Socially, such study strengthened the bonds of religious community (whether conceived at Qumran as *yaḥad* or among the rabbinic sages as *ḥavurah*). As expressed by the Damascus Document (CD xx.10–13), the community inhabited a *beit Torah* ("house/place of Torah"), in which their continual *midrash ha-Torah* ("study/interpretation of Torah") provided the medium for ongoing revelation along a divinely ordained path to redemption (1QS viii.12–16). Similar understandings of *talmud Torah* ("study of Torah") inform early rabbinic self-understandings of how to know and experience God's presence and will in the present while awaiting final (albeit deferred) redemption.

Both communities had a twofold diet of study, however differently denoted and transmitted: for the rabbis, written and oral Torah (Miqra' and Mishnah); for the Qumran sectaries, that which was revealed (*nigleh*) to all Israel (the commonly held "Torah of Moses," by various names) and that which was hidden (*nistar*) from the rest of Israel but revealed to them alone (the community's "statutes," by various names). For both groups, scriptural interpretation was a way of interlinking the two bodies of revelation to one another, thereby engaging them as one.

Yet, once again, acknowledgment of these socially functional similarities between rabbinic *midrash* and Qumran exegetical activity should not distract us from their no less significant differences. The Qumran twofold study curriculum draws no performative distinction, as does rabbinic *midrash*, between "written" and "oral" components. Rabbinic *midrash* stresses that both forms of Torah were revealed through Moses to the whole Israelite people at Mount Sinai, even as the unfolding of the oral Torah was to be continuous throughout subsequent generations. By contrast, Qumran writings suggest that what had previously been hidden (and continued to be hidden from the rest of Israel) was disclosed to the community of the renewed covenant alone, in the period after the destruction of the First Temple, beginning with the Teacher of Righteousness and continuing through the succeeding generations of the community under the guidance of its inspired teachers. While both communities sought to uncover fuller and deeper meanings of the Hebrew scriptures through scriptural study and interpretation, they related this activity to the larger body of Israel and its sacred history quite differently. In the case of rabbinic *midrash*, scripture's progressively uncovered meanings are thought to have been present, at least potentially, already at Mount Sinai and to have been revealed, at least ideally, to all Israel from Mount Sinai on. Among the Qumran sectaries, those meanings were a newly revealed dispensation to the community of the renewed covenant alone at the onset of the End of Days.

[*See also* Interpretation of Scriptures.]

BIBLIOGRAPHY

Baumgarten, Joseph. "The Unwritten Law in the Pre-Rabbinic Period." *Journal for the Study of Judaism* 3 (1972), 7–29. Contrasts the rabbinic emphasis on the oral nature of rabbinic teaching with the relative absence of such a doctrine among the rabbinic antecedents, especially as evidenced in the Dead Sea Scrolls.

Bernstein, Moshe J. "Introductory Formulas for Citation and Re-Citation of Biblical Verses in the Qumran Pesharim: Observations on a Pesher Technique." *Dead Sea Discoveries* 1 (1994), 30–70.

Bernstein, Moshe J. "The Employment and Interpretation of Scripture in 4QMMT." In *Reading 4QMMT: New Perspectives on Qumran Law and History*, edited by John Kampen and Moshe J. Bernstein, pp. 29–51. Atlanta, 1996. Considers the nature and forms of scriptural interpretation in the recently published Miqtsat Ma'asei ha-Torah.

Brooke, George J. *Exegesis at Qumran: 4QFlorilegium in Its Jewish Context*. Journal for the Study of the Old Testament Supplement Series, 29. Sheffield, 1985. In chapter 1, analogies are drawn between early rabbinic *midrash* and Qumran exegesis.

Brownlee, William H. "Biblical Interpretation among the Sectarians of the Dead Sea Scrolls." *Biblical Archaeologist* 14 (1951), 54–76.

Campbell, Jonathan G. *The Use of Scripture in the Damascus Document 1–8, 19–20*. Beihefte zur Zeitschrift für die alttestamentliche Wissenschaft, 228. Berlin, 1995. Limits examination of scriptural exegesis in the Damascus Document to its hortatory, nonlegal sections.

Dimant, Devorah. "The Hebrew Bible in the Dead Sea Scrolls: The Torah Quotations in the *Damascus Document*." In *"Sha'arei Talmon": Studies in the Bible, Qumran, and the Ancient Near East Presented to Shemaryahu Talmon*, edited by Michael Fishbane, Emanuel Tov, and Weston W. Fields, pp. 113–122 (Hebrew section). Winona Lake, Ind., 1992. Argues that explicit legal *midrash* in the Damascus Document is specifically employed for sectarian rules that are at polemical odds with those of other groups (e.g., the Pharisees).

Fishbane, Michael. "The Qumran-Pesher and Traits of Ancient Hermeneutics." In *Proceedings of the Sixth World Congress of Jewish Studies*, vol. 1, pp. 97–114. Jerusalem, 1977.

Fishbane, Michael. "Use, Authority and Interpretation of Mikra at Qumran." In *Mikra: Text, Translation, Reading and Interpretation of the Hebrew Bible in Ancient Judaism and Early Chritianity*, edited by Martin Jan Mulder, pp. 339–377. Compendia Rerum Iudaicarum ad Novum Testamentum. Section Two: The Literature of the Jewish People in the Period of the Second Temple and Talmud, 1. Assen, 1988. Provides an excellent overview.

Fitzmyer, Joseph A. "The Use of Explicit Old Testament Quotations in Qumran Literature and in the New Testament." In *Essays on the Semitic Background of the New Testament*, pp. 3–58. Society of Biblical Literature Sources for Biblical Study, 5. Missoula, Mont., 1974. Originally published in *New Testament Studies* 7 (1960–1961), 297–333. Detailed study of the terminology of scriptural citation in the Dead Sea Scrolls.

Fraade, Steven D. *From Tradition to Commentary: Torah and Its Interpretation in the Midrash Sifre to Deuteronomy*. Albany, N.Y., 1991. See, especially, chapter 1, for a comparison of rabbinic and Qumran forms of scriptural commentary, and chapter 3, for the social role of midrashic interpretation in the self-understanding of the rabbinic sages.

Fraade, Steven D. "Interpretive Authority in the Studying Community at Qumran." *Journal of Jewish Studies* 44 (1993), 46–49. Discusses the place of scriptural study and interpretation in the Qumran community, with comparisons to rabbinic *midrash*.

Fraade, Steven D. "Looking for Legal Midrash at Qumran." In *Biblical Perspectives: Early Use and Interpretation of the Bible in Light of the Dead Sea Scrolls*, edited by Michael E. Stone and Esther Chazon, pp. 59–79. Leiden, 1998. Discusses the relative absence of explicit legal *midrash* in the Dead Sea Scrolls.

Horgan, Maurya P. *Pesharim: Qumran Interpretations of Biblical Books*. Catholic Biblical Quarterly Monograph Series, 8. Washington, D.C., 1979.

Schiffman, Lawrence H. *Reclaiming the Dead Sea Scrolls: The History of Judaism, the Background of Christianity, the Lost Library of Qumran*. Philadelphia and Jerusalem, 1994. See, especially, chapters 13–14 for an excellent survey of scriptural interpretation and the *pesharim* among the Dead Sea Scrolls.

Silberman, Lou H. "Unriddling the Riddle: A Study in the Structure and Language of the Habakkuk Pesher (1 QpHab)." *Revue de Qumrân* 3 (1961), 323–364.

Swanson, Dwight D. *The Temple Scroll and the Bible: The Methodology of 11QT*. Studies on the Texts of the Desert of Judah, 14. Leiden, 1995.

Vermes, Geza. "Bible Interpretation at Qumran." In *Eretz-Israel: Archaeological, Historical and Geographical Studies. Vol. 20: Yigael Yadin Memorial Volume*, edited by Amnon Ben-Tor, Jonas C. Greenfield, and Abraham Malamat, pp. 184–191. Jerusalem, 1989.

Vermes, Geza. "Biblical Proof-Texts in Qumran Literature." *Journal of Semitic Studies* 34 (1989), 493–508.

STEVEN D. FRAADE

MILIK, JÓZEF T. (1922–), Franco-Polish Orientalist and editor of the Dead Sea Scrolls. Born on 24 March 1922 in Seroczyn, Poland, Milik studied at the Boleslaw Prus Lyceum in Siedlce and then at the Major Seminary of Płock and Warsaw. In 1944 he began his studies of ancient and modern languages at the Catholic Institute of Lublin. From 1946 to 1951 he studied at the Pontifical Oriental Institute and Pontifical Biblical Institute in Rome.

In 1950 Milik published a series of scholarly notes on the spelling, phonetic, and textual variants of the biblical manuscripts among the Dead Sea Scrolls, in particular Isaiah[a] and [b] from Cave 1 at Qumran (1QIsa[a–b]). In 1951, he was one of the first to publish a translation, in Latin, of the Rule of the Community from Cave 1 at Qumran (1QS), of which he later published the text in volume 1 of Discoveries in the Judaean Desert (Oxford, 1955). He identified one fragment as belonging either to the end of *1 Enoch* or to the beginning of *Noah*; in fact it was the largest fragment of a work that, in the *editio princeps*, by Milik himself, is called Noah (1Q19).

These scholarly studies attracted the notice of Roland de Vaux, director of the École Biblique et Archéologique Française, president of the Trustees of the Palestine Archeological Museum and codirector of the excavations of Cave 1 and Khirbet Qumran. De Vaux invited Milik to Jerusalem to participate in the study of the hundreds of manuscript fragments from Cave 1. In 1952 Milik worked with Dominique Barthélemy in organizing, distributing, and classifying manuscript fragments found in Cave 1 during the excavations or purchased on the antiquities market.

In 1952 Cave 3 was discovered by the team of Roland de Vaux, to which Milik belonged. This increased Milik's on-site work and complemented his work as an epigraphist. He took part in excavating Cave 4 and unearthed hundreds of fragments. He also took part in the discovery of Cave 5 and excavating Caves 5 and 6, while workers from the University of Louvain excavated the nearby site at Khirbet Mird. [*See* Mird, Khirbet.]

Naturalized as a French citizen, Milik was admitted as a researcher to the Centre National de la Recherche Scientifique in Paris, an institution of which he was a member until his retirement in 1987. At first detached to work in Jerusalem, other researchers later joined him, working on an international and interdenominational team recruited by de Vaux. But all concurred that Milik was the most active, quick, and effective member in the work of grouping, classifying, and deciphering the fragments. He was the scholar who developed the universally accepted system of *sigla*, by which the manuscripts are cited (Barthélemy and Milik, 1955, pp. 46–48). De Vaux made him the pillar of the team and entrusted to him the publication of the fragmentary and extremely difficult manuscripts from the caves of Wadi Murabbaʿat. [*See* Murabbaʿat, Wadi, *article on* Written Material.] (Benoit, Milik, and de Vaux, 1961).

Milik deciphered the hitherto unknown Aramaic cursive script. De Vaux entrusted to him the most important lot of manuscripts from Cave 4 (apocryphal works and compositions of the Community), the manuscripts from Cave 5, and the Copper Scroll from Cave 3 (3Q15; Baillet, Milik, and de Vaux, 1962).

During the nine years he spent at the École Biblique et Archéologique Française de Jérusalem and in the "scrollery" of the Palestine Archaeological Museum, doing painstaking and austere work, Milik published in French (1957) a first synthesis of the main contributions of these discoveries to our knowledge of the Bible and Oriental studies (Milik, 1957). [*See* École Biblique et Archéologique Française; Palestine Archaeological Museum.] This work appeared in Italian that same year; it was updated and translated into English by John Strugnell in 1959. Although this work is intended for a wide audience in addition to scholars, it is still authoritative because the author is an expert who knows better than anybody else the places and texts. Having participated in the excavations, Milik could have a personal view and approach, having in mind the fragments which he was progressively identifying and deciphering. From the outset, Milik defended the identification of the Wicked Priest with Jonathan, and he stuck to this solution as the only one that could account for all the data gathered. [*See* Wicked Priest.] This solution was adopted by a majority of scholars and even by de Vaux himself (1973, pp. 5, 116f.), although de Vaux still could not make up his mind between Simon and Jonathan.

Endowed with a prodigious memory, Milik remembered everything he deciphered. He also had a gift for minute observation, and noted the quality of the leather, its preparation as a support for the writing, the scribe's handwriting, the ink, the language and vocabulary, the subjects treated, the shape of the breaks, that is, anything that individualizes a fragment in order to link up fragments, even at a distance, or to determine whether a fragment belonged to another sheet or manuscript. He excelled in this art of reconstruction. The members of the international team remember the story of his decipherment of the cryptic writing—the time of their lunch!

In addition to the excavations at Qumran, Milik and Frank Moore Cross led a surface exploration in the Buqeia in an attempt to understand the toponymy (placenames) of the region. [*See* Buqeia.] Milik's linguistic skills gave him the opportunity to publish and to study a number of inscriptions, whether in Greek or in a Semitic language, and to complete researches on Palestinian topography, largely of the Holy City, mainly because of the Copper Scroll from Cave 3. [*See* Copper Scroll.] Again and again, Milik showed his erudition. The first to join the team, he is also, by far, the one who has edited the greatest number of texts, drawing value from even the tiniest fragment to rediscover precisely a literary, historical, and religious context for works for which the complete text has been forever lost. Finally, he played a crucial role in completing the "manual concordance" at the Palestine Archaeological Museum, which was intended to help editors find places where texts or expressions may overlap.

While based in Jerusalem, Milik had the chance to explore many subjects. He made friends with the Samaritan priests in Nablus, who permitted him to record their recitation of biblical books. This served his editions, for example, of the phylacteries from Cave 4 (de Vaux and Milik, 1977, pp. 39–46).

After another long stay in Rome during the 1960s, Milik came back to Paris where he continued to publish (Milik, 1976, Attridge et al., 1994), sharing the results of his research with the youngest members of the team, and, thereby, the benefit of his work that was already considerably advanced on a number of fragmentary manuscripts. As a master of decipherment he is frequently consulted, since his is the only living memory of the first work done on the site and on the original texts. The editors of Discoveries in the Judaean Desert, 22, acknowledge their indebtedness for finishing an edition for which Milik contributed his decipherment and notes (Brooke, et al., 1997).

In March 1991, the Complutensian University of Madrid honored this man of genius in epigraphy and decipherment by a medal.

The *Revue de Qumrân*, which includes Milik on its editorial committee, dedicated an entire volume to him on the occasion of his seventy-fifth birthday, in 1997. [*See* Revue de Qumrân.] Milik is and shall remain the greatest master of his generation in deciphering the Dead Sea Scrolls; a researcher of integrity, uninvolved in the plots and passionate debates of the last decade, and devoted to science, philology, and history.

[*See also biographies of Barthélemy; de Vaux.*]

BIBLIOGRAPHY

Attridge, Harold, et al. *Qumran Cave 4: Parabiblical Texts, Part 1*. Discoveries in the Judaean Desert, 13. Oxford, 1994.

Baillet, Maurice, J. T. Milik, and Roland de Vaux. *Les 'Petites Grottes' de Qumrân*. Discoveries in the Judaean Desert, 3. Oxford, 1962.

Barthélemy, D., and J. T. Milik. *Qumran Cave 1*. Discoveries in the Judaean Desert, 1. Oxford, 1955.

Baumgarten, J. M., and J. T. Milik. *Qumran Cave 4. XII, The Damascus Document (4Q266–273)*. Discoveries in the Judaean Desert, 18. Oxford, 1996.

Benoit, P., J. T. Milik, and Roland de Vaux. *Les Grottes de Murabbaʿat*. Discoveries in the Judaean Desert, 2. Oxford, 1961.

Brooke, George, et al. *Qumran Cave 4: Parabiblical Texts, Part 3*. Discoveries in the Judaean Desert, 22. Oxford, 1997.

de Vaux, Roland. *Archaeology and the Dead Sea Scrolls*, rev. ed. Oxford, 1973.

de Vaux, Roland, and Milik, J. T. *Qumrân Grotte 4: Archéologie-Tefil-*

lin, Mezuzot et Targums 4Q128–4Q157. Discoveries in the Judaean Desert, 6. Oxford, 1977.

García Martínez, Florentino. "Bibliographie qumrânienne de Józef Tadeusz Milik." In *Hommage a Jósef T. Milik*, edited by Florentino García Martínez and Émile Puech. *Revue de Qumrân* 17 (1996), 11–20.

Milik, J. T. *Dix Ans de découvertes dans le désert de Juda*. Paris, 1957.

Milik, J. T. *The Books of Enoch. Aramaic Fragments of Qumrân Cave 4*. Oxford, 1976.

Milik, J. T. *Ten years of Discovery in the Wilderness of Judaea*. SBT, 26. London, 1959.

Puech, Émile. "Jósef Tadeusz Milik." In *Hommage a Jósef T. Milik*, edited by Florentino García Martínez and Émile Puech. *Revue de Qumrân* 17 (1996), 5–10.

ÉMILE PUECH

Translated from French by Robert E. Shillenn

MILKI-RESHAʿ. *See* Demons.

MILLSTONES, generally made of basalt quarried in the Golan and Hauran, were used for turning grain into flour. The process involved several steps. Husked grains were first pounded, and then the kernels were broken and finally ground. Naked grains were then grated between two stone surfaces to yield flour.

The simplest and oldest milling equipment was the mortar (*mortarium*) and pestle (*pilum*), yet, while they had been used to pound husked grains for a long time, they were unsuitable for large quantities and ineffective in grinding. Like the common clay *mortaria*, stone mortars were used for pounding and breaking up spices and herbs. The basalt mortar was an open flat dish with low sides set on three feet, while the shape of the pestles varied; a representative group of them came to light in the Herodian mansions of Jerusalem (Avigad, 1983, p. 127, illus. 123; p. 182, illus. 209.4).

In the course of time, however, the development led from the mortar and pestle to the hand-operated simple saddle quern, a primitive hand-turned grain mill, and then to the technically advanced animal- and water-powered rotary mill. The application of rotary motion was a great improvement. Not found in Israel before 100 BCE, it was the prevailing type used from then on.

In the settlement of Qumran, remains of a grain mill and a baking oven were discovered in the workshop area, indicating that flour was produced by its inhabitants. In de Vaux's opinion it was unlikely that grain was bought from outside the area for that purpose, but rather that corn or barley was grown in the plain of the Buqeiʿa to the west of Qumran, the sites being connected by an ancient pathway. The installation consists of a circular raised base for the millstones; in a pit nearby two intact basalt stones and two broken ones were found (de Vaux, 1973, pp. 28–29, pl. XX). The type is the turning- or rotary grain mill (*mola versatilis*).

The earliest dated examples are known from El Sec (Mallorca) and Morgantina (Sicily) from the fourth century BCE. While scholars agree that the rotary grain mill was invented in the West, it is not clear when the type was introduced into the East; the theory that it was brought by the Roman legions to Greece in the first century BCE and from there further East might be due to insufficient research and the lack of stratified archaeological finds.

The mill consists of two stones, a lower one shaped like a bell (*meta*) and a hollow double-conic upper one shaped like an hourglass (*catillus*) with two central handles. The lower stone remained stationary on a platform, while the upper stone was rotated by turning it with a horizontal wooden handle. Depending on its size, the mill could be worked by a single person or by two people, one turning on each side.

A further development was the so-called Pompeian mill, a type employed in the commercial bakeries at Pompei, Herculaneum, and Ostia. It was too heavy to be turned by human power, but was drawn by a mule, donkey, or horse fastened to its handlebar (*mola asinaria*). The simplest form of rotary hand mill (*mola manuaria*), easy to transport, consists of a pair of round flat stones, later a pair of lower convex stone and an upper concave stone, held in place by a vertical wooden handle.

BIBLIOGRAPHY

Avigad, Nahman. *Discovering Jerusalem*. Nashville, 1983. A well-illustrated account of the excavations in the Jewish Quarter.

Bar-Adon, Pesach. "Another Settlement of the Judean Desert Sect at ʿEin el-Ghuweir on the Shores of the Dead Sea." *Bulletin of the American Schools of Oriental Research* 227 (1977), 1–25.

Benoit, P., J. T. Milik, and R. de Vaux. *Les grottes de Murabbaʿat*. Discoveries in the Judaean Desert, 2. Oxford, 1961.

de Vaux, Roland. *Archaeology and the Dead Sea Scrolls: The Schweich Lectures of the British Academy*. London, 1973.

Moritz, L. A. *Grain-Mills and Flour in Classical Antiquity*. Oxford, 1958. A detailed study of written and archaeological sources.

White, K. D. *Greek and Roman Technology*, pp. 63–67. London, 1984. A summary on food technology.

RENATE ROSENTHAL-HEGINBOTTOM

MINOR PROPHETS. The manuscripts of the Minor Prophets from the Judean Desert vary in date and in textual affiliation. This article will survey the textual witnesses for the Twelve Minor Prophets from the Judean Desert and describe the contribution they make to our understanding of the text of the Twelve at this stage of scholarship.

As is well known by now, the biblical manuscripts from the Judean Desert have demonstrated that the text of the Hebrew scriptures was still evolving in the third through the first centuries BCE and into the first century CE. The consonantal text of the Hebrew scriptures was probably "standardized" by the end of the second century CE. In the case of the Minor Prophets in Hebrew, our evidence stretches from approximately 150 BCE to 50–100 CE, a period of 200–250 years covering a crucial phase in the history of the text and the collection of the Twelve. From the beginning of this period there exist manuscripts which show definite variation from the type of Hebrew text which is ancestral to the Masoretic Text. Likewise the ancestor of Masoretic Text is also attested. The picture which emerges is similar to that for other sections of the Hebrew scriptures. There is textual diversity and there is no unambiguous evidence that any one type of text was favored over another, although such theories have been proposed. For the Book of the Twelve we are extremely fortunate also to have a manuscript in Greek from the last half of the first century BCE which has been demonstrated to be a recension of the Septuagint (8Ḥev 1). This recension is closely aligned with later Greek versions which are known to be attempts to produce a Greek translation that was close to the Hebrew text. The existence of this early recension may be taken as evidence of the desire on the part of a community to revise the text of their Bible. Because the text of this recension, Greek Minor Prophets (8Ḥev 1), was based on the Septuagint translation, but stood closer to the proto-masoretic form of the text, scholars have assumed that the revision was done in order to bring the Septuagint closer to the current form of the Hebrew text. If this assumption were correct, then it would follow that there existed at that time a form of the Hebrew text which was viewed as more authentic or more authoritative than other forms of the Hebrew text which we know also existed at that time, some of which corresponded closely to the Septuagint. If this line of reasoning is accurate, then the theory which maintains that the proto-masoretic form of the text was more highly valued even in this period would be indirectly supported. There might have been additional reasons for a community to commission a revision of their scripture. We should not ignore the idea that revisions of translations might be desired to make the language current or up to date. This has not been explored as one of the possible motives for the production of the Greek recension of the Twelve.

Because the manuscript evidence from the Judean Desert is often fragmentary, it is not always possible to be certain of the textual affiliation of a witness. This uncertainty must always be kept in mind and should moderate generalizations based on this evidence.

In the following section are summarized the data regarding the agreements and disagreements among the versions, the ancient manuscripts, and the *pesharim*. The data are discussed book by book, following the order in the Hebrew canon. Disagreements which are due to orthographic differences, including the so-called longer suffixes, have not been included in the discussion.

Although in the Book of the Twelve the Septuagint may be somewhat expansionistic in general in comparison with the Masoretic Text, it is essential to keep in mind that the Masoretic Text also preserves later interpolations in addition to many incomprehensible readings. It is necessary for the textual critic and/or biblical exegete to review all evidence for each individual passage before deciding on the best reading.

Hebrew Biblical Manuscripts: Qumran Cave 4. Minor Prophets (4Q76) is one of the oldest biblical manuscripts from the Qumran caves, dating to approximately 150 BCE. It is written in an irregular semicursive script, which is rare in the biblical manuscripts recovered from the Judean Desert. This, along with its age, raises the possibility that it was not copied at Qumran, but rather imported into the community. Minor Prophets[a] is a nonaligned manuscript in terms of its textual affiliation. It agrees sometimes with the Masoretic Text, sometimes with G, and frequently does not resemble either.

Minor Prophets[b] (4Q77) is a neatly written manuscript in a semiformal hand from the middle of the second century BCE, roughly contemporary with Minor Prophets[a]. It stands relatively close to the proto-masoretic textual tradition in the readings, which are preserved. Minor Prophets[b] is also noteworthy because it preserves the transition between the "book" of *Zephaniah* and the "book" of Haggai, which allows insight into early scribal practices in copying biblical manuscripts.

Minor Prophets[c] (4Q78) is a manuscript written in a semiformal hand, which dates from approximately 75 BCE. It stands relatively close to the textual tradition represented by the Septuagint. It exhibits a "full" orthography, which Tov has described as the "Qumran Practice."

Minor Prophets[d] (4Q79) is a poorly copied manuscript written in a "rustic" semicursive script which is extremely difficult to date precisely; it may come from the second half of the first century BCE. In the few readings from the *Book of Hosea* which have been preserved, Minor Prophets[d] seems to stand relatively close to the proto-masoretic textual tradition. The lower fragment of this manuscript preserves an uninscribed section of leather which probably wrapped around the scroll when the scroll was rolled from the end.

Minor Prophets[e] (4Q80) is written in a minuscule, semiformal hand dating from approximately 75 BCE. There are several erasures and corrections evident in this manuscript. In the readings which are preserved, Minor Prophets[e] stands very close to the textual tradition represented by the Septuagint.

Minor Prophets[f] (4Q81) is preserved in only five fragments from the *Book of Jonah*. Like Minor Prophets[b], it varies little from the Masoretic Text, but since so little is preserved, it is not possible to reach a conclusion regarding its textual affiliation.

Minor Prophets[g] (4Q82) is a poorly preserved and extremely fragmentary manuscript in most of the Book of the Twelve. It is written in a semiformal hand dating from the last half of the first century BCE. Although 4QXII[g] disagrees frequently with both the Masoretic Text and the Septuagint, it stands close to the proto-masoretic textual tradition in most readings.

Murabbaʿat Minor Prophets Scroll. The Hebrew manuscript evidence also includes the Murabbaʿat Minor Prophets scroll, which dates to the second half of the first century CE. It has been described as virtually identical to the Masoretic Text. In the terminology of Emanuel Tov, which he uses in his book on the textual criticism of the Hebrew scriptures, Minor Prophets (Mur 88) is a proto-masoretic text. In comparison with the sometimes strong variation from the Masoretic Text among the seven Minor Prophets scrolls from cave four at Qumran, Minor Prophets (Mur 88) shows relatively little variation from the Masoretic Text (only one time in agreement with Septuagint against the Masoretic Text). The largest differences in comparison to the Masoretic Text are omissions where the omitted word or phrase was added interlinearly. These additions or "corrections" occur seven times and always correct the text of Minor Prophets (Mur 88) to agree with the reading of the consonantal text of the Masoretic Text. This correction of the text of Minor Prophets (Mur 88) may be indicative of the process of standardization. The consonantal text dates from the first century CE and has been described as a proto-masoretic text.

The textual situation in the Books of the Twelve. The Hebrew text of the *Book of Hosea* is attested in three biblical manuscripts and three *pesharim*. 4QXII[c] and 4QpHos[a] both seem to stand closer to the textual tradition represented by the Septuagint. 4QXII[d] and 4QXII[g] stand closer to the proto-masoretic tradition. In 4QpIsa[c] the form of the citation of *Hosea* 6.9 in this commentary may be the result of the replacement of an archaic verbal form with a form which was more frequent at the time it was copied—a form of modernizing. 4QpHos[b] agrees with the Septuagint against the proto-masoretic text in the single reading which seems to indicate an unambiguous variant, but there is too little text preserved to be certain of the textual affiliation of this manuscript. The other materials do not preserve enough text to know where to place them textually. The situation was mixed, but by the second half of the first century BCE it seems that the proto-masoretic tradition is better attested.

The Hebrew text of the *Book of Joel* is attested in three biblical manuscripts and in one nonbiblical composition. Once again 4QXII[c] emerges as an independent witness which stands closest to the textual tradition also preserved in the Septuagint. The ancient versions frequently had difficulty with *Joel* because of the higher frequency of rare terms. 4QXII[g] stands in the tradition of the proto-masoretic text, while Minor Prophets (Mur 88) is surprisingly quite independent in *Joel*. Catena[a] (4Q106) preserves only one citation of *Joel* (2.20) which disagrees with the Masoretic Text and is not reflected in other witnesses.

The Hebrew text of the *Book of Amos* is attested in three biblical manuscripts, one *pesher*, and two nonbiblical compositions. 4QXII[c], the earliest manuscript, is quite independent in *Amos*, although probably closer to the Septuagint. In contrast, 4QXII[g] is quite close to the Masoretic Text. Minor Prophets (Mur 88), although in general quite close to the Masoretic Text, varies somewhat in *Amos*. 5QAmos disagrees with the Masoretic Text twice. Florilegium disagrees with the Masoretic Text once in agreement with the citation of *Amos* 9.11 in the Damascus Document (CD vii.16).

The Hebrew text of *Obadiah* is attested in only two biblical manuscripts. As usual, 4QXII[g] stands quite close to the Masoretic Text. Minor Prophets Scroll (Mur 88) is somewhat independent.

The Hebrew text of the *Book of Jonah* is partially preserved in four biblical manuscripts. Greek Minor Prophets (8Ḥev 1) also preserves parts of the revised Greek text of the Septuagint. In the *Book of Jonah*, the texts of the Masoretic Text and the Septuagint are not far apart from each other. 4QXII[a] is independent. 4QXII[f], while small, may be proto-masoretic, as is 4QXII[g]. Minor Prophets (Mur 88) disagrees with the Masoretic Text twice.

The Hebrew text of the *Book of Micah* is attested in two biblical manuscripts and in two *pesharim*. Greek Minor Prophets preserves fragments of the revised text of the Septuagint. Witnesses both early and late preserve disagreements with the Masoretic Text in the *Book of Micah*. As usual, 4QXII[g] agrees with the proto-masoretic textual tradition against the Septuagint. 4QMic is a single, small fragment written in a script very similar to that of 4QXII[f]. It preserves a single unique reading which may be the result of exegetical activity. Minor Prophets (Mur 88) preserves two unique readings where the Septuagint and the proto-masoretic text agree with each other, and agrees with the Septuagint once against the proto-masoretic text in what is probably a secondary reading. Pesher Micah (1Q14) disagrees with both the proto-masoretic text and the Septuagint, which are in agreement. Pesher Micah? (4Q168) preserves only orthographic differences from the Masoretic Text. Catena[a] preserves only one reading where it disagrees with both the Masoretic Text and the Septuagint.

The Hebrew text of the *Book of Nahum* is attested in two biblical manuscripts and in one *pesher*. Parts of the revised text of the Septuagint are preserved in Greek Minor Prophets (8Ḥev 1). The two earliest witnesses to the Hebrew text of *Nahum*, 4QXII[g] and Minor Prophets (Mur 88), agree more frequently with the proto-masoretic tradition than with the Septuagint but all three witnesses preserve some variation from the Masoretic Text. Minor Prophets (Mur 88) was frequently corrected to agree with the Masoretic Text. Pesher Nahum (4Q169) disagrees with the Masoretic Text some thirty-two times. Some disagreements may originally have had a basis in orthographic differences, but developed beyond that. At least six times, Pesher Nahum (4Q169) agrees with the Septuagint and the Masoretic Text. There is also a pattern of corrections toward the Masoretic Text by a second hand.

The Hebrew text of the *Book of Habakkuk* is preserved partially in Minor Prophets (Mur 88) and in the pesher on *Habakkuk* found in Cave 1 near Qumran. Greek Minor Prophets (8Ḥev 1) also preserves part of the revised Septuagint text. There are few significant variants preserved in Minor Prophets (Mur 88). The reading in 3.10 (= Ps. 77.18) is well known. In his study of the text of Pesher Habakkuk (1QpHab), Brownlee examined over 160 variants. Many were orthographic in nature, but several were important variants although unsupported by other witnesses. The text of the Masoretic Text can be difficult and in some places is corrupt. Both of the Hebrew witnesses preserve some useful readings. Pesher Habukkuk is of great importance for the study of the biblical interpretation of the Qumran community.

The Hebrew text of the *Book of Zephaniah* is partially preserved in four biblical manuscripts and two *pesharim*. Greek Minor Prophets (8Ḥev 1) also preserves part of the revised Septuagint text. Both 4QXII[b] and 4QXII[g] stand closest to the proto-masoretic textual tradition in *Zephaniah*. In 4QXII[c] no significant variants are preserved. Minor Prophets (Mur 88) stands closer to the textual tradition found also in the Septuagint. The reading of Pesher Zephaniah (1Q15) is uncertain and the reading of the *pesher* in Cave 4 (4Q170) may reflect a variation in orthography.

The Hebrew text of the *Book of Haggai* is attested in three biblical manuscripts. 4QXII[b] preserves no variants. 4QXII[e] stands very close to the textual tradition found in the Septuagint. Minor Prophets (Mur 88) disagrees with both the Masoretic Text and the Septuagint once.

The Hebrew text of the *Book of Zechariah* is attested in three biblical manuscripts and in three commentaries. Greek Minor Prophets also preserves part of the revision of the Septuagint for *Zechariah*. The Hebrew text of *Zechariah* preserved in the Masoretic Text is relatively free of problems; however, the ancient manuscripts of the book are of value. 4QXII[e], the most ancient witness to the text, does offer some useful readings. It also illustrates the sometimes complex web of agreements and disagreements between manuscripts. The remaining witnesses are important for the history of exegesis.

The Hebrew text of the *Book of Malachi* is attested in two biblical manuscripts and in one *pesher*. 4QXII[a] is a somewhat idiosyncratic witness which is unaffiliated with either the Masoretic Text or the Septuagint. In *Malachi* it occasionally preserves readings of value in reconstructing an older form of the Hebrew text, as well as understanding the ancient exegesis of *Malachi*. Both 4QXII[c] and 5QpMal are of little interest or text-critical value.

There is a gap of nearly eight hundred years between Minor Prophets (Mur 88) and the next manuscript of the Twelve, the Cairo Codex. The Cairo Codex is a masoretic manuscript of the Ben Asher family. It includes vowels, accents, and Masora. The Aleppo Codex is only slightly younger (925 CE).

BIBLIOGRAPHY

Brownlee, William H. *The Midrash Pesher of Habakkuk*. SBLMS, 24. Missoula, Mont., 1979.

Cross, Frank Moore. *The Ancient Library of Qumran*. 3d ed. Minneapolis, 1995. A classic and valuable introduction to the study of Qumran and the importance of the manuscripts for the study of the Hebrew scriptures, early Judaism, and Christianity.

Fuller, Russell Earl. "The Minor Prophets Manuscripts from Qumran, Cave IV." In *Qumran Cave 4, X: The Prophets*, edited by E. Ulrich et al. Discoveries in the Judaean Desert, 15. Oxford, 1997.

Fuller, Russell Earl. "Text-Critical Problems in Malachi 2.10–16." *JBL* 110/1 (1991), 47–57.

Fuller, Russell Earl. "A Critical Note on Hosea 12.10 and 13.4" *Revue biblique* 98 (1991), 343–357.

Fuller, Russell Earl. "Textual Traditions in the Book of Hosea and the Minor Prophets." In *The Madrid Qumran Congress*, vol. 1. Edited by Julio Trebolle Barrera and Luis Vegas Montaner. Leiden, 1992.

Fuller, Russell Earl. "4QMicah: A Small Fragment of a Manuscript from Qumran, Cave IV." *Revue de Qumrân* 62 (1993), 193–202.

García Martínez, Florentino. *The Dead Sea Scrolls Translated*. 2d ed. Leiden, 1996.

Horgan, Maurya P. *Pesharim: Qumran Interpretations of Biblical Books*. Catholic Biblical Quarterly Monograph Series, 8. Washington, D.C., 1979. A thorough study of nearly all the *pesharim* with Hebrew text and analysis.

Tov, Emanuel. *The Greek Minor Prophets Scroll from Naḥal Ḥever (8ḤevXIIgr)*. Discoveries in the Judaean Desert, 8. Oxford, 1990.

Tov, Emanuel. *The Textual Criticism of the Hebrew Bible*. Minneapolis, 1992. An excellent reference work for the textual criticism of the Hebrew scriptures which takes account of the manuscripts from the Judean Desert.

RUSSELL FULLER

MIQTSAT MAʿASEI HA-TORAH (also known as the Halakhic Letter and by its abbreviation 4QMMT) purports to be a document sent by the leaders of the Qumran sect to the leaders of the priestly establishment in Jerusalem. The title of this text, which may be translated as "Some Precepts of the Torah," or "Some Rulings Pertaining to the Torah," was assigned by its editors as a description of its contents, based on phrases found at the beginning and the end of the text. As is the case with almost all the Qumran manuscripts, the text itself bears no title. This text, found in Cave 4 in six fragmentary manuscripts, outlines some twenty laws regarding sacrificial laws, priestly gifts, ritual purity, and other matters over which the writers disagree with the Jerusalem authorities. Stated in a polemical manner, these laws clearly represent the views of the founders of the sect as opposed to those of their opponents whom the sect calls upon to accept their views. The laws are set within a framework that may allow us to learn much about the ideology of those who authored the text and about the very origins of the Qumran sect itself.

Miqtsat Maʿasei ha-Torah (4QMMT) may be an actual document dating to the earliest days of the Qumran group, or it may have been written later to justify the sectarian schism with the Jerusalem establishment. The existence of six manuscripts of this composition testifies to the importance of this text to the sectarians. The earliest manuscripts date from the late Hasmonean to early Herodian period, that is, from the second half of the first century BCE.

The document played a particular role in the recent history of Dead Sea Scrolls research. The text had been known under the title 4QMishnique only, from a short quotation of one law by J. T. Milik (Discoveries in the Judaean Desert, 3, 1962, p. 225), until it was announced at the International Congress on Biblical Archaeology held in Jerusalem in 1984. Its announcement and description there by Elisha Qimron (Qimron and Strugnell, *Biblical Archaeology Today*), who had worked on the text with J. Strugnell, sparked immense interest and drove home the point that enormously important material still awaited scholarly discussion in the unpublished corpus of Qumran manuscripts. Ultimately, this announcement was a major factor stimulating the demand for release of the scrolls.

The unauthorized publication of Qimron and Strugnell's transcription and restoration of this text (Shanks, 1991, p. xxxi) led Qimron to sue Herschel Shanks, editor of the *Biblical Archaeology Review*. The lawsuit also focused attention on the significance of this text and on the issues of intellectual property surrounding the scrolls and other ancient texts.

The structure of the document can be divided into three parts: an introductory sentence stating the nature of the letter, a section listing the halakhic disagreements between the sect and the Jerusalem authorities, and a conclusion. In at least one of the manuscripts, this text was attached to a copy of the 364-day solar calendar known from other Qumran scrolls, such as *1 Enoch* and *Jubilees*. [*See* Calendars and Mishmarot].

The Calendar. It is questionable whether the calendar is really integral to the text of MMT, an issue that is connected with the physical reconstruction of the manuscript. A calendar was also attached to one of the manuscripts of the Rule of the Community from Cave 4. It is apparent that this calendrical list was not composed by the author of the MMT text but was imported as a unit into the text. The calendar mentions, in addition to the solar months, the specific extra day added after three months of thirty days at the equinoxes and solstices, and is organized in ninety-one-day quarters, which are the basic division of the year. It also mentions some extra festivals, such as the Festival of the New Wine on the third day of the fifth month, the Festival of the Fresh Oil on the twenty-second day of the sixth month, and the Festival of the Wood offering on the twenty-third day of the same month. All these are among the festivals associated with the solar calendar in the Temple Scroll.

The Introduction. The initial introductory sentence states that what follows are some of "our words" that are legal rulings "we hold to." These rulings concern only two topics, only one of which is legible—that is, the laws of ritual purity. The other topic, from the later list of laws, appears to introduce sacrificial offerings in the Temple.

List of Laws. In this section, the authors list about twenty matters of Jewish law that, they insist, are being violated by the Jerusalem establishment and have caused them to withdraw from Jerusalem and form their sect. This letter is proof that the major conflicts of Second Temple Judaism did not arise from theological disagreements such as messianism but from conflicts about the proper way to carry out Jewish law.

The following *halakhot* or halakhic topics are mentioned in the extant fragments of MMT:

1. Gentile wheat may not be brought into the Temple.
2. A fragmentary *halakhah* about the cooking of offerings.
3. Gentile sacrifices, also fragmentary.
4. Cereal offerings may not be left overnight.
5. The purity of those preparing the red cow.
6. The purity of hides.
7. The place of slaughtering and offering sacrifices.
8. Prohibition of the slaughter of pregnant animals.

9. Forbidden sexual unions.
10. The exclusion of the blind and deaf from the "purity of the Temple."
11. Impurity of liquid streams poured from one vessel into another.
12. Dogs may not enter Jerusalem.
13. The fruit of the fourth year is to be given to the priests.
14. The cattle tithe is to be given to the priests.
15. Purification rituals of the leper.
16. Impurity of human bones.
17. Marriages between priests and Israelites are forbidden.

The views of the author of MMT are representative of Sadducean *halakhah*. Some of the same laws are reported in the Mishnah (tractate *Yadayim*), and the views of our text are there attributed to the Sadducees. These *halakhot* are usually stricter than those of the Pharisees and later rabbis, and the author excoriates those who do not accept the sectarians' view.

Conclusion. Here the authors state that because of their strict observance of the previous laws according to their own opinion, they have separated themselves from the majority of the Jewish people and from their observances. The sectarians write the addressee in the singular form asking him to investigate the words of the Torah and see that they must be observed according to the sectarian interpretation. For he must know that the biblical kings were blessed when they followed the word of God and cursed when they transgressed. The addressee is urged to repent and spare his nation misfortune.

To whom is this letter addressed? The text alternates between the second person singular and the plural. When in the second person singular, the manuscript assumes that it is addressing a leader who can, by virtue of his position, identify with the kings of Israel. It appears that the head of the Jerusalem establishment with such status must be the high priest during Hasmonean times.

Miqtsat Maʿasei ha-Torah has wide ramifications for the history of Judaism in the Hasmonean period. In the disputes mentioned in the letter, the opinions of the opponents of the sect are those attributed in rabbinic literature to the Pharisees or the *tanna'im* (Mishnaic rabbis). When tannaitic texts preserve a Pharisee–Sadducee conflict mentioned in MMT, the view of the sectarians coincides with that of the Sadducees. For example, the specifics of the required state of purity of the one who prepared the ashes of the red cow according to our text are mentioned in rabbinic sources as being the custom of the Sadducean priests in the Temple. This phenomenon can be explained by seeing the earliest members of the sect as Sadducees who were unwilling to accept the suppression of the Zadokite high priests in the aftermath of the Maccabean Revolt (168–164 BCE). Some of the disaffected Zadokites separated from the high priests in Jerusalem and formed the sect. The sect often refers to itself as the Sons of Zadok. The polemics of the Halakhic Letter are addressed to their Sadducean brethren who stayed in the Jerusalem Temple and accepted the new order, following the Pharisaic rulings, and no longer practiced the old Sadducean teachings. This document dates from the earliest stage of the development of the Qumran sect at which time the sectarians still hoped to reconcile with the Jerusalem priesthood. Later on, sectarian writings, having abandoned that hope, are filled with radical tendencies, animated polemics, and hatred for outsiders.

The Halakhic Letter demonstrates that the sect is not linked to the Hasidim, supposedly a second-century BCE group that was opposed to Hellenism and was devoted to the strict observance of ritual law. Any attempt to see the sect as emerging from some subgroup of the Pharisees must also be rejected. Similarly, they cannot be placed at the center of the Judaism of the Second Temple but are definitely a particular sect. The dominant Essene hypothesis must take into account the originally Sadducean sectarians who perhaps had gone through a process of radicalization and became a distinct sect.

There is no question that the origin of the community that collected these scrolls was in a sectarian conflict that sustained the community throughout its existence. Miqtsat Maʿasei ha-Torah preserves evidence that this conflict was with those in control of the Jerusalem Temple under Hasmonean rule. The library at Qumran was collected by a subgroup of society in opposition to the political and religious authorities of the time.

From MMT we learn the reasons for the schism. Up to now we had no explicit evidence on this subject. Josephus gives the impression that the sects were primarily divided over theological questions, but his explanation was designed to appeal to Greek and Roman readers. Only matters of practice are mentioned in MMT. This list of *halakhot* proves how important were matters of Jewish law, particularly purity regulations, as sources of schism within Judaism of the period.

The contribution of MMT to our knowledge of the history and character of the *halakhah* of the various groups in the period is of the highest importance. The text polemicizes strongly against another group that is the predecessor of the rabbis, hence probably the Pharisees. It helps to prove that some Pharisaic laws are older than once thought. This text allows us to date a number of practices known only from later rabbinic literature in the Second Temple period.

Relationship to Other Dead Sea Scrolls. The text of Miqtsat Ma'asei ha-Torah has much in common with various documents of the Qumran corpus. Its appearance along with the 364-day sectarian calendar of solar months and solar years gives the impression that the authors of MMT accepted this calendar. MMT shares a variety of sacrificial laws and the same ritual calendar with the Temple Scroll. These parallels are no doubt to be traced to the common Sadducean legal substratum that they share, although these texts are not literarily interdependent. The Damascus Document also shares many common principles with the legal section of MMT. Here again, no literary relationship can be shown, only a relationship of content.

The Florilegium from Cave 4 also preserves some common legal rulings with Miqtsat Ma'asei ha-Torah, although they are not literarily dependent on one another. Miqtsat Ma'asei ha-Torah exhibits no parallels with the Rule of the Community or other such documents representing the teachings of the sect after it reached maturity.

These conclusions are consistent with the view that Miqtsat Ma'asei ha-Torah reflects the formative period of the Qumran sect. It therefore shares legal rulings with the sources of the Temple Scroll and the early laws of the Damascus Document. At the same time, it reflects the ideology of parts of the Temple Scroll. While the earlier Miqtsat Ma'asei ha-Torah and the Temple Scroll lack the language of sectarian antagonism, this tone is found in the Damascus Document, which was completed after the split was final and which reflects the sectarian animus that would characterize the later documents of the Qumran group.

Language. Another important area of research regarding discovery, which stems from the fact that 4QMMT represents the early history of the Qumran sect, is the analysis of its language. Milik, in discussing the Hebrew of the Copper Scroll, identified the language of this text as being Mishnaic Hebrew (Discoveries in the Judaean Desert, 3, p. 222), as a result of the large number of nouns found in it that are known from tannaitic usage. In actuality, this is an oversimplification, since the morphology and syntax resemble in many respects that of the Qumran sectarian texts. Accordingly, we can state that this document indicates that much of the halakhic vocabulary known from later tannaitic texts was already known in this period, even to those who used Qumran linguistic forms, and that certain of the characteristic elements of Mishnaic Hebrew already existed at an earlier period and influenced the usage even of the sectarians.

BIBLIOGRAPHY

Baumgarten, Joseph M. "The Pharisaic-Sadducean Controversies about Purity and the Qumran Texts." *Journal of Jewish Studies* 31 (1980), 157–170. The first study to identify a parallel between MMT and Sadducean law.

Baumgarten, Joseph M. "The 'Halakha' in Miqṣat Ma'ase ha-Torah (MMT)." *Journal of the American Oriental Society* 116 (1996), 512–516. Review essay on Qimron and Strugnell, *Qumran Cave 4, V.* Discoveries in the Judaean Desert, 10.

Qimron, Elisha, and John Strugnell. "An Unpublished Halakhic Letter from Qumran." In *Biblical Archaeology Today: Proceedings of the International Congress on Biblical Archaeology, Jerusalem, April 1984*, edited by Janet Amitai, pp. 400–407. Jerusalem, 1985. First announcement of the character and significance of MMT.

Qimron, Elisha, and John Strugnell. "An Unpublished Halakhic Letter from Qumran." *Israel Museum Journal* 4 (1985), 9–12. Popular report on Miqtsat Ma'asei ha-Torah and its importance.

Qimron, Elisha, and John Strugnell. *Qumran Cave 4, V: Miqṣat Ma'aśe ha-Torah.* Discoveries in the Judaean Desert, 10. Oxford, 1994. Official edition and thorough study of the text, its law, language, and historical significance.

Reading 4QMMT: New Perspectives on Qumran Law and History, edited by John Kampen and Moshe J. Bernstein. SBL Symposium series, 2. Atlanta, 1996. Volume of important studies showing direction in which research on this text can be expected to go.

Schiffman, Lawrence H. "Miqṣat Ma'ase ha-Torah and the Temple Scroll." *Revue de Qumrân* 14 (1990), 435–457. Detailed comparison of parallel laws in 4QMMT and 11QT showing the shared halakhic heritage of these works.

Schiffman, Lawrence H. "The New Halakhic Letter (4QMMT) and the Origins of the Dead Sea Sect." *Biblical Archaeologist* 53 (1990), 64–73. Significance of Miqtsat Ma'asei ha-Torah for history of the Qumran sect.

Shanks, Hershel. "Publisher's Forward." In *A Facsimile Edition of the Dead Sea Scrolls*, prepared with an introduction and index by Robert H. Eisenman and James M. Robinson, pp. xii–xlv. Washington, D.C., 1991. Publication of 4QMMT in the edition of Qimran and Strugnell without permission or attribution to Qimron, sparking lawsuit.

Sussman, Yaakov. "Ḥeqer Toledot ha-Halakhah u-Megillot Midbar Yehudah: Hirhurim Talmudiyim Rishonim le-'Or Megillat Miqtsat Ma'ase ha-Torah." *Tarbiz* 59 (1989/90), 11–77. Pioneering study of the *halakhah* of Miqtsat Ma'asei ha-Torah and its significance for history of Jewish law in the Second Temple period. English translation in Discoveries in the Judaean Desert, 10, pp. 179–200.

LAWRENCE H. SCHIFFMAN

MIQVA'OT. Man-made installations constructed according to several regulations, *miqva'ot* ("ritual baths"; singular, *miqveh* [literally, "a gathering of water"]) were made to enable the observant Jew to purify himself, when necessary, through full immersion (*ṭevilah*) of the nude body in water. This ritual act was different from the simple process of washing or cleansing the body (which was performed in a bathtub situated in the bathroom), although at a certain time, washing of the body before the *ṭevilah* became a prerequisite, as a measure taken in order to keep the immersion waters as clean as possible.

The earliest practical regulations concerning ritual purity are presented, in a somewhat condensed manner, in *Leviticus* (especially chapters 11–15), dating perhaps to early postexilic times. As the requirements for purification were limited and the population small, natural water sources, like springs and sporadic water concentrations that formed after heavy rains, satisfied the needs of the Jewish population. About the mid-second century BCE, when these purification locations were not sufficient, the *miqveh* was introduced in Judea.

The main written sources for this subject in the rabbinic (Pharisaic) literature are the tractates *Miqva'ot* in the Mishnah and Tosefta. These *halakhot* ("laws") are not composed as a manual to instruct the builder of a *miqveh* but are discussions of solved problems relating to the use of these installations.

Physical Characteristics. Attention was drawn to this type of installation in the excavations carried out in the Jewish quarter of Jerusalem (1969 onward), where in the bathrooms located in the basements of every private house, plastered and stepped water installations were discovered, dated to the first centuries BCE and the first century CE, down to 70 CE. My recent study has demonstrated their identification with the *miqva'ot* known from the rabbinic literature.

So that the waters of the *miqveh* would possess the intrinsic power of purification, they had to meet a number of regulations. The waters had to be gathered in the *miqveh* without direct human intervention (waters from "divine hands"). This implies rainwater flowing by gravity from the roof and courtyard of a house into a *miqveh*. Rainwater drawn with a bucket from a nearby cistern and poured into a *miqveh* does not qualify for purification, as it is in the "hands of man." For this reason, *miqva'ot* were cut or built into the ground and were not precast vessels. A minimum water volume of 40 *se'ah* (estimates fall between 0.5 and 1.0 cubic meters) was required with a minimum depth of 3 cubits (approximately 1.2 to 1.5 meters [4.0 to 4.9 feet]).

That the waters in the *miqveh* should be stationary, that is, not flowing, implied that no leakage through cracks in the walls should have occurred. This last requirement was clearly met with multiple coatings of plaster, so typical of the excavated *miqva'ot*. Tractate *Miqva'ot* neither refers to the provision for steps (which are, in fact, a common architectural element in the excavated installations, as such a requirement is self-evident) nor mentions any hint of a fixed number of steps.

Rainwater with a volume greater than 40 *se'ah* was regarded by the Pharisaic *halakhah* as possessing the power to purify people, vessels (with the exception of pottery vessels), and even impure (i.e., drawn) waters. This regulation is of a somewhat axiomatic nature, and it meant that these waters were not susceptible to any sort of impurity as long as they maintained the natural features of water and their volume did not diminish below 40 *se'ah*.

A man-made water installation is one in which the lower part is cut in bedrock while the upper part is built and roofed over with a barrel-shaped vault, or, alternatively, hewn completely out of bedrock. Its average measurements are 2 by 4 meters (6.6 by 13.1 feet). The steps, which usually occupy the entire width of the installation, have a comfortable height of approximately 25 to 30 centimeters (9.8 to 11.7 inches), with the exception of the lowest step, which descends to the bottom and has a height of 60 to 70 centimeters (23.4 to 27.3 inches). To overcome this elevation, one, two, or three small auxiliary steps were provided at the bottom. The tread of the steps varies in depth. In many cases, a deep step of 0.5 to 0.7 meters (1.6 feet to 2.3 feet) alternates with two or three steps of normal (0.3 meter [1 foot]) depth. Another type of installation (common at Jericho) has a narrow staircase attached to one or two sides of the basin. Rainwater was collected from the roof or stone-paved courtyard and diverted directly into these installations, either through the opening or by means of a gutter that pierced the built vault. Another means of providing a *miqveh* on a permanent basis was by spring waters, as in Hasmonean Jericho, or with winter runoff rain water as in Qumran, both using an aqueduct as means of conveyance. [*See* Qumran, *article on* Archaeology.]

A certain type of stepped and plastered water installation has been excavated in large numbers (over three hundred known, over one hundred fifty of them from Jerusalem) in sites dating to the Second Temple period. Domestic *miqva'ot* excavated in Jerusalem have been found in each private house. Others have been revealed in the palaces and mansions of the Hasmonean and Herodian dynasties in Jericho, Masada, and Herodium, as well as in other locations. [*See* Herodium; Masada, *article on* Archaeology.] Also in Jerusalem a large number of *miqva'ot* were found adjacent to the gates located on the southern and western walls of the Temple mount, made for the public who were entering the mount on the Jewish holidays and were obliged to do so in compliance with the purity regulations. [*See* Jerusalem.]

Another location in which *miqva'ot* were anticipated, in the light of rabbinic sources, was within rural areas with evidence of agricultural industry. Indeed, stepped installations are often discovered in very close proximity to ancient oil or wine presses dating to the Second Temple period. It is the strict observance of regulations related to the handling of fruits that calls for extreme purity: fruits that were picked and pressed to yield fluids (oil, wine) become susceptible to ritual impurity. Also, priestly families could consume tithes only in a state of purity.

In addition to the standard *miqveh*, several variant types evolved, one of which deserves special mention: a *miqveh* that was equipped with two adjacent openings, instead of the normal single opening and/or a low partition (10 to 30 centimeters [3.9 to 11.7 inches] high), built or cut from bedrock, dividing the staircase into two lanes separating the descending impure person from undesired contact with the ascending pure person (cf. M. *Sheq.* 2.8).

The chief operational problem in maintaining a *miqveh* was to guarantee a constant supply of pure waters for immersion throughout the year. With a long rainless season prevailing at least from April to November, this poses a very grave difficulty in the Land of Israel. The *miqva'ot* are filled with rainwater during the first rainstorms of the year. However, as a minimal volume of 40 *se'ah* has the intrinsic power to purify persons, most utensils, and also drawn waters, an easy solution to maintain the pure waters was simply to add drawn waters to the *miqveh* on occasion, provided that the water level at the moment of addition was higher than 40 *se'ah*. In this case, any new amount of drawn, and therefore impure, waters would have been purified instantaneously. It is my opinion that this was the common way to tackle this problem, although it is not evident in the archaeological record.

When the waters of a *miqveh* became dirty or stagnant (which does not necessarily imply that they are impure) to such an extent that even the addition of drawn water would not improve their quality, they had to be changed. As there is no direct way to feed an empty *miqveh* with pure waters drawn from a nearby cistern (although the cistern water is in effect rainwater), this becomes an acute problem. In the large private houses and mansions in Jerusalem, which usually included several *miqva'ot*, a defiled *miqveh* did not raise any problem. The other installations would have sufficed through the dry season.

In several sites in the Judean Desert, which could afford only a small number of *miqva'ot*, an operational device was introduced based on the principle mentioned in the Mishnah that any body of water linked to the waters of a valid *miqveh* becomes equally pure. In several sites (Masada, Herodium, Jericho, and a few cases in Jerusalem) a pair of *miqva'ot* were excavated, linked at their rim by a pipe or channel initially filled with pure rainwater. One installation was not used for ritual immersion (in later times this installation was termed *otsar* ["treasury"]). When the waters of the other frequently used installation became filthy, they were simply drawn out of the *miqveh*. Clean waters were drawn from a nearby cistern and poured into the *miqveh*. The moment the stopper was pulled from the pipe connecting the installations and a momentary contact occurred between the two bodies of water, the *miqveh* became valid. It was the waters of the treasury, which possess the power to purify additional amounts of drawn waters, that purified the freshly drawn waters. This procedure could be repeated as often as required. It made it possible for those who used *miqva'ot* regularly in an arid area to use waters that were as clean and pure as possible. This method, which was only rarely used in the Second Temple period, is obligatory today.

As common as *miqva'ot* were in private houses of the Second Temple period, they were completely absent in contemporary non-Jewish private houses of the same period. Apart from Jewish inscriptions and symbols, the *miqveh* was the only architectural element within the private house that might point to the Jewish identity of the owners.

After the destruction of Jerusalem and the Temple in 70 CE, the needs for ritual purity were minimized considerably, resulting in the sharp decline in the number of *miqva'ot* in use, as attested by the archaeological record. From an average frequency of two to three installations per private house, as found in Jerusalem, the number declined to one to two *miqva'ot* per village or neighborhood. This relatively small number also was present later, in the Jewish neighborhoods in the towns of medieval Europe.

Miqva'ot at Khirbet Qumran. The architectural element at Khirbet Qumran that catches the eye more than anything else is the seeming abundance of water installations, sealed with watertight plaster. These installations were fed with runoff waters collected in the winter from the nearby Wadi Qumran and diverted to the settlement by an aqueduct. [*See* Water Systems.]

De Vaux, in the French edition of his book on Qumran (1961), defined all water installations as functioning for storage. In the English edition (1973) he concluded that installations 138 and 68 (following de Vaux's numbers) were used as baths but not for a ritualistic immersion. All the rest were still considered installations for storage. Wood (1984) has demonstrated that the volume of the stepless installations (numbers 58, 91, and 110) was sufficient to support a population of approximately two hundred persons and their livestock, and he has concluded that the stepped installations were constructed for a "nonutilitarian purpose," that is, cultic immersion. [*See* Cisterns and Reservoirs.]

At least ten stepped water installations were excavated in Qumran, six of which (138, 118, 117, 56, 48, and 71) are very similar (in plan, architectural details, and workmanship) to installations found in Jerusalem, Judea, and Galilee that undoubtedly served as *miqva'ot*. This analogy proves clearly that the Qumran installations were a local type or adaptation of the standard *miqveh*. Moreover, the Qumran installations resemble more closely the Jerusalem type than the type frequently used in the neighboring town of Jericho, meaning that they follow a Jerusalem architectural tradition.

Despite the resemblance there are some technical differences. The Qumran installations are considerably larger (at least twice the volume) than the Jerusalem installations, and some are provided with two to four vertical, parallel, small partitions on the upper part of their staircases (versus a single central partition, if at all, in Jerusalem). Four other installations (85, 83, 68, and 69) are also stepped installations but of a smaller size and somewhat irregular shape. They might have been used for ritual immersion of a different type (of household utensils?).

The abundance of installations is not unique to Qumran. It is of the same order of magnitude found in Jerusalem (in the private houses of the Upper City and near the gates of the Temple mount). It should also be taken into account that not all installations were used simultaneously but reflect a long period of time in which they were built and might have been used consecutively (e.g., number 48 went out of use due to the severe crack caused by an earthquake).

In the event that Qumran was indeed the site of the sect of the scrolls, it should be stressed that few *halakhot* mentioned in the scrolls refer directly to the practical and perhaps technical aspects of ritual immersion. The Rule of the Community (1QS v.13) mentions the use of water purification, and the verb used, *bo'* (to "enter" the water), alludes to a total immersion. The Damascus Document (CD x.10–11) regulates that a ritual immersion (using the root *rḥts*) is prohibited in filthy water. It also requires that the immersion be total (the body should be covered), which differs from the Pharisaic requirement that included definite minimal measurements of water for purification. It further prohibits the use of "vessel waters" (i.e., water drawn with the help of a vessel) and suggests that immersion was carried out in waters gathered in a natural cavity (*geve'*; CD x.11–12). The different types of waters mentioned in the Rule of the Community (1QS iii.4–5) might indicate that in addition to the waters of seas and rivers, the purification waters were termed *mei raḥats*. [*See* Damascus Document *and* Rule of the Community.]

[*See also* Archaeology.]

BIBLIOGRAPHY

Avigad, Nahman. *Discovering Jerusalem*. Nashville, 1983. See especially pages 139–143. Describes the *miqva'ot* discovered in the private houses of the Upper City of Jerusalem from the Second Temple period.

de Vaux, Roland. *L'archéologique et les manuscrits de la Mer Morte*. London, 1961.

de Vaux, Roland. *Archaeology and the Dead Sea Scrolls*. London, 1973.

Netzer, Ehud. "Ancient Ritual Baths (Miqva'ot) in Jericho." *Jerusalem Cathedra* 2 (1982), 106–119. Describes the ritual baths found in the Hasmonean and Herodian palaces excavated in Jericho.

Reich, Ronny. "The Hot Bath-House (*balneum*), the Miqweh and the Jewish Community in the Second Temple Period." *Journal of Jewish Studies* 39 (1988), 102–107. Describes the introduction of both institutions, bathhouse and ritual bath, into the Jewish community and their interrelations.

Reich, Ronny. *Miqwa'ot (Jewish Ritual Immersion Baths) in Eretz-Israel in the Second Temple and Mishnah and Talmud Periods*. Jerusalem, 1990 (3 vols., in Hebrew with English abstract). First comprehensive study on the subject, including corpus of installations. Ph.D. dissertation.

Wood, B. G. "To Dip or to Sprinkle? The Qumran Cisterns in Perspective." *Bulletin of the American Schools of Oriental Research* 256 (1984), 45–60. Offers a quantitative analysis of the water installations of Qumran in relation to its population, and defines some of these as used for cultic purposes.

RONNY REICH

MIRD, KHIRBET. The name of a ruin located on top of an isolated hill in the Judean Desert, 248 meters above sea level and some 200 meters above Buqeia, Khirbet Mird (el Mird [Ar.]) is approached from the west along a saddle that was narrowed by rock cutting. The saddle carried a path and an aqueduct. The literary designation of el Mird is a corruption of the Syriac-Aramaic word *marda*, meaning "fortress," synonymous with the Greek Kastellion, the name of a famous Byzantine monastery erected in the late fifth century over the ruined Hasmonean-Herodian fortress of Hyrcania. This fortress gave the ruin its later names: Kastellion, Marda, and el Mird. The Greek Kastellion is derived from *castellum*, the Latin term for "fortress." The identification of Khirbet Mird with Hyrcania and Kastellion was first suggested by K. Furrer in 1880 and was accepted by most scholars.

History. Hyrcania is first mentioned by Josephus (*Jewish Antiquities* XIII, 417) as one of the three fortresses retained by Shelamzion Alexandra (r. 76–67 BCE). It may have been erected by Alexander Jannaeus or perhaps even in the time of his father, John Hyrcanus I, after whom the fortress was named. It was destroyed by Gabinius, the Roman governor of Syria, in 57 BCE (*Antiquities* XIV, 89; *The Jewish War* I, 160–170); Herod captured the fortress in 34 BCE, rebuilt it, and made it into a detention site for his political opponents, many of whom were executed and buried there, including his son Antipater (*The Jewish War* I, 364,664; *Antiquities* XV, 365–367, XVI, 13). The name Hyrcania does not appear in the literary sources after the death of Herod.

In 492 CE a *coenobium* ("monastery"), called Kastellion, was erected on the site by Saint Sabas. [*See* Monasteries.] Our chief sources for the history of this monastery in the late fifth and sixth centuries are the hagiographies, mainly *The Life of Euthymius* and *The Life of Sabas*, written by Cyril of Scythopolis (died ca. 559). Kastellion was a dependency of the Great Laura of Saint Sabas (today Mar Saba) in the Kidron Valley (Wadi en-Nar), and it was headed by an administrator (*dioiketes*) and his assistant, who had succeeded him in the administration. The administrators up to the year 559 were Paul, Theodore, Sergius, and another Paul, successively. John Moschus (*Leimonarion* 167, 3033) mentions Abba Agathonicus, an abbot of Kastellion. The site was a *coenobium* for older monks who excelled in their way of life and a place where monks who misbehaved were sent. The monastery had a stable and beasts of burden, and it owned two hostelries, purchased by Sabas, one in Jericho and a second in Jerusalem. Papyri dating from the seventh to tenth centuries discovered at the site attest that it survived the Persian invasion of 614 and the Arab conquest of 638. The monastery is mentioned in the eighth-century *Life of Stephen the Sabaite*, indicating that to the end of the eighth century it was still an active monastery. In approximately 749 is was headed for a short while by Zacharias, the uncle of Stephen and a monk of the Great Laura. In 1355 an icon was brought to Mar Saba from Kastellion as is attested by a Greek inscription on the back of that icon. However, it is doubtful whether a community of monks, rather than a single anchorite, was still occupying the site at such a late date. John Phocas, who had passed close to Khirbet Mird on his way to Mar Saba in 1185, did not mention this monastery.

In 1923, the site was reoccupied by monks from the Mar Saba monastery. They cleared the ruins of the church and set up a chapel in an ancient burial cave. They, in turn, abandoned the site in 1931 because of security problems, and their buildings were destroyed by bedouin.

Exploration. Khirbet Mird/Hyrcania has not yet been excavated. Data concerning its ruins are based on surveys and mapping. The site was first surveyed by the British Palestine Exploration Fund in 1873. In 1877, Conrad Schick prepared a map of the site and its surroundings. A. E. Mader studied the frescoes in the Christian burial cave during five visits to the site between 1913 and 1927 and also published various finds discovered there (1929 and 1937). Following the discovery by bedouin in July 1952 of inscribed papyri, a Belgian expedition from Louvain University, headed by R. de Langhe, arrived at the site in the spring of 1953. The expedition discovered texts written on papyrus and parchment in Palestinian Aramaic, Greek, and Arabic. In April 1960, an expedition headed by G. R. H. Wright investigated the site, measured the structures on the hilltop, and excavated some of the burials found at the foot of the hill east of Hyrcania, as well as a watchtower incorporated into the fortress's circumvallation (Wright, 1961). This circumvallation was reidentified and surveyed in 1973 by Zeev Meshel, on behalf of the Institute of Archaeology at Tel Aviv University. The water supply system was studied in 1971 by Yosef Feldman, on behalf of the Society for the Protection of Nature in Israel. As part of the survey of the Mar Saba region, on behalf of the Archaeological Survey of Israel, I further investigated the site and the water supply system, and resurveyed the structures on the hilltop.

Remains. The structure on the hilltop was erected on a leveled area (25 meters by 40 meters) supported by subterranean vaults used as cisterns. The structure consists of rooms located on the north, east, and west around a central courtyard. The bottom courses of the walls, preserved in the east and north, were ashlars with drafted margins and a smoothed face laid as headers and stretchers. These are typical Herodian features at the site. Some stones also have a prominent central boss characteristic of Hasmonean masonry. The base of a heart-shaped column also was found. On the south, the boundary is a Herodian retaining wall, with several monastic cells abutting its eastern edge. The fence enclosing the hilltop today is from a later period, but under it a mass of stones set into mortar is visible, especially on the west. These stones probably belong to a glacis that was part of the fortress defenses. A cemetery from the Herodian period was found at the foot of the hill on the east, and an Aramaic inscription, published by Joseph Naveh, may have come from there. The circumvallation is well preserved, especially on the south, west, and east. Meshel is of the opinion that it was built during Herod's siege of Hyrcania, which had been taken by a sister of Antigonus (Josephus, *The Jewish War* I, 364).

The Byzantine monks settled in the structure on the hilltop and transformed its northeastern part into a chapel (5.5 meters by 16 meters) with a white mosaic floor and a roof supported by two arches. The room south of the chapel was paved with a colorful mosaic. The square central panel (2.4 meters by 2.4 meters) bears a floral design of leaflets forming diamonds. This is framed by a guilloche and running wave motifs 0.52 meters wide. A smaller panel has birds. The western wing of the summit structure, which had two openings to the courtyard, is still full of debris. Presumably this was the refectory. A Byzantine burial cave was excavated on the west side on a lower level. Eight pit graves were recorded under its white mosaic floor. Additional graves were built into the walls of the cave. The cave's plastered walls are covered with frescoes depicting thirty-six saints, most of them monks from the Judean Desert. Twenty-five can be identified by Greek inscriptions flanking their heads. On the west wall are Saints Euthymius, Athanasius, Thallelaius, and Martyrius; on the south wall Lazarus, Basilius, Arsenius, Timotheus, Symeon, Palladius, Johannes, Theoctistus, and Georgius Chozibites; on the east wall Abraamius, Marcianus, Theoctistus, Macarius, Moises, Theodosius, Paulus, Stephanus, Isidorus, and Arcadius; and on the north wall Johannes and Xenophon. Mader and other scholars had suggested that these frescoes should be dated to the eleventh or twelfth century CE, but since there is no evidence that the monastery continued to exist so late, they might be attributed to a time as early as the sixth or early seventh century. Also found on the walls are graffiti in Greek, Arabic, and Syriac. There also is a burial inscription engraved on a tombstone for a monk named Andraos.

The finds in the monastery included a baptismal font that was discovered south of the chapel, along with three marble screen posts, decorated with vine tendrils, issuing from an amphora, and fragments of two screen plates, one ornamented with lilies between its branches, surrounded by an acanthus wreath, and the other with a relief of a deer. Also found were a fragment of an altar post, a Byzantine stone sundial, and the cover of a reliquary. An icon kept in the Mar Saba monastery depicts Jesus as Pantokrator with Mary and John the Baptist flanking him and the twelve Apostles around them. On its back it bears a Greek inscription that records that it was brought there in 1355 from Kastellion by a monk named Paulus. This is the latest evidence of a monk's residing in or visiting Kastellion. The papyri found in cistern K1 and graffiti on the walls of several cisterns indicate that the monks turned them into dwelling cells.

Written Documents. There are two sets of Arabic papyri, two sets of Greek papyri, and a smaller group of Greek and Syriac (or Christian Palestinian Aramaic) documents written on papyri or parchment. The Arabic papyri have been published by Adolf Grohmann (1963), who took them from thirty-one plates in the Palestine Archaeological Museum (Rockefeller Museum) and thirty-six plates found by the Belgian Archaeological Mission. They consist of one hundred texts from the first two centuries of the Hegira, most of them fragmentary, including a passage from the Koran. They are designated APHM 1 through 100. Yet many of the smaller fragments remain unpublished. Most of the texts were written by Muslims, and only four were written by or intended for Christians. Thematically the texts are divided into seven groups: APHM 1 through 7 are protocols, three of them bilingual; APHM 8 and 9 are legal texts; and APHM 10 through 32 are official letters, APHM 23 being a letter to the governor. APHM 35 through 41 are economic texts, and APHM 42 through 70 are private letters, 45 and 46 being correspondence between Anba Magnille, possibly the abbot of Kastellion, and a Muslim named Habban ibn Yusuf. These letters indicate the close relations between the monks and the Muslim population of the area. APHM 71 through 73 are literary texts, and the rest, APHM 74 through 99, are minor fragments of various kinds. APHM 100 is a fragment of a drawing. Of the Syriac or Christian Palestinian Aramaic papyri, only a letter (papMird A), written in the seventh century by a monk named Gabriel to the head of the Mar Saba laura (*lwr* in the Syriac script), a magic amulet (MirdAmul cpa), and two fragments from the *Acts of the Apostles* (Mird Acts cpa; *Acts* 10.28–29, 10.32–41) have been published. Among the other Christian Palestinian Aramaic texts reported are fragments from the *Gospel of Luke* (3.1, 3.3–4), the *Gospel of Matthew* (21.30–34), the *Acts of the Apostles* (10.36–41), the *Letter to the Colossians* (1.16–18, 1.20–21), and the *Book of Joshua* (22.6–7, 22.9–10). The last three hitherto were unknown in Syriac. The publication of the Greek texts found by the Belgian mission was assigned by de Langhe to J. van Haelst, who has published five texts. The Greek documents include passages from *Matthew* (20.23–25, 20.30–31), *Mark* (2.3–5, 2.8–9, 6.30–31, 6.33–34, 6.36–37, 6.39–41), *John* (17.3, 17.7–8), *Acts of the Apostles* (11.29–12.5), and a monastic letter. Five plates of fragmentary documents in the archives of the Rockefeller Museum in Jerusalem, designated Nar 1 through 5 (Wadi En-Nar), perhaps originated at Khirbet Mird.

Water Supply System. Of the twenty-one rock-cut cisterns, six are on the hilltop, three are on the eastern slope, and twelve are on the southern slope, eight on the upper level and four on the lower level. One of the summit cisterns, with a wide staircase and a vault, presumably served as a *miqveh*. Another graded and more spacious *miqveh* was on the southern slope. Two open water reservoirs are situated at the foot of the fortress to the west, north of the aqueduct bridge. Another reservoir may have been dug south of the bridge. The cisterns and reservoirs are plastered with white lime and fine gravel plaster laid directly on bedrock. Their combined capacity was 20,000 square meters. Rows of rock-cut benches above the east side of the northernmost reservoir suggest that it may also have functioned as a swimming pool. Water was supplied from the west by two aqueducts, plastered along their entire length, that collected runoff water. The course of both aqueducts followed the contours of the hill; some parts were rock cut and some were masonry built or supported by retaining walls. The shorter aqueduct, coming from the northwest, was probably built in the Hasmonean period. It issued from a dam in Wadi Abu Shu'ala (Naḥal Sakekah) that drains the eastern slope of el-Muntar, the highest peak in the Judean Desert, and is approximately 1,950 meters long. A cross is carved in the rock near the dam, suggesting that this line was reused by the monks. The longer aqueduct, arriving from the southwest, begins in Naḥal Kidron and meanders 9 kilometers, crossing some deep ravines on high bridges on its way. Both aqueducts merge into a single channel on a saddle 750 meters west of Hyrcania; beyond that point, the aqueduct runs along another three bridges crossing the three saddles. The most impressive and highest of these is the eastern one, which is built with the isodomic technique of identical courses that are graded upward. The four lower courses, which are visible on the north side and date to the Hasmonean period, are built headers above stretchers and have drafted margins and a central boss. The upper courses, laid as alternating headers and stretchers, have drafted margins and a smoothed face, typical of Herodian masonry.

The Byzantine aqueduct is identifiable by its reddish plaster. Sections of this aqueduct were exposed next to the westernmost of the three bridges west of Khirbet Mird and at the head of the easternmost bridge (which in the Byzantine period was lower by 6.3 meters than in the Second Temple period). Between these two points, the aqueduct runs along a course parallel to the earlier one, but on a lower level and to the north of it. Thus, the Byzantine aqueduct could fill only the cisterns of the lower level. Indeed, in the excavation carried out next to the steps of cistern C, on the upper level, fragments of Herodian jars and lamps were recovered, together with a coin of the same period, but no later shards were found.

BIBLIOGRAPHY

Baillet, Maurice. "Un livret magique en christo-palestinien à l'Université de Louvain." *Muséon* 76 (1963), 375–401.

Grohmann, Adolf. *Arabic Papyri from Ḫirbet el-Mird*. In *Bibliothèque du Muséon*, vol. 52. Louvain, 1963.

Haelst, J. Van. "Cinq Texts Provenant de Khirbet Mird." *Ancient History* 22 (1991), 297–317.

Kister, Menahem J. "On a Fragment of a Private Letter of the First Century A.H." *Jerusalem Studies in Arabic and Islam* 3 (1981–1982), 237–240.

Kister, Menahem J. "On an Early Fragment of the Quran." In *Studies in Judaica, Karaitica and Islamica Presented to L. Nemoy*, pp. 163–166. Ramat-Gan, Israel, 1982.

Mader, A. E. "Sechsunddreissig Heiligengemälde in einer Gräberhöhle von Khirbet el-Merd in der Wüste Judäa." *Das Heilige Land* 72 (1928), 33–52, Taf.I.

Mader, A. E. "Conical Sundials and Ikon Inscription from the Kastellion Monastery on Khirbet el-Merd in the Wilderness of Juda." *Journal of the Palestine Oriental Society* (1929), 122–135.

Mader, A. E. "Ein Bilderzyklus in der Gräberhöhle der St. Euthymios-Laura auf Mardes (Chirbet el-Mard) in der Wüste Judäa." *Oriens Christianus* 34 (1937), 27–58, 192–212.

Marti, Karl. "Mittheilungen von Baurath C. Schick über die alten Lauren und Klöster in der Wüste Juda." *Zeitschrift des Deutschen Palästina-Vereins* 3 (1880), 1–43.

Milik, Józef T. "Une inscription et une lettre en arameén christo-palestinien." *Revue biblique* 60 (1953), 26–39.

Milik, Józef T. "The Monastery of Kastellion." *Biblica* 48 (1961), 21–27.

Patrich, Joseph. "Hyrcania." In *The New Encyclopedia of Archaeological Excavations in the Holy Land*, edited by E. Stern, pp. 639–641. Jerusalem, 1995.

Patrich, Joseph. *Archaeological Survey in Judaea and Samaria. Map of Deir Mar Saba (109/7)*. Jerusalem, 1995. See pp. 59–60.

Patrich, Joseph. *Sabas, Leader of Palestinian Monasticism. A Comparative Study in Eastern Monasticism, Fourth to Seventh Centuries*. In Dumbarton Oaks Studies XXXII, pp. 137–145. Washington, D.C., 1995.

Patrich, Joseph. "The Aqueducts of Hyrcania." In *The Ancient Aqueducts of Judaea-Palaestina*, edited by David Amit, Joseph Patrich, and Yizhar Hirschfeld. Journal of Roman Archaeology Supplement Series. (forthcoming).

Perrot, Ch. "Un fragment christo-palestinien découvert à Khirbet Mird (Actes des Apôtres X, 28–29, 32–41)." *Revue biblique* 70 (1963), 506–555.

Reed, S. A., M. J. Lundberg, and M. B. Phelps. *The Dead Sea Scrolls Catalogue: Documents, Photographs and Museum Inventory Numbers*, pp. xxxvii–xxxix, 217–225. SBL Resources for Biblical Study, 32. Atlanta, 1994.

Wright, G. R. H. "The Archaeological Remains of el-Mird in the Wilderness of Judaea." *Biblica* 42 (1961), 1–21.

JOSEPH PATRICH

MIRIAM, the sister of Moses and Aaron, one of the leaders of the Israelites in the wilderness. In *Exodus* 15.20–21 she is described as a female prophet who leads the Israelite women in a victory song after the defeat of the Egyptians at the Sea of Reeds. Unfortunately, the text of Miriam's song is not given. In *Numbers* 12 she is stricken with leprosy after she and her brother Aaron challenge the supremacy of Moses, and *Numbers* 20.1 describes her death and burial. Miriam is also traditionally identified as the unnamed sister (*Ex.* 2.4–10), who watches over Moses after he has been cast adrift in the bulrushes by his mother. In later biblical tradition, Miriam retains her identification as one of the leaders of Israel during the wilderness period (*Mi.* 6.4).

In the literature of the Second Temple period and in rabbinic literature, Miriam's biblical functions are mentioned (e.g., *Jub.* 47.4), but her role as a prophet is emphasized (she does not appear in the New Testament). In Pseudo-Philo's *Biblical Antiquities*, she prophesies that the child Moses will redeem Israel (*P.-Ph.* 9.9–10). Targum Yerushalmi highlights Miriam's role in leading the singing of the Israelite women at the Sea of Reeds. It is in this role that Miriam appears in the Qumran text, Reworked Pentateuch^{c} (4Q365).

Reworked Pentateuch^{c}, which is dated paleographically between 75 and 50 BCE, is one of five manuscripts (all found in Cave 4 at Qumran) that reflect a text of the Pentateuch (or Torah) that has been thoroughly reworked. In particular, it contains material not found in any other known version of the Pentateuch. This is illustrated by the so-called Song of Miriam (4Q365 6a.ii.1–7), the fragmentary remains of a poetic text that appears to be missing in the received text of Exodus. This additional material appears to belong between *Exodus* 15.21, where Miriam sings the opening words of the Song of the Sea found in *Exodus* 15.1–18, and 15.22, where the narrative continues. The Song of Miriam tells of God's victory over the enemy at the Sea of Reeds in language that is reminiscent of, but not identical to, the Song of the Sea. Whether Miriam's song found in Reworked Pentateuch[c] is from a different and hitherto unknown tradition or is an addition to the received text by an unknown author is not clear, but the song fills a gap in the narrative and serves to bring the shadowy figure of Miriam, who is all but lost in later tradition, into sharper focus.

[*See also* Reworked Pentateuch.]

BIBLIOGRAPHY

Brooke, George J. "Power to the Powerless—A Long-Lost Song of Miriam." *Biblical Archaeology Review* 20.3 (1994): 62–65.

Tov, Emanuel, and Sidnie A. White. "4QReworked Pentateuch." In *Qumran Cave 4: Parabiblical Texts, Part 1*, edited by Emanuel Tov et al., pp. 255–308. Discoveries in the Judaean Desert, 13. Oxford, 1994. *Editio princeps* of the text of 4Q365.

White, Sidnie A. "4Q364 & 365: A Preliminary Report." In *The Madrid Qumran Congress: Proceedings of the International Congress on the Dead Sea Scrolls, Madrid, 18–21 March 1991*, edited by Julio Trebolle Barrera and Luis Vegas Montaner, pp. 217–228. Studies on the Texts of the Desert of Judah, 11. Leiden, 1992.

SIDNIE WHITE CRAWFORD

MISHMAR, NAḤAL.

[*This entry consists of two articles:* Chalcolithic Hoard *and* Roman Period.]

Chalcolithic Hoard

The "Judean Desert Treasure," also known as the Naḥal Mishmar hoard, is unique in its size, in the quality of its contents, and in its excellent preservation (Bar-Adon, 1980). It was found in a natural niche in the Cave of the Treasure, blocked by a large stone (90 by 120 centimeters [35 by 47 inches]). The 429 objects were partially wrapped in a reed (Cyperus) mat (80 by 120 centimeters [31 by 47 inches]) and partially spread on the ground in no apparent order. All objects were made of copper, except for six ivory and six hematite artifacts and one made of limestone. Comparative stylistic studies of the artifacts and recent carbon-14 dating of the organic material recovered with the hoard place it in the local Chalcolithic culture, best attested in the northern Negev. The hoard is now dated to the first part of the fourth millennium, not later than 3500 BCE.

Ivory Objects. Five flat, perforated objects made of hippopotamus ivory are sickle shaped, curved like the animal's tusk itself. They are 45.5–57.5 centimeters long (17–22.6 inches) and 484–800 grams (17–28 ounces) in weight. The perforations are arranged in three rows over the entire surface of each object. The central perforation is larger and surrounded by a raised rim. Most objects also have small holes at their wide end; a piece of a linen thread was preserved in one of these holes. These objects may have been used as ceremonial standards, carried on wooden poles inserted into the central perforations. A sixth object, made of elephant ivory, is a large elongated container, slightly curved and oval in shape, 38.3 centimeters long (15.1 inches) and 1150 grams (41 ounces) in weight.

Stone Objects. Six plain hematite mace heads were found in the hoard. They are globular or elongated, similar in shape to the most common copper mace heads of the hoard. There was only one limestone mace head in the hoard, typologically similar to the hematite ones.

Metal Objects. The 240 copper mace heads form the largest group of metal artifacts, comprising well over half of the hoard's components. Most are globular or elongated, devoid of any decoration; eleven are disk shaped, also plain; five are cone or barrel shaped, their surfaces covered with rows of small knobs. One mace head is surmounted by twin ibexes and two tool-like projections. All are hollow lengthwise and could be mounted on wooden poles.

Maces (in the excavator's nomenclature, "standards"), made in their entirety of copper, form the second largest category. They have disk-shaped rims; short necks; globular, elongated, or disk-shaped heads; long straight shafts; and splaying base rims. Almost all have decorated heads and shafts. All maces are hollow lengthwise and the majority could be mounted on wooden poles. Fragments of such poles were actually preserved in a few shafts, and a piece of cloth (used for securing such a pole?) was found in one.

The remaining groups of copper artifacts are smaller. There are ten large, open cylinders termed *crowns* because of their shape, but their actual use is unknown. All but three are decorated, and one is highly ornate. There are also six long, ornate scepters (43–77 centimeters [17–30 inches] long). Unlike the maces, these scepters have solid shafts. Three objects are horn shaped, hollow at the wide end and decorated, each with two suspension holes beneath the rim; one still had a piece of twisted string threaded through the holes. Only five objects could serve as receptacles for liquids or solids: these are three small vessels with basket handles (situlae), one bottle, and one in the shape of a deep, open bowl. All are decorated.

The artifacts listed above are commonly considered to have been ceremonial. Their shapes are unusual, they are made of costly raw materials that had to be imported, and they were produced by complex technology that required considerable expertise and equipment. Their decoration is mostly based on geometric elements: horizontal, vertical, or diagonal lines, either raised or grooved, often forming a continuous design. Only the most outstanding objects contain figurative ornaments: representations of ibexes, ibex heads with bent, grooved horns, or just horns possibly symbolizing the complete animal. One standard is shaped in the form of a vulture, and figures of birds are superimposed on the rims of a few objects. Floral motifs are rare. Anthropomorphic heads with round eyes and prominent noses appear only twice: on a mace and on a crown.

The hoard contains a group of nineteen copper tools: twelve ax and adz blades and one hammer. In addition, there are three long, thin ax-blades and three socketed ax-blades, among them one decorated with an intricate rope design. These objects may have been designated for ceremonial rather than practical use.

Metallurgy. The Naḥal Mishmar hoard produced decisive proof of the existence of highly developed Chalcolithic metallurgy in the Levant. All copper objects were produced by casting. Except for the six scepters and most of the tools, all artifacts were cast over a core, in the lost-wax casting technique. Gamma-ray inspection and thermal neutron radiography showed that each object was cast in its entirety, with all the details of ornamentation already existent in the mold. However, the quality of casting varies. As no two objects are identical, each must have been cast in an individual mold. After casting, all the objects were extensively smoothed and polished, obliterating exterior defects and obtaining shining surfaces.

The elemental composition of about 10 percent of the copper objects was determined. Twenty-eight samples were subjected to chemical, neutron activation and lead isotope analyses (Tadmor, 1995). The results show that the tools are made of pure copper of a type that could be obtained in the copper mines of Feinan (Biblical Punon) in the Wadi Arabah (Jordan). A few of the ceremonial objects also are made of pure copper, but most are made of antimony-arsenic-rich copper; while a few are made of nickel-rich arsenical copper. Both types of these complex metals are nonexistent in the Wadi Arabah mines and could be obtained only in the distant regions of central Asia, the Caucasus, or the Iranian plateau.

Several theories have been put forward to explain the enigmatic location of the Naḥal Mishmar hoard. Ussishkin (1971) claimed that originally the hoard had belonged to the Chalcolithic temple at ʿEin-Gedi and was hidden in the cave in time of danger. I believe that the hoard belonged to traders or trader-smiths who lived in the desert caves. They served as intermediaries between the Arabah mines and the Negev villages and, possibly, as importers of ores or ingots and distributors of finished products (Tadmor, 1989). Still another theory suggests that the hoard was buried in the cave in a "ritual burial" (Garfinkel, 1994).

The connection between the Naḥal Mishmar hoard and the local Chalcolithic culture was ascertained by similar copper, ivory, and stone artifacts that were unearthed in excavations in contemporary settlements and caves. Copper axes and adzes, maces and mace heads were found in private houses in Chalcolithic villages in the northern Negev, mostly in association with small-scale copper smelting and melting of Arabah copper. Similar objects were also deposited in burial caves in the Judean and Samaria Deserts and in other parts of the country: one mace was excavated in a cave at Palmaḥim on the Mediterranean coast; an assemblage of similar artifacts, together with eight gold and electrum rings (ingots?) was found in the Naḥal Qanah Cave in the central hill country. Similar copper finds also were unearthed in a cave at Peqiʿin in Upper Galilee and in caves and pits at Givat Ha'oranim (Naḥal Bameget) at the foothills of western Samaria. None has yet been found in a Chalcolithic temple. The local character of the Naḥal Mishmar hoard has been confirmed by the occurrence of local stylistic elements, for example, round eyes and prominent noses in anthropomorphic images and the many representations of ibex horns.

The exceptionally high quality of the Naḥal Mishmar hoard indicates the existence of specialized local trading systems in prestige goods in the Chalcolithic period. The use of ivory, hematite, and, especially, complex ores suggests interregional and long-distance connections. The hoard also proves that in the local Chalcolithic society there were ruling authorities capable of safeguarding the supply of raw materials and distribution of finished products as well as elites who used such artifacts in cult and ceremony (Moorey, 1988; Levy, 1995).

BIBLIOGRAPHY

Bar-Adon, Pessah. *The Cave of the Treasure.* Jerusalem, 1980.

Garfinkel, Yosef. "Ritual Burial of Cultic Objects: The Earliest Evidence." *Cambridge Archaeological Journal* 4 (1994), 159–188.

Levy, Thomas E. "Cult, Metallurgy, and Rank Societies: Chalcolithic Period (ca. 4500–3500 BCE)." In *The Archaeology of Society in the Holy Land*, edited by Thomas Evan Levy, pp. 226–243. London, 1995.

Moorey, P. R. S. "The Chalcolithic Hoard from Naḥal Mishmar, Israel, in Context." *World Archaeology* 20 (1988), 171–189.

Tadmor, Miriam. "The Judean Desert Treasure from Naḥal Mishmar: A Chalcolithic Traders' Hoard?" In *Essays in Ancient Civilization Presented to Helene J. Kantor*, edited by Albert Leonard Jr. and Bruce Beyer Williams, pp. 250–261. Chicago, 1989.

Tadmor, Miriam, et al. "The Naḥal Mishmar Hoard from the Judean Desert: Technology, Composition, and Provenance." *ʿAtiqot* 27 (1995), 95–148.

Ussishkin, David. "The 'Ghassulian' Temple in ʿEin Gedi and the Origin of the Hoard from Naḥal Mishmar." *Biblical Archaeologist* 34 (1971), 23–29.

MIRIAM TADMOR

Roman Period

In 1955 Yohanan Aharoni discovered two structures at the crest of the cliff above Naḥal Mishmar, but did not excavate the caves under these structures. Under the aegis of the Judean Desert Expeditions in 1960 and 1961 Naḥal Mishmar was excavated by Pessah Bar-Adon. In the first season following the excavation of the caves in the valley, the archaeologists concentrated upon a large cave that, until then, had been nicknamed the Scouts Cave. This cave was found above two small springs. A natural cave with a wide opening, it comprises two chambers with a few niches and tunnels. Outside of the Scouts Cave the excavators found remnants of a narrow path that led to the cave in ancient times. Many segments of this path have eroded, and the descent to the cave became dangerous. For this reason the bedouin did not conduct excavations in it.

The first visit to the cave yielded pottery from the Chalcolithic period and the Roman period, glass vessels, and strips of fabric. Two fragments of documents written upon a papyrus were also found. In an additional cave (Cave 2), located approximately 15 meters northeast of the Scouts Cave, skeletons from the Chalcolithic period and pottery from the Roman period were found.

Bar-Adon returned to the Scouts Cave in 1961 and found a variety of items, including 429 vessels from the Chalcolithic period. On account of this discovery the name of the cave was changed from the Scouts Cave to the Cave of the Treasure. The third season of excavation was conducted in the Cave of the Treasure and in Naḥal Mishmar in 1962. During this time a number of additional caves in Naḥal Mishmar were excavated. In Cave 4, a small cave (4 meters in diameter) situated southwest of the Cave of the Treasure, were found sherds of pottery from the Iron Age II and from the Roman period. Also, a knife similar to the knives that Yigael Yadin had found in the Cave of the Letters in Naḥal Ḥever was found in Cave 4. [*See* Naḥal Ḥever, *article on* Archaeology.] This cave served only as a temporary place for shepherds to stay and not as an extended dwelling. In 1962 Bar-Adon also excavated the two structures at the crest of the cliff, and it was ascertained that one was a public structure from the Chalcolithic period, and the other was an army camp from the Roman period. The Roman camp is located directly above the Cave of the Treasure; from it there is an excellent view of the full length of Naḥal Mishmar.

In the Cave of the Treasure and in Cave 2 a large group of pottery characteristic of the era of the Bar Kokhba Revolt was found. [*See* Bar Kokhba Revolt.] In this collection the following were recovered: storage jars with flat rims that were popular during the second century CE, as well as bottles and jars, crockery, and two types of oil lamp (one with a splayed nozzle and a round Roman oil lamp). Also found in the Cave of the Treasure were many sherds of glass vessels, among these a greenish juglet shaped with a high folded handle. The bottles are characteristic of the second century CE. Similar glass bottles were discovered in the Cave of Horror in Naḥal Ḥever. In the Cave of the Treasure, stoneware, such as a measuring cup and mortar and pestle, as well as remnants of clothing and sandals, various straw items, and a ball of fine linen thread wound around a small stone also were found. [*See* Archaeology; Qumran, *article on* Archaeology.]

In the Cave of the Treasure three small fragments of documents written upon papyri and four ostraca were found. Two of the ostraca were found erased and are not legible. The first papyrus (fragment of an official document, 1Mish 1) was discovered at the entrance to the cave. It is a very small fragment upon which the Hebrew word for "were given" remains. This is possibly a fragment of a deed of gift. The second papyrus (list of personal names, 1Mish 2) was located in the inner chamber; a list of names in Greek is written on both sides of the papyrus. [*See* Names and Naming.] Next to each name appears the Greek word for "brother," a practice also attested in one of the documents found by Aharoni in Naḥal Ṣe'elim. [*See* Ṣe'elim, Naḥal, *article on* Written Material.] The third papyrus (1Mish 3) was found in the inner chamber. It is a portion of a document on which a few of the signatures remain. Three people signed in Aramaic, and the last witness signed in Greek. In the first line the words "He wrote it for himself" remain and therefore on this line one of the parties mentioned in the document signed. This man also wrote the document. On the second and third lines witnesses signed in Aramaic, while on the fourth line a Greek signature appears. The first ostracon was found in the outer chamber, and on it the word *zuzin* was written; on the second ostracon, which was found in the inner chamber, there are three Greek letters.

BIBLIOGRAPHY

Bar-Adon, Pessah. "Expedition C." *Israel Exploration Journal* 11 (1961), 25–35.

Bar-Adon, Pessah. "Expedition C—The Cave of the Treasure." *Israel Exploration Journal* 12 (1961), 215–226.

Bar-Adon, Pessah. *The Cave of the Treasure: The Finds from the Caves in Nahal Mishmar*. Jerusalem, 1980.

Lifshitz, B. "The Greek Documents from Naḥal Se'elim and Naḥal Mishmar." *Israel Exploration Journal* 11 (1961), 53–62.

HANAN ESHEL

Translated from Hebrew from Daphna Krupp

MISHNAH AND TOSEFTA. Literally, "oral teaching" from Hebrew *sh-n-h*, "to repeat," Mishnah refers to a collection of laws, which rapidly became standard for Talmudic Judaism. Tosefta (literally, "addition") refers to a collection of teachings which, while perhaps predating the Mishnah, now are in part arranged as a commentary on the Mishnah. Some elements of these collections seem to date back to Second Temple and Pharisaic times. Overwhelmingly, however, the term *the Mishnah* refers to the collection compiled in the first quarter of the third century in Palestine, and attributed to Rabbi Judah the Prince (d. 220) by later rabbinic authorities (B.T., *Yev.*, 65a). It is thus the earliest rabbinic legal code of any scope that has come down to us.

The Mishnah contains material that is conventionally dated by tannaitic "generation," the *tannaim* being the sages whose work makes up a large part of both the Mishnah, Tosefta, the halakhic *midrashim*, and various and sundry "external" *baraitot* cited in both Talmuds. They are conventionally dated to six or seven "generations," or clusters of sages who are seen to interact, or share a common program, or take opposite sides in disputes on rabbinic law. All these compilations are composed in Middle Hebrew I, a dialect related to, but not identical with, that of the Bar Kokhba letters, and quite distinct from Qumran Hebrew. Middle Hebrew I, as represented in the Mishnah, Tosefta, and most halakhic *midrashim*, may be dated linguistically to before the middle of the fourth century, while the latest of the halakhic *midrashim*, the so-called *Mekhilta de-Rav Shimʿon bar Yoḥai*, contains redactional material that seems to date to the beginning of the fifth century and perhaps later.

Closely related to the Mishnah, at least as currently structured, is a parallel compilation known as Tosefta. Like the Mishnah, various collections of *tosefata* (plural of *tosefta*) seem to have circulated in rabbinic circles, but again, like the Mishnah, only one version has been preserved in its entirety. In its current form, it serves to present tannaitic material parallel to, and occasionally divergent from, the Mishnah. It also contains sections that are independent of the Mishnah, covering topics not included in the Mishnah. Because of its relation to the Mishnah, we can occasionally discern the seams between its constituent collections, when two such collections overlap.

While some or even most of its constituent elements may predate the Mishnah's redaction, and while it belongs to the same stratum of Middle Hebrew as the Mishnah itself, recent research indicates that it may be dated (on linguistic grounds) as slightly later than the Mishnah, and earlier than its parallels in the Palestinian and Babylonian Talmuds.

The Qumran Halakah. In regard to the use of these collections in the study of Qumran *halakhah* and related matters, it should be noted that since the Tosefta is both a larger and more heterogenous collection than the Mishnah, it contains some references to sectarian *halakhah* not to be found in the latter, as for example to discussion of "heterodox practices" (*derekh aḥeret*) in T., *Berakhot* 7.6 and T., *Terumot* 7.11, or to the "Morning Bathers" (hemerobaptists) in the Vienna manuscript of T., *Yadayim* 2.20. On the other hand, the compiler(s) did not always have traditions independent of, or supplementary to, the Mishnah. Thus, the parallel Tosefta to Mishnah *Yadayim* 4.6–8 contains hardly any such traditions to add to our knowledge of this important source of Sadducee-Pharisee history.

For purposes of research into the early history of *halakhah*, and thus into rabbinic parallels to Qumran legal texts, the essential question is the reliability of rabbinic traditions for the period before the destruction of the Second Temple, and on this there is no consensus, at least from the point of view of method. The school founded by Jacob Neusner maintains that the Mishnah as a whole must be viewed as a product of the generation before c.220 CE, while nearly all Israeli scholars, and others as well, view the Mishnah as the product of generations of compilatory work. One striking difference between the two schools involves the dating of the anonymous redactional material. The Neusnerian school, while acknowledging that some of this material may be quite early, maintains that the methodologically "safe," and therefore, correct, approach, is to consider all of it as redactional. The Israeli school sees in this anonymous material some very old traditions, indeed, some of which date to the period in which the influence of Biblical Hebrew was still felt in the formulation of rabbinic traditions.

However, when we examine specific texts, the differences in approach become much narrower, especially when we limit our investigation to texts that may provide parallels to Qumran material. This is because much of the anonymous Mishnaic material involves issues that are not represented in our Qumran corpus, but also because the two modern scholarly schools, in the end, often agree on the dating of material for which the Mishnah provides attributions.

As currently organized, both the Mishnah and Tosefta are divided into six *sedarim*, "orders," named Zeraʿim, Moʿed, Nashim, Neziqin, Qodashim, and Tohorot. Roughly speaking, each is primarily devoted to one or two topics. In order, these are liturgical and agricultural rules, the laws of Sabbath and festivals, laws affecting the status of women, civil law, laws relating to the Temple service, and laws of ritual purity. The last two are the largest orders, comprising some 40 percent of the total; they, along with Neziqin, contain the largest proportion of anonymous material. Except for relatively minor parts of Qodashim, however, little of these orders finds parallels in the Qumran legal or cultic material, though of late some significant texts relating to minor parts of Tohorot have been published.

Nevertheless, it is clear that some of this material is closely related to Qumran *halakhah*. The most striking case involves the Pharisaic-Sadducee debates of Mishnah *Yadayim* 4.6–8, which both in form and substance echo parts of Miqtsat Maʿasei ha-Torah. Both texts seem to reflect a halakhic dispute between the Pharisees and their antagonists. In the Mishnah these are identified with the Sadducees; in Miqtsat Maʿasei ha-Torah, the interlocutor(s) are unnamed, but in two cases, at least, their halakhic stance may be identical to that of the Sadducees of the Mishnah *Yadayim* passage. It is this parallel that has led some scholars, most prominently Lawrence H. Schiffman, to identify the Qumran sect not with the Essenes, but as an outgrowth of the Sadducees, though others consider such an identification as premature.

Another case relates to the question of whether the ceremony of the Red Heifer may be carried out by a *ṭevul yom*, that is, one who has undergone the requisite purificatory rites—sacrifice(s) and/or immersion in a ritual bath—but whose complete purification awaits sunset. According to Mishnah *Parah* 3.7, the Sadducees prohibit this, and the precursors of the *tannaim* went out of their way to ensure that their view would be followed, to the extent of causing impurity to the one assigned the task of burning the heifer, so that he would become a *ṭevul yom*. In the parallel toseftan text (T., *Par.* 3.5) it is Rabban Yohannan b. Zakkai who did this to an unnamed high priest.

Another tannaitic text that deals explicitly with legal disputes between the Pharisees and their opponents, in this case the Boethusians, is to be found in T., *Sukkah* 3.1 (with a parallel at T., *Suk.* 43b). According to the view of the sages, and apparently the priests as well, the willow branch ceremony at the Temple at the end of the Sukkot festival overrode Sabbath restrictions; according to the Boethusians, it did not. Most interestingly, the latter are reported as having attempted to prevent the willow branches from being brought in on the Sabbath, but were outwitted by the common people. Another case, in Mishnah *Menaḥot* 10.3 and T., *Menaḥot* 10.23, involves the date of the reaping of the *ʿomer*, though the nature of the dispute between the sages and the Boethusians is not clear. It is, however, difficult to avoid associating this dispute with the major calendrical disagreement between the Pharisees and the sectarians, a disagreement of longstanding, and one that would have made a shared celebration of the festivals impossible. In this case, it may even be that the sectarians' literal understanding of "on the morrow of the Sabbath" of *Leviticus* 23.15, on which the date of the Festival of Weeks depends, also served to preclude the reaping of the *ʿomer* on the Sabbath itself. But it must be noted that the rabbinic material is hardly clear on this point.

It is true that the relationships between the Boethusians, the Sadducees, the Essenes, the Qumran sect, and other contemporaneous sects known only by name, are not well understood, and may never be, unless documents that can be clearly linked to each of these sects have survived and will be discovered. However, the existence of works of a non-Qumranic provenance, which were nonetheless preserved and presumably studied at Qumran, indicates that sectarian lines were fluid, at least to some extent. There is also the possibility, raised by Yaakov Sussman, that the very names that have been preserved in rabbinic literature (Boethusians, Sadducees, "Morning Bathers," and so forth) were not sharply defined in the first place.

Given the predilection of the sectarians for biblicizing style, this is all the more important when the Qumran Hebrew term has greater affinities with the later rabbinic term than its Biblical Hebrew cognate. For example, the rabbinic term for the ash and water combination of the red heifer, which serves to purify those made impure by corpse-impurity, is *mei ḥaṭaʾt*, as opposed to the Biblical Hebrew *mei niddah*. While the biblical term appears several times in non-halakhic contexts in Qumran literature, the appearance of the "rabbinic" term in 4QMMT serves to antedate the origin of this term by several centuries. It also serves to indicate the distance that Qumran halakhic terminology had traveled from its biblical roots by the middle of the second century BCE. As E. Qimron has pointed out, the coexistence of the two terms in Qumran Hebrew, along with its near total disappearance in rabbinic texts, even alongside a biblical proof text, situates the two terms on an almost linear linguistic continuum.

Second Temple–Period Sects. Though the Mishnah and Tosefta are the earliest rabbinic compilations that have come down to us, and contain earlier materials, they are far from providing us with anything resembling a complete, or even coherent, view of the positions of the various sects that existed in Second Temple times. Their compilers were interested in these sects only to the extent that they impinged on issues important to later rabbinic law, and to the extent that traditions regarding these questions had come down to them. Moreover, even matters of interest and importance to the rabbinic movement as a whole do not necessarily find their place in these two compilations. As an indication of the partial nature of evidence available from them, it is sufficient to point to the absence from the Mishnah or the Tosefta of any clear reference to that sectarian dispute that perhaps would have been considered of paramount importance in the Second Temple period: the nature of the calendar.

To the extent to which this question makes its appearance in rabbinic literature, we must seek it not in these early compilations, but rather in the Babylonian Talmud. According to the consensus opinion, which equates these calendars with the view attributed to the Boethusians in

B.T., *Menaḥot* 65a–b, the Boethusians and the Sadducees shared the sectarian calendar. Again, however, the relation of this to the question of the identification of the sect with those groups known from rabbinic literature is not altogether clear. Whatever the true contours of this dispute, it is important to note that it is absent from our earliest rabbinic sources, and the sectarian position is far from clear where it does appear, in the Babylonian Talmud. Though rabbinic sources can provide important data, which help clarify some of the sectarian issues in contention between the Pharisees and other Second Temple groups, great care must be taken in their use.

This is all the more relevant in matters on which there is little or no dispute between the sects. The rabbis, as successors to the Pharisees, hardly dwell on such matters. As is often the case, sectarian hostility tends to magnify sectarian differences, ignoring matters on which there was substantial agreement. Thus, while rabbinic literature contains many parallels to the rules contained in the so-called Qumran "Sabbath Code" of Damascus Document, CD x–xi, from these parallels alone it would be difficult to conclude that the sectarians observed the Sabbath in much the same way as the Pharisees did. And were we dependent on rabbinic literature alone, we would hardly guess that rabbinic and sectarian Sabbath laws are very similar in this area, even when there is no clear biblical source for the law in question. As we might well expect, where the two groups' practices were similar, and no polemic intent was meant, the sectarians' codificatory efforts would hardly relate to their opponents' views. But it does indeed appear to be the case that in this major area of concern to Second Temple Judaism, the two groups differed but little. Thus, both groups ushered in the Sabbath before sunset on Friday (*tosefet Shabbat* in rabbinic terminology), set strict limits on walking beyond the city limits (*teḥum Shabbat*), forbade labor to be done by a non-Jew for the sake of a Jew, and forbade the handling of materials or objects of no conceivable use on the Sabbath, such as rocks and earth (*muqtseh*). Such quintessential rabbinic conceptions turn out to be not solely tannaitic/rabbinic at all, but apparently common to sects that in other respects were at daggers drawn.

However, the parallels are seldom direct; the individual cases may differ slightly, and we have few general statements to guide us. It is therefore difficult to extrapolate from the individual cases to the general system of Qumran *halakhah*. Because of that, it is difficult to state with certainty that a particular rule, even when similar, has the same resonance in the two systems.

Laws of Purities. Rabbinic literature on the laws of purities, even when restricted to the Mishnah and Tosefta, is both extensive and complex in its ramifications and interconnections. It is for this reason one of the areas of rabbinic law that perhaps demonstrably existed as a system in tannaitic times, that is, as a consistent set of principles and applications.

Bearing this in mind, it is all the more telling that one of the most interesting, compelling, and apparently inevitable parallels adduced between the rabbinic system of purities and a section of Miqtsat Maʿasei ha-Torah (4QMMT), the matter of *nitsoq-mutsaqot*, raises a number of difficulties. This is because that single equation of *nitsoq-mutsaqot*, when viewed systemically, together with the generally accepted view that Qumran *halakhah* is always more stringent than the rabbinic parallel, yields contradictory consequences. According to 4QMMT B 55–58,

> concerning (unbroken) streams of a liquid (poured from a clean vessel into an unclean vessel): we are of the opinion that they are not pure, and that these streams do not act as a separative between impure and pure liquids, for the liquid of the streams and that of the vessel which receives them are alike, being a single liquid.

If we equate Miqtsat Maʿasei ha-Torah's *mutsaqot* with the rabbinic *nitsoq* as it appears in Mishnah *Yadayim* 4.7, we have a clear partial parallel between the two documents, at least as concerns the ruling in Miqtsat Maʿasei ha-Torah on transmitting impurity ("impure liquids"), in which the Qumran rule is more strict. However, Miqtsat Maʿasei ha-Torah also rules that pure liquids follow the same rule. While it is difficult to determine the exact application of this rule, it is certainly more permissive than the rabbinic rule, which denies that *nitsoq* can be a connective for either purity or impurity. Similar difficulties have been raised on the rabbinic side of the parallel.

Again, there is no evidence that the Qumran sect accepted the tannaitic system of degrees of ritual impurity, which plays so large a part in the rabbinic system of purities, though it seems to have recognized the existence of different stages of purification. Again, their system of purities was extremely sensitive to the dangers of contact with non-sectarians, similar to the early rabbinic traditions. However, when we examine the respective systems in detail, the differences are more impressive than the similarities. Nevertheless, this argument from silence must be viewed with a great deal of caution, so long as we lack a large corpus of halakhic texts from Qumran.

In Context of the Rabbinic System. This brings us to a central issue in the interpretation of Qumran *halakhah* against the background of the rabbinic system. From the earliest days of research on the Genizah fragments of Damascus Document (CD) before World War I, it has generally been accepted that "all the halakhot in the Dead Sea scrolls which are at variance with Pharisaic halakha are stricter than the corresponding Pharisaic rulings," as

Yaakov Sussman put it in his remarks on 4QMMT (Qimron and Strugnell, 1994, p. 197). An examination of the available evidence does not bear out this judgment in the extreme manner in which it is typically expressed.

For example, Temple Scroll[a] (11Q119 1.4–7) rules that contact with the bone or blood of dead person defiles, but not, it would appear, the amputated bone of a living person.

> As for any man who shall touch upon the surface of the field a bone of a dead human or one killed by the sword, or a dead person, or the blood of a dead human or a grave, he shall be purified according to this ordinance.

As Yigael Yadin (1983) rightly noted, the inclusion of the word *met* ("corpse") modifying *ʿetsem adam* ("human bone") and *dam adam* ("human blood") clearly points to a concern on the part of the drafter of the Temple Scroll to exclude amputated ("living") limbs from this law. But rabbinic *halakhah* clearly rules to the contrary, as Yadin already noted, and as Hannah K. Harrington (1993) observes in her comparison of the two systems of purities. Thus the Temple Scroll in this instance is less stringent than the rabbis. The drafter has employed what Jacob Milgrom (1989) has called "homogenization," in this case similar to the rabbinic forms of analogical reasoning which we may subsume under the heading of *heqqesh* ("argument by analogy"), to define the limbs and blood of *Numbers* 19.18 as issuing from a corpse rather than a living person, since the verse deals with "one killed by the sword or a dead person." The latter terms modify the former in the direction of a more limited application of the resultant rule, that is, in the direction of leniency!

Perhaps the most important single contribution of rabbinic sources, then, is the setting of a context for the sectarian writings of Qumran and related literature, though they may disagree on many details large and small. Even when the two systems do *not* intersect, and no parallel can be found on one side or the other, a comparative study of the two will yield important results, which will enhance our understanding of both. For example, rabbinic law defines limits, quantities; in Qumran, the definition of the onset of the Sabbath and the *teḥum Shabbat* stand out as anomalous. The Mishnah wishes to define not only the Sabbath-walk limit, but also the amount of various materials the carrying of which will require a sin-offering, the precise criteria for defining the various categories of Sabbath-territories. There is no indication that such jurisprudential activity was at all of interest to the sectarians. This is not to say that Qumran *halakhah* is totally bereft of quantification. Even if the original locus of *teḥum Shabbat* lay outside Qumran, we still have the agricultural laws of Damascus Document[e] (4Q270), recently studied by Joseph M. Baumgarten, in which the amount of *leqeṭ* ("gleanings"), *ʿolelot* ("single grapes"), and the like are defined. But this attempt proceeds ineluctably from the need to translate the biblical text into reality. In rabbinic law quantification acquires its own momentum, whether it was a practical necessity or not.

To some extent, the difference in elaboration in halakhic detail may merely be a function of history. Qumran *halakhah* is simply earlier, just as the Palestinian Talmud, earlier than the Babylonian by more than a century, is less developed than the latter. But some amount—again, still undefined—of this lack of articulation is certainly due to the different vectors of Qumran and rabbinic law.

As Lawrence H. Schiffman pointed out long ago, the sects of the Second Temple period shared a halakhic universe of discourse; the important disputes were over minutae of the law even more than theological issues. If we want entree into that shared universe, rabbinic literature, and the Mishnah and Tosefta in particular, properly understood and applied, can provide it.

BIBLIOGRAPHY

Baumgarten, Joseph M. *Studies in Qumran Law.* Leiden, 1977.

Baumgarten, Joseph M. "The Pharisaic-Sadducean Controversies about Purity, and the Qumran Texts." *Journal of Jewish Studies* 31 (1980), 157–170.

Elman, Yaakov. *Authority and Tradition: Toseftan Baraitot in Talmudic Babylonia.* New York, 1994.

Elman, Yaakov. "Some Remarks on 4QMMT and the Rabbinic Tradition, Or, When Is a Parallel Not a Parallel?" In *Reading 4QMMT: New Perspectives on Qumran Law and History,* edited by Moshe J. Bernstein and John Kampen, pp. 99–128. Symposia 2. Atlanta, 1996.

Harrington, Hannah K. *The Impurity Systems of Qumran and the Rabbis: Biblical Foundations.* Atlanta, 1993.

Milgrom, Jacob. "The Qumran Cult: Its Exegetical Principles." In *Temple Scroll Studies,* edited by George Brooke, pp. 165–180. Journal for the Study of Pseudepigrapha Supplement, 7. Sheffield, 1989.

Neusner, Jacob. *Eliezer ben Hyrcanus: The Tradition and the Man: Part 2, Analysis of the Tradition, the Man.* Leiden, 1973.

Neusner, Jacob. *A History of the Mishnaic Law of Purities.* Leiden, 1977.

Neusner, Jacob. *In Search of Talmudic Biography: The Problem of the Attributed Saying.* Chico, Calif., 1984.

Neusner, Jacob. *Judaism: The Evidence of the Mishnah.* Chicago, 1981.

Qimron, E., and J. Strugnell. *Qumran Cave 4, V: Miqṣat Maʿaśe ha-Torah,* Yaakov Sussman consulting editor. Discoveries in the Judaean Desert, 10. Oxford, 1994.

Rabin, Chaim. *Qumran Studies.* Oxford, 1957.

Schiffman, Lawrence H. *The Halakhah at Qumran.* Leiden, 1975.

Schiffman, Lawrence H. "Legislation Concerning Relations with Non-Jews in the Zadokite Fragments and in the Tannaitic Literature." *Revue de Qumrân* 11 (1983), 379–389.

Schiffman, Lawrence H. "The Temple Scroll and the System of Jewish Law of the Second Temple Period." In *Temple Scroll Studies,* edited by George Brooke, pp. 239–255. Journal for the Study of Pseudepigraphic Studies, 7. Sheffield, 1989.

Schiffman, Lawrence H. "*Miqṣat Maʿaseh Ha-Torah* and the Temple Scroll." *Revue de Qumrân* 14 (1990), 435–458.

Schiffman, Lawrence H. "Qumran and Rabbinic Halakhah." In *Jew-*

ish Civilization in the Hellenistic-Roman Period, pp. 138–146. Journal for the Study of Pseudepigrapha Supplement 10. Sheffield, 1991.

Schwartz, Daniel R. "Laws and Truth: On Qumran-Sadducean and Rabbinic Views of Law." In *The Dead Sea Scrolls: Forty Years of Research,* edited by D. Dimant and V. Rappaport, pp. 229–240. Leiden and Jerusalem, 1992.

Slomovic, E. "Toward an Understanding of the Exegesis in the Dead Sea Scrolls." *Revue de Qumrân* 6 (1969), 3–15.

Yadin, Yigael. *The Temple Scroll.* Jerusalem, 1983.

YAAKOV ELMAN

MMT. *See* Miqtsat Maʿasei ha-Torah.

MONASTERIES. The most important literary sources pertaining to monasticism in the Judean Desert are the seven hagiographies by Cyril of Scythopolis (died ca. 560), including those of the prominent desert Fathers Euthymius, Sabas, and Theodosius. Stories and anecdotes from the lives of the monks were assembled in the late sixth and early seventh centuries by John Moschus in his *Leimonarion*. Other contemporary sources are the anonymous lives of Chariton and Gerasimus, the life of George of Choziba by Anthony of Choziba, and *The Miracles of the Holy Virgin in Choziba* by the same author.

The major studies concerning the history and archaeology of the monasteries are those of Simon Vialhé (1990), Darews Chitty (1966), and more recently Yizhar Hirschfeld (1992, 1993) and Joseph Patrich (1993). Hirschfeld (in Bottini, Di Segri, and Alliata, 1990) had recorded ruins of some sixty monasteries and monastic installations. Some—Khirbet el Murasas, Khirbet ed-Deir, Khan el Ahmar, Khirbet el Kiliya, and five monasteries on the fringes of the desert, adjacent to Bethlehem—were entirely excavated, and all the others were surveyed comprehensively.

Institutionally and architecturally the monasteries were divided into two main types, the *laura* and the *coenobium*. The different ways of life in each of them dictated their different physical structures. The *laura* was a community of hermits. During the week, each monk lived in solitude in his cell, and only on the weekends would all assemble for a communal prayer and a communal meal. In a *coenobium*, on the other hand, the monks would live and work together and meet daily with each other in the church and in the dining room. Monastic life in the sixth century in *coenobia* and *laurae* alike was governed by fixed rules that controlled the daily and weekly routine; times of prayer and their contents; the monk's food, drink and clothing; his work in his cell; and the utensils he was allowed to keep there.

The founder of monasticism in the Judean Desert was Chariton, a native of Iconium in Asia Minor. Chariton established his first monastery, Pharan, near ʿEin-Fara, the westernmost and most abundant perennial spring of Wadi Qilt, to the northeast of Jerusalem, in about 330 CE. At that time anchorites also lived among the reeds of the Jordan River. Later Chariton established two other monasteries: Douka, overlooking Jericho, on the site of the Hasmonean fortress of Duq-Dagon (c. 340); and Souka, not far from Thecoa (c. 345). From the beginning the *laura* had been the most prevalent type of monastic settlement in the Judean Desert and near the Jordan River. In 406 Euthymius, a native of the Roman province of Armenia, had settled in Pharan, and in 411 he and his colleague Theoctistus founded the first *coenobium* in the Judean Desert, the monastery of Theoctistus (Deir Muqallik) on the cliffs of Naḥal Og. A second *coenobium* was established by Euthymius in 425 near Capharbaricha, and in 428 his *laura* (Khan el Ahmar) was inaugurated. The disciples of Euthymius founded other monasteries, all of them *coenobia*, and eventually occupied important posts in the Church of Palestine. Two of them, Martyrius and Elias, became patriarchs of Jerusalem. Romanus and Marcianus were two mid-fifth-century monastic leaders. The first established his monastery (Khirbet er-Rubeia) near Thecoa, and the second his monastery (Siyar el-Ghanam) near Bethlehem (454). In about 455 Gerasimus, a native of Lycia in Asia Minor, organized the individual anchorites living along the Jordan in an ordered community by setting up a *laura* with a *coenobium* at its center (Deir Hajla). At that time the nearby *laura* of Calamon (ʿEin-Hajla) was established based on a similar pattern. The *coenobium* of Choziba was established near ʿEin-Qilt by John of Choziba in about 480; previously five Syrian anchorites had lived there in succession. Pilgrimage to the site of baptism on the Jordan was institutionalized when Emperor Anastasius I (491–518) established the Church of Saint John the Baptist (Qast el-Yahud) near the Jordan River and settled monks there who received a permanent yearly allowance of six gold coins (*solidi*).

The monastic movement reached its peak under the leadership of Theodosius and Sabas. Theodosius headed a large *coenobium* (Deir Dosi) founded in 479, while Sabas headed the Great Laura (Mar Saba), founded in 483. In the late fifth and early sixth centuries Sabas and his disciples established six other *laurae* and six *coenobia*, populating the entire desert with monks. In the sixth century the Great Laura and the Laura of Gerasimus were the leading *laurae* in the desert of Jerusalem and the desert near the Jordan, respectively. The leading *coenobia* were those of Theodosius and of Martyrius.

Architecturally, the *coenobium* was an enclosed monastery, with all its components confined within its walls. It had a gate and a two-or three-storied tower with a cross on its top. The Monastery of Martyrius (Khirbet el Murasas) is the best representative of this type (Magen and Talgam, 1990). In *coenobia*, generally each monk lived separately, but a cell might have been shared by two or three monks or there might have been larger dormitories, in accordance with the regulations for the monks legislated by Emperor Justinian.

The *laura*, by contrast, was composed of dispersed cells, connected to each other and to the communal buildings by a network of paths that converted the scattered elements into an integral architectural entity. The Great Laura of Saint Sabas (Mar Saba) was the most elaborate example of this type (Patrich, 1995). Its remains are distributed along two kilometers of the ravine.

The *laura* hermitages were of various types. The simplest cells had a single room and a courtyard, while the complex ones consisted of several rooms, including a private chapel or a prayer niche. Cooking installations and utensils were sometimes found in the cells. All cells had one or several water cisterns.

Two main church types were common in the desert monasteries—the cave church and the built chapel; a true basilica was rare. The communal buildings in a *coenobium* consisted of one or more churches, a refectory, a kitchen and bakery, storerooms, stables, and sometimes a hostel for the lodging of pilgrims and guests. There also might be a hospital or cells furnished with stone beds for the care of the sick, and even a bathhouse, as in the Monastery of Martyrius. Rainwater was collected by means of a most efficient and well cared for system of plastered channels and gutters leading into large water cisterns constructed under the courtyard. Special reservoirs were constructed for the irrigation of the garden of the monastery. Open spaces and passages were paved by flagstones. In some instances, the large halls—the monastic chapel, refectory, and the rooms adjoining them—were paved by colorful mosaic floors with various patterns. There also were burial chapels and cemeteries, in which the monks were interred according to their inner hierarchy: abbots apart, priests and deacons in another group, and unordained monks in a third. The tomb of the founding father was sometimes marked by a special building, or he was buried in the cave in which he had spent his life. The tomb could become a focal point for the veneration of monks and pilgrims.

Almost all of the communal buildings found in a *coenobium* also were present in the core of a *laura*, except that the latter had no walls or gates. Typologically both kinds of monasteries could be constructed on a plain, on a moderately hilly area, or upon steep cliffs. Monasteries also were established among the ruins of the Hasmonean/Herodian desert fortresses like Masada (*laura*) and Hyrcania and Herodium (*coenobia*) (Hirschfeld, 1992; Patrich, 1995).

BIBLIOGRAPHY

Bottini, G. C., Leah Di Segni, and Eugenio Alliata, eds. *Christian Archaeology in the Holy Land. New Discoveries*. Jerusalem, 1990.

Chitty, Darews J. *The Desert a City*. Oxford, 1966.

Goldfus, Haim, Benny Arubas, and Eugenio Alliata. "The Monastery of St. Theoctistus (Deir Muqallik)." *Liber Annuus* 45 (1995), 247–292; pls. 5–24.

Hirschfeld, Yizhar. *The Judean Desert Monasteries in the Byzantine Period*. New Haven and London, 1992.

Hirschfeld, Yizhar. "Euthymius and His Monastery in the Judean Desert." *Liber Annuus* 43 (1993), 339–371; pls. 19–24.

Hirschfeld, Yizhar, and Rivka Birger. "Chronique Archéologique: Khirbet ed-Deir (Désert de Juda)—1981–1984." *Revue biblique* 93 (1986), 276–284.

Magen, Yizhak, and Rina Talgam. "The Monastery of Martyrius at Maale Adumim (Khirbet el-Murassas) and Its Mosaics." In *Christian Archaeology in the Holy Land. New Discoveries*, edited by G. C. Bottini et al., pp. 91–152. Jerusalem, 1990.

Patrich, Joseph. "Chapels and Hermitages of St. Sabas Monastery." In *Ancient Churches Revealed*, edited by Yoram Tsafrir, pp. 233–243. Jerusalem, 1993.

Patrich, Joseph. *Sabas, Leader of Palestinian Monasticism. A Comparative Study in Eastern Monasticism, Fourth to Seventh Centuries*. Dumbarton Oaks Studies XXXII. Washington, D.C., 1995.

Sion, Ofer. "The Monasteries of the 'Desert of the Jordan.'" *Liber Annuus* 46 (1996), 245–264; pls. 1–4.

Vailhé, Simon. "Répertoire alphabétique des monastères de Palestine." *Révue de l'Orient Chretien* 4 (1989), 512–542; 5 (1990), 19–48, 272–292. A comprehensive catalog of 116 Palestinian monasteries according to the literary sources with reference to numerous other studies by the author on particular monasteries in the Judean Desert.

JOSEPH PATRICH

MOSAICS. The intensive archaeological fieldwork conducted at the Hasmonean and Herodian fortresses of the Judean Desert, which began in the 1960s, has yielded rich evidence of mosaic art from the late Hellenistic and Roman periods. As a whole, the mosaics of the Hasmonean and Herodian periods found in the Judean Desert exemplify the Jewish art tradition of avoiding the representation of living creatures, rather, making use of geometric and floral motifs. The earliest mosaic floor was found in the bathhouse of the Hasmonean palace near the mound Tulul Abu el-Alayiq at Jericho (second to the first century BCE). White tesserae (small evenly cut cubes of stone) form the background for a rectangular panel divided into three sections by two rows of black tesserae. In the center, a checkerboard pattern frames a square, surrounded by a saw-toothed pattern and filled with a smaller checkerboard pattern of angular white and black tesserae.

Other early mosaic floors dating to the first century BCE, were discovered by Yigael Yadin in the royal palaces of the Herodian fortress of Masada. Simple geometrical patterns decorate the floors of the living quarters of the upper terrace of the Northern Palace: for example, a rectangle formed by rows of black tesserae on a background of white tesserae and a pattern of adjacent hexagons of black tesserae on a white background. Traces of a mosaic border are visible along the walls of the lower terrace in the same palace. Outside the southern wall, a mosaic floor had been laid in the court of the public bathroom. An isolated row of black tesserae decorates the perimeter of the court. On a background of white tesserae, a second row of the same width surrounds a frame of adjacent hexagons of black tesserae for a central circular geometric composition later destroyed.

Rooms of the residential wing of the Western Palace at Masada are decorated with polychrome mosaics. For instance, the entrance hall to the throne room has an elaborate composition in white, black, and red. A row of red tesserae followed by a saw-toothed pattern of black tesserae forms the perimeter of the decorated area. On a white background, a double row of black tesserae arranged in an inverted wave pattern surrounds a composition of segmented meander motif in red and black tesserae, which in turn frames the central composition on a background of red tesserae. Stems and opposed shoots with white berries encircle a simple ivy scroll in white and red tesserae, the white ivy leaves alternate with red vine leaves and single pomegranates. The central medallion is composed of intersecting circles with alternating sections in red and black tesserae. The corners of the central square are decorated with floral motifs.

A small private bathroom and the corridor leading to it in the same northeastern section of the palace are paved with a polychrome mosaic. The corridor is decorated with a square panel of red and black tesserae on a white background filled with the geometric pattern of the main composition, apart from the center of the composition where a radial pattern of leaves formed by white and red tesserae crossed by a double blue line appears.

The partial destruction of the mosaic floors in the Northern and Western Palaces provides an opportunity to see the process followed by their makers in laying the floors. They scratched the main lines of the composition in the wet plaster of the *rudus* (bottom floor) as guides for bedding the tesserae.

In Upper Herodium near Bethlehem traces of the mosaic floor can be seen along the wall of the *caldarium* ("hot room") in the bathhouse of the royal palace. A still intact composition was found in the *tepidarium* of the central bathhouse of Lower Herodium in the southwest corner of the pool complex. A row of black tesserae decorates the white background of the room. The central composition is a square panel enclosed in a frame of black tesserae. A three-strand guilloche forms the inner circular medallion, which surrounds a series of intersecting circles creating a pattern of rosettes. Single and multiple pomegranates decorate the corner of the square panel. The *laconicum*, too, had been paved with mosaic; only an isolated section of the circular frame of ivy scrolls on a white background remains.

In the fortress of Cypros near Jericho, the mosaic floor of the *apodyterium* ("disrobing room") of the lower bathhouse has survived. The floor is decorated with a square panel composed of intersecting circles on a square grid, forming an orthogonal row of white quatrefoils alternating with concave squares.

The small mosaic sections found in the *apodyterium* of the Royal Palace atop the fortress of Machaerus in Perea, in the rich mansions of Jerusalem, in the villa on the shore at Caesarea, and on the floors of the royal fortresses of the Judean Desert constitute a homogenous group.

Stylistically, the mosaics can be divided into two groups. The polychrome mosaics of the Western Palace at Masada are better placed in the context of the Oriental Hellenistic tradition. The more simple mosaic compositions in black and white found in the Northern Palace and in the public bath, as in the fortress of Cypros, are typical of Italian mosaics and support the idea that artisans were sent from the center of the empire to decorate the royal palaces of King Herod.

BIBLIOGRAPHY

Balty, Janine. "La mosäique antique au Proche-Orient, I: Des origines à la Tétrarchie." In *Aufstieg und Niedergang der Römischen Welt*, vol. 12, edited by Hildebard Temporini, pp. 348–429. Berlin, 1981. See especially "Époque d'Hérode" on pages 357–360.

Netzer, Ehud. *Herodium: An Archaeological Guide.* Jerusalem, 1987.

Netzer, Ehud. *Masada III, The Buildings: Stratigraphy and Architecture*. Jerusalem, 1991.

Netzer, Ehud. "Cypros." In *The New Encyclopedia of Archaeological Excavations in the Holy Land*, vol. 1, edited by Ephraim Stern, pp. 315–317. New York, 1993.

Netzer, Ehud. "Jericho: Hellenistic to Early Arab Period." In *The New Encyclopedia of Archaeological Excavations in the Holy Land*, vol. 2, edited by Ephraim Stern, pp. 681–691. New York, 1993.

Yadin, Yigael. *Masada: Herod's Fortress and the Zealots' Last Stand.* London, 1966.

MICHELE PICCIRILLO

MOSES. In the Bible, Moses is primarily a deliverer, leader, mediator, and judge, and secondarily a prophet and priest. In Jewish literature of the Second Temple period there are two main trends. First, Moses' biblical roles are amplified (especially in *Jubilees* and the *Testament of Moses*): he is predestined from creation to be mediator, continually intercedes for Israel, and is a prophetic lawgiver who receives revelation from God about all things to the last days. Second, in the apologetic of Jewish Greek writers (especially Aristobulus, Artapanus, Philo, and Josephus), Moses conforms to Greek ideals: the great civilizer, philosopher, and inventor; the ideal king embodying the offices of legislator, high priest, and prophet; and, perhaps, a "divine man."

In the Dead Sea Scrolls the character of Moses is developed in the manner of the former category. There is no reference to Moses as king, and his priestly role of atonement receives only brief mention in a prayer (Words of the Luminaries[a] 4Q504 1–2, ii.9–10). Moses is above all a lawgiver, associated with the Torah through formulas such as "Moses said," "as God said/commanded by the hand of Moses," "as it is written in the book of Moses," and "the Torah of Moses." In the two sectarian rule books Damascus Document (CD; 4Q266–273; 5Q12; 6Q15) and Rule of the Community (1QS; 4Q255–264a; 5Q11), joining the community is tantamount to "taking upon oneself (an oath) to return to the Torah of Moses" (CD xv.9, 12; xvi.2, 5; 1QS v.8). [*See* Damascus Document, Rule of the Community.] Any deliberate or negligent breach of the Torah of Moses is punishable by permanent expulsion (see Apocryphon of Moses C, 4Q377 2.ii). [*See* Community Organization.] Oaths by the Torah of Moses, as with the divine name, are banned (CD xv.2; cf. Josephus's comment about the Essenes [*The Jewish War* 2.145]: "after God, they hold most in awe the name of their lawgiver, any blasphemer of whom is punished with death"). [*See* Essenes; Josephus Flavius.]

Moses' mediatory role is particularly enhanced in the Rewritten Bible/pseudepigraphal narratives. [*See* Apocrypha and Pseudepigrapha; Rewritten Bible.] Moses' authority as God's spokesperson and the promise of a future prophet like Moses are grounded in the biblical account (*Ex*. 20.18–21 and *Dt*. 5.23–31) that the people shrank in fear from God's presence at Mount Sinai and requested that Moses mediate between them and God (4Q377 2.ii; Reworked Pentateuch[a] 4Q158 6). [*See* Reworked Pentateuch.] Moses is the "man of God," a "great and upright man," one who knows the knowledge of the most high, sees the vision of the Almighty, and whose voice is heard in the council of the most high (Apocryphon of Joshua[a] 4Q378 3, 26). He is covered by the cloud because of his sanctity and is an incomparable herald of glad tidings through whom God would speak "as though he were an angel" (4Q377 2.ii). Moses' intercession serves as the model for a prayer of confession (4Q393 3; cf. *Jub*. 1).

But it is in Moses' role as prophet par excellence that the distinctiveness of this literature is especially apparent. Along with the writings of other prophets, the Torah of Moses is regarded as foretelling the sins and punishment of the Israelites until the last days, (4Q504 1–2.iii.11–14; cf. 1QS i.3; 4Q397 14–21; 4Q398 14–17.i–ii, 11–13 C; Words of Moses 1Q22 1.7–11; Commentary on Genesis A 4Q252 1.iv.2; Florilegium 4Q174 1–3.i.2–3 and 1–3.ii.2–3; Jubilees[a] 4Q216 1–4). In the sectarian rules, the "Torah of Moses" embraces the extrabiblical ordinances of the community (4Q266 11.6 parallels 4Q270 7.i.20), "for in it everything is specified" (CD xvi.2). This too is tied up with the idea of Moses as a prophet and recipient of all revelation: inherent in his Torah are the "hidden things" that are discernible only by inspired exegesis (see also the halakhic works Miqtsat Maʿasei ha-Torah and juridical text 2Q25, Temple Scroll[a] 11Q19 and Reworked Pentateuch[c] 4Q365 23.4). Although in the Bible he is neither anointed nor given the title, Moses is called God's "anointed one" in the Apocryphon of Moses C (4Q377 2.ii), presumably to highlight his role as one of the prophets who are designated "anointed ones" (War Scroll 1QM xi.7; CD ii.12, vi.1). Furthermore, the future prophet described in *Deuteronomy* 18.15–19 as "like" Moses is regarded as an eschatological figure accompanying the Messiahs of Aaron and Israel at Qumran (Testimonia 4Q175; 1QS ix.11; cf. Melchizedek, 11Q13 ii.17–18) and the royal Messiah in rabbinic literature. The historical Teacher of Righteousness mentioned in the sectarian scrolls is modeled as a prophet like Moses—authoritative lawgiver and leader of a new Israel in the wilderness in the last days—but seemingly not the prophet to accompany the messiahs. None of this is directly parallel to the portrayal of Moses as Israel's ideal king in Philo and rabbinic literature, nor to the combination of prophet and king in Johannine Christology.

[*See also* Moses, Texts of.]

BIBLIOGRAPHY

Abrahams, Israel et al. "Moses." In *Encyclopaedia Judaica*, vol. 12, cols. 371–411. Extensive survey on Moses in the Bible, Jewish Greek writings, and rabbinic literature, but does not treat the Dead Sea Scrolls.

Jeremias, J. "Mouses." In *Theological Dictionary of the New Testament*, vol. 4, pp. 848–878. A technical survey of the figure of Moses in writings of the Second Temple period (including the Damascus Document) and rabbinic Judaism compared with the New Testament.

Meeks, Wayne A. *The Prophet-King: Moses Traditions and the Johannine Christology*. Novum Testamentum Supplements 14. Leiden, 1967. A detailed examination of the role of Moses in Jewish literature of the Second Temple period—including the Dead Sea Scrolls, rabbinic literature, Samaritan and Mandean sources, and the *Gospel of John*.

DANIEL K. FALK

MOSES, TEXTS OF. As the greatest figure within Judaism, Moses inspired an extensive body of extrabiblical literature, but the vast majority consists of anecdotes or citations of his authority in larger works. Relatively few works composed in the Second Temple period survive that were devoted primarily to the purpose of developing traditions about Moses either as the central subject or as purported author. In contrast with the rich cycles of literature associated with Enoch, Baruch, Ezra, and Daniel, one can cite *Jubilees*, *Testament of Moses*, and Philo's *De Vita Mosis*. Taking the Dead Sea Scrolls into account, this body of texts is richly enhanced, testifying to a very high regard for Moses among those who cherished these documents.

All the following works survive at Qumran only in Hebrew, the original language of composition. The connection of several of the works with Moses is disputable, and the first three works are mentioned here only briefly because they receive detailed discussion in specific articles.

Jubilees. Fourteen or fifteen copies and three or four related works attest to the importance of this work at Qumran, although it is clearly a pre-Qumran work and also was preserved elsewhere. [*See* Jubilees, Book of.] Chapter 1 supplements the biblical account of Moses receiving the law on Mount Sinai: an angel dictates the revelation to Moses; God foretells the sins of Israel analogously to his final revelation to Moses in *Deuteronomy* 31.16–21, but adding calendrical error and defilement of the sanctuary to the biblical mention of idolatry; and while still on the mountain, Moses intercedes for the people with a nonbiblical prayer based on *Deuteronomy* 9.26–29 and Psalm 51, which may in turn have been the inspiration for a communal confession from Cave 4 at Qumran (liturgical work 4Q393). Chapters 2 through 46 describe the story of the Book of Genesis being dictated to Moses on Mount Sinai, and chapters 47 through 50 concern Moses' life from birth to the Sinai revelation.

Temple Scroll. It is not entirely certain whether this very large work intends to be a new *torah*, given directly without Mosaic mediation or a rewritten *torah*, attempting to elucidate the true meaning of the laws received by Moses. [*See* Temple Scroll.] The reference to "sons of Aaron your brother" and the setting of divine revelation on a mountain (Temple Scroll[a] 11Q19 xliv.5, li.6–7) suggest but do not necessarily imply that Moses is the assumed recipient. In either case, the author's effort to remove every mention of Moses and to portray God as speaking in the first person means that although the author conjures Moses' authority for extrabiblical laws, Moses himself remains invisible.

Reworked Pentateuch[a–e]. Five copies (4Q158, 364–365, and 366–367) survive of this reordered, harmonized, and supplemented narrative, which seems to encompass Pentateuchal traditions broadly. [*See* Reworked Pentateuch.] Moses appears in fragments dealing with the Exodus, but there is no special emphasis on him as either author or central subject. The reworking of several passages emphasizes Moses' authority as God's spokesperson and that this role and the promise of a future prophet like Moses derive from the people's request. (See similarly Apocryphon of Moses C 4Q377).

Words of Moses. Thirty-two small fragments preserve a large proportion of the first four columns of the scroll (1Q22). Both form and content indicate that it was intended as a rewritten *Deuteronomy*, harmonized with other Pentateuchal traditions. It consists of an introduction similar to *Deuteronomy*, giving the same setting for the following Mosaic discourse; an admonition by Moses to the congregation of Israel to keep God's commandments, warning against apostasy and the consequent judgment, and instruction to appoint wise men to teach God's laws; and laws for sabbatical years and Yom Kippur. The content and extent of the rest of the manuscript are unknown.

The author's use of biblical phrasing, above all that of *Deuteronomy*, has been termed *anthological* in style, but the retelling is more purposeful than is suggested by that term. First, the author emphasizes Moses' authority as God's spokesperson. Second, calendrical violation is added to the sin of idolatry from *Deuteronomy* 4.25–28 as grounds for the foretold destruction, as in *Jubilees* 1.10–14. Third, by having Eleazar and Joshua accompany Moses on the mountain and making them mediators of the instruction along with the Levitical leaders and priests, the author may endorse the successors to Mosaic authority as a normative model of leadership. Similar idealization of Moses' successors appears in Josephus (*Jewish Antiquities* 4.218) and probably underlies certain authority structures in the sectarian scrolls (e.g., priest, overseer, and judges/elders/council). Fourth, Yom Kippur rituals are on behalf of the land as well as the people, a concern that is emphasized in the sectarian scrolls (e.g., Rule of the Community 1QS viii.6, viii.10, ix.4–5; Rule of the Congregation 1Q28a i.3). [*See* Rule of the Community; Rule of the Congregation; *and* Yom Kippur.]

Thus, a rewritten *Deuteronomy* is used to demonstrate concerns about calendar, submission to the community's teachers, and atonement. These are common concerns of the Qumran sectarian literature, but distinctive features pointing to a Qumran origin are lacking. On the basis of paleography, one may conclude that this manuscript was probably copied no later than the early first century BCE.

Apocryphon of Moses B[a] and [b] and Liturgy of the Three Tongues of Fire. Liturgy of the Three Tongues of Fire (1Q29; seventeen very small fragments) was titled after the phrase "three tongues of fire" (2.3) in the context of what appears to be a ritual led by the priest involving a "right hand stone." The same ritual almost certainly appears in Apocryphon of Moses B[b] (4Q376; one long narrow fragment and possibly another small fragment), originally given the same title. A ritual involving a priest and a "left hand stone," which emits flashes of fire, is preceded by sacrifices similar to those on Yom Kippur and followed by matters concerning the Prince of the Congregation in battle.

Because of a shared mention of "the anointed priest," sacrifices reminiscent of Yom Kippur, and similar movements of the priest, it is probable that Apocryphon of Moses B[b] and Liturgy of Three Tongues of Fire are the same work as Apocryphon of Moses B[a] (4Q375). John Strugnell (1995) suggested that Words of Moses may be another copy of this work, but the similarity is not compelling.

Apocryphon of Moses B[a] (one large and one small fragment) contains an address by an individual to a group based on *Deuteronomy* 13.1–6, urging the people to adhere to everything that God commands "by the mouth of the prophet" but to put to death the prophet who preaches apostasy. Next, the text details an unprecedented procedure of adjudication for dealing with a case not raised in the Bible: What to do if a prophet's tribe appeals an accusation against him, claiming that he is a truthful and faithful prophet? The tribe, elders, and judges assemble before the high priest, who carries out a ritual of discernment involving sacrifices reminiscent of Yom Kippur (*Lv.* 16), study of "hidden" laws in the secrecy of the Holy of Holies, and a presentation before the assembly.

The rest of the ritual is lost from Apocryphon of Moses B[a], but if Apocryphon of Moses B[b] and Liturgy of Three Tongues of Fire are indeed copies of the same work, it involved an oracular use of two stones. Probably after some sort of test or ordeal and his private study, the high priest was to lead the prophet out before the people. While he delivered his verdict, one of the stones would shine forth, presumably either to indicate a judgment or to confirm the priest's verdict. The two stones were certainly the shoulder stones of the high priest's breastplate (*Ex.* 28.9–12), apparently confused with the Urim and Thummim, as is the case in a remarkably analogous passage in Josephus (*Jewish Antiquities* 3.214–15). In both cases, a description of the oracle's use in times of war seems to follow (cf. *Nm.* 27.21).

One can only speculate as to the genre and setting of such a fragmentary work. Gershon Brin's (1994) suggestion that it is a polemic by the Qumran community against the rejection of their Teacher of Righteousness is unconvincing. [*See* Teacher of Righteousness.] Strugnell also pauses to speculate on a possible Qumran setting: The Teacher of Righteousness, who may have served as high priest during the supposed interregnum of 159 to 152 BCE, took the oracular stones from the breastplate with him in his retreat to Qumran. Strugnell is correct, however, to hesitate to posit a Qumran origin. Apart from the singular "Prince of all the Congregation," which is a familiar messianic title in several of the sectarian scrolls, the work lacks terminology and content distinctive to the sectarian literature of Qumran. [*See* Prince of the Congregation.] Furthermore, its use of the Tetragrammaton would be unusual in a Qumran composition. It is only possible to conclude that the work originated no later than about the middle of the first century BCE, since Apocryphon of Moses B[b] is written in a late Hasmonean hand and Liturgy of Three Tongues of Fire and Apocryphon of Moses B[a] are early Herodian.

Strugnell concludes that the work is probably a general legal text on the discernment of prophecy and the use of oracle stones, which were operative in the writer's time. Expectation of renewed prophetic activity in the last days and concern over identifying true (e.g., *1 Mc.* 4.46 and 14.41) and false (e.g., *Mk.* 13.22, *Mt.* 24.11, *Rev.* 19.20) prophets were certainly alive in the later Second Temple period, but Strugnell's conviction that the work assumes current use of oracle stones is questionable. The seeming confusion of the shoulder stones with the Urim and Thummim suggests rather an idealized speculation on the use of objects no longer understood.

Assuming Strugnell's probable reconstruction and the heavy reliance on Pentateuchal language, the composition can perhaps best be understood as a rewritten Pentateuch text attempting to explain the use of the mysterious Urim and Thummim in the guise of Mosaic instruction. Its purpose could be to assert priestly primacy, whether or not the prophet and prince represent eschatological figures.

Pseudo-Moses[a–e]. Strugnell originally classified Pseudo-Moses[a–e] (4Q385a, 387a, 388–389, and 390) as six copies of one work titled Pseudo-Ezekiel, then Second-Ezekiel. Devorah Dimant, the current editor, has discerned in these fragments parts of three different works of different character: Apocryphon of Jeremiah, Pseudo-Ezekiel, and Pseudo-Moses. Here the concern is only with those fragments that Dimant attributes to Pseudo-Moses: Pseudo-Moses[a] 13, 20, 40–42, and 44; Pseudo-Moses[b] 1–3, and 5; Pseudo-Moses[c] 4, 6, 9, 17, and 19; Pseudo-Moses[d] 1–2, 8–9; and all seven fragments of Pseudo-Moses[e].

In a manner common in apocalyptic literature, Pseudo-Moses[e] presents a schematized history of Israel's sin and divine punishment as a sequence of periods (jubilees, weeks of years, seventy years) in the guise of revelation by God spoken in the first person singular to an unnamed leader in the second person singular. [*See* Apocalyptic Texts.] Considering his role as lawgiver and mediator and the similar style and language to the divine addresses in *Deuteronomy* and *Jubilees* 1, the addressee is almost certainly Moses.

Neither the progression of periods nor the order of fragments is certain. Fragment 1 of Pseudo-Moses[e] begins with the return from Babylonian captivity but assumes the concept of an extended exile lasting 490 years or ten jubilees (see 4Q387[a] 3–4), characterized as a time of escalating sin and divine wrath. Only the first returnees are evaluated positively as receptive to God and penitent for their sins. The special laxity in the "seventh jubilee," when the people will forget "ordinance and appointed time, and sabbath and covenant" might refer to the Hellenistic assimilation of the third century BCE under Ptolemaic control of Palestine. God delivers them up to enemy armies and the angels of Mastemah but preserves a remnant.

If fragment 2 of Pseudo-Moses[e] follows (Dimant, 1992), it seems to concern the even greater apostasy under the Seleucids: violation of all of God's laws and commandments, factional disputes, hoarding of unjust wealth, defilement of the Temple, corrupt priests, and intermarriage or incest. The last three sins correspond to the "three nets of Belial," with which the Damascus Document (CD iv.17) also characterizes this time. These generations, too, are consigned to the rule of Belial and the angels of Mastemah. Alternatively, if fragment 2 precedes fragment 1 (Florentino García Martínez, 1991; Michael Knibb, 1992), it concerns sins of the divided kingdom.

Extensive overlaps among Pseudo-Moses[a–d] indicate that these are copies of a single work. The style and general content correspond so remarkably to Pseudo-Moses[e] that Dimant plausibly argues that they are the same Pseudo-Moses text. On the other hand, there is no exact overlap with Pseudo-Moses[e] and no second person singular address, but rather a few cases of second person plural. In the absence of more concrete evidence, the possibility must be kept open that Pseudo-Moses[a–d] represent copies of a variant version of a closely related work.

In one fragment (4Q389 2) God speaks in the past tense of his care for the Israelites in having led them out of Egypt and through the wilderness to the Promised Land, but he also addresses a group in the second person plural. If this is in fact a Pseudo-Moses text, it must then be regarded as a divine discourse to Moses with other leaders shortly before the crossing of the Jordan—exactly the situation depicted in Words of Moses, discussed above.

Most of the preserved content concerns the extended exile under God's wrath until the end of "ten jubilees of years." It is tempting to suggest that a large passage that can be reconstructed from overlapping fragments (4Q385a 41, 44; 4Q387a 2, 3.i–iii; 4Q388a 1.i–ii; 4Q389 1.i–ii; see Wacholder and Abegg, 1995, pp. xvii–xviii) describes the returnees who try to serve God, the downfall of the Persian empire, the conquests of Alexander the Great (a "blasphemer"), the subsequent division of his kingdom, and, later, the Seleucid Antiochus IV Epiphanes as a second "blasphemer" who plunders Egypt and Israel (see *Dn.* 11.25–28, 42–43; *1 Mc.* 1.16–28) and in whose time Jerusalem priests apostatize. [*See* Antiochus IV Epiphanes.] This is far from certain, but if correct, then this work—represented by Pseudo-Moses[a–d]—could not be the same as Pseudo-Moses[e], since it gives a different portrayal of the same chronology.

The schematized framework of history that Pseudo-Moses[e] shares with Pseudo-Moses[a–d], in which sin and punishment escalate throughout an extended exile under the rule of evil angels, belongs to a rich tradition in apocalyptic literature. [*See* Angels.] *Daniel* 9.20–27, the Animal Apocalypse (*1 Enoch* 89), Melchizedek (11Q13), and, possibly, Ages of Creation (4Q180–181) all share a framework of ten jubilees or seventy weeks (equal to 490 years), and similar schemes appear in *Jubilees*, the Apocalypse of Weeks (*1 En.* 93), and the *Testament of Levi*. The catalog of sins with which Israel is charged finds very close verbal parallels in *Jubilees* and the Damascus Document, and, to a lesser extent, in the *Testament of Levi* and the *Testament of Moses*. *Jubilees* furthermore shares the illusion of a discourse to Moses as a venue for a forecast, as do the *Testament of Moses* and Words of Moses. [*See* Enoch, Books of; Testaments.]

There is no use of distinctive language that could concretely indicate a Qumran provenance, and the positive evaluation of the first generation of returnees may speak against it (cf. CD iii.10b–12a). The comparable literature and the enumerated sins point to a circle with priestly and apocalyptic concerns, probably pre-Qumran. If these manuscripts represent a single work, paleography suggests that it could not have been composed later than about the middle of the first century BCE, since Pseudo-Moses[e] is written in a Herodian hand and the rest in late Hasmonean or early Herodian hands. [*See* Paleography.] On the basis of historical allusions, Dimant tentatively suggests a date of composition no later than the reign of the Hasmonean John Hyrcanus (134–104 BCE). [*See* John Hyrcanus.]

Apocryphon of Moses? Two small fragments (2Q21) written in a Herodian script preserve a scrap of discourse addressed to someone in the second person singular, in which the sons of Aaron apparently are appointed to administer justice, followed by a nonbiblical prayer of Moses. Whether this was a rewritten Pentateuch text, a narrative section in a Moses pseudepigraph, or merely part of a broader narrative, remains open. Nor is it clear whether the discourse is spoken by Moses to Israel, God to Moses, or God to Israel. In the Pentateuch, Aaron's four sons are appointed to serve as priests. Their judicial role here may be deduced from the association of Nadab and Abihu with the seventy elders (*Ex.* 24.1, 24.9) and

Eleazar's function as judge after Moses' death (*Dt.* 17.9, 17.12). Possibly it relates to the judicial role that priests exercise in the Qumran rule books, but there are no clues to the provenance of these fragments. [*See* Priests.]

Discourse on the Exodus/Conquest Tradition. One medium-sized and fifteen small fragments remain of this text (4Q374), copied in an early Herodian hand. It contains a discourse on the Exodus and the conquest in the manner of numerous historical recitals dependent on Deuteronomic theology whose purpose is normally hortatory. It is unlikely that Moses is the speaker, as earlier believed (the text originally was entitled Apocryphon of Moses A), because the text alludes to the conquest in the past tense and seems to describe Joshua's mourning for Moses. The speaker is more likely Joshua or a later prophet. It lacks distinctive indicators of Qumran sectarian origin, and use of the Tetragrammaton may suggest a non-Qumran origin.

Apocryphon of Moses C. The work (4Q377) survives in one large and one small fragment, copied in a Herodian hand. The lack of distinctive Qumran language and a free use of the Tetragrammaton do not suggest a Qumran origin. Unlike the other Moses texts reviewed here, this is the only one that clearly speaks about Moses as its subject. In contrast to the "congregation of YHVH," which shrank from God's glory revealed on Mount Sinai, Moses is eulogized as "his anointed one," through whose mouth God would speak "as an angel."

All the texts surveyed here make implicit authoritative claims on the basis of the figure Moses. [*See* Moses.] Although there is no proof that any of these texts were composed at Qumran, the number of manuscripts found there and the interrelationships with sectarian compositions suggest the authority attributed to them at Qumran. This is wholly consonant with a community that envisaged and organized itself on the model of the wilderness congregation under Mosaic leadership, applying in a practical way the idea of a prophetic *torah* to be uncovered by inspired interpretation. [*See* Community Organization.] Rabbinic Judaism's concept of the oral Torah is a different means of drawing on the figure Moses to assert legal authority. When the early church portrayed Jesus in continuity with Moses (e.g., *Mk.* 9.4 and parallels), as a second Moses (e.g., *Mt.* 5–7, *Acts* 3.22), or one greater than Moses (e.g., *Heb.* 3.1–6, *Jn.* 1.17), it expressed an analogous impulse: these are assertions of the authority of Jesus' teaching.

BIBLIOGRAPHY

TEXTS

Dimant, Devorah. "New Light from Qumran on the Jewish Pseudepigrapha: 4Q390." In *The Madrid Qumran Congress: Proceedings of the International Congress on the Dead Sea Scrolls, Madrid, 18–21 March 1991*, edited by Julio Trebolle Barrera and Luis Vegas Montaner, vol. 2, pp. 405–448. Studies on the Texts of the Desert of Judah, 11. Leiden, 1992. A preliminary publication of Pseudo-Moses[e].

Newsom, Carol. "Discourse on the Exodus/Conquest Tradition." In *Qumran Cave 4: Parabiblical Texts, Part 2*, by Magen Broshi et al., pp. 85–110. Discoveries in the Judaean Desert, 19. Oxford, 1995. The official publication of Discourse on the Exodus/Conquest Tradition.

Strugnell, John. "Apocryphon of Moses." In *Qumran Cave 4: Parabiblical Texts, Part 2*, by Magen Broshi et al., pp. 111–136. Discoveries in the Judaean Desert, 19. Oxford, 1995. The official publication of Apocryphon of Moses B[a–b].

Wacholder, Ben Zion, and Martin G. Abegg. *A Preliminary Edition of the Unpublished Dead Sea Scrolls, The Hebrew and Aramaic Texts from Cave Four, Fascicle Three*, pp. 155–166, 228–244, 248–266. Washington, D.C., 1995. Preliminary transcriptions of 4Q374, 4Q375, 4Q376, 4Q377, 4Q385a, 4Q387a, 4Q388a, 4Q389, and 4Q390. Discourse on the Exodus/Conquest Tradition, Apocryphon of Moses B[a–b], Apocryphon of Moses C, and Pseudo-Moses [a–e].

STUDIES

Brin, Gershon. "Issues Concerning Prophets (Studies in 4Q375)." In *Studies in Biblical Law: From the Hebrew Bible to the Dead Sea Scrolls*, pp. 128–163. Journal for the Study of the Old Testament Supplement Series, 176. Sheffield, 1994. A detailed commentary on Apocryphon of Moses B[a].

García Martínez, Florentino. "Nuevos textos no bíblicos procedentes de Qumrán (I)." *Estudios Bíbliocos* 49 (1991), 97–134. Survey and evaluation of Pseudo-Moses texts, pp. 123–132; proposes a different order of fragments for Pseudo-Moses[e].

Knibb, Michael A. "A Note on *4Q372* and *4Q390*." In *The Scriptures and the Scrolls. Studies in Honour of A. S. van der Woude on the Occasion of His 65th Birthday*, edited by Florentino García Martínez, A. Hilhorst, and C. J. Labuschagne, pp. 164–177. Supplements to Vetus Testamentum, 49. Leiden, 1992. An alternative interpretation of Pseudo-Moses[e].

DANIEL K. FALK

MURABBAʿAT, WADI. [*This entry is divided into two articles:* Archaeology *and* Written Material.]

Archaeology

The caves of Wadi Murabbaʿat lie in a deep ravine descending from the Judean Desert to the Dead Sea and are situated approximately 18 kilometers (11 miles) south of Khirbet Qumran and 25 kilometers (15.5 miles) southeast of Jerusalem. First discovered by the bedouin, the area was then subjected to controlled excavations and survey, revealing the remains from the Chalcolithic period onward and, most importantly, from the time of the Bar Kokhba Revolt (132–135 CE). [*See* Bar Kokhba Revolt.]

Four caves were examined in 1952 by Gerald L. Harding, Roland de Vaux, and Dominique Barthélemy (de Vaux, Benoit, and Milik, 1961). During an extensive survey in 1968, another cave was excavated by P. Bar Adon, who traced the remains of a Roman road from one cave to another (Greenhut, 1984). A cemetery which resembles the one at Qumran was discovered by Hanan Eshel and Z. Greenhut in 1993. [*See* Cemeteries.] In that year, another survey was carried out by the Israel Antiquities Authority, but no results have yet been published. [*See* Israel Antiquities Authority.]

The site, Mispeh Shalem, extends across two hills and a terrace that faces the Judean Desert eastward, between the Wadi Murabbaʿat and the Metsoqui Derogot. Several ravines separate the different parts of the site; a wall built of large stones joins two areas of the site. All areas reveal burnt layers. Area A, on a flat hilltop, yielded a two-room structure, where a hearth, silos, ashes, and pottery sherds were found. Area B is the main part of the site, located on a terrace on the lower slope. Two platforms or halls were discovered here. In Area C, indications of the production of flint tools were discerned. The tools comprise a unique assemblage including over four hundred complete and broken tabular scrapers, over eighty of which bear incisions. Pottery includes numerous tiny votive vessels and large, coarse vessels were found. Petrographic analysis show three sources of clay, one being from Transjordan. The nature of the archaeological remains indicates that the site must have served as a cult center serving nomadic groups who wandered between Transjordan and southern Palestine.

Chalcolithic Period. The excavators distinguished two phases at Wadi Murabbaʿat: the Middle Chalcolithic (c. mid-fourth millennium BCE) and the Late Chalcolithic. It cannot be determined whether the occupation was seasonal or continuous.

The Chalcolithic period finds were discovered in Caves 1 and 2 and consist of handmade coarse ware with only a small amount of tempering added. Common types are reconstructed from the sherds as few vessels were found complete: cornets, chalices, goblets, deep bowls with straight sides, holemouth jars, several jugs with lug handles, and several thumb-indented ledge handles. Several of the bases bear mat impressions. Some complete vessels were burnished. Three types of decoration were used: red or brown wash; incised decoration, usually in a herringbone pattern; and relief decoration, formed by a rope or thumb-indented clay strip. [*See* Pottery.] The flint assemblage consisted mostly of scrapers. Blades, knives, axes, and several arrowheads were also found. The bone artifacts include awls, needles, and several spindle whorls. Stoneware includes two basalt whetstones and a small limestone bowl with four rectangular projections around the rim. [*See* Stoneware.]

The Bronze Age and the Iron Age. As the finds from the Middle Bronze Age II are relatively scarce, the excavators believe that Cave 2 served as a brief temporary settlement. The Hyksos scarab found in Cave 2 invites special attention; it is dated to the fifteenth dynasty. Two wooden combs have exact parallels in the Middle Bronze Age II tombs at Jericho and from thirteenth-dynasty tombs in Egypt.

During the Iron Age, on the basis of the small amount of pottery dated to the eighth and seventh centuries BCE, the excavators have concluded that the site again served as a temporary refuge rather than as a permanent settlement.

Roman. Most of the finds are dated to the Roman period. A large amount of pottery of all types was dated through parallel pieces at Khirbet Qumran and Jerusalem to the second and early third centuries. Weapons are particularly abundant, including the blade of a *pilum*, the javelin used by the Roman legionnaires. Among wooden artifacts was a stamp with a Latin inscription *C/enturia Annaii/Gargiliu*[*s*] ("Gargilius of the Anaiian century"). The first name is Latin; the second, an African name that was especially common in the first and second centuries CE.

Many wooden and stone spindle whorls were found. The textile fragments were wool, linen, and cotton—some dyed and some decorated. An unusual find was a set of implements believed by the excavators to have been used by a doctor. [*See* Textiles; Wooden Artifacts.]

Coins were discovered by the bedouin, which the excavators purchased. They are believed to be authentic (Milik and Seyrig, 1958). This hoard of silver coins includes 149 Nabatean drachmas, 51 imperial dinars, and 33 tetradrachmas of Trajan. The others were minted locally, the majority in Antioch. One coin was from the First Jewish Revolt (69–70 CE), and nine coins were from the Bar Kokhba Revolt. Two coins had the emblem of the Tenth Legion Fretensis. [*See* Numismatics.]

The excavators took into account the evidence in the caves, especially the written documents, some of which were dated, and concluded that the caves were settled temporarily from the first century BCE onward. A larger and more developed settlement existed during the Bar Kokhba Revolt, when the area served as a refuge for the fleeing rebels and their families (suggested by a child's sandal). The site was eventually overrun by Roman army units, whose belongings—the legionnaire's *pilum* and the military wooden stamp—survived. A small unit continued to be stationed in the area until the end of the second century CE (one of the documents is attributed to the days of Commodus [180–192 CE]).

Caves 1 and 2 were also used in the Arab period. Two lamps dating from the eighth to ninth century CE; several inscriptions, one of which mentions the years 938–939 CE; and a coin from Cave 1, minted in Ramla in the eighth century CE, are from this period. Fragments of Arab pottery were dated to the fourteenth and fifteenth century CE.

BIBLIOGRAPHY

de Vaux, Roland. "Les grottes de Murabbʿât et leurs documents." *Revue biblique* 60 (1953), 244–267.

de Vaux, Roland. "Wady el Murabbaʿât." *Annual of the Department of Antiquities of Jordan* 2 (1953), 85.

de Vaux, Roland, P. Benoit, and J. T. Milik, eds. *Les grottes de Murabbaʿât*. Discoveries in the Judaean Desert, 2. Oxford, 1961.

Eshel, Ḥanan, Zvi Greenhut, and Ḥiam El-Sagha. "A Cemetery of the Qumran Type, Judaean Desert." *Revue biblique* 100 (1993), 252–259.

Greenhut, Z., ed. "P. Bar Adon Excavations in the Judaean Desert." *Atiqot* 9 (Hebrew Series) (1984), 50–82.

Harding, G. L. "Khirbet Qumran and Wadi Murabbaʿât." *Palestine Exploration Quarterly* 84 (1952), 104–109.

Kochavi, M., ed. *Judea Samaria and Golan Archaeological Survey 1967–1968* (Hebrew), p. 36. Jerusalem, 1972.

Milik, J. T., and H. Seyrig. "Tresor Monetair de Murabbaʿât." *Revue numismatique* 6 (1958), 11–26.

EPHRAIM STERN

Written Material

Written documents dated to various periods, beginning with the First Temple era and ending with the Middle Ages, were discovered at Wadi Murabbaʿat. In the following survey I will treat the most significant documents discovered in Wadi Murabbaʿat in chronological order.

Document of the First Temple Period. Palimpsest: letter; list of personal names (Mur 17) was written on papyrus. The palimpsest (a document that was written twice, meaning that after there was no longer a need for the first document, the scribe erased the ink from the document and used the papyrus again) is from the seventh century BCE. [*See* Scribal Practices.] In the first stage a list of names typical of the end of the First Temple era was written on the papyrus, while in the second stage the papyrus was used for writing a letter. It is possible that this document indicates that there were people in Judea who fled to Wadi Murabbaʿat during the Babylonian campaigns in Judea at the beginning of the sixth century BCE.

Documents of the Second Temple Period. A number of important documents from the Second Temple period were found in the caves of Wadi Murabbaʿat. The most ancient among them is a document recording the decisions of a court on an ostracon (Mur 72). This document was dated according to paleographic considerations to the years between 125 and 100 BCE. Regarding the two decisions that a certain court made, the document's mention of Masada is significant. This is one of the proofs that Masada was built during the Hasmonean period. [*See* Masada.]

An additional document from the Second Temple period is the debt acknowledgment (Mur 18) from the year 55/6 CE. This document was written in Tsoba, which is near Jerusalem, and in it Zekhariah ben Yehoḥanan from Kislon says that he owes Avshalom ben Ḥanun twenty silver zuz (meaning twenty Roman dinars) for items he had purchased from Avshalom. [*See* Deeds of Sale.] A third document, which should probably be dated to the end of the Second Temple period, is a writ of divorce (*geṭ*) written during the year 6 in Masada (Mur 19). [*See* Marriage and Divorce.] In this document Yehosef son of Naksan, who lives in Masada, divorces of his own free will Miryam daughter of Yehonatan, who also resides in Masada. Milik thinks that the document is dated by the era of the Roman province of Arabia, which was founded by Trajan in 106 CE, and therefore the document is from 111 CE. Yadin (1961), however, claimed that since the formula "according to the era of Provincia Arabia" does not appear in the document, one cannot suppose that the date is according to the era of Provincia of Arabia. He believed that the document was from the days of the First Jewish Revolt, from 71 CE, and that Miryam left Masada in 71 CE and took her writ of divorce with her to Wadi Murabbaʿat. [*See* First Jewish Revolt.] Yadin assumed that the Jewish rebels living in Masada after the destruction of Jerusalem continued to count the years according to the era of the First Jewish Revolt even after the destruction of Jerusalem, but they could not write: "in the sixth year of the freedom of Israel" or "freedom of Jerusalem," only "in the sixth year." Hence, the sixth year in the document under discussion is the sixth year of the First Jewish Revolt. The latest coin so far discovered in Masada is from the year 112 CE, hence, it is not impossible that the document is from 111 CE (Roman soldiers remained at Masada at least until 112). However, it is not likely that the Romans permitted the Jews to stay in Masada during those years. Therefore it seems that Yadin's suggestion that the document is from 71 CE is more convincing than Milik's later dating.

The debt acknowledgment (Mur 18) and perhaps the writ of divorce (Mur 19), as well as additional documents—deeds of sale of land (Mur 22, 25), deed of sale (Mur 29), and deed of sale of plot (Mur 30)—prove that there were Jewish refugees who escaped to Wadi Murabbaʿat at the end of the First Jewish Revolt, and in light of document Mur 18 it is apparent that some of them fled from the Jerusalem area. If Yadin is correct in his theory regarding the date of document Mur 19, it appears that a woman from Masada moved to Wadi Murabbaʿat after the fall of Jerusalem.

Documents of the Bar Kokhba Period. The majority of the documents found in the caves of Wadi Murabbaʿat were brought to the desert at the end of the Bar Kokhba Revolt (c.132–135 CE). A group of people seeking refuge in the caves of Wadi Murabbaʿat at the end of the rebellion escaped from the region of Herodium (east of Bethlehem). These refugees brought with them to the caves fragments of leather scrolls upon which were written religious texts, as well as papyri upon which were written financial documents and letters. Among the scrolls, mention should be made of the book of Deuteronomy (Mur 2) discovered in Cave 1 at Murabbaʿat (portions of chapters 10 through 15 were preserved) and a scroll of the Minor Prophets (Mur 88) that was found in Cave 5 (portions of *Joel, Amos, Obadiah, Jonah, Micah, Nahum, Habakkuk, Zephaniah,* and *Haggai* were preserved). [*See* Deuteronomy, Book of Minor Prophets.] The remaining scrolls and documents were found in Cave 2. Fragments from a scroll (from which portions of Genesis [Mur 1: 1–3], Exodus [Mur 1:4–5], and Numbers [Mur 1:6–7] were preserved) that possibly contained the entire Torah were found in Cave 1 as well as a small excerpt of a scroll that contained portions of the book of Isaiah (Mur 3; the surviving part is from *Isaiah* 1). [*See* Genesis, Book of; Exodus, Book of; Isaiah, Book of; *and* Numbers, Book of.] Also, phylacteries containing paragraphs from *Exodus* and *Deuteronomy* and a *mezuzah*, the writing upon which cannot be identified, were found in Cave 2. Besides the biblical documents, a small segment of a prayer mentioning Zion (unclassified text Mur 6) was also discovered in Wadi Murabbaʿat.

Fiscal and administrative documents. The fiscal and administrative documents from Wadi Murabbaʿat all were found in Cave 2. The fiscal documents must be divided into those written prior to the Bar Kokhba Revolt and those written during the course of the rebellion. Among the documents written before the Bar Kokhba Revolt are four marriage contracts. Two marriage contracts are written in Aramaic and formulated in a very similar way to those documented in the Mishnah (Mur 20 and Mur 21; Milik suggests that Mur 20 should be dated to the year 117 CE). Both of the other documents are written in Greek (Mur 115, 116). The most significant among them (remarriage contract Mur 115) is dated to 124 CE, and in it a man by the name of Elias son of Simon, born in the village of Gludah in the district of Akrabah, remarried his divorced wife Salome daughter of Vanus Galgulah, whose family lived in the village Beit Betzi in the district of Herodium (this place is mentioned in *1 Maccabees* 9.62–65). [*See* Herodium.] Elias built his house in the district of Gofnah. This document confirms that the division of districts in effect during the Second Temple period and documented in Pliny (*Historia naturalis* 5.70) and Josephus (*The Jewish War* 3.54–56) continued to function until the Bar Kokhba Revolt.

Highly significant among the documents written during the rebellion are farming contracts (Mur 24) written in Hebrew. In them were copied a series of transactions signed in the winter of "year two of the redemption of Israel by Shimʿon ben Kosibaʾ [Bar Kokhba] in a camp situated in Herodion." [*See* Bar Kokhba, Shimʿon.] In these transactions plots of land were leased by the administrator Hillel ben Garis to various people in the city of Naḥash. The payment for the lease was not to be made in money but with grain, which the lessees had to weigh on the roof of the treasury of Herodium. In all, Hillel had leased on that day a dozen different plots in the city of Naḥash.

Bar Kokhba Revolt. Four documents discovered at Wadi Murabbaʿat are of considerable importance for clarifying the problem of the rebels taking control of Jerusalem and the dating of the end of the Bar Kokhba Revolt. The text, entitled deed of sale of land (Mur 25), was written in the third year of the liberation of Jerusalem. A deed of sale (Mur 29) from the second year of the redemption of Israel was signed in Jerusalem. Both of the deeds were poorly preserved, and therefore the details of the transactions documented in them are not known; however, it is clear that in both of them immovable property was sold. The text called deed of sale of plot (Mur 30) was written on the twenty-second day of Tishrei in the fourth year of the liberation of Israel in Jerusalem, meaning that this document was written on the last day of Sukkot, and in it a man by the name of Dustus sold a field to a man whose name is not preserved. The fact that the document is from the fourth year and was written in Jerusalem is of great significance for clarifying the course of the rebellion. A deed of sale of land (Mur 22) was written on the fourteenth day of Marḥeshvan in the fourth year of the redemption of Israel, that is, a month after Sukkot. In these documents the formula "of the liberation of Israel by Bar Kokhba" does not appear, and, therefore, the possibility that these documents under discussion are from the period of the First Jewish Revolt must be considered. During archaeological excavations conducted in Jerusalem, coins from the period of the Bar Kokhba Revolt were not found, and, therefore, the excavators assumed that Jerusalem did not fall into the hands of the rebels. The question of dating the end of the Bar Kokhba Revolt also is complicated. The rabbis asserted that the duration of the rebellion was three and a half years while, according to the Mishnah, Betar fell on Tishʿah be-ʾAv, in the summer, two months prior to Sukkot. If these traditions reflect a historical kernel it cannot be assumed that in the fourth year fields were still being sold. Furthermore, it is difficult to assume that Jerusalem remained in the hands of the rebels after the fall of Betar. Hence, the possibility that the documents are from the days of the First Jewish Revolt, that is, from the years 67 through 69 CE, should not be discounted.

One interesting document has an intermediate status between a letter and a fiscal document. This is the letter from Beit-Mashiko to Yeshuʿa son of Galgula (Mur 42), in which both administrators of the village Beit-Mashiko wrote to Yeshuʿa son of Galgula, who bore the title of head of the camp, and verified that Ariston's cow, which a man by the name of Yosef confiscated, belongs to Yaʿaqov ben Yehudah. What is interesting about this document is that the administrators attempted to write Hebrew, but they integrated Aramaic words and Aramaic syntax into this Hebrew document. This document attests to how difficult it was for some of the people of Judea to express themselves in Hebrew during the course of the rebellion. The administrators also mention that if it were not for the Romans being in close proximity to their dwelling place, they themselves would have come before Yeshuʿa son of Galgula and clarified the incident regarding the cow. Unfortunately, the document is not dated, and, therefore, the time of the arrival of the Romans in the region of Yeshuʿa is unknown.

Two letters from Shimʿon bar Kokhba to Yeshuʿa son of Galgula (Mur 43, 44) were found at Wadi Murabbaʿat. In the first letter Bar Kokhba vows that he will imprison Yeshuʿa son of Galgula in shackles if the Galileans in the region that is under the command of Yeshuʿa are injured in any way. In order to explain to Yeshuʿa that the threat is serious, Bar Kokhba explains that whoever harms the Galileans will be dealt with in the same manner as a man named Ben ʿAflul. Unfortunately, we do not know what transgression Ben ʿAflul committed or what his punishment was, but it can be assumed that the details were known to Yeshuʿa son of Galgula. Some have claimed that these are people from the Galilee or that the people under discussion were Christians whom Bar Kokhba dubbed Galileans. The second letter deals with the supplying of grain, and from it one can learn that Bar Kokhba's warriors observed the Sabbath, since Bar Kokhba requests Yeshuʿa to accommodate on the Sabbath the people who were coming to gather the wheat (Mur 44). The remainder of the letters found at Wadi Murabbaʿat are fragmentary. Particularly important is the letter sent from ʿEin-Gedi (Mur 46), which probably was written by Yonatan son of Baʿayar, the commander of ʿEin-Gedi (whose letters were found in the Cave of the Letters in Naḥal Ḥever), to a man by the name of Yosef. [*See* ʿEin-Gedi, Ḥever, Naḥal.] In another fragmentary letter (Mur 45) Milik read Maṣad Ḥasidin and claimed that it referred to Qumran; however, this reading is doubtful.

In summary, the scrolls, documents, and letters discovered at Wadi Murabbaʿat are of significance for clarifying the details concerning the Bar Kokhba Revolt. The scrolls attest that in the first and second centuries CE all the biblical scrolls were written according to the version now found in the Masoretic Text, and no Hebrew scrolls that reflect a different biblical version were found. The documents and letters prove that at the end of the Bar Kokhba Revolt a group of people from Herodium escaped to Wadi Murabbaʿat. The military commander of Herodium during the period of the rebellion was Yeshuʿa son of Galgula, whose family lived in the village of Beit Betzi near Herodium. An administrator by the name of Hillel son of Garis was appointed to the region of Herodium, as well. The administrator was responsible for civil matters, such as leasing Bar Kokhba's land and receiving agricultural products as compensation for it. Even small places, such as Beit-Mashiko, had administrators, and when the need arose they turned to the military commander of the region (and not to the administrator) to solve civil problems. The letters found at Wadi Murabbaʿat bear witness that Bar Kokhba was meticulous in the performance of precepts and also testify to the tension between the people of Judea and the Galileans.

Documents of the Roman Period. Apparently after the Bar Kokhba Revolt the Roman army kept a presence at Wadi Murabbaʿat. It should be assumed that military units of the tenth legion lingered in the area during the winter months, thereby preventing the Jewish rebels from seeking refuge in the caves during those years when there was still a lack of peace in Judea. A wooden imprint of Gargiliu(s) Centuria Annaii was found in the caves. Gargilius most likely was the commander of the Annaiian unit of the tenth legion. Recognition of debt (Mur 114) is a Greek document containing an acknowledgment of a debt (IOU) conducted between two Roman soldiers. This promissory note is dated either to the year 141 or 171 CE. Extracts from official ordinances (Mur 117) is a synopsis of an official regulation mentioning Caesar Commodus, who ruled between the years 180 and 192 CE, as well as serving as governor of Egypt during the years 183/4 to 185 CE. This is the latest document from the Roman era found in the caves, and it should be assumed that Roman presence there ceased at the end of the second century.

Documents from the Middle Ages. In the Middle Ages as well, during the eleventh century, people found refuge in the caves of Wadi Murabbaʿat and also brought with them to the caves documents in Greek and Arabic. From this period a Christian prayer in Greek (the Horologion, prayers for the hours of the day), which served monks during that period, was found there. Arabic documents were found, as well, among them two receipts—a complete one from the year 938 CE (Mur 169) and a fragment of sales contract (Mur 170)—and three magical texts. The complete magical text is an amulet (Mur 173) written in Arabic and Greek (its Greek side was given the number Mur 157 [fragment of magical text] that promises a safe journey to its bearer). The other two are a fragment of magical text (Mur 171) and a religious or magical text (Mur 172), which contains Arabic magical documents. [*See* Magic and Magical Texts.]

[*See also* Aramaic; Hebrew; Names and Naming.]

BIBLIOGRAPHY

Benoit, P., J. T. Milik, and Roland de Vaux, eds. *Les Grottes de Murabbaʿat (Texte)*. Discoveries in the Judaean Desert, 2. Oxford, 1961.

Koffmahn, E. *Die Doppelurkunden aus der Wüste Juda: Recht und Praxis der jüdischen Papyri des 1. und 2. Jahrhunderts*. Studies on the Texts of the Desert of Judah, 5. Leiden, 1968.

Yadin, Yigael. "Expedition D." *Israel Exploration Journal* 11 (1961), 36–52. See pages 51 through 52.

HANAN ESHEL

Translated from Hebrew by Daphna Krupp

MUSEUMS AND COLLECTIONS. Written materials and other artifacts from the Judean Desert that are connected with them are housed primarily in Jerusalem at the Palestine Archaeological Museum and the Shrine of the Book. [*See* Palestine Archaeological Museum; Shrine of the Book.] Two fragments are kept at the Franciscan Museum in Jerusalem. Outside Jerusalem, a small number are in Amman, Jordan, at the National Museum of the Department of Antiquities; in Paris, at the Bibliothèque Nationale de France; in private collections in France, Switzerland, and Norway; and in university collections at Heidelberg (Germany), Louvain (Belgium), and Chicago (USA). There are also fragments at the Museum Bible et Terre Sainte, Paris; the Syrian Orthodox Cathedral, Teaneck, New Jersey (USA); and possibly in Beirut.

Museums. Founded in 1936 through an endowment from John D. Rockefeller, Jr., the Palestinian Archaeological Museum in East Jerusalem was nationalized by the Hashemite Kingdom of Jordan early in 1967, and renamed the Rockefeller Museum after its capture by Israel during the 1967 Six Day War. [*See* Palestine Archaeological Museum.] It remains the primary repository for fragments of the Dead Sea Scrolls studied and published by the International Committee, and artifacts connected especially with Qumran, for example, some storage jars found in nearby caves. As the headquarters for the Department of Antiquities of Jordan during the 1950s and 1960s, this building was the center for scrolls acquisition and reconstruction. The scrolls listed below are stored in a basement room known as the "Scrollery," located near the scrolls conservation laboratory of the Israel Antiquities Authority. [*See* Department of Antiquities of Jordan; Israeli Antiquities Authority.] Scrolls located here include 1Q5, 8 (partial), 9–12; 21; 28, 28b, 29; 41–49; 69; 2Q1–33, 2QX1; 3Q1–14, 3QX1–6; 4Q1–21, 22 (except one plate), 23–108, 110–161, 163–174, 176–575; 5Q1–25, X–1; 6Q1–31, X1–2; 7Q1–19; 8Q1–5, X1–3; 9Q; 10Q; 11Q1–18, 20–23; Mur 1–173; 8Ḥev 1–6; XḤev/Se 1–48; sem, Nab. 1–6, Gr. 1–6; Mas 1–951; Sdeir 1–4; 5/6Ḥev 1–64; XḤev/Se gr. 7; 34Se 1–8; 1Mish 1–8; Ghweir? 1–2; Nar 1–5; WDSP1–28; Khirbet Mird APHM1–54, 56–93, 95–98, 100, Josh 22cpa, Mt. 21cpa, Lk. 3cpa, Acts cpa, Col. 1, papMird A, plaster with Syriac, pap. frag; all Ketef Jericho Aramaic and Greek documents.

A division of the Israel Museum, the Shrine of the Book, is located in West Jerusalem. [*See* Shrine of the Book.] The Shrine was built specially to house the Cave 1 scrolls bought by Sukenik and later Yadin. [*See* Discovery and Purchase.] Underwritten by the Samuel Gottesman family (who also paid for the Cave 1 scrolls), the Shrine consists of a large exhibition room where an Isaiah scroll replica and other large scrolls are on permanent display, as well as artifacts from the Bar Kokhba caves. Scrolls located at the Shrine include 1QIsa[a], 1QpHab, 1QS, 1QIsa[b], 1QapGen, 1QM, 1QH[a], and 11Q10 (one plate).

The Amman National Museum, Department of Antiquities of Jordan, houses the Copper Scroll. [*See* Amman Museum.] Other scrolls are stored under the original glass plates from the work of the International Team in Jerusalem during the 1950s. Most of the Jordanian collection is displayed in the main exhibition hall, but a few plates, containing more fragmentary remains, are usually kept in the museum vault.

Bibliothèque Nationale de Paris contains scrolls from Cave 1 at Qumran originally allotted to the École Biblique et Archeólogique Français in Jerusalem. [*See* Bibliotheque Nationale de France; École Biblique et Archeologique Française.] The Franciscan Museum at the Church of the Flagellation, Jerusalem, has two fragments (4Q475) and the Museum Bible et Terre Sainte, Paris, one (4Q98).

Private Collections. Various scrolls have made their way into private collections: Georges Roux (France), the Schøyen Collection, Oslo, Norway, and the Syrian Orthodox Cathedral, Teaneck, NJ, USA.

University Collections. Various universities bought and retain certain scroll fragments, such as the University of Heidelberg, Germany, the University of Louvain, Belgium, and the Oriental Institute, University of Chicago.

Artifacts. Most artifacts from the Dead Sea caves and the Qumran excavations are housed in Jerusalem at the École Biblique et Archéologique Française (center of much of the early study of the scrolls), the Shrine of the Book, the Rockefeller Museum, and the Albright Institute of Archaeology, Jerusalem (formerly the American Schools of Oriental Research). [*See* American Schools of Oriental Research.] Small quantities of artifacts are in private collections elsewhere.

Photographic Negatives. Most of the photographic negatives of the scrolls are stored in a temperature-controlled environment at the IAA facility at Har Haṣophim (Jerusalem). Additional collections of negatives are found in California at the Ancient Biblical Manuscript Center in Claremont, California, at the Huntington Library in San

Marino, California, in England, at Oxford University, and at Hebrew Union College-Jewish Institute of Religion, in Cincinnati, Ohio. The latter collection is for security only, and is not open for consultation.

BIBLIOGRAPHY

Shor, Penina. Personal consultation, the Rockefeller Museum, Jerusalem, March, 1998.

Tov, Emanuel, with the collaboration of Stephen J. Pfann. *Companion Volume to the Dead Sea Scrolls Microfiche Edition*. 2d rev. ed. Leiden, 1995.

WESTON W. FIELDS

MYSTERIES. This work is represented by at least three manuscripts at Qumran: Mysteries from Cave 1 at Qumran (1Q27) and Mysteries[a] and Mysteries[b] from Cave 4 (4Q299–300). Józef T. Milik identified Mysteries[c] (4Q301) as a fourth copy, but the correctness of this identification has been questioned by Lawrence Schiffman. He notes that while Mysteries (1Q27) and Mysteries[a] and Mysteries[b] all overlap textually, Mysteries[c] does not overlap with any of the other manuscripts and contains parallels with the Heikhalot literature not found in the other three. Nevertheless, given the fragmentary nature of the texts, one should probably not make too much of the lack of overlap or the presence or absence of parallels with Heikhalot texts. Moreover, clear terminological similarities between Mysteries[c] and the other manuscripts appear to favor Milik's identification.

All the Mysteries texts are written in Hebrew, and some of the fragments reveal a poetic structure. In spelling, the manuscripts contain a somewhat strange mixture of both full and defective forms. Paleographically, the earliest of the texts is Mysteries from Cave 1, which is written in a hand dating to the end of the first century BCE or the beginning of the first century CE. This date thus provides a *terminus ante quem* for the composition of Mysteries. Of the Cave 4 copies, Mysteries[a] is written in a developed Herodian hand, and Mysteries[b] and Mysteries[c] are late Herodian (c.50–68 CE).

Contents and Ideology. Mysteries is so named because the *raz* ("mystery") figures prominently in the preserved fragments. This word is used both alone and in phrases such as "mysteries of iniquity" (1Q27 1.i.2), "mystery of that which is coming into being" (1Q27 1.i.3–4), "marvelous mysteries" (1Q27 1.i.7), "mysteries of the deep" (1Q27 13.3), "mysteries of eternity" (4Q299 2b.5), and "mysteries of light" (4Q299 5.2). It appears from this that the term *mystery* is used in a variety of ways to describe both the natural and moral order of God's creation.

The most extensive run of continuous text is provided by fragment 1 of Mysteries. The first column of this fragment contains an almost prophetic indictment against those who did not consider the "former things" and who did not know something called the "mystery of that which is coming into being," or *raz nihyeh* (1Q27 1.i.3–4). In Mysteries, the contrast in the text between the "former things" and the *raz nihyeh* indicates that the latter carries eschatological overtones, though the same phrase is used without eschatological significance in Sapiential Work A[e] (4Q423 3.5 and 5.10) in a section dealing with agricultural matters.

The author of Mysteries proceeds to tell his readers, directly addressed as "you" in the second person plural, that the disappearance of wickedness before righteousness will be a sign that the *raz nihyeh* is about to come to pass. At that time will come the destruction of all the adherents of the "marvelous mysteries" (1Q27 1.i.7), the latter phrase clearly being used euphemistically for something like "mysteries of iniquity" (cf. 1Q27 1.i.2; elsewhere in the scrolls "marvelous mysteries" is used only in a positive sense). The truth of this "oracle" may be seen in that iniquity abounds in all peoples and nations.

Everywhere in Mysteries the sinfulness and shortcomings of human beings stand in sharp contrast to the character of God. Indeed, according to one restoration of Mysteries[a] 3.ii.3, even the deeds of the seemingly righteous person are unclean. Line 8 of this same fragment highlights the authority of God over mankind by referring to him as the Creator (cf. 4Q299 5 and 6.i) and then foretells the destruction of those who violate his commands (cf. the theme of judgment in 4Q299 frgs. 53 and 59 and 4Q301 3a–b. 4–5). This leads into an exhortation in lines 9 through 16, probably addressed to those who hold fast to God's secrets, to recognize the omnipotence of the God who exists from before eternity and causes all things. The teaching of predestination here is somewhat reminiscent of Rule of the Community from Cave 1 at Qumran (hereafter, 1QRule of the Community, 1QS) and Hodayot[a] from Cave 1 at Qumran (hereafter, 1QHodayot[a], 1QH[a]).

Nowhere is the distinction between God and humanity clearer than in the matter of wisdom and knowledge. Twice God is referred to as "the God of knowledge" (4Q299 35.1 and 73.3.). One fairly well preserved section, Mysteries[b] 1a.ii–b and its parallel in Mysteries[a] 3c, contains an indictment against certain magicians, directly addressed in the second person plural, who under a pretense of wisdom actually teach transgression. The vision and the eternal secrets are closed to them.

Such is not the case, however, with the author of Mysteries. In Mysteries[c] 1.1, he states that he will speak freely and apportion his words to his hearers according to their "kinds." Although the meaning of the next several lines is not totally clear, the reference to various kinds of hearers seems to indicate that only those who are diligent in their search for wisdom will truly understand the author's message. According to Mysteries[a] 8, however, even the quest for wisdom will fail unless God gives understanding. Thus, the writer of Mysteries says, "He opened our ear that we should hear."

Genre. Milik originally had suggested that Mysteries was a pseudepigraphic work containing revelations attributed to some biblical patriarch. However, although both Abraham and Aaron are mentioned in the fragments (cf. 4Q299 102 and 75, respectively), this suggestion seems unlikely since there is no real indication of any kind of historical narrative framework that might serve as the setting of the entire composition.

A better case can be made for associating Mysteries with the genre of writing commonly called wisdom literature. Throughout Mysteries, for instance, one finds typical wisdom terminology such as *daʿat* ("knowledge"), *śekhel* ("understanding"), *binah* ("insight"), *ḥokhmah* ("wisdom"), *ʾivvelet* ("foolishness"), and *kesel* ("folly"). There also is an abundant use of rhetorical questions designed to lead the addressees to affirm for themselves certain viewpoints that were important to the author's overall message. Both parallelism and antithesis are used to good effect. In general, the style is not so much the stringing together of disconnected maxims found in *Proverbs* 10.1–22.16 but more the discursive style of writing found in *Proverbs* 1–9 and *Ben Sira*. In common with the latter work, Mysteries also contains some halakhic material.

Nevertheless, despite the foregoing similarities, one difference that distinguishes Mysteries from both *Proverbs* and *Ben Sira* is the material in Mysteries that is eschatological in character. In this respect, as well as others, there are clear similarities between Mysteries and the so-called sapiential works found at Qumran. Daniel Harrington (1996, p. 41) has pointed out that fragment 1 of Sapiential Work A[b] (4Q416) likely preserves the beginning of the work and sets the entire composition in a framework that is both cosmic and eschatological. Interestingly, fragment 1 of Mysteries, which Milik concluded must have come near the beginning of the Mysteries composition, also is eschatological in nature. The mixture of wisdom, *halakhah*, and eschatology in one work is a striking combination that shows again the richness and diversity of Second Temple literature.

Origin and Authorship. The ideology, language, and orthography of the Mysteries texts show some similarities to certain works believed to have been authored by the Qumran sect. This has led Schiffman to conclude that they share a common authorship. Armin Lange disputes this, maintaining that, despite certain general parallels, there are no specific theological ideas or vocabulary that indicate authorship by the Qumran sect.

Even before the full publication of Mysteries, Isaac Rabinowitz suggested that Mysteries was written by a Teacher of Righteousness of the Qumran sect (he thought there were several such teachers). Rabinowitz believed that the origins of the sect lay in the group known as the Hasideans, and he even suggested that the author of Mysteries specifically could be identified as Mattathias, the patriarch of the Maccabean dynasty.

Although Rabinowitz's theory of Qumran origins has found little support, his suggestion that the text was authored by a sectarian leader is still possible. Many texts for which there is good evidence of Qumran authorship tell of mysteries to which the writer has been made privy. Thus, in 1QHodayot[a] the author(s) makes frequent reference to the fact that God had revealed mysteries to him (1QH ix[i].21, xii[iv].27, xv[vii].27, xx[xii].13). Likewise, 1QRule of the Community often mentions that the members of the Qumran community possess insight into God's mysteries (1QS iv.6, ix.18, xi.3, xi.5, xi.19). Indeed, 1QRule of the Community xi.3 specifically refers to the "mystery of that which is coming into being," which also is found in Mysteries. Although this by itself does not prove sectarian authorship for Mysteries (Sapiential Work A also uses *raz nihyeh* but may not be sectarian), it is suggestive of it, as is the teaching about predestination.

BIBLIOGRAPHY

Brown, Raymond E. *The Semitic Background of the Term "Mystery" in the New Testament*. Facet Books, Biblical Series, 21. Philadelphia, 1968. A classic study on the term *mystery*.

Harrington, Daniel J. *Wisdom Texts from Qumran*. London, 1996. An excellent recent introduction to the wisdom literature at Qumran.

Lange, Armin. *Weisheit und Prädestination: Weisheitliche Urordnung und Prädestination in den Textfunden von Qumran*. Studies on the Texts of the Desert of Judah, 18. Leiden, 1995.

Lange, Amin. "Wisdom and Predestination in the Dead Sea Scrolls." *Dead Sea Discoveries* 2 (1995), 340–355.

Milik, Józef T. "Livre des mystères." In *Qumran Cave 1*, edited by D. Barthélemy and J. T. Milik. Discoveries in the Judaean Desert, 1, pp. 102–107. Oxford, 1955. *Editio princeps* of Mysteries. Recently reprinted.

Rabinowitz, Isaac. "The Authorship, Audience and Date of the De Vaux Fragment of an Unknown Work." *Journal of Biblical Literature* 71 (1952), 19–32.

Schiffman, Lawrence H. "Mysteries." In *Qumran Cave 4: The Sapiential Texts, Part 1*, edited by T. Elgvin et al., pp. 31–123. Discoveries in the Judaean Desert, 20. Oxford, 1997. Official publication of Mysteries[a–c].

Schiffman, Lawrence H. "4QMysteries[b], A Preliminary Edition." *Revue de Qumrân* 62 (1993), 203–223.

Schiffman, Lawrence H. "4QMysteries[a]: A Preliminary Edition and Translation." In *Solving Riddles and Untying Knots: Biblical, Epigraphic, and Semitic Studies in Honor of Jonas C. Greenfield*, edited by Z. Zevit, S. Gitin, and M. Sokoloff, pp. 207–259. Winona Lake, Ind., 1995.

Erik W. Larson

MYSTERY. The most prominent term for "mystery" in the Qumran writings is *raz*, which is generally regarded as a Persian loanword taken over into Aramaic and Hebrew. The biblical Greek translation of *raz* is *mysterion*, though there is little need to assume a connection with the Greek mystery religions in the Greek Bible versions or at Qumran. Two Hebrew terms associated with *raz* are *sod* and *nistarot*. The word *sod* carries the ambiguity of "council" (an assembly gathered to give advice or make decisions) and "counsel" (the content of the advice or decision). The idea of the heavenly council has a rich background in ancient Near Eastern and biblical literature, and it was an easy step to use *sod* for the divine decrees. The word *nistarot* ("secrets") derives from the Hebrew root *str* ("hide," "conceal") and refers to what has been "hidden away." All three terms—*raz*, *sod*, and *nistarot*—convey the idea of the essential knowledge of heavenly or historical matters known to God and granted to humans only by divine revelation.

Biblical Usage. The biblical occurrences of *raz* are confined to the Aramaic sections of *Daniel* (2 and 4), a book that is well represented at Qumran both in the form it takes in the Hebrew scriptures and in writings related to it in language and content. The Qumran uses of *raz*, however, need not be regarded as directly dependent on *Daniel* as their source. They are probably better taken as parallels, though attention to the use of *raz* in *Daniel* illumines greatly the pertinent Qumran texts.

According to *Daniel* 2, the Babylonian king Nebuchadrezzar demanded that his court sages tell him both his dream and its interpretation. The content of his challenge is called a *raz*, and it transcends the powers of human understanding (see *Daniel* 2.18, 2.27, 4.6). The Jewish courtier Daniel comes to understand and explain the *raz* only because the mystery was revealed to him in a "vision of the night" (*Dn*. 2.19). The dream concerned a great statue and its destruction, and its interpretation (*pesher*) concerned the four empires (Babylonia, Persia, Media, and Greece) and their destruction as well as the indestructible and everlasting kingdom to be established by God for God's people, Israel. Daniel gives credit to God ("for there is a God in heaven who reveals mysteries," *Dn*. 2.28), and even the gentile king comes to celebrate the God of Israel as "a revealer of mysteries" (*Dn*. 2.47). The episode in *Daniel* 2 is important for understanding *raz* in the Qumran writings because in it *raz* pertains to the future course of history, transcends human understanding, and requires a revelation from God.

Usage in Qumran Texts. The Pesher Habakkuk (1QpHab) uses the term *raz* to refer to the words of the prophet in *Habakkuk* 2.2–3 and asserts that God has made known to the Teacher of Righteousness "all the mysteries of the words of his servants the prophets" (1QpHab vii.4–5). Just as God revealed to Daniel the king's dream and its interpretation (*pesher*), so God revealed to the Teacher the true meaning of the biblical prophecies. The text goes on to attribute the delay of the "last time" to the astounding character of the mysteries of God (1QpHab vii.8) and to affirm that "all the times of God shall come to pass as he has decreed in the mysteries of his prudence" (1QpHab vii.13–14). As in *Daniel*, the word *raz* has a connection with the end of the present phase in human history and the establishment of God's reign in its fullness. But it transcends human understanding and needs divine revelation to be understood.

In the "Treatise on the Two Spirits" in the Rule of the Community from Qumran Cave 1 (hereafter, 1QRule of the Community; 1QS iii.13–iv.25), the *maskil* explains the present success of the Angel of Darkness and those under his control as being "in accord with the mysteries of God" (1QS iii.23). But he also promises that God "in the mysteries of his understanding and in his glorious wisdom" has determined to destroy iniquity at the time of his visitation" (1QS iv.18). In the poem of the *maskil* near the end of the work, the speaker (1QS xi.3, 5) claims to have been illumined with the knowledge of the "mystery to be [come]" (*raz nihyeh*) and the "mysteries of his wonder" (or, "God's marvelous mysteries"). The content of these mysteries is clarified somewhat by parallel expressions in 1QRule of the Community: "your counsel . . . your holy design . . . the depth of your mysteries . . . the power of your might" (1QS xi.18–20). One of the *maskil*'s duties is to instruct members of the community "in the mysteries of wonder and truth" so that they may "walk perfectly together, each with his neighbor, in everything revealed to them" (1QS ix.18–19). It appears that knowing the divine mysteries has an effect on how one behaves in the present, that is, one's ethical activity. That this knowledge has an esoteric character in the sense of not being intended for everyone, especially not the wicked, is suggested by the description of the children of light as displaying "prudence with respect to the truth of the mysteries of knowledge" (1QS iv.6).

In the War Scroll the trumpets of ambush are inscribed with the slogan "the mysteries of God are to destroy wickedness" (1QM iii.9)—an expression of the group's hope for the outcome of the cosmic and eschatological battle described in the work as a whole. The present success of Belial is attributed to "the mysteries of his enmity" (1QM xiv.9). Whether the permissive will of God or Satan's (limited) power is meant, the assumption is that all things, including the suffering and death of the righteous in the battle against Belial, take place in accord with the "mysteries of God" (1QM xvi.11). In "his marvelous mysteries" (1QM xiv.14) God can raise up (humans?) from the dust and expel heavenly beings from the divine council. Thus, in the exhortation to courage in the War Scroll (1QM xvii.4–9), the "sons of the covenant" are promised that "his mysteries will uphold you until he shakes his hand and fills up his crucibles" (1QM xvii.9).

The Hodayot scrolls connect the "mysteries" to God's activity in creating the heavenly lights (1QH[a] ix.11, 13 [i.9, 11]) and in allowing humans to proclaim God's glory and to praise his name (1QH[a] ix.29 [i.27]). But the most distinctive contribution made by this work to our understanding of "mystery" at Qumran comes in those passages in which the speaker relates himself to the divine mysteries. Whether the "I" is the Teacher of Righteousness, the collective representation of the community, or some other figure is not clear. At any rate, the speaker claims to know the secrets of creation "from your knowledge because you have revealed to me marvelous mysteries" (1QH[a] ix.21 [i.19]). He identifies himself as a "knowing interpreter in marvelous mysteries" (1QH[a] x.13 [ii.11]). With regard to the speaker's role vis-à-vis the community, he affirms that "you gave me knowledge of your marvelous mysteries" (1QH[a] xii.27 [iv.26]; see also 1QH[a] xv.17 [vii.24]).

The concept of mystery is also used in Hodayot to deal with suffering and sin. The speaker claims that his opponents have rebelled and murmured against him "concerning the mystery you have hidden within me" (1QH[a] xiii.25 [v.23]). He attributes their success against him to the "mysteries of transgression" (1QH[a] xiii.36 [v.34]). The idea seems to be that God, in his wisdom, permits the children of darkness to do their sinful deeds. The speaker interprets his personal sufferings as a divine discipline: "For by the mystery of your wisdom you have chastised me" (1QH[a] xvii.23 [ix.23]). Through the speaker, God has made known special knowledge to the "children of your good pleasure": "For you gave them knowledge in the council/counsel [*sod*] of your truth, and in your marvelous mysteries you taught them" (1QH[a] xix.10 [xi.7]). As the recipient of the "mystery of your teaching" (1QH[a] xx.13 [xii.10]), the speaker has the task of teaching others to understand "all your mysteries" (1QH[a] xx.20 [xii.17]) and to make known God's glory "in the mysteries of your insight" (1QH[a] xiii.13 [v.11]).

In these core documents from Qumran, the term *mystery* involves creation, the present, and the future. It is the divine plan or economy and has cosmic, ethical, and eschatological dimensions. It is a special knowledge revealed by God to his chosen ones through the instructor and/or the Teacher of Righteousness. It helps to explain the temporary success of the Angel of Darkness and his minions in the present, and it holds out hope of the ultimate vindication of the righteous. Knowledge of this mystery serves to guide and direct the behavior of the righteous in the present.

Raz Nihyeh. The expression *raz nihyeh* occurs about thirty times in Sapiential Work A—a wisdom instruction preserved in the wisdom apocryphon (1Q26) and Sapiential Work A from Qumran Cave 4 (4Q415–418, 423). The second element of the phrase (which is also found in 1QS xi.3–4) is the *niphal* participle of the verb "be" (*hayah*). The expression appears to have a future sense and should be translated "the mystery that is to be [come]."

In many cases *raz nihyeh* is prefaced by the preposition *b*, but it is difficult to determine whether this has an instrumental ("by") or local ("in" or "on") sense. The expression often appears with verbs in the singular imperative, usually in the context of the instructor's advice to his pupil: "test" (*bḥn*), "study" (*drsh*), "meditate" (*hgh*), "understand" (*lqḥ*), and "look at" (*nbt*).

The content of *raz nihyeh* can be clarified to some extent by attending to its parallel expressions in Sapiential Work A: "all the ways of truth, and all the roots of iniquity" (Sapiential Work A[b], 4Q416 2.iii.14); "the birth time of salvation, and who is to inherit glory and iniquity" (Sapiential Work A[c], 4Q417 i.10–11); and "the inheritance of everything that lives" (Sapiential Work A[a], 4Q418 2.i.18). Meditating on *raz nihyeh* will help one to understand "the generations of mankind" (4Q418 77.2) and the "weight of the times and the measure" (4Q418 77.4). Such phrases indicate that the *raz nihyeh* involves creation, ethics, and eschatology. Applying oneself to it will give one knowledge about how to live in the present: "in righteousness you shall walk" (4Q416 iii.9); and "you shall know to discern between good and evil" (4Q417 2.i.7).

The parallel expressions suggest that the *raz nihyeh* is a body of teaching concerning the cosmos, proper behavior, and eschatology. Thus, it may have been a compendium such as the "Treatise on the Two Spirits" (1QS iii.13–iv.26), the "Book of Meditation" of the Rule of the Congregation (1Q28a i.6–8), or something like Book of Mysteries (1Q27, 4Q299–301), which uses the expression *raz nihyeh* in similar ways.

In Mysteries the future sense of the *raz nihyeh* is supported by the antithetically parallel phrase "the former things" and the synonymous expression "what will come upon them" (1Q27 1.i.3–4 and parallels). The use of the word *raz* with reference to the mystery of evil in the present occurs in the expressions "mysteries of transgression" (1Q27 1.i.2 and parallels) and "mysteries of Belial" (1Q27 1.i.6 and parallels). As in other Qumran texts, such phrases seem to refer to the permissive will of God in allowing evil to exist and even to flourish in the present. The "magicians skilled in transgression" who are challenged in Mysteries[b] (4Q300 1.ii.1–5) are criticized for not applying themselves to the eternal mysteries: "For the seal of vision has been sealed up from you, and on the eternal mysteries you have not looked, and you have not come to understand knowledge" (4Q300 1.ii.2).

Mystery in *1 Enoch*. That many manuscripts of *1 Enoch* were discovered at Qumran indicates its popularity there. This work also uses the terms *mystery* and *hidden things* to refer to the phenomena of the cosmos (*1 En.* 60.11, 71.4). It explains the existence of evil in the world by attributing to the wicked and rebellious angels the revelation of the "everlasting secrets" to their earthly mistresses (*1 En*. 9.6; see *Gn*. 6.1–4). Enoch, having been granted access to the heavenly mysteries and having seen the holy writings (*1 En*. 103.2; see 4Q417 2.i.14–18), proclaims that he knows "this mystery"—the destinies of the righteous and the wicked at the last judgment. As in Sapiential Work A and the Mysteries, knowledge of the divine mystery serves as a guide for conduct in the present.

Mystery in the New Testament. The New Testament term *mysterion* shows many affinities with the uses of *raz* in the Qumran scrolls. In some cases *mysterion* refers to a puzzle or riddle to be solved (*Rv*. 1.20, 17.5; *Eph*. 5.32; *1 Cor*. 14.2), as in *Daniel* 2 and Pesher Habakkuk (1QpHab vii.4–5). The most common use of *mysterion* is with regard to the divine plan or economy (see *Col*. 1.26–27, 2.2; *Eph*. 1.9; *Rom*. 16.25; *Rv*. 17.7). Often it is synonymous with the "gospel" (*Col*. 4.3; *1 Tm*. 3.9, 3.16; *Eph*. 6.19), and sometimes it points toward a future (eschatological) action of God (*Rom*. 11.25; *1 Cor*. 15.51; *Eph*. 3.3). There is an esoteric aspect to the New Testament *mysterion*: "To you [Jesus' disciples] has been given the mystery of the kingdom of God" (*Mk*. 4.11). Paul describes himself and his co-workers as speaking "the wisdom of God hidden in mystery" (*1 Cor*. 2.7) and as "stewards of the mysteries of God" (*1 Cor*. 4.1). The use of the word *mystery* to describe God's allowing the presence of evil in the world is termed in *2 Thessalonians* 2.7 "the mystery of lawlessness."

Though there are many verbal and conceptual parallels with the Qumran "mystery" texts, the New Testament occurrences of *mysterion* also reflect the distinctively Christian theological conviction that in Jesus' person, and especially in his death and resurrection, there has been a decisive unfolding of the divine mystery in history. Nevertheless, the Qumran texts and related writings (*Daniel* and *1 Enoch*) provide a much more appropriate framework for understanding the New Testament "mystery" texts than do the Greek "mystery" religions.

[*See also* Creation; Enoch, Books of; Hodayot; Mysteries; Pesher Habakkuk; Rule of the Community; Sapiential Work; Secrecy; Teacher of Righteousness; War of the Sons of Light against the Sons of Darkness; *and* Wisdom Texts.]

BIBLIOGRAPHY

Brown, Raymond E. *The Semitic Background of the Term "Mystery" in the New Testament*. Philadelphia, 1968. The best treatment of the topic, though now dated.

Coppens, Joseph. "'Mystery' in the Theology of Saint Paul and Its Parallels at Qumran." In *Paul and the Dead Sea Scrolls*, edited by Jerome Murphy-O'Connor and James H. Charlesworth, pp. 132–158. New York, 1990.

Harrington, Daniel J. "The *Raz Nihyeh* in a Qumran Wisdom Text (1Q26, 4Q415–418, 423)." *Revue de Qumrân* 65–68 (1996), 549–553.

Holm-Nielsen, Sven. *Hodayot: Psalms from Qumran*. Aarhus, 1960. A rich biblical-theological study.

Horgan, Maurya P. *Pesharim: Qumran Interpretations of Biblical Books*. Catholic Biblical Quarterly Monograph Series, 8. Washington, D.C., 1979. Important for the interpretive terminology in the *pesharim*.

Leaney, A. R. C. *The Rule of Qumran and Its Meaning*. Philadelphia, 1966. A literary-theological commentary on 1QRule of the Community.

Rigaux, Beda. "Révélation des mystères et perfection à Qumran et dans le Nouveau Testament." *New Testament Studies* 4 (1957–1958), 237–262. An early attempt to use Qumran "mystery" texts to illumine New Testament texts.

Ringgren, Helmer. *The Faith of Qumran: Theology of the Dead Sea Scrolls*. Expanded ed. New York, 1955. Contains a section on "mysteries" (pp. 60–63).

Schiffman, Lawrence H. "4QMysteries^{b}: A Preliminary Edition." *Revue de Qumrân* 16 (1993), 203–223.

Schiffman, Lawrence H. *Reclaiming the Dead Sea Scrolls: The History of Judaism, the Background of Christianity, the Lost Library of Qumran*. Philadelphia and Jerusalem, 1994. A good discussion of the Book of Mysteries (pp. 206–210).

DANIEL J. HARRINGTON

MYSTICISM. A term notoriously difficult to define, for purposes of this article *mysticism* is taken to refer to a type of religious praxis in which an individual engages in techniques specifically designed to give ecstatic access to the realm of the divine. In this narrow sense there is no evidence of mystical praxis in the communities represented by the literature of the Dead Sea Scrolls. Nevertheless, several texts from Qumran bear on related phenomena (the visionary ascents characteristic of many apocalypses, liturgical communion with angelic worshipers, and the disclosure of the mysteries of the chariot-throne of God). [*See* Apocalyptic Texts; Heaven; *and* Throne.]

Visionary Ascents. In ancient Jewish apocalypses the visionary often records an experience of ascent from earth into heaven, where he may be accompanied by an angelic guide, see the various structures and beings who occupy heaven (or multiple heavens), come into the presence of God, and receive a revelation, usually about the course of future events (e.g., *1 Enoch*, *2 Baruch*, *Apocalypse of Abraham*, *Testament of Levi*). [*See* Angels.] The oldest of these texts is *1 Enoch*, copies of which were found at Qumran, including portions of the text that describes Enoch's ascent to heaven (*1 En*. 13–16, Enoch^{c} 4Q204 vi). Enoch's ascent is presented as an intentionally cultivated experience. Having been asked by the fallen Watchers to take their petition to heaven, he sits next to "the waters of Dan" and reads the petitions until he falls asleep, whereupon he has a dream vision in which he ascends to heaven. The practice of incubating revelatory dreams at a holy place is attested already in second-millennium BCE literary texts (e.g., the Kirtu legend from Ugarit). Dan, the site of one of the ancient sanctuaries in northern Israel, would be such a holy place. [*See* Archaeology.] Rivers also are often mentioned in connection with mystical experiences (cf. the occurrence of Ezekiel's vision "by the river Chebar," *Ezek.* 1.1). Although the significance of rivers as a propitious site for incubating visions is debated, it may be that waters were thought to reflect the heavens above and so to provide a means of gazing into the mysteries of heaven. Enoch's ecstatic ascent is described as a "summoning" by clouds and mist, as he is carried by winds and hastened along by lightning flashes. The numinous quality of the heavenly palace is suggested by the description of it as composed of fire and hailstones, snow, and water, simultaneously hot and cold. Characteristically, Enoch is terrified to find himself in the divine presence (cf. *Ezek.* 1.28) and has to be lifted up by the divine command.

Three other texts from Qumran (like *1 Enoch*, in Aramaic) contain accounts of revelatory dream visions, although only in one case does the vision apparently include an ascent. The Apocryphon of Jacob (4Q537) recounts a dream vision, presumably occurring at Bethel (cf. *Gn.* 28), in which an angel shows Jacob heavenly tablets concerning his future and the Temple that is to be built at Jerusalem, not Bethel. [*See* Jacob.] In the Visions of Amram[a–f(?)](4Q543–548), Amram sees two angelic beings, Melchiresha‘ and (presumably) Melchizedek, quarreling over him and receives instruction concerning the dualistic division of humankind into children of light and darkness. [*See* Amram, Visions of Amram.] In neither of these texts, however, is there an indication that the dream vision is intentionally brought about or incubated, or that it involves the transportation of the visionary to heaven. By contrast, the Aramaic Levi texts (1Q21, 4Q213–214b, 4Q540–541), although fragmentary, appear to refer to techniques of incubation (prayer, followed by sleep). [*See* Levi, Aramaic.] Although the mechanism of transportation to heaven is not described, there is reference to a mountain (Mount Zion?) upon which Levi stands, a mountain that reaches to heaven, where gates are opened and Levi presumably enters. [*See* Levi.]

All these texts are literary fictions describing the experiences of ancient and legendary characters and as such cannot be used as direct evidence for the existence of mystical praxis in late–Second Temple Judaism. However, Paul's reference to his own mystical ascent to Paradise where he heard "things that are not to be told, that no mortal is permitted to repeat" (*2 Cor.* 12.2–4) is clear evidence that such ascents were part of actual religious experience at least in some segments of Judaism. No evidence exists, however, for such practice at Qumran. The Aramaic texts discussed above are generally considered to be literature read but not composed by the Qumran community. In the texts composed by the Qumran community there are references to a sense of communion with angels but no language that suggests the practice of ascent.

Liturgical Communion. Several passages in texts composed by members of the Qumran community speak of an experience of entering into communion "with the congregation of the sons of heaven" (Hodayot[a] from Cave 1 at Qumran, 1QH[a] xi.19–23 [iii.18–22], xix.11–13 [xi.8–11]; Rule of the Community from Cave 1 at Qumran, 1QS xi.7–8). [*See* Hodayot; Rule of the Community.] In one instance the language used to express this conviction echoes that of visionary ascent, as the speaker describes being lifted up from Sheol and Abaddon "to an everlasting height" (1QH[a], xi.19–20 [iii.18–19]); but the description appears to be figurative rather than literal, as in Paul's account. These passages probably refer less to specific experiences than to convictions about the status of the sect as an elect body integrated into the lot of the angelic hosts. The Damascus Document, for instance, excludes the physically and mentally impaired from the community "because the holy angels are in its midst" (Damascus Document CD xv.15–17, Rule of the Congregation 1Q28a ii.3–9; cf. War Scroll, 1QM vii.3–7). [*See* War Scroll.] This language is dependent upon *Leviticus* 21.16–21, which refers to qualifications for priestly service in the sacrificial cult.

A somewhat more vivid account of access to the heavens is found in a hymn of self-glorification (War Scroll[a] 4Q491), part of a copy of the War Scroll from Cave 4 at Qumran. In this text the speaker asserts that he has been given "a mighty throne in the council of the gods," where he claims to have "taken my seat in the [counc]il in heaven." Although Morton Smith (1990, pp. 187–188) has argued that the text should be understood in relation to visionary ascent traditions, War Scroll[a] says nothing about the techniques of ascent or about the revelations characteristically given to such visionaries. Instead, analogously to the 1QHodayot[a], the text uses heavenly enthronement imagery to assert a claim about the status of the speaker, who may plausibly be the priestly Messiah who officiates in the eschatological war (see Collins, 1995, pp. 148–149). [*See* Messiahs.]

The analogy between the community and the priests who serve in the Temple suggests that the distinctive sense of communion with the angelic hosts in the Qumran community is developed not so much from the apocalyptic ascent tradition as from priestly and temple traditions. [*See* Temple.] Johann Maier (1964) argues that there was a tradition of priestly mysticism based on the understanding of the Temple as the place of God's presence and so, uniquely, the place where heaven and earth intersect. Already in the prophetic vision in *Isaiah* 6 there is an ambiguity or, perhaps better, a blurring of the heavenly or earthly locus of the temple in which the vision occurs. Little evidence exists, however, to substantiate the existence of a developed tradition of priestly mysticism, although numerous texts assert the correspondence between earthly and angelic priests (e.g., *Jub.* 31.13–14; *Testament of Levi* 2–5, 8) and common service with the Angels of the Presence in the heavenly temple is part of the eschatological expectation at Qumran (see Rule of the Blessings 1Q28b). [*See* Priests; Rule of the Blessings.]

Liturgical traditions, however, do provide a basis for the experience of common worship with angels and thus for a type of quasi-mystical praxis. Already in biblical psalmody, references occur to the joining of angelic and human praise (Psalm 148, Psalm 150; The *Song of the Three Children*). Later, the Qedushah de-Yotser in the synagogue liturgy explicitly incorporates a vivid description of the praise uttered by the ministering angels, the celestial *'ofannim* (wheels), the holy *ḥayyot* (creatures), and the seraphim as part of the human act of praise, thus creating an experience of common worship with the heavenly beings. Such a cultivation of liturgical communion with the angels is extensively developed in the Songs of the Sabbath Sacrifice, a text found in multiple copies at Qumran (4Q400–407, 11Q17) and in one at Masada (Maslk). Probably a presectarian composition, the Songs of the Sabbath Sacrifice comprise a liturgical cycle for the first thirteen Sabbaths of the year, to be recited presumably at the time of the Sabbath Musaf offering. The tradition of coordinating song with sacrifice is attested in *Chronicles* (*2 Chr.* 29.27–28). Since the boundary between heaven and earth was considered to be especially "permeable" at the time when the smoke of offerings went up to God, it was considered a propitious time for prayer (see *Jdt.* 9.1, *Lk.* 1.10, Josephus, *Against Apion* 2.23; B.T., *Ber.* 26b). Similarly, it would be a suitable time for an act of worship that cultivated a sense of being present in the heavenly temple and witnessing angelic worship. Moreover, the Sabbath itself, as a holy day observed by the angels and by Israel (*Jub.* 2.18), was considered the distinctive occasion for common praise with the angels (Words of the Luminaries[a–c] 4Q504–506). [*See* Sabbath; Words of the Luminaries.]

Since there is no indication that the Songs of the Sabbath Sacrifice functioned as a technique for ecstatic or dissociative experience, they are not, technically speaking, mystical texts. Nevertheless, they are crafted, both individually and as a cycle, to produce an intense religious-aesthetic experience of worship in the heavenly temple. Each song begins with a call to praise God addressed to the angels, so that human praise and angelic praise are intimately interrelated. Within the cycle three distinct sections occur, songs 1 through 5, songs 6 through 8, and songs 9 through 13, each section distinguished both by content and by style. The first five songs describe and praise the angels who serve as priests in the heavenly temple. The style is characteristic of late–Second Temple poetry, parallelistic, but somewhat more free than biblical poetry. The central songs, 6 through 8, which form an initial climax for the cycle, contain highly repetitious and formulaic structures. The sixth and eighth songs are constructed of long formulaic accounts of the praises and blessings offered successively by each of the "seven chief princes" and the "seven deputy princes," each account highlighting the number seven in its formulas. The central, seventh song begins with a call to praise addressed to each of seven angelic councils, followed by an account of the animate heavenly temple itself bursting into praise, and concluding with an account of the inner shrine of the heavenly temple, the throne of God, and the praises uttered by the chariot thrones and their attendant cherubim and *'ofannim* (wheels). The final group of songs, 9 through 13, contains a progressive description of the heavenly temple and the praise uttered by its various structures, culminating in a description of the divine chariot-throne and the angelic high priests. This section of the Songs of the Sabbath Sacrifice is written in a style that features long construct chains in nominal or participial sentences, with few finite verbs, apparently an attempt to create a numinous style befitting the subject.

The fascination with angelic worship so evident in the Songs of the Sabbath Sacrifice is attested also in apocalypses that recount descriptions of angelic attendance upon God and the hymns sung by the angels (e.g., *1 En.* 39; *Apocalypse of Abraham* 17). Although little is known about liturgical and ritual practices by which human worshipers attempted to experience such angelic ceremonies, it may be such practices that Paul refers to when he cautions the Colossians not to be "disqualified by the decisions of people who go in for self-mortification and angel worship and access to some visionary world" (*Col.* 2.18).

Chariot-Throne. Late antique and early medieval Jewish communities did give rise to a genuine mystical literature, known as *merkavah* ("chariot") or *heikhalot* ("palaces") mysticism (see esp. *Ma'aseh Merkavah* and *Heikhalot Rabbati*). Although the extent to which this was a literary phenomenon or a genuine religious praxis is still debated, it seems certain that there was some systematic attempt to cultivate ecstatic experiences of the heavenly realm, particularly the immediate presence of God, which was imaged in terms elaborated from Ezekiel's vision of the chariot-throne. Although it is not possible to trace a direct line of influence from the description of the *merkavah* in the Songs of the Sabbath Sacrifice to later *merkavah* texts, these compositions nevertheless belong to the same complex stream of religious tradition. Certain types of general continuity may be indicated. Much of the early Jewish literature concerning the *merkavah*, for instance, reflects exegetical interpretation of Ezekiel's vision of the chariot-throne, concerned in particular with the way in which the creatures of the *merkavah* generate the sounds of praise. So, too, the description of the *merkavah* in the twelfth of the Songs of the Sabbath Sacrifice is largely generated by a systematic attempt to explicate how the creatures of the *merkavah* praise God.

As striking as the similarities, however, are the differences. One of the distinctive features of the *merkavah* or *heikhalot* tradition as it is found in the Similitudes of Enoch (*1 Enoch* 37–71), in the synagogue liturgy (the Qedushah de-Yotser and the Qedushah de-ʿAmidah), and in *Maʿaseh Merkavah* and *Heikhalot Rabbati*, is the interest in the hymns sung by the angels and by the attendants of the chariot throne. It is just this feature, however, that indicates the complexity of the relationship between the Songs of the Sabbath Sacrifice from Qumran and the later mystical literature. The Qedushah, the angelic hymn based on *Isaiah* 6.3 and usually complemented by the blessing from *Ezekiel* 3.12 ("Holy, holy, holy is the Lord of Hosts . . . ; blessed be the Glory of the Lord from His place"), is the centerpiece of the heavenly worship as described in *1 Enoch* 39 and in the synagogue liturgy, and it is a regular feature of the angelic hymns cited in the *heikhalot* literature. Yet the Qedushah is conspicuous by its absence from the Songs of the Sabbath Sacrifice. Nor is there any other indication of elements from Isaiah's vision in the Songs of the Sabbath Sacrifice: no seraphim and no description of the throne as "high and lifted up," a formula that appears often in *heikhalot* hymns. Such differences are scarcely accidental. At the least it points to two divergent streams of tradition and possibly to a polemical rejection by the authors of Songs of the Sabbath Sacrifice of the tradition that set the recitation of the Qedushah at the center of the representation of angelic song.

The Songs of the Sabbath Sacrifice also have different emphases than do other *heikhalot* texts. The representation of heaven as a temple served by angelic priests, central to the Songs of the Sabbath Sacrifice, is not prominent in later *heikhalot* texts. Whereas the *heikhalot* tradition contains the texts of long hymns praising God, Songs of the Sabbath Sacrifice are much more concerned with describing the angels in the act of praising God than they are with quoting the words of praise uttered by the angels. Stylistically, although some general comparisons can be drawn, the techniques of composition are not strikingly similar between the Qumran Songs of the Sabbath Sacrifice and the later *heikhalot* hymns.

[*See* Psalms, Hymns, and Prayers; Religious Beliefs, Qumran Sect.]

BIBLIOGRAPHY

Collins, John J. *The Scepter and the Star: The Messiahs of the Dead Sea Scrolls and Other Ancient Literature.* New York, 1995.

Francis, Fred. "Humility and Angelic Worship in Col. 2.18." *Studia Theologica* 16 (1962), 109–134.

Gruenwald, Ithamar. *Apocalyptic and Merkavah Mysticism.* Arbeiten zur Geschichte des antiken Judentums und des Urchristentums, 14. Leiden, 1980.

Halperin, David. *The Merkabah in Rabbinic Literature.* American Oriental Series, 62. Philadelphia, 1980.

Halperin, David. "Merkabah Midrash in the Septuagint." *Journal of Biblical Literature* 101 (1982), 351–363.

Halperin, David. *The Faces of the Chariot: Early Jewish Responses to Ezekiel's Vision.* Texte und Studien zum Antiken Judentum, 16. Tübingen, 1988.

Kuhn, H. W. *Enderwartung und gegenwärtiges Heil.* Studien zur Umwelt des Neuen Testaments, 4. Göttingen, 1966.

Maier, Johann. *Vom Kultus zur Gnosis.* Religionswissenschaftliche Studien, 1. Salzburg, 1964.

Newsom, Carol A. *Songs of the Sabbath Sacrifice: A Critical Edition.* Harvard Semitic Studies, 27. Atlanta, 1985.

Newsom, Carol A. "Merkabah Exegesis in the Qumran Sabbath Shirot." *Journal of Jewish Studies* 38 (1987), 11–30.

Nitzan, Bilha. "Harmonic and Mystical Characteristics in Poetic and Liturgical Writings from Qumran." *Jewish Quarterly Review* 85 (1994), 163–183.

Rowland, Christopher. *The Open Heaven: A Study of Apocalyptic in Judaism and Early Christianity.* New York, 1982.

Schäfer, Peter, ed. *Synopse zur Hekhalot-Literatur.* Texte und Studien zum Antiken Judentum, 2. Tübingen, 1981.

Scholem, Gershom. *Jewish Gnosticism, Merkabah Mysticism, and Talmudic Tradition.* 2nd ed. New York, 1965.

Smith, Morton. "Ascent to the Heavens and Deification in 4QM^{a}." In *Archaeology and History in the Dead Sea Scrolls: The New York University Conference in Memory of Yigael Yadin*, edited by Lawrence H. Schiffman, pp. 181–188. Journal for the Study of the Pseudepigrapha Supplement Series, 8; Journal for the Study of the Old Testament/American Schools of Oriental Research Monograph Series, 2. Sheffield, 1990.

Wolfson, Elliot R. "Mysticism and the Poetic-Liturgical Compositions from Qumran." *Jewish Quarterly Review* (1994), 185–202.

CAROL A. NEWSOM